KU-051-851

PHILIP'S

WORLD ATLAS
& GAZETTEER

West Dunbartonshire Libraries

Reference Department

This book is provided for use in the
Reference Department only. It **must not** be
taken away.

Books should be used with great care, and
not injured or defaced in any way.

Class	Location	Accession
Ref 912	~~Gavinburn~~ Main	C 02 0131226

TITLE

WEST
DUNBARTONSHIRE
LIBRARIES

PRICE   SUPPLIER
£7.99   Camder

LOCATION   CLASS   Ref
Gen.Ref   912

INVOICE DATE
5-00

ACCESSION NUMBER
C 02 0131226

The Gazetteer of Nations
Text
Keith Lye

The World in Focus
Cartography by Philip's

Picture Acknowledgements
Page 14
Science Photo Library/NOAA

Illustrations
Stefan Chabluk

CONSULTANTS

Philip's are grateful to the following people for acting as specialist geography consultants on '*The World in Focus*' front section:

Professor D. Brunsden, Kings College, University of London, UK
Dr C. Clarke, Oxford University, UK
Dr I. S. Evans, Durham University, UK
Professor P. Haggett, University of Bristol, UK
Professor K. McLachlan, University of London, UK
Professor M. Monmonier, Syracuse University, New York, USA
Professor M-L. Hsu, University of Minnesota, Minnesota, USA
Professor M. J. Tooley, University of St Andrews, UK
Dr T. Unwin, Royal Holloway, University of London, UK

Published in Great Britain in 1999
by George Philip Limited,
a division of Octopus Publishing Group Limited,
2–4 Heron Quays, London E14 4JP

Copyright © 1999 George Philip Limited

Cartography by Philip's

ISBN 0–540–07709–7

A CIP catalogue record for this book is available from the British Library.

All rights reserved. Apart from any fair dealing for the purpose of private study, research, criticism or review, as permitted under the Copyright, Designs and Patents Act, 1988, no part of this publication may be reproduced, stored in a retrieval system, or transmitted in any form or by any means, electronic, electrical, chemical, mechanical, optical, photocopying, recording, or otherwise, without prior written permission. All enquiries should be addressed to the Publisher.

Printed in China

Details of other Philip's titles and services can be found on our website at: www.philips-maps.co.uk

Philip's is proud to announce that its World Atlases are now published in association with The Royal Geographical Society (with The Institute of British Geographers).

The Society was founded in 1830 and given a Royal Charter in 1859 for 'the advancement of geographical science'. It holds historical collections of national and international importance, many of which relate to the Society's association with and support for scientific exploration and research from the 19th century onwards. It was pivotal in establishing geography as a teaching and research discipline in British universities close to the turn of the century, and has played a key role in geographical and environmental education ever since.

Today the Society is a leading world centre for geographical learning – supporting education, teaching, research and expeditions, and promoting public understanding of the subject.

The Society welcomes those interested in geography as members. For further information, please visit the website at: www.rgs.org

PHILIP'S

WORLD ATLAS
& GAZETTEER

SEVENTH EDITION

WEST DUNBARTONSHIRE LIBRARIES

IN ASSOCIATION WITH
THE ROYAL GEOGRAPHICAL SOCIETY
WITH THE INSTITUTE OF BRITISH GEOGRAPHERS

Contents

v

World Statistics: Countries

This alphabetical list includes all the countries and territories of the world. If a territory is not completely independent, then the country it is associated with is named. The area figures give the total area of land, inland water and ice. The population figures are 1998 estimates. The annual income is the Gross National Product per capita in US dollars. The figures are the latest available, usually 1997.

Country/Territory	Area km² Thousands	Area miles² Thousands	Population Thousands	Capital	Annual Income US $
Adélie Land (France)	432	167	0.03	–	–
Afghanistan	652	252	24,792	Kabul	600
Albania	28.8	11.1	3,331	Tirana	750
Algeria	2,382	920	30,481	Algiers	1,490
American Samoa (US)	0.20	0.08	62	Pago Pago	2,600
Andorra	0.45	0.17	75	Andorra La Vella	16,200
Angola	1,247	481	11,200	Luanda	340
Anguilla (UK)	0.1	0.04	11	The Valley	6,800
Antigua & Barbuda	0.44	0.17	64	St John's	7,330
Argentina	2,767	1,068	36,265	Buenos Aires	8,750
Armenia	29.8	11.5	3,422	Yerevan	530
Aruba (Netherlands)	0.19	0.07	69	Oranjestad	15,890
Ascension Is. (UK)	0.09	0.03	1.5	Georgetown	–
Australia	7,687	2,968	18,613	Canberra	20,540
Austria	83.9	32.4	8,134	Vienna	27,980
Azerbaijan	86.6	33.4	7,856	Baku	510
Azores (Portugal)	2.2	0.87	238	Ponta Delgada	–
Bahamas	13.9	5.4	280	Nassau	11,940
Bahrain	0.68	0.26	616	Manama	7,840
Bangladesh	144	56	125,000	Dhaka	270
Barbados	0.43	0.17	259	Bridgetown	6,560
Belarus	207.6	80.1	10,409	Minsk	2,150
Belgium	30.5	11.8	10,175	Brussels	26,420
Belize	23	8.9	230	Belmopan	2,700
Benin	113	43	6,101	Porto-Novo	380
Bermuda (UK)	0.05	0.02	62	Hamilton	31,870
Bhutan	47	18.1	1,908	Thimphu	390
Bolivia	1,099	424	7,826	La Paz/Sucre	950
Bosnia-Herzegovina	51	20	3,366	Sarajevo	300
Botswana	582	225	1,448	Gaborone	4,381
Brazil	8,512	3,286	170,000	Brasília	4,720
British Indian Ocean Terr. (UK)	0.08	0.03	0	–	–
Brunei	5.8	2.2	315	Bandar Seri Begawan	15,800
Bulgaria	111	43	8,240	Sofia	1,140
Burkina Faso	274	106	11,266	Ouagadougou	240
Burma (= Myanmar)	677	261	47,305	Rangoon	1,790
Burundi	27.8	10.7	5,531	Bujumbura	180
Cambodia	181	70	11,340	Phnom Penh	300
Cameroon	475	184	15,029	Yaoundé	650
Canada	9,976	3,852	30,675	Ottawa	19,290
Canary Is. (Spain)	7.3	2.8	1,494	Las Palmas/Santa Cruz	–
Cape Verde Is.	4	1.6	399	Praia	1,010
Cayman Is. (UK)	0.26	0.10	35	George Town	20,000
Central African Republic	623	241	3,376	Bangui	320
Chad	1,284	496	7,360	Ndjaména	240
Chatham Is. (NZ)	0.96	0.37	0.05	Waitangi	–
Chile	757	292	14,788	Santiago	5,020
China	9,597	3,705	1,236,915	Beijing	860
Christmas Is. (Australia)	0.14	0.05	2	The Settlement	–
Cocos (Keeling) Is. (Australia)	0.01	0.005	1	West Island	–
Colombia	1,139	440	38,581	Bogotá	2,280
Comoros	2.2	0.86	545	Moroni	450
Congo	342	132	2,658	Brazzaville	660
Congo (= Zaïre)	2,345	905	49,001	Kinshasa	110
Cook Is. (NZ)	0.24	0.09	20	Avarua	900
Costa Rica	51.1	19.7	3,605	San José	2,640
Croatia	56.5	21.8	4,672	Zagreb	4,610
Cuba	111	43	11,051	Havana	1,300
Cyprus	9.3	3.6	749	Nicosia	13,420
Czech Republic	78.9	30.4	10,286	Prague	5,200
Denmark	43.1	16.6	5,334	Copenhagen	32,500
Djibouti	23.2	9	650	Djibouti	850
Dominica	0.75	0.29	78	Roseau	3,090
Dominican Republic	48.7	18.8	7,999	Santo Domingo	1,670
Ecuador	284	109	12,337	Quito	1,590
Egypt	1,001	387	66,050	Cairo	1,180
El Salvador	21	8.1	5,752	San Salvador	1,810
Equatorial Guinea	28.1	10.8	454	Malabo	530
Eritrea	94	36	3,842	Asmara	570
Estonia	44.7	17.3	1,421	Tallinn	3,330
Ethiopia	1,128	436	58,390	Addis Ababa	110
Falkland Is. (UK)	12.2	4.7	2	Stanley	–
Faroe Is. (Denmark)	1.4	0.54	41	Tórshavn	23,660
Fiji	18.3	7.1	802	Suva	2,470
Finland	338	131	5,149	Helsinki	24,080
France	552	213	58,805	Paris	26,050
French Guiana (France)	90	34.7	162	Cayenne	10,580
French Polynesia (France)	4	1.5	237	Papeete	7,500
Gabon	268	103	1,208	Libreville	4,230
Gambia, The	11.3	4.4	1,292	Banjul	320
Georgia	69.7	26.9	5,109	Tbilisi	840
Germany	357	138	82,079	Berlin/Bonn	28,260
Ghana	239	92	18,497	Accra	370
Gibraltar (UK)	0.007	0.003	29	Gibraltar Town	5,000
Greece	132	51	10,662	Athens	12,010
Greenland (Denmark)	2,176	840	59	Nuuk (Godthåb)	15,500
Grenada	0.34	0.13	96	St George's	2,880
Guadeloupe (France)	1.7	0.66	416	Basse-Terre	9,200
Guam (US)	0.55	0.21	149	Agana	6,000
Guatemala	109	42	12,008	Guatemala City	1,500
Guinea	246	95	7,477	Conakry	570
Guinea-Bissau	36.1	13.9	1,206	Bissau	240
Guyana	215	83	820	Georgetown	690
Haiti	27.8	10.7	6,781	Port-au-Prince	330
Honduras	112	43	5,862	Tegucigalpa	700
Hong Kong (China)	1.1	0.40	6,707	–	22,990
Hungary	93	35.9	10,208	Budapest	4,430
Iceland	103	40	271	Reykjavik	26,580
India	3,288	1,269	984,000	New Delhi	390
Indonesia	1,905	735	212,942	Jakarta	1,110
Iran	1,648	636	64,411	Tehran	4,700
Iraq	438	169	21,722	Baghdad	2,000
Ireland	70.3	27.1	3,619	Dublin	18,280
Israel	27	10.3	5,644	Jerusalem	15,810
Italy	301	116	56,783	Rome	20,120
Ivory Coast (Côte d'Ivoire)	322	125	15,446	Yamoussoukro	690
Jamaica	11	4.2	2,635	Kingston	1,560
Jan Mayen Is. (Norway)	0.38	0.15	1	–	–
Japan	378	146	125,932	Tokyo	37,850
Johnston Is. (US)	0.002	0.0009	1	–	–
Jordan	89.2	34.4	4,435	Amman	1,570
Kazakstan	2,717	1,049	16,847	Astana	1,340
Kenya	580	224	28,337	Nairobi	330
Kerguelen Is. (France)	7.2	2.8	0.7	–	–
Kermadec Is. (NZ)	0.03	0.01	0.1	–	–
Kiribati	0.72	0.28	85	Tarawa	920
Korea, North	121	47	21,234	Pyŏngyang	1,000
Korea, South	99	38.2	46,417	Seoul	10,550
Kuwait	17.8	6.9	1,913	Kuwait City	17,390
Kyrgyzstan	198.5	76.6	4,522	Bishkek	440
Laos	237	91	5,261	Vientiane	400
Latvia	65	25	2,385	Riga	2,430
Lebanon	10.4	4	3,506	Beirut	3,350

Country/Territory	Area km² Thousands	Area miles² Thousands	Population Thousands	Capital	Annual Income US $
Lesotho	30.4	11.7	2,090	Maseru	670
Liberia	111	43	2,772	Monrovia	770
Libya	1,760	679	4,875	Tripoli	6,510
Liechtenstein	0.16	0.06	32	Vaduz	33,000
Lithuania	65.2	25.2	3,600	Vilnius	2,230
Luxembourg	2.6	1	425	Luxembourg	45,360
Macau (China)	0.02	0.006	429	Macau	7,500
Macedonia	25.7	9.9	2,009	Skopje	1,090
Madagascar	587	227	14,463	Antananarivo	250
Madeira (Portugal)	0.81	0.31	253	Funchal	–
Malawi	118	46	9,840	Lilongwe	220
Malaysia	330	127	20,993	Kuala Lumpur	4,680
Maldives	0.30	0.12	290	Malé	1,080
Mali	1,240	479	10,109	Bamako	260
Malta	0.32	0.12	379	Valletta	12,000
Marshall Is.	0.18	0.07	63	Dalap-Uliga-Darrit	1,890
Martinique (France)	1.1	0.42	407	Fort-de-France	10,000
Mauritania	1,030	412	2,511	Nouakchott	450
Mauritius	2.0	0.72	1,168	Port Louis	3,800
Mayotte (France)	0.37	0.14	141	Mamoundzou	1,430
Mexico	1,958	756	98,553	Mexico City	3,680
Micronesia, Fed. States of	0.70	0.27	127	Palikir	2,070
Midway Is. (US)	0.005	0.002	2	–	–
Moldova	33.7	13	4,458	Chişinău	540
Monaco	0.002	0.0001	32	Monaco	25,000
Mongolia	1,567	605	2,579	Ulan Bator	390
Montserrat (UK)	0.10	0.04	12	Plymouth	4,500
Morocco	447	172	29,114	Rabat	1,250
Mozambique	802	309	18,641	Maputo	90
Namibia	825	318	1,622	Windhoek	2,220
Nauru	0.02	0.008	12	Yaren District	10,000
Nepal	141	54	23,698	Katmandu	210
Netherlands	41.5	16	15,731	Amsterdam/The Hague	25,820
Netherlands Antilles (Neths)	0.99	0.38	210	Willemstad	10,400
New Caledonia (France)	18.6	7.2	192	Nouméa	8,000
New Zealand	269	104	3,625	Wellington	16,480
Nicaragua	130	50	4,583	Managua	410
Niger	1,267	489	9,672	Niamey	200
Nigeria	924	357	110,532	Abuja	260
Niue (NZ)	0.26	0.10	2	Alofi	–
Norfolk Is. (Australia)	0.03	0.01	2	Kingston	–
Northern Mariana Is. (US)	0.48	0.18	50	Saipan	11,500
Norway	324	125	4,420	Oslo	36,090
Oman	212	82	2,364	Muscat	4,950
Pakistan	796	307	135,135	Islamabad	490
Palau	0.46	0.18	18	Koror	5,000
Panama	77.1	29.8	2,736	Panama City	3,080
Papua New Guinea	463	179	4,600	Port Moresby	940
Paraguay	407	157	5,291	Asunción	2,010
Peru	1,285	496	26,111	Lima	2,460
Philippines	300	116	77,736	Manila	1,220
Pitcairn Is. (UK)	0.03	0.01	0.05	Adamstown	–
Poland	313	121	38,607	Warsaw	3,590
Portugal	92.4	35.7	9,928	Lisbon	10,450
Puerto Rico (US)	9	3.5	3,860	San Juan	7,800
Qatar	11	4.2	697	Doha	11,600
Queen Maud Land (Norway)	2,800	1,081	0	–	–
Réunion (France)	2.5	0.97	705	Saint-Denis	4,500
Romania	238	92	22,396	Bucharest	1,420
Russia	17,075	6,592	146,861	Moscow	2,740
Rwanda	26.3	10.2	7,956	Kigali	210
St Helena (UK)	0.12	0.05	7	Jamestown	–
St Kitts & Nevis	0.36	0.14	42	Basseterre	5,870
St Lucia	0.62	0.24	150	Castries	3,500
St Pierre & Miquelon (France)	0.24	0.09	7	Saint Pierre	–
St Vincent & Grenadines	0.39	0.15	120	Kingstown	2,370
San Marino	0.06	0.02	25	San Marino	20,000
São Tomé & Príncipe	0.96	0.37	150	São Tomé	330
Saudi Arabia	2,150	830	20,786	Riyadh	6,790
Senegal	197	76	9,723	Dakar	550
Seychelles	0.46	0.18	79	Victoria	6,850
Sierra Leone	71.7	27.7	5,080	Freetown	200
Singapore	0.62	0.24	3,490	Singapore	32,940
Slovak Republic	49	18.9	5,393	Bratislava	3,700
Slovenia	20.3	7.8	1,972	Ljubljana	9,680
Solomon Is.	28.9	11.2	441	Honiara	900
Somalia	638	246	6,842	Mogadishu	500
South Africa	1,220	471	42,835	C. Town/Pretoria/Bloem.	3,400
South Georgia (UK)	3.8	1.4	0.05	–	–
Spain	505	195	39,134	Madrid	14,510
Sri Lanka	65.6	25.3	18,934	Colombo	800
Sudan	2,506	967	33,551	Khartoum	800
Surinam	163	63	427	Paramaribo	1,000
Svalbard (Norway)	62.9	24.3	4	Longyearbyen	–
Swaziland	17.4	6.7	966	Mbabane	1,210
Sweden	450	174	8,887	Stockholm	26,220
Switzerland	41.3	15.9	7,260	Bern	44,220
Syria	185	71	16,673	Damascus	1,150
Taiwan	36	13.9	21,908	Taipei	12,400
Tajikistan	143.1	55.2	6,020	Dushanbe	330
Tanzania	945	365	30,609	Dodoma	210
Thailand	513	198	60,037	Bangkok	2,800
Togo	56.8	21.9	4,906	Lomé	330
Tokelau (NZ)	0.01	0.005	2	Nukunonu	–
Tonga	0.75	0.29	107	Nuku'alofa	1,790
Trinidad & Tobago	5.1	2	1,117	Port of Spain	4,230
Tristan da Cunha (UK)	0.11	0.04	0.33	Edinburgh	–
Tunisia	164	63	9,380	Tunis	2,090
Turkey	779	301	64,568	Ankara	3,130
Turkmenistan	488.1	188.5	4,298	Ashkhabad	630
Turks & Caicos Is. (UK)	0.43	0.17	16	Cockburn Town	5,000
Tuvalu	0.03	0.01	10	Fongafale	600
Uganda	236	91	22,167	Kampala	320
Ukraine	603.7	233.1	50,125	Kiev	1,040
United Arab Emirates	83.6	32.3	2,303	Abu Dhabi	17,360
United Kingdom	243.3	94	58,970	London	20,710
United States of America	9,373	3,619	270,290	Washington, DC	28,740
Uruguay	177	68	3,285	Montevideo	6,020
Uzbekistan	447.4	172.7	23,784	Tashkent	1,010
Vanuatu	12.2	4.7	185	Port-Vila	1,290
Vatican City	0.0004	0.0002	1	–	–
Venezuela	912	352	22,803	Caracas	3,450
Vietnam	332	127	76,236	Hanoi	320
Virgin Is. (UK)	0.15	0.06	13	Road Town	–
Virgin Is. (US)	0.34	0.13	118	Charlotte Amalie	12,000
Wake Is.	0.008	0.003	0.3	–	–
Wallis & Futuna Is. (France)	0.20	0.08	15	Mata-Utu	–
Western Sahara	266	103	280	El Aaiún	300
Western Samoa	2.8	1.1	224	Apia	1,170
Yemen	528	204	16,388	Sana	270
Yugoslavia	102.3	39.5	10,500	Belgrade	2,000
Zambia	753	291	9,461	Lusaka	380
Zimbabwe	391	151	11,044	Harare	750

World Statistics: Physical Dimensions

Each topic list is divided into continents and within a continent the items are listed in order of size. The bottom part of many of the lists is selective in order to give examples from as many different countries as possible. The order of the continents is the same as in the atlas, beginning with Europe and ending with South America. The figures are rounded as appropriate.

World, Continents, Oceans

	km^2	$miles^2$	%
The World	509,450,000	196,672,000	–
Land	149,450,000	57,688,000	29.3
Water	360,000,000	138,984,000	70.7
Asia	44,500,000	17,177,000	29.8
Africa	30,302,000	11,697,000	20.3
North America	24,241,000	9,357,000	16.2
South America	17,793,000	6,868,000	11.9
Antarctica	14,100,000	5,443,000	9.4
Europe	9,957,000	3,843,000	6.7
Australia & Oceania	8,557,000	3,303,000	5.7
Pacific Ocean	179,679,000	69,356,000	49.9
Atlantic Ocean	92,373,000	35,657,000	25.7
Indian Ocean	73,917,000	28,532,000	20.5
Arctic Ocean	14,090,000	5,439,000	3.9

Ocean Depths

Atlantic Ocean	m	ft
Puerto Rico (Milwaukee) Deep	9,220	30,249
Cayman Trench	7,680	25,197
Gulf of Mexico	5,203	17,070
Mediterranean Sea	5,121	16,801
Black Sea	2,211	7,254
North Sea	660	2,165
Indian Ocean	m	ft
Java Trench	7,450	24,442
Red Sea	2,635	8,454
Pacific Ocean	m	ft
Mariana Trench	11,022	36,161
Tonga Trench	10,882	35,702
Japan Trench	10,554	34,626
Kuril Trench	10,542	34,587
Arctic Ocean	m	ft
Molloy Deep	5,608	18,399

Mountains

Europe		m	ft
Elbrus	*Russia*	5,642	18,510
Mont Blanc	*France/Italy*	4,807	15,771
Monte Rosa	*Italy/Switzerland*	4,634	15,203
Dom	*Switzerland*	4,545	14,911
Liskamm	*Switzerland*	4,527	14,852
Weisshorn	*Switzerland*	4,505	14,780
Taschorn	*Switzerland*	4,490	14,730
Matterhorn/Cervino	*Italy/Switzerland*	4,478	14,691
Mont Maudit	*France/Italy*	4,465	14,649
Dent Blanche	*Switzerland*	4,356	14,291
Nadelhorn	*Switzerland*	4,327	14,196
Grandes Jorasses	*France/Italy*	4,208	13,806
Jungfrau	*Switzerland*	4,158	13,642
Grossglockner	*Austria*	3,797	12,457
Mulhacén	*Spain*	3,478	11,411
Zugspitze	*Germany*	2,962	9,718
Olympus	*Greece*	2,917	9,570
Triglav	*Slovenia*	2,863	9,393
Gerlachovka	*Slovak Republic*	2,655	8,711
Galdhöpiggen	*Norway*	2,468	8,100
Kebnekaise	*Sweden*	2,117	6,946
Ben Nevis	*UK*	1,343	4,406
Asia		m	ft
Everest	*China/Nepal*	8,848	29,029
K2 (Godwin Austen)	*China/Kashmir*	8,611	28,251
Kanchenjunga	*India/Nepal*	8,598	28,208
Lhotse	*China/Nepal*	8,516	27,939
Makalu	*China/Nepal*	8,481	27,824
Cho Oyu	*China/Nepal*	8,201	26,906
Dhaulagiri	*Nepal*	8,172	26,811
Manaslu	*Nepal*	8,156	26,758
Nanga Parbat	*Kashmir*	8,126	26,660
Annapurna	*Nepal*	8,078	26,502
Gasherbrum	*China/Kashmir*	8,068	26,469
Broad Peak	*China/Kashmir*	8,051	26,414
Xixabangma	*China*	8,012	26,286
Kangbachen	*India/Nepal*	7,902	25,925
Trivor	*Pakistan*	7,720	25,328
Pik Kommunizma	*Tajikistan*	7,495	24,590
Demavend	*Iran*	5,604	18,386
Ararat	*Turkey*	5,165	16,945
Gunong Kinabalu	*Malaysia (Borneo)*	4,101	13,455
Fuji-San	*Japan*	3,776	12,388
Africa		m	ft
Kilimanjaro	*Tanzania*	5,895	19,340
Mt Kenya	*Kenya*	5,199	17,057
Ruwenzori (Margherita)	*Ug./Congo (Z.)*	5,109	16,762
Ras Dashan	*Ethiopia*	4,620	15,157
Meru	*Tanzania*	4,565	14,977
Karisimbi	*Rwanda/Congo (Zaïre)*	4,507	14,787
Mt Elgon	*Kenya/Uganda*	4,321	14,176
Batu	*Ethiopia*	4,307	14,130
Toubkal	*Morocco*	4,165	13,665
Mt Cameroon	*Cameroon*	4,070	13,353
Oceania		m	ft
Puncak Jaya	*Indonesia*	5,029	16,499
Puncak Trikora	*Indonesia*	4,750	15,584
Puncak Mandala	*Indonesia*	4,702	15,427
Mt Wilhelm	*Papua New Guinea*	4,508	14,790
Mauna Kea	*USA (Hawaii)*	4,205	13,796
Mauna Loa	*USA (Hawaii)*	4,170	13,681
Mt Cook (Aoraki)	*New Zealand*	3,753	12,313
Mt Kosciuszko	*Australia*	2,237	7,339
North America		m	ft
Mt McKinley (Denali)	*USA (Alaska)*	6,194	20,321
Mt Logan	*Canada*	5,959	19,551
Citlaltepetl	*Mexico*	5,700	18,701
Mt St Elias	*USA/Canada*	5,489	18,008
Popocatepetl	*Mexico*	5,452	17,887
Mt Foraker	*USA (Alaska)*	5,304	17,401
Ixtaccihuatl	*Mexico*	5,286	17,342
Lucania	*Canada*	5,227	17,149
Mt Steele	*Canada*	5,073	16,644
Mt Bona	*USA (Alaska)*	5,005	16,420
Mt Whitney	*USA*	4,418	14,495
Tajumulco	*Guatemala*	4,220	13,845
Chirripó Grande	*Costa Rica*	3,837	12,589
Pico Duarte	*Dominican Rep.*	3,175	10,417
South America		m	ft
Aconcagua	*Argentina*	6,960	22,834
Bonete	*Argentina*	6,872	22,546
Ojos del Salado	*Argentina/Chile*	6,863	22,516
Pissis	*Argentina*	6,779	22,241
Mercedario	*Argentina/Chile*	6,770	22,211
Huascaran	*Peru*	6,768	22,204
Llullaillaco	*Argentina/Chile*	6,723	22,057
Nudo de Cachi	*Argentina*	6,720	22,047
Yerupaja	*Peru*	6,632	21,758
Sajama	*Bolivia*	6,542	21,463
Chimborazo	*Ecuador*	6,267	20,561
Pico Colon	*Colombia*	5,800	19,029
Pico Bolivar	*Venezuela*	5,007	16,427
Antarctica		m	ft
Vinson Massif		4,897	16,066
Mt Kirkpatrick		4,528	14,855

Rivers

Europe		km	miles
Volga	*Caspian Sea*	3,700	2,300
Danube	*Black Sea*	2,850	1,770
Ural	*Caspian Sea*	2,535	1,575
Dnepr (Dnipro)	*Black Sea*	2,285	1,420
Kama	*Volga*	2,030	1,260
Don	*Black Sea*	1,990	1,240
Petchora	*Arctic Ocean*	1,790	1,110
Oka	*Volga*	1,480	920
Dnister (Dniester)	*Black Sea*	1,400	870
Vyatka	*Kama*	1,370	850
Rhine	*North Sea*	1,320	820
N. Dvina	*Arctic Ocean*	1,290	800
Elbe	*North Sea*	1,145	710
Asia		km	miles
Yangtze	*Pacific Ocean*	6,380	3,960
Yenisey–Angara	*Arctic Ocean*	5,550	3,445
Huang He	*Pacific Ocean*	5,464	3,395
Ob–Irtysh	*Arctic Ocean*	5,410	3,360
Mekong	*Pacific Ocean*	4,500	2,795
Amur	*Pacific Ocean*	4,400	2,730
Lena	*Arctic Ocean*	4,400	2,730
Irtysh	*Ob*	4,250	2,640
Yenisey	*Arctic Ocean*	4,090	2,540
Ob	*Arctic Ocean*	3,680	2,285
Indus	*Indian Ocean*	3,100	1,925
Brahmaputra	*Indian Ocean*	2,900	1,800
Syrdarya	*Aral Sea*	2,860	1,775
Salween	*Indian Ocean*	2,800	1,740
Euphrates	*Indian Ocean*	2,700	1,675
Amudarya	*Aral Sea*	2,540	1,575
Africa		km	miles
Nile	*Mediterranean*	6,670	4,140
Congo	*Atlantic Ocean*	4,670	2,900
Niger	*Atlantic Ocean*	4,180	2,595
Zambezi	*Indian Ocean*	3,540	2,200
Oubangi/Uele	*Congo (Zaïre)*	2,250	1,400
Kasai	*Congo (Zaïre)*	1,950	1,210
Shaballe	*Indian Ocean*	1,930	1,200
Orange	*Atlantic Ocean*	1,860	1,155
Cubango	*Okavango Swamps*	1,800	1,120
Limpopo	*Indian Ocean*	1,600	995
Senegal	*Atlantic Ocean*	1,600	995
Australia		km	miles
Murray–Darling	*Indian Ocean*	3,750	2,330
Darling	*Murray*	3,070	1,905
Murray	*Indian Ocean*	2,575	1,600
Murrumbidgee	*Murray*	1,690	1,050
North America		km	miles
Mississippi–Missouri	*Gulf of Mexico*	6,020	3,740
Mackenzie	*Arctic Ocean*	4,240	2,630
Mississippi	*Gulf of Mexico*	3,780	2,350
Missouri	*Mississippi*	3,780	2,350
Yukon	*Pacific Ocean*	3,185	1,980
Rio Grande	*Gulf of Mexico*	3,030	1,880
Arkansas	*Mississippi*	2,340	1,450
Colorado	*Pacific Ocean*	2,330	1,445
Red	*Mississippi*	2,040	1,270
Columbia	*Pacific Ocean*	1,950	1,210
Saskatchewan	*Lake Winnipeg*	1,940	1,205
South America		km	miles
Amazon	*Atlantic Ocean*	6,450	4,010
Paraná–Plate	*Atlantic Ocean*	4,500	2,800
Purus	*Amazon*	3,350	2,080
Madeira	*Amazon*	3,200	1,990
São Francisco	*Atlantic Ocean*	2,900	1,800
Paraná	*Plate*	2,800	1,740
Tocantins	*Atlantic Ocean*	2,750	1,710
Paraguay	*Paraná*	2,550	1,580
Orinoco	*Atlantic Ocean*	2,500	1,550
Pilcomayo	*Paraná*	2,500	1,550
Araguaia	*Tocantins*	2,250	1,400

Lakes

Europe		km^2	$miles^2$
Lake Ladoga	*Russia*	17,700	6,800
Lake Onega	*Russia*	9,700	3,700
Saimaa system	*Finland*	8,000	3,100
Vänern	*Sweden*	5,500	2,100
Asia		km^2	$miles^2$
Caspian Sea	*Asia*	371,800	143,550
Lake Baykal	*Russia*	30,500	11,780
Aral Sea	*Kazakstan/Uzbekistan*	28,687	11,086
Tonlé Sap	*Cambodia*	20,000	7,700
Lake Balqash	*Kazakstan*	18,500	7,100
Africa		km^2	$miles^2$
Lake Victoria	*East Africa*	68,000	26,000
Lake Tanganyika	*Central Africa*	33,000	13,000
Lake Malawi/Nyasa	*East Africa*	29,600	11,430
Lake Chad	*Central Africa*	25,000	9,700
Lake Turkana	*Ethiopia/Kenya*	8,500	3,300
Lake Volta	*Ghana*	8,500	3,300
Australia		km^2	$miles^2$
Lake Eyre	*Australia*	8,900	3,400
Lake Torrens	*Australia*	5,800	2,200
Lake Gairdner	*Australia*	4,800	1,900
North America		km^2	$miles^2$
Lake Superior	*Canada/USA*	82,350	31,800
Lake Huron	*Canada/USA*	59,600	23,010
Lake Michigan	*USA*	58,000	22,400
Great Bear Lake	*Canada*	31,800	12,280
Great Slave Lake	*Canada*	28,500	11,000
Lake Erie	*Canada/USA*	25,700	9,900
Lake Winnipeg	*Canada*	24,400	9,400
Lake Ontario	*Canada/USA*	19,500	7,500
Lake Nicaragua	*Nicaragua*	8,200	3,200
South America		km^2	$miles^2$
Lake Titicaca	*Bolivia/Peru*	8,300	3,200
Lake Poopo	*Peru*	2,800	1,100

Islands

Europe		km^2	$miles^2$
Great Britain	*UK*	229,880	88,700
Iceland	*Atlantic Ocean*	103,000	39,800
Ireland	*Ireland/UK*	84,400	32,600
Novaya Zemlya (N.)	*Russia*	48,200	18,600
Sicily	*Italy*	25,500	9,800
Corsica	*France*	8,700	3,400
Asia		km^2	$miles^2$
Borneo	*Southeast Asia*	744,360	287,400
Sumatra	*Indonesia*	473,600	182,860
Honshu	*Japan*	230,500	88,980
Sulawesi (Celebes)	*Indonesia*	189,000	73,000
Java	*Indonesia*	126,700	48,900
Luzon	*Philippines*	104,700	40,400
Hokkaido	*Japan*	78,400	30,300
Africa		km^2	$miles^2$
Madagascar	*Indian Ocean*	587,040	226,660
Socotra	*Indian Ocean*	3,600	1,400
Réunion	*Indian Ocean*	2,500	965
Oceania		km^2	$miles^2$
New Guinea	*Indonesia/Papua NG*	821,030	317,000
New Zealand (S.)	*Pacific Ocean*	150,500	58,100
New Zealand (N.)	*Pacific Ocean*	114,700	44,300
Tasmania	*Australia*	67,800	26,200
Hawaii	*Pacific Ocean*	10,450	4,000
North America		km^2	$miles^2$
Greenland	*Atlantic Ocean*	2,175,600	839,800
Baffin Is.	*Canada*	508,000	196,100
Victoria Is.	*Canada*	212,200	81,900
Ellesmere Is.	*Canada*	212,000	81,800
Cuba	*Caribbean Sea*	110,860	42,800
Hispaniola	*Dominican Rep./Haiti*	76,200	29,400
Jamaica	*Caribbean Sea*	11,400	4,400
Puerto Rico	*Atlantic Ocean*	8,900	3,400
South America		km^2	$miles^2$
Tierra del Fuego	*Argentina/Chile*	47,000	18,100
Falkland Is. (E.)	*Atlantic Ocean*	6,800	2,600

Philip's World Maps

The reference maps which form the main body of this atlas have been prepared in accordance with the highest standards of international cartography to provide an accurate and detailed representation of the Earth. The scales and projections used have been carefully chosen to give balanced coverage of the world, while emphasizing the most densely populated and economically significant regions. A hallmark of Philip's mapping is the use of hill shading and relief colouring to create a graphic impression of landforms: this makes the maps exceptionally easy to read. However, knowledge of the key features employed in the construction and presentation of the maps will enable the reader to derive the fullest benefit from the atlas.

Map sequence

The atlas covers the Earth continent by continent: first Europe; then its land neighbour Asia (mapped north before south, in a clockwise sequence), then Africa, Australia and Oceania, North America and South America. This is the classic arrangement adopted by most cartographers since the 16th century. For each continent, there are maps at a variety of scales. First, physical relief and political maps of the whole continent; then a series of larger-scale maps of the regions within the continent, each followed, where required, by still larger-scale maps of the most important or densely populated areas. The governing principle is that by turning the pages of the atlas, the reader moves steadily from north to south through each continent, with each map overlapping its neighbours. A key map showing this sequence, and the area covered by each map, can be found on the endpapers of the atlas.

Map presentation

With very few exceptions (e.g. for the Arctic and Antarctica), the maps are drawn with north at the top, regardless of whether they are presented upright or sideways on the page. In the borders will be found the map title; a locator diagram showing the area covered and the page numbers for maps of adjacent areas; the scale; the projection used; the degrees of latitude and longitude; and the letters and figures used in the index for locating place names and geographical features. Physical relief maps also have a height reference panel identifying the colours used for each layer of contouring.

Map symbols

Each map contains a vast amount of detail which can only be conveyed clearly and accurately by the use of symbols. Points and circles of varying sizes locate and identify the relative importance of towns and cities; different styles of type are employed for administrative, geographical and regional place names. A variety of pictorial symbols denote features such as glaciers and marshes, as well

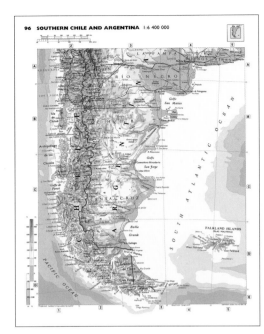

as man-made structures including roads, railways, airports and canals. International borders are shown by red lines. Where neighbouring countries are in dispute, for example in the Middle East, the maps show the *de facto* boundary between nations, regardless of the legal or historical situation. The symbols are explained on the first page of the World Maps section of the atlas.

Map scales

The scale of each map is given in the numerical form known as the 'representative fraction'. The first figure is always one, signifying one unit of distance on the map; the second figure, usually in millions, is the number by which the map unit must be multiplied to give the equivalent distance on the Earth's surface. Calculations can easily be made in centimetres and kilometres, by dividing the Earth units figure by 100 000 (i.e. deleting the last five 0s). Thus 1:1 000 000 means 1 cm = 10 km. The calculation for inches and miles is more laborious, but 1 000 000 divided by 63 360 (the number of inches in a mile) shows that the ratio 1:1 000 000 means approximately 1 inch = 16 miles. The table below provides distance equivalents for scales down to 1:50 000 000.

LARGE SCALE		
1:1 000 000	1 cm = 10 km	1 inch = 16 miles
1:2 500 000	1 cm = 25 km	1 inch = 39.5 miles
1:5 000 000	1 cm = 50 km	1 inch = 79 miles
1:6 000 000	1 cm = 60 km	1 inch = 95 miles
1:8 000 000	1 cm = 80 km	1 inch = 126 miles
1:10 000 000	1 cm = 100 km	1 inch = 158 miles
1:15 000 000	1 cm = 150 km	1 inch = 237 miles
1:20 000 000	1 cm = 200 km	1 inch = 316 miles
1:50 000 000	1 cm = 500 km	1 inch = 790 miles
SMALL SCALE		

Measuring distances

Although each map is accompanied by a scale bar, distances cannot always be measured with confidence because of the distortions involved in portraying the curved surface of the Earth on a flat page. As a general rule, the larger the map scale (i.e. the lower the number of Earth units in the representative fraction), the more accurate and reliable will be the distance measured. On small-scale maps such as those of the world and of entire continents, measurement may only be accurate along the 'standard parallels', or central axes, and should not be attempted without considering the map projection.

Latitude and longitude

Accurate positioning of individual points on the Earth's surface is made possible by reference to the geometrical system of latitude and longitude. Latitude *parallels* are drawn west–east around the Earth and numbered by degrees north and south of the Equator, which is designated 0° of latitude. Longitude *meridians* are drawn north–south and numbered by degrees east and west of the *prime meridian*, 0° of longitude, which passes through Greenwich in England. By referring to these co-ordinates and their subdivisions of minutes ($1/60$th of a degree) and seconds ($1/60$th of a minute), any place on Earth can be located to within a few hundred metres. Latitude and longitude are indicated by blue lines on the maps; they are straight or curved according to the projection employed. Reference to these lines is the easiest way of determining the relative positions of places on different maps, and for plotting compass directions.

Name forms

For ease of reference, both English and local name forms appear in the atlas. Oceans, seas and countries are shown in English throughout the atlas; country names may be abbreviated to their commonly accepted form (e.g. Germany, not The Federal Republic of Germany). Conventional English forms are also used for place names on the smaller-scale maps of the continents. However, local name forms are used on all large-scale and regional maps, with the English form given in brackets only for important cities – the large-scale map of Russia and Central Asia thus shows Moskva (Moscow). For countries which do not use a Roman script, place names have been transcribed according to the systems adopted by the British and US Geographic Names Authorities. For China, the Pin Yin system has been used, with some more widely known forms appearing in brackets, as with Beijing (Peking). Both English and local names appear in the index, the English form being cross-referenced to the local form.

The
GAZETTEER
OF NATIONS

Index to Countries

Notes

The countries are arranged alphabetically, with Afghanistan as the first entry and Zimbabwe as the last. Information is given for all countries and territories, except for some of the smallest and near uninhabited islands. The form of names for all the countries follows the conventions used in all Philip's world atlases.

The statistical data is the latest available, usually for 1997–8. In the statistics boxes: Country area includes inland water and land areas covered in ice, as in Greenland and Canada, for example. City populations are usually those of the 'urban agglomerations' rather than within the legal city boundaries.

AFGHANISTAN

GEOGRAPHY The Republic of Afghanistan is a landlocked, mountainous country in southern Asia. The central highlands reach a height of more than 7,000 m [22,966 ft] in the east and make up nearly three-quarters of Afghanistan. The main range is the Hindu Kush, which is cut by deep, fertile valleys.

The height of the land and the country's remote position have a great effect on the climate. In winter, northerly winds bring cold, snowy weather to the mountains, but summers are hot and dry.

POLITICS & ECONOMY The modern history of Afghanistan began in 1747, when the various tribes in the area united for the first time. In the 19th century, Russia and Britain struggled for control of the country. Following Britain's withdrawal in 1919, Afghanistan became fully independent. Soviet troops invaded Afghanistan in 1979 to support a socialist regime in Kabul, but, facing fierce opposition from Muslim groups, they withdrew in 1989. But Muslim factions continued to fight each other. By early 1999 a group called Taliban ('Islamic students') controlled most of the country apart from the north.

Afghanistan is one of the world's poorest countries. About 60% of the people live by farming. Many people are semi-nomadic herders. Natural gas is produced, together with some coal, copper, gold, precious stones and salt.

AREA 652,090 sq km [251,772 sq mls]
POPULATION 24,792,000
CAPITAL (POPULATION) Kabul (1,565,000)
GOVERNMENT Islamic republic
ETHNIC GROUPS Pashtun ('Pathan') 52%, Tajik 20%, Uzbek 9%, Hazara 9%, Chahar 3%, Turkmen 2%, Baluchi 1%
LANGUAGES Pashto, Dari / Persian (both official), Uzbek
RELIGIONS Islam (Sunni Muslim 74%, Shiite Muslim 25%)
CURRENCY Afghani = 100 puls

ALBANIA

GEOGRAPHY The Republic of Albania lies in the Balkan peninsula, facing the Adriatic Sea. About 70% of the land is mountainous, but most Albanians live in the west on the coastal lowlands.

The coastal areas of Albania have a typical Mediterranean climate, with fairly dry, sunny summers and cool, moist winters. The mountains have a severe climate, with heavy winter snowfalls.

POLITICS & ECONOMY Albania is Europe's poorest country. Formerly a Communist regime, Albania introduced a multiparty system in the early 1990s. The transition to a market economy was traumatic, but, following elections in 1997, a socialist government committed to a market system took office. In 1999, problems arose with the arrival of ethnic Albanian refugees from Kosovo, Yugoslavia, following the NATO offensive against Serbia.

In the early 1990s, agriculture employed 56% of the people. The land was divided into large collective and state farms, but private ownership has been encouraged since 1991. Albania has some minerals and chromite, copper and nickel are exported.

AREA 28,750 sq km [11,100 sq mls]
POPULATION 3,331,000
CAPITAL (POPULATION) Tirana (251,000)
GOVERNMENT Multiparty republic
ETHNIC GROUPS Albanian 98%, Greek 1.8%, Macedonian, Montenegrin, Gypsy
LANGUAGES Albanian (official)
RELIGIONS Many people say they are non-believers; of the believers, 65% follow Islam and 33% follow Christianity (Orthodox 20%, Roman Catholic 13%)
CURRENCY Lek = 100 qindars

ALGERIA

GEOGRAPHY The People's Democratic Republic of Algeria is Africa's second largest country after Sudan. Most Algerians live in the north, on the fertile coastal plains and hill country bordering the Mediterranean Sea. Four-fifths of Algeria is in the Sahara. The coast has a Mediterranean climate, but the arid Sahara is hot by day and cool at night.

POLITICS & ECONOMY France ruled Algeria from 1830 until 1962, when the socialist FLN (National Liberation Front) formed a one-party government. Following the recognition of opposition parties in 1989, a Muslim group, the FIS (Islamic Salvation Front), won an election in 1991. The FLN cancelled the elections and civil conflict broke out. About 75,000 people were killed between 1991 and 1998. Presidential elections in 1999 did little to calm the situation, when the six anti-army candidates withdrew, alleging fraud. This resulted in a hollow victory for Abjulaziz Bouteflika, who was assumed to be the candidate favoured by the army.

Algeria is a developing country, whose chief resources are oil and natural gas. The natural gas reserves are among the world's largest, and gas and oil account for 90% of Algeria's exports. Cement, iron and steel, textiles and vehicles are manufactured.

AREA 2,381,740 sq km [919,590 sq mls]
POPULATION 30,481,000
CAPITAL (POPULATION) Algiers (1,722,000)
GOVERNMENT Socialist republic
ETHNIC GROUPS Arab 83%, Berber 16%
LANGUAGES Arabic (official), Berber, French
RELIGIONS Sunni Muslim 98%
CURRENCY Algerian dinar = 100 centimes

AMERICAN SAMOA

An 'unincorporated territory' of the United States, American Samoa lies in the south-central Pacific Ocean. **AREA** 200 sq km [77 sq mls]; **POPULATION** 62,000; **CAPITAL** Pago Pago.

ANDORRA

A mini-state situated in the Pyrenees Mountains, Andorra is a co-principality whose main activity is tourism. Most Andorrans live in the six valleys (the Valls) that drain into the River Valira. **AREA** 453 sq km [175 sq mls]; **POPULATION** 75,000; **CAPITAL** Andorra La Vella.

ANGOLA

GEOGRAPHY The Republic of Angola is a large country in south-western Africa. Most of the country is part of the plateau that forms most of southern Africa, with a narrow coastal plain in the west.

Angola has a tropical climate, with temperatures of over 20°C [68°F] throughout the year, though the highest areas are cooler. The coastal regions are dry, but the rainfall increases to the north and east.

POLITICS & ECONOMY A former Portuguese colony, Angola gained its independence in 1975, after which rival nationalist forces began a struggle for power. A long-running civil war developed, finally ending with a peace treaty in 1994, which led to a coalition government in 1997. However, civil war again broke out in 1999.

Angola is a developing country, where 70% of the people are poor farmers. The main food crops are cassava and maize. Coffee is exported. Angola has much economic potential. It has oil reserves near Luanda and in the Cabinda enclave, which is separated from Angola by a strip of land belonging to Congo (Zaïre). Oil is the leading export. Angola also produces diamonds and has reserves of copper, manganese and phosphates.

AREA 1,246,700 sq km [481,351 sq mls]
POPULATION 11,200,000
CAPITAL (POPULATION) Luanda (2,250,000)
GOVERNMENT Multiparty republic
ETHNIC GROUPS Ovimbundu 37%, Mbundu 22%, Kongo 13%, Luimbe-Nganguela 5%, Nyaneka-Humbe 5%, Chokwe, Luvale, Luchazi
LANGUAGES Portuguese (official), many others
RELIGIONS Christianity (Roman Catholic 69%, Protestant 20%), traditional beliefs 10%
CURRENCY Kwanza = 100 lwei

ANGUILLA

Formerly part of St Kitts and Nevis, Anguilla became a British dependency (now a British overseas territory) in 1980. The main source of revenue is now tourism, although lobster still accounts for half the island's exports. **AREA** 96 sq km [37 sq mls]; **POPULATION** 11,000; **CAPITAL** The Valley.

ANTIGUA AND BARBUDA

A former British dependency in the Caribbean, Antigua and Barbuda became independent in 1981. Tourism is the main industry. **AREA** 440 sq km [170 sq mls]; **POPULATION** 64,000; **CAPITAL** St John's.

ARGENTINA

GEOGRAPHY The Argentine Republic is South America's second largest and the world's eighth largest country. The high Andes range in the west contains Mount Aconcagua, the highest peak in the Americas. In southern Argentina, the Andes Mountains overlook Patagonia, a plateau region. In east-central Argentina lies a fertile plain called the *pampas*.

The climate varies from subtropical in the north to temperate in the south. Rainfall is abundant in the north-east, but is lower to the west and south. Patagonia is a dry region, crossed by rivers that rise in the Andes.

POLITICS & ECONOMY Argentina became independent from Spain in the early 19th century, but it later suffered from instability and periods of military rule. In 1982, Argentina invaded the Falkland (Malvinas) islands, but Britain regained the islands later in the year. Elections were held in 1983 and constitutional government was restored.

According to the World Bank, Argentina is an 'upper-middle-income' developing country. Large areas are fertile and the main agricultural products are beef, maize and wheat. But about 87% of the people live in cities and towns, where many work in factories that process farm products. Other industries include the manufacture of cars, electrical equipment and textiles. Oil is the leading mineral resource. The leading exports include meat, wheat, maize, vegetable oils, hides and skins, and wool. In 1991, Argentina, Brazil, Paraguay and Uruguay set up Mercosur, an alliance aimed at creating a common market.

AREA 2,766,890 sq km [1,068,296 sq mls]
POPULATION 36,265,000
CAPITAL (POPULATION) Buenos Aires (10,990,000)
GOVERNMENT Federal republic
ETHNIC GROUPS European 85%, Mestizo, Amerindian
LANGUAGES Spanish (official)
RELIGIONS Christianity (Roman Catholic 92%)
CURRENCY Peso = 10,000 australs

ARMENIA

GEOGRAPHY The Republic of Armenia is a landlocked country in south-western Asia. Most of Armenia consists of a rugged plateau, criss-crossed by long faults (cracks). Movements along the faults cause earthquakes. The highest point is Mount Aragats, at 4,090 m [13,419 ft] above sea level.

The height of the land, which averages 1,500 m [4,920 ft] above sea level gives rise to severe winters and cool summers. The highest peaks are snow-capped, but the total yearly rainfall is generally low.

POLITICS & ECONOMY In 1920, Armenia became a Communist republic and, in 1922, it became, with Azerbaijan and Georgia, part of the Transcaucasian Republic within the Soviet Union. But the three territories became separate Soviet Socialist Republics in 1936. After the break-up of the Soviet Union in 1991, Armenia became an independent republic. Fighting broke out over Nagorno-Karabakh, an area enclosed by Azerbaijan where the majority of the people are Armenians. In 1992, Armenia occupied the territory between it and Nagorno-Karabakh. A cease-fire agreed in 1994 left Armenia in control of about 20% of Azerbaijan's land area.

The World Bank classifies Armenia as a 'lower-middle-income economy'. The conflict has badly damaged the economy, but the government has encouraged free enterprise, selling farmland and government-owned businesses.

AREA 29,800 sq km [11,506 sq mls]
POPULATION 3,422,000
CAPITAL (POPULATION) Yerevan (1,226,000)
GOVERNMENT Multiparty republic
ETHNIC GROUPS Armenian 93%, Azerbaijani 3%, Russian, Kurd
LANGUAGES Armenian (official)
RELIGIONS Christianity (Armenian Apostolic)
CURRENCY Dram = 100 couma

ARUBA

Formerly part of the Netherlands Antilles, Aruba became a separate self-governing Dutch territory in 1986. **AREA** 193 sq km [75 sq mls]; **POPULATION** 69,000; **CAPITAL** Oranjestad.

AUSTRALIA

GEOGRAPHY The Commonwealth of Australia, the world's sixth largest country, is also a continent. Australia is the flattest of the continents and the main highland area is in the east. Here the Great Dividing Range separates the eastern coastal plains from the Central Plains. This range extends from the Cape York Peninsula to Victoria in the far south. The longest rivers, the Murray and Darling, drain the south-eastern part of the Central Plains. The Western Plateau makes up two-thirds of Australia. A few mountain ranges break the monotony of the generally flat landscape.

Only 10% of Australia has an average yearly rainfall of more than 1,000 mm [39 in]. These areas include the tropical north, where Darwin is situated, the north-east coast, and the south-east, where Sydney is located. The interior is dry, and water is quickly evaporated in the heat.

POLITICS & ECONOMY The Aboriginal people of Australia entered the continent from South-east Asia more than 50,000 years ago. The first European explorers were Dutch in the 17th century, but they did not settle. In 1770, the British Captain Cook explored the east coast and, in 1788, the first British settlement was established for convicts on the site of what is now Sydney. Australia has strong ties with the British Isles. But in the last 50 years, people from other parts of Europe and, most recently, from Asia have settled in Australia. Ties with Britain were also weakened by Britain's membership of the European Union. Many Australians now believe that they should become more involved with the nations of eastern Asia and the Americas rather than with Europe. By the late 1990s, many people thought that Australia should become a republic, with a president replacing the British monarch as head of state.

Australia is a prosperous country. Crops can be grown on only 6% of the land, though dry pasture covers another 58%. Yet the country remains a major producer and exporter of farm products, particularly cattle, wheat and wool. Grapes grown for wine-making are also important. The country is also rich in natural resources. It is a major producer of minerals, including bauxite, coal, copper, diamonds, gold, iron ore, manganese, nickel, silver, tin, tungsten and zinc. Australia also produces some oil and natural gas. Metals, minerals and farm products account for the bulk of exports. Australia's imports are mostly manufactured products, although the country makes many factory products, especially consumer goods, such as foods and household articles. Major imports include machinery and other goods used by factories.

AREA 7,686,850 sq km [2,967,893 sq mls]
POPULATION 18,613,000
CAPITAL (POPULATION) Canberra (325,000)
GOVERNMENT Federal constitutional monarchy
ETHNIC GROUPS White 95%, Aboriginal 1.5%, Asian 1.3%
LANGUAGES English (official)
RELIGIONS Christianity (Roman Catholic 26%, Anglican 24%, others 20%), Islam, Buddhism, Judaism
CURRENCY Australian dollar = 100 cents

AUSTRIA

GEOGRAPHY The Republic of Austria is a landlocked country in the heart of Europe. Northern Austria contains the valley of the River Danube, which flows from Germany to the Black Sea, and the Vienna basin – Austria's main farming regions. Southern Austria contains ranges of the Alps, which reach their highest point at Grossglockner, at 3,797 m [12,457 ft] above sea level.

The climate of Austria is influenced both by westerly and easterly winds. The moist westerly winds bring rain and snow. They also moderate the temperatures. But dry easterly winds bring cold weather in winter and hot weather in summer.

POLITICS & ECONOMY Formerly part of the powerful monarchy of Austria-Hungary, which collapsed in 1918, Austria was annexed by Germany in 1938. After World War II, the Allies partitioned and occupied the country until 1955, when Austria became a neutral federal republic. Austria joined the European Union on 1 January 1995.

Austria is a prosperous country. It has plenty of hydroelectric power, as well as some oil, gas and coal reserves. The country's leading economic activity is manufacturing metals and metal products. Crops are grown on 18% of the land and another 24% is pasture. Dairy and livestock farming are the leading activities. Major crops include barley, potatoes, rye, sugar beet and wheat. Tourism is a major activity in this scenic country.

AREA 83,850 sq km [32,374 sq mls]
POPULATION 8,134,000
CAPITAL (POPULATION) Vienna (1,560,000)
GOVERNMENT Federal republic
ETHNIC GROUPS Austrian 93%, Yugoslav 2%, Turkish, German
LANGUAGES German (official)
RELIGIONS Christianity (Roman Catholic 78%, Protestant 6%), Islam
CURRENCY Euro; Schilling = 100 Groschen

AZERBAIJAN

GEOGRAPHY The Azerbaijani Republic is a country in the south-west of Asia, facing the Caspian Sea to the east. It includes an area called the Naxçivan Autonomous Republic, which is completely cut off from the rest of Azerbaijan by Armenian territory. The Caucasus Mountains border Russia in the north.

Azerbaijan has hot summers and cool winters, with low rainfall on the plains and much higher rainfall in the highlands.

POLITICS & ECONOMY After the Russian Revolution of 1917, attempts were made to form a Transcaucasian Federation made up of Armenia, Azerbaijan and Georgia. When this failed, Azerbaijanis set up an independent state. But Russian forces occupied the area in 1920. In 1922, the Communists set up a Transcaucasian Republic consisting of Armenia, Azerbaijan and Georgia under Russian control. In 1936, the three areas became separate Soviet Socialist Republics within the Soviet Union. In 1991, following the break-up of the Soviet Union, Azerbaijan became an independent nation. After independence, the country's economic progress was slow, partly because of the conflict with Armenia over the enclave of Nagorno-Karabakh, a region in Azerbaijan where the majority of people are Armenians. A cease-fire in 1994 left Armenia in control of about 20% of Azerbaijan's area, including Nagorno-Karabakh.

In the mid-1990s, the World Bank classified Azerbaijan as a 'lower-middle-income' economy. Yet by the late 1990s, the enormous oil reserves in the Baku area, on the Caspian Sea and in the sea itself, held out great promise for the future. Oil extraction and manufacturing, including oil refining and the production of chemicals, machinery and textiles, are now the most valuable activities.

AREA 86,600 sq km [33,436 sq mls]
POPULATION 7,856,000
CAPITAL (POPULATION) Baku (1,081,000)
GOVERNMENT Federal multiparty republic
ETHNIC GROUPS Azerbaijani 83%, Russian 6%, Armenian 6%, Lezgin, Avar, Ukrainian, Tatar
LANGUAGES Azerbaijani (official)
RELIGIONS Islam
CURRENCY Manat = 100 gopik

BAHAMAS

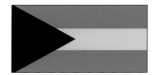

A coral-limestone archipelago off the coast of Florida, the Bahamas became independent from Britain in 1973, and has since developed strong ties with the United States. Tourism and banking are major activities. **AREA** 13,880 sq km [5,359 sq mls]; **POPULATION** 280,000; **CAPITAL** Nassau.

BAHRAIN

The Emirate of Bahrain, an island nation in the Gulf, became independent from the UK in 1971. Oil accounts for 80% of the country's exports. **AREA** 678 sq km [262 sq mls]; **POPULATION** 616,000; **CAPITAL** Manama.

BANGLADESH

GEOGRAPHY The People's Republic of Bangladesh is one of the world's most densely populated countries. Apart from hilly regions in the far north-east and south-east, most of the land is flat and covered by fertile alluvium spread over the land by the Ganges, Brahmaputra and Meghna rivers. These rivers overflow when they are swollen by the annual monsoon rains. Floods also occur along the coast, 575 km [357 mls] long, when cyclones (hurricanes) drive sea-water inland. Bangladesh has a tropical monsoon climate. Dry northerly winds blow in winter, but, in summer, moist winds from the south bring monsoon rains. Heavy monsoon rains cause floods. In 1998, about two-thirds of the entire country was submerged, causing great suffering.

POLITICS & ECONOMY In 1947, British India was partitioned between the mainly Hindu India and the Muslim Pakistan. Pakistan consisted of two parts, West and East Pakistan, which were separated by about 1,600 km [1,000 mls] of Indian territory. Differences developed between West and East Pakistan. In 1971, the East Pakistanis rebelled. After a nine-month civil war, they declared East Pakistan to be a separate nation named Bangladesh.

Bangladesh is one of the world's poorest countries. Its economy depends mainly on agriculture, which employs over half the population. Bangladesh is the world's fourth largest producer of rice.

AREA 144,000 sq km [55,598 sq mls]
POPULATION 125,000,000
CAPITAL (POPULATION) Dhaka (6,105,000)
GOVERNMENT Multiparty republic
ETHNIC GROUPS Bengali 98%, tribal groups
LANGUAGES Bengali, English (both official)
RELIGIONS Islam 87%, Hinduism 12%, Buddhism, Christianity
CURRENCY Taka = 100 paisas

BARBADOS

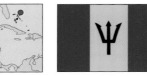

The most easterly Caribbean country, Barbados became independent from the UK in 1960. A densely populated island, Barbados is prosperous by comparison with most Caribbean countries. **AREA** 430 sq km [166 sq mls]; **POPULATION** 259,000; **CAPITAL** Bridgetown.

BELARUS

GEOGRAPHY The Republic of Belarus is a landlocked country in Eastern Europe. The land is low-lying and mostly flat. In the south, much of the land is marshy and this area contains Europe's largest marsh and peat bog, the Pripet Marshes.

The climate of Belarus is affected by both the moderating influence of the Baltic Sea and continental conditions to the east. The winters are cold and the summers warm.

POLITICS & ECONOMY In 1918, Belarus (White Russia) became an independent republic, but Russia invaded the country and, in 1919, a Communist state was set up. In 1922, Belarus became a founder republic of the Soviet Union. In 1991, after the break-up of the Soviet Union, Belarus again became an independent republic, though it retained ties with Russia through an organization called the Commonwealth of Independent States. In 1998, Belarus and Russia set up a 'union state', with plans to have a common currency, a customs union, and common foreign and defence policies. But any surrender of sovereignty was not anticipated.

The World Bank classifies Belarus as an 'upper-middle-income' economy. Like other former republics of the Soviet Union, it faces many problems in turning from Communism to a free-market economy.

AREA 297,600 sq km [80,154 sq mls]
POPULATION 10,409,000
CAPITAL (POPULATION) Minsk (1,700,000)
GOVERNMENT Multiparty republic
ETHNIC GROUPS Belarussian 80%, Russian, Polish
LANGUAGES Belarussian, Russian (both official)
RELIGIONS Christianity (mainly Belarussian Orthodox, with Roman Catholics in the west)
CURRENCY Belarussian rouble = 100 kopecks

BELGIUM

GEOGRAPHY The Kingdom of Belgium is a densely populated country in western Europe. Behind the coastline on the North Sea, which is 63 km [39 mls] long, lie its coastal plains. Central Belgium consists of low plateaux and the only highland region is the Ardennes in the south-east.

Belgium has a cool, temperate climate. Moist winds from the Atlantic Ocean bring fairly heavy rain, especially in the Ardennes. In January and February much snow falls on the Ardennes.

POLITICS & ECONOMY In 1815, Belgium and the Netherlands united as the 'low countries', but Belgium became independent in 1830. Belgium's economy was weakened by the two World Wars, but, from 1945, the country recovered quickly, first through collaboration with the Netherlands and Luxembourg, which formed a customs union called Benelux, and later through its membership of the European Union.

A central political problem in Belgium has been the tension between the Dutch-speaking Flemings and the French-speaking Walloons. In the 1970s, the government divided the country into three economic regions: Dutch-speaking Flanders, French-speaking Wallonia and bilingual Brussels. In 1993, Belgium adopted a federal system of government. Each of the regions now has its own parliament, which is responsible for local matters. Elections under this new system were held in 1995.

Belgium is a major trading nation, with a highly developed economy. Its main products include chemicals, processed food and steel. The textile industry is also important and has existed since medieval times in the Belgium province of Flanders.

Agriculture employs only 3% of the people, but Belgian farmers produce most of the food needed by the people. Barley and wheat are the chief crops, followed by flax, hops, potatoes and sugar beet, but the most valuable activities are dairy farming and livestock rearing.

> **AREA** 30,510 sq km [11,780 sq mls]
> **POPULATION** 10,175,000
> **CAPITAL (POPULATION)** Brussels (952,000)
> **GOVERNMENT** Federal constitutional monarchy
> **ETHNIC GROUPS** Belgian 91% (Fleming 55%, Walloon 32%), Italian, French, Dutch, Turkish, Moroccan
> **LANGUAGES** Dutch, French, German (all official)
> **RELIGIONS** Christianity (Roman Catholic 90%), Islam
> **CURRENCY** Euro; Belgian franc = 100 centimes

BELIZE

GEOGRAPHY Behind the swampy coastal plain in the south, the land rises to the low Maya Mountains, which reach a height of 1,120 m [3,674 ft] at Victoria Peak. The north is mostly low-lying and swampy.

Belize has a tropical, humid climate. Temperatures are high throughout the year and the average yearly rainfall ranges from 1,300 mm [51 in] in the north to over 3,800 mm [150 in] in the south.

POLITICS & ECONOMY From 1862, Belize (then called British Honduras) was a British colony. Full independence was achieved in 1981, but Guatemala, which had claimed the area since the early 19th century, opposed Belize's independence and British troops remained to prevent a possible invasion. In 1983, Guatemala reduced its claim to the southern fifth of Belize. Improved relations in the early 1990s led Guatemala to recognize Belize's independence and, in 1992, Britain agreed to withdraw its troops from the country.

The World Bank classifies Belize as a 'lower-middle-income' developing country. Its economy is based on agriculture and sugar cane is the chief commercial crop and export. Other crops include bananas, beans, citrus fruits, maize and rice. Forestry, fishing and tourism are other important activities.

> **AREA** 22,960 sq km [8,865 sq mls]
> **POPULATION** 230,000
> **CAPITAL (POPULATION)** Belmopan (44,000)
> **GOVERNMENT** Constitutional monarchy
> **ETHNIC GROUPS** Mestizo (Spanish-Indian) 44%, Creole (mainly African American) 30%, Mayan Indian 11%, Garifuna (Black-Carib Indian) 7%, White 4%, East Indian 3%
> **LANGUAGES** English (official), Creole, Spanish
> **RELIGIONS** Christianity (Roman Catholic 58%, Protestant 29%), Hinduism 2%
> **CURRENCY** Belize dollar = 100 cents

BENIN

GEOGRAPHY The Republic of Benin is one of Africa's smallest countries. It extends north–south for about 620 km [390 mls]. Lagoons line the short coastline, and the country has no natural harbours.

Benin has a hot, wet climate. The average annual temperature on the coast is about 25°C [77°F], and the average rainfall is about 1,330 mm [52 in]. The inland plains are wetter than the coast.

POLITICS & ECONOMY After slavery was ended in the 19th century, the French began to gain influence in the area. Benin became self-governing in 1958 and fully independent in 1960. After much instability and many changes of government, a military group took over in 1972. The country, renamed Benin in 1975, became a one-party socialist state. Socialism was abandoned in 1989, and multiparty elections were held in 1991 and 1996.

Benin is a developing country. About 70% of the people earn their living by farming, though many remain at subsistence level. The chief exports include cotton, petroleum and palm products.

> **AREA** 112,620 sq km [43,483 sq mls]
> **POPULATION** 6,101,000
> **CAPITAL (POPULATION)** Porto-Novo (179,000)
> **GOVERNMENT** Multiparty republic
> **ETHNIC GROUPS** Fon, Adja, Bariba, Yoruba, Fulani
> **LANGUAGES** French (official), Fon, Adja, Yoruba
> **RELIGIONS** Traditional beliefs 60%, Christianity 23%, Islam 15%
> **CURRENCY** CFA franc = 100 centimes

BERMUDA

A group of about 150 small islands situated 920 km [570 mls] east of the USA. Bermuda remains Britain's oldest overseas territory, but it has a long tradition of self-government. **AREA** 53 sq km [20 sq mls]; **POPULATION** 62,000; **CAPITAL** Hamilton.

BHUTAN

GEOGRAPHY A mountainous, isolated Himalayan country located between India and Tibet. The climate is similar to that of Nepal, being dependent on altitude and affected by monsoonal winds.

POLITICS & ECONOMY The monarch of Bhutan is head of both state and government and this predominantly Buddhist country remains, even in the Asian context, both conservative and poor. Bhutan is the world's most 'rural' country, with over 90% of the population dependent on agriculture and only 6% living in towns.

> **AREA** 47,000 sq km [18,147 sq mls]
> **POPULATION** 1,908,000
> **CAPITAL (POPULATION)** Thimphu [30,000]
> **GOVERNMENT** Constitutional monarchy
> **ETHNIC GROUPS** Bhutanese, Nepali
> **LANGUAGES** Dzongkha (official)
> **RELIGIONS** Buddhism 75%, Hindu
> **CURRENCY** Ngultrum = 100 chetrum

BOLIVIA

GEOGRAPHY The Republic of Bolivia is a land-locked country which straddles the Andes Mountains in central South America. The Andes rise to a height of 6,542 m [21,464 ft] at Nevado Sajama in the west.

About 40% of Bolivians live on a high plateau called the Altiplano in the Andean region, while the sparsely populated east is essentially a vast lowland plain.

The Bolivian climate is greatly affected by altitude, with the Andean peaks permanently snow-covered, while the eastern plains remain hot and humid.

POLITICS & ECONOMY American Indians have lived in Bolivia for at least 10,000 years. The main groups today are the Aymara and Quechua people.

In the last 50 years, Bolivia, an independent country since 1825, has been ruled by a succession of civilian and military governments, which violated human rights. Constitutional government was restored in 1982, but Bolivia faced many problems, including high inflation and poverty.

Bolivia is one of the poorest countries in South America. It has several natural resources, including tin, silver and natural gas, but the chief activity is agriculture, which employs 47% of the people. But experts believe that the main export may be coca, which is used to make the drug cocaine. Coca is exported illegally. The government is trying to stamp out this growing industry.

> **AREA** 1,098,580 sq km [424,162 sq mls]
> **POPULATION** 7,826,000
> **CAPITAL (POPULATION)** La Paz (1,126,000)
> **GOVERNMENT** Multiparty republic
> **ETHNIC GROUPS** Mestizo 31%, Quechua 25%, Aymara 17%, White 15%
> **LANGUAGES** Spanish, Aymara, Quechua (all official)
> **RELIGIONS** Christianity (Roman Catholic 94%)
> **CURRENCY** Boliviano = 100 centavos

BOSNIA-HERZEGOVINA

GEOGRAPHY The Republic of Bosnia-Herzegovina is one of the five republics to emerge from the former Federal People's Republic of Yugoslavia. Much of the country is mountainous or hilly, with an arid limestone plateau in the south-west. The River Sava, which forms most of the northern border with Croatia, is a tributary of the River Danube. Because of the country's odd shape, the coastline is limited to a short stretch of 20 km [13 mls] on the Adriatic coast.

A Mediterranean climate, with dry, sunny summers and moist, mild winters, prevails only near the coast. Inland, the weather becomes more severe, with hot, dry summers and bitterly cold, snowy winters.

POLITICS & ECONOMY In 1918, Bosnia-Herzegovina became part of the Kingdom of the Serbs, Croats and Slovenes, which was renamed Yugoslavia in 1929. Germany occupied the area during World War II (1939–45). From 1945, Communist governments ruled Yugoslavia as a federation containing six republics, one of which was Bosnia-Herzegovina. In the 1980s, the country faced problems as Communist policies proved unsuccessful and differences arose between ethnic groups.

In 1990, free elections were held in Bosnia-Herzegovina and the non-Communists won a majority. A Muslim, Alija Izetbegovic, was elected president. In 1991, Croatia and Slovenia, other parts of the former Yugoslavia, declared themselves independent. In 1992, Bosnia-Herzegovina held a vote on independence. Most Bosnian Serbs boycotted the vote, while the Muslims and Bosnian Croats voted in favour. Many Bosnian Serbs, opposed to independence, started a war against the non-Serbs. They soon occupied more than two-thirds of the land. The Bosnian Serbs were accused of 'ethnic cleansing' – that is, the killing or expulsion of other ethnic groups from Serb-occupied areas. The war was later extended when Croat forces seized other parts of the country.

In 1995, the warring parties agreed to a solution to the conflict. This involved keeping the present boundaries of Bosnia-Herzegovina, but dividing it into two self-governing provinces, one Bosnian Serb and the other Muslim-Croat, under a central, unified, multi-ethnic government. Elections were held in 1996 under this new arrangement.

The economy of Bosnia-Herzegovina, the least developed of the six republics of the former Yugoslavia apart from Macedonia, was shattered by the war in the early 1990s. Before the war, manufactures were the main exports, including electrical equipment, machinery and transport equipment, and textiles. Farm products include fruits, maize, tobacco, vegetables and wheat, but the country has to import food.

AREA 51,129 sq km [19,745 sq mls]
POPULATION 3,366,000
CAPITAL (POPULATION) Sarajevo (526,000)
GOVERNMENT Transitional
ETHNIC GROUPS Muslim 49%, Serb 31%, Croat 17%
LANGUAGES Serbo-Croatian
RELIGIONS Islam 40%, Christianity (Serbian Orthodox 31%, Roman Catholic 15%, Protestant 4%)
CURRENCY Convertible mark = 100 paras

BOTSWANA

GEOGRAPHY The Republic of Botswana is a landlocked country in southern Africa. The Kalahari, a semi-desert area covered mostly by grasses and thorn scrub, covers much of the country. Most of the south has no permanent streams. But large depressions in the north are inland drainage basins. In one of them, the Okavango River, which rises in Angola, forms a large, swampy delta.

Temperatures are high in the summer months (October to April), but the winter months are much cooler. In winter, night-time temperatures sometimes drop below freezing point. The average annual rainfall ranges from over 400 mm [16 in] in the east to less than 200 mm [8 in] in the south-west.

POLITICS & ECONOMY The earliest inhabitants of the region were the San, who are also called Bushmen. They had a nomadic way of life, hunting wild animals and collecting wild plant foods.

Britain ruled the area as the Bechuanaland Protectorate between 1885 and 1966. When the country became independent, it adopted the name of Botswana. Since then, unlike many African countries, Botswana has been a stable multiparty democracy.

In 1966, Botswana was one of Africa's poorest countries, depending on meat and live cattle for its exports. But the discovery of minerals, including coal, cobalt, copper, diamonds and nickel, has boosted the economy. However, more than 40% of the people still work as farmers, raising cattle and growing crops, such as millet, maize, beans and vegetables. Botswana also has some food-processing plants and factories producing such things as soap and textiles.

AREA 581,730 sq km [224,606 sq mls]
POPULATION 1,448,000
CAPITAL (POPULATION) Gaborone (133,000)
GOVERNMENT Multiparty republic
ETHNIC GROUPS Tswana 75%, Shona 12%, San (Bushmen) 3%
LANGUAGES English (official), Setswana
RELIGIONS Traditional beliefs 49%, Christianity 50%
CURRENCY Pula = 100 thebe

BRAZIL

GEOGRAPHY The Federative Republic of Brazil is the world's fifth largest country. It contains three main regions. The Amazon basin in the north covers more than half of Brazil. The Amazon, the world's second longest river, has a far greater volume than any other river. The second region, the north-east, consists of a coastal plain and the *sertão*, which is the name for the inland plateaux and hill country. The main river in this region is the São Francisco.

The third region is made up of the plateaux in the south-east. This region, which covers about a quarter of the country, is the most developed and densely populated part of Brazil. Its main river is the Paraná, which flows south through Argentina.

Manaus has high temperatures all through the year. The rainfall is heavy, though the period from June to September is drier than the rest of the year. The capital, Brasília, and the city Rio de Janeiro also have tropical climates, with much more marked dry seasons than Manaus. The far south has a temperate climate. The north-eastern interior is the driest region, with an average annual rainfall of only 250 mm [10 in] in places. The rainfall is also unreliable and severe droughts are common in this region.

POLITICS & ECONOMY The Portuguese explorer Pedro Alvarez Cabral claimed Brazil for Portugal in 1500. With Spain occupied in western South America, the Portuguese began to develop their colony, which was more than 90 times as big as Portugal. To do this, they enslaved many local Amerindian people and introduced about 4 million African slaves to work on their plantations and in the mines. Brazil declared itself an independent empire in 1822 and a republic in 1889. From the 1930s, Brazil faced many problems, including corruption and spells of dictatorial military government. Civilian government was restored in 1985 and Brazil adopted a new constitution in 1988.

The United Nations has described Brazil as a 'Rapidly Industrializing Country', or RIC. Its total volume of production is one of the largest in the world. But many people, including poor farmers and residents of the *favelas* (city slums), do not share in the country's fast economic growth. Widespread poverty, together with high inflation and unemployment, cause political problems.

By the early 1990s, industry was the most valuable activity, employing 25% of the people. Brazil is among the world's top producers of bauxite, chrome, diamonds, gold, iron ore, manganese and tin. It is also a major manufacturing country. Its products include aircraft, cars, chemicals, processed food, including raw sugar, iron and steel, paper and textiles.

Brazil is one of the world's leading farming countries and agriculture employs 28% of the people. Coffee is a major export. Other leading products include bananas, citrus fruits, cocoa, maize, rice, soya beans and sugar cane. Brazil is also the top producer of eggs, meat and milk in South America.

Forestry is a major industry, though many people fear that the exploitation of the rainforests, with 1.5% to 4% of Brazil's forest being destroyed every year, is a disaster for the entire world.

AREA 8,511,970 sq km [3,286,472 sq mls]
POPULATION 170,000,000
CAPITAL (POPULATION) Brasília (1,596,000)
GOVERNMENT Federal republic
ETHNIC GROUPS White 53%, Mulatto 22%, Mestizo 12%, African American 11%, Japanese 1%, Amerindian 0.1%
LANGUAGES Portuguese (official)
RELIGIONS Christianity (Roman Catholic 88%)
CURRENCY Real = 100 centavos

BRUNEI

The Islamic Sultanate of Brunei, a British protectorate until 1984, lies on the north coast of Borneo. The climate is tropical and rainforests cover large areas. Brunei is a prosperous country because of its oil and natural gas production, and the Sultan is said to be among the world's richest men. **AREA** 5,770 sq km [2,228 sq mls]; **POPULATION** 315,000; **CAPITAL** Bandar Seri Begawan.

BURUNDI

BULGARIA

GEOGRAPHY The Republic of Bulgaria is a country in the Balkan peninsula, facing the Black Sea in the east. The heart of Bulgaria is mountainous. The main ranges are the Balkan Mountains in the centre and the Rhodope (or Rhodopi) Mountains in the south.

Summers are hot and winters are cold, though seldom severe. The rainfall is moderate throughout the year.

POLITICS & ECONOMY Ottoman Turks ruled Bulgaria from 1396 and ethnic Turks still form a sizeable minority in the country. In 1879, Bulgaria became a monarchy, and in 1908 it became fully independent. Bulgaria was an ally of Germany in World War I (1914–18) and again in World War II (1939–45). In 1944, Soviet troops invaded Bulgaria and, after the war, the monarchy was abolished and the country became a Communist ally of the Soviet Union. In the late 1980s, reforms in the Soviet Union led Bulgaria's government to introduce a multiparty system in 1990. A non-Communist government was elected in 1991, the first free elections in 44 years. Since 1991, Bulgaria has faced problems in trying to transform the old Communist economy into a new one based on private enterprise.

According to the World Bank, Bulgaria in the 1990s was a 'lower-middle-income' developing country. Bulgaria has some deposits of minerals, including brown coal, manganese and iron ore. But manufacturing is the leading economic activity, though problems arose in the early 1990s, because much industrial technology is outdated. The main products are chemicals, processed foods, metal products, machinery and textiles. Manufactures are the leading exports. Bulgaria trades mainly with countries in Eastern Europe.

AREA 110,910 sq km [42,822 sq mls]
POPULATION 8,240,000
CAPITAL (POPULATION) Sofia (1,117,000)
GOVERNMENT Multiparty republic
ETHNIC GROUPS Bulgarian 86%, Turkish 10%, Gypsy 3%, Macedonian, Armenian, Romanian, Greek
LANGUAGES Bulgarian (official), Turkish
RELIGIONS Christianity (Eastern Orthodox 87%), Islam 13%
CURRENCY Lev = 100 stotinki

BURKINA FASO

GEOGRAPHY The Democratic People's Republic of Burkina Faso is a landlocked country, a little larger than the United Kingdom, in West Africa. But Burkina Faso has only one-sixth of the population of the UK. The country consists of a plateau, between about 300 m and 700 m [650 ft to 2,300 ft] above sea level. The plateau is cut by several rivers.

The capital city, Ouagadougou, in central Burkina Faso, has high temperatures throughout the year. Most of the rain falls between May and September, but the rainfall is erratic and droughts are common.

POLITICS & ECONOMY The people of Burkina Faso are divided into two main groups. The Voltaic group includes the Mossi, who form the largest single group, and the Bobo. The French conquered the Mossi capital of Ouagadougou in 1897 and they made the area a protectorate. In 1919, the area became a French colony called Upper Volta. After independence in 1960, Upper Volta became a one-party state. But it was unstable – military groups seized power several times and a number of political killings took place.

In 1984, the country's name was changed to Burkina Faso. Elections were held in 1991 – for the first time in more than ten years – but the military kept an important role in the government.

Burkina Faso is one of the world's 20 poorest countries and has become very dependent on foreign aid. Most of Burkina Faso is dry with thin soils. The country's main food crops are beans, maize, millet, rice and sorghum. Cotton, groundnuts and shea nuts, whose seeds produce a fat used to make cooking oil and soap, are grown for sale abroad. Livestock are also an important export.

The country has few resources and manufacturing is on a small scale. There are some deposits of manganese, zinc, lead and nickel in the north of the country, but there is not yet a good enough transport system there. Many young men seek jobs abroad in Ghana and Ivory Coast. The money they send home to their families is important to the country's economy.

AREA 274,200 sq km [105,869 sq mls]
POPULATION 11,266,000
CAPITAL (POPULATION) Ouagadougou (690,000)
GOVERNMENT Multiparty republic
ETHNIC GROUPS Mossi 48%, Mande 9%, Fulani 8%, Bobo 7%
LANGUAGES French (official), Mossi, Fulani
RELIGIONS Traditional beliefs 45%, Islam 43%, Christianity 12%
CURRENCY CFA franc = 100 centimes

BURMA (MYANMAR)

GEOGRAPHY The Union of Burma is now officially known as the Union of Myanmar; its name was changed in 1989. Mountains border the country in the east and west, with the highest mountains in the north. Burma's highest mountain is Hkakabo Razi, which is 5,881 m [19,294 ft] high. Between these ranges is central Burma, which contains the fertile valleys of the Irrawaddy and Sittang rivers. The Irrawaddy delta on the Bay of Bengal is one of the world's leading rice-growing areas. Burma also includes the long Tenasserim coast in the south-east.

Burma has a tropical monsoon climate. There are three seasons. The rainy season runs from late May to mid-October. A cool, dry season follows, between late October and the middle part of February. The hot season lasts from late February to mid-May, though temperatures remain high during the humid rainy season.

POLITICS & ECONOMY Many groups settled in Burma in ancient times. Some, called the hill peoples, live in remote mountain areas where they have retained their own cultures. The ancestors of the country's main ethnic group today, the Burmese, arrived in the 9th century AD.

Britain conquered Burma in the 19th century and made it a province of British India. But, in 1937, the British granted Burma limited self-government. Japan conquered Burma in 1942, but the Japanese were driven out in 1945. Burma became a fully independent country in 1948.

Revolts by Communists and various hill people led to instability in the 1950s. In 1962, Burma became a military dictatorship and, in 1974, a one-party state. Attempts to control minority liberation movements and the opium trade led to repressive rule. The National League for Democracy led by Aung San Suu Kyi won the elections in 1990, but the military ignored the result and continued their repressive rule. They earned Burma the reputation for having one of the world's worst records on human rights. Burma's internal political problems have helped to make it one of the world's poorest countries. Its admission to ASEAN (Association of South-east Asian Nations) in 1997 may have implied regional recognition of the regime, but the European Union continues to voice its concern over human rights abuses.

Agriculture is the main activity, employing 64% of the people. The chief crop is rice. Maize, pulses, oilseeds and sugar cane are other major products. Forestry is important. Teak and rice together make up about two-thirds of the total value of the exports. Burma has many mineral resources, though they are mostly undeveloped, but the country is famous for its precious stones, especially rubies. Manufacturing is mostly on a small scale.

AREA 676,577 sq km [261,228 sq mls]
POPULATION 47,305,000
CAPITAL (POPULATION) Rangoon (2,513,000)
GOVERNMENT Military regime
ETHNIC GROUPS Burman 69%, Shan 9%, Karen 6%, Rakhine 5%, Mon 2%, Kachin 1%
LANGUAGES Burmese (official), Shan, Karen, Rakhine, Mon, Kachin, English, Chin
RELIGIONS Buddhism 89%, Christianity, Islam
CURRENCY Kyat = 100 pyas

BURUNDI

GEOGRAPHY The Republic of Burundi is the fifth smallest country in mainland Africa. It is also the second most densely populated after its northern neighbour, Rwanda. Part of the Great African Rift Valley, which runs throughout eastern Africa into south-western Asia, lies in western Burundi. It includes part of Lake Tanganyika.

Bujumbura, the capital city, lies on the shore of Lake Tanganyika. It has a warm climate. A dry season occurs from June to September, but the other months are fairly rainy. The mountains and plateaux to the east are cooler and wetter, but the rainfall generally decreases to the east.

POLITICS & ECONOMY The Twa, a pygmy people, were the first known inhabitants of Burundi. About 1,000 years ago, the Hutu, a people who speak a Bantu language, gradually began to settle the area, pushing the Twa into remote areas.

From the 15th century, the Tutsi, a cattle-owning people from the north-east, gradually took over the country. The Hutu, although greatly outnumbering the Tutsi, were forced to serve the Tutsi overlords.

Germany conquered the area that is now Burundi and Rwanda in the late 1890s. The area, called

Ruanda-Urundi, was taken by Belgium during World War I (1914–18). In 1961, the people of Urundi voted to become a monarchy, while the people of Ruanda voted to become a republic. The two territories became fully independent as Burundi and Rwanda in 1962. After 1962, the rivalries between the Hutu and Tutsi led to periodic outbreaks of fighting. The Tutsi monarchy was ended in 1966 and Burundi became a republic. Instability continued with coups in 1976, 1987, 1993 and 1996, with periodic massacres of thousands of people as Tutsis and Hutus fought for power.

Burundi is one of the world's ten poorest countries. About 92% of the people are farmers, who mostly grow little more than they need to feed their own families. The main food crops are beans, cassava, maize and sweet potatoes. Cattle, goats and sheep are raised, while fish are an important supplement to people's diets. However, Burundi has to import food.

> **AREA** 27,830 sq km [10,745 sq mls]
> **POPULATION** 5,531,000
> **CAPITAL (POPULATION)** Bujumbura (300,000)
> **GOVERNMENT** Republic
> **ETHNIC GROUPS** Hutu 85%, Tutsi 14%, Twa (pygmy) 1%
> **LANGUAGES** French and Kirundi (both official)
> **RELIGIONS** Christianity 85% (Roman Catholic 78%), traditional beliefs 13%
> **CURRENCY** Burundi franc = 100 centimes

CAMBODIA

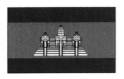

GEOGRAPHY The Kingdom of Cambodia is a country in South-east Asia. Low mountains border the country except in the south-east. But most of Cambodia consists of plains drained by the River Mekong, which enters Cambodia from Laos in the north and exits through Vietnam in the south-east. The north-west contains Tonlé Sap (or Great Lake). In the dry season, this lake drains into the River Mekong. But in the wet season, the level of the Mekong rises and water flows in the opposite direction from the river into Tonlé Sap – the lake then becomes the largest freshwater lake in Asia.

Cambodia has a tropical monsoon climate, with high temperatures all through the year. The dry season, when winds blow from the north or north-east, runs from November to April. During the rainy season, from May to October, moist winds blow from the south or south-east. The high humidity and heat often make conditions unpleasant. The rainfall is heaviest near the coast, and rather lower inland.

POLITICS & ECONOMY From 802 to 1432, the Khmer people ruled a great empire, which reached its peak in the 12th century. The Khmer capital was at Angkor. The Hindu stone temples built there and at nearby Angkor Wat form the world's largest group of religious buildings. France ruled the country between 1863 and 1954, when the country became an independent monarchy. But the monarchy was abolished in 1970 and Cambodia became a republic.

In 1970, US and South Vietnamese troops entered Cambodia but left after destroying North Vietnamese Communist camps in the east. The country became involved in the Vietnamese War, and then in a civil war as Cambodian Communists of the Khmer Rouge organization fought for power. The Khmer Rouge took over Cambodia in 1975 and launched a reign of terror in which between 1 million and 2.5 million people were killed. In 1979, Vietnamese and Cambodian troops overthrew the Khmer Rouge government. But fighting continued between several factions. Vietnam withdrew in 1989, and in 1991 Prince Sihanouk was recognized as head of state. Elections were held in May 1993, and in September 1993 the monarchy was restored. Sihanouk again became king. In 1997, the prime minister, Prince Norodom Ranariddh, was deposed, so ending four years of democratic rule. This led to Cambodia's application to join the Association of South-east Asian Nations to be put on hold.

Cambodia is a poor country whose economy has been wrecked by war. Until the 1970s, the country's farmers produced most of the food needed by the people. But by 1986, it was only able to supply 80% of its needs. Farming is the main activity and rice, rubber and maize are major products. Manufacturing is almost non-existent, apart from rubber processing and a few factories producing items for sale in Cambodia.

> **AREA** 181,040 sq km [69,900 sq mls]
> **POPULATION** 11,340,000
> **CAPITAL (POPULATION)** Phnom Penh (920,000)
> **GOVERNMENT** Constitutional monarchy
> **ETHNIC GROUPS** Khmer 94%, Chinese 3%, Cham 2%, Thai, Lao, Kola, Vietnamese
> **LANGUAGES** Khmer (official)
> **RELIGIONS** Buddhism 88%, Islam 2%
> **CURRENCY** Riel = 100 sen

CAMEROON

GEOGRAPHY The Republic of Cameroon in West Africa got its name from the Portuguese word *camarões*, or prawns. This name was used by Portuguese explorers who fished for prawns along the coast. Behind the narrow coastal plains on the Gulf of Guinea, the land rises to a series of plateaux, with a mountainous region in the south-west where the volcano Mount Cameroon is situated. In the north, the land slopes down towards the Lake Chad basin.

The rainfall is heavy, especially in the highlands. The rainiest months near the coast are June to September. The rainfall decreases to the north and the far north has a hot, dry climate. Temperatures are high on the coast, whereas the inland plateaux are cooler.

POLITICS & ECONOMY Germany lost Cameroon during World War I (1914–18). The country was then divided into two parts, one ruled by Britain and the other by France. In 1960, French Cameroon became the independent Cameroon Republic. In 1961, after a vote in British Cameroon, part of the territory joined the Cameroon Republic to become the Federal Republic of Cameroon. The other part joined Nigeria. In 1972, Cameroon became a unitary state called the United Republic of Cameroon. It adopted the name Republic of Cameroon in 1984, but the country had two official languages. In 1995, partly to placate English-speaking people, Cameroon became the 52nd member of the Commonwealth.

Like most countries in tropical Africa, Cameroon's economy is based on agriculture, which employs 73% of the people. The chief food crops include cassava, maize, millet, sweet potatoes and yams. The country also has plantations to produce such crops as cocoa and coffee for export.

Cameroon is fortunate in having some oil, the country's chief export, and bauxite. Although Cameroon has few manufacturing and processing industries, its mineral exports and its self-sufficiency in food production make it one of the better-off countries in tropical Africa.

> **AREA** 475,440 sq km [183,567 sq mls]
> **POPULATION** 15,029,000
> **CAPITAL (POPULATION)** Yaoundé (750,000)
> **GOVERNMENT** Multiparty republic
> **ETHNIC GROUPS** Fang 20%, Bamileke and Bamum 19%, Duala, Luanda and Basa 15%, Fulani 10%
> **LANGUAGES** French and English (both official)
> **RELIGIONS** Christianity 53%, traditional beliefs 25%, Islam 22%
> **CURRENCY** CFA franc = 100 centimes

CANADA

GEOGRAPHY Canada is the world's second largest country after Russia. It is thinly populated, however, with much of the land too cold or too mountainous for human settlement. Most Canadians live within 300 km [186 mls] of the southern border.

Western Canada is rugged. It includes the Pacific ranges and the mighty Rocky Mountains. East of the Rockies are the interior plains. In the north lie the bleak Arctic islands, while to the south lie the densely populated lowlands around lakes Erie and Ontario and in the St Lawrence River valley.

Canada has a cold climate. In winter, temperatures fall below freezing point throughout most of Canada. But the south-western coast has a relatively mild climate. Along the Arctic Circle, mean temperatures are below freezing for seven months a year.

Western and south-eastern Canada experience high rainfall, but the prairies are dry with 250 mm to 500 mm [10 in to 20 in] of rain every year.

POLITICS & ECONOMY Canada's first people, the ancestors of the Native Americans, or Indians, arrived in North America from Asia around 40,000 years ago. Later arrivals were the Inuit (Eskimos), who also came from Asia. Europeans reached the Canadian coast in 1497 and a race began between Britain and France for control of the territory.

France gained an initial advantage, and the French founded Québec in 1608. But the British later occupied eastern Canada. In 1867, Britain passed the British North America Act, which set up the Dominion of Canada, which was made up of Québec, Ontario, Nova Scotia and New Brunswick. Other areas were added, the last being Newfoundland in 1949. Canada fought alongside Britain in both World Wars and many Canadians feel close ties with Britain. Canada is a constitutional monarchy. The head of state is Queen Elizabeth II, though the country is governed by a prime minister, a cabinet and an elected, two-chamber parliament.

Rivalries between French- and English-speaking Canadians continue. In 1995, Québeckers voted against a move to make Québec a sovereign state. The majority was less than 1% and this issue seems unlikely to disappear. Another problem concerns the future of the Native Americans, who would like to have more say in the running of their own affairs. To this end, a new territory, Nunavut, was created for the Inuit population in 1999. It occupies the eastern part of Northern Territories.

Canada is a highly developed and prosperous country. Although farmland covers only 8% of the country, Canadian farms are highly productive. Canada is one of the world's leading producers of barley, wheat, meat and milk. Forestry and fishing are other important industries. It is rich in natural resources, especially oil and natural gas, and is a major exporter of minerals. The country also produces copper, gold, iron ore, uranium and zinc. Manufacturing is highly developed, especially in the cities where 77% of the people live. Canada has many factories that process farm and mineral products. It also produces cars, chemicals, electronic goods, machinery, paper and timber products.

AREA 9,976,140 sq km [3,851,788 sq mls]
POPULATION 30,675,000
CAPITAL (POPULATION) Ottawa (1,010,000)
GOVERNMENT Federal multiparty constitutional monarchy
ETHNIC GROUPS British 34%, French 26%, German 4%, Italian 3%, Ukrainian 2%, Native American (Amerindian/Inuit) 1.5%, Chinese
LANGUAGES English and French (both official)
RELIGIONS Christianity (Roman Catholic 47%, Protestant 41%), Judaism, Islam, Hinduism
CURRENCY Canadian dollar = 100 cents

CAPE VERDE

Cape Verde consists of ten large and five small islands, and is situated 560 km [350 mls] west of Dakar in Senegal. The islands have a tropical climate, with high temperatures all year round. Cape Verde became independent from Portugal in 1975 and is rated as a 'low-income' developing country by the World Bank. AREA 4,030 sq km [1,556 sq mls]; POPULATION 399,000; CAPITAL Praia.

CAYMAN ISLANDS

The Cayman Islands are an overseas territory of the UK, consisting of three low-lying islands. Financial services are the main economic activity and the islands offer a secret tax haven to many companies and banks. AREA 259 sq km [100 sq mls]; POPULATION 35,000; CAPITAL George Town.

CENTRAL AFRICAN REPUBLIC

GEOGRAPHY The Central African Republic is a remote, landlocked country in the heart of Africa. It consists mostly of a plateau lying between 600 m and 800 m [1,970 ft to 2,620 ft] above sea level. The Ubangi drains the south, while the Chari (or Shari)

River flows from the north to the Lake Chad basin.

Bangui, the capital, lies in the south-west of the country on the Ubangi River. The climate is warm throughout the year, with average yearly rainfall totalling 1,574 mm [62 in]. The north is drier, with an average yearly rainfall of about 800 mm [31 in].

POLITICS & ECONOMY France set up an outpost at Bangui in 1899 and ruled the country as a colony from 1894. Known as Ubangi-Shari, the country was ruled by France as part of French Equatorial Africa until it gained independence in 1960.

Central African Republic became a one-party state in 1962, but army officers seized power in 1966. The head of the army, Jean-Bedel Bokassa, made himself emperor in 1976. The country was renamed the Central African Empire, but after a brutal and tyrannical reign, Bokassa was overthrown by a military group in 1979. As a result, the monarchy was abolished and the country again became a republic.

The country adopted a new, multiparty constitution in 1991. Elections were held in 1993. An army rebellion was put down in 1996 with help from French troops.

The World Bank classifies Central African Republic as a 'low-income' developing country. Over 80% of the people are farmers, and most of them produce little more than they need to feed their families. The main crops are bananas, maize, manioc, millet and yams. Coffee, cotton, timber and tobacco are produced for export, mainly on commercial plantations. The country's development has been impeded by its remote position, its poor transport system and its untrained workforce. The country depends heavily on aid, especially from France.

AREA 622,980 sq km [240,533 sq mls]
POPULATION 3,376,000
CAPITAL (POPULATION) Bangui (706,000)
GOVERNMENT Multiparty republic
ETHNIC GROUPS Banda 29%, Baya 25%, Ngbandi 11%, Azande 10%, Sara 7%, Mbaka 4%
LANGUAGES French and Sango (both official)
RELIGIONS Traditional beliefs 57%, Christianity 35%, Islam 8%
CURRENCY CFA franc = 100 centimes

CHAD

GEOGRAPHY The Republic of Chad is a landlocked country in north-central Africa. It is Africa's fifth largest country and is more than twice as big as France, the country which once ruled it as a colony.

Ndjamena in central Chad has a hot, tropical climate, with a marked dry season from November to April. The south of the country is wetter, with an average yearly rainfall of around 1,000 mm [39 in]. The burning-hot desert in the north has an average yearly rainfall of less than 130 mm [5 in].

POLITICS & ECONOMY Chad straddles two worlds. The north is populated by Muslim Arab and Berber peoples, while black Africans, who follow traditional beliefs or who have converted to Christianity, live in the south.

French explorers were active in the area in the late 19th century. France finally made Chad a colony in 1902. After becoming independent in 1960, Chad has been hit by ethnic conflict. In the 1970s, civil war, frequent coups and intervention in the north by Libya retarded the country's economic development. Chad

and Libya agreed a truce in 1987 and, in 1994, the International Court of Justice ruled that Libya had no claim on the Aozou Strip in the far north.

Hit by drought and civil war, Chad is one of the world's poorest countries. Farming, fishing and livestock raising employ 83% of the people. Groundnuts, millet, rice and sorghum are major food crops in the wetter south, but the most valuable crop in export terms is cotton. The country has few natural resources and very few manufacturing industries.

AREA 1,284,000 sq km [495,752 sq mls]
POPULATION 7,360,000
CAPITAL (POPULATION) Ndjaména (530,000)
GOVERNMENT Transitional
ETHNIC GROUPS Bagirmi, Kreish and Sara 31%, Sudanic Arab 26%, Teda 7%, Mbum 6%
LANGUAGES French and Arabic (both official)
RELIGIONS Islam 40%, Christianity 33%, traditional beliefs 27%
CURRENCY CFA franc = 100 centimes

CHILE

GEOGRAPHY The Republic of Chile stretches about 4,260 km [2,650 mls] from north to south, although the maximum east–west distance is only about 430 km [267 mls]. The high Andes Mountains form Chile's eastern borders with Argentina and Bolivia. To the west are basins and valleys, with coastal uplands overlooking the shore. Most people live in the central valley, where Santiago is situated.

Santiago, Chile's capital, has a Mediterranean climate, with hot, dry summers from November to March and mild, moist winters from April to October. However, the Atacama Desert in the north is one of the world's driest places, while southern Chile is cold and stormy.

POLITICS & ECONOMY Amerindian people reached the southern tip of South America at least 8,000 years ago. In 1520, the Portuguese navigator Ferdinand Magellan became the first European to sight Chile, but the country became a Spanish colony in the 1540s. Chile became independent in 1818 and, during a war (1879–83), it gained mineral-rich areas from Peru and Bolivia.

In 1970, Salvador Allende became the first Communist leader ever to be elected democratically. He was overthrown in 1973 by army officers, who were supported by the CIA. General Augusto Pinochet then ruled as a dictator. A new constitution was introduced in 1981 and elections were held in 1989.

The World Bank classifies Chile as a 'lower-middle-income' developing country. Mining is important, especially copper production. Minerals dominate Chile's exports. But the most valuable activity is manufacturing; products include processed foods, metals, iron and steel, wood products, transport equipment and textiles.

AREA 756,950 sq km [292,258 sq mls]
POPULATION 14,788,000
CAPITAL (POPULATION) Santiago (5,077,000)
GOVERNMENT Multiparty republic
ETHNIC GROUPS Mestizo 92%, Amerindian 7%
LANGUAGES Spanish (official)
RELIGIONS Christianity (Roman Catholic 81%)
CURRENCY Peso = 100 centavos

CHINA

CHINA

GEOGRAPHY The People's Republic of China is the world's third largest country. It is also the only country with more than 1,000 million people. Most people live in the east – on the coastal plains or in the fertile valleys of the Huang He (Hwang Ho or Yellow River), the Chang Jiang (Yangtze Kiang), which is Asia's longest river at 6,380 km [3,960 mls], and the Xi Jiang (Si Kiang).

Western China is thinly populated. It includes the bleak Tibetan plateau which is bounded by the Himalaya, the world's highest mountain range. Other ranges include the Kunlun Shan, the Altun Shan and the Tian Shan. Deserts include the Gobi desert along the Mongolian border and the Taklimakan desert in the far west.

Beijing in north-eastern China has cold winters and warm summers, with a moderate rainfall. Shanghai, in the east-central region of China, has milder winters and more rain. The south-east has a wet, subtropical climate. In the west, the climate is severe. Lhasa has very cold winters and a low rainfall.

POLITICS & ECONOMY China is one of the world's oldest civilizations, going back 3,500 years. Under the Han dynasty (202 BC to AD 220), the Chinese empire was as large as the Roman empire. Mongols conquered China in the 13th century, but Chinese rule was restored in 1368. The Manchu people of Mongolia ruled the country from 1644 to 1912, when the country became a republic.

War with Japan (1937–45) was followed by civil war between the nationalists and the Communists. The Communists triumphed in 1949, setting up the People's Republic of China.

In the 1980s, following the death of the revolutionary leader Mao Zedong (Mao Tse-tung) in 1976, China introduced reforms. It encouraged private enterprise and foreign investment, formerly forbidden policies. But the Communist leaders have not permitted political freedom. Opponents of the regime continue to be harshly treated, while attempts to negotiate some degree of autonomy for Tibet were firmly rejected in 1998.

China's economy, which is one of the world's largest, has expanded rapidly since the late 1970s. This is partly the result of the gradual abandonment of some fundamental Communist policies, including the setting up of many private manufacturing industries in the east. China's sheer size, combined with its rapid economic growth, have led to predictions that China will soon become a superpower. It was forecast in 1996 that China would become the world's biggest economy 'within a generation'. This was made more likely by the return of Hong Kong in July 1997 and, to a much lesser extent, by the return of Macau in December 1999.

In the early 1990s, agriculture employed about 70% of the people, although only 10% of the land is used for crops. Major products include rice, sweet potatoes, tea and wheat, together with many fruits and vegetables. Livestock farming is also important. Pork is a popular meat and China has more than a third of the world's pigs.

China's resources include coal, oil, iron ore and various other metals. China has huge steel industries and manufactures include cement, chemicals, fertilizers, machinery, telecommunications and recording equipment, and textiles. Consumer goods, such as bicycles and radios, are becoming increasingly important.

AREA 9,596,960 sq km [3,705,386 sq mls]
POPULATION 1,236,915,000
CAPITAL (POPULATION) Beijing (12,362,000)
GOVERNMENT Single-party Communist republic
ETHNIC GROUPS Han Chinese 92%, 55 minority groups
LANGUAGES Mandarin Chinese (official)
RELIGIONS Atheist 50%, Confucian 20%
CURRENCY Renminbi yuan = 10 jiao = 100 fen

COLOMBIA

GEOGRAPHY The Republic of Colombia, in north-eastern South America, is the only country in the continent to have coastlines on both the Pacific and the Caribbean Sea. Colombia also contains the northernmost ranges of the Andes Mountains.

There is a tropical climate in the lowlands. But the altitude greatly affects the climate of the Andes. The capital, Bogotá, which stands on a plateau in the eastern Andes at about 2,800 m [9,200 ft] above sea level, has mild temperatures throughout the year. The rainfall is heavy, especially on the Pacific coast

POLITICS & ECONOMY Amerindian people have lived in Colombia for thousands of years. But today, only a small proportion of the people are of unmixed Amerindian ancestry. Mestizos (people of mixed white and Amerindian ancestry) form the largest group, followed by whites and mulattos (people of mixed European and African ancestry).

Spaniards opened up the area in the early 16th century and they set up a territory known as the Viceroyalty of the New Kingdom of Granada, which included Colombia, Ecuador, Panama and Venezuela. In 1819, the area became independent, but Ecuador and Venezuela soon split away, followed by Panama in 1903. Colombia's recent history has been very unstable. Rivalries between the main political parties led to civil wars in 1899–1902 and 1949–57, when the parties agreed to form a coalition. The coalition government ended in 1986 when the Liberal Party was elected. Colombia faces many economic problems, as well as the difficulty of controlling a large illicit drug industry run by violent dealers. Colombia exports coal and oil, and it also produces emeralds and gold.

AREA 1,138,910 sq km [439,733 sq mls]
POPULATION 38,581,000
CAPITAL (POPULATION) Bogotá (5,026,000)
GOVERNMENT Multiparty republic
ETHNIC GROUPS Mestizo 58%, White 20%, Mulatto 14%, Black 4%
LANGUAGES Spanish (official)
RELIGIONS Christianity (Roman Catholic 93%)
CURRENCY Peso = 100 centavos

COMOROS

The Federal Islamic Republic of the Comoros consists of three large islands and some smaller ones,

lying at the north end of the Mozambique Channel in the Indian Ocean. The country became independent from France in 1974, but the people on a fourth island, Mayotte, voted to remain French. In 1997, secessionists on the island of Anjouan, who favoured a return to French rule, defeated forces from Grand Comore and, in 1998, they voted overwhelmingly to break away from the Comoros. Most people are subsistence farmers, although cash crops such as coconuts, coffee, cocoa and spices are also produced. The main exports are cloves, perfume oils and vanilla. **AREA** 2,230 sq km [115 sq mls]; **POPULATION** 545,000; **CAPITAL** Moroni.

CONGO

GEOGRAPHY The Republic of Congo is a country on the River Congo in west-central Africa. The Equator runs through the centre of the country. Congo has a narrow coastal plain on which its main port, Pointe Noire, stands. Behind the plain are uplands through which the River Niari has carved a fertile valley. Central Congo consists of high plains. The north contains large swampy areas in the valleys of rivers that flow into the River Congo and its large tributary, the Oubangi.

Congo has a hot, wet equatorial climate. Brazzaville and its environs experience a dry season between June and September. The coastal plain is drier and cooler than the rest of the country because a cold ocean current, the Benguela, flows northwards along the coast.

POLITICS & ECONOMY Part of the huge Kongo kingdom between the 15th and 18th centuries, the coast of the Congo later became a centre of the European slave trade. The area came under French protection in 1880. It was later governed as part of a larger region called French Equatorial Africa. The country remained under French control until 1960.

Congo became a one-party state in 1964 and a military group took over the government in 1968. In 1970, Congo declared itself a Communist country, though it continued to seek aid from Western countries. The government officially abandoned its Communist policies in 1990. Multiparty elections were held in 1992, but the elected president, Pascal Lissouba, was overthrown in 1997 by former president, Denis Sassou-Nguesso.

The World Bank classifies Congo as a 'lower-middle-income' developing country. Agriculture is the most important activity, employing more than 60% of the people. But many farmers produce little more than they need to feed their families. Major food crops include bananas, cassava, maize and rice, while the leading cash crops are coffee and cocoa. Congo's main exports are oil (which makes up 70% of the total) and timber. Manufacturing is relatively unimportant at the moment, still hampered by poor transport links, but it is gradually being developed.

AREA 342,000 sq km [132,046 sq mls]
POPULATION 2,658,000
CAPITAL (POPULATION) Brazzaville (938,000)
GOVERNMENT Military regime
ETHNIC GROUPS Kongo 52%, Teke 17%, Mboshi 12%, Mbete 5%
LANGUAGES French (official), Kongo, Teke
RELIGIONS Christianity (Roman Catholic 54%, Protestant 25%, African Christians 14%
CURRENCY CFA franc = 100 centimes

CONGO (ZAÏRE)

GEOGRAPHY The Democratic Republic of the Congo, formerly known as Zaïre, is the world's 12th largest country. Much of the country lies within the drainage basin of the huge River Congo. The river reaches the sea along the country's coastline, which is 40 km [25 mls] long. Mountains rise in the east, where the country's borders run through lakes Tanganyika, Kivu, Edward and Albert. These lakes lie on the floor of an arm of the Great Rift Valley.

The equatorial region has high temperatures and heavy rainfall throughout the year. In the subtropical south, where the town of Lubumbashi is situated, there is a marked wet and dry season.

POLITICS & ECONOMY Pygmies were the first inhabitants of the region, with Portuguese navigators not reaching the coast until 1482, but the interior was not explored until the late 19th century. In 1885, the country, called Congo Free State, became the personal property of King Léopold II of Belgium. In 1908, the country became a Belgian colony.

The Belgian Congo became independent in 1960 and was renamed Zaïre in 1971. Ethnic rivalries caused instability until 1965, when the country became a one-party state, ruled by President Mobutu. The government allowed the formation of political parties in 1990, but elections were repeatedly postponed. In 1996, fighting broke out in eastern Zaïre, as the Tutsi–Hutu conflict in Burundi and Rwanda spilled over. The rebel leader Laurent Kabila took power in 1997, ousting Mobutu and renaming the country. A rebellion against Kabila broke out in 1998. Rwanda and Uganda supported the rebels, while Angola, Chad, Namibia and Zimbabwe sent troops to assist Kabila.

The World Bank classifies the Democratic Republic of the Congo as a 'low-income' developing country, despite its reserves of copper, the main export, and other minerals. Agriculture, mainly at subsistence level, employs 71% of the people.

AREA 2,344,885 sq km [905,365 sq mls]
POPULATION 49,001,000
CAPITAL (POPULATION) Kinshasa (3,804,000)
GOVERNMENT Single-party republic
ETHNIC GROUPS Luba 18%, Kongo 16%, Mongo 14%, Rwanda 10%, Azande 6%, Bandi and Ngale 6%, Rundi 4%, Teke, Boa, Chokwe, Lugbara, Banda
LANGUAGES French (official), tribal languages
RELIGIONS Christianity (Roman Catholic 48%, Protestant 29%, indigenous Christian churches 17%), traditional beliefs 3%, Islam 1%
CURRENCY Congolese franc

COSTA RICA

GEOGRAPHY The Republic of Costa Rica in Central America has coastlines on both the Pacific Ocean and also on the Caribbean Sea. Central Costa Rica consists of mountain ranges and plateaux with many volcanoes.

The coolest months are December and January. The north-east trade winds bring heavy rain to the Caribbean coast. There is less rainfall in the highlands and on the Pacific coastlands.

POLITICS & ECONOMY Christopher Columbus reached the Caribbean coast in 1502 and rumours of treasure soon attracted many Spaniards to settle in the country. Spain ruled the country until 1821, when Spain's Central American colonies broke away to join Mexico in 1822. In 1823, the Central American states broke with Mexico and set up the Central American Federation. Later, this large union broke up and Costa Rica became fully independent in 1838. From the late 19th century, Costa Rica experienced a number of revolutions, with periods of dictatorship and periods of democracy. In 1948, following a revolt, the armed forces were abolished. Since 1948, Costa Rica has enjoyed a long period of stable democracy, which many in Latin America admire and envy.

Costa Rica is classified by the World Bank as a 'lower-middle-income' developing country and one of the most prosperous countries in Central America. There are high educational standards and a high life expectancy (to an average of 73.5 years). Agriculture employs 24% of the people.

The country's resources include its forests, but it lacks minerals apart from some bauxite and manganese. Manufacturing is increasing. The United States is Costa Rica's chief trading partner. Tourism is a growing industry.

AREA 51,100 sq km [19,730 sq mls]
POPULATION 3,605,000
CAPITAL (POPULATION) San José (1,186,000)
GOVERNMENT Multiparty republic
ETHNIC GROUPS White 85%, Mestizo 8%, Black and Mulatto 3%, East Asian (mostly Chinese) 3%
LANGUAGES Spanish (official)
RELIGIONS Christianity (Roman Catholic 81%)
CURRENCY Colón = 100 céntimos

CROATIA

GEOGRAPHY The Republic of Croatia was one of the six republics that made up the former Communist country of Yugoslavia until it became independent in 1991. The region bordering the Adriatic Sea is called Dalmatia. It includes the coastal ranges, which contain large areas of bare limestone. Most of the rest of the country consists of the fertile Pannonian plains.

The coastal area has a typical Mediterranean climate, with hot, dry summers and mild, moist winters. Inland, the climate becomes more continental. Winters are cold, while temperatures often soar to 38°C [100°F] in the summer months.

POLITICS & ECONOMY Slav people settled in the area around 1,400 years ago. In 803, Croatia became part of the Holy Roman Empire and the Croats soon adopted Christianity. Croatia was an independent kingdom in the 10th and 11th centuries. In 1102, the king of Hungary also became king of Croatia, creating a union that lasted 800 years. In 1526, part of Croatia came under the Turkish Ottoman empire, while the rest came under the Austrian Habsburgs.

After Austria-Hungary was defeated in World War I (1914–18), Croatia became part of the new Kingdom of the Serbs, Croats and Slovenes. This kingdom was renamed Yugoslavia in 1929. Germany occupied

Yugoslavia during World War II (1939–45). Croatia was proclaimed independent, but it was really ruled by the invaders.

After the war, Communists took power with Josip Broz Tito as the country's leader. Despite ethnic differences between the people, Tito held Yugoslavia together until his death in 1980. In the 1980s, economic and ethnic problems, including a deterioration in relations with Serbia, threatened stability. In the 1990s, Yugoslavia split into five nations, one of which was Croatia, which declared itself independent in 1991.

After Serbia supplied arms to Serbs living in Croatia, war broke out between the two republics, causing great damage. Croatia lost more than 30% of its territory. But in 1992, the United Nations sent a peacekeeping force to Croatia, which effectively ended the war with Serbia.

In 1992, when war broke out in Bosnia-Herzegovina, Bosnian Croats occupied parts of the country. But in 1994, Croatia helped to end Croat–Muslim conflict in Bosnia-Herzegovina and, in 1995, after retaking some areas occupied by Serbs, it helped to draw up the Dayton Peace Accord which ended the civil war there.

The wars of the early 1990s disrupted Croatia's economy, which had been quite prosperous before the disturbances. Tourism on the Dalmatian coast had been a major industry. Croatia also had major manufacturing industries, and manufactures remain the chief exports.

AREA 56,538 sq km [21,824 sq mls]
POPULATION 4,672,000
CAPITAL (POPULATION) Zagreb (931,000)
GOVERNMENT Multiparty republic
ETHNIC GROUPS Croat 78%, Serb 12%, Bosnian
LANGUAGES Serbo-Croatian
RELIGIONS Christianity (Roman Catholic 77%, Eastern Orthodox 11%), Islam 1%
CURRENCY Kuna = 100 lipas

CUBA

GEOGRAPHY The Republic of Cuba is the largest island country in the Caribbean Sea. It consists of one large island, Cuba, the Isle of Youth (Isla de la Juventud) and about 1,600 small islets. Mountains and hills cover about a quarter of Cuba. The highest mountain range, the Sierra Maestra in the south-east, reaches 2,000 m [6,562 ft] above sea level. The rest of the land consists of gently rolling country or coastal plains, crossed by fertile valleys carved by the short, mostly shallow and narrow rivers.

Cuba lies in the tropics. But sea breezes moderate the temperature, warming the land in winter and cooling it in summer.

POLITICS & ECONOMY Christopher Columbus discovered the island in 1492 and Spaniards began to settle there from 1511. Spanish rule ended in 1898, when the United States defeated Spain in the Spanish-American War. American influence in Cuba remained strong until 1959, when revolutionary forces under Fidel Castro overthrew the dictatorial government of Fulgencio Batista.

The United States opposed Castro's policies, when he turned to the Soviet Union for assistance. In 1961, Cuban exiles attempting an invasion were defeated. In 1962, the US learned that nuclear missile bases

armed by the Soviet Union had been established in Cuba. The US ordered the Soviet Union to remove the missiles and bases and, after a few days, when many people feared that a world war might break out, the Soviet Union agreed to the American demands.

Cuba's relations with the Soviet Union remained strong until 1991, when the Soviet Union was broken up. The loss of Soviet aid greatly damaged Cuba's economy, but Castro continued the country's left-wing policies. Elections in February 1993 showed a continuing high level of support from the people for Castro.

The government runs Cuba's economy and owns 70% of the farmland. Agriculture is important and sugar is the chief export, followed by refined nickel ore. Other exports include cigars, citrus fruits, fish, medical products and rum.

Before 1959, US companies owned most of Cuba's manufacturing industries. But under Fidel Castro, they became government property. After the collapse of Communist governments in the Soviet Union and its allies, Cuba worked to increase its trade with Latin America and China.

AREA 110,860 sq km [42,803 sq mls]
POPULATION 11,051,000
CAPITAL (POPULATION) Havana (2,241,000)
GOVERNMENT Socialist republic
ETHNIC GROUPS White 66%, Mulatto 22%, Black 12%
LANGUAGES Spanish (official)
RELIGIONS Christianity (Roman Catholic 40%, Protestant 3%)
CURRENCY Cuban peso = 100 centavos

CYPRUS

GEOGRAPHY The Republic of Cyprus is an island nation in the north-eastern Mediterranean Sea. Geographers regard it as part of Asia, but it resembles southern Europe in many ways.

Cyprus has scenic mountain ranges, including the Kyrenia range in the north and the Troodos Mountains in the south, which rise to 1,951 m [6,401 ft] at Mount Olympus. The island also contains several fertile lowlands, including the broad Mesaoria plain between the Kyrenia and Troodos mountains.

Cyprus has a Mediterranean climate, with hot, dry summers and mild, moist winters. But the summers are hotter than in the western Mediterranean lands; this is because Cyprus lies close to the hot mainland of south-western Asia.

POLITICS & ECONOMY Greeks settled on Cyprus around 3,200 years ago. From AD 330, the island was part of the Byzantine empire. In the 1570s, Cyprus became part of the Turkish Ottoman empire. Turkish rule continued until 1878 when Cyprus was leased to Britain. Britain annexed the island in 1914 and proclaimed it a colony in 1925.

In the 1950s, Greek Cypriots, who made up four-fifths of the population, began a campaign for enosis (union) with Greece. Their leader was the Greek Orthodox Archbishop Makarios. A secret guerrilla force called EOKA attacked the British, who exiled Makarios. Cyprus became an independent country in 1960, although Britain retained two military bases. Independent Cyprus had a constitution which provided for power-sharing between the Greek and Turkish Cypriots. But the constitution

proved unworkable and fighting broke out between the two communities. In 1964, the United Nations sent in a peacekeeping force. Communal clashes recurred in 1967.

In 1974, Cypriot forces led by Greek officers overthrew Makarios. This led Turkey to invade northern Cyprus, a territory occupying about 40% of the island. Many Greek Cypriots fled from the Turkish-occupied area, which, in 1979, was proclaimed to be a self-governing region. In 1983, the Turkish Cypriots declared the north to be an independent state called the Turkish Republic of Northern Cyprus. But only Turkey recognizes this state. The UN regards Cyprus as a single nation under the Greek Cypriot government in the south.

Cyprus got its name from the Greek word *kypros*, meaning copper. But little copper remains and the chief minerals today are asbestos and chromium. However, the most valuable activity in Cyprus is tourism. In the early 1990s, the United Nations reclassified Cyprus as a developed rather than a developing country. But the economy of the Turkish-Cypriot north lags behind that of the more prosperous Greek-Cypriot south.

AREA 9,250 sq km [3,571 sq mls]
POPULATION 749,000
CAPITAL (POPULATION) Nicosia (189,000)
GOVERNMENT Multiparty republic
ETHNIC GROUPS Greek Cypriot 81%, Turkish Cypriot 19%
LANGUAGES Greek and Turkish (both official)
RELIGIONS Christianity (Greek Orthodox), Islam
CURRENCY Cyprus pound = 100 cents

CZECH REPUBLIC

GEOGRAPHY The Czech Republic is the western three-fifths of the former country of Czechoslovakia. It contains two regions: Bohemia in the west and Moravia in the east. Mountains border much of the country in the west. The Bohemian basin in the north-centre is a fertile lowland region, with Prague, the capital city, as its main centre. Highlands cover much of the centre of the country, with lowlands in the south-east.

The climate is influenced by its landlocked position in east-central Europe. Prague has warm, sunny summers and cold winters. The average rainfall is moderate, with 500 mm to 750 mm [20 in to 30 in] every year in lowland areas.

POLITICS & ECONOMY After World War I (1914–18), Czechoslovakia was created. Germany seized the country in World War II (1939–45). In 1948, Communist leaders took power and Czechoslovakia was allied to the Soviet Union. When democratic reforms were introduced in the Soviet Union in the late 1980s, the Czechs also demanded reforms. Free elections were held in 1990, but differences between the Czechs and Slovaks and a resurgence of Slovak nationalism led the government to agree in 1992 to the partitioning of the country on 1 January 1993. The break was peaceful. In 1999, the Czech Republic became a member of NATO.

Under Communist rule the Czech Republic became one of the most industrialized parts of Eastern Europe. The country has deposits of coal, uranium, iron ore, magnesite, tin and zinc. Manufacturing employs about 40% of the Czech Republic's entire

workforce. Farming is also important. Under Communism, the government owned the land, but private ownership is now being restored. The country was admitted into the OECD in 1995.

AREA 78,864 sq km [30,449 sq mls]
POPULATION 10,286,000
CAPITAL (POPULATION) Prague (1,213,000)
GOVERNMENT Multiparty republic
ETHNIC GROUPS Czech 81%, Moravian 13%, Slovak 3%, Polish, German, Silesian, Gypsy, Hungarian, Ukrainian
LANGUAGES Czech (official), Moravian
RELIGIONS Christianity (Roman Catholic 39%, Protestant 4%)
CURRENCY Czech koruna = 100 haler

DENMARK

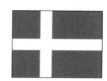

GEOGRAPHY The Kingdom of Denmark is the smallest country in Scandinavia. It consists of a peninsula, called Jutland (or Jylland), which is joined to Germany, and more than 400 islands, 89 of which are inhabited.

The land is flat and mostly covered by rocks dropped there by huge ice-sheets during the last Ice Age. The highest point in Denmark is on Jutland. It is only 173 m [568 ft] above sea level.

Denmark has a cool but pleasant climate, except during cold spells in the winter when The Sound between Sjælland and Sweden may freeze over. Summers are warm. Rainfall occurs all through the year.

POLITICS & ECONOMY Danish Vikings terrorized much of Western Europe for about 300 years after AD 800. Danish kings ruled England in the 11th century. In the late 14th century, Denmark formed a union with Norway and Sweden (which included Finland). Sweden broke away in 1523, while Denmark lost Norway to Sweden in 1814.

After 1945, Denmark played an important part in European affairs, becoming a member of the North Atlantic Treaty Organization (NATO). In 1973, Denmark joined the European Union, although it remains one of its least enthusiastic members. The Danes now enjoy some of the world's highest living standards, although the extensive social welfare provisions exert a considerable cost.

Denmark has few natural resources apart from some oil and gas from wells deep under the North Sea. But the economy is highly developed. Manufacturing industries, which employ about 27% of all workers, produce a wide variety of products, including furniture, processed food, machinery, television sets and textiles. Farms cover about three-quarters of the land. Farming employs only 4% of the workers, but it is highly scientific and productive. Meat and dairy farming are the chief activities.

AREA 43,070 sq km [16,629 sq mls]
POPULATION 5,334,000
CAPITAL (POPULATION) Copenhagen (1,353,000)
GOVERNMENT Parliamentary monarchy
ETHNIC GROUPS Danish 97%
LANGUAGES Danish (official)
RELIGIONS Christianity (Lutheran 91%, Roman Catholic 1%)
CURRENCY Krone = 100 øre

DJIBOUTI

GEOGRAPHY The Republic of Djibouti is a small country in eastern Africa which occupies a strategic position where the Red Sea meets the Gulf of Aden. Behind the coastal plain on the northern side of the Gulf of Tadjoura is a highland region, the Mabla Mountains, rising to 1,783 m [5,850 ft] above sea level. Djibouti also contains Lake Assal, the lowest point on land in Africa.

Djibouti has one of the world's hottest and driest climates. Summer days are very hot with recorded temperatures of more than 44°C [112°F]. On average, it rains on only 26 days every year.

POLITICS & ECONOMY Islam was introduced into the area which is now Djibouti in the 9th century AD. The conversion of the Afars led to conflict between them and the Christian Ethiopians who lived in the interior. By the 19th century, the Issas, who are Somalis, had moved north and occupied much of the traditional grazing land of the Afars. France gained influence in the area in the second half of the 19th century and, in 1888, they set up a territory called French Somaliland. The capital of the territory, Djibouti, became important when the Ethiopian emperor, Menelik II, decided to build a railway to it from Addis Ababa, thus making it the main port handling Ethiopian trade.

In 1967, the people voted to retain their links with France, though most of the Issas favoured independence. The country was renamed the French Territory of the Afars and Issas, but it was named Djibouti when it became fully independent in 1977.

Djibouti became a one-party state in 1981, but a new constitution was introduced in 1992, permitting four parties which must maintain a balance between the ethnic groups in the country. However, in 1992 and 1993, tensions between the Afars and Issas flared up when Afars launched an uprising which was put down by government troops.

Djibouti is a poor country. Its economy is based mainly on money it gets for use of its port and the railway that links it to Addis Ababa. Most of the food the country needs has to be imported.

AREA 23,200 sq km [8,958 sq mls]
POPULATION 650,000
CAPITAL (POPULATION) Djibouti (383,000)
GOVERNMENT Multiparty republic
ETHNIC GROUPS Issa 47%, Afar 37%, Arab 6%
LANGUAGES Arabic and French (both official)
RELIGIONS Islam 96%, Christianity 4%
CURRENCY Djibouti franc = 100 centimes

DOMINICA

The Commonwealth of Dominica, a former British colony, became independent in 1978. The island has a mountainous spine and less than 10% of the land is cultivated. Yet agriculture employs more than 60% of the people. Manufacturing, mining and tourism are other minor activities. **AREA** 751 sq km [290 sq mls]; **POPULATION** 78,000; **CAPITAL** Roseau.

DOMINICAN REPUBLIC

GEOGRAPHY Second largest of the Caribbean nations in both area and population, the Dominican Republic shares the island of Hispaniola with Haiti. The country is mountainous, and the generally hot and humid climate eases with altitude.

POLITICS & ECONOMY The Dominican Republic has chaotic origins, having been held by Spain, France, Haiti and the USA at various times. Civil war broke out in 1966 but soon ended after US intervention. Joaquín Balaguer, elected president in 1966 under a new constitution, stood down in 1996 and was replaced by Leonel Fernández.

AREA 48,730 sq km [18,815 sq mls]
POPULATION 7,999,000
CAPITAL (POPULATION) Santo Domingo (2,135,000)
GOVERNMENT Multiparty republic
ETHNIC GROUPS Mulatto 73%, White 16%, Black 11%
LANGUAGES Spanish (official)
RELIGIONS Roman Catholic 93%
CURRENCY Peso = 100 centavos

ECUADOR

GEOGRAPHY The Republic of Ecuador straddles the Equator on the west coast of South America. Three ranges of the high Andes Mountains form the backbone of the country. Between the towering, snow-capped peaks of the mountains, some of which are volcanoes, lie a series of high plateaux, or basins. Nearly half of Ecuador's population lives on these plateaux.

The climate in Ecuador depends on the height above sea level. Though the coastline is cooled by the cold Peruvian Current, temperatures are between 23°C and 25°C [73°F to 77°F] all through the year. In Quito, at 2,500 m [8,200 ft] above sea level, temperatures are 14°C to 15°C [57°F to 59°F], though the city is just south of the Equator.

POLITICS & ECONOMY The Inca people of Peru conquered much of what is now Ecuador in the late 15th century. They introduced their language, Quechua, which is widely spoken today. Spanish forces defeated the Incas in 1533 and took control of Ecuador. The country became independent in 1822, following the defeat of a Spanish force in a battle near Quito. In the 19th and 20th centuries, Ecuador suffered from political instability, while successive governments failed to tackle the country's social and economic problems. A war with Peru in 1941 led to a loss of territory, and border disputes continued, with the most recent conflict occurring in 1995. An agreement was eventually signed in January 1998. Civilian governments have ruled Ecuador since multiparty elections took place in 1979.

The World Bank classifies Ecuador as a 'lower-middle-income' developing country. Agriculture employs 30% of the people and bananas, cocoa and coffee are all important crops. Fishing, forestry, mining and manufacturing are other activities.

AREA 283,560 sq km [109,483 sq mls]
POPULATION 12,337,000
CAPITAL (POPULATION) Quito (1,101,000)
GOVERNMENT Multiparty republic
ETHNIC GROUPS Mestizo (mixed White and Amerindian) 40%, Amerindian 40%, White 15%, Black 5%
LANGUAGES Spanish (official), Quechua
RELIGIONS Christianity (Roman Catholic 92%)
CURRENCY Sucre = 100 centavos

EGYPT

GEOGRAPHY The Arab Republic of Egypt is Africa's second largest country by population after Nigeria, though it ranks 13th in area. Most of Egypt is desert. Almost all the people live either in the Nile Valley and its fertile delta or along the Suez Canal, the artificial waterway between the Mediterranean and Red seas. This canal shortens the sea journey between the United Kingdom and India by 9,700 km [6,027 mls]. Recent attempts have been made to irrigate parts of the western desert and thus redistribute the rapidly growing Egyptian population into previously uninhabited regions.

Apart from the Nile Valley, Egypt has three other main regions. The Western and Eastern deserts are parts of the Sahara. The Sinai peninsula (Es Sina), to the east of the Suez Canal, is a mountainous desert region, geographically within Asia. It contains Egypt's highest peak, Gebel Katherina (2,637 m [8,650 ft]); few people live in this area.

Egypt is a dry country. The low rainfall occurs, if at all, in winter and the country is one of the sunniest places on Earth.

POLITICS & ECONOMY Ancient Egypt, which was founded about 5,000 years ago, was one of the great early civilizations. Throughout the country, pyramids, temples and richly decorated tombs are memorials to its great achievements.

After Ancient Egypt declined, the country came under successive foreign rulers. Arabs occupied Egypt in AD 639–42. They introduced the Arabic language and Islam. Their influence was so great that most Egyptians now regard themselves as Arabs.

Egypt came under British rule in 1882, but it gained partial independence in 1922, becoming a monarchy. The monarchy was abolished in 1952, when Egypt became a republic. The creation of Israel in 1948 led Egypt into a series of wars in 1948–9, 1956, 1967 and 1973. Since the late 1970s, Egypt has sought for peace. In 1979, Egypt signed a peace treaty with Israel and regained the Sinai region which it had lost in a war in 1967. Extremists opposed contacts with Israel and, in 1981, President Sadat, who had signed the treaty, was assassinated.

While Egypt is important in foreign affairs, most people are poor. Some groups within the country dislike Western influences on their way of life and favour a return to the fundamental principles of Islam. In the 1990s, attacks on foreign visitors caused a decline in the valuable tourist industry. In 1997, 62 people, mostly foreign tourists, were killed by Islamic terrorists near Luxor.

Egypt is Africa's second most industrialized country after South Africa, but it remains a developing country and income levels remain low for the vast majority of Egyptian people. Oil and textiles are the chief exports.

EL SALVADOR

AREA 1,001,450 sq km [386,660 sq mls]
POPULATION 66,050,000
CAPITAL (POPULATION) Cairo (9,656,000)
GOVERNMENT Republic
ETHNIC GROUPS Egyptian 99%
LANGUAGES Arabic (official), French, English
RELIGIONS Islam (Sunni Muslim 94%),
Christianity (mainly Coptic Christian 6%)
CURRENCY Pound = 100 piastres

EL SALVADOR

GEOGRAPHY The Republic of El Salvador is the only country in Central America which does not have a coast on the Caribbean Sea. El Salvador has a narrow coastal plain along the Pacific Ocean. Behind the coastal plain, the coastal range is a zone of rugged mountains, including volcanoes, which overlooks a densely populated inland plateau. Beyond the plateau, the land rises to the sparsely populated interior highlands.

The coast has a hot, tropical climate. Inland, the climate is moderated by the altitude. Rain falls on practically every afternoon between May and October.

POLITICS & ECONOMY Amerindians have lived in El Salvador for thousands of years. The ruins of Mayan pyramids built between AD 100 and 1000 are still found in the western part of the country. Spanish soldiers conquered the area in 1524 and 1525, and Spain ruled until 1821. In 1823, all the Central American countries, except for Panama, set up a Central American Federation. But El Salvador withdrew in 1840 and declared its independence in 1841. El Salvador suffered from instability throughout the 19th century. The 20th century saw a more stable government, but from 1931 military dictatorships alternated with elected governments and the country remained poor.

In the 1970s, El Salvador was plagued by conflict as protesters demanded that the government introduce reforms to help the poor. Kidnappings and murders committed by left- and right-wing groups caused instability. A civil war broke out in 1979 between the US-backed, right-wing government forces and left-wing guerrillas in the FMLN (Farabundo Marti National Liberation Front). In 12 years, more than 750,000 people died and hundreds of thousands were made homeless. A cease-fire was agreed on 1 February 1992 and elections were held in 1994. With its economy shattered by war, El Salvador remains a 'lower-middle-income' economy, according to the World Bank. Farmland and pasture cover about three-quarters of the country. Coffee, grown in the highlands, is the main export, followed by sugar and cotton, which grow on the coastal lowlands. Fishing for lobsters and shrimps is important, but manufacturing is on a small scale.

AREA 21,040 sq km [8,124 sq mls]
POPULATION 5,752,000
CAPITAL (POPULATION) San Salvador (1,522,000)
GOVERNMENT Republic
ETHNIC GROUPS Mestizo (mixed White and
Amerindian) 89%, Amerindian 10%, White 1%
LANGUAGES Spanish (official)
RELIGIONS Christianity (Roman Catholic 94%)
CURRENCY Colón = 100 centavos

EQUATORIAL GUINEA

GEOGRAPHY The Republic of Equatorial Guinea is a small republic in west-central Africa. It consists of a mainland territory which makes up 90% of the land area, called Mbini (or Rio Muni), between Cameroon and Gabon, and five offshore islands in the Bight of Bonny, the largest of which is Bioko. The island of Annobon lies 560 km [350 mls] south-west of Mbini. Mbini consists mainly of hills and plateaux behind the coastal plains.

The climate is hot and humid. Bioko is mountainous, with the land rising to 3,008 m [9,869 ft], and hence it is particularly rainy. But there is a marked dry season between the months of December and February. Mainland Mbini has a similar climate, though the rainfall diminishes inland.

POLITICS & ECONOMY Portuguese navigators reached the area in 1471. In 1778, Portugal granted Bioko, together with rights over Mbini, to Spain.

In 1959, Spain made Bioko and Mbini provinces of overseas Spain and, in 1963, it gave the provinces a degree of self-government. Equatorial Guinea became independent in 1968.

The first president of Equatorial Guinea, Francisco Macias Nguema, proved to be a tyrant. He was overthrown in 1979 and a group of officers, led by Lt.-Col. Teodoro Obiang Nguema Mbasogo, set up a Supreme Military Council to rule the country. In 1991, the people voted to set up a multiparty democracy. Elections were held in 1993 and 1996, amid many allegations of intimidation and fraud.

Equatorial Guinea is a poor country. Agriculture employs up to 66% of the people. The main food crops are bananas, cassava and sweet potatoes, but the most valuable crop is cocoa, grown on Bioko.

AREA 28,050 sq km [10,830 sq mls]
POPULATION 454,000
CAPITAL (POPULATION) Malabo (35,000)
GOVERNMENT Multiparty republic (transitional)
ETHNIC GROUPS Fang 83%, Bubi 10%, Ndowe 4%
LANGUAGES Spanish (official), Fang, Bubi
RELIGIONS Christianity 89%, traditional beliefs 5%
CURRENCY CFA franc = 100 centimes

ERITREA

GEOGRAPHY The State of Eritrea consists of a hot, dry coastal plain facing the Red Sea, with a fairly mountainous area in the centre. Most people live in the cooler highland area.

POLITICS & ECONOMY Eritrea, which was an Italian colony from the 1880s, was part of Ethiopia from 1952 until 1993, when it became a fully independent nation. National reconstruction was hampered by conflict with Yemen over three islands in the Red Sea, while in 1998 and 1999, clashes with Ethiopia flared up along the countries' borders.

Farming and nomadic livestock rearing are the main activities in this poor, war-ravaged territory. Eritrea has a few manufacturing industries, based mainly in Asmara.

AREA 94,000 sq km [36,293 sq mls]
POPULATION 3,842,000
CAPITAL (POPULATION) Asmara (367,500)
GOVERNMENT Transitional government
ETHNIC GROUPS Tigrinya 49%, Tigre 32%, Afar
4%, Beja 3%, Saho 3%, Kunama 3%, Nara 2%
LANGUAGES Arabic, English, Tigrinya, Tigre, Saho
RELIGIONS Coptic Christian 50%, Muslim 50%
CURRENCY Nakfa

ESTONIA

GEOGRAPHY The Republic of Estonia is the smallest of the three states on the Baltic Sea, which were formerly part of the Soviet Union, but which became independent in the early 1990s. Estonia consists of a generally flat plain which was covered by ice-sheets during the Ice Age. The land is strewn with moraine (rocks deposited by the ice).

The country is dotted with more than 1,500 small lakes, and water, including the large Lake Peipus (Chudskoye Ozero) and the River Narva, makes up much of Estonia's eastern border with Russia. Estonia has more than 800 islands, which together make up about a tenth of the country. The largest island is Saaremaa (Sarema).

Despite its northerly position, Estonia has a fairly mild climate because of its nearness to the sea. This is because sea winds tend to warm the land in winter and cool it in summer.

POLITICS & ECONOMY The ancestors of the Estonians, who are related to the Finns, settled in the area several thousand years ago. German crusaders, known as the Teutonic Knights, introduced Christianity in the early 13th century. By the 16th century, German noblemen owned much of the land in Estonia. In 1561, Sweden took the northern part of the country and Poland the south. From 1625, Sweden controlled the entire country until Sweden handed it over to Russia in 1721.

Estonian nationalists campaigned for their independence from around the mid-19th century. Finally, Estonia was proclaimed independent in 1918. In 1919, the government began to break up the large estates and distribute land among the peasants.

In 1939, Germany and the Soviet Union agreed to take over parts of Eastern Europe. In 1940, Soviet forces occupied Estonia, but they were driven out by the Germans in 1941. Soviet troops returned in 1944 and Estonia became one of the 15 Soviet Socialist Republics of the Soviet Union. The Estonians strongly opposed Soviet rule. Many of them were deported to Siberia.

Political changes in the Soviet Union in the late 1980s led to renewed demands for freedom. In 1990, the Estonian government declared the country independent and, finally, the Soviet Union recognized this act in September 1991, shortly before the Soviet Union was dissolved. Estonia adopted a new constitution in 1992, when multiparty elections were held for a new national assembly. In 1993, Estonia negotiated an agreement with Russia to withdraw its troops.

Under Soviet rule, Estonia was the most prosperous of the three Baltic states. Since 1988, Estonia has begun to change its government-dominated economy to one based on private enterprise, and the country has started to strengthen its links with the rest of Europe. Estonia's resources include oil shale and its

FRANCE

forests. Industries produce fertilizers, machinery, petrochemical products, machinery, processed food, wood products and textiles. Agriculture and fishing are also important.

AREA 44,700 sq km [17,300 sq mls]
POPULATION 1,421,000
CAPITAL (POPULATION) Tallinn (435,000)
GOVERNMENT Multiparty republic
ETHNIC GROUPS Estonian 62%, Russian 30%, Ukrainian 3%, Belarussian 2%, Finnish 1%
LANGUAGES Estonian (official), Russian
RELIGIONS Christianity (Lutheran, with Orthodox and Baptist minorities)
CURRENCY Kroon = 100 sents

ETHIOPIA

GEOGRAPHY Ethiopia is a landlocked country in north-eastern Africa. The land is mainly mountainous, though there are extensive plains in the east, bordering southern Eritrea, and in the south, bordering Somalia. The highlands are divided into two blocks by an arm of the Great Rift Valley which runs throughout eastern Africa. North of the Rift Valley, the land is especially rugged, rising to 4,620 m [15,157 ft] at Ras Dashen. South-east of Ras Dashen is Lake Tana, source of the River Abay (Blue Nile).

The climate in Ethiopia is greatly affected by the altitude. Addis Ababa, at 2,450 m [8,000 ft], has an average yearly temperature of 20°C [68°F]. The rainfall is generally more than 1,000 mm [39 in]. But the lowlands bordering the Eritrean coast are hot.

POLITICS & ECONOMY Ethiopia was the home of an ancient monarchy, which became Christian in the 4th century. In the 7th century, Muslims gained control of the lowlands, but Christianity survived in the highlands. In the 19th century, Ethiopia resisted attempts to colonize it. Italy invaded Ethiopia in 1935, but Ethiopian and British troops defeated the Italians in 1941.

In 1952, Eritrea, on the Red Sea coast, was federated with Ethiopia. But in 1961, Eritrean nationalists demanded their freedom and began a struggle that ended in their independence in 1993. Relations with Eritrea gradually soured and border clashes occurred in 1998 and 1999. Ethnic diversity in Ethiopia has led to demands by several minorities for self-government. As a result, in 1995, Ethiopia was divided into nine provinces, each province with its own regional assembly.

Ethiopia is one of the world's poorest countries, particularly in the 1970s and 1980s when it was plagued by civil war and famine caused partly by long droughts. Many richer countries have sent aid (money and food) to help the Ethiopian people. Agriculture remains the leading activity.

AREA 1,128,000 sq km [435,521 sq mls]
POPULATION 58,390,000
CAPITAL (POPULATION) Addis Ababa (2,316,000)
GOVERNMENT Federation of nine provinces
ETHNIC GROUPS Amharic 38%, Galla 35%, Tigrinya 9%, Guage 3%, 60 others
LANGUAGES Amharic (official), 280 others
RELIGIONS Ethiopian Orthodox 53%, Sunni Muslim 31%, animist beliefs 11%
CURRENCY Birr = 100 cents

FALKLAND ISLANDS

Comprising two main islands and over 200 small islands, the Falkland Islands lie 480 km [300 mls] from South America. Sheep farming is the main activity, though the search for oil and diamonds holds out hope for the future of this harsh and virtually treeless environment. **AREA** 12,170 sq km [4,699 sq mls]; **POPULATION** 2,000; **CAPITAL** Stanley.

FAROE ISLANDS

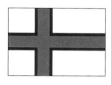

The Faroe Islands are a group of 18 volcanic islands and some reefs in the North Atlantic Ocean. The islands have been Danish since the 1380s, but they became largely self-governing in 1948. In 1998, the government of the Faroes announced its intention to become independent of Denmark. **AREA** 1,400 sq km [541 sq mls]; **POPULATION** 41,000; **CAPITAL** Torshávn.

FIJI

The Republic of Fiji comprises more than 800 Melanesian islands, the biggest being Viti Levu and Vanua Levu. The climate is tropical, with south-east trade winds blowing throughout the year. A former British colony, Fiji became independent in 1970. Its membership of the Commonwealth lapsed in 1987 after the enactment of discriminatory legislation against the country's Indian population. Fiji rejoined the Commonwealth in 1997 following changes in the constitution. **AREA** 18,270 sq km [7,054 sq mls]; **POPULATION** 802,000; **CAPITAL** Suva.

FINLAND

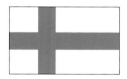

GEOGRAPHY The Republic of Finland is a beautiful country in northern Europe. In the south, behind the coastal lowlands where most Finns live, lies a region of sparkling lakes worn out by ice-sheets in the Ice Age. The thinly populated northern uplands cover about two-fifths of the country.

Helsinki, the capital city, has warm summers, but the average temperatures between the months of December and March are below freezing point. Snow covers the land in winter. The north has less precipitation than the south, but it is much colder.

POLITICS & ECONOMY Between 1150 and 1809, Finland was under Swedish rule. The close links between the countries continue today. Swedish

remains an official language in Finland and many towns have Swedish as well as Finnish names.

In 1809, Finland became a grand duchy of the Russian empire. It finally declared itself independent in 1917, after the Russian Revolution and the collapse of the Russian empire. But during World War II (1939–45), the Soviet Union declared war on Finland and took part of Finland's territory. Finland allied itself with Germany, but it lost more land to the Soviet Union at the end of the war.

After World War II, Finland became a neutral country and negotiated peace treaties with the Soviet Union. Finland also strengthened its relations with other northern European countries and became an associate member of the European Free Trade Association (EFTA) in 1961. Finland became a full member of EFTA in 1986, but in 1992, along with most of its fellow EFTA members, it applied for membership of the European Union. In 1994, the Finnish people voted in favour of membership of the EU. Finland officially joined on 1 January 1995.

Forests are Finland's most valuable resource, and forestry accounts for about 35% of the country's exports. The chief manufactures are wood products, pulp and paper. Since World War II, Finland has set up many other industries, producing such things as machinery and transport equipment. Its economy has expanded rapidly, but there has been a large increase in the number of unemployed people.

AREA 338,130 sq km [130,552 sq mls]
POPULATION 5,149,000
CAPITAL (POPULATION) Helsinki (525,000)
GOVERNMENT Multiparty republic
ETHNIC GROUPS Finnish 93%, Swedish 6%
LANGUAGES Finnish and Swedish (both official)
RELIGIONS Christianity (Evangelical Lutheran 88%)
CURRENCY Euro; Markka = 100 penniä

FRANCE

GEOGRAPHY The Republic of France is the largest country in Western Europe. The scenery is extremely varied. The Vosges Mountains overlook the Rhine valley in the north-east, the Jura Mountains and the Alps form the borders with Switzerland and Italy in the south-east, while the Pyrenees straddle France's border with Spain. The only large highland area entirely within France is the Massif Central in southern France.

Brittany (Bretagne) and Normandy (Normande) form a scenic hill region. Fertile lowlands cover most of northern France, including the densely populated Paris basin. Another major lowland area, the Aquitanian basin, is in the south-west, while the Rhône-Saône valley and the Mediterranean lowlands are in the south-east.

The climate of France varies from west to east and from north to south. The west comes under the moderating influence of the Atlantic Ocean, giving generally mild weather. To the east, summers are warmer and winters colder. The climate also becomes warmer as one travels from north to south. The Mediterranean Sea coast has hot, dry summers and mild, moist winters. The Alps, Jura and Pyrenees mountains have snowy winters. Winter sports centres are found in all three areas. Large glaciers occupy high valleys in the Alps.

FRANCE

POLITICS & ECONOMY The Romans conquered France (then called Gaul) in the 50s BC. Roman rule began to decline in the fifth century AD and, in 486, the Frankish realm (as France was called) became independent under a Christian king, Clovis. In 800, Charlemagne, who had been king since 768, became emperor of the Romans. He extended France's boundaries, but, in 843, his empire was divided into three parts and the area of France contracted. After the Norman invasion of England in 1066, large areas of France came under English rule, but this was finally ended in 1453.

France later became a powerful monarchy. But the French Revolution (1789–99) ended absolute rule by French kings. In 1799, Napoleon Bonaparte took power and fought a series of brilliant military campaigns before his final defeat in 1815. The monarchy was restored until 1848, when the Second Republic was founded. In 1852, Napoleon's nephew became Napoleon III, but the Third Republic was established in 1875. France was the scene of much fighting during World War I (1914–18) and World War II (1939–45), causing great loss of life and much damage to the economy.

In 1946, France adopted a new constitution, establishing the Fourth Republic. But political instability and costly colonial wars slowed France's post-war recovery. In 1958, Charles de Gaulle was elected president and he introduced a new constitution, giving the president extra powers and inaugurating the Fifth Republic.

Since the 1960s, France has made rapid economic progress, becoming one of the most prosperous nations in the European Union. But France's government faced a number of problems, including unemployment, pollution and the growing number of elderly people, who find it difficult to live when inflation rates are high. One social problem concerns the presence in France of large numbers of immigrants from Africa and southern Europe, many of whom live in poor areas.

A socialist government under Lionel Jospin was elected in June 1997. Jospin pledged to take France into the European single currency, but also increased the minimum wage and shortened the working week. The French system of high social security taxes and inflexible labour laws seems set to continue, although the economy continues to develop, with exports booming and inflation negligible.

France is one of the world's most developed countries. Its natural resources include its fertile soil, together with deposits of bauxite, coal, iron ore, oil and natural gas, and potash. France is also one of the world's top manufacturing nations, and it has often innovated in bold and imaginative ways. The TGV, Concorde and hypermarkets are all typical examples. Paris is a world centre of fashion industries, but France has many other industrial towns and cities. Major manufactures include aircraft, cars, chemicals, electronic products, machinery, metal products, processed food, steel and textiles.

Agriculture employs about 7% of the people, but France is the largest producer of farm products in Western Europe, producing most of the food it needs. Wheat is the leading crop and livestock farming is of major importance. Fishing and forestry are leading industries, while tourism is a major activity.

AREA 551,500 sq km [212,934 sq mls]
POPULATION 58,805,000
CAPITAL (POPULATION) Paris (9,469,000)
GOVERNMENT Multiparty republic
ETHNIC GROUPS French 93%, Arab, German
LANGUAGES French (official), Breton, Occitan
RELIGIONS Roman Catholic 86%, Islam 3%
CURRENCY Euro; Franc = 100 centimes

FRENCH GUIANA

GEOGRAPHY French Guiana is the smallest country in mainland South America. The coastal plain is swampy in places, but some dry areas are cultivated. Inland lies a plateau, with the low Tumachumac Mountains in the south. Most of the rivers run north towards the Atlantic Ocean.

French Guiana has a hot, equatorial climate, with high temperatures throughout the year. The rainfall is heavy, especially between December and June, but it is dry between August and October. The north-east trade winds blow constantly across the country.

POLITICS & ECONOMY The first people to live in what is now French Guiana were Amerindians. Today, only a few of them survive in the interior. The first Europeans to explore the coast arrived in 1500, and they were followed by adventurers seeking El Dorado, the mythical city of gold. Cayenne was founded in 1637 by a group of French merchants. The area became a French colony in the late 17th century.

France used the colony as a penal settlement for political prisoners from the times of the French Revolution in the 1790s. From the 1850s to 1945, the country became notorious as a place where prisoners were harshly treated. Many of them died, unable to survive in the tropical conditions.

In 1946, French Guiana became an overseas department of France, and in 1974 it also became an administrative region. An independence movement developed in the 1980s, but most people want to retain their links with France and continue to obtain financial aid to develop their territory.

Although it has rich forest and mineral resources, such as bauxite (aluminium ore), French Guiana is a developing country. It depends greatly on France for money to run its services and the government is the country's biggest employer. Since 1968, Kourou in French Guiana, the European Space Agency's rocket-launching site, has earned money for France by sending communications satellites into space.

AREA 90,000 sq km [34,749 sq mls]
POPULATION 162,000
CAPITAL (POPULATION) Cayenne (42,000)
GOVERNMENT Overseas department of France
ETHNIC GROUPS Creole 42%, Chinese 14%, French 10%, Haitian 7%
LANGUAGES French (official)
RELIGIONS Christianity (Roman Catholic 80%, Protestant 4%)
CURRENCY French franc = 100 centimes

FRENCH POLYNESIA

French Polynesia consists of 130 islands, scattered over 4 million sq km [1.5 million sq mls] of the Pacific Ocean. Tribal chiefs in the area agreed to a French protectorate in 1843. They gained increased autonomy in 1984, but the links with France ensure a high standard of living. **AREA** 3,941 sq km [1,520 sq mls]; **POPULATION** 237,000; **CAPITAL** Papeete.

GABON

GEOGRAPHY The Gabonese Republic lies on the Equator in west-central Africa. In area, it is a little larger than the United Kingdom, with a coastline 800 km [500 mls] long. Behind the narrow, partly lagoon-lined coastal plain, the land rises to hills, plateaux and mountains divided by deep valleys carved by the River Ogooué and its tributaries.

Most of Gabon has an equatorial climate, with high temperatures and humidity throughout the year. The rainfall is heavy and the skies are often cloudy.

POLITICS & ECONOMY Gabon became a French colony in the 1880s, but it achieved full independence in 1960. In 1964, an attempted coup was put down when French troops intervened and crushed the revolt. Gabon became a one-party state in 1968. Opposition parties were legalized in 1990 and elections took place amid allegations of fraud. The Gabonese Democratic Party, formerly the only party, won a majority in the National Assembly.

Gabon's abundant natural resources include its forests, oil and gas deposits near Port Gentil, together with manganese and uranium. These mineral deposits make Gabon one of Africa's better-off countries. But agriculture still employs about 75% of the population and many farmers produce little more than they need to support their families.

AREA 267,670 sq km [103,347 sq mls]
POPULATION 1,208,000
CAPITAL (POPULATION) Libreville (418,000)
GOVERNMENT Multiparty republic
ETHNIC GROUPS Fang 36%, Mpongwe 15%, Mbete 14%, Punu 12%
LANGUAGES French (official), Bantu languages
RELIGIONS Christianity (Roman Catholic 65%, Protestant 19%, African churches 12%), traditional beliefs 3%, Islam 2%
CURRENCY CFA franc = 100 centimes

GAMBIA, THE

GEOGRAPHY The Republic of The Gambia is the smallest country in mainland Africa. It consists of a narrow strip of land bordering the River Gambia. The Gambia is almost entirely enclosed by Senegal, except along the short Atlantic coastline.

The Gambia has hot and humid summers, but the winter temperatures (November to May) drop to around 16°C [61°F]. In the summer, moist south-westerlies bring rain, which is heaviest on the coast.

POLITICS & ECONOMY English traders bought rights to trade on the River Gambia in 1588, and in 1664 the English established a settlement on an island in the river estuary. In 1765, the British founded a colony called Senegambia, which included parts of The Gambia and Senegal. In 1783, Britain handed this colony over to France.

In the 1860s and 1870s, Britain and France discussed the exchange of The Gambia for some other French territory. But no agreement was reached and Britain made The Gambia a British

colony in 1888. It remained under British rule until it achieved full independence in 1965. In 1970, The Gambia became a republic. Relations between the English-speaking Gambians and the French-speaking Senegalese form a major political issue. In 1981, an attempted coup in The Gambia was put down with the help of Senegalese troops. In 1982, The Gambia and Senegal set up a defence alliance, called the Confederation of Senegambia. But this alliance was dissolved in 1989. In July 1994, a military group overthrew the president, Sir Dawda Jawara, who fled into exile. Captain Yahya Jammeh, who took power, was elected president in 1996.

Agriculture employs more than 80% of the people. The main food crops include cassava, millet and sorghum, but groundnuts and groundnut products are the chief exports. Tourism is a growing industry.

AREA 11,300 sq km [4,363 sq mls]
POPULATION 1,292,000
CAPITAL (POPULATION) Banjul (171,000)
GOVERNMENT Military regime
ETHNIC GROUPS Mandinka (also called Mandingo or Malinke) 40%, Fulani (also called Peul) 19%, Wolof 15%, Dyola 10%, Soninke 8%
LANGUAGES English (official), Mandinka, Fula
RELIGIONS Islam 95%, Christianity 4%, traditional beliefs 1%
CURRENCY Dalasi = 100 butut

GEORGIA

GEOGRAPHY Georgia is a country on the borders of Europe and Asia, facing the Black Sea. The land is rugged with the Caucasus Mountains forming its northern border. The highest mountain in this range, Mount Elbrus (5,633 m [18,481 ft]), lies over the border in Russia.

The Black Sea plains have hot summers and mild winters, when the temperatures seldom drop below freezing point. The rainfall is heavy, but inland Tbilisi has moderate rainfall, with the heaviest rains in the spring and early summer.

POLITICS & ECONOMY The first Georgian state was set up nearly 2,500 years ago. But for much of its history, the area was ruled by various conquerors. Christianity was introduced in AD 330. Georgia freed itself of foreign rule in the 11th and 12th centuries, but Mongol armies attacked in the 13th century. From the 16th to the 18th centuries, Iran and the Turkish Ottoman empire struggled for control of the area, and in the late 18th century Georgia sought the protection of Russia and, by the early 19th century, Georgia was part of the Russian empire. After the Russian Revolution of 1917, Georgia declared itself independent and was recognized by the League of Nations. But Russian troops invaded and made Georgia part of the Soviet regime.

In 1991, following reforms in the Soviet Union, Georgia declared itself independent. It became a separate country when the Soviet Union was dissolved in December 1991.

Georgia contains three regions containing minority peoples: Abkhazia in the north-west, South Ossetia in north-central Georgia, and Adjaria (also spelled Adzharia) in the south-west. Communal conflict in the early 1990s led to outbreaks of civil war in South Ossetia and Abkhazia, where the people expressed the wish to set up their own independent countries.

Georgia is a developing country. Agriculture is important. Major products include barley, citrus fruits, grapes for wine-making, maize, tea, tobacco and vegetables. Food processing and silk and perfume-making are other important activities. Sheep and cattle are reared.

AREA 69,700 sq km [26,910 sq mls]
POPULATION 5,109,000
CAPITAL (POPULATION) Tbilisi (1,279,000)
GOVERNMENT Multiparty republic
ETHNIC GROUPS Georgian 70%, Armenian 8%, Russian 6%, Azerbaijani 6%, Ossetes 3%, Greek 2%, Abkhazian 2%, others 3%
LANGUAGES Georgian (official)
RELIGIONS Christianity (Georgian Orthodox 65%, Russian Orthodox 10%, Armenian Orthodox 8%), Islam 11%
CURRENCY Lari

GERMANY

GEOGRAPHY The Federal Republic of Germany is the fourth largest country in Western Europe, after France, Spain and Sweden. The North German plain borders the North Sea in the north-west and the Baltic Sea in the north-east. Major rivers draining the plain include the Weser, Elbe and Oder.

The central highlands contain plateaux and highlands, including the Harz Mountains, the Thuringian Forest (Thüringer Wald), the Ore Mountains (Erzgebirge), and the Bohemian Forest (Böhmerwald) on the Czech border. South Germany is largely hilly, but the land rises in the south to the Bavarian Alps, which contain Germany's highest peak, Zugspitze, at 2,963 m [9,721 ft] above sea level. The scenic Black Forest (Scharzwald) overlooks the River Rhine, which flows through a rift valley in the south-west. The Black Forest contains the source of the River Danube.

North-western Germany has a mild climate, but the Baltic coastlands are cooler. To the south, the climate becomes more continental, especially in the highlands. The precipitation is greatest on the uplands, many of which are snow-capped in winter.

POLITICS & ECONOMY Germany and its allies were defeated in World War I (1914–18) and the country became a republic. Adolf Hitler came to power in 1933 and ruled as a dictator. His order to invade Poland led to the start of World War II (1939–45), which ended with Germany in ruins.

In 1945, Germany was divided into four military zones. In 1949, the American, British and French zones were amalgamated to form the Federal Republic of Germany (West Germany), while the Soviet zone became the German Democratic Republic (East Germany), a Communist state. Berlin, which had also been partitioned, became a divided city. West Berlin was part of West Germany, while East Berlin became the capital of East Germany. Bonn was the capital of West Germany.

Tension between East and West mounted during the Cold War, but West Germany rebuilt its economy quickly. In East Germany, the recovery was less rapid. In the late 1980s, reforms in the Soviet Union led to unrest in East Germany. Free elections were held in East Germany in 1990 and, on 3 October 1990, Germany was reunited.

The united Germany adopted West Germany's official name, the Federal Republic of Germany. Elections in December 1990 returned Helmut Kohl, West Germany's Chancellor (head of government) since 1982, to power. His government faced many problems, especially the restructuring of the economy of the former East Germany. Kohl was defeated in elections in 1998 and was succeeded as Chancellor by Social Democrat Gerhard Schröder. In 1999, Germany's parliament moved from Bonn to the reconstructed Reichstag building in Berlin.

West Germany's 'economic miracle' after the destruction of World War II was greatly helped by foreign aid. Today, despite all the problems caused by reunification, Germany is one of the world's greatest economic and trading nations.

Manufacturing is the most valuable part of Germany's economy and manufactured goods make up the bulk of the country's exports. Cars and other vehicles, cement, chemicals, computers, electrical equipment, processed food, machinery, scientific instruments, ships, steel, textiles and tools are among the leading manufactures. Germany has some coal, lignite, potash and rock salt deposits. But it imports many of the raw materials needed by its industries.

Germany also imports food. Major agricultural products include fruits, grapes for wine-making, potatoes, sugar beet and vegetables. Beef and dairy cattle are raised, together with many other livestock.

AREA 356,910 sq km [137,803 sq mls]
POPULATION 82,079,000
CAPITAL (POPULATION) Berlin (3,472,000) / Bonn (293,000)
GOVERNMENT Federal multiparty republic
ETHNIC GROUPS German 93%, Turkish 2%, Yugoslav 1%, Italian 1%, Greek, Polish, Spanish
LANGUAGES German (official)
RELIGIONS Christianity (Protestant, mainly Lutheran 45%, Roman Catholic 37%), Islam 2%
CURRENCY Euro; Deutschmark = 100 Pfennig

GHANA

GEOGRAPHY The Republic of Ghana faces the Gulf of Guinea in West Africa. This hot country, just north of the Equator, was formerly called the Gold Coast. Behind the thickly populated southern coastal plains, which are lined with lagoons, lies a plateau region in the south-west.

Accra has a hot, tropical climate. Rain occurs all through the year, though Accra is drier than areas inland.

POLITICS & ECONOMY Portuguese explorers reached the area in 1471 and named it the Gold Coast. The area became a centre of the slave trade in the 17th century. The slave trade was ended in the 1860s and, gradually, the British took control of the area. After independence in 1957, attempts were made to develop the economy by creating large state-owned manufacturing industries. But debt and corruption, together with falls in the price of cocoa, the chief export, caused economic problems. This led to instability and frequent coups. In 1981, power was invested in a Provisional National Defence Council, led by Flight-Lieutenant Jerry Rawlings.

The government steadied the economy and introduced several new policies, including the relaxation of government controls. In 1992, the

GIBRALTAR

government introduced a new constitution, which allowed for multiparty election, and Rawlings was re-elected later that year.

The World Bank classifies Ghana as a 'low-income' developing country. Most people are poor and farming employs 59% of the population.

AREA 238,540 sq km [92,100 sq mls]
POPULATION 18,497,000
CAPITAL (POPULATION) Accra (1,781,000)
GOVERNMENT Republic
ETHNIC GROUPS Akan 54%, Mossi 16%, Ewe 12%, Ga-Adangame 8%, Gurma 3%
LANGUAGES English (official), Akan, Mossi
RELIGIONS Christianity 62%, traditional beliefs 21%, Islam 16%
CURRENCY Cedi = 100 pesewas

GIBRALTAR

Gibraltar occupies a strategic position on the south coast of Spain where the Mediterranean meets the Atlantic. It was recognized as a British possession in 1713 and, despite Spanish claims, its population has consistently voted to retain its contacts with Britain. AREA 6.5 sq km [2.5 sq mls]; POPULATION 29,000; CAPITAL Gibraltar Town.

GREECE

GEOGRAPHY The Hellenic Republic, as Greece is officially called, is a rugged country situated at the southern end of the Balkan peninsula. Olympus, at 2,917 m [9,570 ft] is the highest peak. Islands make up about a fifth of the land.

Low-lying areas in Greece have mild, moist winters and hot, dry summers. The east coast has more than 2,700 hours of sunshine a year and only about half of the rainfall of the west. The mountains have a much more severe climate, with snow on the higher slopes in winter.

POLITICS & ECONOMY After World War II (1939–45), when Germany had occupied Greece, a civil war broke out between Communist and nationalist forces. This war ended in 1949. A military dictatorship took power in 1967. The monarchy was abolished in 1973 and democratic government was restored in 1974. Greece joined the European Community in 1981. But despite efforts to develop the economy, Greece remains one of the poorest nations in the European Union and, in 1998, it failed to qualify for the adoption of the euro.

Manufacturing is important. Products include processed food, cement, chemicals, metal products, textiles and tobacco. Greece also mines lignite (brown coal), bauxite and chromite.

Farmland covers about a third of the country, and grazing land another 40%. Major crops include barley, grapes for wine-making, dried fruits, olives, potatoes, sugar beet and wheat. Poultry, sheep, goats, pigs and cattle are raised. Greece's beaches and ancient ruins make it a major tourist destination.

AREA 131,990 sq km [50,961 sq mls]
POPULATION 10,662,000
CAPITAL (POPULATION) Athens (3,097,000)
GOVERNMENT Multiparty republic
ETHNIC GROUPS Greek 96%, Macedonian 2%, Turkish 1%, Albanian, Slav
LANGUAGES Greek (official)
RELIGIONS Christianity (Eastern Orthodox 97%)
CURRENCY Drachma = 100 lepta

GREENLAND

Greenland is the world's largest island. Settlements are confined to the coast, because an ice-sheet covers four-fifths of the land. Greenland became a Danish possession in 1380. Full internal self-government was granted in 1981 and, in 1997, Danish place names were superseded by Inuit forms. However, Greenland remains heavily dependent on Danish subsidies. AREA 2,175,600 sq km [838,999 sq mls]; POPULATION 59,000; CAPITAL Nuuk (Godthaab).

GRENADA

The most southerly of the Windward Islands in the Caribbean Sea, Grenada became independent from the UK in 1974. A military group seized power in 1983, when the prime minister was killed. US troops intervened and restored order and constitutional government. AREA 344 sq km [133 sq mls]; POPULATION 96,000; CAPITAL St George's.

GUADELOUPE

Guadeloupe is a French overseas department which includes seven Caribbean islands, the largest of which is Basse-Terre. French aid has helped to mantain a reasonable standard of living for the people. AREA 1,710 sq km [660 sq mls]; POPULATION 416,000; CAPITAL Basse-Terre.

GUAM

Guam, a strategically important 'unincorporated territory' of the USA, is the largest of the Mariana Islands in the Pacific Ocean. It is composed of a coralline limestone plateau. AREA 541 sq km [209 sq mls]; POPULATION 149,000; CAPITAL Agana.

GUATEMALA

GEOGRAPHY The Republic of Guatemala in Central America contains a thickly populated mountain region, with fertile soils. The mountains, which run in an east–west direction, contain many volcanoes, some of which are active. Volcanic eruptions and earthquakes are common in the highlands. South of the mountains lie the thinly populated Pacific coastlands, while a large inland plain occupies the north.

Guatemala lies in the tropics. The lowlands are hot and rainy. But the central mountain region is cooler and drier. Guatemala City, at about 1,500 m [5,000 ft] above sea level, has a pleasant, warm climate, with a marked dry season between November and April.

POLITICS & ECONOMY In 1823, Guatemala joined the Central American Federation. But it became fully independent in 1839. Since independence, Guatemala has been plagued by instability and periodic violence.

Guatemala has a long-standing claim over Belize, but this was reduced in 1983 to the southern fifth of the country. Violence became widespread in Guatemala from the early 1960s, because of conflict between left-wing groups, including many Amerindians, and government forces. Talks were held to end the war in 1993, but by then the conflict had claimed an estimated 100,000 lives.

The World Bank classifies Guatemala as a 'lower-middle-income' developing country. Agriculture employs nearly half of the population and coffee, sugar, bananas and beef are the leading exports. Other important crops include the spice cardamom and cotton, while maize is the chief food crop. But Guatemala still has to import food to feed the people.

AREA 108,890 sq km [42,042 sq mls]
POPULATION 12,008,000
CAPITAL (POPULATION) Guatemala City (1,814,000)
GOVERNMENT Republic
ETHNIC GROUPS Amerindian 45%, Ladino (mixed Hispanic and Amerindian) 45%, White 5%, Black 2%, others including Chinese 3%
LANGUAGES Spanish (official), Mayan languages
RELIGIONS Christianity (Roman Catholic 75%, Protestant 25%)
CURRENCY Guatemalan quetzal = 100 centavos

GUINEA

GEOGRAPHY The Republic of Guinea faces the Atlantic Ocean in West Africa. A flat, swampy plain borders the coast. Behind this plain, the land rises to a plateau region called Fouta Djalon. The Upper Niger plains, named after one of Africa's longest rivers, the Niger, which rises there, are in the north-east.

Guinea has a tropical climate and Conakry, on the coast, has heavy rains between May and November. This is also the coolest period in the year. During the dry season, hot, dry harmattan winds blow south-westwards from the Sahara Desert.

POLITICS & ECONOMY Guinea became independent in 1958. The first president, Sékou Touré, followed socialist policies, but most people remained poor and Touré had to introduce repressive policies to hold on to power. After his death in 1984, military leaders took over. Colonel Lansana Conté became president and his government introduced free enterprise policies. In 1993, Conté won a presidential election.

The World Bank classifies Guinea as a 'low-income' developing country. It has several natural resources, including bauxite (aluminium ore), diamonds, gold, iron ore and uranium. Bauxite and alumina (processed bauxite) account for 90% of the value of the exports. Agriculture, however, employs 78% of the people, many of whom produce little more than they need for their own families. Guinea has some manufacturing industries. Products include alumina, processed food and textiles.

> **AREA** 245,860 sq km [94,927 sq mls]
> **POPULATION** 7,477,000
> **CAPITAL (POPULATION)** Conakry (1,508,000)
> **GOVERNMENT** Multiparty republic
> **ETHNIC GROUPS** Fulani 40%, Malinke 26%, Susu 11%, Kissi 7%, Kpelle 5%
> **LANGUAGES** French (official), Fulani, Malinke
> **RELIGIONS** Islam 85%, traditional beliefs 5%
> **CURRENCY** Guinean franc = 100 cauris

GUINEA-BISSAU

GEOGRAPHY The Republic of Guinea-Bissau, formerly known as Portuguese Guinea, is a small country in West Africa. The land is mostly low-lying, with a broad, swampy coastal plain and many flat offshore islands, including the Bijagós Archipelago.

The country has a tropical climate, with one dry season (December to May) and a rainy season from June to November.

POLITICS & ECONOMY Portugal appointed a governor to administer Guinea-Bissau and the Cape Verde Islands in 1836, but in 1879 the two territories were separated and Guinea-Bissau became a colony, then called Portuguese Guinea. But development was slow, partly because the territory did not attract settlers on the same scale as Portugal's much healthier African colonies of Angola and Mozambique.

In 1956, African nationalists in Portuguese Guinea and Cape Verde founded the African Party for the Independence of Guinea and Cape Verde (PAIGC). Because Portugal seemed determined to hang on to its overseas territories, the PAIGC began a guerrilla war in 1963. By 1968, it held two-thirds of the country. In 1972, a rebel National Assembly, elected by the people in the PAIGC-controlled area, voted to make the country independent as Guinea-Bissau.

In 1974, newly independent Guinea-Bissau faced many problems arising from its under-developed economy and its lack of trained people to work in the administration. One objective of the leaders of Guinea-Bissau was to unite their country with Cape Verde. But, in 1980, army leaders overthrew Guinea-Bissau's government. The Revolutionary Council, which took over, opposed unification with Cape Verde. Guinea-Bissau ceased to be a one-party state in 1991 and multiparty elections were held in 1994. However, a government of national unity was set up after a short civil war in 1998.

Guinea-Bissau is a poor country. Agriculture employs more than 80% of the people, but most farming is at subsistence level. Major crops include beans, coconuts, groundnuts, maize, palm kernels and rice, the staple food.

> **AREA** 36,120 sq km [13,946 sq mls]
> **POPULATION** 1,206,000
> **CAPITAL (POPULATION)** Bissau (145,000)
> **GOVERNMENT** Multiparty republic
> **ETHNIC GROUPS** Balante 27%, Fulani (or Peul) 23%, Malinke 12%, Mandyako 11%, Pepel 10%
> **LANGUAGES** Portuguese (official), Crioulo
> **RELIGIONS** Traditional beliefs 54%, Islam 38%
> **CURRENCY** CFA franc = 100 centimes

GUYANA

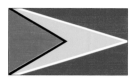

GEOGRAPHY The Co-operative Republic of Guyana is a country facing the Atlantic Ocean in north-eastern South America. The coastal plain is flat and much of it is below sea level.

The climate is hot and humid, though the interior highlands are cooler than the coast. The rainfall is heavy, occurring on more than 200 days a year.

POLITICS & ECONOMY British Guiana became independent in 1966. A black lawyer, Forbes Burnham, became the first prime minister. Under a new constitution adopted in 1980, the powers of the president were increased. Burnham became president until his death in 1985. He was succeeded by Hugh Desmond Hoyte. Hoyte was defeated in presidential elections in 1993 by Cheddli Jagan. Following Jagan's death in 1997, his wife Janet was elected president.

Guyana is a poor, developing country. Its resources include gold, bauxite (aluminium ore) and other minerals, and its forests and fertile soils. Agriculture employs 27% of the people. Sugar cane and rice are the leading crops. Electric power is in short supply, although the country has great potential for producing hydroelectricity from its many rivers.

> **AREA** 214,970 sq km [83,000 sq mls]
> **POPULATION** 820,000
> **CAPITAL (POPULATION)** Georgetown (200,000)
> **GOVERNMENT** Multiparty republic
> **ETHNIC GROUPS** Asian Indian 49%, Black 36%, Mixed 7%, Amerindian 7%, Portuguese, Chinese
> **LANGUAGES** English (official)
> **RELIGIONS** Christianity (Protestant 34%, Roman Catholic 18%), Hinduism 34%, Islam 9%
> **CURRENCY** Guyana dollar = 100 cents

HAITI

GEOGRAPHY The Republic of Haiti occupies the western third of Hispaniola in the Caribbean. The land is mainly mountainous. The climate is hot and humid, though the northern highlands, with about 200 mm [79 in], have more than twice as much rainfall as the southern coast.

POLITICS & ECONOMY Visited by Christopher Columbus in 1492, Haiti was later developed by the French to become the richest territory in the Caribbean region. The African slaves revolted in 1791 and the country became independent in 1804. Since independence, Haiti has suffered from instability, violence and dictatorial governments. Elections in 1990 returned Jean-Bertrand Aristide as president. But he was overthrown in 1991. Following US intervention, Aristide returned in 1994. In 1995, René Preval was elected president.

> **AREA** 27,750 sq km [10,714 sq mls]
> **POPULATION** 6,781,000
> **CAPITAL (POPULATION)** Port-au-Prince (1,402,000)
> **GOVERNMENT** Multiparty republic
> **ETHNIC GROUPS** Black 95%, Mulatto 5%
> **LANGUAGES** French (official), Creole
> **RELIGIONS** Roman Catholic 80%, Voodoo
> **CURRENCY** Gourde = 100 centimes

HONDURAS

GEOGRAPHY The Republic of Honduras is the second largest country in Central America. The northern coast on the Caribbean Sea extends more than 600 km [373 mls], but the Pacific coast in the south-east is only about 80 km [50 mls] long.

Honduras has a tropical climate, but the highlands, where the capital Tegucigalpa is situated, have a cooler climate than the hot coastal plains. The months between May and November are the rainiest and the north coast is sometimes hit by fierce hurricanes that cause great damage.

POLITICS & ECONOMY In the 1890s, American companies developed plantations in Honduras to grow bananas, which soon became the country's chief source of income. The companies exerted great political influence in Honduras and the country became known as a 'banana republic', a name that was later applied to several other Latin American nations. Instability has continued to mar the country's progress. In 1969, Honduras fought the short 'Soccer War' with El Salvador. The war was sparked off by the treatment of fans during a World Cup soccer series. But the real reason was that Honduras had forced Salvadoreans in Honduras to give up their land. In 1980, the countries signed a peace agreement.

Honduras is a developing country – one of the poorest in the Americas. It has few resources besides some silver, lead and zinc, and agriculture dominates the economy. Bananas and coffee are the leading exports, and maize is the main food crop.

Honduras is the least industrialized country in Central America. Manufactures include processed food, textiles, and a wide variety of wood products.

> **AREA** 112,090 sq km [43,278 sq mls]
> **POPULATION** 5,862,000
> **CAPITAL (POPULATION)** Tegucigalpa (739,000)
> **GOVERNMENT** Republic
> **ETHNIC GROUPS** Mestizo 90%, Amerindian 7%, Black (including Black Carib) 2%, White 1%
> **LANGUAGES** Spanish (official)
> **RELIGIONS** Christianity (Roman Catholic 85%)
> **CURRENCY** Honduran lempira = 100 centavos

HONG KONG

HONG KONG

Hong Kong, or Xianggang as it is known in Chinese, was a British dependency until 1 July 1997. It is now a Special Administrative Region of China. It consists of 236 islands, part of the mainland, and is home to over six million people. Hong Kong is a major financial and industrial centre, the world's biggest container port, and a major producer of textiles. **AREA** 1,071 sq km [413 sq mls]; **POPULATION** 6,707,000.

HUNGARY

GEOGRAPHY The Hungarian Republic is a land-locked country in central Europe. The land is mostly low-lying and drained by the Danube (Duna) and its tributary, the Tisza. Most of the land east of the Danube belongs to a region called the Great Plain (Nagyalföld), which covers about half of Hungary.

Hungary lies far from the moderating influence of the sea. As a result, summers are warmer and sunnier, and the winters colder than in Western Europe.

POLITICS & ECONOMY Hungary entered World War II (1939–45) in 1941, as an ally of Germany, but the Germans occupied the country in 1944. The Soviet Union invaded Hungary in 1944 and, in 1946, the country became a republic. The Communists gradually took over the government, taking complete control in 1949. From 1949, Hungary was an ally of the Soviet Union. In 1956, Soviet troops crushed an anti-Communist revolt. But in the 1980s, reforms in the Soviet Union led to the growth of anti-Communist groups in Hungary.

In 1989, Hungary adopted a new constitution making it a multiparty state. Elections held in 1990 led to a victory for the non-Communist Democratic Forum. In 1994, the Hungarian Socialist Party, composed of ex-Communists who had renounced Communism, won a majority in new elections and, in 1999, Hungary became a member of NATO.

Before World War II, Hungary's economy was based mainly on agriculture. But the Communists set up many manufacturing industries. The new factories were owned by the government, as also was most of the land. However, from the late 1980s, the government has worked to increase private ownership. This change of policy caused many problems, including inflation and high rates of unemployment. Manufacturing is the chief activity. Major products include aluminium, chemicals, and electrical and electronic goods.

AREA 93,030 sq km [35,919 sq mls]
POPULATION 10,208,000
CAPITAL (POPULATION) Budapest (1,909,000)
GOVERNMENT Multiparty republic
ETHNIC GROUPS Magyar (Hungarian) 98%, Gypsy, German, Croat, Romanian, Slovak
LANGUAGES Hungarian (official)
RELIGIONS Christianity (Roman Catholic 64%, Protestant 23%, Orthodox 1%), Judaism 1%
CURRENCY Forint = 100 fillér

ICELAND

GEOGRAPHY The Republic of Iceland, in the North Atlantic Ocean, is closer to Greenland than Scotland. Iceland sits astride the Mid-Atlantic Ridge. It is slowly getting wider as the ocean is being stretched apart by continental drift.

Iceland has around 200 volcanoes and eruptions are frequent. An eruption under the Vatnajökull ice-cap in 1996 created a subglacial lake which subsequently burst, causing severe flooding. Geysers and hot springs are other common volcanic features. Ice-caps and glaciers cover about an eighth of the land. The only habitable regions are the coastal lowlands.

Although it lies far to the north, Iceland's climate is moderated by the warm waters of the Gulf Stream. The port of Reykjavik is ice-free all the year round.

POLITICS & ECONOMY Norwegian Vikings colonized Iceland in AD 874, and in 930 the settlers founded the world's oldest parliament, the Althing.

Iceland united with Norway in 1262. But when Norway united with Denmark in 1380, Iceland came under Danish rule. Iceland became a self-governing kingdom, united with Denmark, in 1918. It became a fully independent republic in 1944, following a referendum in which 97% of the people voted to break their country's ties with Denmark.

Iceland has played an important part in European affairs. It is a member of the North Atlantic Treaty Organization, though it has been involved in disputes with the United Kingdom over fishing rights. In 1977, the UK agreed not to fish within Iceland's 370 km [200 nautical mls] fishing limits.

Iceland has few resources besides the fishing grounds which surround it. Fishing and fish processing are major industries which dominate Iceland's overseas trade. Barely 1% of the land is used to grow crops, mainly root vegetables and fodder for livestock. But 23% of the country is used for grazing sheep and cattle.

AREA 103,000 sq km [39,768 sq mls]
POPULATION 271,000
CAPITAL (POPULATION) Reykjavik (103,000)
GOVERNMENT Multiparty republic
ETHNIC GROUPS Icelandic 97%, Danish 1%
LANGUAGES Icelandic (official)
RELIGIONS Christianity (Evangelical Lutheran 92%, other Lutheran 3%, Roman Catholic 1%)
CURRENCY Króna = 100 aurar

INDIA

GEOGRAPHY The Republic of India is the world's seventh largest country. In population, it ranks second only to China. The north is mountainous, with mountains and foothills of the Himalayan range. Rivers, such as the Brahmaputra and Ganges (Ganga), rise in the Himalaya and flow across the fertile northern plains. Southern India consists of a large plateau, called the Deccan. The Deccan is bordered by two mountain ranges, the Western Ghats and the Eastern Ghats.

India has three main seasons. The cool season runs from October to February. The hot season runs from March to June. The rainy monsoon season starts in the middle of June and continues into September. Delhi has a moderate rainfall, with about 640 mm [25 in] a year. The south-western coast and the north-east have far more rain. Darjeeling in the north-east has an average annual rainfall of 3,040 mm [120 in]. But parts of the Thar Desert in the north-west have only 50 mm [2 in] of rain per year.

POLITICS & ECONOMY In southern India, most people are descendants of the dark-skinned Dravidians, who were among India's earliest people. Most northerners are descendants of lighter-skinned Aryans who arrived around 3,500 years ago.

India was the birthplace of several major religions, including Hinduism, Buddhism and Sikhism. Islam was introduced from about AD 1000. The Muslim Mughal empire was founded in 1526. From the 17th century, Britain began to gain influence. From 1858 to 1947, India was ruled as part of the British Empire. Independence in 1947 led to the break-up of British India into India and Muslim Pakistan.

Although India has 15 major languages and hundreds of minor ones, together with many religions, the country remains the world's largest democracy. It has faced many problems, especially with Pakistan, over the disputed territory of Jammu and Kashmir. Tension arose again in 1998 when both India and Pakistan tested nuclear devices.

Economic development has been a major problem and, according to the World Bank, India is a 'low-income' developing country. Socialist policies have failed to raise the living standards of the poor and, in the early 1990s, the government introduced private enterprise policies to stimulate growth.

Farming employs more than 60% of the people. The main food crops are rice, wheat, millet and sorghum, together with beans and peas. India has more cattle than any other country. These animals provide milk, but Hindus do not eat beef. India's large mineral reserves include coal, iron ore and oil, and manufacturing has expanded greatly since 1947. Products include iron and steel, machinery, refined petroleum, textiles and transport equipment.

AREA 3,287,590 sq km [1,269,338 sq mls]
POPULATION 984,000,000
CAPITAL (POPULATION) New Delhi (part of Delhi, 301,000)
GOVERNMENT Multiparty federal republic
ETHNIC GROUPS Indo-Aryan (Caucasoid) 72%, Dravidian (Aboriginal) 25%, other (mainly Mongoloid) 3%
LANGUAGES Hindi 30% and English (both official), Telugu 8%, Bengali 8%, Marati 8%, Urdu 5%, Tamil, many local languages
RELIGIONS Hinduism 83%, Islam (Sunni Muslim) 11%, Christianity 2%, Sikhism 2%, Buddhism 1%
CURRENCY Rupee = 100 paisa

INDONESIA

GEOGRAPHY The Republic of Indonesia is an island nation in South-east Asia. In all, Indonesia contains about 13,600 islands, less than 6,000 of which are inhabited. Three-quarters of the country is made up of five main areas: the islands of Sumatra, Java and Sulawesi (Celebes), together with

Kalimantan (southern Borneo) and Irian Jaya (western New Guinea). The islands are generally mountainous and Indonesia has more active volcanoes than any other country. The larger islands have extensive coastal lowlands.

Indonesia lies on the Equator and temperatures are high throughout the year. The climate is also humid. The rainfall is generally heavy, and only Java and the Sunda Islands have a relatively dry season. The highlands are cooler than the lowlands.

POLITICS & ECONOMY Indonesia is the world's most populous Muslim nation, though Islam was introduced as recently as the 15th century. The Dutch became active in the area in the early 17th century and Indonesia became a Dutch colony in 1799. After a long struggle, the Netherlands recognized Indonesia's independence in 1949. Despite instability, the economy has expanded, although a general depression hit the economies of most nations in eastern Asia in 1997. The removal from office of the autocratic President Suharto in 1998 held out hopes for a more democratic system and the resolution of the disputed status of East (formerly Portuguese) Timor, which Indonesia had annexed in 1976.

Indonesia is a developing country. Its resources include oil, natural gas, tin and other minerals, its fertile volcanic soils and its forests. Oil and gas are major exports. Timber, textiles, rubber, coffee and tea are also exported. The chief food crop is rice. Manufacturing is increasing, especially on Java.

> **AREA** 1,904,570 sq km [735,354 sq mls]
> **POPULATION** 212,942,000
> **CAPITAL (POPULATION)** Jakarta (11,500,000)
> **GOVERNMENT** Multiparty republic
> **ETHNIC GROUPS** Javanese 39%, Sundanese 16%, Indonesian (Malay) 12%, Madurese 4%, more than 300 others
> **LANGUAGES** Bahasa Indonesian (official), others
> **RELIGIONS** Islam 87%, Christianity 10% (Roman Catholic 6%), Hinduism 2%, Buddhism 1%
> **CURRENCY** Indonesian rupiah = 100 sen

IRAN

GEOGRAPHY The Republic of Iran contains a barren central plateau which covers about half of the country. It includes the Dasht-e-Kavir (Great Salt Desert) and the Dasht-e-Lut (Great Sand Desert). The Elburz Mountains north of the plateau contain Iran's highest peak, Damavand, while narrow lowlands lie between the mountains and the Caspian Sea. West of the plateau are the Zagros Mountains, beyond which the land descends to the plains bordering the Gulf.

Much of Iran has a severe, dry climate, with hot summers and cold winters. In Tehran, rain falls on only about 30 days in the year and the annual temperature range is more than 25°C [45°F]. The climate in the lowlands, however, is generally milder.

POLITICS & ECONOMY Iran was called Persia until 1935. The empire of Ancient Persia flourished between 550 and 350 BC, when it fell to Alexander the Great. Islam was introduced in AD 641.

Britain and Russia competed for influence in the area in the 19th century, and in the early 20th century the British began to develop the country's oil resources. In 1925, the Pahlavi family took power.

Reza Khan became shah (king) and worked to modernize the country. The Pahlavi dynasty was ended in 1979 when a religious leader, Ayatollah Ruhollah Khomeini, made Iran an Islamic republic. In 1980–8, Iran and Iraq fought a war over disputed borders. Khomeini died in 1989, but his fundamentalist views and anti-Western attitudes continued to influence many Muslims around the world. In 1995, Iran's alleged support for such terrorist groups as the Palestinian Hamas led the United States to impose trade sanctions.

Iran's prosperity is based on its oil production and oil accounts for 95% of the country's exports. However, the economy was severely damaged by the Iran–Iraq war in the 1980s. Oil revenues have been used to develop a growing manufacturing sector. Agriculture is important even though farms cover only a tenth of the land. The main crops are wheat and barley. Livestock farming and fishing are other important activities, although Iran has to import much of the food it needs.

> **AREA** 1,648,000 sq km [636,293 sq mls]
> **POPULATION** 64,411,000
> **CAPITAL (POPULATION)** Tehran (6,750,000)
> **GOVERNMENT** Islamic republic
> **ETHNIC GROUPS** Persian 46%, Azerbaijani 17%, Kurdish 9%, Gilaki 5%, Luri, Mazandarani, Baluchi, Arab
> **LANGUAGES** Farsi/Persian (official), Kurdish
> **RELIGIONS** Islam 99%
> **CURRENCY** Rial = 100 dinars

IRAQ

GEOGRAPHY The Republic of Iraq is a south-west Asian country at the head of The Gulf. Rolling deserts cover western and south-western Iraq, with mountains in the north-east. The northern plains, across which flow the rivers Euphrates (Nahr al Furat) and Tigris (Nahr Dijlah), are dry. But the southern plains, including Mesopotamia, and the delta of the Shatt al Arab, the river formed south of Al Qurnah by the combined Euphrates and Tigris, contain irrigated farmland, together with marshes.

The climate of Iraq varies from temperate in the north to subtropical in the south and east. Baghdad, in central Iraq, has cool winters, with occasional frosts, and hot summers. The rainfall is generally low.

POLITICS & ECONOMY Mesopotamia was the home of several great civilizations, including Sumer, Babylon and Assyria. It later became part of the Persian empire. Islam was introduced in AD 637 and Baghdad became the brilliant capital of the powerful Arab empire. But Mesopotamia declined after the Mongols invaded it in 1258. From 1534, Mesopotamia became part of the Turkish Ottoman empire. Britain invaded the area in 1916. In 1921, Britain renamed the country Iraq and set up an Arab monarchy. Iraq finally became independent in 1932.

By the 1950s, oil dominated Iraq's economy. In 1952, Iraq agreed to take 50% of the profits of the foreign oil companies. This revenue enabled the government to pay for welfare services and development projects. But many Iraqis felt that they should benefit more from their oil.

Since 1958, when army officers killed the king and made Iraq a republic, the country has undergone turbulent times. In the 1960s, the Kurds, who live in

northern Iraq and also in Iran, Turkey, Syria and Armenia, asked for self-rule. The government rejected their demands and war broke out. A peace treaty was signed in 1975, but conflict has continued.

In 1979, Saddam Hussein became Iraq's president. Under his leadership, Iraq invaded Iran in 1980, starting an eight-year war. During this war, Iraqi Kurds supported Iran and the Iraqi government attacked Kurdish villages with poison gas.

In 1990, Iraqi troops occupied Kuwait but an international force drove them out in 1991. Since 1991, Iraqi troops have attacked Shiite Marsh Arabs and Kurds. In 1996, the government aided the forces of the Kurdish Democratic Party in an offensive against the Patriotic Union of Kurdistan, a rival Kurdish faction. In 1998, Iraq's failure to permit UNSCOM, the UN body charged with disposing of Iraq's deadliest weapons, access to all suspect sites led to Western bombardment of military sites.

Civil war, war damage, UN sanctions and economic mismanagement have all contributed to economic chaos in the 1990s. Oil remains Iraq's main resource, but a UN trade embargo in 1990 halted oil exports. Farmland, including pasture, covers about a fifth of the land. Products include barley, cotton, dates, fruit, livestock, wheat and wool, but Iraq still has to import food. Industries include oil refining and the manufacture of petrochemicals and consumer goods.

> **AREA** 438,320 sq km [169,235 sq mls]
> **POPULATION** 21,722,000
> **CAPITAL (POPULATION)** Baghdad (3,841,000)
> **GOVERNMENT** Republic
> **ETHNIC GROUPS** Arab 77%, Kurdish 19%, Turkmen, Persian, Assyrian
> **LANGUAGES** Arabic (official), Kurdish (official in Kurdish areas)
> **RELIGIONS** Islam 96%, Christianity 4%
> **CURRENCY** Iraqi dinar = 20 dirhams = 1,000 fils

IRELAND

GEOGRAPHY The Republic of Ireland occupies five-sixths of the island of Ireland. The country consists of a large lowland region surrounded by a broken rim of low mountains. The uplands include the Mountains of Kerry where Carrauntoohill, Ireland's highest peak at 1,041 m [3,415 ft], is situated. The River Shannon is the longest in the British Isles. It flows through three large lakes, loughs Allen, Ree and Derg.

Ireland has a mild, damp climate greatly influenced by the warm Gulf Stream current that washes its shores. The effects of the Gulf Stream are greatest in the west. Dublin in the east is cooler than places on the west coast. Rain occurs throughout the year.

POLITICS & ECONOMY In 1801, the Act of Union created the United Kingdom of Great Britain and Ireland. But Irish discontent intensified in the 1840s when a potato blight caused a famine in which a million people died and nearly a million emigrated. Britain was blamed for not having done enough to help. In 1916, an uprising in Dublin was crushed, but between 1919 and 1922 civil war occurred. In 1922, the Irish Free State was created as a Dominion in the British Commonwealth. But Northern Ireland remained part of the UK.

Ireland became a republic in 1949. Since then, Irish governments have sought to develop the economy,

and it was for this reason that Ireland joined the European Community in 1973. In 1998, Ireland took part in the negotiations to produce a constitutional settlement in Northern Ireland. As part of the agreement, Ireland agreed to give up its constitutional claim on Northern Ireland.

Major farm products in Ireland include barley, cattle and dairy products, pigs, potatoes, poultry, sheep, sugar beet and wheat, while fishing provides another valuable source of food. Farming is now profitable, aided by European Union grants, but manufacturing is the leading economic sector. Many factories produce food and beverages. Chemicals and pharmaceuticals, electronic equipment, machinery, paper and textiles are also important.

AREA 70,280 sq km [27,135 sq mls]
POPULATION 3,619,000
CAPITAL (POPULATION) Dublin (1,024,000)
GOVERNMENT Multiparty republic
ETHNIC GROUPS Irish 94%
LANGUAGES Irish and English (both official)
RELIGIONS Christianity (Roman Catholic 93%, Protestant 3%)
CURRENCY Euro; Irish pound = 100 new pence

ISRAEL

GEOGRAPHY The State of Israel is a small country in the eastern Mediterranean. It includes a fertile coastal plain, where Israel's main industrial cities, Haifa (Hefa) and Tel Aviv–Jaffa are situated. Inland lie the Judaeo-Galilean highlands, which run from northern Israel to the northern tip of the Negev Desert in the south. To the east lies part of the Great Rift Valley which runs through East Africa into Asia. In Israel, the Rift Valley contains the River Jordan, the Sea of Galilee and the Dead Sea.

Israel has hot, dry, sunny summers. Winters are mild and moist on the coast, but the total rainfall decreases from west to east and also from north to south, where the Dead Sea region has only 70 mm [2.5 in] a year.

POLITICS & ECONOMY Israel is part of a region called Palestine. Some Jews have always lived in the area, though most modern Israelis are descendants of immigrants who began to settle there from the 1880s. Britain ruled Palestine from 1917. Large numbers of Jews escaping Nazi persecution arrived in the 1930s, provoking an Arab uprising against British rule. In 1947, the UN agreed to partition Palestine into an Arab and a Jewish state. Fighting broke out after Arabs rejected the plan. The State of Israel came into being in May 1948, but fighting continued into 1949. Other Arab–Israeli wars in 1956, 1967 and 1973 led to land gains for Israel.

In 1978, Israel signed a treaty with Egypt which led to the return of the occupied Sinai peninsula to Egypt in 1979. But conflict continued between Israel and the PLO (Palestine Liberation Organization). In 1993, the PLO and Israel agreed to establish Palestinian self-rule in two areas: the occupied Gaza Strip, and in the town of Jericho in the occupied West Bank. The agreement was extended in 1995 to include more than 30% of the West Bank. Israel's prime minister, Yitzhak Rabin, was assassinated in 1995 and his successor, Simon Peres, was narrowly defeated in elections in 1996. His right-wing successor, Benjamin Netanyahu, who resigned in

1999, favoured a more hardline policy towards Palestinians and the peace process became stalled. His successor, the left-wing challenger, Ehud Barak, vows to continue the peace process.

Israel's most valuable activity is manufacturing and the country's products include chemicals, electronic equipment, fertilizers, military equipment, plastics, processed food, scientific instruments and textiles. Fruits and vegetables are leading exports.

AREA 26,650 sq km [10,290 sq mls]
POPULATION 5,644,000
CAPITAL (POPULATION) Jerusalem (591,000)
GOVERNMENT Multiparty republic
ETHNIC GROUPS Jewish 82%, Arab and others 18%
LANGUAGES Hebrew and Arabic (both official)
RELIGIONS Judaism 82%, Islam 14%, Christianity 2%, Druse and others 2%
CURRENCY New Israeli sheqel = 100 agorat

ITALY

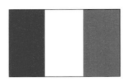

GEOGRAPHY The Republic of Italy is famous for its history and traditions, its art and culture, and its beautiful scenery. Northern Italy is bordered in the north by the high Alps, with their many climbing and skiing resorts. The Alps overlook the northern plains – Italy's most fertile and densely populated region – drained by the River Po. The rugged Apennines form the backbone of southern Italy. Bordering the range are scenic hilly areas and coastal plains.

Southern Italy contains a string of volcanoes, stretching from Vesuvius, near Naples (Nápoli), through the Lipari Islands, to Mount Etna on Sicily. Sicily is the largest island in the Mediterranean. Sardinia is also part of Italy.

Milan (Milano), in the north, has cold, often snowy winters. But the summer months are warm and sunny. Rainfall is plentiful, with brief but powerful thunderstorms in summer. Southern Italy has mild, moist winters and warm, dry summers.

POLITICS & ECONOMY Magnificent ruins throughout Italy testify to the glories of the ancient Roman Empire, which was founded, according to legend, in 753 BC. It reached its peak in the AD 100s. It finally collapsed in the 400s, although the Eastern Roman Empire, also called the Byzantine Empire, survived for another 1,000 years.

In the Middle Ages, Italy was split into many tiny states. But they made a great contribution to the revival of art and learning, called the Renaissance, in the 14th to 16th centuries. Beautiful cities, such as Florence (Firenze) and Venice (Venézia), testify to the artistic achievements of this period.

Italy finally became a united kingdom in 1861, although the Papal Territories (a large area ruled by the Roman Catholic Church) was not added until 1870. The Pope and his successors disputed the take-over of the Papal Territories. The dispute was finally resolved in 1929, when the Vatican City was set up in Rome as a fully independent state.

Italy fought in World War I (1914–18) alongside the Allies – Britain, France and Russia. In 1922, the dictator Benito Mussolini, leader of the Fascist party, took power. Under Mussolini, Italy conquered Ethiopia. During World War II (1939–45), Italy at first fought on Germany's side against the Allies. But in late 1943, Italy declared war on Germany. Italy became a republic in 1946. It has played an

important part in European affairs. It was a founder member of the North Atlantic Treaty Organization (NATO) in 1949 and also of what has now become the European Union in 1958.

After the setting up of the European Union, Italy's economy developed quickly. But the country faced many problems. For example, much of the economic development was in the north. This forced many people to leave the poor south to find jobs in the north or abroad. Social problems, corruption at high levels of society, and a succession of weak coalition governments all contributed to instability. Elections in 1996 were won by the left-wing Olive Tree alliance led by Romano Prodi. After losing a confidence vote in October 1998, Prodi was replaced as prime minister by an ex-Communist, Massimo D'Alema.

Only 50 years ago, Italy was a mainly agricultural society. But today it is a leading industrial power. It lacks mineral resources, and imports most of the raw materials used in industry. Manufactures include textiles and clothing, processed food, machinery, cars and chemicals. The chief industrial region is in the north-west.

Farmland covers around 42% of the land, pasture 17%, and forest and woodland 22%. Major crops include citrus fruits, grapes which are used to make wine, olive oil, sugar beet and vegetables. Livestock farming is important, though meat is imported.

AREA 301,270 sq km [116,320 sq mls]
POPULATION 56,783,000
CAPITAL (POPULATION) Rome (2,688,000)
GOVERNMENT Multiparty republic
ETHNIC GROUPS Italian 94%, German, French, Albanian, Ladino, Slovenian, Greek
LANGUAGES Italian 94% (official)
RELIGIONS Christianity (Roman Catholic) 83%
CURRENCY Euro; Lira = 100 centesimi

IVORY COAST

GEOGRAPHY The Republic of the Ivory Coast, in West Africa, is officially known as Côte d'Ivoire. The south-east coast is bordered by sand bars that enclose lagoons, on one of which the former capital and chief port of Abidjan is situated. But the south-western coast is lined by rocky cliffs.

Ivory Coast has a hot and humid tropical climate, with high temperatures throughout the year. The south of the country has two distinct rainy seasons: between May and July, and from October to November. Inland, the rainfall decreases and the north has one dry and one rainy season.

POLITICS & ECONOMY From 1895, Ivory Coast was governed as part of French West Africa, a massive union which also included what are now Benin, Burkina Faso, Guinea, Mali, Mauritania, Niger and Senegal. In 1946, Ivory Coast became a territory in the French Union.

Ivory Coast became fully independent in 1960 and its first president, Félix Houphouët-Boigny, became the longest serving head of state in Africa with an uninterrupted period in office which ended with his death in 1993. Houphouët-Boigny was a paternalistic, pro-Western leader, who made his country a one-party state. In 1983, the National Assembly agreed to move the capital from Abidjan to Yamoussoukro, the president's birthplace.

Agriculture employs about two-thirds of the people,

and farm products, notably cocoa beans, coffee, cotton and cotton cloth, make up nearly half of the value of the exports. Manufacturing has grown in importance since 1960; products include fertilizers, processed food, refined oil, textiles and timber.

> **AREA** 322,460 sq km [124,502 sq mls]
> **POPULATION** 15,446,000
> **CAPITAL (POPULATION)** Yamoussoukro (120,000)
> **GOVERNMENT** Multiparty republic
> **ETHNIC GROUPS** Akan 41%, Kru 17%, Voltaic 16%, Malinke 15%, Southern Mande 10%
> **LANGUAGES** French (official), Akan, Voltaic
> **RELIGIONS** Islam 38%, Christianity 28%, traditional beliefs 17%
> **CURRENCY** CFA franc = 100 centimes

JAMAICA

GEOGRAPHY Third largest of the Caribbean islands, half of Jamaica lies above 300 m [1,000 ft] and moist south-east trade winds bring rain to the central mountain range.

The 'cockpit country' in the north-west of the island is an inaccessible limestone area of steep broken ridges and isolated basins.

POLITICS & ECONOMY Britain took Jamaica from Spain in the 17th century, and the island did not gain its independence until 1962. Some economic progress was made by the socialist government in the 1980s, but migration and unemployment remain high. Farming is the leading activity and sugar cane is the main crop, though bauxite production provides much of the country's income. Jamaica has some industries and tourism is a major industry.

> **AREA** 10,990 sq km [4,243 sq mls]
> **POPULATION** 2,635,000
> **CAPITAL (POPULATION)** Kingston (644,000)
> **GOVERNMENT** Constitutional monarchy
> **ETHNIC GROUPS** Black 76%, Afro-European 15%, East Indian 3%, White 3%
> **LANGUAGES** English (official), Creole, Hindi, Spanish, Chinese
> **RELIGIONS** Protestant 70%, Roman Catholic 8%
> **CURRENCY** Dollar = 100 cents

JAPAN

GEOGRAPHY Japan's four largest islands – Honshu, Hokkaido, Kyushu and Shikoku – make up 98% of the country. But Japan contains thousands of small islands. The four largest islands are mainly mountainous, while many of the small islands are the tips of volcanoes. Japan has more than 150 volcanoes, about 60 of which are active. Volcanic eruptions, earthquakes and tsunamis (destructive sea waves triggered by underwater earthquakes and eruptions) are common because the islands lie in an unstable part of our planet, where continental plates are always on the move. One powerful recent earthquake

killed more than 5,000 people in Kobe in 1995.

The climate of Japan varies greatly from north to south. Hokkaido in the north has cold, snowy winters. At Sapporo, temperatures below –20°C [4°F] have been recorded between December and March. But summers are warm, with temperatures sometimes exceeding 30°C [86°F]. Rain falls throughout the year, though Hokkaido is one of the driest parts of Japan.

Tokyo has higher rainfall and temperatures, though frosts may occur as late as April when north-westerly winds are blowing. The southern islands of Shikoku and Kyushu have warm temperate climates. Summers are long and hot. Winters are mild.

POLITICS & ECONOMY In the late 19th century, Japan began a programme of modernization. Under its new imperial leaders, it began to look for lands to conquer. In 1894–5, it fought a war with China and, in 1904–5, it defeated Russia. Soon its overseas empire included Korea and Taiwan. In 1930, Japan invaded Manchuria (north-east China) and, in 1937, it began a war against China. In 1941, Japan launched an attack on the US base at Pearl Harbor in Hawaii. This drew both Japan and the United States into World War II.

Japan surrendered in 1945 when the Americans dropped atomic bombs on two cities, Hiroshima and Nagasaki. The United States occupied Japan until 1952. During this period, Japan adopted a democratic constitution. The emperor, who had previously been regarded as a god, became a constitutional monarch. Power was vested in the prime minister and cabinet, who are chosen from the Diet (elected parliament).

From the 1960s, Japan experienced many changes as the country rapidly built up new industries. By the early 1990s, Japan had become the world's second richest economic power after the US. But economic success has brought problems. For example, the rapid growth of cities has led to housing shortages and pollution. Another problem is that the proportion of people over 65 years of age is steadily increasing.

Japan has the world's second highest gross domestic product (GDP) after the United States. [The GDP is the total value of all goods and services produced in a country in one year.] The most important sector of the economy is industry. Yet Japan has to import most of the raw materials and fuels it needs for its industries. Its success is based on its use of the latest technology, its skilled and hard-working labour force, its vigorous export policies and its comparatively small government spending on defence. Manufactures dominate its exports, which include machinery, electrical and electronic equipment, vehicles and transport equipment, iron and steel, chemicals, textiles and ships.

Japan is one of the world's top fishing nations and fish is an important source of protein. Because the land is so rugged, only 15% of the country can be farmed. Yet Japan produces about 70% of the food it needs. Rice is the chief crop, taking up about half of the total farmland. Other major products include fruits, sugar beet, tea and vegetables. Livestock farming has increased since the 1950s.

> **AREA** 377,800 sq km [145,869 sq mls]
> **POPULATION** 125,932,000
> **CAPITAL (POPULATION)** Tokyo (26,836,000)
> **GOVERNMENT** Constitutional monarchy
> **ETHNIC GROUPS** Japanese 99%, Chinese, Korean, Ainu
> **LANGUAGES** Japanese (official)
> **RELIGIONS** Shintoism 93%, Buddhism 74%, Christianity 1% (most Japanese consider themselves to be both Shinto and Buddhist)
> **CURRENCY** Yen = 100 sen

JORDAN

GEOGRAPHY The Hashemite Kingdom of Jordan is an Arab country in south-western Asia. The Great Rift Valley in the west contains the River Jordan and the Dead Sea, which Jordan shares with Israel. East of the Rift Valley is the Transjordan plateau, where most Jordanians live. To the east and south lie vast areas of desert.

Amman has a much lower rainfall and longer dry season than the Mediterranean lands to the west. The Transjordan plateau, on which Amman stands, is a transition zone between the Mediterranean climate zone to the west and the desert climate to the east.

POLITICS & ECONOMY In 1921, Britain created a territory called Transjordan east of the River Jordan. In 1923, Transjordan became self-governing, but Britain retained control of its defences, finances and foreign affairs. This territory became fully independent as Jordan in 1946.

Jordan has suffered from instability arising from the Arab–Israeli conflict since the creation of the State of Israel in 1948. After the first Arab–Israeli War in 1948–9, Jordan acquired East Jerusalem and a fertile area called the West Bank. In 1967, Israel occupied this area. In Jordan, the presence of Palestinian refugees led to civil war in 1970–1.

In 1974, Arab leaders declared that the PLO (Palestine Liberation Organization) was the sole representative of the Palestinian people. In 1988, King Hussein of Jordan renounced his country's claims to the West Bank and passed responsibility for it to the PLO. In 1991, opposition parties were legalized and multiparty elections were held in 1993.

In October 1994, Jordan and Israel signed a peace treaty ending a state of war which had been going on for over 40 years. Jordan's King Hussein continued to command respect by playing an important role in Middle Eastern affairs until his death in 1999.

Jordan lacks natural resources, apart from phosphates and potash, and the country's economy depends substantially on aid. The World Bank classifies Jordan as a 'lower-middle-income' developing country. Less than 6% of the land is farmed or used as pasture. Jordan has an oil refinery and manufactures include cement, pharmaceuticals, processed food, fertilizers and textiles.

> **AREA** 89,210 sq km [34,444 sq mls]
> **POPULATION** 4,435,000
> **CAPITAL (POPULATION)** Amman (1,300,000)
> **GOVERNMENT** Constitutional monarchy
> **ETHNIC GROUPS** Arab 99%, of which Palestinians make up roughly half
> **LANGUAGES** Arabic (official)
> **RELIGIONS** Islam 93%, Christianity 5%
> **CURRENCY** Jordan dinar = 1,000 fils

KAZAKSTAN

GEOGRAPHY Kazakstan is a large country in west-central Asia. In the west, the Caspian Sea lowlands include the Karagiye depression, which

KENYA

reaches 132 m [433 ft] below sea level. The lowlands extend eastwards through the Aral Sea area. The north contains high plains, but the highest land is along the eastern and southern borders. These areas include parts of the Altai and Tian Shan mountain ranges.

Eastern Kazakstan contains several freshwater lakes, the largest of which is Lake Balkhash. The water in the rivers has been used for irrigation, causing ecological problems. For example, the Aral Sea, deprived of water, shrank from 66,900 sq km [25,830 sq mls] in 1960 to 33,642 sq km [12,989 sq mls] in 1993. Areas which once provided fish have dried up and are now barren desert.

The climate reflects Kazakstan's position in the heart of Asia, far from the moderating influence of the oceans. Winters are cold and snow covers the land for about 100 days, on average, at Almaty. The rainfall is generally low.

POLITICS & ECONOMY After the Russian Revolution of 1917, many Kazaks wanted to make their country independent. But the Communists prevailed and in 1936 Kazakstan became a republic of the Soviet Union, called the Kazak Soviet Socialist Republic. During World War II and also after the war, the Soviet government moved many people from the west into Kazakstan. From the 1950s, people were encouraged to work on a 'Virgin Lands' project, which involved bringing large areas of grassland under cultivation.

Reforms in the Soviet Union in the 1980s led to the break-up of the country in December 1991. Kazakstan kept contacts with Russia and most of the other republics in the former Soviet Union by joining the Commonwealth of Independent States (CIS), and in 1995 Kazakstan announced that its army would unite with that of Russia. In December 1997, the government moved the capital from Almaty to Aqmola (later renamed Astana), a town in the Russian-dominated north. It was hoped that this move would bring some Kazak identity to the area.

The World Bank classifies Kazakstan as a 'lower-middle-income' developing country. Livestock farming, especially sheep and cattle, is an important activity, and major crops include barley, cotton, rice and wheat. The country is rich in mineral resources, including coal and oil reserves, together with bauxite, copper, lead, tungsten and zinc. Manufactures include chemicals, food products, machinery and textiles. Oil is exported via a pipeline through Russia, though, to reduce dependence on Russia, Kazakstan signed an agreement in 1997 to build a new pipeline to China. Other exports include metals, chemicals, grain, wool and meat.

AREA 2,717,300 sq km [1,049,150 sq mls]
POPULATION 16,847,000
CAPITAL (POPULATION) Astana (280,000)
GOVERNMENT Multiparty republic
ETHNIC GROUPS Kazak 40%, Russian 38%, German 6%, Ukrainian 5%, Uzbek, Tatar
LANGUAGES Kazak (official); Russian, the former official language, is widely spoken
RELIGIONS Mainly Islam, with a Christian minority
CURRENCY Tenge

KENYA

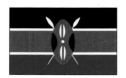

GEOGRAPHY The Republic of Kenya is a country in East Africa which straddles the Equator. It is slightly larger in area than France. Behind the narrow coastal plain on the Indian Ocean, the land rises to high plains and highlands, broken by volcanic mountains, including Mount Kenya, the country's highest peak at 5,199 m [17,057 ft]. Crossing the country is an arm of the Great Rift Valley, on the floor of which are several lakes, including Baringo, Magadi, Naivasha, Nakuru and, on the northern frontier, Lake Turkana (formerly Lake Rudolf).

Mombasa on the coast is hot and humid. But inland, the climate is moderated by the height of the land. As a result, Nairobi, in the thickly populated south-western highlands, has summer temperatures which are 10°C [18°F] lower than Mombasa. Nights can be cool, but temperatures do not fall below freezing. Nairobi's main rainy season is from April to May, with 'little rains' in November and December. However, only about 15% of the country has a reliable rainfall of 800 mm [31 in].

POLITICS & ECONOMY The Kenyan coast has been a trading centre for more than 2,000 years. Britain took over the coast in 1895 and soon extended its influence inland. In the 1950s, a secret movement, called Mau Mau, launched an armed struggle against British rule. Although Mau Mau was eventually defeated, Kenya became independent in 1963.

Many Kenyan leaders felt that the division of the population into 40 ethnic groups might lead to instability. They argued that Kenya should have a strong central government and it was a one-party state for much of the time since independence. Multiparty democracy was restored in the early 1990s and elections were held in 1992 and 1997, each resulting in a victory for the ruling president Daniel Arap Moi.

According to the United Nations, Kenya is a 'low-income' developing country. Agriculture employs about 80% of the people, but many Kenyans are subsistence farmers, growing little more than they need to support their families. The chief food crop is maize. The main cash crops and leading exports are coffee and tea. Manufactures include chemicals, leather and footwear, processed food, petroleum products and textiles.

AREA 580,370 sq km [224,081 sq mls]
POPULATION 28,337,000
CAPITAL (POPULATION) Nairobi (2,000,000)
GOVERNMENT Multiparty republic
ETHNIC GROUPS Kikuyu 21%, Luhya 14%, Luo 13%, Kamba 11%, Kalenjin 11%
LANGUAGES Swahili and English (both official)
RELIGIONS Christianity (Roman Catholic 27%, Protestant 19%, others 27%), traditional beliefs 19%, Islam 6%
CURRENCY Kenya shilling = 100 cents

KIRIBATI

The Republic of Kiribati comprises three groups of corall atolls scattered over about 5 million sq km [2 million sq mls]. Kiribati straddles the equator and temperatures are high and the rainfall is abundant.

Formerly part of the British Gilbert and Ellice Islands, Kiribati became independent in 1979. The main export is copra and the country depends heavily on foreign aid. AREA 728 sq km [281 sq mls]; POPULATION 85,000; CAPITAL Tarawa.

KOREA, NORTH

GEOGRAPHY The Democratic People's Republic of Korea occupies the northern part of the Korean peninsula which extends south from north-eastern China. Mountains form the heart of the country, with the highest peak, Paektu-san, reaching 2,744 m [9,003 ft] on the northern border.

North Korea has a fairly severe climate, with bitterly cold winters when winds blow from across central Asia, bringing snow and freezing conditions. In summer, moist winds from the oceans bring rain.

POLITICS & ECONOMY North Korea was created in 1945, when the peninsula, a Japanese colony since 1910, was divided into two parts. Soviet forces occupied the north, with US forces in the south. Soviet occupation led to a Communist government being established in 1948 under the leadership of Kim Il Sung. He initiated a Stalinist regime in which he assumed the role of dictator, and a personality cult developed around him. He was to become the world's most durable Communist leader.

The Korean War began in June 1950 when North Korean troops invaded the south. North Korea, aided by China and the Soviet Union, fought with South Korea, which was supported by troops from the United States and other UN members. The war ended in July 1953. An armistice was signed but no permanent peace treaty was agreed. After the war, North Korea adopted a hostile policy towards South Korea in pursuit of its policy of reunification. At times, the situation grew so tense that it became a matter of international concern.

The ending of the Cold War in the late 1980s eased the situation and both North and South Korea joined the United Nations in 1991. The two countries made several agreements, including one in which they agreed not to use force against each other.

As Communism collapsed in the Soviet Union, however, North Korea remained as isolated as ever, pursuing the overriding principle of self-reliance.

In 1993, North Korea began a new international crisis by announcing that it was withdrawing from the Nuclear Non-Proliferation Treaty. This led to suspicions that North Korea, which had signed the Treaty in 1985, was developing its own nuclear weapons. Kim Il Sung, who had ruled as a virtual dictator from 1948 until his death in 1994, was succeeded by his son, Kim Jong Il.

North Korea has considerable resources, including coal, copper, iron ore, lead, tin, tungsten and zinc. Under Communism, North Korea has concentrated on developing heavy, state-owned industries. Manufactures include chemicals, iron and steel, machinery, processed food and textiles. Agriculture employs about a third of the people of North Korea and rice is the leading crop. Economic decline and mis-management, aggravated by three successive crop failures caused by floods in 1995 and 1996 and a drought in 1997, led to famine on a large scale.

AREA 120,540 sq km [46,540 sq mls]
POPULATION 21,234,000
CAPITAL (POPULATION) Pyŏngyang (2,639,000)
GOVERNMENT Single-party people's republic
ETHNIC GROUPS Korean 99%
LANGUAGES Korean (official)
RELIGIONS Traditional beliefs 16%, Chondogyo 14%, Buddhism 2%, Christianity 1%
CURRENCY North Korean won = 100 chon

KOREA, SOUTH

GEOGRAPHY The Republic of Korea, as South Korea is officially known, occupies the southern part of the Korean peninsula. Mountains cover much of the country. The southern and western coasts are major farming regions. Many islands are found along the west and south coasts. The largest is Cheju-do, which contains South Korea's highest peak, which rises to 1,950 m [6,398 ft].

Like North Korea, South Korea is chilled in winter by cold, dry winds blowing from central Asia. Snow often covers the mountains in the east. The summers are hot and wet, especially in July and August.

POLITICS & ECONOMY After Japan's defeat in World War II (1939–45), North Korea was occupied by troops from the Soviet Union, while South Korea was occupied by United States forces. Attempts to reunify Korea failed and, in 1948, a National Assembly was elected in South Korea. This Assembly created the Republic of Korea, while North Korea became a Communist state. North Korean troops invaded the South in June 1950, sparking off the Korean War (1950–3).

In the 1950s, South Korea had a weak economy, which had been further damaged by the destruction caused by the Korean War. From the 1960s to the 1980s, South Korean governments worked to industrialize the economy. The governments were dominated by military leaders, who often used authoritarian methods, imprisoning opponents and restricting freedom of speech. In 1987, a new constitution was approved, enabling presidential elections to be held every five years.

In 1991, both South and North Korea became members of the United Nations. The two countries signed several agreements, including one in which they agreed not to use force against each other. But tensions between them continued.

The World Bank classifies South Korea as an 'upper-middle-income' developing country. It is also one of the world's fastest growing industrial economies. The country's resources include coal and tungsten, and its main manufactures are processed food and textiles. Since partition, heavy industries have been built up, making chemicals, fertilizers, iron and steel, and ships. South Korea has also developed the production of such things as computers, cars and television sets. In late 1997, however, the dramatic expansion of the economy was halted by a market crash which affected many of the booming economies of Asia. In an effort to negate the economic and social turmoil that resulted, tough reforms were demanded by the International Monetary Fund and an agreement was reached to restructure much of the short-term debt faced by the government.

Farming remains important in South Korea. Rice is the chief crop, together with fruit, grains and vegetables, while fishing provides a major source of protein.

AREA 99,020 sq km [38,232 sq mls]
POPULATION 46,417,000
CAPITAL (POPULATION) Seoul (11,641,000)
GOVERNMENT Multiparty republic
ETHNIC GROUPS Korean 99%
LANGUAGES Korean (official)
RELIGIONS Buddhism 28%, Christianity (Protestant 19%, Roman Catholic 6%)
CURRENCY South Korean won = 100 chon

KUWAIT

The State of Kuwait at the north end of the Gulf is largely made up of desert. Temperatures are high and the rainfall low. Kuwait became independent from Britain in 1961 and revenues from its oil wells have made it highly prosperous. Iraq invaded Kuwait in 1990 and much damage was inflicted in the ensuing conflict in 1991 when Kuwait was liberated. **AREA** 17,820 sq km [6,880 sq mls]; **POPULATION** 1,913,000; **CAPITAL** Kuwait City.

KYRGYZSTAN

GEOGRAPHY The Republic of Kyrgyzstan is a landlocked country between China, Tajikistan, Uzbekistan and Kazakstan. The country is mountainous, with spectacular scenery. The highest mountain, Pik Pobedy in the Tian Shan range, reaches 7,439 m [24,406 ft] in the east.

The lowlands of Kyrgyzstan have warm summers and cold winters. But the altitude influences the climate in the mountains, where the January temperatures plummet to –28°C [–18°F]. Far from any sea, Kyrgyzstan has a low annual rainfall.

POLITICS & ECONOMY In 1876, Kyrgyzstan became a province of Russia and Russian settlement in the area began. In 1916, Russia crushed a rebellion among the Kyrgyz, and many subsequently fled to China. In 1922, the area became an autonomous *oblast* (self-governing region) of the newly formed Soviet Union but, in 1936, it became one of the Soviet Socialist Republics. Under Communist rule, nomads were forced to work on government-run farms, while local customs and religious worship were suppressed. However, there were concurrent improvements in education and health.

In 1991, Kyrgyzstan became an independent country following the break-up of the Soviet Union. The Communist party was dissolved, but the country maintained ties with Russia through an organization called the Commonwealth of Independent States. Kyrgyzstan adopted a new constitution in 1994 and parliamentary elections were held in 1995.

In the early 1990s, when Kyrgyzstan was working to reform its economy, the World Bank classified it as a 'lower-middle-income' developing country. Agriculture, especially livestock rearing, is the chief activity. The chief products include cotton, eggs, fruits, grain, tobacco, vegetables and wool. But food must be imported. Industries are mainly concentrated around the capital Bishkek.

AREA 198,500 sq km [76,640 sq mls]
POPULATION 4,522,000
CAPITAL (POPULATION) Bishkek (584,000)
GOVERNMENT Multiparty republic
ETHNIC GROUPS Kyrgyz 52%, Russian 22%, Uzbek 13%, Ukrainian 3%, German 2%, Tatar 2%
LANGUAGES Kyrgyz (official), Russian, Uzbek
RELIGIONS Islam
CURRENCY Som = 100 tyiyn

LAOS

GEOGRAPHY The Lao People's Democratic Republic is a landlocked country in South-east Asia. Mountains and plateaux cover much of the country.

Most people live on the plains bordering the River Mekong and its tributaries. This river, one of Asia's longest, forms much of the country's north-western and south-western borders.

Laos has a tropical monsoon climate. Winters are dry and sunny, with winds blowing in from the north-east. The temperatures rise until April, when the wind directions are reversed and moist south-westerly winds reach Laos, heralding the start of the wet monsoon season.

POLITICS & ECONOMY France made Laos a protectorate in the late 19th century and ruled it as part of French Indo-China, a region which also included Cambodia and Vietnam. Laos became a member of the French Union in 1948 and an independent kingdom in 1954.

After independence, Laos suffered from instability caused by a long power struggle between royalist government forces and a pro-Communist group called the Pathet Lao. A civil war broke out in 1960 and continued into the 1970s. The Pathet Lao took control in 1975 and the king abdicated. Laos then came under the influence of Communist Vietnam, which had used Laos as a supply base during the Vietnam War (1957–75). However, from the late 1980s, Laos began to introduce economic reforms, including the encouragement of private enterprise.

Laos is one of the world's poorest countries. Agriculture employs about 76% of the people, as compared with 7% in industry and 17% in services. Rice is the main crop, and timber and coffee are both exported. But the most valuable export is electricity, which is produced at hydroelectric power stations on the River Mekong and is exported to Thailand. Laos also produces opium. In the early 1990s, Laos was thought to be the world's third biggest source of this illegal drug.

AREA 236,800 sq km [91,428 sq mls]
POPULATION 5,261,000
CAPITAL (POPULATION) Vientiane (449,000)
GOVERNMENT Single-party republic
ETHNIC GROUPS Lao 67%, Mon-Khmer 17%, Tai 8%
LANGUAGES Lao (official), Khmer, Tai, Miao
RELIGIONS Buddhism 58%, traditional beliefs 34%, Christianity 2%, Islam 1%
CURRENCY Kip = 100 at

LATVIA

GEOGRAPHY The Republic of Latvia is one of three states on the south-eastern corner of the Baltic Sea which were ruled as parts of the Soviet Union between 1940 and 1991. Latvia consists mainly of flat plains separated by low hills, composed of moraine (ice-worn rocks).

Riga has warm summers, but the winter months

LEBANON

(from December to March) are subzero. In the winter, the sea often freezes over. The rainfall is moderate and it occurs throughout the year, with light snow in winter.

POLITICS & ECONOMY In 1800, Russia was in control of Latvia, but Latvians declared their independence after World War I. In 1940, under a German-Soviet pact, Soviet troops occupied Latvia, but they were driven out by the Germans in 1941. Soviet troops returned in 1944 and Latvia became part of the Soviet Union. Under Soviet rule, many Russian immigrants settled in Latvia and many Latvians feared that the Russians would become the dominant ethnic group.

In the late 1980s, when reforms were being introduced in the Soviet Union, Latvia's government ended absolute Communist rule and made Latvian the official language. In 1990, it declared the country to be independent, an act which was finally recognized by the Soviet Union in September 1991.

Latvia held its first free elections to its parliament (the Saeima) in 1993. Voting was limited only to citizens of Latvia on 17 June 1940 and their descendants. This meant that about 34% of Latvian residents were unable to vote. In 1994, Latvia restricted the naturalization of non-Latvians, including many Russian settlers, who were not allowed to vote or own land. However, in 1998, the government agreed that all children born since independence should have automatic citizenship regardless of the status of their parents.

The World Bank classifies Latvia as a 'lower-middle-income' country and, in the 1990s, it faced many problems in turning its economy into a free-market system. Products include electronic goods, farm machinery, fertilizers, processed food, plastics, radios and vehicles. Latvia produces only about a tenth of the electricity it needs. It imports the rest from Belarus, Russia and Ukraine.

AREA 64,589 sq km [24,938 sq mls]
POPULATION 2,385,000
CAPITAL (POPULATION) Riga (840,000)
GOVERNMENT Multiparty republic
ETHNIC GROUPS Latvian 53%, Russian 34%, Belarussian 4%, Ukrainian 3%, Polish 2%, Lithuanian, Jewish
LANGUAGES Latvian (official), Russian
RELIGIONS Christianity (including Lutheran, Russian Orthodox and Roman Catholic)
CURRENCY Lats = 10 santimi

LEBANON

GEOGRAPHY The Republic of Lebanon is a country on the eastern shores of the Mediterranean Sea. Behind the coastal plain are the rugged Lebanon Mountains (Jabal Lubnan), which rise to 3,088 m [10,131 ft]. Another range, the Anti-Lebanon Mountains (Al Jabal Ash Sharqi), form the eastern border with Syria. Between the two ranges is the Bekaa (Beqaa) Valley, a fertile farming region.

The Lebanese coast has the hot, dry summers and mild, wet winters that are typical of many Mediterranean lands. Inland, onshore winds bring heavy rain to the western slopes of the mountains in the winter months, with snow at the higher altitudes.

POLITICS & ECONOMY Lebanon was ruled by Turkey from 1516 until World War I. France ruled the country from 1923, but Lebanon became independent in 1946. After independence, the Muslims and Christians agreed to share power, and Lebanon made rapid economic progress. But from the late 1950s, development was slowed by periodic conflict between Sunni and Shia Muslims, Druze and Christians. The situation was further complicated by the presence of Palestinian refugees who used bases in Lebanon to attack Israel.

In 1975, civil war broke out as private armies representing the many factions struggled for power. This led to intervention by Israel in the south and Syria in the north. UN peacekeeping forces arrived in 1978, but bombings, assassinations and kidnappings became almost everyday events in the 1980s. From 1991, Lebanon enjoyed an uneasy peace. However, Israel continued to occupy an area in the south and, periodically, Israel launched attacks on pro-Iranian (Shia) Hezbollah guerrilla bases in Lebanon.

Lebanon's civil war almost destroyed the valuable trade and financial services which had been Lebanon's chief source of income, together with tourism. The manufacturing industry, formerly another major activity, was also badly hit and many factories were damaged.

AREA 10,400 sq km [4,015 sq mls]
POPULATION 3,506,000
CAPITAL (POPULATION) Beirut (1,500,000)
GOVERNMENT Multiparty republic
ETHNIC GROUPS Arab (Lebanese 80%, Palestinian 12%), Armenian 5%, Syrian, Kurdish
LANGUAGES Arabic (official)
RELIGIONS Islam 58%, Christianity 27%, Druse
CURRENCY Lebanese pound = 100 piastres

LESOTHO

GEOGRAPHY The Kingdom of Lesotho is a landlocked country, completely enclosed by South Africa. The land is mountainous, rising to 3,482 m [11,424 ft] on the north-eastern border. The Drakensberg range covers most of the country.

The climate of Lesotho is greatly affected by the altitude, because most of the country lies above 1,500 m [4,921 ft]. Maseru has warm summers, but the temperatures fall below freezing in the winter. The mountains are colder. The rainfall varies, averaging around 700 mm [28 in].

POLITICS & ECONOMY The Basotho nation was founded in the 1820s by King Moshoeshoe I, who united various groups fleeing from tribal wars in southern Africa. Britain made the area a protectorate in 1868 and, in 1971, placed it under the British Cape Colony in South Africa. But in 1884, Basutoland, as the area was called, was reconstituted as a British protectorate, where whites were not allowed to own land.

The country finally became independent in 1966 as the Kingdom of Lesotho, with Moshoeshoe II, great-grandson of Moshoeshoe I, as its king. Since independence, Lesotho has suffered instability. The military seized power in 1986 and stripped Moshoeshoe II of his powers in 1990, installing his son, Letsie III, as monarch. After elections in 1993, Moshoeshoe II was restored to office in 1995. But after his death in a car crash in 1996, Letsie III again became king. In 1998, an army revolt, following an election in which the ruling party won 79 out of the 80 seats, caused much damage to the economy, despite the intervention of a South African force intended to maintain order.

Lesotho is a 'low-income' developing country. It lacks natural resources. Agriculture, mainly at subsistence level, light manufacturing and money sent home by Basotho working abroad are the main sources of income.

AREA 30,350 sq km [11,718 sq mls]
POPULATION 2,090,000
CAPITAL (POPULATION) Maseru (130,000)
GOVERNMENT Constitutional monarchy
ETHNIC GROUPS Sotho 99%
LANGUAGES Sesotho and English (both official)
RELIGIONS Christianity 93% (Roman Catholic 44%), traditional beliefs 6%
CURRENCY Loti = 100 lisente

LIBERIA

GEOGRAPHY The Republic of Liberia is a country in West Africa. Behind the coastline, 500 km [311 mls] long, lies a narrow coastal plain. Beyond, the land rises to a plateau region, with the highest land along the border with Guinea.

Liberia has a tropical climate with high temperatures and high humidity all through the year. The rainfall is abundant all year round, but there is a particularly wet period from June to November. The rainfall generally increases from east to west.

POLITICS & ECONOMY In the late 18th century, some white Americans in the United States wanted to help freed black slaves to return to Africa. In 1816, they set up the American Colonization Society, which bought land in what is now Liberia.

In 1822, the Society landed former slaves at a settlement on the coast which they named Monrovia. In 1847, Liberia became a fully independent republic with a constitution much like that of the United States. For many years, the Americo-Liberians controlled the country's government. US influence remained strong and the American Firestone Company, which ran Liberia's rubber plantations, was especially influential. Foreign companies were also involved in exploiting Liberia's mineral resources, including its huge iron-ore deposits.

In 1980, a military group composed of people from the local population killed the Americo-Liberian president, William R. Tolbert. An army sergeant, Samuel K. Doe, was made president of Liberia. Elections held in 1985 resulted in victory for Doe.

From 1989, the country was plunged into civil war between various ethnic groups. Doe was assassinated in 1990, but his successor, Amos Sawyer, continued to struggle with rebel groups. Peacekeeping forces from other West African countries arrived in Liberia, but the fighting continued. In 1995, a cease-fire was agreed and a council of state, composed of former warlords, was set up. In 1997, one of the warlords, Charles Taylor, was elected president.

Liberia's civil war devastated its economy. Three out of every four people depend on agriculture, though many of them grow little more than they need to feed their families. The chief food crops include cassava, rice and sugar cane, while rubber, cocoa and coffee are grown for export. But the most valuable export is iron ore.

Liberia also obtains revenue from its 'flag of

convenience', which is used by about one-sixth of the world's commercial shipping, exploiting low taxes.

AREA 111,370 sq km [43,000 sq mls]
POPULATION 2,772,000
CAPITAL (POPULATION) Monrovia (490,000)
GOVERNMENT Multiparty republic
ETHNIC GROUPS Kpelle 19%, Bassa 14%, Grebo 9%, Gio 8%, Kru 7%, Mano 7%
LANGUAGES English (official), Mande, Mel, Kwa
RELIGIONS Christianity 68%, Islam 14%, traditional beliefs and others 18%
CURRENCY Liberian dollar = 100 cents

LIBYA

GEOGRAPHY The Socialist People's Libyan Arab Jamahiriya, as Libya is officially called, is a large country in North Africa. Most people live on the coastal plains in the north-east and north-west. The Sahara, the world's largest desert which occupies 95% of Libya, reaches the Mediterranean coast along the Gulf of Sidra (Khalij Surt).

The coastal plains in the north-east and north-west of the country have Mediterranean climates, with hot, dry summers and mild winters, with some rain in the winter months. Inland, the average yearly rainfall drops to 100 mm [4 in] or less.

POLITICS & ECONOMY Italy took over Libya in 1911, but lost it during World War II. Britain and France then jointly ruled Libya until 1951, when the country became an independent kingdom.

In 1969, a military group headed by Colonel Muammar Gaddafi deposed the king and set up a military government. Under Gaddafi, the government took control of the economy and used money from oil exports to finance welfare services and development projects. Gaddafi has attracted international criticism for his support for radical movements, such as the PLO (Palestine Liberation Organization) and various terrorist groups. In 1986, his policies led the United States to bomb installations in the capital. Libya has disputes with its neighbours, including Chad, where it sent troops to intervene in a civil war. In 1994, the International Court of Justice ruled against Libya's claim for territory in the Aozou Strip in northern Chad.

The discovery of oil and natural gas in 1959 led to the transformation of Libya's economy. Formerly one of the world's poorest countries, it has become Africa's richest in terms of its per capita income. But it remains a developing country because of its dependence on oil, which accounts for nearly all of its export revenues.

Agriculture is important, although Libya has to import food. Crops include barley, citrus fruits, dates, olives, potatoes and wheat. Cattle, sheep and poultry are raised. Libya has oil refineries and petrochemical plants. Other manufactures include cement and steel.

AREA 1,759,540 sq km [679,358 sq mls]
POPULATION 4,875,000
CAPITAL (POPULATION) Tripoli (960,000)
GOVERNMENT Single-party socialist state
ETHNIC GROUPS Libyan Arab and Berber 89%
LANGUAGES Arabic (official), Berber
RELIGIONS Islam
CURRENCY Libyan dinar = 1,000 dirhams

LIECHTENSTEIN

The tiny Principality of Liechtenstein is sandwiched between Switzerland and Austria. The River Rhine flows along its western border, while Alpine peaks rise in the east and south. The climate is relatively mild. Since 1924, Liechtenstein has been in a customs union with Switzerland and, like its neighbour, it is extremely prosperous. Taxation is low and, as a result, the country has become a haven for international companies. AREA 157 sq km [61 sq mls]; POPULATION 32,000; CAPITAL Vaduz.

LITHUANIA

GEOGRAPHY The Republic of Lithuania is the southernmost of the three Baltic states which were ruled as part of the Soviet Union between 1940 and 1991. Much of the land is flat or gently rolling, with the highest land in the south-east.

Winters are cold. January's temperatures average –3°C [27°F] in the west and –6°C [21°F] in the east. Summers are warm, with average temperatures in July of 17°C [63°F]. The average rainfall in the west is about 630 mm [25 in]. Inland areas are drier.

POLITICS & ECONOMY The Lithuanian people were united into a single nation in the 12th century, and later joined a union with Poland. In 1795, Lithuania came under Russian rule. After World War I (1914–18), Lithuania declared itself independent, and in 1920 it signed a peace treaty with the Russians, though Poland held Vilnius until 1939. In 1940, the Soviet Union occupied Lithuania, but the Germans invaded in 1941. Soviet forces returned in 1944, and Lithuania was integrated into the Soviet Union. In 1988, when the Soviet Union was introducing reforms, the Lithuanians demanded independence. Their language is one of the oldest in the world, and the country was always the most homogenous of the Baltic states, staunchly Catholic and resistant of attempts to suppress their culture. Pro-independence groups won the national elections in 1990 and, in 1991, the Soviet Union recognized Lithuania's independence.

After independence, Lithuania faced many problems as it sought to reform its economy and introduce a private enterprise system. In 1998, Valdas Adamkus, a Lithuanian-American who had fled the country in 1944, was elected president.

The World Bank classifies Lithuania as a 'lower-middle-income' developing country. Lithuania lacks natural resources, but manufacturing, based on imported materials, is the most valuable activity.

AREA 65,200 sq km [25,200 sq mls]
POPULATION 3,600,000
CAPITAL (POPULATION) Vilnius (576,000)
GOVERNMENT Multiparty republic
ETHNIC GROUPS Lithuanian 80%, Russian 9%, Polish 7%, Belarussian 2%
LANGUAGES Lithuanian (official), Russian, Polish
RELIGIONS Christianity (mainly Roman Catholic)
CURRENCY Litas = 100 centai

LUXEMBOURG

GEOGRAPHY The Grand Duchy of Luxembourg is one of the smallest and oldest countries in Europe. The north belongs to an upland region which includes the Ardenne in Belgium and Luxembourg, and the Eifel highlands in Germany.

Luxembourg has a temperate climate. The south has warm summers and autumns, when grapes ripen in sheltered south-eastern valleys. Winters are sometimes severe, especially in upland areas.

POLITICS & ECONOMY Germany occupied Luxembourg in World Wars I and II. In 1944–5, northern Luxembourg was the scene of the famous Battle of the Bulge. In 1948, Luxembourg joined Belgium and the Netherlands in a union called Benelux and, in the 1950s, it was one of the six founders of what is now the European Union. Luxembourg has played a major role in Europe. Its capital contains the headquarters of several international agencies, including the European Coal and Steel Community and the European Court of Justice. The city is also a major financial centre.

Luxembourg has iron-ore reserves and is a major steel producer. It also has many high-technology industries, producing electronic goods and computers. Steel and other manufactures, including chemicals, rubber products, glass and aluminium, dominate the country's exports. Other major activities include tourism and financial services.

AREA 2,590 sq km [1,000 sq mls]
POPULATION 425,000
CAPITAL (POPULATION) Luxembourg (76,000)
GOVERNMENT Constitutional monarchy (Grand Duchy)
ETHNIC GROUPS Luxembourger 71%, Portuguese 10%, Italian 5%, French 3%, Belgian 3%
LANGUAGES Letzeburgish/Luxembourgian (official), French, German
RELIGIONS Christianity (Roman Catholic 95%)
CURRENCY Euro; Luxem. franc = 100 centimes

MACAU

Macau is a small peninsula at the head of the Zhu Jiang (Pearl) River, west of Hong Kong. A Portuguese colony since 1557, Macau was returned to China in 1999. Its main industries are textiles, gambling and tourism. AREA 16 sq km [6 sq mls]; POPULATION 429,000; CAPITAL Macau.

MACEDONIA

GEOGRAPHY The Republic of Macedonia is a country in south-eastern Europe, which was once one

of the six republics that made up the former Federal People's Republic of Yugoslavia. This landlocked country is largely mountainous or hilly.

Macedonia has hot summers, though highland areas are cooler. Winters are cold and snowfalls are often heavy. The climate is fairly continental in character and rain occurs throughout the year.

POLITICS & ECONOMY Between 1912 and 1913, the area called Macedonia was divided between Serbia, Bulgaria, which took a small area in the east, and Greece, which gained the south. At the end of World War I, Serbian Macedonia became part of the Kingdom of the Serbs, Croats and Slovenes, which was renamed Yugoslavia in 1929. After World War II, Yugoslavia became a Communist regime.

Tito died in 1980 and, in the early 1990s, the country broke up into five separate republics. Macedonia declared its independence in September 1991. Greece objected to this territory using the name Macedonia, which it considered to be a Greek name. It also objected to a symbol on Macedonia's flag and a reference in the constitution to the desire to reunite the three parts of the old Macedonia.

Macedonia adopted a new clause in its constitution rejecting any Macedonian claims on Greek territory and, in 1993, the United Nations accepted the new republic as a member under the name of The Former Yugoslav Republic of Macedonia (FYROM).

By the end of 1993, all the countries of the European Union, except Greece, were establishing diplomatic relations with the FYROM. Greece barred Macedonian trade in 1994, but lifted the ban in 1995 when Macedonia agreed to redesign its flag and remove all territorial claims from its constitution.

In 1999, Macedonia faced new problems caused by the influx of ethnic Albanian refugees from neighbouring Kosovo, Yugoslavia.

The World Bank describes Macedonia as a 'lower-middle-income' developing country. Manufactures dominate the country's exports. Macedonia mines coal, but imports all its oil and natural gas. The country is self-sufficient in its basic food needs.

AREA 25,710 sq km [9,927 sq mls]
POPULATION 2,009,000
CAPITAL (POPULATION) Skopje (541,000)
GOVERNMENT Multiparty republic
ETHNIC GROUPS Macedonian 65%, Albanian 21%, Turkish 5%, Romanian 3%, Serb 2%
LANGUAGES Macedonian (official), Albanian
RELIGIONS Christianity (mainly Eastern Orthodox, with Macedonian Orthodox and Roman Catholic communities), Islam
CURRENCY Dinar = 100 paras

MADAGASCAR

GEOGRAPHY The Democratic Republic of Madagascar, in south-eastern Africa, is an island nation, which has a larger area than France. Behind the narrow coastal plains in the east lies a highland zone, mostly between 610 m and 1,220 m [2,000 ft to 4,000 ft] above sea level. Broad plains border the Mozambique Channel in the west.

Temperatures in the highlands are moderated by the altitude. The winters (from April to September) are dry, but heavy rains occur in summer. The eastern coastlands are warm and humid. The west is drier and the south and south-west are hot and dry.

POLITICS & ECONOMY People from South-east Asia began to settle on Madagascar around 2,000 years ago. Subsequent influxes from Africa and Arabia added to the island's diverse heritage, culture and language.

French troops defeated a Malagasy army in 1895 and Madagascar became a French colony. In 1960, it achieved full independence as the Malagasy Republic. In 1972, army officers seized control and, in 1975, under the leadership of Lt-Commander Didier Ratsiraka, the country was renamed Madagascar. Parliamentary elections were held in 1977, but Ratsiraka remained president of a one-party socialist state. The government resigned in 1991 following huge demonstrations. In 1992–3, Ratsiraka was defeated by opposition leader, Albert Zafy. But Ratsiraka returned to power following presidential elections in 1996.

Madagascar is one of the world's poorest countries. The land has been badly eroded because of the cutting down of the forests and overgrazing of the grasslands. Farming, fishing and forestry employ about 80% of the people. The country's food crops include bananas, cassava, rice and sweet potatoes. Coffee is the leading export.

AREA 587,040 sq km [226,656 sq mls]
POPULATION 14,463,000
CAPITAL (POPULATION) Antananarivo (1,053,000)
GOVERNMENT Republic
ETHNIC GROUPS Merina 27%, Betsimisaraka 15%, Betsileo 11%, Tsimihety 7%, Sakalava 6%
LANGUAGES Malagasy, French (both official)
RELIGIONS Christianity 51%, traditional beliefs 47%, Islam 2%
CURRENCY Malagasy franc = 100 centimes

MALAWI

GEOGRAPHY The Republic of Malawi includes part of Lake Malawi, which is drained by the River Shire, a tributary of the River Zambezi. The land is mostly mountainous. The highest peak, Mulanje, reaches 3,000 m [9,843 ft] in the south-east.

While the low-lying areas of Malawi are hot and humid all year round, the uplands have a pleasant climate. Lilongwe, at about 1,100 m [3,609 ft] above sea level, has a warm and sunny climate. Frosts sometimes occur in July and August, in the middle of the long dry season.

POLITICS & ECONOMY Malawi, then called Nyasaland, became a British protectorate in 1891. In 1953, Britain established the Federation of Rhodesia and Nyasaland, which also included what are now Zambia and Zimbabwe. Black African opposition, led in Nyasaland by Dr Hastings Kamuzu Banda, led to the dissolution of the federation in 1963. In 1964, Nyasaland became independent as Malawi, with Banda as prime minister. Banda became president when the country became a republic in 1966 and, in 1971, he was made president for life. Banda ruled autocratically through the only party, the Malawi Congress Party. However, a multiparty system was restored in 1993, and in elections in 1994, Banda and his party were defeated and Bakili Muluzi became president. Banda died in 1997.

Malawi is one of the world's poorest countries. More than 80% of the people are farmers, but many grow little more than they need to feed their families.

AREA 118,480 sq km [45,745 sq mls]
POPULATION 9,840,000
CAPITAL (POPULATION) Lilongwe (395,000)
GOVERNMENT Multiparty republic
ETHNIC GROUPS Maravi (Chewa, Nyanja, Tonga, Tumbuka) 58%, Lomwe 18%, Yao 13%, Ngoni 7%
LANGUAGES Chichewa and English (both official)
RELIGIONS Christianity (Protestant 34%, Roman Catholic 28%), traditional beliefs 21%, Islam 16%
CURRENCY Kwacha = 100 tambala

MALAYSIA

GEOGRAPHY The Federation of Malaysia consists of two main parts. Peninsular Malaysia, which is joined to mainland Asia, contains about 80% of the population. The other main regions, Sabah and Sarawak, are in northern Borneo, an island which Malaysia shares with Indonesia. Much of the land is mountainous, with coastal lowlands bordering the rugged interior. The highest peak, Kinabalu, reaches 4,101 m [13,455 ft] in Sabah.

Malaysia has a hot equatorial climate. The temperatures are high all through the year, though the mountains are much cooler than the lowland areas. The rainfall is heavy throughout the year.

POLITICS & ECONOMY Japan occupied what is now Malaysia during World War II, but British rule was re-established in 1945. In the 1940s and 1950s, British troops fought a war against Communist guerrillas, but Peninsular Malaysia (then called Malaya) became independent in 1957. Malaysia was created in 1963, when Malaya, Singapore, Sabah and Sarawak agreed to unite, but Singapore withdrew in 1965.

From the 1970s, Malaysia achieved rapid economic progress and, by the mid-1990s, it was playing a major part in regional affairs, especially through its membership of ASEAN (Association of South-east Asian Nations). However, together with several other countries in eastern Asia, Malaysia was hit by economic recession in 1997, including a major fall in stock market values. In response to the crisis, the government ordered the repatriation of many temporary foreign workers and initiated a series of austerity measures aimed at restoring confidence and avoiding the chronic debt problems affecting some other Asian countries.

The World Bank classifies Malaysia as an 'upper-middle-income' developing country. Malaysia is a leading producer of palm oil, rubber and tin.

Manufacturing now plays a major part in the economy. Manufactures are diverse, including cars, chemicals, a wide range of electronic goods, plastics, textiles, rubber and wood products.

AREA 329,750 sq km [127,316 sq mls]
POPULATION 20,993,000
CAPITAL (POPULATION) Kuala Lumpur (1,145,000)
GOVERNMENT Federal constitutional monarchy
ETHNIC GROUPS Malay and other indigenous groups 62%, Chinese 30%, Indian 8%
LANGUAGES Malay (official), Chinese, Iban
RELIGIONS Islam 53%, Buddhism 17%, Chinese folk religionist 12%, Hinduism 7%, Christianity 6%
CURRENCY Ringgit (Malaysian dollar) = 100 cents

MALDIVES

The Republic of the Maldives consists of about 1,200 low-lying coral islands, south of India. The highest point is 24 m [79 ft], but most of the land is only 1.8 m [6 ft] above sea level. The islands became a British territory in 1887 and independence was achieved in 1965. Tourism and fishing are the main industries. **AREA** 298 sq km [115 sq mls]; **POPULATION** 290,000; **CAPITAL** Malé.

MALI

GEOGRAPHY The Republic of Mali is a landlocked country in northern Africa. The land is generally flat, with the highest land in the Adrar des Iforhas on the border with Algeria.

Northern Mali is part of the Sahara, with a hot, practically rainless climate. But the south has enough rain for farming.

POLITICS & ECONOMY France ruled the area, then known as French Sudan, from 1893 until the country became independent as Mali in 1960.

The first socialist government was overthrown in 1968 by an army group led by Moussa Traoré, but he was ousted in 1991. Multiparty democracy was restored in 1992 and Alpha Oumar Konaré was elected president. The new government agreed a pact providing for a special administration for the Tuareg minority in the north.

Mali is one of the world's poorest countries and 70% of the land is desert or semi-desert. Only about 2% of the land is used for growing crops, while 25% is used for grazing animals. Despite this, agriculture employs more than 80% of the people, many of whom still subsist by nomadic livestock rearing.

AREA 1,240,190 sq km [478,837 sq mls]
POPULATION 10,109,000
CAPITAL (POPULATION) Bamako (746,000)
GOVERNMENT Multiparty republic
ETHNIC GROUPS Bambara 32%, Fulani (or Peul) 14%, Senufo 12%, Soninke 9%, Tuareg 7%, Songhai 7%, Malinke (Mandingo or Mandinke) 7%
LANGUAGES French (official), Voltaic languages
RELIGIONS Islam 90%, traditional beliefs 9%, Christianity 1%
CURRENCY CFA franc = 100 centimes

MALTA

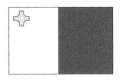

GEOGRAPHY The Republic of Malta consists of two main islands, Malta and Gozo, a third, much smaller island called Comino lying between the two large islands, and two tiny islets.

Malta's climate is typically Mediterranean, with hot and dry summers and mild and wet winters. The sirocco, a hot wind that blows from North Africa, may raise temperatures considerably during the spring.

POLITICS & ECONOMY During World War I (1914–18) Malta was an important naval base. In World War II (1939–45), Italian and German aircraft bombed the islands. In recognition of the bravery of the Maltese, the British King George VI awarded the George Cross to Malta in 1942. In 1953, Malta became a base for NATO (North Atlantic Treaty Organization). Malta became independent in 1964, and in 1974 it became a republic. In 1979, Britain's military agreement with Malta expired, and Malta ceased to be a military base when all the British forces withdrew. In the 1980s, the people declared Malta a neutral country. In the 1990s, Malta applied to join the European Union. The application was scrapped when the Labour Party won the elections in 1996, but, following the Labour Party's defeat in elections in 1998, the situation changed yet again.

The World Bank classifies Malta as an 'upper-middle-income' developing country. It lacks natural resources, and most people work in the former naval dockyards, which are now used for commercial shipbuilding and repair, in manufacturing industries and in the tourist industry.

Manufactures include chemicals, processed food and chemicals. Farming is difficult, because of the rocky soils. Crops include barley, fruits, potatoes and wheat. Malta also has a small fishing industry.

AREA 316 sq km [122 sq mls]
POPULATION 379,000
CAPITAL (POPULATION) Valletta (102,000)
GOVERNMENT Multiparty republic
ETHNIC GROUPS Maltese 96%, British 2%
LANGUAGES Maltese and English (both official)
RELIGIONS Christianity (Roman Catholic 99%)
CURRENCY Maltese lira = 100 cents

MARSHALL ISLANDS

The Republic of the Marshall Islands, a former US territory, became fully independent in 1991. This island nation, lying north of Kiribati in a region known as Micronesia, is heavily dependent on US aid. The main activities are agriculture and tourism. **AREA** 181 sq km [70 sq mls]; **POPULATION** 63,000; **CAPITAL** Dalap-Uliga-Darrit, on Majuro island.

MARTINIQUE

Martinique, a volcanic island nation in the Caribbean, was colonized by France in 1635. It became a French overseas department in 1946. Tourism and agriculture are major activities. About 70% of Martinique's Gross Domestic Product is provided by the French government, allowing for a good standard of living. **AREA** 1,100 sq km [425 sq mls]; **POPULATION** 407,000; **CAPITAL** Fort-de-France.

MAURITANIA

GEOGRAPHY The Islamic Republic of Mauritania in north-western Africa is nearly twice the size of France. But France has more than 26 times as many people. Part of the world's largest desert, the Sahara, covers northern Mauritania and most Mauritanians live in the south-west.

The amount of rainfall and the length of the rainy season increase from north to south. Much of the land is desert, with dry north-east and easterly winds throughout the year. But south-westerly winds bring summer rain to the south.

POLITICS & ECONOMY Originally part of the great African empires of Ghana and Mali, France set up a protectorate in Mauritania in 1903, attempting to exploit the trade in gum arabic. The country became a territory of French West Africa and a French colony in 1920. French West Africa was a huge territory, which included present-day Benin, Burkina Faso, Guinea, Ivory Coast, Mali, Niger and Senegal, as well as Mauritania. In 1958, Mauritania became a self-governing territory in the French Union and it became fully independent in 1960.

In 1976, Spain withdrew from Spanish (now Western) Sahara, a territory bordering Mauritania to the north. Morocco occupied the northern two-thirds of this territory, while Mauritania took the rest. But Saharan guerrillas belonging to POLISARIO (the Popular Front for the Liberation of Saharan Territories) began an armed struggle for independence. In 1979, Mauritania withdrew from the southern part of Western Sahara, which was then occupied by Morocco. In 1991, the country adopted a new constitution when the people voted to create a multiparty government. Multiparty elections were held in 1992 and 1996-7.

The World Bank classifies Mauritania as a 'low-income' developing country. Agriculture employs 69% of the people. Some are herders who move around with herds of cattle and sheep, though recent droughts forced many farmers to seek aid in the cities.

AREA 1,030,700 sq km [397,953 sq mls]
POPULATION 2,511,000
CAPITAL (POPULATION) Nouakchott (600,000)
GOVERNMENT Multiparty Islamic republic
ETHNIC GROUPS Moor (Arab-Berber) 70%, Wolof 7%, Tukulor 5%, Soninke 3%, Fulani 1%
LANGUAGES Arabic (official), Wolof, French
RELIGIONS Islam 99%
CURRENCY Ouguiya = 5 khoums

MAURITIUS

The Republic of Mauritius, an Indian Ocean nation lying east of Madagascar, was previously ruled by France and Britain until it achieved independence in 1968. It became a republic in 1992. Sugar is the main export, but tourism is now vital to the economy. **AREA** 1,860 sq km [718 sq mls]; **POPULATION** 1,168,000; **CAPITAL** Port Louis.

MEXICO

GEOGRAPHY The United Mexican States, as Mexico is officially named, is the world's most populous Spanish-speaking country. Much of the land is mountainous, although most people live on the central plateau. Mexico contains two large peninsulas, Lower (or Baja) California in the north-west and the flat Yucatán peninsula in the south-east.

The climate varies according to the altitude. The resort of Acapulco on the south-west coast has a dry and sunny climate. Mexico City, at about 2,300 m [7,546 ft] above sea level, is much cooler. Most rain occurs between June and September. The rainfall decreases north of Mexico City and northern Mexico is mainly arid.

POLITICS & ECONOMY In the mid-19th century, Mexico lost land to the United States, and between 1910 and 1921 violent revolutions created chaos.

Reforms were introduced in the 1920s and, in 1929, the Institutional Revolutionary Party (PRI) was formed. The PRI dominated Mexican politics, though it lost its overall majority in the Chamber of Deputies in 1997. Mexico faces many problems, including unemployment and rapid urbanization especially around Mexico City, demands for indigenous rights by Amerindian groups, and illegal emigration to the USA.

The World Bank classifies Mexico as an 'upper-middle-income' developing country. Agriculture is important. Food crops include beans, maize, rice and wheat, while cash crops include coffee, cotton, fruits and vegetables. Beef cattle, dairy cattle and other livestock are raised and fishing is also important.

But oil and oil products are the chief exports, while manufacturing is the most valuable activity. Many factories near the northern border assemble goods, such as car parts and electrical products, for US companies. These factories are called *maquiladoras*. Hope for the future lies in increasing economic co-operation with the USA and Canada through NAFTA (North American Free Trade Association), which came into being on 1 January 1994.

> **AREA** 1,958,200 sq km [756,061 sq mls]
> **POPULATION** 98,553,000
> **CAPITAL (POPULATION)** Mexico City (15,643,000)
> **GOVERNMENT** Federal republic
> **ETHNIC GROUPS** Mestizo 60%, Amerindian 30%, European 9%
> **LANGUAGES** Spanish (official)
> **RELIGIONS** Christianity (Roman Catholic 90%, Protestant 5%)
> **CURRENCY** New peso = 100 centavos

MICRONESIA

The Federated States of Micronesia, a former US territory covering a vast area in the western Pacific Ocean, became fully independent in 1991. The main export is copra. Fishing and tourism are also important. **AREA** 705 sq km [272 sq mls]; **POPULATION** 127,000; **CAPITAL** Palikir.

MOLDOVA

GEOGRAPHY The Republic of Moldova is a small country sandwiched between Ukraine and Romania. It was formerly one of the 15 republics that made up the Soviet Union. Much of the land is hilly and the highest areas are near the centre of the country.

Moldova has a moderately continental climate, with warm summers and fairly cold winters when temperatures dip below freezing point. Most of the rain comes in the warmer months.

POLITICS & ECONOMY In the 14th century, the Moldavians formed a state called Moldavia. It included part of Romania and Bessarabia (now the modern country of Moldova). The Ottoman Turks took the area in the 16th century, but in 1812 Russia took over Bessarabia. In 1861, Moldavia and Walachia united to form Romania. Russia retook southern Bessarabia in 1878.

After World War I (1914–18), all of Bessarabia was returned to Romania, but the Soviet Union did not recognize this act. From 1944, the Moldovan Soviet Socialist Republic was part of the Soviet Union.

In 1989, the Moldovans asserted their independence and ethnicity by making Romanian the official language and, at the end of 1991, Moldova became an independent country. In 1992, fighting occurred between Moldovans and Russians in Trans-Dniester, a mainly Russian-speaking area east of the River Dniester. This region was given a special status within Moldova in 1996. The first multiparty elections were held in 1994, when a proposal to unite with Romania was decisively rejected.

Moldova is a fertile country in which agriculture remains central to the economy. Major products include fruits, maize, tobacco and wine.

There are few natural resources within Moldova, and the government imports materials and fuels for its industries. Light industries, such as food processing and the manufacturing of household appliances, are gradually expanding.

> **AREA** 33,700 sq km [13,010 sq mls]
> **POPULATION** 4,458,000
> **CAPITAL (POPULATION)** Chisinau (700,000)
> **GOVERNMENT** Multiparty republic
> **ETHNIC GROUPS** Moldovan 65%, Ukrainian 14%, Russian 13%, Gagauz 4%, Jewish 2%, Bulgarian
> **LANGUAGES** Moldovan/Romanian (official)
> **RELIGIONS** Christianity (Eastern Orthodox)
> **CURRENCY** Leu = 100 bani

MONACO

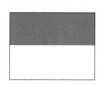

The tiny Principality of Monaco consists of a narrow strip of coastline and a rocky peninsula on the French Riviera. Its considerable wealth is derived largely from banking, finance, gambling and tourism. Monaco's citizens do not pay any state tax. Its attractions include the Monte Carlo casino and such sporting events as the Monte Carlo Rally and the Monaco Grand Prix. **AREA** 1.5 sq km [0.6 sq mls]; **POPULATION** 32,000; **CAPITAL** Monaco.

MONGOLIA

GEOGRAPHY The State of Mongolia is the world's largest landlocked country. It consists mainly of high plateaux, with the Gobi desert in the south-east.

Ulan Bator lies on the northern edge of a desert plateau in the heart of Asia. It has bitterly cold winters. In the summer months, the temperatures are moderated by the height of the land.

POLITICS & ECONOMY In the 13th century, Genghis Khan united the Mongolian peoples and built up a great empire. Under his grandson, Kublai Khan, the Mongol empire extended from Korea and China to eastern Europe and present-day Iraq.

The Mongol empire broke up in the late 14th century. In the early 17th century, Inner Mongolia came under Chinese control, and by the late 17th century Outer Mongolia had become a Chinese province. In 1911, the Mongolians drove the Chinese out of Outer Mongolia and made the area a Buddhist kingdom. But in 1924, under Russian influence, the Communist Mongolian People's Republic was set up. From the 1950s, Mongolia supported the Soviet Union in its disputes with China. In 1990, the people demonstrated for more freedom and free elections in June 1990 resulted in victory for the Mongolian People's Revolutionary Party, which was composed of Communists. But Communist rule finally ended in 1996 when the elections were won by the opposition Democratic Union coalition.

The World Bank classifies Mongolia as a 'lower-middle-income' developing country. Most people were once nomads, who moved around with their herds of sheep, cattle, goats and horses. Under Communist rule, most people were moved into permanent homes on government-owned farms. But livestock and animal products remain leading exports. The Communists also developed industry, especially the mining of coal, copper, gold, molybdenum, tin and tungsten, and manufacturing. Minerals and fuels now account for around half of Mongolia's exports.

> **AREA** 1,566,500 sq km [604,826 sq mls]
> **POPULATION** 2,579,000
> **CAPITAL (POPULATION)** Ulan Bator (619,000)
> **GOVERNMENT** Multiparty republic
> **ETHNIC GROUPS** Khalkha Mongol 79%, Kazak 6%
> **LANGUAGES** Khalkha Mongolian (official), Kazak
> **RELIGIONS** Tibetan Buddhist (Lamaist)
> **CURRENCY** Tugrik = 100 möngös

MONTSERRAT

Monserrat is a British overseas territory in the Caribbean Sea. The climate is tropical and hurricanes often cause much damage. Intermittent eruptions of the Soufrière Hills volcano between 1995 and 1998 led to the emigration of many of the inhabitants and the virtual destruction of Plymouth, the capital, in the southern part of the island. **AREA** 1,100 sq km [39 sq mls]; **POPULATION** (prior to the volcanic activity) 12,000; **CAPITAL** Plymouth.

MOROCCO

GEOGRAPHY The Kingdom of Morocco lies in north-western Africa. Its name comes from the Arabic Maghreb-el-Aksa, meaning 'the farthest west'. Behind the western coastal plain the land rises to a broad plateau and ranges of the Atlas Mountains. The High (Haut) Atlas contains the highest peak, Djebel Toubkal, at 4,165 m [13,665 ft]. East of the mountains, the land descends to the arid Sahara.

The Atlantic coast of Morocco is cooled by the Canaries Current. Inland, summers are hot and dry. The winters are mild. In winter, between October and April, south-westerly winds from the Atlantic Ocean bring moderate rainfall, and snow often falls on the High Atlas Mountains.

POLITICS & ECONOMY The original people of Morocco were the Berbers. But in the 680s, Arab invaders introduced Islam and the Arabic language. By the early 20th century, France and Spain controlled Morocco, but Morocco became an independent kingdom in 1956. Although Morocco is a constitutional monarchy, King Hassan II has ruled the country in a generally authoritarian way since coming to the throne in 1961. Since 1979, Morocco has occupied the whole of Western (formerly Spanish) Sahara. UN attempts to hold a referendum on the territory's future have failed because of the difficulty of drawing up an agreed voters' register.

Morocco is classified as a 'lower-middle-income' developing country. It is the world's third largest producer of phosphate rock, which is used to make fertilizer. One reason why Morocco wants to keep Western Sahara is that it, too, has large phosphate reserves. Farming employs 44% of Moroccans. Tourism is also important.

AREA 446,550 sq km [172,413 sq mls]
POPULATION 29,114,000
CAPITAL (POPULATION) Rabat (1,220,000)
GOVERNMENT Constitutional monarchy
ETHNIC GROUPS Arab 70%, Berber 30%
LANGUAGES Arabic (official), Berber, French
RELIGIONS Islam 99%, Christianity 1%
CURRENCY Moroccan dirham = 100 centimes

MOZAMBIQUE

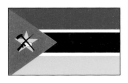

GEOGRAPHY The Republic of Mozambique borders the Indian Ocean in south-eastern Africa. The coastal plains are narrow in the north but broaden in the south. Inland lie plateaux and hills, which make up another two-fifths of Mozambique.

Mozambique has a mostly tropical climate. The capital Maputo, which lies outside the tropics, has hot and humid summers, though the winters are mild and fairly dry.

POLITICS & ECONOMY In 1885, when the European powers divided Africa, Mozambique was recognized as a Portuguese colony. But black African opposition to European rule gradually increased. In 1961, the Front for the Liberation of Mozambique (FRELIMO) was founded to oppose Portuguese rule.

In 1964, FRELIMO launched a guerrilla war, which continued for ten years. Mozambique became independent in 1975.

After independence, Mozambique became a one-party state. Its government aided African nationalists in Rhodesia (now Zimbabwe) and South Africa. But the white governments of these countries helped an opposition group, the Mozambique National Resistance Movement (RENAMO) to lead an armed struggle against Mozambique's government. The civil war, combined with severe droughts, caused much human suffering in the 1980s. In 1989, FRELIMO declared that it had dropped its Communist policies and ended one-party rule. The war officially ended in 1992 and multiparty elections in 1994 heralded more stable conditions. In 1995 Mozambique became the 53rd member of the Commonwealth, joining its English-speaking allies in southern Africa.

According to the World Bank, Mozambique is one of the world's five poorest countries. Agriculture employs 85% of the people, though many farmers grow little more than they need to feed their families. Crops include cassava, cotton, cashew nuts, fruits, maize, rice, sugar cane and tea.

AREA 801,590 sq km [309,494 sq mls]
POPULATION 18,641,000
CAPITAL (POPULATION) Maputo (2,000,000)
GOVERNMENT Multiparty republic
ETHNIC GROUPS Makua 47%, Tsonga 23%, Malawi 12%, Shona 11%, Yao 4%, Swahili 1%, Makonde 1%
LANGUAGES Portuguese (official), many others
RELIGIONS Traditional beliefs 48%, Christianity (Roman Catholic 31%, others 9%), Islam 13%
CURRENCY Metical = 100 centavos

NAMIBIA

GEOGRAPHY The Republic of Namibia was formerly ruled by South Africa, who called it South West Africa. The country became independent in 1990. The coastal region contains the arid Namib Desert, which is virtually uninhabited. Inland is a central plateau, bordered by a rugged spine of mountains stretching north–south. Eastern Namibia contains part of the Kalahari desert.

Namibia is a warm and mostly arid country. Lying at 1,700 m [5,500 ft] above sea level, Windhoek has an average annual rainfall of about 370 mm [15 in], often occurring during thunderstorms in the hot summer months.

POLITICS & ECONOMY During World War I, South African troops defeated the Germans who ruled what is now Namibia. After World War II, many people challenged South Africa's right to govern the territory and a civil war began in the 1960s between African guerrillas and South African troops. A cease-fire was agreed in 1989 and the country became independent in 1990. After winning independence, the government pursued a successful policy of 'national reconciliation'. A small area on Namibia's coast, called Walvis Bay (Walvisbaai), remained part of South Africa until 1994, when South Africa transferred it to Namibia.

Namibia is rich in mineral reserves, including diamonds, uranium, zinc and copper. Minerals make up 90% of the exports. But farming employs about two out of every five Namibians. Sea fishing is also

important, though overfishing has reduced the yields of the country's fishing fleet. The country has few industries, but tourism is increasing.

AREA 825,414 sq km [318,434 sq mls], including Walvis Bay, a former South African territory
POPULATION 1,622,000
CAPITAL (POPULATION) Windhoek (126,000)
GOVERNMENT Multiparty republic
ETHNIC GROUPS Ovambo 50%, Kavango 9%, Herero 7%, Damara 7%, White 6%, Nama 5%
LANGUAGES English (official), Ovambo
RELIGIONS Christianity 90% (Lutheran 51%)
CURRENCY Namibian dollar = 100 cents

NAURU

Nauru is the world's smallest republic, located in the western Pacific Ocean, close to the equator. Independent since 1968, Nauru's prosperity is based on phosphate mining, but the reserves are running out. **AREA** 21 sq km [8 sq mls]; **POPULATION** 12,000; **CAPITAL** Yaren.

NEPAL

GEOGRAPHY Over three-quarters of Nepal lies in the Himalayan mountain heartland, culminating in the world's highest peak (Mount Everest, or Chomolongma in Nepali) at 8,848 m [29,029 ft]. The far lower Siwalik Range overlooks the Ganges plain.

As a result, there is a wide range of climatic conditions from tropical forest to the permanently glaciated landscape of the high Himalaya.

POLITICS & ECONOMY Nepal was united in the late 18th century, although its complex topography has ensured that it remains a diverse patchwork of peoples. From the mid-19th century to 1951, power was held by the royal Rana family. Attempts to introduce a democratic system in the 1950s failed and political parties were banned in 1962. The first democratic elections for 32 years were held in 1991.

Agriculture remains the chief activity in this overwhelmingly rural country and the government is heavily dependent on aid. Tourism, centred around the high Himalaya, grows in importance year by year, although Nepal was closed to foreigners until 1951. There are also ambitious plans to exploit the hydroelectric potential offered by the ferocious Himalayan rivers.

AREA 140,880 sq km [54,363 sq mls]
POPULATION 23,698,000
CAPITAL (POPULATION) Katmandu (535,000)
GOVERNMENT Constitutional monarchy
ETHNIC GROUPS Nepalese 53%, Bihari 18%, Tharu 5%, Tamang 5%, Newar 3%
LANGUAGES Nepali (official), local languages
RELIGIONS Hindu 86%, Buddhist 8%, Muslim 4%
CURRENCY Nepalese rupee = 100 paisa

NETHERLANDS

GEOGRAPHY The Netherlands lies at the western end of the North European Plain, which extends to the Ural Mountains in Russia. Except for the far south-eastern corner, the Netherlands is flat and about 40% lies below sea level at high tide. To prevent flooding, the Dutch have built dykes (sea walls) to hold back the waves. Large areas which were once under the sea, but which have been reclaimed, are called polders.

Because of its position on the North Sea, the Netherlands has a temperate climate. The winters are mild, with rain coming from the Atlantic depressions which pass over the country.

POLITICS & ECONOMY Before the 16th century, the area that is now the Netherlands was under a succession of foreign rulers, including the Romans, the Germanic Franks, the French and the Spanish. The Dutch declared their independence from Spain in 1581 and their status was finally recognized by Spain in 1648. In the 17th century, the Dutch built up a great overseas empire, especially in South-east Asia. But in the early 18th century, the Dutch lost control of the seas to England.

France controlled the Netherlands from 1795 to 1813. In 1815, the Netherlands, then containing Belgium and Luxembourg, became an independent kingdom. Belgium broke away in 1830 and Luxembourg followed in 1890.

The Netherlands was neutral in World War I (1914–18), but was occupied by Germany in World War II (1939–45). After the war, the Netherlands Indies became independent as Indonesia. The Netherlands became active in West European affairs. With Belgium and Luxembourg, it formed a customs union called Benelux in 1948. In 1949, it joined NATO (the North Atlantic Treaty Organization), and the European Coal and Steel Community (ECSC) in 1953. In 1957, it became a founder member of the European Economic Community (now the European Union), and its economy prospered. Although the economy was based on private enterprise, the government introduced many social welfare programmes.

The Netherlands is a highly industrialized country and industry and commerce are the most valuable activities. Its resources include natural gas, some oil, salt and china clay. But the Netherlands imports many of the materials needed by its industries and it is, therefore, a major trading country. Industrial products are wide-ranging, including aircraft, chemicals, electronic equipment, machinery, textiles and vehicles. Agriculture employs only 5% of the people, but scientific methods are used and yields are high. Dairy farming is the leading farming activity. Major products include barley, flowers and bulbs, potatoes, sugar beet and wheat.

AREA 41,526 sq km [16,033 sq mls]
POPULATION 15,731,000
CAPITAL (POPULATION) Amsterdam (1,100,000)
GOVERNMENT Constitutional monarchy
ETHNIC GROUPS Netherlander 95%, Indonesian, Turkish, Moroccan, German
LANGUAGES Dutch (official), Frisian
RELIGIONS Christianity (Roman Catholic 34%, Dutch Reformed Church 17%, Calvinist 8%), Islam 3%
CURRENCY Euro; Guilder = 100 cents

NETHERLANDS ANTILLES

The Netherlands Antilles consists of two different island groups; one off the coast of Venezuela, and the other at the northern end of the Leeward Islands, some 800 km [500 mls] away. They remain a self-governing Dutch territory. The island of Aruba was once part of the territory, but it broke away in 1986. Oil refining and tourism are important activities. **AREA** 993 sq km [383 sq mls]; **POPULATION** 210,000; **CAPITAL** Willemstad.

NEW CALEDONIA

New Caledonia is the most southerly of the Melanesian countries in the Pacific. A French possession since 1853 and an Overseas Territory since 1958. In 1998, France announced an agreement with local Melanesians that a vote on independence would be postponed for 15 years. The country is rich in mineral resources, especially nickel. **AREA** 18,580 sq km [7,174 sq mls]; **POPULATION** 192,000; **CAPITAL** Nouméa.

NEW ZEALAND

GEOGRAPHY New Zealand lies about 1,600 km [994 mls] south-east of Australia. It consists of two main islands and several other small ones. Much of North Island is volcanic. Active volcanoes include Ngauruhoe and Ruapehu. Hot springs and geysers are common, and steam from the ground is used to produce electricity. The Southern Alps, which contain the country's highest peak Mount Cook (Aoraki), at 3,753 m [12,313 ft] form the backbone of South Island. The island also has some large, fertile plains.

Auckland in the north has a warm, humid climate throughout the year. Wellington has cooler summers, while in Dunedin, in the south-east, temperatures sometimes dip below freezing in winter. The rainfall is heaviest on the western highlands.

POLITICS & ECONOMY Evidence suggests that early Maori settlers arrived in New Zealand more than 1,000 years ago. The Dutch navigator Abel Tasman reached New Zealand in 1642, but his discovery was not followed up. In 1769, the British Captain James Cook rediscovered the islands. In the early 19th century, British settlers arrived and, in 1840, under the Treaty of Waitangi, Britain took possession of the islands. Clashes occurred with the Maoris in the 1860s but, from the 1870s, the Maoris were gradually integrated into society.

In 1907, New Zealand became a self-governing dominion in the British Commonwealth. The country's economy developed quickly and the people became increasingly prosperous. However, after

Britain joined the European Economic Community in 1973, New Zealand's exports to Britain shrank and the country had to reassess its economic and defence strategies and seek new markets. The world economic recession also led the government to cut back on its spending on welfare services in the 1990s. Maori rights and the preservation of Maori culture are other major political issues.

New Zealand's economy has traditionally depended on agriculture, but manufacturing now employs twice as many people as agriculture. Meat and dairy products are the most valuable items produced on farms. The country has more than 48 million sheep, 4 million dairy cattle and 5 million beef cattle.

AREA 268,680 sq km [103,737 sq mls]
POPULATION 3,625,000
CAPITAL (POPULATION) Wellington (329,000)
GOVERNMENT Constitutional monarchy
ETHNIC GROUPS New Zealand European 74%, New Zealand Maori 10%, Polynesian 4%
LANGUAGES English and Maori (both official)
RELIGIONS Christianity (Anglican 21%, Presbyterian 16%, Roman Catholic 15%)
CURRENCY New Zealand dollar = 100 cents

NICARAGUA

GEOGRAPHY The Republic of Nicaragua is the second largest country in Central America. In the east is a broad plain bordering the Caribbean Sea. The plain is drained by rivers that flow from the Central Highlands. The fertile western Pacific region contains about 40 volcanoes, many of which are active, and earthquakes are common.

Nicaragua has a tropical climate. Managua is hot throughout the year and there is a marked rainy season from May to October. The Central Highlands and Caribbean region are cooler and wetter. The wettest region is the humid Caribbean plain.

POLITICS & ECONOMY In 1502, Christopher Columbus claimed the area for Spain, which ruled Nicaragua until 1821. By the early 20th century, the United States had considerable influence in the country and, in 1912, US forces entered Nicaragua to protect US interests. From 1927 to 1933, rebels under General Augusto César Sandino, tried to drive US forces out of the country. In 1933, US marines set up a Nicaraguan army, the National Guard, to help to defeat the rebels. Its leader, Anastasio Somoza Garcia, had Sandino murdered in 1934 and, from 1937, Somoza ruled as a dictator.

In the mid-1970s, many people began to protest against Somoza's rule. Many joined a guerrilla force, called the Sandinista National Liberation Front, named after General Sandino. The rebels defeated the Somoza regime in 1979. In the 1980s, the US-supported forces, called the 'Contras', launched a campaign against the Sandinista government. The US government opposed the Sandinista regime, under Daniel José Ortega Saavedra, claiming that it was a Communist dictatorship. A coalition, the National Opposition Union, defeated the Sandinistas in elections in 1990. In 1996, the Sandinistas were again defeated and Arnoldo Alemán, leader of the Liberal Alliance Party, became president.

In the early 1990s, Nicaragua faced many problems in rebuilding its shattered economy. Agriculture is the main activity, employing nearly half of the people.

OMAN

Coffee, cotton, sugar and bananas are grown for export, while rice is the main food crop.

AREA 130,000 sq km [50,193 sq mls]
POPULATION 4,583,000
CAPITAL (POPULATION) Managua (974,000)
GOVERNMENT Multiparty republic
ETHNIC GROUPS Mestizo 77%, White 10%, Black 9%, Amerindian 4%
LANGUAGES Spanish (official), Misumalpan
RELIGIONS Christianity (Roman Catholic 91%, others 9%)
CURRENCY Córdoba oro (gold córdoba) = 100 centavos

NIGER

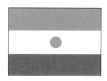

GEOGRAPHY The Republic of Niger is a landlocked nation in north-central Africa. The northern plateaux lie in the Sahara Desert, while Central Niger contains the rugged Aïr Mountains, but the most fertile and densely populated region is the narrow Niger valley in the south-west.

Niger has a tropical climate and the south has a rainy season between June and September. The hot harmattan wind blows from the Sahara between March and May. The north is practically rainless.

POLITICS & ECONOMY Since independence in 1960, Niger, a French territory from 1900, has suffered several droughts. Food shortages and the collapse of the traditional nomadic way of life of some of Niger's people have caused political instability. After a period of military rule, a multiparty constitution was adopted in 1992, but the military again seized power in 1996. Later that year, the coup leader Col. Ibrahim Barre Mainassara, was elected president.

Niger's chief resource is uranium and it is the fourth largest producer in the world. Some tin and tungsten are also mined, though other mineral resources are largely untouched.

Despite its resources, Niger is one of the world's poorest countries. Farming employs 85% of the population, though only 3% of the land can be used for crops and 7% for grazing.

AREA 1,267,000 sq km [489,189 sq mls]
POPULATION 9,672,000
CAPITAL (POPULATION) Niamey (398,000)
GOVERNMENT Multiparty republic
ETHNIC GROUPS Hausa 53%, Zerma-Songhai 21%, Tuareg 11%, Fulani (or Peul) 10%
LANGUAGES French (official), Hausa, Songhai
RELIGIONS Islam 98%
CURRENCY CFA franc = 100 centimes

NIGERIA

GEOGRAPHY The Federal Republic of Nigeria is the most populous nation in Africa. The country's main rivers are the Niger and Benue, which meet in central Nigeria. North of the two river valleys are high plains and plateaus. The Lake Chad basin is in the north-east, with the Sokoto plains in the north-west. Southern Nigeria contains hilly uplands and broad coastal plains, including the swampy Niger delta.

The south has high temperatures and rain throughout the year. The north is drier and often hotter than the south.

POLITICS & ECONOMY Nigeria has a long artistic tradition. Major cultures include the Nok (500 BC to AD 200), Ife, which developed about 1,000 years ago, and Benin, which flourished between the 15th and 17th centuries. Britain gradually extended its influence over the area in the second half of the 19th century. Nigeria became independent in 1960 and a federal republic in 1963. A federal constitution dividing the country into regions was necessary because Nigeria contains more than 250 ethnic and linguistic groups, as well as several religious ones. Local rivalries have long been a threat to national unity, and six new states were created in 1996 in an attempt to overcome this. Civil war occurred between 1967 and 1970, when the people of the south-east attempted unsuccessfully to secede during the Biafran War. Between 1960 and 1998, Nigeria had only nine years of civilian government. However, in 1998-9, Nigeria held elections at state and national level aimed at restoring civilian rule. The former general, Olusegun Obasanjo, was elected president.

Nigeria is a developing country, with great economic potential. Its greatest natural resource is oil, which accounts for the bulk of its exports. But agriculture employs 43% of the people. The country is a major producer of cocoa, palm oil and palm kernels, groundnuts and rubber.

AREA 923,770 sq km [356,668 sq mls]
POPULATION 110,532,000
CAPITAL (POPULATION) Abuja (339,000)
GOVERNMENT Federal republic
ETHNIC GROUPS Hausa 21%, Yoruba 21%, Ibo (or Igbo) 19%, Fulani 11%, Ibibio 6%
LANGUAGES English (official), Hausa, Yoruba, Ibo
RELIGIONS Christianity (Protestant 26%, Roman Catholic 12%, others 11%), Islam 45%
CURRENCY Naira = 100 kobo

NORTHERN MARIANA ISLANDS

The Commonwealth of the Northern Mariana Islands contains 16 mountainous islands north of Guam in the western Pacific Ocean. In a 1975 plebiscite, the islanders voted for Commonwealth status in union with the USA and, in 1986, they were granted US citizenship. AREA 477 sq km [184 sq mls]; POPULATION 50,000; CAPITAL Saipan.

NORWAY

GEOGRAPHY The Kingdom of Norway forms the western part of the rugged Scandinavian peninsula. The deep inlets along the highly indented coastline were worn out by glaciers during the Ice Age.

The warm North Atlantic Drift off the coast of Norway moderates the climate, with mild winters and cool summers. Nearly all the ports are ice-free throughout the year. Inland, winters are colder and snow cover lasts for at least three months a year.

POLITICS & ECONOMY Under a treaty in 1814, Denmark handed Norway over to Sweden, but it kept Norway's colonies – Greenland, Iceland and the Faroe Islands. Norway briefly became independent, but Swedish forces defeated the Norwegians and Norway had to accept Sweden's king as its ruler.

The union between Norway and Sweden ended in 1903. During World War II (1939–45), Germany occupied Norway. Norway's economy developed quickly after the war and the country now enjoys one of the world's highest standards of living. In 1960, Norway, together with six other countries, formed the European Free Trade Association (EFTA). In 1994, the Norwegians voted against joining the EU.

Norway's chief resources and exports are oil and natural gas which come from wells under the North Sea. Farmland covers only 3% of the land. Dairy farming and meat production are important, but Norway has to import food. Norway has many industries powered by cheap hydroelectricity.

AREA 323,900 sq km [125,050 sq mls]
POPULATION 4,420,000
CAPITAL (POPULATION) Oslo (714,000)
GOVERNMENT Constitutional monarchy
ETHNIC GROUPS Norwegian 97%
LANGUAGES Norwegian (official), Lappish, Finnish
RELIGIONS Christianity (Lutheran 88%)
CURRENCY Krone = 100 ore

OMAN

GEOGRAPHY The Sultanate of Oman occupies the south-eastern corner of the Arabian peninsula. It also includes the tip of the Musandam peninsula, overlooking the strategic Strait of Hormuz.

Oman has a hot tropical climate. In Muscat, temperatures may reach 47°C [117°F] in summer.

POLITICS & ECONOMY British influence in Oman dates back to the end of the 18th century, but the country became fully independent in 1971. Since then, using revenue from oil, which was discovered in 1964, the government has sought to modernize and develop the country.

The World Bank classifies Oman as an 'upper-middle-income' developing country. Its economy is based on oil production and oil accounts for more than 90% of Oman's export revenues. But agriculture still provides a living for half of the people. Major crops include alfalfa, bananas, coconuts, dates, limes, tobacco, vegetables and wheat. Some farmers raise cattle, and fishing, especially for sardines, is also important, though Oman still has to import food.

AREA 212,460 sq km [82,031 sq mls]
POPULATION 2,364,000
CAPITAL (POPULATION) Muscat (350,000)
GOVERNMENT Monarchy with consultative council
ETHNIC GROUPS Omani Arab 74%, Pakistani 21%
LANGUAGES Arabic (official), Baluchi, English
RELIGIONS Islam (Ibadiyah) 86%, Hinduism 13%
CURRENCY Omani rial = 100 baizas

PAKISTAN

PAKISTAN

GEOGRAPHY The Islamic Republic of Pakistan contains high mountains, fertile plains and rocky deserts. The Karakoram range, which contains K2, the world's second highest peak, lies in the northern part of Jammu and Kashmir, which is occupied by Pakistan but claimed by India. Other mountains rise in the west. Plains, drained by the River Indus and its tributaries, occupy much of eastern Pakistan. The Thar Desert is in the south-east and the dry Baluchistan plateau is in the south-west.

The mountains have cold, snowy winters. But most of Pakistan has hot summers and cool winters. The rainfall is sparse throughout much of the country. Most of it comes between July and September, when south-west monsoon winds blow.

POLITICS & ECONOMY Pakistan was the site of the Indus Valley civilization which developed about 4,500 years ago. But Pakistan's modern history dates from 1947, when British India was divided into India and Pakistan. Muslim Pakistan was divided into two parts: East and West Pakistan, but East Pakistan broke away in 1971 to become Bangladesh. In 1948–9, 1965 and 1971, Pakistan and India clashed over the disputed territory of Kashmir. In 1998, Pakistan responded in kind to a series of Indian nuclear weapon tests, provoking global controversy.

Pakistan has been subject to several periods of military rule, but elections held in 1988 led to Benazir Bhutto, daughter of a former prime minister and president, Zulfikar Ali Bhutto, becoming prime minister. Benazir Bhutto was removed from office in 1990 but she again became prime minister in 1993, until she was dismissed in 1996. Following elections in 1997, Nawaz Sharif became prime minister.

According to the World Bank, Pakistan is a 'low-income' developing country. The economy is based on farming or rearing goats and sheep. Agriculture employs nearly half the people. Major crops, grown mainly on irrigated land, include cotton, fruits, rice, sugar cane and, most important of all, wheat.

AREA 796,100 sq km [307,374 sq mls]
POPULATION 135,135,000
CAPITAL (POPULATION) Islamabad (204,000)
GOVERNMENT Federal republic
ETHNIC GROUPS Punjabi 60%, Sindhi 12%, Pushtun 13%, Baluch, Muhajir
LANGUAGES Urdu (official), many others
RELIGIONS Islam 97%, Christianity, Hinduism
CURRENCY Pakistan rupee = 100 paisa

PALAU

The Republic of Palau became fully independent in 1994, after the USA refused to accede to a 1979 referendum that declared this island nation a nuclear-free zone. The economy relies on US aid, tourism, fishing and subsistence agriculture. The main crops include cassava, coconuts and copra.
AREA 458 sq km [177 sq mls]; **POPULATION** 18,000; **CAPITAL** Koror.

PANAMA

GEOGRAPHY The Republic of Panama forms an isthmus linking Central America to South America. The Panama Canal, which is 81.6 km [50.7 mls] long, cuts across the isthmus. It has made the country a major transport centre.

Panama has a tropical climate. Temperatures are high, though the mountains are much cooler than the coastal plains. The main rainy season is between May and December.

POLITICS & ECONOMY Christopher Columbus landed in Panama in 1502 and Spain soon took control of the area. In 1821, Panama became independent from Spain and a province of Colombia.

In 1903, Colombia refused a request by the United States to build a canal. Panama then revolted against Colombia, and became independent. The United States then began to build the canal, which was opened in 1914. The United States administered the Panama Canal Zone, a strip of land along the canal. But many Panamanians resented US influence and, in 1979, the Canal Zone was returned to Panama. The USA also agreed to hand over control of the Canal to Panama on 31 December 1999.

Panama's government has changed many times since independence, and there have been periods of military dictatorships. In 1983, General Manuel Antonio Noriega became Panama's leader. In 1988, two US grand juries in Florida indicted Noriega on charges of drug trafficking. In 1989, Noriega was apparently defeated in a presidential election, but the government declared the election invalid. After the killing of a US marine, US troops entered Panama and arrested Noriega, who was convicted by a Miami court of drug offences in 1992. Elections in 1994 were won the Democratic Revolutionary Party, led by Ernesto Pérez Balladares.

The World Bank classifies Panama as a 'lower-middle-income' developing country. The Panama Canal is an important source of revenue and it generates many jobs in commerce, trade, manufacturing and transport. Away from the Canal, the main activity is agriculture, which employs 27% of the people.

AREA 77,080 sq km [29,761 sq mls]
POPULATION 2,736,000
CAPITAL (POPULATION) Panama City (452,000)
GOVERNMENT Multiparty republic
ETHNIC GROUPS Mestizo 60%, Black and Mulatto 20%, White 10%, Amerindian 8%, Asian 2%
LANGUAGES Spanish (official)
RELIGIONS Christianity (Roman Catholic 84%, Protestant 5%), Islam 5%
CURRENCY Balboa = 100 centésimos

PAPUA NEW GUINEA

GEOGRAPHY Papua New Guinea is an independent country in the Pacific Ocean, north of Australia. It is part of a Pacific island region called Melanesia. Papua New Guinea includes the eastern part of New Guinea, the Bismarck Archipelago, the northern Solomon Islands, the D'Entrecasteaux Islands and the Louisiade Archipelago. The land is largely mountainous.

Papua New Guinea has a tropical climate, with high temperatures throughout the year. Most of the rain occurs during the monsoon season (from December to April), when the north-westerly winds blow. Winds blow from the south-east during the dry season.

POLITICS & ECONOMY The Dutch took western New Guinea (now part of Indonesia) in 1828, but it was not until 1884 that Germany took north-eastern New Guinea and Britain the south-east. In 1906, Britain handed the south-east over to Australia. It then became known as the Territory of Papua. When World War I broke out in 1914, Australia took German New Guinea and, in 1921, the League of Nations gave Australia a mandate to rule the area, which was named the Territory of New Guinea.

Japan invaded New Guinea in 1942, but the Allies reconquered the area in 1944. In 1949, Papua and New Guinea were combined into the Territory of Papua and New Guinea. Papua New Guinea became fully independent in 1975.

Since independence, the government of Papua New Guinea has worked to develop its mineral reserves. One of the most valuable mines was on Bougainville, in the northern Solomon Islands. But the people of Bougainville demanded a larger share in the profits of the mine. Conflict broke out, the mine was closed and the Bougainville Revolutionary Army proclaimed the island independent. But their attempted secession was not recognized internationally. An agreement to end the conflict was finally signed in New Zealand in January 1998.

The World Bank classifies Papua New Guinea as a 'lower-middle-income' developing country. Agriculture employs three out of every four people, many of whom produce little more than they need to feed their families. But minerals, notably copper and gold, are the most valuable exports.

AREA 462,840 sq km [178,703 sq mls]
POPULATION 4,600,000
CAPITAL (POPULATION) Port Moresby (174,000)
GOVERNMENT Constitutional monarchy
ETHNIC GROUPS Papuan 84%, Melanesian 1%
LANGUAGES English (official), about 800 others
RELIGIONS Christianity (Protestant 58%, Roman Catholic 33%, Anglican 5%), traditional beliefs 3%
CURRENCY Kina = 100 toea

PARAGUAY

GEOGRAPHY The Republic of Paraguay is a land-locked country and rivers, notably the Paraná, Pilcomayo (Brazo Sur) and Paraguay, form most of its borders. A flat region called the Gran Chaco lies in the north-west, while the south-east contains plains, hills and plateaux.

Northern Paraguay lies in the tropics, while the south is subtropical. Most of the country has a warm, humid climate.

POLITICS & ECONOMY In 1776, Paraguay became part of a large colony called the Vice-royalty of La Plata, with Buenos Aires as the capital. Paraguayans opposed this move and the country declared its independence in 1811.

For many years, Paraguay was torn by internal strife and conflict with its neighbours. A war against Brazil, Argentina and Uruguay (1865–70) led to the deaths of more than half of Paraguay's population, and a great loss of territory.

General Alfredo Stroessner took power in 1954 and ruled as a dictator. His government imprisoned many opponents. Stroessner was overthrown in 1989. Free multiparty elections were held in 1993 and 1998. However, the return of democracy frequently seemed precarious because of rivalries between politicians and army leaders.

The World Bank classifies Paraguay as a 'lower-middle-income' developing country. Agriculture and forestry are the leading activities, employing 48% of the population. The country has abundant hydroelectricity and it exports power to Argentina and Brazil.

AREA 406,750 sq km [157,046 sq mls]
POPULATION 5,291,000
CAPITAL (POPULATION) Asunción (945,000)
GOVERNMENT Multiparty republic
ETHNIC GROUPS Mestizo 90%, Amerindian 3%
LANGUAGES Spanish and Guaraní (both official)
RELIGIONS Christianity (Roman Catholic 96%, Protestant 2%)
CURRENCY Guaraní = 100 céntimos

PERU

GEOGRAPHY The Republic of Peru lies in the tropics in western South America. A narrow coastal plain borders the Pacific Ocean in the west. Inland are ranges of the Andes Mountains, which rise to 6,768 m [22,205 ft] at Mount Huascarán, an extinct volcano. East of the Andes, the land descends to the Amazon basin.

Lima, on the coastal plain, has an arid climate. The coastal region is chilled by the cold, offshore Humboldt Current. The rainfall increases inland and many mountains in the high Andes are snow-capped.
POLITICS & ECONOMY Spanish conquistadors conquered Peru in the 1530s. In 1820, an Argentinian, José de San Martín, led an army into Peru and declared it independent. But Spain still held large areas. In 1823, the Venezuelan Simon Bolívar led another army into Peru and, in 1824, one of his generals defeated the Spaniards at Ayacucho. The Spaniards surrendered in 1826. Peru suffered much instability throughout the 19th century.

Instability continued in the 20th century. In 1980, when civilian rule was restored, a left-wing group called the Sendero Luminoso, or the 'Shining Path', began guerrilla warfare against the government. In 1990, Alberto Fujimori, son of Japanese immigrants, became president. In 1992, he suspended the constitution and dismissed the legislature. The guerrilla leader, Abimael Guzmán, was arrested in 1992, but instability continued. A new constitution was introduced in 1993, giving increased power to the president, who faced many problems in rebuilding the shattered economy.

The World Bank classifies Peru as a 'lower-middle-income' developing country. Agriculture employs 35% of the people and major food crops include beans, maize, potatoes and rice. Fish products are exported, but the most valuable export is copper. Peru also produces lead, silver, zinc and iron ore.

AREA 1,285,220 sq km [496,223 sq mls]
POPULATION 26,111,000
CAPITAL (POPULATION) Lima (Lima-Callao, 6,601,000)
GOVERNMENT Transitional republic
ETHNIC GROUPS Quechua 47%, Mestizo 32%, White 12%, Aymara 5%
LANGUAGES Spanish and Quechua (both official), Aymara
RELIGIONS Christianity (Roman Catholic 93%, Protestant 6%)
CURRENCY New sol = 100 centavos

PHILIPPINES

GEOGRAPHY The Republic of the Philippines is an island country in south-eastern Asia. It includes about 7,100 islands, of which 2,770 are named and about 1,000 are inhabited. Luzon and Mindanao, the two largest islands, make up more than two-thirds of the country. The land is mainly mountainous and lacks large lowlands.

The country has a tropical climate, with high temperatures all through the year. The dry season runs from December to April. The rest of the year is wet. The high rainfall is associated with typhoons which periodically strike the east coast.
POLITICS & ECONOMY The first European to reach the Philippines was the Portuguese navigator Ferdinand Magellan in 1521. Spanish explorers claimed the region in 1565 when they established a settlement on Cebu. The Spaniards ruled the country until 1898, when the United States took over at the end of the Spanish–American War. Japan invaded the Philippines in 1941, but US forces returned in 1944. The country became fully independent as the Republic of the Philippines in 1946.

Since independence, the country's problems have included armed uprisings by left-wing guerrillas demanding land reform, and Muslim separatist groups, crime, corruption and unemployment. The dominant figure in recent times was Ferdinand Marcos, who ruled in a dictatorial manner from 1965 to 1986. His successor was Corazon Aquino, widow of an assassinated opponent of Marcos. Aquino did not stand in the presidential elections in 1992. Her successor was General Fidel Ramos.

The Philippines is a developing country with a lower-middle-income economy. Agriculture employs 45% of the people. The main foods are rice and maize, while such crops as bananas, cocoa, coconuts, coffee, sugar cane and tobacco are grown commercially. Manufacturing now plays an increasingly important role in the economy.

AREA 300,000 sq km [115,300 sq mls]
POPULATION 77,736,000
CAPITAL (POPULATION) Manila (Metro Manila, 9,280,000)
GOVERNMENT Multiparty republic
ETHNIC GROUPS Tagalog 30%, Cebuano 24%, Ilocano 10%, Hiligaynon Ilongo 9%, Bicol 6%
LANGUAGES Pilipino (Tagalog) and English (both official), Spanish, many others
RELIGIONS Christianity (Roman Catholic 84%, Philippine Independent Church or Aglipayan 6%, Protestant 4%), Islam 4%
CURRENCY Philippine peso = 100 centavos

PITCAIRN ISLANDS

Pitcairn Island is a British overseas territory in the Pacific Ocean. Its inhabitants are descendants of the original settlers – nine mutineers from *HMS Bounty* and 18 Tahitians who arrived in 1790. **AREA** 48 sq km [19 sq mls]; **POPULATION** 60; **CAPITAL** Adamstown.

POLAND

GEOGRAPHY The Republic of Poland faces the Baltic Sea and, behind its lagoon-fringed coast, lies a broad plain. The land rises to a plateau region in the south-east, while the Sudeten Highlands straddle part of the border with the Czech Republic. Part of the Carpathian range (the Tatra) lies on the south-eastern border with the Slovak Republic.

Poland's climate is influenced by its position in Europe. Warm, moist air masses come from the west, while cold air masses come from the north and east. Summers are warm, but winters are cold and snowy.
POLITICS & ECONOMY Poland's boundaries have changed several times in the last 200 years, partly as a result of its geographical location between the powers of Germany and Russia. It disappeared from the map in the late 18th century, when a Polish state called the Grand Duchy of Warsaw was set up. But in 1815, the country was partitioned, between Austria, Prussia and Russia. Poland became independent in 1918, but in 1939 it was divided between Germany and the Soviet Union. The country again became independent in 1945, when it lost land to Russia but gained some from Germany. Communists took power in 1948, but opposition mounted and eventually became focused through an organization called Solidarity.

Solidarity was led by a trade unionist, Lech Walesa. A coalition government was formed between Solidarity and the Communists in 1989. In 1990, the Communist party was dissolved and Walesa became president. But Walesa faced many problems in turning Poland towards a market economy. In presidential elections in 1995, Walesa was defeated by ex-Communist Aleksander Kwasniewski. However, Kwasniewski continued to follow westward-looking policies and, in 1999, it joined NATO. Poland seemed likely to be among the first eastern European countries to join an expanded EU.

Poland has large reserves of coal and deposits of various minerals which are used in its factories. Manufactures include chemicals, processed food, machinery, ships, steel and textiles.

AREA 312,680 sq km [120,726 sq mls]
POPULATION 38,607,000
CAPITAL (POPULATION) Warsaw (1,638,000)
GOVERNMENT Multiparty republic
ETHNIC GROUPS Polish 98%, Ukrainian 1%, German 1%
LANGUAGES Polish (official)
RELIGIONS Christianity (Roman Catholic 94%, Orthodox 2%)
CURRENCY Zloty = 100 groszy

PORTUGAL

GEOGRAPHY The Republic of Portugal is the most westerly of Europe's mainland countries. The land rises from the coastal plains on the Atlantic Ocean to the western edge of the huge plateau, or Meseta, which occupies most of the Iberian peninsula. Portugal also contains two autonomous regions, the Azores and Madeira island groups.

The climate is moderated by winds blowing from the Atlantic Ocean. Summers are cooler and winters are milder than in other Mediterranean lands.

POLITICS & ECONOMY Portugal became a separate country, independent of Spain, in 1143. In the 15th century, Portugal led the 'Age of European Exploration'. This led to the growth of a large Portuguese empire, with colonies in Africa, Asia and, most valuable of all, Brazil in South America. Portuguese power began to decline in the 16th century and, between 1580 and 1640, Portugal was ruled by Spain. Portugal lost Brazil in 1822 and, in 1910, Portugal became a republic. Instability hampered progress and army officers seized power in 1926. In 1928, they chose Antonio de Salazar to be minister of finance. He became prime minister in 1932 and ruled as a dictator from 1933.

Salazar ruled until 1968, but his successor, Marcello Caetano, was overthrown in 1974 by a group of army officers. The new government made most of Portugal's remaining colonies independent. Free elections were held in 1978. Portugal joined the European Community (now the European Union) in 1986. But despite great efforts to increase economic growth, Portugal remains one of its poorest members.

Agriculture and fishing were the mainstays of the economy until the mid-20th century. But manufacturing is now the most valuable sector.

AREA 92,390 sq km [35,670 sq mls]
POPULATION 9,928,000
CAPITAL (POPULATION) Lisbon (2,561,000)
GOVERNMENT Multiparty republic
ETHNIC GROUPS Portuguese 99%, Cape Verdean, Brazilian, Spanish, British
LANGUAGES Portuguese (official)
RELIGIONS Christianity (Roman Catholic 95%, other Christians 2%)
CURRENCY Euro; Escudo = 100 centavos

PUERTO RICO

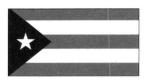

The Commonwealth of Puerto Rico, a mainly mountainous island, is the easternmost of the Greater Antilles chain. The climate is hot and wet. Puerto Rico is a dependent territory of the USA and the people are US citizens. In 1998, 50.2% of the population voted in a referendum on possible statehood to maintain the status quo. Puerto Rico is the most industrialized country in the Caribbean. Tax exemptions attract US companies to the island and manufacturing is expanding. **AREA** 8,900 sq km [3,436 sq km]; **POPULATION** 3,860,000; **CAPITAL** San Juan.

QATAR

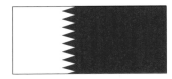

The State of Qatar occupies a low, barren peninsula that extends northwards from the Arabian peninsula into the Gulf. The climate is hot and dry. Qatar became a British protectorate in 1916, but it became fully independent in 1971. Oil, first discovered in 1939, is the mainstay of the economy of this prosperous nation. **AREA** 11,000 sq km [4,247 sq mls]; **POPULATION** 697,000; **CAPITAL** Doha.

RÉUNION

Réunion is a French overseas department in the Indian Ocean. The land is mainly mountainous, though the lowlands are intensely cultivated. Sugar and sugar products are the main exports, but French aid, given to the island in return for its use as a military base, is important to the economy. **AREA** 2,510 sq km [969 sq mls]; **POPULATION** 705,000; **CAPITAL** Saint-Denis.

ROMANIA

GEOGRAPHY Romania is a country on the Black Sea in eastern Europe. Eastern and southern Romania form part of the Danube river basin. The delta region, near the mouths of the Danube, where the river flows into the Black Sea, is one of Europe's finest wetlands. The southern part of the coast contains several resorts. The heart of the country is called Transylvania. It is ringed in the east, south and west by scenic mountains which are part of the Carpathian mountain system.

Romania has hot summers and cold winters. The rainfall is heaviest in spring and early summer, when thundery showers are common.

POLITICS & ECONOMY From the late 18th century, the Turkish empire began to break up. The modern history of Romania began in 1861 when Walachia and Moldavia united. After World War I (1914–18), Romania, which had fought on the side of the victorious Allies, obtained large areas, including Transylvania, where most people were Romanians. This almost doubled the country's size and population. In 1939, Romania lost territory to Bulgaria, Hungary and the Soviet Union. Romania fought alongside Germany in World War II, and Soviet troops occupied the country in 1944. Hungary returned northern Transylvania to Romania in 1945, but Bulgaria and the Soviet Union kept former Romanian territory. In 1947, Romania officially became a Communist country.

In 1990, Romania held its first free elections since the end of World War II. The National Salvation Front, led by Ion Iliescu and containing many former Communist leaders, won a large majority. A new constitution, approved in 1991, made the country a democratic republic. Elections held under this constitution in 1992 again resulted in victory for Ion Iliescu, whose party was renamed the Party of Social Democracy (PDSR) in 1993. But the government faced many problems as it tried to reform the economy. In 1996, the PDSR was defeated in elections by the centre-right Democratic Convention led by Emil Constantinescu.

According to the World Bank, Romania is a 'lower-middle-income' economy. Under Communist rule, industry, including mining and manufacturing, became more important than agriculture.

AREA 237,500 sq km [91,699 sq mls]
POPULATION 22,396,000
CAPITAL (POPULATION) Bucharest (2,061,000)
GOVERNMENT Multiparty republic
ETHNIC GROUPS Romanian 89%, Hungarian 7%, Gypsy 2%
LANGUAGES Romanian (official), Hungarian
RELIGIONS Christianity (Romanian Orthodox 87%, Roman Catholic 5%, Greek Orthodox 4%)
CURRENCY Romanian leu = 100 bani

RUSSIA

GEOGRAPHY Russia is the world's largest country. About 25% lies west of the Ural Mountains in European Russia, where 80% of the population lives. It is mostly flat or undulating, but the land rises to the Caucasus Mountains in the south, where Russia's highest peak, Elbrus, at 5,633 m [18,481 ft], is found. Asian Russia, or Siberia, contains vast plains and plateaux, with mountains in the east and south. The Kamchatka peninsula in the far east has many active volcanoes. Russia contains many of the world's longest rivers, including the Yenisey-Angara and the Ob-Irtysh. It also includes part of the world's largest inland body of water, the Caspian Sea, and Lake Baikal, the world's deepest lake.

Moscow has a continental climate with cold and snowy winters and warm summers. Krasnoyarsk in south-central Siberia has a harsher, drier climate, but it is not as severe as parts of northern Siberia.

POLITICS & ECONOMY In the 9th century AD, a state called Kievan Rus was formed by a group of people called the East Slavs. Kiev, now capital of Ukraine, became a major trading centre, but, in 1237, Mongol armies conquered Russia and destroyed Kiev. Russia was part of the Mongol empire until the late 15th century. Under Mongol rule, Moscow became the leading Russian city.

In the 16th century, Moscow's grand prince was retitled 'tsar'. The first tsar, Ivan the Terrible, expanded Russian territory. In 1613, after a period of civil war, Michael Romanov became tsar, founding a dynasty which ruled until 1917. In the early 18th century, Tsar Peter the Great began to westernize Russia and, by 1812, when Napoleon failed to conquer the country, Russia was a major European power. But during the 19th century, many Russians demanded reforms and discontent was widespread.

In World War I (1914–18), the Russian people suffered great hardships and, in 1917, Tsar Nicholas II was forced to abdicate. In November 1917, the Bolsheviks seized power under Vladimir Lenin. In 1922, the Bolsheviks set up a new nation, the Union

SAUDI ARABIA

of Soviet Socialist Republics (also called the USSR or the Soviet Union).

From 1924, Joseph Stalin introduced a socialist economic programme, suppressing all opposition. In 1939, the Soviet Union and Germany signed a non-aggression pact, but Germany invaded the Soviet Union in 1941. Soviet forces pushed the Germans back, occupying eastern Europe. They reached Berlin in May 1945. From the late 1940s, tension between the Soviet Union and its allies and Western nations developed into a 'Cold War'. This continued until 1991, when the Soviet Union was dissolved.

The Soviet Union collapsed because of the failure of its economic policies. From 1991, its new leader, Boris Yeltsin, worked to develop democratic systems, reform the economy and increase private ownership. Russia kept contacts with 11 of the republics in the former Soviet Union through the Commonwealth of Independent States. But fighting in Chechenia in the 1990s showed that Russia's diverse population makes national unity difficult to achieve.

Russia's economy was thrown into disarray after the collapse of the Soviet Union, and in the early 1990s the World Bank described Russia as a 'lower-middle-income' economy. Russia was admitted to the Council of Europe in 1997, essentially to discourage instability in the Caucasus. More significantly still, Boris Yeltsin was invited to attend the G7 summit in Denver in 1997. The summit became known as 'the Summit of the Eight' and it appeared that Russia will now be included in future meetings of the world's most powerful economies. Industry is the most valuable activity, though, under Communist rule, manufacturing was less efficient than in the West and the emphasis was on heavy industry. Today, light industries producing consumer goods are becoming important. Russia's adundant resources include oil and natural gas, coal, timber, metal ores and hydroelectric power.

Most farmland is still government-owned or run as collectives. Russia is a major producer of farm products, though it imports grains. Major crops include barley, flax, fruits, oats, rye, potatoes, sugar beet, sunflower seeds, vegetables and wheat. Livestock farming is also important.

AREA 17,075,000 sq km [6,592,800 sq mls]
POPULATION 146,861,000
CAPITAL (POPULATION) Moscow (9,233,000)
GOVERNMENT Federal multiparty republic
ETHNIC GROUPS Russian 82%, Tatar 4%, Ukrainian 3%, Chuvash 1%, more than 100 other nationalities
LANGUAGES Russian (official), many others
RELIGIONS Christianity (mainly Russian Orthodox, with Roman Catholic and Protestant minorities), Islam, Judaism
CURRENCY Russian rouble = 100 kopeks

RWANDA

GEOGRAPHY The Republic of Rwanda is a small, landlocked country in east-central Africa. Lake Kivu and the River Ruzizi in the Great African Rift Valley form the country's western border.

Kigali stands on the central plateau of Rwanda. Here, temperatures are moderated by the altitude. The rainfall is abundant, but much heavier rain falls on the western mountains.

POLITICS & ECONOMY Germany conquered the

area, called Ruanda-Urundi, in the 1890s. But Belgium occupied the region during World War I (1914–18) and ruled it until 1961, when the people of Ruanda voted for their country to become a republic, called Rwanda. This decision followed a rebellion by the majority Hutu people against the Tutsi monarchy. About 150,000 deaths resulted from this conflict. Many Tutsis fled to Uganda, where they formed a rebel army. Burundi became independent as a monarchy, though it became a republic in 1966. Relations between Hutus and Tutsis continued to cause friction. Civil war broke out in 1994 and in 1996 the conflict spilled over into Congo (then Zaïre), where Tutsis clashes with government troops.

According to the World Bank, Rwanda is a 'low-income' developing country. Most people are poor farmers, who produce little more than they need to feed their families. Food crops include bananas, beans, cassava and sorghum. Some cattle are raised.

AREA 26,340 sq km [10,170 sq mls]
POPULATION 7,956,000
CAPITAL (POPULATION) Kigali (235,000)
GOVERNMENT Republic
ETHNIC GROUPS Hutu 90%, Tutsi 9%, Twa 1%
LANGUAGES French, English and Kinyarwanda (all official)
RELIGIONS Christianity 74% (Roman Catholic 65%), traditional beliefs 17%, Islam 9%
CURRENCY Rwanda franc = 100 centimes

ST HELENA

St Helena, which became a British colony in 1834, is an isolated volcanic island in the south Atlantic Ocean. Now a British overseas territory, it is also the administrative centre of Ascension and Tristan da Cunha. AREA 122 sq km [47 sq mls]; POPULATION 8,200; CAPITAL Jamestown.

ST KITTS AND NEVIS

The Federation of St Kitts and Nevis became independent from Britain in 1983. In 1998, a vote for the secession of Nevis fell short of the two-thirds required. AREA 360 sq km [139 sq mls]; POPULATION 42,000; CAPITAL Basseterre.

ST LUCIA

St Lucia, which became independent from Britain in 1979, is a mountainous, forested island of extinct volcanoes. It exports bananas and coconuts, and now attracts many tourists. AREA 610 sq km [236 sq mls]; POPULATION 150,000; CAPITAL Castries.

ST VINCENT AND THE GRENADINES

St Vincent and the Grenadines achieved its independence from Britain in 1979. Tourism is growing, but the territory is less prosperous than its neighbours. AREA 388 sq km [150 sq mls]; POPULATION 120,000; CAPITAL Kingstown.

SAN MARINO

The 'Most Serene Republic of San Marino', as this tiny state in northern Italy is officially called, has been independent since 885 and a republic since the 14th century. This makes it the world's oldest republic. AREA 61 sq km [24 sq mls]; POPULATION 25,000; CAPITAL San Marino

SÃO TOMÉ AND PRÍNCIPE

The Democratic Republic of São Tomé and Príncipe, a mountainous island territory west of Gabon, became a Portuguese colony in 1522. Following independence in 1975, the islands became a one-party Marxist state, but multiparty elections were held in 1991. Cocoa is the main product. AREA 964 sq km [372 sq mls]; POPULATION 150,000; CAPITAL Sao Tome.

SAUDI ARABIA

GEOGRAPHY The Kingdom of Saudi Arabia occupies about three-quarters of the Arabian peninsula in south-west Asia. Deserts cover most of the land. Mountains border the Red Sea plains in the west. In the north is the sandy Nafud Desert (An Nafud). In the south is the Rub' al Khali (the 'Empty Quarter'), one of the world's bleakest deserts.

Saudi Arabia has a hot, dry climate. In the summer months, the temperatures in Riyadh often exceed 40°C [104°F], though the nights are cool.

POLITICS & ECONOMY Saudi Arabia contains the two holiest places in Islam – Mecca (or Makka), the birthplace of the Prophet Muhammad in AD 570, and Medina (Al Madinah) where Muhammad went in 622. These places are visited by many pilgrims.

Saudi Arabia was poor until the oil industry began to operate on the eastern plains in 1933. Oil revenues have been used to develop the country and Saudi Arabia has given aid to poorer Arab nations. The monarch has supreme authority and Saudi Arabia

SENEGAL

has no formal constitution. In the first Gulf War (1980-88), Saudi Arabia supported Iraq against Iran. But when Iraq invaded Kuwait in 1990, it joined the international alliance to drive Iraq's forces out of Kuwait in 1991.

Saudi Arabia has about 25% of the world's known oil reserves, and oil and oil products make up 85% of its exports. But agriculture still employs 48% of the people, including nomadic herders who rear cattle, goats, sheep, and other animals. Crops grown in the south-western highlands and at oases include dates and other fruits, vegetables and wheat. Modern irrigation and desalination schemes have greatly increased crop production in recent years. The government continues to encourage the development of modern agriculture and new industries as a method of diversifying the economy.

AREA 2,149,690 sq km [829,995 sq mls]
POPULATION 20,786,000
CAPITAL (POPULATION) Riyadh (2,000,000)
GOVERNMENT Absolute monarchy with consultative assembly
ETHNIC GROUPS Arab (Saudi 82%, Yemeni 10%, other Arab 3%)
LANGUAGES Arabic (official)
RELIGIONS Islam 99%, Christianity 1%
CURRENCY Saudi riyal = 100 halalas

SENEGAL

GEOGRAPHY The Republic of Senegal is on the north-west coast of Africa. The volcanic Cape Verde (Cap Vert), on which Dakar stands, is the most westerly point in Africa. Plains cover most of Senegal, though the land rises gently in the south-east.

Dakar has a tropical climate, with a short rainy season between July and October when moist winds blow from the south-west.
POLITICS & ECONOMY In 1882, Senegal became a French colony, and from 1895 it was ruled as part of French West Africa, the capital of which, Dakar, developed as a major port and city.

In 1959, Senegal joined French Sudan (now Mali) to form the Federation of Mali. But Senegal withdrew in 1960 and became the separate Republic of Senegal. Its first president, Léopold Sédar Senghor, was a noted African poet. He continued in office until 1981, when he was succeeded by the prime minister, Abdou Diouf.

Senegal and The Gambia have always enjoyed close relations despite their differing French and British traditions. In 1981, Senegalese troops put down an attempted coup in The Gambia and, in 1982, the two countries set up a defence alliance, called the Confederation of Senegambia. But this confederation was dissolved in 1989.

According to the World Bank, Senegal is a 'lower-middle-income' developing country. It was badly hit in the 1960s and 1970s by droughts, which caused starvation. Agriculture still employs 81% of the population though many farmers produce little more than they need to feed their families. Food crops include groundnuts, millet and rice. Phosphates are the country's chief resource, but Senegal also refines oil which it imports from Gabon and Nigeria. Dakar is a busy port and has many industries.

Senegal exports fish products, groundnuts, oil products and phosphates.

AREA 196,720 sq km [75,954 sq mls]
POPULATION 9,723,000
CAPITAL (POPULATION) Dakar (1,729,000)
GOVERNMENT Multiparty republic
ETHNIC GROUPS Wolof 44%, Fulani-Tukulor 24%, Serer 15%
LANGUAGES French (official), tribal languages
RELIGIONS Islam 94%, Christianity (mainly Roman Catholic) 5%, traditional beliefs and others 1%
CURRENCY CFA franc = 100 centimes

SEYCHELLES

The Republic of Seychelles in the western Indian Ocean achieved independence from Britain in 1976. Coconuts are the main cash crop and fishing and tourism are important. AREA 455 sq km [176 sq mls]; POPULATION 79,000; CAPITAL Victoria.

SIERRA LEONE

GEOGRAPHY The Republic of Sierra Leone in West Africa is about the same size as the Republic of Ireland. The coast contains several deep estuaries in the north, with lagoons in the south. The most prominent feature is the mountainous Freetown (or Sierra Leone) peninsula. North of the peninsula is the River Rokel estuary, West Africa's best natural harbour.

Sierra Leone has a tropical climate, with heavy rainfall between April and November.
POLITICS & ECONOMY After independence, Sierra Leone became a monarchy. Its head of state was the British monarch, who was represented in the country by a governor-general. But after a military government took power in 1968, Sierra Leone became a republic in 1971 and a one-party state in 1978. In 1991, a majority of the people voted for the restoration of democracy but, in 1992, a military group seized power. In 1994 and 1995, civil war caused a collapse of law and order in some areas. Elections were held in 1996, but another military coup occurred in 1997. In 1998, the West Africa Peace Force restored the elected President Ahmed Tejan Kabbah to power, but conflict continued.

The World Bank classifies Sierra Leone among the 'low-income' economies. Agriculture provides a living for 70% of the people, though farming is mainly at subsistence level. The most valuable exports are minerals, including diamonds, bauxite and rutile (titanium ore). The country has few manufacturing industries.

AREA 71,740 sq km [27,699 sq mls]
POPULATION 5,080,000
CAPITAL (POPULATION) Freetown (505,000)
GOVERNMENT Single-party republic
ETHNIC GROUPS Mende 35%, Temne 37%
LANGUAGES English (official), Mande, Temne
RELIGIONS Traditional beliefs 51%, Islam 39%
CURRENCY Leone = 100 cents

SINGAPORE

GEOGRAPHY The Republic of Singapore is an island country at the southern tip of the Malay peninsula. It consists of the large Singapore Island and 58 small islands, 20 of which are inhabited.

Singapore has a hot and humid climate, typical of places near the Equator. The temperatures are high and the rainfall is heavy throughout the year.
POLITICS & ECONOMY Singapore's modern history began in 1819 when Sir Thomas Stamford Raffles (1781–1826), agent of the British East India Company, made a treaty with the Sultan of Johor. This treaty allowed the British to build a settlement on Singapore Island. Singapore soon became the leading British trading centre in South-east Asia and it later became a naval base. Japanese forces seized the island in 1942, but British rule was restored in 1945.

In 1963, Singapore became part of the Federation of Malaysia, which also included Malaya and the territories of Sabah and Sarawak on the island of Borneo. But, in 1965, Singapore broke away from the Federation and became an independent country.

The People's Action Party (PAP) has ruled Singapore since 1959. Its leader, Lee Kuan Yew, served as prime minister from 1959 until 1990, when he resigned and was succeeded by Goh Chok Tong. Under the PAP, the economy has expanded rapidly, though some people consider that the PAP's rule has been rather dictatorial and oversensitive to criticism.

The World Bank classifies Singapore as a 'high-income' economy. Its highly skilled workforce has created one of the world's fastest growing economies, though the recession in East Asia in 1997–8 was a setback. Trade and finance are leading activities and manufactures include chemicals, electronic products, machinery, metal products, paper, scientific instruments, ships and textiles. Singapore has a large oil refinery and petroleum products and manufactures are the main exports.

AREA 618 sq km [239 sq mls]
POPULATION 3,490,000
CAPITAL (POPULATION) Singapore City (2,874,000)
GOVERNMENT Multiparty republic
ETHNIC GROUPS Chinese 78%, Malay 14%, Indian 7%
LANGUAGES Chinese, Malay, Tamil and English (all official)
RELIGIONS Buddhism, Taoism and other traditional beliefs 54%, Islam 15%, Christianity 13%, Hinduism 4%
CURRENCY Singapore dollar = 100 cents

SLOVAK REPUBLIC

GEOGRAPHY The Slovak Republic is a predominantly mountainous country, consisting of part of the Carpathian range. The highest peak is Gerlachovka in the Tatra Mountains, which reaches 2,655 m [8,711 ft]. The south is a fertile lowland drained by the River Danube.

The Slovak Republic has cold winters and warm summers. Kosice, in the east, has average temperatures ranging from –3°C [27°F] in January to 20°C [68°F] in July. The highland areas are much colder. Snow or rain falls throughout the year. Kosice has an average annual rainfall of 600 mm [24 in], the wettest months being July and August.

POLITICS & ECONOMY Slavic peoples settled in the region in the 5th century AD. They were subsequently conquered by Hungary; the beginning of a millennium of Hungarian rule and concurrent suppression of Slovak culture.

In 1867, Hungary and Austria united to form Austria-Hungary, of which the present-day Slovak Republic was a part. Austria-Hungary collapsed at the end of World War I (1914–18). The Czech and Slovak people then united to form a new nation, Czechoslovakia, but Czech domination of the union led to resentment by many Slovaks. In 1939, the Slovak Republic declared itself independent, but Germany occupied the entire country. At the end of World War II, the Slovak Republic again became part of Czechoslovakia.

The Communist party took control in 1948. In the 1960s, many Czechs and Slovaks sought to reform the Communist system, but the Russians crushed the reformers. However, in the late 1980s, demands for democracy mounted as Soviet reformers began to question Communist policies. Elections in Czechoslovakia in 1992 led to victory for the Movement for a Democratic Slovakia, led by a former Communist and nationalist, Vladimir Meciar. In September 1992, the Slovak National Council voted to create a separate, independent Slovak Republic on 1 January 1994.

After independence, the Slovaks maintained close relations with the Czech Republic, although occasional diplomatic spats occurred. Relations with Hungary were damaged in 1996 when the Slovak government initiated eight new administrative regions which the Hungarian minority claimed under-represented them politically. In addition, a law was convened to make Slovak the only official language.

Before 1948, the Slovak Republic's economy was based on farming, but Communist governments developed manufacturing industries, producing such things as chemicals, machinery, steel and weapons. Since the late 1980s, many state-run businesses have been handed over to private owners.

AREA 49,035 sq km [18,932 sq mls]
POPULATION 5,393,000
CAPITAL (POPULATION) Bratislava (451,000)
GOVERNMENT Multiparty republic
ETHNIC GROUPS Slovak, Hungarian, with small groups of Czechs, Germans, Gypsies, Poles, Russians and Ukrainians
LANGUAGES Slovak (official), Hungarian
RELIGIONS Christianity (Roman Catholic 60%, Protestant 6%, Orthodox 3%)
CURRENCY Koruna = 100 halierov

SLOVENIA

GEOGRAPHY The Republic of Slovenia was one of the six republics which made up the former Yugoslavia. Much of the land is mountainous, rising to 2,863 m [9,393 ft] at Mount Triglav in the Julian Alps (Julijske Alpe) in the north-west. Central Slovenia contains the limestone Karst region. The Postojna caves near Ljubljana are among the largest in Europe.

The coast has a mild Mediterranean climate, but inland the climate is more continental. The mountains are snow-capped in winter.

POLITICS & ECONOMY In the last 2,000 years, the Slovene people have been independent as a nation for less than 50 years. The Austrian Habsburgs ruled over the region from the 13th century until World War I. Slovenia became part of the Kingdom of the Serbs, Croats and Slovenes (later called Yugoslavia) in 1918. During World War II, Slovenia was invaded and partitioned between Italy, Germany and Hungary but, after the war, Slovenia again became part of Yugoslavia.

From the late 1960s, some Slovenes demanded independence, but the central government opposed the break-up of the country. In 1990, when Communist governments had collapsed throughout Eastern Europe, elections were held and a non-Communist coalition government was set up. Slovenia then declared itself independent. This led to fighting between Slovenes and the federal army, but Slovenia did not become a battlefield like other parts of the former Yugoslavia. The European Community recognized Slovenia's independence in 1992 and elections were held. A coalition government led by the Liberal Democrats was set up.

The reform of the economy, formerly run by the government, and the fighting in areas to the south have caused problems for Slovenia, although it remains one of the fastest growing economies in Europe. In 1992, the World Bank classified Slovenia as an 'upper-middle-income' developing country, and it is expected to be among the first countries to join an expanded European Union.

Manufacturing is the leading activity and manufactures are the principal exports. Manufactures include chemicals, machinery and transport equipment, metal goods and textiles. Agriculture employs 8% of the people. Fruits, maize, potatoes and wheat are major crops, while many farmers raise cattle, pigs and sheep.

AREA 20,251 sq km [7,817 sq mls]
POPULATION 1,972,000
CAPITAL (POPULATION) Ljubljana (280,000)
GOVERNMENT Multiparty republic
ETHNIC GROUPS Slovene 88%, Croat 3%, Serb 2%, Bosnian 1%
LANGUAGES Slovene (official), Serbo-Croat
RELIGIONS Christianity (mainly Roman Catholic)
CURRENCY Tolar = 100 stotin

SOLOMON ISLANDS

The Solomon Islands, a chain of mainly volcanic islands south of the equator in the Pacific Ocean, were a British territory between 1893 and 1978. The chain extends for some 2,250 km [1,400 mls]. They were the scene of fierce fighting during World War II. Most people are Melanesians, and the islands have a very young population profile, with half the people aged under 20. Fish, coconuts and cocoa are leading products, although development is hampered by the mountainous, densely forested terrain. **AREA** 29,900 sq km [11,158 sq mls]; **POPULATION** 441,000; **CAPITAL** Honiara.

SOMALIA

GEOGRAPHY The Somali Democratic Republic, or Somalia, is in a region known as the 'Horn of Africa'. It is more than twice the size of Italy, the country which once ruled the southern part of Somalia. The most mountainous part of the country is in the north, behind the narrow coastal plains that border the Gulf of Aden.

Rainfall is light throughout Somalia. The wettest regions are the south and the northern mountains, but droughts often occur. Temperatures are high on the low plateaux and plains.

POLITICS & ECONOMY European powers became interested in the Horn of Africa in the 19th century. In 1884, Britain made the northern part of what is now Somalia a protectorate, while Italy took the south in 1905. The new boundaries divided the Somalis into five areas: the two Somalilands, Djibouti (which was taken by France in the 1880s), Ethiopia and Kenya. Since then, many Somalis have longed for reunification in a Greater Somalia.

Italy entered World War II in 1940 and invaded British Somaliland. But British forces conquered the region in 1941 and ruled both Somalilands until 1950, when the United Nations asked Italy to take over the former Italian Somaliland for ten years. In 1960, both Somalilands became independent and united to become Somalia.

Somalia has faced many problems since independence. Economic problems led a military group to seize power in 1969. In the 1970s, Somalia supported an uprising of Somali-speaking people in the Ogaden region of Ethiopia. But Ethiopian forces prevailed and, in 1988, Somalia signed a peace treaty with Ethiopia. The cost of the fighting weakened Somalia's economy.

Further problems occurred when people in the north fought to secede from Somalia. In 1991, they set up the 'Somaliland Republic', with its capital at Hargeisa. But the new state was recognized neither internationally nor by Somalia's government. Fighting continued and US troops sent by the UN in 1993 had to withdraw in 1994. By 1995, Somalia was divided into three main regions – the north, the north-east and the south. The country had no effective national government.

Somalia is a developing country, whose economy has been shattered by drought and war. Catastrophic flooding in late 1997 displaced tens of thousands of people, further damaging the country's infrastrucure and destroying the slender hope of an economic recovery.

Many Somalis are nomads who raise livestock. Live animals, meat and hides and skins are major exports, followed by bananas grown in the wetter south. Other crops include citrus fruits, cotton, maize and sugar cane. Mining and manufacturing remain relatively unimportant in the economy.

AREA 637,660 sq km [246,201 sq mls]
POPULATION 6,842,000
CAPITAL (POPULATION) Mogadishu (1,000,000)
GOVERNMENT Single-party republic, military dominated
ETHNIC GROUPS Somali 98%, Arab 1%
LANGUAGES Somali and Arabic (both official), English, Italian
RELIGIONS Islam 99%
CURRENCY Somali shilling = 100 cents

SOUTH AFRICA

SOUTH AFRICA

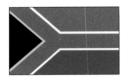

GEOGRAPHY The Republic of South Africa is made up largely of the southern part of the huge plateau which makes up most of southern Africa. The highest peaks are in the Drakensberg range, which is formed by the uptilted rim of the plateau. In the south-west lie the folded Cape Mountain ranges. The coastal plains are mostly narrow. The Namib Desert is in the north-west.

Most of South Africa has a mild, sunny climate. Much of the coastal strip, including the city of Cape Town, has warm, dry summers and mild, rainy winters, just like the Mediterranean lands in northern Africa. Inland, large areas are arid.

POLITICS & ECONOMY Early inhabitants in South Africa were the Khoisan. In the last 2,000 years, Bantu-speaking people moved into the area. Their descendants include the Zulu, Xhosa, Sotho and Tswana. The Dutch founded a settlement at the Cape in 1652, but Britain took over in the early 19th century, making the area a colony. The Dutch, called Boers or Afrikaners, resented British rule and moved inland. Rivalry between the groups led to Anglo-Boer Wars in 1880–1 and 1899–1902.

In 1910, the country was united as the Union of South Africa. In 1948, the National Party won power and introduced a policy known as apartheid, under which non-whites had no votes and their human rights were strictly limited. In 1990, Nelson Mandela, leader of the banned African National Congress (ANC), was released after serving 28 years as a political prisoner. Under a new constitution, multi-racial elections were held in 1994. They resulted in victory for the ANC and Mandela became president. A new constitution was adopted in 1996.

South Africa is Africa's most developed country. But most of the black people are poor, with low standards of living. Natural resources include diamonds, gold and many other metals. Mining and manufacturing are the most valuable activities.

AREA 1,219,916 sq km [470,566 sq mls]
POPULATION 42,835,000
CAPITAL (POPULATION) Cape Town (legislative, 2,350,000); Pretoria (administrative, 1,080,000); Bloemfontein (judiciary, 300,000)
GOVERNMENT Multiparty republic
ETHNIC GROUPS Black 76%, White 13%, Coloured 9%, Asian 2%
LANGUAGES Afrikaans, English, Ndebele, North Sotho, South Sotho, Swazi, Tsonga, Tswana, Venda, Xhosa, Zulu (all official)
RELIGIONS Christianity 68%, Hinduism 1%, Islam 1%
CURRENCY Rand = 100 cents

SPAIN

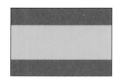

GEOGRAPHY The Kingdom of Spain is the second largest country in Western Europe after France. It shares the Iberian peninsula with Portugal. A large plateau, called the Meseta, covers most of Spain.

Much of the Meseta is flat, but it is crossed by several mountain ranges, called sierras.

The northern highlands include the Cantabrian Mountains (Cordillera Cantabrica) and the high Pyrenees, which form Spain's border with France. But Mulhacén, the highest peak on the Spanish mainland, is in the Sierra Nevada in the south-east. Spain also contains fertile coastal plains. Other major lowlands are the Ebro river basin in the north-east and the Guadalquivir river basin in the south-west. Spain also includes the Balearic Islands in the Mediterranean Sea and the Canary Islands off the north-west coast of Africa.

The Meseta has a continental climate, with hot summers and cold winters, when temperatures often fall below freezing point. Snow often covers the mountain ranges on the Meseta. The Mediterranean coastal regions also have hot, dry summers, but the winters are mild.

POLITICS & ECONOMY In the 16th century, Spain became a world power. At its peak, it controlled much of Central and South America, parts of Africa and the Philippines in Asia. Spain began to decline in the late 16th century. Its sea power was destroyed by a British fleet in the Battle of Trafalgar (1805). By the 20th century, it was a poor country.

Spain became a republic in 1931, but the republicans were defeated in the Spanish Civil War (1936–9). General Francisco Franco (1892–1975) became the country's dictator, though, technically, it was a monarchy. When Franco died, the monarchy was restored. Prince Juan Carlos became king.

Spain has several groups with their own languages and cultures. Some of these people want to run their own regional affairs. In the northern Basque region, some nationalists have waged a terrorist campaign, though a truce was declared in September 1998.

Since the late 1970s, a regional parliament with a considerable degree of autonomy has been set up in the Basque Country (called Euskadi in the indigenous tongue and Pais Vasco in Spanish). Similar parliaments have been initiated in Catalonia in the north-east and Galicia in the north-west. All these regions have their own languages.

The revival of Spain's economy, which was shattered by the Civil War, began in the 1950s and 1960s, especially through the growth of tourism and manufacturing. Since the 1950s, Spain has changed from a poor country, dependent on agriculture, to a fairly prosperous industrial nation.

By the early 1990s, agriculture employed 10% of the people, as compared with industry 35% and services, including tourism, 55%. Farmland, including pasture, makes up about two-thirds of the land, with forest making up most of the rest. Major crops include barley, citrus fruits, grapes for wine-making, olives, potatoes and wheat. Sheep are the leading livestock.

Spain has some high-grade iron ore in the north, though otherwise it lacks natural resources. But it has many manufacturing industries. Manufactures include cars, chemicals, clothing, electronics, processed food, metal goods, steel and textiles. The leading manufacturing centres are Barcelona, Bilbao and Madrid.

AREA 504,780 sq km [194,896 sq mls]
POPULATION 39,134,000
CAPITAL (POPULATION) Madrid (3,041,000)
GOVERNMENT Constitutional monarchy
ETHNIC GROUPS Castilian Spanish 72%, Catalan 16%, Galician 8%, Basque 2%
LANGUAGES Castilian Spanish (official), Catalan, Galician, Basque
RELIGIONS Christianity (Roman Catholic 97%)
CURRENCY Euro; Peseta = 100 céntimos

SRI LANKA

GEOGRAPHY The Democratic Socialist Republic of Sri Lanka is an island nation, separated from the south-east coast of India by the Palk Strait. The land is mostly low-lying, but a mountain region dominates the south-central part of the country.

The western part of Sri Lanka has a wet equatorial climate. Temperatures are high and the rainfall is heavy. Eastern Sri Lanka is drier than the west.

POLITICS & ECONOMY From the early 16th century, Ceylon (as Sri Lanka was then known) was ruled successively by the Portuguese, Dutch and British. Independence was achieved in 1948 and the country was renamed Sri Lanka in 1972.

After independence, rivalries between the two main ethnic groups, the Sinhalese and Tamils, marred progress. In the 1950s, the government made Sinhala the official language. Following protests, the prime minister made provisions for Tamil to be used in some areas. In 1959, the prime minister was assassinated by a Sinhalese extremist and he was succeeded by Sirimavo Bandanaraike, who became the world's first woman prime minister.

Conflict between Tamils and Sinhalese continued in the 1970s and 1980s. In 1987, India helped to engineer a cease-fire. Indian troops arrived to enforce the agreement, but withdrew in 1990 after failing to subdue the main guerrilla group, the Tamil Tigers, who wanted to set up an independent Tamil home-land in northern Sri Lanka. In 1993, the country's president was assassinated by a suspected Tamil separatist. Offensives against the Tamil Tigers continued through the 1990s.

The World Bank classifies Sri Lanka as a 'low-income' developing country. Agriculture employs half of the workforce and coconuts, rubber and tea are exported.

AREA 65,610 sq km [25,332 sq mls]
POPULATION 18,934,000
CAPITAL (POPULATION) Colombo (1,863,000)
GOVERNMENT Multiparty republic
ETHNIC GROUPS Sinhalese 74%, Tamil 18%, Sri Lankan Moor 7%
LANGUAGES Sinhala and Tamil (both official)
RELIGIONS Buddhism 69%, Hinduism 16%, Islam 8%, Christianity 7%
CURRENCY Sri Lankan rupee = 100 cents

SUDAN

GEOGRAPHY The Republic of Sudan is the largest country in Africa. From north to south, it spans a vast area extending from the arid Sahara in the north to the wet equatorial region in the south. The land is mostly flat, with the highest mountains in the far south. The main physical feature is the River Nile.

The climate of Khartoum represents a transition between the virtually rainless northern deserts and the equatorial lands in the south. Some rain falls in Khartoum in summer.

POLITICS & ECONOMY In the 19th century, Egypt

gradually took over Sudan. In 1881, a Muslim religious teacher, the Mahdi ('divinely appointed guide'), led an uprising. Britain and Egypt put the rebellion down in 1898. In 1899, they agreed to rule Sudan jointly as a condominium.

After independence in 1952, the black Africans in the south, who were either Christians or followers of traditional beliefs, feared domination by the Muslim northerners. For example, they objected to the government declaring that Arabic was the only official language. In 1964, civil war broke out and continued until 1972, when the south was given regional self-government, though executive power was still vested in the military government in Khartoum.

In 1983, the government established Islamic law throughout the country. This sparked off further conflict when the Sudan People's Liberation Army in the south launched attacks on government installations. Despite attempts to restore order, the fighting continued into the late 1990s. The problems of food shortages and the displacement of people who became refugees added to Sudan's difficulties. By 1998, the situation had become critical. Widespread famine in southern Sudan attracted global attention and humanitarian aid.

AREA 2,505,810 sq km [967,493 sq mls]
POPULATION 33,551,000
CAPITAL (POPULATION) Khartoum (925,000)
GOVERNMENT Military regime
ETHNIC GROUPS Sudanese Arab 49%, Dinka 12%, Nuba 8%, Beja 6%, Nuer 5%, Azande 3%
LANGUAGES Arabic (official), Nubian, Dinka
RELIGIONS Islam 73%, traditional beliefs 17%, Christianity (Roman Catholic 4%, Protestant 2%)
CURRENCY Dinar = 10 Sudanese pounds

SURINAM

GEOGRAPHY The Republic of Surinam is sandwiched between French Guiana and Guyana in north-eastern South America. The narrow coastal plain was once swampy, but it has been drained and now consists mainly of farmland. Inland lie hills and low mountains, which rise to 1,280 m [4,199 ft].

Surinam has a hot, wet and humid climate. Temperatures are high throughout the year.
POLITICS & ECONOMY In 1667, the British handed Surinam to the Dutch in return for New Amsterdam, an area that is now the state of New York. Slave revolts and Dutch neglect hampered development. In the early 19th century, Britain and the Netherlands disputed the ownership of the area. The British gave up their claims in 1813. Slavery was abolished in 1863 and, soon afterwards, Indian and Indonesian labourers were introduced to work on the plantations. Surinam became fully independent in 1975, but the economy was weakened when thousands of skilled people emigrated from Surinam to the Netherlands.

In 1992, the government negotiated a peace agreement with the *boschneger*, descendants of African slaves, who had launched a struggle against the government in 1986. This rebellion had disrupted the area where bauxite, the main export, was mined. But instability continued, especially among the military. In 1993, the Netherlands stopped financial aid after an EC report stated that Surinam had failed to reform the economy and control inflation.

The World Bank classifies Surinam as an 'upper-middle-income' developing country. Its economy is based on mining and metal processing. Surinam is a leading producer of bauxite, from which the metal aluminium is made.

AREA 163,270 sq km [63,039 sq mls]
POPULATION 427,000
CAPITAL (POPULATION) Paramaribo (201,000)
GOVERNMENT Multiparty republic
ETHNIC GROUPS Asian Indian 37%, Creole (mixed White and Black), 31%, Indonesian 14%, Black 9%, Amerindian 3%, Chinese 3%, Dutch 1%
LANGUAGES Dutch (official), Sranantonga
RELIGIONS Christianity (Roman Catholic 23%, Protestant 19%), Hinduism 27%, Islam 20%
CURRENCY Surinam guilder = 100 cents

SWAZILAND

GEOGRAPHY The Kingdom of Swaziland is a small, landlocked country in southern Africa. The country has four regions which run north-south. In the west, the Highveld, with an average height of 1,200 m [3,937 ft], makes up 30% of Swaziland. The Middleveld, between 350 m and 1,000 m [1,148 ft to 3,281 ft], covers 28% of the country. The Lowveld, with an average height of 270 m [886 ft], covers another 33%. Finally, the Lebombo Mountains reach 800 m [2,600 ft] along the eastern border.

The Lowveld is almost tropical, with an average temperature of 22°C [72°F] and low rainfall. The altitude moderates the climate in the west of the country. Mbabane has a climate typical of the Highveld with warm summers and cool winters.
POLITICS & ECONOMY In 1894, Britain and the Boers of South Africa agreed to put Swaziland under the control of the South African Republic (the Transvaal). But at the end of the Anglo-Boer War (1899–1902), Britain took control of the country. In 1968, when Swaziland became fully independent as a constitutional monarchy, the head of state was King Sobhuza II. Sobhuza died in 1982 after a reign of 82 years. In 1983, one of his sons, Prince Makhosetive (born 1968), was chosen as his heir. In 1986, he was installed as King Mswati III. In 1993, Swaziland held its first-ever multiparty elections.

The World Bank classifies Swaziland as a 'lower-middle-income' developing country. Agriculture employs 74% of the people, and farm products and processed foods, including soft drink concentrates, sugar, wood pulp, citrus fruits and canned fruit, are the leading exports. Many farmers live at subsistence level, producing little more than they need to feed their own families. Swaziland is heavily dependent on South Africa and the two countries are linked through a customs union.

AREA 17,360 sq km [6,703 sq mls]
POPULATION 966,000
CAPITAL (POPULATION) Mbabane (42,000)
GOVERNMENT Monarchy
ETHNIC GROUPS Swazi 84%, Zulu 10%, Tsonga 2%
LANGUAGES Siswati and English (both official)
RELIGIONS Christianity 77%, traditional beliefs
CURRENCY Lilangeni = 100 cents

SWEDEN

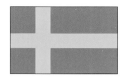

GEOGRAPHY The Kingdom of Sweden is the largest of the countries of Scandinavia in both area and population. It shares the Scandinavian peninsula with Norway. The western part of the country, along the border with Norway, is mountainous. The highest point is Kebnekaise, which reaches 2,117 m [6,946 ft] in the north-west.

The climate of Sweden becomes more severe from south to north. Stockholm has cold winters and cool summers. The far south is much milder.
POLITICS & ECONOMY Swedish Vikings plundered areas to the south and east between the 9th and 11th centuries. Sweden, Denmark and Norway were united in 1397, but Sweden regained its independence in 1523. In 1809, Sweden lost Finland to Russia, but, in 1814, it gained Norway from Denmark. The union between Sweden and Norway was dissolved in 1905. Sweden was neutral in World Wars I and II. Since 1945, Sweden has become a prosperous country. It was a founder member of the European Free Trade Association, but in 1994 the people voted to join the European Union on 1 January 1995.

Sweden has wide-ranging welfare services. But many people are concerned about the high cost of these services and the high taxes they must pay. In 1991, the Social Democrats, who had built up the welfare state, were defeated by a coalition of centre and right-wing parties, though a minority Social Democrat government took office in 1994.

Sweden is a highly developed industrial country. Major products include steel and steel goods. Steel is used in the engineering industry to manufacture aircraft, cars, machinery and ships. Sweden has some of the world's richest iron ore deposits. They are located near Kiruna in the far north. But most of this ore is exported, and Sweden imports most of the materials needed by its industries. In 1996, a decision was taken to decommission all of Sweden's nuclear power stations. This is said to be one of the boldest and most expensive environmental pledges ever made by a government.

AREA 449,960 sq km [173,730 sq mls]
POPULATION 8,887,000
CAPITAL (POPULATION) Stockholm (1,553,000)
GOVERNMENT Constitutional monarchy
ETHNIC GROUPS Swedish 91%, Finnish 3%
LANGUAGES Swedish (official), Finnish
RELIGIONS Christianity (Lutheran 89%, Roman Catholic 2%)
CURRENCY Swedish krona = 100 öre

SWITZERLAND

GEOGRAPHY The Swiss Confederation is a landlocked country in Western Europe. Much of the land is mountainous. The Jura Mountains lie along Switzerland's western border with France, while the Swiss Alps make up about 60% of the country in the south and east. Four-fifths of the people of

Switzerland live on the fertile Swiss plateau, which contains most of Switzerland's large cities.

The climate of Switzerland varies greatly according to the height of the land. The plateau region has a central European climate with warm summers, but cold and snowy winters. Rain occurs all through the year. The rainiest months are in summer.

POLITICS & ECONOMY In 1291, three small cantons (states) united to defend their freedom against the Habsburg rulers of the Holy Roman Empire. They were Schwyz, Uri and Unterwalden, and they called the confederation they formed 'Switzerland'. Switzerland expanded and, in the 14th century, defeated Austria in three wars of independence. After a defeat by the French in 1515, the Swiss adopted a policy of neutrality, which they still follow. In 1815, the Congress of Vienna expanded Switzerland to 22 cantons and guaranteed its neutrality. Switzerland's 23rd canton, Jura, was created in 1979 from part of Bern. Neutrality combined with the vigour and independence of its people have made Switzerland prosperous. In 1993, the Swiss people voted against joining the European Union.

Although lacking in natural resources, Switzerland is a wealthy, industrialized country. Many workers are highly skilled. Major products include chemicals, electrical equipment, machinery and machine tools, precision instruments, processed food, watches and textiles. Farmers produce about three-fifths of the country's food – the rest is imported. Livestock raising, especially dairy farming, is the chief agricultural activity. Crops include fruits, potatoes and wheat. Tourism and banking are also important. Swiss banks attract investors from all over the world.

> **AREA** 41,290 sq km [15,942 sq mls]
> **POPULATION** 7,260,000
> **CAPITAL (POPULATION)** Bern (324,000)
> **GOVERNMENT** Federal republic
> **ETHNIC GROUPS** German 64%, French 19%, Italian 8%, Yugoslav 3%, Spanish 2%, Romansch 1%
> **LANGUAGES** French, German, Italian, Romansch (all official)
> **RELIGIONS** Christianity (Roman Catholic 46%, Protestant 40%)
> **CURRENCY** Swiss franc = 100 centimes

SYRIA

GEOGRAPHY The Syrian Arab Republic is a country in south-western Asia. The narrow coastal plain is overlooked by a low mountain range which runs north–south. Another range, the Jabal ash Sharqi, runs along the border with Lebanon. South of this range is the Golan Heights, which Israel has occupied since 1967.

The coast has a Mediterranean climate, with dry, warm summers and wet, mild winters. The low mountains cut off Damascus from the sea. It has less rainfall than the coastal areas. To the east, the land becomes drier.

POLITICS & ECONOMY After the collapse of the Turkish Ottoman empire in World War I, Syria was ruled by France. Since independence in 1946, Syria has been involved in the Arab–Israeli wars and, in 1967, it lost a strategic border area, the Golan Heights, to Israel. In 1970, Lieutenant-General

Hafez al-Assad took power, establishing a stable but repressive regime which attracted international criticism. In the mid-1990s, Syria had talks with Israel over the future of the Golan Heights, but the negotiations were suspended after the election of Benjamin Netanyahu's right-wing government in Israel in 1996.

The World Bank classifies Syria as a 'lower-middle-income' developing country. But it has great potential for development. Its main resources are oil, hydro-electricity from the dam at Lake Assad, and fertile land. Oil is the main export; farm products, textiles and phosphates are also important. Agriculture employs about 26% of the workforce.

> **AREA** 185,180 sq km [71,498 sq mls]
> **POPULATION** 16,673,000
> **CAPITAL (POPULATION)** Damascus (2,230,000)
> **GOVERNMENT** Multiparty republic
> **ETHNIC GROUPS** Arab 89%, Kurd 6%
> **LANGUAGES** Arabic (official)
> **RELIGIONS** Islam 90%, Christianity 9%
> **CURRENCY** Syrian pound = 100 piastres

TAIWAN

GEOGRAPHY High mountain ranges run down the length of the island, with dense forest in many areas.

The climate is warm, moist and suitable for agriculture.

POLITICS & ECONOMY Chinese settlers occupied Taiwan from the 7th century. In 1895, Japan seized the territory from the Portuguese, who had named it Isla Formosa, or 'beautiful island'. China regained the island after World War II. In 1949, it became the refuge of the Nationalists who had been driven out of China by the Communists. They set up the Republic of China, which, with US help, launched an ambitious programme of economic development. Today, it produces a wide range of manufactured goods. Mainland China regards Taiwan as one of its provinces, though reunification seems unlikely in the foreseeable future.

> **AREA** 36,000 sq km [13,900 sq mls]
> **POPULATION** 21,908,000
> **CAPITAL (population)** Taipei (2,653,000)
> **GOVERNMENT** Unitary multiparty republic
> **ETHNIC GROUPS** Taiwanese (Han Chinese) 84%, mainland Chinese 14%
> **LANGUAGES** Mandarin (official), Min, Hakka
> **RELIGIONS** Buddhist 43%, Taoist & Confucian 49%
> **CURRENCY** New Taiwan dollar = 100 cents

TAJIKISTAN

GEOGRAPHY The Republic of Tajikistan is one of the five central Asian republics that formed part of the former Soviet Union. Only 7% of the land is below 1,000 m [3,280 ft], while almost all of eastern

Tajikistan is above 3,000 m [9,840 ft]. The highest point is Communism Peak (Pik Kommunizma), which reaches 7,495 m [24,590 ft].

Tajikistan has a severe continental climate. Summers are hot and dry in the lower valleys, and winters are long and bitterly cold in the mountains.

POLITICS & ECONOMY Russia conquered parts of Tajikistan in the late 19th century and, by 1920, Russia took complete control. In 1924, Tajikistan became part of the Uzbek Soviet Socialist Republic, but, in 1929, it was expanded, taking in some areas populated by Uzbeks, becoming the Tajik Soviet Socialist Republic.

While the Soviet Union began to introduce reforms in the 1980s, many Tajiks demanded freedom. In 1989, the Tajik government made Tajik the official language instead of Russian and, in 1990, it stated that its local laws overruled Soviet laws. Tajikistan became fully independent in 1991, following the break-up of the Soviet Union. As the poorest of the ex-Soviet republics, Tajikistan faced many problems in trying to introduce a free-market system.

In 1992, civil war broke out between the government, which was run by former Communists, and an alliance of democrats and Islamic forces. The government maintained control, but it relied heavily on aid from the Commonwealth of Independent States, the organization through which most of the former republics of the Soviet Union kept in contact.

The World Bank classifies Tajikistan as a 'low-income' developing country. Agriculture, mainly on irrigated land, is the main activity and cotton is the chief product. Other crops include fruits, grains and vegetables. The country has large hydroelectric power resources and it produces aluminium.

> **AREA** 143,100 sq km [55,520 sq mls]
> **POPULATION** 6,020,000
> **CAPITAL (POPULATION)** Dushanbe (524,000)
> **GOVERNMENT** Transitional democracy
> **ETHNIC GROUPS** Tajik 62%, Uzbek 24%, Russian 8%, Tatar, Kyrgyz, Ukrainian, German
> **LANGUAGES** Tajik (official), Uzbek, Russian
> **RELIGIONS** Islam
> **CURRENCY** Tajik rouble = 100 tanga

TANZANIA

GEOGRAPHY The United Republic of Tanzania consists of the former mainland country of Tanganyika and the island nation of Zanzibar, which also includes the island of Pemba. Behind a narrow coastal plain, most of Tanzania is a plateau, which is broken by arms of the Great African Rift Valley. In the west, this valley contains lakes Nyasa and Tanganyika. The highest peak is Kilimanjaro, Africa's tallest mountain.

The coast has a hot and humid climate, with the greatest rainfall in April and May. The inland plateaux and mountains are cooler and less humid.

POLITICS & ECONOMY Mainland Tanganyika became a German territory in the 1880s, while Zanzibar and Pemba became a British protectorate in 1890. Following Germany's defeat in World War I, Britain took over Tanganyika, which remained a British territory until its independence in 1961. In 1964, Tanganyika and Zanzibar united to form the United Republic of Tanzania. The country's president, Julius Nyerere, pursued socialist policies of

self-help (*ujamaa*) and egalitarianism. Many of its social reforms were successful, but the country failed to make economic progress. Nyerere resigned as president in 1985 and his successors introduced more liberal economic policies.

Tanzania is one of the world's poorest countries. Although crops are grown on only 5% of the land, agriculture employs 85% of the people. Most farmers grow only enough to feed their families. Food crops include bananas, cassava, maize, millet, rice and vegetables.

AREA 945,090 sq km [364,899 sq mls]
POPULATION 30,609,000
CAPITAL (POPULATION) Dodoma (204,000)
GOVERNMENT Multiparty republic
ETHNIC GROUPS Nyamwezi and Sukuma 21%, Swahili 9%, Hehet and Bena 7%, Makonde 6%, Haya 6%
LANGUAGES Swahili and English (both official)
RELIGIONS Christianity (mostly Roman Catholic) 34%, Islam 33% (99% in Zanzibar), traditional beliefs and others 33%
CURRENCY Tanzanian shilling = 100 cents

THAILAND

GEOGRAPHY The Kingdom of Thailand is one of the ten countries in South-east Asia. The highest land is in the north, where Doi Inthanon, the highest peak, reaches 2,595 m [8,514 ft]. The Khorat Plateau, in the north-east, makes up about 30% of the country and is the most heavily populated part of Thailand. In the south, Thailand shares the finger-like Malay Peninsula with Burma and Malaysia.

Thailand has a tropical climate. Monsoon winds from the south-west bring heavy rains between the months of May and October. The rainfall in Bangkok is lower than in many other parts of South-east Asia, because mountains shelter the central plains from the rain-bearing winds.
POLITICS & ECONOMY The first Thai state was set up in the 13th century. By 1350, it included most of what is now Thailand. European contact began in the early 16th century. But, in the late 17th century, the Thais, fearing interference in their affairs, forced all Europeans to leave. This policy continued for 150 years. In 1782, a Thai General, Chao Phraya Chakkri, became king, founding a dynasty which continues today. The country became known as Siam, and Bangkok became its capital. From the mid-19th century, contacts with the West were restored. In World War I, Siam supported the Allies against Germany and Austria-Hungary. But in 1941, the country was conquered by Japan and became its ally. But, after the end of World War II, it became an ally of the United States.

Since 1967, when Thailand became a member of ASEAN (the Association of South-east Asian Nations), its economy has grown, especially its manufacturing and service industries. However, in 1997, it suffered recession along with other eastern Asian countries. Despite its rapid progress, the World Bank classifies the country as a 'lower-middle-income' developing country. Manufactures, including food products, machinery, timber products and textiles, are exported, but agriculture still employs two-thirds of the people. Rice is the main food, while other major crops include cassava, cotton, maize, pineapples,

rubber, sugar cane and tobacco. Thailand also mines tin and other minerals, and tourism is a major source of income.

AREA 513,120 sq km [198,116 sq mls]
POPULATION 60,037,000
CAPITAL (POPULATION) Bangkok (5,876,000)
GOVERNMENT Constitutional monarchy
ETHNIC GROUPS Thai 80%, Chinese 12%, Malay 4%, Khmer 3%
LANGUAGES Thai (official), Chinese, Malay
RELIGIONS Buddhism 94%, Islam 4%, Christianity 1%
CURRENCY Thai baht = 100 satang

TOGO

GEOGRAPHY The Republic of Togo is a long, narrow country in West Africa. From north to south, it extends about 500 km [311 mls]. Its coastline on the Gulf of Guinea is only 64 km [40 mls] long and it is only 145 km [90 mls] at its widest point.

Togo has high temperatures all through the year. The main wet season is from March to July, with a minor wet season in October and November.
POLITICS & ECONOMY Togo became a German protectorate in 1884 but, in 1919, Britain took over the western third of the territory, while France took over the eastern two-thirds. In 1956, the people of British Togoland voted to join Ghana, while French Togoland became an independent republic in 1960.

Local rivalries, especially between the northerners and southerners, are important political factors, and, in 1963, a group of army officers from the north assassinated the president, a southerner. In 1967, Gnassingbé Eyadéma, one of the officers responsible for the 1963 coup, took power and suspended the constitution. Constitutional government was restored in 1980 and multiparty elections were held in 1994.

Togo is a poor developing country. Farming employs 65% of the people, but most farmers grow little more than they need to feed their families. Major food crops include cassava, maize, millet and yams. The leading export is phosphate rock, which is used to make fertilizers.

AREA 56,790 sq km [21,927 sq mls]
POPULATION 4,906,000
CAPITAL (POPULATION) Lomé (590,000)
CAPITAL Multiparty republic
ETHNIC GROUPS Ewe-Adja 43%, Tem-Kabre 26%, Gurma 16%
LANGUAGES French (official), Ewe, Kabiye
RELIGIONS Traditional beliefs 50%, Christianity 35%, Islam 15%
CURRENCY CFA franc = 100 centimes

TONGA

The Kingdom of Tonga, a former British protectorate, became independent in 1970. Situated in the

South Pacific Ocean, it contains more than 170 islands, 36 of which are inhabited. Agriculture is the main activity; coconuts, copra, fruits and fish are leading products. **AREA** 75 sq km [290 sq mls]; **POPULATION** 107,000; **CAPITAL** Nuku'alofa.

TRINIDAD AND TOBAGO

The Republic of Trinidad and Tobago became independent from Britain in 1962. These tropical islands, populated by people of African, Asian (mainly Indian) and European origin, are hilly and forested, though there are some fertile plains. Oil production is the main sector of the economy. **AREA** 5,130 sq km [1,981 sq mls]; **POPULATION** 1,117,000; **CAPITAL** Port-of-Spain.

TUNISIA

GEOGRAPHY The Republic of Tunisia is the smallest country in North Africa. The mountains in the north are an eastwards and comparatively low extension of the Atlas Mountains. To the north and east of the mountains lie fertile plains, especially between Sfax, Tunis and Bizerte. In the south, low-lying regions contain a vast salt pan, called the Chott Djerid, and part of the Sahara Desert.

Northern Tunisia has a Mediterranean climate, with dry, sunny summers, and mild winters with a moderate rainfall. The average yearly rainfall decreases towards the south.
POLITICS & ECONOMY In 1881, France established a protectorate over Tunisia and ruled the country until 1956. The new parliament abolished the monarchy and declared Tunisia to be a republic in 1957, with the nationalist leader, Habib Bourguiba, as president. His government introduced many reforms, including votes for women, but various problems arose, including unemployment among the middle class and fears that Western values introduced by tourists might undermine Muslim values. In 1987, the prime minister Zine el Abidine Ben Ali removed Bourguiba from office and succeeded him as president. He was elected in 1989 and again in 1994.

The World Bank classifies Tunisia as a 'middle-income' developing country. The main resources and chief exports are phosphates and oil. Most industries are concerned with food processing. Agriculture employs 22% of the people; major crops being barley, dates, grapes, olives and wheat. Fishing is important, as is tourism. Almost four million tourists visited Tunisia in 1994.

AREA 163,610 sq km [63,170 sq mls]
POPULATION 9,380,000
CAPITAL (POPULATION) Tunis (1,827,000)
CAPITAL Multiparty republic
ETHNIC GROUPS Arab 98%, Berber 1%, French
LANGUAGES Arabic (official), French
RELIGIONS Islam 99%
CURRENCY Dinar = 1,000 millimes

TURKEY

TURKEY

GEOGRAPHY The Republic of Turkey lies in two continents. The European section lies west of a waterway between the Black and Mediterranean seas. European Turkey, also called Thrace, is a fertile, hilly region. Most of the Asian part of Turkey consists of plateaux and mountains, which rise to 5,165 m [16,945 ft] at Mount Ararat (Agri Dagi) near the border with Armenia.

Central Turkey has a dry climate, with hot, sunny summers and cold winters. The driest part of the central plateau lies south of the city of Ankara, around Lake Tuz. Western Turkey has a Mediterranean climate, while the Black Sea coast has cooler summers.

POLITICS & ECONOMY In AD 330, the Roman empire moved its capital to Byzantium, which it renamed Constantinople. Constantinople became capital of the East Roman (or Byzantine) empire in 395. Muslim Seljuk Turks from central Asia invaded Anatolia in the 11th century. In the 14th century, another group of Turks, the Ottomans, conquered the area. In 1435, the Ottoman Turks took Constantinople, which they called Istanbul.

The Ottoman Turks built up a large empire which finally collapsed during World War I (1914–18). In 1923, Turkey became a republic. Its leader Mustafa Kemal, or Atatürk ('father of the Turks'), launched policies to modernize and secularize the country.

Since the 1940s, Turkey has sought to strengthen its ties with Western powers. It joined NATO (North Atlantic Treaty Organization) in 1951 and it applied to join the European Economic Community in 1987. But Turkey's conflict with Greece, together with its invasion of northern Cyprus in 1974, have led many Europeans to treat Turkey's aspirations with caution. Political instability, military coups, conflict with Kurdish nationalists in eastern Turkey and concern about the country's record on human rights are other problems. Turkey has enjoyed democracy since 1983, though, in 1998, the government banned the Islamist Welfare Party, which it accused of violating secular principles. In 1999, the Muslim Virtue Party (successor to Islamist Welfare Party) lost ground. The largest numbers of parliamentary seats were won by the ruling Democratic Left Party and the far-right National Action Party.

The World Bank classifies Turkey as a 'lower-middle-income' developing country. Agriculture employs 47% of the people, and barley, cotton, fruits, maize, tobacco and wheat are major crops. Livestock farming is important and wool is a leading product.

Turkey produces chromium, but manufacturing is the chief activity. Manufactures include processed farm products and textiles, cars, fertilizers, iron and steel, machinery, metal products and paper products. Over nine million tourists visited Turkey in 1998. But, in 1999, tourism was threatened by Kurdish bombings in Ankara and Istanbul.

AREA 779,450 sq km [300,946 sq mls]
POPULATION 64,568,000
CAPITAL (POPULATION) Ankara (3,028,000)
GOVERNMENT Multiparty republic
ETHNIC GROUPS Turkish 86%, Kurdish 11%, Arab 2%
LANGUAGES Turkish (official), Kurdish
RELIGIONS Islam 99%
CURRENCY Turkish lira = 100 kurus

TURKMENISTAN

GEOGRAPHY The Republic of Turkmenistan is one of the five central Asian republics which once formed part of the former Soviet Union. Most of the land is low-lying, with mountains lying on the southern and south-western borders. In the west lies the salty Caspian Sea. Most of Turkmenistan is arid and the Garagum, Asia's largest sand desert, covers about 80% of the country. Turkmenistan has a continental climate, with average annual rainfall varying from 80 mm [3 in] in the desert to 300 mm [12 in] in the mountains. Summer months are hot but winter temperatures drop well below freezing point.

POLITICS & ECONOMY Just over 1,000 years ago, Turkic people settled in the lands east of the Caspian Sea and the name 'Turkmen' comes from this time. Mongol armies conquered the area in the 13th century and Islam was introduced in the 14th century. Russia took over the area in the 1870s and 1880s. After the Russian Revolution of 1917, the area came under Communist rule and, in 1924, it became the Turkmen Soviet Socialist Republic. The Communists strictly controlled all aspects of life and, in particular, they discouraged religious worship. But they also improved such services as education, health, housing and transport.

In the 1980s, when the Soviet Union began to introduce reforms, the Turkmen began to demand more freedom. In 1990, the Turkmen government stated that its laws overruled Soviet laws. In 1991, Turkmenistan became fully independent after the break-up of the Soviet Union. But the country kept ties with Russia through the Commonwealth of Independent States (CIS).

In 1992, Turkmenistan adopted a new constitution, allowing for the setting up of political parties, providing that they were not ethnic or religious in character. But, effectively, Turkmenistan remained a one-party state and, in 1992, Saparmurad Niyazov, the former Communist and now Democratic party leader, was the only candidate. In 1994, 99.5% of the voters in a referendum were in favour of prolonging Niyazov's term of office to 2002.

Faced with many economic problems, Turkmenistan began to look south rather than to the CIS for support. As part of this policy, it joined the Economic Co-operation Organization which had been set up in 1985 by Iran, Pakistan and Turkey. In 1996, the completion of a rail link from Turkmenistan to the Iranian coast was seen both as a revival of the traditions of the ancient silk road, and as a highly significant step for the future economic development of Central Asia.

Turkmenistan's chief resources are oil and natural gas, but the main activity is agriculture, with cotton, grown on irrigated land, as the main crop. Grain and vegetables are also important. Manufactures include cement, glass, petrochemicals and textiles.

AREA 488,100 sq km [188,450 sq mls]
POPULATION 4,298,000
CAPITAL (POPULATION) Ashgabat (407,000)
GOVERNMENT Single-party republic
ETHNIC GROUPS Turkmen 72%, Russian 10%, Uzbek 9%, Kazak 3%, Tatar
LANGUAGES Turkmen (official), Russian, Uzbek, Kazak
RELIGIONS Islam
CURRENCY Manat = 100 tenesi

TURKS AND CAICOS ISLANDS

The Turks and Caicos Islands, a British territory in the Caribbean since 1776, are a group of about 30 islands. Fishing and tourism are major activities. **AREA** 430 sq km [166 sq mls]; **POPULATION** 16,000; **CAPITAL** Cockburn Town.

TUVALU

Tuvalu, formerly called the Ellice Islands, was a British territory from the 1890s until it became independent in 1978. It consists of nine low-lying coral atolls in the southern Pacific Ocean. Copra is the chief export. **AREA** 24 sq km [9 sq mls]; **POPULATION** 10,000; **CAPITAL** Fongafale.

UGANDA

GEOGRAPHY The Republic of Uganda is a land-locked country on the East African plateau. It contains part of Lake Victoria, Africa's largest lake and a source of the River Nile, which occupies a shallow depression in the plateau.

The equator runs through Uganda and the country is warm throughout the year, though the high altitude moderates the temperature. The wettest regions are the lands to the north of Lake Victoria, where Kampala is situated, and the western mountains, especially the high Ruwenzori range.

POLITICS & ECONOMY Little is known of the early history of Uganda. When Europeans first reached the area in the 19th century, many of the people were organized in kingdoms, the most powerful of which was Buganda, the home of the Baganda people. Britain took over the country between 1894 and 1914, and ruled it until independence in 1962.

In 1967, Uganda became a republic and Buganda's Kabaka (king), Sir Edward Mutesa II, was made president. But tensions between the Kabaka and the prime minister, Apollo Milton Obote, led to the dismissal of the Kabaka in 1966. Obote also abolished the traditional kingdoms, including Buganda. Obote was overthrown in 1971 by an army group led by General Idi Amin Dada. Amin ruled as a dictator. He forced most of the Asians who lived in Uganda to leave the country and had many of his opponents killed.

In 1978, a border dispute between Uganda and Tanzania led Tanzanian troops to enter Uganda. With help from Ugandan opponents of Amin, they overthrew Amin's government. In 1980, Obote led his party to victory in national elections. But after charges of fraud, Obote's opponents began guerrilla warfare. A military group overthrew Obote in 1985, but strife continued until 1986, when Yoweri

Museveni's National Resistance Movement seized power. In 1993, Museveni restored the traditional kingdoms, including Buganda where a new Kabaka was crowned. Museveni also held national elections in 1994 but political parties were not permitted. Museveni was elected president in 1996.

The strife in Uganda since the 1960s has greatly damaged the economy. By 1991 Uganda was, according to the World Bank, among the world's five poorest countries. Agriculture dominates the economy, employing 86% of the people. The chief export is coffee.

AREA 235,880 sq km [91,073 sq mls]
POPULATION 22,167,000
CAPITAL (POPULATION) Kampala (773,000)
GOVERNMENT Republic in transition
ETHNIC GROUPS Baganda 18%, Banyoro 14%, Teso 9%, Banyan 8%, Basoga 8%, Bagisu 7%, Bachiga 7%, Lango 6%, Acholi 5%
LANGUAGES English and Swahili (both official)
RELIGIONS Christianity (Roman Catholic 40%, Protestant 29%), traditional beliefs 18%, Islam 7%
CURRENCY Uganda shilling = 100 cent

UKRAINE

GEOGRAPHY Ukraine is the second largest country in Europe after Russia. It was formerly part of the Soviet Union, which split apart in 1991. This mostly flat country faces the Black Sea in the south. The Crimean peninsula includes a highland region overlooking Yalta.

Ukraine has warm summers, but the winters are cold, becoming more severe from west to east. In the summer, the east of the country is often warmer than the west. The heaviest rainfall occurs in the summer.
POLITICS & ECONOMY Kiev was the original capital of the early Slavic civilization known as Kievan Rus. In the 17th and 18th centuries, parts of Ukraine came under Polish and Russian rule. But Russia gained most of Ukraine in the late 18th century. In 1918, Ukraine became independent, but in 1922 it became part of the Soviet Union. Millions of people died in the 1930s as the result of Soviet policies, while millions more died during the Nazi occupation (1941–4).

In the 1980s, Ukrainian people demanded more say over their affairs. The country finally became independent when the Soviet Union broke up in 1991. Ukraine continued to work with Russia through the Commonwealth of Independent States. But Ukraine differed with Russia on some issues, including control over Crimea. In 1999, a treaty ratifying Ukraine's present boundaries failed to get the approval of Russia's upper house.

The World Bank classifies Ukraine as a 'lower-middle-income' economy. Agriculture is important. Crops include wheat and sugar beet, which are the major exports, together with barley, maize, potatoes, sunflowers and tobacco. Livestock rearing and fishing are also important industries.

Manufacturing is the chief economic activity. Major manufactures include iron and steel, machinery and vehicles. The country has large coalfields. The country imports oil and natural gas, but it has hydro-electric and nuclear power stations. In 1986, an accident at the Chernobyl nuclear power plant caused widespread nuclear radiation.

AREA 603,700 sq km [233,100 sq mls]
POPULATION 50,125,000
CAPITAL (POPULATION) Kiev (2,630,000)
GOVERNMENT Multiparty republic
ETHNIC GROUPS Ukrainian 73%, Russian 22%, Jewish 1%, Belarussian 1%, Moldovan, Bulgarian, Polish
LANGUAGES Ukrainian (official), Russian
RELIGIONS Christianity (mostly Ukrainian Orthodox)
CURRENCY Hryvna

UNITED ARAB EMIRATES

The United Arab Emirates were formed in 1971 when the seven Trucial States of the Gulf (Abu Dhabi, Dubai, Sharjah, Ajman, Umm al Qawayn, Ra's al Khaymah and Al Fujayrah) opted to join together and form an independent country. The economy of this hot and dry country depends on oil production, and oil revenues give the United Arab Emirates one of the highest per capita GNPs in Asia.
AREA 83,600 sq km [32,278 sq mls]; **POPULATION** 2,303,000; **CAPITAL** Abu Dhabi.

UNITED KINGDOM

GEOGRAPHY The United Kingdom (or UK) is a union of four countries. Three of them – England, Scotland and Wales – make up Great Britain. The fourth country is Northern Ireland. The Isle of Man and the Channel Islands, including Jersey and Guernsey, are not part of the UK. They are self-governing British dependencies.

The land is highly varied. Much of Scotland and Wales is mountainous, and the highest peak is Scotland's Ben Nevis at 1,343 m [4,406 ft]. England has some highland areas, including the Cumbrian Mountains (or Lake District) and the Pennine range in the north. But England also has large areas of fertile lowland. Northern Ireland is also a mixture of lowlands and uplands. It contains the UK's largest lake, Lough Neagh.

The UK has a mild climate, influenced by the warm Gulf Stream which flows across the Atlantic from the Gulf of Mexico, then past the British Isles. Moist winds from the south-west bring rain, but the rainfall decreases from west to east. Winds from the east and north bring cold weather in winter.
POLITICS & ECONOMY In ancient times, Britain was invaded by many peoples, including Iberians, Celts, Romans, Angles, Saxons, Jutes, Norsemen, Danes, and Normans, who arrived in 1066. The evolution of the United Kingdom spanned hundreds of years. The Normans finally overcame Welsh resistance in 1282, when King Edward I annexed Wales and united it with England. Union with Scotland was achieved by the Act of Union of 1707. This created a country known as the United Kingdom of Great Britain.

Ireland came under Norman rule in the 11th century, and much of its later history was concerned with a struggle against English domination. In 1801, Ireland became part of the United Kingdom of Great Britain and Ireland. But in 1921, southern Ireland broke away to become the Irish Free State. Most of the people in the Irish Free State were Roman Catholics. In Northern Ireland, where the majority of the people were Protestants, most people wanted to remain citizens of the United Kingdom. As a result, the country's official name changed to the United Kingdom of Great Britain and Northern Ireland.

The modern history of the UK began in the 18th century when the British empire began to develop, despite the loss in 1783 of its 13 North American colonies which became the core of the modern United States. The other major event occurred in the late 18th century, when the UK became the first country to industrialize its economy.

The British empire broke up after World War II (1939–45), though the UK still administers many small, mainly island, territories around the world. The empire was transformed into the Commonwealth of Nations, a free association of independent countries which numbered 54 in 1999.

But while the UK retained a world role through the Commonwealth and the United Nations, it recognized that its economic future lay within Europe. As a result, it became a member of the European Economic Community (now the European Union) in 1973. In the 1990s, most people accepted the importance of the European Union to the UK's economic future. But some feared a loss of British identity should the European Union evolve into a political federation. In 1999, the UK began to decentralize power away from London as people in Scotland and Wales elected regional assemblies, while referendums on city mayors were planned.

The UK is a major industrial and trading nation. It lacks natural resources apart from coal, iron ore, oil and natural gas, and has to import most of the materials it needs for its industries. The UK also has to import food, because it produces only about two-thirds of the food it needs.

In the first half of the 20th century, the UK became known for exporting such products as cars, ships, steel and textiles. However, many traditional industries have suffered from increased competition from other countries, whose lower labour costs enable them to produce goods more cheaply. Today, a growing number of industries use sophisticated high-technology in order to compete on the world market.

The UK is one of the world's most urbanized countries, and agriculture employs only 2% of the people. Yet production is high because farms use scientific methods and modern machinery. Major crops include barley, potatoes, sugar beet and wheat. Sheep are the leading livestock, but beef cattle, dairy cattle, pigs and poultry are also important. Fishing is another major activity.

Service industries play a major part in the UK's economy. Financial and insurance services bring in much-needed foreign exchange, while tourism has become a major earner.

AREA 243,368 sq km [94,202 sq mls]
POPULATION 58,970,000
CAPITAL (POPULATION) London (8,089,000)
GOVERNMENT Constitutional monarchy
ETHNIC GROUPS White 94%, Asian Indian 1%, Pakistani 1%, West Indian 1%
LANGUAGES English (official), Welsh, Gaelic
RELIGIONS Christianity (Anglican 57%, Roman Catholic 13%, Presbyterian 7%, Methodist 4%, Baptist 1%), Islam 1%, Judaism, Hinduism, Sikhism
CURRENCY Pound sterling = 100 pence

UNITED STATES OF AMERICA

GEOGRAPHY The United States of America is the world's fourth largest country in area and the third largest in population. It contains 50 states, 48 of which lie between Canada and Mexico, plus Alaska in north-western North America, and Hawaii, a group of volcanic islands in the North Pacific Ocean. Densely populated coastal plains lie to the east and south of the Appalachian Mountains. The central lowlands drained by the Mississippi–Missouri rivers stretch from the Appalachians to the Rocky Mountains in the west. The Pacific region contains fertile valleys, separated by mountain ranges.

The climate varies greatly, ranging from the Arctic cold of Alaska to the intense heat of Death Valley, a bleak desert in California. Of the 48 states between Canada and Mexico, winters are cold and snowy in the north, but mild in the south, a region which is often called the 'Sun Belt'.

POLITICS & ECONOMY The first people in North America, the ancestors of the Native Americans (or American Indians) arrived perhaps 40,000 years ago from Asia. Although Vikings probably reached North America 1,000 years ago, European exploration proper did not begin until the late 15th century.

The first Europeans to settle in large numbers were the British, who founded settlements on the eastern coast in the early 17th century. British rule ended in the War of Independence (1775–83). The country expanded in 1803 when a vast territory in the south and west was acquired through the Louisiana Purchase, while the border with Mexico was fixed in the mid-19th century.

The Civil War (1861–5) ended the threat that the nation might split in two parts. It also ended slavery for the country's many African Americans. In the late 19th century, the West was opened up, while immigrants flooded in from Europe and elsewhere.

During the late 19th and early 20th centuries, industrialization led to the United States becoming the world's leading economic superpower and a pioneer in science and technology. Because of its economic strength, it has been able to take on the mantle of the champion of the Western world and of democratic government. The fall of Communism and the subsequent break-up of the Soviet Union left the US as the world's only real superpower. While this supremacy may well be challenged by China in time, the USA remains the most powerful voice in global politics.

The United States has the world's largest economy in terms of the total value of its production. Although agriculture employs only 2% of the people, farming is highly mechanized and scientific, and the United States leads the world in farm production. Major products include beef and dairy cattle, together with such crops as cotton, fruits, groundnuts, maize, potatoes, soya beans, tobacco and wheat.

The country's natural resources include oil, natural gas and coal. There are also a wide range of metal ores which are used in manufacturing industries, together with timber, especially from the forests of the Pacific north-west. Manufacturing is the single most important activity, employing about 17% of the population. Major products include vehicles, food products, chemicals, machinery, printed goods, metal products and scientific instruments. California is now the leading manufacturing state. Many southern states, petroleum rich and climatically favoured, have also become highly prosperous in recent years.

AREA 9,372,610 sq km [3,618,765 sq mls]
POPULATION 270,290,000
CAPITAL (POPULATION) Washington, D.C. (4,466,000)
GOVERNMENT Federal republic
ETHNIC GROUPS White 80%, African American 12%, other races 8%
LANGUAGES English (official), Spanish, more than 30 others
RELIGIONS Christianity (Protestant 53%, Roman Catholic 26%, other Christian 8%), Islam 2%, Judaism 2%
CURRENCY US dollar = 100 cents

URUGUAY

GEOGRAPHY Uruguay is South America's second smallest independent country after Surinam. The land consists mainly of flat plains and hills. The River Uruguay, which forms the country's western border, flows into the Río de la Plata, a large estuary which leads into the South Atlantic Ocean.

Uruguay has a mild climate, with rain in every month, though droughts sometimes occur. Summers are pleasantly warm, especially near the coast. The weather remains relatively mild throughout the winter.

POLITICS & ECONOMY In 1726, Spanish settlers founded Montevideo in order to halt the Portuguese gaining influence in the area. By the late 18th century, Spaniards had settled in most of the country. Uruguay became part of a colony called the Viceroyalty of La Plata, which also included Argentina, Paraguay, and parts of Bolivia, Brazil and Chile. In 1820 Brazil annexed Uruguay, ending Spanish rule. In 1825, Uruguayans, supported by Argentina, began a struggle for independence. Finally, in 1828, Brazil and Argentina recognized Uruguay as an independent republic. Social and economic developments were slow in the 19th century, but, from 1903, governments made Uruguay a democratic and stable country.

From the 1950s, economic problems caused unrest. Terrorist groups, notably the Tupumaros, carried out murders and kidnappings. The army crushed the Tupumaros in 1972, but the army took over the government in 1973. Military rule continued until 1984 when elections were held. Julio Maria Sanguinetti, who led Uruguay back to civilian rule, was re-elected president in 1994.

The World Bank classifies Uruguay as an 'upper-middle-income' developing country. Agriculture employs only 5% of the people, but farm products, notably hides and leather goods, beef and wool, are the leading exports, while the leading manufacturing industries process farm products. The main crops include maize, potatoes, wheat and sugar beet.

AREA 177,410 sq km [68,498 sq mls]
POPULATION 3,285,000
CAPITAL (POPULATION) Montevideo (1,326,000)
GOVERNMENT Multiparty republic
ETHNIC GROUPS White 86%, Mestizo 8%, Mulatto or Black 6%
LANGUAGES Spanish (official)
RELIGIONS Christianity (Roman Catholic 66%, Protestant 2%), Judaism 1%
CURRENCY Uruguay peso = 100 centésimos

UZBEKISTAN

GEOGRAPHY The Republic of Uzbekistan is one of the five republics in Central Asia which were once part of the Soviet Union. Plains cover most of western Uzbekistan, with highlands in the east. The main rivers, the Amu (or Amu Darya) and Syr (or Syr Darya), drain into the Aral Sea. So much water has been taken from these rivers to irrigate the land that the Aral Sea shrank from 66,900 sq km [25,830 sq mls] in 1960 to 33,642 sq km [12,989 sq mls] in 1993. The dried-up lake area has become desert, like much of the rest of the country.

Uzbekistan has a continental climate. The winters are cold, but the temperatures soar in the summer months. The west is extremely arid, with an average annual rainfall of about 200 mm [8 in].

POLITICS & ECONOMY Russia took the area in the 19th century. After the Russian Revolution of 1917, the Communists took over and, in 1924, they set up the Uzbek Soviet Socialist Republic. Under Communism, all aspects of Uzbek life were controlled and religious worship was discouraged. But education, health, housing and transport were improved. In the late 1980s, the people demanded more freedom and, in 1990, the government stated that its laws overruled those of the Soviet Union. Uzbekistan became independent in 1991 when the Soviet Union broke up, but it retained links with Russia through the Commonwealth of Independent States. Islam Karimov, leader of the People's Democratic Party (formerly the Communist Party), was elected president in December 1991. In 1992–3, many opposition leaders were arrested because the government said that they threatened national stability. In 1994–5, the PDP won sweeping victories in national elections and, in 1995, a referendum extended Karimov's term in office until 2000.

The World Bank classifies Uzbekistan as a 'lower-middle-income' developing country and the government still controls most economic activity. The country produces coal, copper, gold, oil and natural gas.

AREA 447,400 sq km [172,740 sq mls]
POPULATION 23,784,000
CAPITAL (POPULATION) Tashkent (2,106,000)
GOVERNMENT Socialist republic
ETHNIC GROUPS Uzbek 71%, Russian 8%, Tajik 5%, Kazak 4%, Tatar 2%, Kara-Kalpak 2%
LANGUAGES Uzbek (official), several others
RELIGIONS Islam
CURRENCY Som = 100 tyiyn

VANUATU

The Republic of Vanuatu, formerly the Anglo-French Condominium of the New Hebrides, became independent in 1980. It consists of a chain of 80 islands in the South Pacific Ocean. Its economy is based on agriculture and it exports copra, beef and veal, timber and cocoa. **AREA** 12,190 sq km [4,707 sq mls]; **POPULATION** 185,000; **CAPITAL** Port-Vila.

VATICAN CITY

Vatican City State, the world's smallest independent nation, is an enclave on the west bank of the River Tiber in Rome. It forms an independent base for the Holy See, the governing body of the Roman Catholic Church. **AREA** 0.44 sq km [0.17 sq mls]; **POPULATION** about 1,000.

VENEZUELA

GEOGRAPHY The Republic of Venezuela, in northern South America, contains the Maracaibo lowlands around the oil-rich Lake Maracaibo in the west. Andean ranges enclose the lowlands and extend across most of northern Venezuela. The Orinoco river basin, containing tropical grasslands called *llanos*, lies between the northern highlands and the Guiana Highlands in the south-east.

Venezuela has a tropical climate. Temperatures are high throughout the year on the lowlands, though the mountains are much cooler. The rainfall is heaviest in the mountains. But much of the country has a marked dry season between December and April.

POLITICS & ECONOMY In the early 19th century, Venezuelans, such as Simón Bolívar and Francisco de Miranda, began a struggle against Spanish rule. Venezuela declared its independence in 1811. But it only become truly independent in 1821, when the Spanish were defeated in a battle near Valencia.

The development of Venezuela in the 19th and the first half of the 20th centuries was marred by instability, violence and periods of harsh dictatorial rule. But the country has had elected governments since 1958. The country has greatly benefited from its oil resources which were first exploited in 1917. In 1960, Venezuela helped to form OPEC (the Organization of Petroleum Exporting Countries) and, in 1976, the government of Venezuela took control of the entire oil industry. Money from oil exports has helped Venezuela to raise living standards and diversify the economy.

The World Bank classifies Venezuela as an 'upper-middle-income' developing country. Oil accounts for 80% of the exports. Other exports include bauxite and aluminium, iron ore and farm products. Agriculture employs 13% of the people and cattle ranching is important. The chief industry is petroleum refining. Other manufactures include aluminium, cement, processed food, steel and textiles. The main manufacturing centres include Caracas, Ciudad Guayana (aluminium and steel) and Maracaibo (oil refineries).

AREA 912,050 sq km [352,143 sq mls]
POPULATION 22,803,000
CAPITAL (POPULATION) Caracas (2,784,000)
GOVERNMENT Federal republic
ETHNIC GROUPS Mestizo 67%, White 21%, Black 10%, Amerindian 2%
LANGUAGES Spanish (official), Goajiro
RELIGIONS Christianity (Roman Catholic 94%)
CURRENCY Bolívar = 100 céntimos

VIETNAM

GEOGRAPHY The Socialist Republic of Vietnam occupies an S-shaped strip of land facing the South China Sea in South-east Asia. The coastal plains include two densely populated, fertile delta regions: the Red (Hong) delta facing the Gulf of Tonkin in the north, and the Mekong delta in the south.

Vietnam has a tropical climate, though the driest months of January to March are a little cooler than the wet, hot summer months, when monsoon winds blow from the south-west. Typhoons (cyclones) sometimes hit the coast, causing much damage.

POLITICS & ECONOMY China dominated Vietnam for a thousand years before AD 939, when a Vietnamese state was founded. The French took over the area between the 1850s and 1880s. They ruled Vietnam as part of French Indo-China, which also included Cambodia and Laos.

Japan conquered Vietnam during World War II (1939–45). In 1946, war broke out between a nationalist group, called the Vietminh, and the French colonial government. France withdrew in 1954 and Vietnam was divided into a Communist North Vietnam, led by the Vietminh leader, Ho Chi Minh, and a non-Communist South.

A force called the Viet Cong rebelled against South Vietnam's government in 1957 and a war began, which gradually increased in intensity. The United States aided the South, but after it withdrew in 1975, South Vietnam surrendered. In 1976, the united Vietnam became a Socialist Republic.

Vietnamese troops intervened in Cambodia in 1978 to defeat the Communist Khmer Rouge government, but it withdrew its troops in 1989. In the 1990s, Vietnam began to introduce reforms. In 1995, relations with the US were normalized when the US opened an embassy in Hanoi.

The World Bank classifies Vietnam as a 'low-income' developing country and agriculture employs 67% of the population. The main food crop is rice. The country also produces chromium, oil (which was discovered off the south coast in 1986), phosphates and tin.

AREA 331,689 sq km [128,065 sq mls]
POPULATION 76,236,000
CAPITAL (POPULATION) Hanoi (3,056,000)
GOVERNMENT Socialist republic
ETHNIC GROUPS Vietnamese 87%, Tho (Tay), Chinese (Hoa), Tai, Khmer, Muong, Nung
LANGUAGES Vietnamese (official), Chinese
RELIGIONS Buddhism 55%, Christianity (Roman Catholic 7%)
CURRENCY Dong = 10 hao = 100 xu

VIRGIN ISLANDS, BRITISH

The British Virgin Islands, the most northerly of the Lesser Antilles, are a British overseas territory, with a substantial measure of self-government. **AREA** 153 sq km [59 sq mls]; **POPULATION** 13,000; **CAPITAL** Road Town.

VIRGIN ISLANDS, US

The Virgin Islands of the United States, a group of three islands and 65 small islets, are a self-governing US territory. Purchased from Denmark in 1917, its residents are US citizens and they elect a non-voting delegate to the US House of Representatives. **AREA** 340 sq km [130 sq mls]; **POPULATION** 118,000; **CAPITAL** Charlotte Amalie.

WALLIS AND FUTUNA

Wallis and Futuna, in the South Pacific Ocean, is the smallest and the poorest of France's overseas territories. **AREA** 200 sq km [77 sq mls]; **POPULATION** 15,000; **CAPITAL** Mata-Utu.

WESTERN SAMOA

The Independent State of Western Samoa comprises two islands in the South Pacific Ocean. Governed by New Zealand from 1920, the territory became independent in 1962. Exports include taro, coconut cream and beer. **AREA** 2,840 sq km [1,097 sq mls]; **POPULATION** 224,000; **CAPITAL** Apia.

YEMEN

GEOGRAPHY The Republic of Yemen faces the Red Sea and the Gulf of Aden in the south-western corner of the Arabian peninsula. Behind the narrow coastal plain along the Red Sea, the land rises to a mountain region called High Yemen.

The climate ranges from hot and often humid conditions on the coast to the cooler highlands. Most of the country is arid.

POLITICS & ECONOMY After World War I, northern Yemen, which had been ruled by Turkey, began to evolve into a separate state from the south, where Britain was in control. Britain withdrew in 1967 and a left-wing government took power in the south. In North Yemen, the monarchy was abolished in 1962 and the country became a republic.

Clashes occurred between the traditionalist Yemen Arab Republic in the north and the formerly British Marxist People's Democratic Republic of Yemen but, in 1990, the two Yemens merged to form a single country. Since then, the union has held together, despite a two-month civil war in 1994.

The World Bank classifies Yemen as a 'low-income'

developing country. Agriculture employs up to 63% of the people. Herders raise sheep and other animals, while farmers grow such crops as barley, fruits, wheat and vegetables in highland valleys and around oases. Cash crops include coffee and cotton.

Imported oil is refined at Aden and petroleum extraction began in the north-west in the 1980s. Handicrafts, leather goods and textiles are manufactured. Remittances from Yemenis abroad are a major source of revenue.

> **AREA** 527,970 sq km [203,849 sq mls]
> **POPULATION** 16,388,000
> **CAPITAL (POPULATION)** San'a (972,000)
> **GOVERNMENT** Multiparty republic
> **ETHNIC GROUPS** Arab 96%, Somali 1%
> **LANGUAGES** Arabic (official)
> **RELIGIONS** Islam
> **CURRENCY** Rial = 100 fils

YUGOSLAVIA

GEOGRAPHY The Federal Republic of Yugoslavia consists of Serbia and Montenegro, two of the six republics which made up the former country of Yugoslavia until it broke up in 1991 and 1992. Behind the short coastline along the Adriatic Sea lies a mountainous region, including the Dinaric Alps and part of the Balkan Mountains. The Pannonian Plains make up northern Yugoslavia.

The coast has a Mediterranean climate. The highlands have cold winters and cool summers.

POLITICS & ECONOMY People who became known as the South Slavs began to move into the region around 1,500 years ago. Each group, including the Serbs and Croats, founded its own state. But, by the 15th century, foreign countries controlled the region. Serbia and Montenegro were under the Turkish Ottoman empire.

In the 19th century, many Slavs worked for independence and Slavic unity. In 1914, Austria-Hungary declared war on Serbia, blaming it for the assassination of Archduke Francis Ferdinand of Austria-Hungary. This led to World War I and the defeat of Austria-Hungary. In 1918, the South Slavs united in the Kingdom of the Serbs, Croats and Slovenes, which consisted of Bosnia-Herzegovina, Croatia, Dalmatia, Montenegro, Serbia and Slovenia. The country was renamed Yugoslavia in 1929. Germany occupied Yugoslavia during World War II, but partisans, including a Communist force led by Josip Broz Tito, fought the invaders.

From 1945, the Communists controlled the country, which was called the Federal People's Republic of Yugoslavia. But after Tito's death in 1980, the country faced many problems. In 1990, non-Communist parties were permitted and non-Communists won majorities in elections in all but Serbia and Montenegro, where Socialists (former Communists) won control. Yugoslavia split apart in 1991–2 with Bosnia-Herzegovina, Croatia, Macedonia and Slovenia proclaiming their independence. The two remaining republics of Serbia and Montenegro became the new Yugoslavia.

Fighting broke out in Croatia and Bosnia-Herzegovina as rival groups struggled for power. In 1992, the United Nations withdrew recognition of Yugoslavia because of its failure to halt atrocities committed by Serbs living in Croatia and Bosnia. In

1995, Yugoslavia was involved in the talks that led to the Dayton Peace Accord, which brought peace to Bosnia-Herzegovina. But the issue of Yugoslav repression of minorities flared up again in 1998 in Kosovo, a province where the majority are ethnic Albanians. In response to a developing conflict between Kosovar nationalism and Serb ethnic cleansing, NATO forces launched an aerial offensive against Yugoslavia in March 1999. This accelerated the flight of ethnic Albanians from Kosovo.

Under Communist rule, manufacturing became increasingly important in Yugoslavia. But in the early 1990s, the World Bank classified Yugoslavia as a 'lower-middle-income' economy. Its resources include bauxite, coal, copper and other metals, together with oil and natural gas. Manufactures include aluminium, machinery, plastics, steel, textiles and vehicles. The chief exports are manufactures, but agriculture remains important. Crops include fruits, maize, potatoes, tobacco and wheat. Cattle, pigs and sheep are reared.

> **AREA** 102,170 sq km [39,449 sq mls]
> **POPULATION** 10,500,000
> **CAPITAL (POPULATION)** Belgrade (1,137,000)
> **GOVERNMENT** Federal republic
> **ETHNIC GROUPS** Serb 62%, Albanian 17%, Montenegrin 5%, Hungarian, Muslim, Croat
> **LANGUAGES** Serbo-Croat (official), Albanian
> **RELIGIONS** Christianity (mainly Serbian Orthodox), Islam
> **CURRENCY** Yugoslav new dinar = 100 paras

ZAMBIA

GEOGRAPHY The Republic of Zambia is a landlocked country in southern Africa. Zambia lies on the plateau that makes up most of southern Africa. Much of the land is between 900 m and 1,500 m [2,950 ft to 4,920 ft] above sea level. The Muchinga Mountains in the north-east rise above this flat land.

Zambia lies in the tropics, but temperatures are moderated by the altitude. The rainy season runs from November to March.

POLITICS & ECONOMY European contact with Zambia began in the 19th century, when the explorer David Livingstone crossed the River Zambezi. In the 1890s, the British South Africa Company, set up by Cecil Rhodes (1853–1902), the British financier and statesman, made treaties with local chiefs and gradually took over the area. In 1911, the Company named the area Northern Rhodesia. In 1924, Britain took over the government of the country.

In 1953, Britain formed a federation of Northern Rhodesia, Southern Rhodesia (now Zimbabwe) and Nyasaland (now Malawi). Because of African opposition, the federation was dissolved in 1963 and Northern Rhodesia became independent as Zambia in 1964. Kenneth Kaunda became president and one-party rule was introduced in 1972. However, a new constitution was adopted in 1990 and, in 1991, Kaunda's party was defeated and Frederick Chiluba became president.

Copper is the leading export, accounting for 90% of Zambia's total exports in 1990. Zambia also produces cobalt, lead, zinc and various gemstones. Agriculture accounts for 75% of the workers, as compared with 8% in industry, including mining. Maize is the chief crop. Other crops include cassava, coffee and millet.

> **AREA** 752,614 sq km [290,586 sq mls]
> **POPULATION** 9,461,000
> **CAPITAL (POPULATION)** Lusaka (982,000)
> **GOVERNMENT** Multiparty republic
> **ETHNIC GROUPS** Bemba 36%, Maravi (Nyanja) 18%, Tonga 15%
> **LANGUAGES** English (official), Bemba, Nyanja
> **RELIGIONS** Christianity 68%, traditional beliefs 27%
> **CURRENCY** Kwacha = 100 ngwee

ZIMBABWE

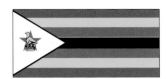

GEOGRAPHY The Republic of Zimbabwe is a landlocked country in southern Africa. Most of the country lies on a high plateau between the Zambezi and Limpopo rivers between 900 m and 1,500 m [2,950 ft to 4,920 ft] above sea level. The highest land is in the east near the Mozambique border.

In the summer, between October and March, the weather is hot and wet. But in the winter, daily temperatures can vary greatly. Frosts have been recorded between June and August. The climate varies according to the altitude.

POLITICS & ECONOMY The Shona people became dominant in the region about 1,000 years ago. They built the impressive Great Zimbabwe, a city of stone buildings. The British South Africa Company, under the statesman Cecil Rhodes (1853–1902), occupied the area in the 1890s, after obtaining mineral rights from local chiefs. The area was named Rhodesia and later Southern Rhodesia. It became a self-governing British colony in 1923. Between 1953 and 1963, Southern and Northern Rhodesia (now Zambia) were joined to Nyasaland (Malawi) in the Central African Federation.

In 1965, the European government of Southern Rhodesia (then called Rhodesia) declared their country independent. But Britain refused to accept Rhodesia's independence. Finally, after a civil war, the country became legally independent in 1980. After independence, rivalries between the Shona and Ndebele people threatened its stability. But order was restored when the Shona prime minister, Robert Mugabe, brought his Ndebele rivals into his government. In 1987, Mugabe became the country's executive president and, in 1991, the government renounced its Marxist ideology. Mugabe was re-elected president in 1990 and 1996.

The World Bank classifies Zimbabwe as a 'low-income' developing country. The country has valuable mineral resources and mining accounts for a fifth of the country's exports. Gold, asbestos, chromium and nickel are all mined. Zimbabwe also has some coal and iron ore, and some metal and food-processing industries. But agriculture employs 68% of working people. Maize is the chief food crop, while export crops include tobacco, cotton and sugar.

> **AREA** 390,579 sq km [150,873 sq mls]
> **POPULATION** 11,044,000
> **CAPITAL (POPULATION)** Harare (1,189,000)
> **GOVERNMENT** Multiparty republic
> **ETHNIC GROUPS** Shona 71%, Ndebele 16%, other Bantu-speaking Africans 11%, White 2%
> **LANGUAGES** English (official), Shona, Ndebele, Nyanja
> **RELIGIONS** Christianity 45%, traditional beliefs 40%
> **CURRENCY** Zimbabwe dollar = 100 cents

The
WORLD IN
FOCUS

Planet Earth

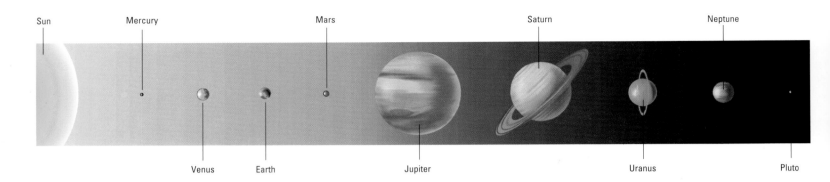

Sun · Mercury · Venus · Earth · Mars · Jupiter · Saturn · Uranus · Neptune · Pluto

The Solar System

A minute part of one of the billions of galaxies (collections of stars) that comprises the Universe, the Solar System lies some 27,000 light-years from the centre of our own galaxy, the 'Milky Way'. Thought to be over 4,700 million years old, it consists of a central sun with nine planets and their moons revolving around it, attracted by its gravitational pull. The planets orbit the Sun in the same direction – anti-clockwise when viewed from the Northern Heavens – and almost in the same plane. Their orbital paths, however, vary enormously.

The Sun's diameter is 109 times that of Earth, and the temperature at its core – caused by continuous thermonuclear fusions of hydrogen into helium – is estimated to be 15 million degrees Celsius. It is the Solar System's only source of light and heat.

Profile of the Planets

	Mean distance from Sun (million km)	Mass (Earth = 1)	Period of orbit (Earth years)	Period of rotation (Earth days)	Equatorial diameter (km)	Number of known satellites
Mercury	57.9	0.055	0.24 years	58.67	4,878	0
Venus	108.2	0.815	0.62 years	243.00	12,104	0
Earth	149.6	1.0	1.00 years	1.00	12,756	1
Mars	227.9	0.107	1.88 years	1.03	6,787	2
Jupiter	778.3	317.8	11.86 years	0.41	142,800	16
Saturn	1,427	95.2	29.46 years	0.43	120,000	20
Uranus	2,871	14.5	84.01 years	0.75	51,118	15
Neptune	4,497	17.1	164.80 years	0.80	49,528	8
Pluto	5,914	0.002	248.50 years	6.39	2,320	1

All planetary orbits are elliptical in form, but only Pluto and Mercury follow paths that deviate noticeably from a circular one. Near perihelion – its closest approach to the Sun – Pluto actually passes inside the orbit of Neptune, an event that last occurred in 1983. Pluto did not regain its station as outermost planet until February 1999.

The Seasons

Seasons occur because the Earth's axis is tilted at a constant angle of 23½°. When the northern hemisphere is tilted to a maximum extent towards the Sun, on 21 June, the Sun is overhead at the Tropic of Cancer (latitude 23½° North). This is midsummer, or the summer solstice, in the northern hemisphere.

On 22 or 23 September, the Sun is overhead at the Equator, and day and night are of equal length throughout the world. This is the autumn equinox in the northern hemisphere. On 21 or 22 December, the Sun is overhead at the Tropic of Capricorn (23½° South), the winter solstice in the northern hemisphere. The overhead Sun then tracks north until, on 21 March, it is overhead at the Equator. This is the spring (vernal) equinox in the northern hemisphere.

In the southern hemisphere, the seasons are the reverse of those in the north.

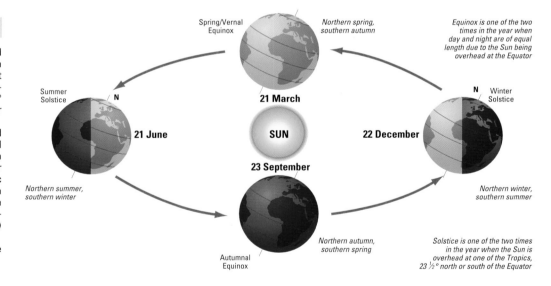

Equinox is one of the two times in the year when day and night are of equal length due to the Sun being overhead at the Equator

Solstice is one of the two times in the year when the Sun is overhead at one of the Tropics, 23 ½° north or south of the Equator

Day and Night

The Sun appears to rise in the east, reach its highest point at noon, and then set in the west, to be followed by night. In reality, it is not the Sun that is moving but the Earth rotating from west to east. The moment when the Sun's upper limb first appears above the horizon is termed sunrise; the moment when the Sun's upper limb disappears below the horizon is sunset.

At the summer solstice in the northern hemisphere (21 June), the Arctic has total daylight and the Antarctic total darkness. The opposite occurs at the winter solstice (21 or 22 December). At the Equator, the length of day and night are almost equal all year.

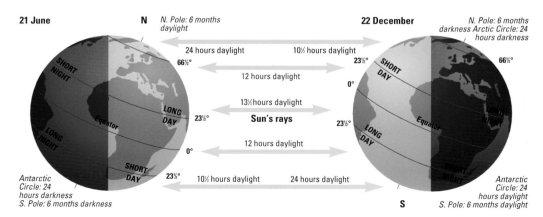

CARTOGRAPHY BY PHILIP'S. COPYRIGHT GEORGE PHILIP LTD

Time

Year: The time taken by the Earth to revolve around the Sun, or 365.24 days.

Leap Year: A calendar year of 366 days, 29 February being the additional day. It offsets the difference between the calendar and the solar year.

Month: The approximate time taken by the Moon to revolve around the Earth. The 12 months of the year in fact vary from 28 (29 in a Leap Year) to 31 days.

Week: An artificial period of 7 days, not based on astronomical time.

Day: The time taken by the Earth to complete one rotation on its axis.

Hour: 24 hours make one day. Usually the day is divided into hours AM (ante meridiem or before noon) and PM (post meridiem or after noon), although most timetables now use the 24-hour system, from midnight to midnight.

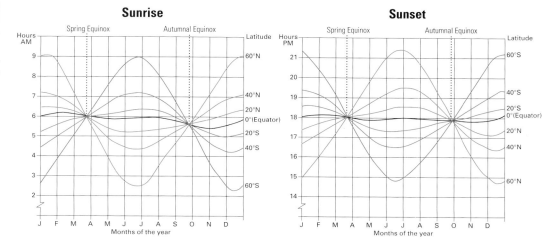

The Moon

The Moon rotates more slowly than the Earth, making one complete turn on its axis in just over 27 days. Since this corresponds to its period of revolution around the Earth, the Moon always presents the same hemisphere or face to us, and we never see 'the dark side'. The interval between one full Moon and the next (and between new Moons) is about 29½ days – a lunar month. The apparent changes in the shape of the Moon are caused by its changing position in relation to the Earth; like the planets, it produces no light of its own and shines only by reflecting the rays of the Sun.

Phases of the Moon

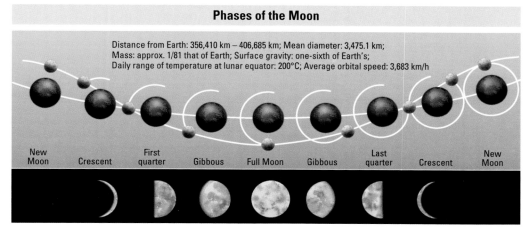

Distance from Earth: 356,410 km – 406,685 km; Mean diameter: 3,475.1 km; Mass: approx. 1/81 that of Earth; Surface gravity: one-sixth of Earth's; Daily range of temperature at lunar equator: 200°C; Average orbital speed: 3,683 km/h

Eclipses

When the Moon passes between the Sun and the Earth it causes a partial eclipse of the Sun (1) if the Earth passes through the Moon's outer shadow (P), or a total eclipse (2) if the inner cone shadow crosses the Earth's surface. In a lunar eclipse, the Earth's shadow crosses the Moon and, again, provides either a partial or total eclipse.

Eclipses of the Sun and the Moon do not occur every month because of the 5° difference between the plane of the Moon's orbit and the plane in which the Earth moves. In the 1990s only 14 lunar eclipses are possible, for example, seven partial and seven total; each is visible only from certain, and variable, parts of the world. The same period witnesses 13 solar eclipses – six partial (or annular) and seven total.

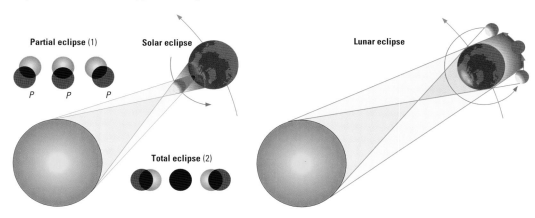

Tides

The daily rise and fall of the ocean's tides are the result of the gravitational pull of the Moon and that of the Sun, though the effect of the latter is only 46.6% as strong as that of the Moon. This effect is greatest on the hemisphere facing the Moon and causes a tidal 'bulge'. When the Sun, Earth and Moon are in line, tide-raising forces are at a maximum and Spring tides occur: high tide reaches the highest values, and low tide falls to low levels. When lunar and solar forces are least coincidental with the Sun and Moon at an angle (near the Moon's first and third quarters), Neap tides occur, which have a small tidal range.

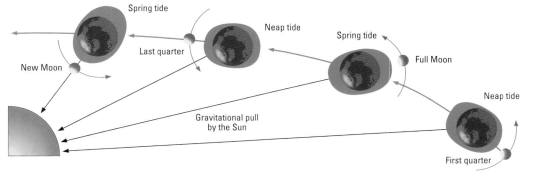

CARTOGRAPHY BY PHILIP'S. COPYRIGHT GEORGE PHILIP LTD

Restless Earth

The Earth's Structure

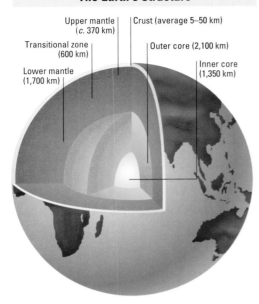

Upper mantle (c. 370 km)
Crust (average 5–50 km)
Transitional zone (600 km)
Outer core (2,100 km)
Lower mantle (1,700 km)
Inner core (1,350 km)

Continental Drift

About 200 million years ago the original Pangaea landmass began to split into two continental groups, which further separated over time to produce the present-day configuration.

180 million years ago

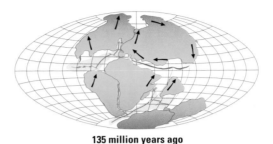

135 million years ago

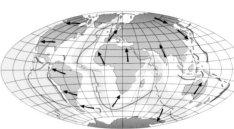

Present day

▬▬ Trench
▬▬ Rift
New ocean floor
▬▬ Zones of slippage

Notable Earthquakes Since 1900

Year	Location	Richter Scale	Deaths
1906	San Francisco, USA	8.3	503
1906	Valparaiso, Chile	8.6	22,000
1908	Messina, Italy	7.5	83,000
1915	Avezzano, Italy	7.5	30,000
1920	Gansu (Kansu), China	8.6	180,000
1923	Yokohama, Japan	8.3	143,000
1927	Nan Shan, China	8.3	200,000
1932	Gansu (Kansu), China	7.6	70,000
1933	Sanriku, Japan	8.9	2,990
1934	Bihar, India/Nepal	8.4	10,700
1935	Quetta, India (now Pakistan)	7.5	60,000
1939	Chillan, Chile	8.3	28,000
1939	Erzincan, Turkey	7.9	30,000
1960	Agadir, Morocco	5.8	12,000
1962	Khorasan, Iran	7.1	12,230
1968	N.E. Iran	7.4	12,000
1970	N. Peru	7.7	66,794
1972	Managua, Nicaragua	6.2	5,000
1974	N. Pakistan	6.3	5,200
1976	Guatemala	7.5	22,778
1976	Tangshan, China	8.2	255,000
1978	Tabas, Iran	7.7	25,000
1980	El Asnam, Algeria	7.3	20,000
1980	S. Italy	7.2	4,800
1985	Mexico City, Mexico	8.1	4,200
1988	N.W. Armenia	6.8	55,000
1990	N. Iran	7.7	36,000
1993	Maharashtra, India	6.4	30,000
1994	Los Angeles, USA	6.6	51
1995	Kobe, Japan	7.2	5,000
1995	Sakhalin Is., Russia	7.5	2,000
1997	N.E. Iran	7.1	2,500
1998	Takhar, Afghanistan	6.1	4,200
1998	Rostaq, Afghanistan	7.0	5,000

The highest magnitude recorded on the Richter scale is 8.9 in Japan on 2 March 1933 which killed 2,990 people.

Earthquakes

Earthquake magnitude is usually rated according to either the Richter or the Modified Mercalli scale, both devised by seismologists in the 1930s. The Richter scale measures absolute earthquake power with mathematical precision: each step upwards represents a tenfold increase in shockwave amplitude. Theoretically, there is no upper limit, but the largest earthquakes measured have been rated at between 8.8 and 8.9. The 12–point Mercalli scale, based on observed effects, is often more meaningful, ranging from I (earthquakes noticed only by seismographs) to XII (total destruction); intermediate points include V (people awakened at night; unstable objects overturned), VII (collapse of ordinary buildings; chimneys and monuments fall) and IX (conspicuous cracks in ground; serious damage to reservoirs).

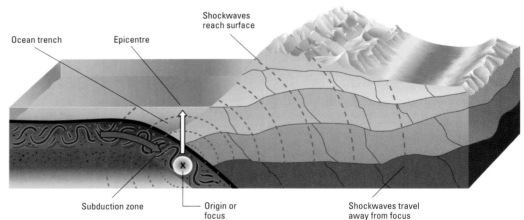

Ocean trench
Epicentre
Shockwaves reach surface
Subduction zone
Origin or focus
Shockwaves travel away from focus

Structure and Earthquakes

Mobile land areas
Submarine zones of mobile land areas
Stable land platforms
Submarine extensions of stable land platforms
Mid-oceanic volcanic ridges
Oceanic platforms

1976○ Principal earthquakes and dates

Earthquakes are a series of rapid vibrations originating from the slipping or faulting of parts of the Earth's crust when stresses within build up to breaking point. They usually happen at depths varying from 8 km to 30 km. Severe earthquakes cause extensive damage when they take place in populated areas, destroying structures and severing communications. Most initial loss of life occurs due to secondary causes such as falling masonry, fires and flooding.

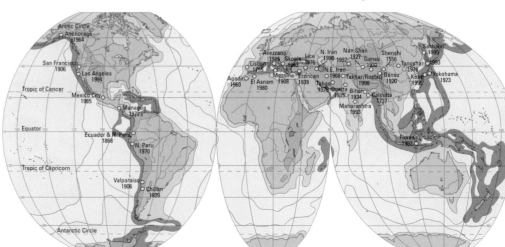

Projection: Interrupted Mollweide

CARTOGRAPHY BY PHILIP'S. COPYRIGHT GEORGE PHILIP LTD

Plate Tectonics

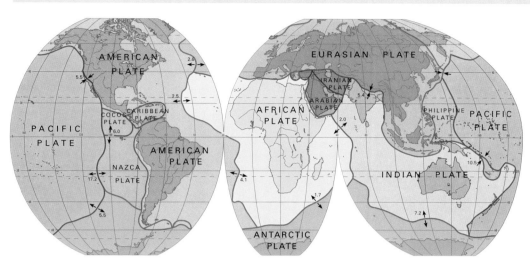

— Plate boundaries   PACIFIC Major plates

➤ Direction of plate movements and rate of movement (cm/year)

The drifting of the continents is a feature that is unique to Planet Earth. The complementary, almost jigsaw-puzzle fit of the coastlines on each side of the Atlantic Ocean inspired Alfred Wegener's theory of continental drift in 1915. The theory suggested that the ancient super-continent, which Wegener named Pangaea, incorporated all of the Earth's landmasses and gradually split up to form today's continents.

The original debate about continental drift was a prelude to a more radical idea: plate tectonics. The basic theory is that the Earth's crust is made up of a series of rigid plates which float on a soft layer of the mantle and are moved about by continental convection currents within the Earth's interior. These plates diverge and converge along margins marked by seismic activity. Plates diverge from mid-ocean ridges where molten lava pushes upwards and forces the plates apart at rates of up to 40 mm [1.6 in] a year.

The three diagrams, left, give some examples of plate boundaries from around the world. Diagram (a) shows sea-floor spreading at the Mid-Atlantic Ridge as the American and African plates slowly diverge. The same thing is happening in (b) where sea-floor spreading at the Mid-Indian Ocean Ridge is forcing the Indian plate to collide into the Eurasian plate. In (c) oceanic crust (sima) is being subducted beneath lighter continental crust (sial).

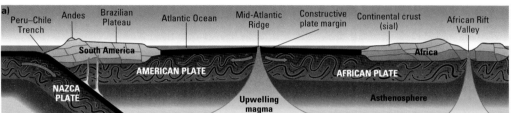

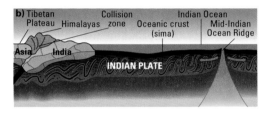

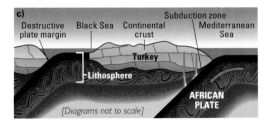

Volcanoes

Volcanoes occur when hot liquefied rock beneath the Earth's crust is pushed up by pressure to the surface as molten lava. Some volcanoes erupt in an explosive way, throwing out rocks and ash, whilst others are effusive and lava flows out of the vent. There are volcanoes which are both, such as Mount Fuji. An accumulation of lava and cinders creates cones of variable size and shape. As a result of many eruptions over centuries, Mount Etna in Sicily has a circumference of more than 120 km [75 miles].

Climatologists believe that volcanic ash, if ejected high into the atmosphere, can influence temperature and weather for several years afterwards. The 1991 eruption of Mount Pinatubo in the Philippines ejected more than 20 million tonnes of dust and ash 32 km [20 miles] into the atmosphere and is believed to have accelerated ozone depletion over a large part of the globe.

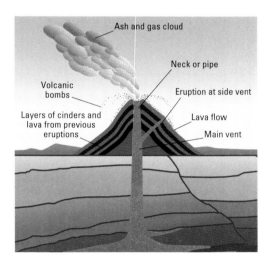

Distribution of Volcanoes

Volcanoes today may be the subject of considerable scientific study but they remain both dramatic and unpredictable: in 1991 Mount Pinatubo, 100 km [62 miles] north of the Philippines capital Manila, suddenly burst into life after lying dormant for more than six centuries. Most of the world's active volcanoes occur in a belt around the Pacific Ocean, on the edge of the Pacific plate, called the 'ring of fire'. Indonesia has the greatest concentration with 90 volcanoes, 12 of which are active. The most famous, Krakatoa, erupted in 1883 with such force that the resulting tidal wave killed 36,000 people and tremors were felt as far away as Australia.

- Submarine volcanoes

▲ Land volcanoes active since 1700

— Boundaries of tectonic plates

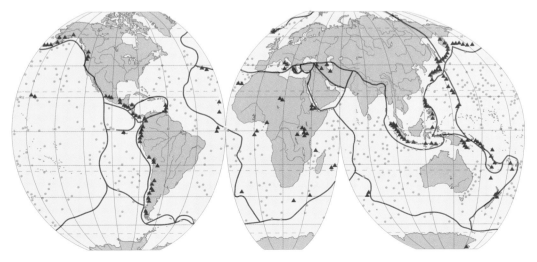

CARTOGRAPHY BY PHILIP'S COPYRIGHT GEORGE PHILIP LTD

Landforms

The Rock Cycle

James Hutton first proposed the rock cycle in the late 1700s after he observed the slow but steady effects of erosion.

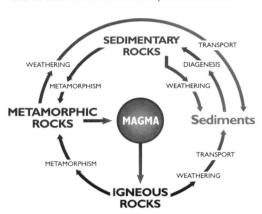

Above and below the surface of the oceans, the features of the Earth's crust are constantly changing. The phenomenal forces generated by convection currents in the molten core of our planet carry the vast segments or 'plates' of the crust across the globe in an endless cycle of creation and destruction. A continent may travel little more than 25 mm [1 in] per year, yet in the vast span of geological time this process throws up giant mountain ranges and creates new land.

Destruction of the landscape, however, begins as soon as it is formed. Wind, water, ice and sea, the main agents of erosion, mount a constant assault that even the most resistant rocks cannot withstand. Mountain peaks may dwindle by as little as a few millimetres each year, but if they are not uplifted by further movements of the crust they will eventually be reduced to rubble and transported away.

Water is the most powerful agent of erosion – it has been estimated that 100 billion tonnes of sediment are washed into the oceans every year. Three

Asian rivers account for 20% of this total, the Huang He, in China, and the Brahmaputra and Ganges in Bangladesh.

Rivers and glaciers, like the sea itself, generate much of their effect through abrasion – pounding the land with the debris they carry with them. But as well as destroying they also create new landforms, many of them spectacular: vast deltas like those of the Mississippi and the Nile, or the deep fjords cut by glaciers in British Columbia, Norway and New Zealand.

Geologists once considered that landscapes evolved from 'young', newly uplifted mountainous areas, through a 'mature' hilly stage, to an 'old age' stage when the land was reduced to an almost flat plain, or peneplain. This theory, called the 'cycle of erosion', fell into disuse when it became evident that so many factors, including the effects of plate tectonics and climatic change, constantly interrupt the cycle, which takes no account of the highly complex interactions that shape the surface of our planet.

Mountain Building

Mountains are formed when pressures on the Earth's crust caused by continental drift become so intense that the surface buckles or cracks. This happens where oceanic crust is subducted by continental crust or, more dramatically, where two tectonic plates collide: the Rockies, Andes, Alps, Urals and Himalayas resulted from such impacts. These are all known as fold mountains because they were formed by the compression of the rocks, forcing the surface to bend and fold like a crumpled rug. The Himalayas are formed from the folded former sediments of the Tethys Sea which was trapped in the collision zone between the Indian and Eurasian plates.

The other main mountain-building process occurs when the crust fractures to create faults, allowing rock to be forced upwards in large blocks; or when the pressure of magma within the crust forces the surface to bulge into a dome, or erupts to form a volcano. Large mountain ranges may reveal a combination of those features; the Alps, for example, have been compressed so violently that the folds are fragmented by numerous faults and intrusions of molten igneous rock.

Over millions of years, even the greatest mountain ranges can be reduced by the agents of erosion (most notably rivers) to a low rugged landscape known as a peneplain.

Types of faults: Faults occur where the crust is being stretched or compressed so violently that the rock strata break in a horizontal or vertical movement. They are classified by the direction in which the blocks of rock have moved. A normal fault results when a vertical movement causes the surface to break apart; compression causes a reverse fault. Horizontal movement causes shearing, known as a strike-slip fault. When the rock breaks in two places, the central block may be pushed up in a horst fault, or sink (creating a rift valley) in a graben fault.

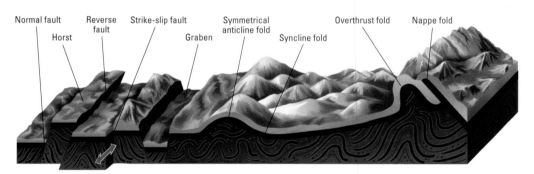

Types of fold: Folds occur when rock strata are squeezed and compressed. They are common therefore at destructive plate margins and where plates have collided, forcing the rocks to buckle into mountain ranges. Geographers give different names to the degrees of fold that result from continuing pressure on the rock. A simple fold may be symmetric, with even slopes on either side, but as the pressure builds up, one slope becomes steeper and the fold becomes asymmetric. Later, the ridge or 'anticline' at the top of the fold may slide over the lower ground or 'syncline' to form a recumbent fold. Eventually, the rock strata may break under the pressure to form an overthrust and finally a nappe fold.

Continental Glaciation

Ice sheets were at their greatest extent about 200,000 years ago. The maximum advance of the last Ice Age was about 18,000 years ago, when ice covered virtually all of Canada and reached as far south as the Bristol Channel in Britain.

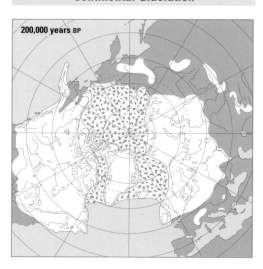

200,000 years BP

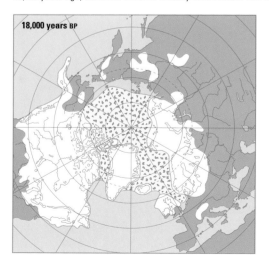

18,000 years BP

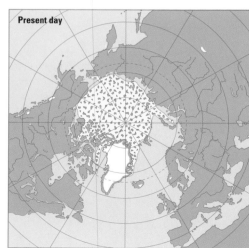

Present day

CARTOGRAPHY BY PHILIP'S. COPYRIGHT GEORGE PHILIP LTD

Natural Landforms

A stylized diagram to show a selection of landforms found in the mid-latitudes.

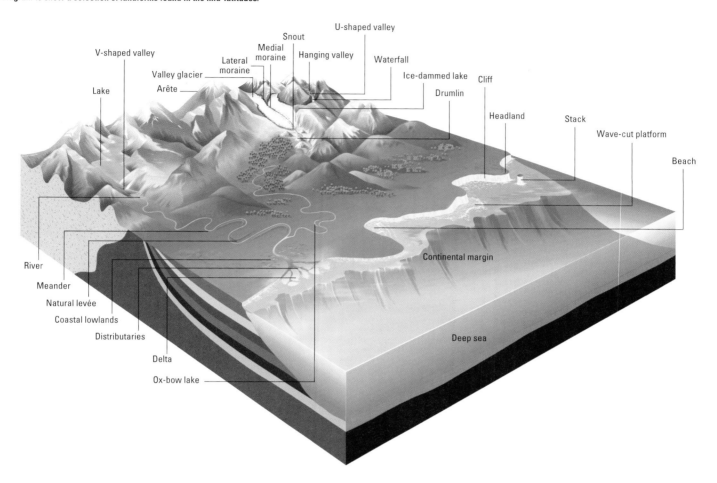

Labels (clockwise): V-shaped valley, Valley glacier, Arête, Lake, Lateral moraine, Medial moraine, Snout, Hanging valley, U-shaped valley, Waterfall, Ice-dammed lake, Drumlin, Cliff, Headland, Stack, Wave-cut platform, Beach, Continental margin, Deep sea, Ox-bow lake, Delta, Distributaries, Coastal lowlands, Natural levée, Meander, River

Desert Landscapes

The popular image that deserts are all huge expanses of sand is wrong. Despite harsh conditions, deserts contain some of the most varied and interesting landscapes in the world. They are also one of the most extensive environments – the hot and cold deserts together cover almost 40% of the Earth's surface.

The three types of hot desert are known by their Arabic names: sand desert, called *erg*, covers only about one-fifth of the world's desert; the rest is divided between *hammada* (areas of bare rock) and *reg* (broad plains covered by loose gravel or pebbles).

In areas of *erg*, such as the Namib Desert, the shape of the dunes reflects the character of local winds. Where winds are constant in direction, crescent-shaped *barchan* dunes form. In areas of bare rock, wind-blown sand is a major agent of erosion. The erosion is mainly confined to within 2 m [6.5 ft] of the surface, producing characteristic, mushroom-shaped rocks.

Erg

Hammada

Reg

Surface Processes

Catastrophic changes to natural landforms are periodically caused by such phenomena as avalanches, landslides and volcanic eruptions, but most of the processes that shape the Earth's surface operate extremely slowly in human terms. One estimate, based on a study in the United States, suggested that 1 m [3 ft] of land was removed from the entire surface of the country, on average, every 29,500 years. However, the time-scale varies from 1,300 years to 154,200 years depending on the terrain and climate.

In hot, dry climates, mechanical weathering, a result of rapid temperature changes, causes the outer layers of rock to peel away, while in cold mountainous regions, boulders are prised apart when water freezes in cracks in rocks. Chemical weathering, at its greatest in warm, humid regions, is responsible for hollowing out limestone caves and decomposing granites.

The erosion of soil and rock is greatest on sloping land and the steeper the slope, the greater the tendency for mass wasting – the movement of soil and rock downhill under the influence of gravity. The mechanisms of mass wasting (ranging from very slow to very rapid) vary with the type of material, but the presence of water as a lubricant is usually an important factor.

Running water is the world's leading agent of erosion and transportation. The energy of a river depends on several factors, including its velocity and volume, and its erosive power is at its peak when it is in full flood. Sea waves also exert tremendous erosive power during storms when they hurl pebbles against the shore, undercutting cliffs and hollowing out caves.

Glacier ice forms in mountain hollows and spills out to form valley glaciers, which transport rocks shattered by frost action. As glaciers move, rocks embedded into the ice erode steep-sided, U-shaped valleys. Evidence of glaciation in mountain regions includes cirques, knife-edged ridges, or arêtes, and pyramidal peaks.

CARTOGRAPHY BY PHILIP'S. COPYRIGHT GEORGE PHILIP LTD

Oceans

Relative sizes of the world's oceans

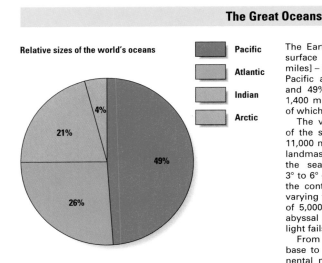

- Pacific
- Atlantic
- Indian
- Arctic

In a strict geographical sense there are only three true oceans – the Atlantic, Indian and Pacific. The legendary 'Seven Seas' would require these to be divided at the Equator and the addition of the Arctic Ocean – which accounts for less than 4% of the total sea area. The International Hydrographic Bureau does not recognize the Antarctic Ocean (even less the 'Southern Ocean') as a separate entity.

The Earth is a watery planet: more than 70% of its surface – over 360,000,000 sq km [140,000,000 sq miles] – is covered by the oceans and seas. The mighty Pacific alone accounts for nearly 36% of the total, and 49% of the sea area. Gravity holds in around 1,400 million cu. km [320 million cu. miles] of water, of which over 97% is saline.

The vast underwater world starts in the shallows of the seaside and plunges to depths of more than 11,000 m [36,000 ft]. The continental shelf, part of the landmass, drops gently to around 200 m [650 ft]; here the seabed falls away suddenly at an angle of 3° to 6° – the continental slope. The third stage, called the continental rise, is more gradual with gradients varying from 1 in 100 to 1 in 700. At an average depth of 5,000 m [16,500 ft] there begins the aptly-named abyssal plain – massive submarine depths where sunlight fails to penetrate and few creatures can survive.

From these plains rise volcanoes which, taken from base to top, rival and even surpass the tallest continental mountains in height. Mount Kea, on Hawaii, reaches a total of 10,203 m [33,400 ft], some 1,355 m [4,500 ft] more than Mount Everest, though scarcely 40% is visible above sea level.

In addition, there are underwater mountain chains up to 1,000 km [600 miles] across, whose peaks sometimes appear above sea level as islands such as Iceland and Tristan da Cunha.

The Ocean Depths

Average and maximum depths of the world's great oceans, in metres

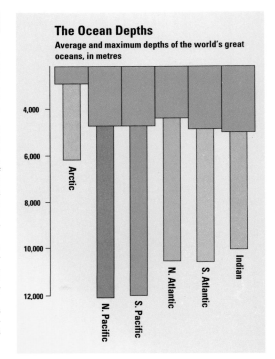

January temperatures and ocean currents

ACTUAL SURFACE TEMPERATURE

°C
30
20
10
0
– 10
– 20
– 30
– 40

OCEAN CURRENTS
Cold   Warm   Speed (knots)
Less than 0.5
0.5 – 1.0
Over 1.0

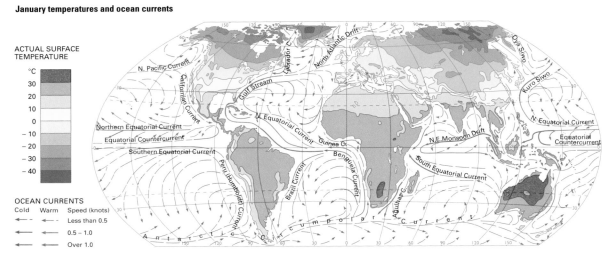

July temperatures and ocean currents

ACTUAL SURFACE TEMPERATURE

°C
30
20
10
0
–10

OCEAN CURRENTS
Cold   Warm   Speed (knots)
Less than 0.5
0.5 – 1.0
Over 1.0

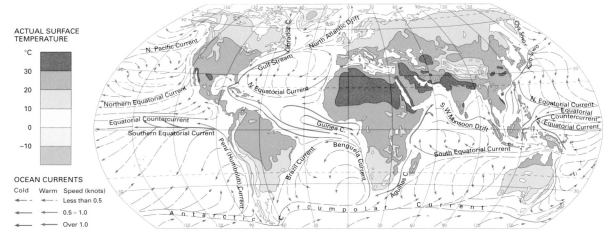

Moving immense quantities of energy as well as billions of tonnes of water every hour, the ocean currents are a vital part of the great heat engine that drives the Earth's climate. They themselves are produced by a twofold mechanism. At the surface, winds push huge masses of water before them; in the deep ocean, below an abrupt temperature gradient that separates the churning surface waters from the still depths, density variations cause slow vertical movements.

The pattern of circulation of the great surface currents is determined by the displacement known as the Coriolis effect. As the Earth turns beneath a moving object – whether it is a tennis ball or a vast mass of water – it appears to be deflected to one side. The deflection is most obvious near the Equator, where the Earth's surface is spinning eastwards at 1,700 km/h [1,050 mph]; currents moving polewards are curved clockwise in the northern hemisphere and anti-clockwise in the southern.

The result is a system of spinning circles known as gyres. The Coriolis effect piles up water on the left of each gyre, creating a narrow, fast-moving stream that is matched by a slower, broader returning current on the right. North and south of the Equator, the fastest currents are located in the west and in the east respectively. In each case, warm water moves from the Equator and cold water returns to it. Cold currents often bring an upwelling of nutrients with them, supporting the world's most economically important fisheries.

Depending on the prevailing winds, some currents on or near the Equator may reverse their direction in the course of the year – a seasonal variation on which Asian monsoon rains depend, and whose occasional failure can bring disaster to millions.

CARTOGRAPHY BY PHILIP'S. COPYRIGHT GEORGE PHILIP LTD

World Fishing Areas

Main commercial fishing areas (numbered FAO regions)

Catch by top marine fishing areas, thousand tonnes (1992)

1. Pacific, NW	[61]	24,199	29.3%
2. Pacific, SE	[87]	13,899	16.8%
3. Atlantic, NE	[27]	11,073	13.4%
4. Pacific, WC	[71]	7,710	9.3%
5. Indian, W	[51]	3,747	4.5%
6. Indian, E	[57]	3,262	4.0%
7. Atlantic, EC	[34]	3,259	3.9%
8. Pacific, NE	[67]	3,149	3.8%

Principal fishing areas

Leading fishing nations

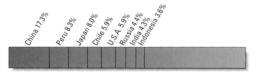

China 17.3% Peru 8.3% Japan 8.0% Chile 5.9% U.S.A. 5.9% Russia 4.4% India 4.3% Indonesia 3.6%

World total (1993): 101,417,500 tonnes
(Marine catch 83.1% Inland catch 16.9%)

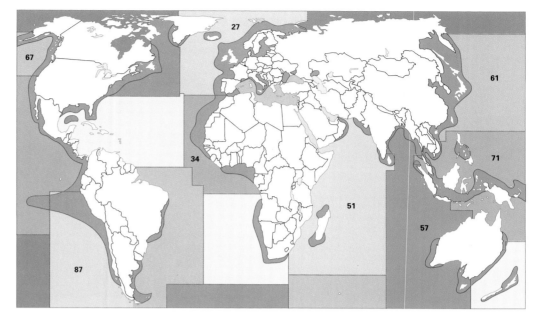

Marine Pollution

Sources of marine oil pollution (latest available year)

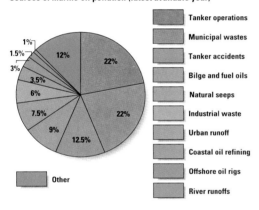

- Tanker operations
- Municipal wastes
- Tanker accidents
- Bilge and fuel oils
- Natural seeps
- Industrial waste
- Urban runoff
- Coastal oil refining
- Offshore oil rigs
- Other
- River runoffs

Oil Spills

Major oil spills from tankers and combined carriers

Year	Vessel	Location	Spill (barrels)**	Cause
1979	Atlantic Empress	West Indies	1,890,000	collision
1983	Castillo De Bellver	South Africa	1,760,000	fire
1978	Amoco Cadiz	France	1,628,000	grounding
1991	Haven	Italy	1,029,000	explosion
1988	Odyssey	Canada	1,000,000	fire
1967	Torrey Canyon	UK	909,000	grounding
1972	Sea Star	Gulf of Oman	902,250	collision
1977	Hawaiian Patriot	Hawaiian Is.	742,500	fire
1979	Independenta	Turkey	696,350	collision
1993	Braer	UK	625,000	grounding
1996	Sea Empress	UK	515,000	grounding

Other sources of major oil spills

Year				
1983	Nowruz oilfield	The Gulf	4,250,000†	war
1979	Ixtoc 1 oilwell	Gulf of Mexico	4,200,000	blow-out
1991	Kuwait	The Gulf	2,500,000†	war

** 1 barrel = 0.136 tonnes/159 lit./35 Imperial gal./42 US gal. † estimated

River Pollution

Sources of river pollution, USA (latest available year)

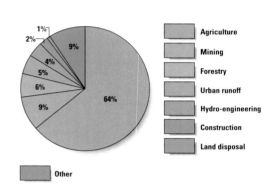

- Agriculture
- Mining
- Forestry
- Urban runoff
- Hydro-engineering
- Construction
- Land disposal
- Other

Water Pollution

- Severely polluted sea areas and lakes
- Polluted sea areas and lakes
- Areas of frequent oil pollution by shipping
- Major oil tanker spills
- Major oil rig blow-outs
- Offshore dumpsites for industrial and municipal waste
- Severely polluted rivers and estuaries

The most notorious tanker spillage of the 1980s occurred when the *Exxon Valdez* ran aground in Prince William Sound, Alaska, in 1989, spilling 267,000 barrels of crude oil close to shore in a sensitive ecological area. This rates as the world's 28th worst spill in terms of volume.

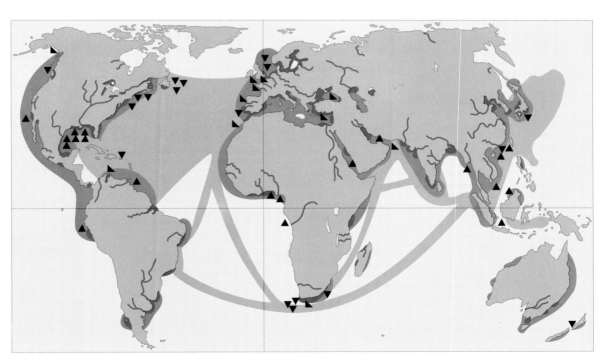

CARTOGRAPHY BY PHILIP'S. COPYRIGHT GEORGE PHILIP LTD

Climate

Climatic Regions

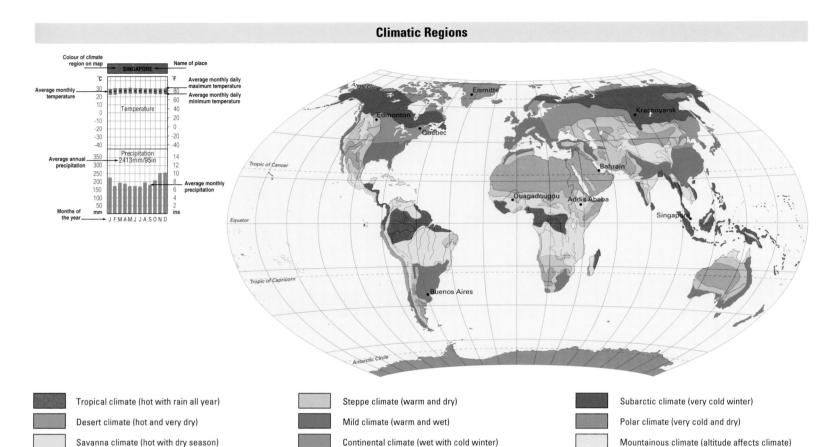

- **Tropical climate** (hot with rain all year)
- **Desert climate** (hot and very dry)
- **Savanna climate** (hot with dry season)
- **Steppe climate** (warm and dry)
- **Mild climate** (warm and wet)
- **Continental climate** (wet with cold winter)
- **Subarctic climate** (very cold winter)
- **Polar climate** (very cold and dry)
- **Mountainous climate** (altitude affects climate)

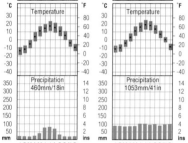
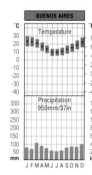
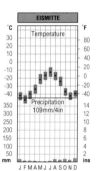
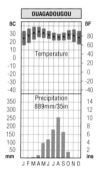
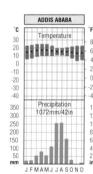
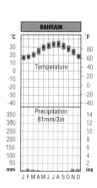
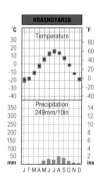

Climate Records

Temperature

Highest recorded shade temperature: Al Aziziyah, Libya, 58°C [136.4°F], 13 September 1922.

Highest mean annual temperature: Dallol, Ethiopia, 34.4°C [94°F], 1960–66.

Longest heatwave: Marble Bar, W. Australia, 162 days over 38°C [100°F], 23 October 1923 to 7 April 1924.

Lowest recorded temperature (outside poles): Verkhoyansk, Siberia, –68°C [–90°F], 6 February 1933.

Lowest mean annual temperature: Plateau Station, Antarctica, –56.6°C [–72.0°F]

Pressure

Longest drought: Calama, N. Chile, no recorded rainfall in 400 years to 1971.

Wettest place (12 months): Cherrapunji, Meghalaya, N. E. India, 26,470 mm [1,040 in], August 1860 to August 1861. Cherrapunji also holds the record for the most rainfall in one month: 2,930 mm [115 in], July 1861.

Wettest place (average): Mawsynram, India, mean annual rainfall 11,873 mm [467.4 in].

Wettest place (24 hours): Cilaos, Réunion, Indian Ocean, 1,870 mm [73.6 in], 15–16 March 1952.

Heaviest hailstones: Gopalganj, Bangladesh, up to 1.02 kg [2.25 lb], 14 April 1986 (killed 92 people).

Heaviest snowfall (continuous): Bessans, Savoie, France, 1,730 mm [68 in] in 19 hours, 5–6 April 1969.

Heaviest snowfall (season/year): Paradise Ranger Station, Mt Rainier, Washington, USA, 31,102 mm [1,224.5 in], 19 February 1971 to 18 February 1972.

Pressure and winds

Highest barometric pressure: Agata, Siberia (at 262 m [862 ft] altitude), 1,083.8 mb, 31 December 1968.

Lowest barometric pressure: Typhoon Tip, Guam, Pacific Ocean, 870 mb, 12 October 1979.

Highest recorded wind speed: Mt Washington, New Hampshire, USA, 371 km/h [231 mph], 12 April 1934. This is three times as strong as hurricane force on the Beaufort Scale.

Windiest place: Commonwealth Bay, Antarctica, where gales frequently reach over 320 km/h [200 mph].

Climate

Climate is weather in the long term: the seasonal pattern of hot and cold, wet and dry, averaged over time (usually 30 years). At the simplest level, it is caused by the uneven heating of the Earth. Surplus heat at the Equator passes towards the poles, levelling out the energy differential. Its passage is marked by a ceaseless churning of the atmosphere and the oceans, further agitated by the Earth's diurnal spin and the motion it imparts to moving air and water. The heat's means of transport – by winds and ocean currents, by the continual evaporation and recondensation of water molecules – is the weather itself. There are four basic types of climate, each of which can be further subdivided: tropical, desert (dry), temperate and polar.

Composition of Dry Air

Nitrogen	78.09%	Sulphur dioxide	trace
Oxygen	20.95%	Nitrogen oxide	trace
Argon	0.93%	Methane	trace
Water vapour	0.2–4.0%	Dust	trace
Carbon dioxide	0.03%	Helium	trace
Ozone	0.00006%	Neon	trace

CARTOGRAPHY BY PHILIP'S. COPYRIGHT GEORGE PHILIP LTD

El Niño

In a normal year, south-easterly trade winds drive surface waters westwards off the coast of South America, drawing cold, nutrient-rich water up from below. In an El Niño year (which occurs every 2–7 years), warm water from the west Pacific suppresses upwelling in the east, depriving the region of nutrients. The water is warmed by as much as 7°C [12°F], disturbing the tropical atmospheric circulation. During an intense El Niño, the south-east trade winds change direction and become equatorial westerlies, resulting in climatic extremes in many regions of the world, such as drought in parts of Australia and India, and heavy rainfall in south-eastern USA. An intense El Niño occurred in 1997–8, with resultant freak weather conditions across the entire Pacific region.

Normal year

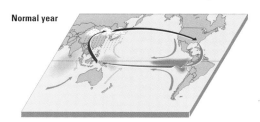

El Niño event

Beaufort Wind Scale

Named after the 19th-century British naval officer who devised it, the Beaufort Scale assesses wind speed according to its effects. It was originally designed as an aid for sailors, but has since been adapted for use on the land.

Scale	Wind speed km/h	mph	Effect
0	0–1	0–1	**Calm** Smoke rises vertically
1	1–5	1–3	**Light air** Wind direction shown only by smoke drift
2	6–11	4–7	**Light breeze** Wind felt on face; leaves rustle; vanes moved by wind
3	12–19	8–12	**Gentle breeze** Leaves and small twigs in constant motion; wind extends small flag
4	20–28	13–18	**Moderate** Raises dust and loose paper; small branches move
5	29–38	19–24	**Fresh** Small trees in leaf sway; wavelets on inland waters
6	39–49	25–31	**Strong** Large branches move; difficult to use umbrellas
7	50–61	32–38	**Near gale** Whole trees in motion; difficult to walk against wind
8	62–74	39–46	**Gale** Twigs break from trees; walking very difficult
9	75–88	47–54	**Strong gale** Slight structural damage
10	89–102	55–63	**Storm** Trees uprooted; serious structural damage
11	103–117	64–72	**Violent storm** Widespread damage
12	118+	73+	**Hurricane**

Conversions

°C = (°F − 32) × 5/9; °F = (°C × 9/5) + 32; 0°C = 32°F

1 in = 25.4 mm; 1 mm = 0.0394 in; 100 mm = 3.94 in

CARTOGRAPHY BY PHILIP'S. COPYRIGHT GEORGE PHILIP LTD

Temperature

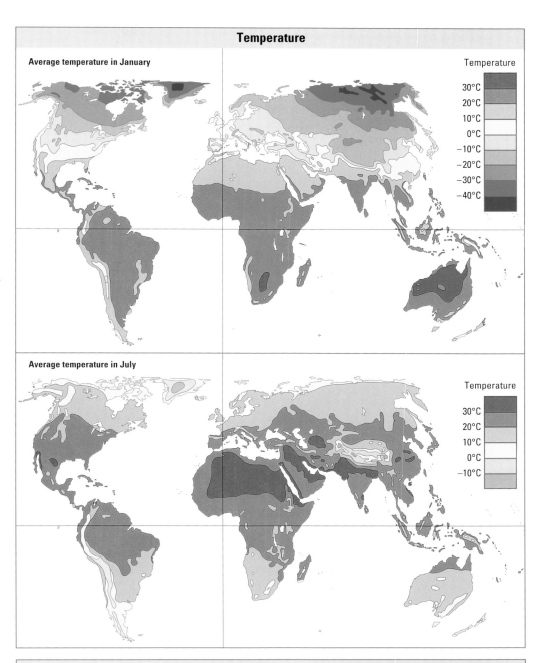

Average temperature in January

Temperature	
	30°C
	20°C
	10°C
	0°C
	−10°C
	−20°C
	−30°C
	−40°C

Average temperature in July

Temperature	
	30°C
	20°C
	10°C
	0°C
	−10°C

Precipitation

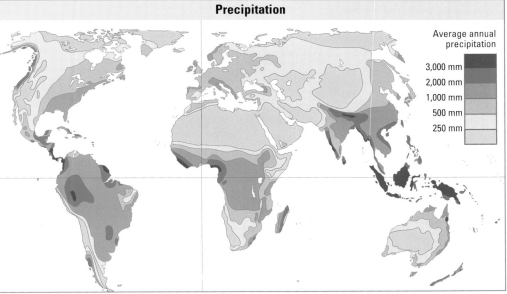

Average annual precipitation	
	3,000 mm
	2,000 mm
	1,000 mm
	500 mm
	250 mm

Water and Vegetation

The Hydrological Cycle

The world's water balance is regulated by the constant recycling of water between the oceans, atmosphere and land. The movement of water between these three reservoirs is known as the hydrological cycle. The oceans play a vital role in the hydrological cycle: 74% of the total precipitation falls over the oceans and 84% of the total evaporation comes from the oceans.

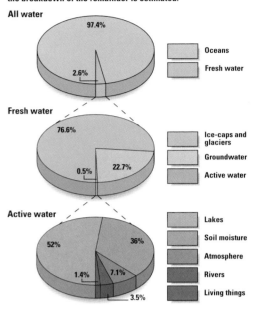

Water Distribution

The distribution of planetary water, by percentage. Oceans and ice-caps together account for more than 99% of the total; the breakdown of the remainder is estimated.

All water
- 97.4% — Oceans
- 2.6% — Fresh water

Fresh water
- 76.6% — Ice-caps and glaciers
- 0.5% — Groundwater
- 22.7% — Active water

Active water
- 52% — Lakes
- 36% — Soil moisture
- 1.4% — Atmosphere
- 7.1% — Rivers
- 3.5% — Living things

Water Utilization

Legend: Domestic | Industrial | Agriculture

The percentage breakdown of water usage by sector, selected countries (1996)

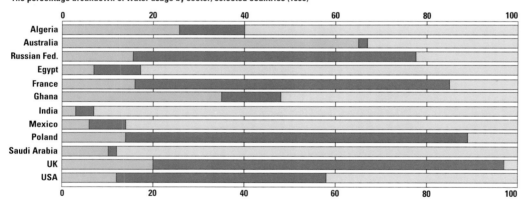

Countries listed: Algeria, Australia, Russian Fed., Egypt, France, Ghana, India, Mexico, Poland, Saudi Arabia, UK, USA

Water Usage

Almost all the world's water is 3,000 million years old, and all of it cycles endlessly through the hydrosphere, though at different rates. Water vapour circulates over days, even hours, deep ocean water circulates over millennia, and ice-cap water remains solid for millions of years.

Fresh water is essential to all terrestrial life. Humans cannot survive more than a few days without it, and even the hardiest desert plants and animals could not exist without some water. Agriculture requires huge quantities of fresh water: without large-scale irrigation most of the world's people would starve. In the USA, agriculture uses 42% and industry 45% of all water withdrawals.

The United States is one of the heaviest users of water in the world. According to the latest figures the average American uses 380 litres a day and the average household uses 415,000 litres a year. This is two to four times more than in Western Europe.

Water Supply

Percentage of total population with access to safe drinking water (1995)

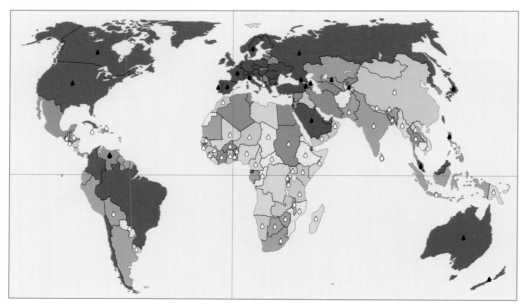

- Over 90% with safe water
- 75 – 90% with safe water
- 60 – 75% with safe water
- 45 – 60% with safe water
- 30 – 45% with safe water
- Under 30% with safe water

- △ Under 80 litres per person per day domestic water consumption
- ◆ Over 320 litres per person per day domestic water consumption

NB: 80 litres of water a day is considered necessary for a reasonable quality of life.

Least well-provided countries

Paraguay	8%	Central Afr. Rep.	18%
Afghanistan	10%	Bhutan	21%
Cambodia	13%	Congo (D. Rep.)	25%

CARTOGRAPHY BY PHILIP'S. COPYRIGHT GEORGE PHILIP LTD

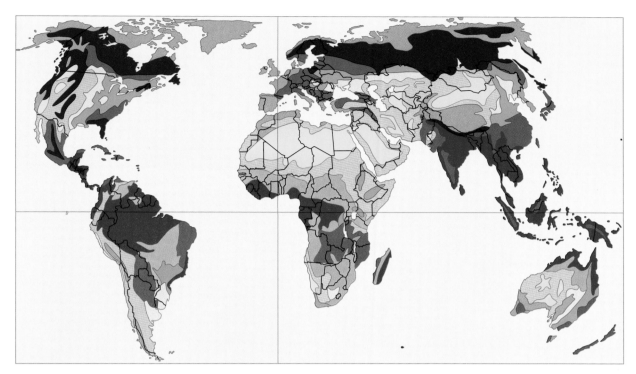

Natural Vegetation

Regional variation in vegetation

- Tundra and mountain vegetation
- Needleleaf evergreen forest
- Mixed needleleaf evergreen & broadleaf deciduous trees
- Broadleaf deciduous woodland
- Mid-latitude grassland
- Evergreen broadleaf and deciduous trees & shrubs
- Semi-desert scrub
- Desert
- Tropical grassland (savanna)
- Tropical broadleaf rainforest and monsoon forest
- Subtropical broadleaf and needleleaf forest

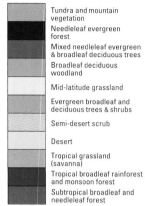

The map shows the natural 'climax vegetation' of regions, as dictated by climate and topography. In most cases, however, agricultural activity has drastically altered the vegetation pattern. Western Europe, for example, lost most of its broadleaf forest many centuries ago, while irrigation has turned some natural semi-desert into productive land.

Land Use by Continent

- Forest
- Permanent pasture and rough grazing
- Permanent crops and plantations
- Arable
- Non-productive

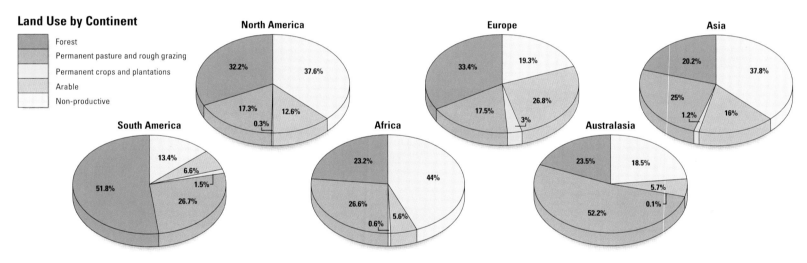

North America: 32.2%, 37.6%, 17.3%, 12.6%, 0.3%

Europe: 33.4%, 19.3%, 17.5%, 26.8%, 3%

Asia: 20.2%, 37.8%, 25%, 1.2%, 16%

South America: 13.4%, 6.6%, 51.8%, 1.5%, 26.7%

Africa: 23.2%, 44%, 26.6%, 0.6%, 5.6%

Australasia: 23.5%, 18.5%, 5.7%, 52.2%, 0.1%

Forestry: Production

Forest and woodland (million hectares)	Annual production (1996, million cubic metres) Fuelwood and charcoal	Industrial roundwood*
World	**3,987.9**	**1,864.8**	**1,489.5**
S. America	829.3	193.0	129.9
N. & C. America	709.8	155.4	600.4
Africa	684.6	519.9	67.9
Asia	131.8	905.2	280.2
Europe	157.3	82.4	369.7
Australasia	157.2	8.7	41.5

Paper and Board

Top producers (1996)**		Top exporters (1996)**	
USA	85,173	Canada	13,393
China	30,253	USA	9,113
Japan	30,014	Finland	8,529
Canada	18,414	Sweden	7,483
Germany	14,733	Germany	6,319

* roundwood is timber as it is felled
** in thousand tonnes

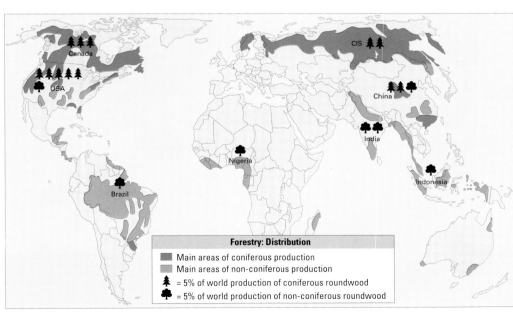

Forestry: Distribution

- Main areas of coniferous production
- Main areas of non-coniferous production
- 🌲 = 5% of world production of coniferous roundwood
- 🌳 = 5% of world production of non-coniferous roundwood

CARTOGRAPHY BY PHILIP'S. COPYRIGHT GEORGE PHILIP LTD

Environment

Humans have always had a dramatic effect on their environment, at least since the development of agriculture almost 10,000 years ago. Generally, the Earth has accepted human interference without obvious ill effects: the complex systems that regulate the global environment have been able to absorb substantial damage while maintaining a stable and comfortable home for the planet's trillions of lifeforms. But advancing human technology and the rapidly-expanding populations it supports are now threatening to overwhelm the Earth's ability to compensate.

Industrial wastes, acid rainfall, desertification and large-scale deforestation all combine to create environmental change at a rate far faster than the great slow cycles of planetary evolution can accommodate. As a result of overcultivation, overgrazing and overcutting of groundcover for firewood, desertification is affecting as much as 60% of the world's croplands. In addition, with fire and chain-saws, humans are destroying more forest in a day than their ancestors could have done in a century, upsetting the balance between plant and animal, carbon dioxide and oxygen, on which all life ultimately depends.

The fossil fuels that power industrial civilization have pumped enough carbon dioxide and other so-called greenhouse gases into the atmosphere to make climatic change a near-certainty. As a result of the combination of these factors, the Earth's average temperature has risen by approximately 0.5°C [1°F] since the beginning of the 20th century, and it is still rising.

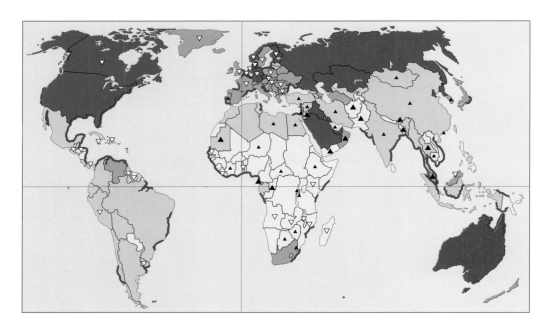

Global Warming

Carbon dioxide emissions in tonnes per person per year (1995)

- Over 10 tonnes of CO_2
- 5 – 10 tonnes of CO_2
- 1 – 5 tonnes of CO_2
- Under 1 tonne of CO_2

Changes in CO_2 emissions 1980–90

- ▲ Over 100% increase in emissions
- ▲ 50–100% increase in emissions
- ▽ Reduction in emissions
- ▬ Coastal areas in danger of flooding from rising sea levels caused by global warming

High atmospheric concentrations of heat-absorbing gases, especially carbon dioxide, appear to be causing a steady rise in average temperatures worldwide – up to 1.5°C [3°F] by the year 2020, according to some estimates. Global warming is likely to bring with it a rise in sea levels that may flood some of the Earth's most densely populated coastal areas.

Greenhouse Power

Relative contributions to the Greenhouse Effect by the major heat-absorbing gases in the atmosphere.

The chart combines greenhouse potency and volume. Carbon dioxide has a greenhouse potential of only 1, but its concentration of 350 parts per million makes it predominate. CFC 12, with 25,000 times the absorption capacity of CO_2, is present only as 0.00044 ppm.

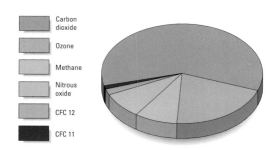

- Carbon dioxide
- Ozone
- Methane
- Nitrous oxide
- CFC 12
- CFC 11

Ozone Layer

The ozone 'hole' over the northern hemisphere on 12 March 1995.

The colours represent Dobson Units (DU). The ozone 'hole' is seen as the dark blue and purple patch in the centre, where ozone values are around 120 DU or lower. Normal levels are around 280 DU. The ozone 'hole' over Antarctica is much larger.

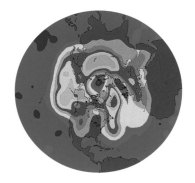

Carbon Dioxide

Carbon dioxide released in millions of tonnes (1992)

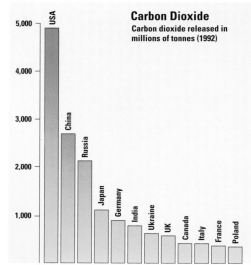

The Greenhouse Effect

Carbon dioxide is increased by burning fossil fuels and cutting forests

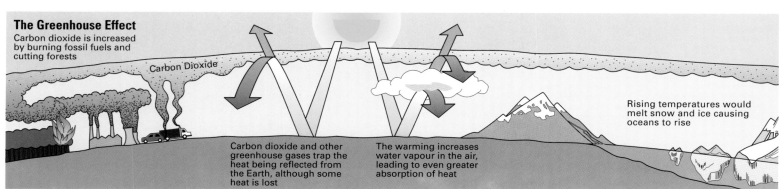

Carbon Dioxide

Carbon dioxide and other greenhouse gases trap the heat being reflected from the Earth, although some heat is lost

The warming increases water vapour in the air, leading to even greater absorption of heat

Rising temperatures would melt snow and ice causing oceans to rise

CARTOGRAPHY BY PHILIP'S. COPYRIGHT GEORGE PHILIP LTD

Desertification

- Existing deserts
- Areas with a high risk of desertification
- Areas with a moderate risk of desertification
- Former areas of rainforest
- Existing rainforest

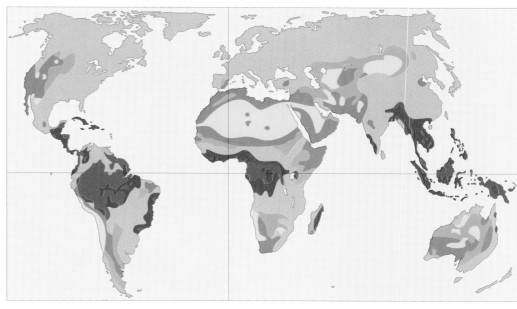

Forest Clearance

Thousands of hectares of forest cleared annually, tropical countries surveyed 1981–85 and 1987–90. Loss as a percentage of remaining stocks is shown in figures on each column.

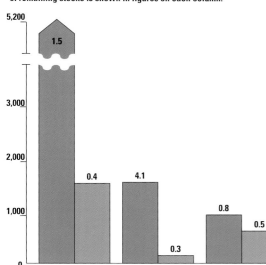

Deforestation

The Earth's remaining forests are under attack from three directions: expanding agriculture, logging, and growing consumption of fuelwood, often in combination. Sometimes deforestation is the direct result of government policy, as in the efforts made to resettle the urban poor in some parts of Brazil; just as often, it comes about despite state attempts at conservation. Loggers, licensed or unlicensed, blaze a trail into virgin forest, often destroying twice as many trees as they harvest. Landless farmers follow, burning away most of what remains to plant their crops, completing the destruction.

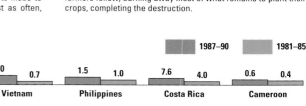

- 1987–90
- 1981–85

Brazil 1.5 / 0.4
India 4.1 / 0.3
Indonesia 0.8 / 0.5
Burma 2.1 / 0.3
Thailand 2.5 / 2.4
Vietnam 2.0 / 0.7
Philippines 1.5 / 1.0
Costa Rica 7.6 / 4.0
Cameroon 0.6 / 0.4

Ozone Depletion

The ozone layer, 25–30 km [15–18 miles] above sea level, acts as a barrier to most of the Sun's harmful ultra-violet radiation, protecting us from the ionizing radiation that can cause skin cancer and cataracts. In recent years, however, two holes in the ozone layer have been observed during winter: one over the Arctic and the other, the size of the USA, over Antarctica. By 1996, ozone had been reduced to around a half of its 1970 amount. The ozone (O_3) is broken down by chlorine released into the atmosphere as CFCs (chlorofluorocarbons) – chemicals used in refrigerators, packaging and aerosols.

Air Pollution

Sulphur dioxide is the main pollutant associated with industrial cities. According to the World Health Organization, at least 600 million people live in urban areas where sulphur dioxide concentrations regularly reach damaging levels. One of the world's most dangerously polluted urban areas is Mexico City, due to a combination of its enclosed valley location, 3 million cars and 60,000 factories. In May 1998, this lethal cocktail was added to by nearby forest fires and the resultant air pollution led to over 20% of the population (3 million people) complaining of respiratory problems.

Acid Rain

Killing trees, poisoning lakes and rivers and eating away buildings, acid rain is mostly produced by sulphur dioxide emissions from industry and volcanic eruptions. By the mid 1990s, acid rain had sterilized 4,000 or more of Sweden's lakes and left 45% of Switzerland's alpine conifers dead or dying, while the monuments of Greece were dissolving in Athens' smog. Prevailing wind patterns mean that the acids often fall many hundred kilometres from where the original pollutants were discharged. In parts of Europe acid deposition has slightly decreased, following reductions in emissions, but not by enough.

World Pollution

Acid rain and sources of acidic emissions (latest available year)

Acid rain is caused by high levels of sulphur and nitrogen in the atmosphere. They combine with water vapour and oxygen to form acids (H_2SO_4 and HNO_3) which fall as precipitation.

- Regions where sulphur and nitrogen oxides are released in high concentrations, mainly from fossil fuel combustion
- Major cities with high levels of air pollution (including nitrogen and sulphur emissions)

Areas of heavy acid deposition

pH numbers indicate acidity, decreasing from a neutral 7. Normal rain, slightly acid from dissolved carbon dioxide, never exceeds a pH of 5.6.

- pH less than 4.0 (most acidic)
- pH 4.0 to 4.5
- pH 4.5 to 5.0
- Areas where acid rain is a potential problem

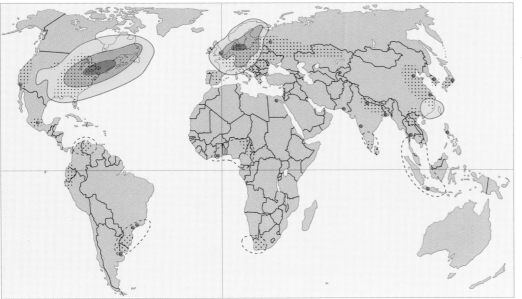

Population

Demographic Profiles

Developed nations such as the UK have populations evenly spread across the age groups and, usually, a growing proportion of elderly people. The great majority of the people in developing nations, how-ever, are in the younger age groups, about to enter their most fertile years. In time, these population profiles should resemble the world profile (even Kenya has made recent progress with reducing its birth rate), but the transition will come about only after a few more generations of rapid population growth.

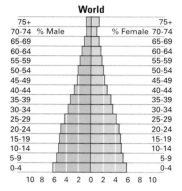

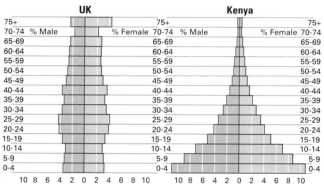

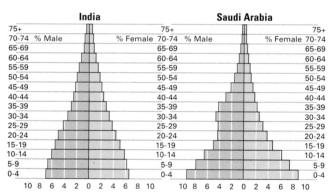

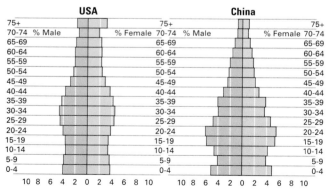

Most Populous Nations [in millions (1998 estimates)]

1.	China	1,237	9. Bangladesh	125	17. Iran	64
2.	India	984	10. Nigeria	111	18. Thailand	60
3.	USA	270	11. Mexico	99	19. France	59
4.	Indonesia	213	12. Germany	82	20. UK	59
5.	Brazil	170	13. Philippines	78	21. Ethiopia	58
6.	Russia	147	14. Vietnam	76	22. Italy	57
7.	Pakistan	135	15. Egypt	66	23. Ukraine	50
8.	Japan	126	16. Turkey	65	24. Congo (=Zaïre)	49

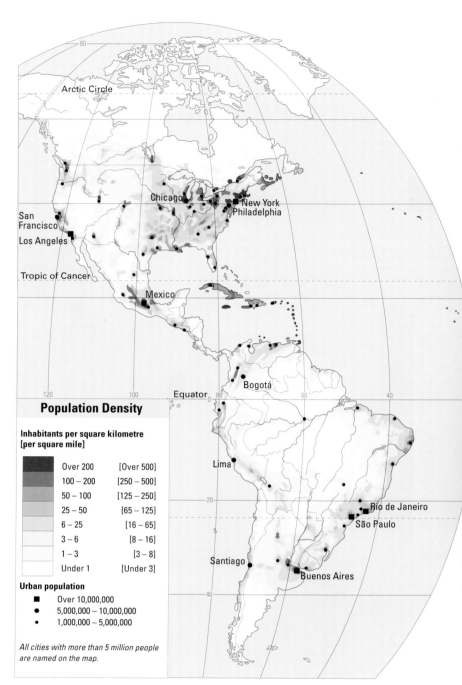

Population Density

Inhabitants per square kilometre [per square mile]

Over 200	[Over 500]
100 – 200	[250 – 500]
50 – 100	[125 – 250]
25 – 50	[65 – 125]
6 – 25	[16 – 65]
3 – 6	[8 – 16]
1 – 3	[3 – 8]
Under 1	[Under 3]

Urban population

■ Over 10,000,000
● 5,000,000 – 10,000,000
• 1,000,000 – 5,000,000

All cities with more than 5 million people are named on the map.

Continental Comparisons

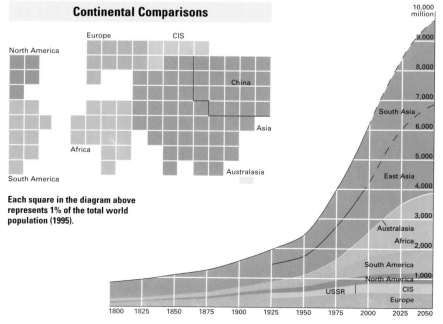

Each square in the diagram above represents 1% of the total world population (1995).

CARTOGRAPHY BY PHILIP'S. COPYRIGHT GEORGE PHILIP LTD

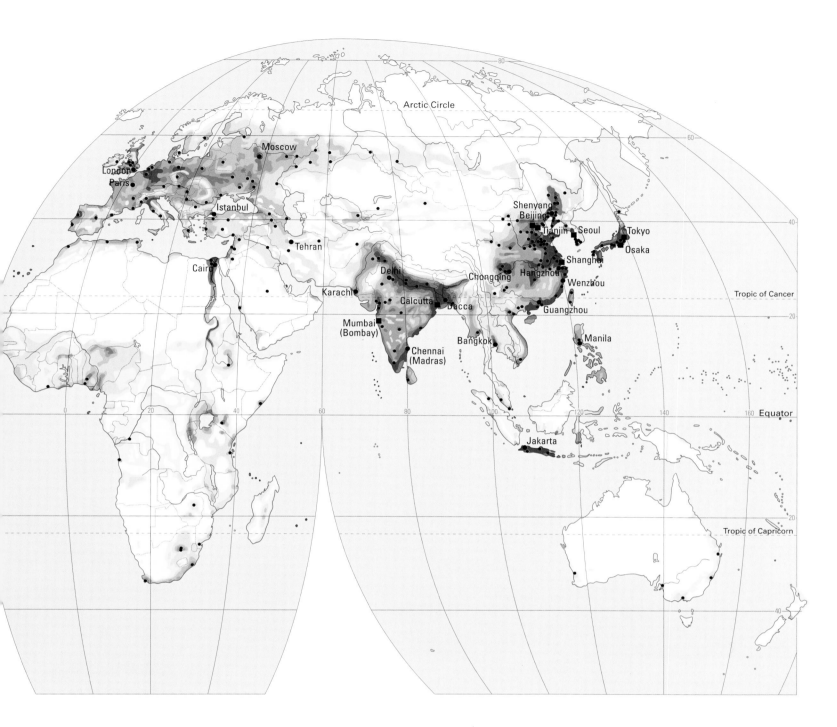

Arctic Circle

Moscow

London
Paris

Istanbul

Tehran

Cairo

Shenyang
Beijing
Tianjin   Seoul   Tokyo
Shanghai   Osaka

Delhi
Karachi   Chongqing   Hangzhou
Calcutta   Wenzhou
Mumbai   Dacca
(Bombay)   Guangzhou

Chennai   Bangkok   Manila
(Madras)

Tropic of Cancer

Equator

Jakarta

Tropic of Capricorn

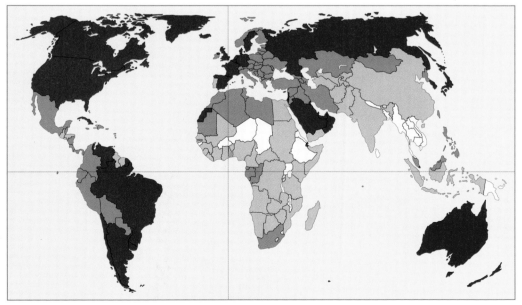

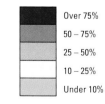

Urban Population

Percentage of total population living in towns and cities (1997)

Over 75%

50 – 75%

25 – 50%

10 – 25%

Under 10%

Most urbanized		Least urbanized	
Singapore	100%	Rwanda	6%
Belgium	97%	Bhutan	8%
Israel	91%	Burundi	8%
Uruguay	91%	Nepal	11%
Netherlands	89%	Swaziland	12%

[UK 89%]

The Human Family

Predominant Languages

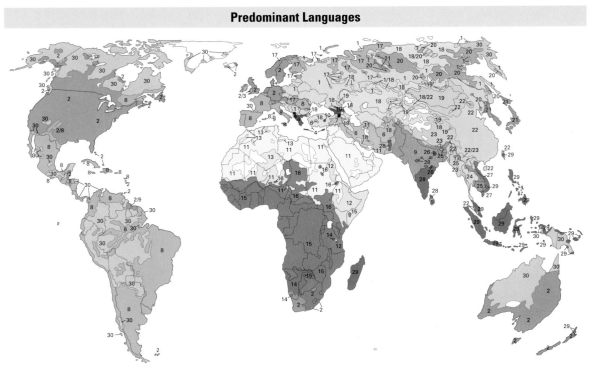

Languages of the World

Language can be classified by ancestry and structure. For example, the Romance and Germanic groups are both derived from an Indo-European language believed to have been spoken 5,000 years ago.

Mother tongues (in millions)
Chinese 1,069 (Mandarin 864), English 443, Hindi 352, Spanish 341, Russian 293, Arabic 197, Bengali 184, Portuguese 173, Malay-Indonesian 142, Japanese 125, French 121, German 118, Urdu 92, Punjabi 84, Korean 71.

Official languages (% of total population)
English 27%, Chinese 19%, Hindi 13.5%, Spanish 5.4%, Russian 5.2%, French 4.2%, Arabic 3.3%, Portuguese 3%, Malay 3%, Bengali 2.9%, Japanese 2.3%.

INDO-EUROPEAN FAMILY

1. Balto-Slavic group (incl. Russian, Ukrainian)
2. Germanic group (incl. English, German)
3. Celtic group
4. Greek
5. Albanian
6. Iranian group
7. Armenian
8. Romance group (incl. Spanish, Portuguese, French, Italian)
9. Indo-Aryan group (incl. Hindi, Bengali, Urdu, Punjabi, Marathi)
10. CAUCASIAN FAMILY

AFRO-ASIATIC FAMILY

11. Semitic group (incl. Arabic)
12. Kushitic group
13. Berber group

14. KHOISAN FAMILY

15. NIGER-CONGO FAMILY

16. NILO-SAHARAN FAMILY

17. URALIC FAMILY

ALTAIC FAMILY

18. Turkic group
19. Mongolian group
20. Tungus-Manchu group
21. Japanese and Korean

SINO-TIBETAN FAMILY

22. Sinitic (Chinese) languages
23. Tibetic-Burmic languages

24. TAI FAMILY

AUSTRO-ASIATIC FAMILY

25. Mon-Khmer group
26. Munda group
27. Vietnamese

28. DRAVIDIAN FAMILY (incl. Telugu, Tamil)

29. AUSTRONESIAN FAMILY (incl. Malay-Indonesian)

30. OTHER LANGUAGES

Predominant Religions

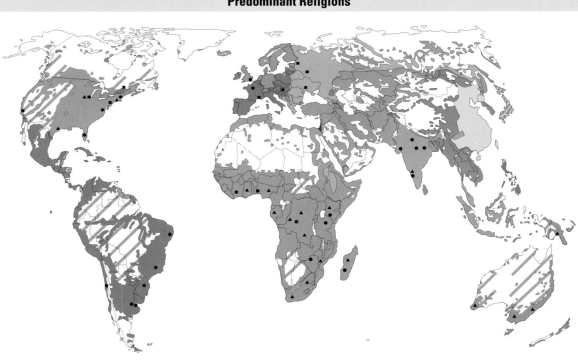

Religious Adherents

Religious adherents in millions:

Christian	1,669	Hindu	663
Roman Catholic	952	Buddhist	312
Protestant	337	Chinese Folk	172
Orthodox	162	Tribal	92
Anglican	70	Jewish	18
Other Christian	148	Sikhs	17
Muslim	966		
Sunni	841		
Shia	125		

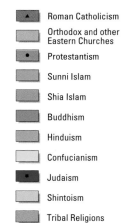

- Roman Catholicism
- Orthodox and other Eastern Churches
- Protestantism
- Sunni Islam
- Shia Islam
- Buddhism
- Hinduism
- Confucianism
- Judaism
- Shintoism
- Tribal Religions

CARTOGRAPHY BY PHILIP'S. COPYRIGHT GEORGE PHILIP LTD

United Nations

Created in 1945 to promote peace and co-operation and based in New York, the United Nations is the world's largest international organization, with 185 members and an annual budget of US $2.6 billion (1996–97). Each member of the General Assembly has one vote, while the permanent members of the 15-nation Security Council – USA, Russia, China, UK and France – hold a veto. The Secretariat is the UN's principal administrative arm. The 54 members of the Economic and Social Council are responsible for economic, social, cultural, educational, health and related matters. The UN has 16 specialized agencies – based in Canada, France, Switzerland and Italy, as well as the USA – which help members in fields such as education (UNESCO), agriculture (FAO), medicine (WHO) and finance (IFC). By the end of 1994, all the original 11 trust territories of the Trusteeship Council had become independent.

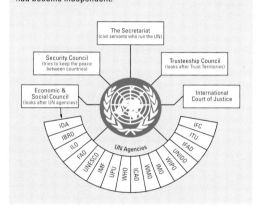

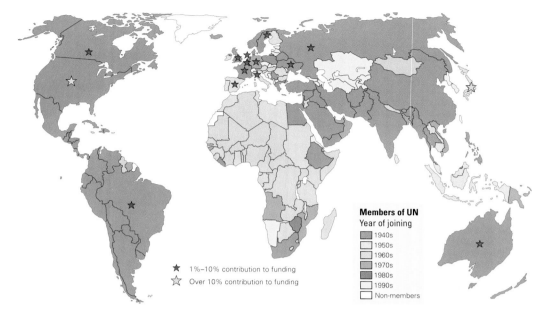

Members of UN
Year of joining
- 1940s
- 1950s
- 1960s
- 1970s
- 1980s
- 1990s
- Non-members

★ 1%–10% contribution to funding
☆ Over 10% contribution to funding

MEMBERSHIP OF THE UN In 1945 there were 51 members; by December 1994 membership had increased to 185 following the admission of Palau. There are 7 independent states which are not members of the UN – Kiribati, Nauru, Switzerland, Taiwan, Tonga, Tuvalu and the Vatican City. All the successor states of the former USSR had joined by the end of 1992. The official languages of the UN are Chinese, English, French, Russian, Spanish and Arabic.

FUNDING The UN budget for 1996–97 was US $2.6 billion. Contributions are assessed by the members' ability to pay, with the maximum 25% of the total, the minimum 0.01%. Contributions for 1996 were: USA 25.0%, Japan 15.4%, Germany 9.0%, France 6.4%, UK 5.3%, Italy 5.2%, Russia 4.5%, Canada 3.1%, Spain 2.4%, Brazil 1.6%, Netherlands 1.6%, Australia 1.5%, Sweden 1.2%, Ukraine 1.1%, Belgium 1.0%.

International Organizations

EU European Union (evolved from the European Community in 1993). The 15 members – Austria, Belgium, Denmark, Finland, France, Germany, Greece, Ireland, Italy, Luxembourg, Netherlands, Portugal, Spain, Sweden and the UK – aim to integrate economies, co-ordinate social developments and bring about political union. These members of what is now the world's biggest market share agricultural and industrial policies and tariffs on trade. The original body, the European Coal and Steel Community (ECSC), was created in 1951 following the signing of the Treaty of Paris.

EFTA European Free Trade Association (formed in 1960). Portugal left the original 'Seven' in 1989 to join what was then the EC, followed by Austria, Finland and Sweden in 1995. Only 4 members remain: Norway, Iceland, Switzerland and Liechtenstein.

ACP African-Caribbean-Pacific (formed in 1963). Members have economic ties with the EU.

NATO North Atlantic Treaty Organization (formed in 1949). It continues after 1991 despite the winding up of the Warsaw Pact. The Czech Republic, Hungary and Poland were the latest members to join in 1999.

OAS Organization of American States (formed in 1948). It aims to promote social and economic co-operation between developed countries of North America and developing nations of Latin America.

ASEAN Association of South-east Asian Nations (formed in 1967). Burma and Laos joined in 1997.

OAU Organization of African Unity (formed in 1963). Its 53 members represent over 94% of Africa's population. Arabic, French, Portuguese and English are recognized as working languages.

LAIA Latin American Integration Association (1980). Its aim is to promote freer regional trade.

OECD Organization for Economic Co-operation and Development (formed in 1961). It comprises the 29 major Western free-market economies. Poland, Hungary and South Korea joined in 1996. 'G8' is its 'inner group' comprising Canada, France, Germany, Italy, Japan, Russia, the UK and the USA.

COMMONWEALTH The Commonwealth of Nations evolved from the British Empire; it comprises 16 Queen's realms, 32 republics and 5 indigenous monarchies, giving a total of 53.

OPEC Organization of Petroleum Exporting Countries (formed in 1960). It controls about three-quarters of the world's oil supply. Gabon left the organization in 1996.

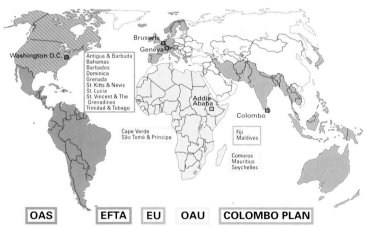

OAS | EFTA | EU | OAU | COLOMBO PLAN

ARAB LEAGUE (formed in 1945). The League's aim is to promote economic, social, political and military co-operation. There are 21 member nations.

COLOMBO PLAN (formed in 1951). Its 26 members aim to promote economic and social development in Asia and the Pacific.

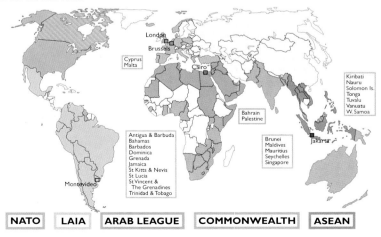

★ G8   OECD | ACP | OPEC | CIS

NATO | LAIA | ARAB LEAGUE | COMMONWEALTH | ASEAN

Wealth

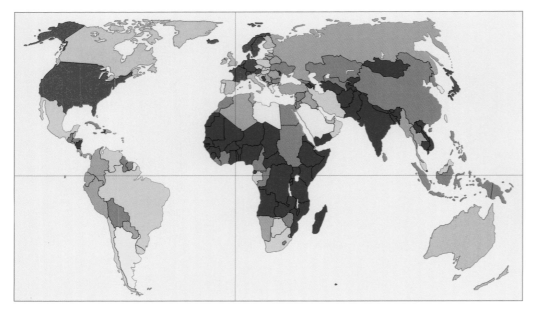

Levels of Income

Gross National Product per capita: the value of total production divided by the population (1997)

- Over 400% of world average
- 200 – 400% of world average
- 100 – 200% of world average

[World average wealth per person US $6,316]

- 50 – 100% of world average
- 25 – 50% of world average
- 10 – 25% of world average
- Under 10% of world average

GNP per capita growth rate (%), selected countries, 1985–94

Thailand	8.2	Brazil	–0.4
Chile	6.9	Zimbabwe	–0.6
Japan	3.2	USA	–1.3
Germany	1.9	UK	–1.4
Australia	1.2	Armenia	–12.9

Wealth Creation

The Gross National Product (GNP) of the world's largest economies, US $ million (1997)

1.	USA	7,690,100	23.	Turkey	199,500
2.	Japan	4,772,300	24.	Denmark	171,400
3.	Germany	2,319,300	25.	Thailand	169,600
4.	France	1,526,400	26.	Hong Kong	164,400
5.	UK	1,220,200	27.	Norway	158,900
6.	Italy	1,155,400	28.	Poland	138,900
7.	China	1,055,400	29.	South Africa	130,200
8.	Brazil	773,400	30.	Saudi Arabia	128,900
9.	Canada	583,900	31.	Greece	126,200
10.	Spain	570,100	32.	Finland	123,800
11.	South Korea	485,200	33.	Portugal	103,900
12.	Russia	403,500	34.	Singapore	101,800
13.	Netherlands	402,700	35.	Malaysia	98,200
14.	Australia	380,000	36.	Philippines	89,300
15.	India	373,900	37.	Israel	87,600
16.	Mexico	348,600	38.	Colombia	86,800
17.	Switzerland	313,500	39.	Venezuela	78,700
18.	Argentina	305,700	40.	Chile	73,300
19.	Belgium	268,400	41.	Egypt	71,200
20.	Sweden	232,000	42.	Pakistan	67,200
21.	Austria	225,900	43.	Ireland	66,400
22.	Indonesia	221,900	44.	Peru	60,800

The Wealth Gap

The world's richest and poorest countries, by Gross National Product per capita in US $ (1997)

1.	Luxembourg	45,360	1.	Mozambique	90
2.	Switzerland	44,220	2.	Ethiopia	110
3.	Japan	37,850	3.	Congo (D. Rep.)	110
4.	Norway	36,090	4.	Burundi	180
5.	Liechtenstein	33,000	5.	Sierra Leone	200
6.	Singapore	32,940	6.	Niger	200
7.	Denmark	32,500	7.	Rwanda	210
8.	Bermuda	31,870	8.	Tanzania	210
9.	USA	28,740	9.	Nepal	210
10.	Germany	28,260	10.	Malawi	220
11.	Austria	27,980	11.	Chad	240
12.	Iceland	26,580	12.	Madagascar	250
13.	Belgium	26,420	13.	Mali	260
14.	Sweden	26,220	14.	Yemen	270
15.	France	26,050	15.	Cambodia	300
16.	Netherlands	25,820	16.	Bosnia-Herzegovina	300
17.	Monaco	25,000	17.	Gambia, The	320
18.	Hong Kong	22,990	18.	Haiti	330
19.	Finland	20,580	19.	Kenya	330
20.	UK	18,700	20.	Angola	340

GNP per capita is calculated by dividing a country's Gross National Product by its total population.

Continental Shares

Shares of population and of wealth (GNP) by continent

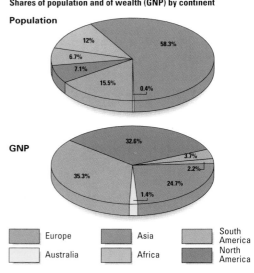

Population

GNP

- Europe
- Asia
- South America
- Australia
- Africa
- North America

Inflation

Average annual rate of inflation (1990–96)

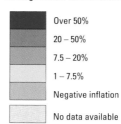

- Over 50%
- 20 – 50%
- 7.5 – 20%
- 1 – 7.5%
- Negative inflation
- No data available

Highest average inflation		Lowest average inflation	
Congo (D. Rep.)	2747%	Oman	–3.0%
Georgia	2279%	Bahrain	–0.5%
Angola	1103%	Brunei	–0.0%
Turkmenistan	1074%	Saudi Araba	1.0%
Armenia	897%	Japan	1.0%

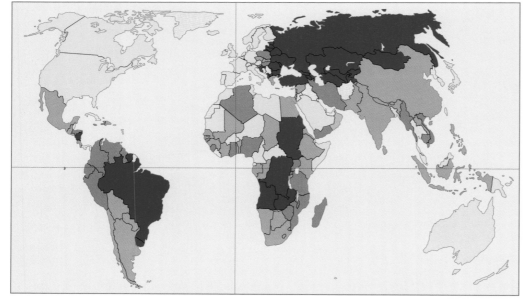

CARTOGRAPHY BY PHILIP'S. COPYRIGHT GEORGE PHILIP LTD

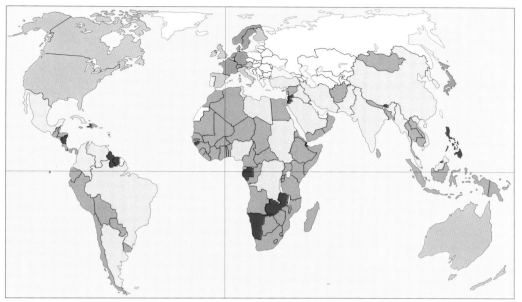

International Aid

Aid provided or received, divided by the total population, in US $ (1995)

Over $100 per person	
$10 – $100 per person	
$0 – $10 per person	Providers
No aid given or received	
$0 – $10 per person	
$10 – $100 per person	Receivers
Over $100 per person	

Top 5 providers per capita (1994)		Top 5 receivers per capita (1994)	
France	$279	São Tomé & P.	$378
Denmark	$260	Cape Verde	$314
Norway	$247	Djibouti	$235
Sweden	$201	Surinam	$198
Germany	$166	Mauritania	$153

Debt and Aid

International debtors and the aid they receive (1996)

Although aid grants make a vital contribution to many of the world's poorer countries, they are usually dwarfed by the burden of debt that the developing economies are expected to repay. In 1992, they had to pay US $160,000 million in debt service charges alone – more than two and a half times the amount of Official Development Assistance (ODA) the developing countries were receiving, and US $60,000 million more than total private flows of aid in the same year. In 1990, the debts of Mozambique, one of the world's poorest countries, were estimated to be 75 times its entire earnings from exports.

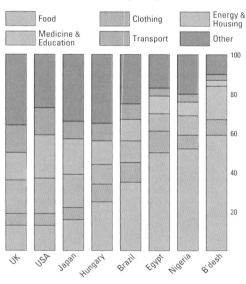

Distribution of Spending

Percentage share of household spending, selected countries

Food · Clothing · Energy & Housing · Medicine & Education · Transport · Other

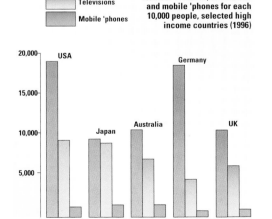

High Income

Number of radios, televisions and mobile 'phones for each 10,000 people, selected high income countries (1996)

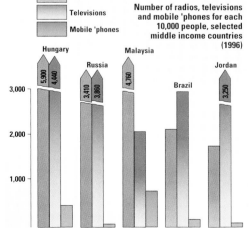

Middle Income

Number of radios, televisions and mobile 'phones for each 10,000 people, selected middle income countries (1996)

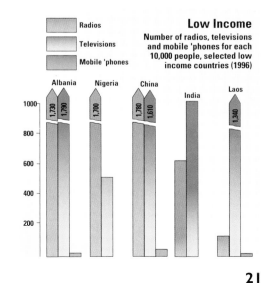

Low Income

Number of radios, televisions and mobile 'phones for each 10,000 people, selected low income countries (1996)

CARTOGRAPHY BY PHILIP'S. COPYRIGHT GEORGE PHILIP LTD

Quality of Life

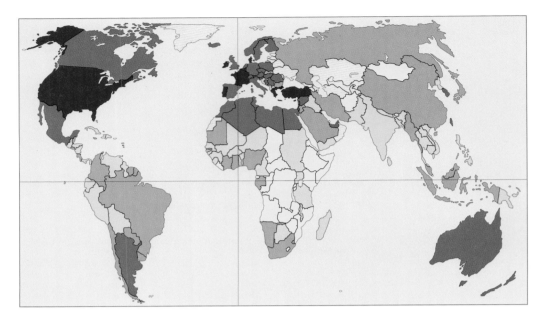

Daily Food Consumption

Average daily food intake in calories per person (1995)

- Over 3,500 calories per person
- 3,000 – 3,500 calories per person
- 2,500 – 3,000 calories per person
- 2,000 – 2,500 calories per person
- Under 2,000 calories per person
- No available data

Top 5 countries		Bottom 5 countries	
Cyprus	3,708 cal.	Congo (D.Rep.)	1,879 cal.
Denmark	3,704 cal.	Djibouti	1,831 cal.
Portugal	3,639 cal.	Togo	1,754 cal.
Ireland	3,638 cal.	Burundi	1,749 cal.
USA	3,603 cal.	Mozambique	1,678 cal.

[UK 3,149 calories]

Hospital Capacity

Hospital beds available for each 1,000 people (1996)

Highest capacity		Lowest capacity	
Switzerland	20.8	Benin	0.2
Japan	16.2	Nepal	0.2
Tajikistan	16.0	Afghanistan	0.3
Norway	13.5	Bangladesh	0.3
Belarus	12.4	Ethiopia	0.3
Kazakstan	12.2	Mali	0.4
Moldova	12.2	Burkina Faso	0.5
Ukraine	12.2	Niger	0.5
Latvia	11.9	Guinea	0.6
Russia	11.8	India	0.6

[UK 4.9] [USA 4.2]

Although the ratio of people to hospital beds gives a good approximation of a country's health provision, it is not an absolute indicator. Raw numbers may mask inefficiency and other weaknesses: the high availability of beds in Kazakstan, for example, has not prevented infant mortality rates over three times as high as in the United Kingdom and the United States.

Life Expectancy

Years of life expectancy at birth, selected countries (1997)

The chart shows combined data for both sexes. On average, women live longer than men worldwide, even in developing countries with high maternal mortality rates. Overall, life expectancy is steadily rising, though the difference between rich and poor nations remains dramatic.

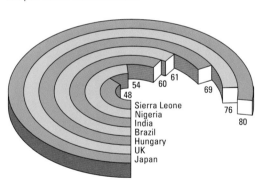

54 Sierra Leone
48
60 Nigeria
61 India
69 Brazil
Hungary
76 UK
80 Japan

Causes of Death

Causes of death for selected countries by % (1992–94)

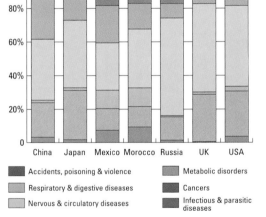

China Japan Mexico Morocco Russia UK USA

- Accidents, poisoning & violence
- Respiratory & digestive diseases
- Nervous & circulatory diseases
- Metabolic disorders
- Cancers
- Infectious & parasitic diseases

Child Mortality

Number of babies who will die under the age of one, per 1,000 births (average 1990–95)

- Over 150 deaths per 1,000 births
- 100 – 150 deaths per 1,000 births
- 50 – 100 deaths per 1,000 births
- 20 – 50 deaths per 1,000 births
- 10 – 20 deaths per 1,000 births
- Under 10 deaths per 1,000 births

Highest child mortality		Lowest child mortality	
Afghanistan	162	Hong Kong	6
Mali	159	Denmark	6
Sierra Leone	143	Japan	5
Guinea-Bissau	140	Iceland	5
Malawi	138	Finland	5

[UK 8 deaths]

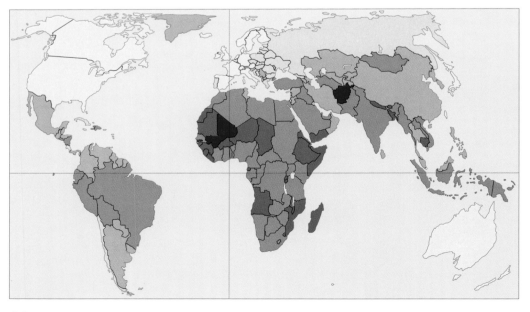

CARTOGRAPHY BY PHILIP'S. COPYRIGHT GEORGE PHILIP LTD

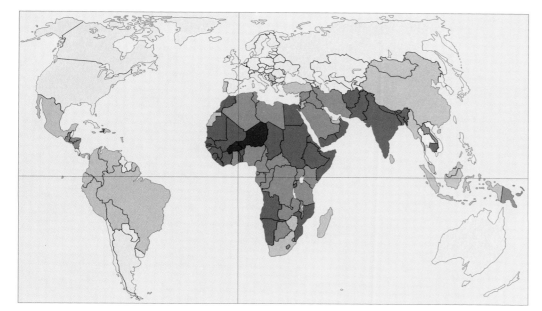

Percentage of the total population unable to read or write (latest available year)

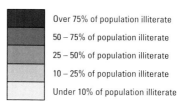

- Over 75% of population illiterate
- 50 – 75% of population illiterate
- 25 – 50% of population illiterate
- 10 – 25% of population illiterate
- Under 10% of population illiterate

Educational expenditure per person (latest available year)

Top 5 countries		Bottom 5 countries	
Sweden	$997	Chad	$2
Qatar	$989	Bangladesh	$3
Canada	$983	Ethiopia	$3
Norway	$971	Nepal	$4
Switzerland	$796	Somalia	$4

Fertility and Education

Fertility rates compared with female education, selected countries (1992–95)

- Percentage of females aged 12–17 in secondary education
- Fertility rate: average number of children borne per woman

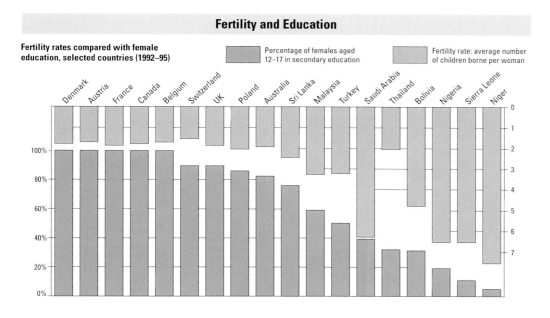

Living Standards

At first sight, most international contrasts in living standards are swamped by differences in wealth. The rich not only have more money, they have more of everything, including years of life. Those with only a little money are obliged to spend most of it on food and clothing, the basic maintenance costs of their existence; air travel and tourism are unlikely to feature on their expenditure lists. However, poverty and wealth are both relative: slum dwellers living on social security payments in an affluent industrial country have far more resources at their disposal than an average African peasant, but feel their own poverty nonetheless. A middle-class Indian lawyer cannot command a fraction of the earnings of a counterpart living in New York, London or Rome; nevertheless, he rightly sees himself as prosperous.

The rich not only live longer, on average, than the poor, they also die from different causes. Infectious and parasitic diseases, all but eliminated in the developed world, remain a scourge in the developing nations. On the other hand, more than two-thirds of the populations of OECD nations eventually succumb to cancer or circulatory disease.

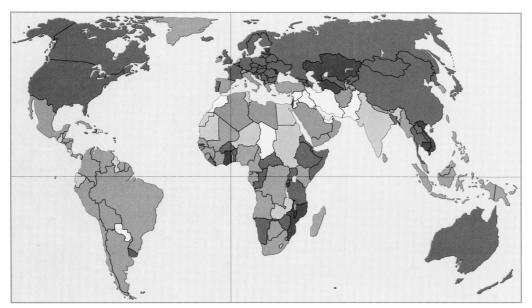

Women in the Workforce

Women in paid employment as a percentage of the total workforce (latest available year)

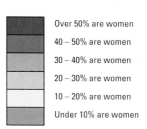

- Over 50% are women
- 40 – 50% are women
- 30 – 40% are women
- 20 – 30% are women
- 10 – 20% are women
- Under 10% are women

Most women in the workforce		Fewest women in the workforce	
Cambodia	56%	Saudi Arabia	4%
Kazakstan	54%	Oman	6%
Burundi	53%	Afghanistan	8%
Mozambique	53%	Algeria	9%
Turkmenistan	52%	Libya	9%

[USA 45] [UK 44]

CARTOGRAPHY BY PHILIP'S. COPYRIGHT GEORGE PHILIP LTD

Energy

Production

[Each square represents 1% of world energy production]

North America

Europe

CIS

Middle East

Africa

Asia

Japan

Australasia

South America

Consumption

[Each square represents 1% of world energy consumption]

North America

Europe

CIS

Middle East

Africa

Asia

Japan

Australasia

South America

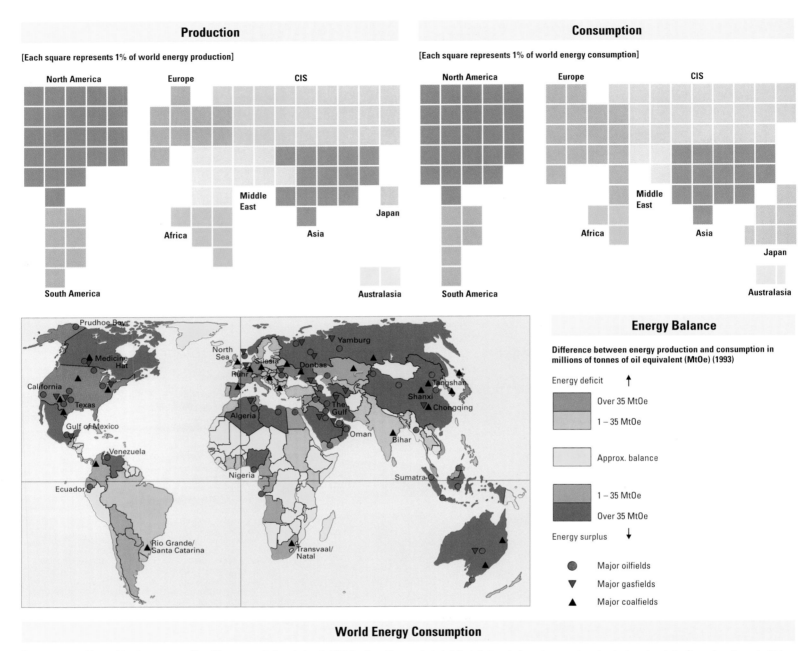

Prudhoe Bay

Medicine Hat

California

Texas

Gulf of Mexico

Venezuela

Ecuador

Rio Grande/Santa Catarina

North Sea

Ruhr

Silesia

Donbas

Algeria

The Gulf

Oman

Nigeria

Transvaal/Natal

Yamburg

Shanxi

Tangshan

Chongqing

Bihar

Sumatra

Energy Balance

Difference between energy production and consumption in millions of tonnes of oil equivalent (MtOe) (1993)

Energy deficit ↑

Over 35 MtOe

1 – 35 MtOe

Approx. balance

1 – 35 MtOe

Over 35 MtOe

Energy surplus ↓

● Major oilfields

▼ Major gasfields

▲ Major coalfields

World Energy Consumption

Energy consumed by world regions, measured in million tonnes of oil equivalent in 1997. Total world consumption was 8,509 MtOe. Only energy from oil, gas, coal, nuclear and hydroelectric sources are included. Excluded are fuels such as wood, peat, animal waste, wind, solar and geothermal which, though important in some countries, are unreliably documented in terms of consumption statistics.

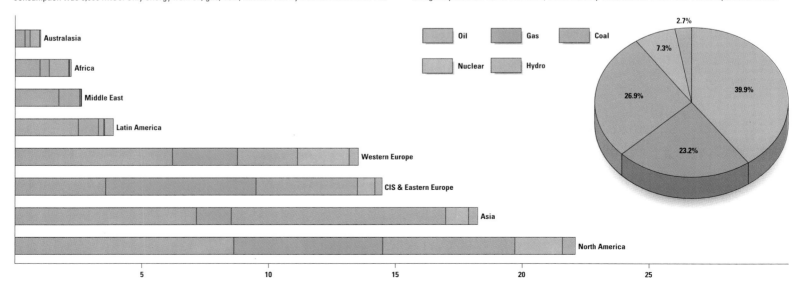

Oil   Gas   Coal

Nuclear   Hydro

Australasia

Africa

Middle East

Latin America

Western Europe

CIS & Eastern Europe

Asia

North America

5   10   15   20   25

2.7%

7.3%

26.9%

39.9%

23.2%

CARTOGRAPHY BY PHILIP'S. COPYRIGHT GEORGE PHILIP LTD

Energy

Energy is used to keep us warm or cool, fuel our industries and our transport systems, and even feed us; high-intensity agriculture, with its use of fertilizers, pesticides and machinery, is heavily energy-dependent. Although we live in a high-energy society, there are vast discrepancies between rich and poor; for example, a North American consumes 13 times as much energy as a Chinese person. But even developing nations have more power at their disposal than was imaginable a century ago.

The distribution of energy supplies, most importantly fossil fuels (coal, oil and natural gas), is very uneven. In addition, the diagrams and map opposite show that the largest producers of energy are not necessarily the largest consumers. The movement of energy supplies around the world is therefore an important component of international trade. In 1995, total world movements in oil amounted to 1,815 million tonnes.

As the finite reserves of fossil fuels are depleted, renewable energy sources, such as solar, hydro-thermal, wind, tidal and biomass, will become increasingly important around the world.

Nuclear Power

Percentage of electricity generated by nuclear power stations, leading nations (1995)

1.	Lithuania...............85%	11.	Spain.....................33%
2.	France..................77%	12.	Finland.................30%
3.	Belgium...............56%	13.	Germany..............29%
4.	Slovak Rep. 49%	14.	Japan...................29%
5.	Sweden................48%	15.	UK........................ 27%
6.	Bulgaria............... 41%	16.	Ukraine................ 27%
7.	Hungary............... 41%	17.	Czech Rep. 22%
8.	Switzerland..........39%	18.	Canada.................19%
9.	Slovenia...............38%	19.	USA......................18%
10.	South Korea........ 33%	20.	Russia..................12%

Although the 1980s were a bad time for the nuclear power industry (major projects ran over budget, and fears of long-term environmental damage were heavily reinforced by the 1986 disaster at Chernobyl), the industry picked up in the early 1990s. However, whilst the number of reactors is still increasing, orders for new plants have shrunk. This is partly due to the increasingly difficult task of disposing of nuclear waste.

Hydroelectricity

Percentage of electricity generated by hydroelectric power stations, leading nations (1995)

1.	Paraguay...........99.9%	11.	Rwanda.............97.6%
2.	Congo (Zaïre)....99.7%	12.	Malawi.............. 97.6%
3.	Bhutan...............99.6%	13.	Cameroon..........96.9%
4.	Zambia...............99.5%	14.	Nepal.................96.7%
5.	Norway............ 99.4%	15.	Laos...................95.3%
6.	Ghana................99.3%	16.	Albania...............95.2%
7.	Congo................99.3%	17.	Iceland...............94.0%
8.	Uganda............ 99.1%	18.	Brazil 92.2%
9.	Burundi.............98.3%	19.	Honduras..........87.6%
10.	Uruguay............98.0%	20.	Tanzania............87.1%

Countries heavily reliant on hydroelectricity are usually small and non-industrial: a high proportion of hydroelectric power more often reflects a modest energy budget than vast hydroelectric resources. The USA, for instance, produces only 9% of power requirements from hydroelectricity; yet that 9% amounts to more than three times the hydropower generated by all of Africa.

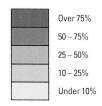

Fuel Exports

Fuels as a percentage of total value of exports (1990–94)

- Over 75%
- 50 – 75%
- 25 – 50%
- 10 – 25%
- Under 10%

Conversion Rates

1 barrel = 0.136 tonnes or 159 litres or 35 Imperial gallons or 42 US gallons

1 tonne = 7.33 barrels or 1,185 litres or 256 Imperial gallons or 261 US gallons

1 tonne oil = 1.5 tonnes hard coal or 3.0 tonnes lignite or 12,000 kWh

1 Imperial gallon = 1.201 US gallons or 4.546 litres or 277.4 cubic inches

Measurements

For historical reasons, oil is traded in 'barrels'. The weight and volume equivalents (shown right) are all based on average-density 'Arabian light' crude oil.

The energy equivalents given for a tonne of oil are also somewhat imprecise: oil and coal of different qualities will have varying energy contents, a fact usually reflected in their price on world markets.

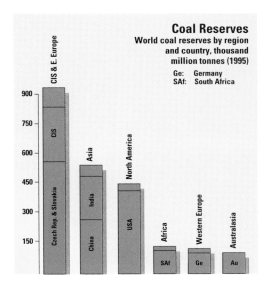

Coal Reserves
World coal reserves by region and country, thousand million tonnes (1995)

Ge: Germany
SAf: South Africa

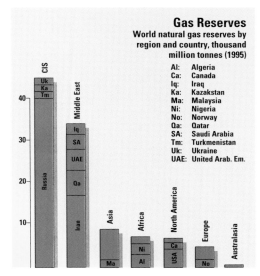

Gas Reserves
World natural gas reserves by region and country, thousand million tonnes (1995)

Al: Algeria
Ca: Canada
Iq: Iraq
Ka: Kazakstan
Ma: Malaysia
Ni: Nigeria
No: Norway
Qa: Qatar
SA: Saudi Arabia
Tm: Turkmenistan
Uk: Ukraine
UAE: United Arab. Em.

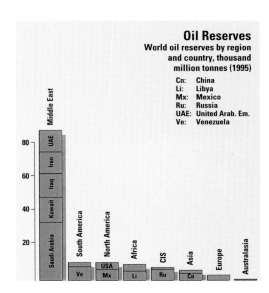

Oil Reserves
World oil reserves by region and country, thousand million tonnes (1995)

Cn: China
Li: Libya
Mx: Mexico
Ru: Russia
UAE: United Arab. Em.
Ve: Venezuela

CARTOGRAPHY BY PHILIP'S. COPYRIGHT GEORGE PHILIP LTD

Production

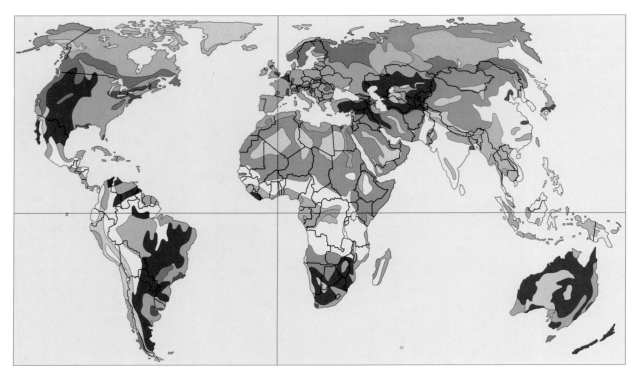

Agriculture

Predominant type of farming or land use.

- Nomadic herding
- Hunting, fishing and gathering
- Subsistence agriculture
- Commercial ranching
- Commercial livestock and grain farming
- Urban areas
- Forestry
- Unproductive land

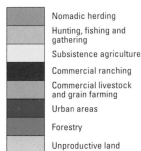

The development of agriculture has transformed human existence more than any other. The whole business of farming is constantly developing: due mainly to the new varieties of rice and wheat, world grain production has increased by over 70% since 1965. New machinery and modern agricultural techniques enable relatively few farmers to produce enough food for the world's 6 billion or so people.

Staple Crops

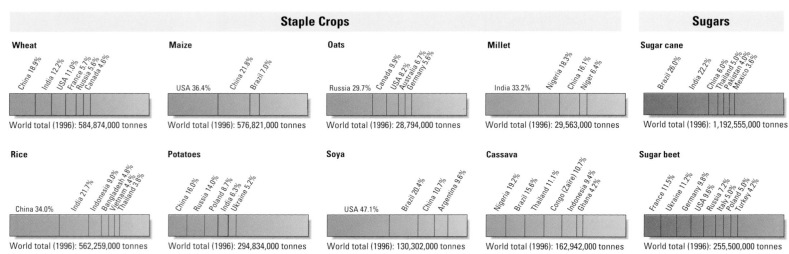

Wheat

China 18.9% · India 12.2% · USA 11.0% · France 5.7% · Russia 5.6% · Canada 4.6%

World total (1996): 584,874,000 tonnes

Maize

USA 36.4% · China 21.8% · Brazil 7.0%

World total (1996): 576,821,000 tonnes

Oats

Russia 29.7% · Canada 9.9% · USA 8.2% · Australia 6.7% · Germany 5.6%

World total (1996): 28,794,000 tonnes

Millet

India 33.2% · Nigeria 18.3% · China 16.1% · Niger 6.4%

World total (1996): 29,563,000 tonnes

Rice

China 34.0% · India 21.7% · Indonesia 9.0% · Bangladesh 4.8% · Vietnam 4.4% · Thailand 3.8%

World total (1996): 562,259,000 tonnes

Potatoes

China 16.0% · Russia 14.0% · Poland 8.7% · India 6.3% · Ukraine 5.2%

World total (1996): 294,834,000 tonnes

Soya

USA 47.1% · Brazil 20.4% · China 10.7% · Argentina 9.6%

World total (1996): 130,302,000 tonnes

Cassava

Nigeria 19.2% · Brazil 15.6% · Thailand 11.1% · Congo (Zaïre) 10.7% · Indonesia 9.4% · Ghana 4.2%

World total (1996): 162,942,000 tonnes

Sugars

Sugar cane

Brazil 26.0% · India 22.2% · China 6.0% · Thailand 5.0% · Pakistan 4.0% · Mexico 3.6%

World total (1996): 1,192,555,000 tonnes

Sugar beet

France 11.5% · Ukraine 11.2% · Germany 9.8% · USA 9.6% · Russia 7.2% · Italy 5.0% · Poland 5.0% · Turkey 4.2%

World total (1996): 255,500,000 tonnes

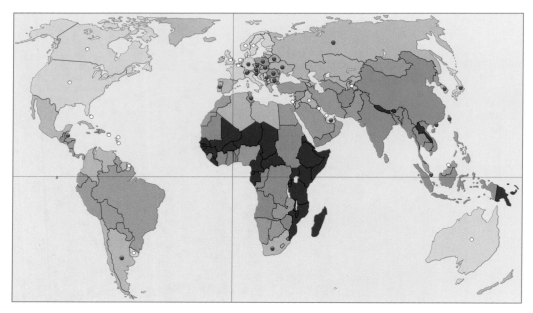

Balance of Employment

Percentage of total workforce employed in agriculture, including forestry and fishing (1990–92)

- Over 75% in agriculture
- 50 – 75% in agriculture
- 25 – 50% in agriculture
- 10 – 25% in agriculture
- Under 10% in agriculture

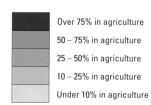

Employment in industry and services

- ● Over a third of total workforce employed in manufacturing

- ○ Over two-thirds of total workforce employed in service industries (work in offices, shops, tourism, transport, construction and government)

CARTOGRAPHY BY PHILIP'S. COPYRIGHT GEORGE PHILIP LTD

Mineral Production

*Figures for aluminium are for refined metal; all other figures refer to ore production.

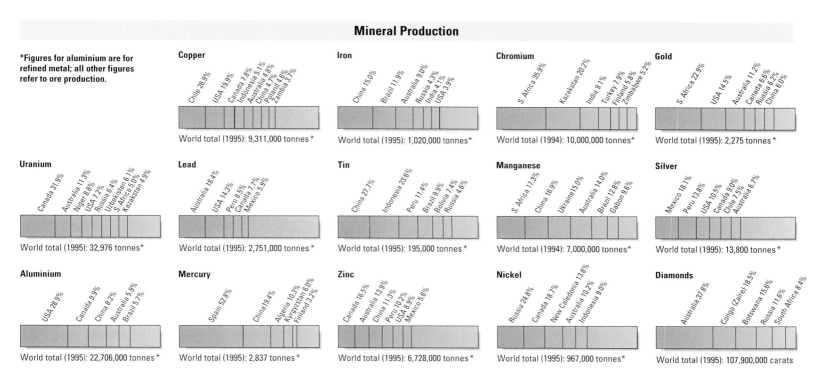

Copper
Chile 26.9% · USA 19.9% · Canada 7.8% · Indonesia 5.1% · Australia 4.8% · China 4.7% · Poland 4.6% · Zambia 3.7%
World total (1995): 9,311,000 tonnes*

Iron
China 15.0% · Brazil 11.9% · Australia 9.0% · Russia 4.3% · India 4.1% · USA 3.9%
World total (1995): 1,020,000 tonnes*

Chromium
S. Africa 35.9% · Kazakstan 20.2% · India 9.1% · Turkey 7.9% · Finland 5.8% · Zimbabwe 5.2%
World total (1994): 10,000,000 tonnes*

Gold
S. Africa 22.9% · USA 14.5% · Australia 11.2% · Canada 6.6% · Russia 6.2% · China 6.0%
World total (1995): 2,275 tonnes*

Uranium
Canada 31.9% · Australia 11.3% · Niger 8.9% · USA 7.2% · Russia 6.4% · Uzbekistan 6.1% · S. Africa 5.0% · Kazakstan 4.9%
World total (1995): 32,976 tonnes*

Lead
Australia 18.4% · USA 14.3% · Peru 8.5% · Canada 7.7% · Mexico 5.9%
World total (1995): 2,751,000 tonnes*

Tin
China 27.7% · Indonesia 23.6% · Peru 11.4% · Brazil 9.9% · Bolivia 7.4% · Russia 4.6%
World total (1995): 195,000 tonnes*

Manganese
S. Africa 17.3% · China 16.9% · Ukraine 15.0% · Australia 14.0% · Brazil 12.8% · Gabon 9.6%
World total (1994): 7,000,000 tonnes*

Silver
Mexico 18.1% · Peru 13.8% · USA 10.5% · Canada 7.5% · Chile 7.5% · Australia 6.7%
World total (1995): 13,800 tonnes*

Aluminium
USA 28.9% · Canada 9.9% · China 8.2% · Australia 5.9% · Brazil 5.7%
World total (1995): 22,706,000 tonnes*

Mercury
Spain 52.8% · China 19.4% · Algeria 10.3% · Kyrgyzstan 6.0% · Finland 3.2%
World total (1995): 2,837 tonnes*

Zinc
Canada 16.5% · Australia 13.9% · China 11.3% · Peru 10.2% · Mexico 5.6%
World total (1995): 6,728,000 tonnes*

Nickel
Russia 24.8% · Canada 18.7% · New Caledonia 13.8% · Australia 10.2% · Indonesia 9.0%
World total (1995): 967,000 tonnes*

Diamonds
Australia 37.8% · Congo (Zaire) 18.5% · Botswana 15.6% · Russia 11.6% · South Africa 8.4%
World total (1995): 107,900,000 carats

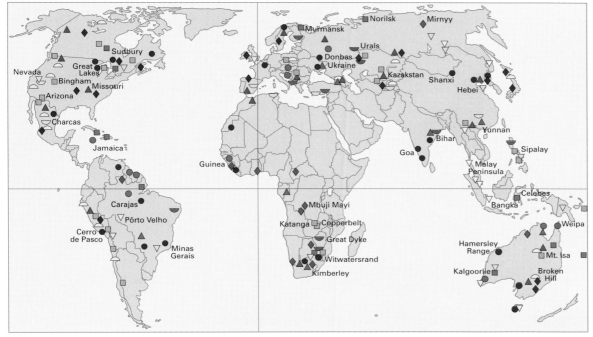

Mineral Distribution

The map shows the richest sources of the most important minerals. Major mineral locations are named.

Light metals
- ● Bauxite

Base metals
- ■ Copper
- ▲ Lead
- ▽ Mercury
- ▽ Tin
- ◆ Zinc

Iron and ferro-alloys
- ● Iron
- ◡ Chrome
- ▲ Manganese
- ■ Nickel

Precious metals
- ▽ Gold
- ◠ Silver

Precious stones
- ◆ Diamonds

The map does not show undersea deposits, most of which are considered inaccessible.

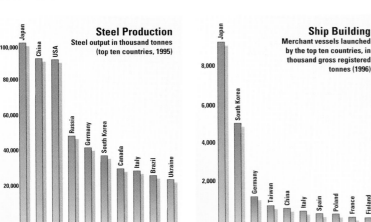

Steel Production
Steel output in thousand tonnes (top ten countries, 1995)

Japan · China · USA · Russia · Germany · South Korea · Canada · Italy · Brazil · Ukraine

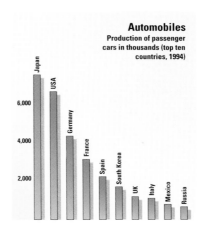

Ship Building
Merchant vessels launched by the top ten countries, in thousand gross registered tonnes (1996)

Japan · South Korea · Germany · Taiwan · China · Italy · Spain · Poland · France · Finland

Automobiles
Production of passenger cars in thousands (top ten countries, 1994)

Japan · USA · Germany · France · Spain · South Korea · UK · Italy · Mexico · Russia

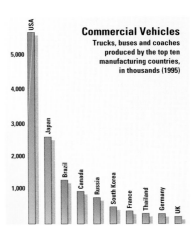

Commercial Vehicles
Trucks, buses and coaches produced by the top ten manufacturing countries, in thousands (1995)

USA · Japan · Brazil · Canada · Russia · South Korea · France · Thailand · Germany · UK

CARTOGRAPHY BY PHILIP'S. COPYRIGHT GEORGE PHILIP LTD

Trade

Share of World Trade

Percentage share of total world exports by value (1996)

- Over 10% of world trade
- 5 – 10% of world trade
- 1 – 5% of world trade
- 0.5 – 1% of world trade
- 0.1 – 0.5% of world trade
- Under 0.1% of world trade

International trade is dominated by a handful of powerful maritime nations. The members of 'G8', the inner circle of OECD (see page 19), and the top seven countries listed in the diagram below, account for more than half the total. The majority of nations – including all but four in Africa – contribute less than one quarter of 1% to the worldwide total of exports; the EU countries account for 40%, the Pacific Rim nations over 35%.

The Main Trading Nations

The imports and exports of the top ten trading nations as a percentage of world trade (1994). Each country's trade in manufactured goods is shown in dark blue.

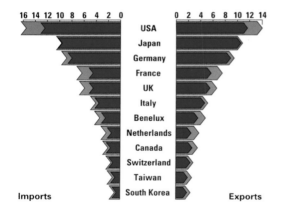

Imports — Exports

USA
Japan
Germany
France
UK
Italy
Benelux
Netherlands
Canada
Switzerland
Taiwan
South Korea

Patterns of Trade

Thriving international trade is the outward sign of a healthy world economy, the obvious indicator that some countries have goods to sell and others the means to buy them. Global exports expanded to an estimated US $3.92 trillion in 1994, an increase due partly to economic recovery in industrial nations but also to export-led growth strategies in many developing nations and lowered regional trade barriers. International trade remains dominated, however, by the rich, industrialized countries of the Organization for Economic Development: between them, OECD members account for almost 75% of world imports and exports in most years. However, continued rapid economic growth in some developing countries is altering global trade patterns. The 'tiger economies' of South-east Asia are particularly vibrant, averaging more than 8% growth between 1992 and 1994. The size of the largest trading economies means that imports and exports usually represent only a small percentage of their total wealth. In export-concious Japan, for example, trade in goods and services amounts to less than 18% of GDP. In poorer countries, trade – often in a single commodity – may amount to 50% of GDP.

Traded Products

Top ten manufactures traded, by value in billions of US $ (latest available year)

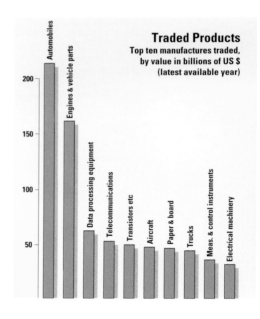

Automobiles
Engines & vehicle parts
Data processing equipment
Telecommunications
Transistors etc
Aircraft
Paper & board
Trucks
Meas. & control instruments
Electrical machinery

Balance of Trade

Value of exports in proportion to the value of imports (1995)

More than 40%	Exports exceed imports by:
10 – 40%	
10% either side	
10 – 40%	
More than 40%	Imports exceed exports by:

The total world trade balance should amount to zero, since exports must equal imports on a global scale. In practice, at least $100 billion in exports go unrecorded, leaving the world with an apparent deficit and many countries in a better position than public accounting reveals. However, a favourable trade balance is not necessarily a sign of prosperity: many poorer countries must maintain a high surplus in order to service debts, and do so by restricting imports below the levels needed to sustain successful economies.

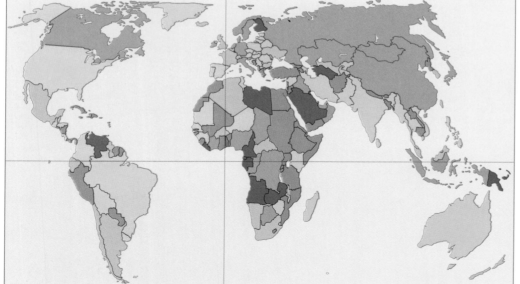

CARTOGRAPHY BY PHILIP'S. COPYRIGHT GEORGE PHILIP LTD

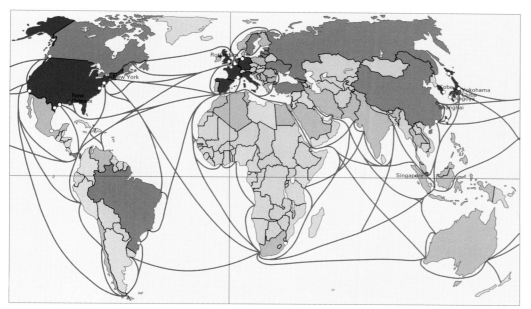

Seaborne Freight

Freight unloaded in millions of tonnes (latest available year)

- Over 100
- 50 – 100
- 10 – 50
- 5 – 10
- Under 5
- Landlocked countries

Major seaports

- ● Over 100 million tonnes per year
- ○ 50–100 million tonnes per year
- ▬ Major shipping routes

Cargoes

Type of seaborne freight

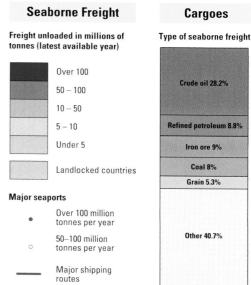

- Crude oil 28.2%
- Refined petroleum 8.8%
- Iron ore 9%
- Coal 8%
- Grain 5.3%
- Other 40.7%

Merchant Fleets

Merchant fleets in thousand gross tonnage (1994). A large number of vessels are registered in Liberia and Panama but they are not part of the national fleet.

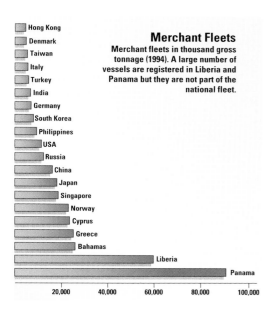

Hong Kong, Denmark, Taiwan, Italy, Turkey, India, Germany, South Korea, Philippines, USA, Russia, China, Japan, Singapore, Norway, Cyprus, Greece, Bahamas, Liberia, Panama

20,000   40,000   60,000   80,000   100,000

The Great Ports

Total Cargo Traffic (1995) '000 tonnes

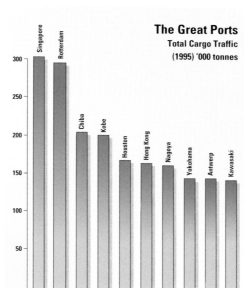

Singapore, Rotterdam, Chiba, Kobe, Houston, Hong Kong, Nagoya, Yokohama, Antwerp, Kawasaki

World Shipping

World merchant fleet by type of vessel and deadweight tonnage (latest available year)

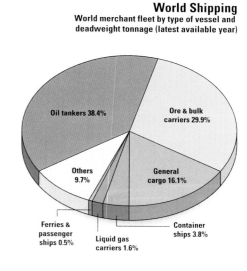

- Oil tankers 38.4%
- Ore & bulk carriers 29.9%
- General cargo 16.1%
- Others 9.7%
- Container ships 3.8%
- Liquid gas carriers 1.6%
- Ferries & passenger ships 0.5%

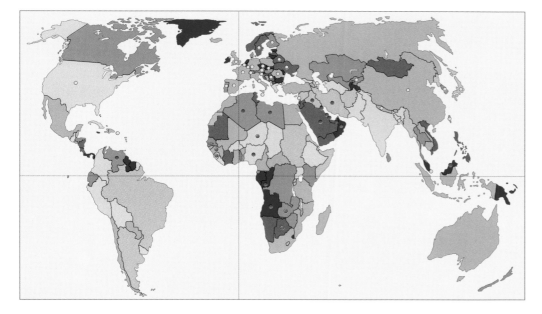

Dependence on Trade

Value of exports as a percentage of Gross Domestic Product (1997)

- Over 50% GDP from exports
- 40 – 50% GDP from exports
- 30 – 40% GDP from exports
- 20 – 30% GDP from exports
- 10 – 20% GDP from exports
- Under 10% GDP from exports

- ○ Most dependent on industrial exports (over 75% of total exports)
- ● Most dependent on fuel exports (over 75% of total exports)
- ● Most dependent on mineral and metal exports (over 75% of total exports)

CARTOGRAPHY BY PHILIP'S. COPYRIGHT GEORGE PHILIP LTD

29

Travel and Tourism

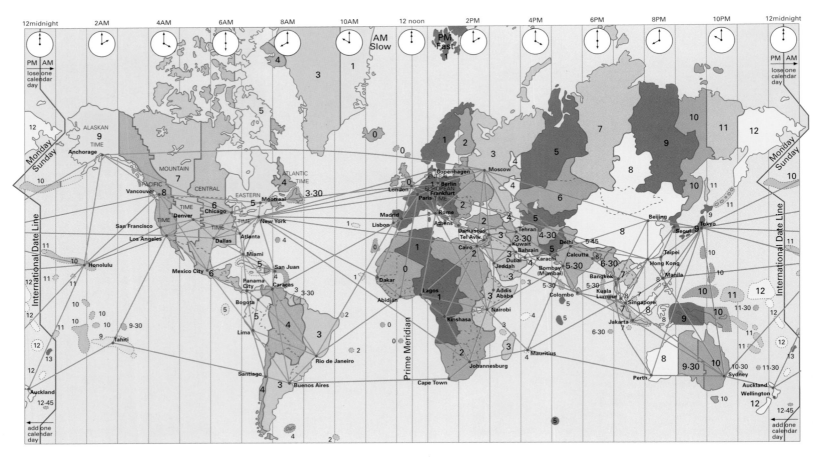

Time Zones

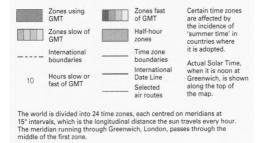

Zones using GMT

Zones slow of GMT

International boundaries

10 — Hours slow or fast of GMT

Zones fast of GMT

Half-hour zones

Time zone boundaries

International Date Line

Selected air routes

Certain time zones are affected by the incidence of 'summer time' in countries where it is adopted.

Actual Solar Time, when it is noon at Greenwich, is shown along the top of the map.

The world is divided into 24 time zones, each centred on meridians at 15° intervals, which is the longitudinal distance the sun travels every hour. The meridian running through Greenwich, London, passes through the middle of the first zone.

Rail and Road: The Leading Nations

Total rail network ('000 km) (1995)	Passenger km per head per year	Total road network ('000 km)	Vehicle km per head per year	Number of vehicles per km of roads
1. USA 235.7	Japan 2,017	USA 6,277.9	USA 12,505	Hong Kong 284
2. Russia 87.4	Belarus 1,880	India 2,962.5	Luxembourg 7,989	Taiwan 211
3. India 62.7	Russia 1,826	Brazil 1,824.4	Kuwait 7,251	Singapore 152
4. China 54.6	Switzerland 1,769	Japan 1,130.9	France 7,142	Kuwait 140
5. Germany 41.7	Ukraine 1,456	China 1,041.1	Sweden 6,991	Brunei 96
6. Australia 35.8	Austria 1,168	Russia 884.0	Germany 6,806	Italy 91
7. Argentina 34.2	France 1,011	Canada 849.4	Denmark 6,764	Israel 87
8. France 31.9	Netherlands 994	France 811.6	Austria 6,518	Thailand 73
9. Mexico 26.5	Latvia 918	Australia 810.3	Netherlands 5,984	Ukraine 73
10. South Africa 26.3	Denmark 884	Germany 636.3	UK 5,738	UK 67
11. Poland 24.9	Slovak Rep. 862	Romania 461.9	Canada 5,493	Netherlands 66
12. Ukraine 22.6	Romania 851	Turkey 388.1	Italy 4,852	Germany 62

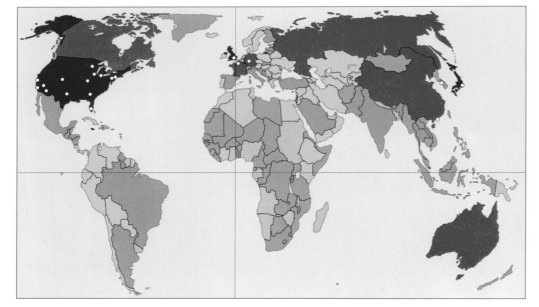

Air Travel

Passenger kilometres (the number of passengers – international and domestic – multiplied by the distance flown by each passenger from the airport of origin) (1996)

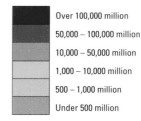

Over 100,000 million

50,000 – 100,000 million

10,000 – 50,000 million

1,000 – 10,000 million

500 – 1,000 million

Under 500 million

○ Major airports (handling over 25 million passengers in 1995)

World's busiest airports (total passengers)		World's busiest airports (international passengers)	
1. Chicago	(O'Hare)	1. London	(Heathrow)
2. Atlanta	(Hatsfield)	2. London	(Gatwick)
3. Dallas	(Dallas/Ft Worth)	3. Frankfurt	(International)
4. Los Angeles	(Intern'l)	4. New York	(Kennedy)
5. London	(Heathrow)	5. Paris	(De Gaulle)

CARTOGRAPHY BY PHILIP'S. COPYRIGHT GEORGE PHILIP LTD

Destinations

- Cultural and historical centres
- Coastal resorts
- Ski resorts
- Centres of entertainment
- Places of pilgrimage
- Places of great natural beauty
- Popular holiday cruise routes

Visitors to the USA

Overseas travellers to the USA, thousands (1997 estimates)

1.	Canada	13,900
2.	Mexico	12,370
3.	Japan	4,640
4.	UK	3,350
5.	Germany	1,990
6.	France	1,030
7.	Taiwan	885
8.	Venezuela	860
9.	South Korea	800
10.	Brazil	785

In 1996, the USA earned the most from tourism, with receipts of more than US $75 billion.

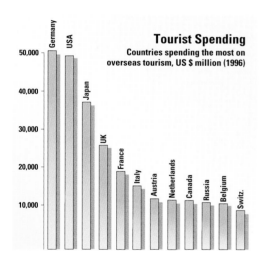

Tourist Spending
Countries spending the most on overseas tourism, US $ million (1996)

Importance of Tourism

		Arrivals from abroad (1996)	% of world total (1996)
1.	France	66,800,000	10.2%
2.	USA	49,038,000	7.5%
3.	Spain	43,403,000	6.6%
4.	Italy	34,087,000	5.2%
5.	UK	25,960,000	3.9%
6.	China	23,770,000	3.6%
7.	Poland	19,514,000	3.0%
8.	Mexico	18,667,000	2.9%
9.	Canada	17,610,000	2.7%
10.	Czech Republic	17,400,000	2.7%
11.	Hungary	17,248,000	2.6%
12.	Austria	16,642,000	2.5%

In 1996, there was a 4.6% rise, to 593 million, in the total number of people travelling abroad. Small economies in attractive areas are often completely dominated by tourism: in some West Indian islands, for example, tourist spending provides over 90% of total income.

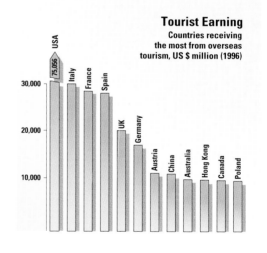

Tourist Earning
Countries receiving the most from overseas tourism, US $ million (1996)

Tourism

Tourism receipts as a percentage of Gross National Product (1994)

- Over 10% of GNP from tourism
- 5 – 10% of GNP from tourism
- 2.5 – 5% of GNP from tourism
- 1 – 2.5% of GNP from tourism
- 0.5 – 1% of GNP from tourism
- Under 0.5% of GNP from tourism

Countries spending the most on promoting tourism, millions of US $ (1996)

Australia	88
Spain	79
UK	79
France	73
Singapore	54

Fastest growing tourist destinations, % change in receipts (1994–5)

South Korea	49%
Czech Republic	27%
India	21%
Russia	19%
Philippines	18%

CARTOGRAPHY BY PHILIP'S. COPYRIGHT GEORGE PHILIP LTD

The World In Focus: Index

WORLD MAPS

SETTLEMENTS

■ PARIS   ■ Berne   ⊙ Livorno   ⊚ Brugge   ⊚ Algeciras   ○ *Frejus*   ○ *Oberammergau*   ○ *Thira*

Settlement symbols and type styles vary according to the scale of each map and indicate the importance
of towns on the map rather than specific population figures

∴ Ruins or Archæological Sites   ⌣ Wells in Desert

ADMINISTRATION

International Boundaries

- - - - - International Boundaries
(Undefined or Disputed)

·········· Internal Boundaries

National Parks

Country Names
NICARAGUA

Administrative
Area Names
KENT
CALABRIA

International boundaries show the *de facto* situation where there are rival claims to territory

COMMUNICATIONS

Principal Roads

Other Roads

┼ - - ┼ Road Tunnels

⤓ Passes

⊕ Airfields

Principal Railways

- - - - Railways
Under Construction

Other Railways

┼ - - ┼ Railway Tunnels

·········· Principal Canals

PHYSICAL FEATURES

Perennial Streams

- - - Intermittent Streams

Perennial Lakes

Intermittent Lakes

Swamps and Marshes

Permanent Ice
and Glaciers

▲ 8848 Elevations in metres

▼ 8500 Sea Depths in metres

1134 Height of Lake Surface
Above Sea Level in metres

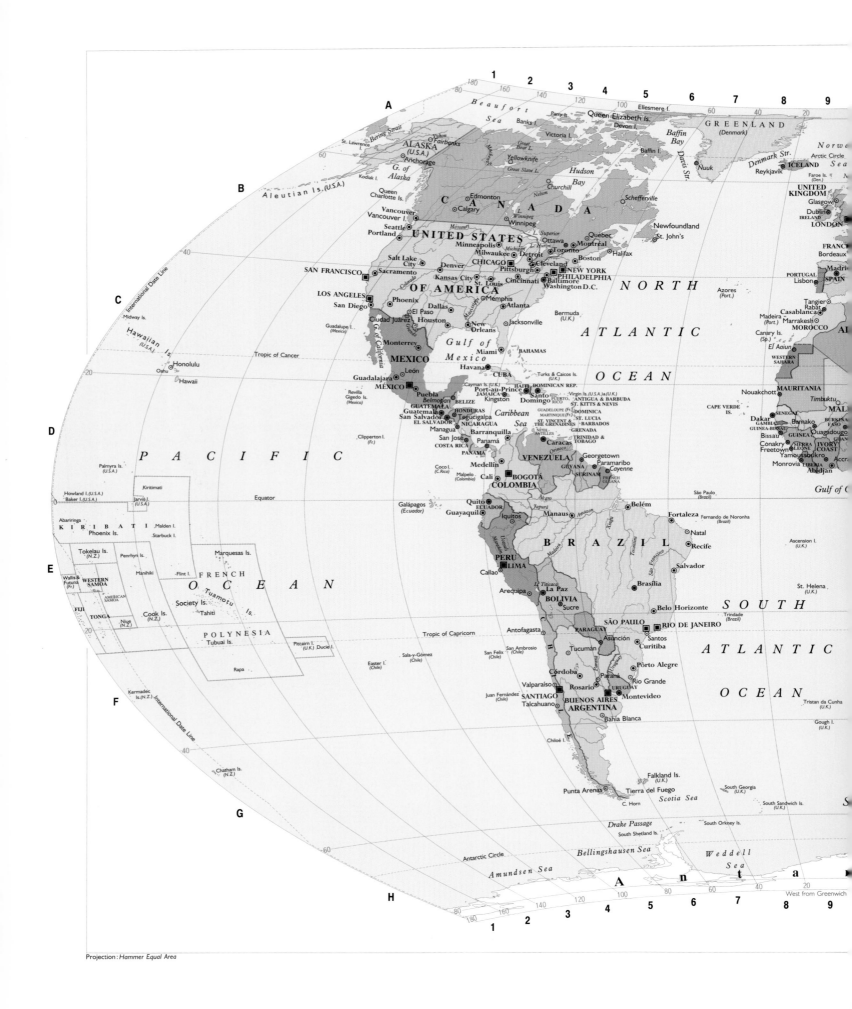

Projection: *Hammer Equal Area*

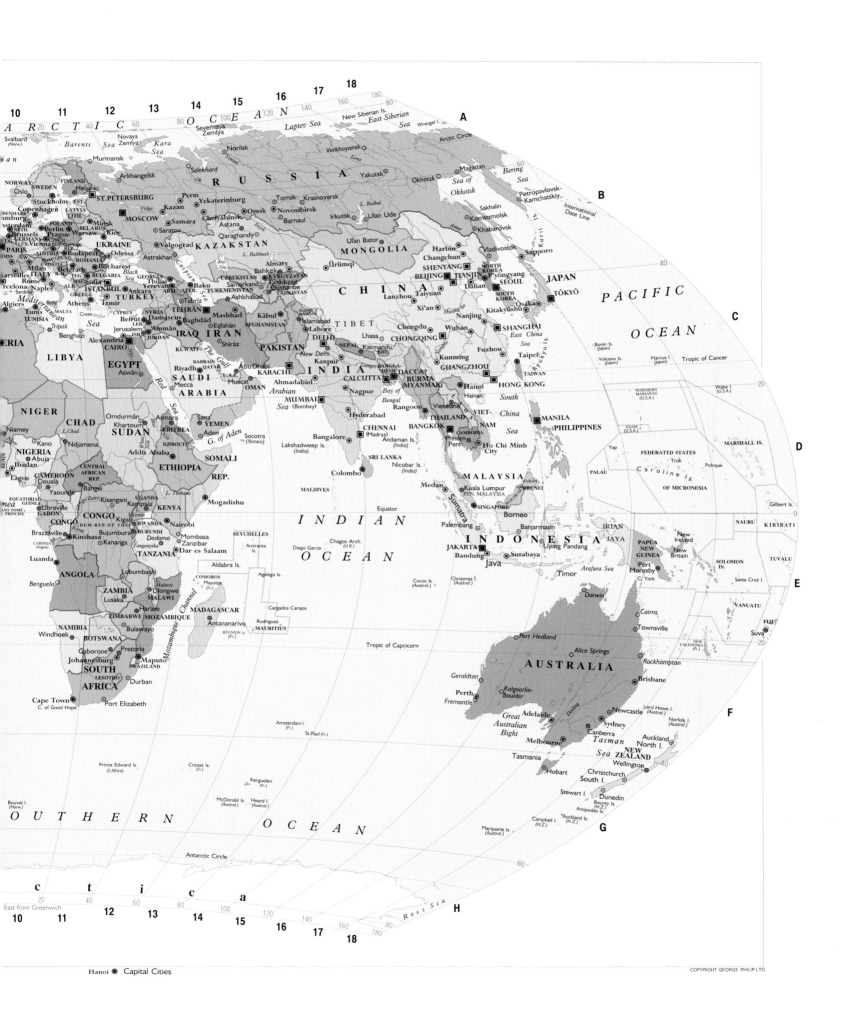

ARCTIC OCEAN

Svalbard *(Nor.)*
Barents Sea
Novaya Zemlya
Kara Sea
Severnaya Zemlya
Laptev Sea
New Siberian Is.
East Siberian Sea
Wrangel I.

A

Arctic Circle

Murmansk
NORWAY SWEDEN FINLAND Helsinki
Oslo Stockholm EST.
DENMARK Copenhagen LATVIA LITH.
ST.PETERSBURG
Perm Yekaterinburg
Arkhangelsk
Salekhard
Norilsk
Yenisey
Ob
RUSSIA
Verkhoyansk
Lena
Yakutsk
Okhotsk
Magadan
Bering Sea
Sea of Okhotsk
Petropavlovsk-Kamchatskiy
International Date Line

B

Hamburg Berlin POLAND MINSK
Amsterdam NETH.
Brussels Prague CZECH. Warsaw
Paris LUX. GERMANY Vienna SLOV.
MOSCOW
Volga Kazan
Samara
Saratov
Tomsk Krasnoyarsk
Omsk Novosibirsk
Irtysh Barnaul
Irkutsk L. Baikal Ulan Ude
Amur Khabarovsk
Komsomolsk
Sakhalin
Vladivostok Sapporo
Kuril Is.

Milan ITALY Belgrade CROATIA ROMANIA Bucharest
Barcelona Rome Naples Sofia BULGARIA Black Sea
Marseilles ALB. GREECE Istanbul TURKEY
Athens Ankara
Mediterranean Sea Crete CYPRUS
Algiers Tunis MALTA TUNISIA Tripoli Benghazi
UKRAINE Odessa Volgograd Astrakhan
Caspian Sea
GEORGIA Tbilisi ARM. AZER. Baku
Yerevan Tabriz
Aral Sea L. Balkhash
KAZAKSTAN
UZBEKISTAN Bishkek KYRGYZSTAN
Samarkand TAJIKISTAN Dushanbe
Almaty Ürümqi
MONGOLIA Ulan Bator
Harbin Changchun SHENYANG NORTH KOREA Pyongyang Vladivostok
BEIJING TIANJIN SEOUL SOUTH KOREA Dalian
JAPAN TŌKYŌ Ōsaka Kitakyūshū
PACIFIC
OCEAN

LIBYA EGYPT Cairo Alexandria
SYRIA Beirut Damascus LEB. Amman ISR. JORDAN
Baghdad IRAQ IRAN TEHRĀN Mashhad
Eşfahān Shīrāz
KUWAIT BAHRAIN QATAR Riyadh
AFGHANISTAN Kābul Islamabad Lahore PAKISTAN
TIBET Lhasa
CHINA Lanzhou Taiyuan Xi'an
Chengdu CHONGQING Wuhan Nanjing SHANGHAI East China Sea
Kunming GUANGZHOU Fuzhou Taipei TAIWAN
HONG KONG
Tropic of Cancer

SAUDI ARABIA Mecca
Red Sea U.A.E. Abu Dhabi Muscat OMAN
Aswān
NIGER CHAD SUDAN Omdurmân Khartoum ERITREA Asmara Sana'a YEMEN Aden
ETHIOPIA Addis Ababa DJIBOUTI SOMALI REP.
Karachi INDIA DELHI New Delhi Kanpur NEPAL Katmandu BHU. DACCA BANGLA. CALCUTTA BURMA (MYANMAR) Rangoon Hanoi Hainan
Ahmadabad Nagpur Bay of Bengal
MUMBAI (Bombay) Hyderabad
Arabian Sea
Bangalore CHENNAI (Madras) Andaman Is. (India) THAILAND BANGKOK VIET-NAM
South China Sea MANILA PHILIPPINES
Vientiane CAMBODIA Phnom Penh Ho Chi Minh City

INDIAN OCEAN

NIGERIA Abuja CAMEROON CENTRAL AFRICAN REP.
Lagos Douala Yaoundé Bangui
EQUATORIAL GUINEA GABON CONGO Brazzaville Kinshasa CONGO DEM. REP. OF THE
Luanda ANGOLA

MALDIVES
Colombo SRI LANKA Nicobar Is. (India)
MALAYSIA Medan Kuala Lumpur SINGAPORE Sumatra Palembang Borneo
BRUNEI Banjarmasin

D

FEDERATED STATES OF MICRONESIA
PALAU Yap Caroline Is. Truk Pohnpei
MARSHALL IS.

Kisangani UGANDA KENYA Nairobi Kampala L. Turkana
RWANDA Kigali BURUNDI Bujumbura Mombasa Zanzibar
TANZANIA Dodoma Dar es Salaam
SEYCHELLES Amirante Is. Aldabra Is.
Equator
Ujung Pandang INDONESIA JAKARTA Bandung Java Surabaya IRIAN JAYA PAPUA NEW GUINEA
NAURU KIRIBATI Gilbert Is.
New Ireland New Britain SOLOMON IS. Santa Cruz I. TUVALU

E

ZAMBIA Lusaka MALAWI Lilongwe
NAMIBIA BOTSWANA ZIMBABWE MOZAMBIQUE
Lubumbashi Benguela
COMOROS Mayotte MADAGASCAR Antananarivo RÉUNION MAURITIUS
Timor Arafura Sea Port Moresby C. York
Darwin
VANUATU NEW CALEDONIA FIJI Suva

Windhoek Gaborone Pretoria Johannesburg
SOUTH AFRICA SWAZILAND LESOTHO Durban Maputo Bulawayo Harare
Tropic of Capricorn
Port Hedland Alice Springs AUSTRALIA Rockhampton Brisbane
Geraldton Perth Fremantle Kalgoorlie-Boulder
Great Australian Bight Adelaide Sydney Canberra Newcastle
Melbourne Tasman Sea NEW ZEALAND
Lord Howe I. Norfolk I. Auckland North I. Wellington

F

Cape Town C. of Good Hope Port Elizabeth
Tasmania Hobart Christchurch South I. Dunedin

Amsterdam I. St.Paul
Prince Edward Is. Crozet Is. Kerguelen McDonald Is. Heard I.
Bouvet I.
SOUTHERN OCEAN
Stewart I. Bounty Is. Antipodes Is. Campbell I. Auckland Is. Macquarie Is.

G

Antarctic Circle
Antarctica
Ross Sea
H

East from Greenwich

Hanoi ● Capital Cities

COPYRIGHT GEORGE PHILIP LTD.

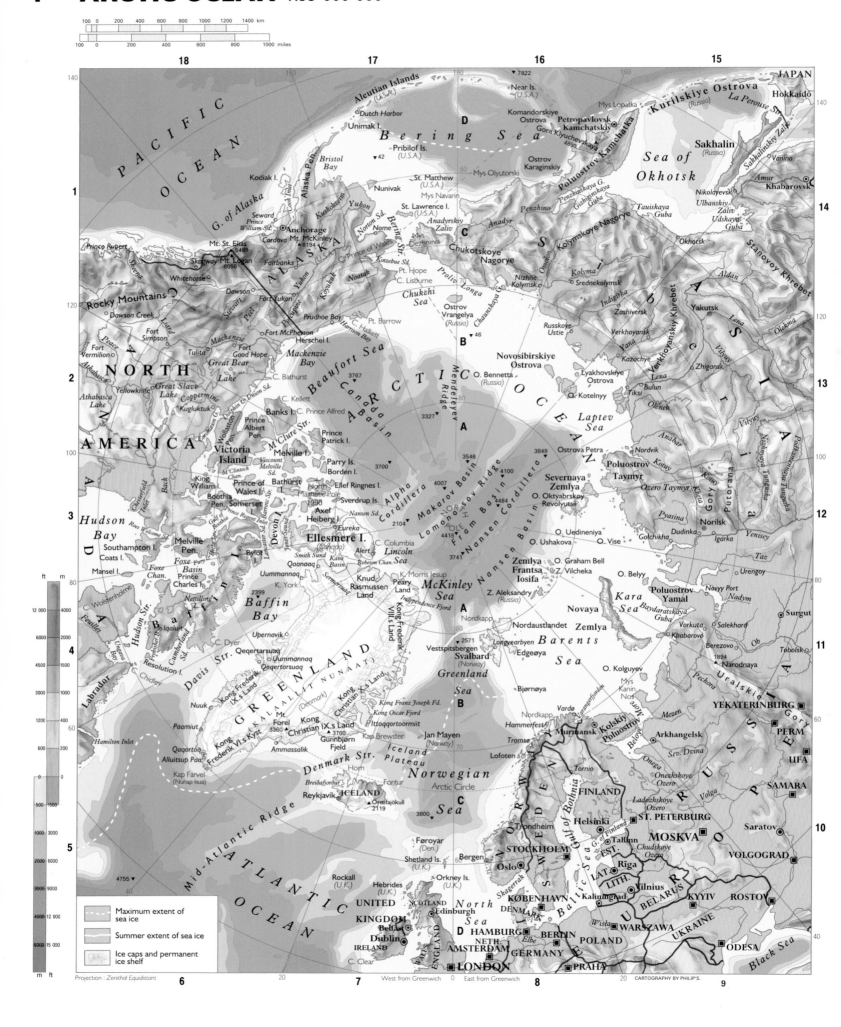

Projection : Zenithal Equidistant   West from Greenwich   East from Greenwich   CARTOGRAPHY BY PHILIP'S.

Maximum extent of sea ice

Summer extent of sea ice

Ice caps and permanent ice shelf

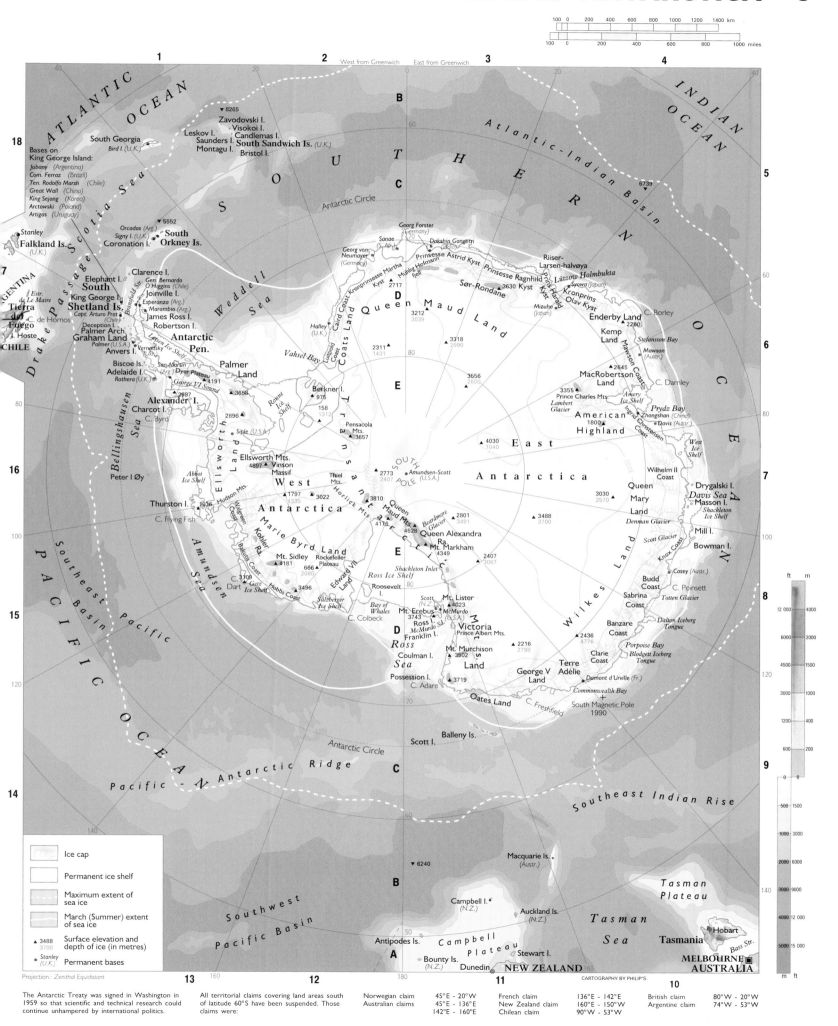

100 0   200 400 600 800 1000 1200 1400 km
100 0   200   400   600   800   1000 miles

1   2   West from Greenwich | East from Greenwich   3   4

ATLANTIC OCEAN

INDIAN OCEAN

B

18

Bases on
King George Island:
Jubany (Argentina)
Com. Ferraz (Brazil)
Ten. Rodolfo Marsh (Chile)
Great Wall (China)
King Sejong (Korea)
Arctowski (Poland)
Artigas (Uruguay)

South Georgia
Bird I. (U.K.)

Zavodovski I.
Visokoi I.
Leskov I.   Candlemas I.
Saunders I.   South Sandwich Is. (U.K.)
Montagu I.   Bristol I.

▼8265

Atlantic–Indian Basin

▲6739

5

S O U T H E R N

Antarctic Circle

Orcadas (Arg.)   ▲5552
Signy I. (U.K.)   South
Coronation I.   Orkney Is.

Georg Forster
(Germany)
Sanae   Dakshin Gangotri
(S. Afr.)   (India)
Georg von   Prinsesse Astrid Kyst
Neumayer   Prinsesse Ragnhild
(Germany)   Kyst
Prinsesse Martha   Mühlig Hofmann   Kyst
Kyst   fjell

Riiser-
Larsen-halvøya

7

ARGENTINA

Stanley
Falkland Is.
(U.K.)

Scotia Sea

Clarence I.
Elephant I.   Gen. Bernardo
South   O'Higgins (Chile)
King George I.   Joinville I.
Shetland Is.   Esperanza (Arg.)
Capt. Arturo Prat   Marambio (Arg.)
(Chile)   James Ross I.
Deception I.   Robertson I.
Palmer Arch.

Coats Land   Kronprinsesse
Caird Coast   ▲2717
Halley   Queen Maud Land
(U.K.)

Sør-Rondane
▲3630 Kyst   Prins Harald
Prins Olav Kyst   Lützow Holmbukta
Syowa (Japan)
Kronprins
Olav Kyst

Enderby Land   C. Borley
▲2280
Kemp
Land   Stefansson Bay

6

Estr.
de Le Maire
Tierra
del
Fuego
I. Hoste
CHILE
C. de Hornos

Drake Passage

Bellingshausen Sea

Graham Land
Palmer (U.S.A.)
Anvers I.   Vernadsky
(U.K.)
Antarctic
Pen.
Palmer
Land
Biscoe Is.   San Martin   Dyer Plateau
Adelaide I.   (Arg.)
Rothera (U.K.)   ▲4191
Alexander I.   ▲2987   ▲3658
Charcot I.   C. Byrd
Peter I Øy   ▲2896

Weddell
Sea

Vahsel Bay   Georg von
Luitpold   3212
Coast   3039

Ronne
Ice
Shelf

▲975
158
1312

Berkner I.
Pensacola
Mts.
▲3657

▲2311   3318
1431   2990

▲3656
2600

Transantarctic

East

▲3355

Prince Charles Mts.
Lambert
Glacier

MacRobertson
Land

American
Highland
1800

▲2645

Mawson (Austr.)
C. Damley

Amery
Ice Shelf

Prydz Bay
Zhongshan (China)
Davis (Austr.)

West Ice Shelf

16

Abbot
Ice Shelf

Ellsworth
Land

Siple (U.S.A.)

Ellsworth Mts.
▲4897   Vinson
Massif

Thiel
Mts.
▲2773   ●Amundsen-Scott
2407   (U.S.A.)

SOUTH
POLE

▲4030
1040

Antarctica

▲3030
2570

Queen
Mary
Land

Wilhelm II
Coast

Drygalski I.
Davis Sea
Masson I.
Shackleton
Ice Shelf

7

15

PACIFIC

Southeast Pacific

Thurston I.   ▲1797   ▲3022
1036   4335
Hudson Mts.
Amundsen
Sea
Walgreen Coast
C. Flying Fish

West
Antarctica

Marie Byrd Land

Kohler Ra.
Bakutis
Coast
Mt. Sidley   Rockefeller
▲4181   666 ▲   Plateau
2080
▲3705   Getz   ▲3496
Dart   Ice Shelf
Hobbs Coast
Sulzberger
Ice Shelf
Edward VII
Land

▲3810
Queen
Maud Mts.
4116
▲4528
Beardmore
Glacier   Queen Alexandra
Ra.
Mt. Markham
▲4349

Horlick Mts.

Shackleton Inlet
Roosevelt
I.
Ross Ice Shelf

Bay of
Whales
C. Colbeck

Scott   Mt. Lister
(N.Z.)   ▲4023
McMurdo
3743   (U.S.A.)
Mt. Erebus
Ross I.
Franklin I.

▲2801
3491

▲3488
3700

▲2407
3087

Scott Glacier

Knox Coast
Totten Glacier

Budd
Coast

Sabrina
Coast

Mill I.
Bowman I.
Casey (Austr.)
C. Poinsett

8

Victoria
Prince Albert Mts.

Coulman I.
Mt. Murchison
▲3502

Possession I.
C. Adare   ▲3719

Ross
Sea

▲2216
2798

Land

George V
Land

Terre
Adélie

▲2436
776

Clarie
Coast

Porpoise Bay
Blodgett Iceberg
Tongue

Dalton Iceberg
Tongue

Banzare
Coast

9

14

Oates Land   C. Freshfield

Balleny Is.

Scott I.

Antarctic Circle

Commonwealth Bay
+ South Magnetic Pole
1990

Dumont d'Urville (Fr.)

Southeast Indian Rise

Pacific – Antarctic Ridge

Macquarie Is.
(Austr.)

Tasman
Plateau

B

▼6240

Campbell I.
(N.Z.)   Auckland Is.
(N.Z.)

Tasman

Sea

Southwest
Pacific Basin

Antipodes Is.
(N.Z.)   Campbell
Plateau
Bounty Is.   Stewart I.
(N.Z.)
Dunedin   NEW ZEALAND

A

Tasmania   Hobart

MELBOURNE
AUSTRALIA   Bass Str.

13   160   12   180   11   160   CARTOGRAPHY BY PHILIP'S   10

ft   m
12 000   4000
6000   2000
4500   1500
3000   1000
1200   400
600   200

500   1500
1000   3000
2000   6000
3000   9000
4000   12 000
5000   15 000
m   ft

Legend:
Ice cap
Permanent ice shelf
Maximum extent of sea ice
March (Summer) extent of sea ice
▲3488 / 3700   Surface elevation and depth of ice (in metres)
●Stanley (U.K.)   Permanent bases

Projection: Zenithal Equidistant

The Antarctic Treaty was signed in Washington in 1959 so that scientific and technical research could continue unhampered by international politics.

All territorial claims covering land areas south of latitude 60°S have been suspended. Those claims were:

Norwegian claim   45°E – 20°W
Australian claims   45°E – 136°E
     142°E – 160°E

French claim   136°E – 142°E
New Zealand claim   160°E – 150°W
Chilean claim   90°W – 53°W

British claim   80°W – 20°W
Argentine claim   74°W – 53°W

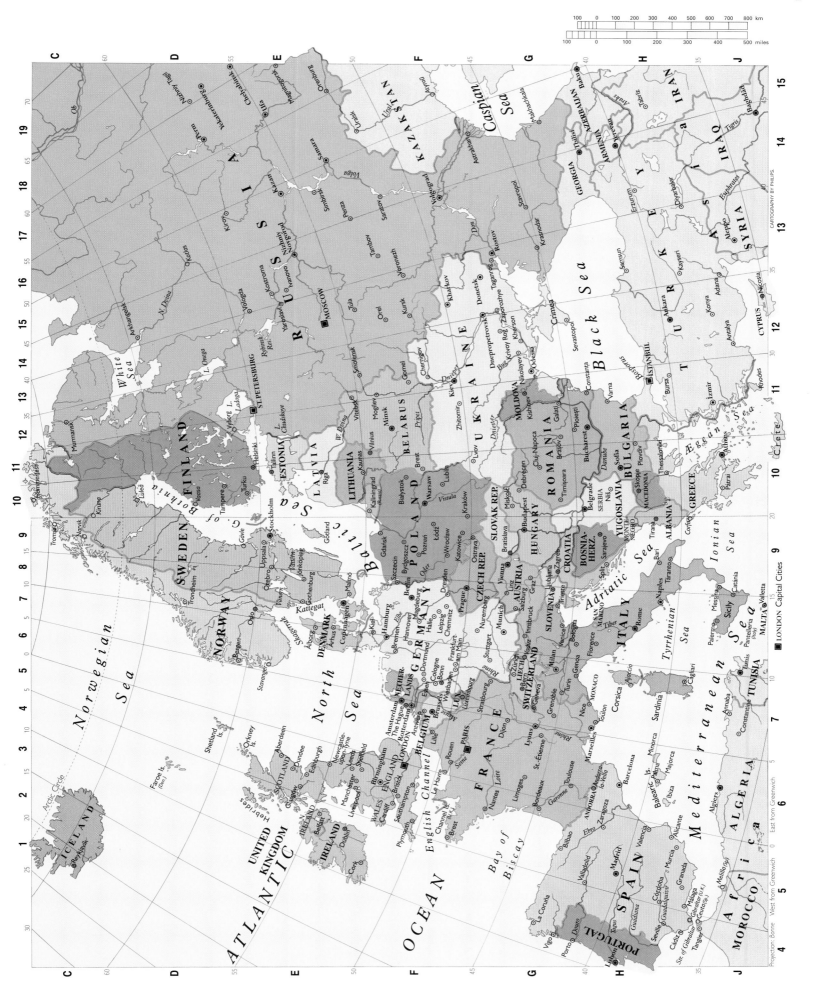

SCANDINAVIA 1:5 000 000

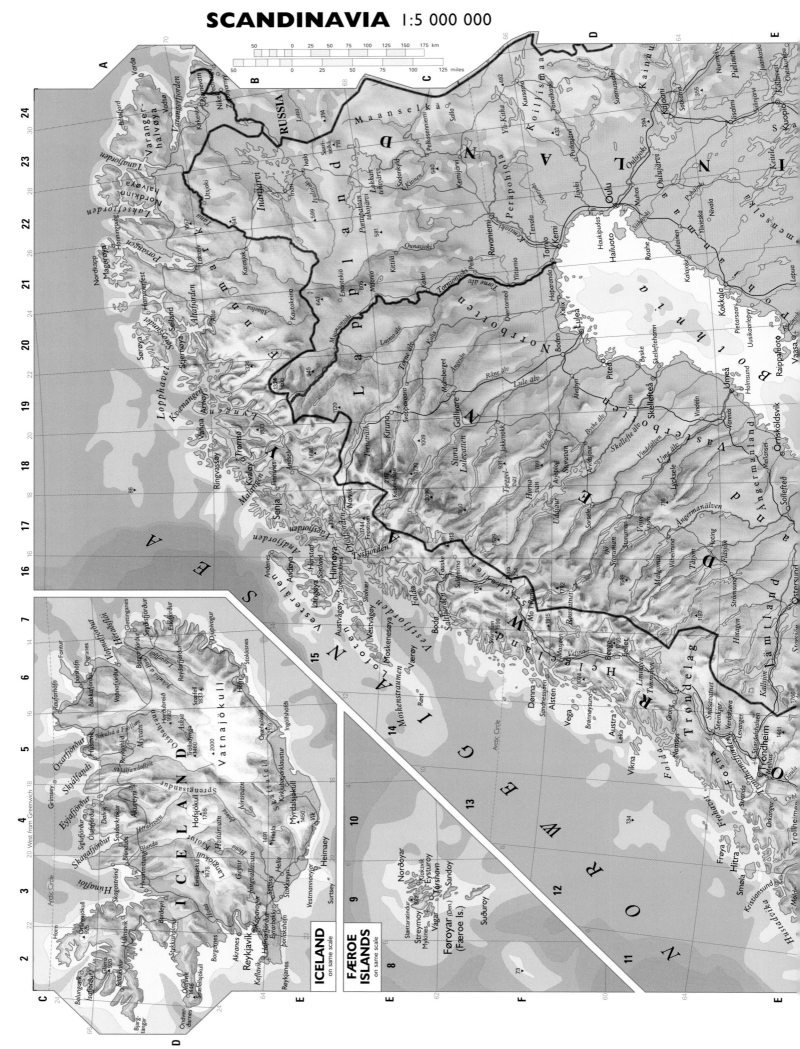

ICELAND
on same scale

FÆROE
ISLANDS
on same scale

COPYRIGHT GEORGE PHILIP LTD

Projection: Conical with two standard parallels

East from Greenwich

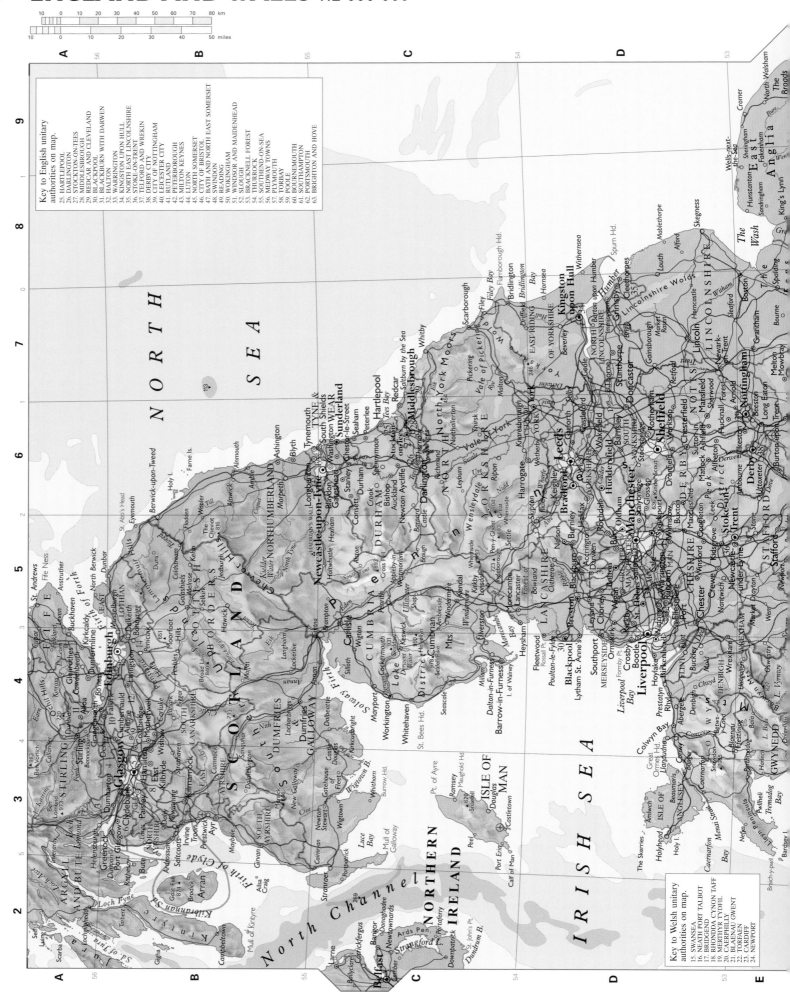

Key to English unitary authorities on map.

25. HARTLEPOOL
26. DARLINGTON
27. STOCKTON-ON-TEES
28. MIDDLESBROUGH
29. REDCAR AND CLEVELAND
30. BLACKPOOL
31. BLACKBURN WITH DARWEN
32. HALTON
33. WARRINGTON
34. KINGSTON UPON HULL
35. NORTH EAST LINCOLNSHIRE
36. STOKE-ON-TRENT
37. TELFORD AND WREKIN
38. DERBY CITY
39. CITY OF NOTTINGHAM
40. LEICESTER CITY
41. RUTLAND
42. PETERBOROUGH
43. MILTON KEYNES
44. LUTON
45. NORTH SOMERSET
46. CITY OF BRISTOL
47. BATH AND NORTH EAST SOMERSET
48. SWINDON
49. READING
50. WOKINGHAM
51. WINDSOR AND MAIDENHEAD
52. SLOUGH
53. BRACKNELL FOREST
54. THURROCK
55. SOUTHEND-ON-SEA
56. MEDWAY TOWNS
57. PLYMOUTH
58. TORBAY
59. POOLE
60. BOURNEMOUTH
61. SOUTHAMPTON
62. PORTSMOUTH
63. BRIGHTON AND HOVE

Key to Welsh unitary authorities on map.

15. SWANSEA
16. NEATH PORT TALBOT
17. BRIDGEND
18. RHONDDA CYNON TAFF
19. MERTHYR TYDFIL
20. CAERPHILLY
21. BLAENAU GWENT
22. TORFAEN
23. CARDIFF
24. NEWPORT

II

ENGLAND

WALES

FRANCE

NORMANDIE

HAUTE-NORMANDIE

SEINE-MARITIME

CALVADOS

MANCHE

Cotentin

ENGLISH CHANNEL

LA MANCHE

Strait of Dover

Bristol Channel

Cardigan Bay

Lyme Bay

Baie de la Seine

Baie de la Somme

CHANNEL ISLANDS (U.K.)

Guernsey

Jersey

Alderney

Sark

Herm

St. Peter Port

St. Helier

ISLE OF WIGHT

CORNWALL

DEVON

DORSET

SOMERSET

WILTSHIRE

HAMPSHIRE

BERKSHIRE

SURREY

KENT

ESSEX

SUFFOLK

NORFOLK

SUSSEX

WEST SUSSEX

EAST SUSSEX

HERTS

BUCKS

OXON

GLOUCS

WORCESTER

HEREFORD

SHROPSHIRE

WARWICK

NORTHAMPTON

LEICESTER

CAMBRIDGE

BEDFORD

NEW FOREST

Exmoor

Dartmoor

Bodmin Moor

POWYS

CEREDIGION

CARMARTHENSHIRE

PEMBROKESHIRE

GLAMORGAN

VALE OF GLAMORGAN

MONMOUTHSHIRE

Brecon Beacons

LONDON

GREATER LONDON

BIRMINGHAM

Cardiff

Swansea

Newport

Bristol

Bath

Gloucester

Cheltenham

Worcester

Hereford

Plymouth

Exeter

Torquay

Bournemouth

Southampton

Portsmouth

Brighton

Hove

Worthing

Eastbourne

Hastings

Dover

Folkestone

Canterbury

Margate

Ramsgate

Deal

Colchester

Ipswich

Cambridge

Peterborough

Northampton

Leicester

Coventry

Oxford

Reading

Swindon

Salisbury

Winchester

Newport (Isle of Wight)

Cherbourg

Le Havre

Rouen

Dieppe

Caen

Boulogne-sur-Mer

Calais

Lisieux

Évreux

Bayeux

COPYRIGHT GEORGE PHILIP LTD.

Projection: Lambert's Conformal Conic

Isles of Scilly
On same scale

Isles of Scilly
St. Mary's
Tresco

East from Greenwich

West from Greenwich

ft m
3000 1000
1500 500
600 200
300 100
0
−50 −150
−200 −600
m ft

10 0 10 20 30 40 50 60 70 80 km
10 0 10 20 30 40 50 miles

Key to Scottish unitary authorities on map
1. CITY OF ABERDEEN
2. DUNDEE CITY
3. WEST DUNBARTONSHIRE
4. EAST DUNBARTONSHIRE
5. CITY OF GLASGOW
6. INVERCLYDE
7. RENFREWSHIRE
8. EAST RENFREWSHIRE
9. NORTH LANARKSHIRE
10. FALKIRK
11. CLACKMANNANSHIRE
12. WEST LOTHIAN
13. CITY OF EDINBURGH
14. MIDLOTHIAN

ORKNEY IS. On same scale
ORKNEY
Mainland
Kirkwall
Stromness
Scapa Flow
Hoy
South Ronaldsay
Westray
Rousay
Sanday
Stronsay
Eday
Papa Westray
North Ronaldsay
Duncansby Head
John o' Groats
Thurso
Dunnet Hd.
Stroma
Sinclair's Bay

SHETLAND IS. On same scale
SHETLAND
Mainland
Lerwick
Unst
Yell
Fetlar
Whalsay
Bressay
Foula
Sumburgh Hd.
St. Magnus Bay

SCOTLAND
Inverness
Aberdeen
Dundee
Perth
Stirling
Glasgow
Edinburgh
Fort William
Oban
Ben Nevis
Loch Ness
HIGHLANDS
Grampian Mountains
Cairngorm Mts.
MORAY
ABERDEENSHIRE
ANGUS
FIFE
PERTH
KINROSS
ARGYLL AND BUTE
NORTH AYRSHIRE
SOUTH AYRSHIRE
EAST AYRSHIRE
SOUTH LANARKSHIRE
SCOTTISH BORDERS
DUMFRIES & GALLOWAY
Southern Uplands
Cheviot Hills
WESTERN ISLES
Lewis
Harris
North Uist
South Uist
Benbecula
Barra
Skye
Mull
Islay
Jura
Arran
Kintyre
Stornoway
Butt of Lewis
C. Wrath
Cape Wrath
Thurso
Wick
Fraserburgh
Peterhead
Stonehaven
Montrose
Arbroath
St. Andrews
Ayr
Stranraer
Dumfries
Carlisle
Berwick-upon-Tweed
Newcastle-upon-Tyne
ENGLAND
NORTHUMBERLAND
CUMBRIA
DURHAM
NORTHERN IRELAND
Belfast
ATLANTIC OCEAN
NORTH SEA
North Channel
Firth of Clyde
Firth of Forth
Moray Firth
Pentland Firth
Solway Firth

ft m scale
Projection: Lambert's Conformal Conic
West from Greenwich
COPYRIGHT GEORGE PHILIP LTD.

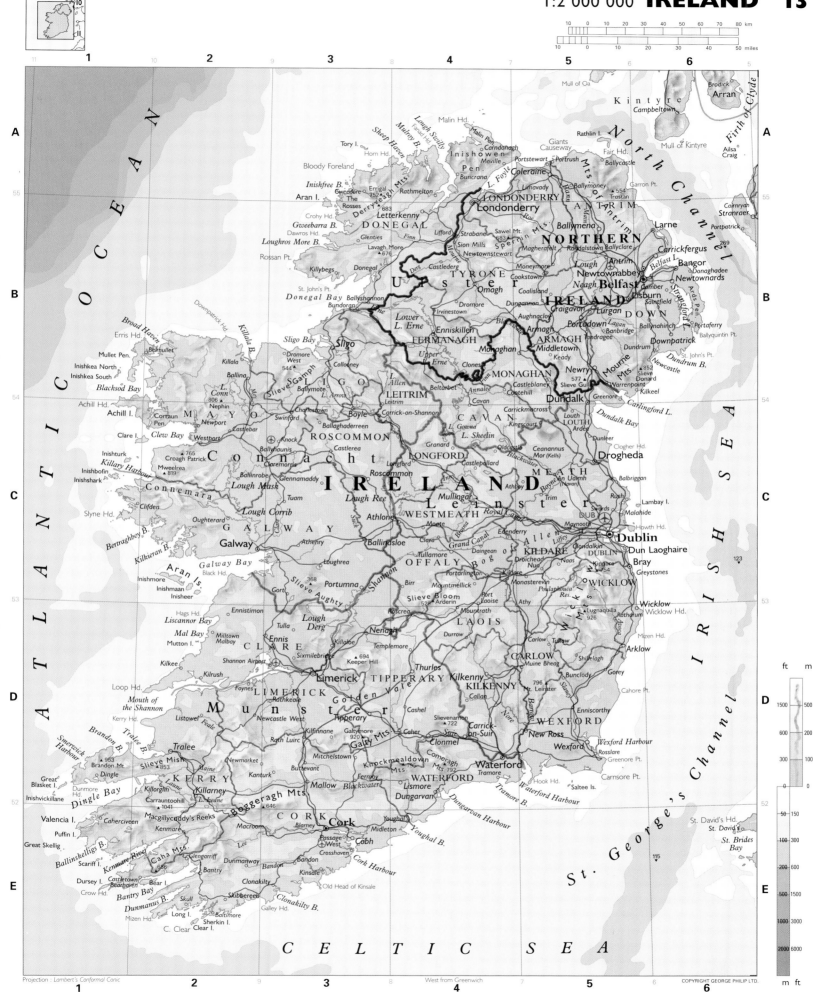

10 0 10 20 30 40 50 60 70 80 km
10 0   10   20   30   40   50 miles

Projection : Lambert's Conformal Conic

West from Greenwich

COPYRIGHT GEORGE PHILIP LTD.

m ft

Underlined towns give their name to the administrative area in which they stand.

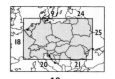

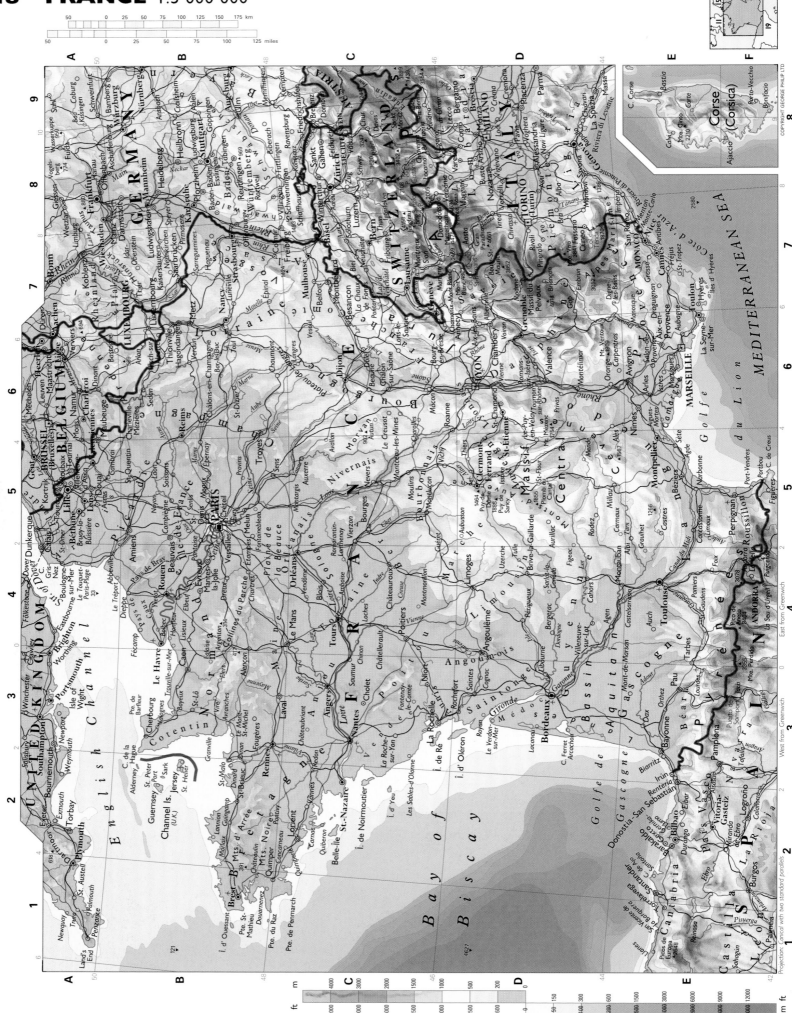

Projection: Conical with two standard parallels

COPYRIGHT GEORGE PHILIP LTD

COPYRIGHT GEORGE PHILIP LTD

Projection: Conical with two standard parallels

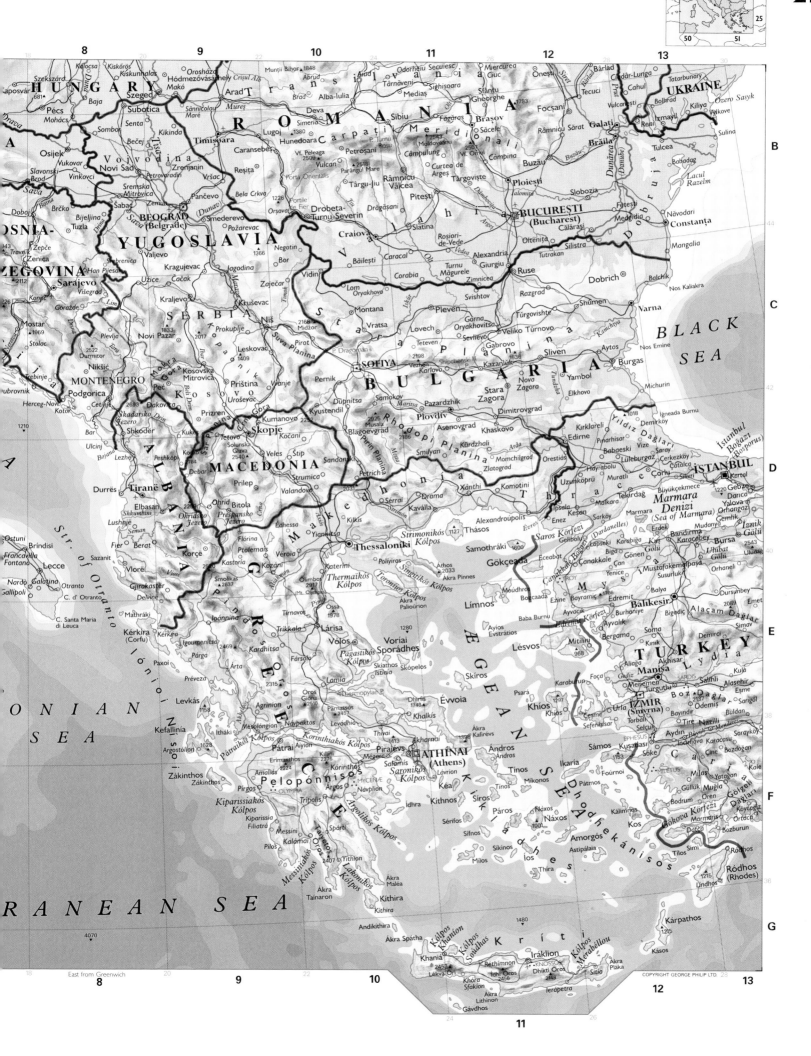

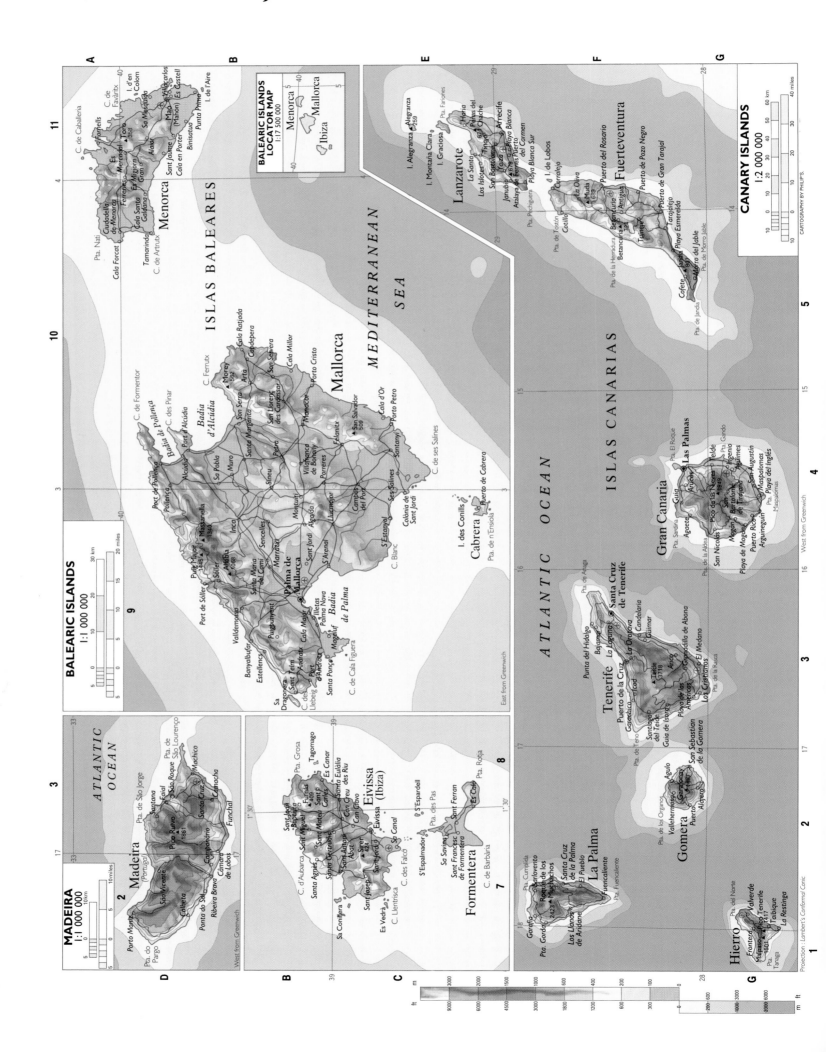

THE BALEARICS, THE CANARIES AND MADEIRA

BALEARIC ISLANDS LOCATOR MAP
1:17 500 000

Menorca
Mallorca
Ibiza

BALEARIC ISLANDS
1:1 000 000

CANARY ISLANDS
1:2 000 000

CARTOGRAPHY BY PHILIP'S.

MADEIRA
1:1 000 000

Projection : Lambert's Conformal Conic

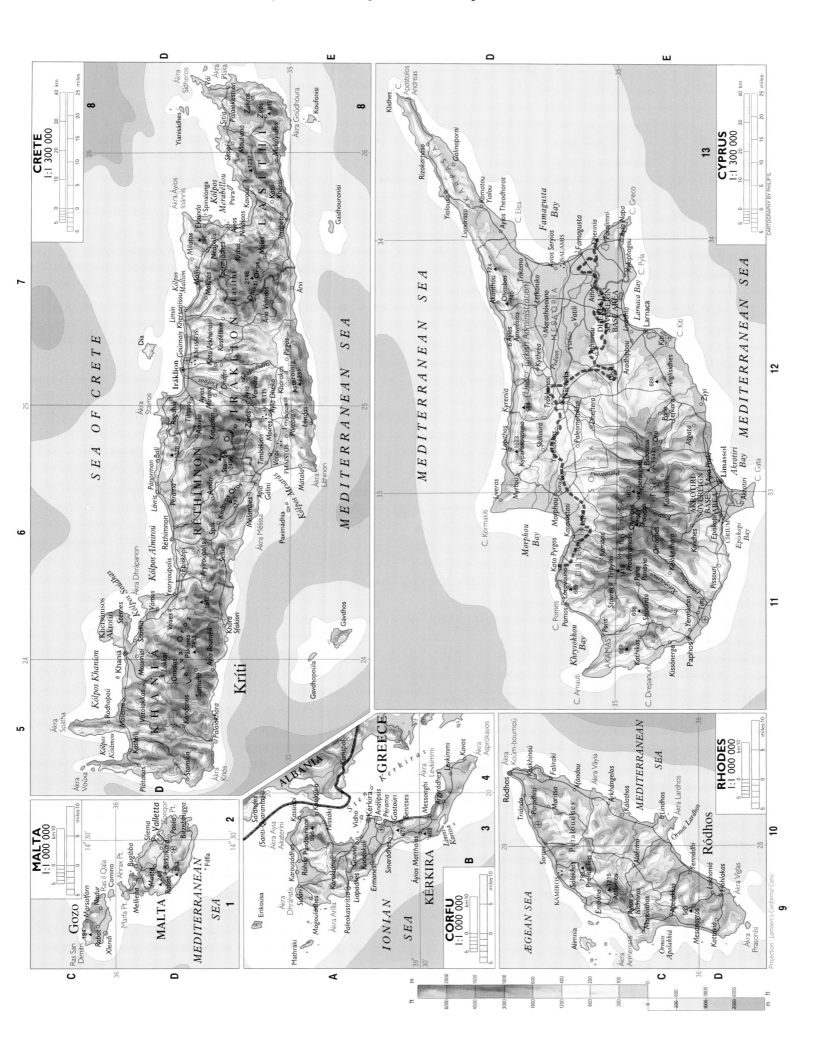

CRETE
1:1 300 000

CYPRUS
1:1 300 000

CARTOGRAPHY BY PHILIP'S

MALTA
1:1 000 000

CORFU
1:1 000 000

RHODES
1:1 000 000

Projection: Lambert's Conformal Conic

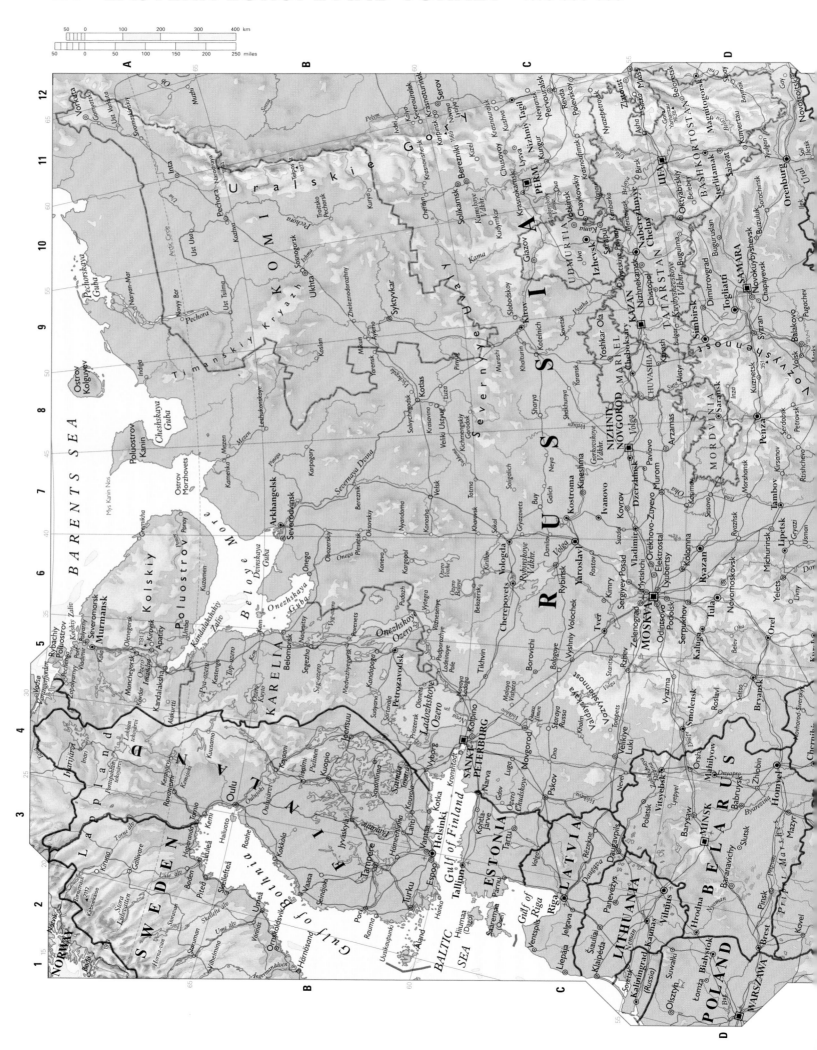

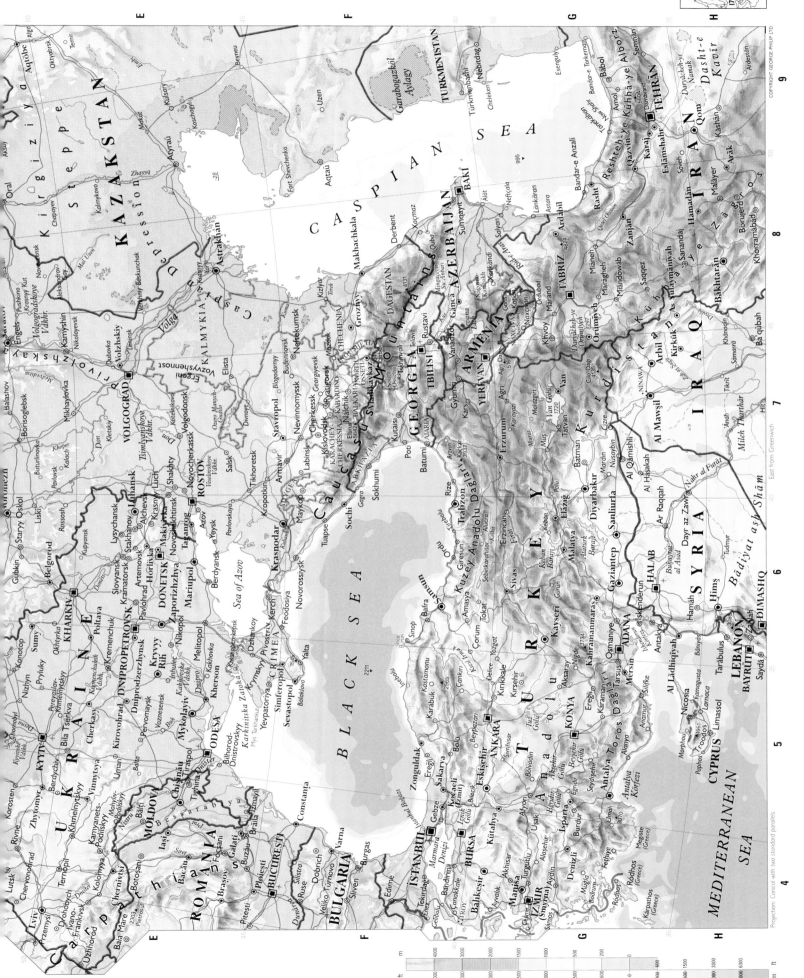

COPYRIGHT GEORGE PHILIP LTD.

9

8

7

6

5

4

East from Greenwich

Projection: Conical with two standard parallels

K A Z A K S T A N

K i r g i z i y a   S t e p p e

C a s p i a n   D e p r e s s i o n

TURKMENISTAN

Garabogazköl Aylagy

C A S P I A N   S E A

AZERBAIJAN

BAKI

I R A N

TEHRĀN

Dasht-e Kavir

GEORGIA

TBILISI

ARMENIA

YEREVAN

DAGESTAN

Caucasus Mountains

VOLGOGRAD

ROSTOV

KHARKIV

U K R A I N E

KYIV

DNIPROPETROVSK

DONETSK

Sea of Azov

CRIMEA

ODESA

MOLDOVA

ROMANIA

BUCUREȘTI

BULGARIA

B L A C K   S E A

T U R K E Y

ANKARA

İSTANBUL

BURSA

İZMİR

A n a t o l i a

KONYA

ADANA

CYPRUS

MEDITERRANEAN SEA

S Y R I A

LEBANON

BAYRŪT

DIMASHQ

I R A Q

Al Mawṣil

Arbil

Kurdistan

TABRĪZ

m / ft

12 000 — 4000

9000 — 3000

6000 — 2000

4500 — 1500

3000 — 1000

1500 — 600

600 — 200

0 — 0

200 — 600

1500 — 3000

6000 — 2000

COPYRIGHT GEORGE PHILIP LTD.

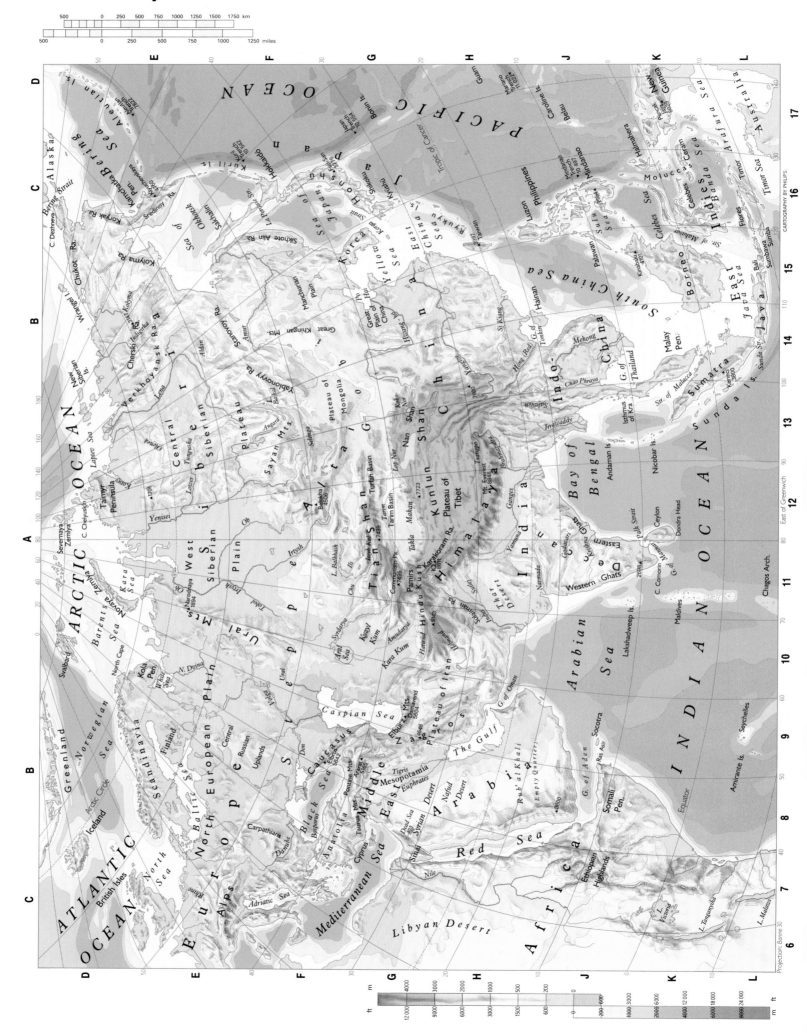

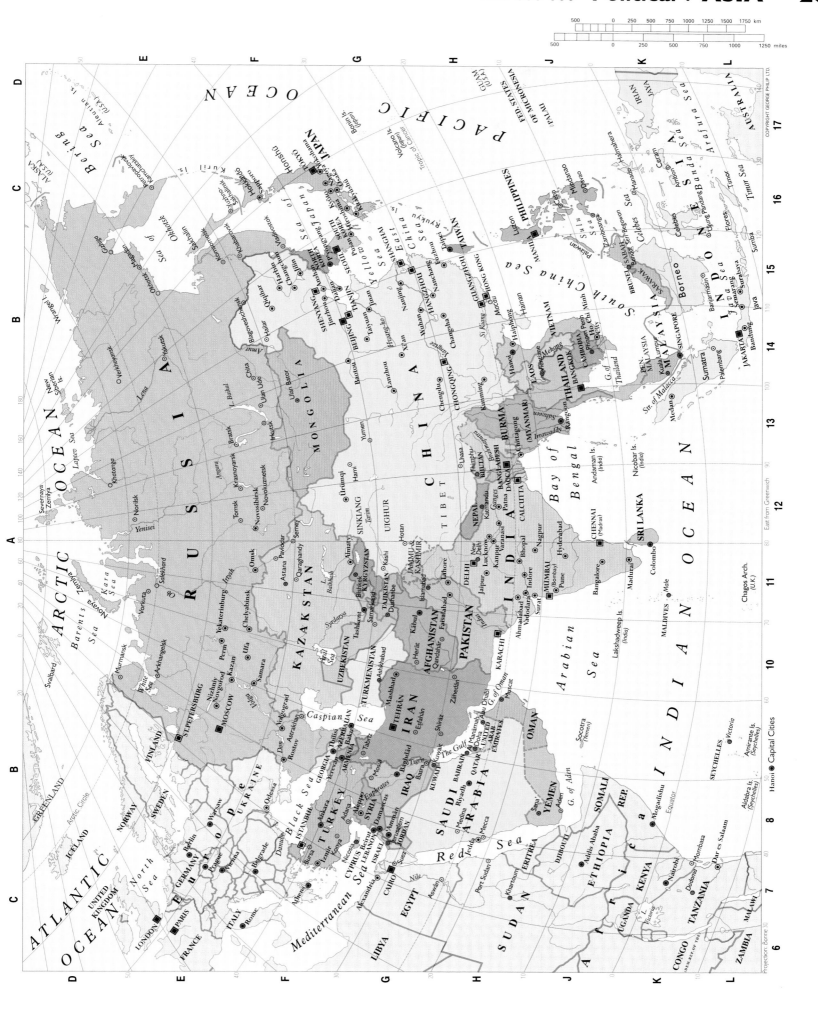

JAPAN 1:5 000 000

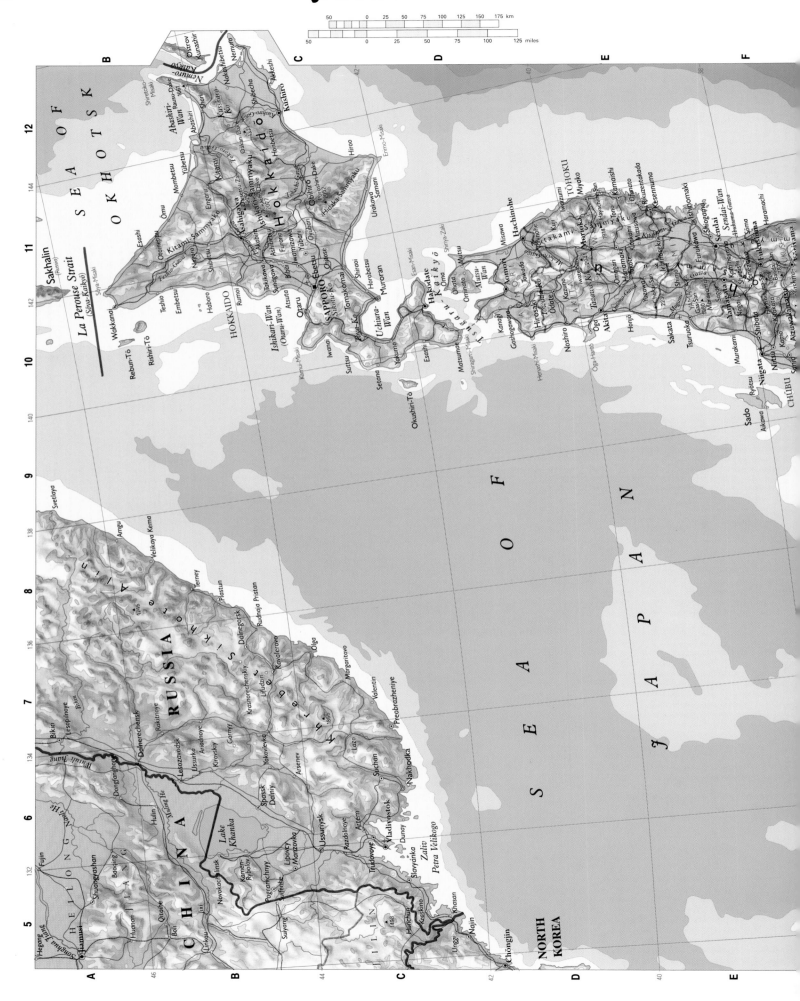

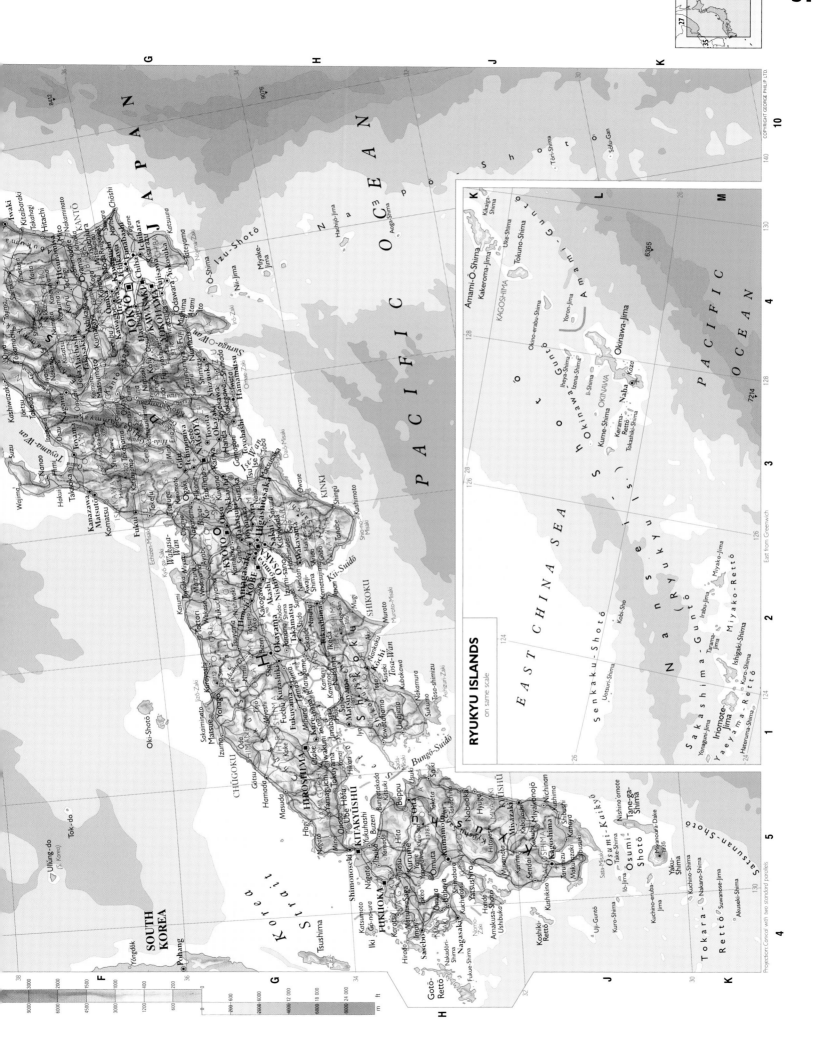

31

RYUKYU ISLANDS
on same scale

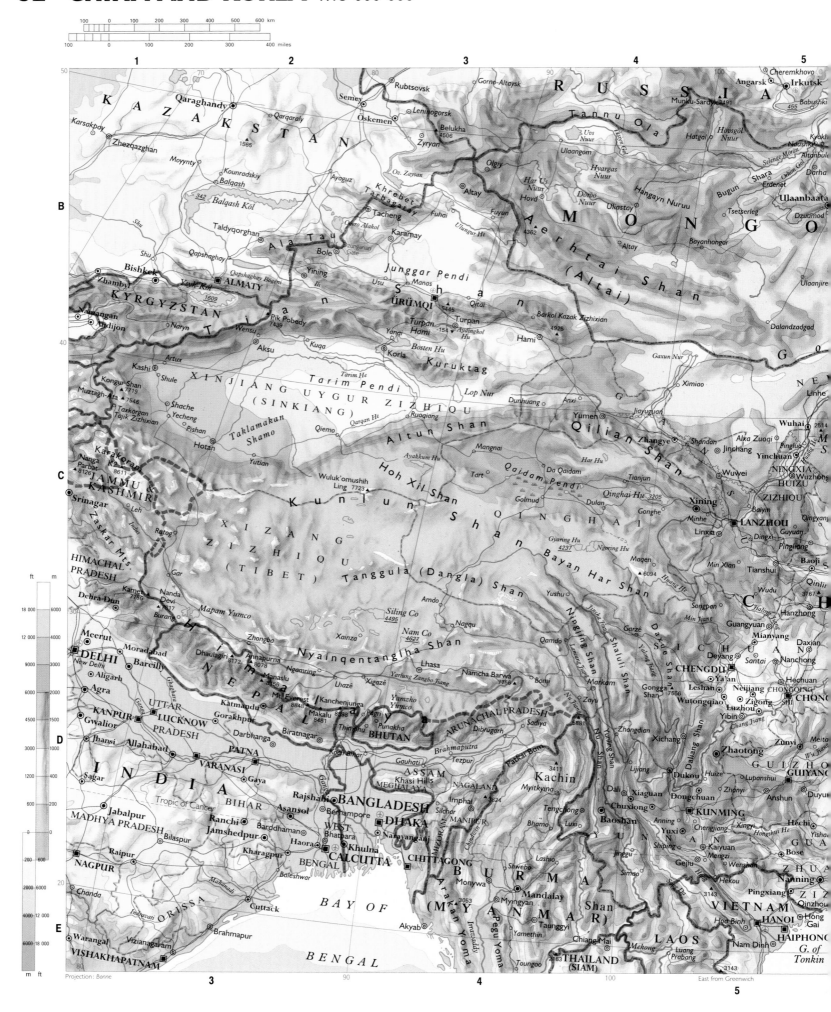

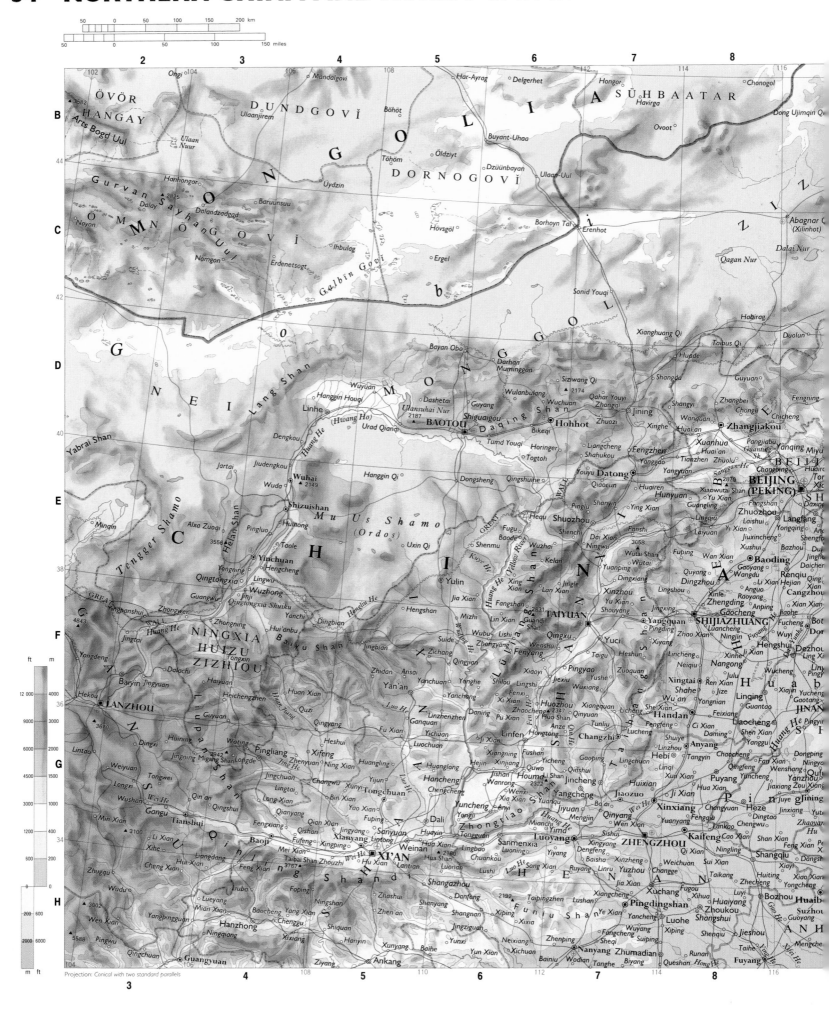

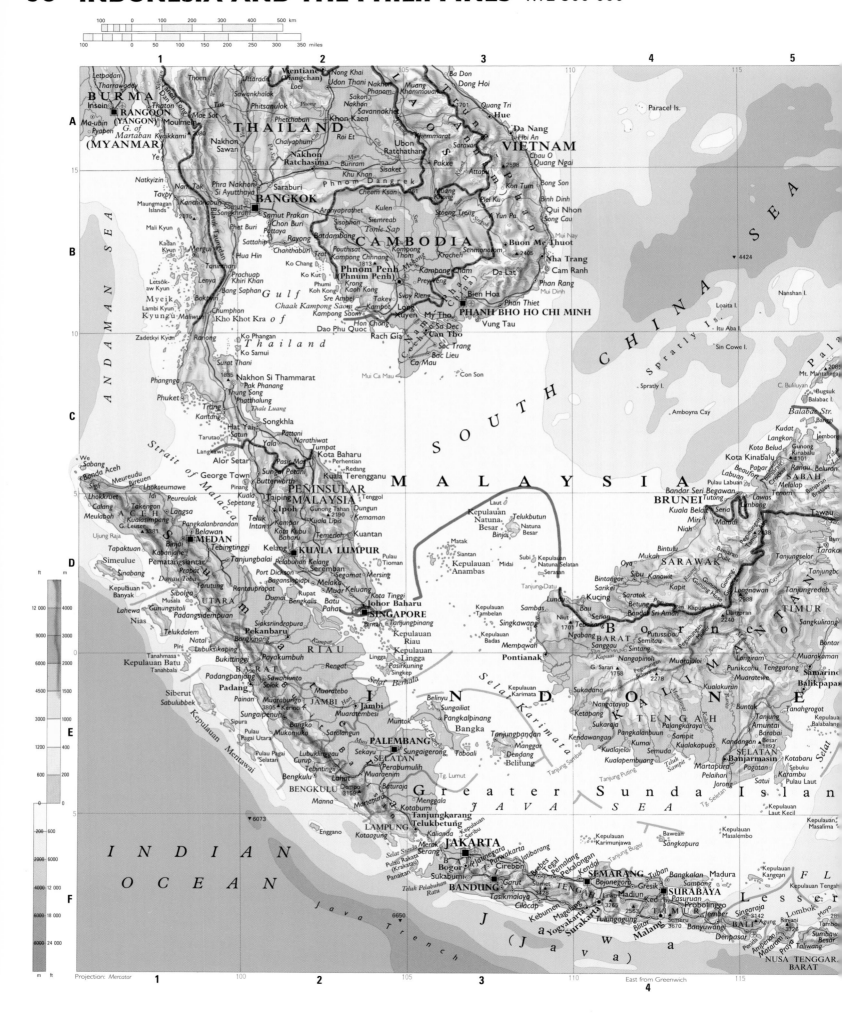

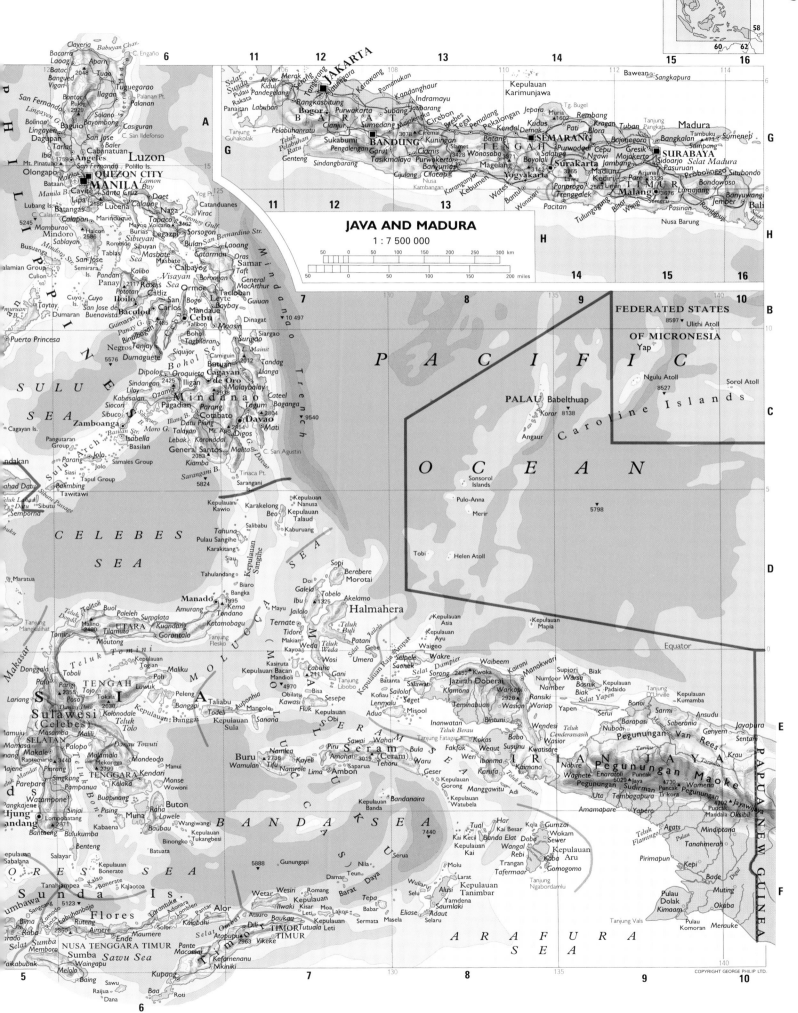

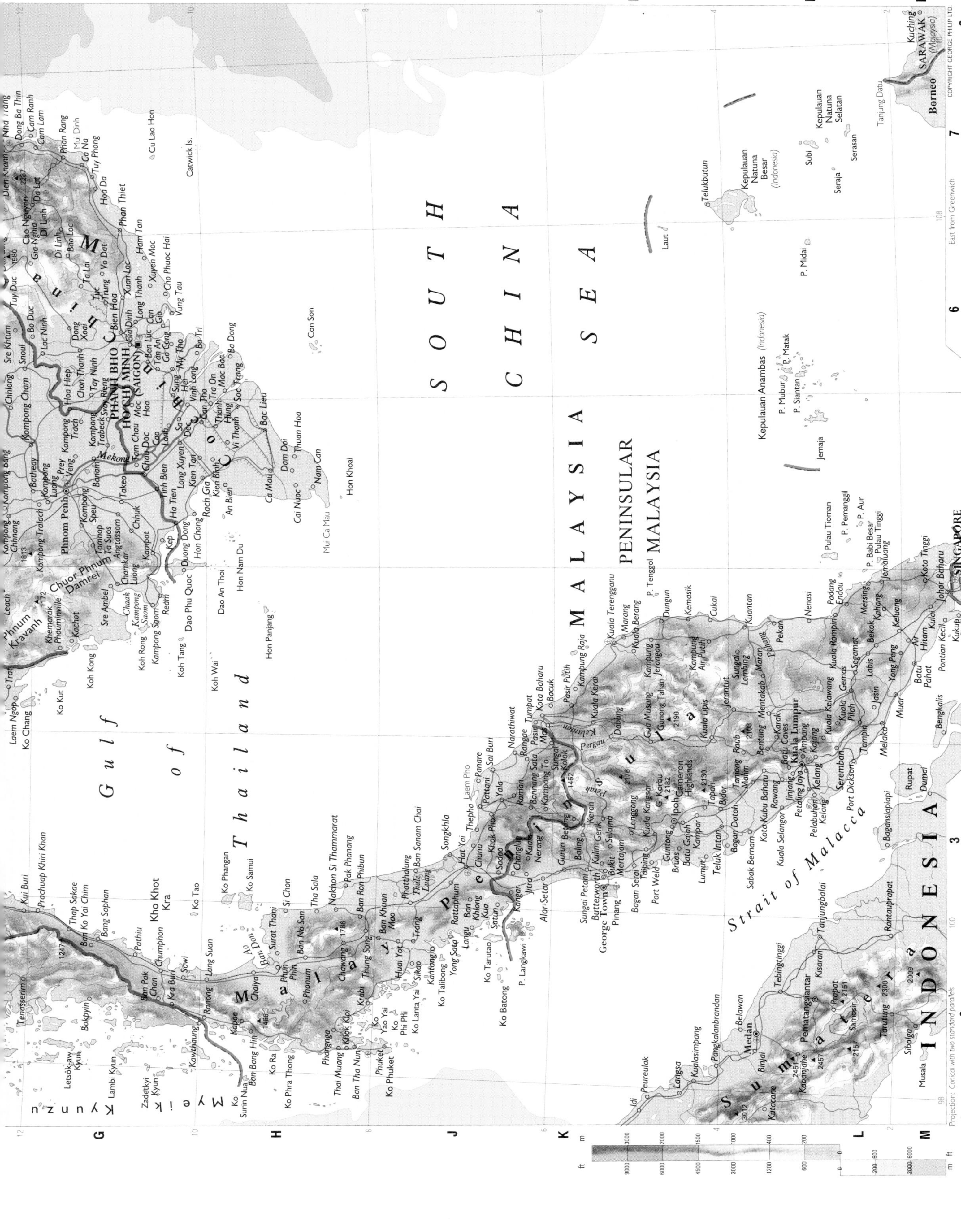

SOUTH CHINA SEA

Gulf of Thailand

Thailand

MALAYSIA

PENINSULAR MALAYSIA

INDONESIA

Sumatera

Strait of Malacca

Borneo

SARAWAK (Malaysia)

Kuching

Singapore

Kuala Lumpur

HO CHI MINH (SAIGON)

PHANOM PENH

Kepulauan Natuna Besar (Indonesia)

Kepulauan Anambas (Indonesia)

COPYRIGHT GEORGE PHILIP LTD.

Projection: Conical with two standard parallels

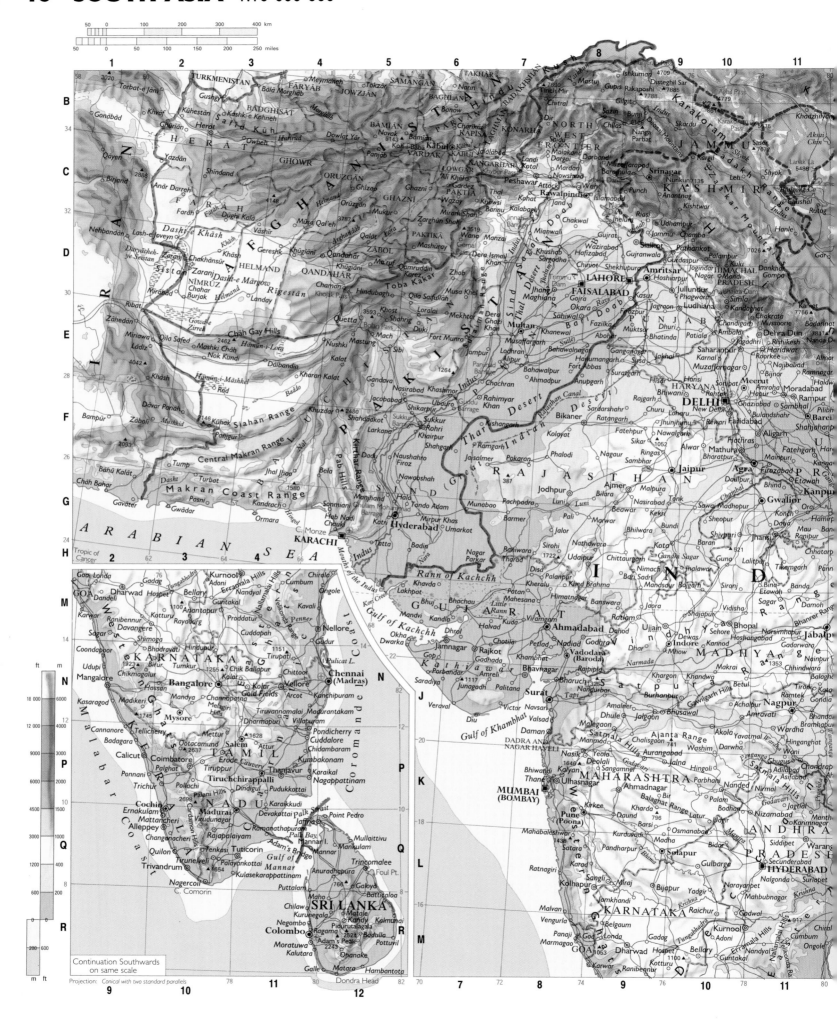

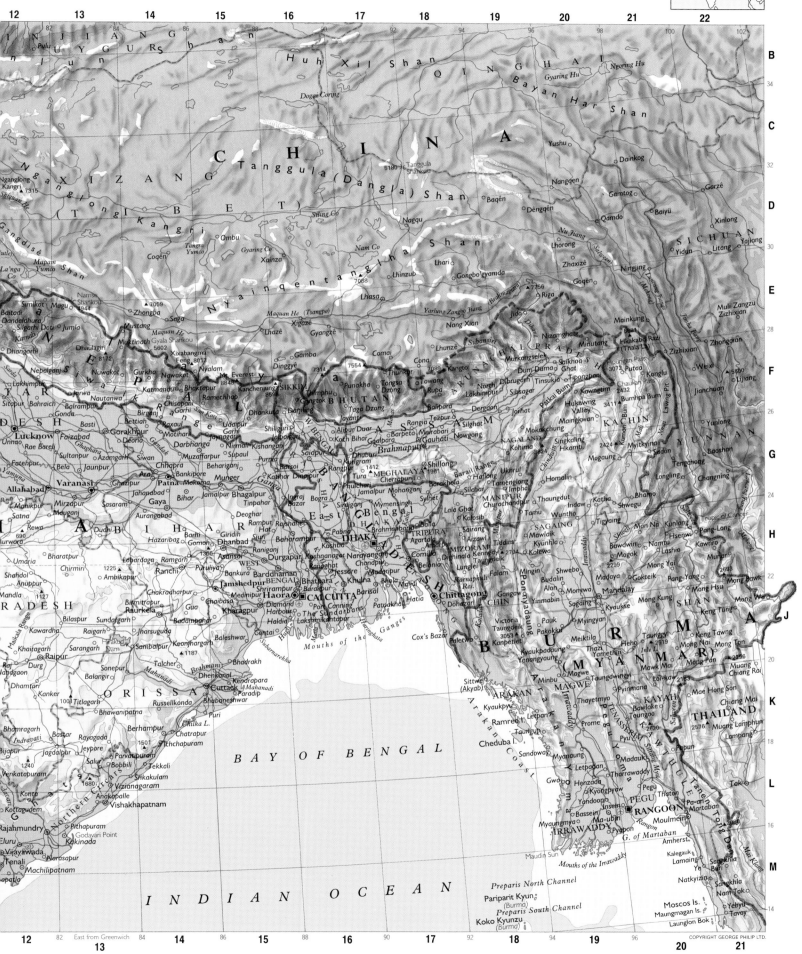

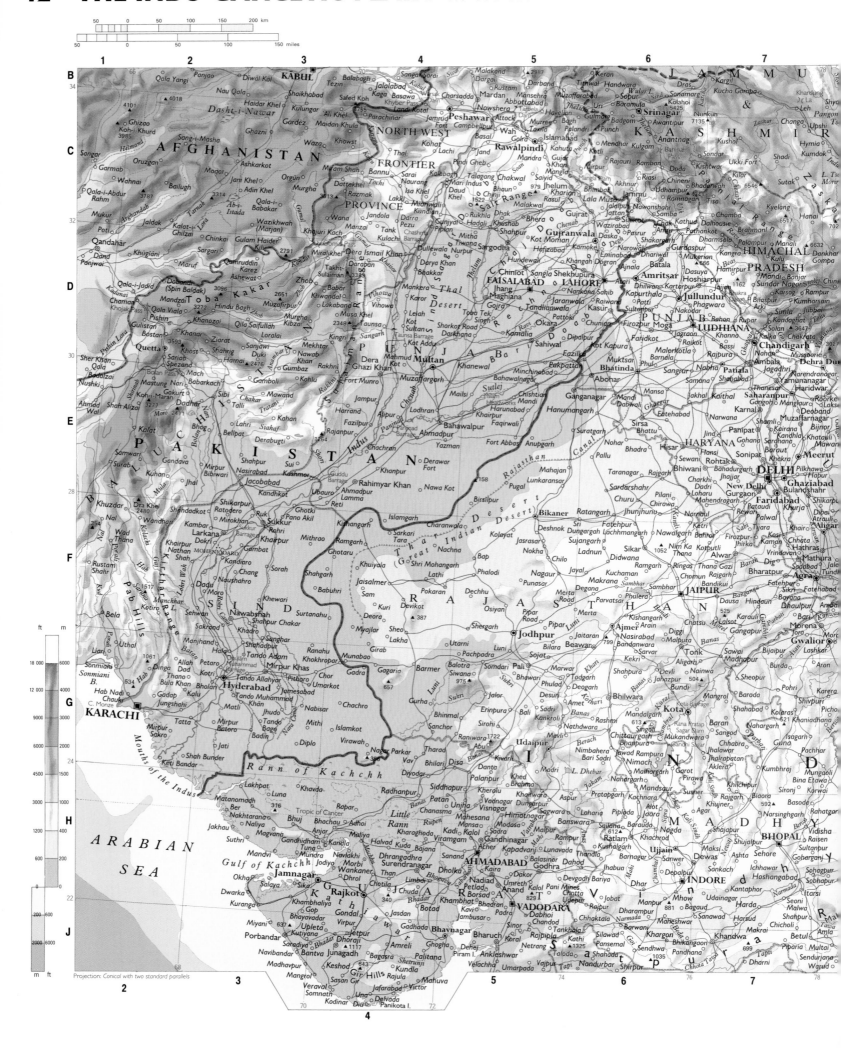

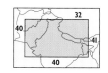

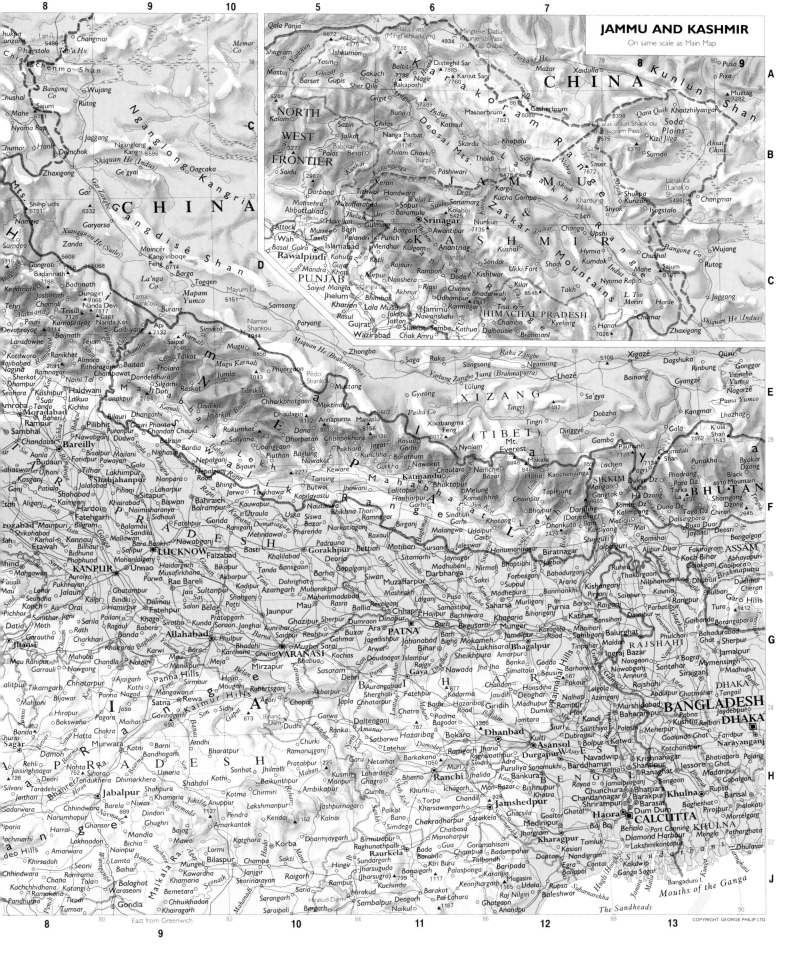

JAMMU AND KASHMIR
On same scale as Main Map

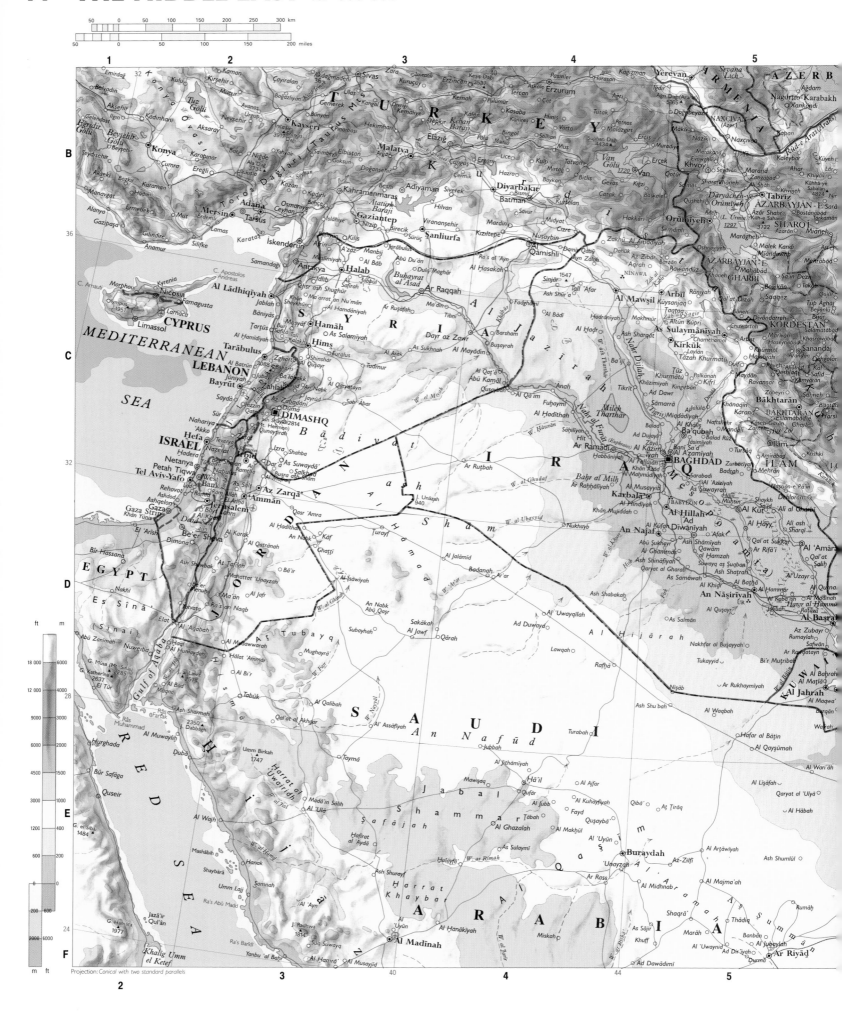

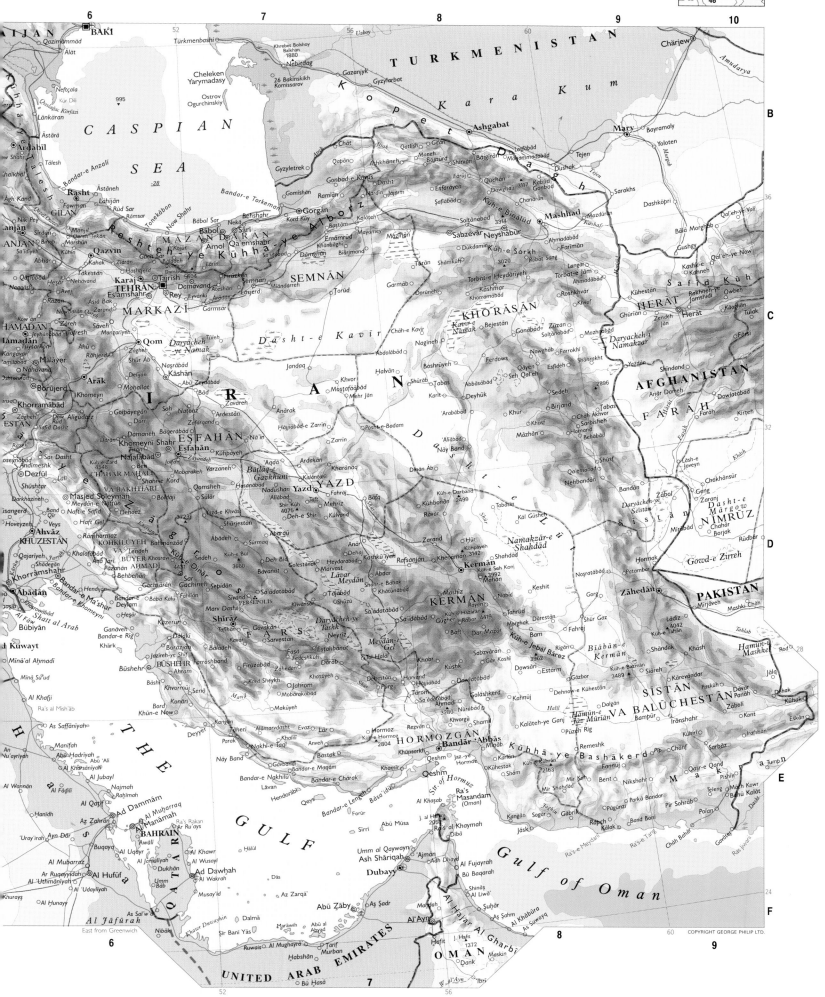

TURKMENISTAN

CASPIAN SEA

IRAN

AFGHANISTAN

PAKISTAN

THE GULF

Gulf of Oman

UNITED ARAB EMIRATES

OMAN

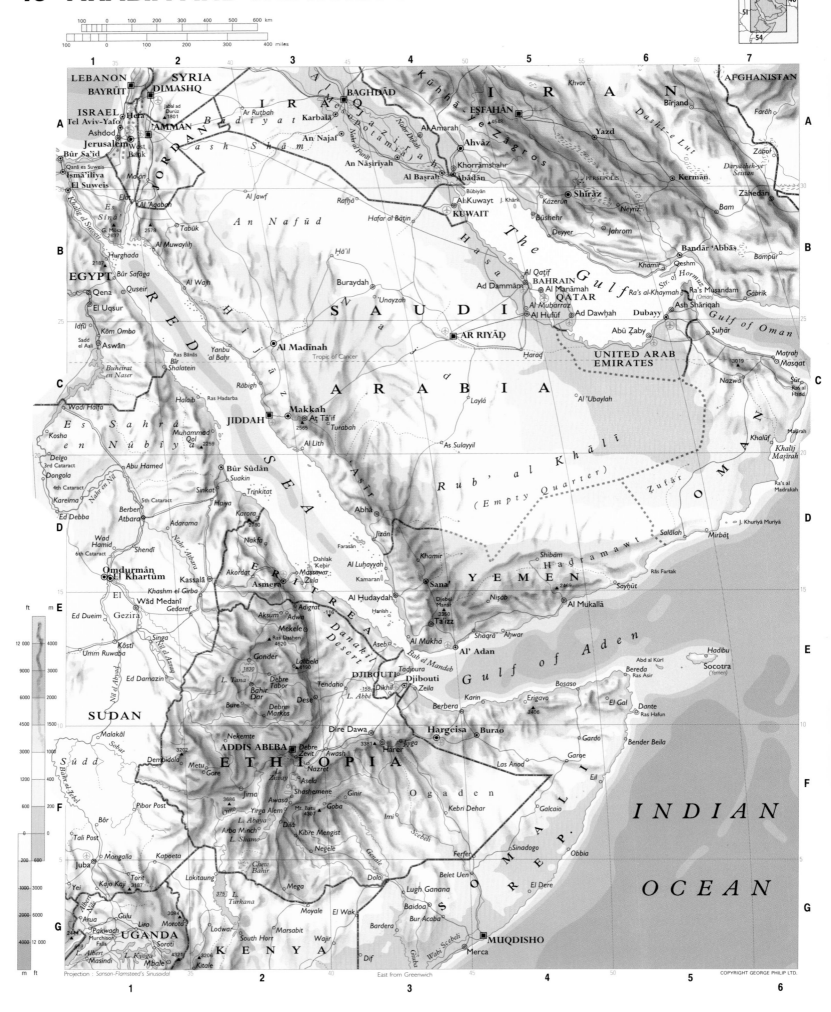

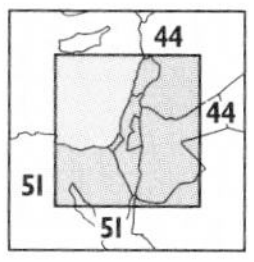

44
44
51
51

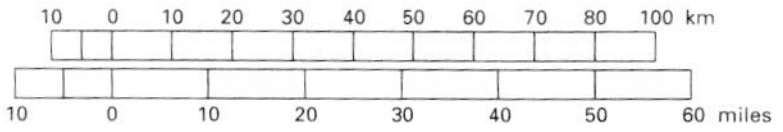

10 0 10 20 30 40 50 60 70 80 100 km
10 0 10 20 30 40 50 60 miles

1 2 3 4 5 6

Paphos
Episkopi
Episkopi Bay
Limassol
Akrotiri Bay
C. Gata
CYPRUS

Al Ḥamīdīyah
Ḥimṣ (Homs)
Tall Kalakh
Shinshār
Furqlus

A

ASH SHAMĀL
Al Minā'
Ṭarābulus (Tripoli)
Zghartā
Qurnat as Sawdā'
3088
Ḥalbā
Al Hirmil
Al Quṣayr
ḤIMṢ
Al Qaryatayn

M E D I T E R R A N E A N
Al Batrūn
Bsharri
2464
Al Burayj

Jubayl
Qartabā
2616
An Nabk
Bi'r Ghadir

S E A
Jūniyah
Ibrāhīm
Bikfayyā
2628 Sannīn
Ba'labakk
Yabrūd

BAYRŪT (Beirut)
Ash Shuwayfāt
Alayh
Zaḥlah
Sirghāyā
SYRIA
Az Zabadānī

B
Ad Dāmūr
Ḥawsh Mūssā
Al Qutayfah
Dumayr
Khān Abū Shāmat

LEBANON
Saydā (Sidon)
Jazzīn
2814 Mt Hermon
Dūmā
DIMASHQ (Damascus)

An Nabaṭīyah at Taḥta
Marj 'Uyūn
Dārayyā
Al Kiswah
Al Ḥājānah

AL JANŪB
Sūr (Tyre)
Qiryat Shemona
Al Khiyām
DIMASHQ
Burāq

Nahariyya
Me'ona
1197
Al Qunayṭirah
Ar Rafīd
As Sanamayn

'Akko (Acre)
Ḥagalil
Zefat
Fiq
Shaykh Miskin
Shahbā'
AS SUWAYDĀ'

C
Mifraẓ Ḥefa
Qiryat Yam
Karmi'el
Yam -210
Teverya (Tiberias)
Kinneret
Saḥam al Jawlān
Dar'ā
As Suwaydā' 1800
Ṣalāh

Ḥefa (Haifa)
Qiryat Ata
Yarmūk
DAR'Ā
Jabal ad Durūz

Dāliyat el Karmel
Nazerat (Nazareth)
ḤAZAFON
Ṭayiba
Ar Ramthā
Buṣrá ash Shām
Salkhad

TEL MEGIDDO
Afula
At Tanība
IRBID

CAESAREA
Umm el Fahm
Janīn
Irbid
Al-Mafraq
Umm al Qittayn

Hadera
Shōmrōn
Bēt She'an
Ailūn

ISRAEL
Ḥanna-Karkur
Ṭulkarm
Tūbās
J. Umm ad Daraj
Jarash

Netanya
SAMARIA
1247
Nahr az Zarqā'

HAMERKAZ
Herzliyya
Nāblus
W. az Zarqā'

Benē Beraq
Kefar Sava
SHILO
AL BALQĀ'
AMMĀN

Tel Aviv-Yafo
Petaḥ Tiqwa
As Salṭ
Az Zarqā

Ramat Gan
West Bank
Wādī as Sīr
Kurama

Bat Yam
-219
Na'ūr
Azraq ash Shīshān

Rishon le Ziyyon
El Arīḥā (Jericho)
At Tunayb

Yavne
Rēhovot
Rām Allāh
'AMMĀN

D
Lod
Ramla
Ma'dabā

Ashdod
Jerusalem (Yerushalayim) (Al Quds)
W. al Ḥaydān
Dhibān

Qiryat Mal'akhi
Bēt Shemesh
Bayt Laḥm (Bethlehem)
Al Ḥadīthah

Ashqelon
Qiryat Gat
TEL LAKHISH
Har Yehuda
-403
Al Qaṭrānah
W. al Ghadaf

Gaza
Az Zāhirīyah
Al Khalīl (Hebron)
W. al Mawjib

Gaza Strip
N. Shiqma
Midbar Yehuda
Al Karak

Khān Yūnis
Sederot
Arad

Rafaḥ
N. Beṣor
Be'er Sheva (Beersheba)
Sedom
1305
Al Mazar

El Daheir
Bor Mashash
Dimona
-333
AL KARAK

Bûr Sa'îd (Port Said)
Bûr Fu'ad
Rās Burūn
El 'Arîsh
W. al Ḥasā

Khalîg el Tîna
Sabkhet el Bardawîl
At Ṭafīlah
W. Bā'ir

Români
Bîr el 'Abd
Bîr Kaseiba
Bîr el Garârât
Bîr Lahfân
HADAROM
JORDAN

E
Bîr el Duweidar
W. al 'Arîsh
Qezi'ot
Bā'ir

El Qantara
Bîr el Jafar
Birein
Sedé Boqér
-121
J. ash Shawmari 1072

Wâḥid
Bîr Madkûr
S Î N Î
Muweilih
Mizpe Ramon

Ismâ'îlîya (Suez)
892
El Quseima
Nijil
Mahattat 'Unayzah

Talâta
Bîr Ḥasana
Bîr Beiḍa
Ḥanegev
Bi'r ad Dabbāghāt
W. Abū Ṣafāt
Qa'el Jafr

Khamsa
G. Yi 'Allaq 1094
Rujm Tal'at al Jamālah
1736
Al Jafr

El Buheirat el Murrat el Kubra (Great Bitter L.)
Bîr el Thamâda
W. el Brûk
El 'Agrûd
N. Paran
PETRA
Ma'ān

Gineifa
E G Y P T
N. Ḥiyyon
MA'ĀN

El Suweis (Suez)
Bûr Taufîq
Mamarr Miṭlā
Bîr Gebel Ḥisn
948 G. el Kabrît
El Kuntilla
Yotvata
Ra's an Naqb
Mahattat ash Shidīyah

F
Adabîya
Uyûn Mûsa
E s S î n â' (S i n a i)
El Thamad
'En 'Avrona
Bi'r al Buṭayyiḥāt
Bi'r al Qaṭṭar

Bîr Bad'
Ain Sudr
Nakhl
Bîr Abu Muḥammad
El Girâfi
1592
Baṭn al Ghûl
SAUDI

Ghubbet el Bûs
1272
Gebel el Tîh
El Wabeira
Bîr el Biarât
Elat
Al 'Aqabah

EL SUWEIS
Bîr Abu Sandûq
W. Abū Ga'da
Shibh Jazîrat Sinâ'
Bîr el Ḥeisi
Bîr Tâba
Gulf of 'Aqaba
W. an Nuweiba
Al Mudawwarah
At Ṭubayq
ARABIA

1165
Ḥaql

Projection: Polyconic
East from Greenwich
COPYRIGHT GEORGE PHILIP LTD.

ft m
9000 3000
6000 2000
4500 1500
3000 1000
1200 400
600 200
200 600
2000 6000
m ft

⬛ ⬛ ⬛ 1974 Cease Fire Lines

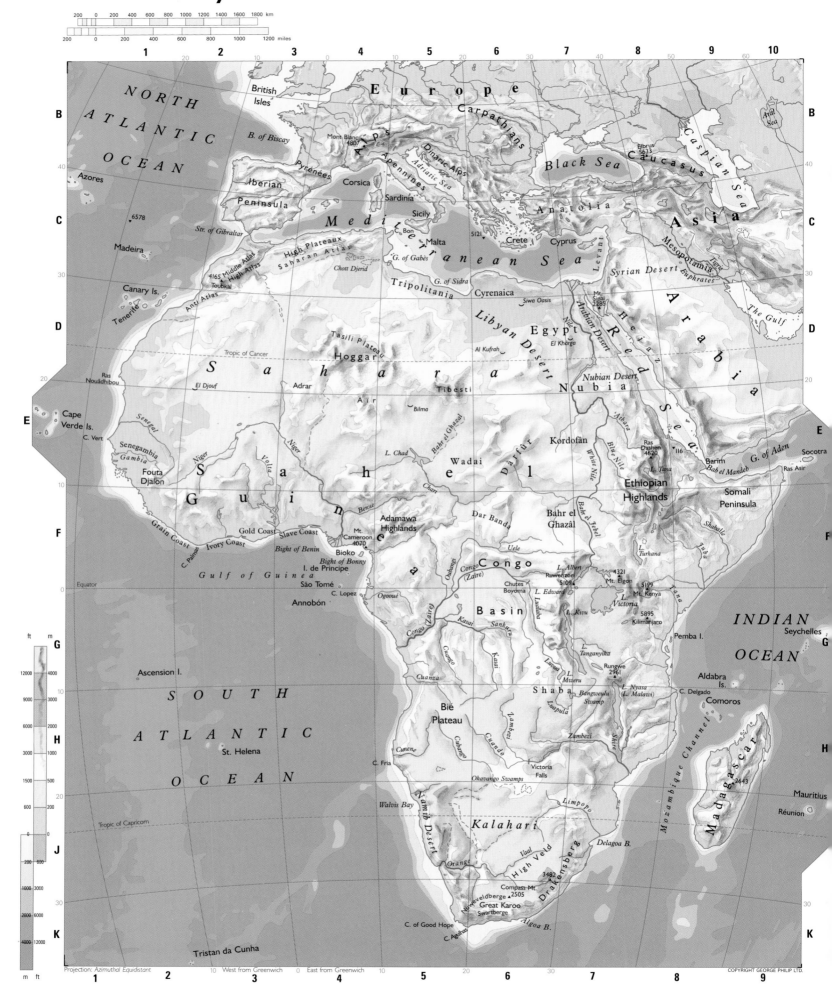

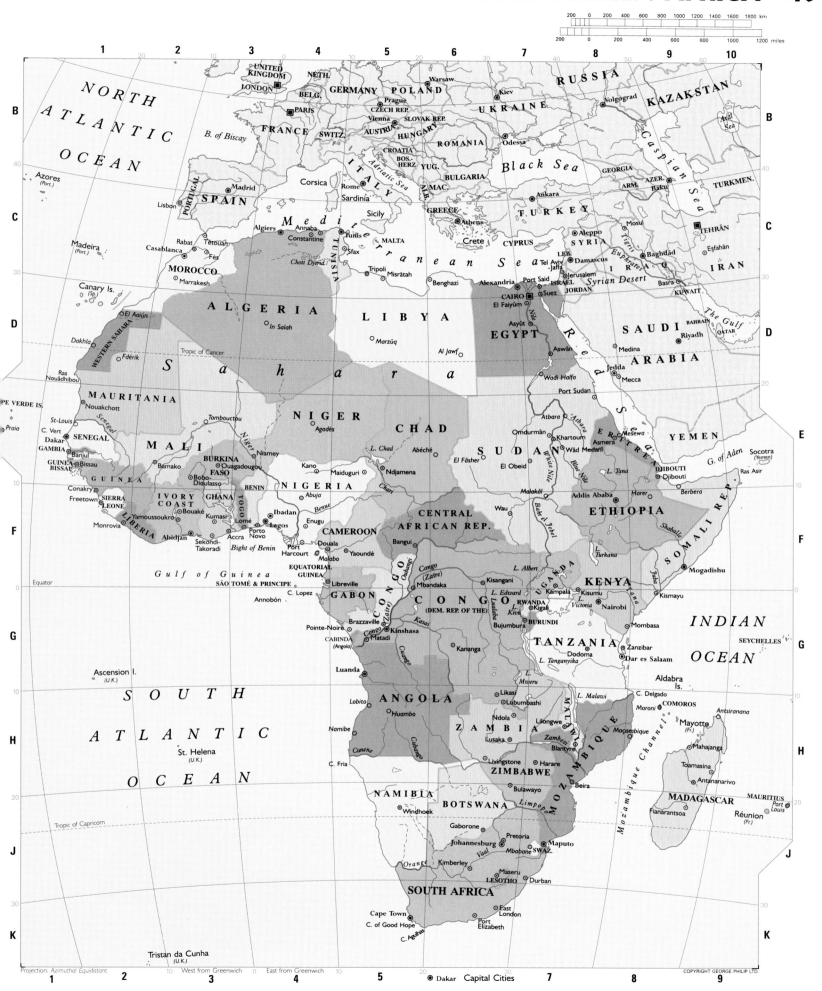

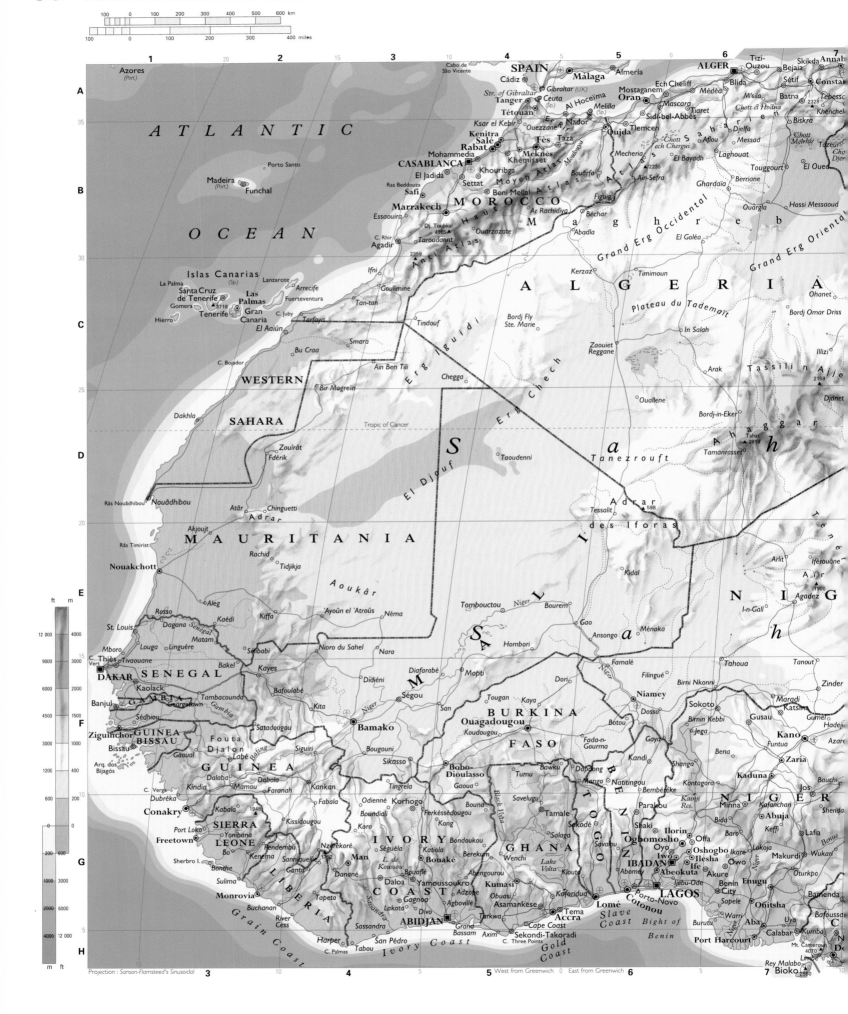

Projection : Sanson-Flamsteed's Sinusoidal

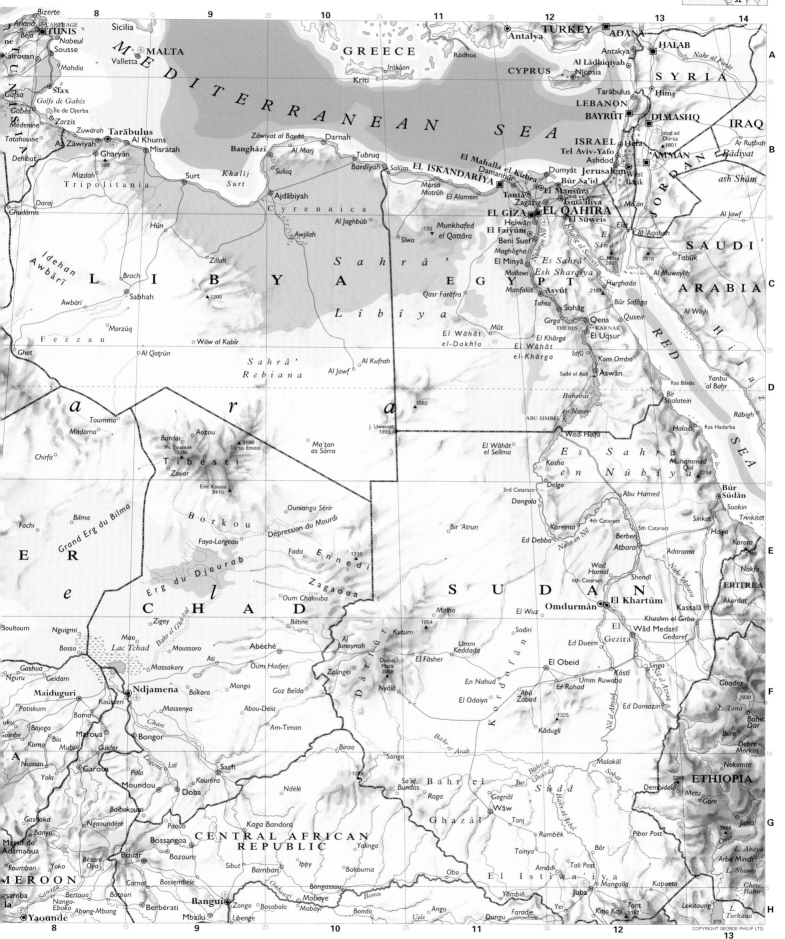

MEDITERRANEAN SEA

GREECE

MALTA

TURKEY
Antalya   ADANA
Antakya
CYPRUS   Al Lādhiqiyah   HALAB
Nicosia   Nahr al Furāt
Tarābulus
LEBANON   Hims
BAYRŪT   DIMASHQ
ISRAEL   Hefa   Jabal ad   IRAQ
Tel Aviv-Yafo   Durūz   Ar Rutbah
Ashdod   AMMAN   Bādiyat
Jerusalem West
Bank   ash Shām
Mā'ān
Al Jawf

Bizerte
Ariana   TUNIS
CARTHAGE
Béja   Nabeul
Kairouan   Sousse
Mahdia
Sfax
Gafsa   Golfe de Gabès
Gabès   Île de Djerba
Médenine   Zarzis
Tatahouine   Zuwārah   Tarābulus
Dehibat   Az Zāwiyah   Al Khums
Gharyān   Misrātah
968
Mizdah
Daraj   Surt
Ghudāmis   Tripolitania

Sicilia
Valletta

Zāwiyat al Baydā   Darnah
Banghāzī   Al Marj
Suluq   Tubruq   Salūm
Khalīj   Bardīyah   EL ISKANDARĪYA
Surt   Marsá   El Mahalla el Kubra
Ajdābiyah   Matrûh   El Alamein   Damanhûr
Cyrenaica   Tanta   Zagazig
-133   El Mansûra
Al Jaghbūb   Munkhafed   Bûr Sa'id
el Qattâra   Qanâ es Suweis
Siwa   EL GĪZA EL QAHIRA   Ismā'īliya
Helwān   El Suweis
Sahrâ'   El Faiyûm   Es
Beni Suef   Sinā'
Maghâgha   G. Mūsa
El Minyâ   2637
Mallawi   Es Sahrâ
Lîbîya   Manfalût   Esh Sharqiya
Asyût   Hurghada
Tahta   Bûr Safâga
Qasr Farâfra   Sohâg
El Wâhât   Girga   2187
el-Dakhla   THEBES   Quseir
Mût   Qena   KARNAK
El Khârga   El Uqsur

SAUDI
ARABIA

Tel Aviv-Yafo
Elat   Al Muwaylih
Al 'Aqabah
2578   Tabûk

Al Wajh

Hurghada
Bûr Safâga
Quseir

RED

El Wâhât   Idfû   Kom Ombo
el-Khârga   Sadd el Aali   Aswân
Buheirat   Ras Bānās
en Naser   Bîr   Yanbu
Shalatein   al Bahr
1082   Râbigh
J. Uweinat   ABU SIMBEL   Halaib   Ras Hadarba
1893   Wâdi Halfa   Muhammad
El Wâhât   Qol   2259
el Selima   Es   Sahrâ
Kosha   en   Nûbîya   Bûr
3rd Cataract   Sûdân
Delgo   Suakin
Dongola   Abu Hamed   Trinkitat
Kareima   Sinkat
4th Cataract   Haiya
5th Cataract   Karora   2780
Ed Debba   Berber
Nahr en Nîl   Atbara   Adarama   Nakfa
Wad   ERITREA
Hamid   Shendî   Akordat
6th Cataract   Nahr 'Atbara
SUDAN
Kassalâ
El Khartûm   Khashm el Girba
Omdurmân   Gedaref

SEA

HIJAZ

Toummo
Madama
Chirfa
Ghat   Al Qatrūn   Wâw al Kabîr
Fezzan

Idehan
Awbārī   Brach
Awbāri
Sabhah
Marzūq
1200

Sahrâ
Rebiana   Al Jawf   Al Kufrah

a   r   a

Bardai   3150
Aozou   Tarso Emissi
Pic Toussidé   3265
3265   Zouâr
Tibesti
Emi Koussi   Ma'tan
3415   as Sarra

Bilma
Fachi   Grand Erg du Bilma
R   Borkou
E   Erg du Djourab
e   Faya-Largeau
Dépression du Mourdi
Fada   Ennedi
1310
Zaghawa
Oum Chalouba

Ouninga Sérir

CHAD

Bir 'Atrun

Ed Debba

EGYPT

SUDAN

El Wuz
Matha
1954   Sodiri
Biltine   Kutum
Al Junaynah   El Fâsher   Umm
Zalingei   Keddada
Djebel   Nyâlâ   En Nahud
Marra   El Obeid   Kôstî
3088   Abū   Er Rahad
Zabad   Umm Ruwaba
El Odaiya   Singa
Ed Dueim   Gonder
El   1830
Gezira
El Wâd Medanî
Gedaref
Ed Damazin
1325   Kâdugli

ETHIOPIA

L. Tana
Bahir
Dar
Bure
Debre
Markos

Boultoum   Zigey   Bahr el Ghazâl
Nguigmi   Mao
Bosso   Lac Tchad   Moussoro
Gashua   Massakory   Ati
Nguru   Geidam   Oum Hadjer
Maiduguri   Abéché
Kousséri   Massenya   Mongo   Goz Beïda
Potiskum   Bama   Bokoro   Am-Timan
Bajoga   Ndjamena   Chari
Gombe   Biu   Guider
Kuma   Maroua   Bongor   Birao
Numan   Mubi
Yola   Garoua   Laï   Sarh   Songa
Gashaka   Moundou   Kourmra   Ndélé   1276
Banyo   Doba   Bossangoa
Massif de   Baibokoum   CENTRAL AFRICAN
Adamaoua   Bétaré   Ngaoundéré   Paoua   REPUBLIC   Yalinga
Oya   Bouar   Bozoum   Sibut
Fombun   Yoko   Carnot   Bossembélé
Abong-Mbang   Bambari   Ippy
MEROON   Sanaga   Berbérati   Bakouma
gsamba   Nanga-   Batouri   Zongo   Bosobolo   Bangassou
la   Eboko   Abong-Mbang   Bonga   Mobaye   Obo
Yaoundé   Mbaïki   Libenge   Uele   Ango   El Istiwa'iya
Faradje

Maroua
Mora
Kuma   Biu

Bahr el
Ghazâl   Nîl Abyad
Kâdugli

3202

Bahr el
Jur   Sûdd
Sa'id
Bundas
Gogriâl   Bahr el Jebel
Raga   Malakâl   Nekemte
Wâw   Tonj   Dembidolo
Ghazâl   Rumbêk   Metu   Gore   Juma
Toinya   3686
Bôr   Arba Minch
Amâdi   Pibor Post   L. Abaya
Tali Post   L. Shamo
Yei   Juba   Torit   Chew
Yambiô   Kajo Kaji   Lokitaung   Bahr
Dungu   Kapoeta   375
Kao Kaji   L.
317   Turkana

MEDITERRANEAN SEA

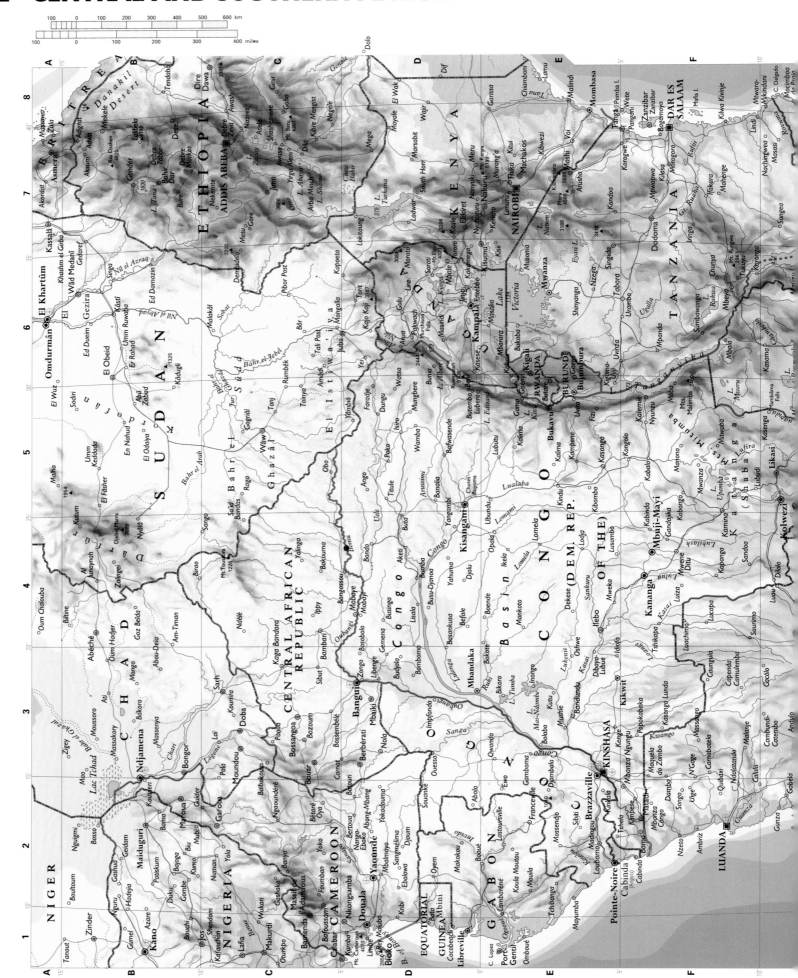

53

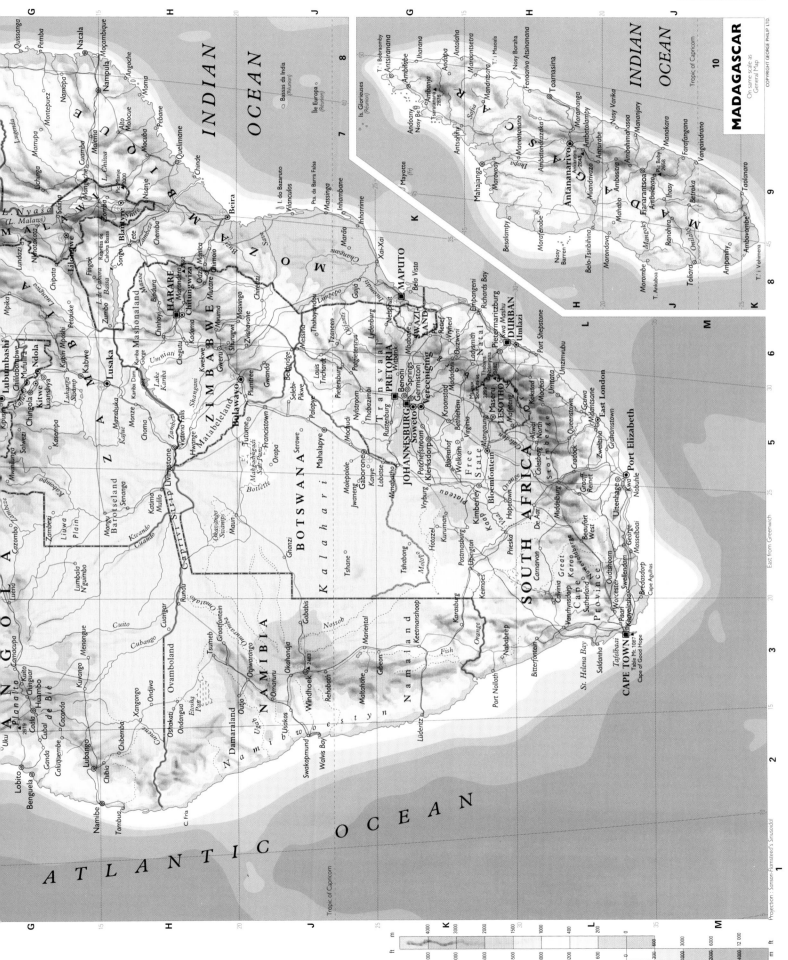

MADAGASCAR

On same scale as
General Map

COPYRIGHT GEORGE PHILIP LTD.

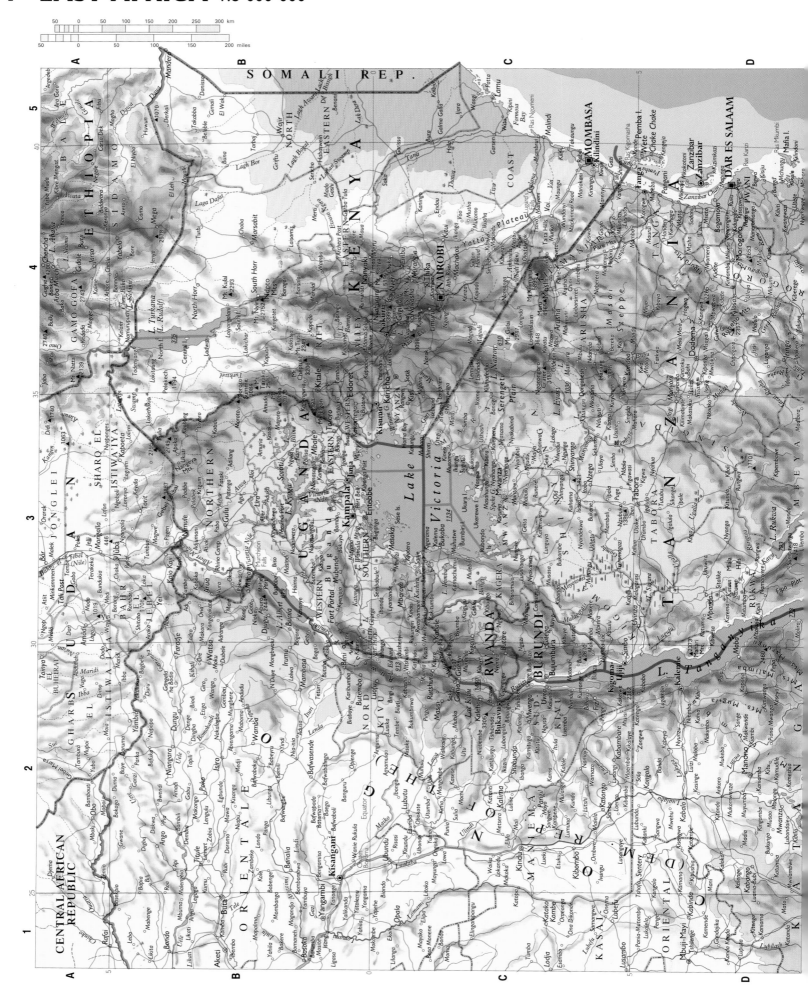

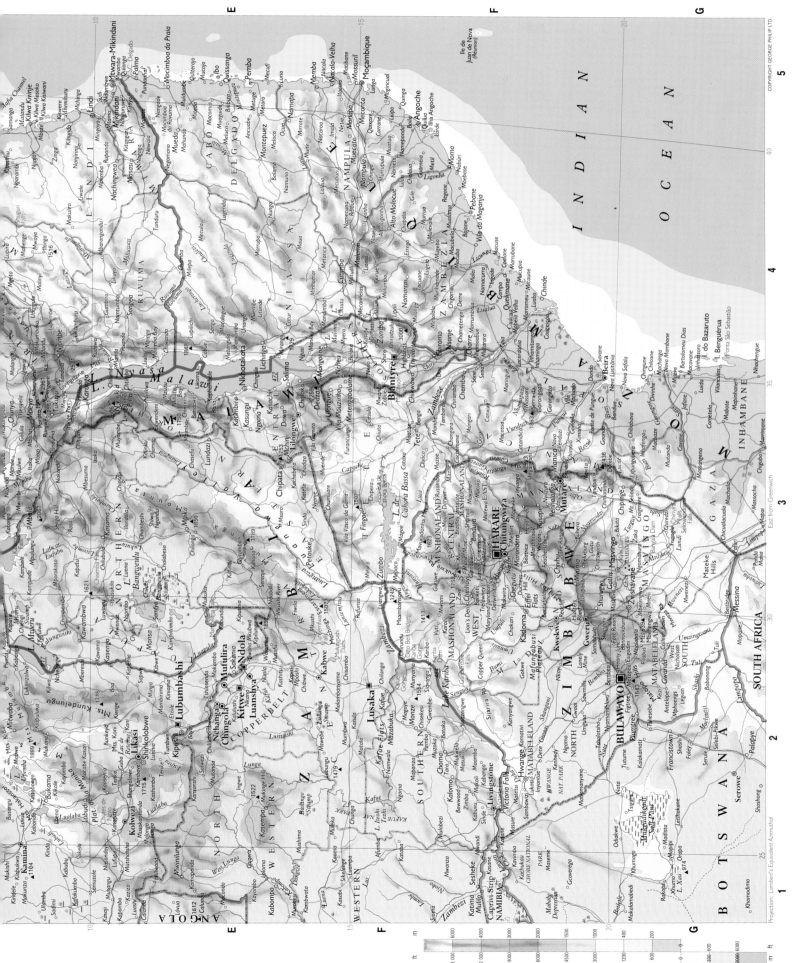

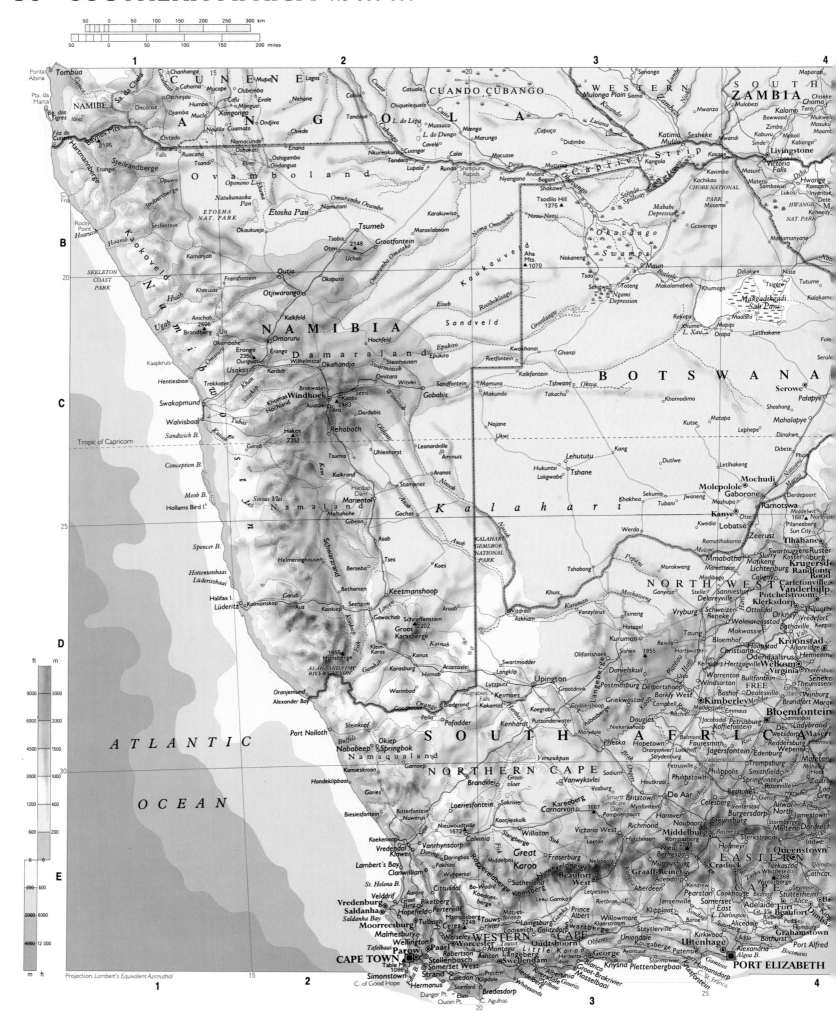

MADAGASCAR

On same scale as General Map

COPYRIGHT GEORGE PHILIP LTD.

East from Greenwich

MOZAMBIQUE CHANNEL

INDIAN OCEAN

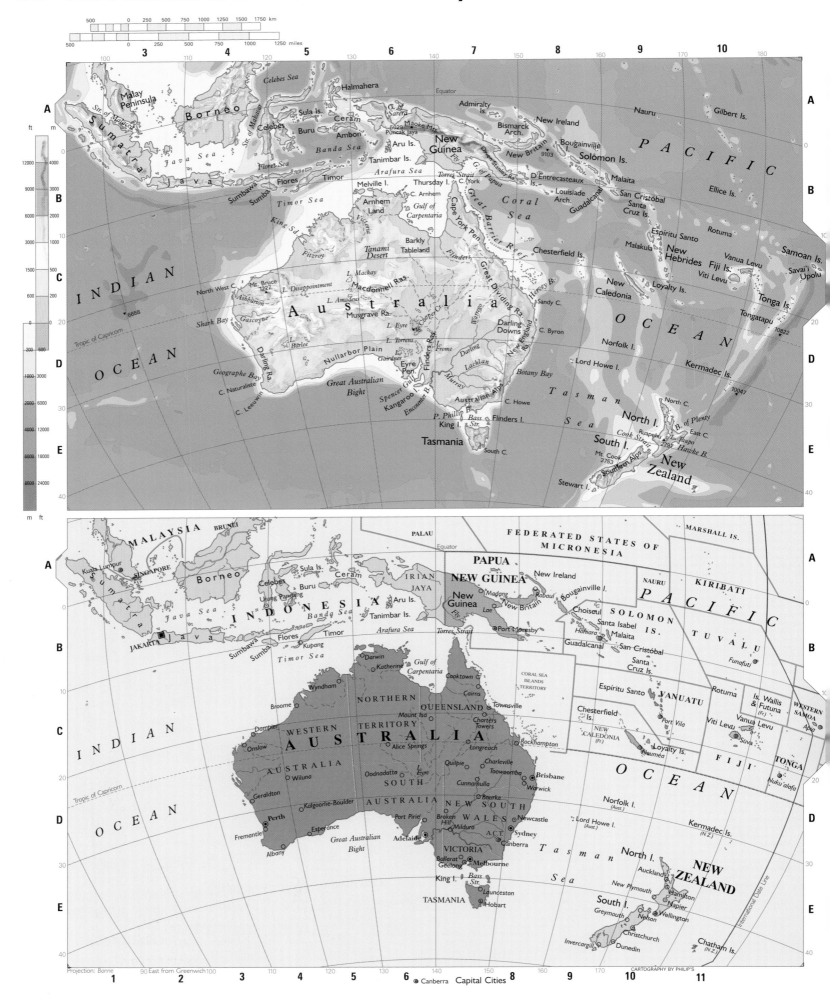

Projection: Bonne

90 East from Greenwich 100

CARTOGRAPHY BY PHILIP'S

Canberra Capital Cities

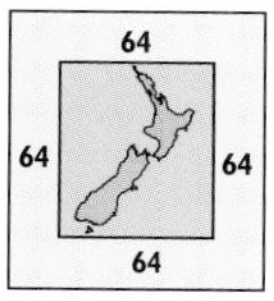

64

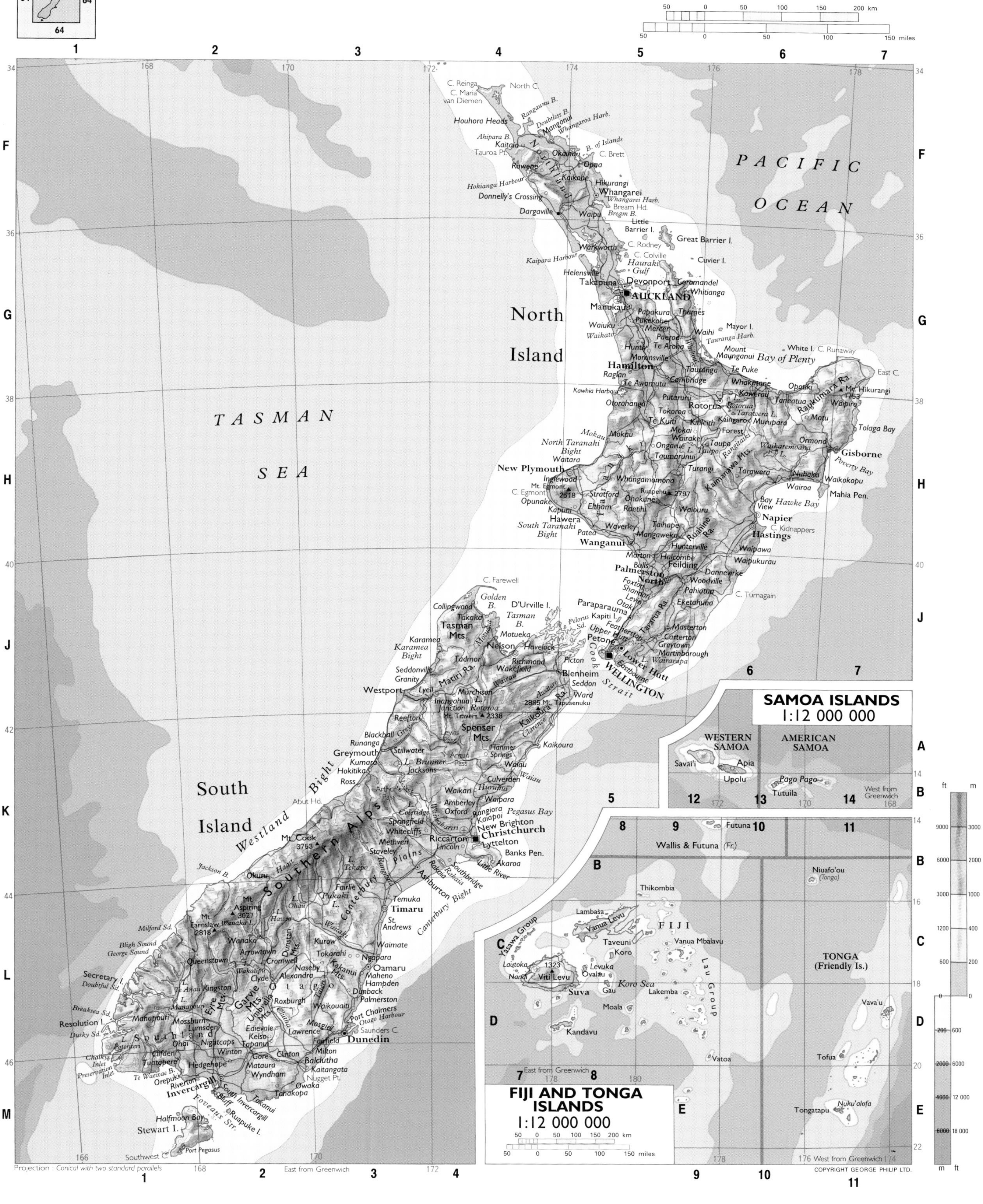

50 0 50 100 150 200 km
50 0 50 100 150 miles

PACIFIC OCEAN

C. Reinga
C. Maria van Diemen
North C.
Rangaunu B.
Houhora Heads
Doubtless B.
Mangonui
Whangaroa Harb.
Ahipara B.
Kaitaia
Okaihau
B. of Islands
C. Brett
Tauroa Pt.
Rawene
Kaikohe
Opua
Hokianga Harbour
Whangarei
Hikurangi
Donnelly's Crossing
Whangarei Harb.
Bream Hd.
Dargaville
Waipu
Bream B.
Little Barrier I.
Great Barrier I.
Workworth
C. Rodney
Helensville
C. Colville
Cuvier I.
Kaipara Harbour
Coromandel
Takapuna
Devonport
Whitianga
Manukau
AUCKLAND
Papakura
Pukekohe
Thames
Waiuku
Mercer
Waihi
Mayor I.
Waikato
Paeroa
Tauranga Harb.
Huntly
Te Aroha
Mount Maunganui
White I.
C. Runaway
Morrinsville
Bay of Plenty
Raglan
Hamilton
Tauranga
Te Awamutu
Cambridge
Whakatane
Opotiki
Kawhia Harbour
Tirau
Kawerau
Taneatua
Mt. Hikurangi
Otorohanga
Putaruru
Rotorua
Kaingaroa
Raukumara Ra.
Wairoa
Te Kuiti
Tokoroa
Rotorua L.
Tarawera L.
Murupara
Motu
Mokau
Mokau
Mokai
Taupo
Forest
Tolaga Bay
North Taranaki Bight
Ongarue
L.
Taupo
Waikaremoana
Waitara
Ormond
New Plymouth
Whangamomona
Turangi
Kaimanawa Mts.
Gisborne
Inglewood
Ruapehu
Tarawera
Poverty Bay
Mt. Egmont 2518
Stratford
Ohakune 2797
Waiouru
Nuhaka
C. Egmont
Opunake
Eltham
Raetihi
Waikokopu
Kapuni
Bay View
Hawera
Waverley
Taihape
Napier
Mahia Pen.
South Taranaki Bight
Patea
Waiouru
Hastings
C. Kidnappers
Wanganui
Mangaweka
Ruahine Ra.
Hunterville
Waipawa
Marton
Halcombe
Waipukurau
Bulls
Feilding
Dannevirke
Palmerston North
Woodville
Foxton
Shannon
Pahiatua
Levin
Eketahuna
C. Turnagain
Otaki
Paraparaumu
Kapiti I.
Masterton
Carterton
Upper Hutt
Greytown
Petone
Martinborough
Lower Hutt
Wairarapa
WELLINGTON
Eastbourne
Cook Strait

North Island

TASMAN SEA

C. Farewell
Collingwood
Golden B.
D'Urville I.
Takaka
Tasman B.
Tasman Mts.
Motueka
Pelorus Sd.
Karamea
Nelson
Picton
Karamea Bight
Tadmor
Havelock
Queen Charlotte Sd.
Seddonville
Richmond
Blenheim
Granity
Wakefield
Seddon
Westport
Lyell
Wairau
Ward
Murchison
Inangahua Junction
Rotoroa L.
2885 Mt. Tapuaenuku
Reefton
Mt. Travers 2338
Spenser Mts.
Kaikoura
Blackball
Grey
Hanmer Springs
Runanga
Clarence
Greymouth
Stillwater
Waiau
Kumara
L. Brunner
Hokitika
Jacksons
Arthur's Pass
Ross
Waikari
Culverden
Amberley
Waipara
Oxford
Pegasus Bay
Coleridge
Rangiora
Kaiapoi
Springfield
New Brighton
Whitecliffs
Riccarton
Christchurch
Mt. Cook 3753
Methven
Lincoln
Lyttelton
Staveley
Banks Pen.
Akaroa
South Island
Fairlie
Southbridge
Rakaia
Tekapo
Rolleston
Lake River
Ashburton
Mt. Aspiring 3027
Pukaki
Ohau
Canterbury Bight
Westland Bight
Abut. Hd.
Mt. Earnslaw 2818
Wanaka L.
Temuka
Timaru
St. Andrews
Jackson B.
Okuru
Hawea
Kurow
Waimate
Milford Sd.
Wanaka
Tokarahi
Ngapara
Bligh Sound
Arrowtown
Cromwell
Maheno
George Sound
Queenstown
Naseby
Hampden
Secretary I.
Wakatipu L.
Clyde
Dunback
Doubtful Sd.
Alexandra
Palmerston
Kingston
Roxburgh
Waikouaiti
Manapouri
Eyre Mts.
Garvie Mts.
Otago
Waihola
Port Chalmers
Manapouri L.
Umbrella Mts.
Lawrence
Mosgiel
Otago Harbour
Breaksea Sd.
Mataura
Clinton
Milton
Dunedin
Resolution I.
Mossburn
Edievale
Kelso
Fairfield
Saunders C.
Dusky Sd.
Lumsden
Gore
Kaitangata
Eyerton
Ohai
Nightcaps
Winton
Balclutha
Chalky Inlet
Clifden
Owaka
Tuatapere
Hedgehope
Nugget Pt.
Te Waewae B.
Orepuki
Riverton
Wyndham
Preservation Inlet
Invercargill
Tokanui
Tahakopa
Bluff
Invercargill
Ruapuke I.
Foveaux Str.
Halfmoon Bay
Port Pegasus
Stewart I.
Southwest C.

Projection: Conical with two standard parallels
East from Greenwich

COPYRIGHT GEORGE PHILIP LTD.

SAMOA ISLANDS 1:12 000 000

WESTERN SAMOA
AMERICAN SAMOA
Savai'i
Apia
Upolu
Pago Pago
Tutuila
West from Greenwich

FIJI AND TONGA ISLANDS 1:12 000 000
50 0 50 100 200 km
50 0 50 100 150 miles

Yasawa Group
Lambasa
Vanua Levu
Thikombia
Niuafo'ou (Tonga)
Taveuni
Vanua Mbalavu
Lautoka
1323
Koro
FIJI
Nandi
Levuka
Viti Levu
Ovalau
Gau
Koro Sea
Lau Group
Lakemba
TONGA (Friendly Is.)
Suva
Moala
Vava'u
Kandavu
Vatoa
Tofua
Tongatapu
Nuku'alofa

ft m
9000 3000
6000 2000
3000 1000
1200 400
600 200
0 0
200 600
2000 6000
4000 12 000
6000 18 000
m ft

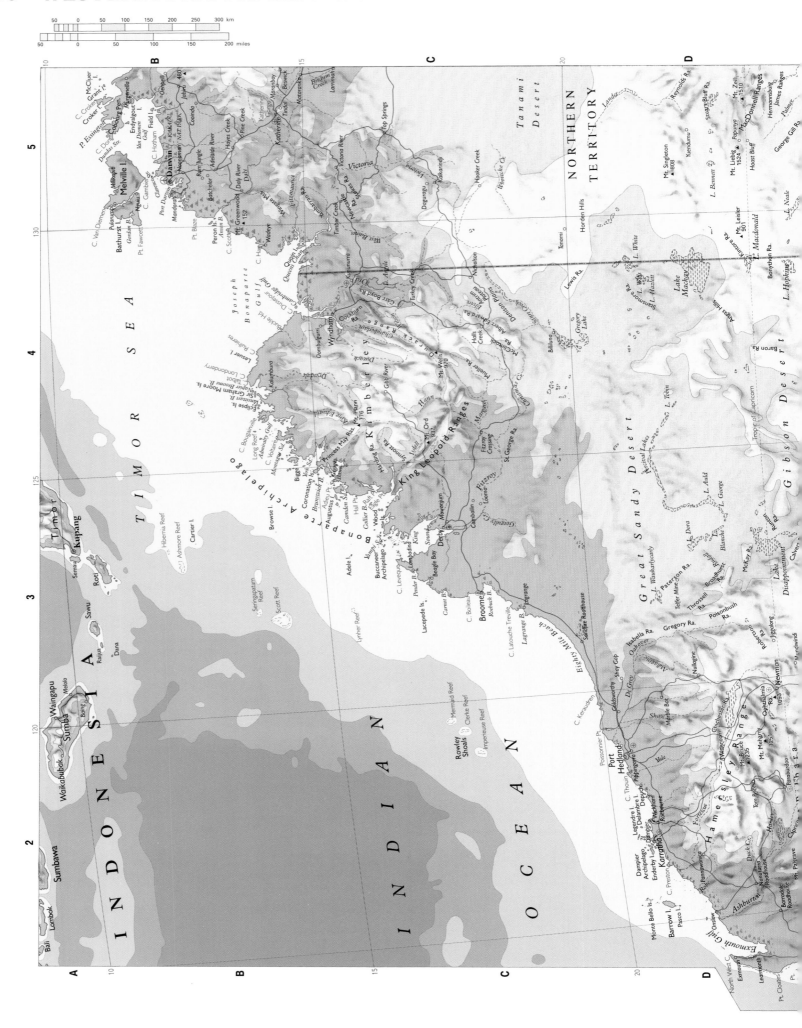

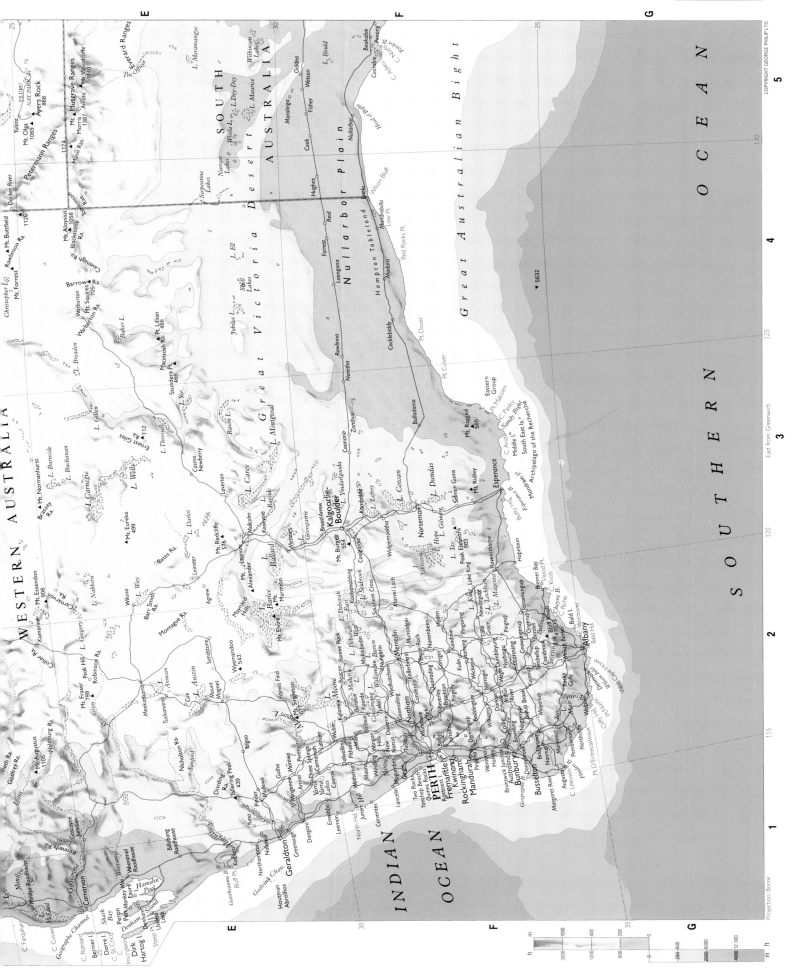

COPYRIGHT GEORGE PHILIP LTD.

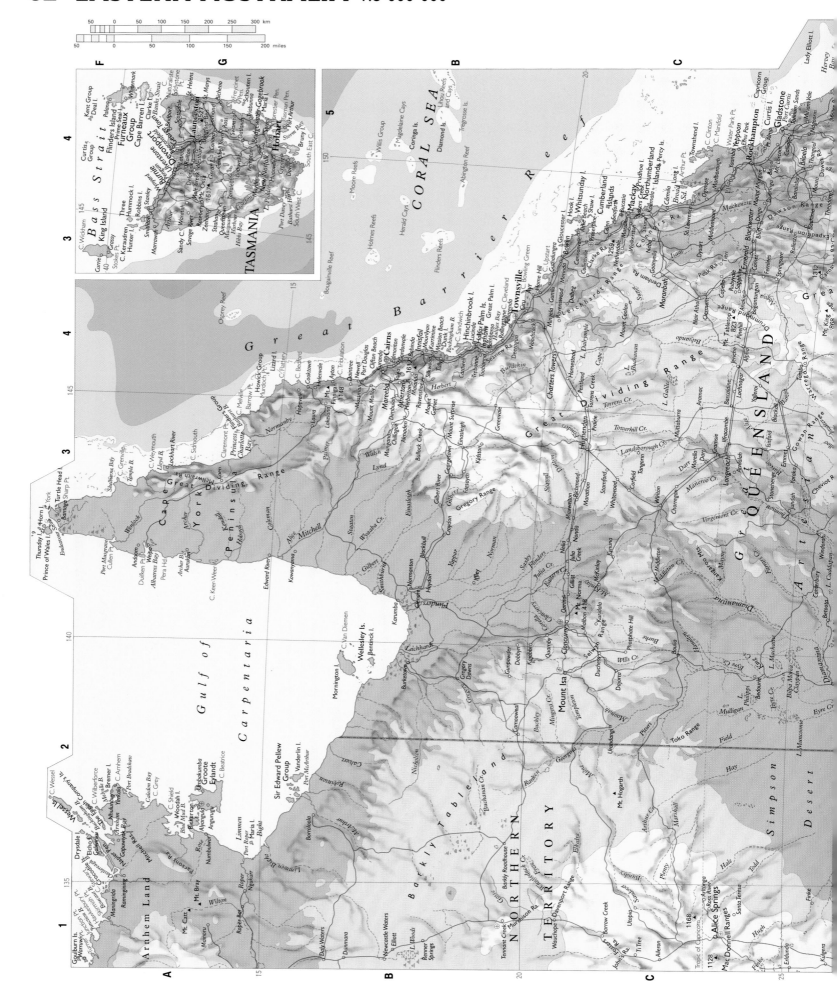

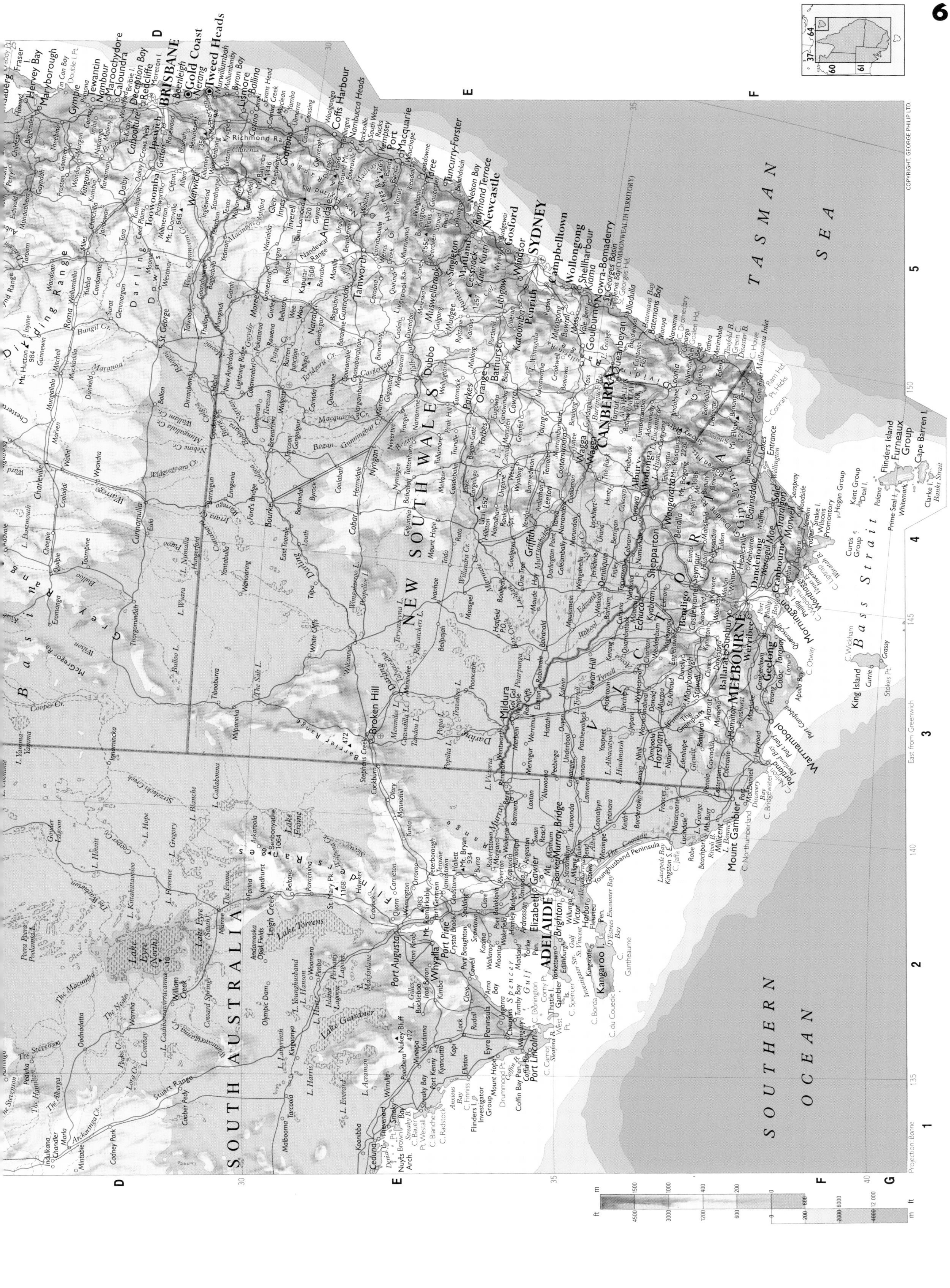

SOUTH AUSTRALIA

NEW SOUTH WALES

VICTORIA

BRISBANE

SYDNEY

CANBERRA

ADELAIDE

MELBOURNE

Gold Coast

Tweed Heads

Newcastle

Wollongong

Geelong

Broken Hill

TASMAN SEA

SOUTHERN OCEAN

Bass Strait

King Island

Flinders Island

Furneaux Group

Cape Barren I.

Great Dividing Range

Darling Range

Flinders Range

Lake Eyre North

Lake Eyre (South)

Lake Torrens

Lake Gairdner

Lake Frome

Spencer Gulf

Gulf St. Vincent

Kangaroo I.

Eyre Peninsula

Yorke Peninsula

Port Augusta

Port Lincoln

Mount Gambier

Warrnambool

East from Greenwich

Projection: Bonne

COPYRIGHT. GEORGE PHILIP LTD.

135   140   145   150

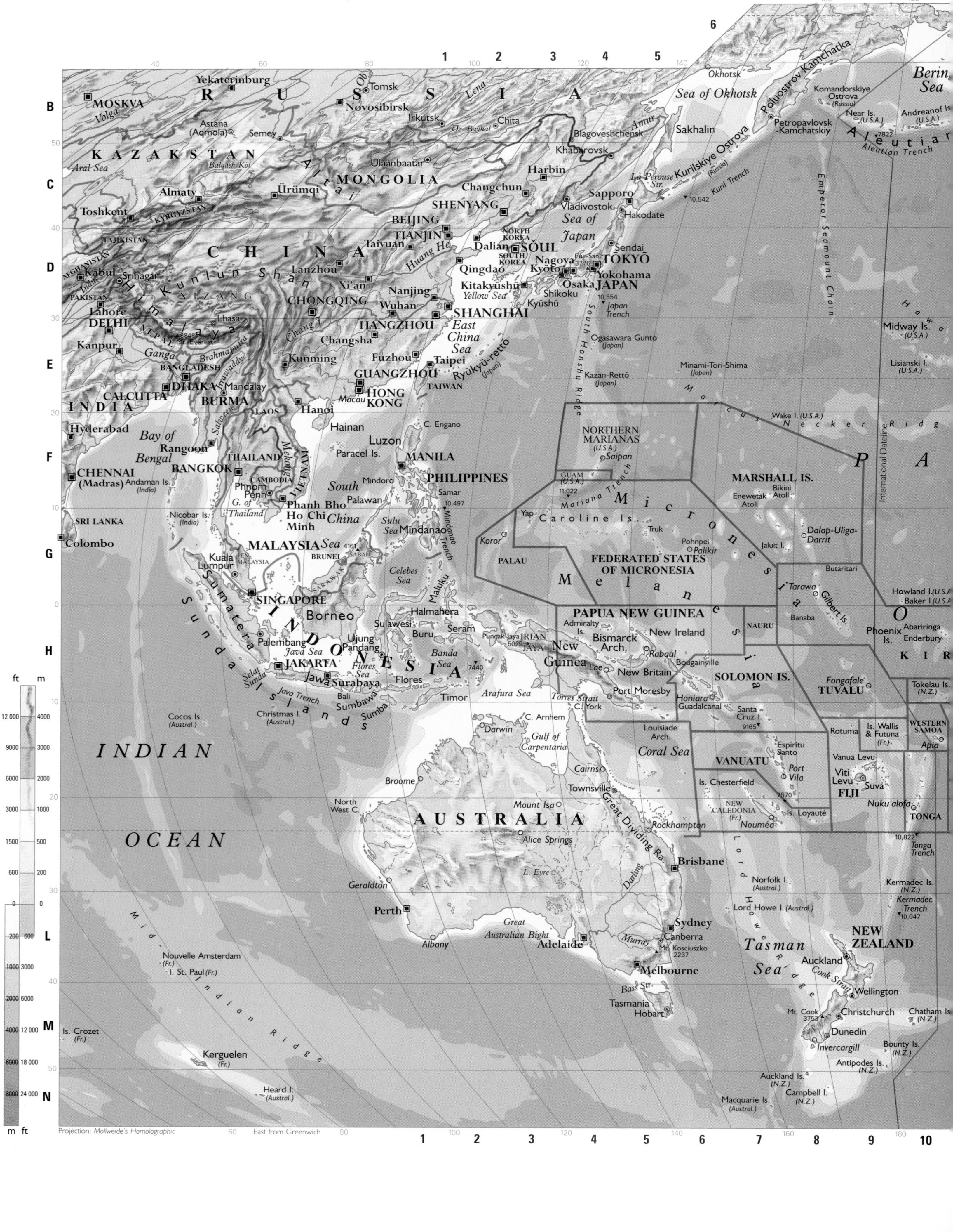

R U S S I A

Yekaterinburg
Tomsk
Novosibirsk
Irkutsk
Chita
MOSKVA
Volga
Ob
Lena
Astana (Aqmola)
Semey
Ulaanbaatar
Blagoveshchensk
Amur
Sea of Okhotsk
Okhotsk
Poluostrov Kamchatka
Bering Sea
Komandorskiye Ostrova (Russia)
Near Is. (U.S.A.)
Andreanof Is. (U.S.A.)

K A Z A K S T A N
Aral Sea
Balqash Köl
Altai
MONGOLIA
Khabarovsk
Sakhalin
Petropavlovsk-Kamchatskiy
7822
Aleutian Trench

Toshkent
Almaty
Ürümqi
Changchun
SHENYANG
Vladivostok
Hakodate
La Perouse Str.
Kurilskiye Ostrova (Russia)
Kuril Trench
10,542
Emperor Seamount Chain

KYRGYZSTAN
TAJIKISTAN
BEIJING
TIANJIN
Taiyuan
NORTH KOREA
Dalian
SOUTH KOREA
SOUL
Sapporo
Sea of Japan
Sendai

AFGHANISTAN
Kabul
Srinagar
Indus
C H I N A
Lanzhou
Kunlun Shan
Xinjiang
Xi'an
Nanjing
Qingdao
SOUTH KOREA
Kyoto
Osaka
JAPAN
TOKYO
Yokohama
Pusan
3776
10,554
Japan Trench

PAKISTAN
Lahore
DELHI
Himalaya
Mt Everest
8848
Lhasa
Brahmaputra
CHONGQING
Wuhan
Kitakyushu
Yellow Sea
Kyūshū
Shikoku
Nagoya

Kanpur
Ganga
Nepal
Changsha
HANGZHOU
SHANGHAI
East China Sea
Ogasawara Gunto (Japan)
Midway Is. (U.S.A.)

BANGLADESH
DHAKA
Mandalay
Kunming
Fuzhou
Taipei
Ryūkyū-retto (Japan)
Minami-Tori-Shima (Japan)
Lisianski I. (U.S.A.)

CALCUTTA
INDIA
BURMA
GUANGZHOU
HONG KONG
Macau
TAIWAN
Kazan-Rettō (Japan)

Hyderabad
Bay of Bengal
Rangoon
Hanoi
LAOS
Hainan
Luzon
Wake I. (U.S.A.)
Necker Ridge
NORTHERN MARIANAS (U.S.A.)
Saipan
Marcus Ridge
Howland
P A

CHENNAI (Madras)
THAILAND
BANGKOK
Andaman Is. (India)
C. Engano
Paracel Is.
MANILA
MARSHALL IS.
Bikini
Micronesia

SRI LANKA
Nicobar Is. (India)
CAMBODIA
Phnom Penh
G. of Thailand
Mindoro
Samar
PHILIPPINES
GUAM (U.S.A.)
Mariana Trench
11,022
Enewetak Atoll

Colombo
Phanh Bho Ho Chi Minh
South China Sea
Palawan
10,497
Yap
Caroline Is.
Truk
Pohnpei
Palikir
Dalap-Uliga-Darrit
Jaluit I.

MALAYSIA
Kuala Lumpur
Sulu Sea
Mindanao
4101
Mindanao Trench
Koror
PALAU
FEDERATED STATES OF MICRONESIA
Butaritari
Tarawa
Gilbert Is.
Howland I.(U.S.A.)
Baker I.(U.S.A.)

SINGAPORE
Borneo
Celebes Sea
Halmahera
Melanesia
NAURU
Banaba
Phoenix Is.
Abariringa
Enderbury
KIR
O

INDONESIA
Palembang
Ujung Pandang
Sulawesi
Buru
Seram
Maluku
Punak Jaya 5029
IRIAN JAYA
Admiralty Is.
Bismarck Arch.
New Ireland
PAPUA NEW GUINEA
Rabaul
Bougainville

Sumatera
Selat Sunda
JAKARTA
Jawa
Surabaya
Java Sea
Bali
Flores Sea
Banda Sea
7440
New Guinea
Lae
New Britain
SOLOMON IS.
Fongafale
TUVALU
Tokelau Is. (N.Z.)
WESTERN SAMOA

Sunda Islands
Java Trench
Flores
Sumbawa
Sumba
Timor
Arafura Sea
Torres Strait
C. York
Port Moresby
Honiara
Guadalcanal
Santa Cruz I.
9165
Rotuma
Is. Wallis & Futuna (Fr.)
Apia

Cocos Is. (Austral.)
Christmas I. (Austral.)
C. Arnhem
Darwin
Gulf of Carpentaria
Cairns
Louisiade Arch.
Coral Sea
VANUATU
Espiritu Santo
Port Vila
Vanua Levu
Viti Levu
Suva
FIJI
Nuku'alofa
TONGA

INDIAN
Broome
North West C.
Mount Isa
Townsville
Great Dividing Ra.
Is. Chesterfield
NEW CALEDONIA (Fr.)
Nouméa
Is. Loyauté
7570
10,822
Tonga Trench

OCEAN
AUSTRALIA
Alice Springs
L. Eyre
Rockhampton
Darling
Brisbane
Norfolk I. (Austral.)
Kermadec Is. (N.Z.)

Geraldton
Great Australian Bight
Murray
Mt Kosciuszko 2237
Sydney
Canberra
Lord Howe I. (Austral.)
Kermadec Trench 10,047

Perth
Albany
Adelaide
Melbourne
Bass Str.
Tasmania
Hobart
Tasman Sea
Auckland
Cook Strait
NEW ZEALAND
Christchurch
Chatham Is. (N.Z.)

Mid-Indian Ridge
Nouvelle Amsterdam (Fr.)
I. St. Paul (Fr.)
Mt Cook 3753
Dunedin
Invercargill
Bounty Is. (N.Z.)

Is. Crozet (Fr.)
Kerguelen (Fr.)
Indian Ridge
Auckland Is. (N.Z.)
Antipodes Is. (N.Z.)

Heard I. (Austral.)
Macquarie Is. (Austral.)
Campbell I. (N.Z.)

Projection: Mollweide's Homolographic   East from Greenwich

ft m
12 000   4000
9000   3000
6000   2000
3000   1000
1500   500
600   200
0   0
200   600
1000   3000
2000   6000
4000   12 000
6000   18 000
8000   24 000
m ft

Arctic Circle

ALASKA
(U.S.A.)
Anchorage

Bristol Bay

Gulf of Alaska

Juneau

15

16 17 18 19 20

ROCKY C A N A D A

Prince of Wales I.
(U.S.A.) Prince Rupert
Queen Charlotte Is.
(Canada)

Edmonton

L. Winnipeg

Calgary

Regina Winnipeg

Newfoundland

N O R T H

Vancouver
Vancouver I. Victoria
Seattle
Portland Boise

St. Lawrence

L. Superior Québec St. John's
Montréal
Minneapolis L. Huron Toronto Ottawa
Detroit L. Ontario Boston
Buffalo
Salt Lake Denver CHICAGO Pittsburgh NEW YORK CITY
City Kansas City L. Erie PHILADELPHIA
Cincinnati Baltimore
SAN FRANCISCO St. Louis Washington D.C.

A T L A N T I C

Sacramento
6741

C. Mendocino

4418

Missouri

UNITED S T A T E S

Oklahoma City Memphis Atlanta
LOS ANGELES Phoenix Dallas C. Hatteras
San Diego Houston Bermuda
Ciudad San Antonio New (U.K.)
Juárez Orleans Jacksonville
Guadalupe Gulf of Mexico Miami
(Mex.) Monterrey BAHAMAS

Sargasso Sea

O C E A N

Tropic of Cancer

Honolulu
Oahu HAWAIIAN IS.
4205 (U.S.A.)
Hawaii

C. San Lucas

Guadalajara

La Habana CUBA West Indies

Canal de Yucatán

MEXICO Mérida HAITI 9200
5700 7680 DOMINICAN REP.
Puebla JAMAICA PUERTO Leeward
Acapulco BELIZE Kingston RICO Is.
(U.S.A.)
Is. Revilla Gigedo GUATEMALA HONDURAS Caribbean Sea
(Mex.) Guatemala BARBADOS
San Salvador NICARAGUA Windward Is.
EL SALVADOR Managua Barranquilla Maracaibo

Johnston I.
(U.S.A.)

C I F I C

Palmyra Is.
(U.S.A.)

I. Clipperton
(Fr.)

COSTA Colón Caracas
RICA San José Panamá Orinoco
I. del Coco PANAMA VENEZUELA
(Costa Rica) Medellín Bogotá

P O L Y N E S I A

Teraina
Tabuaeran
Kiritimati

Equator

Galápagos
(Ecuador)

I. de Malpelo Cali
(Colombia) COLOMBIA

G

Jarvis I.
(U.S.A.)

O C E A N

Quito
ECUADOR

Phoenix Is.

Malden I.

Guayaquil Iquitos
Starbuck I. C. Paliñas Amazonas

KIRIBATI

BRAZIL

H

Tongareva
Pukapuka Caroline I.
Manihiki Vostok I.
Flint I.

Trujillo

6369 PERU

J

MER.
AMOA
U.S.A.

Suwarrow Is. Is. de la
Société Is. Marquises

LIMA Cuzco

Niue
(N.Z.) Cook Is.
(N.Z.) Tahiti
Papeete

Is. Tuamotu

Arequipa Nevada Ancohuma
6550
L. Titicaca
6866 La Paz
Peru- BOLIVIA

F R E N C H   P O L Y N E S I A

Rarotonga Is. Tubuai Mururoa

Iquique Chile
Arica

Tropic of Capricorn

Ducie I.

Pitcairn I.
(U.K.)

Rapa

Antofagasta

PARAGUAY

Asunción

K

Sala-y-Gómez
(Chile)

8050
Trench

San Felix San Ambrosio
(Chile) (Chile)

San Miguel
de Tucumán

Pôrto
Alegre

I. de Pascua
(Chile)

Arch. de Aconcagua Córdoba
Juan Fernández 6960 Rosario URUGUAY
(Chile) Valparaíso Montevideo
SANTIAGO BUENOS Río de la Plata
Concepción AIRES

L

ARGENTINA

SOUTH

40

Chile Rise

ATLANTIC

M

Pacific-Antarctic Ridge

OCEAN
6212

50

Falkland Is.
(U.K.)

N

Punta Arenas Tierra del Fuego South Georgia
Est. de Magallanes (U.K.)
C. de Hornos

COPYRIGHT GEORGE PHILIP LTD.

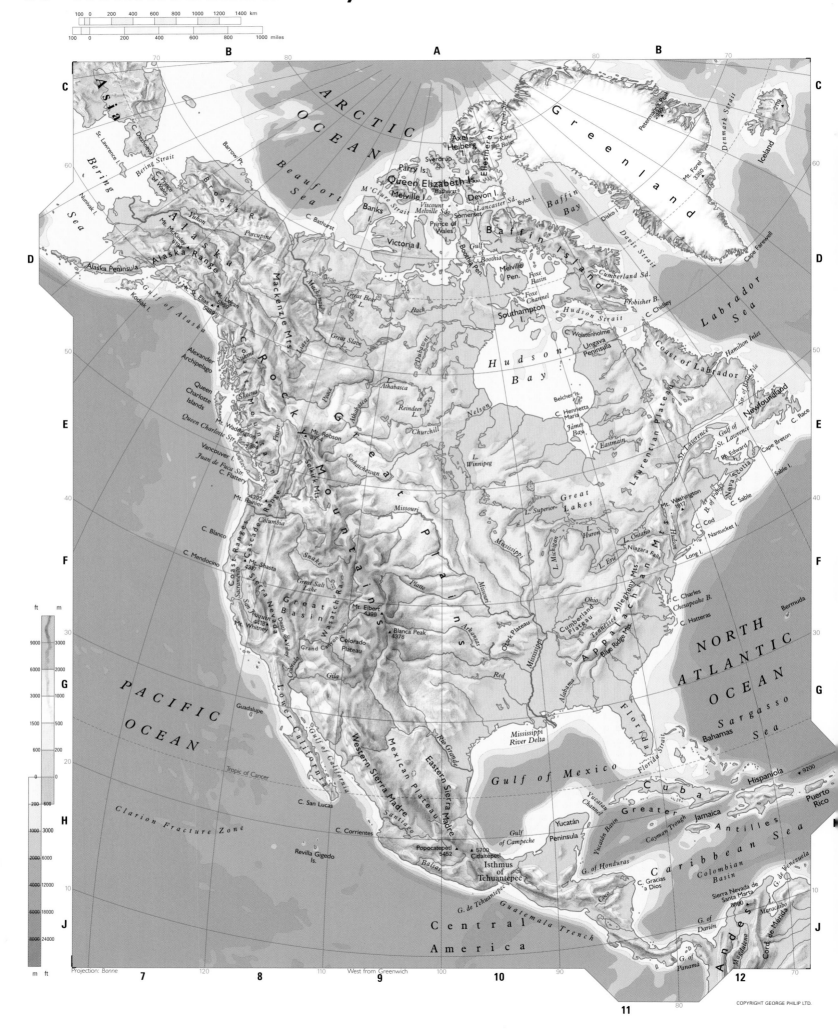

COPYRIGHT GEORGE PHILIP LTD.

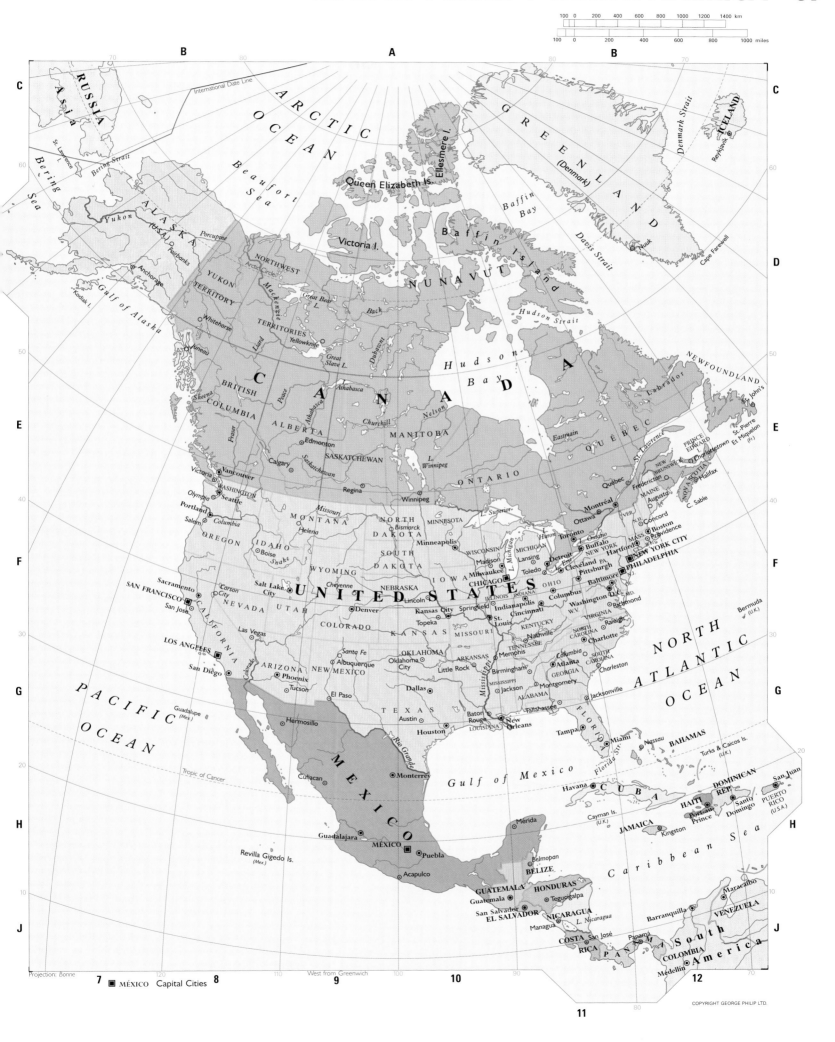

COPYRIGHT GEORGE PHILIP LTD.

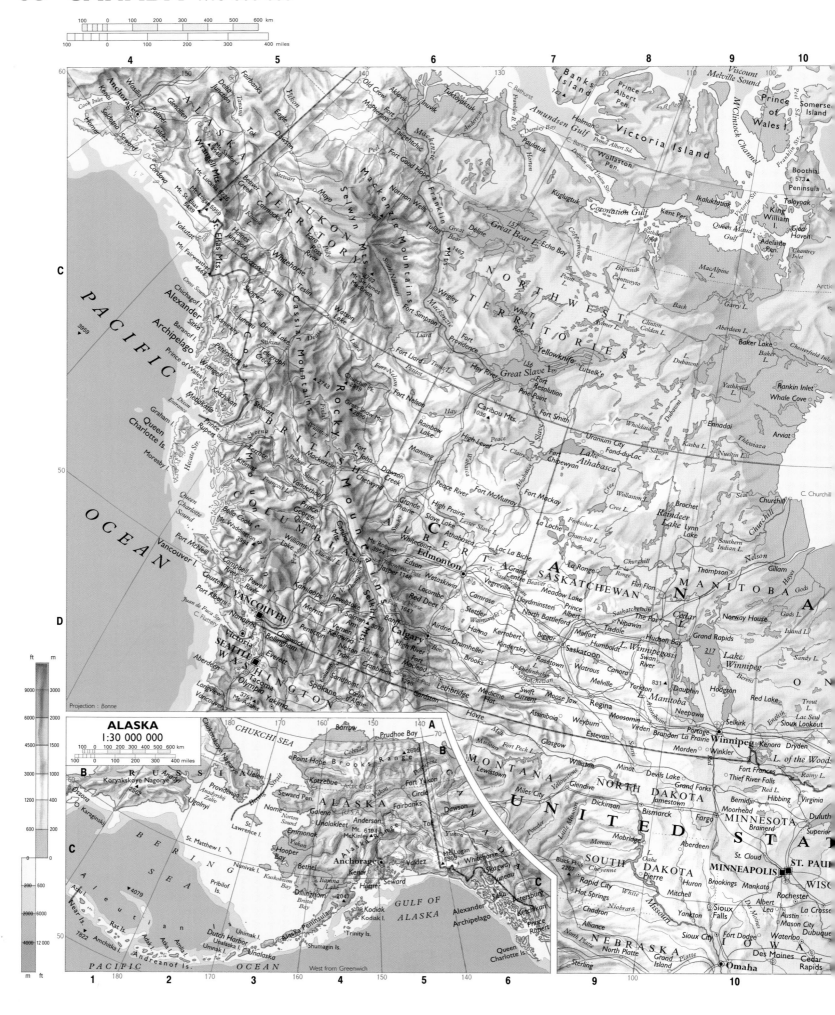

ALASKA
1:30 000 000

Projection : Bonne

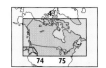

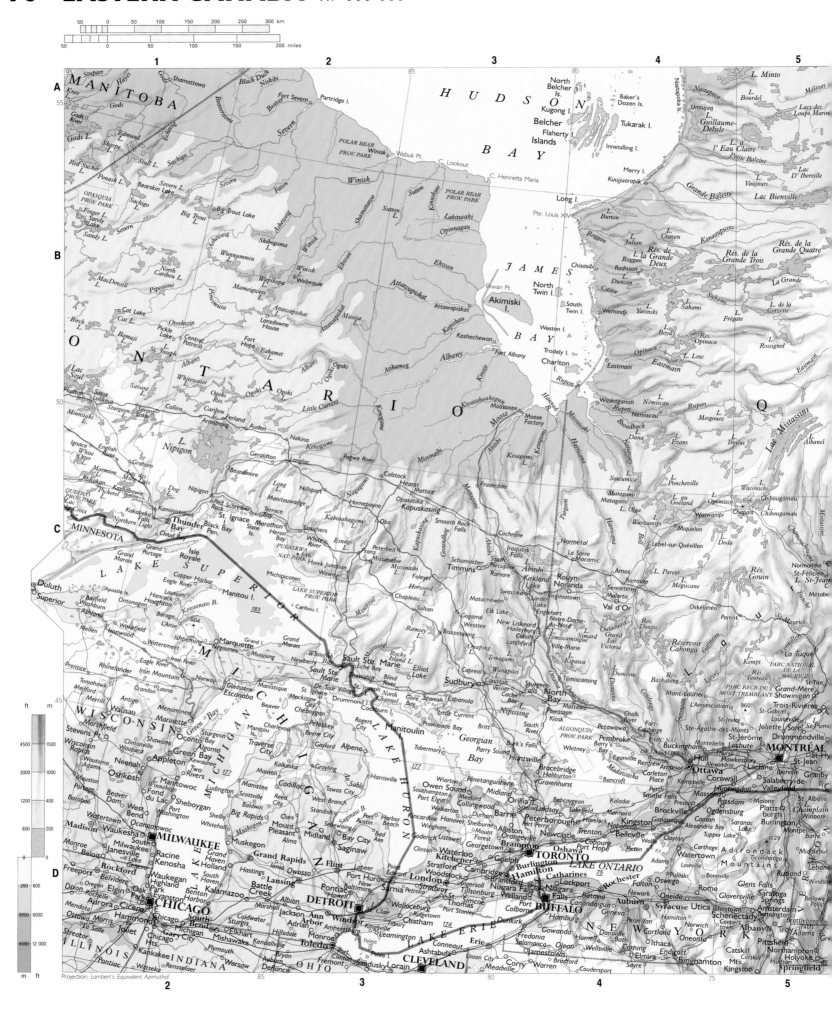

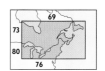

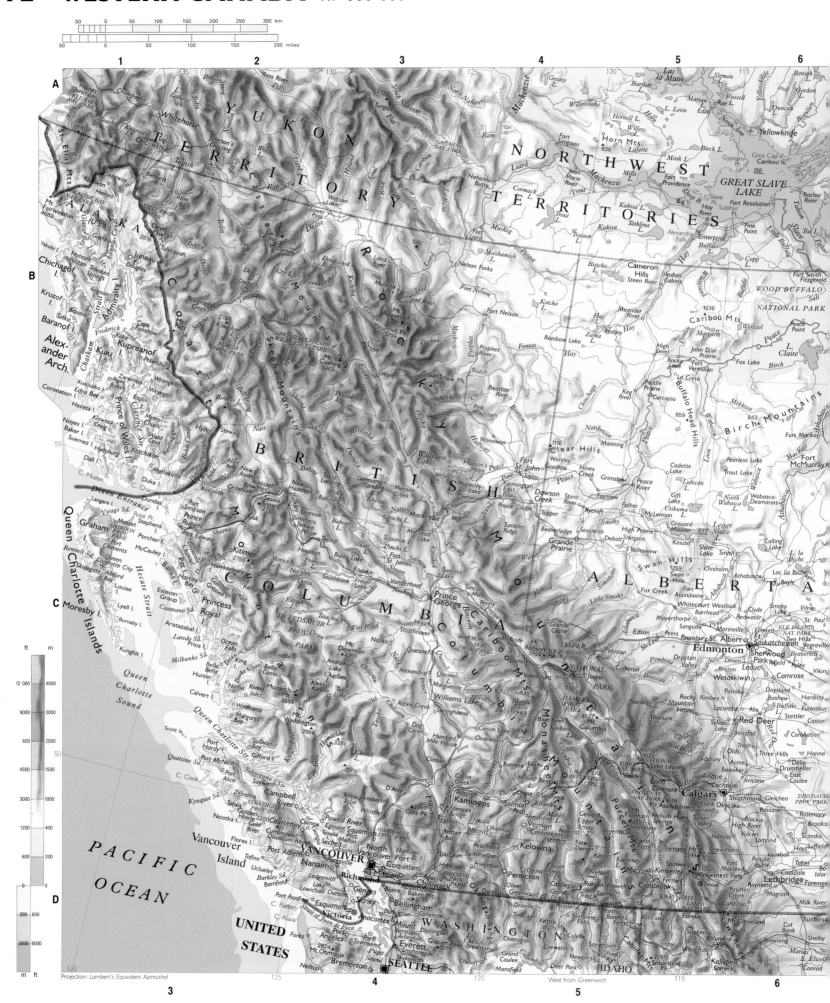

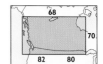

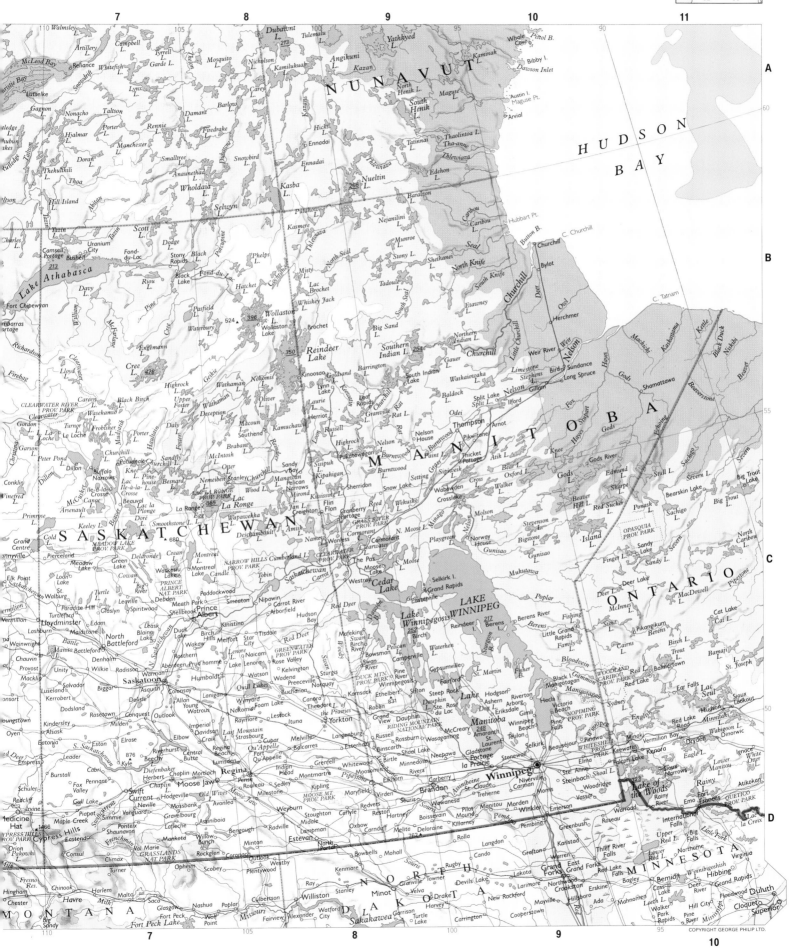

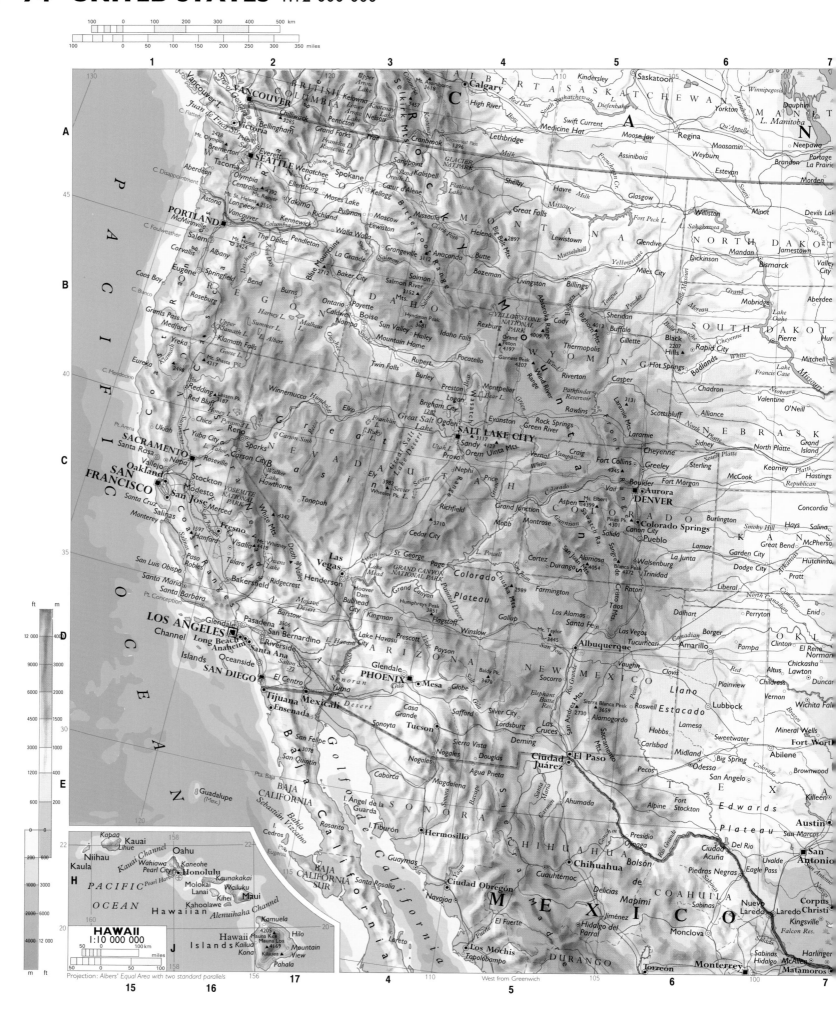

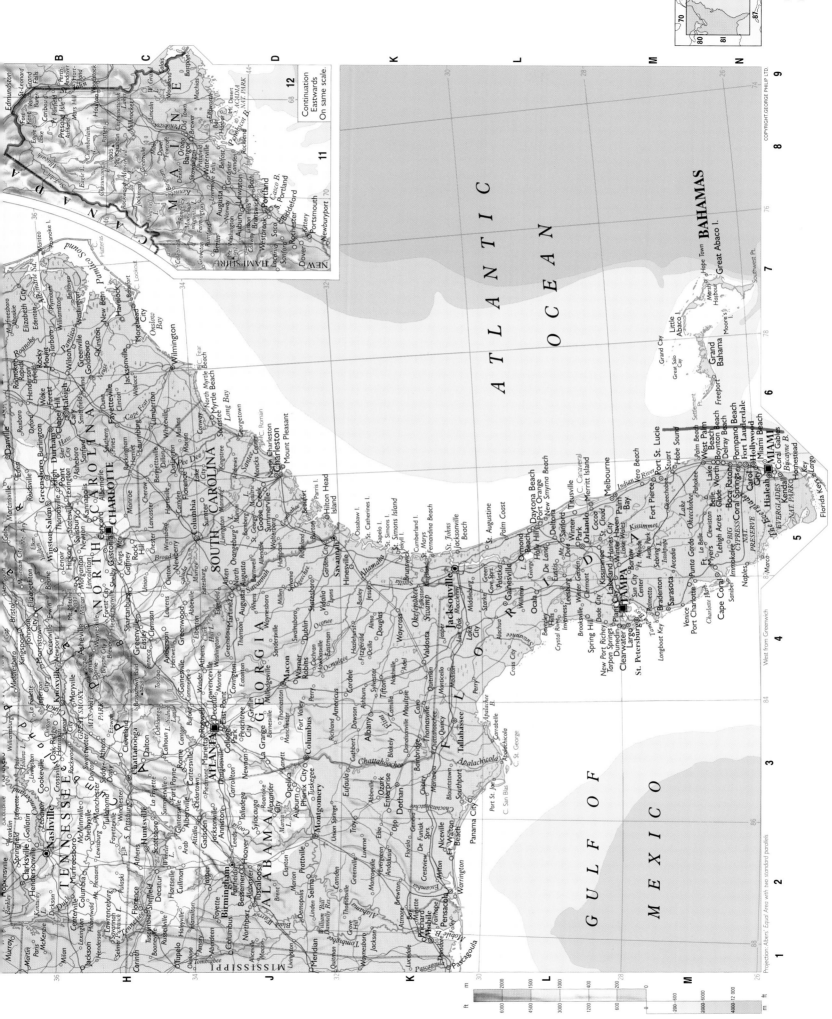

ATLANTIC OCEAN

BAHAMAS

Great Abaco I.

Grand Bahama

GULF OF MEXICO

TENNESSEE

NORTH CAROLINA

SOUTH CAROLINA

GEORGIA

ALABAMA

MISSISSIPPI

FLORIDA

ATLANTA

CHARLOTTE

MIAMI

TAMPA

MAINE

NEW HAMPSHIRE

Continuation
Eastwards
On same scale.

COPYRIGHT GEORGE PHILIP LTD.

Projection: Albers' Equal Area with two standard parallels

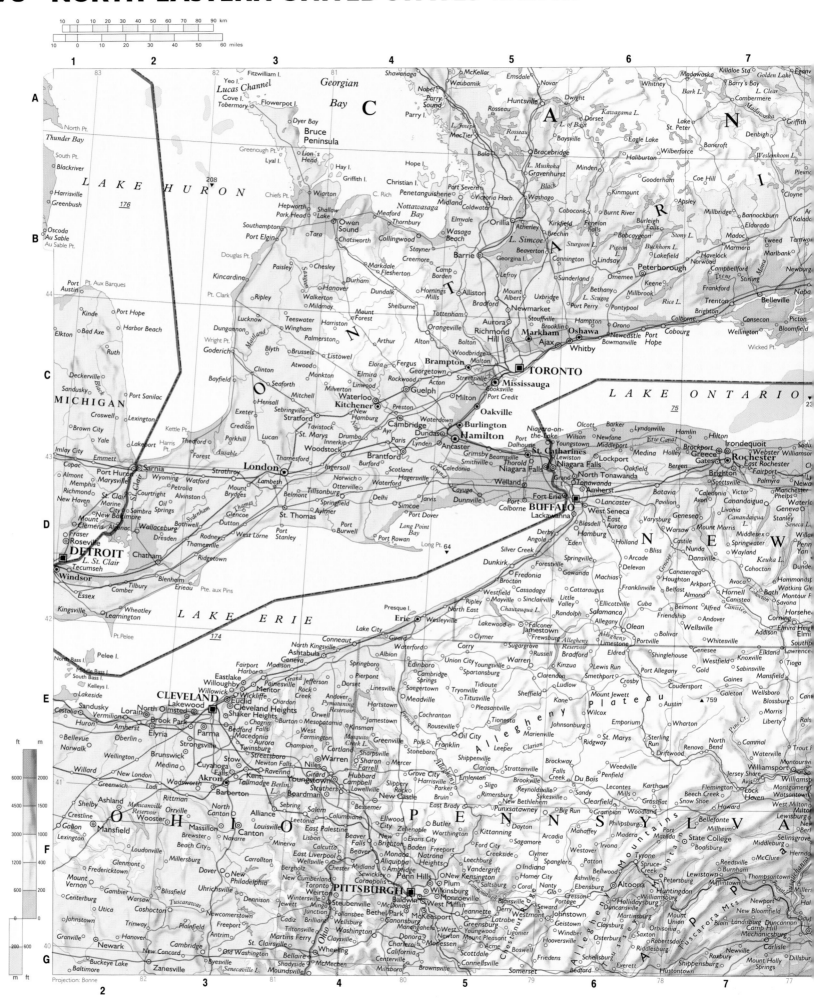

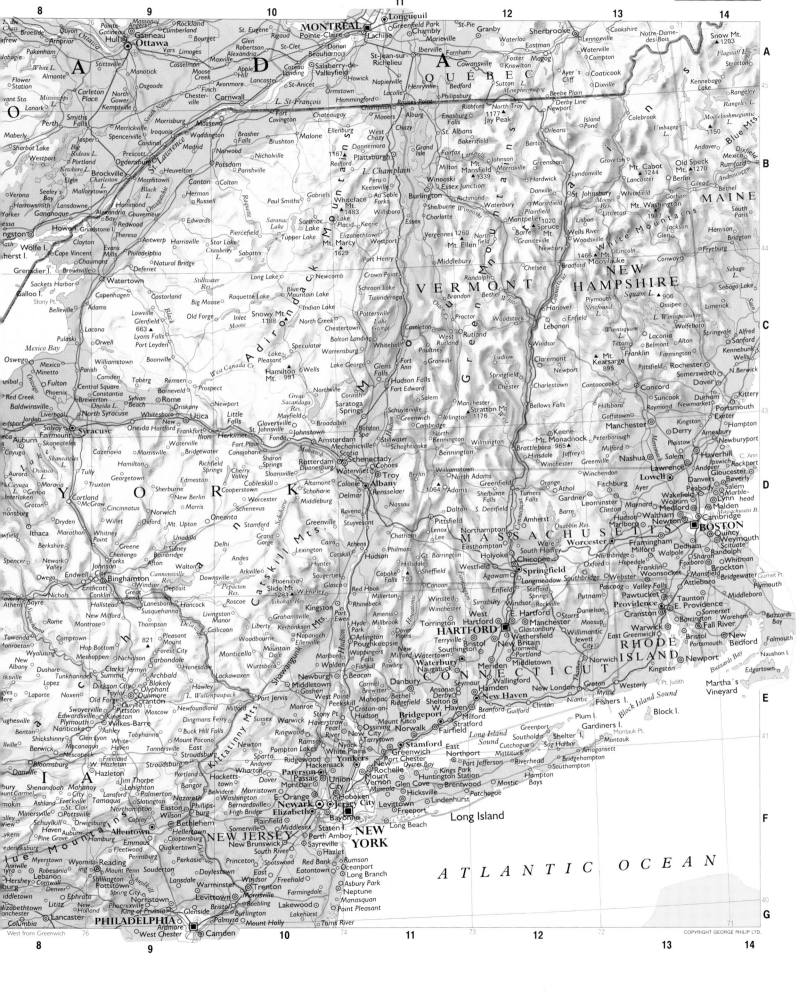

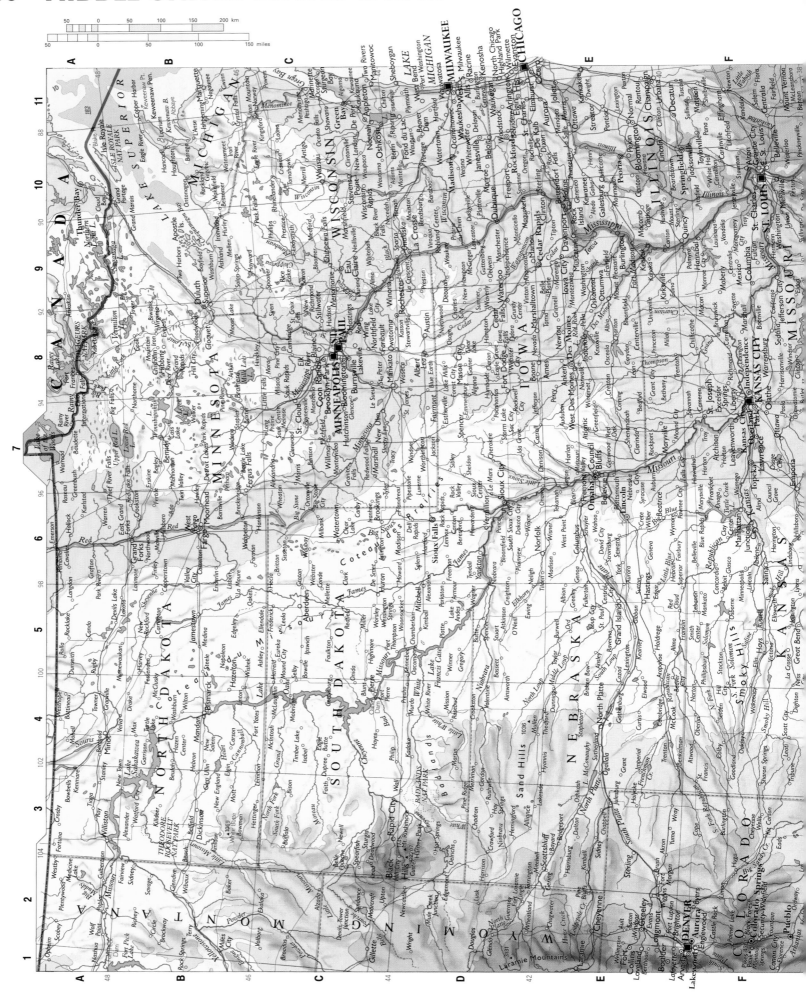

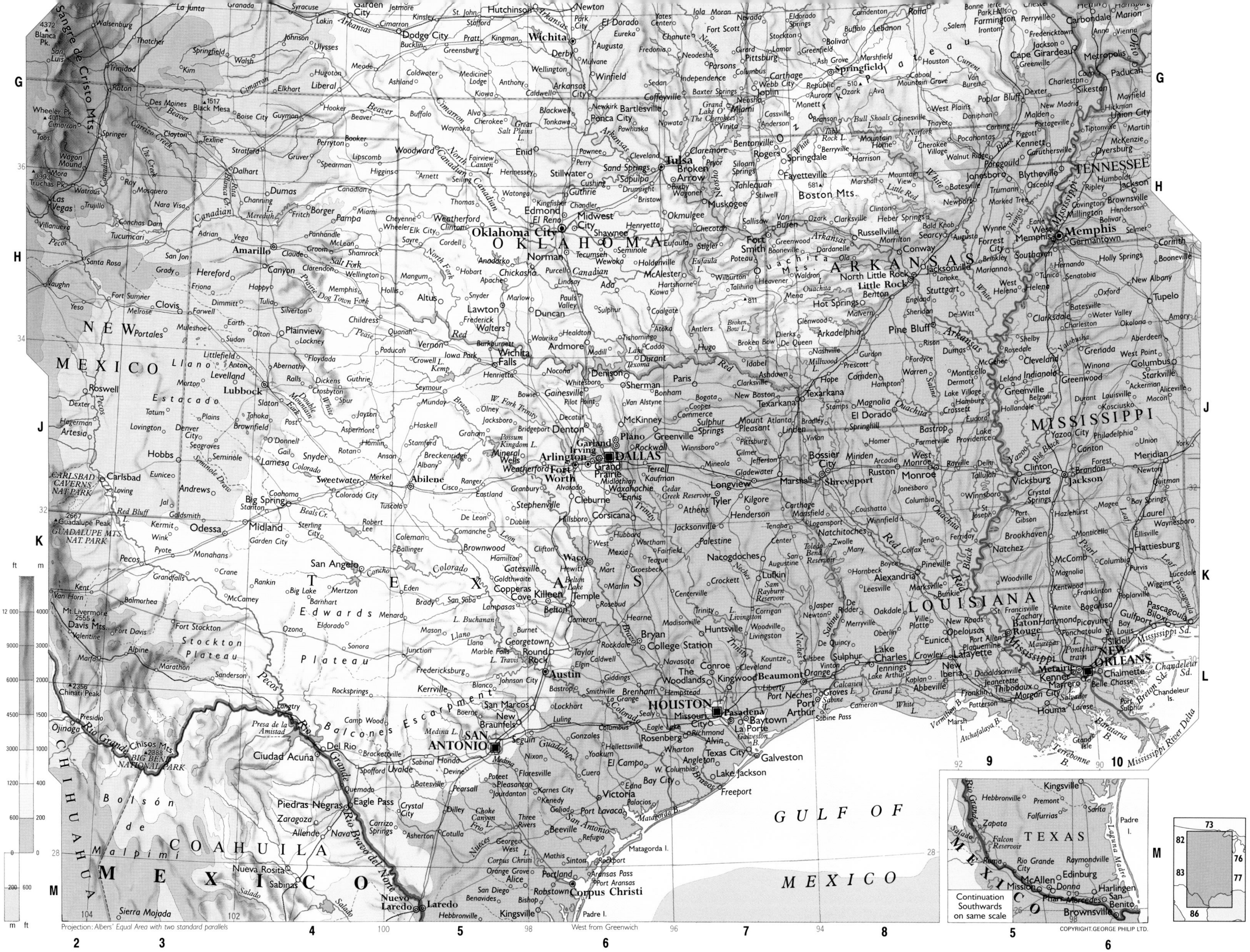

TENNESSEE

MISSISSIPPI

ARKANSAS

LOUISIANA

OKLAHOMA

T E X A S

NEW MEXICO

COAHUILA

CHIHUAHUA

MEXICO

GULF OF MEXICO

Sangre de Cristo Mts.

Boston Mts.

Ouachita Mts.

Edwards Plateau

Llano Estacado

Stockton Plateau

Rio Grande

Rio Bravo del Norte

Laguna Madre

Mississippi River Delta

New Orleans

Houston

San Antonio

Dallas

Fort Worth

Memphis

Tulsa

Oklahoma City

Wichita

Lubbock

Amarillo

Corpus Christi

Nuevo Laredo

Laredo

Continuation Southwards on same scale

Projection: Albers' Equal Area with two standard parallels

West from Greenwich

COPYRIGHT GEORGE PHILIP LTD.

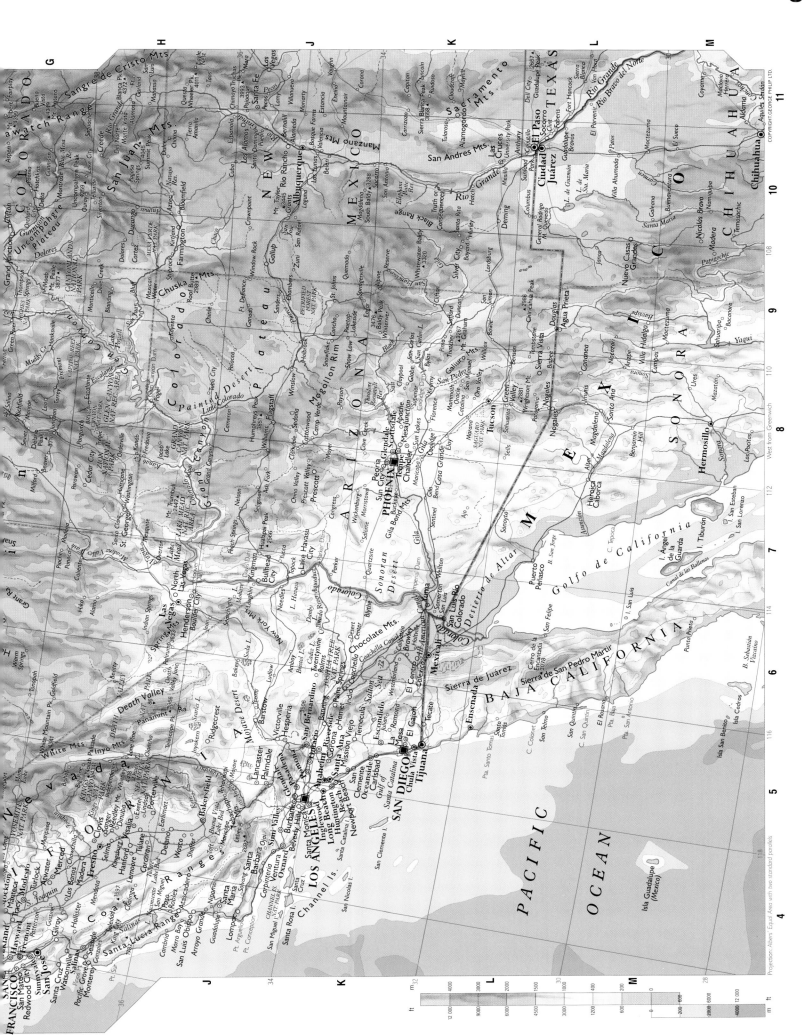

COPYRIGHT GEORGE PHILIP LTD.

Projection: Albers Equal Area with two standard parallels

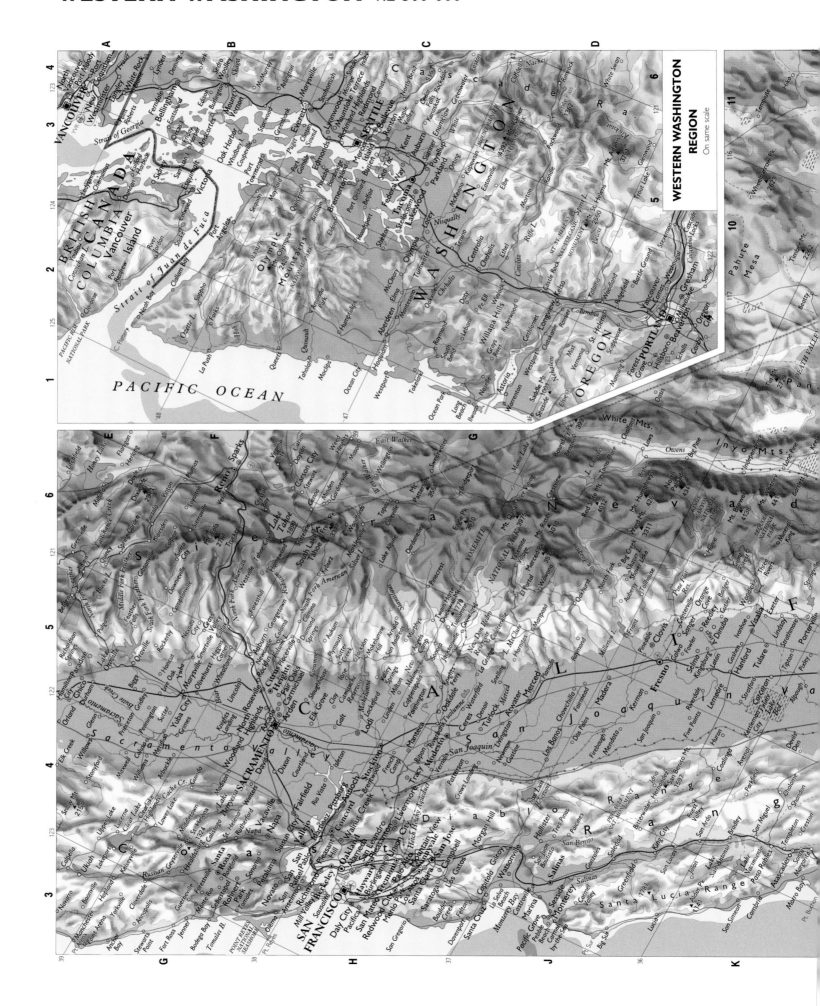

WESTERN WASHINGTON REGION
On same scale

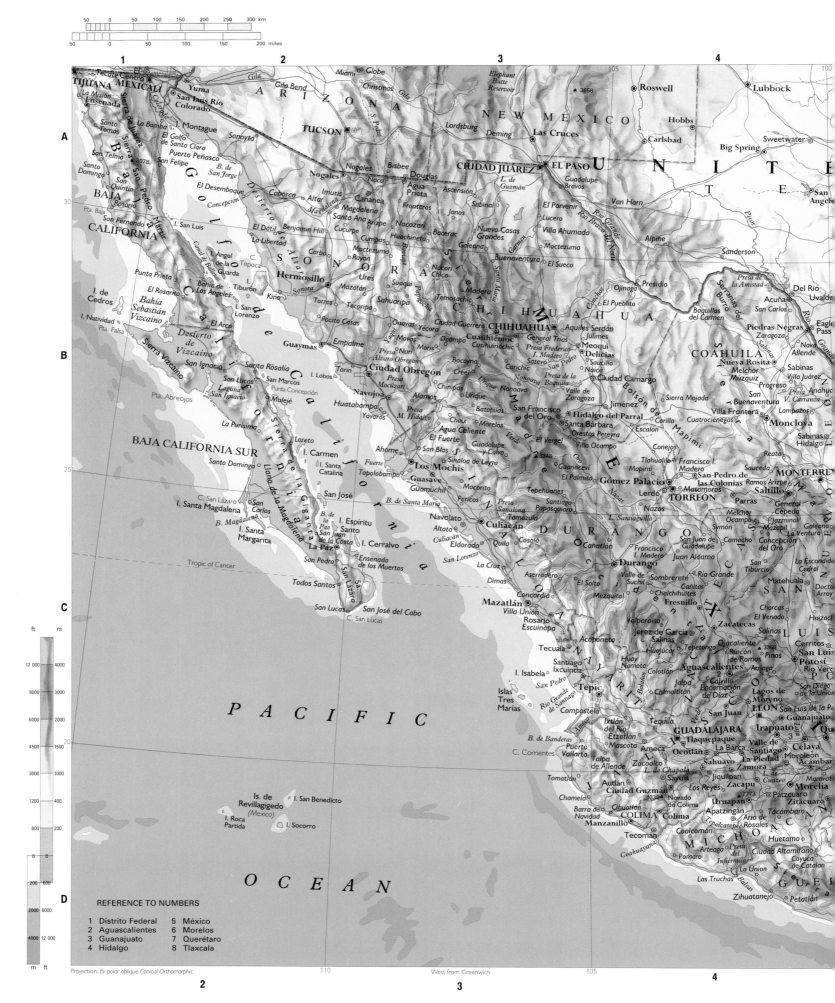

REFERENCE TO NUMBERS

1 Distrito Federal	5 México
2 Aguascalientes	6 Morelos
3 Guanajuato	7 Querétaro
4 Hidalgo	8 Tlaxcala

Projection: Bi-polar oblique Conical Orthomorphic

West from Greenwich

5 **6** **7** **8**

Wichita
Falls
Denison
Sherman
Paris
Red
Hope
Camden
Greenville
Tuscaloosa
Opelika
Columbus
McRae
ARKANSAS
Texarkana
El Dorado
90
MISSISSIPPI
Greenville
ALABAMA
Phenix City
Montgomery
Cordele
Possum
Kingdom
Res.
Brazos
Denton
Greenville
Monroe
Vicksburg
Meridian
Selma
Troy
Americus
Tifton
85
FORT WORTH
DALLAS
Marshall
Longview
Shreveport
Tallulah
Jackson
Alabama
Albany
GEORGIA
Ranger
Cleburne
Tyler
Corsicana
Toledo
Bend
Res.
Natchez
Laurel
Hattiesburg
Flomaton
Dothan
Chattahoochee
Waycross
Valdosta
A
Abilene
Hillsboro
Palestine
Nacogdoches
McComb
Jim Woodruff
Res.
Tallahassee
Lake
City
Brownwood
Waco
Lufkin
San
Rayburn
Reservoir
Alexandria
Baton
Rouge
Bogalusa
Biloxi
MOBILE
Pensacola
Panama City
FLORIDA
30
Temple
Huntsville
Jewett
Sabine
Hammond
Gulfport
Mobile Bay
Apalachee
Bay
Austin
Bryan
Trinity
Lake Charles
Lafayette
NEW
ORLEANS
C. San Blas
Suwannee
Navasota
HOUSTON
Beaumont
Port
Arthur
Atchafalaya
Bay
Breton Sd.
Guadalupe
Rosenberg
Terrebonne Bay
Mississippi
River Delta
Clearwater
B
SAN
ANTONIO
Victoria
Galveston
Dilley
Nueces
Corpus Christi
Alice
GULF
OF
Laredo
Kingsville
Nuevo Laredo
Zapata
Laguna Madre
25
General
Trevino
Presa
Falcon
McAllen
Harlingen
Brownsville
Nuevo
Guerrero
Camargo
Reynosa
Matamoros
M E X I C O
Cadereyta
Presa
M.R.
Gomez
China
Valle
Hermoso
Santa Teresa
Montemorelos
Conchas
Mendez
Laguna Madre
Linares
Villagrán
Hidalgo
Santander Jiménez
San Fernando
Tropic of Cancer
La Esperanza
4064
Zaragoza
La Pesca
Soto la Marina
C
Ciudad
Victoria
Llera
Sierra de Tamaulipas
Pta. Jerez
CUBA
Guane
Tula
Calles
Aldama
Canal de Yucatán
C. San Antonio
La Fé
Ocampo
Ciudad Mante
Altamira
Ciudad Madero
Tampico
I. Desterrada
I. Pérez
(Mexico)
C. Corrientes
TOSI
Cárdenas de Valles
Pánuco
Ozuluama
L. de Tamiahua
Pta.
Yalkukul
Rio Lagartos
C. Catoche
Dzilam
de Bravo
Progreso
Motul
Temax
El Cuyo
Tizimín
Cancún
Puerto Juárez
7
taro
Tempoal
Magozal
C. Rojo
DZIBILCHALTÚN
Mérida
Izamal
Espita
Puerto Morelos
San Juan del Rio
Zimapán
Zacualtipan
Chicontepec
Tantoyuca
Tamazunchale
Tuxpan
Poza Rica
Papantla
MAYAPAN
CHICHEN
ITZA
Sotuta
Valladolid
Cozumel
Isla
Cozumel
20
Huichapan
Pachuca
Huauchinango
Nautla
Misantla
Maxcanú
YUCATÁN
Ticul
Peto
El Oro
Zumpango
Tulancingo
Teziutlán
Jalapa
Enriquez
IZAMAL
Tenabo
Tekax
Vigia Chico
B. de la Ascensión
Tula
MÉXICO
Apizaco
4282
Coatepec
ZEMPOALA
Veracruz
Campeche
Bolonchenticul
Hopelchén
Felipe Carrillo
Puerto
B. del Espíritu Santo
Toluca
Tlaxcala
Amecameca
PUEBLA
Citlaltépetl
5700
Golfo
de
Campeche
Champotón
Chenkán
QUINTANA
ROO
Bacalar
Banco
Chinchorro
Tenancingo
Tenango
Popocatépetl
PUEBLA
Córdoba
Orizaba
CRUZ
Alvarado
Tlacotalpan
Ciudad del
Carmen
L. de
Términos
Matamoros
Chetumal
B. de
Chetumal
D
Cuernavaca
Izúcar de
Matamoros
Tehuacán
Cosamaloapan
San Andrés
Tuxtla
1879
Paraiso
Frontera
Corozal
Taxco
Jojutla
Iguala
Chiautla
Acatlán
Huautla
de Jiménez
Tres Valles
Comalcalco
Palizada
CAMPECHE
Orange Walk
Ambergris Cay
Tlapa
RO
Chilapa
Huajuapan
de León
Asunción
Nochixtlán
Presa
Miguel
Alemán
LA VENTA
Coatzacoalcos
Minatitlán
Cárdenas
TABASCO
Villahermosa
Balancán
Concepción
Hondo
Belize
City
Turneffe Is.
Belmopan
BELIZE
3703
RERO
San Juan Bautista
Silacayoapan
Acayucan
Istmo
de
Macuspana
Tenosique
Uaxactún
San Ignacio
Benque
Viejo
Dangriga
Is. de
la Bahía
Chilpancingo
Coyuca
Tierra Colorada
Oaxaca
Tlacolula
OAXACA
Raudales de
Jesús Carranza
Valle Nacional
Presa
Netzahualcóyotl
Presa Malpaso
Simojovel
Ocosingo
L. Petén Itzá
La Libertad
TIKAL
Flores
Usumacinta
Maya Mts.
Monkey River
Golfo de Honduras
Roatán
Puerto
Castilla
Trujillo
Iriona
Ayutla
OAXACA
Tehuantepec
Tuxtla
Gutiérrez
Chiapa de
Corzo
San Cristóbal
de las Casas
La Independencia
CHIAPAS
San Luis
Punta Gorda
Puerto
Barrios
Livingston
Tela
San Pedro Sula
Belfate
Sava
Balsas
Tlaxiaco
Ocotlán
San Jerónimo
Ixtepec
Matías Romero
Salina
Cruz
Comitán
Sierra
Sebol
La Concordia
L. de Izabal
Gualán
Santa
Barbara
El Progreso
Olanchito
Yoro
HONDURAS
E
Acapulco
Ometepec
Ejutla
Juchitán
Arriaga
Tonalá
3993
Cuchumatanes
Huehuetenango
Cobán
Sierra de las Minas
Zacapa
Santa Rosa
de Copán
L. de
Yojoa
Juticalpa
Catacamas
15
Pinotepa
Nacional
Jamiltepec
Tututepec
Miahuatlán
3139
Tehuantepec
Pijijiapan
Mapastepec
Motozintla
4220
Chiquimula
Comayagua
Tegucigalpa
Danli
Verde
San Pedro
Mixtepec
Pochutla
Puerto
Ángel
Golfo de
Tehuantepec
Puerto
Escondido
Punta
Maldonado
Mar Muerto
Arista
Huixtla
San Marcos
Tapachula
Coatepeque
Mazatenango
Retalhuleu
Totonicapán
Sololá
Jalapa
Antigua
GUATEMALA
Amatitlán
Santa
Ana
La Esperanza
La Paz
Yuscarán
E

5 95 **6** 90 **7**

Golfo de Tehuantepec

COPYRIGHT GEORGE PHILIP LTD.

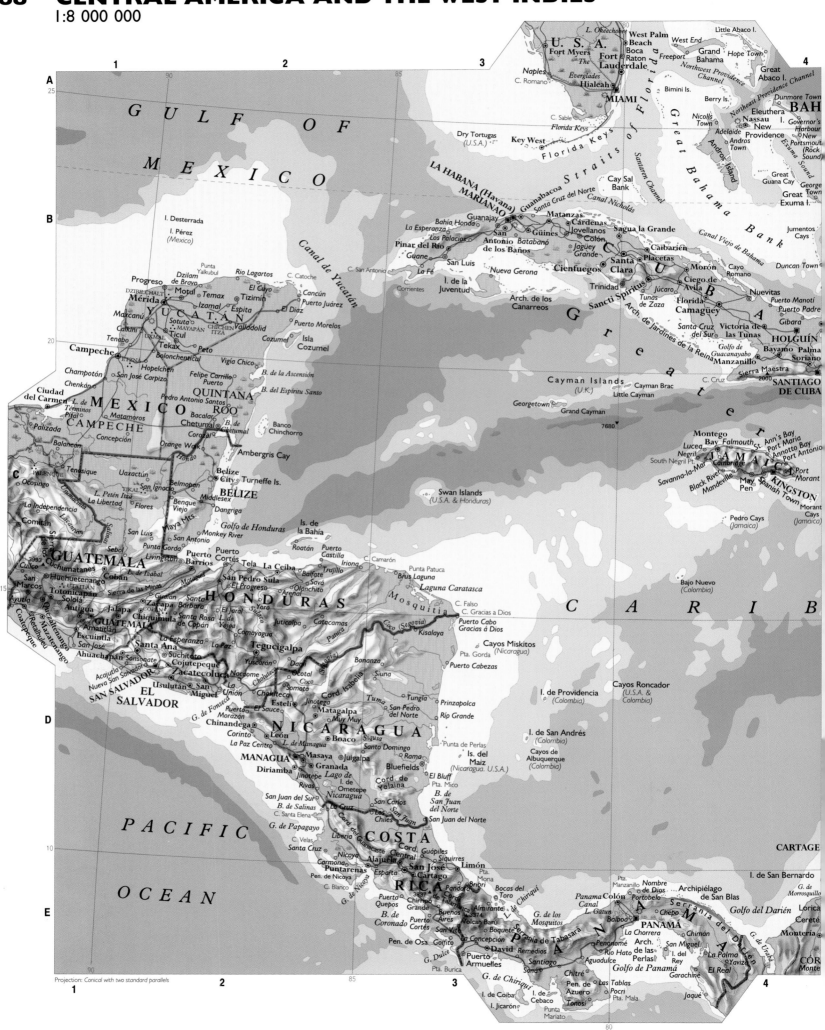

GULF OF MEXICO

PACIFIC OCEAN

U.S.A.

BAH

CUBA

JAMAICA

MEXICO

YUCATÁN

QUINTANA ROO

CAMPECHE

GUATEMALA

BELIZE

HONDURAS

EL SALVADOR

NICARAGUA

COSTA RICA

PANAMA

CARIB

Projection: Conical with two standard parallels

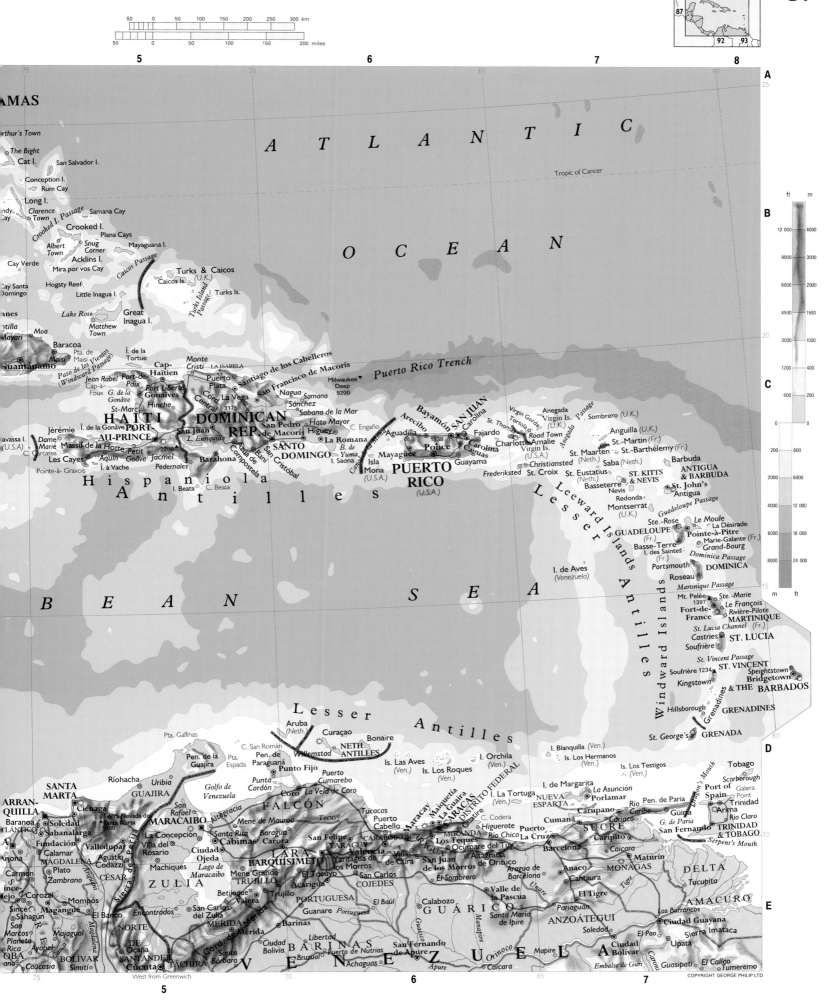

87

92 93

A
25

ATLANTIC

Tropic of Cancer

B

12 000 | 4000

O C E A N

9000 | 3000

6000 | 2000

4500 | 1500

3000 | 1000

C

1200 | 400

600 | 200

Puerto Rico Trench

0 | 0

200 | 600

2000 | 6000

4000 | 12 000

6000 | 18 000

8000 | 24 000

15
m | ft

Milwaukee
Deep
9200

Puerto Rico Trench

AMAS

Arthur's Town

The Bight
Cat I.
San Salvador I.

Conception I.
Rum Cay

Long I.

Clarence
Town
Samana Cay

Andy·
Cay

Crooked I.

Plana Cays

Albert
Town
Snug
Corner
Mayaguana I.

Cay Verde
Acklins I.

Mira por vos Cay

Cay Santa
Domingo

Hogsty Reef.
Little Inagua I.

Turks & Caicos
(U.K.)
Caicos Is.

Turks Is.

anes

Antilla

Lake Rose

Great
Inagua I.

Mayari

Moa

Matthew
Town

Guantánamo

Maisí
Pta. de
Maisí
Î. de la
Tortue

Baracoa

Paso de los Vientos
(Windward Passage)

Cap-
Haïtien
Monte
Cristi
LA ISABELA

Santiago de los Cabelleros

Jean Rabel Port-de-
Paix
Cap-à-
Foux
Fort Liberté
Puerto
Plata
Cord.
Central
La Vega

San Francisco de Macorís

Nagua
Samana

G. de la
Gonâve
Hinche
St-Marc

HAITI
3175

**DOMINICAN
REP**

Sánchez

Sabana de la Mar

Jérémie
Î. de la Gonâve
San Juan
L. Enriquillo

**PORT-
AU-PRINCE**

Hato Mayor

Higüey

C. Engaño

San Pedro
de Macorís

avassa I.
(U.S.A.)
Ste.
Marie
Massif de la Hotte
2280

**SANTO
DOMINGO**

La Romana

B. de
Yuma

Les Cayes
Aquin
Petit
Goâve
Jacmel
Barahona
Azua de
Compostela
San Cristóbal
I. Saona

Pointe-à- Gravois
Î. à Vache
Pedernales

Cavo
Mona
(U.S.A.)

Isla
Mona
(U.S.A.)

**PUERTO
RICO**
(U.S.A.)

Aguadilla
Arecibo
Bayamón
SAN JUAN
Carolina

H i s p a n i o l a
I. Beata
C. Beata

A n t i l l e s

Mayagüez
Ponce
Caguas

Guayama

Virgin Gorda
(U.K.)
Tortola
(U.K.)
St. Thom
Road Town

Anegada
(U.K.)
Virgin Is.

Anegada Passage

Sombrero (U.K.)

Fajardo
Charlotte Amalie
Virgin Is.
(U.S.A.)

St.-Martin (Fr.)
Anguilla (U.K.)

Christiansted
Saba (Neth.)

St.-Barthélemy (Fr.)

Frederiksted St. Croix
St. Eustatius
(Neth.)
**ST. KITTS
& NEVIS**

Barbuda

Basseterre
Nevis

**ANTIGUA
& BARBUDA**

St. John's
Antigua

Redonda
Montserrat
(U.K.)

Ste.-Rose
Le Moule
La Désirade

GUADELOUPE
(Fr.)

Pointe-à-Pitre
(Fr.)

Basse-Terre
I. des Saintes
(Fr.)

Marie-Galante
Grand-Bourg

Guadeloupe Passage

Portsmouth
Roseau

DOMINICA

Dominica Passage

I. de Aves
(Venezuela)

Martinique Passage

C A R I B B E A N   S E A

Mt. Pelée
1397
Fort-de-
France
St. Lucia Channel

Ste.-Marie
Le François
Rivière-Pilote

MARTINIQUE (Fr.)

Castries
Soufrière

ST. LUCIA

St. Vincent Passage

L e s s e r   A n t i l l e s

Soufrière 1234
Kingstown

ST. VINCENT
& THE
GRENADINES

Speightstown
Bridgetown

BARBADOS

Hillsborough

Grenadines
GRENADINES

St. George's
GRENADA

D
60

Pta. Gallinas

Aruba
(Neth.)
Curaçao
Bonaire

Willemstad
**NETH.
ANTILLES**

Is. Las Aves
(Ven.)
Is. Los Roques
(Ven.)

I. Orchila
(Ven.)

I. Blanquilla (Ven.)
Is. Los Hermanos
(Ven.)

Is. Los Testigos
(Ven.)

Tobago
Scarborough

Pen. de la
Guajira
Pta.
Espada
Pen. de
Paraguaná

C. San Román

Punta
Cardón

Punto Fijo

I. de Margarita

I. La Tortuga
(Ven.)

La Asunción
Porlamar

**NUEVA
ESPARTA**

Río
Caribe
Pen. de Paria

Port of
Spain

Galera
Point
Trinidad
Arima
Rio Claro

Ríohacha
Uribia

GUAJIRA

Golfo de
Venezuela

Puerto
Cumarebo

**SANTA
MARTA**
Ciénaga

Sierra Nevada de
Santa Marta
5800
San
Rafael

Coro
La Vela de Coro

Mene de Mauroa

FALCÓN

Maiquetía
La Guaira
CARACAS
DISTRITO
FEDERAL

Cumaná
Carúpano
Güíria

Caribe
G. de Paria

San Fernando
**TRINIDAD
& TOBAGO**

*ARRAN-
QUILLA*

Baranoa
Soledad
ÁNTICO
Sabanalarga

Altagracia
MARACAIBO

Tucacas
Puerto
Cabello

C. Codera
Barcelona

Serpent's Mouth

Fundación
Calamar

La Concepción
Villa del
Rosario

Santa Rita
Baragua
Carora

San Felipe
YARACUY

MIRANDA
Los Teques
Ocumare del Tuy

Puerto
La Cruz

Maturín
MONAGAS

DELTA

Tucupita

Agustín
Codazzi

MAGDALENA
Plato
Zambrano

Ciudad
Ojeda

Mene Grande
LARA

CARABOBO
Valencia
Villa
de Cura
San Juan
de los Morros

Aragua de
Barcelona

Anaco

Caicara

Cantaura

Carmen

Sincé
CÉSAR

Machiques
Lago de
Maracaibo

BARQUISIMETO
El Tocuyo
Yaritagua de
los Morros

San Carlos

El Sombrero

Valle de
la Pascua

El Tigre

Los Barrancos
AMACURO

Corozal
Magangué

El Banco

San Carlos
del Zulia
ZULIA
Betijoque
TRUJILLO
Trujillo

COJEDES

PORTUGUESA
Acarigua

GUÁRICO

Calabozo

Pariaguán

El Pao

Ciudad Guayana
Sierra Imataca

Simití

BOLÍVAR
El Banco
DE
Ocaña
NORTE

SANTANDER
Cúcuta
TÁCHIRA

Mérida
Cord.
de Mérida
MÉRIDA

Barinas
Ciudad
Bolivia

BARINAS
San Fernando
de Apure

Santa María
de Ipire

ANZOÁTEGUI

Soledad
Ciudad
Bolívar

Ciudad
Bolívar

Embalse de Guri

El Callao
Tumeremo

Libertad

Puerto de Nutrias

Bruzual

Achaguas

Apure

Caicara

Mapire

Guasipati

E

75
West from Greenwich
70
6
65
7

COPYRIGHT GEORGE PHILIP LTD

5

50 0 50 100 150 200 250 300 km

50 0 50 100 150 200 miles

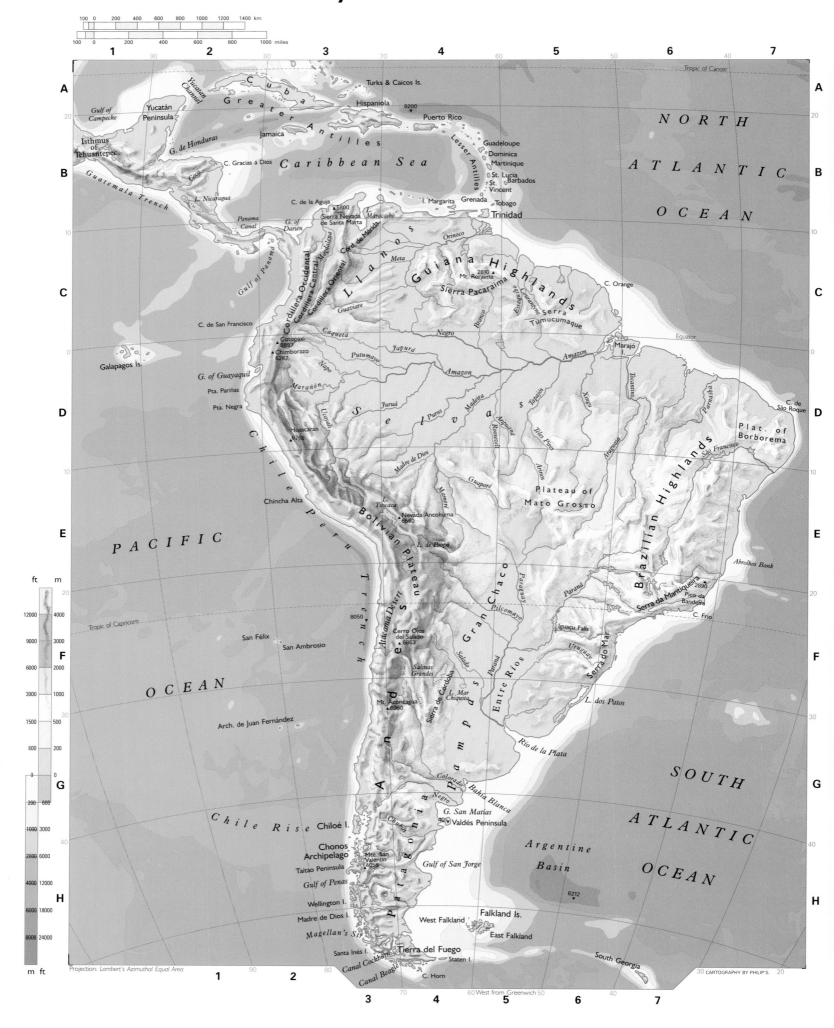

100 0 200 400 600 800 1000 1200 1400 km

100 0 200 400 600 800 1000 miles

1 90 2 80 3 70 4 60 5 50 6 40 7

Tropic of Cancer

A

Yucatán Channel

C u b a

G r e a t e r   A n t i l l e s

Turks & Caicos Is.

Hispaniola

9200

Puerto Rico

N O R T H

Gulf of Campeche

Yucatán Peninsula

B

Isthmus of Tehuantepec

G. de Honduras

Jamaica

Guatemala Trench

Coco

C. Gracias a Dios

Caribbean Sea

Guadeloupe
Dominica
Martinique
St. Lucia
St. Vincent
Barbados
Grenada
Tobago
Trinidad

Lesser Antilles

I. Margarita

A T L A N T I C

O C E A N

L. Nicaragua

Panama Canal

Gulf of Panama

G. of Darién

C. de la Aguja

Sierra Nevada de Santa Marta

5800

L. Maracaibo

Orinoco

Meta

L l a n o s

Guaviare

C

C. de San Francisco

Cord. de Mérida

Cordillera Occidental

Cordillera Central

Cordillera Oriental

G u i a n a   H i g h l a n d s

Mt. Roraima 2810

Sierra Pacaraima

Branco

Caroni

Essequibo

Serra Tumucumaque

C. Orange

Equator

Cotopaxi 5897
Chimborazo 6267

Caquetá

Putumayo

Japurá

Negro

Amazon

Marajó I.

D

Galapagos Is.

G. of Guayaquil

Pta. Pariñas

Pta. Negra

Marañón

Napo

Ucayali

S   e   l

Juruá

Purús

Madeira

v   a

Amazon

Madre de Dios

Roosevelt

Aripuanã

Tapajós

Teles Pires

Xingu

Tocantins

Araguaia

Parnaíba

São Francisco

C. de São Roque

Plat. of Borborema

Huascarán 6768

E

Chincha Alta

P A C I F I C

C h i l e   P e r u   T r e n c h

L. Titicaca

B o l i v i a n   P l a t e a u

Nevada Ancohuma 6550

Mamoré

Guaporé

Plateau of Mato Grosso

Arinos

B r a z i l i a n   H i g h l a n d s

Abrolhos Bank

F

Tropic of Capricorn

San Félix

San Ambrosio

8050

Atacama Desert

Cerro Ojos del Salado 6863

A   n   d   e   s

Salinas Grandes

G r a n   C h a c o

P a m p a s

Paraguay

Pilcomayo

Paraná

Salado

Entre Ríos

Uruguay

S e r r a   d o   M a r

Iguaçu Falls

Serra da Mantiqueira 2890

Pico da Bandeira

C. Frio

O C E A N

G

Arch. de Juan Fernández

Mt. Aconcagua 6960

Sierra de Córdoba

L. Mar Chiquita

P   a   t   a   g   o   n   i   a

Colorado

Negro

L. dos Patos

Río de la Plata

Bahía Blanca

S O U T H

H

C h i l e   R i s e

Chiloé I.

Chubut

G. San Matías

Valdés Peninsula

Argentine Basin

6212

A T L A N T I C

Chonos Archipelago

Taitao Peninsula

Gulf of Penas

Mte. San Valentin 4058

Gulf of San Jorge

Wellington I.

Madre de Dios I.

Magellan's Str.

Santa Inés I.

Canal Cockburn

Tierra del Fuego

Staten I.

West Falkland

East Falkland

Falkland Is.

South Georgia

O C E A N

Canal Beagle

C. Horn

3 70 4 60 West from Greenwich 50 5 6 40 7

ft m
12000 4000
9000 3000
6000 2000
3000 1000
1500 500
600 200
0 0
200 600
1000 3000
2000 6000
4000 12000
6000 18000
8000 24000
m ft

Projection: Lambert's Azimuthal Equal Area

30 CARTOGRAPHY BY PHILIP'S.

100 0 200 400 600 800 1000 1200 1400 km
100 0 200 400 600 800 1000 miles

| 1 | 2 | 3 | 4 | 5 | 6 | 7 |

Tropic of Cancer

A

Havana
CUBA
BAHAMAS
Turks & Caicos Is.
(U.K.)

NORTH

MEXICO
HAITI
DOMINICAN
REP.
Virgin Is.
(U.K.)
San Juan
ST. KITTS
& NEVIS
ANTIGUA &
BARBUDA

ATLANTIC

GUATEMALA
BELIZE
HONDURAS
Tegucigalpa
JAMAICA
Kingston
Port-au-
Prince
PUERTO
RICO
(U.S.A.)
GUADELOUPE
(Fr.)
DOMINICA
MARTINIQUE
(Fr.)

B

Guatemala
San Salvador
EL SALVADOR
NICARAGUA
Managua
Caribbean Sea
Castries
ST. VINCENT
Kingstown
ST. LUCIA
BARBADOS
Bridgetown

OCEAN

COSTA
RICA
San José
Panamá
Aruba
Curaçao
GRENADA
St. George's
Port of
Spain
TRINIDAD &
TOBAGO

C. de
la Aguja
Barranquilla
Cartagena
Maracaibo
Caracas
Valencia

G. of
Darién
Cúcuta
San Cristóbal
Barquisimeto
Orinoco
Ciudad Guayana
Georgetown
Paramaribo
Cayenne
C. Orange

C

Medellín
Bucaramanga
VENEZUELA
GUYANA
SURINAM
FRENCH
GUIANA

Cali
Bogotá
Magdalena
RORAIMA
Essequibo
Branco

COLOMBIA
AMAPÁ

Galapagos Is.
(Ecuador)
Quito
ECUADOR
Napo
Putumayo
Japurá
Equator

D

Guayaquil
G. of Guayaquil
Marañón
Iquitos
Amazon
Manaus
Santarém
Marajó
I.
Belém
São Luís
Fortaleza
C. de
São Roque

Chiclayo
Ucayali
AMAZONAS
Madeira
PARÁ
MARANHÃO
Teresina
Parnaíba
RIO G.
DO NORTE
Natal

Trujillo
Juruá
Purus
Tapajós
Xingu
PARAÍBA
Campina Grande
Recife

Chimbote
ACRE
Pôrto Velho
Tocantins
Araguaia
PIAUÍ
PERNAMBUCO
Maceió

E

PERU
Callao
LIMA
Madre de Dios
RONDÔNIA
BRAZIL
ALAGOAS
SERGIPE
Aracaju

Cuzco
Mamoré
MATO GROSSO
Cuiabá
TOCANTINS
BAHÍA
Salvador

L.
Titicaca
Arequipa
La Paz
BOLIVIA
Cochabamba
Santa Cruz
GOIÁS
DIS. FED.
Brasília
São Francisco

PACIFIC
Sucre
Paraguay
MATO GROSSO
DO SUL
Goiânia
MINAS GERAIS
ESPÍRITO
SANTO

Iquique
Belo
Horizonte
Vitória

F

OCEAN
Antofagasta
PARAGUAY
Pilcomayo
Paraná
Ribeirão
Prêto
SÃO PAULO
Juiz
de Fora
R. DE J.
Campos

Tropic of Capricorn
Salta
Asunción
SÃO
PAULO
Campinas
Niterói
RIO DE
JANEIRO

San Félix
(Chile)
San Ambrosio
(Chile)
San Miguel
de Tucumán
Resistencia
Corrientes
Salado
Uruguay
PARANÁ
Curitiba
SANTA CATARINA

Arch. de Juan Fernández
(Chile)
Córdoba
Santa Fe
Paraná
RIO GRANDE
DO SUL
Pôrto Alegre

Viña del Mar
Valparaíso
San Juan
Mendoza
Rosario
Pelotas
URUGUAY

G

SANTIAGO
Talca
ARGENTINA
Buenos Aires
La Plata
Montevideo
Río de la Plata

Concepción
Bahía
Blanca
Mar del Plata
Colorado

SOUTH

Valdivia
Negro
Viedma

ATLANTIC

Puerto Montt
CHILE
Chubut

H

OCEAN

Comodoro Rivadavia
Gulf of San Jorge

Gulf of Penas
West Falkland
FALKLAND IS.
(U.K.)
Stanley
East Falkland

Magellan's Str.
Punta Arenas
Tierra del Fuego
South Georgia
(U.K.)

C. Horn

Projection: Lambert's Azimuthal Equal Area
LIMA Capital Cities
West from Greenwich
CARTOGRAPHY BY PHILIP'S.

| 1 | 2 | 3 | 4 | 5 | 6 | 7 |

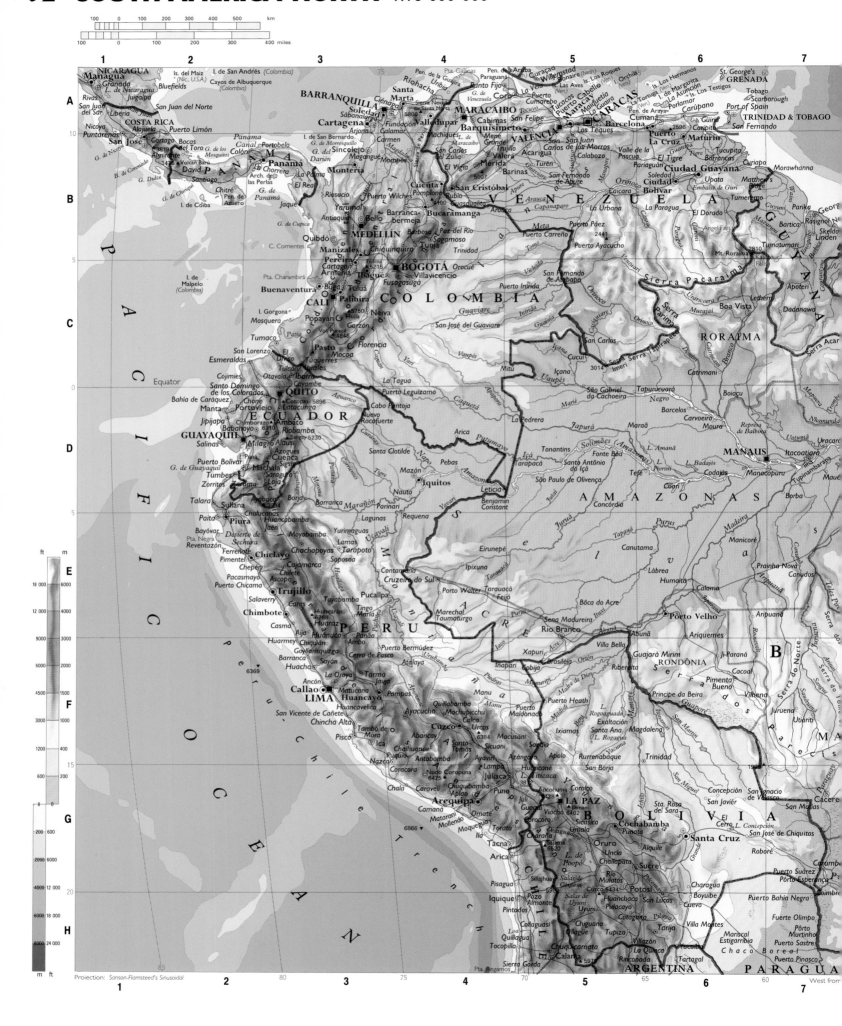

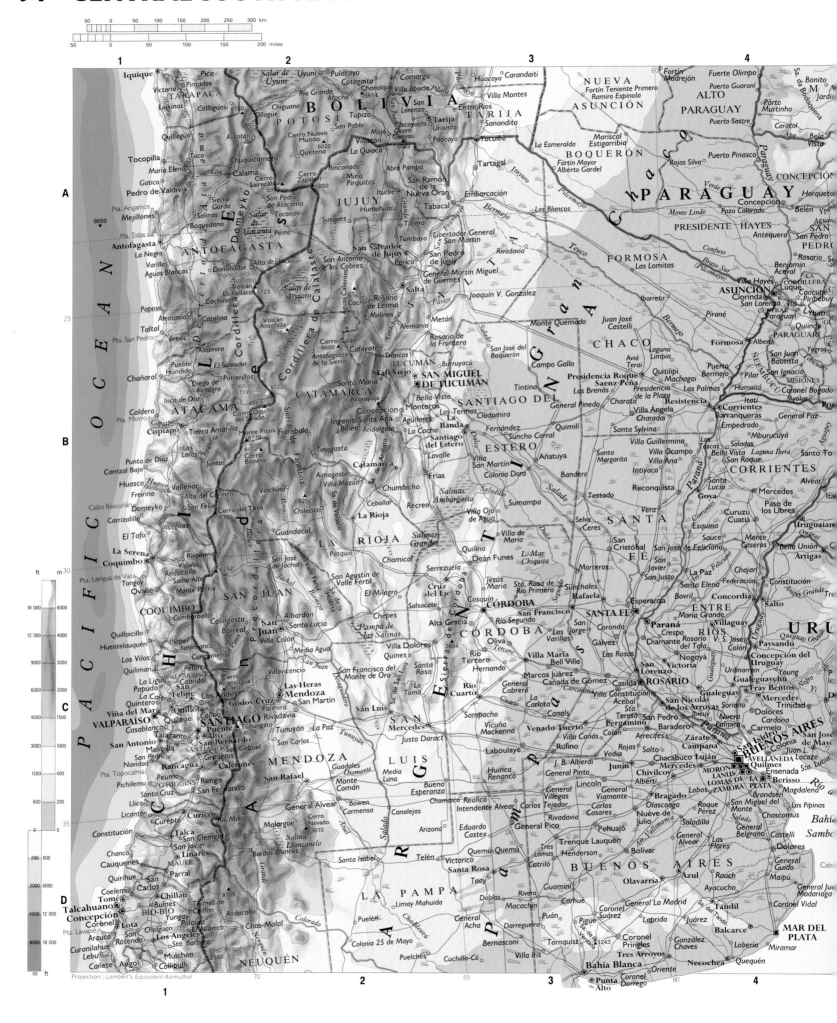

92 93
96

BELO
HORIZONTE
Nova Lima
Itabirito

Vitória
Itaquari
Vila
Velha
Guaraparí

T O G R O S S O
Sidrolândia
Nioaque
ua
y Laguna
ia Lopes
Nova Alvorada
do Sul
Maracaju
Nova Andradina
D O S U L
Dourados
Rio
Brilhante
Ponta Porã
Dourados
Pedro Juan Caballero
Amambay
Capitán
bado

Três Lagoas
Xavantina
Mirandópolis
Panorama
Presidente
Epitácio
Nova
Andradina
Euclides da
Cunha Paulista
Ivinhema
Rosana

Andradina
Araçatuba
Birigui
Penápolis
Lins
Tupã

Mirassol
do Rio Prêto
Catanduva
Taquaritinga
Bebedouro

Olímpia
Novo
Horizonte

Passos
Batatais
São Sebastião
do Paraíso
Guaxupé
Mococa
Casa
Branca

Congonhas
Conselheiro
Lafaiete
Oliveira
Campo Belo
Alfenas
Pouso
Poços de
Caldas

Ouro
Prêto
Lavras
São João
del Rei
Barbacena
Tres
Pontas
Vírginia

Ponte Nova
Ubá
Leopoldina
Juiz de Fora
Cataguases

Pico da
Bandeira
2880
Castelo
Cachoeiro
de Itapemirim
Carangola
Muriaé
Alegre
Itaperuna
Cambuci

S Ã O
Adamantina
Santo
Anastácio
P A U L O
Marília
Paraguaçu
Paulista
Garça
Bauru
Jaú
Rio Claro
Araras
Pinhal
Ouro Fino
Itajubá
Volta
Redonda

Presidente
Prudente
Martinópolis
Rancharia
Assis
Santa Cruz
do Rio Pardo
Piracicaba
Limeira
Americana
Mogi-Mirim
Bragança
Paulista
Cruzeiro
Barra
Mansa
Barra do Piraí
Petrópolis

RIO DE JANEIRO
Nova Friburgo
Macaé

CAMPOS
Cabo de
São Tomé

Pôrto São José
B R A Z I L
Londrina
Maringá
Rolândia
Cambará
Ourinhos
Botucatu
CAMPINAS
Itu
Jundiaí
São José dos
Campos
Taubaté
Jacareí
Moji das Cruzes

NOVA IGUAÇU
DUQUE DE CAXIAS
SÃO GONÇALO
NITERÓI
RIO DE JANEIRO

Cabo Frio

P A R A N Á
Londrina
Cianorte
Nova
Esperança
Mandaguari
Apucarana
Araraquara
São
Carlos
Piracicaba
Tatuí
Sorocaba
São Bernardo
do Campo
Santo André
Santos

Ilha Grande
Angra dos
Reis
La de Araruama

Tropic of Capricorn

Umuarama
Cruzeiro
do Oeste
Campo
Mourão
Candido de Abreu
Ibaiti
Itapetininga
São Vicente
São Paulo

Ilha de São Sebastião
Pta. de Boi

Guaíra
Goio-Erê
Ubiratã
Pitanga
Prudentópolis
Itararé
Itapeva
Itaporanga
Itaí
Apiaí
Itanhaém
Guarujá

Foz do Iguaçu
Ciudad
del Este
Cascavel
Medianeira
Toledo
Sa. das Araras
Guarapuava
Ponta
Grossa
Castro
Tibagi
Serra
Juquiá
Registro
Iguape

Francisco
Beltrão
União da
Vitória
Irati
Lapa
Palmeira
CURITIBA
Antonina
Paranaguá
Matinhos
Guaratuba

Ilha Comprida
Ilha do Cardoso

Bernardo
de Irigoyen
Pato Branco
São Mateus
do Sul
Rio Negro
Mafa
Joinville
São Francisco do Sul

PARANÁ
Eldorado
Palmas
Pôrto União
Caçador
Xanxerê
Blumenau
Santa Cecília
Itajaí
Brusque

TAPUÁ
Pedro
Parana
eral Artigas
mei Corpus
Misiones
Clevelândia
São Miguel
do Oeste
Frederico
Westphalen
Chapecó
Joaçaba
SANTA CATARINA
Curitibanos
Rio do Sul
São José
Ilha de Santa Catarina
Florianópolis

Encarnación
Obera
Candelaria
San
Pedro
Monteagudo
Erechim
Palmeira
das Missões
Passo
Fundo
Campos
Novos
Lajes
São
Joaquim
Vacaria

Leandro N. Alem
Santa Rosa
Carazinho
Lagoa
Vermelha

Apóstoles
São
Javier
São Angelo
Ijuí
Cruz Alta
Guaporé
Bento Gonçalves
Caxias do Sul

Tubarão
Laguna
Cabo Santa Marta Grande
Criciúma
Araranguá

São Borja
Santo Angelo
São Luís
Gonzaga
R I O   G R A N D E
Coxilha Grande
Guaporé
Torres

Santiago
Santa Maria
Santa Cruz
do Sul
Montenegro
Taquara
Nôvo Hamburgo
São
Leopoldo
Osório

Alegrete
sário do Sul
Cachoeira do Sul
Canoas
Viamão
PÔRTO ALEGRE

D O   S U L
São
Gabriel
Santana do
Livramento
Caçapava
do Sul
Sa.
Encantadas
Tapes
Camaquã

Rivera
Dom Pedrito
Camaquã
Bagé
Sa. do Canguçu
Canguçu

São Lourenço
do Sul
Mostardas

A T L A N T I C

Tacuarembó
Pinheiro
Machado
Pelotas
Lagoa dos Patos

Fraile
Muerto
Melo
Jaguarão
Rio Branco
Lagoa Mirim
Rio Grande
São José do Norte

O C E A N

San Gregorio
Blanquillo
Cerro
Chato
Vergara
Santa Vitória do Palmar

José Batlle
y Ordóñez
Lascano
Treinta
y Tres
Chuy

MONTEVIDEO
Minas
Piedras
San Carlos
Maldonado
Castillos
Rocha
Aigua

Plata
bón
Antonio

5304

COPYRIGHT GEORGE PHILIP LTD

West from Greenwich

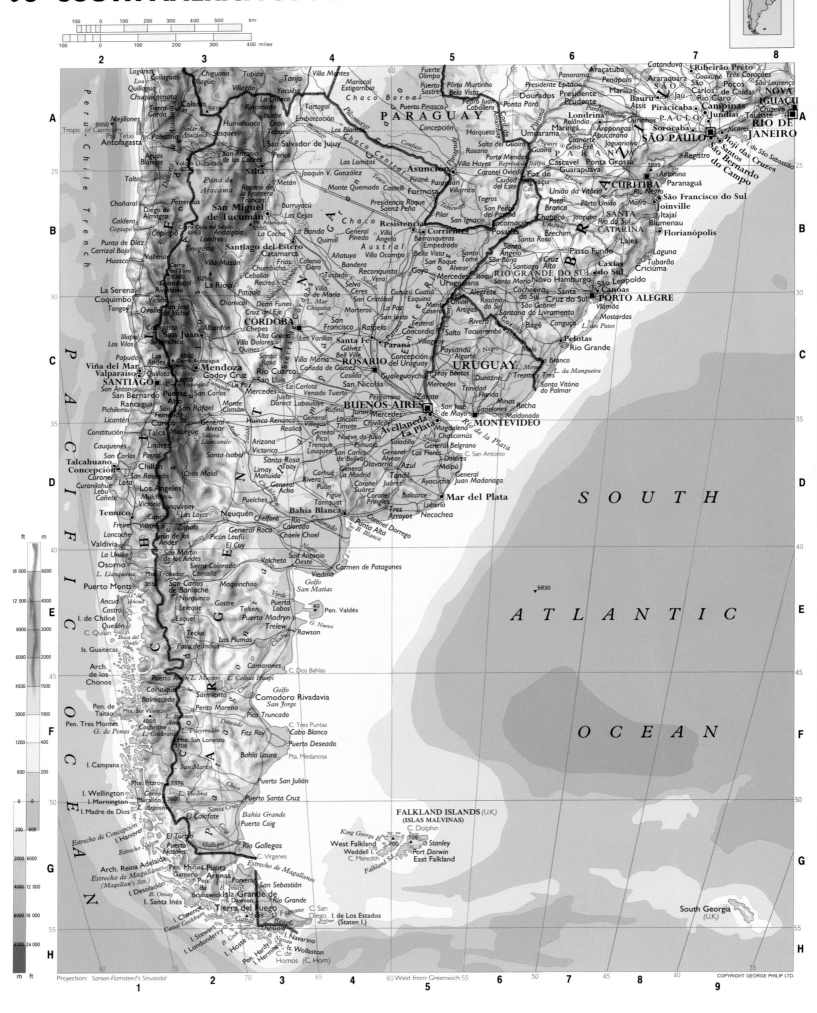

COPYRIGHT GEORGE PHILIP LTD.

Projection: Sanson-Flamsteed's Sinusoidal

INDEX

The index contains the names of all the principal places and features shown on the World Maps. Each name is followed by an additional entry in italics giving the country or region within which it is located. The alphabetical order of names composed of two or more words is governed primarily by the first word and then by the second. This is an example of the rule:

Mīr Kūh, *Iran* . . . . **45 E8** 26 22N 58 55 E
Mīr Shahdād, *Iran* . . . . **45 E8** 26 15N 58 29 E
Mira, *Italy* . . . . **20 B5** 45 26N 12 8 E
Mira por vos Cay, *Bahamas* . **89 B5** 22 9N 74 30W
Miraj, *India* . . . . **40 L9** 16 50N 74 45 E

Physical features composed of a proper name (Erie) and a description (Lake) are positioned alphabetically by the proper name. The description is positioned after the proper name and is usually abbreviated:

Erie, L., *N. Amer.* **78 D4** 42 15N 81 0W

Where a description forms part of a settlement or administrative name however, it is always written in full and put in its true alphabetic position:

Mount Morris, *U.S.A.* **78 D7** 42 44N 77 52W

Names beginning with M' and Mc are indexed as if they were spelled Mac. Names beginning St. are alphabetised under Saint, but Sankt, Sint, Sant', Santa and San are all spelt in full and are alphabetised accordingly. If the same place name occurs two or more times in the index and all are in the same country, each is followed by the name of the administrative subdivision in which it is located. The names are placed in the alphabetical order of the subdivisions. For example:

Jackson, *Ky., U.S.A.* **76 G4** 37 33N 83 23W
Jackson, *Mich., U.S.A.* **76 D3** 42 15N 84 24W
Jackson, *Minn., U.S.A.* **80 D7** 43 37N 95 1W

The number in bold type which follows each name in the index refers to the number of the map page where that feature or place will be found. This is usually the largest scale at which the place or feature appears.

The letter and figure which are in bold type immediately after the page number give the grid square on the map page, within which the feature is situated. The letter represents the latitude and the figure the longitude.

In some cases the feature itself may fall within the specified square, while the name is outside. This is usually the case only with features which are larger than a grid square.

For a more precise location the geographical coordinates which follow the letter/figure references give the latitude and the longitude of each place. The first set of figures represent the latitude which is the distance north or south of the Equator measured as an angle at the centre of the earth. The Equator is latitude 0°, the North Pole is 90°N, and the South Pole 90°S.

The second set of figures represent the longitude, which is the distance East or West of the prime meridian, which runs through Greenwich, England. Longitude is also measured as an angle at the centre of the earth and is given East or West of the prime meridian, from 0° to 180° in either direction.

The unit of measurement for latitude and longitude is the degree, which is subdivided into 60 minutes. Each index entry states the position of a place in degrees and minutes, a space being left between the degrees and the minutes.

The latitude is followed by N(orth) or S(outh) and the longitude by E(ast) or W(est).

Rivers are indexed to their mouths or confluences, and carry the symbol → after their names. A solid square ■ follows the name of a country, while an open square □ refers to a first order administrative area.

Abbreviations used in the index

A.C.T. – Australian Capital Territory
Afghan. – Afghanistan
Ala. – Alabama
Alta. – Alberta
Amer. – America(n)
Arch. – Archipelago
Ariz. – Arizona
Ark. – Arkansas
Atl. Oc. – Atlantic Ocean
B. – Baie, Bahía, Bay, Bucht, Bugt
B.C. – British Columbia
Bangla. – Bangladesh
Barr. – Barrage
Bos.-H. – Bosnia-Herzegovina
C. – Cabo, Cap, Cape, Coast
C.A.R. – Central African Republic
C. Prov. – Cape Province
Calif. – California
Cent. – Central
Chan. – Channel
Colo. – Colorado
Conn. – Connecticut
Cord. – Cordillera
Cr. – Creek
Czech. – Czech Republic
D.C. – District of Columbia
Del. – Delaware
Dep. – Dependency
Des. – Desert
Dist. – District
Dj. – Djebel
Domin. – Dominica
Dom. Rep. – Dominican Republic
E. – East

E. Salv. – El Salvador
Eq. Guin. – Equatorial Guinea
Fla. – Florida
Falk. Is. – Falkland Is.
G. – Golfe, Golfo, Gulf, Guba, Gebel
Ga. – Georgia
Gt. – Great, Greater
Guinea-Biss. – Guinea-Bissau
H.K. – Hong Kong
H.P. – Himachal Pradesh
Hants. – Hampshire
Harb. – Harbor, Harbour
Hd. – Head
Hts. – Heights
I.(s). – Île, Ilha, Insel, Isla, Island, Isle
Ill. – Illinois
Ind. – Indiana
Ind. Oc. – Indian Ocean
Ivory C. – Ivory Coast
J. – Jabal, Jebel, Jazira
Junc. – Junction
K. – Kap, Kapp
Kans. – Kansas
Kep. – Kepulauan
Ky. – Kentucky
L. – Lac, Lacul, Lago, Lagoa, Lake, Limni, Loch, Lough
La. – Louisiana
Liech. – Liechtenstein
Lux. – Luxembourg
Mad. P. – Madhya Pradesh
Madag. – Madagascar
Man. – Manitoba
Mass. – Massachusetts

Md. – Maryland
Me. – Maine
Medit. S. – Mediterranean Sea
Mich. – Michigan
Minn. – Minnesota
Miss. – Mississippi
Mo. – Missouri
Mont. – Montana
Mozam. – Mozambique
Mt.(e) – Mont, Monte, Monti, Montaña, Mountain
N. – Nord, Norte, North, Northern, Nouveau
N.B. – New Brunswick
N.C. – North Carolina
N. Cal. – New Caledonia
N. Dak. – North Dakota
N.H. – New Hampshire
N.I. – North Island
N.J. – New Jersey
N. Mex. – New Mexico
N.S. – Nova Scotia
N.S.W. – New South Wales
N.W.T. – North West Territory
N.Y. – New York
N.Z. – New Zealand
Nebr. – Nebraska
Neths. – Netherlands
Nev. – Nevada
Nfld. – Newfoundland
Nic. – Nicaragua
O. – Oued, Ouadi
Occ. – Occidentale
Okla. – Oklahoma
Ont. – Ontario
Or. – Orientale

Oreg. – Oregon
Os. – Ostrov
Oz. – Ozero
P. – Pass, Passo, Pasul, Pulau
P.E.I. – Prince Edward Island
Pa. – Pennsylvania
Pac. Oc. – Pacific Ocean
Papua N.G. – Papua New Guinea
Pass. – Passage
Pen. – Peninsula, Péninsule
Phil. – Philippines
Pk. – Park, Peak
Plat. – Plateau
Prov. – Province, Provincial
Pt. – Point
Pta. – Ponta, Punta
Pte. – Pointe
Qué. – Québec
Queens. – Queensland
R. – Rio, River
R.I. – Rhode Island
Ra.(s). – Range(s)
Raj. – Rajasthan
Reg. – Region
Rep. – Republic
Res. – Reserve, Reservoir
S. – San, South, Sea
Si. Arabia – Saudi Arabia
S.C. – South Carolina
S. Dak. – South Dakota
S.I. – South Island
S. Leone – Sierra Leone
Sa. – Serra, Sierra
Sask. – Saskatchewan
Scot. – Scotland
Sd. – Sound

Sev. – Severnaya
Sib. – Siberia
Sprs. – Springs
St. – Saint
Sta. – Santa, Station
Ste. – Sainte
Sto. – Santo
Str. – Strait, Stretto
Switz. – Switzerland
Tas. – Tasmania
Tenn. – Tennessee
Tex. – Texas
Tg. – Tanjung
Trin. & Tob. – Trinidad & Tobago
U.A.E. – United Arab Emirates
U.K. – United Kingdom
U.S.A. – United States of America
Ut. P. – Uttar Pradesh
Va. – Virginia
Vdkhr. – Vodokhranilishche
Vf. – Vírful
Vic. – Victoria
Vol. – Volcano
Vt. – Vermont
W. – Wadi, West
W. Va. – West Virginia
Wash. – Washington
Wis. – Wisconsin
Wlkp. – Wielkopolski
Wyo. – Wyoming
Yorks. – Yorkshire
Yug. – Yugoslavia

A Coruña

A

A Coruña, *Spain* **19 A1** 43 20N 8 25W
A Estrada, *Spain* **19 A1** 42 43N 8 27W
A Fonsagrada, *Spain* **19 A2** 43 8N 7 4W
Aachen, *Germany* **16 C4** 50 45N 6 6 E
Aalborg = Ålborg, *Denmark* **9 H13** 57 2N 9 54 E
Aalen, *Germany* **16 D6** 48 51N 10 6 E
Aalst, *Belgium* **15 D4** 50 56N 4 2 E
Aalten, *Neths.* **15 C6** 51 56N 6 35 E
Aalter, *Belgium* **15 C3** 51 5N 3 28 E
Äänekoski, *Finland* **9 E21** 62 36N 25 44 E
Aarau, *Switz.* **18 C8** 47 23N 8 4 E
Aare →, *Switz.* **18 C8** 47 33N 8 14 E
Aarhus = Århus, *Denmark* **9 H14** 56 8N 10 11 E
Aarschot, *Belgium* **15 D4** 50 59N 4 49 E
Aba, *Dem. Rep. of the Congo* **54 B3** 3 58N 30 17 E
Aba, *Nigeria* **50 G7** 5 10N 7 19 E
Ābādān, *Iran* **45 D6** 30 22N 48 20 E
Ābādeh, *Iran* **45 D7** 31 8N 52 40 E
Abadla, *Algeria* **50 B5** 31 2N 2 45W
Abaetetuba, *Brazil* **93 D9** 1 40S 48 50W
Abagnar Qi, *China* **34 C9** 43 52N 116 2 E
Abai, *Paraguay* **95 B4** 25 58S 55 54W
Abakan, *Russia* **27 D10** 53 40N 91 10 E
Abancay, *Peru* **92 F4** 13 35S 72 55W
Abariringa, *Kiribati* **64 H10** 2 50S 171 40W
Abarqū, *Iran* **45 D7** 31 10N 53 20 E
Abashiri, *Japan* **30 C12** 44 0N 144 15 E
Abashiri-Wan, *Japan* **30 C12** 44 0N 144 30 E
Abay, *Kazakstan* **26 E8** 49 38N 72 53 E
Abaya, L., *Ethiopia* **46 F2** 6 30N 37 50 E
Abaza, *Russia* **26 D10** 52 39N 90 6 E
'Abbāsābād, *Iran* **45 C8** 33 34N 58 23 E
Abbay = Nîl el Azraq →, *Sudan* **51 E12** 15 38N 32 31 E
Abbaye, Pt., *U.S.A.* **76 B1** 46 58N 88 8W
Abbé, L., *Ethiopia* **46 E3** 11 8N 41 47 E
Abbeville, *France* **18 A4** 50 6N 1 49 E
Abbeville, *Ala., U.S.A.* **77 K3** 31 34N 85 15W
Abbeville, *La., U.S.A.* **81 L8** 29 58N 92 8W
Abbeville, *S.C., U.S.A.* **77 H4** 34 11N 82 23W
Abbot Ice Shelf, *Antarctica* **5 D16** 73 0S 92 0W
Abbottabad, *Pakistan* **42 B5** 34 10N 73 15 E
Abd al Kūrī, *Ind. Oc.* **46 E5** 12 5N 52 20 E
Ābdar, *Iran* **45 D7** 30 16N 55 19 E
'Abdolābād, *Iran* **45 C8** 34 12N 56 30 E
Abdulpur, *Bangla.* **43 G13** 24 15N 88 59 E
Abéché, *Chad* **51 F10** 13 50N 20 35 E
Abengourou, *Ivory C.* **50 G5** 6 42N 3 27W
Åbenrå, *Denmark* **9 J13** 55 3N 9 25 E
Abeokuta, *Nigeria* **50 G6** 7 3N 3 19 E
Aber, *Uganda* **54 B3** 2 12N 32 25 E
Aberaeron, *U.K.* **11 E3** 52 15N 4 15W
Aberayron = Aberaeron, *U.K.* **11 E3** 52 15N 4 15W
Aberchirder, *U.K.* **12 D6** 57 34N 2 37W
Abercorn = Mbala, *Zambia* **55 D3** 8 46S 31 24 E
Abercorn, *Australia* **63 D5** 25 12S 151 5 E
Aberdare, *U.K.* **11 F4** 51 43N 3 27W
Aberdare Ra., *Kenya* **54 C4** 0 15S 36 50 E
Aberdeen, *Australia* **63 E5** 32 9S 150 56 E
Aberdeen, *Canada* **73 C7** 52 20N 106 8W
Aberdeen, *S. Africa* **56 E3** 32 28S 24 2 E
Aberdeen, *U.K.* **12 D6** 57 9N 2 5W
Aberdeen, *Ala., U.S.A.* **77 J1** 33 49N 88 33W
Aberdeen, *Idaho, U.S.A.* **82 E7** 42 57N 112 50W
Aberdeen, *Md., U.S.A.* **76 F7** 39 31N 76 10W
Aberdeen, *S. Dak., U.S.A.* **80 C5** 45 28N 98 29W
Aberdeen, *Wash., U.S.A.* **84 D3** 46 59N 123 50W
Aberdeen, City of □, *U.K.* **12 D6** 57 10N 2 10W
Aberdeenshire □, *U.K.* **12 D6** 57 17N 2 36W
Aberdovey = Aberdyfi, *U.K.* **11 E3** 52 33N 4 3W
Aberdyfi, *U.K.* **11 E3** 52 33N 4 3W
Aberfeldy, *U.K.* **12 E5** 56 37N 3 51W
Abergavenny, *U.K.* **11 F4** 51 49N 3 1W
Abergele, *U.K.* **10 D4** 53 17N 3 35W
Abernathy, *U.S.A.* **81 J4** 33 50N 101 51W
Abert, L., *U.S.A.* **82 E3** 42 38N 120 14W
Aberystwyth, *U.K.* **11 E3** 52 25N 4 5W
Abhā, *Si. Arabia* **46 D3** 18 0N 42 34 E
Abhar, *Iran* **45 B6** 36 9N 49 13 E
Abhayapuri, *India* **43 F14** 26 24N 90 38 E
Abidjan, *Ivory C.* **50 G5** 5 26N 3 58W
Abilene, *Kans., U.S.A.* **80 F6** 38 55N 97 13W
Abilene, *Tex., U.S.A.* **81 J5** 32 28N 99 43W
Abingdon, *U.K.* **11 F6** 51 40N 1 17W
Abingdon, *U.S.A.* **77 G5** 36 43N 81 59W
Abington Reef, *Australia* **62 B4** 18 0S 149 35 E
Abitau →, *Canada* **73 B7** 59 53N 109 3W
Abitibi →, *Canada* **70 B3** 51 3N 80 55W
Abitibi, L., *Canada* **70 C4** 48 40N 79 40W
Abkhaz Republic = Abkhazia □, *Georgia* **25 F7** 43 12N 41 5 E
Abkhazia □, *Georgia* **25 F7** 43 12N 41 5 E
Abminga, *Australia* **63 D1** 26 8S 134 51 E
Åbo = Turku, *Finland* **9 F20** 60 30N 22 19 E
Abohar, *India* **42 D6** 30 10N 74 10 E
Abolo, *Congo* **52 D2** 0 8N 14 16 E
Abomey, *Benin* **50 G6** 7 10N 2 5 E
Abong-Mbang, *Cameroon* **52 D2** 4 0N 13 8 E
Abou-Deïa, *Chad* **51 F9** 11 20N 19 20 E
Aboyne, *U.K.* **12 D6** 57 4N 2 47W
Abra Pampa, *Argentina* **94 A2** 22 43S 65 42W
Abraham L., *Canada* **72 C5** 52 15N 116 35W
Abreojos, Pta., *Mexico* **86 B2** 26 50N 113 40W
Abrud, *Romania* **17 E12** 46 19N 23 5 E
Absaroka Range, *U.S.A.* **82 D9** 44 45N 109 50W
Abu, *India* **42 G5** 24 41N 72 50 E
Abu al Abyad, *U.A.E.* **45 E7** 24 11N 53 50 E
Abū al Khaşīb, *Iraq* **45 D6** 30 25N 48 0 E
Abū 'Alī, *Si. Arabia* **45 E6** 27 20N 49 27 E
Abū 'Alī →, *Lebanon* **47 A4** 34 25N 35 50 E
Abu Dhabi = Abū Ẓāby, *U.A.E.* **45 E7** 24 28N 54 22 E
Abū Du'ān, *Syria* **44 B3** 36 25N 38 15 E
Abu el Gairi, W. →, *Egypt* **47 F2** 29 35N 33 30 E
Abu Ga'da, W. →, *Egypt* **47 F1** 29 15N 32 53 E
Abū Ḥadrīyah, *Si. Arabia* **45 E6** 27 20N 48 58 E
Abu Hamed, *Sudan* **51 E12** 19 32N 33 13 E
Abū Kamāl, *Syria* **44 C4** 34 30N 41 0 E
Abū Madd, Ra's, *Si. Arabia* **44 E3** 24 50N 37 7 E
Abū Mūsā, *U.A.E.* **45 E7** 25 52N 55 3 E
Abu Şafāt, W. →, *Jordan* **47 E5** 30 24N 36 7 E
Abu Simbel, *Egypt* **51 D12** 22 18N 31 40 E
Abū Şukhayr, *Iraq* **44 D5** 31 54N 44 30 E
Abû Zabad, *Sudan* **51 F11** 12 25N 29 10 E
Abū Ẓāby, *U.A.E.* **45 E7** 24 28N 54 22 E
Abū Zeydābād, *Iran* **45 C6** 33 54N 51 45 E
Abuja, *Nigeria* **50 G7** 9 16N 7 2 E
Abukuma-Gawa →, *Japan* **30 E10** 38 6N 140 52 E
Abukuma-Sammyaku, *Japan* **30 F10** 37 30N 140 45 E
Abunã, *Brazil* **92 E5** 9 40S 65 20W
Abunã →, *Brazil* **92 E5** 9 41S 65 20W
Aburo, *Dem. Rep. of the Congo* **54 B3** 2 4N 30 53 E
Abut Hd., *N.Z.* **59 K3** 43 7S 170 15 E
Acadia National Park, *U.S.A.* **77 C11** 44 20N 68 13W
Açailândia, *Brazil* **93 D9** 4 57S 47 0W
Acajutla, *El Salv.* **88 D2** 13 36N 89 50W
Acámbaro, *Mexico* **86 D4** 20 0N 100 40W
Acaponeta, *Mexico* **86 C3** 22 30N 105 20W
Acapulco, *Mexico* **87 D5** 16 51N 99 56W
Acarai, Serra, *Brazil* **92 C7** 1 50N 57 50W
Acarigua, *Venezuela* **92 B5** 9 33N 69 12W
Acatlán, *Mexico* **87 D5** 18 10N 98 3W
Acayucan, *Mexico* **87 D6** 17 59N 94 58W
Accomac, *U.S.A.* **76 G8** 37 43N 75 40W
Accra, *Ghana* **50 G5** 5 35N 0 6W
Accrington, *U.K.* **10 D5** 53 45N 2 22W
Acebal, *Argentina* **94 C3** 33 20S 60 50W
Aceh □, *Indonesia* **36 D1** 4 15N 97 30 E
Achalpur, *India* **40 J10** 21 22N 77 32 E
Acheng, *China* **35 B14** 45 30N 126 58 E
Acher, *India* **42 H5** 23 10N 72 32 E
Achill Hd., *Ireland* **13 C1** 53 58N 10 15W
Achill I., *Ireland* **13 C1** 53 58N 10 1W
Achinsk, *Russia* **27 D10** 56 20N 90 20 E
Acireale, *Italy* **20 F6** 37 37N 15 10 E
Ackerman, *U.S.A.* **81 J10** 33 19N 89 11W
Acklins I., *Bahamas* **89 B5** 22 30N 74 0W
Acme, *Canada* **72 C6** 51 33N 113 30W
Acme, *U.S.A.* **78 F5** 40 8N 79 26W
Aconcagua, Cerro, *Argentina* **94 C2** 32 39S 70 0W
Aconquija, Mt., *Argentina* **94 B2** 27 0S 66 0W
Açores, Is. dos = Azores, *Atl. Oc.* **50 A1** 38 44N 29 0W
Acraman, L., *Australia* **63 E2** 32 2S 135 23 E
Acre = 'Akko, *Israel* **47 C4** 32 55N 35 4 E
Acre □, *Brazil* **92 E4** 9 1S 71 0W
Acre →, *Brazil* **92 E5** 8 45S 67 22W
Acton, *Canada* **78 C4** 43 38N 80 3W
Acuña, *Mexico* **86 B4** 29 18N 100 55W
Ad Dammām, *Si. Arabia* **45 E6** 26 20N 50 5 E
Ad Dāmūr, *Lebanon* **47 B4** 33 44N 35 27 E
Ad Dawādimī, *Si. Arabia* **44 E5** 24 35N 44 15 E
Ad Dawḩah, *Qatar* **45 E6** 25 15N 51 35 E
Ad Dawr, *Iraq* **44 C4** 34 27N 43 47 E
Ad Dir'īyah, *Si. Arabia* **44 E5** 24 44N 46 35 E
Ad Dīwānīyah, *Iraq* **44 D5** 32 0N 45 0 E
Ad Dujayl, *Iraq* **44 C5** 33 51N 44 14 E
Ad Duwayd, *Si. Arabia* **44 D4** 30 15N 42 17 E
Ada, *Minn., U.S.A.* **80 B6** 47 18N 96 31W
Ada, *Okla., U.S.A.* **81 H6** 34 46N 96 41W
Adabiya, *Egypt* **47 F1** 29 53N 32 28 E
Adair, C., *Canada* **69 A12** 71 31N 71 24W
Adaja →, *Spain* **19 B3** 41 32N 4 52W
Adak I., *U.S.A.* **68 C2** 51 45N 176 45W
Adamaoua, Massif de l', *Cameroon* **52 C2** 7 20N 12 20 E
Adamawa Highlands = Adamaoua, Massif de l', *Cameroon* **52 C2** 7 20N 12 20 E
Adamello, Mte., *Italy* **18 C9** 46 9N 10 30 E
Adaminaby, *Australia* **63 F4** 36 0S 148 45 E
Adams, *Mass., U.S.A.* **79 D11** 42 38N 73 7W
Adams, *N.Y., U.S.A.* **79 C8** 43 49N 76 1W
Adams, *Wis., U.S.A.* **80 D10** 43 57N 89 49W
Adam's Bridge, *Sri Lanka* **40 Q11** 9 15N 79 40 E
Adams L., *Canada* **72 C5** 51 10N 119 40W
Adams Mt., *U.S.A.* **84 D5** 46 12N 121 30W
Adam's Peak, *Sri Lanka* **40 R12** 6 48N 80 30 E
Adana, *Turkey* **25 G6** 37 0N 35 16 E
Adapazarı = Sakarya, *Turkey* **25 F5** 40 48N 30 25 E
Adarama, *Sudan* **51 E12** 17 10N 34 52 E
Adare, C., *Antarctica* **5 D11** 71 0S 171 0 E
Adaut, *Indonesia* **37 F8** 8 8S 131 7 E
Adavale, *Australia* **63 D3** 25 52S 144 32 E
Adda →, *Italy* **18 D8** 45 8N 9 53 E
Addis Ababa = Addis Abeba, *Ethiopia* **46 F2** 9 2N 38 42 E
Addis Abeba, *Ethiopia* **46 F2** 9 2N 38 42 E
Addison, *U.S.A.* **78 D7** 42 1N 77 14W
Addo, *S. Africa* **56 E4** 33 32S 25 45 E
Ādeh, *Iran* **44 B5** 37 42N 45 11 E
Adel, *U.S.A.* **77 K4** 31 8N 83 25W
Adelaide, *Australia* **63 E2** 34 52S 138 30 E
Adelaide, *Bahamas* **88 A4** 25 4N 77 31W
Adelaide, *S. Africa* **56 E4** 32 42S 26 20 E
Adelaide I., *Antarctica* **5 C17** 67 15S 68 30W
Adelaide Pen., *Canada* **68 B10** 68 15N 97 30W
Adelaide River, *Australia* **60 B5** 13 15S 131 7 E
Adelanto, *U.S.A.* **85 L9** 34 35N 117 22W
Adele I., *Australia* **60 C3** 15 32S 123 9 E
Adélie, Terre, *Antarctica* **5 C10** 68 0S 140 0 E
Adélie Land = Adélie, Terre, *Antarctica* **5 C10** 68 0S 140 0 E
Aden = Al 'Adan, *Yemen* **46 E4** 12 45N 45 0 E
Aden, G. of, *Asia* **46 E4** 12 30N 47 30 E
Adendorp, *S. Africa* **56 E3** 32 15S 24 30 E
Adh Dhayd, *U.A.E.* **45 E7** 25 17N 55 53 E
Adhoi, *India* **42 H4** 23 26N 70 32 E
Adi, *Indonesia* **37 E8** 4 15S 133 30 E
Adieu, C., *Australia* **61 F5** 32 0S 132 10 E
Adieu Pt., *Australia* **60 C3** 15 14S 124 35 E
Adige →, *Italy* **20 B5** 45 9N 12 20 E
Adigrat, *Ethiopia* **46 E2** 14 20N 39 26 E
Adilabad, *India* **40 K11** 19 33N 78 20 E
Adin Khel, *Afghan.* **40 C6** 32 45N 68 5 E
Adirondack Mts., *U.S.A.* **79 C10** 44 0N 74 0W
Adjumani, *Uganda* **54 B3** 3 20N 31 50 E
Adlavik Is., *Canada* **71 A8** 55 2N 57 45W
Admiralty G., *Australia* **60 B4** 14 20S 125 55 E
Admiralty I., *U.S.A.* **72 B2** 57 30N 134 30W
Admiralty Is., *Papua N. G.* **64 H6** 2 0S 147 0 E
Adonara, *Indonesia* **37 F6** 8 15S 123 5 E
Adoni, *India* **40 M10** 15 33N 77 18 E
Adour →, *France* **18 E3** 43 32N 1 32W
Adra, *India* **43 H12** 23 30N 86 42 E
Adra, *Spain* **19 D4** 36 43N 3 3W
Adrano, *Italy* **20 F6** 37 40N 14 50 E
Adrar, *Algeria* **48 D4** 27 51N 0 11 E
Adrar, *Mauritania* **50 D3** 20 30N 7 30 E
Adrian, *Mich., U.S.A.* **76 E3** 41 54N 84 2W
Adrian, *Tex., U.S.A.* **81 H3** 35 16N 102 40W
Adriatic Sea, *Medit. S.* **20 C6** 43 0N 16 0 E
Adua, *Indonesia* **37 E7** 1 45S 129 50 E
Adwa, *Ethiopia* **46 E2** 14 15N 38 52 E
Adygea □, *Russia* **25 F7** 45 0N 40 0 E
Adzhar Republic = Ajaria □, *Georgia* **25 F7** 41 30N 42 0 E
Adzopé, *Ivory C.* **50 G5** 6 7N 3 49W
Ægean Sea, *Medit. S.* **21 E11** 38 30N 25 0 E
Aerhtai Shan, *Mongolia* **32 B4** 46 40N 92 45 E
'Afak, *Iraq* **44 C5** 32 4N 45 15 E
Afándou, *Greece* **23 C10** 36 18N 28 12 E
Afghanistan ■, *Asia* **40 C4** 33 0N 65 0 E
Aflou, *Algeria* **50 B6** 34 7N 2 3 E
Africa **48 E6** 10 0N 20 0 E
'Afrīn, *Syria* **44 B3** 36 32N 36 50 E
Afton, *N.Y., U.S.A.* **79 D9** 42 14N 75 32W
Afton, *Wyo., U.S.A.* **82 E8** 42 44N 110 56W
Afuá, *Brazil* **93 D8** 0 15S 50 20W
'Afula, *Israel* **47 C4** 32 37N 35 17 E
Afyon, *Turkey* **25 G5** 38 45N 30 33 E
Afyonkarahisar = Afyon, *Turkey* **25 G5** 38 45N 30 33 E
Agadès = Agadez, *Niger* **50 E7** 16 58N 7 59 E
Agadez, *Niger* **50 E7** 16 58N 7 59 E
Agadir, *Morocco* **50 B4** 30 28N 9 55W
Agaete, *Canary Is.* **22 F4** 28 6N 15 43W
Agar, *India* **42 H7** 23 40N 76 2 E
Agartala, *India* **41 H17** 23 50N 91 23 E
Agassiz, *Canada* **72 D4** 49 14N 121 46W
Agats, *Indonesia* **37 F9** 5 33S 138 0 E
Agawam, *U.S.A.* **79 D12** 42 5N 72 37W
Agboville, *Ivory C.* **50 G5** 5 55N 4 15W
Ağdam, *Azerbaijan* **44 B5** 40 0N 46 58 E
Agde, *France* **18 E5** 43 19N 3 28 E
Agen, *France* **18 D4** 44 12N 0 38 E
Āgh Kand, *Iran* **45 B6** 37 15N 48 4 E
Aginskoye, *Russia* **27 D12** 51 6N 114 32 E
Agnew, *Australia* **61 E3** 28 1S 120 31 E
Agori, *India* **43 G10** 24 33N 82 57 E
Agra, *India* **42 F7** 27 17N 77 58 E
Ağrı, *Turkey* **25 G7** 39 44N 43 3 E
Agri →, *Italy* **20 D7** 40 13N 16 44 E
Ağrı Dağı, *Turkey* **25 G7** 39 50N 44 15 E
Ağrı Karakose = Ağrı, *Turkey* **25 G7** 39 44N 43 3 E
Agrigento, *Italy* **20 F5** 37 19N 13 34 E
Agrínion, *Greece* **21 E9** 38 37N 21 27 E
Agua Caliente, *Baja Calif., Mexico* **85 N10** 32 29N 116 59W
Agua Caliente, *Sinaloa, Mexico* **86 B3** 26 30N 108 20W
Agua Caliente Springs, *U.S.A.* **85 N10** 32 56N 116 19W
Água Clara, *Brazil* **93 H8** 20 25S 52 45W
Agua Hechicero, *Mexico* **85 N10** 32 26N 116 14W
Agua Prieta, *Mexico* **86 A3** 31 20N 109 32W
Aguadilla, *Puerto Rico* **89 C6** 18 26N 67 10W
Aguadulce, *Panama* **88 E3** 8 15N 80 32W
Aguanga, *U.S.A.* **85 M10** 33 27N 116 51W
Aguanish, *Canada* **71 B7** 50 14N 62 2W
Aguanus →, *Canada* **71 B7** 50 13N 62 5W
Aguapey →, *Argentina* **94 B4** 29 7S 56 36W
Aguaray Guazú →, *Paraguay* **94 A4** 24 47S 57 19W
Aguarico →, *Ecuador* **92 D3** 0 59S 75 11W
Aguas Blancas, *Chile* **94 A2** 24 15S 69 55W
Aguas Calientes, Sierra de, *Argentina* **94 B2** 25 26S 66 40W
Aguascalientes, *Mexico* **86 C4** 21 53N 102 12W
Aguascalientes □, *Mexico* **86 C4** 22 0N 102 20W
Aguilares, *Argentina* **94 B2** 27 26S 65 35W
Aguilas, *Spain* **19 D5** 37 23N 1 35W
Agüimes, *Canary Is.* **22 G4** 27 58N 15 27W
Aguja, C. de la, *Colombia* **90 B3** 11 18N 74 12W
Agulhas, C., *S. Africa* **56 E3** 34 52S 20 0 E
Agulo, *Canary Is.* **22 F2** 28 11N 17 12W
Agung, *Indonesia* **36 F5** 8 20S 115 28 E
Agur, *Uganda* **54 B3** 2 28N 32 55 E
Agusan →, *Phil.* **37 C7** 9 0N 125 30 E
Aha Mts., *Botswana* **56 B3** 19 45S 21 0 E
Ahaggar, *Algeria* **50 D7** 23 0N 6 30 E
Ahar, *Iran* **44 B5** 38 35N 47 0 E
Ahipara B., *N.Z.* **59 F4** 35 5S 173 5 E
Ahiri, *India* **40 K12** 19 30N 80 0 E
Ahmad Wal, *Pakistan* **42 E1** 29 18N 65 58 E
Ahmadabad, *India* **42 H5** 23 0N 72 40 E
Aḩmadābād, *Khorāsān, Iran* **45 C9** 35 3N 60 50 E
Aḩmadābād, *Khorāsān, Iran* **45 C8** 35 49N 59 42 E
Aḩmadī, *Iran* **45 E8** 27 56N 56 42 E
Ahmadnagar, *India* **40 K9** 19 7N 74 46 E
Ahmadpur, *Pakistan* **42 E4** 29 12N 71 10 E
Ahmadpur Lamma, *Pakistan* **42 E4** 28 19N 70 3 E
Ahmedabad = Ahmadabad, *India* **42 H5** 23 0N 72 40 E
Ahmednagar = Ahmadnagar, *India* **40 K9** 19 7N 74 46 E
Ahome, *Mexico* **86 B3** 25 55N 109 11W
Ahoskie, *U.S.A.* **77 G7** 36 17N 76 59W
Ahram, *Iran* **45 D6** 28 52N 51 16 E
Ahrax Pt., *Malta* **23 D1** 35 59N 14 22 E
Āhū, *Iran* **45 C6** 34 33N 50 2 E
Ahuachapán, *El Salv.* **88 D2** 13 54N 89 52W
Ahvāz, *Iran* **45 D6** 31 20N 48 40 E
Ahvenanmaa = Åland, *Finland* **9 F19** 60 15N 20 0 E
Aḩwar, *Yemen* **46 E4** 13 30N 46 40 E
Ai →, *India* **43 F14** 26 26N 90 44 E
Aichi □, *Japan* **31 G8** 35 0N 137 15 E
Aigua, *Uruguay* **95 C5** 34 13S 54 46W
Aigues-Mortes, *France* **18 E6** 43 35N 4 12 E
Aihui, *China* **33 A7** 50 10N 127 30 E
Aija, *Peru* **92 E3** 9 50S 77 45W
Aikawa, *Japan* **30 E9** 38 2N 138 15 E
Aiken, *U.S.A.* **77 J5** 33 34N 81 43W
Aileron, *Australia* **62 C1** 22 39S 133 20 E
Aillik, *Canada* **71 A8** 55 11N 59 18W
Ailsa Craig, *U.K.* **12 F3** 55 15N 5 6W
'Ailūn, *Jordan* **47 C4** 32 18N 35 47 E
Aim, *Russia* **27 D14** 59 0N 133 55 E
Aimere, *Indonesia* **37 F6** 8 45S 121 3 E
Aimogasta, *Argentina* **94 B2** 28 33S 66 50W
Aïn Ben Tili, *Mauritania* **50 C4** 25 59N 9 27W
Aïn-Sefra, *Algeria* **50 B5** 32 47N 0 37W
'Ain Sudr, *Egypt* **47 F2** 29 50N 33 6 E
Ainaži, *Latvia* **9 H21** 57 50N 24 24 E
Ainsworth, *U.S.A.* **80 D5** 42 33N 99 52W
Aiquile, *Bolivia* **92 G5** 18 10S 65 10W
Aïr, *Niger* **50 E7** 18 30N 8 0 E
Air Force I., *Canada* **69 B12** 67 58N 74 5W
Air Hitam, *Malaysia* **39 M4** 1 55N 103 11 E
Airdrie, *Canada* **72 C6** 51 18N 114 2W
Airdrie, *U.K.* **12 F5** 55 52N 3 57W
Aire →, *U.K.* **10 D7** 53 43N 0 55W
Aire, I. de l', *Spain* **22 B11** 39 48N 4 16 E
Airlie Beach, *Australia* **62 C4** 20 16S 148 43 E
Aisne →, *France* **18 B5** 49 26N 2 50 E
Ait, *India* **43 G8** 25 54N 79 14 E
Aitkin, *U.S.A.* **80 B8** 46 32N 93 42W
Aiud, *Romania* **17 E12** 46 19N 23 44 E
Aix-en-Provence, *France* **18 E6** 43 32N 5 27 E
Aix-la-Chapelle = Aachen, *Germany* **16 C4** 50 45N 6 6 E
Aix-les-Bains, *France* **18 D6** 45 41N 5 53 E
Aíyion, *Greece* **21 E10** 38 15N 22 5 E
Aizawl, *India* **41 H18** 23 40N 92 44 E
Aizkraukle, *Latvia* **9 H21** 56 36N 25 11 E
Aizpute, *Latvia* **9 H19** 56 43N 21 40 E
Aizuwakamatsu, *Japan* **30 F9** 37 30N 139 56 E
Ajaccio, *France* **18 F8** 41 55N 8 40 E
Ajaigarh, *India* **43 G9** 24 52N 80 16 E
Ajalpan, *Mexico* **87 D5** 18 22N 97 15W
Ajanta Ra., *India* **40 J9** 20 28N 75 50 E
Ajari Rep. = Ajaria □, *Georgia* **25 F7** 41 30N 42 0 E
Ajaria □, *Georgia* **25 F7** 41 30N 42 0 E
Ajax, *Canada* **78 C5** 43 50N 79 1W
Ajdâbiyah, *Libya* **51 B10** 30 54N 20 4 E
Ajka, *Hungary* **17 E9** 47 4N 17 31 E
'Ajmān, *U.A.E.* **45 E7** 25 25N 55 30 E
Ajmer, *India* **42 F6** 26 28N 74 37 E
Ajnala, *India* **42 D6** 31 50N 74 48 E
Ajo, *U.S.A.* **83 K7** 32 22N 112 52W
Ajo, C. de, *Spain* **19 A4** 43 31N 3 35W
Akabira, *Japan* **30 C11** 43 33N 142 5 E
Akamas □, *Cyprus* **23 D11** 35 3N 32 18 E
Akanthou, *Cyprus* **23 D12** 35 22N 33 45 E
Akaroa, *N.Z.* **59 K4** 43 49S 172 59 E
Akashi, *Japan* **31 G7** 34 45N 134 58 E
Akbarpur, *Bihar, India* **43 G10** 24 39N 83 58 E
Akbarpur, *Ut. P., India* **43 F10** 26 25N 82 32 E
Akelamo, *Indonesia* **37 D7** 1 35N 129 40 E
Aketi, *Dem. Rep. of the Congo* **52 D4** 2 38N 23 47 E
Akharnaí, *Greece* **21 E10** 38 5N 23 44 E
Akhelóös →, *Greece* **21 E9** 38 19N 21 7 E
Akhisar, *Turkey* **21 E12** 38 56N 27 48 E
Akhnur, *India* **43 C6** 32 52N 74 45 E
Akhtyrka = Okhtyrka, *Ukraine* **25 D5** 50 25N 35 0 E
Aki, *Japan* **31 H6** 33 30N 133 54 E
Akimiski I., *Canada* **70 B3** 52 50N 81 30W
Akita, *Japan* **30 E10** 39 45N 140 7 E
Akita □, *Japan* **30 E10** 39 40N 140 30 E
Akjoujt, *Mauritania* **50 E3** 19 45N 14 15W
Akkeshi, *Japan* **30 C12** 43 2N 144 51 E
'Akko, *Israel* **47 C4** 32 55N 35 4 E
Aklavik, *Canada* **68 B6** 68 12N 135 0W
Aklera, *India* **42 G7** 24 26N 76 32 E
Akmolinsk = Astana, *Kazakstan* **26 D8** 51 10N 71 30 E
Akō, *Japan* **31 G7** 34 45N 134 24 E
Akola, *India* **40 J10** 20 42N 77 2 E
Akordat, *Eritrea* **46 D2** 15 30N 37 40 E
Akpatok I., *Canada* **69 B13** 60 25N 68 8W
Åkrahamn, *Norway* **9 G11** 59 15N 5 10 E
Akranes, *Iceland* **8 D2** 64 19N 22 5W
Akron, *Colo., U.S.A.* **80 E3** 40 10N 103 13W
Akron, *Ohio, U.S.A.* **78 E3** 41 5N 81 31W
Akrotiri, *Cyprus* **23 E11** 34 36N 32 57 E
Akrotiri Bay, *Cyprus* **23 E12** 34 35N 33 10 E
Aksai Chin, *India* **43 B8** 35 15N 79 55 E
Aksaray, *Turkey* **25 G5** 38 25N 34 2 E
Aksay, *Kazakstan* **25 D9** 51 11N 53 0 E
Akşehir, *Turkey* **44 B1** 38 18N 31 30 E
Akşehir Gölü, *Turkey* **25 G5** 38 30N 31 25 E
Aksu, *China* **32 B3** 41 5N 80 10 E
Aksum, *Ethiopia* **46 E2** 14 5N 38 40 E
Aktogay, *Kazakstan* **26 E8** 46 57N 79 40 E
Aktsyabrski, *Belarus* **17 B15** 52 38N 28 53 E
Aktyubinsk = Aqtöbe, *Kazakstan* **25 D10** 50 17N 57 10 E
Akure, *Nigeria* **50 G7** 7 15N 5 5 E
Akureyri, *Iceland* **8 D4** 65 40N 18 6W
Akuseki-Shima, *Japan* **31 K4** 29 27N 129 37 E
Akyab = Sittwe, *Burma* **41 J18** 20 18N 92 45 E
Al 'Adan, *Yemen* **46 E4** 12 45N 45 0 E
Al Aḩsā = Hasa □, *Si. Arabia* **45 E6** 25 50N 49 0 E
Al Ajfar, *Si. Arabia* **44 E4** 27 26N 43 0 E
Al Amādīyah, *Iraq* **44 B4** 37 5N 43 30 E
Al 'Amārah, *Iraq* **44 D5** 31 55N 47 15 E
Al 'Aqabah, *Jordan* **47 F4** 29 31N 35 0 E
Al Arak, *Syria* **44 C3** 34 38N 38 35 E
Al 'Aramah, *Si. Arabia* **44 E5** 25 30N 46 0 E
Al Arţāwīyah, *Si. Arabia* **44 E5** 26 31N 45 20 E
Al 'Āşimah = 'Ammān □, *Jordan* **47 D5** 31 40N 36 30 E
Al 'Assāfīyah, *Si. Arabia* **44 D3** 28 17N 38 59 E
Al 'Ayn, *Oman* **45 E7** 24 15N 55 45 E
Al 'Ayn, *Si. Arabia* **44 E3** 25 4N 38 6 E
Al 'Aẓamīyah, *Iraq* **44 C5** 33 22N 44 22 E
Al 'Azīzīyah, *Iraq* **44 C5** 32 54N 45 4 E
Al Bāb, *Syria* **44 B3** 36 23N 37 29 E
Al Bad', *Si. Arabia* **44 D2** 28 28N 35 1 E
Al Bādī, *Iraq* **44 C4** 35 56N 41 32 E
Al Baḩrah, *Kuwait* **44 D5** 29 40N 47 52 E
Al Baḩral Mayyit = Dead Sea, *Asia* **47 D4** 31 30N 35 30 E
Al Balqā' □, *Jordan* **47 C4** 32 5N 35 45 E
Al Bārūk, J., *Lebanon* **47 B4** 33 39N 35 40 E
Al Başrah, *Iraq* **44 D5** 30 30N 47 50 E
Al Baţḩā, *Iraq* **44 D5** 31 6N 45 53 E
Al Batrūn, *Lebanon* **47 A4** 34 15N 35 40 E
Al Bayḑā, *Libya* **51 B10** 32 50N 21 44 E
Al Biqā, *Lebanon* **47 A5** 34 10N 36 10 E
Al Bi'r, *Si. Arabia* **44 D3** 28 51N 36 16 E
Al Burayj, *Syria* **47 A5** 34 15N 36 46 E
Al Faḑilī, *Si. Arabia* **45 E6** 26 58N 49 10 E

Amadeus, L.

Al Fallūjah, Iraq 44 C4 33 20N 43 55 E
Al Fāw, Iraq 45 D6 30 0N 48 30 E
Al Fujayrah, U.A.E. 45 E8 25 7N 56 18 E
Al Ghadaf, W. →, Jordan 47 D5 31 26N 36 43 E
Al Ghammās, Iraq 44 D5 31 45N 44 37 E
Al Ghazālah, Si. Arabia 44 E4 26 48N 41 19 E
Al Hābah, Si. Arabia 44 E5 27 10N 47 0 E
Al Ḥadīthah, Iraq 44 C4 34 0N 41 13 E
Al Ḥadīthah, Si. Arabia 47 D6 31 28N 37 8 E
Al Ḥaḍr, Iraq 44 C4 35 35N 42 44 E
Al Ḥājānah, Syria 47 B5 33 20N 36 33 E
Al Hajar al Gharbī, Oman 45 E8 24 10N 56 15 E
Al Ḥāmad, Si. Arabia 44 D3 31 30N 39 30 E
Al Hamdānīyah, Syria 44 C3 35 25N 36 50 E
Al Ḥamīdīyah, Syria 47 A4 34 42N 35 57 E
Al Ḥammār, Iraq 44 D5 30 57N 46 51 E
Al Ḥamrā', Si. Arabia 44 E3 24 2N 38 55 E
Al Ḥanākīyah, Si. Arabia 44 E4 24 51N 40 31 E
Al Harīr, W. →, Syria 47 C4 32 44N 35 59 E
Al Ḥasā, W. →, Jordan 47 D4 31 4N 35 29 E
Al Ḥasakah, Syria 44 B4 36 35N 40 45 E
Al Ḥaydān, W. →, Jordan 47 D4 31 29N 35 34 E
Al Ḥayy, Iraq 44 C5 32 5N 46 5 E
Al Ḥijarah, Asia 44 D4 30 0N 44 0 E
Al Ḥillah, Iraq 44 C5 32 30N 44 25 E
Al Hindīyah, Iraq 44 C5 32 30N 44 10 E
Al Hirmil, Lebanon 47 A5 34 26N 36 24 E
Al Hoceïma, Morocco 50 A5 35 8N 3 58W
Al Ḥudaydah, Yemen 46 E3 14 50N 43 0 E
Al Hufūf, Si. Arabia 45 E6 25 25N 49 45 E
Al Ḥumayḍah, Si. Arabia 44 D2 29 14N 34 56 E
Al Ḥunayy, Si. Arabia 45 E6 25 58N 48 45 E
Al Īsāwīyah, Si. Arabia 44 D3 30 43N 37 59 E
Al Jafr, Jordan 47 E5 30 18N 36 14 E
Al Jāfūrah, Si. Arabia 45 E7 25 0N 50 15 E
Al Jaghbūb, Libya 51 C10 29 42N 24 38 E
Al Jahrah, Kuwait 44 D5 29 25N 47 40 E
Al Jalāmīd, Si. Arabia 44 D3 31 20N 40 6 E
Al Jamalīyah, Qatar 45 E6 25 37N 51 5 E
Al Janūb ☐, Lebanon 47 B4 33 20N 35 20 E
Al Jawf, Libya 51 D10 24 10N 23 24 E
Al Jawf, Si. Arabia 44 D3 29 55N 39 40 E
Al Jazirah, Iraq 44 C5 33 30N 44 0 E
Al Jithāmīyah, Si. Arabia 44 E4 27 41N 41 43 E
Al Jubayl, Si. Arabia 45 E6 27 0N 49 50 E
Al Jubaylah, Si. Arabia 44 E5 24 55N 46 25 E
Al Jubb, Si. Arabia 44 E4 27 11N 42 17 E
Al Junaynah, Sudan 51 F10 13 27N 22 45 E
Al Kabā'ish, Iraq 44 D5 30 58N 47 0 E
Al Karak, Jordan 47 D4 31 11N 35 42 E
Al Karak ☐, Jordan 47 E5 31 0N 36 0 E
Al Kāzim Tyah, Iraq 44 C5 33 22N 44 12 E
Al Khābūra, Oman 45 F8 23 57N 57 5 E
Al Khafji, Si. Arabia 45 E6 28 24N 48 29 E
Al Khalīl, West Bank 47 D4 31 32N 35 6 E
Al Khāliṣ, Iraq 44 C5 33 49N 44 32 E
Al Kharsānīyah, Si. Arabia 45 E6 27 13N 49 18 E
Al Khaṣab, Oman 45 E8 26 14N 56 15 E
Al Khawr, Qatar 45 E6 25 41N 51 30 E
Al Khiḍr, Iraq 44 D5 31 12N 45 33 E
Al Khiyām, Lebanon 47 B4 33 20N 35 36 E
Al Khums, Libya 51 B8 32 40N 14 17 E
Al Kiswah, Syria 47 B5 33 23N 36 14 E
Al Kūfah, Iraq 44 C5 32 2N 44 24 E
Al Kufrah, Libya 51 D10 24 17N 23 15 E
Al Kuhayfīyah, Si. Arabia 44 E4 27 12N 43 3 E
Al Kūt, Iraq 44 C5 32 30N 46 0 E
Al Kuwayt, Kuwait 44 D5 29 30N 48 0 E
Al Labwah, Lebanon 47 A5 34 11N 36 20 E
Al Lādhiqīyah, Syria 44 C2 35 30N 35 45 E
Al Līth, Si. Arabia 46 C3 20 9N 40 15 E
Al Liwā', Oman 45 E8 24 31N 56 36 E
Al Luḥayyah, Yemen 46 D3 15 45N 42 40 E
Al Madīnah, Iraq 44 D5 30 57N 47 16 E
Al Madīnah, Si. Arabia 46 C2 24 35N 39 52 E
Al Mafraq, Jordan 47 C5 32 17N 36 14 E
Al Maḥmūdīyah, Iraq 44 C5 33 3N 44 21 E
Al Majma'ah, Si. Arabia 44 E5 25 57N 45 22 E
Al Makhruq, W. →, Jordan 47 D6 31 28N 37 0 E
Al Makḥūl, Si. Arabia 44 E4 26 37N 42 39 E
Al Manāmah, Bahrain 45 E6 26 10N 50 30 E
Al Maqwa', Kuwait 44 D5 29 10N 47 59 E
Al Marj, Libya 51 B10 32 25N 20 30 E
Al Maṭlā, Kuwait 44 D5 29 24N 47 40 E
Al Mawjib, W. →, Jordan 47 D4 31 28N 35 36 E
Al Mawṣil, Iraq 44 B4 36 15N 43 5 E
Al Mayādin, Syria 44 C4 35 1N 40 27 E
Al Mazār, Jordan 47 D4 31 4N 35 41 E
Al Midhnab, Si. Arabia 44 E5 25 50N 44 18 E
Al Minā', Lebanon 47 A4 34 24N 35 49 E
Al Miqdādīyah, Iraq 44 C5 34 0N 45 0 E
Al Mubarraz, Si. Arabia 45 E6 25 30N 49 40 E
Al Mudawwarah, Jordan 47 F5 29 19N 36 0 E
Al Mughayrā', U.A.E. 45 E7 24 5N 53 32 E
Al Muḥarraq, Bahrain 45 E6 26 15N 50 40 E
Al Mukallā, Yemen 46 E4 14 33N 49 2 E
Al Mukhā, Yemen 46 E3 13 18N 43 15 E
Al Musayjid, Si. Arabia 44 E3 24 5N 39 5 E
Al Musayyib, Iraq 44 C5 32 49N 44 20 E
Al Muwayliḥ, Si. Arabia 44 E2 27 40N 35 30 E
Al Qā'im, Iraq 44 C4 34 21N 41 7 E
Al Qalībah, Si. Arabia 44 D3 28 24N 37 42 E
Al Qāmishli, Syria 44 B4 37 10N 41 10 E
Al Qaryatayn, Syria 47 A6 34 12N 37 13 E
Al Qaṣīm, Si. Arabia 44 E4 26 0N 43 0 E
Al Qaṭ'ā, Syria 44 C4 34 40N 40 48 E
Al Qaṭīf, Si. Arabia 45 E6 26 35N 50 0 E
Al Qaṭrānah, Jordan 47 D5 31 12N 36 6 E
Al Qaṭrūn, Libya 51 D9 24 56N 15 3 E
Al Qayṣūmah, Si. Arabia 44 D5 28 20N 46 7 E
Al Quds = Jerusalem, Israel 47 D4 31 47N 35 10 E
Al Qunayṭirah, Syria 47 C4 32 55N 35 45 E
Al Qurnah, Iraq 44 D5 31 1N 47 25 E
Al Quṣayr, Iraq 44 D5 30 39N 45 50 E
Al Quṣayr, Syria 47 A5 34 31N 36 34 E
Al Quṭayfah, Syria 47 B5 33 44N 36 36 E
Al 'Ubaylah, Si. Arabia 46 C5 21 59N 50 57 E
Al 'Uḍaylīyah, Si. Arabia 45 E6 25 8N 49 18 E
Al 'Ulā, Si. Arabia 44 E3 26 35N 38 0 E
Al 'Uqayr, Si. Arabia 45 E6 25 40N 50 15 E
Al 'Uthmānīyah, Si. Arabia 45 E6 25 5N 49 22 E
Al 'Uwaynid, Si. Arabia 44 E5 24 50N 46 0 E
Al 'Uwayqīlah, Si. Arabia 44 D4 30 30N 42 10 E
Al 'Uyūn, Ḥijāz, Si. Arabia 44 E3 24 33N 39 35 E
Al 'Uyūn, Najd, Si. Arabia 44 E4 26 30N 43 50 E
Al 'Uzayr, Iraq 44 D5 31 19N 47 25 E
Al Wajh, Si. Arabia 44 E3 26 10N 36 30 E
Al Wakrah, Qatar 45 E6 25 10N 51 40 E
Al Wannān, Si. Arabia 45 E6 26 55N 48 24 E
Al Waqbah, Si. Arabia 44 D5 28 48N 45 33 E
Al Wari'āh, Si. Arabia 44 E5 27 51N 47 25 E
Al Wusayl, Qatar 45 E6 25 29N 51 29 E
Ala Dağ, Turkey 44 B2 37 44N 35 9 E
Ala Tau Shankou = Dzungarian Gates, Kazakstan 32 B3 45 0N 82 0 E
Alabama ☐, U.S.A. 77 J2 33 0N 87 0W
Alabama →, U.S.A. 77 K2 31 8N 87 57W
Alabaster, U.S.A. 77 J2 33 15N 86 49W
Alaçam Dağları, Turkey 21 E13 39 18N 28 49 E
Alachua, U.S.A. 77 L4 29 47N 82 30W
Alaérma, Greece 23 C9 36 9N 27 57 E
Alagoa Grande, Brazil 93 E11 7 3S 35 35W
Alagoas ☐, Brazil 93 E11 9 0S 36 0W
Alagoinhas, Brazil 93 F11 12 7S 38 20W
Alaior, Spain 22 B11 39 57N 4 8 E
Alajero, Canary Is. 22 F2 28 3N 17 13W
Alajuela, Costa Rica 88 D3 10 2N 84 8W
Alakamisy, Madag. 57 C8 21 19S 47 14 E
Alaknanda →, India 43 D8 30 8N 78 36 E
Alakurtti, Russia 24 A5 67 0N 30 30 E
Alamarvdasht, Iran 45 E7 27 37N 52 59 E
Alameda, Calif., U.S.A. 84 H4 37 46N 122 15W
Alameda, N. Mex., U.S.A. 83 J10 35 11N 106 37W
Alamo, U.S.A. 85 J11 37 22N 115 10W
Alamo Crossing, U.S.A. 85 L13 34 16N 113 33W
Alamogordo, U.S.A. 83 K11 32 54N 105 57W
Alamos, Mexico 86 B3 27 0N 109 0W
Alamosa, U.S.A. 83 H11 37 28N 105 52W
Åland, Finland 9 F19 60 15N 20 0 E
Ålands hav, Sweden 9 F18 60 0N 19 30 E
Alandur, India 40 N12 13 0N 80 15 E
Alania = North Ossetia ☐, Russia 25 F7 43 30N 44 30 E
Alanya, Turkey 25 G5 36 38N 32 0 E
Alaotra, Farihin', Madag. 57 B8 17 30S 48 30 E
Alapayevsk, Russia 26 D7 57 52N 61 42 E
Alaşehir, Turkey 21 E13 38 23N 28 30 E
Alaska ☐, U.S.A. 68 B5 64 0N 154 0W
Alaska, G. of, Pac. Oc. 68 C5 58 0N 145 0W
Alaska Peninsula, U.S.A. 68 C4 56 0N 159 0W
Alaska Range, U.S.A. 68 B4 62 50N 151 0W
Älät, Azerbaijan 25 G8 39 58N 49 25 E
Alatyr, Russia 24 D8 54 55N 46 35 E
Alausi, Ecuador 92 D3 2 0S 78 50W
Alava, C., U.S.A. 82 B1 48 10N 124 44W
Alavus, Finland 9 E20 62 35N 23 36 E
Alawoona, Australia 63 E3 34 45S 140 30 E
'Alayh, Lebanon 47 B4 33 46N 35 33 E
Alba, Italy 18 D8 44 42N 8 2 E
Alba-Iulia, Romania 17 E12 46 8N 23 39 E
Albacete, Spain 19 C5 39 0N 1 50W
Albacutya, L., Australia 63 F3 35 45S 141 58 E
Albanel, L., Canada 70 B5 50 55N 73 12W
Albania ■, Europe 21 D9 41 0N 20 0 E
Albany, Australia 61 G2 35 1S 117 58 E
Albany, Ga., U.S.A. 77 K3 31 35N 84 10W
Albany, N.Y., U.S.A. 79 D11 42 39N 73 45W
Albany, Oreg., U.S.A. 82 D2 44 38N 123 6W
Albany, Tex., U.S.A. 81 J5 32 44N 99 18W
Albany →, Canada 70 B3 52 17N 81 31W
Albardón, Argentina 94 C2 31 20S 68 30W
Albatross B., Australia 62 A3 12 45S 141 30 E
Albemarle, U.S.A. 77 H5 35 21N 80 11W
Albemarle Sd., U.S.A. 77 H7 36 5N 76 0W
Alberche →, Spain 19 C3 39 58N 4 46W
Alberdi, Paraguay 94 B4 26 14S 58 20W
Albert, L., Australia 63 F2 35 30S 139 10 E
Albert Edward Ra., Australia 60 C4 18 17S 127 57 E
Albert L., Africa 54 B3 1 30N 31 0 E
Albert Lea, U.S.A. 80 D8 43 39N 93 22W
Albert Nile →, Uganda 54 B3 3 36N 32 2 E
Albert Town, Bahamas 89 B5 22 37N 74 33W
Alberta ☐, Canada 72 C6 54 40N 115 0W
Alberti, Argentina 94 D3 35 1S 60 16W
Albertinia, S. Africa 56 E3 34 11S 21 34 E
Alberton, Canada 71 C7 46 50N 64 0W
Albertville = Kalemie, Dem. Rep. of the Congo 54 D2 5 55S 29 9 E
Albertville, France 18 D7 45 40N 6 22 E
Albertville, U.S.A. 77 H2 34 16N 86 13W
Albi, France 18 E5 43 56N 2 9 E
Albia, U.S.A. 80 E8 41 2N 92 48W
Albina, Surinam 93 B8 5 37N 54 15W
Albina, Ponta, Angola 56 B1 15 52S 11 44 E
Albion, Mich., U.S.A. 76 D3 42 15N 84 45W
Albion, Nebr., U.S.A. 80 E6 41 42N 98 0W
Albion, Pa., U.S.A. 78 E4 41 53N 80 22W
Alborán, Medit. S. 19 E4 35 57N 3 0W
Ålborg, Denmark 9 H13 57 2N 9 54 E
Alborz, Reshteh-ye Kūhhā-ye, Iran 45 C7 36 0N 52 0 E
Albuquerque, U.S.A. 83 J10 35 5N 106 39W
Albuquerque, Cayos de, Caribbean 88 D3 12 10N 81 50W
Alburg, U.S.A. 79 B11 44 59N 73 18W
Albury-Wodonga, Australia 63 F4 36 3S 146 56 E
Alcalá de Henares, Spain 19 B4 40 28N 3 22W
Alcalá la Real, Spain 19 D4 37 27N 3 57W
Álcamo, Italy 20 F5 37 59N 12 55 E
Alcañiz, Spain 19 B5 41 2N 0 8W
Alcântara, Brazil 93 D10 2 20S 44 30W
Alcántara, Embalse de, Spain 19 C2 39 44N 6 50W
Alcantarilla, Spain 19 D5 37 59N 1 12W
Alcaraz, Sierra de, Spain 19 C4 38 40N 2 20W
Alcaudete, Spain 19 D3 37 35N 4 5W
Alcázar de San Juan, Spain 19 C4 39 24N 3 12W
Alchevsk, Ukraine 25 E6 48 30N 38 45 E
Alcira = Alzira, Spain 19 C5 39 9N 0 30W
Alcova, U.S.A. 82 E10 42 34N 106 43W
Alcoy, Spain 19 C5 38 43N 0 30W
Alcúdia, Spain 22 B10 39 51N 3 7 E
Alcúdia, B. d', Spain 22 B10 39 47N 3 15 E
Aldabra Is., Seychelles 49 G8 9 22S 46 28 E
Aldama, Mexico 87 C5 23 0N 98 4W
Aldan, Russia 27 D13 58 40N 125 30 E
Aldan →, Russia 27 C13 63 28N 129 35 E
Aldea, Pta. de la, Canary Is. 22 G4 28 0N 15 50W
Aldeburgh, U.K. 11 E9 52 10N 1 37 E
Alder Pk., U.S.A. 84 K5 35 53N 121 22W
Alderney, U.K. 11 H5 49 42N 2 11W
Aldershot, U.K. 11 F7 51 15N 0 44W
Aledo, U.S.A. 80 E9 41 12N 90 45W
Aleg, Mauritania 50 E3 17 3N 13 55W
Alegranza, Canary Is. 22 E6 29 23N 13 32W
Alegranza, I., Canary Is. 22 E6 29 23N 13 32W
Alegre, Brazil 95 A7 20 50S 41 30W
Alegrete, Brazil 95 B4 29 40S 56 0W
Aleisk, Russia 26 D9 52 40N 83 0 E
Aleksandriya = Oleksandriya, Ukraine 17 C14 50 37N 26 19 E
Aleksandrov Gay, Russia 25 D8 50 9N 48 34 E
Aleksandrovsk-Sakhalinskiy, Russia 27 D15 50 50N 142 20 E
Além Paraíba, Brazil 95 A7 21 52S 42 41W
Alemania, Argentina 94 B2 25 40S 65 30W
Alemania, Chile 94 B2 25 10S 69 55W
Alençon, France 18 B4 48 27N 0 4 E
Alenquer, Brazil 93 D8 1 56S 54 46W
Alenuihaha Channel, U.S.A. 74 H17 20 30N 156 0W
Aleppo = Ḥalab, Syria 44 B3 36 10N 37 15 E
Alès, France 18 D6 44 9N 4 5 E
Alessándria, Italy 18 D8 44 54N 8 37 E
Ålesund, Norway 9 E12 62 28N 6 12 E
Aleutian Is., Pac. Oc. 68 C2 52 0N 175 0W
Aleutian Trench, Pac. Oc. 64 C10 48 0N 180 0 E
Alexander, U.S.A. 80 B3 47 51N 103 39W
Alexander, Mt., Australia 61 E3 28 58S 120 16 E
Alexander Arch., U.S.A. 68 C6 56 0N 136 0W
Alexander Bay, S. Africa 56 D2 28 40S 16 30 E
Alexander City, U.S.A. 77 J3 32 56N 85 58W
Alexander I., Antarctica 5 C17 69 0S 70 0W
Alexandra, Australia 63 F4 37 8S 145 40 E
Alexandra, N.Z. 59 L2 45 14S 169 25 E
Alexandra Falls, Canada 72 A5 60 29N 116 18W
Alexandria = El Iskandarîya, Egypt 51 B11 31 13N 29 58 E
Alexandria, B.C., Canada 72 C4 52 35N 122 27W
Alexandria, Ont., Canada 79 A10 45 19N 74 38W
Alexandria, Romania 17 G13 43 57N 25 24 E
Alexandria, S. Africa 56 E4 33 38S 26 28 E
Alexandria, U.K. 12 F4 55 59N 4 35W
Alexandria, La., U.S.A. 81 K8 31 18N 92 27W
Alexandria, Minn., U.S.A. 80 C7 45 53N 95 22W
Alexandria, S. Dak., U.S.A. 80 D6 43 39N 97 47W
Alexandria, Va., U.S.A. 76 F7 38 48N 77 3W
Alexandria Bay, U.S.A. 79 B9 44 20N 75 55W
Alexandrina, L., Australia 63 F2 35 25S 139 10 E
Alexandroúpolis, Greece 21 D11 40 50N 25 54 E
Alexis →, Canada 71 B8 52 33N 56 8W
Alexis Creek, Canada 72 C4 52 10N 123 20W
Alfabia, Spain 22 B9 39 44N 2 44 E
Alfenas, Brazil 95 A6 21 20S 46 10W
Alford, Aberds., U.K. 12 D6 57 14N 2 41W
Alford, Lincs., U.K. 10 D8 53 15N 0 10 E
Alfred, Maine, U.S.A. 79 C14 43 29N 70 43W
Alfred, N.Y., U.S.A. 78 D7 42 16N 77 48W
Alfreton, U.K. 10 D6 53 6N 1 24W
Alga, Kazakstan 25 E10 49 53N 57 20 E
Algaida, Spain 22 B9 39 33N 2 53 E
Ålgård, Norway 9 G11 58 46N 5 53 E
Algarve, Portugal 19 D1 36 58N 8 20W
Algeciras, Spain 19 D3 36 9N 5 28W
Algemesí, Spain 19 C5 39 11N 0 27W
Alger, Algeria 50 A6 36 42N 3 8 E
Algeria ■, Africa 50 C6 28 30N 2 0 E
Alghero, Italy 20 D3 40 33N 8 19 E
Algiers = Alger, Algeria 50 A6 36 42N 3 8 E
Algoa B., S. Africa 56 E4 33 50S 25 45 E
Algoma, U.S.A. 76 C2 44 36N 87 26W
Algona, U.S.A. 80 D7 43 4N 94 14W
Algonac, U.S.A. 78 D2 42 37N 82 32W
Algonquin Prov. Park, Canada 70 C4 45 50N 78 30W
Algorta, Uruguay 96 C5 32 25S 57 23W
Alhambra, U.S.A. 85 L8 34 8N 118 6W
Alhucemas = Al Hoceïma, Morocco 50 A5 35 8N 3 58W
'Alī al Gharbī, Iraq 44 C5 32 30N 46 45 E
'Alī ash Sharqī, Iraq 44 C5 32 7N 46 44 E
'Alī Khēl, Afghan. 42 C3 33 57N 69 43 E
Alī Shāh, Iran 44 B5 38 9N 45 50 E
'Alīābād, Khorāsān, Iran 45 C8 32 30N 57 30 E
'Alīābād, Kordestān, Iran 44 C5 35 4N 46 58 E
'Alīābād, Yazd, Iran 45 D7 31 41N 53 49 E
Aliağa, Turkey 21 E12 38 47N 26 59 E
Aliákmon →, Greece 21 D10 40 30N 22 36 E
Alicante, Spain 19 C5 38 23N 0 30W
Alice, S. Africa 56 E4 32 48S 26 55 E
Alice, U.S.A. 81 M5 27 45N 98 5W
Alice →, Queens., Australia 62 C3 24 2S 144 50 E
Alice →, Queens., Australia 62 B3 15 35S 142 20 E
Alice Arm, Canada 72 B3 55 29N 129 31W
Alice Springs, Australia 62 C1 23 40S 133 50 E
Alicedale, S. Africa 56 E4 33 15S 26 4 E
Aliceville, U.S.A. 77 J1 33 8N 88 9W
Aliganj, India 43 F8 27 30N 79 10 E
Aligarh, Raj., India 42 G7 25 55N 76 15 E
Aligarh, Ut. P., India 42 F8 27 55N 78 10 E
Alīgūdarz, Iran 45 C6 33 25N 49 45 E
Alimnía, Greece 23 C9 36 16N 27 43 E
Alingsås, Sweden 9 H15 57 56N 12 31 E
Alipur, Pakistan 42 E4 29 25N 70 55 E
Alipur Duar, India 41 F16 26 30N 89 35 E
Aliquippa, U.S.A. 78 F4 40 37N 80 15W
Alitus = Alytus, Lithuania 9 J21 54 24N 24 3 E
Aliwal North, S. Africa 56 E4 30 45S 26 45 E
Alix, Canada 72 C6 52 24N 113 11W
Aljustrel, Portugal 19 D1 37 55N 8 10W
Alkmaar, Neths. 15 B4 52 37N 4 45 E
All American Canal, U.S.A. 83 K6 32 45N 115 15W
Allagash →, U.S.A. 77 B11 47 5N 69 3W
Allah Dad, Pakistan 42 G2 25 38N 67 34 E
Allahabad, India 43 G9 25 25N 81 58 E
Allan, Canada 73 C7 51 53N 106 4W
Allanmyo, Burma 41 K19 19 30N 95 17 E
Allanridge, S. Africa 56 D4 27 45S 26 40 E
Allegany, U.S.A. 78 D6 42 6N 78 30W
Allegheny →, U.S.A. 78 F5 40 27N 80 1W
Allegheny Mts., U.S.A. 76 G6 38 15N 80 10W
Allegheny Reservoir, U.S.A. 78 E6 41 50N 79 0W
Allen, Bog of, Ireland 13 C5 53 15N 7 0W
Allen, L., Ireland 13 B3 54 8N 8 4W
Allendale, U.S.A. 77 J5 33 1N 81 18W
Allende, Mexico 86 B4 28 20N 100 50W
Allentown, U.S.A. 79 F9 40 37N 75 29W
Alleppey, India 40 Q10 9 30N 76 28 E
Aller →, Germany 16 B5 52 56N 9 12 E
Alliance, Nebr., U.S.A. 80 D3 42 6N 102 52W
Alliance, Ohio, U.S.A. 78 F3 40 55N 81 6W
Allier →, France 18 C5 46 57N 3 4 E
Alliford Bay, Canada 72 C2 53 12N 131 58W
Alliston, Canada 78 B5 44 9N 79 52W
Alloa, U.K. 12 E5 56 7N 3 47W
Allora, Australia 63 D5 28 2S 152 0 E
Alluitsup Paa = Sydprøven, Greenland 4 C5 60 30N 45 35W
Alma, Canada 71 C5 48 35N 71 40W
Alma, Ga., U.S.A. 77 K4 31 33N 82 28W
Alma, Kans., U.S.A. 80 F6 39 1N 96 17W
Alma, Mich., U.S.A. 76 D3 43 23N 84 39W
Alma, Nebr., U.S.A. 80 E5 40 6N 99 22W
Alma Ata = Almaty, Kazakstan 26 E8 43 15N 76 57 E
Almada, Portugal 19 C1 38 40N 9 9W
Almaden, Australia 62 B3 17 22S 144 40 E
Almadén, Spain 19 C3 38 49N 4 52W
Almanor, L., U.S.A. 82 F3 40 14N 121 9W
Almansa, Spain 19 C5 38 51N 1 5W
Almanzor, Pico, Spain 19 B3 40 15N 5 18W
Almanzora →, Spain 19 D5 37 14N 1 46W
Almaty, Kazakstan 26 E8 43 15N 76 57 E
Almazán, Spain 19 B4 41 30N 2 30W
Almeirim, Brazil 93 D8 1 30S 52 34W
Almelo, Neths. 15 B6 52 22N 6 42 E
Almendralejo, Spain 19 C2 38 41N 6 26W
Almere-Stad, Neths. 15 B5 52 20N 5 15 E
Almería, Spain 19 D4 36 52N 2 27W
Almirante, Panama 88 E3 9 10N 82 30W
Almiroú, Kólpos, Greece 23 D6 35 23N 24 20 E
Almond, U.S.A. 78 D7 42 19N 77 44W
Almont, U.S.A. 78 D1 42 55N 83 3W
Almonte, Canada 79 A8 45 14N 76 12W
Almora, India 43 E8 29 38N 79 40 E
Alness, U.K. 12 D4 57 41N 4 16W
Alnmouth, U.K. 10 B6 55 24N 1 37W
Alnwick, U.K. 10 B6 55 24N 1 42W
Aloi, Uganda 54 B3 2 16N 33 10 E
Alon, Burma 41 H19 22 12N 95 5 E
Alor, Indonesia 37 F6 8 15S 124 30 E
Alor Setar, Malaysia 39 J3 6 7N 100 22 E
Alot, India 42 H6 23 56N 75 40 E
Aloysius, Mt., Australia 61 E4 26 0S 128 38 E
Alpaugh, U.S.A. 84 K7 35 53N 119 29W
Alpena, U.S.A. 76 C4 45 4N 83 27W
Alpha, Australia 62 C4 23 39S 146 37 E
Alphen aan den Rijn, Neths. 15 B4 52 7N 4 40 E
Alpine, Ariz., U.S.A. 83 K9 33 51N 109 9W
Alpine, Calif., U.S.A. 85 N10 32 50N 116 46W
Alpine, Tex., U.S.A. 81 K3 30 22N 103 40W
Alps, Europe 18 C8 46 30N 9 30 E
Alsace, France 18 B7 48 15N 7 25 E
Alsask, Canada 73 C7 51 21N 109 59W
Alsasua, Spain 19 A4 42 54N 2 10W
Alsek →, U.S.A. 72 B1 59 10N 138 12W
Alsten, Norway 8 D15 65 58N 12 40 E
Alston, U.K. 10 C5 54 49N 2 25W
Alta, Norway 8 B20 69 57N 23 10 E
Alta Gracia, Argentina 94 C3 31 40S 64 30W
Alta Sierra, U.S.A. 85 K8 35 42N 118 33W
Altaelva →, Norway 8 B20 69 54N 23 17 E
Altafjorden, Norway 8 A20 70 5N 23 5 E
Altai = Aerhtai Shan, Mongolia 32 B4 46 40N 92 45 E
Altamaha →, U.S.A. 77 K5 31 20N 81 20W
Altamira, Brazil 93 D8 3 12S 52 10W
Altamira, Chile 94 B2 25 47S 69 51W
Altamira, Mexico 87 C5 22 24N 97 55W
Altamont, U.S.A. 79 D10 42 43N 74 3W
Altamura, Italy 20 D7 40 49N 16 33 E
Altanbulag, Mongolia 32 A5 50 16N 106 30 E
Altar, Mexico 86 A2 30 40N 111 50W
Altar, Desierto de, Mexico 86 B2 30 10N 112 0W
Altata, Mexico 86 C3 24 30N 108 0W
Altavista, U.S.A. 76 G6 37 6N 79 17W
Altay, China 32 B3 47 48N 88 10 E
Altea, Spain 19 C5 38 38N 0 2W
Altiplano = Bolivian Plateau, S. Amer. 90 E4 20 0S 67 30W
Alto Araguaia, Brazil 93 G8 17 15S 53 20W
Alto Cuchumatanes = Cuchumatanes, Sierra de los, Guatemala 88 C1 15 35N 91 25W
Alto del Carmen, Chile 94 B1 28 46S 70 30W
Alto del Inca, Chile 94 A2 24 10S 68 10W
Alto Ligonha, Mozam. 55 F4 15 30S 38 11 E
Alto Molocue, Mozam. 55 F4 15 50S 37 35 E
Alto Paraguay ☐, Paraguay 94 A4 21 0S 58 30W
Alto Paraná ☐, Paraguay 95 B5 25 30S 54 50W
Alton, Canada 78 C4 43 54N 80 5W
Alton, U.K. 11 F7 51 9N 0 59W
Alton, Ill., U.S.A. 80 F9 38 53N 90 11W
Alton, N.H., U.S.A. 79 C13 43 27N 71 13W
Altoona, U.S.A. 78 F6 40 31N 78 24W
Altūn Kūprī, Iraq 44 C5 35 45N 44 9 E
Altun Shan, China 32 C3 38 30N 88 0 E
Alturas, U.S.A. 82 F3 41 29N 120 32W
Altus, U.S.A. 81 H5 34 38N 99 20W
Alucra, Turkey 25 F6 40 22N 38 47 E
Alūksne, Latvia 9 H22 57 24N 27 3 E
Alunite, U.S.A. 85 K12 35 59N 114 55W
Alusi, Indonesia 37 F8 7 35S 131 40 E
Alva, U.S.A. 81 G5 36 48N 98 40W
Alvarado, Mexico 87 D5 18 40N 95 50W
Alvarado, U.S.A. 81 J6 32 24N 97 13W
Alvaro Obregón, Presa, Mexico 86 B3 27 55N 109 52W
Alvear, Argentina 94 B4 29 5S 56 30W
Alvesta, Sweden 9 H16 56 54N 14 35 E
Alvin, U.S.A. 81 L7 29 26N 95 15W
Alvinston, Canada 78 D3 42 49N 81 52W
Älvkarleby, Sweden 9 F17 60 34N 17 26 E
Alvord Desert, U.S.A. 82 E4 42 30N 118 25W
Älvsbyn, Sweden 8 D19 65 40N 21 0 E
Alwar, India 42 F7 27 38N 76 34 E
Alxa Zuoqi, China 34 E3 38 50N 105 40 E
Alyangula, Australia 62 A2 13 55S 136 30 E
Alyata = Älät, Azerbaijan 25 G8 39 58N 49 25 E
Alyth, U.K. 12 E5 56 38N 3 13W
Alytus, Lithuania 9 J21 54 24N 24 3 E
Alzada, U.S.A. 80 C2 45 2N 104 25W
Alzira, Spain 19 C5 39 9N 0 30W
Am-Timan, Chad 51 F10 11 0N 20 10 E
Amadeus, L., Australia 61 D5 24 54S 131 0 E

Amadi

Amadi, *Dem. Rep. of the Congo* . **54 B2** 3 40N 26 40 E
Amâdi, *Sudan* . . . . **51 G12** 5 29N 30 25 E
Amadjuak L., *Canada* **69 B12** 65 0N 71 8W
Amagansett, *U.S.A.* **79 F12** 40 59N 72 9W
Amagasaki, *Japan* . . . . **31 G7** 34 42N 135 20 E
Amahai, *Indonesia* . . . . **37 E7** 3 20S 128 55 E
Amakusa-Shotō, *Japan* . . . **31 H5** 32 15N 130 10 E
Åmål, *Sweden* . . . . **9 G15** 59 3N 12 42 E
Amaliás, *Greece* . . . . **21 F9** 37 47N 21 22 E
Amalner, *India* . . . . **40 J9** 21 5N 75 5 E
Amamapare, *Indonesia* . . . **37 E9** 4 53S 136 38 E
Amambaí, *Brazil* **95 A4** 23 5S 55 13W
Amambaí →, *Brazil* **95 A5** 23 22S 53 56W
Amambay □, *Paraguay* . . . **95 A4** 23 0S 56 0W
Amambay, Cordillera de, *S. Amer.* **95 A4** 23 0S 55 45W
Amami-Guntō, *Japan* . . . . . **31 L4** 27 16N 129 21 E
Amami-Ō-Shima, *Japan* . . . **31 L4** 28 0N 129 0 E
Amaná, L., *Brazil* **92 D6** 2 35S 64 40W
Amanat →, *India* . . . . **43 G11** 24 7N 84 4 E
Amanda Park, *U.S.A.* **84 C3** 47 28N 123 55W
Amangeldy, *Kazakstan* . . . . **26 D7** 50 10N 65 10 E
Amapá, *Brazil* **93 C8** 2 5N 50 50W
Amapá □, *Brazil* **93 C8** 1 40N 52 0W
Amarante, *Brazil* **93 E10** 6 14S 42 50W
Amaranth, *Canada* **73 C9** 50 36N 98 43W
Amargosa →, *U.S.A.* **85 J10** 36 14N 116 51W
Amargosa Range, *U.S.A.* . . **85 J10** 36 20N 116 45W
Amári, *Greece* . . . . **23 D6** 35 13N 24 40 E
Amarillo, *U.S.A.* **81 H4** 35 13N 101 50W
Amarkantak, *India* . . . . **43 H9** 22 40N 81 45 E
Amaro, Mte., *Italy* . . . . **20 C6** 42 5N 14 5 E
Amarpur, *India* . . . . **43 G12** 25 5N 87 0 E
Amarwara, *India* . . . . **43 H8** 22 18N 79 10 E
Amasya □, *Turkey* . . . . **25 F6** 40 40N 35 50 E
Amata, *Australia* . . . . **61 E5** 26 9S 131 9 E
Amatikulu, *S. Africa* . . . . . . **57 D5** 29 3S 31 33 E
Amatitlán, *Guatemala* **88 D1** 14 29N 90 38W
Amay, *Belgium* . . . . **15 D5** 50 33N 5 19 E
Amazon = Amazonas →, *S. Amer.* **93 D9** 0 5S 50 0W
Amazonas □, *Brazil* **92 E6** 5 0S 65 0W
Amazonas →, *S. Amer.* . . . **93 D9** 0 5S 50 0W
Ambah, *India* . . . . **42 F8** 26 43N 78 13 E
Ambahakily, *Madag.* . . . . . . **57 C7** 21 36S 43 41 E
Ambala, *India* . . . . **42 D7** 30 23N 76 56 E
Ambalavao, *Madag.* . . . . . . **57 C8** 21 50S 46 56 E
Ambanja, *Madag.* . . . . **57 A8** 13 40S 48 27 E
Ambarchik, *Russia* . . . . **27 C17** 69 40N 162 20 E
Ambarijeby, *Madag.* . . . . . . **57 A8** 14 56S 47 41 E
Ambaro, Helodranon', *Madag.* . . . . **57 A8** 13 23S 48 38 E
Ambato, *Ecuador* **92 D3** 1 5S 78 42W
Ambato, Sierra de, *Argentina* **94 B2** 28 25S 66 10W
Ambato Boeny, *Madag.* . . . . **57 B8** 16 28S 46 43 E
Ambatofinandrahana, *Madag.* . . . . **57 C8** 20 33S 46 48 E
Ambatolampy, *Madag.* . . . . . **57 B8** 19 20S 47 35 E
Ambatondrazaka, *Madag.* . . . **57 B8** 17 55S 48 28 E
Ambatosoratra, *Madag.* . . . . **57 B8** 17 37S 48 31 E
Ambenja, *Madag.* . . . . **57 B8** 15 17S 46 58 E
Amberg, *Germany* . . . . **16 D6** 49 26N 11 52 E
Ambergris Cay, *Belize* **87 D7** 18 0N 88 0W
Amberley, *N.Z.* . . . . **59 K4** 43 9S 172 44 E
Ambikapur, *India* . . . . **43 H10** 23 15N 83 15 E
Ambilobé, *Madag.* . . . . **57 A8** 13 10S 49 3 E
Ambinanindrano, *Madag.* . . . **57 C8** 20 5S 48 23 E
Amble, *U.K.* **10 B6** 55 20N 1 36W
Ambleside, *U.K.* **10 C5** 54 26N 2 58W
Ambo, *Peru* **92 F3** 10 5S 76 10W
Ambodifototra, *Madag.* . . . . . **57 B8** 16 59S 49 52 E
Ambodilazana, *Madag.* . . . . . **57 B8** 18 6S 49 10 E
Ambohimahasoa, *Madag.* . . . **57 C8** 21 7S 47 13 E
Ambohimanga, *Madag.* . . . . . **57 C8** 20 52S 47 36 E
Ambohitra, *Madag.* . . . . **57 A8** 12 30S 49 10 E
Amboise, *France* . . . . **18 C4** 47 24N 1 2 E
Ambon, *Indonesia* . . . . **37 E7** 3 35S 128 20 E
Amboseli, L., *Kenya* . . . . . . **54 C4** 2 40S 37 10 E
Ambositra, *Madag.* . . . . **57 C8** 20 31S 47 25 E
Ambovombe, *Madag.* . . . . . . **57 D8** 25 11S 46 5 E
Amboy, *U.S.A.* **85 L11** 34 33N 115 45W
Amboyna Cay, *S. China Sea* **36 C4** 7 50N 112 50 E
Ambridge, *U.S.A.* **78 F4** 40 36N 80 14W
Ambriz, *Angola* . . . . **52 F2** 7 48S 13 8 E
Amchitka I., *U.S.A.* . . . . **68 C1** 51 32N 179 0 E
Amderma, *Russia* . . . . **26 C7** 69 45N 61 30 E
Amdhi, *India* . . . . **43 H9** 23 51N 81 27 E
Ameca, *Mexico* **86 C4** 20 30N 104 0W
Ameca →, *Mexico* **86 C3** 20 40N 105 15W
Amecameca, *Mexico* **87 D5** 19 7N 98 46W
Ameland, *Neths.* . . . . **15 A5** 53 27N 5 45 E
Amenia, *U.S.A.* **79 E11** 41 51N 73 33W
American Falls, *U.S.A.* **82 E7** 42 47N 112 51W
American Falls Reservoir, *U.S.A.* **82 E7** 42 47N 112 52W
American Fork, *U.S.A.* **82 F8** 40 23N 111 48W
American Highland, *Antarctica* . . . . **5 D6** 73 0S 75 0 E
American Samoa ■, *Pac. Oc.* **59 B13** 14 20S 170 40W
Americana, *Brazil* **95 A6** 22 45S 47 20W
Americus, *U.S.A.* **77 K3** 32 4N 84 14W
Amersfoort, *Neths.* . . . . **15 B5** 52 9N 5 23 E
Amersfoort, *S. Africa* . . . . . **57 D4** 26 59S 29 53 E
Amery Ice Shelf, *Antarctica* **5 C6** 69 30S 72 0 E
Ames, *U.S.A.* **80 E8** 42 2N 93 37W
Amesbury, *U.S.A.* **79 D14** 42 51N 70 56W
Amet, *India* . . . . **42 G5** 25 18N 73 56 E
Amga, *Russia* . . . . **27 C14** 60 50N 132 0 E
Amga →, *Russia* . . . . **27 C14** 62 38N 134 32 E
Amgu, *Russia* . . . . **27 E14** 45 45N 137 15 E
Amgun →, *Russia* . . . . **27 D14** 52 56N 139 38 E
Amherst, *Burma* . . . . **41 L20** 16 2N 97 20 E
Amherst, *Canada* **71 C7** 45 48N 64 8W
Amherst, *Mass., U.S.A.* . . . **79 D12** 42 23N 72 31W
Amherst, *N.Y., U.S.A.* **78 D6** 42 59N 78 48W
Amherst, *Ohio, U.S.A.* **78 E2** 41 24N 82 14W
Amherst I., *Canada* **79 B8** 44 8N 76 43W
Amherstburg, *Canada* **70 D3** 42 6N 83 6W
Amiata, Mte., *Italy* . . . . **20 C4** 42 53N 11 37 E
Amidon, *U.S.A.* **80 B3** 46 29N 103 19W
Amiens, *France* . . . . **18 B5** 49 54N 2 16 E
Amīrābād, *Iran* . . . . **44 C5** 33 20N 46 16 E
Amirante Is., *Seychelles* . . . **28 K9** 6 0S 53 0 E
Amisk L., *Canada* **73 C8** 54 35N 102 15W
Amistad, Presa de la, *Mexico* **86 B4** 29 24N 101 0W
Amite, *U.S.A.* **81 K9** 30 44N 90 30W
Amla, *India* . . . . **42 J8** 21 56N 78 7 E
Amlia I., *U.S.A.* **68 C2** 52 4N 173 30W
Amlwch, *U.K.* **10 D3** 53 24N 4 20W
'Ammān, *Jordan* . . . . **47 D4** 31 57N 35 52 E
'Ammān □, *Jordan* . . . . **47 D5** 31 40N 36 30 E
Ammanford, *U.K.* **11 F4** 51 48N 3 59W
Ammassalik = Angmagssalik, *Greenland* **4 C6** 65 40N 37 20W
Ammon, *U.S.A.* **82 E8** 43 28N 111 58W
Amnat Charoen, *Thailand* . . **38 E5** 15 51N 104 38 E
Amnura, *Bangla.* . . . . **43 G13** 24 37N 88 25 E
Āmol, *Iran* . . . . **45 B7** 36 23N 52 20 E
Amorgós, *Greece* . . . . **21 F11** 36 50N 25 57 E
Amory, *U.S.A.* **77 J1** 33 59N 88 29W
Amos, *Canada* **70 C4** 48 35N 78 5W
Åmot, *Norway* . . . . **9 G13** 59 57N 9 54 E
Amoy = Xiamen, *China* . . . **33 D6** 24 25N 118 4 E
Ampang, *Malaysia* . . . . **39 L3** 3 8N 101 45 E
Ampanihy, *Madag.* . . . . **57 C7** 24 40S 44 45 E
Ampasindava, Helodranon', *Madag.* . . . . **57 A8** 13 40S 48 15 E
Ampasindava, Saikanosy, *Madag.* . . . . **57 A8** 13 42S 47 55 E
Ampenan, *Indonesia* . . . . . . **36 F5** 8 35S 116 13 E
Amper →, *Germany* . . . . . . **16 D6** 48 29N 11 55 E
Ampotaka, *Madag.* . . . . **57 D7** 25 3S 44 41 E
Ampoza, *Madag.* . . . . **57 C7** 22 20S 44 44 E
Amqui, *Canada* **71 C6** 48 28N 67 27W
Amravati, *India* . . . . **40 J10** 20 55N 77 45 E
Amreli, *India* . . . . **42 J4** 21 35N 71 17 E
Amritsar, *India* . . . . **42 D6** 31 35N 74 57 E
Amroha, *India* . . . . **43 E8** 28 53N 78 30 E
Amsterdam, *Neths.* . . . . **15 B4** 52 23N 4 54 E
Amsterdam, *U.S.A.* **79 D10** 42 56N 74 11W
Amsterdam, I., *Ind. Oc.* . . . . **3 F13** 38 30S 77 30 E
Amstetten, *Austria* . . . . **16 D8** 48 7N 14 51 E
Amudarya →, *Uzbekistan* . **26 E6** 43 58N 59 34 E
Amundsen Gulf, *Canada* . . . **68 A7** 71 0N 124 0W
Amundsen Sea, *Antarctica* . . **5 D15** 72 0S 115 0W
Amuntai, *Indonesia* . . . . **36 E5** 2 28S 115 25 E
Amur →, *Russia* . . . . **27 D15** 52 56N 141 10 E
Amurang, *Indonesia* . . . . **37 D6** 1 5N 124 40 E
Amuri Pass, *N.Z.* . . . . **59 K4** 42 31S 172 11 E
Amursk, *Russia* . . . . **27 D14** 50 14N 136 54 E
Amyderya = Amudarya →, *Uzbekistan* . . . . **26 E6** 43 58N 59 34 E
An Bien, *Vietnam* . . . . **39 H5** 9 45N 105 0 E
An Hoa, *Vietnam* . . . . **38 E7** 15 40N 108 5 E
An Nabatīyah at Tahta, *Lebanon* . . . . **47 B4** 33 23N 35 27 E
An Nabk, *Si. Arabia* . . . . . . **44 D3** 31 20N 37 20 E
An Nabk, *Syria* . . . . **47 A5** 34 2N 36 44 E
An Nabk Abū Qaşr, *Si. Arabia* . . . . **44 D3** 30 21N 38 34 E
An Nafūd, *Si. Arabia* . . . . . . **44 D4** 28 15N 41 0 E
An Najaf, *Iraq* . . . . **44 C5** 32 3N 44 15 E
An Nāşirīyah, *Iraq* . . . . **44 D5** 31 0N 46 15 E
An Nhon, *Vietnam* . . . . **38 F7** 13 55N 109 7 E
An Nu'ayrīyah, *Si. Arabia* . . **45 E6** 27 30N 48 30 E
An Nuwayb'ī, W. →, *Si. Arabia* . . . . **47 F3** 29 18N 34 57 E
An Thoi, Dao, *Vietnam* . . . . **39 H5** 9 58N 104 0 E
An Uaimh, *Ireland* **13 C5** 53 39N 6 41W
Anabar →, *Russia* . . . . **27 B12** 73 8N 113 36 E
'Anabtā, *West Bank* . . . . **47 C4** 32 19N 35 7 E
Anaconda, *U.S.A.* **82 C7** 46 8N 112 57W
Anacortes, *U.S.A.* **84 B4** 48 30N 122 37W
Anadarko, *U.S.A.* **81 H5** 35 4N 98 15W
Anadolu, *Turkey* . . . . **25 G5** 39 0N 30 0 E
Anadyr, *Russia* . . . . **27 C18** 64 35N 177 20 E
Anadyr →, *Russia* . . . . **27 C18** 64 55N 176 5 E
Anadyrskiy Zaliv, *Russia* . . . **27 C19** 64 0N 180 0 E
Anaga, Pta. de, *Canary Is.* . . **22 F3** 28 34N 16 9W
'Ānah, *Iraq* . . . . **44 C4** 34 25N 42 0 E
Anaheim, *U.S.A.* **85 M9** 33 50N 117 55W
Anahim Lake, *Canada* **72 C3** 52 28N 125 18W
Anáhuac, *Mexico* **86 B4** 27 14N 100 9W
Anakapalle, *India* . . . . **41 L13** 17 42N 83 6 E
Anakie, *Australia* . . . . **62 C4** 23 32S 147 45 E
Analalava, *Madag.* . . . . **57 A8** 14 35S 48 0 E
Análipsis, *Greece* . . . . **23 A3** 39 36N 19 55 E
Anambar →, *Pakistan* . . . . . **42 D3** 30 15N 68 50 E
Anambas, Kepulauan, *Indonesia* . . . . **39 L6** 3 20N 106 30 E
Anambas Is. = Anambas, Kepulauan, *Indonesia* . . . . **39 L6** 3 20N 106 30 E
Anamosa, *U.S.A.* **80 D9** 42 7N 91 17W
Anamur, *Turkey* . . . . **25 G5** 36 8N 32 58 E
Anan, *Japan* . . . . **31 H7** 33 54N 134 40 E
Anand, *India* . . . . **42 H5** 22 32N 72 59 E
Anantnag, *India* . . . . **43 C6** 33 45N 75 10 E
Ananyiv, *Ukraine* . . . . **17 E15** 47 44N 29 58 E
Anapodhiris →, *Greece* . . . **23 E7** 34 59N 25 20 E
Anápolis, *Brazil* **93 G9** 16 15S 48 50W
Anapu →, *Brazil* **93 D8** 1 53S 50 53W
Anār, *Iran* . . . . **45 D7** 30 55N 55 13 E
Anārak, *Iran* . . . . **45 C7** 33 25N 53 40 E
Anas →, *India* . . . . **42 H5** 23 26N 74 0 E
Anatolia = Anadolu, *Turkey* **25 G5** 39 0N 30 0 E
Anatsogno, *Madag.* . . . . **57 C7** 23 33S 43 46 E
Añatuya, *Argentina* **94 B3** 28 20S 62 50W
Anaunethad L., *Canada* **73 A8** 60 55N 104 25W
Anbyŏn, *N. Korea* . . . . **35 E14** 39 1N 127 35 E
Ancaster, *Canada* **78 C5** 43 13N 79 59W
Anchor Bay, *U.S.A.* **84 G3** 38 48N 123 34W
Anchorage, *U.S.A.* **68 B5** 61 13N 149 54W
Anci, *China* . . . . **34 E9** 39 20N 116 40 E
Ancohuma, Nevada, *Bolivia* **92 G5** 16 0S 68 50W
Ancón, *Peru* **92 F3** 11 50S 77 10W
Ancona, *Italy* . . . . **20 C5** 43 38N 13 30 E
Ancud, *Chile* **96 E2** 42 0S 73 50W
Ancud, G. de, *Chile* **96 E2** 42 0S 73 0W
Anda, *China* . . . . **33 B7** 46 24N 125 19 E
Andacollo, *Argentina* **94 D1** 37 10S 70 42W
Andacollo, *Chile* **94 C1** 30 14S 71 6W
Andalgalá, *Argentina* **94 B2** 27 40S 66 30W
Åndalsnes, *Norway* . . . . **9 E12** 62 35N 7 43 E
Andalucía □, *Spain* **19 D3** 37 35N 5 0W
Andalusia = Andalucía □, *Spain* **19 D3** 37 35N 5 0W
Andalusia, *U.S.A.* **77 K2** 31 18N 86 29W
Andaman Is., *Ind. Oc.* . . . . . **28 H13** 12 30N 92 30 E
Andaman Sea, *Ind. Oc.* . . . . **36 B1** 13 0N 96 0 E
Andamooka Opal Fields, *Australia* . . . . **63 E2** 30 27S 137 9 E
Andapa, *Madag.* . . . . **57 A8** 14 39S 49 39 E
Andara, *Namibia* . . . . **56 B3** 18 2S 21 9 E
Andenes, *Norway* . . . . **8 B17** 69 19N 16 18 E
Andenne, *Belgium* . . . . **15 D5** 50 28N 5 5 E
Anderson, *Alaska, U.S.A.* . . **68 B5** 64 25N 149 15W
Anderson, *Calif., U.S.A.* . . . **82 F2** 40 27N 122 18W
Anderson, *Ind., U.S.A.* **76 E3** 40 10N 85 41W
Anderson, *Mo., U.S.A.* **81 G7** 36 39N 94 27W
Anderson, *S.C., U.S.A.* **77 H4** 34 31N 82 39W
Anderson →, *Canada* **68 B7** 69 42N 129 0W
Andes, *U.S.A.* **79 D10** 42 12N 74 47W
Andes, Cord. de los, *S. Amer.* **92 H5** 20 0S 68 0W
Andfjorden, *Norway* . . . . **8 B17** 69 10N 16 20 E
Andhra Pradesh □, *India* . . **40 L11** 18 0N 79 0 E
Andijon, *Uzbekistan* . . . . . . **26 E8** 41 10N 72 15 E
Andikíthira, *Greece* . . . . **21 G10** 35 52N 23 15 E
Andīmeshk, *Iran* . . . . **45 C6** 32 27N 48 21 E
Andizhan = Andijon, *Uzbekistan* . . . . **26 E8** 41 10N 72 15 E
Andoany, *Madag.* . . . . **57 A8** 13 25S 48 16 E
Andong, *S. Korea* . . . . **35 F15** 36 40N 128 43 E
Andongwei, *China* . . . . **35 G10** 35 6N 119 20 E
Andoom, *Australia* . . . . **62 A3** 12 25S 141 53 E
Andorra ■, *Europe* . . . . **18 E4** 42 30N 1 30 E
Andorra La Vella, *Andorra* . . **18 E4** 42 31N 1 32 E
Andover, *U.K.* **11 F6** 51 12N 1 29W
Andover, *Maine, U.S.A.* **79 B14** 44 38N 70 45W
Andover, *Mass., U.S.A.* **79 D13** 42 40N 71 8W
Andover, *N.J., U.S.A.* **79 F10** 40 59N 74 45W
Andover, *N.Y., U.S.A.* **78 D7** 42 10N 77 48W
Andover, *Ohio, U.S.A.* **78 E4** 41 36N 80 34W
Andøya, *Norway* . . . . **8 B16** 69 10N 15 50 E
Andradina, *Brazil* **93 H8** 20 54S 51 23W
Andrahary, Mt., *Madag.* . . . . **57 A8** 13 37S 49 17 E
Andramasina, *Madag.* . . . . . **57 B8** 19 11S 47 35 E
Andranopasy, *Madag.* . . . . . **57 C7** 21 17S 43 44 E
Andratx, *Spain* . . . . **22 B9** 39 39N 2 25 E
Andreanof Is., *U.S.A.* **68 C2** 51 30N 176 0W
Andrews, *S.C., U.S.A.* **77 J6** 33 27N 79 34W
Andrews, *Tex., U.S.A.* **81 J3** 32 19N 102 33W
Ándria, *Italy* . . . . **20 D7** 41 13N 16 17 E
Andriba, *Madag.* . . . . **57 B8** 17 30S 46 58 E
Androka, *Madag.* . . . . **57 C7** 24 58S 44 2 E
Andropov = Rybinsk, *Russia* **24 C6** 58 5N 38 50 E
Ándros, *Greece* . . . . **21 F11** 37 50N 24 57 E
Andros I., *Bahamas* **88 B4** 24 30N 78 0W
Andros Town, *Bahamas* **88 B4** 24 43N 77 47W
Androscoggin →, *U.S.A.* . . **79 C14** 43 58N 70 0W
Andselv, *Norway* . . . . **8 B18** 69 4N 18 34 E
Andújar, *Spain* **19 C3** 38 3N 4 5W
Andulo, *Angola* . . . . **52 G3** 11 25S 16 45 E
Anegada I., *Virgin Is.* **89 C7** 18 45N 64 20W
Anegada Passage, *W. Indies* **89 C7** 18 15N 63 45W
Aneto, Pico de, *Spain* . . . . . **19 A6** 42 37N 0 40 E
Ang Thong, *Thailand* . . . . . . **38 E3** 14 35N 100 31 E
Angamos, Punta, *Chile* **94 A1** 23 1S 70 32W
Angara →, *Russia* . . . . **27 D10** 58 5N 94 20 E
Angarsk, *Russia* . . . . **27 D11** 52 30N 104 0 E
Angas Hills, *Australia* . . . . . **60 D4** 23 0S 127 50 E
Angaston, *Australia* . . . . . . **63 E2** 34 30S 139 8 E
Angaur I., *Pac. Oc.* . . . . **37 C8** 6 54N 134 9 E
Ånge, *Sweden* . . . . **9 E16** 62 31N 15 35 E
Ángel, Salto = Angel Falls, *Venezuela* **92 B6** 5 57N 62 30W
Ángel de la Guarda, I., *Mexico* **86 B2** 29 30N 113 30W
Angel Falls, *Venezuela* **92 B6** 5 57N 62 30W
Angeles, *Phil.* . . . . **37 A6** 15 9N 120 33 E
Ängelholm, *Sweden* . . . . . . **9 H15** 56 15N 12 58 E
Angels Camp, *U.S.A.* **84 G6** 38 4N 120 32W
Ångermanälven →, *Sweden* . . . . **8 E17** 62 40N 18 0 E
Ångermanland, *Sweden* . . . . **8 E18** 63 36N 17 45 E
Angers, *Canada* **79 A9** 45 31N 75 29W
Angers, *France* **18 C3** 47 30N 0 35W
Ängesån →, *Sweden* . . . . . . **8 C20** 66 16N 22 47 E
Angikuni L., *Canada* **73 A9** 62 0N 100 0W
Angkor, *Cambodia* . . . . **38 F4** 13 22N 103 50 E
Anglesey, *U.K.* **10 D3** 53 17N 4 20W
Anglesey, Isle of □, *U.K.* . . **10 D3** 53 16N 4 18W
Angleton, *U.S.A.* **81 L7** 29 10N 95 26W
Anglisidhes, *Cyprus* . . . . **23 E12** 34 51N 33 27 E
Angmagssalik, *Greenland* . . **4 C6** 65 40N 37 20W
Ango, *Dem. Rep. of the Congo* . **54 B2** 4 10N 26 5 E
Angoche, *Mozam.* . . . . **55 F4** 16 8S 39 55 E
Angoche, I., *Mozam.* . . . . . . **55 F4** 16 20S 39 50 E
Angol, *Chile* **94 D1** 37 56S 72 45W
Angola, *Ind., U.S.A.* **76 E3** 41 38N 85 0W
Angola, *N.Y., U.S.A.* **78 D5** 42 38N 79 2W
Angola ■, *Africa* . . . . **53 G3** 12 0S 18 0 E
Angoulême, *France* . . . . **18 D4** 45 39N 0 10 E
Angoumois, *France* . . . . **18 D3** 45 50N 0 25 E
Angra dos Reis, *Brazil* **95 A7** 23 0S 44 10W
Angren, *Uzbekistan* . . . . **26 E8** 41 1N 70 12 E
Angtassom, *Cambodia* . . . . . **39 G5** 11 1N 104 41 E
Angu, *Dem. Rep. of the Congo* . **54 B1** 3 25N 24 28 E
Anguang, *China* . . . . **35 B12** 45 15N 123 45 E
Anguilla ■, *W. Indies* **89 C7** 18 14N 63 5W
Anguo, *China* . . . . **34 E8** 38 28N 115 15 E
Angurugu, *Australia* . . . . **62 A2** 14 0S 136 25 E
Angus □, *U.K.* **12 E6** 56 46N 2 56W
Anhanduí →, *Brazil* **95 A5** 21 46S 52 9W
Anholt, *Denmark* . . . . **9 H14** 56 42N 11 33 E
Anhui □, *China* . . . . **33 C6** 32 0N 117 0 E
Anhwei = Anhui □, *China* . . **33 C6** 32 0N 117 0 E
Anichab, *Namibia* . . . . **56 C1** 21 0S 14 46 E
Animas →, *U.S.A.* **83 H9** 36 43N 108 13W
Anivorano, *Madag.* . . . . **57 B8** 18 44S 48 58 E
Anjalankoski, *Finland* . . . . . . **9 F22** 60 45N 26 51 E
Anjar, *India* . . . . **42 H4** 23 6N 70 10 E
Anjidiv I., *India* . . . . **40 M9** 14 40N 74 10 E
Anjou, *France* **18 C3** 47 20N 0 15W
Anjozorobe, *Madag.* . . . . **57 B8** 18 22S 47 52 E
Anju, *N. Korea* . . . . **35 E13** 39 36N 125 40 E
Ankaboa, Tanjon, *Madag.* . . **57 C7** 21 58S 43 20 E
Ankang, *China* . . . . **34 H5** 32 40N 109 1 E
Ankara, *Turkey* . . . . **25 G5** 39 57N 32 54 E
Ankaramena, *Madag.* . . . . . . **57 C8** 21 57S 46 39 E
Ankaratra, *Madag.* . . . . **53 H9** 19 25S 47 12 E
Ankazoabo, *Madag.* . . . . **57 C7** 22 18S 44 31 E
Ankazobe, *Madag.* . . . . **57 B8** 18 20S 47 10 E
Ankeny, *U.S.A.* **80 E8** 41 44N 93 36W
Ankisabe, *Madag.* . . . . **57 B8** 19 17S 46 29 E
Ankoro, *Dem. Rep. of the Congo* . **54 D2** 6 45S 26 55 E
Anmyŏn-do, *S. Korea* . . . . . **35 F14** 36 25N 126 25 E
Ann, C., *U.S.A.* **79 D14** 42 38N 70 35W
Ann Arbor, *U.S.A.* **76 D4** 42 17N 83 45W
Anna, *U.S.A.* **81 G10** 37 28N 89 15W
Annaba, *Algeria* . . . . **50 A7** 36 50N 7 46 E
Annalee →, *Ireland* **13 B4** 54 2N 7 24W
Annam, *Vietnam* . . . . **38 E7** 16 0N 108 0 E
Annamitique, Chaîne, *Asia* **38 D6** 17 0N 106 0 E
Annan, *U.K.* **12 G5** 54 59N 3 16W
Annan →, *U.K.* **12 G5** 54 58N 3 16W
Annapolis, *U.S.A.* **76 F7** 38 59N 76 30W
Annapolis Royal, *Canada* . . **71 D6** 44 44N 65 32W
Annapurna, *Nepal* . . . . **43 E10** 28 34N 83 50 E
Annean, L., *Australia* . . . . . **61 E2** 26 54S 118 14 E
Annecy, *France* . . . . **18 D7** 45 55N 6 8 E
Anning, *China* . . . . **32 D5** 24 55N 102 26 E
Anniston, *U.S.A.* **77 J3** 33 39N 85 50W
Annobón, *Atl. Oc.* . . . . **49 G4** 1 25S 5 36 E
Annotto Bay, *Jamaica* **88 C4** 18 17N 76 45W
Annville, *U.S.A.* **79 F8** 40 20N 76 31W
Áno Viánnos, *Greece* . . . . . **23 D7** 35 2N 25 21 E
Anorotsangana, *Madag.* . . . **57 A8** 13 56S 47 55 E
Anóyia, *Greece* . . . . **23 D6** 35 16N 24 52 E
Anping, *Hebei, China* . . . . . **34 E8** 38 15N 115 30 E
Anping, *Liaoning, China* . . . **35 D12** 41 5N 123 30 E
Anqing, *China* . . . . **33 C6** 30 30N 117 3 E
Anqiu, *China* . . . . **35 F10** 36 25N 119 10 E
Ansai, *China* . . . . **34 F5** 36 50N 109 20 E
Ansbach, *Germany* . . . . **16 D6** 49 28N 10 34 E
Anshan, *China* . . . . **35 D12** 41 5N 122 58 E
Anshun, *China* . . . . **32 D5** 26 18N 105 57 E
Ansley, *U.S.A.* **80 E5** 41 18N 99 23W
Anson, *U.S.A.* **81 J5** 32 45N 99 54W
Anson B., *Australia* . . . . **60 B5** 13 20S 130 6 E
Ansongo, *Mali* . . . . **50 E6** 15 25N 0 35 E
Ansonia, *U.S.A.* **79 E11** 41 21N 73 5W
Anstruther, *U.K.* **12 E6** 56 14N 2 41W
Ansudu, *Indonesia* . . . . **37 E9** 2 11S 139 22 E
Antabamba, *Peru* **92 F4** 14 40S 73 0W
Antakya, *Turkey* . . . . **25 G6** 36 14N 36 10 E
Antalaha, *Madag.* . . . . **57 A9** 14 57S 50 20 E
Antalya, *Turkey* . . . . **25 G5** 36 52N 30 45 E
Antalya Körfezi, *Turkey* . . . **25 G5** 36 15N 31 30 E
Antananarivo, *Madag.* . . . . . **57 B8** 18 55S 47 31 E
Antananarivo □, *Madag.* . . . **57 B8** 19 0S 47 0 E
Antanimbaribe, *Madag.* . . . . **57 C7** 21 30S 44 48 E
Antarctic Pen., *Antarctica* . . **5 C18** 67 0S 60 0W
Antarctica . . . . **5 E3** 90 0S 0 0 E
Antelope, *Zimbabwe* . . . . . . **55 G2** 21 2S 28 31 E
Antequera, *Paraguay* **94 A4** 24 8S 57 7W
Antequera, *Spain* **19 D3** 37 5N 4 33W
Antero, Mt., *U.S.A.* **83 G10** 38 41N 106 15W
Anthony, *Kans., U.S.A.* **81 G5** 37 9N 98 2W
Anthony, *N. Mex., U.S.A.* . . **83 K10** 32 0N 106 36W
Anti Atlas, *Morocco* **50 C4** 30 0N 8 30W
Anti-Lebanon = Ash Sharqi, Al Jabal, *Lebanon* . . . . . **47 B5** 33 40N 36 10 E
Antibes, *France* . . . . **18 E7** 43 34N 7 6 E
Anticosti, Î. d', *Canada* . . . **71 C7** 49 30N 63 0W
Antigo, *U.S.A.* **80 C10** 45 9N 89 9W
Antigonish, *Canada* **71 C7** 45 38N 61 58W
Antigua, *Canary Is.* **22 F5** 28 24N 14 1W
Antigua, *W. Indies* **89 C7** 17 0N 61 50W
Antigua & Barbuda ■, *W. Indies* **89 C7** 17 20N 61 48W
Antigua Guatemala, *Guatemala* **88 D1** 14 34N 90 41W
Antilla, *Cuba* **88 B4** 20 40N 75 50W
Antilles = West Indies, *Cent. Amer.* **89 D7** 15 0N 65 0W
Antioch, *U.S.A.* **84 G5** 38 1N 121 48W
Antioquia, *Colombia* **92 B3** 6 40N 75 55W
Antipodes Is., *Pac. Oc.* . . . . **64 M9** 49 45S 178 40 E
Antlers, *U.S.A.* **81 H7** 34 14N 95 37W
Antofagasta, *Chile* **94 A1** 23 50S 70 30W
Antofagasta □, *Chile* **94 A2** 24 0S 69 0W
Antofagasta de la Sierra, *Argentina* **94 B2** 26 5S 67 20W
Antofalla, *Argentina* **94 B2** 25 30S 68 5W
Antofalla, Salar de, *Argentina* **94 B2** 25 40S 67 45W
Anton, *U.S.A.* **81 J3** 33 49N 102 10W
Antongila, Helodrano, *Madag.* . . . . **57 B8** 15 30S 49 50 E
Antonibé, *Madag.* . . . . **57 B8** 15 7S 47 24 E
Antonibé, Presqu'île d', *Madag.* . . . . **57 A8** 14 55S 47 20 E
Antonina, *Brazil* **95 B6** 25 26S 48 42W
Antrim, *U.K.* **13 B5** 54 43N 6 14W
Antrim, *U.S.A.* **78 F3** 40 7N 81 21W
Antrim □, *U.K.* **13 B5** 54 56N 6 25W
Antrim, Mts. of, *U.K.* **13 A5** 55 3N 6 14W
Antrim Plateau, *Australia* . . **60 C4** 18 8S 128 20 E
Antsalova, *Madag.* . . . . **57 B7** 18 40S 44 37 E
Antsirabe, *Madag.* . . . . **57 B8** 19 55S 47 2 E
Antsiranana, *Madag.* . . . . . . **57 A8** 12 25S 49 20 E
Antsohihy, *Madag.* . . . . **57 A8** 14 50S 47 59 E
Antsohimbondrona Seranana, *Madag.* . . . . . . **57 A8** 13 7S 48 48 E
Antu, *China* . . . . **35 C15** 42 30N 128 20 E
Antwerp = Antwerpen, *Belgium* . . . . **15 C4** 51 13N 4 25 E
Antwerp, *U.S.A.* **79 B9** 44 12N 75 37W
Antwerpen, *Belgium* . . . . **15 C4** 51 13N 4 25 E
Antwerpen □, *Belgium* . . . . . **15 C4** 51 15N 4 40 E
Anupgarh, *India* . . . . **42 E5** 29 10N 73 10 E
Anuppur, *India* . . . . **43 H9** 23 6N 81 41 E
Anuradhapura, *Sri Lanka* . . **40 Q12** 8 22N 80 28 E
Anveh, *Iran* . . . . **45 E7** 27 23N 54 11 E
Anvers = Antwerpen, *Belgium* . . . . **15 C4** 51 13N 4 25 E
Anvers I., *Antarctica* **5 C17** 64 30S 63 40W
Anxi, *China* . . . . **32 B4** 40 30N 95 43 E
Anxious B., *Australia* . . . . . **63 E1** 33 24S 134 45 E
Anyang, *China* . . . . **34 F8** 36 5N 114 21 E
Anyer-Kidul, *Indonesia* . . . . **37 G11** 6 4S 105 53 E
Anyi, *China* . . . . **34 G6** 35 2N 111 2 E
Anza, *U.S.A.* **85 M10** 33 35N 116 39W
Anze, *China* . . . . **34 F7** 36 10N 112 12 E
Anzhero-Sudzhensk, *Russia* **26 D9** 56 10N 86 0 E
Ánzio, *Italy* . . . . **20 D5** 41 27N 12 37 E
Aoga-Shima, *Japan* . . . . **31 H9** 32 28N 139 46 E
Aomen = Macau, *China* . . . . **33 D6** 22 16N 113 35 E
Aomori, *Japan* . . . . **30 D10** 40 45N 140 45 E

Asmara

Aomori □, *Japan* **30 D10** 40 45N 140 40 E
Aonla, *India* **43 E8** 28 16N 79 11 E
Aosta, *Italy* **18 D7** 45 45N 7 20 E
Aouker, *Mauritania* **50 E4** 17 40N 10 0W
Aozou, *Chad* **51 D9** 21 45N 17 28 E
Apa →, *S. Amer.* **94 A4** 22 6S 58 2W
Apache, *U.S.A.* **81 H5** 34 54N 98 22W
Apache Junction, *U.S.A.* **83 K8** 33 25N 111 33W
Apalachee B., *U.S.A.* **77 L4** 30 0N 84 0W
Apalachicola, *U.S.A.* **77 L3** 29 43N 84 59W
Apalachicola →, *U.S.A.* **77 L3** 29 43N 84 58W
Apaporis →, *Colombia* **92 D5** 1 23S 69 25W
Aparri, *Phil.* **37 A6** 18 22N 121 38 E
Apatity, *Russia* **24 A5** 67 34N 33 22 E
Apatzingán, *Mexico* **86 D4** 19 0N 102 20W
Apeldoorn, *Neths.* **15 B5** 52 13N 5 57 E
Apennines = Appennini, *Italy* **20 B4** 44 0N 10 0 E
Apia, *W. Samoa* **59 A13** 13 50S 171 50W
Apiacás, Serra dos, *Brazil* **92 E7** 9 50S 57 0W
Apizaco, *Mexico* **87 D5** 19 26N 98 9W
Aplao, *Peru* **92 G4** 16 0S 72 40W
Apo, Mt., *Phil.* **37 C7** 6 53N 125 14 E
Apolakkiá, *Greece* **23 C9** 36 5N 27 48 E
Apolakkiá, Órmos, *Greece* **23 C9** 36 5N 27 45 E
Apollo Bay, *Australia* **63 F3** 38 45S 143 40 E
Apolo, *Bolivia* **92 F5** 14 30S 68 30W
Aporé →, *Brazil* **93 G8** 19 27S 50 57W
Apostle Is., *U.S.A.* **80 B9** 47 0N 90 40W
Apóstoles, *Argentina* **95 B4** 28 0S 56 0W
Apostolos Andreas, C., *Cyprus* **23 D13** 35 42N 34 35 E
Apoteri, *Guyana* **92 C7** 4 2N 58 32W
Appalachian Mts., *U.S.A.* **76 G6** 38 0N 80 0W
Appennini, *Italy* **20 B4** 44 0N 10 0 E
Apple Hill, *Canada* **79 A10** 45 13N 74 46W
Apple Valley, *U.S.A.* **85 L9** 34 32N 117 14W
Appleby-in-Westmorland, *U.K.* **10 C5** 54 35N 2 29W
Appleton, *U.S.A.* **76 C1** 44 16N 88 25W
Approuague →, *Fr. Guiana* **93 C8** 4 30N 51 57W
Aprilia, *Italy* **20 D5** 41 36N 12 39 E
Apsley, *Canada* **78 B6** 44 45N 78 6W
Apucarana, *Brazil* **95 A5** 23 55S 51 33W
Apure →, *Venezuela* **92 B5** 7 37N 66 25W
Apurimac →, *Peru* **92 F4** 12 17S 73 56W
Āqā Jarī, *Iran* **45 D6** 30 42N 49 50 E
Aqaba = Al 'Aqabah, *Jordan* **47 F4** 29 31N 35 0 E
Aqaba, G. of, *Red Sea* **44 D2** 28 15N 33 20 E
'Aqabah, Khalīj al = Aqaba, G. of, *Red Sea* **44 D2** 28 15N 33 20 E
'Aqdā, *Iran* **45 C7** 32 26N 53 37 E
Aqmola = Astana, *Kazakstan* **26 D8** 51 10N 71 30 E
Aqrah, *Iraq* **44 B4** 36 46N 43 45 E
Aqtaū, *Kazakstan* **26 E6** 43 39N 51 12 E
Aqtöbe, *Kazakstan* **25 D10** 50 17N 57 10 E
Aquidauana, *Brazil* **93 H7** 20 30S 55 50W
Aquiles Serdán, *Mexico* **86 B3** 28 37N 105 54W
Aquin, *Haiti* **89 C5** 18 16N 73 24W
Aquitain, Bassin, *France* **18 D3** 44 0N 0 30W
Ar Rachidiya, *Morocco* **50 B5** 31 58N 4 20W
Ar Rafid, *Syria* **47 C4** 32 57N 35 52 E
Ar Raḩḩālīyah, *Iraq* **44 C4** 32 44N 43 23 E
Ar Ramādī, *Iraq* **44 C4** 33 25N 43 20 E
Ar Ramthā, *Jordan* **47 C5** 32 34N 36 0 E
Ar Raqqah, *Syria* **44 C3** 35 59N 39 8 E
Ar Rass, *Si. Arabia* **44 E4** 25 50N 43 40 E
Ar Rifā'ī, *Iraq* **44 D5** 31 50N 46 10 E
Ar Riyāḑ, *Si. Arabia* **46 C4** 24 41N 46 42 E
Ar Ru'ays, *Qatar* **45 E6** 26 8N 51 12 E
Ar Rukhaymīyah, *Iraq* **44 D5** 29 22N 45 38 E
Ar Ruqayyidah, *Si. Arabia* **45 E6** 25 21N 49 34 E
Ar Ruşāfah, *Syria* **44 C3** 35 45N 38 49 E
Ar Ruţbah, *Iraq* **44 C4** 33 0N 40 15 E
Ara, *India* **43 G11** 25 35N 84 32 E
Arab, *U.S.A.* **77 H2** 34 19N 86 30W
'Arab, Bahr el →, *Sudan* **51 G11** 9 0N 29 30 E
'Arabābād, *Iran* **45 C8** 33 2N 57 41 E
Arabia, *Asia* **28 G8** 25 0N 45 0 E
Arabian Desert = Es Sahrâ' Esh Sharqîya, *Egypt* **51 C12** 27 30N 32 30 E
Arabian Gulf = Gulf, The, *Asia* **45 E6** 27 0N 50 0 E
Arabian Sea, *Ind. Oc.* **29 H10** 16 0N 65 0 E
Aracaju, *Brazil* **93 F11** 10 55S 37 4W
Aracati, *Brazil* **93 D11** 4 30S 37 44W
Araçatuba, *Brazil* **95 A5** 21 10S 50 30W
Aracena, *Spain* **19 D2** 37 53N 6 38W
Araçuaí, *Brazil* **93 G10** 16 52S 42 4W
'Arad, *Israel* **47 D4** 31 15N 35 12 E
Arad, *Romania* **17 E11** 46 10N 21 20 E
Arādān, *Iran* **45 C7** 35 21N 52 30 E
Aradhippou, *Cyprus* **23 E12** 34 57N 33 36 E
Arafura Sea, *E. Indies* **37 F9** 9 0S 135 0 E
Aragón □, *Spain* **19 B5** 41 25N 0 40W
Aragón →, *Spain* **19 A5** 42 13N 1 44W
Araguacema, *Brazil* **93 E9** 8 50S 49 20W
Araguaia →, *Brazil* **93 E9** 5 21S 48 41W
Araguaína, *Brazil* **93 E9** 7 12S 48 12W
Araguari, *Brazil* **93 G9** 18 38S 48 11W
Araguari →, *Brazil* **93 C9** 1 15N 49 55W
Arain, *India* **42 F6** 26 27N 75 2 E
Arak, *Algeria* **50 C6** 25 20N 3 45 E
Arāk, *Iran* **45 C6** 34 0N 49 40 E
Arakan Coast, *Burma* **41 K19** 19 0N 94 0 E
Arakan Yoma, *Burma* **41 K19** 20 0N 94 40 E
Araks = Aras, Rūd-e →, *Azerbaijan* **44 B5** 40 5N 48 29 E
Aral, *Kazakstan* **26 E7** 46 41N 61 45 E
Aral Sea, *Asia* **26 E7** 44 30N 60 0 E
Aral Tengizi = Aral Sea, *Asia* **26 E7** 44 30N 60 0 E
Aralsk = Aral, *Kazakstan* **26 E7** 46 41N 61 45 E
Aralskoye More = Aral Sea, *Asia* **26 E7** 44 30N 60 0 E
Aramac, *Australia* **62 C4** 22 58S 145 14 E
Aran I., *Ireland* **13 A3** 55 0N 8 30W
Aran Is., *Ireland* **13 C2** 53 6N 9 38W
Aranda de Duero, *Spain* **19 B4** 41 39N 3 42W
Arandān, *Iran* **44 C5** 35 23N 46 55 E
Aranjuez, *Spain* **19 B4** 40 1N 3 40W
Aranos, *Namibia* **56 C2** 24 9S 19 7 E
Aransas Pass, *U.S.A.* **81 M6** 27 55N 97 9W
Aranyaprathet, *Thailand* **38 F4** 13 41N 102 30 E
Arapahoe, *U.S.A.* **80 E5** 40 18N 99 54W
Arapey Grande →, *Uruguay* **94 C4** 30 55S 57 49W
Arapgir, *Turkey* **44 B3** 39 5N 38 30 E
Arapiraca, *Brazil* **93 E11** 9 45S 36 39W
Arapongas, *Brazil* **95 A5** 23 29S 51 28W
Ar'ar, *Si. Arabia* **44 D4** 30 59N 41 2 E
Araranguá, *Brazil* **95 B6** 29 0S 49 30W
Araraquara, *Brazil* **93 H9** 21 50S 48 0W
Ararás, Serra das, *Brazil* **95 B5** 25 0S 53 10W
Ararat, *Australia* **63 F3** 37 16S 143 0 E
Ararat, Mt. = Ağrı Dağı, *Turkey* **25 G7** 39 50N 44 15 E
Araria, *India* **43 F12** 26 9N 87 33 E
Araripe, Chapada do, *Brazil* **93 E11** 7 20S 40 0W
Araruama, L. de, *Brazil* **95 A7** 22 53S 42 12W
Aras, Rūd-e →, *Azerbaijan* **44 B5** 40 5N 48 29 E
Arauca, *Colombia* **92 B4** 7 0N 70 40W
Arauca →, *Venezuela* **92 B5** 7 24N 66 35W
Arauco, *Chile* **94 D1** 37 16S 73 25W
Araxá, *Brazil* **93 G9** 19 35S 46 55W
Araya, Pen. de, *Venezuela* **92 A6** 10 40N 64 0W
Arba Minch, *Ethiopia* **46 F2** 6 0N 37 30 E
Arbat, *Iraq* **44 C5** 35 25N 45 35 E
Árbatax, *Italy* **20 E3** 39 56N 9 42 E
Arbīl, *Iraq* **44 B5** 36 15N 44 5 E
Arborfield, *Canada* **73 C8** 53 6N 103 39W
Arborg, *Canada* **73 C9** 50 54N 97 13W
Arbroath, *U.K.* **12 E6** 56 34N 2 35W
Arbuckle, *U.S.A.* **84 F4** 39 1N 122 3W
Arcachon, *France* **18 D3** 44 40N 1 10W
Arcade, *Calif., U.S.A.* **85 L8** 34 2N 118 15W
Arcade, *N.Y., U.S.A.* **78 D6** 42 32N 78 25W
Arcadia, *Fla., U.S.A.* **77 M5** 27 13N 81 52W
Arcadia, *La., U.S.A.* **81 J8** 32 33N 92 55W
Arcadia, *Pa., U.S.A.* **78 F6** 40 47N 78 51W
Arcata, *U.S.A.* **82 F1** 40 52N 124 5W
Archangel = Arkhangelsk, *Russia* **24 B7** 64 38N 40 36 E
Archbald, *U.S.A.* **79 E9** 41 30N 75 32W
Archer →, *Australia* **62 A3** 13 28S 141 41 E
Archer B., *Australia* **62 A3** 13 20S 141 30 E
Archers Post, *Kenya* **54 B4** 0 35N 37 35 E
Arches National Park, *U.S.A.* **83 G9** 38 45N 109 25W
Arckaringa Cr. →, *Australia* **63 D2** 28 10S 135 22 E
Arco, *U.S.A.* **82 E7** 43 38N 113 18W
Arcos de la Frontera, *Spain* **19 D3** 36 45N 5 49W
Arcot, *India* **40 N11** 12 53N 79 20 E
Arctic Bay, *Canada* **69 A11** 73 1N 85 7W
Arctic Ocean, *Arctic* **4 B18** 78 0N 160 0W
Arctic Red River = Tsiigehtchic, *Canada* **68 B6** 67 15N 134 0W
Arda →, *Bulgaria* **21 D12** 41 40N 26 30 E
Ardabīl, *Iran* **45 B6** 38 15N 48 18 E
Ardakān = Sepīdān, *Iran* **45 D7** 30 20N 52 5 E
Ardakān, *Iran* **45 C7** 32 19N 53 59 E
Ardee, *Ireland* **13 C5** 53 52N 6 33W
Arden, *Canada* **78 B8** 44 43N 76 56W
Arden, *Calif., U.S.A.* **84 G5** 38 36N 121 33W
Arden, *Nev., U.S.A.* **85 J11** 36 1N 115 14W
Ardenne, *Belgium* **16 D3** 49 50N 5 5 E
Ardennes = Ardenne, *Belgium* **16 D3** 49 50N 5 5 E
Arderin, *Ireland* **13 C4** 53 2N 7 39W
Ardestān, *Iran* **45 C7** 33 20N 52 25 E
Ardivachar Pt., *U.K.* **12 D1** 57 23N 7 26W
Ardlethan, *Australia* **63 E4** 34 22S 146 53 E
Ardmore, *Okla., U.S.A.* **81 H6** 34 10N 97 8W
Ardmore, *Pa., U.S.A.* **79 G9** 39 58N 75 18W
Ardnamurchan, Pt. of, *U.K.* **12 E2** 56 43N 6 14W
Ardnave Pt., *U.K.* **12 F2** 55 53N 6 20W
Ardrossan, *Australia* **63 E2** 34 26S 137 53 E
Ardrossan, *U.K.* **12 F4** 55 39N 4 49W
Ards Pen., *U.K.* **13 B6** 54 33N 5 34W
Arecibo, *Puerto Rico* **89 C6** 18 29N 66 43W
Areia Branca, *Brazil* **93 E11** 5 0S 37 0W
Arena, Pt., *U.S.A.* **84 G3** 38 57N 123 44W
Arenal, *Honduras* **88 C2** 15 21N 86 50W
Arendal, *Norway* **9 G13** 58 28N 8 46 E
Arequipa, *Peru* **92 G4** 16 20S 71 30W
Arévalo, *Spain* **19 B3** 41 3N 4 43W
Arezzo, *Italy* **20 C4** 43 25N 11 53 E
Arga, *Turkey* **44 B3** 38 21N 37 59 E
Arganda, *Spain* **19 B4** 40 19N 3 26W
Argenta, *Canada* **72 C5** 50 11N 116 56W
Argentan, *France* **18 B3** 48 45N 0 1W
Argentário, Mte., *Italy* **20 C4** 42 24N 11 9 E
Argentia, *Canada* **71 C9** 47 18N 53 58W
Argentina ■, *S. Amer.* **96 D3** 35 0S 66 0W
Argentina Is., *Antarctica* **5 C17** 66 0S 64 0W
Argentino, L., *Argentina* **96 G2** 50 10S 73 0W
Argeş →, *Romania* **17 F14** 44 5N 26 38 E
Arghandab →, *Afghan.* **42 D1** 31 30N 64 15 E
Argolikós Kólpos, *Greece* **21 F10** 37 20N 22 52 E
Árgos, *Greece* **21 F10** 37 40N 22 43 E
Argostólion, *Greece* **21 E9** 38 12N 20 33 E
Arguello, Pt., *U.S.A.* **85 L6** 34 35N 120 39W
Arguineguín, *Canary Is.* **22 G4** 27 46N 15 41W
Argun →, *Russia* **27 D13** 53 20N 121 28 E
Argus Pk., *U.S.A.* **85 K9** 35 52N 117 26W
Argyle, L., *Australia* **60 C4** 16 20S 128 40 E
Argyll & Bute □, *U.K.* **12 E3** 56 13N 5 28W
Århus, *Denmark* **9 H14** 56 8N 10 11 E
Ariadnoye, *Russia* **30 B7** 45 8N 134 25 E
Ariamsvlei, *Namibia* **56 D2** 28 9S 19 51 E
Ariana, *Tunisia* **51 A7** 36 52N 10 12 E
Arica, *Chile* **92 G4** 18 32S 70 20W
Arica, *Colombia* **92 D4** 2 0S 71 50W
Arico, *Canary Is.* **22 F3** 28 9N 16 29W
Arid, C., *Australia* **61 F3** 34 1S 123 10 E
Arida, *Japan* **31 G7** 34 5N 135 8 E
Arílla, Ákra, *Greece* **23 A3** 39 43N 19 39 E
Arima, *Trin. & Tob.* **89 D7** 10 38N 61 17W
Arinos →, *Brazil* **92 F7** 10 25S 58 20W
Ario de Rosales, *Mexico* **86 D4** 19 12N 102 0W
Aripuanã, *Brazil* **92 E6** 9 25S 60 30W
Aripuanã →, *Brazil* **92 E6** 5 7S 60 25W
Ariquemes, *Brazil* **92 E6** 9 55S 63 6W
Arisaig, *U.K.* **12 E3** 56 55N 5 51W
Aristazabal I., *Canada* **72 C3** 52 40N 129 10W
Arivonimamo, *Madag.* **57 B8** 19 1S 47 11 E
Arizaro, Salar de, *Argentina* **94 A2** 24 40S 67 50W
Arizona, *Argentina* **94 D2** 35 45S 65 25W
Arizona □, *U.S.A.* **83 J8** 34 0N 112 0W
Arizpe, *Mexico* **86 A2** 30 20N 110 11W
Arjeplog, *Sweden* **8 D18** 66 3N 18 2 E
Arjona, *Colombia* **92 A3** 10 14N 75 22W
Arjuna, *Indonesia* **37 G15** 7 49S 112 34 E
Arka, *Russia* **27 C15** 60 15N 142 0 E
Arkadelphia, *U.S.A.* **81 H8** 34 7N 93 4W
Arkaig, L., *U.K.* **12 E3** 56 59N 5 10W
Arkalyk = Arqalyk, *Kazakstan* **26 D7** 50 13N 66 50 E
Arkansas □, *U.S.A.* **81 H8** 35 0N 92 30W
Arkansas →, *U.S.A.* **81 J9** 33 47N 91 4W
Arkansas City, *U.S.A.* **81 G6** 37 4N 97 2W
Arkaroola, *Australia* **63 E2** 30 20S 139 22 E
Arkhángelos, *Greece* **23 C10** 36 13N 28 7 E
Arkhangelsk, *Russia* **24 B7** 64 38N 40 36 E
Arki, *India* **42 D7** 31 9N 76 58 E
Arklow, *Ireland* **13 D5** 52 48N 6 10W
Arkport, *U.S.A.* **78 D7** 42 24N 77 42W
Arkticheskiy, Mys, *Russia* **27 A10** 81 10N 95 0 E
Arkville, *U.S.A.* **79 D10** 42 9N 74 37W
Arlanzón →, *Spain* **19 A3** 42 3N 4 17W
Arlbergpass, *Austria* **16 E6** 47 9N 10 12 E
Arles, *France* **18 E6** 43 41N 4 40 E
Arlington, *S. Africa* **57 D4** 28 1S 27 53 E
Arlington, *N.Y., U.S.A.* **79 E11** 41 42N 73 54W
Arlington, *Oreg., U.S.A.* **82 D3** 45 43N 120 12W
Arlington, *S. Dak., U.S.A.* **80 C6** 44 22N 97 8W
Arlington, *Tex., U.S.A.* **81 J6** 32 44N 97 7W
Arlington, *Va., U.S.A.* **76 F7** 38 53N 77 7W
Arlington, *Vt., U.S.A.* **79 C11** 43 5N 73 9W
Arlington, *Wash., U.S.A.* **84 B4** 48 12N 122 8W
Arlington Heights, *U.S.A.* **76 D2** 42 5N 87 59W
Arlit, *Niger* **50 E7** 19 0N 7 38 E
Arlon, *Belgium* **15 E5** 49 42N 5 49 E
Arltunga, *Australia* **62 C1** 23 26S 134 41 E
Armagh, *U.K.* **13 B5** 54 21N 6 39W
Armagh □, *U.K.* **13 B5** 54 18N 6 37W
Armavir, *Russia* **25 E7** 45 2N 41 7 E
Armenia, *Colombia* **92 C3** 4 35N 75 45W
Armenia ■, *Asia* **25 F7** 40 20N 45 0 E
Armenistís, Ákra, *Greece* **23 C9** 36 8N 27 42 E
Armidale, *Australia* **63 E5** 30 30S 151 40 E
Armour, *U.S.A.* **80 D5** 43 19N 98 21W
Armstrong, *B.C., Canada* **72 C5** 50 25N 119 10W
Armstrong, *Ont., Canada* **70 B2** 50 18N 89 4W
Arnarfjörður, *Iceland* **8 D2** 65 48N 23 40W
Arnaud →, *Canada* **69 C13** 60 0N 70 0W
Arnauti, C., *Cyprus* **23 D11** 35 6N 32 17 E
Arnett, *U.S.A.* **81 G5** 36 8N 99 46W
Arnhem, *Neths.* **15 C5** 51 58N 5 55 E
Arnhem, C., *Australia* **62 A2** 12 20S 137 30 E
Arnhem B., *Australia* **62 A2** 12 20S 136 10 E
Arnhem Land, *Australia* **62 A1** 13 10S 134 30 E
Arno →, *Italy* **20 C4** 43 41N 10 17 E
Arno Bay, *Australia* **63 E2** 33 54S 136 34 E
Arnold, *U.K.* **10 D6** 53 1N 1 7W
Arnold, *U.S.A.* **84 G6** 38 15N 120 20W
Arnot, *Canada* **73 B9** 55 56N 96 41W
Arnøy, *Norway* **8 A19** 70 9N 20 40 E
Arnprior, *Canada* **79 A8** 45 26N 76 21W
Arnsberg, *Germany* **16 C5** 51 24N 8 5 E
Aroab, *Namibia* **56 D2** 26 41S 19 39 E
Aron, *India* **42 G6** 25 57N 77 56 E
Arqalyk, *Kazakstan* **26 D7** 50 13N 66 50 E
Arrah = Ara, *India* **43 G11** 25 35N 84 32 E
Arran, *U.K.* **12 F3** 55 34N 5 12W
Arras, *France* **18 A5** 50 17N 2 46 E
Arrecife, *Canary Is.* **22 F6** 28 57N 13 37W
Arrecifes, *Argentina* **94 C3** 34 6S 60 9W
Arrée, Mts. d', *France* **18 B2** 48 26N 3 55W
Arriaga, *Chiapas, Mexico* **87 D6** 16 15N 93 52W
Arriaga, *San Luis Potosí, Mexico* **86 C4** 21 55N 101 23W
Arrilalah, *Australia* **62 C3** 23 43S 143 54 E
Arrino, *Australia* **61 E2** 29 30S 115 40 E
Arrow, L., *Ireland* **13 B3** 54 3N 8 19W
Arrowhead, L., *U.S.A.* **85 L9** 34 16N 117 10W
Arrowtown, *N.Z.* **59 L2** 44 57S 168 50 E
Arroyo Grande, *U.S.A.* **85 K6** 35 7N 120 35W
Ars, *Iran* **44 B5** 37 9N 47 46 E
Arsenault L., *Canada* **73 B7** 55 6N 108 32W
Arsenev, *Russia* **30 B6** 44 10N 133 15 E
Árta, *Greece* **21 E9** 39 8N 21 2 E
Artà, *Spain* **22 B10** 39 41N 3 21 E
Arteaga, *Mexico* **86 D4** 18 50N 102 20W
Artem, *Russia* **30 C6** 43 22N 132 13 E
Artemovsk, *Russia* **27 D10** 54 45N 93 35 E
Artemovsk, *Ukraine* **25 E6** 48 35N 38 0 E
Artesia = Mosomane, *Botswana* **56 C4** 24 2S 26 19 E
Artesia, *U.S.A.* **81 J2** 32 51N 104 24W
Arthur, *Canada* **78 C4** 43 50N 80 32W
Arthur →, *Australia* **62 G3** 41 2S 144 40 E
Arthur Cr. →, *Australia* **62 C2** 22 30S 136 25 E
Arthur Pt., *Australia* **62 C5** 22 7S 150 3 E
Arthur River, *Australia* **61 F2** 33 20S 117 2 E
Arthur's Pass, *N.Z.* **59 K3** 42 54S 171 35 E
Arthur's Town, *Bahamas* **89 B4** 24 38N 75 42W
Artigas, *Uruguay* **94 C4** 30 20S 56 30W
Artillery L., *Canada* **73 A7** 63 9N 107 52W
Artois, *France* **18 A5** 50 20N 2 30 E
Artrutx, C. de, *Spain* **22 B10** 39 55N 3 49 E
Artsyz, *Ukraine* **17 E15** 46 4N 29 26 E
Artvin, *Turkey* **25 F7** 41 14N 41 44 E
Aru, Kepulauan, *Indonesia* **37 F8** 6 0S 134 30 E
Aru Is. = Aru, Kepulauan, *Indonesia* **37 F8** 6 0S 134 30 E
Arua, *Uganda* **54 B3** 3 1N 30 58 E
Aruanã, *Brazil* **93 F8** 14 54S 51 10W
Aruba ■, *W. Indies* **89 D6** 12 30N 70 0W
Arucas, *Canary Is.* **22 F4** 28 7N 15 32W
Arun →, *Nepal* **43 F12** 26 55N 87 10 E
Arun →, *U.K.* **11 G7** 50 49N 0 33W
Arunachal Pradesh □, *India* **41 F19** 28 0N 95 0 E
Arusha, *Tanzania* **54 C4** 3 20S 36 40 E
Arusha □, *Tanzania* **54 C4** 4 0S 36 30 E
Arusha Chini, *Tanzania* **54 C4** 3 32S 37 20 E
Aruwimi →, *Dem. Rep. of the Congo* **54 B1** 1 13N 23 36 E
Arvada, *Colo., U.S.A.* **80 F2** 39 48N 105 5W
Arvada, *Wyo., U.S.A.* **82 D10** 44 39N 106 8W
Árvi, *Greece* **23 E7** 34 59N 25 28 E
Arviat, *Canada* **73 A10** 61 6N 93 59W
Arvidsjaur, *Sweden* **8 D18** 65 35N 19 10 E
Arvika, *Sweden* **9 G15** 59 40N 12 36 E
Arvin, *U.S.A.* **85 K8** 35 12N 118 50W
Arwal, *India* **43 G11** 25 15N 84 41 E
Arxan, *China* **33 B6** 47 11N 119 57 E
Aryirádhes, *Greece* **23 B3** 39 27N 19 58 E
Aryiroúpolis, *Greece* **23 D6** 35 17N 24 20 E
Arys, *Kazakstan* **26 E7** 42 26N 68 48 E
Arzamas, *Russia* **24 C7** 55 27N 43 55 E
Aş Şadr, *U.A.E.* **45 E7** 24 40N 54 41 E
Aş Şafā, *Syria* **47 B6** 33 10N 37 0 E
As Saffānīyah, *Si. Arabia* **45 E6** 27 55N 48 50 E
As Safīrah, *Syria* **44 B3** 36 5N 37 21 E
Aş Şahm, *Oman* **45 E8** 24 10N 56 53 E
As Sājir, *Si. Arabia* **44 E5** 25 11N 44 36 E
As Salamīyah, *Syria* **44 C3** 35 1N 37 2 E
As Salmān, *Iraq* **44 D5** 30 30N 44 32 E
As Salţ, *Jordan* **47 C4** 32 2N 35 43 E
As Sal'w'a, *Qatar* **45 E6** 24 23N 50 50 E
As Samāwah, *Iraq* **44 D5** 31 15N 45 15 E
As Sanamayn, *Syria* **47 B5** 33 3N 36 10 E
As Sohar = Şuḩār, *Oman* **45 E8** 24 20N 56 40 E
As Sukhnah, *Syria* **44 C3** 34 52N 38 52 E
As Sulaymānīyah, *Iraq* **44 C5** 35 35N 45 29 E
As Sulaymī, *Si. Arabia* **44 E4** 26 17N 41 21 E
As Sulayyil, *Si. Arabia* **46 C4** 20 27N 45 34 E
As Summān, *Si. Arabia* **44 E5** 25 0N 47 0 E
As Suwaydā', *Syria* **47 C5** 32 40N 36 30 E
As Suwaydā' □, *Syria* **47 C5** 32 45N 36 45 E
As Suwayq, *Oman* **45 F8** 23 51N 57 26 E
As Şuwayrah, *Iraq* **44 C5** 32 55N 45 0 E
Asab, *Namibia* **56 D2** 25 30S 18 0 E
Asad, Buḩayrat al, *Syria* **44 C3** 36 0N 38 15 E
Asahi-Gawa →, *Japan* **31 G6** 34 36N 133 58 E
Asahigawa, *Japan* **30 C11** 43 46N 142 22 E
Asamankese, *Ghana* **50 G5** 5 50N 0 40W
Asan →, *India* **43 F8** 26 37N 78 24 E
Asansol, *India* **43 H12** 23 40N 87 1 E
Asbesberge, *S. Africa* **56 D3** 29 0S 23 0 E
Asbestos, *Canada* **71 C5** 45 47N 71 58W
Asbury Park, *U.S.A.* **79 F10** 40 13N 74 1W
Ascensión, *Mexico* **86 A3** 31 6N 107 59W
Ascensión, B. de la, *Mexico* **87 D7** 19 50N 87 20W
Ascension I., *Atl. Oc.* **49 G2** 8 0S 14 15W
Aschaffenburg, *Germany* **16 D5** 49 58N 9 6 E
Aschersleben, *Germany* **16 C6** 51 45N 11 29 E
Áscoli Piceno, *Italy* **20 C5** 42 51N 13 34 E
Ascope, *Peru* **92 E3** 7 46S 79 8W
Ascotán, *Chile* **94 A2** 21 45S 68 17W
Aseb, *Eritrea* **46 E3** 13 0N 42 40 E
Asela, *Ethiopia* **46 F2** 8 0N 39 0 E
Asenovgrad, *Bulgaria* **21 C11** 42 1N 24 51 E
Aserradero, *Mexico* **86 C3** 23 40N 105 43W
Asgata, *Cyprus* **23 E12** 34 46N 33 15 E
Ash Fork, *U.S.A.* **83 J7** 35 13N 112 29W
Ash Grove, *U.S.A.* **81 G8** 37 19N 93 35W
Ash Shabakah, *Iraq* **44 D4** 30 49N 43 39 E
Ash Shamāl □, *Lebanon* **47 A5** 34 25N 36 0 E
Ash Shāmīyah, *Iraq* **44 D5** 31 55N 44 35 E
Ash Shāriqah, *U.A.E.* **45 E7** 25 23N 55 26 E
Ash Sharmah, *Si. Arabia* **44 D2** 28 1N 35 16 E
Ash Sharqāt, *Iraq* **44 C4** 35 27N 43 16 E
Ash Sharqi, Al Jabal, *Lebanon* **47 B5** 33 40N 36 10 E
Ash Shaţrah, *Iraq* **44 D5** 31 30N 46 10 E
Ash Shawbak, *Jordan* **44 D2** 30 32N 35 34 E
Ash Shawmari, J., *Jordan* **47 E5** 30 35N 36 35 E
Ash Shināfīyah, *Iraq* **44 D5** 31 35N 44 39 E
Ash Shu'bah, *Si. Arabia* **44 D5** 28 54N 44 44 E
Ash Shumlūl, *Si. Arabia* **44 E5** 26 31N 47 20 E
Ash Shūr'a, *Iraq* **44 C4** 35 58N 43 13 E
Ash Shurayf, *Si. Arabia* **44 E3** 25 43N 39 14 E
Ash Shuwayfāt, *Lebanon* **47 B4** 33 45N 35 30 E
Asha, *Russia* **24 D10** 55 0N 57 16 E
Ashau, *Vietnam* **38 D6** 16 6N 107 22 E
Ashbourne, *U.K.* **10 D6** 53 2N 1 43W
Ashburn, *U.S.A.* **77 K4** 31 43N 83 39W
Ashburton, *N.Z.* **59 K3** 43 53S 171 48 E
Ashburton →, *Australia* **60 D1** 21 40S 114 56 E
Ashcroft, *Canada* **72 C4** 50 40N 121 20W
Ashdod, *Israel* **47 D3** 31 49N 34 35 E
Ashdown, *U.S.A.* **81 J7** 33 40N 94 8W
Asheboro, *U.S.A.* **77 H6** 35 43N 79 49W
Ashern, *Canada* **73 C9** 51 11N 98 21W
Asherton, *U.S.A.* **81 L5** 28 27N 99 46W
Asheville, *U.S.A.* **77 H4** 35 36N 82 33W
Ashewat, *Pakistan* **42 D3** 31 22N 68 32 E
Asheweig →, *Canada* **70 B2** 54 17N 87 12W
Ashford, *Australia* **63 D5** 29 15S 151 3 E
Ashford, *U.K.* **11 F8** 51 8N 0 53 E
Ashgabat, *Turkmenistan* **26 F6** 38 0N 57 50 E
Ashibetsu, *Japan* **30 C11** 43 31N 142 11 E
Ashikaga, *Japan* **31 F9** 36 28N 139 29 E
Ashington, *U.K.* **10 B6** 55 11N 1 33W
Ashizuri-Zaki, *Japan* **31 H6** 32 44N 133 0 E
Ashkarkot, *Afghan.* **42 C2** 33 3N 67 58 E
Ashkhabad = Ashgabat, *Turkmenistan* **26 F6** 38 0N 57 50 E
Āshkhāneh, *Iran* **45 B8** 37 26N 56 55 E
Ashland, *Kans., U.S.A.* **81 G5** 37 11N 99 46W
Ashland, *Ky., U.S.A.* **76 F4** 38 28N 82 38W
Ashland, *Mont., U.S.A.* **82 D10** 45 36N 106 16W
Ashland, *Ohio, U.S.A.* **78 F2** 40 52N 82 19W
Ashland, *Oreg., U.S.A.* **82 E2** 42 12N 122 43W
Ashland, *Pa., U.S.A.* **79 F8** 40 45N 76 22W
Ashland, *Va., U.S.A.* **76 G7** 37 46N 77 29W
Ashland, *Wis., U.S.A.* **80 B9** 46 35N 90 53W
Ashley, *N. Dak., U.S.A.* **80 B5** 46 2N 99 22W
Ashley, *Pa., U.S.A.* **79 E9** 41 12N 75 55W
Ashmore Reef, *Australia* **60 B3** 12 14S 123 5 E
Ashmyany, *Belarus* **9 J21** 54 26N 25 52 E
Ashokan Reservoir, *U.S.A.* **79 E10** 41 56N 74 13W
Ashqelon, *Israel* **47 D3** 31 42N 34 35 E
Ashta, *India* **42 H7** 23 1N 76 43 E
Ashtabula, *U.S.A.* **78 E4** 41 52N 80 47W
Ashton, *S. Africa* **56 E3** 33 50S 20 5 E
Ashton, *U.S.A.* **82 D8** 44 4N 111 27W
Ashuanipi, L., *Canada* **71 B6** 52 45N 66 15W
Ashville, *U.S.A.* **78 F6** 40 34N 78 33W
Asia **28 E11** 45 0N 75 0 E
Asia, Kepulauan, *Indonesia* **37 D8** 1 0N 131 13 E
Āsīā Bak, *Iran* **45 C6** 35 19N 50 30 E
Asifabad, *India* **40 K11** 19 20N 79 24 E
Asinara, *Italy* **20 D3** 41 4N 8 16 E
Asinara, G. dell', *Italy* **20 D3** 41 0N 8 30 E
Asino, *Russia* **26 D9** 57 0N 86 0 E
Asipovichy, *Belarus* **17 B15** 53 19N 28 33 E
'Asīr □, *Si. Arabia* **46 D3** 18 40N 42 30 E
Asir, Ras, *Somali Rep.* **46 E5** 11 55N 51 10 E
Askersund, *Sweden* **9 G16** 58 53N 14 55 E
Askham, *S. Africa* **56 D3** 26 59S 20 47 E
Askim, *Norway* **9 G14** 59 35N 11 10 E
Askja, *Iceland* **8 D5** 65 3N 16 48W
Askøy, *Norway* **9 F11** 60 29N 5 10 E
Asmara = Asmera, *Eritrea* **46 D2** 15 19N 38 55 E

Asmera

Asmera, *Eritrea* **46 D2** 15 19N 38 55 E
Åsnen, *Sweden* **9 H16** 56 37N 14 45 E
Aspen, *U.S.A.* **83 G10** 39 11N 106 49W
Aspermont, *U.S.A.* **81 J4** 33 8N 100 14W
Aspiring, Mt., *N.Z.* **59 L2** 44 23S 168 46 E
Asprókavos, Ákra, *Greece* **23 B4** 39 21N 20 6 E
Aspur, *India* **42 H6** 23 58N 74 7 E
Asquith, *Canada* **73 C7** 52 8N 107 13W
Assam □, *India* **41 G18** 26 0N 93 0 E
Asse, *Belgium* **15 D4** 50 24N 4 10 E
Assen, *Neths.* **15 A6** 53 0N 6 35 E
Assiniboia, *Canada* **73 D7** 49 40N 105 59W
Assiniboine →, *Canada* **73 D9** 49 53N 97 8W
Assiniboine, Mt., *Canada* **72 C5** 50 52N 115 39W
Assis, *Brazil* **95 A5** 22 40S 50 20W
Assisi, *Italy* **20 C5** 43 4N 12 37 E
Assynt, L., *U.K.* **12 C3** 58 10N 5 3W
Astana, *Kazakstan* **26 D8** 51 10N 71 30 E
Āstāneh, *Iran* **45 B6** 37 17N 49 59 E
Astara, *Azerbaijan* **25 G8** 38 30N 48 50 E
Asteroúsia, *Greece* **23 E7** 34 59N 25 3 E
Asti, *Italy* **18 D8** 44 54N 8 12 E
Astipálaia, *Greece* **21 F12** 36 32N 26 22 E
Astorga, *Spain* **19 A2** 42 29N 6 8W
Astoria, *U.S.A.* **84 D3** 46 11N 123 50W
Astrakhan, *Russia* **25 E8** 46 25N 48 5 E
Asturias □, *Spain* **19 A3** 43 15N 6 0W
Asunción, *Paraguay* **94 B4** 25 10S 57 30W
Asunción Nochixtlán, *Mexico* **87 D5** 17 28N 97 14W
Aswa →, *Uganda* **54 B3** 3 43N 31 55 E
Aswân, *Egypt* **51 D12** 24 4N 32 57 E
Aswân High Dam = Sadd el Aali, *Egypt* **51 D12** 23 54N 32 54 E
Asyût, *Egypt* **51 C12** 27 11N 31 4 E
At Ţafilah, *Jordan* **47 E4** 30 45N 35 30 E
Aţ Ţā'if, *Si. Arabia* **46 C3** 21 5N 40 27 E
Aţ Ţirāq, *Si. Arabia* **44 E5** 27 19N 44 33 E
Aţ Tubayq, *Si. Arabia* **44 D3** 29 30N 37 0 E
Atacama □, *Chile* **94 B2** 27 30S 70 0W
Atacama, Desierto de, *Chile* **94 A2** 24 0S 69 20W
Atacama, Salar de, *Chile* **94 A2** 23 30S 68 20W
Atalaya, *Peru* **92 F4** 10 45S 73 50W
Atalaya de Femes, *Canary Is.* **22 F6** 28 56N 13 47W
Atami, *Japan* **31 G9** 35 5N 139 4 E
Atapupu, *Indonesia* **37 F6** 9 0S 124 51 E
Atâr, *Mauritania* **50 D3** 20 30N 13 5W
Atari, *Pakistan* **42 D6** 30 56N 74 2 E
Atascadero, *U.S.A.* **84 K6** 35 29N 120 40W
Atasu, *Kazakstan* **26 E8** 48 30N 71 0 E
Atatürk Barajı, *Turkey* **25 G6** 37 28N 38 30 E
Atauro, *Indonesia* **37 F7** 8 10S 125 30 E
Atbara, *Sudan* **51 E12** 17 42N 33 59 E
'Atbara →, *Sudan* **51 E12** 17 40N 33 56 E
Atbasar, *Kazakstan* **26 D7** 51 48N 68 20 E
Atchafalaya B., *U.S.A.* **81 L9** 29 25N 91 25W
Atchison, *U.S.A.* **80 F7** 39 34N 95 7W
Āteshān, *Iran* **45 C7** 35 35N 52 37 E
Ath, *Belgium* **15 D3** 50 38N 3 47 E
Athabasca, *Canada* **72 C6** 54 45N 113 20W
Athabasca →, *Canada* **73 B6** 58 40N 110 50W
Athabasca, L., *Canada* **73 B7** 59 15N 109 15W
Athboy, *Ireland* **13 C5** 53 37N 6 56W
Athenry, *Ireland* **13 C3** 53 18N 8 44W
Athens = Athínai, *Greece* **21 F10** 37 58N 23 46 E
Athens, *Ala., U.S.A.* **77 H2** 34 48N 86 58W
Athens, *Ga., U.S.A.* **77 J4** 33 57N 83 23W
Athens, *N.Y., U.S.A.* **79 D11** 42 16N 73 49W
Athens, *Ohio, U.S.A.* **76 F4** 39 20N 82 6W
Athens, *Pa., U.S.A.* **79 E8** 41 57N 76 31W
Athens, *Tenn., U.S.A.* **77 H3** 35 27N 84 36W
Athens, *Tex., U.S.A.* **81 J7** 32 12N 95 51W
Atherley, *Canada* **78 B5** 44 37N 79 20W
Atherton, *Australia* **62 B4** 17 17S 145 30 E
Athienou, *Cyprus* **23 D12** 35 3N 33 32 E
Athínai, *Greece* **21 F10** 37 58N 23 46 E
Athlone, *Ireland* **13 C4** 53 25N 7 56W
Athna, *Cyprus* **23 D12** 35 3N 33 47 E
Athol, *U.S.A.* **79 D12** 42 36N 72 14W
Atholl, Forest of, *U.K.* **12 E5** 56 51N 3 50W
Atholville, *Canada* **71 C6** 47 59N 66 43W
Áthos, *Greece* **21 D11** 40 9N 24 22 E
Athy, *Ireland* **13 C5** 53 0N 7 0W
Ati, *Chad* **51 F9** 13 13N 18 20 E
Atiak, *Uganda* **54 B3** 3 12N 32 2 E
Atik L., *Canada* **73 B9** 55 15N 96 0W
Atikameg →, *Canada* **70 B3** 52 30N 82 46W
Atikokan, *Canada* **70 C1** 48 45N 91 37W
Atikonak L., *Canada* **71 B7** 52 40N 64 32W
Atka, *Russia* **27 C16** 60 50N 151 48 E
Atka I., *U.S.A.* **68 C2** 52 7N 174 30W
Atkinson, *U.S.A.* **80 D5** 42 32N 98 59W
Atlanta, *Ga., U.S.A.* **77 J3** 33 45N 84 23W
Atlanta, *Tex., U.S.A.* **81 J7** 33 7N 94 10W
Atlantic, *U.S.A.* **80 E7** 41 24N 95 1W
Atlantic City, *U.S.A.* **76 F8** 39 21N 74 27W
Atlantic Ocean **2 E9** 0 0 20 0W
Atlas Mts. = Haut Atlas, *Morocco* **50 B4** 32 30N 5 0W
Atlin, *Canada* **72 B2** 59 31N 133 41W
Atlin, L., *Canada* **72 B2** 59 26N 133 45W
Atlin Prov. Park, *Canada* **72 B2** 59 10N 134 30W
Atmore, *U.S.A.* **77 K2** 31 2N 87 29W
Atoka, *U.S.A.* **81 H6** 34 23N 96 8W
Atolia, *U.S.A.* **85 K9** 35 19N 117 37W
Atrai →, *Bangla.* **43 G13** 24 7N 89 22 E
Atrak = Atrek →, *Turkmenistan* **45 B8** 37 35N 53 58 E
Atrauli, *India* **42 E8** 28 2N 78 20 E
Atrek →, *Turkmenistan* **45 B8** 37 35N 53 58 E
Atsuta, *Japan* **30 C10** 43 24N 141 26 E
Attalla, *U.S.A.* **77 H2** 34 1N 86 6W
Attapu, *Laos* **38 E6** 14 48N 106 50 E
Attáviros, *Greece* **23 C9** 36 12N 27 50 E
Attawapiskat, *Canada* **70 B3** 52 56N 82 24W
Attawapiskat →, *Canada* **70 B3** 52 57N 82 18W
Attawapiskat L., *Canada* **70 B2** 52 18N 87 54W
Attica, *Ind., U.S.A.* **76 E2** 40 18N 87 15W
Attica, *Ohio, U.S.A.* **78 E2** 41 4N 82 53W
Attikamagen L., *Canada* **71 B6** 55 0N 66 30W
Attleboro, *U.S.A.* **79 E13** 41 57N 71 17W
Attock, *Pakistan* **42 C5** 33 52N 72 20 E
Attopeu = Attapu, *Laos* **38 E6** 14 48N 106 50 E
Attu I., *U.S.A.* **68 C1** 52 55N 172 55 E
Attur, *India* **40 P11** 11 35N 78 30 E
Atuel →, *Argentina* **94 D2** 36 17S 66 50W
Åtvidaberg, *Sweden* **9 G17** 58 12N 16 0 E
Atwater, *U.S.A.* **84 H6** 37 21N 120 37W
Atwood, *Canada* **78 C3** 43 40N 81 1W
Atwood, *U.S.A.* **80 F4** 39 48N 101 3W
Atyraū, *Kazakstan* **25 E9** 47 5N 52 0 E
Au Sable, *U.S.A.* **78 B1** 44 25N 83 20W
Au Sable →, *U.S.A.* **76 C4** 44 25N 83 20W
Au Sable Forks, *U.S.A.* **79 B11** 44 27N 73 41W
Au Sable Pt., *U.S.A.* **78 B1** 44 20N 83 20W
Aubagne, *France* **18 E6** 43 17N 5 37 E
Aubarca, C. d', *Spain* **22 B7** 39 4N 1 22 E
Aube →, *France* **18 B5** 48 34N 3 43 E
Auberry, *U.S.A.* **84 H7** 37 7N 119 29W
Auburn, *Ala., U.S.A.* **77 J3** 32 36N 85 29W
Auburn, *Calif., U.S.A.* **84 G5** 38 54N 121 4W
Auburn, *Ind., U.S.A.* **76 E3** 41 22N 85 4W
Auburn, *Maine, U.S.A.* **77 C10** 44 6N 70 14W
Auburn, *N.Y., U.S.A.* **79 D8** 42 56N 76 34W
Auburn, *Nebr., U.S.A.* **80 E7** 40 23N 95 51W
Auburn, *Pa., U.S.A.* **79 F8** 40 36N 76 6W
Auburn, *Wash., U.S.A.* **84 C4** 47 18N 122 14W
Auburn Ra., *Australia* **63 D5** 25 15S 150 30 E
Aubusson, *France* **18 D5** 45 57N 2 11 E
Auch, *France* **18 E4** 43 39N 0 36 E
Auckland, *N.Z.* **59 G5** 36 52S 174 46 E
Auckland Is., *Pac. Oc.* **64 N8** 50 40S 166 5 E
Aude →, *France* **18 E5** 43 13N 3 14 E
Auden, *Canada* **70 B2** 50 14N 87 53W
Audubon, *U.S.A.* **80 E7** 41 43N 94 56W
Augathella, *Australia* **63 D4** 25 48S 146 35 E
Aughnacloy, *U.K.* **13 B5** 54 25N 6 59W
Augrabies Falls, *S. Africa* **56 D3** 28 35S 20 20 E
Augsburg, *Germany* **16 D6** 48 25N 10 52 E
Augusta, *Australia* **61 F2** 34 19S 115 9 E
Augusta, *Italy* **20 F6** 37 13N 15 13 E
Augusta, *Ark., U.S.A.* **81 H9** 35 17N 91 22W
Augusta, *Ga., U.S.A.* **77 J5** 33 28N 81 58W
Augusta, *Kans., U.S.A.* **81 G6** 37 41N 96 59W
Augusta, *Maine, U.S.A.* **69 D13** 44 19N 69 47W
Augusta, *Mont., U.S.A.* **82 C7** 47 30N 112 24W
Augustów, *Poland* **17 B12** 53 51N 23 0 E
Augustus, Mt., *Australia* **61 D2** 24 20S 116 50 E
Augustus I., *Australia* **60 C3** 15 20S 124 30 E
Aukum, *U.S.A.* **84 G6** 38 34N 120 43W
Auld, L., *Australia* **60 D3** 22 25S 123 50 E
Ault, *U.S.A.* **80 E2** 40 35N 104 44W
Aunis, *France* **18 C3** 46 5N 0 50W
Auponhia, *Indonesia* **37 E7** 1 58S 125 27 E
Aur, Pulau, *Malaysia* **39 L5** 2 35N 104 10 E
Auraiya, *India* **43 F8** 26 28N 79 33 E
Aurangabad, *Bihar, India* **43 G11** 24 45N 84 18 E
Aurangabad, *Maharashtra, India* **40 K9** 19 50N 75 23 E
Aurich, *Germany* **16 B4** 53 28N 7 28 E
Aurillac, *France* **18 D5** 44 55N 2 26 E
Aurora, *Canada* **78 C5** 44 0N 79 28W
Aurora, *S. Africa* **56 E2** 32 40S 18 29 E
Aurora, *Colo., U.S.A.* **80 F2** 39 44N 104 52W
Aurora, *Ill., U.S.A.* **76 E1** 41 45N 88 19W
Aurora, *Mo., U.S.A.* **81 G8** 36 58N 93 43W
Aurora, *N.Y., U.S.A.* **79 D8** 42 45N 76 42W
Aurora, *Nebr., U.S.A.* **80 E6** 40 52N 98 0W
Aurora, *Ohio, U.S.A.* **78 E3** 41 21N 81 20W
Aurukun, *Australia* **62 A3** 13 20S 141 45 E
Aus, *Namibia* **56 D2** 26 35S 16 12 E
Ausable →, *Canada* **78 C3** 43 19N 81 46W
Auschwitz = Oświęcim, *Poland* **17 C10** 50 2N 19 11 E
Austin, *Minn., U.S.A.* **80 D8** 43 40N 92 58W
Austin, *Nev., U.S.A.* **82 G5** 39 30N 117 4W
Austin, *Pa., U.S.A.* **78 E6** 41 38N 78 6W
Austin, *Tex., U.S.A.* **81 K6** 30 17N 97 45W
Austin, L., *Australia* **61 E2** 27 40S 118 0 E
Austin I., *Canada* **73 A10** 61 10N 94 0W
Austra, *Norway* **8 D14** 65 8N 11 55 E
Austral Is. = Tubuai Is., *Pac. Oc.* **65 K13** 25 0S 150 0W
Austral Seamount Chain, *Pac. Oc.* **65 K13** 24 0S 150 0W
Australia ■, *Oceania* **64 K5** 23 0S 135 0 E
Australian Capital Territory □, *Australia* **63 F4** 35 30S 149 0 E
Australind, *Australia* **61 F2** 33 17S 115 42 E
Austria ■, *Europe* **16 E8** 47 0N 14 0 E
Austvågøy, *Norway* **8 B16** 68 20N 14 40 E
Autlán, *Mexico* **86 D4** 19 40N 104 30W
Autun, *France* **18 C6** 46 58N 4 17 E
Auvergne, *France* **18 D5** 45 20N 3 15 E
Auvergne, Mts. d', *France* **18 D5** 45 20N 2 55 E
Auxerre, *France* **18 C5** 47 48N 3 32 E
Ava, *U.S.A.* **81 G8** 36 57N 92 40W
Avallon, *France* **18 C5** 47 30N 3 53 E
Avalon, *U.S.A.* **85 M8** 33 21N 118 20W
Avalon Pen., *Canada* **71 C9** 47 30N 53 20W
Avanos, *Turkey* **44 B2** 38 43N 34 51 E
Avaré, *Brazil* **95 A6** 23 4S 48 58W
Avawatz Mts., *U.S.A.* **85 K10** 35 40N 116 30W
Aveiro, *Brazil* **93 D7** 3 10S 55 5W
Aveiro, *Portugal* **19 B1** 40 37N 8 38W
Āvej, *Iran* **45 C6** 35 40N 49 15 E
Avellaneda, *Argentina* **94 C4** 34 50S 58 10W
Avellino, *Italy* **20 D6** 40 54N 14 47 E
Avenal, *U.S.A.* **84 K6** 36 0N 120 8W
Aversa, *Italy* **20 D6** 40 58N 14 12 E
Avery, *U.S.A.* **82 C6** 47 15N 115 49W
Aves, Is. las, *Venezuela* **89 D6** 12 0N 67 30W
Avesta, *Sweden* **9 F17** 60 9N 16 10 E
Avezzano, *Italy* **20 C5** 42 2N 13 25 E
Aviá Terai, *Argentina* **94 B3** 26 45S 60 50W
Aviemore, *U.K.* **12 D5** 57 12N 3 50W
Avignon, *France* **18 E6** 43 57N 4 50 E
Ávila, *Spain* **19 B3** 40 39N 4 43W
Avila Beach, *U.S.A.* **85 K6** 35 11N 120 44W
Avilés, *Spain* **19 A3** 43 35N 5 57W
Avis, *U.S.A.* **78 E7** 41 11N 77 19W
Avoca, *U.S.A.* **78 D7** 42 25N 77 25W
Avoca →, *Australia* **63 F3** 35 40S 143 43 E
Avoca →, *Ireland* **13 D5** 52 48N 6 10W
Avola, *Canada* **72 C5** 51 45N 119 19W
Avola, *Italy* **20 F6** 36 56N 15 7 E
Avon, *U.S.A.* **78 D7** 42 55N 77 45W
Avon →, *Australia* **61 F2** 31 40S 116 7 E
Avon →, *Bristol, U.K.* **11 F5** 51 29N 2 41W
Avon →, *Dorset, U.K.* **11 G6** 50 44N 1 46W
Avon →, *Warks., U.K.* **11 E5** 52 0N 2 8W
Avon Park, *U.S.A.* **77 M5** 27 36N 81 31W
Avondale, *Zimbabwe* **55 F3** 17 43S 30 58 E
Avonlea, *Canada* **73 D8** 50 0N 105 0W
Avonmore, *Canada* **79 A10** 45 10N 74 58W
Avranches, *France* **18 B3** 48 40N 1 20W
A'waj →, *Syria* **47 B5** 33 23N 36 20 E
Awaji-Shima, *Japan* **31 G7** 34 30N 134 50 E
'Awālī, *Bahrain* **45 E6** 26 0N 50 30 E
Awantipur, *India* **43 C6** 33 55N 75 3 E
Awasa, *Ethiopia* **46 F2** 7 3N 38 28 E
Awash, *Ethiopia* **46 F3** 9 1N 40 10 E
Awatere →, *N.Z.* **59 J5** 41 37S 174 10 E
Awbārī, *Libya* **51 C8** 26 46N 12 57 E
Awe, L., *U.K.* **12 E3** 56 17N 5 16W
Awjilah, *Libya* **51 C10** 29 8N 21 7 E
Axe →, *U.K.* **11 F5** 50 42N 3 4W
Axel Heiberg I., *Canada* **4 B3** 80 0N 90 0W
Axim, *Ghana* **50 H5** 4 51N 2 15W
Axiós →, *Greece* **21 D10** 40 57N 22 35 E
Axminster, *U.K.* **11 G4** 50 46N 3 0W
Ayabaca, *Peru* **92 D3** 4 40S 79 53W
Ayabe, *Japan* **31 G7** 35 20N 135 20 E
Ayacucho, *Argentina* **94 D4** 37 5S 58 20W
Ayacucho, *Peru* **92 F4** 13 0S 74 0W
Ayaguz, *Kazakstan* **26 E9** 48 10N 80 10 E
Ayamonte, *Spain* **19 D2** 37 12N 7 24W
Ayan, *Russia* **27 D14** 56 30N 138 16 E
Ayaviri, *Peru* **92 F4** 14 50S 70 35W
Aydın, *Turkey* **21 F12** 37 51N 27 51 E
Aydin □, *Turkey* **25 G4** 37 50N 28 0 E
Ayer, *U.S.A.* **79 D13** 42 34N 71 35W
Ayer's Cliff, *Canada* **79 A12** 45 10N 72 3W
Ayers Rock, *Australia* **61 E5** 25 23S 131 5 E
Ayia Aikateríni, Ákra, *Greece* **23 A3** 39 50N 19 50 E
Ayia Dhéka, *Greece* **23 D6** 35 3N 24 58 E
Ayia Gálini, *Greece* **23 D6** 35 6N 24 41 E
Ayia Napa, *Cyprus* **23 E13** 34 59N 34 0 E
Ayia Phyla, *Cyprus* **23 E12** 34 43N 33 1 E
Ayia Varvára, *Greece* **23 D7** 35 8N 25 1 E
Áyios Amvrósios, *Cyprus* **23 D12** 35 20N 33 35 E
Áyios Evstrátios, *Greece* **21 E11** 39 34N 24 58 E
Áyios Ioánnis, Ákra, *Greece* **23 D7** 35 20N 25 40 E
Áyios Isidhoros, *Greece* **23 C9** 36 9N 27 51 E
Áyios Matthaíos, *Greece* **23 B3** 39 30N 19 47 E
Áyios Nikólaos, *Greece* **23 D7** 35 11N 25 41 E
Áyios Seryios, *Cyprus* **23 D12** 35 12N 33 53 E
Ayios Theodhoros, *Cyprus* **23 D13** 35 22N 34 1 E
Aykino, *Russia* **24 B8** 62 15N 49 56 E
Aylesbury, *U.K.* **11 F7** 51 49N 0 49W
Aylmer, *Canada* **78 D4** 42 46N 80 59W
Aylmer, L., *Canada* **68 B8** 64 0N 110 8W
'Ayn, Wādī al, *Oman* **45 F7** 22 15N 55 28 E
Ayn Dār, *Si. Arabia* **45 E7** 25 55N 49 10 E
Ayn Zālah, *Iraq* **44 B4** 36 45N 42 35 E
Ayolas, *Paraguay* **94 B4** 27 10S 56 59W
Ayon, Ostrov, *Russia* **27 C17** 69 50N 169 0 E
'Ayoûn el 'Atroûs, *Mauritania* **50 E4** 16 40N 9 37W
Ayr, *Australia* **62 B4** 19 35S 147 25 E
Ayr, *Canada* **78 C4** 43 17N 80 27W
Ayr, *U.K.* **12 F4** 55 28N 4 38W
Ayr →, *U.K.* **12 F4** 55 28N 4 38W
Ayre, Pt. of, *U.K.* **10 C3** 54 25N 4 21W
Ayton, *Australia* **62 B4** 15 56S 145 22 E
Aytos, *Bulgaria* **21 C12** 42 42N 27 16 E
Ayu, Kepulauan, *Indonesia* **37 D8** 0 35N 131 5 E
Ayutla, *Guatemala* **88 D1** 14 40N 92 10W
Ayutla, *Mexico* **87 D5** 16 58N 99 17W
Ayvacık, *Turkey* **21 E12** 39 36N 26 24 E
Ayvalık, *Turkey* **21 E12** 39 20N 26 46 E
Az Zabadānī, *Syria* **47 B5** 33 43N 36 5 E
Az̧ Z̧āhirīyah, *West Bank* **47 D3** 31 25N 34 58 E
Az̧ Z̧ahrān, *Si. Arabia* **45 E6** 26 10N 50 7 E
Az Zarqā, *Jordan* **47 C5** 32 5N 36 4 E
Az Zarqā', *U.A.E.* **45 E7** 24 53N 53 4 E
Az Zāwiyah, *Libya* **51 B8** 32 52N 12 56 E
Az Zībār, *Iraq* **44 B5** 36 52N 44 4 E
Az-Zilfī, *Si. Arabia* **44 E5** 26 12N 44 52 E
Az Zubayr, *Iraq* **44 D5** 30 26N 47 40 E
Azamgarh, *India* **43 F10** 26 5N 83 13 E
Azangaro, *Peru* **92 F4** 14 55S 70 13W
Āzār Shahr, *Iran* **44 B5** 37 45N 45 59 E
Azārān, *Iran* **44 B5** 37 25N 47 16 E
Azärbayjan = Azerbaijan ■, *Asia* **25 F8** 40 20N 48 0 E
Āzarbāyjān-e Gharbī □, *Iran* **44 B5** 37 0N 44 30 E
Āzarbāyjān-e Sharqī □, *Iran* **44 B5** 37 20N 47 0 E
Azare, *Nigeria* **50 F8** 11 55N 10 10 E
A'zāz, *Syria* **44 B3** 36 36N 37 4 E
Azbine = Aïr, *Niger* **50 E7** 18 30N 8 0 E
Azerbaijan ■, *Asia* **25 F8** 40 20N 48 0 E
Azerbaijchan = Azerbaijan ■, *Asia* **25 F8** 40 20N 48 0 E
Azimganj, *India* **43 G13** 24 14N 88 16 E
Azogues, *Ecuador* **92 D3** 2 35S 78 0W
Azores, *Atl. Oc.* **50 A1** 38 44N 29 0W
Azov, *Russia* **25 E6** 47 3N 39 25 E
Azov, Sea of, *Europe* **25 E6** 46 0N 36 30 E
Azovskoye More = Azov, Sea of, *Europe* **25 E6** 46 0N 36 30 E
Azraq ash Shīshān, *Jordan* **47 D5** 31 50N 36 49 E
Aztec, *U.S.A.* **83 H10** 36 49N 107 59W
Azúa de Compostela, *Dom. Rep.* **89 C5** 18 25N 70 44W
Azuaga, *Spain* **19 C3** 38 16N 5 39W
Azuero, Pen. de, *Panama* **88 E3** 7 30N 80 30W
Azul, *Argentina* **94 D4** 36 42S 59 43W
Azusa, *U.S.A.* **85 L9** 34 8N 117 52W

B

Ba Don, *Vietnam* **38 D6** 17 45N 106 26 E
Ba Dong, *Vietnam* **39 H6** 9 40N 106 33 E
Ba Ngoi = Cam Lam, *Vietnam* **39 G7** 11 54N 109 10 E
Ba Tri, *Vietnam* **39 G6** 10 2N 106 36 E
Ba Xian = Bazhou, *China* **34 E9** 39 8N 116 22 E
Baa, *Indonesia* **37 F6** 10 50S 123 0 E
Baarle-Nassau, *Belgium* **15 C4** 51 27N 4 56 E
Bab el Mandeb, *Red Sea* **46 E3** 12 35N 43 25 E
Baba Burnu, *Turkey* **21 E12** 39 29N 26 2 E
Bābā Kalū, *Iran* **45 D6** 30 7N 50 49 E
Babadag, *Romania* **17 F15** 44 53N 28 44 E
Babadayhan, *Turkmenistan* **26 F7** 37 42N 60 23 E
Babaeski, *Turkey* **21 D12** 41 26N 27 6 E
Babahoyo, *Ecuador* **92 D3** 1 40S 79 30W
Babai = Sarju →, *India* **43 F9** 27 21N 81 23 E
Babar, *Indonesia* **37 F7** 8 0S 129 30 E
Babar, *Pakistan* **42 D3** 31 7N 69 32 E
Babarkach, *Pakistan* **42 E3** 29 45N 68 0 E
Babb, *U.S.A.* **82 B7** 48 51N 113 27W
Babelthuap, *Pac. Oc.* **37 C8** 7 30N 134 30 E
Baberu, *India* **43 G9** 25 33N 80 43 E
Babi Besar, Pulau, *Malaysia* **39 L4** 2 25N 103 59 E
Babinda, *Australia* **62 B4** 17 20S 145 56 E
Babine, *Canada* **72 B3** 55 22N 126 37W
Babine →, *Canada* **72 B3** 55 45N 127 44W
Babine L., *Canada* **72 C3** 54 48N 126 0W
Babo, *Indonesia* **37 E8** 2 30S 133 30 E
Bābol, *Iran* **45 B7** 36 40N 52 50 E
Bābol Sar, *Iran* **45 B7** 36 45N 52 45 E
Babruysk, *Belarus* **17 B15** 53 10N 29 15 E
Babuhri, *India* **42 F3** 26 49N 69 43 E
Babusar Pass, *Pakistan* **43 B5** 35 12N 73 59 E
Babuyan Chan., *Phil.* **37 A6** 18 40N 121 30 E
Babylon, *Iraq* **44 C5** 32 34N 44 22 E
Bac Lieu, *Vietnam* **39 H5** 9 17N 105 43 E
Bac Phan, *Vietnam* **38 B5** 22 0N 105 0 E
Bacabal, *Brazil* **93 D10** 4 15S 44 45W
Bacalar, *Mexico* **87 D7** 18 50N 87 27W
Bacan, Kepulauan, *Indonesia* **37 E7** 0 35S 127 30 E
Bacarra, *Phil.* **37 A6** 18 15N 120 37 E
Bacău, *Romania* **17 E14** 46 35N 26 55 E
Bacerac, *Mexico* **86 A3** 30 18N 108 50W
Bach Long Vi, Dao, *Vietnam* **38 B6** 20 10N 107 40 E
Bachelina, *Russia* **26 D7** 57 45N 67 20 E
Bachhwara, *India* **43 G11** 25 35N 85 54 E
Back →, *Canada* **68 B9** 65 10N 104 0W
Bacolod, *Phil.* **37 B6** 10 40N 122 57 E
Bacuk, *Malaysia* **39 J4** 6 4N 102 25 E
Bād, *Iran* **45 C7** 33 41N 52 1 E
Bad →, *U.S.A.* **80 C4** 44 21N 100 22W
Bad Axe, *U.S.A.* **78 C2** 43 48N 83 0W
Bad Ischl, *Austria* **16 E7** 47 44N 13 38 E
Bad Kissingen, *Germany* **16 C6** 50 11N 10 4 E
Bad Lands, *U.S.A.* **80 D3** 43 40N 102 10W
Bada Barabil, *India* **43 H11** 22 7N 85 24 E
Badagara, *India* **40 P9** 11 35N 75 40 E
Badajós, L., *Brazil* **92 D6** 3 15S 62 50W
Badajoz, *Spain* **19 C2** 38 50N 6 59W
Badalona, *Spain* **19 B7** 41 26N 2 15 E
Badalzai, *Afghan.* **42 E1** 29 50N 65 35 E
Badampahar, *India* **41 H15** 22 10N 86 10 E
Badanah, *Si. Arabia* **44 D4** 30 58N 41 30 E
Badarinath, *India* **43 D8** 30 45N 79 30 E
Badas, Kepulauan, *Indonesia* **36 D3** 0 45N 107 5 E
Baddo →, *Pakistan* **40 F4** 28 0N 64 20 E
Bade, *Indonesia* **37 F9** 7 10S 139 35 E
Baden, *Austria* **16 D9** 48 1N 16 13 E
Baden, *U.S.A.* **78 F4** 40 38N 80 14W
Baden-Baden, *Germany* **16 D5** 48 44N 8 13 E
Baden-Württemberg □, *Germany* **16 D5** 48 20N 8 40 E
Badgastein, *Austria* **16 E7** 47 7N 13 9 E
Badger, *Canada* **71 C8** 49 0N 56 4W
Badger, *U.S.A.* **84 J7** 36 38N 119 1W
Bādghīsāt □, *Afghan.* **40 B3** 35 0N 63 0 E
Badgom, *India* **43 B6** 34 1N 74 45 E
Badin, *Pakistan* **42 G3** 24 38N 68 54 E
Badlands National Park, *U.S.A.* **80 D3** 43 38N 102 56W
Badrah, *Iraq* **44 C5** 33 6N 45 58 E
Badrinath, *India* **43 D8** 30 44N 79 29 E
Badulla, *Sri Lanka* **40 R12** 7 1N 81 7 E
Baena, *Spain* **19 D3** 37 37N 4 20W
Baeza, *Spain* **19 D4** 37 57N 3 25W
Baffin B., *Canada* **4 B4** 72 0N 64 0W
Baffin I., *Canada* **69 B12** 68 0N 75 0W
Bafing →, *Mali* **50 F3** 13 49N 10 50W
Bafliyūn, *Syria* **44 B3** 36 37N 36 59 E
Bafoulabé, *Mali* **50 F3** 13 50N 10 55W
Bafoussam, *Cameroon* **52 C2** 5 28N 10 25 E
Bāfq, *Iran* **45 D7** 31 40N 55 25 E
Bafra, *Turkey* **25 F6** 41 34N 35 54 E
Bāft, *Iran* **45 D8** 29 15N 56 38 E
Bafwasende, *Dem. Rep. of the Congo* **54 B2** 1 3N 27 5 E
Bagamoyo, *Tanzania* **54 D4** 6 28S 38 55 E
Bagan Datoh, *Malaysia* **39 L3** 3 59N 100 47 E
Bagan Serai, *Malaysia* **39 K3** 5 1N 100 32 E
Baganga, *Phil.* **37 C7** 7 34N 126 33 E
Bagani, *Namibia* **56 B3** 18 7S 21 41 E
Bagansiapiapi, *Indonesia* **36 D2** 2 12N 100 50 E
Bagasra, *India* **42 J4** 21 30N 71 0 E
Bagaud, *India* **42 H6** 22 19N 75 53 E
Bagdad, *U.S.A.* **85 L11** 34 35N 115 53W
Bagdarin, *Russia* **27 D12** 54 26N 113 36 E
Bagé, *Brazil* **95 C5** 31 20S 54 15W
Bagenalstown = Muine Bheag, *Ireland* **13 D5** 52 42N 6 58W
Baggs, *U.S.A.* **82 F10** 41 2N 107 39W
Bagh, *Pakistan* **43 C5** 33 59N 73 45 E
Baghain →, *India* **43 G9** 25 32N 81 1 E
Baghdād, *Iraq* **44 C5** 33 20N 44 30 E
Bagheria, *Italy* **20 E5** 38 5N 13 30 E
Baghlān, *Afghan.* **40 A6** 36 12N 69 0 E
Bagley, *U.S.A.* **80 B7** 47 32N 95 24W
Bagodar, *India* **43 G11** 24 5N 85 52 E
Bagrationovsk, *Russia* **9 J19** 54 23N 20 39 E
Baguio, *Phil.* **37 A6** 16 26N 120 34 E
Bah, *India* **43 F8** 26 53N 78 36 E
Bahadurganj, *India* **43 F12** 26 16N 87 49 E
Bahadurgarh, *India* **42 E7** 28 40N 76 57 E
Bahama, Canal Viejo de, *W. Indies* **88 B4** 22 10N 77 30W
Bahamas ■, *N. Amer.* **89 B5** 24 0N 75 0W
Baharampur, *India* **43 G13** 24 2N 88 27 E
Bahawalnagar, *Pakistan* **42 E5** 30 0N 73 15 E
Bahawalpur, *Pakistan* **42 E4** 29 24N 71 40 E
Baheri, *India* **43 E8** 28 45N 79 34 E
Bahgul →, *India* **43 F8** 27 45N 79 36 E
Bahi, *Tanzania* **54 D4** 5 58S 35 21 E
Bahi Swamp, *Tanzania* **54 D4** 6 10S 35 0 E
Bahia = Salvador, *Brazil* **93 F11** 13 0S 38 30W
Bahia □, *Brazil* **93 F10** 12 0S 42 0W
Bahía, Is. de la, *Honduras* **88 C2** 16 45N 86 15W
Bahía Blanca, *Argentina* **94 D3** 38 35S 62 13W
Bahía de Caráquez, *Ecuador* **92 D2** 0 40S 80 27W
Bahía Honda, *Cuba* **88 B3** 22 54N 83 10W
Bahía Laura, *Argentina* **96 F3** 48 10S 66 30W
Bahía Negra, *Paraguay* **92 H7** 20 5S 58 5W

Bardstown

Bahir Dar, *Ethiopia* **46 E2** 11 37N 37 10 E
Bahmanzād, *Iran* **45 D6** 31 15N 51 47 E
Bahr el Ghazâl □, *Sudan* **51 G11** 7 0N 28 0 E
Bahraich, *India* **43 F9** 27 38N 81 37 E
Bahrain ■, *Asia* **45 E6** 26 0N 50 35 E
Bahror, *India* **42 F7** 27 51N 76 20 E
Bāhū Kalāt, *Iran* **45 E9** 25 43N 61 25 E
Bai Bung, Mui = Ca Mau, Mui, *Vietnam* **39 H5** 8 38N 104 44 E
Bai Duc, *Vietnam* **38 C5** 18 3N 105 49 E
Bai Thuong, *Vietnam* **38 C5** 19 54N 105 23 E
Baia Mare, *Romania* **17 E12** 47 40N 23 35 E
Baião, *Brazil* **93 D9** 2 40S 49 40W
Baïbokoum, *Chad* **51 G9** 7 46N 15 43 E
Baicheng, *China* **35 B12** 45 38N 122 42 E
Baidoa, *Somali Rep.* **46 G3** 3 8N 43 30 E
Baie Comeau, *Canada* **71 C6** 49 12N 68 10W
Baie-St-Paul, *Canada* **71 C5** 47 28N 70 32W
Baie Trinité, *Canada* **71 C6** 49 25N 67 20W
Baie Verte, *Canada* **71 C8** 49 55N 56 12W
Baihar, *India* **43 H9** 22 6N 80 33 E
Baihe, *China* **34 H6** 32 50N 110 5 E
Ba'ījī, *Iraq* **44 C4** 35 0N 43 30 E
Baijnath, *India* **43 E8** 29 55N 79 37 E
Baikal, L. = Baykal, Oz., *Russia* **27 D11** 53 0N 108 0 E
Baikunthpur, *India* **43 H10** 23 15N 82 33 E
Baile Atha Cliath = Dublin, *Ireland* **13 C5** 53 21N 6 15W
Băileşti, *Romania* **17 F12** 44 1N 23 20 E
Bainbridge, *Ga., U.S.A.* **77 K3** 30 55N 84 35W
Bainbridge, *N.Y., U.S.A.* **79 D9** 42 18N 75 29W
Baing, *Indonesia* **37 F6** 10 14S 120 34 E
Bainiu, *China* **34 H7** 32 50N 112 15 E
Bā'ir, *Jordan* **47 E5** 30 45N 36 55 E
Bairin Youqi, *China* **35 C10** 43 30N 118 35 E
Bairin Zuoqi, *China* **35 C10** 43 58N 119 15 E
Bairnsdale, *Australia* **63 F4** 37 48S 147 36 E
Baisha, *China* **34 G7** 34 20N 112 32 E
Baitadi, *Nepal* **43 E9** 29 35N 80 25 E
Baiyin, *China* **34 F3** 36 45N 104 14 E
Baiyu Shan, *China* **34 F4** 37 15N 107 30 E
Baj Baj, *India* **43 H13** 22 30N 88 5 E
Baja, *Hungary* **17 E10** 46 12N 18 59 E
Baja, Pta., *Mexico* **86 B1** 29 50N 116 0W
Baja California, *Mexico* **86 A1** 31 10N 115 12W
Baja California □, *Mexico* **86 B2** 30 0N 115 0W
Baja California Sur □, *Mexico* **86 B2** 25 50N 111 50W
Bajag, *India* **43 H9** 22 40N 81 21 E
Bajamar, *Canary Is.* **22 F3** 28 33N 16 20W
Bajana, *India* **42 H4** 23 7N 71 49 E
Bājgīrān, *Iran* **45 B8** 37 36N 58 24 E
Bajimba, Mt., *Australia* **63 D5** 29 17S 152 6 E
Bajo Nuevo, *Caribbean* **88 C4** 15 40N 78 50W
Bajoga, *Nigeria* **51 F8** 10 57N 11 20 E
Bajool, *Australia* **62 C5** 23 40S 150 35 E
Bakel, *Senegal* **50 F3** 14 56N 12 20W
Baker, *Calif., U.S.A.* **85 K10** 35 16N 116 4W
Baker, *Mont., U.S.A.* **80 B2** 46 22N 104 17W
Baker, L., *Canada* **68 B10** 64 0N 96 0W
Baker City, *U.S.A.* **82 D5** 44 47N 117 50W
Baker I., *Pac. Oc.* **64 G10** 0 10N 176 35W
Baker I., *U.S.A.* **72 B2** 55 20N 133 40W
Baker L., *Australia* **61 E4** 26 54S 126 5 E
Baker Lake, *Canada* **68 B10** 64 20N 96 3W
Baker Mt., *U.S.A.* **82 B3** 48 50N 121 49W
Bakers Creek, *Australia* **62 C4** 21 13S 149 7 E
Baker's Dozen Is., *Canada* **70 A4** 56 45N 78 45W
Bakersfield, *Calif., U.S.A.* **85 K8** 35 23N 119 1W
Bakersfield, *Vt., U.S.A.* **79 B12** 44 45N 72 48W
Bākhtarān, *Iran* **44 C5** 34 23N 47 0 E
Bākhtarān □, *Iran* **44 C5** 34 0N 46 30 E
Bakı, *Azerbaijan* **25 F8** 40 29N 49 56 E
Bakkafjörður, *Iceland* **8 C6** 66 2N 14 48W
Bakony, *Hungary* **17 E9** 47 10N 17 30 E
Bakony Forest = Bakony, *Hungary* **17 E9** 47 10N 17 30 E
Bakouma, *C.A.R.* **52 C4** 5 40N 22 56 E
Bakswaho, *India* **43 G8** 24 15N 79 18 E
Baku = Bakı, *Azerbaijan* **25 F8** 40 29N 49 56 E
Bakutis Coast, *Antarctica* **5 D15** 74 0S 120 0W
Baky = Bakı, *Azerbaijan* **25 F8** 40 29N 49 56 E
Bala, *Canada* **78 A5** 45 1N 79 37W
Bala, *U.K.* **10 E4** 52 54N 3 36W
Bala, L., *U.K.* **10 E4** 52 53N 3 37W
Balabac I., *Phil.* **36 C5** 8 0N 117 0 E
Balabac Str., *E. Indies* **36 C5** 7 53N 117 5 E
Balabagh, *Afghan.* **42 B4** 34 25N 70 12 E
Ba'labakk, *Lebanon* **47 B5** 34 0N 36 10 E
Balabalangan, Kepulauan, *Indonesia* **36 E5** 2 20S 117 30 E
Balad, *Iraq* **44 C5** 34 1N 44 9 E
Balad Rūz, *Iraq* **44 C5** 33 42N 45 5 E
Bālādeh, *Fārs, Iran* **45 D6** 29 17N 51 56 E
Bālādeh, *Māzandaran, Iran* **45 B6** 36 12N 51 48 E
Balaghat, *India* **40 J12** 21 49N 80 12 E
Balaghat Ra., *India* **40 K10** 18 50N 76 30 E
Balaguer, *Spain* **19 B6** 41 50N 0 50 E
Balaklava, *Ukraine* **25 F5** 44 30N 33 30 E
Balakovo, *Russia* **24 D8** 52 4N 47 55 E
Balamau, *India* **43 F9** 27 10N 80 21 E
Balancán, *Mexico* **87 D6** 17 48N 91 32W
Balashov, *Russia* **25 D7** 51 30N 43 10 E
Balasinor, *India* **42 H5** 22 57N 73 23 E
Balasore = Baleshwar, *India* **41 J15** 21 35N 87 3 E
Balaton, *Hungary* **17 E9** 46 50N 17 40 E
Balbina, Represa de, *Brazil* **92 D7** 2 0S 59 30W
Balboa, *Panama* **88 E4** 8 57N 79 34W
Balbriggan, *Ireland* **13 C5** 53 37N 6 11W
Balcarce, *Argentina* **94 D4** 38 0S 58 10W
Balcarres, *Canada* **73 C8** 50 50N 103 35W
Balchik, *Bulgaria* **21 C13** 43 28N 28 11 E
Balclutha, *N.Z.* **59 M2** 46 15S 169 45 E
Balcones Escarpment, *U.S.A.* **81 L5** 29 30N 99 15W
Bald Hd., *Australia* **61 G2** 35 6S 118 1 E
Bald I., *Australia* **61 F2** 34 57S 118 27 E
Bald Knob, *U.S.A.* **81 H9** 35 19N 91 34W
Baldock L., *Canada* **73 B9** 56 33N 97 57W
Baldwin, *Mich., U.S.A.* **76 D3** 43 54N 85 51W
Baldwin, *Pa., U.S.A.* **78 F5** 40 23N 79 59W
Baldwinsville, *U.S.A.* **79 C8** 43 10N 76 20W
Baldy Mt., *U.S.A.* **82 B9** 48 9N 109 39W
Baldy Peak, *U.S.A.* **83 K9** 33 54N 109 34W
Baleares, Is., *Spain* **22 B10** 39 30N 3 0 E
Balearic Is. = Baleares, Is., *Spain* **22 B10** 39 30N 3 0 E
Baleine = Whale →, *Canada* **71 A6** 58 15N 67 40W
Baler, *Phil.* **37 A6** 15 46N 121 34 E
Baleshare, *U.K.* **12 D1** 57 31N 7 22W
Baleshwar, *India* **41 J15** 21 35N 87 3 E
Balfate, *Honduras* **88 C2** 15 48N 86 25W
Bali, *Greece* **23 D6** 35 25N 24 47 E
Bali, *India* **42 G5** 25 11N 73 17 E
Bali □, *Indonesia* **36 F5** 8 20S 115 0 E
Bali, Selat, *Indonesia* **37 H16** 8 18S 114 25 E
Baliapal, *India* **43 J12** 21 40N 87 17 E
Balikeşir, *Turkey* **21 E12** 39 39N 27 53 E
Balikpapan, *Indonesia* **36 E5** 1 10S 116 55 E
Balimbing, *Phil.* **37 C5** 5 5N 119 58 E
Baling, *Malaysia* **39 K3** 5 41N 100 55 E
Balipara, *India* **41 F18** 26 50N 92 45 E
Balkan Mts. = Stara Planina, *Bulgaria* **21 C10** 43 15N 23 0 E
Balkhash = Balqash, *Kazakstan* **26 E8** 46 50N 74 50 E
Balkhash, Ozero = Balqash Köl, *Kazakstan* **26 E8** 46 0N 74 50 E
Balla, *Bangla.* **41 G17** 24 10N 91 35 E
Ballachulish, *U.K.* **12 E3** 56 41N 5 8W
Balladonia, *Australia* **61 F3** 32 27S 123 51 E
Ballaghaderreen, *Ireland* **13 C3** 53 55N 8 34W
Ballarat, *Australia* **63 F3** 37 33S 143 50 E
Ballard, L., *Australia* **61 E3** 29 20S 120 40 E
Ballater, *U.K.* **12 D5** 57 3N 3 3W
Ballenas, Canal de, *Mexico* **86 B2** 29 10N 113 45W
Balleny Is., *Antarctica* **5 C11** 66 30S 163 0 E
Ballia, *India* **43 G11** 25 46N 84 12 E
Ballina, *Australia* **63 D5** 28 50S 153 31 E
Ballina, *Ireland* **13 B2** 54 7N 9 9W
Ballinasloe, *Ireland* **13 C3** 53 20N 8 13W
Ballinger, *U.S.A.* **81 K5** 31 45N 99 57W
Ballinrobe, *Ireland* **13 C2** 53 38N 9 13W
Ballinskelligs B., *Ireland* **13 E1** 51 48N 10 13W
Ballston Spa, *U.S.A.* **79 D11** 43 0N 73 51W
Ballycastle, *U.K.* **13 A5** 55 12N 6 15W
Ballyclare, *U.K.* **13 B5** 54 46N 6 0W
Ballyhaunis, *Ireland* **13 C3** 53 46N 8 46W
Ballymena, *U.K.* **13 B5** 54 52N 6 17W
Ballymoney, *U.K.* **13 A5** 55 5N 6 31W
Ballymote, *Ireland* **13 B3** 54 5N 8 31W
Ballynahinch, *U.K.* **13 B6** 54 24N 5 54W
Ballyquintin Pt., *U.K.* **13 B6** 54 20N 5 30W
Ballyshannon, *Ireland* **13 B3** 54 30N 8 11W
Balmaceda, *Chile* **96 F2** 46 0S 71 50W
Balmertown, *Canada* **73 C10** 51 4N 93 41W
Balmoral, *Australia* **63 F3** 37 15S 141 48 E
Balmorhea, *U.S.A.* **81 K3** 30 59N 103 45W
Balonne →, *Australia* **63 D4** 28 47S 147 56 E
Balotra, *India* **42 G5** 25 50N 72 14 E
Balqash, *Kazakstan* **26 E8** 46 50N 74 50 E
Balqash Köl, *Kazakstan* **26 E8** 46 0N 74 50 E
Balrampur, *India* **43 F10** 27 30N 82 20 E
Balranald, *Australia* **63 E3** 34 38S 143 33 E
Balsas, *Mexico* **87 D5** 18 0N 99 40W
Balsas →, *Brazil* **93 E9** 7 15S 44 35W
Balsas →, *Mexico* **86 D4** 17 55N 102 10W
Balston Spa, *U.S.A.* **79 D11** 43 0N 73 52W
Balta, *Ukraine* **17 D15** 48 2N 29 45 E
Bălţi, *Moldova* **17 E14** 47 48N 27 58 E
Baltic Sea, *Europe* **9 H18** 57 0N 19 0 E
Baltimore, *Ireland* **13 E2** 51 29N 9 22W
Baltimore, *Md., U.S.A.* **76 F7** 39 17N 76 37W
Baltimore, *Ohio, U.S.A.* **78 G2** 39 51N 82 36W
Baltit, *Pakistan* **43 A6** 36 15N 74 40 E
Baltiysk, *Russia* **9 J18** 54 41N 19 58 E
Baluchistan □, *Pakistan* **40 F4** 27 30N 65 0 E
Balurghat, *India* **43 G13** 25 15N 88 44 E
Balvi, *Latvia* **9 H22** 57 8N 27 15 E
Balya, *Turkey* **21 E12** 39 44N 27 35 E
Bam, *Iran* **45 D8** 29 7N 58 14 E
Bama, *Nigeria* **51 F8** 11 33N 13 41 E
Bamaga, *Australia* **62 A3** 10 50S 142 25 E
Bamaji L., *Canada* **70 B1** 51 9N 91 25W
Bamako, *Mali* **50 F4** 12 34N 7 55W
Bambari, *C.A.R.* **52 C4** 5 40N 20 35 E
Bambaroo, *Australia* **62 B4** 18 50S 146 10 E
Bamberg, *Germany* **16 D6** 49 54N 10 54 E
Bamberg, *U.S.A.* **77 J5** 33 18N 81 2W
Bambili, *Dem. Rep. of the Congo* **54 B2** 3 40N 26 0 E
Bamenda, *Cameroon* **52 C1** 5 57N 10 11 E
Bamfield, *Canada* **72 D3** 48 45N 125 10W
Bāmīān □, *Afghan.* **40 B5** 35 0N 67 0 E
Bamiancheng, *China* **35 C13** 43 15N 124 2 E
Bampūr, *Iran* **45 E9** 27 15N 60 21 E
Ban Ban, *Laos* **38 C4** 19 31N 103 30 E
Ban Bang Hin, *Thailand* **39 H2** 9 32N 98 35 E
Ban Chiang Klang, *Thailand* **38 C3** 19 25N 100 55 E
Ban Chik, *Laos* **38 D4** 17 15N 102 22 E
Ban Choho, *Thailand* **38 E4** 15 2N 102 9 E
Ban Dan Lan Hoi, *Thailand* **38 D2** 17 0N 99 35 E
Ban Don = Surat Thani, *Thailand* **39 H2** 9 6N 99 20 E
Ban Don, *Vietnam* **38 F6** 12 53N 107 48 E
Ban Don, Ao →, *Thailand* **39 H2** 9 20N 99 25 E
Ban Dong, *Thailand* **38 C3** 19 30N 100 59 E
Ban Hong, *Thailand* **38 C2** 18 18N 98 50 E
Ban Kaeng, *Thailand* **38 D3** 17 29N 100 7 E
Ban Kantang, *Thailand* **39 J2** 7 25N 99 31 E
Ban Keun, *Laos* **38 C4** 18 22N 102 35 E
Ban Khai, *Thailand* **38 F3** 12 46N 101 18 E
Ban Kheun, *Laos* **38 B3** 20 13N 101 7 E
Ban Khlong Kua, *Thailand* **39 J3** 6 57N 100 8 E
Ban Khuan Mao, *Thailand* **39 J2** 7 50N 99 37 E
Ban Ko Yai Chim, *Thailand* **39 G2** 11 17N 99 26 E
Ban Kok, *Thailand* **38 D4** 16 40N 103 40 E
Ban Laem, *Thailand* **38 F2** 13 13N 99 59 E
Ban Lao Ngam, *Laos* **38 E6** 15 28N 106 10 E
Ban Le Kathe, *Thailand* **38 E2** 15 49N 98 53 E
Ban Mae Chedi, *Thailand* **38 C2** 19 11N 99 31 E
Ban Mae Laeng, *Thailand* **38 B2** 20 1N 99 17 E
Ban Mae Sariang, *Thailand* **38 C1** 18 10N 97 56 E
Ban Mê Thuôt = Buon Ma Thuot, *Vietnam* **38 F7** 12 40N 108 3 E
Ban Mi, *Thailand* **38 E3** 15 3N 100 32 E
Ban Muong Mo, *Laos* **38 C4** 19 4N 103 58 E
Ban Na Mo, *Laos* **38 D5** 17 7N 105 40 E
Ban Na San, *Thailand* **39 H2** 8 53N 99 52 E
Ban Na Tong, *Laos* **38 B3** 20 56N 101 47 E
Ban Nam Bac, *Laos* **38 B4** 20 38N 102 20 E
Ban Nam Ma, *Laos* **38 A3** 22 2N 101 37 E
Ban Ngang, *Laos* **38 E6** 15 59N 106 11 E
Ban Nong Bok, *Laos* **38 D5** 17 5N 104 48 E
Ban Nong Boua, *Laos* **38 E6** 15 40N 106 33 E
Ban Nong Pling, *Thailand* **38 E3** 15 40N 100 10 E
Ban Pak Chan, *Thailand* **39 G2** 10 32N 98 51 E
Ban Phai, *Thailand* **38 D4** 16 4N 102 44 E
Ban Pong, *Thailand* **38 F2** 13 50N 99 55 E
Ban Ron Phibun, *Thailand* **39 H2** 8 9N 99 51 E
Ban Sanam Chai, *Thailand* **39 J3** 7 33N 100 25 E
Ban Sangkha, *Thailand* **38 E4** 14 37N 103 52 E
Ban Tak, *Thailand* **38 D2** 17 2N 99 4 E
Ban Tako, *Thailand* **38 E4** 14 5N 102 40 E
Ban Tha Dua, *Thailand* **38 D2** 17 59N 98 39 E
Ban Tha Li, *Thailand* **38 D3** 17 37N 101 25 E
Ban Tha Nun, *Thailand* **39 H2** 8 12N 98 18 E
Ban Thahine, *Laos* **38 E5** 14 12N 105 33 E
Ban Xien Kok, *Laos* **38 B3** 20 54N 100 39 E
Ban Yen Nhan, *Vietnam* **38 B6** 20 57N 106 2 E
Banaba, *Kiribati* **64 H8** 0 45S 169 50 E
Banalia, *Dem. Rep. of the Congo* **54 B2** 1 32N 25 5 E
Banam, *Cambodia* **39 G5** 11 20N 105 17 E
Bananal, I. do, *Brazil* **93 F8** 11 30S 50 30W
Banaras = Varanasi, *India* **43 G10** 25 22N 83 0 E
Banas →, *Gujarat, India* **42 H4** 23 45N 71 25 E
Banas →, *Mad. P., India* **43 G9** 24 15N 81 30 E
Bânâs, Ras, *Egypt* **51 D13** 23 57N 35 59 E
Banbān, *Si. Arabia* **44 E5** 25 1N 46 35 E
Banbridge, *U.K.* **13 B5** 54 22N 6 16W
Banbury, *U.K.* **11 E6** 52 4N 1 20W
Banchory, *U.K.* **12 D6** 57 3N 2 29W
Bancroft, *Canada* **78 A7** 45 3N 77 51W
Band Bonī, *Iran* **45 E8** 25 30N 59 33 E
Band Qīr, *Iran* **45 D6** 31 39N 48 53 E
Banda, *India* **43 G9** 25 30N 80 26 E
Banda, *Mad. P., India* **43 G8** 24 3N 78 57 E
Banda, Kepulauan, *Indonesia* **37 E7** 4 37S 129 50 E
Banda Aceh, *Indonesia* **36 C1** 5 35N 95 20 E
Banda Banda, Mt., *Australia* **63 E5** 31 10S 152 28 E
Banda Elat, *Indonesia* **37 F8** 5 40S 133 5 E
Banda Is. = Banda, Kepulauan, *Indonesia* **37 E7** 4 37S 129 50 E
Banda Sea, *Indonesia* **37 F8** 6 0S 130 0 E
Bandai-San, *Japan* **30 F10** 37 36N 140 4 E
Bandān, *Iran* **45 D9** 31 23N 60 44 E
Bandanaira, *Indonesia* **37 E7** 4 32S 129 54 E
Bandanwara, *India* **42 F6** 26 9N 74 38 E
Bandar = Machilipatnam, *India* **41 L12** 16 12N 81 8 E
Bandār 'Abbās, *Iran* **45 E8** 27 15N 56 15 E
Bandar-e Anzalī, *Iran* **45 B6** 37 30N 49 30 E
Bandar-e Bushehr = Būshehr, *Iran* **45 D6** 28 55N 50 55 E
Bandar-e Chārak, *Iran* **45 E7** 26 45N 54 20 E
Bandar-e Deylam, *Iran* **45 D6** 30 5N 50 10 E
Bandar-e Khomeynı, *Iran* **45 D6** 30 30N 49 5 E
Bandar-e Lengeh, *Iran* **45 E7** 26 35N 54 58 E
Bandar-e Maqām, *Iran* **45 E7** 26 56N 53 29 E
Bandar-e Ma'shur, *Iran* **45 D6** 30 35N 49 10 E
Bandar-e Nakhīlū, *Iran* **45 E7** 26 58N 53 30 E
Bandar-e Rīg, *Iran* **45 D6** 29 29N 50 38 E
Bandar-e Torkeman, *Iran* **45 B7** 37 0N 54 10 E
Bandar Maharani = Muar, *Malaysia* **39 L4** 2 3N 102 34 E
Bandar Penggaram = Batu Pahat, *Malaysia* **39 M4** 1 50N 102 56 E
Bandar Seri Begawan, *Brunei* **36 D5** 4 52N 115 0 E
Bandar Sri Aman, *Malaysia* **36 D4** 1 15N 111 32 E
Bandawe, *Malawi* **55 E3** 11 58S 34 5 E
Bandeira, Pico da, *Brazil* **95 A7** 20 26S 41 47W
Bandera, *Argentina* **94 B3** 28 55S 62 20W
Banderas, B. de, *Mexico* **86 C3** 20 40N 105 30W
Bandhogarh, *India* **43 H9** 23 40N 81 2 E
Bandi →, *India* **42 F6** 26 12N 75 47 E
Bandikui, *India* **42 F7** 27 3N 76 34 E
Bandırma, *Turkey* **21 D13** 40 20N 28 0 E
Bandon, *Ireland* **13 E3** 51 44N 8 44W
Bandon →, *Ireland* **13 E3** 51 43N 8 37W
Bandula, *Mozam.* **55 F3** 19 0S 33 7 E
Bandundu, *Dem. Rep. of the Congo* **52 E3** 3 15S 17 22 E
Bandung, *Indonesia* **37 G12** 6 54S 107 36 E
Bāneh, *Iran* **44 C5** 35 59N 45 53 E
Banes, *Cuba* **89 B4** 21 0N 75 42W
Banff, *Canada* **72 C5** 51 10N 115 34W
Banff, *U.K.* **12 D6** 57 40N 2 33W
Banff Nat. Park, *Canada* **72 C5** 51 30N 116 15W
Bang Fai →, *Laos* **38 D5** 16 57N 104 45 E
Bang Hieng →, *Laos* **38 D5** 16 10N 105 10 E
Bang Krathum, *Thailand* **38 D3** 16 34N 100 18 E
Bang Lamung, *Thailand* **38 F3** 13 3N 100 56 E
Bang Mun Nak, *Thailand* **38 D3** 16 2N 100 23 E
Bang Pa In, *Thailand* **38 E3** 14 14N 100 35 E
Bang Rakam, *Thailand* **38 D3** 16 45N 100 7 E
Bang Saphan, *Thailand* **39 G2** 11 14N 99 28 E
Bangaduni I., *India* **43 J13** 21 34N 88 52 E
Bangala Dam, *Zimbabwe* **55 G3** 21 7S 31 25 E
Bangalore, *India* **40 N10** 12 59N 77 40 E
Banganga →, *India* **42 F6** 27 6N 77 25 E
Bangaon, *India* **43 H13** 23 0N 88 47 E
Bangassou, *C.A.R.* **52 D4** 4 55N 23 7 E
Banggai, *Indonesia* **37 E6** 1 34S 123 30 E
Banggai, Kepulauan, *Indonesia* **37 E6** 1 40S 123 30 E
Banggai Arch. = Banggai, Kepulauan, *Indonesia* **37 E6** 1 40S 123 30 E
Banggi, *Malaysia* **36 C5** 7 17N 117 12 E
Banghāzī, *Libya* **51 B10** 32 11N 20 3 E
Bangka, *Sulawesi, Indonesia* **37 D7** 1 50N 125 5 E
Bangka, *Sumatera, Indonesia* **36 E3** 2 0S 105 50 E
Bangka, Selat, *Indonesia* **36 E3** 2 30S 105 30 E
Bangkalan, *Indonesia* **37 G15** 7 2S 112 46 E
Bangkinang, *Indonesia* **36 D2** 0 18N 101 5 E
Bangko, *Indonesia* **36 E2** 2 5S 102 9 E
Bangkok, *Thailand* **38 F3** 13 45N 100 35 E
Bangladesh ■, *Asia* **41 H17** 24 0N 90 0 E
Bangong Co, *India* **43 B8** 35 50N 79 20 E
Bangor, *Down, U.K.* **13 B6** 54 40N 5 40W
Bangor, *Gwynedd, U.K.* **10 D3** 53 14N 4 8W
Bangor, *Maine, U.S.A.* **69 D13** 44 48N 68 46W
Bangor, *Pa., U.S.A.* **79 F9** 40 52N 75 13W
Bangued, *Phil.* **37 A6** 17 40N 120 37 E
Bangui, *C.A.R.* **52 D3** 4 23N 18 35 E
Banguru, *Dem. Rep. of the Congo* **54 B2** 0 30N 27 10 E
Bangweulu, L., *Zambia* **55 E3** 11 0S 30 0 E
Bangweulu Swamp, *Zambia* **55 E3** 11 20S 30 15 E
Bani, *Dom. Rep.* **89 C5** 18 16N 70 22W
Banī Sa'd, *Iraq* **44 C5** 33 34N 44 32 E
Banihal Pass, *India* **43 C6** 33 30N 75 12 E
Bāniyās, *Syria* **44 C3** 35 10N 36 0 E
Banja Luka, *Bos.-H.* **20 B7** 44 49N 17 11 E
Banjar, *India* **42 D7** 31 38N 77 21 E
Banjar →, *India* **43 H9** 22 36N 80 22 E
Banjarmasin, *Indonesia* **36 E4** 3 20S 114 35 E
Banjul, *Gambia* **50 F2** 13 28N 16 40W
Banka, *India* **43 G12** 24 53N 86 55 E
Banket, *Zimbabwe* **55 F3** 17 27S 30 19 E
Bankipore, *India* **41 G14** 25 35N 85 10 E
Banks I., *B.C., Canada* **72 C3** 53 20N 130 0W
Banks I., *N.W.T., Canada* **68 A7** 73 15N 121 30W
Banks Pen., *N.Z.* **59 K4** 43 45S 173 15 E
Banks Str., *Australia* **62 G4** 40 40S 148 10 E
Bankura, *India* **43 H12** 23 11N 87 18 E
Banmankhi, *India* **43 G12** 25 53N 87 11 E
Bann →, *Arm., U.K.* **13 B5** 54 30N 6 31W
Bann →, *L'derry., U.K.* **13 A5** 55 8N 6 41W
Bannang Sata, *Thailand* **39 J3** 6 16N 101 16 E
Banning, *U.S.A.* **85 M10** 33 56N 116 53W
Banningville = Bandundu, *Dem. Rep. of the Congo* **52 E3** 3 15S 17 22 E
Bannockburn, *Canada* **78 B7** 44 39N 77 33W
Bannockburn, *U.K.* **12 E5** 56 5N 3 55W
Bannockburn, *Zimbabwe* **55 G2** 20 17S 29 48 E
Bannu, *Pakistan* **40 C7** 33 0N 70 18 E
Bano, *India* **43 H11** 22 40N 84 55 E
Bansgaon, *India* **43 F10** 26 33N 83 21 E
Banská Bystrica, *Slovak Rep.* **17 D10** 48 46N 19 14 E
Banswara, *India* **42 H6** 23 32N 74 24 E
Bantaeng, *Indonesia* **37 F5** 5 32S 119 56 E
Bantry, *Ireland* **13 E2** 51 41N 9 27W
Bantry B., *Ireland* **13 E2** 51 37N 9 44W
Bantul, *Indonesia* **37 G14** 7 55S 110 19 E
Bantva, *India* **42 J4** 21 29N 70 12 E
Banu, *Afghan.* **40 B6** 35 35N 69 5 E
Banyak, Kepulauan, *Indonesia* **36 D1** 2 10N 97 10 E
Banyalbufar, *Spain* **22 B9** 39 42N 2 31 E
Banyo, *Cameroon* **52 C2** 6 52N 11 45 E
Banyumas, *Indonesia* **37 G13** 7 32S 109 18 E
Banyuwangi, *Indonesia* **37 H16** 8 13S 114 21 E
Banzare Coast, *Antarctica* **5 C9** 68 0S 125 0 E
Banzyville = Mobayi, *Dem. Rep. of the Congo* **52 D4** 4 15N 21 8 E
Bao Lac, *Vietnam* **38 A5** 22 57N 105 40 E
Bao Loc, *Vietnam* **39 G6** 11 32N 107 48 E
Baocheng, *China* **34 H4** 33 12N 106 56 E
Baode, *China* **34 E6** 39 1N 111 5 E
Baodi, *China* **35 E9** 39 38N 117 20 E
Baoding, *China* **34 E8** 38 50N 115 28 E
Baoji, *China* **34 G4** 34 20N 107 5 E
Baoshan, *China* **32 D4** 25 10N 99 5 E
Baotou, *China* **34 D6** 40 32N 110 2 E
Baoying, *China* **35 H10** 33 17N 119 20 E
Bap, *India* **42 F5** 27 23N 72 18 E
Bapatla, *India* **41 M12** 15 55N 80 30 E
Bāqerābād, *Iran* **45 C6** 33 2N 51 58 E
Ba'qūbah, *Iraq* **44 C5** 33 45N 44 50 E
Baquedano, *Chile* **94 A2** 23 20S 69 52W
Bar, *Montenegro, Yug.* **21 C8** 42 8N 19 6 E
Bar, *Ukraine* **17 D14** 49 4N 27 40 E
Bar Bigha, *India* **43 G11** 25 21N 85 47 E
Bar Harbor, *U.S.A.* **77 C11** 44 23N 68 13W
Bar-le-Duc, *France* **18 B6** 48 47N 5 10 E
Bara, *India* **43 G9** 25 16N 81 43 E
Bara Banki, *India* **43 F9** 26 55N 81 12 E
Barabai, *Indonesia* **36 E5** 2 32S 115 34 E
Baraboo, *U.S.A.* **80 D10** 43 28N 89 45W
Baracoa, *Cuba* **89 B5** 20 20N 74 30W
Baradā →, *Syria* **47 B5** 33 33N 36 34 E
Baradero, *Argentina* **94 C4** 33 52S 59 29W
Baradine, *Australia* **63 E4** 30 56S 149 4 E
Baraga, *U.S.A.* **80 B10** 46 47N 88 30W
Barah →, *India* **42 F6** 27 42N 77 5 E
Barahona, *Dom. Rep.* **89 C5** 18 13N 71 7W
Barail Range, *India* **41 G18** 25 15N 93 20 E
Barakaldo, *Spain* **19 A4** 43 18N 2 59W
Barakar →, *India* **43 G12** 24 7N 86 14 E
Barakhola, *India* **41 G18** 25 0N 92 45 E
Barakot, *India* **43 J11** 21 33N 84 59 E
Barakpur, *India* **43 H13** 22 44N 88 30 E
Baralaba, *Australia* **62 C4** 24 13S 149 50 E
Baralzon L., *Canada* **73 B9** 60 0N 98 3W
Baramula, *India* **43 B6** 34 15N 74 20 E
Baran, *India* **42 G7** 25 9N 76 40 E
Baran →, *Pakistan* **42 G3** 25 13N 68 17 E
Baranavichy, *Belarus* **17 B14** 53 10N 26 0 E
Baranof, *U.S.A.* **72 B2** 57 5N 134 50W
Baranof I., *U.S.A.* **68 C6** 57 0N 135 0W
Barapasi, *Indonesia* **37 E9** 2 15S 137 5 E
Barasat, *India* **43 H13** 22 46N 88 31 E
Barat Daya, Kepulauan, *Indonesia* **37 F7** 7 30S 128 0 E
Barataria B., *U.S.A.* **81 L10** 29 20N 89 55W
Barauda, *India* **42 H6** 23 33N 75 15 E
Baraut, *India* **42 E7** 29 13N 77 7 E
Barbacena, *Brazil* **95 A7** 21 15S 43 56W
Barbados ■, *W. Indies* **89 D8** 13 10N 59 30W
Barbària, C. de, *Spain* **22 C7** 38 39N 1 24 E
Barbastro, *Spain* **19 A6** 42 2N 0 5 E
Barberton, *S. Africa* **57 D5** 25 42S 31 2 E
Barberton, *U.S.A.* **78 E3** 41 0N 81 39W
Barbosa, *Colombia* **92 B4** 5 57N 73 37W
Barbourville, *U.S.A.* **77 G4** 36 52N 83 53W
Barbuda, *W. Indies* **89 C7** 17 30N 61 40W
Barcaldine, *Australia* **62 C4** 23 43S 145 6 E
Barcellona Pozzo di Gotto, *Italy* **20 E6** 38 9N 15 13 E
Barcelona, *Spain* **19 B7** 41 21N 2 10 E
Barcelona, *Venezuela* **92 A6** 10 10N 64 40W
Barcelos, *Brazil* **92 D6** 1 0S 63 0W
Barcoo →, *Australia* **62 D3** 25 30S 142 50 E
Bardaï, *Chad* **51 D9** 21 25N 17 0 E
Bardas Blancas, *Argentina* **94 D2** 35 49S 69 45W
Barddhaman, *India* **43 H12** 23 14N 87 39 E
Bardejov, *Slovak Rep.* **17 D11** 49 18N 21 15 E
Bardera, *Somali Rep.* **46 G3** 2 20N 42 27 E
Bardīyah, *Libya* **51 B10** 31 45N 25 5 E
Bardsey I., *U.K.* **10 E3** 52 45N 4 47W
Bardstown, *U.S.A.* **76 G3** 37 49N 85 28W

Bareilly

Bareilly, *India* **43 E8** 28 22N 79 27 E
Barela, *India* **43 H9** 23 6N 80 3 E
Barents Sea, *Arctic* **4 B9** 73 0N 39 0 E
Barfleur, Pte. de, *France* **18 B3** 49 42N 1 16W
Bargara, *Australia* **62 C5** 24 50S 152 25 E
Barguzin, *Russia* **27 D11** 53 37N 109 37 E
Barh, *India* **43 G11** 25 29N 85 46 E
Barhaj, *India* **43 F10** 26 18N 83 44 E
Barham, *Australia* **63 F3** 35 36S 144 8 E
Barharwa, *India* **43 G12** 24 52N 87 47 E
Barhi, *India* **43 G11** 24 15N 85 25 E
Bari, *India* **42 F7** 26 39N 77 39 E
Bari, *Italy* **20 D7** 41 8N 16 51 E
Bari Doab, *Pakistan* **42 D5** 30 20N 73 0 E
Bari Sadri, *India* **42 G6** 24 28N 74 30 E
Barīdī, Ra's, *Si. Arabia* **44 E3** 24 17N 37 31 E
Barīm, *Yemen* **48 E8** 12 39N 43 25 E
Barinas, *Venezuela* **92 B4** 8 36N 70 15W
Baring, C., *Canada* **68 B8** 70 0N 117 30W
Baringo, *Kenya* **54 B4** 0 47N 36 16 E
Baringo, L., *Kenya* **54 B4** 0 47N 36 16 E
Barisal, *Bangla.* **41 H17** 22 45N 90 20 E
Barisan, Bukit, *Indonesia* **36 E2** 3 30S 102 15 E
Barito →, *Indonesia* **36 E4** 4 0S 114 50 E
Bark L., *Canada* **78 A7** 45 27N 77 51W
Barkakana, *India* **43 H11** 23 37N 85 29 E
Barker, *U.S.A.* **78 C6** 43 20N 78 33W
Barkley, L., *U.S.A.* **77 G2** 37 1N 88 14W
Barkley Sound, *Canada* **72 D3** 48 50N 125 10W
Barkly East, *S. Africa* **56 E4** 30 58S 27 33 E
Barkly Roadhouse, *Australia* **62 B2** 19 52S 135 50 E
Barkly Tableland, *Australia* **62 B2** 17 50S 136 40 E
Barkly West, *S. Africa* **56 D3** 28 5S 24 31 E
Barkol Kazak Zizhixian, *China* **32 B4** 43 37N 93 2 E
Bârlad, *Romania* **17 E14** 46 15N 27 38 E
Bârlad →, *Romania* **17 F14** 45 38N 27 32 E
Barlee, L., *Australia* **61 E2** 29 15S 119 30 E
Barlee, Mt., *Australia* **61 D4** 24 38S 128 13 E
Barletta, *Italy* **20 D7** 41 19N 16 17 E
Barlovento, *Canary Is.* **22 F2** 28 48N 17 48W
Barlow L., *Canada* **73 A8** 62 0N 103 0W
Barmedman, *Australia* **63 E4** 34 9S 147 21 E
Barmer, *India* **42 G4** 25 45N 71 20 E
Barmera, *Australia* **63 E3** 34 15S 140 28 E
Barmouth, *U.K.* **10 E3** 52 44N 4 4W
Barna →, *India* **43 G10** 25 21N 83 3 E
Barnagar, *India* **42 H6** 23 7N 75 19 E
Barnala, *India* **42 D6** 30 23N 75 33 E
Barnard Castle, *U.K.* **10 C6** 54 33N 1 55W
Barnaul, *Russia* **26 D9** 53 20N 83 40 E
Barnesville, *U.S.A.* **77 J3** 33 3N 84 9W
Barnet, *U.K.* **11 F7** 51 38N 0 9W
Barneveld, *Neths.* **15 B5** 52 7N 5 36 E
Barneveld, *U.S.A.* **79 C9** 43 16N 75 14W
Barnhart, *U.S.A.* **81 K4** 31 8N 101 10W
Barnsley, *U.K.* **10 D6** 53 34N 1 27W
Barnstaple, *U.K.* **11 F3** 51 5N 4 4W
Barnstaple Bay = Bideford Bay, *U.K.* **11 F3** 51 5N 4 20W
Barnsville, *U.S.A.* **80 B6** 46 43N 96 28W
Barnwell, *U.S.A.* **77 J5** 33 15N 81 23W
Baro, *Nigeria* **50 G7** 8 35N 6 18 E
Baroda = Vadodara, *India* **42 H5** 22 20N 73 10 E
Baroda, *India* **42 G7** 25 29N 76 35 E
Baroe, *S. Africa* **56 E3** 33 13S 24 33 E
Baron Ra., *Australia* **60 D4** 23 30S 127 45 E
Barotseland, *Zambia* **53 H4** 15 0S 24 0 E
Barpeta, *India* **41 F17** 26 20N 91 10 E
Barques, Pt. Aux, *U.S.A.* **78 B2** 44 4N 82 58W
Barquisimeto, *Venezuela* **92 A5** 10 4N 69 19W
Barr Smith Range, *Australia* **61 E3** 27 4S 120 20 E
Barra, *Brazil* **93 F10** 11 5S 43 10W
Barra, *U.K.* **12 E1** 57 0N 7 29W
Barra, Sd. of, *U.K.* **12 D1** 57 4N 7 25W
Barra de Navidad, *Mexico* **86 D4** 19 12N 104 41W
Barra do Corda, *Brazil* **93 E9** 5 30S 45 10W
Barra do Piraí, *Brazil* **95 A7** 22 30S 43 50W
Barra Falsa, Pta. da, *Mozam.* **57 C6** 22 58S 35 37 E
Barra Hd., *U.K.* **12 E1** 56 47N 7 40W
Barra Mansa, *Brazil* **95 A7** 22 35S 44 12W
Barraba, *Australia* **63 E5** 30 21S 150 35 E
Barrackpur = Barakpur, *India* **43 H13** 22 44N 88 30 E
Barradale Roadhouse, *Australia* **60 D1** 22 42S 114 58 E
Barraigh = Barra, *U.K.* **12 E1** 57 0N 7 29W
Barranca, *Lima, Peru* **92 F3** 10 45S 77 50W
Barranca, *Loreto, Peru* **92 D3** 4 50S 76 50W
Barrancabermeja, *Colombia* **92 B4** 7 0N 73 50W
Barrancas, *Venezuela* **92 B6** 8 55N 62 5W
Barrancos, *Portugal* **19 C2** 38 10N 6 58W
Barranqueras, *Argentina* **94 B4** 27 30S 59 0W
Barranquilla, *Colombia* **92 A4** 11 0N 74 50W
Barraute, *Canada* **70 C4** 48 26N 77 38W
Barre, *Mass., U.S.A.* **79 D12** 42 25N 72 6W
Barre, *Vt., U.S.A.* **79 B12** 44 12N 72 30W
Barreal, *Argentina* **94 C2** 31 33S 69 28W
Barreiras, *Brazil* **93 F10** 12 8S 45 0W
Barreirinhas, *Brazil* **93 D10** 2 30S 42 50W
Barreiro, *Portugal* **19 C1** 38 40N 9 6W
Barren, Nosy, *Madag.* **57 B7** 18 25S 43 40 E
Barretos, *Brazil* **93 H9** 20 30S 48 35W
Barrhead, *Canada* **72 C6** 54 10N 114 24W
Barrie, *Canada* **78 B5** 44 24N 79 40W
Barrier Ra., *Australia* **63 E3** 31 0S 141 30 E
Barrière, *Canada* **72 C4** 51 12N 120 7W
Barrington, *U.S.A.* **79 E13** 41 44N 71 18W
Barrington L., *Canada* **73 B8** 56 55N 100 15W
Barrington Tops, *Australia* **63 E5** 32 6S 151 28 E
Barringun, *Australia* **63 D4** 29 1S 145 41 E
Barro do Garças, *Brazil* **93 G8** 15 54S 52 16W
Barron, *U.S.A.* **80 C9** 45 24N 91 51W
Barrow, *U.S.A.* **68 A4** 71 18N 156 47W
Barrow →, *Ireland* **13 D5** 52 25N 6 58W
Barrow Creek, *Australia* **62 C1** 21 30S 133 55 E
Barrow I., *Australia* **60 D2** 20 45S 115 20 E
Barrow-in-Furness, *U.K.* **10 C4** 54 7N 3 14W
Barrow Pt., *Australia* **62 A3** 14 20S 144 40 E
Barrow Pt., *U.S.A.* **66 B4** 71 24N 156 29W
Barrow Ra., *Australia* **61 E4** 26 0S 127 40 E
Barrow Str., *Canada* **4 B3** 74 20N 95 0W
Barry, *U.K.* **11 F4** 51 24N 3 16W
Barry's Bay, *Canada* **78 A7** 45 29N 77 41W
Barsat, *Pakistan* **43 A5** 36 10N 72 45 E
Barsham, *Syria* **44 C4** 35 21N 40 33 E
Barsi, *India* **40 K9** 18 10N 75 50 E
Barsoi, *India* **41 G15** 25 48N 87 57 E
Barstow, *U.S.A.* **85 L9** 34 54N 117 1W
Barthélemy, Col, *Vietnam* **38 C5** 19 26N 104 6 E
Bartica, *Guyana* **92 B7** 6 25N 58 40W
Bartlesville, *U.S.A.* **81 G7** 36 45N 95 59W
Bartlett, *U.S.A.* **84 J8** 36 29N 118 2W
Bartlett, L., *Canada* **72 A5** 63 5N 118 20W
Bartolomeu Dias, *Mozam.* **55 G4** 21 10S 35 8 E
Barton, *U.S.A.* **79 B12** 44 45N 72 11W
Barton upon Humber, *U.K.* **10 D7** 53 41N 0 25W
Bartow, *U.S.A.* **77 M5** 27 54N 81 50W
Barú, Volcan, *Panama* **88 E3** 8 55N 82 35W
Barumba, *Dem. Rep. of the Congo* **54 B1** 1 3N 23 37 E
Baruunsuu, *Mongolia* **34 C3** 43 43N 105 35 E
Barwani, *India* **42 H6** 22 2N 74 57 E
Barysaw, *Belarus* **17 A15** 54 17N 28 28 E
Barzān, *Iraq* **44 B5** 36 55N 44 3 E
Bāsa'idū, *Iran* **45 E7** 26 35N 55 20 E
Basal, *Pakistan* **42 C5** 33 33N 72 13 E
Basankusa, *Dem. Rep. of the Congo* **52 D3** 1 5N 19 50 E
Basarabeasca, *Moldova* **17 E15** 46 21N 28 58 E
Basawa, *Afghan.* **42 B4** 34 15N 70 50 E
Bascuñán, C., *Chile* **94 B1** 28 52S 71 35W
Basel, *Switz.* **18 C7** 47 35N 7 35 E
Bashākerd, Kūhhā-ye, *Iran* **45 E8** 26 42N 58 35 E
Bashaw, *Canada* **72 C6** 52 35N 112 58W
Bāshī, *Iran* **45 D6** 28 41N 51 4 E
Bashkir Republic = Bashkortostan □, *Russia* **24 D10** 54 0N 57 0 E
Bashkortostan □, *Russia* **24 D10** 54 0N 57 0 E
Basilan, *Phil.* **37 C6** 6 35N 122 0 E
Basilan Str., *Phil.* **37 C6** 6 50N 122 0 E
Basildon, *U.K.* **11 F8** 51 34N 0 28 E
Basim = Washim, *India* **40 J10** 20 3N 77 0 E
Basin, *U.S.A.* **82 D9** 44 23N 108 2W
Basingstoke, *U.K.* **11 F6** 51 15N 1 5W
Baskatong, Rés., *Canada* **70 C4** 46 46N 75 50W
Basle = Basel, *Switz.* **18 C7** 47 35N 7 35 E
Basoda, *India* **42 H7** 23 52N 77 54 E
Basoka, *Dem. Rep. of the Congo* **54 B1** 1 16N 23 40 E
Basque Provinces = País Vasco □, *Spain* **19 A4** 42 50N 2 45W
Basra = Al Başrah, *Iraq* **44 D5** 30 30N 47 50 E
Bass Str., *Australia* **62 F4** 39 15S 146 30 E
Bassano, *Canada* **72 C6** 50 48N 112 20W
Bassano del Grappa, *Italy* **20 B4** 45 46N 11 44 E
Bassas da India, *Ind. Oc.* **53 J7** 22 0S 39 0 E
Basse-Terre, *Guadeloupe* **89 C7** 16 0N 61 44W
Bassein, *Burma* **41 L19** 16 45N 94 30 E
Basseterre, *St. Kitts & Nevis* **89 C7** 17 17N 62 43W
Bassett, *U.S.A.* **80 D5** 42 35N 99 32W
Bassi, *India* **42 D7** 30 44N 76 21 E
Bastak, *Iran* **45 E7** 27 15N 54 25 E
Baştām, *Iran* **45 B7** 36 29N 55 4 E
Bastar, *India* **41 K12** 19 15N 81 40 E
Basti, *India* **43 F10** 26 52N 82 55 E
Bastia, *France* **18 E8** 42 40N 9 30 E
Bastogne, *Belgium* **15 D5** 50 1N 5 43 E
Bastrop, *La., U.S.A.* **81 J9** 32 47N 91 55W
Bastrop, *Tex., U.S.A.* **81 K6** 30 7N 97 19W
Bat Yam, *Israel* **47 C3** 32 2N 34 44 E
Bata, *Eq. Guin.* **52 D1** 1 57N 9 50 E
Bataan, *Phil.* **37 B6** 14 40N 120 25 E
Batabanó, *Cuba* **88 B3** 22 40N 82 20W
Batabanó, G. de, *Cuba* **88 B3** 22 30N 82 30W
Batac, *Phil.* **37 A6** 18 3N 120 34 E
Batagai, *Russia* **27 C14** 67 38N 134 38 E
Batala, *India* **42 D6** 31 48N 75 12 E
Batama, *Dem. Rep. of the Congo* **54 B2** 0 58N 26 33 E
Batamay, *Russia* **27 C13** 63 30N 129 15 E
Batang, *Indonesia* **37 G13** 6 55S 109 45 E
Batangas, *Phil.* **37 B6** 13 35N 121 10 E
Batanta, *Indonesia* **37 E8** 0 55S 130 40 E
Batatais, *Brazil* **95 A6** 20 54S 47 37W
Batavia, *U.S.A.* **78 D6** 43 0N 78 11W
Batchelor, *Australia* **60 B5** 13 4S 131 1 E
Batdambang, *Cambodia* **38 F4** 13 7N 103 12 E
Bateman's B., *Australia* **63 F5** 35 40S 150 12 E
Batemans Bay, *Australia* **63 F5** 35 44S 150 11 E
Bates Ra., *Australia* **61 E3** 27 27S 121 5 E
Batesburg, *U.S.A.* **77 J5** 33 54N 81 33W
Batesville, *Ark., U.S.A.* **81 H9** 35 46N 91 39W
Batesville, *Miss., U.S.A.* **81 H10** 34 19N 89 57W
Batesville, *Tex., U.S.A.* **81 L5** 28 58N 99 37W
Bath, *Canada* **79 B8** 44 11N 76 47W
Bath, *U.K.* **11 F5** 51 23N 2 22W
Bath, *Maine, U.S.A.* **77 D11** 43 55N 69 49W
Bath, *N.Y., U.S.A.* **78 D7** 42 20N 77 19W
Bath & North East Somerset □, *U.K.* **11 F5** 51 21N 2 27W
Batheay, *Cambodia* **39 G5** 11 59N 104 57 E
Bathurst = Banjul, *Gambia* **50 F2** 13 28N 16 40W
Bathurst, *Australia* **63 E4** 33 25S 149 31 E
Bathurst, *Canada* **71 C6** 47 37N 65 43W
Bathurst, *S. Africa* **56 E4** 33 30S 26 50 E
Bathurst, C., *Canada* **68 A7** 70 34N 128 0W
Bathurst B., *Australia* **62 A3** 14 16S 144 25 E
Bathurst Harb., *Australia* **62 G4** 43 15S 146 10 E
Bathurst I., *Australia* **60 B5** 11 30S 130 10 E
Bathurst I., *Canada* **4 B2** 76 0N 100 30W
Bathurst Inlet, *Canada* **68 B9** 66 50N 108 1W
Batlow, *Australia* **63 F4** 35 31S 148 9 E
Batman, *Turkey* **25 G7** 37 55N 41 5 E
Baţn al Ghūl, *Jordan* **47 F4** 29 36N 35 56 E
Batna, *Algeria* **50 A7** 35 34N 6 15 E
Batoka, *Zambia* **55 F2** 16 45S 27 15 E
Baton Rouge, *U.S.A.* **81 K9** 30 27N 91 11W
Batong, Ko, *Thailand* **39 J2** 6 32N 99 12 E
Batopilas, *Mexico* **86 B3** 27 0N 107 45W
Batouri, *Cameroon* **52 D2** 4 30N 14 25 E
Båtsfjord, *Norway* **8 A23** 70 38N 29 39 E
Battambang = Batdambang, *Cambodia* **38 F4** 13 7N 103 12 E
Batticaloa, *Sri Lanka* **40 R12** 7 43N 81 45 E
Battipáglia, *Italy* **20 D6** 40 37N 14 58 E
Battle, *U.K.* **11 G8** 50 55N 0 30 E
Battle →, *Canada* **73 C7** 52 43N 108 15W
Battle Creek, *U.S.A.* **76 D3** 42 19N 85 11W
Battle Ground, *U.S.A.* **84 E4** 45 47N 122 32W
Battle Harbour, *Canada* **71 B8** 52 16N 55 35W
Battle Lake, *U.S.A.* **80 B7** 46 17N 95 43W
Battle Mountain, *U.S.A.* **82 F5** 40 38N 116 56W
Battlefields, *Zimbabwe* **55 F2** 18 37S 29 47 E
Battleford, *Canada* **73 C7** 52 45N 108 15W
Batu, Kepulauan, *Indonesia* **36 E1** 0 30S 98 25 E
Batu, Mt., *Ethiopia* **46 F2** 6 55N 39 45 E
Batu Caves, *Malaysia* **39 L3** 3 15N 101 40 E
Batu Gajah, *Malaysia* **39 K3** 4 28N 101 3 E
Batu Is. = Batu, Kepulauan, *Indonesia* **36 E1** 0 30S 98 25 E
Batu Pahat, *Malaysia* **39 M4** 1 50N 102 56 E
Batuata, *Indonesia* **37 F6** 6 12S 122 42 E
Batumi, *Georgia* **25 F7** 41 39N 41 44 E
Baturaja, *Indonesia* **36 E2** 4 11S 104 15 E
Baturité, *Brazil* **93 D11** 4 28S 38 45W
Bau, *Malaysia* **36 D4** 1 25N 110 9 E
Baubau, *Indonesia* **37 F6** 5 25S 122 38 E
Bauchi, *Nigeria* **50 F7** 10 22N 9 48 E
Baudette, *U.S.A.* **80 A7** 48 43N 94 36W
Bauer, C., *Australia* **63 E1** 32 44S 134 4 E
Bauhinia, *Australia* **62 C4** 24 35S 149 18 E
Baukau, *Indonesia* **37 F7** 8 27S 126 27 E
Bauld, C., *Canada* **69 C14** 51 38N 55 26W
Bauru, *Brazil* **95 A6** 22 10S 49 0W
Bausi, *India* **43 G12** 24 48N 87 1 E
Bauska, *Latvia* **9 H21** 56 24N 24 15 E
Bautzen, *Germany* **16 C8** 51 10N 14 26 E
Bavānāt, *Iran* **45 D7** 30 28N 53 27 E
Bavaria = Bayern □, *Germany* **16 D6** 48 50N 12 0 E
Bavispe →, *Mexico* **86 B3** 29 30N 109 11W
Bawdwin, *Burma* **41 H20** 23 5N 97 20 E
Bawean, *Indonesia* **36 F4** 5 46S 112 35 E
Bawku, *Ghana* **50 F5** 11 3N 0 19W
Bawlake, *Burma* **41 K20** 19 11N 97 21 E
Baxley, *U.S.A.* **77 K4** 31 47N 82 21W
Baxter, *U.S.A.* **80 B7** 46 21N 94 17W
Baxter Springs, *U.S.A.* **81 G7** 37 2N 94 44W
Bay City, *Mich., U.S.A.* **76 D4** 43 36N 83 54W
Bay City, *Tex., U.S.A.* **81 L7** 28 59N 95 58W
Bay Minette, *U.S.A.* **77 K2** 30 53N 87 46W
Bay Roberts, *Canada* **71 C9** 47 36N 53 16W
Bay St. Louis, *U.S.A.* **81 K10** 30 19N 89 20W
Bay Springs, *U.S.A.* **81 K10** 31 59N 89 17W
Bay View, *N.Z.* **59 H6** 39 25S 176 50 E
Baya, *Dem. Rep. of the Congo* **55 E2** 11 53S 27 25 E
Bayamo, *Cuba* **88 B4** 20 20N 76 40W
Bayamón, *Puerto Rico* **89 C6** 18 24N 66 10W
Bayan Har Shan, *China* **32 C4** 34 0N 98 0 E
Bayan Hot = Alxa Zuoqi, *China* **34 E3** 38 50N 105 40 E
Bayan Obo, *China* **34 D5** 41 52N 109 59 E
Bayan-Ovoo = Erdenetsogt, *Mongolia* **34 C4** 42 55N 106 5 E
Bayana, *India* **42 F7** 26 55N 77 18 E
Bayanaūyl, *Kazakstan* **26 D8** 50 45N 75 45 E
Bayandalay, *Mongolia* **34 C2** 43 30N 103 29 E
Bayanhongor, *Mongolia* **32 B5** 46 8N 102 43 E
Bayard, *N. Mex., U.S.A.* **83 K9** 32 46N 108 8W
Bayard, *Nebr., U.S.A.* **80 E3** 41 45N 103 20W
Baybay, *Phil.* **37 B6** 10 40N 124 55 E
Bayern □, *Germany* **16 D6** 48 50N 12 0 E
Bayeux, *France* **18 B3** 49 17N 0 42W
Bayfield, *Canada* **78 C3** 43 34N 81 42W
Bayfield, *U.S.A.* **80 B9** 46 49N 90 49W
Bayındır, *Turkey* **21 E12** 38 13N 27 39 E
Baykal, Oz., *Russia* **27 D11** 53 0N 108 0 E
Baykan, *Turkey* **44 B4** 38 7N 41 44 E
Baykonur = Bayqongyr, *Kazakstan* **26 E7** 47 48N 65 50 E
Baymak, *Russia* **24 D10** 52 36N 58 19 E
Baynes Mts., *Namibia* **56 B1** 17 15S 13 0 E
Bayombong, *Phil.* **37 A6** 16 30N 121 10 E
Bayonne, *France* **18 E3** 43 30N 1 28W
Bayonne, *U.S.A.* **79 F10** 40 40N 74 7W
Bayovar, *Peru* **92 E2** 5 50S 81 0W
Bayqongyr, *Kazakstan* **26 E7** 47 48N 65 50 E
Bayram-Ali = Bayramaly, *Turkmenistan* **26 F7** 37 37N 62 10 E
Bayramaly, *Turkmenistan* **26 F7** 37 37N 62 10 E
Bayramiç, *Turkey* **21 E12** 39 48N 26 36 E
Bayreuth, *Germany* **16 D6** 49 56N 11 35 E
Bayrūt, *Lebanon* **47 B4** 33 53N 35 31 E
Bays, L. of, *Canada* **78 A5** 45 15N 79 4W
Baysville, *Canada* **78 A5** 45 9N 79 7W
Bayt Lahm, *West Bank* **47 D4** 31 43N 35 12 E
Baytown, *U.S.A.* **81 L7** 29 43N 94 59W
Baza, *Spain* **19 D4** 37 30N 2 47W
Bazaruto, I. do, *Mozam.* **57 C6** 21 40S 35 28 E
Bazhou, *China* **34 E9** 39 8N 116 22 E
Bazmān, Kūh-e, *Iran* **45 D9** 28 4N 60 1 E
Beach, *U.S.A.* **80 B3** 46 58N 104 0W
Beach City, *U.S.A.* **78 F3** 40 39N 81 35W
Beachport, *Australia* **63 F3** 37 29S 140 0 E
Beachy Hd., *U.K.* **11 G8** 50 44N 0 15 E
Beacon, *Australia* **61 F2** 30 26S 117 52 E
Beacon, *U.S.A.* **79 E11** 41 30N 73 58W
Beaconsfield, *Australia* **62 G4** 41 11S 146 48 E
Beagle, Canal, *S. Amer.* **96 H3** 55 0S 68 30W
Beagle Bay, *Australia* **60 C3** 16 58S 122 40 E
Bealanana, *Madag.* **57 A8** 14 33S 48 44 E
Beals Cr. →, *U.S.A.* **81 J4** 32 10N 100 51W
Beamsville, *Canada* **78 C5** 43 12N 79 28W
Bear →, *Calif., U.S.A.* **84 G5** 38 56N 121 36W
Bear →, *Utah, U.S.A.* **74 B4** 41 30N 112 8W
Bear I., *Ireland* **13 E2** 51 38N 9 50W
Bear L., *Canada* **73 B9** 55 8N 96 0W
Bear L., *U.S.A.* **82 F8** 41 59N 111 21W
Beardmore, *Canada* **70 C2** 49 36N 87 57W
Beardmore Glacier, *Antarctica* **5 E11** 84 30S 170 0 E
Beardstown, *U.S.A.* **80 F9** 40 1N 90 26W
Bearma →, *India* **43 G8** 24 20N 79 51 E
Béarn, *France* **18 E3** 43 20N 0 30W
Bearpaw Mts., *U.S.A.* **82 B9** 48 12N 109 30W
Bearskin Lake, *Canada* **70 B1** 53 58N 91 2W
Beas →, *India* **42 D6** 31 10N 74 59 E
Beata, C., *Dom. Rep.* **89 C5** 17 40N 71 30W
Beata, I., *Dom. Rep.* **89 C5** 17 34N 71 31W
Beatrice, *U.S.A.* **80 E6** 40 16N 96 45W
Beatrice, *Zimbabwe* **55 F3** 18 15S 30 55 E
Beatrice, C., *Australia* **62 A2** 14 20S 136 55 E
Beatton →, *Canada* **72 B4** 56 15N 120 45W
Beatton River, *Canada* **72 B4** 57 26N 121 20W
Beatty, *U.S.A.* **84 J10** 36 54N 116 46W
Beauce, Plaine de la, *France* **18 B4** 48 10N 1 45 E
Beauceville, *Canada* **71 C5** 46 13N 70 46W
Beaudesert, *Australia* **63 D5** 27 59S 153 0 E
Beaufort, *Malaysia* **36 C5** 5 30N 115 40 E
Beaufort, *N.C., U.S.A.* **77 H7** 34 43N 76 40W
Beaufort, *S.C., U.S.A.* **77 J5** 32 26N 80 40W
Beaufort Sea, *Arctic* **4 B1** 72 0N 140 0W
Beaufort West, *S. Africa* **56 E3** 32 18S 22 36 E
Beauharnois, *Canada* **79 A11** 45 20N 73 52W
Beaulieu →, *Canada* **72 A6** 62 3N 113 11W
Beauly, *U.K.* **12 D4** 57 30N 4 28W
Beauly →, *U.K.* **12 D4** 57 29N 4 27W
Beaumaris, *U.K.* **10 D3** 53 16N 4 6W
Beaumont, *Belgium* **15 D4** 50 15N 4 14 E
Beaumont, *U.S.A.* **81 K7** 30 5N 94 6W
Beaune, *France* **18 C6** 47 2N 4 50 E
Beaupré, *Canada* **71 C5** 47 3N 70 54W
Beauraing, *Belgium* **15 D4** 50 7N 4 57 E
Beauséjour, *Canada* **73 C9** 50 5N 96 35W
Beauvais, *France* **18 B5** 49 25N 2 8 E
Beauval, *Canada* **73 B7** 55 9N 107 37W
Beaver, *Okla., U.S.A.* **81 G4** 36 49N 100 31W
Beaver, *Pa., U.S.A.* **78 F4** 40 42N 80 19W
Beaver, *Utah, U.S.A.* **83 G7** 38 17N 112 38W
Beaver →, *B.C., Canada* **72 B4** 59 52N 124 20W
Beaver →, *Ont., Canada* **70 A2** 55 55N 87 48W
Beaver →, *Sask., Canada* **73 B7** 55 26N 107 45W
Beaver →, *U.S.A.* **81 G5** 36 35N 99 30W
Beaver City, *U.S.A.* **80 E5** 40 8N 99 50W
Beaver Creek, *Canada* **68 B5** 63 0N 141 0W
Beaver Dam, *U.S.A.* **80 D10** 43 28N 88 50W
Beaver Falls, *U.S.A.* **78 F4** 40 46N 80 20W
Beaver Hill L., *Canada* **73 C10** 54 5N 94 50W
Beaver I., *U.S.A.* **76 C3** 45 40N 85 33W
Beaverhill L., *Canada* **72 C6** 53 27N 112 32W
Beaverlodge, *Canada* **72 B5** 55 11N 119 29W
Beaverstone →, *Canada* **70 B2** 54 59N 89 25W
Beaverton, *Canada* **78 B5** 44 26N 79 9W
Beaverton, *U.S.A.* **84 E4** 45 29N 122 48W
Beawar, *India* **42 F6** 26 3N 74 18 E
Bebedouro, *Brazil* **95 A6** 21 0S 48 25W
Beboa, *Madag.* **57 B7** 17 22S 44 33 E
Beccles, *U.K.* **11 E9** 52 27N 1 35 E
Bečej, *Serbia, Yug.* **21 B9** 45 36N 20 3 E
Béchar, *Algeria* **50 B5** 31 38N 2 18W
Beckley, *U.S.A.* **76 G5** 37 47N 81 11W
Beddouza, Ras, *Morocco* **50 B4** 32 33N 9 9W
Bedford, *Canada* **79 A12** 45 7N 72 59W
Bedford, *S. Africa* **56 E4** 32 40S 26 10 E
Bedford, *U.K.* **11 E7** 52 8N 0 28W
Bedford, *Ind., U.S.A.* **76 F2** 38 52N 86 29W
Bedford, *Iowa, U.S.A.* **80 E7** 40 40N 94 44W
Bedford, *Ohio, U.S.A.* **78 E3** 41 23N 81 32W
Bedford, *Pa., U.S.A.* **78 F6** 40 1N 78 30W
Bedford, *Va., U.S.A.* **76 G6** 37 20N 79 31W
Bedford, C., *Australia* **62 B4** 15 14S 145 21 E
Bedfordshire □, *U.K.* **11 E7** 52 4N 0 28W
Bedourie, *Australia* **62 C2** 24 30S 139 30 E
Bedum, *Neths.* **15 A6** 53 18N 6 36 E
Beebe Plain, *Canada* **79 A12** 45 1N 72 9W
Beech Creek, *U.S.A.* **78 E7** 41 5N 77 36W
Beenleigh, *Australia* **63 D5** 27 43S 153 10 E
Be'er Menuha, *Israel* **44 D2** 30 19N 35 8 E
Be'er Sheva, *Israel* **47 D3** 31 15N 34 48 E
Beersheba = Be'er Sheva, *Israel* **47 D3** 31 15N 34 48 E
Beeston, *U.K.* **10 E6** 52 56N 1 14W
Beeville, *U.S.A.* **81 L6** 28 24N 97 45W
Befale, *Dem. Rep. of the Congo* **52 D4** 0 25N 20 45 E
Befandriana, *Madag.* **57 C7** 21 55S 44 0 E
Befotaka, *Madag.* **57 C8** 23 49S 47 0 E
Bega, *Australia* **63 F4** 36 41S 149 51 E
Begusarai, *India* **43 G12** 25 24N 86 9 E
Behābād, *Iran* **45 C8** 32 24N 59 47 E
Behala, *India* **43 H13** 22 30N 88 20 E
Behara, *Madag.* **57 C8** 24 55S 46 20 E
Behbehān, *Iran* **45 D6** 30 30N 50 15 E
Behm Canal, *U.S.A.* **72 B2** 55 10N 131 0W
Behshahr, *Iran* **45 B7** 36 45N 53 35 E
Bei Jiang →, *China* **33 D6** 23 2N 112 58 E
Bei'an, *China* **33 B7** 48 10N 126 20 E
Beihai, *China* **33 D5** 21 28N 109 6 E
Beijing, *China* **34 E9** 39 55N 116 20 E
Beijing □, *China* **34 E9** 39 55N 116 20 E
Beilen, *Neths.* **15 B6** 52 52N 6 27 E
Beilpajah, *Australia* **63 E3** 32 54S 143 52 E
Beinn na Faoghla = Benbecula, *U.K.* **12 D1** 57 26N 7 21W
Beipiao, *China* **35 D11** 41 52N 120 32 E
Beira, *Mozam.* **55 F3** 19 50S 34 52 E
Beirut = Bayrūt, *Lebanon* **47 B4** 33 53N 35 31 E
Beiseker, *Canada* **72 C6** 51 23N 113 32W
Beitaolaizhao, *China* **35 B13** 44 58N 125 58 E
Beitbridge, *Zimbabwe* **55 G3** 22 12S 30 0 E
Beizhen = Binzhou, *China* **35 F10** 37 20N 118 2 E
Beizhen, *China* **35 D11** 41 38N 121 54 E
Beizhengzhen, *China* **35 B12** 44 31N 123 30 E
Beja, *Portugal* **19 C2** 38 2N 7 53W
Béja, *Tunisia* **51 A7** 36 43N 9 12 E
Bejaia, *Algeria* **50 A7** 36 42N 5 2 E
Béjar, *Spain* **19 B3** 40 23N 5 46W
Bejestān, *Iran* **45 C8** 34 30N 58 5 E
Békéscsaba, *Hungary* **17 E11** 46 40N 21 5 E
Bekily, *Madag.* **57 C8** 24 13S 45 19 E
Bekok, *Malaysia* **39 L4** 2 20N 103 7 E
Bela, *India* **43 G10** 25 50N 82 0 E
Bela, *Pakistan* **42 F2** 26 12N 66 20 E
Bela Crkva, *Serbia, Yug.* **21 B9** 44 55N 21 27 E
Bela Vista, *Brazil* **94 A4** 22 12S 56 20W
Bela Vista, *Mozam.* **57 D5** 26 10S 32 44 E
Belan →, *India* **43 G9** 24 2N 81 45 E
Belarus ■, *Europe* **17 B14** 53 30N 27 0 E
Belau = Palau ■, *Pac. Oc.* **28 J17** 7 30N 134 30 E
Belavenona, *Madag.* **57 C8** 24 50S 47 4 E
Belawan, *Indonesia* **36 D1** 3 33N 98 32 E
Belaya →, *Russia* **24 C9** 54 40N 56 0 E
Belaya Tserkov = Bila Tserkva, *Ukraine* **17 D16** 49 45N 30 10 E
Belcher Is., *Canada* **70 A3** 56 15N 78 45W
Belden, *U.S.A.* **84 E5** 40 2N 121 17W
Belebey, *Russia* **24 D9** 54 7N 54 7 E
Belém, *Brazil* **93 D9** 1 20S 48 30W
Belén, *Argentina* **94 B2** 27 40S 67 5W
Belén, *Paraguay* **94 A4** 23 30S 57 6W
Belen, *U.S.A.* **83 J10** 34 40N 106 46W
Belet Uen, *Somali Rep.* **46 G4** 4 30N 45 5 E
Belev, *Russia* **24 D6** 53 50N 36 5 E
Belfair, *U.S.A.* **84 C4** 47 27N 122 50W
Belfast, *S. Africa* **57 D5** 25 42S 30 2 E
Belfast, *U.K.* **13 B6** 54 37N 5 56W

Big Timber

Belfast, Maine, U.S.A. 77 C11 44 26N 69 1W
Belfast, N.Y., U.S.A. 78 D6 42 21N 78 7W
Belfast L., U.K. 13 B6 54 40N 5 50W
Belfield, U.S.A. 80 B3 46 53N 103 12W
Belfort, France 18 C7 47 38N 6 50 E
Belfry, U.S.A. 82 D9 45 9N 109 1W
Belgaum, India 40 M9 15 55N 74 35 E
Belgium ■, Europe 15 D4 50 30N 5 0 E
Belgorod, Russia 25 D6 50 35N 36 35 E
Belgorod-Dnestrovskiy = Bilhorod-Dnistrovskyy, Ukraine 25 E5 46 11N 30 23 E
Belgrade = Beograd, Serbia, Yug. 21 B9 44 50N 20 37 E
Belgrade, U.S.A. 82 D8 45 47N 111 11W
Belhaven, U.S.A. 77 H7 35 33N 76 37W
Beli Drim →, Europe 21 C9 42 6N 20 25 E
Belinyu, Indonesia 36 E3 1 35S 105 50 E
Beliton Is. = Belitung, Indonesia 36 E3 3 10S 107 50 E
Belitung, Indonesia 36 E3 3 10S 107 50 E
Belize ■, Cent. Amer. 87 D7 17 0N 88 30W
Belize City, Belize 87 D7 17 25N 88 0W
Belkovskiy, Ostrov, Russia 27 B14 75 32N 135 44 E
Bell →, Canada 70 C4 49 48N 77 38W
Bell I., Canada 71 B8 50 46N 55 35W
Bell-Irving →, Canada 72 B3 56 12N 129 5W
Bell Peninsula, Canada 69 B11 63 50N 82 0W
Bell Ville, Argentina 94 C3 32 40S 62 40W
Bella Bella, Canada 72 C3 52 10N 128 10W
Bella Coola, Canada 72 C3 52 25N 126 40W
Bella Unión, Uruguay 94 C4 30 15S 57 40W
Bella Vista, Corrientes, Argentina 94 B4 28 33S 59 0W
Bella Vista, Tucuman, Argentina 94 B2 27 10S 65 25W
Bellaire, U.S.A. 78 F4 40 1N 80 45W
Bellary, India 40 M10 15 10N 76 56 E
Bellata, Australia 63 D4 29 53S 149 46 E
Belle-Chasse, U.S.A. 81 L10 29 51N 89 59W
Belle Fourche, U.S.A. 80 C3 44 40N 103 51W
Belle Fourche →, U.S.A. 80 C3 44 26N 102 18W
Belle Glade, U.S.A. 77 M5 26 41N 80 40W
Belle-Île, France 18 C2 47 20N 3 10W
Belle Isle, Canada 71 B8 51 57N 55 25W
Belle Isle, Str. of, Canada 71 B8 51 30N 56 30W
Belle Plaine, U.S.A. 80 E8 41 54N 92 17W
Bellefontaine, U.S.A. 76 E4 40 22N 83 46W
Bellefonte, U.S.A. 78 F7 40 55N 77 47W
Belleoram, Canada 71 C8 47 31N 55 25W
Belleville, Canada 78 B7 44 10N 77 23W
Belleville, Ill., U.S.A. 80 F10 38 31N 89 59W
Belleville, Kans., U.S.A. 80 F6 39 50N 97 38W
Belleville, N.Y., U.S.A. 79 C8 43 46N 76 10W
Bellevue, Canada 72 D6 49 35N 114 22W
Bellevue, Idaho, U.S.A. 82 E6 43 28N 114 16W
Bellevue, Nebr., U.S.A. 80 E7 41 8N 95 53W
Bellevue, Ohio, U.S.A. 78 E2 41 17N 82 51W
Bellevue, Wash., U.S.A. 84 C4 47 37N 122 12W
Bellin = Kangirsuk, Canada 69 C13 60 0N 70 0W
Bellingen, Australia 63 E5 30 25S 152 50 E
Bellingham, U.S.A. 68 D7 48 46N 122 29W
Bellingshausen Sea, Antarctica 5 C17 66 0S 80 0W
Bellinzona, Switz. 18 C8 46 11N 9 1 E
Bello, Colombia 92 B3 6 20N 75 33W
Bellows Falls, U.S.A. 79 C12 43 8N 72 27W
Bellpat, Pakistan 42 E3 29 0N 68 5 E
Belluno, Italy 20 A5 46 9N 12 13 E
Bellwood, U.S.A. 78 F6 40 36N 78 20W
Belmont, Canada 78 D3 42 53N 81 5W
Belmont, S. Africa 56 D3 29 28S 24 22 E
Belmont, U.S.A. 78 D6 42 14N 78 2W
Belmonte, Brazil 93 G11 16 0S 39 0W
Belmopan, Belize 87 D7 17 18N 88 30W
Belmullet, Ireland 13 B2 54 14N 9 58W
Belo Horizonte, Brazil 93 G10 19 55S 43 56W
Belo-sur-Mer, Madag. 57 C7 20 42S 44 0 E
Belo-Tsiribihina, Madag. 57 B7 19 40S 44 30 E
Belogorsk, Russia 27 D13 51 0N 128 20 E
Beloha, Madag. 57 D8 25 10S 45 3 E
Beloit, Kans., U.S.A. 80 F5 39 28N 98 6W
Beloit, Wis., U.S.A. 80 D10 42 31N 89 2W
Belokorovichi, Ukraine 17 C15 51 7N 28 2 E
Belomorsk, Russia 24 B5 64 35N 34 54 E
Belonia, India 41 H17 23 15N 91 30 E
Beloretsk, Russia 24 D10 53 58N 58 24 E
Belorussia = Belarus ■, Europe 17 B14 53 30N 27 0 E
Belovo, Russia 26 D9 54 30N 86 0 E
Beloye, Ozero, Russia 24 B6 60 10N 37 35 E
Beloye More, Russia 24 A6 66 30N 38 0 E
Belozersk, Russia 24 B6 60 1N 37 45 E
Belpre, U.S.A. 76 F5 39 17N 81 34W
Belrain, India 43 E9 28 23N 80 55 E
Belt, U.S.A. 82 C8 47 23N 110 55W
Beltana, Australia 63 E2 30 48S 138 25 E
Belterra, Brazil 93 D8 2 45S 55 0W
Belton, U.S.A. 81 K6 31 3N 97 28W
Belton L., U.S.A. 81 K6 31 8N 97 32W
Beltsy = Bălţi, Moldova 17 E14 47 48N 27 58 E
Belturbet, Ireland 13 B4 54 6N 7 26W
Belukha, Russia 26 E9 49 50N 86 50 E
Beluran, Malaysia 36 C5 5 48N 117 35 E
Belvidere, Ill., U.S.A. 80 D10 42 15N 88 50W
Belvidere, N.J., U.S.A. 79 F9 40 50N 75 5W
Belyando →, Australia 62 C4 21 38S 146 50 E
Belyy, Ostrov, Russia 26 B8 73 30N 71 0 E
Belyy Yar, Russia 26 D9 58 26N 84 39 E
Belzoni, U.S.A. 81 J9 33 11N 90 29W
Bemaraha, Lembalemban' i, Madag. 57 B7 18 40S 44 45 E
Bemarivo, Madag. 57 C7 21 45S 44 45 E
Bemarivo →, Madag. 57 B8 15 27S 47 40 E
Bemavo, Madag. 57 C8 21 33S 45 25 E
Bembéréke, Benin 50 F6 10 11N 2 43 E
Bembesi, Zimbabwe 55 G2 20 0S 28 58 E
Bembesi →, Zimbabwe 55 F2 18 57S 27 47 E
Bemetara, India 43 J9 21 42N 81 32 E
Bemidji, U.S.A. 80 B7 47 28N 94 53W
Ben, Iran 45 C6 32 32N 50 45 E
Ben Cruachan, U.K. 12 E3 56 26N 5 8W
Ben Dearg, U.K. 12 D4 57 47N 4 56W
Ben Hope, U.K. 12 C4 58 25N 4 36W
Ben Lawers, U.K. 12 E4 56 32N 4 14W
Ben Lomond, N.S.W., Australia 63 E5 30 1S 151 43 E
Ben Lomond, Tas., Australia 62 G4 41 38S 147 42 E
Ben Lomond, U.K. 12 E4 56 11N 4 38W
Ben Luc, Vietnam 39 G6 10 39N 106 29 E
Ben Macdhui, U.K. 12 D5 57 4N 3 40W
Ben Mhor, U.K. 12 D1 57 15N 7 18W
Ben More, Arg. & Bute, U.K. 12 E2 56 26N 6 1W
Ben More, Stirl., U.K. 12 E4 56 23N 4 32W
Ben More Assynt, U.K. 12 C4 58 8N 4 52W
Ben Nevis, U.K. 12 E3 56 48N 5 1W
Ben Quang, Vietnam 38 D6 17 3N 106 55 E
Ben Vorlich, U.K. 12 E4 56 21N 4 14W
Ben Wyvis, U.K. 12 D4 57 40N 4 35W
Bena, Nigeria 50 F7 11 20N 5 50 E
Benalla, Australia 63 F4 36 30S 146 0 E
Benares = Varanasi, India 43 G10 25 22N 83 0 E
Benavente, Spain 19 A3 42 2N 5 43W
Benavides, U.S.A. 81 M5 27 36N 98 25W
Benbecula, U.K. 12 D1 57 26N 7 21W
Benbonyathe, Australia 63 E2 30 25S 139 11 E
Bend, U.S.A. 82 D3 44 4N 121 19W
Bendemeer, Australia 63 E5 30 53S 151 8 E
Bender Beila, Somali Rep. 46 F5 9 30N 50 48 E
Bendery = Tighina, Moldova 17 E15 46 50N 29 30 E
Bendigo, Australia 63 F3 36 40S 144 15 E
Bené Beraq, Israel 47 C3 32 6N 34 51 E
Benenitra, Madag. 57 C8 23 27S 45 5 E
Benevento, Italy 20 D6 41 8N 14 45 E
Benga, Mozam. 55 F3 16 11S 33 40 E
Bengal, Bay of, Ind. Oc. 41 M17 15 0N 90 0 E
Bengbu, China 35 H9 32 58N 117 20 E
Benghazi = Banghāzī, Libya 51 B10 32 11N 20 3 E
Bengkalis, Indonesia 36 D2 1 30N 102 10 E
Bengkulu, Indonesia 36 E2 3 50S 102 12 E
Bengkulu □, Indonesia 36 E2 3 48S 102 16 E
Bengough, Canada 73 D7 49 25N 105 10W
Benguela, Angola 53 G2 12 37S 13 25 E
Benguérua, I., Mozam. 57 C6 21 58S 35 28 E
Beni, Dem. Rep. of the Congo 54 B2 0 30N 29 27 E
Beni →, Bolivia 92 F5 10 23S 65 24W
Beni Mellal, Morocco 50 B4 32 21N 6 21W
Beni Suef, Egypt 51 C12 29 5N 31 6 E
Beniah L., Canada 72 A6 63 23N 112 17W
Benicia, U.S.A. 84 G4 38 3N 122 9W
Benidorm, Spain 19 C5 38 33N 0 9W
Benin ■, Africa 50 G6 10 0N 2 0 E
Benin, Bight of, W. Afr. 50 H6 5 0N 3 0 E
Benin City, Nigeria 50 G7 6 20N 5 31 E
Benitses, Greece 23 A3 39 32N 19 55 E
Benjamin Aceval, Paraguay 94 A4 24 58S 57 34W
Benjamin Constant, Brazil 92 D4 4 40S 70 15W
Benjamin Hill, Mexico 86 A2 30 10N 111 10W
Benkelman, U.S.A. 80 E4 40 3N 101 32W
Bennett, Canada 72 B2 59 56N 134 53W
Bennett, L., Australia 60 D5 22 50S 131 2 E
Bennetta, Ostrov, Russia 27 B15 76 21N 148 56 E
Bennettsville, U.S.A. 77 H6 34 37N 79 41W
Bennington, N.H., U.S.A. 79 D11 43 0N 71 55W
Bennington, Vt., U.S.A. 79 D11 42 53N 73 12W
Benoni, S. Africa 57 D4 26 11S 28 18 E
Benque Viejo, Belize 87 D7 17 5N 89 8W
Benson, Ariz., U.S.A. 83 L8 31 58N 110 18W
Benson, Minn., U.S.A. 80 C7 45 19N 95 36W
Bent, Iran 45 E8 26 20N 59 31 E
Benteng, Indonesia 37 F6 6 10S 120 30 E
Bentinck I., Australia 62 B2 17 3S 139 35 E
Bento Gonçalves, Brazil 95 B5 29 10S 51 31W
Benton, Ark., U.S.A. 81 H8 34 34N 92 35W
Benton, Calif., U.S.A. 84 H8 37 48N 118 32W
Benton, Ill., U.S.A. 80 G10 38 0N 88 55W
Benton, Pa., U.S.A. 79 E8 41 12N 76 23W
Benton Harbor, U.S.A. 76 D2 42 6N 86 27W
Bentonville, U.S.A. 81 G7 36 22N 94 13W
Bentung, Malaysia 39 L3 3 31N 101 55 E
Benue →, Nigeria 50 G7 7 48N 6 46 E
Benxi, China 35 D12 41 20N 123 48 E
Beo, Indonesia 37 D7 4 25N 126 50 E
Beograd, Serbia, Yug. 21 B9 44 50N 20 37 E
Beppu, Japan 31 H5 33 15N 131 30 E
Beqaa Valley = Al Biqā, Lebanon 47 A5 34 10N 36 10 E
Ber Mota, India 42 H3 23 27N 68 34 E
Berach →, India 42 G6 25 15N 75 2 E
Berati, Albania 21 D8 40 43N 19 59 E
Berau, Teluk, Indonesia 37 E8 2 30S 132 30 E
Berber, Sudan 51 E12 18 0N 34 0 E
Berbera, Somali Rep. 46 E4 10 30N 45 2 E
Berbérati, C.A.R. 52 D3 4 15N 15 40 E
Berbice →, Guyana 92 B7 6 20N 57 32W
Berdichev = Berdychiv, Ukraine 17 D15 49 57N 28 30 E
Berdsk, Russia 26 D9 54 47N 83 2 E
Berdyansk, Ukraine 25 E6 46 45N 36 50 E
Berdychiv, Ukraine 17 D15 49 57N 28 30 E
Berea, U.S.A. 76 G3 37 34N 84 17W
Berebere, Indonesia 37 D7 2 25N 128 45 E
Bereda, Somali Rep. 46 E5 11 45N 51 0 E
Berehove, Ukraine 17 D12 48 15N 22 35 E
Berekum, Ghana 50 G5 7 29N 2 34W
Berens →, Canada 73 C9 52 25N 97 2W
Berens I., Canada 73 C9 52 18N 97 18W
Berens River, Canada 73 C9 52 25N 97 0W
Beresford, U.S.A. 80 D6 43 5N 96 47W
Berestechko, Ukraine 17 C13 50 22N 25 5 E
Berevo, Mahajanga, Madag. 57 B7 17 14S 44 17 E
Berevo, Toliara, Madag. 57 B7 19 44S 44 58 E
Bereza, Belarus 17 B13 52 31N 24 51 E
Berezhany, Ukraine 17 D13 49 26N 24 58 E
Berezina = Byarezina →, Belarus 17 B16 52 33N 30 14 E
Bereznik, Russia 24 B7 62 51N 42 40 E
Berezniki, Russia 24 C10 59 24N 56 46 E
Berezovo, Russia 26 C7 64 0N 65 0 E
Berga, Spain 19 A6 42 6N 1 48 E
Bergama, Turkey 21 E12 39 8N 27 11 E
Bérgamo, Italy 18 D8 45 41N 9 43 E
Bergen, Neths. 15 B4 52 40N 4 43 E
Bergen, Norway 9 F11 60 20N 5 20 E
Bergen, U.S.A. 78 C7 43 5N 77 57W
Bergen op Zoom, Neths. 15 C4 51 28N 4 18 E
Bergerac, France 18 D4 44 51N 0 30 E
Bergholz, U.S.A. 78 F4 40 31N 80 53W
Bergisch Gladbach, Germany 15 D7 50 59N 7 8 E
Bergville, S. Africa 57 D4 28 52S 29 18 E
Berhala, Selat, Indonesia 36 E2 1 0S 104 15 E
Berhampore = Baharampur, India 43 G13 24 2N 88 27 E
Berhampur = Brahmapur, India 41 K14 19 15N 84 54 E
Bering Sea, Pac. Oc. 68 C1 58 0N 171 0 E
Bering Strait, Pac. Oc. 68 B3 65 30N 169 0W
Beringovskiy, Russia 27 C18 63 3N 179 19 E
Berisso, Argentina 94 C4 34 56S 57 50W
Berja, Spain 19 D4 36 50N 2 56W
Berkeley, U.S.A. 84 H4 37 52N 122 16W
Berkner I., Antarctica 5 D18 79 30S 50 0W
Berkshire, U.S.A. 79 D8 42 19N 76 11W
Berkshire Downs, U.K. 11 F6 51 33N 1 29W
Berlin, Germany 16 B7 52 30N 13 25 E
Berlin, Md., U.S.A. 76 F8 38 20N 75 13W
Berlin, N.H., U.S.A. 79 B13 44 28N 71 11W
Berlin, N.Y., U.S.A. 79 D11 42 42N 73 23W
Berlin, Wis., U.S.A. 76 D1 43 58N 88 57W
Berlin L., U.S.A. 78 E4 41 3N 81 0W
Bermejo →, Formosa, Argentina 94 B4 26 51S 58 23W
Bermejo →, San Juan, Argentina 94 C2 32 30S 67 30W
Bermen, L., Canada 71 B6 53 35N 68 55W
Bermuda ■, Atl. Oc. 66 F13 32 45N 65 0W
Bern, Switz. 18 C7 46 57N 7 28 E
Bernalillo, U.S.A. 83 J10 35 18N 106 33W
Bernardo de Irigoyen, Argentina 95 B5 26 15S 53 40W
Bernardo O'Higgins □, Chile 94 C1 34 15S 70 45W
Bernardsville, U.S.A. 79 F10 40 43N 74 34W
Bernasconi, Argentina 94 D3 37 55S 63 44W
Bernburg, Germany 16 C6 51 47N 11 44 E
Berne = Bern, Switz. 18 C7 46 57N 7 28 E
Berneray, U.K. 12 D1 57 43N 7 11W
Bernier I., Australia 61 D1 24 50S 113 12 E
Bernina, Piz, Switz. 18 C8 46 20N 9 54 E
Beroroha, Madag. 57 C8 21 40S 45 10 E
Beroun, Czech Rep. 16 D8 49 57N 14 5 E
Berri, Australia 63 E3 34 14S 140 35 E
Berriane, Algeria 50 B6 32 50N 3 46 E
Berrigan, Australia 63 F4 35 38S 145 49 E
Berry, Australia 63 E5 34 46S 150 43 E
Berry, France 18 C5 46 50N 2 0 E
Berry Is., Bahamas 88 A4 25 40N 77 50W
Berryessa L., U.S.A. 84 G4 38 31N 122 6W
Berryville, U.S.A. 81 G8 36 22N 93 34W
Bershad, Ukraine 17 D15 48 22N 29 31 E
Berthold, U.S.A. 80 A4 48 19N 101 44W
Berthoud, U.S.A. 80 E2 40 19N 105 5W
Bertoua, Cameroon 52 D2 4 30N 13 45 E
Bertraghboy B., Ireland 13 C2 53 22N 9 54W
Berwick, U.S.A. 79 E8 41 3N 76 14W
Berwick-upon-Tweed, U.K. 10 B6 55 46N 2 0W
Berwyn Mts., U.K. 10 E4 52 54N 3 26W
Besal, Pakistan 43 B5 35 4N 73 56 E
Besalampy, Madag. 57 B7 16 43S 44 29 E
Besançon, France 18 C7 47 15N 6 2 E
Besar, Indonesia 36 E5 2 40S 116 0 E
Besnard L., Canada 73 B7 55 25N 106 0W
Besni, Turkey 44 B3 37 41N 37 52 E
Besor, N. →, Egypt 47 D3 31 28N 34 22 E
Bessarabiya, Moldova 17 E15 47 0N 28 10 E
Bessarabka = Basarabeasca, Moldova 17 E15 46 21N 28 58 E
Bessemer, Ala., U.S.A. 77 J2 33 24N 86 58W
Bessemer, Mich., U.S.A. 80 B9 46 29N 90 3W
Bessemer, Pa., U.S.A. 78 F4 40 59N 80 30W
Beswick, Australia 60 B5 14 34S 132 53 E
Bet She'an, Israel 47 C4 32 30N 35 30 E
Bet Shemesh, Israel 47 D4 31 44N 35 0 E
Betafo, Madag. 57 B8 19 50S 46 51 E
Betancuria, Canary Is. 22 F5 28 25N 14 3W
Betanzos, Spain 19 A1 43 15N 8 12W
Bétaré Oya, Cameroon 52 C2 5 40N 14 5 E
Bethal, S. Africa 57 D4 26 27S 29 28 E
Bethanien, Namibia 56 D2 26 31S 17 8 E
Bethany, Canada 78 B6 44 11N 78 34W
Bethany, U.S.A. 80 E7 40 16N 94 2W
Bethel, Alaska, U.S.A. 68 B3 60 48N 161 45W
Bethel, Conn., U.S.A. 79 E11 41 22N 73 25W
Bethel, Maine, U.S.A. 79 B14 44 25N 70 47W
Bethel, Vt., U.S.A. 79 C12 43 50N 72 38W
Bethel Park, U.S.A. 78 F4 40 20N 80 1W
Bethlehem = Bayt Lahm, West Bank 47 D4 31 43N 35 12 E
Bethlehem, S. Africa 57 D4 28 14S 28 18 E
Bethlehem, U.S.A. 79 F9 40 37N 75 23W
Bethulie, S. Africa 56 E4 30 30S 25 59 E
Béthune, France 18 A5 50 30N 2 38 E
Betioky, Madag. 57 C7 23 48S 44 20 E
Betong, Thailand 39 K3 5 45N 101 5 E
Betoota, Australia 62 D3 25 45S 140 42 E
Betroka, Madag. 57 C8 23 16S 46 0 E
Betsiamites, Canada 71 C6 48 56N 68 40W
Betsiamites →, Canada 71 C6 48 56N 68 38W
Betsiboka →, Madag. 57 B8 16 3S 46 36 E
Bettendorf, U.S.A. 80 E9 41 32N 90 30W
Bettiah, India 43 F11 26 48N 84 33 E
Betul, India 40 J10 21 58N 77 59 E
Betung, Malaysia 36 D4 1 24N 111 31 E
Betws-y-Coed, U.K. 10 D4 53 5N 3 48W
Beulah, Mich., U.S.A. 76 C2 44 38N 86 6W
Beulah, N. Dak., U.S.A. 80 B4 47 16N 101 47W
Beveren, Belgium 15 C4 51 12N 4 16 E
Beverley, Australia 61 F2 32 9S 116 56 E
Beverley, U.K. 10 D7 53 51N 0 26W
Beverley Hills, U.S.A. 77 L4 28 56N 82 28W
Beverly, U.S.A. 79 D14 42 33N 70 53W
Beverly Hills, U.S.A. 85 L8 34 4N 118 25W
Bewas →, India 43 H8 23 59N 79 21 E
Bexhill, U.K. 11 G8 50 51N 0 29 E
Beyānlū, Iran 44 C5 36 0N 47 51 E
Beyneu, Kazakstan 25 E10 45 18N 55 9 E
Beypazarı, Turkey 25 F5 40 10N 31 56 E
Beyşehir Gölü, Turkey 25 G5 37 41N 31 33 E
Béziers, France 18 E5 43 20N 3 12 E
Bezwada = Vijayawada, India 41 L12 16 31N 80 39 E
Bhabua, India 43 G10 25 3N 83 37 E
Bhachau, India 40 H7 23 20N 70 16 E
Bhadar →, Gujarat, India 42 H5 22 17N 72 20 E
Bhadar →, Gujarat, India 42 J3 21 27N 69 47 E
Bhadarwah, India 43 C6 32 58N 75 46 E
Bhadohi, India 43 G10 25 25N 82 34 E
Bhadra, India 42 E6 29 8N 75 14 E
Bhadrakh, India 41 J15 21 10N 86 30 E
Bhadran, India 42 H5 22 19N 72 6 E
Bhadravati, India 40 N9 13 49N 75 40 E
Bhag, Pakistan 42 E2 29 2N 67 49 E
Bhagalpur, India 43 G12 25 10N 87 0 E
Bhagirathi →, Ut. P., India 43 D8 30 8N 78 35 E
Bhagirathi →, W. Bengal, India 43 H13 23 25N 88 23 E
Bhakkar, Pakistan 42 D4 31 40N 71 5 E
Bhakra Dam, India 42 D7 31 30N 76 45 E
Bhamo, Burma 41 G20 24 15N 97 15 E
Bhandara, India 40 J11 21 5N 79 42 E
Bhanpura, India 42 G6 24 31N 75 44 E
Bhanrer Ra., India 43 H8 23 40N 79 45 E
Bhaptiahi, India 43 F12 26 19N 86 44 E
Bharat = India ■, Asia 40 K11 20 0N 78 0 E
Bharatpur, Mad. P., India 43 H9 23 44N 81 46 E
Bharatpur, Raj., India 42 F7 27 15N 77 30 E
Bharno, India 43 H11 23 14N 84 53 E
Bhatinda, India 42 D6 30 15N 74 57 E
Bhatpara, India 43 H13 22 50N 88 25 E
Bhattu, India 42 E6 29 36N 75 19 E
Bhaun, Pakistan 42 C5 32 55N 72 40 E
Bhaunagar = Bhavnagar, India 40 J8 21 45N 72 10 E
Bhavnagar, India 40 J8 21 45N 72 10 E
Bhawanipatna, India 41 K12 19 55N 80 10 E
Bhawari, India 42 G5 25 42N 73 4 E
Bhayavadar, India 42 J4 21 51N 70 15 E
Bhera, Pakistan 42 C5 32 29N 72 57 E
Bhikangaon, India 42 J6 21 52N 75 57 E
Bhilsa = Vidisha, India 42 H7 23 28N 77 53 E
Bhilwara, India 42 G6 25 25N 74 38 E
Bhima →, India 40 L10 16 25N 77 17 E
Bhimavaram, India 41 L12 16 30N 81 30 E
Bhimbar, Pakistan 43 C6 32 59N 74 3 E
Bhind, India 43 F8 26 30N 78 46 E
Bhinga, India 43 F9 27 43N 81 56 E
Bhinmal, India 42 G5 25 0N 72 15 E
Bhiwandi, India 40 K8 19 20N 73 0 E
Bhiwani, India 42 E7 28 50N 76 9 E
Bhogava →, India 42 H5 22 26N 72 20 E
Bhola, Bangla. 41 H17 22 45N 90 35 E
Bholari, Pakistan 42 G3 25 19N 68 13 E
Bhopal, India 42 H7 23 20N 77 30 E
Bhubaneshwar, India 41 J14 20 15N 85 50 E
Bhuj, India 42 H3 23 15N 69 49 E
Bhusaval, India 40 J9 21 3N 75 46 E
Bhutan ■, Asia 41 F17 27 25N 90 30 E
Biafra, B. of = Bonny, Bight of, Africa 52 D1 3 30N 9 20 E
Biak, Indonesia 37 E9 1 10S 136 6 E
Biała Podlaska, Poland 17 B12 52 4N 23 6 E
Białogard, Poland 16 A8 54 2N 15 58 E
Białystok, Poland 17 B12 53 10N 23 10 E
Biaora, India 42 H7 23 56N 76 56 E
Bīārjmand, Iran 45 B7 36 6N 55 53 E
Biaro, Indonesia 37 D7 2 5N 125 26 E
Biarritz, France 18 E3 43 29N 1 33W
Bibai, Japan 30 C10 43 19N 141 52 E
Bibby I., Canada 73 A10 61 55N 93 0W
Biberach, Germany 16 D5 48 5N 9 47 E
Bibungwa, Dem. Rep. of the Congo 54 C2 2 40S 28 15 E
Bic, Canada 71 C6 48 20N 68 41W
Bicester, U.K. 11 F6 51 54N 1 9W
Bicheno, Australia 62 G4 41 52S 148 18 E
Bichia, India 43 H9 22 27N 80 42 E
Bickerton I., Australia 62 A2 13 45S 136 10 E
Bida, Nigeria 50 G7 9 3N 5 58 E
Bidar, India 40 L10 17 55N 77 35 E
Biddeford, U.S.A. 77 D10 43 30N 70 28W
Bideford, U.K. 11 F3 51 1N 4 13W
Bideford Bay, U.K. 11 F3 51 5N 4 20W
Bidhuna, India 43 F8 26 49N 79 31 E
Bidor, Malaysia 39 K3 4 6N 101 15 E
Bié, Planalto de, Angola 53 G3 12 0S 16 0 E
Bieber, U.S.A. 82 F3 41 7N 121 8W
Biel, Switz. 18 C7 47 8N 7 14 E
Bielefeld, Germany 16 B5 52 1N 8 33 E
Biella, Italy 18 D8 45 34N 8 3 E
Bielsk Podlaski, Poland 17 B12 52 47N 23 12 E
Bielsko-Biała, Poland 17 D10 49 50N 19 2 E
Bien Hoa, Vietnam 39 G6 10 57N 106 49 E
Bienne = Biel, Switz. 18 C7 47 8N 7 14 E
Bienville, L., Canada 70 A5 55 5N 72 40W
Biesiesfontein, S. Africa 56 E2 30 57S 17 58 E
Big →, Canada 71 B8 54 50N 58 55W
Big B., Canada 71 A7 55 43N 60 35W
Big Bear City, U.S.A. 85 L10 34 16N 116 51W
Big Bear Lake, U.S.A. 85 L10 34 15N 116 56W
Big Belt Mts., U.S.A. 82 C8 46 30N 111 25W
Big Bend, Swaziland 57 D5 26 50S 31 58 E
Big Bend National Park, U.S.A. 81 L3 29 20N 103 5W
Big Black →, U.S.A. 81 K9 32 3N 91 4W
Big Blue →, U.S.A. 80 F6 39 35N 96 34W
Big Creek, U.S.A. 84 H7 37 11N 119 14W
Big Cypress National Preserve, U.S.A. 77 M5 26 0N 81 10W
Big Cypress Swamp, U.S.A. 77 M5 26 12N 81 10W
Big Falls, U.S.A. 80 A8 48 12N 93 48W
Big Fork →, U.S.A. 80 A8 48 31N 93 43W
Big Horn Mts. = Bighorn Mts., U.S.A. 82 D10 44 30N 107 30W
Big I., Canada 72 A5 61 7N 116 45W
Big Lake, U.S.A. 81 K4 31 12N 101 28W
Big Moose, U.S.A. 79 C10 43 49N 74 58W
Big Muddy Cr. →, U.S.A. 80 A2 48 8N 104 36W
Big Pine, U.S.A. 84 H8 37 10N 118 17W
Big Piney, U.S.A. 82 E8 42 32N 110 7W
Big Rapids, U.S.A. 76 D3 43 42N 85 29W
Big Rideau L., Canada 79 B8 44 40N 76 15W
Big River, Canada 73 C7 53 50N 107 0W
Big Run, U.S.A. 78 F6 40 57N 78 55W
Big Sable Pt., U.S.A. 76 C2 44 3N 86 1W
Big Salmon →, Canada 72 A2 61 52N 134 55W
Big Sand L., Canada 73 B9 57 45N 99 45W
Big Sandy, U.S.A. 82 B8 48 11N 110 7W
Big Sandy →, U.S.A. 76 F4 38 25N 82 36W
Big Sandy Cr. →, U.S.A. 80 F3 38 7N 102 29W
Big Sioux →, U.S.A. 80 D6 42 29N 96 27W
Big Spring, U.S.A. 81 J4 32 15N 101 28W
Big Stone City, U.S.A. 80 C6 45 18N 96 28W
Big Stone Gap, U.S.A. 77 G4 36 52N 82 47W
Big Stone L., U.S.A. 80 C6 45 30N 96 35W
Big Sur, U.S.A. 84 J5 36 15N 121 48W
Big Timber, U.S.A. 82 D9 45 50N 109 57W

Cárdenas

Cabora Bassa Dam = Cahora Bassa, Reprêsa de, *Mozam.* **55 F3** 15 20S 32 50 E
Caborca, *Mexico* **86 A2** 30 40N 112 10W
Cabot, Mt., *U.S.A.* **79 B13** 44 30N 71 25W
Cabot Hd., *Canada* **78 A3** 45 14N 81 17W
Cabot Str., *Canada* **71 C8** 47 15N 59 40W
Cabra, *Spain* **19 D3** 37 30N 4 28W
Cabrera, *Spain* **22 B9** 39 8N 2 57 E
Cabri, *Canada* **73 C7** 50 35N 108 25W
Cabriel →, *Spain* **19 C5** 39 14N 1 3W
Caçador, *Brazil* **95 B5** 26 47S 51 0W
Čačak, *Serbia, Yug.* **21 C9** 43 54N 20 20 E
Caçapava do Sul, *Brazil* **95 C5** 30 30S 53 30W
Cáceres, *Brazil* **92 G7** 16 5S 57 40W
Cáceres, *Spain* **19 C2** 39 26N 6 23W
Cache Bay, *Canada* **70 C4** 46 22N 80 0W
Cache Cr. →, *U.S.A.* **84 G5** 38 42N 121 42W
Cache Creek, *Canada* **72 C4** 50 48N 121 19W
Cachi, *Argentina* **94 B2** 25 5S 66 10W
Cachimbo, Serra do, *Brazil* **93 E7** 9 30S 55 30W
Cachinal de la Sierra, *Chile* **94 A2** 24 58S 69 32W
Cachoeira, *Brazil* **93 F11** 12 30S 39 0W
Cachoeira de Itapemirim, *Brazil* **95 A7** 20 51S 41 7W
Cachoeira do Sul, *Brazil* **95 C5** 30 3S 52 53W
Cacoal, *Brazil* **92 F6** 11 32S 61 18W
Cacólo, *Angola* **52 G3** 10 9S 19 21 E
Caconda, *Angola* **53 G3** 13 48S 15 8 E
Caddo, *U.S.A.* **81 H6** 34 7N 96 16W
Cader Idris, *U.K.* **11 E4** 52 42N 3 53W
Cadereyta, *Mexico* **86 B5** 25 36N 100 0W
Cadibarrawirracanna, L., *Australia* **63 D2** 28 52S 135 27 E
Cadillac, *U.S.A.* **76 C3** 44 15N 85 24W
Cadiz, *Phil.* **37 B6** 10 57N 123 15 E
Cádiz, *Spain* **19 D2** 36 30N 6 20W
Cadiz, *Calif., U.S.A.* **85 L11** 34 30N 115 28W
Cadiz, *Ohio, U.S.A.* **78 F4** 40 22N 81 0W
Cádiz, G. de, *Spain* **19 D2** 36 40N 7 0W
Cadiz L., *U.S.A.* **83 J6** 34 18N 115 24W
Cadney Park, *Australia* **63 D1** 27 55S 134 3 E
Cadomin, *Canada* **72 C5** 53 2N 117 20W
Cadotte Lake, *Canada* **72 B5** 56 26N 116 23W
Cadoux, *Australia* **61 F2** 30 46S 117 7 E
Caen, *France* **18 B3** 49 10N 0 22W
Caernarfon, *U.K.* **10 D3** 53 8N 4 16W
Caernarfon B., *U.K.* **10 D3** 53 4N 4 40W
Caernarvon = Caernarfon, *U.K.* **10 D3** 53 8N 4 16W
Caerphilly, *U.K.* **11 F4** 51 35N 3 13W
Caerphilly □, *U.K.* **11 F4** 51 37N 3 12W
Caesarea, *Israel* **47 C3** 32 30N 34 53 E
Caetité, *Brazil* **93 F10** 13 50S 42 32W
Cafayate, *Argentina* **94 B2** 26 2S 66 0W
Cafu, *Angola* **56 B2** 16 30S 15 8 E
Cagayan de Oro, *Phil.* **37 C6** 8 30N 124 40 E
Cagayan Is., *Phil.* **37 C5** 9 40N 121 16 E
Cágliari, *Italy* **20 E3** 39 13N 9 7 E
Cágliari, G. di, *Italy* **20 E3** 39 8N 9 11 E
Caguán →, *Colombia* **92 D4** 0 8S 74 18W
Caguas, *Puerto Rico* **89 C6** 18 14N 66 2W
Caha Mts., *Ireland* **13 E2** 51 45N 9 40W
Cahama, *Angola* **56 B1** 16 17S 14 19 E
Caher, *Ireland* **13 D4** 52 22N 7 56W
Caherciveen, *Ireland* **13 E1** 51 56N 10 14W
Cahora Bassa, Reprêsa de, *Mozam.* **55 F3** 15 20S 32 50 E
Cahore Pt., *Ireland* **13 D5** 52 33N 6 12W
Cahors, *France* **18 D4** 44 27N 1 27 E
Cahul, *Moldova* **17 F15** 45 50N 28 15 E
Cai Nuoc, *Vietnam* **39 H5** 8 56N 105 1 E
Caia, *Mozam.* **55 F4** 17 51S 35 24 E
Caianda, *Angola* **55 E1** 11 2S 23 31 E
Caibarién, *Cuba* **88 B4** 22 30N 79 30W
Caicara, *Venezuela* **92 B5** 7 38N 66 10W
Caicó, *Brazil* **93 E11** 6 20S 37 0W
Caicos Is., *W. Indies* **89 B5** 21 40N 71 40W
Caicos Passage, *W. Indies* **89 B5** 22 45N 72 45W
Caird Coast, *Antarctica* **5 D1** 75 0S 25 0W
Cairn Gorm, *U.K.* **12 D5** 57 7N 3 39W
Cairngorm Mts., *U.K.* **12 D5** 57 6N 3 42W
Cairnryan, *U.K.* **12 G3** 54 59N 5 1W
Cairns, *Australia* **62 B4** 16 57S 145 45 E
Cairns L., *Canada* **73 C10** 51 42N 94 30W
Cairo = El Qâhira, *Egypt* **51 B12** 30 1N 31 14 E
Cairo, *Ga., U.S.A.* **77 K3** 30 52N 84 13W
Cairo, *Ill., U.S.A.* **81 G10** 37 0N 89 11W
Cairo, *N.Y., U.S.A.* **79 D11** 42 18N 74 0W
Caithness, Ord of, *U.K.* **12 C5** 58 8N 3 36W
Cajamarca, *Peru* **92 E3** 7 5S 78 28W
Cajàzeiras, *Brazil* **93 E11** 6 52S 38 30W
Cala d'Or, *Spain* **22 B10** 39 23N 3 14 E
Cala en Porter, *Spain* **22 B11** 39 52N 4 8 E
Cala Figuera, C. de, *Spain* **22 B9** 39 27N 2 31 E
Cala Forcat, *Spain* **22 B10** 40 0N 3 47 E
Cala Major, *Spain* **22 B9** 39 33N 2 37 E
Cala Mezquida = Sa Mesquida, *Spain* **22 B11** 39 55N 4 16 E
Cala Millor, *Spain* **22 B10** 39 35N 3 22 E
Cala Ratjada, *Spain* **22 B10** 39 43N 3 27 E
Cala Santa Galdana, *Spain* **22 B10** 39 56N 3 58 E
Calabar, *Nigeria* **50 H7** 4 57N 8 20 E
Calabogie, *Canada* **79 A8** 45 18N 76 43W
Calabozo, *Venezuela* **92 B5** 9 0N 67 28W
Calábria □, *Italy* **20 E7** 39 0N 16 30 E
Calafate, *Argentina* **96 G2** 50 19S 72 15W
Calahorra, *Spain* **19 A5** 42 18N 1 59W
Calais, *France* **18 A4** 50 57N 1 56 E
Calais, *U.S.A.* **77 C12** 45 11N 67 17W
Calalaste, Cord. de, *Argentina* **94 B2** 25 0S 67 0W
Calama, *Brazil* **92 E6** 8 0S 62 50W
Calama, *Chile* **94 A2** 22 30S 68 55W
Calamar, *Colombia* **92 A4** 10 15N 74 55W
Calamian Group, *Phil.* **37 B5** 11 50N 119 55 E
Calamocha, *Spain* **19 B5** 40 50N 1 17W
Calang, *Indonesia* **36 D1** 4 37N 95 37 E
Calapan, *Phil.* **37 B6** 13 25N 121 7 E
Călăraşi, *Romania* **17 F14** 44 12N 27 20 E
Calatayud, *Spain* **19 B5** 41 20N 1 40W
Calauag, *Phil.* **37 B6** 13 55N 122 15 E
Calavite, C., *Phil.* **37 B6** 13 26N 120 20 E
Calbayog, *Phil.* **37 B6** 12 4N 124 38 E
Calca, *Peru* **92 F4** 13 22S 72 0W
Calcasieu L., *U.S.A.* **81 L8** 29 55N 93 18W
Calcutta, *India* **43 H13** 22 36N 88 24 E
Calcutta, *U.S.A.* **78 F4** 40 40N 80 34W
Caldas da Rainha, *Portugal* **19 C1** 39 24N 9 8W
Calder →, *U.K.* **10 D6** 53 44N 1 22W
Caldera, *Chile* **94 B1** 27 5S 70 55W
Caldwell, *Idaho, U.S.A.* **82 E5** 43 40N 116 41W
Caldwell, *Kans., U.S.A.* **81 G6** 37 2N 97 37W
Caldwell, *Tex., U.S.A.* **81 K6** 30 32N 96 42W
Caledon, *S. Africa* **56 E2** 34 14S 19 26 E
Caledon →, *S. Africa* **56 E4** 30 31S 26 5 E
Caledon B., *Australia* **62 A2** 12 45S 137 0 E
Caledonia, *Canada* **78 C5** 43 7N 79 58W
Caledonia, *U.S.A.* **78 D7** 42 58N 77 51W
Calemba, *Angola* **56 B2** 16 0S 15 44 E
Calen, *Australia* **62 C4** 20 56S 148 48 E
Caletones, *Chile* **94 C1** 34 6S 70 27W
Calexico, *U.S.A.* **85 N11** 32 40N 115 30W
Calf of Man, *U.K.* **10 C3** 54 3N 4 48W
Calgary, *Canada* **72 C6** 51 0N 114 10W
Calheta, *Madeira* **22 D2** 32 44N 17 11W
Calhoun, *U.S.A.* **77 H3** 34 30N 84 57W
Cali, *Colombia* **92 C3** 3 25N 76 35W
Calicut, *India* **40 P9** 11 15N 75 43 E
Caliente, *U.S.A.* **83 H6** 37 37N 114 31W
California, *Mo., U.S.A.* **80 F8** 38 38N 92 34W
California, *Pa., U.S.A.* **78 F5** 40 4N 79 54W
California □, *U.S.A.* **84 H7** 37 30N 119 30W
California, Baja, *Mexico* **86 A1** 32 10N 115 12W
California, Baja, T.N. = Baja California □, *Mexico* **86 B2** 30 0N 115 0W
California, Baja, T.S. = Baja California Sur □, *Mexico* **86 B2** 25 50N 111 50W
California, G. de, *Mexico* **86 B2** 27 0N 111 0W
California City, *U.S.A.* **85 K9** 35 10N 117 55W
California Hot Springs, *U.S.A.* **85 K8** 35 51N 118 41W
Calingasta, *Argentina* **94 C2** 31 15S 69 30W
Calipatria, *U.S.A.* **85 M11** 33 8N 115 31W
Calistoga, *U.S.A.* **84 G4** 38 35N 122 35W
Calitzdorp, *S. Africa* **56 E3** 33 33S 21 42 E
Callabonna, L., *Australia* **63 D3** 29 40S 140 5 E
Callan, *Ireland* **13 D4** 52 32N 7 24W
Callander, *U.K.* **12 E4** 56 15N 4 13W
Callao, *Peru* **92 F3** 12 0S 77 0W
Calles, *Mexico* **87 C5** 23 2N 98 42W
Callicoon, *U.S.A.* **79 E9** 41 46N 75 3W
Calling Lake, *Canada* **72 B6** 55 15N 113 12W
Calliope, *Australia* **62 C5** 24 0S 151 16 E
Calne, *U.K.* **11 F6** 51 26N 2 0W
Calola, *Angola* **56 B2** 16 25S 17 48 E
Caloundra, *Australia* **63 D5** 26 45S 153 10 E
Calpella, *U.S.A.* **84 F3** 39 14N 123 12W
Calpine, *U.S.A.* **84 F6** 39 40N 120 27W
Calstock, *Canada* **70 C3** 49 47N 84 9W
Caltagirone, *Italy* **20 F6** 37 14N 14 31 E
Caltanissetta, *Italy* **20 F6** 37 29N 14 4 E
Calulo, *Angola* **52 G2** 10 1S 14 56 E
Caluquembe, *Angola* **53 G2** 13 47S 14 44 E
Calvert →, *Australia* **62 B2** 16 17S 137 44 E
Calvert I., *Canada* **72 C3** 51 30N 128 0W
Calvert Ra., *Australia* **60 D3** 24 0S 122 30 E
Calvi, *France* **18 E8** 42 34N 8 45 E
Calviá, *Spain* **19 C7** 39 34N 2 31 E
Calvillo, *Mexico* **86 C4** 21 51N 102 43W
Calvinia, *S. Africa* **56 E2** 31 28S 19 45 E
Calwa, *U.S.A.* **84 J7** 36 42N 119 46W
Cam →, *U.K.* **11 E8** 52 21N 0 16 E
Cam Lam, *Vietnam* **39 G7** 11 54N 109 10 E
Cam Ranh, *Vietnam* **39 G7** 11 54N 109 12 E
Cam Xuyen, *Vietnam* **38 C6** 18 15N 106 0 E
Camabatela, *Angola* **52 F3** 8 20S 15 26 E
Camacha, *Madeira* **22 D3** 32 41N 16 49W
Camacho, *Mexico* **86 C4** 24 25N 102 18W
Camacupa, *Angola* **53 G3** 11 58S 17 22 E
Camagüey, *Cuba* **88 B4** 21 20N 78 0W
Camaná, *Peru* **92 G4** 16 30S 72 50W
Camanche Reservoir, *U.S.A.* **84 G6** 38 14N 121 1W
Camaquã, *Brazil* **95 C5** 30 51S 51 49W
Camaquã →, *Brazil* **95 C5** 31 17S 51 47W
Câmara de Lobos, *Madeira* **22 D3** 32 39N 16 59W
Camargo, *Mexico* **87 B5** 26 19N 98 50W
Camargue, *France* **18 E6** 43 34N 4 34 E
Camarillo, *U.S.A.* **85 L7** 34 13N 119 2W
Camarón, C., *Honduras* **88 C2** 16 0N 85 5W
Camarones, *Argentina* **96 E3** 44 50S 65 40W
Camas, *U.S.A.* **84 E4** 45 35N 122 24W
Camas Valley, *U.S.A.* **82 E2** 43 2N 123 40W
Camballin, *Australia* **60 C3** 17 59S 124 12 E
Cambará, *Brazil* **95 A5** 23 2S 50 5W
Cambay = Khambhat, *India* **42 H5** 22 23N 72 33 E
Cambay, G. of = Khambhat, G. of, *India* **40 J8** 20 45N 72 30 E
Cambodia ■, *Asia* **38 F5** 12 15N 105 0 E
Camborne, *U.K.* **11 G2** 50 12N 5 19W
Cambrai, *France* **18 A5** 50 11N 3 14 E
Cambria, *U.S.A.* **84 K5** 35 34N 121 5W
Cambrian Mts., *U.K.* **11 E4** 52 3N 3 57W
Cambridge, *Canada* **78 C4** 43 23N 80 15W
Cambridge, *Jamaica* **88 C4** 18 18N 77 54W
Cambridge, *N.Z.* **59 G5** 37 54S 175 29 E
Cambridge, *U.K.* **11 E8** 52 12N 0 8 E
Cambridge, *Mass., U.S.A.* **79 D13** 42 22N 71 6W
Cambridge, *Md., U.S.A.* **75 C11** 38 34N 76 5W
Cambridge, *Minn., U.S.A.* **80 C8** 45 34N 93 13W
Cambridge, *N.Y., U.S.A.* **79 C11** 43 2N 73 22W
Cambridge, *Nebr., U.S.A.* **80 E4** 40 17N 100 10W
Cambridge, *Ohio, U.S.A.* **78 F3** 40 2N 81 35W
Cambridge Bay = Ikaluktutiak, *Canada* **68 B9** 69 10N 105 0W
Cambridge G., *Australia* **60 B4** 14 55S 128 15 E
Cambridge Springs, *U.S.A.* **78 E4** 41 48N 80 4W
Cambridgeshire □, *U.K.* **11 E7** 52 25N 0 7W
Cambuci, *Brazil* **95 A7** 21 35S 41 55W
Cambundi-Catembo, *Angola* **52 G3** 10 10S 17 35 E
Camden, *Ala., U.S.A.* **77 K2** 31 59N 87 17W
Camden, *Ark., U.S.A.* **81 J8** 33 35N 92 50W
Camden, *Maine, U.S.A.* **77 C11** 44 13N 69 4W
Camden, *N.J., U.S.A.* **79 G9** 39 56N 75 7W
Camden, *N.Y., U.S.A.* **79 C9** 43 20N 75 45W
Camden, *S.C., U.S.A.* **77 H5** 34 16N 80 36W
Camden Sd., *Australia* **60 C3** 15 27S 124 25 E
Camdenton, *U.S.A.* **81 F8** 38 1N 92 45W
Cameron, *Ariz., U.S.A.* **83 J8** 35 53N 111 25W
Cameron, *La., U.S.A.* **81 L8** 29 48N 93 20W
Cameron, *Mo., U.S.A.* **80 F7** 39 44N 94 14W
Cameron, *Tex., U.S.A.* **81 K6** 30 51N 96 59W
Cameron Highlands, *Malaysia* **39 K3** 4 27N 101 22 E
Cameron Hills, *Canada* **72 B5** 59 48N 118 0W
Cameroon ■, *Africa* **52 C2** 6 0N 12 30 E
Cameroun, Mt., *Cameroon* **52 D1** 4 13N 9 10 E
Cametá, *Brazil* **93 D9** 2 12S 49 30W
Camiguin I., *Phil.* **37 C6** 18 56N 121 55 E
Camilla, *U.S.A.* **77 K3** 31 14N 84 12W
Caminha, *Portugal* **19 B1** 41 50N 8 50W
Camino, *U.S.A.* **84 G6** 38 44N 120 41W
Camira Creek, *Australia* **63 D5** 29 15S 152 58 E
Cammal, *U.S.A.* **78 E7** 41 24N 77 28W
Camocim, *Brazil* **93 D10** 2 55S 40 50W
Camooweal, *Australia* **62 B2** 19 56S 138 7 E
Camopi, *Fr. Guiana* **93 C8** 3 12N 52 17W
Camp Borden, *Canada* **78 B5** 44 18N 79 56W
Camp Hill, *U.S.A.* **78 F8** 40 14N 76 55W
Camp Nelson, *U.S.A.* **85 J8** 36 8N 118 39W
Camp Pendleton, *U.S.A.* **85 M9** 33 16N 117 23W
Camp Verde, *U.S.A.* **83 J8** 34 34N 111 51W
Camp Wood, *U.S.A.* **81 L5** 29 40N 100 1W
Campana, *Argentina* **94 C4** 34 10S 58 55W
Campana, I., *Chile* **96 F1** 48 20S 75 20W
Campanário, *Madeira* **22 D2** 32 39N 17 2W
Campánia □, *Italy* **20 D6** 41 0N 14 30 E
Campbell, *S. Africa* **56 D3** 28 48S 23 44 E
Campbell, *Calif., U.S.A.* **84 H5** 37 17N 121 57W
Campbell, *Ohio, U.S.A.* **78 E4** 41 5N 80 37W
Campbell I., *Pac. Oc.* **64 N8** 52 30S 169 0 E
Campbell L., *Canada* **73 A7** 63 14N 106 55W
Campbell River, *Canada* **72 C3** 50 5N 125 20W
Campbell Town, *Australia* **62 G4** 41 52S 147 30 E
Campbellford, *Canada* **78 B7** 44 18N 77 48W
Campbellpur, *Pakistan* **42 C5** 33 46N 72 26 E
Campbellsville, *U.S.A.* **76 G3** 37 21N 85 20W
Campbellton, *Canada* **71 C6** 47 57N 66 43W
Campbelltown, *Australia* **63 E5** 34 4S 150 49 E
Campbeltown, *U.K.* **12 F3** 55 26N 5 36W
Campeche, *Mexico* **87 D6** 19 50N 90 32W
Campeche □, *Mexico* **87 D6** 19 50N 90 32W
Campeche, Golfo de, *Mexico* **87 D6** 19 30N 93 0W
Camperdown, *Australia* **63 F3** 38 14S 143 9 E
Camperville, *Canada* **73 C8** 51 59N 100 9W
Câmpina, *Romania* **17 F13** 45 10N 25 45 E
Campina Grande, *Brazil* **93 E11** 7 20S 35 47W
Campinas, *Brazil* **95 A6** 22 50S 47 0W
Campo Grande, *Brazil* **93 H8** 20 25S 54 40W
Campo Maior, *Brazil* **93 D10** 4 50S 42 12W
Campo Mourão, *Brazil* **95 A5** 24 3S 52 22W
Campobasso, *Italy* **20 D6** 41 34N 14 39 E
Campos, *Brazil* **95 A7** 21 50S 41 20W
Campos Belos, *Brazil* **93 F9** 13 10S 47 3W
Campos del Puerto, *Spain* **22 B10** 39 26N 3 1 E
Campos Novos, *Brazil* **95 B5** 27 21S 51 50W
Camptonville, *U.S.A.* **84 F5** 39 27N 121 3W
Camptown, *U.S.A.* **79 E8** 41 44N 76 14W
Câmpulung, *Romania* **17 F13** 45 17N 25 3 E
Camrose, *Canada* **72 C6** 53 0N 112 50W
Camsell Portage, *Canada* **73 B7** 59 37N 109 15W
Çan, *Turkey* **21 D12** 40 2N 27 3 E
Can Clavo, *Spain* **22 C7** 38 57N 1 27 E
Can Creu, *Spain* **22 C7** 38 58N 1 28 E
Can Gio, *Vietnam* **39 G6** 10 25N 106 58 E
Can Tho, *Vietnam* **39 G5** 10 2N 105 46 E
Canaan, *U.S.A.* **79 D11** 42 2N 73 20W
Canada ■, *N. Amer.* **68 C10** 60 0N 100 0W
Cañada de Gómez, *Argentina* **94 C3** 32 40S 61 30W
Canadian, *U.S.A.* **81 H4** 35 55N 100 23W
Canadian →, *U.S.A.* **81 H7** 35 28N 95 3W
Canajoharie, *U.S.A.* **79 D10** 42 54N 74 35W
Çanakkale, *Turkey* **21 D12** 40 8N 26 24 E
Çanakkale Boğazı, *Turkey* **21 D12** 40 17N 26 32 E
Canal Flats, *Canada* **72 C5** 50 10N 115 48W
Canalejas, *Argentina* **94 D2** 35 15S 66 34W
Canals, *Argentina* **94 C3** 33 35S 62 53W
Canandaigua, *U.S.A.* **78 D7** 42 54N 77 17W
Canandaigua L., *U.S.A.* **78 D7** 42 47N 77 19W
Cananea, *Mexico* **86 A2** 31 0N 110 20W
Canarias, Is., *Atl. Oc.* **22 F4** 28 30N 16 0W
Canarreos, Arch. de los, *Cuba* **88 B3** 21 35N 81 40W
Canary Is. = Canarias, Is., *Atl. Oc.* **22 F4** 28 30N 16 0W
Canaseraga, *U.S.A.* **78 D7** 42 27N 77 45W
Canatlán, *Mexico* **86 C4** 24 31N 104 47W
Canaveral, C., *U.S.A.* **77 L5** 28 27N 80 32W
Canavieiras, *Brazil* **93 G11** 15 39S 39 0W
Canberra, *Australia* **63 F4** 35 15S 149 8 E
Canby, *Calif., U.S.A.* **82 F3** 41 27N 120 52W
Canby, *Minn., U.S.A.* **80 C6** 44 43N 96 16W
Canby, *Oreg., U.S.A.* **84 E4** 45 16N 122 42W
Cancún, *Mexico* **87 C7** 21 8N 86 44W
Candelaria, *Argentina* **95 B4** 27 29S 55 44W
Candelaria, *Canary Is.* **22 F3** 28 22N 16 22W
Candelo, *Australia* **63 F4** 36 47S 149 43 E
Candia = Iráklion, *Greece* **23 D7** 35 20N 25 12 E
Candle L., *Canada* **73 C7** 53 50N 105 18W
Candlemas I., *Antarctica* **5 B1** 57 3S 26 40W
Cando, *U.S.A.* **80 A5** 48 32N 99 12W
Canea = Khaniá, *Greece* **23 D6** 35 30N 24 4 E
Canelones, *Uruguay* **95 C4** 34 32S 56 17W
Cañete, *Chile* **94 D1** 37 50S 73 30W
Cañete, *Peru* **92 F3** 13 8S 76 30W
Cangas de Narcea, *Spain* **19 A2** 43 10N 6 32W
Canguaretama, *Brazil* **93 E11** 6 20S 35 5W
Canguçu, *Brazil* **95 C5** 31 22S 52 43W
Canguçu, Serra do, *Brazil* **95 C5** 31 20S 52 40W
Cangzhou, *China* **34 E9** 38 19N 116 52 E
Caniapiscau →, *Canada* **71 A6** 56 40N 69 30W
Caniapiscau Rés. de, *Canada* **71 B6** 54 10N 69 55W
Canicattì, *Italy* **20 F5** 37 21N 13 51 E
Canim Lake, *Canada* **72 C4** 51 47N 120 54W
Canindeyu □, *Paraguay* **95 A5** 24 10S 55 0W
Canisteo, *U.S.A.* **78 D7** 42 16N 77 36W
Canisteo →, *U.S.A.* **78 D7** 42 7N 77 8W
Cañitas, *Mexico* **86 C4** 23 36N 102 43W
Çankırı, *Turkey* **25 F5** 40 40N 33 37 E
Cankuzo, *Burundi* **54 C3** 3 10S 30 31 E
Canmore, *Canada* **72 C5** 51 7N 115 18W
Cann River, *Australia* **63 F4** 37 35S 149 7 E
Canna, *U.K.* **12 D2** 57 3N 6 33W
Cannanore, *India* **40 P9** 11 53N 75 27 E
Cannes, *France* **18 E7** 43 32N 7 1 E
Canning Town = Port Canning, *India* **43 H13** 22 23N 88 40 E
Cannington, *Canada* **78 B5** 44 20N 79 2W
Cannock, *U.K.* **11 E5** 52 41N 2 1W
Cannon Ball →, *U.S.A.* **80 B4** 46 20N 100 38W
Cannondale Mt., *Australia* **62 D4** 25 13S 148 57 E
Cannonsville Reservoir, *U.S.A.* **79 D9** 42 4N 75 22W
Cannonvale, *Australia* **62 C4** 20 17S 148 43 E
Canoas, *Brazil* **95 B5** 29 56S 51 11W
Canoe L., *Canada* **73 B7** 55 10N 108 15W
Canon City, *U.S.A.* **80 F2** 38 27N 105 14W
Canora, *Canada* **73 C8** 51 40N 102 30W
Canowindra, *Australia* **63 E4** 33 35S 148 38 E
Canso, *Canada* **71 C7** 45 20N 61 0W
Cantabria □, *Spain* **19 A4** 43 10N 4 0W
Cantabrian Mts. = Cantábrica, Cordillera, *Spain* **19 A3** 43 0N 5 10W
Cantábrica, Cordillera, *Spain* **19 A3** 43 0N 5 10W
Cantal, Plomb du, *France* **18 D5** 45 3N 2 45 E
Canterbury, *Australia* **62 D3** 25 23S 141 53 E
Canterbury, *U.K.* **11 F9** 51 16N 1 6 E
Canterbury □, *N.Z.* **59 K3** 43 45S 171 19 E
Canterbury Bight, *N.Z.* **59 L3** 44 16S 171 55 E
Canterbury Plains, *N.Z.* **59 K3** 43 55S 171 22 E
Cantil, *U.S.A.* **85 K9** 35 18N 117 58W
Canton = Guangzhou, *China* **33 D6** 23 5N 113 10 E
Canton, *Ga., U.S.A.* **77 H3** 34 14N 84 29W
Canton, *Ill., U.S.A.* **80 E9** 40 33N 90 2W
Canton, *Miss., U.S.A.* **81 J9** 32 37N 90 2W
Canton, *Mo., U.S.A.* **80 E9** 40 8N 91 32W
Canton, *N.Y., U.S.A.* **79 B9** 44 36N 75 10W
Canton, *Ohio, U.S.A.* **78 F3** 40 48N 81 23W
Canton, *Pa., U.S.A.* **78 E8** 41 39N 76 51W
Canton, *S. Dak., U.S.A.* **80 D6** 43 18N 96 35W
Canton L., *U.S.A.* **81 G5** 36 6N 98 35W
Canudos, *Brazil* **92 E7** 7 13S 58 5W
Canumã →, *Brazil* **92 D7** 3 55S 59 10W
Canutama, *Brazil* **92 E6** 6 30S 64 20W
Canutillo, *U.S.A.* **83 L10** 31 55N 106 36W
Canvey, *U.K.* **11 F8** 51 31N 0 37 E
Canyon, *U.S.A.* **81 H4** 34 59N 101 55W
Canyonlands National Park, *U.S.A.* **83 G9** 38 15N 110 0W
Canyonville, *U.S.A.* **82 E2** 42 56N 123 17W
Cao He →, *China* **35 D13** 40 10N 124 32 E
Cao Lanh, *Vietnam* **39 G5** 10 27N 105 38 E
Cao Xian, *China* **34 G8** 34 50N 115 35 E
Cap-aux-Meules, *Canada* **71 C7** 47 23N 61 52W
Cap-Chat, *Canada* **71 C6** 49 6N 66 40W
Cap-de-la-Madeleine, *Canada* **70 C5** 46 22N 72 31W
Cap-Haïtien, *Haiti* **89 C5** 19 40N 72 20W
Capac, *U.S.A.* **78 C2** 43 1N 82 56W
Capanaparo →, *Venezuela* **92 B5** 7 1N 67 7W
Cape →, *Australia* **62 C4** 20 59S 146 51 E
Cape Barren I., *Australia* **62 G4** 40 25S 148 15 E
Cape Breton Highlands Nat. Park, *Canada* **71 C7** 46 50N 60 40W
Cape Breton I., *Canada* **71 C7** 46 0N 60 30W
Cape Charles, *U.S.A.* **76 G8** 37 16N 76 1W
Cape Coast, *Ghana* **50 G5** 5 5N 1 15W
Cape Coral, *U.S.A.* **77 M5** 26 33N 81 57W
Cape Dorset, *Canada* **69 B12** 64 14N 76 32W
Cape Fear →, *U.S.A.* **77 H6** 33 53N 78 1W
Cape Girardeau, *U.S.A.* **81 G10** 37 19N 89 32W
Cape May, *U.S.A.* **76 F8** 38 56N 74 56W
Cape May Point, *U.S.A.* **75 C12** 38 56N 74 58W
Cape Province □, *S. Africa* **53 L3** 32 0S 23 0 E
Cape Tormentine, *Canada* **71 C7** 46 8N 63 47W
Cape Town, *S. Africa* **56 E2** 33 55S 18 22 E
Cape Verde Is. ■, *Atl. Oc.* **49 E1** 17 10N 25 20W
Cape Vincent, *U.S.A.* **79 B8** 44 8N 76 20W
Cape York Peninsula, *Australia* **62 A3** 12 0S 142 30 E
Capela, *Brazil* **93 F11** 10 30S 37 0W
Capella, *Australia* **62 C4** 23 2S 148 1 E
Capenda Camulemba, *Angola* **52 F3** 9 24S 18 27 E
Capim →, *Brazil* **93 D9** 1 40S 47 47W
Capitan, *U.S.A.* **83 K11** 33 35N 105 35W
Capitol Reef National Park, *U.S.A.* **83 G8** 38 15N 111 10W
Capitola, *U.S.A.* **84 J5** 36 59N 121 57W
Capoche →, *Mozam.* **55 F3** 15 35S 33 0 E
Capraia, *Italy* **18 E8** 43 2N 9 50 E
Capreol, *Canada* **70 C3** 46 43N 80 56W
Capri, *Italy* **20 D6** 40 33N 14 14 E
Capricorn Group, *Australia* **62 C5** 23 30S 151 55 E
Capricorn Ra., *Australia* **60 D2** 23 20S 116 50 E
Caprivi Strip, *Namibia* **56 B3** 18 0S 23 0 E
Captain's Flat, *Australia* **63 F4** 35 35S 149 27 E
Caquetá →, *Colombia* **92 D5** 1 15S 69 15W
Caracal, *Romania* **17 F13** 44 8N 24 22 E
Caracas, *Venezuela* **92 A5** 10 30N 66 55W
Caracol, *Brazil* **94 A4** 22 18S 57 1W
Caracol, *Piauí, Brazil* **93 E10** 9 15S 43 22W
Carajas, *Brazil* **93 E8** 6 5S 50 23W
Carajás, Serra dos, *Brazil* **93 E8** 6 0S 51 30W
Carangola, *Brazil* **95 A7** 20 44S 42 5W
Caransebeş, *Romania* **17 F12** 45 28N 22 18 E
Caraquet, *Canada* **71 C6** 47 48N 64 57W
Caras, *Peru* **92 E3** 9 3S 77 47W
Caratasca, L., *Honduras* **88 C3** 15 20N 83 40W
Caratinga, *Brazil* **93 G10** 19 50S 42 10W
Caraúbas, *Brazil* **93 E11** 5 43S 37 33W
Caravaca = Caravaca de la Cruz, *Spain* **19 C5** 38 8N 1 52W
Caravaca de la Cruz, *Spain* **19 C5** 38 8N 1 52W
Caravelas, *Brazil* **93 G11** 17 45S 39 15W
Caraveli, *Peru* **92 G4** 15 45S 73 25W
Caràzinho, *Brazil* **95 B5** 28 16S 52 46W
Carballo, *Spain* **19 A1** 43 13N 8 41W
Carberry, *Canada* **73 D9** 49 50N 99 25W
Carbó, *Mexico* **86 B2** 29 42N 110 58W
Carbonara, C., *Italy* **20 E3** 39 6N 9 31 E
Carbondale, *Colo., U.S.A.* **82 G10** 39 24N 107 13W
Carbondale, *Ill., U.S.A.* **81 G10** 37 44N 89 13W
Carbondale, *Pa., U.S.A.* **79 E9** 41 35N 75 30W
Carbonear, *Canada* **71 C9** 47 42N 53 13W
Carbónia, *Italy* **20 E3** 39 10N 8 30 E
Carcajou, *Canada* **72 B5** 57 47N 117 6W
Carcarana →, *Argentina* **94 C3** 32 27S 60 48W
Carcasse, C., *Haiti* **89 C5** 18 30N 74 28W
Carcassonne, *France* **18 E5** 43 13N 2 20 E
Carcross, *Canada* **72 A2** 60 13N 134 45W
Cardamon Hills, *India* **40 Q10** 9 30N 77 15 E
Cárdenas, *Cuba* **88 B3** 23 0N 81 30W
Cárdenas, *San Luis Potosí, Mexico* **87 C5** 22 0N 99 41W

Cárdenas

110

Chinchorro, Banco

Chinchorro, Banco, *Mexico* **87 D7** 18 35N 87 20W
Chinchou = Jinzhou, *China* **35 D11** 41 5N 121 3 E
Chincoteague, *U.S.A.* **76 G8** 37 56N 75 23W
Chinde, *Mozam.* **55 F4** 18 35S 36 30 E
Chindo, *S. Korea* **35 G14** 34 28N 126 15 E
Chindwin →, *Burma* **41 J19** 21 26N 95 15 E
Chineni, *India* **43 C6** 33 2N 75 15 E
Chinga, *Mozam.* **55 F4** 15 13S 38 35 E
Chingola, *Zambia* **55 E2** 12 31S 27 53 E
Chingole, *Malawi* **55 E3** 13 4S 34 17 E
Ch'ingtao = Qingdao, *China* **35 F11** 36 5N 120 20 E
Chinguar, *Angola* **53 G3** 12 25S 16 45 E
Chinguetti, *Mauritania* **50 D3** 20 25N 12 24W
Chingune, *Mozam.* **57 C5** 20 33S 34 58 E
Chinhae, *S. Korea* **35 G15** 35 9N 128 47 E
Chinhanguanine, *Mozam.* **57 D5** 25 21S 32 30 E
Chinhoyi, *Zimbabwe* **55 F3** 17 20S 30 8 E
Chini, *India* **42 D8** 31 32N 78 15 E
Chiniot, *Pakistan* **42 D5** 31 45N 73 0 E
Chínipas, *Mexico* **86 B3** 27 22N 108 32W
Chinji, *Pakistan* **42 C5** 32 42N 72 22 E
Chinju, *S. Korea* **35 G15** 35 12N 128 2 E
Chinle, *U.S.A.* **83 H9** 36 9N 109 33W
Chinnampo = Namp'o, *N. Korea* **35 E13** 38 52N 125 10 E
Chino, *Japan* **31 G9** 35 59N 138 9 E
Chino, *U.S.A.* **85 L9** 34 1N 117 41W
Chino Valley, *U.S.A.* **83 J7** 34 45N 112 27W
Chinon, *France* **18 C4** 47 10N 0 15 E
Chinook, *U.S.A.* **82 B9** 48 35N 109 14W
Chinsali, *Zambia* **55 E3** 10 30S 32 2 E
Chióggia, *Italy* **20 B5** 45 13N 12 17 E
Chíos = Khíos, *Greece* **21 E12** 38 27N 26 9 E
Chipata, *Zambia* **55 E3** 13 38S 32 28 E
Chipinge, *Zimbabwe* **55 G3** 20 13S 32 28 E
Chipley, *U.S.A.* **77 K3** 30 47N 85 32W
Chipman, *Canada* **71 C6** 46 6N 65 53W
Chipoka, *Malawi* **55 E3** 13 57S 34 28 E
Chippenham, *U.K.* **11 F5** 51 27N 2 6W
Chippewa →, *U.S.A.* **80 C8** 44 25N 92 5W
Chippewa Falls, *U.S.A.* **80 C9** 44 56N 91 24W
Chipping Norton, *U.K.* **11 F6** 51 56N 1 32W
Chiputneticook Lakes, *U.S.A.* **77 C11** 45 35N 67 35W
Chiquián, *Peru* **92 F3** 10 10S 77 0W
Chiquimula, *Guatemala* **88 D2** 14 51N 89 37W
Chiquinquira, *Colombia* **92 B4** 5 37N 73 50W
Chirala, *India* **40 M12** 15 50N 80 26 E
Chiramba, *Mozam.* **55 F3** 16 55S 34 39 E
Chirawa, *India* **42 E6** 28 14N 75 42 E
Chirchiq, *Uzbekistan* **26 E7** 41 29N 69 35 E
Chiredzi, *Zimbabwe* **57 C5** 21 0S 31 38 E
Chirfa, *Niger* **51 D8** 20 55N 12 22 E
Chiricahua Peak, *U.S.A.* **83 L9** 31 51N 109 18W
Chiriquí, G. de, *Panama* **88 E3** 8 0N 82 10W
Chiriquí, L. de, *Panama* **88 E3** 9 10N 82 0W
Chirivira Falls, *Zimbabwe* **55 G3** 21 10S 32 12 E
Chirmiri, *India* **41 H13** 23 15N 82 20 E
Chirripó Grande, Cerro, *Costa Rica* **88 E3** 9 29N 83 29W
Chisamba, *Zambia* **55 E2** 14 55S 28 20 E
Chisapani Garhi, *Nepal* **41 F14** 27 30N 84 2 E
Chisasibi, *Canada* **70 B4** 53 50N 79 0W
Chisholm, *Canada* **72 C6** 54 55N 114 10W
Chisholm, *U.S.A.* **80 B8** 47 29N 92 53W
Chishtian Mandi, *Pakistan* **42 E5** 29 50N 72 55 E
Chisimaio, *Somali Rep.* **49 G8** 0 22S 42 32 E
Chisimba Falls, *Zambia* **55 E3** 10 12S 30 56 E
Chişinău, *Moldova* **17 E15** 47 2N 28 50 E
Chisos Mts., *U.S.A.* **81 L3** 29 5N 103 15W
Chistopol, *Russia* **24 C9** 55 25N 50 38 E
Chita, *Russia* **27 D12** 52 0N 113 35 E
Chitipa, *Malawi* **55 D3** 9 41S 33 19 E
Chitose, *Japan* **30 C10** 42 49N 141 39 E
Chitral, *Pakistan* **40 B7** 35 50N 71 56 E
Chitré, *Panama* **88 E3** 7 59N 80 27W
Chittagong, *Bangla.* **41 H17** 22 19N 91 48 E
Chittagong □, *Bangla.* **41 G17** 24 5N 91 0 E
Chittaurgarh, *India* **42 G6** 24 52N 74 38 E
Chittoor, *India* **40 N11** 13 15N 79 5 E
Chitungwiza, *Zimbabwe* **55 F3** 18 0S 31 6 E
Chiusi, *Italy* **20 C4** 43 1N 11 57 E
Chivasso, *Italy* **18 D7** 45 11N 7 53 E
Chivhu, *Zimbabwe* **55 F3** 19 2S 30 52 E
Chivilcoy, *Argentina* **94 C4** 34 55S 60 0W
Chiwanda, *Tanzania* **55 E3** 11 23S 34 55 E
Chizera, *Zambia* **55 E2** 13 10S 25 0 E
Chkalov = Orenburg, *Russia* **24 D10** 51 45N 55 6 E
Chloride, *U.S.A.* **85 K12** 35 25N 114 12W
Cho-do, *N. Korea* **35 E13** 38 30N 124 40 E
Cho Phuoc Hai, *Vietnam* **39 G6** 10 26N 107 18 E
Choba, *Kenya* **54 B4** 2 30N 38 5 E
Chobe National Park, *Botswana* **56 B4** 18 0S 25 0 E
Choch'iwŏn, *S. Korea* **35 F14** 36 37N 127 18 E
Chocolate Mts., *U.S.A.* **85 M11** 33 15N 115 15W
Choctawatchee →, *U.S.A.* **77 K3** 30 25N 86 8W
Choctawhatchee B., *U.S.A.* **75 D9** 30 20N 86 20W
Choele Choel, *Argentina* **96 D3** 39 11S 65 40W
Choix, *Mexico* **86 B3** 26 40N 108 23W
Chojnice, *Poland* **17 B9** 53 42N 17 32 E
Chōkai-San, *Japan* **30 E10** 39 6N 140 3 E
Choke Canyon L., *U.S.A.* **81 L5** 28 30N 98 20W
Chokurdakh, *Russia* **27 B15** 70 38N 147 55 E
Cholame, *U.S.A.* **84 K6** 35 44N 120 18W
Cholet, *France* **18 C3** 47 4N 0 52W
Cholguan, *Chile* **94 D1** 37 10S 72 3W
Choluteca, *Honduras* **88 D2** 13 20N 87 14W
Choluteca →, *Honduras* **88 D2** 13 0N 87 20W
Chom Bung, *Thailand* **38 F2** 13 37N 99 36 E
Chom Thong, *Thailand* **38 C2** 18 25N 98 41 E
Choma, *Zambia* **55 F2** 16 48S 26 59 E
Chomun, *India* **42 F6** 27 15N 75 40 E
Chomutov, *Czech Rep.* **16 C7** 50 28N 13 23 E
Chon Buri, *Thailand* **38 F3** 13 21N 101 1 E
Chon Thanh, *Vietnam* **39 G6** 11 24N 106 36 E
Ch'onan, *S. Korea* **35 F14** 36 48N 127 9 E
Chone, *Ecuador* **92 D3** 0 40S 80 0W
Chong Kai, *Cambodia* **38 F4** 13 57N 103 35 E
Chong Mek, *Thailand* **38 E5** 15 10N 105 27 E
Chŏngdo, *S. Korea* **35 G15** 35 38N 128 42 E
Chŏngha, *S. Korea* **35 F15** 36 12N 129 21 E
Chŏngjin, *N. Korea* **35 D15** 41 47N 129 50 E
Chŏngju, *S. Korea* **35 F14** 36 39N 127 27 E
Chŏngju, *N. Korea* **35 E13** 39 40N 125 5 E
Chongli, *China* **34 D8** 40 58N 115 15 E
Chongqing, *China* **32 D5** 29 35N 106 25 E
Chongqing □, *China* **32 C5** 30 0N 108 0 E
Chŏngŭp, *S. Korea* **35 G14** 35 35N 126 50 E
Chŏnju, *S. Korea* **35 G14** 35 50N 127 4 E
Chonos, Arch. de los, *Chile* **96 F2** 45 0S 75 0W
Chop, *Ukraine* **17 D12** 48 26N 22 12 E
Chopim →, *Brazil* **95 B5** 25 35S 53 5W
Chor, *Pakistan* **42 G3** 25 31N 69 46 E
Chorbat La, *India* **43 B7** 34 42N 76 37 E
Chorley, *U.K.* **10 D5** 53 39N 2 38W
Chornobyl, *Ukraine* **17 C16** 51 20N 30 15 E
Chorolque, Cerro, *Bolivia* **94 A2** 20 59S 66 5W
Chorregon, *Australia* **62 C3** 22 40S 143 32 E
Chortkiv, *Ukraine* **17 D13** 49 2N 25 46 E
Ch'ŏrwon, *S. Korea* **35 E14** 38 15N 127 10 E
Chorzów, *Poland* **17 C10** 50 18N 18 57 E
Chos-Malal, *Argentina* **94 D1** 37 20S 70 15W
Ch'osan, *N. Korea* **35 D13** 40 50N 125 47 E
Choszczno, *Poland* **16 B8** 53 7N 15 25 E
Choteau, *U.S.A.* **82 C7** 47 49N 112 11W
Chotila, *India* **42 H4** 22 23N 71 15 E
Chotta Udepur, *India* **42 H6** 22 19N 74 1 E
Chowchilla, *U.S.A.* **84 H6** 37 7N 120 16W
Choybalsan, *Mongolia* **33 B6** 48 4N 114 30 E
Christchurch, *N.Z.* **59 K4** 43 33S 172 47 E
Christchurch, *U.K.* **11 G6** 50 44N 1 47W
Christian I., *Canada* **78 B4** 44 50N 80 12W
Christiana, *S. Africa* **56 D4** 27 52S 25 8 E
Christiansted, *Virgin Is.* **89 C7** 17 45N 64 42W
Christie B., *Canada* **73 A6** 62 32N 111 10W
Christina →, *Canada* **73 B6** 56 40N 111 3W
Christmas Cr. →, *Australia* **60 C4** 18 29S 125 23 E
Christmas I. = Kiritimati, *Kiribati* **65 G12** 1 58N 157 27W
Christmas I., *Ind. Oc.* **64 J2** 10 30S 105 40 E
Christopher L., *Australia* **61 D4** 24 49S 127 42 E
Chtimba, *Malawi* **55 E3** 10 35S 34 13 E
Chu = Shu, *Kazakstan* **26 E8** 43 36N 73 42 E
Chu = Shu →, *Kazakstan* **28 E10** 45 0N 67 44 E
Chu →, *Vietnam* **38 C5** 19 53N 105 45 E
Chu Lai, *Vietnam* **38 E7** 15 28N 108 45 E
Ch'uanchou = Quanzhou, *China* **33 D6** 24 55N 118 34 E
Chuankou, *China* **34 G6** 34 20N 110 59 E
Chubbuck, *U.S.A.* **82 E7** 42 55N 112 28W
Chūbu □, *Japan* **31 F8** 36 45N 137 30 E
Chubut →, *Argentina* **96 E3** 43 20S 65 5W
Chuchi L., *Canada* **72 B4** 55 12N 124 30W
Chuda, *India* **42 H4** 22 29N 71 41 E
Chudskoye, Ozero, *Russia* **9 G22** 58 13N 27 30 E
Chūgoku □, *Japan* **31 G6** 35 0N 133 0 E
Chūgoku-Sanchi, *Japan* **31 G6** 35 0N 133 0 E
Chugwater, *U.S.A.* **80 E2** 41 46N 104 50W
Chukchi Sea, *Russia* **27 C19** 68 0N 175 0W
Chukotskoye Nagorye, *Russia* **27 C18** 68 0N 175 0 E
Chula Vista, *U.S.A.* **85 N9** 32 39N 117 5W
Chulucanas, *Peru* **92 E2** 5 8S 80 10W
Chulym →, *Russia* **26 D9** 57 43N 83 51 E
Chum Phae, *Thailand* **38 D4** 16 40N 102 6 E
Chum Saeng, *Thailand* **38 E3** 15 55N 100 15 E
Chumar, *India* **43 C8** 32 40N 78 35 E
Chumbicha, *Argentina* **94 B2** 29 0S 66 10W
Chumikan, *Russia* **27 D14** 54 40N 135 10 E
Chumphon, *Thailand* **39 G2** 10 35N 99 14 E
Chumuare, *Mozam.* **55 E3** 14 31S 31 50 E
Chumunjin, *S. Korea* **35 F15** 37 55N 128 54 E
Chuna →, *Russia* **27 D10** 57 47N 94 37 E
Ch'unch'ŏn, *S. Korea* **35 F14** 37 58N 127 44 E
Chunchura, *India* **43 H13** 22 53N 88 27 E
Chunga, *Zambia* **55 F2** 15 0S 26 2 E
Chunggang-ŭp, *N. Korea* **35 D14** 41 48N 126 48 E
Chunghwa, *N. Korea* **35 E13** 38 52N 125 47 E
Ch'ungju, *S. Korea* **35 F14** 36 58N 127 58 E
Chungking = Chongqing, *China* **32 D5** 29 35N 106 25 E
Ch'ungmu, *S. Korea* **35 G15** 34 50N 128 20 E
Chungt'iaoshan = Zhongtiao Shan, *China* **34 G6** 35 0N 111 10 E
Chunian, *Pakistan* **42 D6** 30 57N 74 0 E
Chunya, *Tanzania* **55 D3** 8 30S 33 27 E
Chunyang, *China* **35 C15** 43 38N 129 23 E
Chuquibamba, *Peru* **92 G4** 15 47S 72 44W
Chuquicamata, *Chile* **94 A2** 22 15S 69 0W
Chur, *Switz.* **18 C8** 46 52N 9 32 E
Churachandpur, *India* **41 G18** 24 20N 93 40 E
Churchill, *Canada* **73 B10** 58 47N 94 11W
Churchill →, *Man., Canada* **73 B10** 58 47N 94 12W
Churchill →, *Nfld., Canada* **71 B7** 53 19N 60 10W
Churchill, C., *Canada* **73 B10** 58 46N 93 12W
Churchill Falls, *Canada* **71 B7** 53 36N 64 19W
Churchill L., *Canada* **73 B7** 55 55N 108 20W
Churchill Pk., *Canada* **72 B3** 58 10N 125 10W
Churki, *India* **43 H10** 23 50N 83 12 E
Churu, *India* **42 E6** 28 20N 74 50 E
Churún Merú = Angel Falls, *Venezuela* **92 B6** 5 57N 62 30W
Chushal, *India* **43 C8** 33 40N 78 40 E
Chuska Mts., *U.S.A.* **83 H9** 36 15N 108 50W
Chusovoy, *Russia* **24 C10** 58 22N 57 50 E
Chute-aux-Outardes, *Canada* **71 C6** 49 7N 68 24W
Chuuronjang, *N. Korea* **35 D15** 41 35N 129 40 E
Chuvash Republic = Chuvashia □, *Russia* **24 C8** 55 30N 47 0 E
Chuvashia □, *Russia* **24 C8** 55 30N 47 0 E
Chuwārtah, *Iraq* **44 C5** 35 43N 45 34 E
Chuy, *Uruguay* **95 C5** 33 41S 53 27W
Ci Xian, *China* **34 F8** 36 20N 114 25 E
Ciadâr-Lunga, *Moldova* **17 E15** 46 3N 28 51 E
Ciamis, *Indonesia* **37 G13** 7 20S 108 21 E
Cianjur, *Indonesia* **37 G12** 6 49S 107 8 E
Cianorte, *Brazil* **95 A5** 23 37S 52 37W
Cibola, *U.S.A.* **85 M12** 33 17N 114 42W
Cicero, *U.S.A.* **76 E2** 41 48N 87 48W
Ciechanów, *Poland* **17 B11** 52 52N 20 38 E
Ciego de Avila, *Cuba* **88 B4** 21 50N 78 50W
Ciénaga, *Colombia* **92 A4** 11 1N 74 15W
Cienfuegos, *Cuba* **88 B3** 22 10N 80 30W
Cieszyn, *Poland* **17 D10** 49 45N 18 35 E
Cieza, *Spain* **19 C5** 38 17N 1 23W
Cihuatlán, *Mexico* **86 D4** 19 14N 104 35W
Cijara, Embalse de, *Spain* **19 C3** 39 18N 4 52W
Cijulang, *Indonesia* **37 G13** 7 42S 108 27 E
Cilacap, *Indonesia* **37 G13** 7 43S 109 0 E
Cill Chainnigh = Kilkenny, *Ireland* **13 D4** 52 39N 7 15W
Cilo Dağı, *Turkey* **25 G7** 37 28N 43 55 E
Cima, *U.S.A.* **85 K11** 35 14N 115 30W
Cimarron, *Kans., U.S.A.* **81 G4** 37 48N 100 21W
Cimarron, *N. Mex., U.S.A.* **81 G2** 36 31N 104 55W
Cimarron →, *U.S.A.* **81 G6** 36 10N 96 17W
Cimişlia, *Moldova* **17 E15** 46 34N 28 44 E
Cimone, Mte., *Italy* **20 B4** 44 12N 10 42 E
Cinca →, *Spain* **19 B6** 41 26N 0 21 E
Cincar, *Bos.-H.* **20 C7** 43 55N 17 5 E
Cincinnati, *U.S.A.* **76 F3** 39 6N 84 31W
Cincinnatus, *U.S.A.* **79 D9** 42 33N 75 54W
Çine, *Turkey* **21 F13** 37 37N 28 2 E
Ciney, *Belgium* **15 D5** 50 18N 5 5 E
Cinto, Mte., *France* **18 E8** 42 24N 8 54 E
Circle, *Alaska, U.S.A.* **68 B5** 65 50N 144 4W
Circle, *Mont., U.S.A.* **80 B2** 47 25N 105 35W
Circleville, *U.S.A.* **76 F4** 39 36N 82 57W
Cirebon, *Indonesia* **37 G13** 6 45S 108 32 E
Ciremai, *Indonesia* **37 G13** 6 55S 108 27 E
Cirencester, *U.K.* **11 F6** 51 43N 1 57W
Cirium, *Cyprus* **23 E11** 34 40N 32 53 E
Cisco, *U.S.A.* **81 J5** 32 23N 98 59W
Citlaltépetl, *Mexico* **87 D5** 19 0N 97 20W
Citrus Heights, *U.S.A.* **84 G5** 38 42N 121 17W
Citrusdal, *S. Africa* **56 E2** 32 35S 19 0 E
Città di Castello, *Italy* **20 C5** 43 27N 12 14 E
City of Edinburgh □, *U.K.* **12 F5** 55 57N 3 17W
City of Glasgow □, *U.K.* **12 F4** 55 51N 4 12W
Ciudad Altamirano, *Mexico* **86 D4** 18 20N 100 40W
Ciudad Bolívar, *Venezuela* **92 B6** 8 5N 63 36W
Ciudad Camargo, *Mexico* **86 B3** 27 41N 105 10W
Ciudad de Valles, *Mexico* **87 C5** 22 0N 99 0W
Ciudad del Carmen, *Mexico* **87 D6** 18 38N 91 50W
Ciudad del Este, *Paraguay* **95 B5** 25 30S 54 50W
Ciudad Delicias = Delicias, *Mexico* **86 B3** 28 10N 105 30W
Ciudad Guayana, *Venezuela* **92 B6** 8 0N 62 30W
Ciudad Guerrero, *Mexico* **86 B3** 28 33N 107 28W
Ciudad Guzmán, *Mexico* **86 D4** 19 40N 103 30W
Ciudad Juárez, *Mexico* **86 A3** 31 40N 106 28W
Ciudad Madero, *Mexico* **87 C5** 22 19N 97 50W
Ciudad Mante, *Mexico* **87 C5** 22 50N 99 0W
Ciudad Obregón, *Mexico* **86 B3** 27 28N 109 59W
Ciudad Real, *Spain* **19 C4** 38 59N 3 55W
Ciudad Rodrigo, *Spain* **19 B2** 40 35N 6 32W
Ciudad Trujillo = Santo Domingo, *Dom. Rep.* **89 C6** 18 30N 69 59W
Ciudad Victoria, *Mexico* **87 C5** 23 41N 99 9W
Ciudadela, *Spain* **22 B10** 40 0N 3 50 E
Civitanova Marche, *Italy* **20 C5** 43 18N 13 44 E
Civitavécchia, *Italy* **20 C4** 42 6N 11 48 E
Cizre, *Turkey* **25 G7** 37 19N 42 10 E
Clackmannanshire □, *U.K.* **12 E5** 56 10N 3 43W
Clacton-on-Sea, *U.K.* **11 F9** 51 47N 1 11 E
Claire, L., *Canada* **72 B6** 58 35N 112 5W
Clairton, *U.S.A.* **78 F5** 40 18N 79 53W
Clallam Bay, *U.S.A.* **84 B2** 48 15N 124 16W
Clanton, *U.S.A.* **77 J2** 32 51N 86 38W
Clanwilliam, *S. Africa* **56 E2** 32 11S 18 52 E
Clara, *Ireland* **13 C4** 53 21N 7 37W
Claraville, *U.S.A.* **85 K8** 35 24N 118 20W
Clare, *Australia* **63 E2** 33 50S 138 37 E
Clare, *U.S.A.* **76 D3** 43 49N 84 46W
Clare □, *Ireland* **13 D3** 52 45N 9 0W
Clare →, *Ireland* **13 C2** 53 20N 9 2W
Clare I., *Ireland* **13 C1** 53 49N 10 0W
Claremont, *Calif., U.S.A.* **85 L9** 34 6N 117 43W
Claremont, *N.H., U.S.A.* **79 C12** 43 23N 72 20W
Claremont Pt., *Australia* **62 A3** 14 1S 143 41 E
Claremore, *U.S.A.* **81 G7** 36 19N 95 36W
Claremorris, *Ireland* **13 C3** 53 45N 9 0W
Clarence →, *Australia* **63 D5** 29 25S 153 22 E
Clarence →, *N.Z.* **59 K4** 42 10S 173 56 E
Clarence, I., *Chile* **96 G2** 54 0S 72 0W
Clarence I., *Antarctica* **5 C18** 61 10S 54 0W
Clarence Str., *Australia* **60 B5** 12 0S 131 0 E
Clarence Town, *Bahamas* **89 B5** 23 6N 74 59W
Clarendon, *Pa., U.S.A.* **78 E5** 41 47N 79 6W
Clarendon, *Tex., U.S.A.* **81 H4** 34 56N 100 53W
Clarenville, *Canada* **71 C9** 48 10N 54 1W
Claresholm, *Canada* **72 D6** 50 0N 113 33W
Clarie Coast, *Antarctica* **5 C9** 68 0S 135 0 E
Clarinda, *U.S.A.* **80 E7** 40 44N 95 2W
Clarion, *Iowa, U.S.A.* **80 D8** 42 44N 93 44W
Clarion, *Pa., U.S.A.* **78 E5** 41 13N 79 23W
Clarion →, *U.S.A.* **78 E5** 41 7N 79 41W
Clark, *U.S.A.* **80 C6** 44 53N 97 44W
Clark, Pt., *Canada* **78 B3** 44 4N 81 45W
Clark Fork, *U.S.A.* **82 B5** 48 9N 116 11W
Clark Fork →, *U.S.A.* **82 B5** 48 9N 116 15W
Clark Hill L., *U.S.A.* **77 J4** 33 40N 82 12W
Clarkdale, *U.S.A.* **83 J7** 34 46N 112 3W
Clarke City, *Canada* **71 B6** 50 12N 66 38W
Clarke I., *Australia* **62 G4** 40 32S 148 10 E
Clarke Ra., *Australia* **62 C4** 20 40S 148 30 E
Clark's Fork →, *U.S.A.* **82 D9** 45 39N 108 43W
Clark's Harbour, *Canada* **71 D6** 43 25N 65 38W
Clarks Summit, *U.S.A.* **79 E9** 41 30N 75 42W
Clarksburg, *U.S.A.* **76 F5** 39 17N 80 30W
Clarksdale, *U.S.A.* **81 H9** 34 12N 90 35W
Clarksville, *Ark., U.S.A.* **81 H8** 35 28N 93 28W
Clarksville, *Tenn., U.S.A.* **77 G2** 36 32N 87 21W
Clarksville, *Tex., U.S.A.* **81 J7** 33 37N 95 3W
Clatskanie, *U.S.A.* **84 D3** 46 6N 123 12W
Claude, *U.S.A.* **81 H4** 35 7N 101 22W
Claveria, *Phil.* **37 A6** 18 37N 121 4 E
Clay, *U.S.A.* **84 G5** 38 17N 121 10W
Clay Center, *U.S.A.* **80 F6** 39 23N 97 8W
Claypool, *U.S.A.* **83 K8** 33 25N 110 51W
Claysburg, *U.S.A.* **78 F6** 40 17N 78 27W
Claysville, *U.S.A.* **78 F4** 40 7N 80 25W
Clayton, *N. Mex., U.S.A.* **81 G3** 36 27N 103 11W
Clayton, *N.Y., U.S.A.* **79 B8** 44 14N 76 5W
Clear, C., *Ireland* **13 E2** 51 25N 9 32W
Clear, L., *Canada* **78 A7** 45 26N 77 12W
Clear Hills, *Canada* **72 B5** 56 40N 119 30W
Clear I., *Ireland* **13 E2** 51 26N 9 30W
Clear L., *U.S.A.* **84 F4** 39 2N 122 47W
Clear Lake, *Iowa, U.S.A.* **80 D8** 43 8N 93 23W
Clear Lake, *S. Dak., U.S.A.* **80 C6** 44 45N 96 41W
Clear Lake Reservoir, *U.S.A.* **82 F3** 41 56N 121 5W
Clearfield, *Pa., U.S.A.* **78 E6** 41 2N 78 27W
Clearfield, *Utah, U.S.A.* **82 F8** 41 7N 112 2W
Clearlake, *U.S.A.* **82 G2** 38 57N 122 38W
Clearlake Highlands, *U.S.A.* **84 G4** 38 57N 122 38W
Clearwater, *Canada* **72 C4** 51 38N 120 2W
Clearwater, *U.S.A.* **77 M4** 27 58N 82 48W
Clearwater →, *Alta., Canada* **72 C6** 52 22N 114 57W
Clearwater →, *Alta., Canada* **73 B6** 56 44N 111 23W
Clearwater L., *Canada* **73 C9** 53 34N 99 49W
Clearwater Mts., *U.S.A.* **82 C6** 46 5N 115 20W
Clearwater Prov. Park, *Canada* **73 C8** 54 0N 101 0W
Clearwater River Prov. Park, *Canada* **73 B7** 56 55N 109 10W
Cleburne, *U.S.A.* **81 J6** 32 21N 97 23W
Clee Hills, *U.K.* **11 E5** 52 26N 2 35W
Cleethorpes, *U.K.* **10 D7** 53 33N 0 3W
Cleeve Cloud, *U.K.* **11 F6** 51 56N 2 0W
Clemson, *U.S.A.* **77 H4** 34 41N 82 50W
Clerke Reef, *Australia* **60 C2** 17 22S 119 20 E
Clermont, *Australia* **62 C4** 22 49S 147 39 E
Clermont, *U.S.A.* **77 L5** 28 33N 81 46W
Clermont-Ferrand, *France* **18 D5** 45 46N 3 4 E
Clervaux, *Lux.* **15 D6** 50 4N 6 2 E
Cleve, *Australia* **63 E2** 33 43S 136 30 E
Clevedon, *U.K.* **11 F5** 51 26N 2 52W
Cleveland, *Miss., U.S.A.* **81 J9** 33 45N 90 43W
Cleveland, *Ohio, U.S.A.* **78 E3** 41 30N 81 42W
Cleveland, *Okla., U.S.A.* **81 G6** 36 19N 96 28W
Cleveland, *Tenn., U.S.A.* **77 H3** 35 10N 84 53W
Cleveland, *Tex., U.S.A.* **81 K7** 30 21N 95 5W
Cleveland, C., *Australia* **62 B4** 19 11S 147 1 E
Cleveland, Mt., *U.S.A.* **82 B7** 48 56N 113 51W
Cleveland Heights, *U.S.A.* **78 E3** 41 30N 81 34W
Clevelândia, *Brazil* **95 B5** 26 24S 52 23W
Clew B., *Ireland* **13 C2** 53 50N 9 49W
Clewiston, *U.S.A.* **77 M5** 26 45N 80 56W
Clifden, *Ireland* **13 C1** 53 29N 10 1W
Clifden, *N.Z.* **59 M1** 46 1S 167 42 E
Cliffdell, *U.S.A.* **84 D5** 46 56N 121 5W
Cliffy Hd., *Australia* **61 G2** 35 1S 116 29 E
Clifton, *Australia* **63 D5** 27 59S 151 53 E
Clifton, *Ariz., U.S.A.* **83 K9** 33 3N 109 18W
Clifton, *Colo., U.S.A.* **83 G9** 39 7N 108 25W
Clifton, *Tex., U.S.A.* **81 K6** 31 47N 97 35W
Clifton Beach, *Australia* **62 B4** 16 46S 145 39 E
Climax, *Canada* **73 D7** 49 10N 108 20W
Clinch →, *U.S.A.* **77 H3** 35 53N 84 29W
Clingmans Dome, *U.S.A.* **77 H4** 35 34N 83 30W
Clint, *U.S.A.* **83 L10** 31 35N 106 14W
Clinton, *B.C., Canada* **72 C4** 51 6N 121 35W
Clinton, *Ont., Canada* **78 C3** 43 37N 81 32W
Clinton, *N.Z.* **59 M2** 46 12S 169 23 E
Clinton, *Ark., U.S.A.* **81 H8** 35 36N 92 28W
Clinton, *Conn., U.S.A.* **79 E12** 41 17N 72 32W
Clinton, *Ill., U.S.A.* **80 E10** 40 9N 88 57W
Clinton, *Ind., U.S.A.* **76 F2** 39 40N 87 24W
Clinton, *Iowa, U.S.A.* **80 E9** 41 51N 90 12W
Clinton, *Mass., U.S.A.* **79 D13** 42 25N 71 41W
Clinton, *Miss., U.S.A.* **81 J9** 32 20N 90 20W
Clinton, *Mo., U.S.A.* **80 F8** 38 22N 93 46W
Clinton, *N.C., U.S.A.* **77 H6** 35 0N 78 22W
Clinton, *Okla., U.S.A.* **81 H5** 35 31N 98 58W
Clinton, *S.C., U.S.A.* **77 H5** 34 29N 81 53W
Clinton, *Tenn., U.S.A.* **77 G3** 36 6N 84 8W
Clinton, *Wash., U.S.A.* **84 C4** 47 59N 122 21W
Clinton C., *Australia* **62 C5** 22 30S 150 45 E
Clinton Colden L., *Canada* **68 B9** 63 58N 107 27W
Clintonville, *U.S.A.* **80 C10** 44 37N 88 46W
Clipperton, I., *Pac. Oc.* **65 F17** 10 18N 109 13W
Clisham, *U.K.* **12 D2** 57 57N 6 49W
Clitheroe, *U.K.* **10 D5** 53 53N 2 22W
Clo-oose, *Canada* **84 B2** 48 39N 124 49W
Cloates, Pt., *Australia* **60 D1** 22 43S 113 40 E
Clocolan, *S. Africa* **57 D4** 28 55S 27 34 E
Clodomira, *Argentina* **94 B3** 27 35S 64 14W
Clogher Hd., *Ireland* **13 C5** 53 48N 6 14W
Clonakilty, *Ireland* **13 E3** 51 37N 8 53W
Clonakilty B., *Ireland* **13 E3** 51 35N 8 51W
Cloncurry, *Australia* **62 C3** 20 40S 140 28 E
Cloncurry →, *Australia* **62 B3** 18 37S 140 40 E
Clondalkin, *Ireland* **13 C5** 53 19N 6 25W
Clones, *Ireland* **13 B4** 54 11N 7 15W
Clonmel, *Ireland* **13 D4** 52 21N 7 42W
Cloquet, *U.S.A.* **80 B8** 46 43N 92 28W
Clorinda, *Argentina* **94 B4** 25 16S 57 45W
Cloud Bay, *Canada* **70 C2** 48 5N 89 26W
Cloud Peak, *U.S.A.* **82 D10** 44 23N 107 11W
Cloudcroft, *U.S.A.* **83 K11** 32 58N 105 45W
Cloverdale, *U.S.A.* **84 G4** 38 48N 123 1W
Clovis, *Calif., U.S.A.* **84 J7** 36 49N 119 42W
Clovis, *N. Mex., U.S.A.* **81 H3** 34 24N 103 12W
Cloyne, *Canada* **78 B7** 44 49N 77 11W
Cluj-Napoca, *Romania* **17 E12** 46 47N 23 38 E
Clunes, *Australia* **63 F3** 37 20S 143 45 E
Clutha →, *N.Z.* **59 M2** 46 20S 169 49 E
Clwyd →, *U.K.* **10 D4** 53 19N 3 31W
Clyde, *Canada* **72 C6** 54 9N 113 39W
Clyde, *N.Z.* **59 L2** 45 12S 169 20 E
Clyde, *U.S.A.* **78 C8** 43 5N 76 52W
Clyde →, *U.K.* **12 F4** 55 55N 4 30W
Clyde, Firth of, *U.K.* **12 F3** 55 22N 5 1W
Clyde River, *Canada* **69 A13** 70 30N 68 30W
Clydebank, *U.K.* **12 F4** 55 54N 4 23W
Clymer, *N.Y., U.S.A.* **78 D5** 42 1N 79 37W
Clymer, *Pa., U.S.A.* **78 D5** 40 40N 79 1W
Coachella, *U.S.A.* **85 M10** 33 41N 116 10W
Coachella Canal, *U.S.A.* **85 N12** 32 43N 114 57W
Coahoma, *U.S.A.* **81 J4** 32 18N 101 18W
Coahuayana →, *Mexico* **86 D4** 18 41N 103 45W
Coahuila □, *Mexico* **86 B4** 27 0N 103 0W
Coal →, *Canada* **72 B3** 59 39N 126 57W
Coalane, *Mozam.* **55 F4** 17 48S 37 2 E
Coalcomán, *Mexico* **86 D4** 18 40N 103 10W
Coaldale, *Canada* **72 D6** 49 45N 112 35W
Coalgate, *U.S.A.* **81 H6** 34 32N 96 13W
Coalinga, *U.S.A.* **84 J6** 36 9N 120 21W
Coalisland, *U.K.* **13 B5** 54 33N 6 42W
Coalville, *U.K.* **10 E6** 52 44N 1 23W
Coalville, *U.S.A.* **82 F8** 40 55N 111 24W
Coari, *Brazil* **92 D6** 4 8S 63 7W
Coast □, *Kenya* **54 C4** 2 40S 39 45 E
Coast Mts., *Canada* **72 C3** 55 0N 129 20W
Coast Ranges, *U.S.A.* **84 G4** 39 0N 123 0W
Coatbridge, *U.K.* **12 F4** 55 52N 4 6W
Coatepec, *Mexico* **87 D5** 19 27N 96 58W
Coatepeque, *Guatemala* **88 D1** 14 46N 91 55W
Coatesville, *U.S.A.* **76 F8** 39 59N 75 50W
Coaticook, *Canada* **79 A13** 45 10N 71 46W
Coats I., *Canada* **69 B11** 62 30N 83 0W
Coats Land, *Antarctica* **5 D1** 77 0S 25 0W
Coatzacoalcos, *Mexico* **87 D6** 18 7N 94 25W
Cobalt, *Canada* **70 C4** 47 25N 79 42W

Corrientes

Corrientes □, *Argentina* **94 B4** 28 0S 57 0W
Corrientes →, *Argentina* **94 C4** 30 42S 59 38W
Corrientes →, *Peru* **92 D4** 3 43S 74 35W
Corrientes, C., *Colombia* **92 B3** 5 30N 77 34W
Corrientes, C., *Cuba* **88 B3** 21 43N 84 30W
Corrientes, C., *Mexico* **86 C3** 20 25N 105 42W
Corrigan, *U.S.A.* **81 K7** 31 0N 94 52W
Corrigin, *Australia* **61 F2** 32 20S 117 53 E
Corry, *U.S.A.* **78 E5** 41 55N 79 39W
Corryong, *Australia* **63 F4** 36 12S 147 53 E
Corse, *France* **18 F8** 42 0N 9 0 E
Corse, C., *France* **18 E8** 43 1N 9 25 E
Corsica = Corse, *France* **18 F8** 42 0N 9 0 E
Corsicana, *U.S.A.* **81 J6** 32 6N 96 28W
Corte, *France* **18 E8** 42 19N 9 11 E
Cortez, *U.S.A.* **83 H9** 37 21N 108 35W
Cortland, *N.Y., U.S.A.* **79 D8** 42 36N 76 11W
Cortland, *Ohio, U.S.A.* **78 E4** 41 20N 80 44W
Çorum, *Turkey* **25 F5** 40 30N 34 57 E
Corumbá, *Brazil* **92 G7** 19 0S 57 30W
Corunna = A Coruña, *Spain* **19 A1** 43 20N 8 25W
Corvallis, *U.S.A.* **82 D2** 44 34N 123 16W
Corvette, L. de la, *Canada* **70 B5** 53 25N 74 3W
Corydon, *U.S.A.* **80 E8** 40 46N 93 19W
Cosalá, *Mexico* **86 C3** 24 28N 106 40W
Cosamaloapan, *Mexico* **87 D5** 18 23N 95 50W
Cosenza, *Italy* **20 E7** 39 18N 16 15 E
Coshocton, *U.S.A.* **78 F3** 40 16N 81 51W
Cosmo Newberry, *Australia* **61 E3** 28 0S 122 54 E
Coso Junction, *U.S.A.* **85 J9** 36 3N 117 57W
Coso Pk., *U.S.A.* **85 J9** 36 13N 117 44W
Cosquín, *Argentina* **94 C3** 31 15S 64 30W
Costa Blanca, *Spain* **19 C5** 38 25N 0 10W
Costa Brava, *Spain* **19 B7** 41 30N 3 0 E
Costa del Sol, *Spain* **19 D3** 36 30N 4 30W
Costa Dorada, *Spain* **19 B6** 41 12N 1 15 E
Costa Mesa, *U.S.A.* **85 M9** 33 38N 117 55W
Costa Rica ■, *Cent. Amer.* **88 E3** 10 0N 84 0W
Cosumnes →, *U.S.A.* **84 G5** 38 16N 121 26W
Cotabato, *Phil.* **37 C6** 7 14N 124 15 E
Cotagaita, *Bolivia* **94 A2** 20 45S 65 40W
Côte d'Azur, *France* **18 E7** 43 25N 7 10 E
Côte-d'Ivoire = Ivory Coast ■, *Africa* **50 G4** 7 30N 5 0W
Coteau des Prairies, *U.S.A.* **80 C6** 45 20N 97 50W
Coteau du Missouri, *U.S.A.* **80 B4** 47 0N 100 0W
Coteau Landing, *Canada* **79 A10** 45 15N 74 13W
Cotentin, *France* **18 B3** 49 15N 1 30W
Cotillo, *Canary Is.* **22 F5** 28 41N 14 1W
Cotonou, *Benin* **50 G6** 6 20N 2 25 E
Cotopaxi, *Ecuador* **92 D3** 0 40S 78 30W
Cotswold Hills, *U.K.* **11 F5** 51 42N 2 10W
Cottage Grove, *U.S.A.* **82 E2** 43 48N 123 3W
Cottbus, *Germany* **16 C8** 51 45N 14 20 E
Cottonwood, *U.S.A.* **83 J7** 34 45N 112 1W
Cotulla, *U.S.A.* **81 L5** 28 26N 99 14W
Coudersport, *U.S.A.* **78 E6** 41 46N 78 1W
Couedic, C. du, *Australia* **63 F2** 36 5S 136 40 E
Coulee City, *U.S.A.* **82 C4** 47 37N 119 17W
Coulman I., *Antarctica* **5 D11** 73 35S 170 0 E
Coulonge →, *Canada* **70 C4** 45 52N 76 46W
Coulterville, *U.S.A.* **84 H6** 37 43N 120 12W
Council, *U.S.A.* **82 D5** 44 44N 116 26W
Council Bluffs, *U.S.A.* **80 E7** 41 16N 95 52W
Council Grove, *U.S.A.* **80 F6** 38 40N 96 29W
Coupeville, *U.S.A.* **84 B4** 48 13N 122 41W
Courantyne →, *S. Amer.* **92 B7** 5 55N 57 5W
Courcelles, *Belgium* **15 D4** 50 28N 4 22 E
Courtenay, *Canada* **72 D4** 49 45N 125 0W
Courtland, *U.S.A.* **84 G5** 38 20N 121 34W
Courtrai = Kortrijk, *Belgium* **15 D3** 50 50N 3 17 E
Courtright, *Canada* **78 D2** 42 49N 82 28W
Coushatta, *U.S.A.* **81 J8** 32 1N 93 21W
Coutts Crossing, *Australia* **63 D5** 29 49S 152 55 E
Couvin, *Belgium* **15 D4** 50 3N 4 29 E
Cove I., *Canada* **78 A3** 45 17N 81 44W
Coventry, *U.K.* **11 E6** 52 25N 1 28W
Covilhã, *Portugal* **19 B2** 40 17N 7 31W
Covington, *Ga., U.S.A.* **77 J4** 33 36N 83 51W
Covington, *Ky., U.S.A.* **76 F3** 39 5N 84 31W
Covington, *Okla., U.S.A.* **81 G6** 36 18N 97 35W
Covington, *Tenn., U.S.A.* **81 H10** 35 34N 89 39W
Covington, *Va., U.S.A.* **76 G5** 37 47N 79 59W
Cowal, L., *Australia* **63 E4** 33 40S 147 25 E
Cowan, L., *Australia* **61 F3** 31 45S 121 45 E
Cowan L., *Canada* **73 C7** 54 0N 107 15W
Cowangie, *Australia* **63 F3** 35 12S 141 26 E
Cowansville, *Canada* **79 A12** 45 14N 72 46W
Coward Springs, *Australia* **63 D2** 29 24S 136 49 E
Cowcowing Lakes, *Australia* **61 F2** 30 55S 117 20 E
Cowdenbeath, *U.K.* **12 E5** 56 7N 3 21W
Cowell, *Australia* **63 E2** 33 39S 136 56 E
Cowes, *U.K.* **11 G6** 50 45N 1 18W
Cowichan L., *Canada* **84 B2** 48 53N 124 17W
Cowlitz →, *U.S.A.* **84 D4** 46 6N 122 55W
Cowra, *Australia* **63 E4** 33 49S 148 42 E
Coxilha Grande, *Brazil* **95 B5** 28 18S 51 30W
Coxim, *Brazil* **93 G8** 18 30S 54 55W
Cox's Bazar, *Bangla.* **41 J17** 21 26N 91 59 E
Coyote Wells, *U.S.A.* **85 N11** 32 44N 115 58W
Coyuca de Benítez, *Mexico* **87 D4** 17 1N 100 8W
Coyuca de Catalan, *Mexico* **86 D4** 18 18N 100 41W
Cozad, *U.S.A.* **80 E5** 40 52N 99 59W
Cozumel, *Mexico* **87 C7** 20 31N 86 55W
Cozumel, Isla, *Mexico* **87 C7** 20 30N 86 40W
Cracow = Kraków, *Poland* **17 C10** 50 4N 19 57 E
Cracow, *Australia* **63 D5** 25 17S 150 17 E
Cradock, *Australia* **63 E2** 32 6S 138 31 E
Cradock, *S. Africa* **56 E4** 32 8S 25 36 E
Craig, *U.S.A.* **82 F10** 40 31N 107 33W
Craigavon, *U.K.* **13 B5** 54 27N 6 23W
Craigmore, *Zimbabwe* **55 G3** 20 28S 32 50 E
Craik, *Canada* **73 C7** 51 3N 105 49W
Crailsheim, *Germany* **16 D6** 49 8N 10 5 E
Craiova, *Romania* **17 F12** 44 21N 23 48 E
Cramsie, *Australia* **62 C3** 23 20S 144 15 E
Cranberry L., *U.S.A.* **79 B10** 44 11N 74 50W
Cranberry Portage, *Canada* **73 C8** 54 35N 101 23W
Cranbrook, *Australia* **61 F2** 34 18S 117 33 E
Cranbrook, *Canada* **72 D5** 49 30N 115 46W
Crandon, *U.S.A.* **80 C10** 45 34N 88 54W
Crane, *Oreg., U.S.A.* **82 E4** 43 25N 118 35W
Crane, *Tex., U.S.A.* **81 K3** 31 24N 102 21W
Cranston, *U.S.A.* **79 E13** 41 47N 71 26W
Crater L., *U.S.A.* **82 E2** 42 56N 122 6W
Crater Lake National Park, *U.S.A.* **82 E2** 42 55N 122 10W
Crateús, *Brazil* **93 E10** 5 10S 40 39W
Crato, *Brazil* **93 E11** 7 10S 39 25W
Craven, L., *Canada* **70 B4** 54 20N 76 56W
Crawford, *U.S.A.* **80 D3** 42 41N 103 25W
Crawfordsville, *U.S.A.* **76 E2** 40 2N 86 54W
Crawley, *U.K.* **11 F7** 51 7N 0 11W
Crazy Mts., *U.S.A.* **82 C8** 46 12N 110 20W
Crean L., *Canada* **73 C7** 54 5N 106 9W
Crediton, *Canada* **78 C3** 43 17N 81 33W
Cree →, *Canada* **73 B7** 58 57N 105 47W
Cree →, *U.K.* **12 G4** 54 55N 4 25W
Cree L., *Canada* **73 B7** 57 30N 106 30W
Creede, *U.S.A.* **83 H10** 37 51N 106 56W
Creekside, *U.S.A.* **78 F5** 40 40N 79 11W
Creel, *Mexico* **86 B3** 27 45N 107 38W
Creemore, *Canada* **78 B4** 44 19N 80 6W
Creighton, *Canada* **73 C8** 54 45N 101 54W
Creighton, *U.S.A.* **80 D6** 42 28N 97 54W
Crema, *Italy* **18 D8** 45 22N 9 41 E
Cremona, *Italy* **18 D9** 45 7N 10 2 E
Cres, *Croatia* **16 F8** 44 58N 14 25 E
Crescent City, *U.S.A.* **82 F1** 41 45N 124 12W
Crespo, *Argentina* **94 C3** 32 2S 60 19W
Cresson, *U.S.A.* **78 F6** 40 28N 78 36W
Crestline, *Calif., U.S.A.* **85 L9** 34 14N 117 18W
Crestline, *Ohio, U.S.A.* **78 F2** 40 47N 82 44W
Creston, *Canada* **72 D5** 49 10N 116 31W
Creston, *Calif., U.S.A.* **84 K6** 35 32N 120 33W
Creston, *Iowa, U.S.A.* **80 E7** 41 4N 94 22W
Crestview, *Calif., U.S.A.* **84 H8** 37 46N 118 58W
Crestview, *Fla., U.S.A.* **77 K2** 30 46N 86 34W
Crete = Kríti, *Greece* **23 D7** 35 15N 25 0 E
Crete, *U.S.A.* **80 E6** 40 38N 96 58W
Créteil, *France* **18 B5** 48 47N 2 28 E
Creus, C. de, *Spain* **19 A7** 42 20N 3 19 E
Creuse →, *France* **18 C4** 47 0N 0 34 E
Crewe, *U.K.* **10 D5** 53 6N 2 26W
Crewkerne, *U.K.* **11 G5** 50 53N 2 48W
Criciúma, *Brazil* **95 B6** 28 40S 49 23W
Crieff, *U.K.* **12 E5** 56 22N 3 50W
Crimea □, *Ukraine* **25 E5** 45 30N 33 10 E
Crimean Pen. = Krymskyy Pivostriv, *Ukraine* **25 F5** 45 0N 34 0 E
Crişul Alb →, *Romania* **17 E11** 46 42N 21 17 E
Crişul Negru →, *Romania* **17 E11** 46 42N 21 16 E
Crna →, *Macedonia* **21 D9** 41 33N 21 59 E
Crna Gora = Montenegro □, *Yugoslavia* **21 C8** 42 40N 19 20 E
Crna Gora, *Macedonia* **21 C9** 42 10N 21 30 E
Crna Reka = Crna →, *Macedonia* **21 D9** 41 33N 21 59 E
Croagh Patrick, *Ireland* **13 C2** 53 46N 9 40W
Croatia ■, *Europe* **16 F9** 45 20N 16 0 E
Crocker, Banjaran, *Malaysia* **36 C5** 5 40N 116 30 E
Crockett, *U.S.A.* **81 K7** 31 19N 95 27W
Crocodile = Krokodil →, *Mozam.* **57 D5** 25 14S 32 18 E
Crocodile Is., *Australia* **62 A1** 12 3S 134 58 E
Crohy Hd., *Ireland* **13 B3** 54 55N 8 26W
Croix, L. La, *Canada* **70 C1** 48 20N 92 15W
Croker, C., *Australia* **60 B5** 10 58S 132 35 E
Croker, C., *Canada* **78 B4** 44 58N 80 59W
Croker I., *Australia* **60 B5** 11 12S 132 32 E
Cromarty, *U.K.* **12 D4** 57 40N 4 2W
Cromer, *U.K.* **10 E9** 52 56N 1 17 E
Cromwell, *N.Z.* **59 L2** 45 3S 169 14 E
Cromwell, *U.S.A.* **79 E12** 41 36N 72 39W
Crook, *U.K.* **10 C6** 54 43N 1 45W
Crooked →, *Canada* **72 C4** 54 50N 122 54W
Crooked →, *U.S.A.* **82 D3** 44 32N 121 16W
Crooked I., *Bahamas* **89 B5** 22 50N 74 10W
Crooked Island Passage, *Bahamas* **89 B5** 23 0N 74 30W
Crookston, *Minn., U.S.A.* **80 B6** 47 47N 96 37W
Crookston, *Nebr., U.S.A.* **80 D4** 42 56N 100 45W
Crookwell, *Australia* **63 E4** 34 28S 149 24 E
Crosby, *U.K.* **10 D4** 53 30N 3 3W
Crosby, *U.S.A.* **78 E6** 41 45N 78 23W
Crosbyton, *U.S.A.* **81 J4** 33 40N 101 14W
Cross City, *U.S.A.* **77 L4** 29 38N 83 7W
Cross Fell, *U.K.* **10 C5** 54 43N 2 28W
Cross L., *Canada* **73 C9** 54 45N 97 30W
Cross Lake, *Canada* **73 C9** 54 37N 97 47W
Cross Sound, *U.S.A.* **68 C6** 58 0N 135 0W
Crossett, *U.S.A.* **81 J9** 33 8N 91 58W
Crosshaven, *Ireland* **13 E3** 51 47N 8 17W
Crossville, *U.S.A.* **77 G3** 35 57N 85 2W
Croswell, *U.S.A.* **78 C2** 43 16N 82 37W
Croton-on-Hudson, *U.S.A.* **79 E11** 41 12N 73 55W
Crotone, *Italy* **20 E7** 39 5N 17 8 E
Crow →, *Canada* **72 B4** 59 41N 124 20W
Crow Agency, *U.S.A.* **82 D10** 45 36N 107 28W
Crow Hd., *Ireland* **13 E1** 51 35N 10 9W
Crowell, *U.S.A.* **81 J5** 33 59N 99 43W
Crowley, *U.S.A.* **81 K8** 30 13N 92 22W
Crowley, L., *U.S.A.* **84 H8** 37 35N 118 42W
Crown Point, *Ind., U.S.A.* **76 E2** 41 25N 87 22W
Crown Point, *N.Y., U.S.A.* **79 C11** 43 57N 73 26W
Crownpoint, *U.S.A.* **83 J9** 35 41N 108 9W
Crows Landing, *U.S.A.* **84 H5** 37 23N 121 6W
Crows Nest, *Australia* **63 D5** 27 16S 152 4 E
Crowsnest Pass, *Canada* **72 D6** 49 40N 114 40W
Croydon, *Australia* **62 B3** 18 13S 142 14 E
Croydon, *U.K.* **11 F7** 51 22N 0 5W
Crozet Is., *Ind. Oc.* **3 G12** 46 27S 52 0 E
Cruz, C., *Cuba* **88 C4** 19 50N 77 50W
Cruz Alta, *Brazil* **95 B5** 28 45S 53 40W
Cruz del Eje, *Argentina* **94 C3** 30 45S 64 50W
Cruzeiro, *Brazil* **95 A7** 22 33S 45 0W
Cruzeiro do Oeste, *Brazil* **95 A5** 23 46S 53 4W
Cruzeiro do Sul, *Brazil* **92 E4** 7 35S 72 35W
Cry L., *Canada* **72 B3** 58 45N 129 0W
Crystal Bay, *U.S.A.* **84 F7** 39 15N 120 0W
Crystal Brook, *Australia* **63 E2** 33 21S 138 12 E
Crystal City, *U.S.A.* **81 L5** 28 41N 99 50W
Crystal Falls, *U.S.A.* **76 B1** 46 5N 88 20W
Crystal River, *U.S.A.* **77 L4** 28 54N 82 35W
Crystal Springs, *U.S.A.* **81 K9** 31 59N 90 21W
Csongrád, *Hungary* **17 E11** 46 43N 20 12 E
Cu Lao Hon, *Vietnam* **39 G7** 10 54N 108 18 E
Cua Rao, *Vietnam* **38 C5** 19 16N 104 27 E
Cuácua →, *Mozam.* **55 F4** 17 54S 37 0 E
Cuamato, *Angola* **56 B2** 17 2S 15 7 E
Cuamba, *Mozam.* **55 E4** 14 45S 36 22 E
Cuando →, *Angola* **53 H4** 17 30S 23 15 E
Cuando Cubango □, *Angola* **56 B3** 16 25S 20 0 E
Cuangar, *Angola* **56 B2** 17 36S 18 39 E
Cuanza →, *Angola* **52 F2** 9 2S 13 30 E
Cuarto →, *Argentina* **94 C3** 33 25S 63 2W
Cuatrociénegas, *Mexico* **86 B4** 26 59N 102 5W
Cuauhtémoc, *Mexico* **86 B3** 28 25N 106 52W
Cuba, *N. Mex., U.S.A.* **83 J10** 36 1N 107 4W
Cuba, *N.Y., U.S.A.* **78 D6** 42 13N 78 17W
Cuba ■, *W. Indies* **88 B4** 22 0N 79 0W
Cubal, *Angola* **53 G2** 12 26S 14 3 E
Cubango →, *Africa* **56 B3** 18 50S 22 25 E
Cuchumatanes, Sierra de los, *Guatemala* **88 C1** 15 35N 91 25W
Cuckfield, *U.K.* **11 F7** 51 1N 0 8W
Cucuí, *Brazil* **92 C5** 1 12N 66 50W
Cucurpe, *Mexico* **86 A2** 30 20N 110 43W
Cúcuta, *Colombia* **92 B4** 7 54N 72 31W
Cuddalore, *India* **40 P11** 11 46N 79 45 E
Cuddapah, *India* **40 M11** 14 30N 78 47 E
Cuddapan, L., *Australia* **62 D3** 25 45S 141 26 E
Cue, *Australia* **61 E2** 27 25S 117 54 E
Cuenca, *Ecuador* **92 D3** 2 50S 79 9W
Cuenca, *Spain* **19 B4** 40 5N 2 10W
Cuenca, Serranía de, *Spain* **19 C5** 39 55N 1 50W
Cuernavaca, *Mexico* **87 D5** 18 55N 99 15W
Cuero, *U.S.A.* **81 L6** 29 6N 97 17W
Cuevas del Almanzora, *Spain* **19 D5** 37 18N 1 58W
Cuevo, *Bolivia* **92 H6** 20 15S 63 30W
Cuiabá, *Brazil* **93 G7** 15 30S 56 0W
Cuiabá →, *Brazil* **93 G7** 17 5S 56 36W
Cuijk, *Neths.* **15 C5** 51 44N 5 50 E
Cuilco, *Guatemala* **88 C1** 15 24N 91 58W
Cuillin Hills, *U.K.* **12 D2** 57 13N 6 15W
Cuillin Sd., *U.K.* **12 D2** 57 4N 6 20W
Cuito →, *Angola* **56 B3** 18 1S 20 48 E
Cuitzeo, L. de, *Mexico* **86 D4** 19 55N 101 5W
Cukai, *Malaysia* **39 K4** 4 13N 103 25 E
Culbertson, *U.S.A.* **80 A2** 48 9N 104 31W
Culcairn, *Australia* **63 F4** 35 41S 147 3 E
Culgoa →, *Australia* **63 D4** 29 56S 146 20 E
Culiacán, *Mexico* **86 C3** 24 50N 107 23W
Culiacán →, *Mexico* **86 C3** 24 30N 107 42W
Culion, *Phil.* **37 B6** 11 54N 119 58 E
Cullarin Ra., *Australia* **63 E4** 34 30S 149 30 E
Cullen, *U.K.* **12 D6** 57 42N 2 49W
Cullen Pt., *Australia* **62 A3** 11 57S 141 54 E
Cullera, *Spain* **19 C5** 39 9N 0 17W
Cullman, *U.S.A.* **77 H2** 34 11N 86 51W
Culpeper, *U.S.A.* **76 F7** 38 30N 78 0W
Culuene →, *Brazil* **93 F8** 12 56S 52 51W
Culver, Pt., *Australia* **61 F3** 32 54S 124 43 E
Culverden, *N.Z.* **59 K4** 42 47S 172 49 E
Cumaná, *Venezuela* **92 A6** 10 30N 64 5W
Cumberland, *B.C., Canada* **72 D4** 49 40N 125 0W
Cumberland, *Ont., Canada* **79 A9** 45 29N 75 24W
Cumberland, *U.S.A.* **76 F6** 39 39N 78 46W
Cumberland →, *U.S.A.* **77 G2** 36 15N 87 0W
Cumberland I., *U.S.A.* **77 G3** 36 57N 84 55W
Cumberland L., *U.S.A.* **77 K5** 30 50N 81 25W
Cumberland Is., *Australia* **62 C4** 20 35S 149 10 E
Cumberland L., *Canada* **73 C8** 54 3N 102 18W
Cumberland Pen., *Canada* **69 B13** 67 0N 64 0W
Cumberland Plateau, *U.S.A.* **77 H3** 36 0N 85 0W
Cumberland Sd., *Canada* **69 B13** 65 30N 66 0W
Cumbernauld, *U.K.* **12 F5** 55 57N 3 58W
Cumborah, *Australia* **63 D4** 29 40S 147 45 E
Cumbria □, *U.K.* **10 C5** 54 42N 2 52W
Cumbrian Mts., *U.K.* **10 C5** 54 30N 3 0W
Cumbum, *India* **40 M11** 15 40N 79 10 E
Cuminá →, *Brazil* **93 D7** 1 30S 56 0W
Cummings Mt., *U.S.A.* **85 K8** 35 2N 118 34W
Cummins, *Australia* **63 E2** 34 16S 135 43 E
Cumnock, *Australia* **63 E4** 32 59S 148 46 E
Cumnock, *U.K.* **12 F4** 55 28N 4 17W
Cumpas, *Mexico* **86 B3** 30 0N 109 48W
Cumplida, Pta., *Canary Is.* **22 F2** 28 50N 17 48W
Cunco, *Chile* **96 D2** 38 55S 72 2W
Cuncumén, *Chile* **94 C1** 31 53S 70 38W
Cunderdin, *Australia* **61 F2** 31 37S 117 12 E
Cunene →, *Angola* **56 B1** 17 20S 11 50 E
Cúneo, *Italy* **18 D7** 44 23N 7 32 E
Çüngüş, *Turkey* **44 B3** 38 13N 39 17 E
Cunillera, I. = Sa Conillera, *Spain* **22 C7** 38 59N 1 13 E
Cunnamulla, *Australia* **63 D4** 28 2S 145 38 E
Cupar, *Canada* **73 C8** 50 57N 104 10W
Cupar, *U.K.* **12 E5** 56 19N 3 1W
Cupica, G. de, *Colombia* **92 B3** 6 25N 77 30W
Curaçao, *Neth. Ant.* **89 D6** 12 10N 69 0W
Curanilahue, *Chile* **94 D1** 37 29S 73 28W
Curaray →, *Peru* **92 D4** 2 20S 74 5W
Curepto, *Chile* **94 D1** 35 8S 72 1W
Curiapo, *Venezuela* **92 B6** 8 33N 61 5W
Curicó, *Chile* **94 C1** 34 55S 71 20W
Curitiba, *Brazil* **95 B6** 25 20S 49 10W
Curitibanos, *Brazil* **95 B5** 27 18S 50 36W
Currabubula, *Australia* **63 E5** 31 16S 150 44 E
Currais Novos, *Brazil* **93 E11** 6 13S 36 30W
Curralinho, *Brazil* **93 D9** 1 45S 49 46W
Currant, *U.S.A.* **82 G6** 38 51N 115 32W
Current →, *U.S.A.* **81 G9** 36 15N 90 55W
Currie, *Australia* **62 F3** 39 56S 143 53 E
Currie, *U.S.A.* **82 F6** 40 16N 114 45W
Curtea de Argeş, *Romania* **17 F13** 45 12N 24 42 E
Curtis, *U.S.A.* **80 E4** 40 38N 100 31W
Curtis Group, *Australia* **62 F4** 39 30S 146 37 E
Curtis I., *Australia* **62 C5** 23 35S 151 10 E
Curuápanema →, *Brazil* **93 D7** 2 25S 55 2W
Curuçá, *Brazil* **93 D9** 0 43S 47 50W
Curuguaty, *Paraguay* **95 A4** 24 31S 55 42W
Curup, *Indonesia* **36 E2** 4 26S 102 13 E
Cururupu, *Brazil* **93 D10** 1 50S 44 50W
Curuzú Cuatiá, *Argentina* **94 B4** 29 50S 58 5W
Curvelo, *Brazil* **93 G10** 18 45S 44 27W
Cushing, *U.S.A.* **81 H6** 35 59N 96 46W
Cushing, Mt., *Canada* **72 B3** 57 35N 126 57W
Cusihuiriáchic, *Mexico* **86 B3** 28 10N 106 50W
Custer, *U.S.A.* **80 D3** 43 46N 103 36W
Cut Bank, *U.S.A.* **82 B7** 48 38N 112 20W
Cutchogue, *U.S.A.* **79 E12** 41 1N 72 30W
Cuthbert, *U.S.A.* **77 K3** 31 46N 84 48W
Cutler, *U.S.A.* **84 J7** 36 31N 119 17W
Cuttaburra →, *Australia* **63 D3** 29 43S 144 22 E
Cuttack, *India* **41 J14** 20 25N 85 57 E
Cuvier, C., *Australia* **61 D1** 23 14S 113 22 E
Cuvier I., *N.Z.* **59 G5** 36 27S 175 50 E
Cuxhaven, *Germany* **16 B5** 53 51N 8 41 E
Cuyahoga Falls, *U.S.A.* **78 E3** 41 8N 81 29W
Cuyo, *Phil.* **37 B6** 10 50N 121 5 E
Cuyuni →, *Guyana* **92 B7** 6 23N 58 41W
Cuzco, *Bolivia* **92 H5** 20 0S 66 50W
Cuzco, *Peru* **92 F4** 13 32S 72 0W
Cwmbran, *U.K.* **11 F4** 51 39N 3 2W
Cyangugu, *Rwanda* **54 C2** 2 29S 28 54 E
Cyclades = Kikládhes, *Greece* **21 F11** 37 0N 24 30 E
Cygnet, *Australia* **62 G4** 43 8S 147 1 E
Cynthiana, *U.S.A.* **76 F3** 38 23N 84 18W
Cypress Hills, *Canada* **73 D7** 49 40N 109 30W
Cypress Hills Prov. Park, *Canada* **73 D7** 49 40N 109 30W
Cyprus ■, *Asia* **23 E12** 35 0N 33 0 E
Cyrenaica, *Libya* **51 C10** 27 0N 23 0 E
Czar, *Canada* **73 C6** 52 27N 110 50W
Czech Rep. ■, *Europe* **16 D8** 50 0N 15 0 E
Częstochowa, *Poland* **17 C10** 50 49N 19 7 E

D

Da Hinggan Ling, *China* **33 B7** 48 0N 121 0 E
Da Lat, *Vietnam* **39 G7** 11 56N 108 25 E
Da Nang, *Vietnam* **38 D7** 16 4N 108 13 E
Da Qaidam, *China* **32 C4** 37 50N 95 15 E
Da Yunhe →, *China* **35 G11** 34 25N 120 5 E
Da'an, *China* **35 B13** 45 30N 124 7 E
Daba Shan, *China* **33 C5** 32 0N 109 0 E
Dabbagh, Jabal, *Si. Arabia* **44 E2** 27 52N 35 45 E
Dabhoi, *India* **42 H5** 22 10N 73 20 E
Dabo = Pasirkuning, *Indonesia* **36 E2** 0 30S 104 33 E
Dabola, *Guinea* **50 F3** 10 50N 11 5W
Dabung, *Malaysia* **39 K4** 5 23N 102 1 E
Dacca = Dhaka, *Bangla.* **43 H14** 23 43N 90 26 E
Dacca = Dhaka □, *Bangla.* **43 G14** 24 25N 90 25 E
Dachau, *Germany* **16 D6** 48 15N 11 26 E
Dadanawa, *Guyana* **92 C7** 2 50N 59 30W
Dade City, *U.S.A.* **77 L4** 28 22N 82 11W
Dadhar, *Pakistan* **42 E2** 29 28N 67 39 E
Dadra & Nagar Haveli □, *India* **40 J8** 20 5N 73 0 E
Dadri = Charkhi Dadri, *India* **42 E7** 28 37N 76 17 E
Dadu, *Pakistan* **42 F2** 26 45N 67 45 E
Daet, *Phil.* **37 B6** 14 2N 122 55 E
Dagana, *Senegal* **50 E2** 16 30N 15 35W
Dagestan □, *Russia* **25 F8** 42 30N 47 0 E
Daggett, *U.S.A.* **85 L10** 34 52N 116 52W
Daghestan Republic = Dagestan □, *Russia* **25 F8** 42 30N 47 0 E
Dağlıq Qarabağ = Nagorno-Karabakh, *Azerbaijan* **25 F8** 39 55N 46 45 E
Dagö = Hiiumaa, *Estonia* **9 G20** 58 50N 22 45 E
Dagu, *China* **35 E9** 38 59N 117 40 E
Dagupan, *Phil.* **37 A6** 16 3N 120 20 E
Daguragu, *Australia* **60 C5** 17 33S 130 30 E
Dahlak Kebir, *Eritrea* **46 D3** 15 50N 40 10 E
Dahlonega, *U.S.A.* **77 H4** 34 32N 83 59W
Dahod, *India* **42 H6** 22 50N 74 15 E
Dahomey = Benin ■, *Africa* **50 G6** 10 0N 2 0 E
Dahūk, *Iraq* **44 B3** 36 50N 43 1 E
Dai Hao, *Vietnam* **38 C6** 18 1N 106 25 E
Dai-Sen, *Japan* **31 G6** 35 22N 133 32 E
Dai Xian, *China* **34 E7** 39 4N 112 58 E
Daicheng, *China* **34 E9** 38 42N 116 38 E
Daingean, *Ireland* **13 C4** 53 18N 7 17W
Daintree, *Australia* **62 B4** 16 20S 145 20 E
Daiō-Misaki, *Japan* **31 G8** 34 15N 136 45 E
Daisetsu-Zan, *Japan* **30 C11** 43 30N 142 57 E
Dajarra, *Australia* **62 C2** 21 42S 139 30 E
Dak Dam, *Cambodia* **38 F6** 12 20N 107 21 E
Dak Nhe, *Vietnam* **38 E6** 15 28N 107 48 E
Dak Pek, *Vietnam* **38 E6** 15 4N 107 44 E
Dak Song, *Vietnam* **39 F6** 12 19N 107 35 E
Dak Sui, *Vietnam* **38 E6** 14 55N 107 43 E
Dakar, *Senegal* **50 F2** 14 34N 17 29W
Dakhla, *W. Sahara* **50 D2** 23 50N 15 53W
Dakhla, El Wâhât el-, *Egypt* **51 C11** 25 30N 28 50 E
Dakor, *India* **42 H5** 22 45N 73 11 E
Dakota City, *U.S.A.* **80 D6** 42 25N 96 25W
Đakovica, *Yugoslavia* **21 C9** 42 22N 20 26 E
Dalachi, *China* **34 F3** 36 48N 105 0 E
Dalai Nur, *China* **34 C9** 43 20N 116 45 E
Dālakī, *Iran* **45 D6** 29 26N 51 17 E
Dalälven, *Sweden* **9 F17** 60 12N 16 43 E
Dalaman →, *Turkey* **21 F13** 36 41N 28 43 E
Dalandzadgad, *Mongolia* **34 C3** 43 27N 104 30 E
Dalap-Uliga-Darrit, *Marshall Is.* **64 G9** 7 7N 171 24 E
Dalarna, *Sweden* **9 F16** 61 0N 14 0 E
Dālbandīn, *Pakistan* **40 E4** 29 0N 64 23 E
Dalbeattie, *U.K.* **12 G5** 54 56N 3 50W
Dalbeg, *Australia* **62 C4** 20 16S 147 18 E
Dalby, *Australia* **63 D5** 27 10S 151 17 E
Dale City, *U.S.A.* **76 F7** 38 38N 77 18W
Dale Hollow L., *U.S.A.* **77 G3** 36 32N 85 27W
Dalgān, *Iran* **45 E8** 27 31N 59 19 E
Dalhart, *U.S.A.* **81 G3** 36 4N 102 31W
Dalhousie, *Canada* **71 C6** 48 5N 66 26W
Dalhousie, *India* **42 C6** 32 38N 75 58 E
Dali, *Shaanxi, China* **34 G5** 34 48N 109 58 E
Dali, *Yunnan, China* **32 D5** 25 40N 100 10 E
Dalian, *China* **35 E11** 38 50N 121 40 E
Daliang Shan, *China* **32 D5** 28 0N 102 45 E
Daling He →, *China* **35 D11** 40 55N 121 40 E
Dāliyat el Karmel, *Israel* **47 C4** 32 43N 35 2 E
Dalkeith, *U.K.* **12 F5** 55 54N 3 4W
Dallas, *Oreg., U.S.A.* **82 D2** 44 55N 123 19W
Dallas, *Tex., U.S.A.* **81 J6** 32 47N 96 49W
Dalmā, *U.A.E.* **45 E7** 24 30N 52 20 E
Dalmacija, *Croatia* **20 C7** 43 20N 17 0 E
Dalmas, L., *Canada* **71 B5** 53 30N 71 50W
Dalmatia = Dalmacija, *Croatia* **20 C7** 43 20N 17 0 E
Dalmau, *India* **43 F9** 26 4N 81 2 E
Dalmellington, *U.K.* **12 F4** 55 19N 4 23W
Dalnegorsk, *Russia* **27 E14** 44 32N 135 33 E
Dalnerechensk, *Russia* **27 E14** 45 50N 133 40 E
Daloa, *Ivory C.* **50 G4** 7 0N 6 30W
Dalry, *U.K.* **12 F4** 55 42N 4 43W
Dalrymple, L., *Australia* **62 C4** 20 40S 147 0 E
Dalsland, *Sweden* **9 G14** 58 50N 12 15 E
Daltenganj, *India* **43 H11** 24 0N 84 4 E
Dalton, *Ga., U.S.A.* **77 H3** 34 46N 84 58W

Desolación, I.

Dalton, *Mass., U.S.A.* **79 D11** 42 28N 73 11W
Dalton, *Nebr., U.S.A.* **80 E3** 41 25N 102 58W
Dalton Iceberg Tongue, *Antarctica* **5 C9** 66 15S 121 30 E
Dalton-in-Furness, *U.K.* **10 C4** 54 10N 3 11W
Dalvík, *Iceland* **8 D4** 65 58N 18 32W
Dalwallinu, *Australia* **61 F2** 30 17S 116 40 E
Daly →, *Australia* **60 B5** 13 35S 130 19 E
Daly City, *U.S.A.* **84 H4** 37 42N 122 28W
Daly L., *Canada* **73 B7** 56 32N 105 39W
Daly River, *Australia* **60 B5** 13 46S 130 42 E
Daly Waters, *Australia* **62 B1** 16 15S 133 24 E
Dam Doi, *Vietnam* **39 H5** 8 50N 105 12 E
Dam Ha, *Vietnam* **38 B6** 21 21N 107 36 E
Daman, *India* **40 J8** 20 25N 72 57 E
Dāmaneh, *Iran* **45 C6** 33 1N 50 29 E
Damanhûr, *Egypt* **51 B12** 31 0N 30 30 E
Damant L., *Canada* **73 A7** 61 45N 105 5W
Damanzhuang, *China* **34 E9** 38 5N 116 35 E
Damar, *Indonesia* **37 F7** 7 7S 128 40 E
Damaraland, *Namibia* **56 C2** 20 0S 15 0 E
Damascus = Dimashq, *Syria* **47 B5** 33 30N 36 18 E
Damāvand, *Iran* **45 C7** 35 47N 52 0 E
Damāvand, Qolleh-ye, *Iran* **45 C7** 35 56N 52 10 E
Damba, *Angola* **52 F3** 6 44S 15 20 E
Dâmboviţa →, *Romania* **17 F14** 44 12N 26 26 E
Dame Marie, *Haiti* **89 C5** 18 36N 74 26W
Dāmghān, *Iran* **45 B7** 36 10N 54 17 E
Damiel, *Spain* **19 C4** 39 4N 3 37W
Damietta = Dumyât, *Egypt* **51 B12** 31 24N 31 48 E
Daming, *China* **34 F8** 36 15N 115 6 E
Damīr Qābū, *Syria* **44 B4** 36 58N 41 51 E
Dammam = Ad Dammām, *Si. Arabia* **45 E6** 26 20N 50 5 E
Damodar →, *India* **43 H12** 23 17N 87 35 E
Damoh, *India* **43 H8** 23 50N 79 28 E
Dampier, *Australia* **60 D2** 20 41S 116 42 E
Dampier, Selat, *Indonesia* **37 E8** 0 40S 131 0 E
Dampier Arch., *Australia* **60 D2** 20 38S 116 32 E
Damrei, Chuor Phnum, *Cambodia* **39 G4** 11 30N 103 0 E
Dan Xian, *China* **38 C7** 19 31N 109 33 E
Dana, *Indonesia* **37 F6** 11 0S 122 52 E
Dana, L., *Canada* **70 B4** 50 53N 77 20W
Dana, Mt., *U.S.A.* **84 H7** 37 54N 119 12W
Danakil Depression, *Ethiopia* **46 E3** 12 45N 41 0 E
Danané, *Ivory C.* **50 G4** 7 16N 8 9W
Danau Poso, *Indonesia* **37 E6** 1 52S 120 35 E
Danbury, *U.S.A.* **79 E11** 41 24N 73 28W
Danby L., *U.S.A.* **83 J6** 34 13N 115 5W
Dand, *Afghan.* **42 D1** 31 28N 65 32 E
Dandeldhura, *Nepal* **43 E9** 29 20N 80 35 E
Dandeli, *India* **40 M9** 15 5N 74 30 E
Dandenong, *Australia* **63 F4** 38 0S 145 15 E
Dandong, *China* **35 D13** 40 10N 124 20 E
Danfeng, *China* **34 H6** 33 45N 110 25 E
Danger Is. = Pukapuka, *Cook Is.* **65 J11** 10 53S 165 49W
Danger Pt., *S. Africa* **56 E2** 34 40S 19 17 E
Dangla Shan = Tanggula Shan, *China* **32 C4** 32 40N 92 10 E
Dangrek, Phnom, *Thailand* **38 E5** 14 15N 105 0 E
Dangriga, *Belize* **87 D7** 17 0N 88 13W
Dangshan, *China* **34 G9** 34 27N 116 22 E
Daniel, *U.S.A.* **82 E8** 42 52N 110 4W
Daniel's Harbour, *Canada* **71 B8** 50 13N 57 35W
Danielskuil, *S. Africa* **56 D3** 28 11S 23 33 E
Danielson, *U.S.A.* **79 E13** 41 48N 71 53W
Danilov, *Russia* **24 C7** 58 16N 40 13 E
Daning, *China* **34 F6** 36 28N 110 45 E
Danissa, *Kenya* **54 B5** 3 15N 40 58 E
Dank, *Oman* **45 F8** 23 33N 56 16 E
Dankhar Gompa, *India* **40 C11** 32 10N 78 10 E
Danlí, *Honduras* **88 D2** 14 4N 86 35W
Dannemora, *U.S.A.* **79 B11** 44 43N 73 44W
Dannevirke, *N.Z.* **59 J6** 40 12S 176 8 E
Dannhauser, *S. Africa* **57 D5** 28 0S 30 3 E
Dansville, *U.S.A.* **78 D7** 42 34N 77 42W
Danta, *India* **42 G5** 24 11N 72 46 E
Dantan, *India* **43 J12** 21 57N 87 20 E
Dante, *Somali Rep.* **46 E5** 10 25N 51 16 E
Danube = Dunărea →, *Europe* **17 F15** 45 20N 29 40 E
Danvers, *U.S.A.* **79 D14** 42 34N 70 56W
Danville, *Ill., U.S.A.* **76 E2** 40 8N 87 37W
Danville, *Ky., U.S.A.* **76 G3** 37 39N 84 46W
Danville, *Pa., U.S.A.* **79 F8** 40 58N 76 37W
Danville, *Va., U.S.A.* **77 G6** 36 36N 79 23W
Danville, *Vt., U.S.A.* **79 B12** 44 25N 72 9W
Danzig = Gdańsk, *Poland* **17 A10** 54 22N 18 40 E
Dapaong, *Togo* **50 F6** 10 55N 0 16 E
Daqing Shan, *China* **34 D6** 40 40N 111 0 E
Dar Banda, *Africa* **48 F6** 8 0N 23 0 E
Dar el Beida = Casablanca, *Morocco* **50 B4** 33 36N 7 36W
Dar es Salaam, *Tanzania* **54 D4** 6 50S 39 12 E
Dar Mazār, *Iran* **45 D8** 29 14N 57 20 E
Dar'ā, *Syria* **47 C5** 32 36N 36 7 E
Dar'ā □, *Syria* **47 C5** 32 55N 36 10 E
Dārāb, *Iran* **45 D7** 28 50N 54 30 E
Daraban, *Pakistan* **42 D4** 31 44N 70 20 E
Daraj, *Libya* **51 B8** 30 10N 10 28 E
Dārān, *Iran* **45 C6** 32 59N 50 24 E
Dārayyā, *Syria* **47 B5** 33 28N 36 15 E
Darband, *Pakistan* **42 B5** 34 20N 72 50 E
Darband, Kūh-e, *Iran* **45 D8** 31 34N 57 8 E
Darbhanga, *India* **43 F11** 26 15N 85 55 E
D'Arcy, *Canada* **72 C4** 50 27N 122 35W
Dardanelle, *Ark., U.S.A.* **81 H8** 35 13N 93 9W
Dardanelle, *Calif., U.S.A.* **84 G7** 38 20N 119 50W
Dardanelles = Çanakkale Boğazı, *Turkey* **21 D12** 40 17N 26 32 E
Dārestān, *Iran* **45 D8** 29 9N 58 42 E
Dârfûr, *Sudan* **51 F10** 13 40N 24 0 E
Dargai, *Pakistan* **42 B4** 34 25N 71 55 E
Dargan Ata, *Uzbekistan* **26 E7** 40 29N 62 10 E
Dargaville, *N.Z.* **59 F4** 35 57S 173 52 E
Darhan, *Mongolia* **32 B5** 49 37N 106 21 E
Darhan Muminggan Lianheqi, *China* **34 D6** 41 40N 110 28 E
Darıca, *Turkey* **21 D13** 40 45N 29 23 E
Darién, G. del, *Colombia* **92 B3** 9 0N 77 0W
Dariganga = Ovoot, *Mongolia* **34 B7** 45 21N 113 45 E
Darjeeling = Darjiling, *India* **43 F13** 27 3N 88 18 E
Darjiling, *India* **43 F13** 27 3N 88 18 E
Darkan, *Australia* **61 F2** 33 20S 116 43 E
Darkhana, *Pakistan* **42 D5** 30 39N 72 11 E
Darkhazīneh, *Iran* **45 D6** 31 54N 48 39 E
Darkot Pass, *Pakistan* **43 A5** 36 45N 73 26 E
Darling →, *Australia* **63 E3** 34 4S 141 54 E
Darling Downs, *Australia* **63 D5** 27 30S 150 30 E
Darling Ra., *Australia* **61 F2** 32 30S 116 0 E
Darlington, *U.K.* **10 C6** 54 32N 1 33W
Darlington, *U.S.A.* **77 H6** 34 18N 79 52W
Darlington □, *U.K.* **10 C6** 54 32N 1 33W
Darlington, L., *S. Africa* **56 E4** 33 10S 25 9 E
Darlington Point, *Australia* **63 E4** 34 37S 146 1 E
Darlot, L., *Australia* **61 E3** 27 48S 121 35 E
Darłowo, *Poland* **16 A9** 54 25N 16 25 E
Darmstadt, *Germany* **16 D5** 49 51N 8 39 E
Darnah, *Libya* **51 B10** 32 45N 22 45 E
Darnall, *S. Africa* **57 D5** 29 23S 31 18 E
Darnley, C., *Antarctica* **5 C6** 68 0S 69 0 E
Darnley B., *Canada* **68 B7** 69 30N 123 30W
Darr →, *Australia* **62 C3** 23 39S 143 50 E
Darra Pezu, *Pakistan* **42 C4** 32 19N 70 44 E
Darrequeira, *Argentina* **94 D3** 37 42S 63 10W
Darrington, *U.S.A.* **82 B3** 48 15N 121 36W
Dart →, *U.K.* **11 G4** 50 24N 3 39W
Dart, C., *Antarctica* **5 D14** 73 6S 126 20W
Dartford, *U.K.* **11 F8** 51 26N 0 13 E
Dartmoor, *U.K.* **11 G4** 50 38N 3 57W
Dartmouth, *Canada* **71 D7** 44 40N 63 30W
Dartmouth, *U.K.* **11 G4** 50 21N 3 36W
Dartmouth, L., *Australia* **63 D4** 26 4S 145 18 E
Dartuch, C. = Artrutx, C. de, *Spain* **22 B10** 39 55N 3 49 E
Darvaza, *Turkmenistan* **26 E6** 40 11N 58 24 E
Darvel, Teluk = Lahad Datu, Teluk, *Malaysia* **37 D5** 4 50N 118 20 E
Darwen, *U.K.* **10 D5** 53 42N 2 29W
Darwha, *India* **40 J10** 20 15N 77 45 E
Darwin, *Australia* **60 B5** 12 25S 130 51 E
Darwin, *U.S.A.* **85 J9** 36 15N 117 35W
Darya Khan, *Pakistan* **42 D4** 31 48N 71 6 E
Daryoi Amu = Amudarya →, *Uzbekistan* **26 E6** 43 58N 59 34 E
Dās, *U.A.E.* **45 E7** 25 20N 53 30 E
Dashetai, *China* **34 D5** 41 0N 109 5 E
Dashhowuz, *Turkmenistan* **26 E6** 41 49N 59 58 E
Dashköpri, *Turkmenistan* **45 B9** 36 16N 62 8 E
Dasht, *Iran* **45 B8** 37 17N 56 7 E
Dasht →, *Pakistan* **40 G2** 25 10N 61 40 E
Dasht-e Mārgow, *Afghan.* **40 D3** 30 40N 62 30 E
Dasht-i-Nawar, *Afghan.* **42 C3** 33 52N 68 0 E
Daska, *Pakistan* **42 C6** 32 20N 74 20 E
Dasuya, *India* **42 D6** 31 49N 75 38 E
Datça, *Turkey* **21 F12** 36 46N 27 40 E
Datia, *India* **43 G8** 25 39N 78 27 E
Datong, *China* **34 D7** 40 6N 113 18 E
Dattakhel, *Pakistan* **42 C3** 32 54N 69 46 E
Datu, Tanjung, *Indonesia* **36 D3** 2 5N 109 39 E
Datu Piang, *Phil.* **37 C6** 7 2N 124 30 E
Daud Khel, *Pakistan* **42 C4** 32 53N 71 34 E
Daudnagar, *India* **43 G11** 25 2N 84 24 E
Daugava →, *Latvia* **9 H21** 57 4N 24 3 E
Daugavpils, *Latvia* **9 J22** 55 53N 26 32 E
Daulpur, *India* **42 F7** 26 45N 77 59 E
Dauphin, *Canada* **73 C8** 51 9N 100 5W
Dauphin, *U.S.A.* **78 F8** 40 22N 76 56W
Dauphin L., *Canada* **73 C9** 51 20N 99 45W
Dauphiné, *France* **18 D6** 45 15N 5 25 E
Dausa, *India* **42 F7** 26 52N 76 20 E
Davangere, *India* **40 M9** 14 25N 75 55 E
Davao, *Phil.* **37 C7** 7 0N 125 40 E
Davao, G. of, *Phil.* **37 C7** 6 30N 125 48 E
Dāvar Panāh, *Iran* **45 E9** 27 25N 62 15 E
Davenport, *Calif., U.S.A.* **84 H4** 37 1N 122 12W
Davenport, *Iowa, U.S.A.* **80 E9** 41 32N 90 35W
Davenport, *Wash., U.S.A.* **82 C4** 47 39N 118 9W
Davenport Ra., *Australia* **62 C1** 20 28S 134 0 E
Daventry, *U.K.* **11 E6** 52 16N 1 10W
David, *Panama* **88 E3** 8 30N 82 30W
David City, *U.S.A.* **80 E6** 41 15N 97 8W
David Gorodok = Davyd Haradok, *Belarus* **17 B14** 52 4N 27 8 E
Davidson, *Canada* **73 C7** 51 16N 105 59W
Davis, *U.S.A.* **84 G5** 38 33N 121 44W
Davis Dam, *U.S.A.* **85 K12** 35 11N 114 34W
Davis Inlet, *Canada* **71 A7** 55 50N 60 59W
Davis Mts., *U.S.A.* **81 K2** 30 50N 103 55W
Davis Sea, *Antarctica* **5 C7** 66 0S 92 0 E
Davis Str., *N. Amer.* **69 B14** 65 0N 58 0W
Davos, *Switz.* **18 C8** 46 48N 9 49 E
Davy L., *Canada* **73 B7** 58 53N 108 18W
Davyd Haradok, *Belarus* **17 B14** 52 4N 27 8 E
Dawei, *Burma* **38 E2** 14 2N 98 12 E
Dawes Ra., *Australia* **62 C5** 24 40S 150 40 E
Dawlish, *U.K.* **11 G4** 50 35N 3 28W
Dawros Hd., *Ireland* **13 B3** 54 50N 8 33W
Dawson, *Canada* **68 B6** 64 10N 139 30W
Dawson, *U.S.A.* **77 K3** 31 46N 84 27W
Dawson, I., *Chile* **96 G2** 53 50S 70 50W
Dawson B., *Canada* **73 C8** 52 53N 100 49W
Dawson Creek, *Canada* **72 B4** 55 45N 120 15W
Dawson Inlet, *Canada* **73 A10** 61 50N 93 25W
Dawson Ra., *Australia* **62 C4** 24 30S 149 48 E
Dax, *France* **18 E3** 43 44N 1 3W
Daxian, *China* **32 C5** 31 15N 107 23 E
Daxindian, *China* **35 F11** 37 30N 120 50 E
Daxinggou, *China* **35 C15** 43 25N 129 40 E
Daxue Shan, *China* **32 C5** 30 30N 101 30 E
Daylesford, *Australia* **63 F3** 37 21S 144 9 E
Dayr az Zawr, *Syria* **44 C4** 35 20N 40 5 E
Daysland, *Canada* **72 C6** 52 50N 112 20W
Dayton, *Nev., U.S.A.* **84 F7** 39 14N 119 36W
Dayton, *Ohio, U.S.A.* **76 F3** 39 45N 84 12W
Dayton, *Pa., U.S.A.* **78 F5** 40 53N 79 15W
Dayton, *Tenn., U.S.A.* **77 H3** 35 30N 85 1W
Dayton, *Wash., U.S.A.* **82 C4** 46 19N 117 59W
Dayton, *Wyo., U.S.A.* **82 D10** 44 53N 107 16W
Daytona Beach, *U.S.A.* **77 L5** 29 13N 81 1W
Dayville, *U.S.A.* **82 D4** 44 28N 119 32W
De Aar, *S. Africa* **56 E3** 30 39S 24 0 E
De Funiak Springs, *U.S.A.* **77 K2** 30 43N 86 7W
De Grey →, *Australia* **60 D2** 20 12S 119 13 E
De Haan, *Belgium* **15 C3** 51 16N 3 2 E
De Kalb, *U.S.A.* **80 E10** 41 56N 88 46W
De Land, *U.S.A.* **77 L5** 29 2N 81 18W
De Leon, *U.S.A.* **81 J5** 32 7N 98 32W
De Panne, *Belgium* **15 C2** 51 6N 2 34 E
De Pere, *U.S.A.* **76 C1** 44 27N 88 4W
De Queen, *U.S.A.* **81 H7** 34 2N 94 21W
De Quincy, *U.S.A.* **81 K8** 30 27N 93 26W
De Ridder, *U.S.A.* **81 K8** 30 51N 93 17W
De Smet, *U.S.A.* **80 C6** 44 23N 97 33W
De Soto, *U.S.A.* **80 F9** 38 8N 90 34W
De Tour Village, *U.S.A.* **76 C4** 46 0N 83 56W
De Witt, *U.S.A.* **81 H9** 34 18N 91 20W
Dead Sea, *Asia* **47 D4** 31 30N 35 30 E
Deadwood, *U.S.A.* **80 C3** 44 23N 103 44W
Deadwood L., *Canada* **72 B3** 59 10N 128 30W
Deal, *U.K.* **11 F9** 51 13N 1 25 E
Deal I., *Australia* **62 F4** 39 30S 147 20 E
Dealesville, *S. Africa* **56 D4** 28 41S 25 44 E
Dean →, *Canada* **72 C3** 52 49N 126 58W
Dean, Forest of, *U.K.* **11 F5** 51 45N 2 33W
Dean Chan., *Canada* **72 C3** 52 30N 127 15W
Deán Funes, *Argentina* **94 C3** 30 20S 64 20W
Dease →, *Canada* **72 B3** 59 56N 128 32W
Dease L., *Canada* **72 B2** 58 40N 130 5W
Dease Lake, *Canada* **72 B2** 58 25N 130 6W
Death Valley, *U.S.A.* **85 J10** 36 15N 116 50W
Death Valley Junction, *U.S.A.* **85 J10** 36 20N 116 25W
Death Valley National Park, *U.S.A.* **85 J10** 36 45N 117 15W
Debar, *Macedonia* **21 D9** 41 31N 20 30 E
Debden, *Canada* **73 C7** 53 30N 106 50W
Dębica, *Poland* **17 C11** 50 2N 21 25 E
Debolt, *Canada* **72 B5** 55 12N 118 1W
Deborah East, L., *Australia* **61 F2** 30 45S 119 0 E
Deborah West, L., *Australia* **61 F2** 30 45S 118 50 E
Debre Markos, *Ethiopia* **46 E2** 10 20N 37 40 E
Debre Tabor, *Ethiopia* **46 E2** 11 50N 38 26 E
Debre Zeyit, *Ethiopia* **46 F2** 11 48N 38 30 E
Debrecen, *Hungary* **17 E11** 47 33N 21 42 E
Decatur, *Ala., U.S.A.* **77 H2** 34 36N 86 59W
Decatur, *Ga., U.S.A.* **77 J3** 33 47N 84 18W
Decatur, *Ill., U.S.A.* **80 F10** 39 51N 88 57W
Decatur, *Ind., U.S.A.* **76 E3** 40 50N 84 56W
Decatur, *Tex., U.S.A.* **81 J6** 33 14N 97 35W
Deccan, *India* **40 L11** 18 0N 79 0 E
Deception Bay, *Australia* **63 D5** 27 10S 153 5 E
Deception L., *Canada* **73 B8** 56 33N 104 13W
Dechhu, *India* **42 F5** 26 46N 72 20 E
Děčín, *Czech Rep.* **16 C8** 50 47N 14 12 E
Deckerville, *U.S.A.* **78 C2** 43 32N 82 44W
Decorah, *U.S.A.* **80 D9** 43 18N 91 48W
Dedéagach = Alexandroúpolis, *Greece* **21 D11** 40 50N 25 54 E
Dedham, *U.S.A.* **79 D13** 42 15N 71 10W
Dedza, *Malawi* **55 E3** 14 20S 34 20 E
Dee →, *Aberds., U.K.* **12 D6** 57 9N 2 5W
Dee →, *Dumf. & Gall., U.K.* **12 G4** 54 51N 4 3W
Dee →, *Wales, U.K.* **10 D4** 53 22N 3 17W
Deep B., *Canada* **72 A5** 61 15N 116 35W
Deepwater, *Australia* **63 D5** 29 25S 151 51 E
Deer →, *Canada* **73 B10** 58 23N 94 13W
Deer L., *Canada* **73 C10** 52 40N 94 20W
Deer Lake, *Nfld., Canada* **71 C8** 49 11N 57 27W
Deer Lake, *Ont., Canada* **73 C10** 52 36N 94 20W
Deer Lodge, *U.S.A.* **82 C7** 46 24N 112 44W
Deer Park, *U.S.A.* **82 C5** 47 57N 117 28W
Deer River, *U.S.A.* **80 B8** 47 20N 93 48W
Deeragun, *Australia* **62 B4** 19 16S 146 33 E
Deerdepoort, *S. Africa* **56 C4** 24 37S 26 27 E
Deferiet, *U.S.A.* **79 B9** 44 2N 75 41W
Defiance, *U.S.A.* **76 E3** 41 17N 84 22W
Degana, *India* **42 F6** 26 50N 74 20 E
Dégelis, *Canada* **71 C6** 47 30N 68 35W
Deggendorf, *Germany* **16 D7** 48 50N 12 57 E
Degh →, *Pakistan* **42 D5** 31 3N 73 21 E
Deh Bīd, *Iran* **45 D7** 30 39N 53 11 E
Deh-e Shīr, *Iran* **45 D7** 31 29N 53 45 E
Dehaj, *Iran* **45 D7** 30 42N 54 53 E
Dehak, *Iran* **45 E9** 27 11N 62 37 E
Dehdez, *Iran* **45 D6** 31 43N 50 17 E
Dehej, *India* **42 J5** 21 44N 72 40 E
Dehestān, *Iran* **45 D7** 28 30N 55 35 E
Dehgolān, *Iran* **44 C5** 35 17N 47 25 E
Dehi Titan, *Afghan.* **40 C3** 33 45N 63 50 E
Dehibat, *Tunisia* **51 B8** 32 0N 10 47 E
Dehlorān, *Iran* **44 C5** 32 41N 47 16 E
Dehnow-e Kūhestān, *Iran* **45 E8** 27 58N 58 32 E
Dehra Dun, *India* **42 D8** 30 20N 78 4 E
Dehri, *India* **43 G11** 24 50N 84 15 E
Dehui, *China* **35 B13** 44 30N 125 40 E
Deinze, *Belgium* **15 D3** 50 59N 3 32 E
Dej, *Romania* **17 E12** 47 10N 23 52 E
Dekese, *Dem. Rep. of the Congo* **52 E4** 3 24S 21 24 E
Del Mar, *U.S.A.* **85 N9** 32 58N 117 16W
Del Norte, *U.S.A.* **83 H10** 37 41N 106 21W
Del Rio, *U.S.A.* **81 L4** 29 22N 100 54W
Delambre I., *Australia* **60 D2** 20 26S 117 5 E
Delano, *U.S.A.* **85 K7** 35 46N 119 15W
Delano Peak, *U.S.A.* **83 G7** 38 22N 112 22W
Delareyville, *S. Africa* **56 D4** 26 41S 25 26 E
Delaronde L., *Canada* **73 C7** 54 3N 107 3W
Delavan, *U.S.A.* **80 D10** 42 38N 88 39W
Delaware, *U.S.A.* **76 E4** 40 18N 83 4W
Delaware □, *U.S.A.* **76 F8** 39 0N 75 20W
Delaware →, *U.S.A.* **79 G9** 39 15N 75 20W
Delaware B., *U.S.A.* **76 F8** 39 0N 75 10W
Delay →, *Canada* **71 A5** 56 56N 71 28W
Delegate, *Australia* **63 F4** 37 4S 148 56 E
Delevan, *U.S.A.* **78 D6** 42 29N 78 29W
Delft, *Neths.* **15 B4** 52 1N 4 22 E
Delfzijl, *Neths.* **15 A6** 53 20N 6 55 E
Delgado, C., *Mozam.* **55 E5** 10 45S 40 40 E
Delgerhet, *Mongolia* **34 B6** 45 50N 110 30 E
Delgo, *Sudan* **51 D12** 20 6N 30 40 E
Delhi, *Canada* **78 D4** 42 51N 80 30W
Delhi, *India* **42 E7** 28 38N 77 17 E
Delhi, *La., U.S.A.* **81 J9** 32 28N 91 30W
Delhi, *N.Y., U.S.A.* **79 D10** 42 17N 74 55W
Delia, *Canada* **72 C6** 51 38N 112 23W
Delice, *Turkey* **25 G5** 39 54N 34 2 E
Delicias, *Mexico* **86 B3** 28 10N 105 30W
Delījān, *Iran* **45 C6** 33 59N 50 40 E
Déline, *Canada* **68 B7** 65 10N 123 30W
Delisle, *Canada* **73 C7** 51 55N 107 8W
Dell City, *U.S.A.* **83 L11** 31 56N 105 12W
Dell Rapids, *U.S.A.* **80 D6** 43 50N 96 43W
Delmar, *U.S.A.* **79 D11** 42 37N 73 47W
Delmenhorst, *Germany* **16 B5** 53 3N 8 37 E
Delong, Ostrova, *Russia* **27 B15** 76 40N 149 20 E
Deloraine, *Australia* **62 G4** 41 30S 146 40 E
Deloraine, *Canada* **73 D8** 49 15N 100 29W
Delphi, *U.S.A.* **76 E2** 40 36N 86 41W
Delphos, *U.S.A.* **76 E3** 40 51N 84 21W
Delportshoop, *S. Africa* **56 D3** 28 22S 24 20 E
Delray Beach, *U.S.A.* **77 M5** 26 28N 80 4W
Delta, *Colo., U.S.A.* **83 G9** 38 44N 108 4W
Delta, *Utah, U.S.A.* **82 G7** 39 21N 112 35W
Delta Junction, *U.S.A.* **68 B5** 64 2N 145 44W
Deltona, *U.S.A.* **77 L5** 28 54N 81 16W
Delungra, *Australia* **63 D5** 29 39S 150 51 E
Delvada, *India* **42 J4** 20 46N 71 2 E
Delvinë, *Albania* **21 E9** 39 59N 20 6 E
Demak, *Indonesia* **37 G14** 6 53S 110 38 E
Demanda, Sierra de la, *Spain* **19 A4** 42 15N 3 0W
Demavand = Damāvand, *Iran* **45 C7** 35 47N 52 0 E
Dembia, *Dem. Rep. of the Congo* **54 B2** 3 33N 25 48 E
Dembidolo, *Ethiopia* **46 F1** 8 34N 34 50 E
Demchok, *India* **43 C8** 32 42N 79 29 E
Demer →, *Belgium* **15 D4** 50 57N 4 42 E
Deming, *N. Mex., U.S.A.* **83 K10** 32 16N 107 46W
Deming, *Wash., U.S.A.* **84 B4** 48 50N 122 13W
Demini →, *Brazil* **92 D6** 0 46S 62 56W
Demirci, *Turkey* **21 E13** 39 2N 28 38 E
Demirköy, *Turkey* **21 D12** 41 49N 27 45 E
Demopolis, *U.S.A.* **77 J2** 32 31N 87 50W
Dempo, *Indonesia* **36 E2** 4 2S 103 15 E
Den Burg, *Neths.* **15 A4** 53 3N 4 47 E
Den Chai, *Thailand* **38 D3** 17 59N 100 4 E
Den Haag = 's-Gravenhage, *Neths.* **15 B4** 52 7N 4 17 E
Den Helder, *Neths.* **15 B4** 52 57N 4 45 E
Den Oever, *Neths.* **15 B5** 52 56N 5 2 E
Denair, *U.S.A.* **84 H6** 37 32N 120 48W
Denau, *Uzbekistan* **26 F7** 38 16N 67 54 E
Denbigh, *Canada* **78 A7** 45 8N 77 15W
Denbigh, *U.K.* **10 D4** 53 12N 3 25W
Denbighshire □, *U.K.* **10 D4** 53 8N 3 22W
Dendang, *Indonesia* **36 E3** 3 7S 107 56 E
Dendermonde, *Belgium* **15 C4** 51 2N 4 5 E
Dengfeng, *China* **34 G7** 34 25N 113 2 E
Dengkou, *China* **34 D4** 40 18N 106 55 E
Denham, *Australia* **61 E1** 25 56S 113 31 E
Denham Ra., *Australia* **62 C4** 21 55S 147 46 E
Denham Sd., *Australia* **61 E1** 25 45S 113 15 E
Denholm, *Canada* **73 C7** 52 39N 108 1W
Denia, *Spain* **19 C6** 38 49N 0 8 E
Denial B., *Australia* **63 E1** 32 14S 133 32 E
Deniliquin, *Australia* **63 F3** 35 30S 144 58 E
Denison, *Iowa, U.S.A.* **80 E7** 42 1N 95 21W
Denison, *Tex., U.S.A.* **81 J6** 33 45N 96 33W
Denison Plains, *Australia* **60 C4** 18 35S 128 0 E
Denizli, *Turkey* **25 G4** 37 42N 29 2 E
Denman Glacier, *Antarctica* **5 C7** 66 45S 99 25 E
Denmark, *Australia* **61 F2** 34 59S 117 25 E
Denmark ■, *Europe* **9 J13** 55 45N 10 0 E
Denmark Str., *Atl. Oc.* **4 C6** 66 0N 30 0W
Dennison, *U.S.A.* **78 F3** 40 24N 81 19W
Denny, *U.K.* **12 E5** 56 1N 3 55W
Denpasar, *Indonesia* **36 F5** 8 45S 115 14 E
Denton, *Mont., U.S.A.* **82 C9** 47 19N 109 57W
Denton, *Tex., U.S.A.* **81 J6** 33 13N 97 8W
D'Entrecasteaux, Pt., *Australia* **61 F2** 34 50S 115 57 E
Denver, *Colo., U.S.A.* **80 F2** 39 44N 104 59W
Denver, *Pa., U.S.A.* **79 F8** 40 14N 76 8W
Denver City, *U.S.A.* **81 J3** 32 58N 102 50W
Deoband, *India* **42 E7** 29 42N 77 43 E
Deogarh, *India* **42 G5** 25 32N 73 54 E
Deoghar, *India* **43 G12** 24 30N 86 42 E
Deolali, *India* **40 K8** 19 58N 73 50 E
Deoli = Devli, *India* **42 G6** 25 50N 75 20 E
Deora, *India* **42 F4** 26 22N 70 55 E
Deori, *India* **43 H8** 23 24N 79 1 E
Deoria, *India* **43 F10** 26 31N 83 48 E
Deosai Mts., *Pakistan* **43 B6** 35 40N 75 0 E
Deosri, *India* **43 F14** 26 46N 90 29 E
Depalpur, *India* **42 H6** 22 51N 75 33 E
Deping, *China* **35 F9** 37 25N 116 58 E
Deposit, *U.S.A.* **79 D9** 42 4N 75 25W
Depuch I., *Australia* **60 D2** 20 37S 117 44 E
Deputatskiy, *Russia* **27 C14** 69 18N 139 54 E
Dera Ghazi Khan, *Pakistan* **42 D4** 30 5N 70 43 E
Dera Ismail Khan, *Pakistan* **42 D4** 31 50N 70 50 E
Derabugti, *Pakistan* **42 E3** 29 2N 69 9 E
Derawar Fort, *Pakistan* **42 E4** 28 46N 71 20 E
Derbent, *Russia* **25 F8** 42 5N 48 15 E
Derby, *Australia* **60 C3** 17 18S 123 38 E
Derby, *U.K.* **10 E6** 52 56N 1 28W
Derby, *Conn., U.S.A.* **79 E11** 41 19N 73 5W
Derby, *Kans., U.S.A.* **81 G6** 37 33N 97 16W
Derby, *N.Y., U.S.A.* **78 D6** 42 41N 78 58W
Derby City □, *U.K.* **10 E6** 52 56N 1 28W
Derby Line, *U.S.A.* **79 B12** 45 0N 72 6W
Derbyshire □, *U.K.* **10 D6** 53 11N 1 38W
Derg →, *U.K.* **13 B4** 54 44N 7 26W
Derg, L., *Ireland* **13 D3** 53 0N 8 20W
Dergaon, *India* **41 F19** 26 45N 94 0 E
Dermott, *U.S.A.* **81 J9** 33 32N 91 26W
Derry = Londonderry, *U.K.* **13 B4** 55 0N 7 20W
Derry = Londonderry □, *U.K.* **13 B4** 55 0N 7 20W
Derry, *N.H., U.S.A.* **79 D13** 42 53N 71 19W
Derry, *Pa., U.S.A.* **78 F5** 40 20N 79 18W
Derryveagh Mts., *Ireland* **13 B3** 54 56N 8 11W
Derwent →, *Cumb., U.K.* **10 C4** 54 39N 3 33W
Derwent →, *Derby, U.K.* **10 E6** 52 57N 1 28W
Derwent →, *N. Yorks., U.K.* **10 D7** 53 45N 0 58W
Derwent Water, *U.K.* **10 C4** 54 35N 3 9W
Des Moines, *Iowa, U.S.A.* **80 E8** 41 35N 93 37W
Des Moines, *N. Mex., U.S.A.* **81 G3** 36 46N 103 50W
Des Moines →, *U.S.A.* **80 E9** 40 23N 91 25W
Desaguadero →, *Argentina* **94 C2** 34 30S 66 46W
Desaguadero →, *Bolivia* **92 G5** 16 35S 69 5W
Descanso, Pta., *Mexico* **85 N9** 32 21N 117 3W
Deschaillons, *Canada* **71 C5** 46 32N 72 7W
Deschambault L., *Canada* **73 C8** 54 50N 103 30W
Deschutes →, *U.S.A.* **82 D3** 45 38N 120 55W
Dese, *Ethiopia* **46 E2** 11 5N 39 40 E
Deseado →, *Argentina* **96 F3** 47 45S 65 54W
Desert Center, *U.S.A.* **85 M11** 33 43N 115 24W
Desert Hot Springs, *U.S.A.* **85 M10** 33 58N 116 30W
Deshnok, *India* **42 F5** 27 48N 73 21 E
Desna →, *Ukraine* **17 C16** 50 33N 30 32 E
Desolación, I., *Chile* **96 G2** 53 0S 74 0W

Despeñaperros, Paso

Despeñaperros, Paso, *Spain* **19 C4** 38 24N 3 30W
Dessau, *Germany* **16 C7** 51 51N 12 14 E
Dessye = Dese, *Ethiopia* **46 E2** 11 5N 39 40 E
D'Estrees B., *Australia* **63 F2** 35 55S 137 45 E
Desuri, *India* **42 G5** 25 18N 73 35 E
Det Udom, *Thailand* **38 E5** 14 54N 105 5 E
Dete, *Zimbabwe* **55 F2** 18 38S 26 50 E
Detmold, *Germany* **16 C5** 51 56N 8 52 E
Detour, Pt., *U.S.A.* **76 C2** 45 40N 86 40W
Detroit, *U.S.A.* **78 D1** 42 20N 83 3W
Detroit Lakes, *U.S.A.* **80 B7** 46 49N 95 51W
Deurne, *Neths.* **15 C5** 51 27N 5 49 E
Deutsche Bucht, *Germany* **16 A5** 54 15N 8 0 E
Deva, *Romania* **17 F12** 45 53N 22 55 E
Devakottai, *India* **40 Q11** 9 55N 78 45 E
Devaprayag, *India* **43 D8** 30 13N 78 35 E
Deventer, *Neths.* **15 B6** 52 15N 6 10 E
Deveron →, *U.K.* **12 D6** 57 41N 2 32W
Devgadh Bariya, *India* **42 H5** 22 40N 73 55 E
Devikot, *India* **42 F4** 26 42N 71 12 E
Devils Den, *U.S.A.* **84 K7** 35 46N 119 58W
Devils Lake, *U.S.A.* **80 A5** 48 7N 98 52W
Devils Paw, *Canada* **72 B2** 58 47N 134 0W
Devils Tower Junction, *U.S.A.* **80 C2** 44 31N 104 57W
Devine, *U.S.A.* **81 L5** 29 8N 98 54W
Devizes, *U.K.* **11 F6** 51 22N 1 58W
Devli, *India* **42 G6** 25 50N 75 20 E
Devon, *Canada* **72 C6** 53 24N 113 44W
Devon □, *U.K.* **11 G4** 50 50N 3 40W
Devon I., *Canada* **4 B3** 75 10N 85 0W
Devonport, *Australia* **62 G4** 41 10S 146 22 E
Devonport, *N.Z.* **59 G5** 36 49S 174 49 E
Dewas, *India* **42 H7** 22 59N 76 3 E
Dewetsdorp, *S. Africa* **56 D4** 29 33S 26 39 E
Dexter, *Maine, U.S.A.* **77 C11** 45 1N 69 18W
Dexter, *Mo., U.S.A.* **81 G10** 36 48N 89 57W
Dexter, *N. Mex., U.S.A.* **81 J2** 33 12N 104 22W
Dey-Dey, L., *Australia* **61 E5** 29 12S 131 4 E
Deyhūk, *Iran* **45 C8** 33 15N 57 30 E
Deyyer, *Iran* **45 E6** 27 55N 51 55 E
Dezadeash L., *Canada* **72 A1** 60 28N 136 58W
Dezfūl, *Iran* **45 C6** 32 20N 48 30 E
Dezhneva, Mys, *Russia* **27 C19** 66 5N 169 40W
Dezhou, *China* **34 F9** 37 26N 116 18 E
Dhadhar →, *India* **43 G11** 24 56N 85 24 E
Dháfni, *Greece* **23 D7** 35 13N 25 3 E
Dhahiriya = Aẕ Ẕāhirīyah, *West Bank* **47 D3** 31 25N 34 58 E
Dhahran = Aẓ Ẓahrān, *Si. Arabia* **45 E6** 26 10N 50 7 E
Dhak, *Pakistan* **42 C5** 32 25N 72 33 E
Dhaka, *Bangla.* **43 H14** 23 43N 90 26 E
Dhaka □, *Bangla.* **43 G14** 24 25N 90 25 E
Dhali, *Cyprus* **23 D12** 35 1N 33 25 E
Dhampur, *India* **43 E8** 29 19N 78 33 E
Dhamtari, *India* **41 J12** 20 42N 81 35 E
Dhanbad, *India* **43 H12** 23 50N 86 30 E
Dhangarhi, *Nepal* **41 E12** 28 55N 80 40 E
Dhankuta, *Nepal* **43 F12** 26 55N 87 40 E
Dhar, *India* **42 H6** 22 35N 75 26 E
Dharampur, *India* **42 H6** 22 13N 75 18 E
Dharamsala = Dharmsala, *India* **42 C7** 32 16N 76 23 E
Dhariwal, *India* **42 D6** 31 57N 75 19 E
Dharla →, *Bangla.* **43 G13** 25 46N 89 42 E
Dharmapuri, *India* **40 N11** 12 10N 78 10 E
Dharmjaygarh, *India* **43 H10** 22 28N 83 13 E
Dharmsala, *India* **42 C7** 32 16N 76 23 E
Dharni, *India* **42 J7** 21 33N 76 53 E
Dhasan →, *India* **43 G8** 25 48N 79 24 E
Dhaulagiri, *Nepal* **43 E10** 28 39N 83 28 E
Dhebar, L., *India* **42 G6** 24 10N 74 0 E
Dheftera, *Cyprus* **23 D12** 35 5N 33 16 E
Dhenkanal, *India* **41 J14** 20 45N 85 35 E
Dherinia, *Cyprus* **23 D12** 35 3N 33 57 E
Dhiarrizos →, *Cyprus* **23 E11** 34 41N 32 34 E
Dhībān, *Jordan* **47 D4** 31 30N 35 46 E
Dhíkti Óros, *Greece* **23 D7** 35 8N 25 30 E
Dhilwan, *India* **42 D6** 31 31N 75 21 E
Dhimarkhera, *India* **43 H9** 23 28N 80 22 E
Dhírfis = Dhírfis Óros, *Greece* **21 E10** 38 40N 23 54 E
Dhírfis Óros, *Greece* **21 E10** 38 40N 23 54 E
Dhodhekánisos, *Greece* **21 F12** 36 35N 27 0 E
Dholka, *India* **42 H5** 22 44N 72 29 E
Dhoraji, *India* **42 J4** 21 45N 70 37 E
Dhráhstis, Ákra, *Greece* **23 A3** 39 48N 19 40 E
Dhrangadhra, *India* **42 H4** 22 59N 71 31 E
Dhrápanon, Ákra, *Greece* **23 D6** 35 28N 24 14 E
Dhrol, *India* **42 H4** 22 33N 70 25 E
Dhuburi, *India* **41 F16** 26 2N 89 59 E
Dhule, *India* **40 J9** 20 58N 74 50 E
Di Linh, *Vietnam* **39 G7** 11 35N 108 4 E
Di Linh, Cao Nguyen, *Vietnam* **39 G7** 11 30N 108 0 E
Día, *Greece* **23 D7** 35 28N 25 14 E
Diablo, Mt., *U.S.A.* **84 H5** 37 53N 121 56W
Diablo Range, *U.S.A.* **84 J5** 37 20N 121 25W
Diafarabé, *Mali* **50 F5** 14 9N 4 57W
Diamante, *Argentina* **94 C3** 32 5S 60 40W
Diamante →, *Argentina* **94 C2** 34 30S 66 46W
Diamantina, *Brazil* **93 G10** 18 17S 43 40W
Diamantina →, *Australia* **63 D2** 26 45S 139 10 E
Diamantino, *Brazil* **93 F7** 14 30S 56 30W
Diamond Bar, *U.S.A.* **85 L9** 34 1N 117 48W
Diamond Harbour, *India* **43 H13** 22 11N 88 14 E
Diamond Is., *Australia* **62 B5** 17 25S 151 5 E
Diamond Mts., *U.S.A.* **82 G6** 39 50N 115 30W
Diamond Springs, *U.S.A.* **84 G6** 38 42N 120 49W
Dībā, *Oman* **45 E8** 25 45N 56 16 E
Dibai, *India* **42 E8** 28 13N 78 15 E
Dibaya-Lubue, *Dem. Rep. of the Congo* **52 E3** 4 12S 19 54 E
Dibete, *Botswana* **56 C4** 23 45S 26 32 E
Dibrugarh, *India* **41 F19** 27 29N 94 55 E
Dickens, *U.S.A.* **81 J4** 33 37N 100 50W
Dickinson, *U.S.A.* **80 B3** 46 53N 102 47W
Dickson = Dikson, *Russia* **26 B9** 73 40N 80 5 E
Dickson, *U.S.A.* **77 G2** 36 5N 87 23W
Dickson City, *U.S.A.* **79 E9** 41 29N 75 40W
Didiéni, *Mali* **50 F4** 13 53N 8 6W
Didsbury, *Canada* **72 C6** 51 35N 114 10W
Didwana, *India* **42 F6** 27 23N 74 36 E
Diefenbaker, L., *Canada* **73 C7** 51 0N 106 55W
Diego de Almagro, *Chile* **94 B1** 26 22S 70 3W
Diego Garcia, *Ind. Oc.* **3 E13** 7 50S 72 50 E
Diekirch, *Lux.* **15 E6** 49 52N 6 10 E
Dien Ban, *Vietnam* **38 E7** 15 53N 108 16 E
Dien Khanh, *Vietnam* **39 F7** 12 15N 109 6 E
Dieppe, *France* **18 B4** 49 54N 1 4 E
Dierks, *U.S.A.* **81 H8** 34 7N 94 1W
Diest, *Belgium* **15 D5** 50 58N 5 4 E
Dif, *Somali Rep.* **46 G3** 0 59N 0 56 E
Differdange, *Lux.* **15 E5** 49 31N 5 54 E
Dig, *India* **42 F7** 27 28N 77 20 E
Digba, *Dem. Rep. of the Congo* **54 B2** 4 25N 25 48 E
Digby, *Canada* **71 D6** 44 38N 65 50W
Diggi, *India* **42 F6** 26 22N 75 26 E
Dighinala, *Bangla.* **41 H18** 23 15N 92 5 E
Dighton, *U.S.A.* **80 F4** 38 29N 100 28W
Digne-les-Bains, *France* **18 D7** 44 5N 6 12 E
Digos, *Phil.* **37 C7** 6 45N 125 20 E
Digranes, *Iceland* **8 C6** 66 4N 14 44W
Digul →, *Indonesia* **37 F9** 7 7S 138 42 E
Dihang →, *India* **41 F19** 27 48N 95 30 E
Dijlah, Nahr →, *Asia* **44 D5** 31 0N 47 25 E
Dijon, *France* **18 C6** 47 20N 5 3 E
Dikkil, *Djibouti* **46 E3** 11 8N 42 20 E
Dikomu di Kai, *Botswana* **56 C3** 24 58S 24 36 E
Diksmuide, *Belgium* **15 C2** 51 2N 2 52 E
Dikson, *Russia* **26 B9** 73 40N 80 5 E
Dila, *Ethiopia* **46 F2** 6 21N 38 22 E
Dili, *Indonesia* **37 F7** 8 39S 125 34 E
Dilley, *U.S.A.* **81 L5** 28 40N 99 10W
Dillingham, *U.S.A.* **68 C4** 59 3N 158 28W
Dillon, *Canada* **73 B7** 55 56N 108 35W
Dillon, *Mont., U.S.A.* **82 D7** 45 13N 112 38W
Dillon, *S.C., U.S.A.* **77 H6** 34 25N 79 22W
Dillon →, *Canada* **73 B7** 55 56N 108 56W
Dillsburg, *U.S.A.* **78 F7** 40 7N 77 2W
Dilolo, *Dem. Rep. of the Congo* **52 G4** 10 28S 22 18 E
Dimas, *Mexico* **86 C3** 23 43N 106 47W
Dimashq, *Syria* **47 B5** 33 30N 36 18 E
Dimashq □, *Syria* **47 B5** 33 30N 36 30 E
Dimbaza, *S. Africa* **57 E4** 32 50S 27 14 E
Dimboola, *Australia* **63 F3** 36 28S 142 7 E
Dîmboviţa = Dâmboviţa →, *Romania* **17 F14** 44 12N 26 26 E
Dimbulah, *Australia* **62 B4** 17 8S 145 4 E
Dimitrovgrad, *Bulgaria* **21 C11** 42 5N 25 35 E
Dimitrovgrad, *Russia* **24 D8** 54 14N 49 39 E
Dimitrovo = Pernik, *Bulgaria* **21 C10** 42 35N 23 2 E
Dimmitt, *U.S.A.* **81 H3** 34 33N 102 19W
Dimona, *Israel* **47 D4** 31 2N 35 1 E
Dinagat, *Phil.* **37 B7** 10 10N 125 40 E
Dinajpur, *Bangla.* **41 G16** 25 33N 88 43 E
Dinan, *France* **18 B2** 48 28N 2 2W
Dīnān Āb, *Iran* **45 C8** 32 4N 56 49 E
Dinant, *Belgium* **15 D4** 50 16N 4 55 E
Dinapur, *India* **43 G11** 25 38N 85 5 E
Dīnār, Kūh-e, *Iran* **45 D6** 30 42N 51 46 E
Dinara Planina, *Croatia* **20 C7** 44 0N 16 30 E
Dinard, *France* **18 B2** 48 38N 2 6W
Dinaric Alps = Dinara Planina, *Croatia* **20 C7** 44 0N 16 30 E
Dindigul, *India* **40 P11** 10 25N 78 0 E
Dindori, *India* **43 H9** 22 57N 81 5 E
Ding Xian = Dingzhou, *China* **34 E8** 38 30N 114 59 E
Dinga, *Pakistan* **42 G2** 25 26N 67 10 E
Dingbian, *China* **34 F4** 37 35N 107 32 E
Dingle, *Ireland* **13 D1** 52 9N 10 17W
Dingle B., *Ireland* **13 D1** 52 3N 10 20W
Dingmans Ferry, *U.S.A.* **79 E10** 41 13N 74 55W
Dingo, *Australia* **62 C4** 23 38S 149 19 E
Dingtao, *China* **34 G8** 35 5N 115 35 E
Dingwall, *U.K.* **12 D4** 57 36N 4 26W
Dingxi, *China* **34 G3** 35 30N 104 33 E
Dingxiang, *China* **34 E7** 38 30N 112 58 E
Dingzhou, *China* **34 E8** 38 30N 114 59 E
Dinh, Mui, *Vietnam* **39 G7** 11 22N 109 1 E
Dinokwe, *Botswana* **56 C4** 23 29S 26 37 E
Dinorwic, *Canada* **73 D10** 49 41N 92 30W
Dinosaur National Monument, *U.S.A.* **82 F9** 40 30N 108 45W
Dinosaur Prov. Park, *Canada* **72 C6** 50 47N 111 30W
Dinuba, *U.S.A.* **84 J7** 36 32N 119 23W
Dipalpur, *Pakistan* **42 D5** 30 40N 73 39 E
Diplo, *Pakistan* **42 G3** 24 35N 69 35 E
Dipolog, *Phil.* **37 C6** 8 36N 123 20 E
Dir, *Pakistan* **40 B7** 35 8N 71 59 E
Dire Dawa, *Ethiopia* **46 F3** 9 35N 41 45 E
Diriamba, *Nic.* **88 D2** 11 51N 86 19W
Dirk Hartog I., *Australia* **61 E1** 25 50S 113 5 E
Dirranbandi, *Australia* **63 D4** 28 33S 148 17 E
Disa, *India* **42 G5** 24 18N 72 10 E
Disappointment, C., *U.S.A.* **82 C2** 46 18N 124 5W
Disappointment, L., *Australia* **60 D3** 23 20S 122 40 E
Disaster B., *Australia* **63 F4** 37 15S 149 58 E
Discovery B., *Australia* **63 F3** 38 10S 140 40 E
Disko, *Greenland* **4 C5** 69 45N 53 30W
Disko Bugt, *Greenland* **4 C5** 69 10N 52 0W
Diss, *U.K.* **11 E9** 52 23N 1 7 E
Disteghil Sar, *Pakistan* **43 A6** 36 20N 75 12 E
Distrito Federal □, *Brazil* **93 G9** 15 45S 47 45W
Distrito Federal □, *Mexico* **87 D5** 19 15N 99 10W
Diu, *India* **42 J4** 20 45N 70 58 E
Dīvāndarreh, *Iran* **44 C5** 35 55N 47 2 E
Divide, *U.S.A.* **82 D7** 45 45N 112 45W
Dividing Ra., *Australia* **61 E2** 27 45S 116 0 E
Divinópolis, *Brazil* **93 H10** 20 10S 44 54W
Divnoye, *Russia* **25 E7** 45 55N 43 21 E
Divo, *Ivory C.* **50 G4** 5 48N 5 15W
Dīwāl Kol, *Afghan.* **42 B2** 34 23N 67 52 E
Dixie Mt., *U.S.A.* **84 F6** 39 55N 120 16W
Dixon, *Calif., U.S.A.* **84 G5** 38 27N 121 49W
Dixon, *Ill., U.S.A.* **80 E10** 41 50N 89 29W
Dixon Entrance, *U.S.A.* **68 C6** 54 30N 132 0W
Dixville, *Canada* **79 A13** 45 4N 71 46W
Diyālā →, *Iraq* **44 C5** 33 14N 44 31 E
Diyarbakır, *Turkey* **25 G7** 37 55N 40 18 E
Diyodar, *India* **42 G4** 24 8N 71 50 E
Djakarta = Jakarta, *Indonesia* **37 G12** 6 9S 106 49 E
Djamba, *Angola* **56 B1** 16 45S 13 58 E
Djambala, *Congo* **52 E2** 2 32S 14 30 E
Djanet, *Algeria* **50 D7** 24 35N 9 32 E
Djawa = Jawa, *Indonesia* **37 G14** 7 0S 110 0 E
Djelfa, *Algeria* **50 B6** 34 40N 3 15 E
Djema, *C.A.R.* **54 A2** 6 3N 25 15 E
Djerba, I. de, *Tunisia* **51 B8** 33 50N 10 48 E
Djerid, Chott, *Tunisia* **50 B7** 33 42N 8 30 E
Djibouti, *Djibouti* **46 E3** 11 30N 43 5 E
Djibouti ■, *Africa* **46 E3** 12 0N 43 0 E
Djolu, *Dem. Rep. of the Congo* **52 D4** 0 35N 22 5 E
Djoum, *Cameroon* **52 D2** 2 41N 12 35 E
Djourab, Erg du, *Chad* **51 E9** 16 40N 18 50 E
Djugu, *Dem. Rep. of the Congo* **54 B3** 1 55N 30 35 E
Djúpivogur, *Iceland* **8 D6** 64 39N 14 17W
Dmitriya Lapteva, Proliv, *Russia* **27 B15** 73 0N 140 0 E
Dnepr = Dnipro →, *Ukraine* **25 E5** 46 30N 32 18 E
Dneprodzerzhinsk = Dniprodzerzhynsk, *Ukraine* **25 E5** 48 32N 34 37 E
Dnepropetrovsk = Dnipropetrovsk, *Ukraine* **25 E6** 48 30N 35 0 E
Dnestr = Dnister →, *Europe* **17 E16** 46 18N 30 17 E
Dnestrovski = Belgorod, *Russia* **25 D6** 50 35N 36 35 E
Dnieper = Dnipro →, *Ukraine* **25 E5** 46 30N 32 18 E
Dniester = Dnister →, *Europe* **17 E16** 46 18N 30 17 E
Dnipro →, *Ukraine* **25 E5** 46 30N 32 18 E
Dniprodzerzhynsk, *Ukraine* **25 E5** 48 32N 34 37 E
Dnipropetrovsk, *Ukraine* **25 E6** 48 30N 35 0 E
Dnister →, *Europe* **17 E16** 46 18N 30 17 E
Dnistrovskyy Lyman, *Ukraine* **17 E16** 46 15N 30 17 E
Dno, *Russia* **24 C4** 57 50N 29 58 E
Dnyapro = Dnipro →, *Ukraine* **25 E5** 46 30N 32 18 E
Doaktown, *Canada* **71 C6** 46 33N 66 8W
Doba, *Chad* **51 G9** 8 40N 16 50 E
Dobandi, *Pakistan* **42 D2** 31 13N 66 50 E
Dobbyn, *Australia* **62 B3** 19 44S 140 2 E
Dobele, *Latvia* **9 H20** 56 37N 23 16 E
Doberai, Jazirah, *Indonesia* **37 E8** 1 25S 133 0 E
Doblas, *Argentina* **94 D3** 37 5S 64 0W
Dobo, *Indonesia* **37 F8** 5 45S 134 15 E
Doboj, *Bos.-H.* **21 B8** 44 46N 18 4 E
Dobreta-Turnu Severin, *Romania* **17 F12** 44 39N 22 41 E
Dobrich, *Bulgaria* **21 C12** 43 37N 27 49 E
Dobruja, *Europe* **17 F15** 44 30N 28 15 E
Dobrush, *Belarus* **17 B16** 52 25N 31 22 E
Doc, Mui, *Vietnam* **38 D6** 17 58N 106 30 E
Docker River, *Australia* **61 D4** 24 52S 129 5 E
Doctor Arroyo, *Mexico* **86 C4** 23 40N 100 11W
Doda, *India* **43 C6** 33 10N 75 34 E
Doda, L., *Canada* **70 C4** 49 25N 75 13W
Dodecanese = Dhodhekánisos, *Greece* **21 F12** 36 35N 27 0 E
Dodge City, *U.S.A.* **81 G5** 37 45N 100 1W
Dodge L., *Canada* **73 B7** 59 50N 105 36W
Dodgeville, *U.S.A.* **80 D9** 42 58N 90 8W
Dodoma, *Tanzania* **54 D4** 6 8S 35 45 E
Dodoma □, *Tanzania* **54 D4** 6 0S 36 0 E
Dodsland, *Canada* **73 C7** 51 50N 108 45W
Dodson, *U.S.A.* **82 B9** 48 24N 108 15W
Doesburg, *Neths.* **15 B6** 52 1N 6 9 E
Doetinchem, *Neths.* **15 C6** 51 59N 6 18 E
Dog Creek, *Canada* **72 C4** 51 35N 122 14W
Dog L., *Man., Canada* **73 C9** 51 2N 98 31W
Dog L., *Ont., Canada* **70 C2** 48 48N 89 30W
Dogi, *Afghan.* **40 C3** 32 20N 62 50 E
Dogran, *Pakistan* **42 D5** 31 48N 73 35 E
Doğubayazıt, *Turkey* **44 B5** 39 31N 44 5 E
Doha = Ad Dawḩah, *Qatar* **45 E6** 25 15N 51 35 E
Dohazari, *Bangla.* **41 H18** 22 10N 92 5 E
Dohrighat, *India* **43 F10** 26 16N 83 31 E
Doi, *Indonesia* **37 D7** 2 14N 127 49 E
Doi Luang, *Thailand* **38 C3** 18 30N 101 0 E
Doi Saket, *Thailand* **38 C2** 18 52N 99 9 E
Dois Irmãos, Sa., *Brazil* **93 E10** 9 0S 42 30W
Dokkum, *Neths.* **15 A5** 53 20N 5 59 E
Dokri, *Pakistan* **42 F3** 27 25N 68 7 E
Dolak, Pulau, *Indonesia* **37 F9** 8 0S 138 30 E
Dolbeau, *Canada* **71 C5** 48 53N 72 18W
Dole, *France* **18 C6** 47 7N 5 31 E
Dolgellau, *U.K.* **10 E4** 52 45N 3 53W
Dolgelley = Dolgellau, *U.K.* **10 E4** 52 45N 3 53W
Dollard, *Neths.* **15 A7** 53 20N 7 10 E
Dolo, *Ethiopia* **46 G3** 4 11N 42 3 E
Dolomites = Dolomiti, *Italy* **20 A4** 46 23N 11 51 E
Dolomiti, *Italy* **20 A4** 46 23N 11 51 E
Dolores, *Argentina* **94 D4** 36 20S 57 40W
Dolores, *Uruguay* **94 C4** 33 34S 58 15W
Dolores, *U.S.A.* **83 H9** 37 28N 108 30W
Dolores →, *U.S.A.* **83 G9** 38 49N 109 17W
Dolphin, C., *Falk. Is.* **96 G5** 51 10S 59 0W
Dolphin and Union Str., *Canada* **68 B8** 69 5N 114 45W
Dom Pedrito, *Brazil* **95 C5** 31 0S 54 40W
Domariaganj →, *India* **43 F10** 26 17N 83 44 E
Domasi, *Malawi* **55 F4** 15 15S 35 22 E
Dombarovskiy, *Russia* **26 D6** 50 46N 59 32 E
Dombås, *Norway* **9 E13** 62 4N 9 8 E
Domel I. = Letsôk-aw Kyun, *Burma* **39 G2** 11 30N 98 25 E
Domeyko, *Chile* **94 B1** 29 0S 71 0W
Domeyko, Cordillera, *Chile* **94 A2** 24 30S 69 0W
Dominador, *Chile* **94 A2** 24 21S 69 20W
Dominica ■, *W. Indies* **89 C7** 15 20N 61 20W
Dominica Passage, *W. Indies* **89 C7** 15 10N 61 20W
Dominican Rep. ■, *W. Indies* **89 C5** 19 0N 70 30W
Domodóssola, *Italy* **18 C8** 46 7N 8 17 E
Domville, Mt., *Australia* **63 D5** 28 1S 151 15 E
Don →, *Russia* **25 E6** 47 4N 39 18 E
Don →, *Aberds., U.K.* **12 D6** 57 11N 2 5W
Don →, *S. Yorks., U.K.* **10 D7** 53 41N 0 52W
Don, C., *Australia* **60 B5** 11 18S 131 46 E
Don Benito, *Spain* **19 C3** 38 53N 5 51W
Dona Ana = Nhamaabué, *Mozam.* **55 F4** 17 25S 35 5 E
Donaghadee, *U.K.* **13 B6** 54 39N 5 33W
Donald, *Australia* **63 F3** 36 23S 143 0 E
Donaldsonville, *U.S.A.* **81 K9** 30 6N 90 59W
Donalsonville, *U.S.A.* **77 K3** 31 3N 84 53W
Donau = Dunărea →, *Europe* **17 F15** 45 20N 29 40 E
Donau →, *Austria* **15 D3** 48 10N 17 0 E
Donauwörth, *Germany* **16 D6** 48 43N 10 47 E
Doncaster, *U.K.* **10 D6** 53 32N 1 6W
Dondo, *Mozam.* **55 F3** 19 33S 34 46 E
Dondo, Teluk, *Indonesia* **37 D6** 0 50N 120 30 E
Dondra Head, *Sri Lanka* **40 S12** 5 55N 80 40 E
Donegal, *Ireland* **13 B3** 54 39N 8 5W
Donegal □, *Ireland* **13 B4** 54 53N 8 0W
Donegal B., *Ireland* **13 B3** 54 31N 8 49W
Donets →, *Russia* **25 E7** 47 33N 40 55 E
Donetsk, *Ukraine* **25 E6** 48 0N 37 45 E
Dong Ba Thin, *Vietnam* **39 F7** 12 8N 109 13 E
Dong Giam, *Vietnam* **38 C5** 19 25N 105 31 E
Dong Ha, *Vietnam* **38 D6** 16 55N 107 8 E
Dong Hene, *Laos* **38 D5** 16 40N 105 18 E
Dong Hoi, *Vietnam* **38 D6** 17 29N 106 36 E
Dong Khe, *Vietnam* **38 A6** 22 26N 106 27 E
Dong Ujimqin Qi, *China* **34 B9** 45 32N 116 55 E
Dong Van, *Vietnam* **38 A5** 23 16N 105 22 E
Dong Xoai, *Vietnam* **39 G6** 11 32N 106 55 E
Dongara, *Australia* **61 E1** 29 14S 114 57 E
Dongbei, *China* **35 D13** 45 0N 125 0 E
Dongchuan, *China* **32 D5** 26 8N 103 1 E
Dongfang, *China* **38 C7** 18 50N 108 33 E
Dongfeng, *China* **35 C13** 42 40N 125 34 E
Donggala, *Indonesia* **37 E5** 0 30S 119 40 E
Donggou, *China* **35 E13** 39 52N 124 10 E
Dongguang, *China* **34 F9** 37 50N 116 30 E
Dongjingcheng, *China* **35 B15** 44 5N 129 10 E
Dongning, *China* **35 B16** 44 2N 131 5 E
Dongola, *Sudan* **51 E12** 19 9N 30 22 E
Dongping, *China* **34 G9** 35 55N 116 20 E
Dongsheng, *China* **34 E6** 39 50N 110 0 E
Dongtai, *China* **35 H11** 32 51N 120 21 E
Dongting Hu, *China* **33 D6** 29 18N 112 45 E
Donington, C., *Australia* **63 E2** 34 45S 136 0 E
Doniphan, *U.S.A.* **81 G9** 36 37N 90 50W
Dønna, *Norway* **8 C15** 66 6N 12 30 E
Donna, *U.S.A.* **81 M5** 26 9N 98 4W
Donnaconna, *Canada* **71 C5** 46 41N 71 41W
Donnelly's Crossing, *N.Z.* **59 F4** 35 42S 173 38 E
Donnybrook, *Australia* **61 F2** 33 34S 115 48 E
Donnybrook, *S. Africa* **57 D4** 29 59S 29 48 E
Donora, *U.S.A.* **78 F5** 40 11N 79 52W
Donostia = Donostia-San Sebastián, *Spain* **19 A5** 43 17N 1 58W
Donostia-San Sebastián, *Spain* **19 A5** 43 17N 1 58W
Doon →, *U.K.* **12 F4** 55 27N 4 39W
Dora, L., *Australia* **60 D3** 22 0S 123 0 E
Dora Báltea →, *Italy* **18 D8** 45 11N 8 3 E
Doran L., *Canada* **73 A7** 61 13N 108 6W
Dorchester, *U.K.* **11 G5** 50 42N 2 27W
Dorchester, C., *Canada* **69 B12** 65 27N 77 27W
Dordogne →, *France* **18 D3** 45 2N 0 36W
Dordrecht, *Neths.* **15 C4** 51 48N 4 39 E
Dordrecht, *S. Africa* **56 E4** 31 20S 27 3 E
Doré L., *Canada* **73 C7** 54 46N 107 17W
Doré Lake, *Canada* **73 C7** 54 38N 107 36W
Dori, *Burkina Faso* **50 F5** 14 3N 0 2W
Doring →, *S. Africa* **56 E2** 31 54S 18 39 E
Doringbos, *S. Africa* **56 E2** 31 59S 19 16 E
Dorion, *Canada* **79 A10** 45 23N 74 3W
Dornbirn, *Austria* **16 E5** 47 25N 9 45 E
Dornie, *U.K.* **12 D3** 57 17N 5 31W
Dornoch, *U.K.* **12 D4** 57 53N 4 2W
Dornoch Firth, *U.K.* **12 D4** 57 51N 4 4W
Dornogovĭ □, *Mongolia* **34 C6** 44 0N 110 0 E
Dorohoi, *Romania* **17 E14** 47 56N 26 23 E
Döröö Nuur, *Mongolia* **32 B4** 48 0N 93 0 E
Dorr, *Iran* **45 C6** 33 17N 50 38 E
Dorre I., *Australia* **61 E1** 25 13S 113 12 E
Dorrigo, *Australia* **63 E5** 30 20S 152 44 E
Dorris, *U.S.A.* **82 F3** 41 58N 121 55W
Dorset, *Canada* **78 A6** 45 14N 78 54W
Dorset, *U.S.A.* **78 E4** 41 40N 80 40W
Dorset □, *U.K.* **11 G5** 50 45N 2 26W
Dortmund, *Germany* **16 C4** 51 30N 7 28 E
Doruma, *Dem. Rep. of the Congo* **54 B2** 4 42N 27 33 E
Dorūneh, *Iran* **45 C8** 35 10N 57 18 E
Dos Bahías, C., *Argentina* **96 E3** 44 58S 65 32W
Dos Hermanas, *Spain* **19 D3** 37 16N 5 55W
Dos Palos, *U.S.A.* **84 J6** 36 59N 120 37W
Dosso, *Niger* **50 F6** 13 0N 3 13 E
Dothan, *U.S.A.* **77 K3** 31 13N 85 24W
Doty, *U.S.A.* **84 D3** 46 38N 123 17W
Douai, *France* **18 A5** 50 21N 3 4 E
Douala, *Cameroon* **52 D1** 4 0N 9 45 E
Douarnenez, *France* **18 B1** 48 6N 4 21W
Double Island Pt., *Australia* **63 D5** 25 56S 153 11 E
Double Mountain Fork →, *U.S.A.* **81 J4** 33 16N 100 0W
Doubs →, *France* **18 C6** 46 53N 5 1 E
Doubtful Sd., *N.Z.* **59 L1** 45 20S 166 49 E
Doubtless B., *N.Z.* **59 F4** 34 55S 173 26 E
Douglas, *S. Africa* **56 D3** 29 4S 23 46 E
Douglas, *U.K.* **10 C3** 54 10N 4 28W
Douglas, *Ariz., U.S.A.* **83 L9** 31 21N 109 33W
Douglas, *Ga., U.S.A.* **77 K4** 31 31N 82 51W
Douglas, *Wyo., U.S.A.* **80 D2** 42 45N 105 24W
Douglas Chan., *Canada* **72 C3** 53 40N 129 20W
Douglas Pt., *Canada* **78 B3** 44 19N 81 37W
Douglasville, *U.S.A.* **77 J3** 33 45N 84 45W
Dounreay, *U.K.* **12 C5** 58 35N 3 44W
Dourada, Serra, *Brazil* **93 F9** 13 10S 48 45W
Dourados, *Brazil* **95 A5** 22 9S 54 50W
Dourados →, *Brazil* **95 A5** 21 58S 54 18W
Dourados, Serra dos, *Brazil* **95 A5** 23 30S 53 30W
Douro →, *Europe* **19 B1** 41 8N 8 40W
Dove →, *U.K.* **10 E6** 52 51N 1 36W
Dove Creek, *U.S.A.* **83 H9** 37 46N 108 54W
Dover, *Australia* **62 G4** 43 18S 147 2 E
Dover, *U.K.* **11 F9** 51 7N 1 19 E
Dover, *Del., U.S.A.* **76 F8** 39 10N 75 32W
Dover, *N.H., U.S.A.* **79 C14** 43 12N 70 56W
Dover, *N.J., U.S.A.* **79 F10** 40 53N 74 34W
Dover, *Ohio, U.S.A.* **78 F3** 40 32N 81 29W
Dover, Pt., *Australia* **61 F4** 32 32S 125 32 E
Dover, Str. of, *Europe* **11 G9** 51 0N 1 30 E
Dover-Foxcroft, *U.S.A.* **77 C11** 45 11N 69 13W
Dover Plains, *U.S.A.* **79 E11** 41 43N 73 35W
Dovey = Dyfi →, *U.K.* **11 E3** 52 32N 4 3W
Dovrefjell, *Norway* **9 E13** 62 15N 9 33 E
Dow Rūd, *Iran* **45 C6** 33 28N 49 4 E
Dowa, *Malawi* **55 E3** 13 38S 33 58 E
Dowagiac, *U.S.A.* **76 E2** 41 59N 86 6W

Eddystone Pt.

Dowerin, *Australia* .... **61 F2** 31 12S 117 2 E
Dowgha'i, *Iran* .... **45 B8** 36 54N 58 32 E
Dowlatābād, *Iran* .... **45 D8** 28 20N 56 40 E
Down □, *U.K.* **13 B5** 54 23N 6 2W
Downey, *Calif., U.S.A.* **85 M8** 33 56N 118 7W
Downey, *Idaho, U.S.A.* **82 E7** 42 26N 112 7W
Downham Market, *U.K.* ... **11 E8** 52 37N 0 23 E
Downieville, *U.S.A.* **84 F6** 39 34N 120 50W
Downpatrick, *U.K.* **13 B6** 54 20N 5 43W
Downpatrick Hd., *Ireland* .. **13 B2** 54 20N 9 21W
Downsville, *U.S.A.* **79 D10** 42 5N 74 50W
Downton, Mt., *Canada* **72 C4** 52 42N 124 52W
Dowsārī, *Iran* .... **45 D8** 28 25N 57 59 E
Doyle, *U.S.A.* **84 E6** 40 2N 120 6W
Doylestown, *U.S.A.* **79 F9** 40 21N 75 10W
Dozois, Rés., *Canada* **70 C4** 47 30N 77 5W
Dra Khel, *Pakistan* ...... **42 F2** 27 58N 66 45 E
Drachten, *Neths.* .... **15 A6** 53 7N 6 5 E
Drăgăşani, *Romania* ...... **17 F13** 44 39N 24 17 E
Dragichyn, *Belarus* .... **17 B13** 52 15N 25 8 E
Dragoman, Prokhod,
Bulgaria .... **21 C10** 42 58N 22 53 E
Draguignan, *France* ...... **18 E7** 43 32N 6 27 E
Drain, *U.S.A.* **82 E2** 43 40N 123 19W
Drake, *U.S.A.* **80 B4** 47 55N 100 23W
Drake Passage, *S. Ocean* .. **5 B17** 58 0S 68 0W
Drakensberg, *S. Africa* ... **57 E4** 31 0S 28 0 E
Dráma, *Greece* .... **21 D11** 41 9N 24 10 E
Drammen, *Norway* .... **9 G14** 59 42N 10 12 E
Drangajökull, *Iceland* **8 C2** 66 9N 22 15W
Dras, *India* .... **43 B6** 34 25N 75 48 E
Drau = Drava ⟶, *Croatia* **21 B8** 45 33N 18 55 E
Drava ⟶, *Croatia* .... **21 B8** 45 33N 18 55 E
Drayton Valley, *Canada* ... **72 C6** 53 12N 114 58W
Drenthe □, *Neths.* .... **15 B6** 52 52N 6 40 E
Drepanum, C., *Cyprus* .... **23 E11** 34 54N 32 19 E
Dresden, *Canada* **78 D2** 42 35N 82 11W
Dresden, *Germany* .... **16 C7** 51 3N 13 44 E
Dreux, *France* .... **18 B4** 48 44N 1 23 E
Driffield, *U.K.* **10 C7** 54 0N 0 26W
Driftwood, *U.S.A.* **78 E6** 41 20N 78 8W
Driggs, *U.S.A.* **82 E8** 43 44N 111 6W
Drina ⟶, *Bos.-H.* .... **21 B8** 44 53N 19 21 E
Drini ⟶, *Albania* .... **21 C8** 42 1N 19 38 E
Drøbak, *Norway* .... **9 G14** 59 39N 10 39 E
Drochia, *Moldova* .... **17 D14** 48 2N 27 48 E
Drogheda, *Ireland* **13 C5** 53 43N 6 22W
Drogichin = Dragichyn,
Belarus .... **17 B13** 52 15N 25 8 E
Drogobych = Drohobych,
Ukraine .... **17 D12** 49 20N 23 30 E
Drohobych, *Ukraine* ...... **17 D12** 49 20N 23 30 E
Droichead Atha =
Drogheda, *Ireland* **13 C5** 53 43N 6 22W
Droichead Nua, *Ireland* ... **13 C5** 53 11N 6 48W
Droitwich, *U.K.* **11 E5** 52 16N 2 8W
Dromedary, C., *Australia* . **63 F5** 36 17S 150 10 E
Dromore, *U.K.* **13 B4** 54 31N 7 28W
Dromore West, *Ireland* **13 B3** 54 15N 8 52W
Dronfield, *U.K.* **10 D6** 53 19N 1 27W
Dronten, *Neths.* .... **15 B5** 52 32N 5 43 E
Drumbo, *Canada* **78 C4** 43 16N 80 35W
Drumheller, *Canada* **72 C6** 51 25N 112 40W
Drummond, *U.S.A.* **82 C7** 46 40N 113 9W
Drummond I., *U.S.A.* **76 C4** 46 1N 83 39W
Drummond Pt., *Australia* . **63 E2** 34 9S 135 16 E
Drummond Ra., *Australia* . **62 C4** 23 45S 147 10 E
Drummondville, *Canada* .. **70 C5** 45 55N 72 25W
Drumright, *U.S.A.* **81 H6** 35 59N 96 36W
Druskininkai, *Lithuania* .... **9 J20** 54 3N 23 58 E
Drut ⟶, *Belarus* .... **17 B16** 53 8N 30 5 E
Druzhina, *Russia* .... **27 C15** 68 14N 145 18 E
Dry Tortugas, *U.S.A.* **88 B3** 24 38N 82 55W
Dryden, *Canada* **73 D10** 49 47N 92 50W
Dryden, *U.S.A.* **79 D8** 42 30N 76 18W
Drygalski I., *Antarctica* .... **5 C7** 66 0S 92 0 E
Drysdale ⟶, *Australia* ... **60 B4** 13 59S 126 51 E
Drysdale I., *Australia* .... **62 A2** 11 41S 136 0 E
Du Bois, *U.S.A.* **78 E6** 41 8N 78 46W
Du Gué ⟶, *Canada* **70 A5** 57 21N 70 45W
Du Quoin, *U.S.A.* **80 G10** 38 1N 89 14W
Duanesburg, *U.S.A.* **79 D10** 42 45N 74 11W
Duaringa, *Australia* ...... **62 C4** 23 42S 149 42 E
Ḑubā, *Si. Arabia* .... **44 E2** 27 10N 35 40 E
Dubai = Dubayy, *U.A.E.* ... **45 E7** 25 18N 55 20 E
Dubăsari, *Moldova* .... **17 E15** 47 15N 29 10 E
Dubăsari Vdkhr., *Moldova* . **17 E15** 47 30N 29 0 E
Dubawnt ⟶, *Canada* **73 A8** 64 33N 100 6W
Dubawnt, L., *Canada* **73 A8** 63 4N 101 42W
Dubayy, *U.A.E.* .... **45 E7** 25 18N 55 20 E
Dubbo, *Australia* .... **63 E4** 32 11S 148 35 E
Dubele,
Dem. Rep. of the Congo . **54 B2** 2 56N 29 35 E
Dublin, *Ireland* **13 C5** 53 21N 6 15W
Dublin, *Ga., U.S.A.* **77 J4** 32 32N 82 54W
Dublin, *Tex., U.S.A.* **81 J5** 32 5N 98 21W
Dublin □, *Ireland* **13 C5** 53 24N 6 20W
Dubno, *Ukraine* .... **17 C13** 50 25N 25 45 E
Dubois, *U.S.A.* **82 D7** 44 10N 112 14W
Dubossary = Dubăsari,
Moldova .... **17 E15** 47 15N 29 10 E
Dubossary Vdkhr. =
Dubăsari Vdkhr., *Moldova* **17 E15** 47 30N 29 0 E
Dubovka, *Russia* .... **25 E7** 49 5N 44 50 E
Dubrajpur, *India* .... **43 H12** 23 48N 87 25 E
Dubréka, *Guinea* **50 G3** 9 46N 13 31W
Dubrovitsa = Dubrovytsya,
Ukraine .... **17 C14** 51 31N 26 35 E
Dubrovnik, *Croatia* .... **21 C8** 42 39N 18 6 E
Dubrovytsya, *Ukraine* .... **17 C14** 51 31N 26 35 E
Dubuque, *U.S.A.* **80 D9** 42 30N 90 41W
Duchesne, *U.S.A.* **82 F8** 40 10N 110 24W
Duchess, *Australia* ...... **62 C2** 21 20S 139 50 E
Ducie I., *Pac. Oc.* **65 K15** 24 40S 124 48W
Duck ⟶, *U.S.A.* **77 G2** 36 2N 87 52W
Duck Cr. ⟶, *Australia* ... **60 D2** 22 37S 116 53 E
Duck Lake, *Canada* **73 C7** 52 50N 106 16W
Duck Mountain Prov. Park,
Canada **73 C8** 51 45N 101 0W
Duckwall, Mt., *U.S.A.* **84 H6** 37 58N 120 7W
Dudhi, *India* .... **41 G13** 24 15N 83 10 E
Dudinka, *Russia* .... **27 C9** 69 30N 86 13 E
Dudley, *U.K.* **11 E5** 52 31N 2 5W
Dudwa, *India* .... **43 E9** 28 30N 80 41 E
Duero = Douro ⟶, *Europe* **19 B1** 41 8N 8 40W
Dufftown, *U.K.* **12 D5** 57 27N 3 8W
Dugi Otok, *Croatia* .... **16 G8** 44 0N 15 3 E
Duifken Pt., *Australia* ..... **62 A3** 12 33S 141 38 E
Duisburg, *Germany* ...... **16 C4** 51 26N 6 45 E
Duiwelskloof, *S. Africa* .... **57 C5** 23 42S 30 10 E
Dūkdamīn, *Iran* .... **45 C8** 35 59N 57 43 E
Dukelský Průsmyk,
Slovak Rep. .... **17 D11** 49 25N 21 42 E
Dukhān, *Qatar* .... **45 E6** 25 25N 50 50 E
Duki, *Pakistan* .... **40 D6** 30 14N 68 25 E
Duku, *Nigeria* .... **51 F8** 10 43N 10 43 E
Dulce, *U.S.A.* **83 H10** 36 56N 107 0W
Dulce ⟶, *Argentina* **94 C3** 30 32S 62 33W
Dulce, G., *Costa Rica* **88 E3** 8 40N 83 20W
Dulf, *Iraq* .... **44 C5** 35 7N 45 51 E
Dulit, Banjaran, *Malaysia* .. **36 D4** 3 15N 114 30 E
Duliu, *China* .... **34 E9** 39 2N 116 55 E
Dullewala, *Pakistan* ...... **42 D4** 31 50N 71 25 E
Dulq Maghār, *Syria* .... **44 B3** 36 22N 38 39 E
Duluth, *U.S.A.* **80 B8** 46 47N 92 6W
Dum Dum, *India* .... **43 H13** 22 39N 88 33 E
Dum Duma, *India* .... **41 F19** 27 40N 95 40 E
Dūmā, *Syria* .... **47 B5** 33 34N 36 24 E
Dumaguete, *Phil.* .... **37 C6** 9 17N 123 15 E
Dumai, *Indonesia* .... **36 D2** 1 35N 101 28 E
Dumaran, *Phil.* .... **37 B5** 10 33N 119 50 E
Dumas, *Ark., U.S.A.* **81 J9** 33 53N 91 29W
Dumas, *Tex., U.S.A.* **81 H4** 35 52N 101 58W
Ḑumayr, *Syria* .... **47 B5** 33 39N 36 42 E
Dumbarton, *U.K.* **12 F4** 55 57N 4 33W
Dumbleyung, *Australia* .... **61 F2** 33 17S 117 42 E
Dumfries, *U.K.* **12 F5** 55 4N 3 37W
Dumfries & Galloway □,
U.K. **12 F5** 55 9N 3 58W
Dumka, *India* .... **43 G12** 24 12N 87 15 E
Dumoine ⟶, *Canada* **70 C4** 46 13N 77 51W
Dumoine, L., *Canada* **70 C4** 46 55N 77 55W
Dumraon, *India* .... **43 G11** 25 33N 84 8 E
Dumyât, *Egypt* .... **51 B12** 31 24N 31 48 E
Dún Dealgan = Dundalk,
Ireland **13 B5** 54 1N 6 24W
Dun Laoghaire, *Ireland* ... **13 C5** 53 17N 6 8W
Duna = Dunărea ⟶,
Europe .... **17 F15** 45 20N 29 40 E
Dunagiri, *India* .... **43 D8** 30 31N 79 52 E
Dunaj = Dunărea ⟶,
Europe .... **17 F15** 45 20N 29 40 E
Dunakeszi, *Hungary* ...... **17 E10** 47 37N 19 8 E
Dunărea ⟶, *Europe* ..... **17 F15** 45 20N 29 40 E
Dunaújváros, *Hungary* .... **17 E10** 46 58N 18 57 E
Dunav = Dunărea ⟶,
Europe .... **17 F15** 45 20N 29 40 E
Dunay, *Russia* .... **30 C6** 42 52N 132 22 E
Dunback, *N.Z.* .... **59 L3** 45 23S 170 36 E
Dunbar, *U.K.* **12 E6** 56 0N 2 31W
Dunblane, *U.K.* **12 E5** 56 11N 3 58W
Duncan, *Canada* **72 D4** 48 45N 123 40W
Duncan, *Ariz., U.S.A.* **83 K9** 32 43N 109 6W
Duncan, *Okla., U.S.A.* **81 H6** 34 30N 97 57W
Duncan, L., *Canada* **70 B4** 53 29N 77 58W
Duncan L., *Canada* **72 A6** 62 51N 113 58W
Duncan Town, *Bahamas* .. **88 B4** 22 15N 75 45W
Duncannon, *U.S.A.* **78 F7** 40 23N 77 2W
Duncansby Head, *U.K.* **12 C5** 58 38N 3 1W
Duncansville, *U.S.A.* **78 F6** 40 25N 78 26W
Dundalk, *Canada* **78 B4** 44 10N 80 24W
Dundalk, *Ireland* **13 B5** 54 1N 6 24W
Dundalk, *U.S.A.* **76 F7** 39 16N 76 32W
Dundalk Bay, *Ireland* **13 C5** 53 55N 6 15W
Dundas, *Canada* **78 C5** 43 17N 79 59W
Dundas, L., *Australia* ..... **61 F3** 32 35S 121 50 E
Dundas I., *Canada* **72 C2** 54 30N 130 50W
Dundas Str., *Australia* .... **60 B5** 11 15S 131 35 E
Dundee, *S. Africa* .... **57 D5** 28 11S 30 15 E
Dundee, *U.K.* **12 E6** 56 28N 2 59W
Dundee, *U.S.A.* **78 D8** 42 32N 76 59W
Dundee City □, *U.K.* **12 E6** 56 30N 2 58W
Dundgovĭ □, *Mongolia* .... **34 B4** 45 10N 106 0 E
Dundrum, *U.K.* **13 B6** 54 16N 5 52W
Dundrum B., *U.K.* **13 B6** 54 13N 5 47W
Dunedin, *N.Z.* .... **59 L3** 45 50S 170 33 E
Dunedin, *U.S.A.* **77 L4** 28 1N 82 47W
Dunedoo, *Australia* ...... **63 E4** 32 0S 149 25 E
Dunfermline, *U.K.* **12 E5** 56 5N 3 27W
Dungannon, *Canada* **78 C3** 43 51N 81 36W
Dungannon, *U.K.* **13 B5** 54 31N 6 46W
Dungarpur, *India* .... **42 H5** 23 52N 73 45 E
Dungarvan, *Ireland* **13 D4** 52 5N 7 37W
Dungarvan Harbour, *Ireland* **13 D4** 52 4N 7 35W
Dungeness, *U.K.* .... **11 G8** 50 54N 0 59 E
Dungo, L. do, *Angola* .... **56 B2** 17 15S 19 0 E
Dungog, *Australia* .... **63 E5** 32 22S 151 46 E
Dungu,
Dem. Rep. of the Congo . **54 B2** 3 40N 28 32 E
Dungun, *Malaysia* .... **39 K4** 4 45N 103 25 E
Dunhua, *China* .... **35 C15** 43 20N 128 14 E
Dunhuang, *China* .... **32 B4** 40 8N 94 36 E
Dunk I., *Australia* .... **62 B4** 17 59S 146 29 E
Dunkeld, *Australia* .... **63 E4** 33 25S 149 29 E
Dunkeld, *U.K.* **12 E5** 56 34N 3 35W
Dunkerque, *France* .... **18 A5** 51 2N 2 20 E
Dunkery Beacon, *U.K.* **11 F4** 51 9N 3 36W
Dunkirk = Dunkerque,
France .... **18 A5** 51 2N 2 20 E
Dunkirk, *U.S.A.* **78 D5** 42 29N 79 20W
Dúnleary = Dun Laoghaire,
Ireland **13 C5** 53 17N 6 8W
Dunleer, *Ireland* **13 C5** 53 50N 6 24W
Dunmanus B., *Ireland* **13 E2** 51 31N 9 50W
Dunmanway, *Ireland* **13 E2** 51 43N 9 6W
Dunmara, *Australia* ...... **62 B1** 16 42S 133 25 E
Dunmore, *U.S.A.* **79 E9** 41 25N 75 38W
Dunmore Hd., *Ireland* **13 D1** 52 10N 10 35W
Dunmore Town, *Bahamas* . **88 A4** 25 30N 76 39W
Dunn, *U.S.A.* **77 H6** 35 19N 78 37W
Dunnet Hd., *U.K.* **12 C5** 58 40N 3 21W
Dunning, *U.S.A.* **80 E4** 41 50N 100 6W
Dunnville, *Canada* **78 D5** 42 54N 79 36W
Dunolly, *Australia* .... **63 F3** 36 51S 143 44 E
Dunoon, *U.K.* **12 F4** 55 57N 4 56W
Dunphy, *U.S.A.* **82 F5** 40 42N 116 31W
Duns, *U.K.* **12 F6** 55 47N 2 20W
Dunseith, *U.S.A.* **80 A4** 48 50N 100 3W
Dunsmuir, *U.S.A.* **82 F2** 41 13N 122 16W
Dunstable, *U.K.* **11 F7** 51 53N 0 32W
Dunstan Mts., *N.Z.* .... **59 L2** 44 53S 169 35 E
Dunster, *Canada* **72 C5** 53 8N 119 50W
Dunvegan L., *Canada* **73 A7** 60 8N 107 10W
Duolun, *China* .... **34 C9** 42 12N 116 28 E
Duong Dong, *Vietnam* .... **39 G4** 10 13N 103 58 E
Dupree, *U.S.A.* **80 C4** 45 4N 101 35W
Dupuyer, *U.S.A.* **82 B7** 48 13N 112 30W
Duque de Caxias, *Brazil* ... **95 A7** 22 45S 43 19W
Durack ⟶, *Australia* ..... **60 C4** 15 33S 127 52 E
Durack Ra., *Australia* ..... **60 C4** 16 50S 127 40 E
Durance ⟶, *France* ..... **18 E6** 43 55N 4 45 E
Durand, *U.S.A.* **80 C9** 44 38N 91 58W
Durango, *Mexico* **86 C4** 24 3N 104 39W
Durango, *U.S.A.* **83 H10** 37 16N 107 53W
Durango □, *Mexico* **86 C4** 25 0N 105 0W
Durant, *Miss., U.S.A.* **81 J10** 33 4N 89 51W
Durant, *Okla., U.S.A.* **81 J6** 33 59N 96 25W
Durazno, *Uruguay* **94 C4** 33 25S 56 31W
Durazzo = Durrësi, *Albania* **21 D8** 41 19N 19 28 E
Durban, *S. Africa* .... **57 D5** 29 49S 31 1 E
Durbuy, *Belgium* .... **15 D5** 50 21N 5 28 E
Düren, *Germany* .... **16 C4** 50 48N 6 29 E
Durg, *India* .... **41 J12** 21 15N 81 22 E
Durgapur, *India* .... **43 H12** 23 30N 87 20 E
Durham, *Canada* **78 B4** 44 10N 80 49W
Durham, *U.K.* **10 C6** 54 47N 1 34W
Durham, *Calif., U.S.A.* **84 F5** 39 39N 121 48W
Durham, *N.C., U.S.A.* **77 H6** 35 59N 78 54W
Durham, *N.H., U.S.A.* **79 C14** 43 8N 70 56W
Durham □, *U.K.* **10 C6** 54 42N 1 45W
Ḑurmā, *Si. Arabia* .... **44 E5** 24 37N 46 8 E
Durmitor, *Montenegro, Yug.* **21 C8** 43 10N 19 0 E
Durness, *U.K.* **12 C4** 58 34N 4 45W
Durrësi, *Albania* .... **21 D8** 41 19N 19 28 E
Durrow, *Ireland* **13 D4** 52 51N 7 24W
Dursey I., *Ireland* **13 E1** 51 36N 10 12W
Dursunbey, *Turkey* .... **21 E13** 39 35N 28 37 E
Duru,
Dem. Rep. of the Congo . **54 B2** 4 14N 28 50 E
Durūz, Jabal ad, *Jordan* ... **47 C5** 32 35N 36 40 E
D'Urville, Tanjung,
Indonesia .... **37 E9** 1 28S 137 54 E
D'Urville I., *N.Z.* .... **59 J4** 40 50S 173 55 E
Duryea, *U.S.A.* **79 E9** 41 20N 75 45W
Dushak, *Turkmenistan* .... **26 F7** 37 13N 60 1 E
Dushanbe, *Tajikistan* ..... **26 F7** 38 33N 68 48 E
Dushore, *U.S.A.* **79 E8** 41 31N 76 24W
Dusky Sd., *N.Z.* .... **59 L1** 45 47S 166 30 E
Dussejour, C., *Australia* ... **60 B4** 14 45S 128 13 E
Düsseldorf, *Germany* ..... **16 C4** 51 14N 6 47 E
Dutch Harbor, *U.S.A.* **68 C3** 53 53N 166 32W
Dutlwe, *Botswana* .... **56 C3** 23 58S 23 46 E
Dutton, *Canada* **78 D3** 42 39N 81 30W
Dutton ⟶, *Australia* ..... **62 C3** 20 44S 143 10 E
Duwayhin, Khawr, *U.A.E.* .. **45 E6** 24 20N 51 25 E
Duyun, *China* .... **32 D5** 26 18N 107 29 E
Duzdab = Zāhedān, *Iran* .. **45 D9** 29 30N 60 50 E
Dvina, Severnaya ⟶,
Russia .... **24 B7** 64 32N 40 30 E
Dvinsk = Daugavpils, *Latvia* **9 J22** 55 53N 26 32 E
Dvinskaya Guba, *Russia* ... **24 B6** 65 0N 39 0 E
Dwarka, *India* .... **42 H3** 22 18N 69 8 E
Dwellingup, *Australia* .... **61 F2** 32 43S 116 4 E
Dwight, *Canada* **78 A5** 45 20N 79 1W
Dwight, *U.S.A.* **76 E1** 41 5N 88 26W
Dyatlovo = Dzyatlava,
Belarus .... **17 B13** 53 28N 25 28 E
Dyce, *U.K.* **12 D6** 57 13N 2 12W
Dyer, C., *Canada* **69 B13** 66 40N 61 0W
Dyer Bay, *Canada* **78 A3** 45 10N 81 20W
Dyer Plateau, *Antarctica* .. **5 D17** 70 45S 65 30W
Dyersburg, *U.S.A.* **81 G10** 36 3N 89 23W
Dyfi ⟶, *U.K.* **11 E3** 52 32N 4 3W
Dymer, *Ukraine* .... **17 C16** 50 47N 30 18 E
Dysart, *Australia* .... **62 C4** 22 32S 148 23 E
Dzamin Üüd = Borhoyn Tal,
Mongolia .... **34 C6** 43 50N 111 58 E
Dzerzhinsk, *Russia* .... **24 C7** 56 14N 43 30 E
Dzhalinda, *Russia* .... **27 D13** 53 26N 124 0 E
Dzhambul = Zhambyl,
Kazakstan .... **26 E8** 42 54N 71 22 E
Dzhankoy, *Ukraine* .... **25 E5** 45 40N 34 20 E
Dzhezkazgan =
Zhezqazghan, *Kazakstan* . **26 E7** 47 44N 67 40 E
Dzhizak = Jizzakh,
Uzbekistan .... **26 E7** 40 6N 67 50 E
Dzhugdzur, Khrebet, *Russia* **27 D14** 57 30N 138 0 E
Dzhungarskiye Vorota =
Dzungarian Gates,
Kazakstan .... **32 B3** 45 0N 82 0 E
Działdowo, *Poland* .... **17 B11** 53 15N 20 15 E
Dzibilchaltun, *Mexico* **87 C7** 21 5N 89 36W
Dzierżoniów, *Poland* ...... **17 C9** 50 45N 16 39 E
Dzilam de Bravo, *Mexico* .. **87 C7** 21 24N 88 53W
Dzungaria = Junggar Pendi,
China .... **32 B3** 44 30N 86 0 E
Dzungarian Gates,
Kazakstan .... **32 B3** 45 0N 82 0 E
Dzuumod, *Mongolia* ...... **32 B5** 47 45N 106 58 E
Dzyarzhynsk, *Belarus* ..... **17 B14** 53 40N 27 1 E
Dzyatlava, *Belarus* .... **17 B13** 53 28N 25 28 E

E

Eabamet L., *Canada* **70 B2** 51 30N 87 46W
Eads, *U.S.A.* **80 F3** 38 29N 102 47W
Eagar, *U.S.A.* **83 J9** 34 6N 109 17W
Eagle, *Alaska, U.S.A.* **68 B5** 64 47N 141 12W
Eagle, *Colo., U.S.A.* **82 G10** 39 39N 106 50W
Eagle ⟶, *Canada* **71 B8** 53 36N 57 26W
Eagle Butte, *U.S.A.* **80 C4** 45 0N 101 10W
Eagle Grove, *U.S.A.* **80 D8** 42 40N 93 54W
Eagle L., *Canada* **73 D10** 49 42N 93 13W
Eagle L., *Calif., U.S.A.* **82 F3** 40 39N 120 45W
Eagle L., *Maine, U.S.A.* ... **77 B11** 46 20N 69 22W
Eagle Lake, *Canada* **78 A6** 45 8N 78 29W
Eagle Lake, *Maine, U.S.A.* . **77 B11** 47 3N 68 36W
Eagle Lake, *Tex., U.S.A.* ... **81 L6** 29 35N 96 20W
Eagle Mountain, *U.S.A.* ... **85 M11** 33 49N 115 27W
Eagle Nest, *U.S.A.* **83 H11** 36 33N 105 16W
Eagle Pass, *U.S.A.* **81 L4** 28 43N 100 30W
Eagle Pk., *U.S.A.* **84 G7** 38 10N 119 25W
Eagle Pt., *Australia* ...... **60 C3** 16 11S 124 23 E
Eagle River, *Mich., U.S.A.* . **76 B1** 47 24N 88 18W
Eagle River, *Wis., U.S.A.* .. **80 C10** 45 55N 89 15W
Eaglehawk, *Australia* ..... **63 F3** 36 44S 144 15 E
Eagles Mere, *U.S.A.* **79 E8** 41 25N 76 33W
Ealing, *U.K.* **11 F7** 51 31N 0 20W
Ear Falls, *Canada* **73 C10** 50 38N 93 13W
Earle, *U.S.A.* **81 H9** 35 16N 90 28W
Earlimart, *U.S.A.* **85 K7** 35 53N 119 16W
Earn ⟶, *U.K.* **12 E5** 56 21N 3 18W
Earn, L., *U.K.* **12 E4** 56 23N 4 13W
Earnslaw, Mt., *N.Z.* ...... **59 L2** 44 32S 168 27 E
Earth, *U.S.A.* **81 H3** 34 14N 102 24W
Easley, *U.S.A.* **77 H4** 34 50N 82 36W
East Anglia, *U.K.* .... **10 E9** 52 30N 1 0 E
East Angus, *Canada* **71 C5** 45 30N 71 40W
East Aurora, *U.S.A.* **78 D6** 42 46N 78 37W
East Ayrshire □, *U.K.* **12 F4** 55 26N 4 11W
East Bengal, *Bangla.* ...... **41 H17** 24 0N 90 0 E
East Beskids = Vychodné
Beskydy, *Europe* .... **17 D11** 49 20N 22 0 E
East Brady, *U.S.A.* **78 F5** 40 59N 79 36W
East C., *N.Z.* .... **59 G7** 37 42S 178 35 E
East Chicago, *U.S.A.* **76 E2** 41 38N 87 27W
East China Sea, *Asia* ...... **33 D7** 30 0N 126 0 E
East Coulee, *Canada* **72 C6** 51 23N 112 27W
East Dereham, *U.K.* ...... **11 E8** 52 41N 0 57 E
East Dunbartonshire □, *U.K.* **12 F4** 55 57N 4 13W
East Falkland, *Falk. Is.* ... **96 G5** 51 30S 58 30W
East Grand Forks, *U.S.A.* .. **80 B6** 47 56N 97 1W
East Greenwich, *U.S.A.* ... **79 E13** 41 40N 71 27W
East Grinstead, *U.K.* ...... **11 F8** 51 7N 0 0 E
East Hartford, *U.S.A.* **79 E12** 41 46N 72 39W
East Helena, *U.S.A.* **82 C8** 46 35N 111 56W
East Indies, *Asia* .... **28 K15** 0 0 120 0 E
East Kilbride, *U.K.* **12 F4** 55 47N 4 11W
East Lansing, *U.S.A.* **76 D3** 42 44N 84 29W
East Liverpool, *U.S.A.* **78 F4** 40 37N 80 35W
East London, *S. Africa* .... **57 E4** 33 0S 27 55 E
East Lothian □, *U.K.* **12 F6** 55 58N 2 44W
East Main = Eastmain,
Canada **70 B4** 52 10N 78 30W
East Northport, *U.S.A.* **79 F11** 40 53N 73 20W
East Orange, *U.S.A.* **79 F10** 40 46N 74 13W
East Pacific Ridge, *Pac. Oc.* **65 J17** 15 0S 110 0W
East Palestine, *U.S.A.* **78 F4** 40 50N 80 33W
East Pine, *Canada* **72 B4** 55 48N 120 12W
East Point, *U.S.A.* **77 J3** 33 41N 84 27W
East Providence, *U.S.A.* .. **79 E13** 41 49N 71 23W
East Pt., *Canada* **71 C7** 46 27N 61 58W
East Renfrewshire □, *U.K.* . **12 F4** 55 46N 4 21W
East Retford = Retford, *U.K.* **10 D7** 53 19N 0 56W
East Riding of Yorkshire □,
U.K. **10 D7** 53 55N 0 30W
East Rochester, *U.S.A.* ... **78 C7** 43 7N 77 29W
East St. Louis, *U.S.A.* **80 F9** 38 37N 90 9W
East Schelde =
Oosterschelde ⟶, *Neths.* **15 C4** 51 33N 4 0 E
East Siberian Sea, *Russia* . **27 B17** 73 0N 160 0 E
East Stroudsburg, *U.S.A.* .. **79 E9** 41 1N 75 11W
East Sussex □, *U.K.* ...... **11 G8** 50 56N 0 19 E
East Tawas, *U.S.A.* **76 C4** 44 17N 83 29W
East Timor = Timor
Timur □, *Indonesia* ..... **37 F7** 9 0S 125 0 E
East Toorale, *Australia* .... **63 E4** 30 27S 145 28 E
East Walker ⟶, *U.S.A.* ... **84 G7** 38 52N 119 10W
East Windsor, *U.S.A.* **79 F10** 40 17N 74 34W
Eastbourne, *N.Z.* .... **59 J5** 41 19S 174 55 E
Eastbourne, *U.K.* .... **11 G8** 50 46N 0 18 E
Eastend, *Canada* **73 D7** 49 32N 108 50W
Easter I. = Pascua, I. de,
Pac. Oc. **65 K17** 27 0S 109 0W
Eastern □, *Kenya* .... **54 C4** 0 0 38 30 E
Eastern □, *Uganda* .... **54 B3** 1 50N 33 45 E
Eastern Cape □, *S. Africa* . **56 E4** 32 0S 26 0 E
Eastern Cr. ⟶, *Australia* . **62 C3** 20 40S 141 35 E
Eastern Ghats, *India* ...... **40 N11** 14 0N 78 50 E
Eastern Group = Lau Group,
Fiji **59 C9** 17 0S 178 30W
Eastern Group, *Australia* .. **61 F3** 33 30S 124 30 E
Eastern Transvaal =
Mpumalanga □, *S. Africa* **57 B5** 26 0S 30 0 E
Easterville, *Canada* **73 C9** 53 8N 99 49W
Easthampton, *U.S.A.* **79 D12** 42 16N 72 40W
Eastlake, *U.S.A.* **78 E3** 41 40N 81 26W
Eastland, *U.S.A.* **81 J5** 32 24N 98 49W
Eastleigh, *U.K.* **11 G6** 50 58N 1 21W
Eastmain, *Canada* **70 B4** 52 10N 78 30W
Eastmain ⟶, *Canada* **70 B4** 52 27N 78 26W
Eastman, *Canada* **79 A12** 45 18N 72 19W
Eastman, *U.S.A.* **77 J4** 32 12N 83 11W
Easton, *Md., U.S.A.* **76 F7** 38 47N 76 5W
Easton, *Pa., U.S.A.* **79 F9** 40 41N 75 13W
Easton, *Wash., U.S.A.* **84 C5** 47 14N 121 11W
Eastpointe, *U.S.A.* **78 D2** 42 27N 82 56W
Eastport, *U.S.A.* **77 C12** 44 56N 67 0W
Eastsound, *U.S.A.* **84 B4** 48 42N 122 55W
Eaton, *U.S.A.* **80 E2** 40 32N 104 42W
Eatonia, *Canada* **73 C7** 51 13N 109 25W
Eatonton, *U.S.A.* **77 J4** 33 20N 83 23W
Eatontown, *U.S.A.* **79 F10** 40 19N 74 4W
Eatonville, *U.S.A.* **84 D4** 46 52N 122 16W
Eau Claire, *U.S.A.* **80 C9** 44 49N 91 30W
Eau Claire, L. à l', *Canada* . **70 A5** 56 10N 74 25W
Ebbw Vale, *U.K.* **11 F4** 51 46N 3 12W
Ebeltoft, *Denmark* .... **9 H14** 56 12N 10 41 E
Ebensburg, *U.S.A.* **78 F6** 40 29N 78 44W
Eberswalde-Finow, *Germany* **16 B7** 52 50N 13 49 E
Ebetsu, *Japan* .... **30 C10** 43 7N 141 34 E
Ebolowa, *Cameroon* ...... **52 D2** 2 55N 11 10 E
Ebro ⟶, *Spain* .... **19 B6** 40 43N 0 54 E
Eceabat, *Turkey* .... **21 D12** 40 11N 26 21 E
Ech Cheliff, *Algeria* ...... **50 A6** 36 10N 1 20 E
Echigo-Sammyaku, *Japan* . **31 F9** 36 50N 139 50 E
Echizen-Misaki, *Japan* ... **31 G7** 35 59N 135 57 E
Echo Bay, *N.W.T., Canada* . **68 B8** 66 5N 117 55W
Echo Bay, *Ont., Canada* ... **70 C3** 46 29N 84 4W
Echoing ⟶, *Canada* **70 B1** 55 51N 92 5W
Echternach, *Lux.* .... **15 E6** 49 49N 6 25 E
Echuca, *Australia* .... **63 F3** 36 10S 144 20 E
Ecija, *Spain* **19 D3** 37 30N 5 10W
Eclipse Is., *Australia* ..... **60 B4** 13 54S 126 19 E
Eclipse Sd., *Canada* **69 A11** 72 38N 79 0W
Ecuador ■, *S. Amer.* **92 D3** 2 0S 78 0W
Ed Damazin, *Sudan* .... **51 F12** 11 46N 34 21 E
Ed Debba, *Sudan* .... **51 E12** 18 0N 30 51 E
Ed Dueim, *Sudan* .... **51 F12** 14 0N 32 10 E
Edam, *Canada* **73 C7** 53 11N 108 46W
Edam, *Neths.* .... **15 B5** 52 31N 5 3 E
Eday, *U.K.* **12 B6** 59 11N 2 47W
Eddrachillis B., *U.K.* **12 C3** 58 17N 5 14W
Eddystone Pt., *Australia* ... **62 G4** 40 59S 148 20 E

Ede, Neths. 15 B5 52 4N 5 40 E
Edehon L., Canada 73 A9 60 25N 97 15W
Eden, Australia 63 F4 37 3S 149 55 E
Eden, N.C., U.S.A. 77 G6 36 29N 79 53W
Eden, N.Y., U.S.A. 78 D6 42 39N 78 55W
Eden, Tex., U.S.A. 81 K5 31 13N 99 51W
Eden →, U.K. 10 C4 54 57N 3 1W
Edenburg, S. Africa 56 D4 29 43S 25 58 E
Edendale, S. Africa 57 D5 29 39S 30 18 E
Edenderry, Ireland 13 C4 53 21N 7 4W
Edenhope, Australia 63 F3 37 4S 141 19 E
Edenton, U.S.A. 77 G7 36 4N 76 39W
Edenville, S. Africa 57 D4 27 37S 27 34 E
Eder →, Germany 16 C5 51 12N 9 28 E
Edgar, U.S.A. 80 E6 40 22N 97 58W
Edgartown, U.S.A. 79 E14 41 23N 70 31W
Edge Hill, U.K. 11 E6 52 8N 1 26W
Edgefield, U.S.A. 77 J5 33 47N 81 56W
Edgeley, U.S.A. 80 B5 46 22N 98 43W
Edgemont, U.S.A. 80 D3 43 18N 103 50W
Edgeøya, Svalbard 4 B9 77 45N 22 30 E
Édhessa, Greece 21 D10 40 48N 22 5 E
Edievale, N.Z. 59 L2 45 49S 169 22 E
Edina, U.S.A. 80 E8 40 10N 92 11W
Edinboro, U.S.A. 78 E4 41 52N 80 8W
Edinburg, U.S.A. 81 M5 26 18N 98 10W
Edinburgh, U.K. 12 F5 55 57N 3 13W
Edineţ, Moldova 17 D14 48 9N 27 18 E
Edirne, Turkey 21 D12 41 40N 26 34 E
Edison, U.S.A. 84 B4 48 33N 122 27W
Edithburgh, Australia 63 F2 35 5S 137 43 E
Edmeston, U.S.A. 79 D9 42 42N 75 15W
Edmond, U.S.A. 81 H6 35 39N 97 29W
Edmonds, U.S.A. 84 C4 47 49N 122 23W
Edmonton, Australia 62 B4 17 2S 145 46 E
Edmonton, Canada 72 C6 53 30N 113 30W
Edmund L., Canada 70 B1 54 45N 93 17W
Edmundston, Canada 71 C6 47 23N 68 20W
Edna, U.S.A. 81 L6 28 59N 96 39W
Edremit, Turkey 21 E12 39 34N 27 0 E
Edremit Körfezi, Turkey 21 E12 39 30N 26 45 E
Edson, Canada 72 C5 53 35N 116 28W
Eduardo Castex, Argentina 94 D3 35 50S 64 18W
Edward →, Australia 63 F3 35 5S 143 30 E
Edward, L., Africa 54 C2 0 25S 29 40 E
Edward River, Australia 62 A3 14 59S 141 26 E
Edward VII Land, Antarctica 5 E13 80 0S 150 0W
Edwards, Calif., U.S.A. 85 L9 34 55N 117 51W
Edwards, N.Y., U.S.A. 79 B9 44 20N 75 15W
Edwards Air Force Base, U.S.A. 85 L9 34 50N 117 40W
Edwards Plateau, U.S.A. 81 K4 30 45N 101 20W
Edwardsville, U.S.A. 79 E9 41 15N 75 56W
Edzo, Canada 72 A5 62 49N 116 4W
Eeklo, Belgium 15 C3 51 11N 3 33 E
Effingham, U.S.A. 76 F1 39 7N 88 33W
Égadi, Ísole, Italy 20 F5 37 55N 12 16 E
Egan Range, U.S.A. 82 G6 39 35N 114 55W
Eganville, Canada 78 A7 45 32N 77 5W
Eger = Cheb, Czech Rep. 16 C7 50 9N 12 28 E
Eger, Hungary 17 E11 47 53N 20 27 E
Egersund, Norway 9 G12 58 26N 6 1 E
Egg L., Canada 73 B7 55 5N 105 30W
Éghezée, Belgium 15 D4 50 35N 4 55 E
Egmont, Canada 72 D4 49 45N 123 56W
Egmont, C., N.Z. 59 H4 39 16S 173 45 E
Egmont, Mt., N.Z. 59 H5 39 17S 174 5 E
Egra, India 43 J12 21 54N 87 32 E
Eğridir, Turkey 25 G5 37 52N 30 51 E
Eğridir Gölü, Turkey 25 G5 37 53N 30 50 E
Egvekinot, Russia 27 C19 66 19N 179 50W
Egypt ■, Africa 51 C12 28 0N 31 0 E
Ehime □, Japan 31 H6 33 30N 132 40 E
Ehrenberg, U.S.A. 85 M12 33 36N 114 31W
Eibar, Spain 19 A4 43 11N 2 28W
Eidsvold, Australia 63 D5 25 25S 151 12 E
Eidsvoll, Norway 9 F14 60 19N 11 14 E
Eifel, Germany 16 C4 50 15N 6 50 E
Eiffel Flats, Zimbabwe 55 F3 18 20S 30 0 E
Eigg, U.K. 12 E2 56 54N 6 10W
Eighty Mile Beach, Australia 60 C3 19 30S 120 40 E
Eil, Somali Rep. 46 F4 8 0N 49 50 E
Eil, L., U.K. 12 E3 56 51N 5 16W
Eildon, Australia 63 F4 37 14S 145 55 E
Eildon, L., Australia 63 F4 37 10S 146 0 E
Einasleigh, Australia 62 B3 18 32S 144 5 E
Einasleigh →, Australia 62 B3 17 30S 142 17 E
Eindhoven, Neths. 15 C5 51 26N 5 28 E
Eire = Ireland ■, Europe 13 C4 53 50N 7 52W
Eiríksjökull, Iceland 8 D3 64 46N 20 24W
Eirunepé, Brazil 92 E5 6 35S 69 53W
Eisenach, Germany 16 C6 50 58N 10 19 E
Eisenerz, Austria 16 E8 47 32N 14 54 E
Eivissa, Spain 22 C7 38 54N 1 26 E
Ejutla, Mexico 87 D5 16 34N 96 44W
Ekalaka, U.S.A. 80 C2 45 53N 104 33W
Eketahuna, N.Z. 59 J5 40 38S 175 43 E
Ekibastuz, Kazakstan 26 D8 51 50N 75 10 E
Ekoli, Dem. Rep. of the Congo 54 C1 0 23S 24 13 E
Eksjö, Sweden 9 H16 57 40N 14 58 E
Ekwan →, Canada 70 B3 53 12N 82 15W
Ekwan Pt., Canada 70 B3 53 16N 82 7W
El Aaiún, W. Sahara 50 C3 27 9N 13 12W
El Abanico, Chile 94 D1 37 20S 71 31W
El 'Agrûd, Egypt 47 E3 30 14N 34 24 E
El Alamein, Egypt 51 B11 30 48N 28 58 E
El 'Aqaba, W. →, Egypt 47 E2 30 7N 33 54 E
El Arīḥā, West Bank 47 D4 31 52N 35 27 E
El 'Arîsh, Egypt 47 D2 31 8N 33 50 E
El 'Arîsh, W. →, Egypt 47 D2 31 8N 33 47 E
El Asnam = Ech Cheliff, Algeria 50 A6 36 10N 1 20 E
El Bayadh, Algeria 50 B6 33 40N 1 1 E
El Bluff, Nic. 88 D3 11 59N 83 40W
El Brûk, W. →, Egypt 47 E2 30 15N 33 50 E
El Cajon, U.S.A. 85 N10 32 48N 116 58W
El Campo, U.S.A. 81 L6 29 12N 96 16W
El Centro, U.S.A. 85 N11 32 48N 115 34W
El Cerro, Bolivia 92 G6 17 30S 61 40W
El Compadre, Mexico 85 N10 32 20N 116 14W
El Cuy, Argentina 96 D3 39 55S 68 25W
El Cuyo, Mexico 87 C7 21 30N 87 40W
El Daheir, Egypt 47 D3 31 13N 34 10 E
El Dátil, Mexico 86 B2 30 7N 112 15W
El Dere, Somali Rep. 46 G4 3 50N 47 8 E
El Descanso, Mexico 85 N10 32 12N 116 58W
El Desemboque, Mexico 86 A2 30 30N 112 57W
El Diviso, Colombia 92 C3 1 22N 78 14W
El Djouf, Mauritania 50 D4 20 0N 9 0W
El Dorado, Ark., U.S.A. 81 J8 33 12N 92 40W
El Dorado, Kans., U.S.A. 81 G6 37 49N 96 52W
El Dorado, Venezuela 92 B6 6 55N 61 37W
El Escorial, Spain 19 B3 40 35N 4 7W
El Faiyûm, Egypt 51 C12 29 19N 30 50 E
El Fâsher, Sudan 51 F11 13 33N 25 26 E
El Ferrol = Ferrol, Spain 19 A1 43 29N 8 15W
El Fuerte, Mexico 86 B3 26 30N 108 40W
El Gal, Somali Rep. 46 E5 10 58N 50 20 E
El Geneina = Al Junaynah, Sudan 51 F10 13 27N 22 45 E
El Gîza, Egypt 51 C12 30 0N 31 10 E
El Goléa, Algeria 50 B6 30 30N 2 50 E
El Iskandarîya, Egypt 51 B11 31 13N 29 58 E
El Istiwa'iya, Sudan 51 G11 5 0N 28 0 E
El Jadida, Morocco 50 B4 33 11N 8 17W
El Jardal, Honduras 88 D2 14 54N 88 50W
El Kabrît, G., Egypt 47 F2 29 42N 33 16 E
El Khârga, Egypt 51 C12 25 30N 30 33 E
El Khartûm, Sudan 51 E12 15 31N 32 35 E
El Kuntilla, Egypt 47 E3 30 1N 34 45 E
El Maestrazgo, Spain 19 B5 40 30N 0 25W
El Mahalla el Kubra, Egypt 51 B12 31 0N 31 0 E
El Mansûra, Egypt 51 B12 31 0N 31 19 E
El Medano, Canary Is. 22 F3 28 3N 16 32W
El Milagro, Argentina 94 C2 30 59S 65 59W
El Minyâ, Egypt 51 C12 28 7N 30 33 E
El Monte, U.S.A. 85 L8 34 4N 118 1W
El Obeid, Sudan 51 F12 13 8N 30 10 E
El Odaiya, Sudan 51 F11 12 8N 28 12 E
El Oro, Mexico 87 D4 19 48N 100 8W
El Oued, Algeria 50 B7 33 20N 6 58 E
El Palmito, Presa, Mexico 86 B3 25 40N 105 30W
El Paso, U.S.A. 83 L10 31 45N 106 29W
El Paso Robles, U.S.A. 84 K6 35 38N 120 41W
El Portal, U.S.A. 84 H7 37 41N 119 47W
El Porvenir, Mexico 86 A3 31 15N 105 51W
El Prat de Llobregat, Spain 19 B7 41 18N 2 3 E
El Progreso, Honduras 88 C2 15 26N 87 51W
El Pueblito, Mexico 86 B3 29 3N 105 4W
El Pueblo, Canary Is. 22 F2 28 36N 17 47W
El Puerto de Santa María, Spain 19 D2 36 36N 6 13W
El Qâhira, Egypt 51 B12 30 1N 31 14 E
El Qantara, Egypt 47 E1 30 51N 32 20 E
El Quseima, Egypt 47 E3 30 40N 34 15 E
El Real, Panama 92 B3 8 0N 77 40W
El Reno, U.S.A. 81 H6 35 32N 97 57W
El Rio, U.S.A. 85 L7 34 14N 119 10W
El Roque, Pta., Canary Is. 22 F4 28 10N 15 25W
El Rosarito, Mexico 86 B2 28 38N 114 4W
El Saheira, W. →, Egypt 47 E2 30 5N 33 25 E
El Salto, Mexico 86 C3 23 47N 105 22W
El Salvador ■, Cent. Amer. 88 D2 13 50N 89 0W
El Sauce, Nic. 88 D2 13 0N 86 40W
El Sueco, Mexico 86 B3 29 54N 106 24W
El Suweis, Egypt 51 C12 29 58N 32 31 E
El Tamarâni, W. →, Egypt 47 E3 30 7N 34 43 E
El Thamad, Egypt 47 F3 29 40N 34 28 E
El Tigre, Venezuela 92 B6 8 44N 64 15W
El Tîh, Gebal, Egypt 47 F2 29 40N 33 50 E
El Tîna, Khalîg, Egypt 47 D1 31 10N 32 40 E
El Tofo, Chile 94 B1 29 22S 71 18W
El Tránsito, Chile 94 B1 28 52S 70 17W
El Tûr, Egypt 44 D2 28 14N 33 36 E
El Turbio, Argentina 96 G2 51 45S 72 5W
El Uqsur, Egypt 51 C12 25 41N 32 38 E
El Venado, Mexico 86 C4 22 56N 101 10W
El Vergel, Mexico 86 B3 26 28N 106 22W
El Vigía, Venezuela 92 B4 8 38N 71 39W
El Wabeira, Egypt 47 F2 29 34N 33 6 E
El Wak, Kenya 54 B5 2 49N 40 56 E
El Wuz, Sudan 51 E12 15 5N 30 7 E
Elat, Israel 47 F3 29 30N 34 56 E
Elâzığ, Turkey 25 G6 38 37N 39 14 E
Elba, Italy 20 C4 42 46N 10 17 E
Elba, U.S.A. 77 K2 31 25N 86 4W
Elbasani, Albania 21 D9 41 9N 20 9 E
Elbe, U.S.A. 84 D4 46 45N 122 10W
Elbe →, Europe 16 B5 53 50N 9 0 E
Elbert, Mt., U.S.A. 83 G10 39 7N 106 27W
Elberton, U.S.A. 77 H4 34 7N 82 52W
Elbeuf, France 18 B4 49 17N 1 2 E
Elbidtan, Turkey 44 B3 38 13N 37 12 E
Elbing = Elbląg, Poland 17 A10 54 10N 19 25 E
Elbląg, Poland 17 A10 54 10N 19 25 E
Elbow, Canada 73 C7 51 7N 106 35W
Elbrus, Asia 25 F7 43 21N 42 30 E
Elburz Mts. = Alborz, Reshteh-ye Kūhhā-ye, Iran 45 C7 36 0N 52 0 E
Elche, Spain 19 C5 38 15N 0 42W
Elcho I., Australia 62 A2 11 55S 135 45 E
Elda, Spain 19 C5 38 29N 0 47W
Elde →, Germany 16 B6 53 7N 11 15 E
Eldon, Mo., U.S.A. 80 F8 38 21N 92 35W
Eldon, Wash., U.S.A. 84 C3 47 33N 123 3W
Eldora, U.S.A. 80 D8 42 22N 93 5W
Eldorado, Argentina 95 B5 26 28S 54 43W
Eldorado, Canada 78 B7 44 35N 77 31W
Eldorado, Mexico 86 C3 24 20N 107 22W
Eldorado, Ill., U.S.A. 76 G1 37 49N 88 26W
Eldorado, Tex., U.S.A. 81 K4 30 52N 100 36W
Eldorado Springs, U.S.A. 81 G8 37 52N 94 1W
Eldoret, Kenya 54 B4 0 30N 35 17 E
Eldred, U.S.A. 78 E6 41 58N 78 23W
Elea, C., Cyprus 23 D13 35 19N 34 4 E
Eleanora, Pk., Australia 61 F3 32 57S 121 9 E
Electra, U.S.A. 74 D7 34 2N 98 55W
Elefantes →, Mozam. 57 C5 24 10S 32 40 E
Elektrostal, Russia 24 C6 55 41N 38 32 E
Elephant Butte Reservoir, U.S.A. 83 K10 33 9N 107 11W
Elephant I., Antarctica 5 C18 61 0S 55 0W
Eleuthera, Bahamas 88 B4 25 0N 76 20W
Elgin, Canada 79 B8 44 36N 76 13W
Elgin, U.K. 12 D5 57 39N 3 19W
Elgin, Ill., U.S.A. 76 D1 42 2N 88 17W
Elgin, N. Dak., U.S.A. 80 B4 46 24N 101 51W
Elgin, Oreg., U.S.A. 82 D5 45 34N 117 55W
Elgin, Tex., U.S.A. 81 K6 30 21N 97 22W
Elgon, Mt., Africa 54 B3 1 10N 34 30 E
Eliase, Indonesia 37 F8 8 21S 130 48 E
Elim, S. Africa 56 E2 34 35S 19 45 E
Elisabethville = Lubumbashi, Dem. Rep. of the Congo 55 E2 11 40S 27 28 E
Elista, Russia 25 E7 46 16N 44 14 E
Elizabeth, Australia 63 E2 34 42S 138 41 E
Elizabeth, N.J., U.S.A. 79 F10 40 39N 74 13W
Elizabeth, N.J., U.S.A. 79 F10 40 40N 74 13W
Elizabeth City, U.S.A. 77 G7 36 18N 76 14W
Elizabethton, U.S.A. 77 G4 36 21N 82 13W
Elizabethtown, Ky., U.S.A. 76 G3 37 42N 85 52W
Elizabethtown, N.Y., U.S.A. 79 B11 44 13N 73 36W
Elizabethtown, Pa., U.S.A. 79 F8 40 9N 76 36W
Ełk, Poland 17 B12 53 50N 22 21 E
Elk →, Canada 72 C5 49 11N 115 14W
Elk →, U.S.A. 77 H2 34 46N 87 16W
Elk City, U.S.A. 81 H5 35 25N 99 25W
Elk Creek, U.S.A. 84 F4 39 36N 122 32W
Elk Grove, U.S.A. 84 G5 38 25N 121 22W
Elk Island Nat. Park, Canada 72 C6 53 35N 112 59W
Elk Lake, Canada 70 C3 47 40N 80 25W
Elk Point, Canada 73 C6 53 54N 110 55W
Elk River, Idaho, U.S.A. 82 C5 46 47N 116 11W
Elk River, Minn., U.S.A. 80 C8 45 18N 93 35W
Elkedra →, Australia 62 C2 21 8S 136 22 E
Elkhart, Ind., U.S.A. 76 E3 41 41N 85 58W
Elkhart, Kans., U.S.A. 81 G4 37 0N 101 54W
Elkhorn, Canada 73 D8 49 59N 101 14W
Elkhorn →, U.S.A. 80 E6 41 8N 96 19W
Elkhovo, Bulgaria 21 C12 42 10N 26 35 E
Elkin, U.S.A. 77 G5 36 15N 80 51W
Elkins, U.S.A. 76 F6 38 55N 79 51W
Elkland, U.S.A. 78 E7 41 59N 77 19W
Elko, Canada 72 D5 49 20N 115 10W
Elko, U.S.A. 82 F6 40 50N 115 46W
Elkton, U.S.A. 78 C1 43 49N 83 11W
Ell, L., Australia 61 E4 29 13S 127 46 E
Ellef Ringnes I., Canada 4 B2 78 30N 102 2W
Ellen, Mt., U.S.A. 79 B12 44 9N 72 56W
Ellenburg, U.S.A. 79 B11 44 54N 73 48W
Ellendale, U.S.A. 80 B5 46 0N 98 32W
Ellensburg, U.S.A. 82 C3 46 59N 120 34W
Ellenville, U.S.A. 79 E10 41 43N 74 24W
Ellery, Mt., Australia 63 F4 37 28S 148 47 E
Ellesmere, L., N.Z. 59 M4 47 47S 172 28 E
Ellesmere I., Canada 4 B4 79 30N 80 0W
Ellesmere Port, U.K. 10 D5 53 17N 2 54W
Ellice Is. = Tuvalu ■, Pac. Oc. 64 H9 8 0S 178 0 E
Ellicottville, U.S.A. 78 D6 42 17N 78 40W
Elliot, Australia 62 B1 17 33S 133 32 E
Elliot, S. Africa 57 E4 31 22S 27 48 E
Elliot Lake, Canada 70 C3 46 25N 82 35W
Elliotdale = Xhora, S. Africa 57 E4 31 55S 28 38 E
Ellis, U.S.A. 80 F5 38 56N 99 34W
Elliston, Australia 63 E1 33 39S 134 53 E
Ellisville, U.S.A. 81 K10 31 36N 89 12W
Ellon, U.K. 12 D6 57 22N 2 4W
Ellore = Eluru, India 41 L12 16 48N 81 8 E
Ellsworth, Kans., U.S.A. 80 F5 38 44N 98 14W
Ellsworth, Maine, U.S.A. 77 C11 44 33N 68 25W
Ellsworth Land, Antarctica 5 D16 76 0S 89 0W
Ellsworth Mts., Antarctica 5 D16 78 30S 85 0W
Ellwood City, U.S.A. 78 F4 40 52N 80 17W
Elma, Canada 73 D9 49 52N 95 55W
Elma, U.S.A. 84 D3 47 0N 123 25W
Elmalı, Turkey 25 G4 36 44N 29 56 E
Elmhurst, U.S.A. 76 E2 41 53N 87 56W
Elmira, Canada 78 C4 43 36N 80 33W
Elmira, U.S.A. 78 D8 42 6N 76 48W
Elmira Heights, U.S.A. 78 D8 42 8N 76 50W
Elmore, Australia 63 F3 36 30S 144 37 E
Elmore, U.S.A. 85 M11 33 7N 115 49W
Elmshorn, Germany 16 B5 53 43N 9 40 E
Elmvale, Canada 78 B5 44 35N 79 52W
Elora, Canada 78 C4 43 41N 80 26W
Eloúnda, Greece 23 D7 35 16N 25 42 E
Eloy, U.S.A. 83 K8 32 45N 111 33W
Elrose, Canada 73 C7 51 12N 108 0W
Elsie, U.S.A. 84 E3 45 52N 123 36W
Elsinore = Helsingør, Denmark 9 H15 56 2N 12 35 E
Eltham, N.Z. 59 H5 39 26S 174 19 E
Eluru, India 41 L12 16 48N 81 8 E
Elvas, Portugal 19 C2 38 50N 7 10W
Elverum, Norway 9 F14 60 53N 11 34 E
Elvire →, Australia 60 C4 17 51S 128 11 E
Elvire, Mt., Australia 61 E2 29 22S 119 36 E
Elwell, L., U.S.A. 82 B8 48 22N 111 17W
Elwood, Ind., U.S.A. 76 E3 40 17N 85 50W
Elwood, Nebr., U.S.A. 80 E5 40 36N 99 52W
Elx = Elche, Spain 19 C5 38 15N 0 42W
Ely, U.K. 11 E8 52 24N 0 16 E
Ely, Minn., U.S.A. 80 B9 47 55N 91 51W
Ely, Nev., U.S.A. 82 G6 39 15N 114 54W
Elyria, U.S.A. 78 E2 41 22N 82 7W
Emāmrūd, Iran 45 B7 36 30N 55 0 E
Emba, Kazakstan 26 E6 48 50N 58 8 E
Emba →, Kazakstan 25 E9 46 55N 53 28 E
Embarcación, Argentina 94 A3 23 10S 64 0W
Embarras Portage, Canada 73 B6 58 27N 111 28W
Embetsu, Japan 30 B10 44 44N 141 47 E
Embi = Emba, Kazakstan 26 E6 48 50N 58 8 E
Embi = Emba →, Kazakstan 25 E9 46 55N 53 28 E
Embóna, Greece 23 C9 36 13N 27 51 E
Embrun, France 18 D7 44 34N 6 30 E
Embu, Kenya 54 C4 0 32S 37 38 E
Emden, Germany 16 B4 53 21N 7 12 E
Emerald, Australia 62 C4 23 32S 148 10 E
Emerson, Canada 73 D9 49 0N 97 10W
Emet, Turkey 21 E13 39 20N 29 15 E
Emi Koussi, Chad 51 E9 19 45N 18 55 E
Eminabad, Pakistan 42 C6 32 2N 74 8 E
Emine, Nos, Bulgaria 21 C12 42 40N 27 56 E
Emlenton, U.S.A. 78 E5 41 11N 79 43W
Emmaus, U.S.A. 79 F9 40 32N 75 30W
Emmeloord, Neths. 15 B5 52 44N 5 46 E
Emmen, Neths. 15 B6 52 48N 6 57 E
Emmet, Australia 62 C3 24 45S 144 30 E
Emmetsburg, U.S.A. 80 D7 43 7N 94 41W
Emmett, Idaho, U.S.A. 82 E5 43 52N 116 30W
Emmett, Mich., U.S.A. 78 D2 42 59N 82 46W
Emmonak, U.S.A. 68 B3 62 46N 164 30W
Emo, Canada 73 D10 48 38N 93 50W
Empalme, Mexico 86 B2 28 1N 110 49W
Empangeni, S. Africa 57 D5 28 50S 31 52 E
Empedrado, Argentina 94 B4 28 0S 58 46W
Emperor Seamount Chain, Pac. Oc. 64 D9 40 0N 170 0 E
Emporia, Kans., U.S.A. 80 F6 38 25N 96 11W
Emporia, Va., U.S.A. 77 G7 36 42N 77 32W
Emporium, U.S.A. 78 E6 41 31N 78 14W
Empress, Canada 73 C7 50 57N 110 0W
Empty Quarter = Rub' al Khālī, Si. Arabia 46 D4 18 0N 48 0 E
Ems →, Germany 16 B4 53 20N 7 12 E
Emsdale, Canada 78 A5 45 32N 79 19W
Emu, China 35 C15 43 40N 128 6 E
Emu Park, Australia 62 C5 23 13S 150 50 E
'En 'Avrona, Israel 47 F4 29 43N 35 0 E
En Nahud, Sudan 51 F11 12 45N 28 25 E
Ena, Japan 31 G8 35 25N 137 25 E
Enana, Namibia 56 B2 17 30S 16 23 E
Enaratoli, Indonesia 37 E9 3 55S 136 21 E
Enard B., U.K. 12 C3 58 5N 5 20W
Enare = Inarijärvi, Finland 8 B22 69 0N 28 0 E
Encampment, U.S.A. 82 F10 41 12N 106 47W
Encantadas, Serra, Brazil 95 C5 30 40S 53 0W
Encarnación, Paraguay 95 B4 27 15S 55 50W
Encarnación de Diaz, Mexico 86 C4 21 30N 102 13W
Encinitas, U.S.A. 85 M9 33 3N 117 17W
Encino, U.S.A. 83 J11 34 39N 105 28W
Encounter B., Australia 63 F2 35 45S 138 45 E
Endako, Canada 72 C3 54 6N 125 2W
Ende, Indonesia 37 F6 8 45S 121 40 E
Endeavour Str., Australia 62 A3 10 45S 142 0 E
Enderbury I., Kiribati 64 H10 3 8S 171 5W
Enderby, Canada 72 C5 50 35N 119 10W
Enderby I., Australia 60 D2 20 35S 116 30 E
Enderby Land, Antarctica 5 C5 66 0S 53 0 E
Enderlin, U.S.A. 80 B6 46 38N 97 36W
Endicott, U.S.A. 79 D8 42 6N 76 4W
Endwell, U.S.A. 79 D8 42 6N 76 2W
Endyalgout I., Australia 60 B5 11 40S 132 35 E
Eneabba, Australia 61 E2 29 49S 115 16 E
Enewetak Atoll, Marshall Is. 64 F8 11 30N 162 15 E
Enez, Turkey 21 D12 40 45N 26 5 E
Enfield, Canada 71 D7 44 56N 63 32W
Enfield, Conn., U.S.A. 79 E12 41 58N 72 36W
Enfield, N.H., U.S.A. 79 C12 43 39N 72 9W
Engadin, Switz. 18 C9 46 45N 10 10 E
Engaño, C., Dom. Rep. 89 C6 18 30N 68 20W
Engaño, C., Phil. 37 A6 18 35N 122 23 E
Engaru, Japan 30 B11 44 3N 143 31 E
Engcobo, S. Africa 57 E4 31 37S 28 0 E
Engels, Russia 25 D8 51 28N 46 6 E
Engemann L., Canada 73 B7 58 0N 106 55W
Enggano, Indonesia 36 F2 5 20S 102 40 E
England, U.S.A. 81 H9 34 33N 91 58W
England □, U.K. 10 D7 53 0N 2 0W
Englee, Canada 71 B8 50 45N 56 5W
Englehart, Canada 70 C4 47 49N 79 52W
Englewood, U.S.A. 80 F2 39 39N 104 59W
English →, Canada 73 C10 50 35N 93 30W
English Bazar = Ingraj Bazar, India 43 G13 24 58N 88 10 E
English Channel, Europe 11 G6 50 0N 2 0W
English River, Canada 70 C1 49 14N 91 0W
Enid, U.S.A. 81 G6 36 24N 97 53W
Enkhuizen, Neths. 15 B5 52 42N 5 17 E
Enna, Italy 20 F6 37 34N 14 16 E
Ennadai, Canada 73 A8 61 8N 100 53W
Ennadai L., Canada 73 A8 61 0N 101 0W
Ennedi, Chad 51 E10 17 15N 22 0 E
Enngonia, Australia 63 D4 29 21S 145 50 E
Ennis, Ireland 13 D3 52 51N 8 59W
Ennis, Mont., U.S.A. 82 D8 45 21N 111 44W
Ennis, Tex., U.S.A. 81 J6 32 20N 96 38W
Enniscorthy, Ireland 13 D5 52 30N 6 34W
Enniskillen, U.K. 13 B4 54 21N 7 39W
Ennistimon, Ireland 13 D2 52 57N 9 17W
Enns →, Austria 16 D8 48 14N 14 32 E
Enontekiö, Finland 8 B20 68 23N 23 37 E
Enosburg Falls, U.S.A. 79 B12 44 55N 72 48W
Enriquillo, L., Dom. Rep. 89 C5 18 20N 72 5W
Enschede, Neths. 15 B6 52 13N 6 53 E
Ensenada, Argentina 94 C4 34 55S 57 55W
Ensenada, Mexico 86 A1 31 50N 116 50W
Ensenada de los Muertos, Mexico 86 C2 23 59N 109 50W
Ensiola, Pta. de n', Spain 22 B9 39 7N 2 55 E
Entebbe, Uganda 54 B3 0 4N 32 28 E
Enterprise, Canada 72 A5 60 47N 115 45W
Enterprise, Ala., U.S.A. 77 K3 31 19N 85 51W
Enterprise, Oreg., U.S.A. 82 D5 45 25N 117 17W
Entre Ríos, Bolivia 94 A3 21 30S 64 25W
Entre Ríos □, Argentina 94 C4 30 30S 58 30W
Entroncamento, Portugal 19 C1 39 28N 8 28W
Enugu, Nigeria 50 G7 6 20N 7 30 E
Enumclaw, U.S.A. 84 C5 47 12N 121 59W
Eólie, Ís., Italy 20 E6 38 30N 14 57 E
Epe, Neths. 15 B5 52 21N 5 59 E
Épernay, France 18 B5 49 3N 3 56 E
Ephesus, Turkey 21 F12 37 55N 27 22 E
Ephraim, U.S.A. 82 G8 39 22N 111 35W
Ephrata, Pa., U.S.A. 79 F8 40 11N 76 11W
Ephrata, Wash., U.S.A. 82 C4 47 19N 119 33W
Épinal, France 18 B7 48 10N 6 27 E
Episkopi, Cyprus 23 E11 34 40N 32 54 E
Episkopí, Greece 23 D6 35 20N 24 20 E
Episkopi Bay, Cyprus 23 E11 34 35N 32 50 E
Epsom, U.K. 11 F7 51 19N 0 16W
Epukiro, Namibia 56 C2 21 40S 19 9 E
Equatorial Guinea ■, Africa 52 D1 2 0N 8 0 E
Er Rahad, Sudan 51 F12 12 45N 30 32 E
Er Rif, Morocco 50 A5 35 1N 4 1W
Erāwadī Myit = Irrawaddy →, Burma 41 M19 15 50N 95 6 E
Erbil = Arbīl, Iraq 44 B5 36 15N 44 5 E
Erçek, Turkey 44 B4 38 39N 43 36 E
Erciyaş Dağı, Turkey 25 G6 38 30N 35 30 E
Érd, Hungary 17 E10 47 22N 18 56 E
Erdao Jiang →, China 35 C14 43 0N 127 0 E
Erdek, Turkey 21 D12 40 23N 27 47 E
Erdene = Ulaan-Uul, Mongolia 34 B6 44 13N 111 10 E
Erdenetsogt, Mongolia 34 C4 42 55N 106 5 E
Erebus, Mt., Antarctica 5 D11 77 35S 167 0 E
Erechim, Brazil 95 B5 27 35S 52 15W
Ereğli, Konya, Turkey 25 G5 37 31N 34 4 E
Ereğli, Zonguldak, Turkey 25 F5 41 15N 31 24 E
Erenhot, China 34 C7 43 48N 112 2 E
Eresma →, Spain 19 B3 41 26N 4 45W
Erewadi Myitwanya, Burma 41 M19 15 30N 95 0 E

Felipe Carrillo Puerto

Felipe Carrillo Puerto, Mexico 87 D7 19 38N 88 3W
Felixstowe, U.K. 11 F9 51 58N 1 23 E
Felton, U.S.A. 84 H4 37 3N 122 4W
Femer Bælt = Fehmarn Bælt, Europe 9 J14 54 35N 11 20 E
Femunden, Norway 9 E14 62 10N 11 53 E
Fen He →, China 34 G6 35 36N 110 42 E
Fenelon Falls, Canada 78 B6 44 32N 78 45W
Feng Xian, Jiangsu, China 34 G9 34 43N 116 35 E
Feng Xian, Shaanxi, China 34 H4 33 54N 106 40 E
Fengcheng, China 35 D13 40 28N 124 5 E
Fengfeng, China 34 F8 36 28N 114 8 E
Fengjie, China 33 C5 31 5N 109 36 E
Fengning, China 34 D9 41 10N 116 33 E
Fengqiu, China 34 G8 35 2N 114 25 E
Fengrun, China 35 E10 39 48N 118 8 E
Fengtai, China 34 E9 39 50N 116 18 E
Fengxiang, China 34 G4 34 29N 107 25 E
Fengyang, China 35 H9 32 51N 117 29 E
Fengzhen, China 34 D7 40 25N 113 2 E
Fenoarivo Afovoany, Madag. 57 B8 18 26S 46 34 E
Fenoarivo Atsinanana, Madag. 57 B8 17 22S 49 25 E
Fens, The, U.K. 10 E7 52 38N 0 2W
Fenton, U.S.A. 76 D4 42 48N 83 42W
Fenxi, China 34 F6 36 40N 111 31 E
Fenyang, China 34 F6 37 18N 111 48 E
Feodosiya, Ukraine 25 E6 45 2N 35 16 E
Ferdows, Iran 45 C8 33 58N 58 2 E
Ferfer, Somali Rep. 46 F4 5 4N 45 9 E
Fergana = Farghona, Uzbekistan 26 E8 40 23N 71 19 E
Fergus, Canada 78 C4 43 43N 80 24W
Fergus Falls, U.S.A. 80 B6 46 17N 96 4W
Ferkéssédougou, Ivory C. 50 G4 9 35N 5 6W
Ferland, Canada 70 B2 50 19N 88 27W
Fermanagh □, U.K. 13 B4 54 21N 7 40W
Fermo, Italy 20 C5 43 9N 13 43 E
Fermont, Canada 71 B6 52 47N 67 5W
Fermont, Qué., Canada 69 C13 50 28N 67 29W
Fermoy, Ireland 13 D3 52 9N 8 16W
Fernández, Argentina 94 B3 27 55S 63 50W
Fernandina Beach, U.S.A. 77 K5 30 40N 81 27W
Fernando de Noronha, Brazil 93 D12 4 0S 33 10W
Fernando Póo = Bioko, Eq. Guin. 52 D1 3 30N 8 40 E
Ferndale, U.S.A. 84 B4 48 51N 122 36W
Fernie, Canada 72 D5 49 30N 115 5W
Fernlees, Australia 62 C4 23 51S 148 7 E
Fernley, U.S.A. 82 G4 39 36N 119 15W
Ferozepore = Firozpur, India 42 D6 30 55N 74 40 E
Ferrara, Italy 20 B4 44 50N 11 35 E
Ferreñafe, Peru 92 E3 6 42S 79 50W
Ferrerías, Spain 22 B11 39 59N 4 1 E
Ferret, C., France 18 D3 44 38N 1 15W
Ferriday, U.S.A. 81 K9 31 38N 91 33W
Ferrol, Spain 19 A1 43 29N 8 15W
Ferron, U.S.A. 83 G8 39 5N 111 8W
Ferrutx, C., Spain 22 B10 39 47N 3 21 E
Ferryland, Canada 71 C9 47 2N 52 53W
Fertile, U.S.A. 80 B6 47 32N 96 17W
Fès, Morocco 50 B5 34 0N 5 0W
Fessenden, U.S.A. 80 B5 47 39N 99 38W
Festus, U.S.A. 80 F9 38 13N 90 24W
Feteşti, Romania 17 F14 44 22N 27 51 E
Fethiye, Turkey 25 G4 36 36N 29 6 E
Fetlar, U.K. 12 A8 60 36N 0 52W
Feuilles →, Canada 69 C12 58 47N 70 4W
Fez = Fès, Morocco 50 B5 34 0N 5 0W
Fezzan, Libya 51 C8 27 0N 13 0 E
Fiambalá, Argentina 94 B2 27 45S 67 37W
Fianarantsoa, Madag. 57 C8 21 26S 47 5 E
Fianarantsoa □, Madag. 57 B8 19 30S 47 0 E
Ficksburg, S. Africa 57 D4 28 51S 27 53 E
Field →, Australia 62 C2 23 48S 138 0 E
Field I., Australia 60 B5 12 5S 132 23 E
Fieri, Albania 21 D8 40 43N 19 33 E
Fife □, U.K. 12 E5 56 16N 3 1W
Fife Ness, U.K. 12 E6 56 17N 2 35W
Fifth Cataract, Sudan 51 E12 18 23N 33 47 E
Figeac, France 18 D5 44 37N 2 2 E
Figtree, Zimbabwe 55 G2 20 22S 28 20 E
Figueira da Foz, Portugal 19 B1 40 7N 8 54W
Figueres, Spain 19 A7 42 18N 2 58 E
Figuig, Morocco 50 B5 32 5N 1 11W
Fihaonana, Madag. 57 B8 18 36S 47 12 E
Fiherenana, Madag. 57 B8 18 29S 48 24 E
Fiherenana →, Madag. 57 C7 23 19S 43 37 E
Fiji ■, Pac. Oc. 59 C8 17 20S 179 0 E
Filey, U.K. 10 C7 54 12N 0 18W
Filey B., U.K. 10 C7 54 12N 0 15W
Filfla, Malta 23 D1 35 47N 14 24 E
Filiatrá, Greece 21 F9 37 9N 21 35 E
Filingué, Niger 50 F6 14 21N 3 22 E
Filipstad, Sweden 9 G16 59 43N 14 9 E
Fillmore, Calif., U.S.A. 85 L8 34 24N 118 55W
Fillmore, Utah, U.S.A. 83 G7 38 58N 112 20W
Finch, Canada 79 A9 45 11N 75 7W
Findhorn →, U.K. 12 D5 57 38N 3 38W
Findlay, U.S.A. 76 E4 41 2N 83 39W
Finger L., Canada 70 B1 53 33N 93 30W
Finger Lakes, U.S.A. 79 D8 42 40N 76 30W
Fingoè, Mozam. 55 E3 14 55S 31 50 E
Finisterre, C. = Fisterra, C., Spain 19 A1 42 50N 9 19W
Finke, Australia 62 D1 25 34S 134 35 E
Finland ■, Europe 8 E22 63 0N 27 0 E
Finland, G. of, Europe 9 G21 60 0N 26 0 E
Finlay →, Canada 72 B3 57 0N 125 10W
Finley, Australia 63 F4 35 38S 145 35 E
Finley, U.S.A. 80 B6 47 31N 97 50W
Finn →, Ireland 13 B4 54 51N 7 28W
Finnigan, Mt., Australia 62 B4 15 49S 145 17 E
Finniss, C., Australia 63 E1 33 8S 134 51 E
Finnmark, Norway 8 B20 69 37N 23 57 E
Finnsnes, Norway 8 B18 69 14N 18 0 E
Finspång, Sweden 9 G16 58 43N 15 47 E
Fiora →, Italy 20 C4 42 20N 11 34 E
Fiq, Syria 47 C4 32 46N 35 41 E
Firat = Furāt, Nahr al →, Asia 44 D5 31 0N 47 25 E
Firebag →, Canada 73 B6 57 45N 111 21W
Firebaugh, U.S.A. 84 J6 36 52N 120 27W
Firedrake L., Canada 73 A8 61 25N 104 30W
Firenze, Italy 20 C4 43 46N 11 15 E
Firk →, Iraq 44 D5 30 59N 44 34 E
Firozabad, India 43 F8 27 10N 78 25 E
Firozpur, India 42 D6 30 55N 74 40 E
Firozpur-Jhirka, India 42 F7 27 48N 76 57 E
Fīrūzābād, Iran 45 D7 28 52N 52 35 E
Fīrūzkūh, Iran 45 C7 35 50N 52 50 E
Firvale, Canada 72 C3 52 27N 126 13W
Fish →, Namibia 56 D2 28 7S 17 10 E
Fish →, S. Africa 56 E3 31 30S 20 16 E
Fisher, Australia 61 F5 30 30S 131 0 E
Fisher B., Canada 73 C9 51 35N 97 13W
Fishers I., U.S.A. 79 E13 41 15N 72 0W
Fishguard, U.K. 11 E3 52 0N 4 58W
Fishing L., Canada 73 C9 52 10N 95 24W
Fishkill, U.S.A. 79 E11 41 32N 73 53W
Fisterra, C., Spain 19 A1 42 50N 9 19W
Fitchburg, U.S.A. 79 D13 42 35N 71 48W
Fitz Roy, Argentina 96 F3 47 0S 67 0W
Fitzgerald, Canada 72 B6 59 51N 111 36W
Fitzgerald, U.S.A. 77 K4 31 43N 83 15W
Fitzmaurice →, Australia 60 B5 14 45S 130 5 E
Fitzroy →, Queens., Australia 62 C5 23 32S 150 52 E
Fitzroy →, W. Austral., Australia 60 C3 17 31S 123 35 E
Fitzroy, Mte., Argentina 96 F2 49 17S 73 5W
Fitzroy Crossing, Australia 60 C4 18 9S 125 38 E
Fitzwilliam I., Canada 78 A3 45 30N 81 45W
Fiume = Rijeka, Croatia 16 F8 45 20N 14 21 E
Five Points, U.S.A. 84 J6 36 26N 120 6W
Fizi, Dem. Rep. of the Congo 54 C2 4 17S 28 55 E
Flagstaff, U.S.A. 83 J8 35 12N 111 39W
Flagstaff L., Maine, U.S.A. 77 C10 45 12N 70 19W
Flagstaff L., Maine, U.S.A. 79 A14 45 12N 70 18W
Flaherty I., Canada 70 A4 56 15N 79 15W
Flåm, Norway 9 F12 60 50N 7 7 E
Flambeau →, U.S.A. 80 C9 45 18N 91 14W
Flamborough Hd., U.K. 10 C7 54 7N 0 5W
Flaming Gorge Reservoir, U.S.A. 82 F9 41 10N 109 25W
Flamingo, Teluk, Indonesia 37 F9 5 30S 138 0 E
Flanders = Flandre, Europe 18 A5 50 50N 2 30 E
Flandre, Europe 18 A5 50 50N 2 30 E
Flandre Occidentale = West-Vlaanderen □, Belgium 15 D2 51 0N 3 0 E
Flandre Orientale = Oost-Vlaanderen □, Belgium 15 C3 51 5N 3 50 E
Flandreau, U.S.A. 80 C6 44 3N 96 36W
Flanigan, U.S.A. 84 E7 40 10N 119 53W
Flannan Is., U.K. 12 C1 58 9N 7 52W
Flåsjön, Sweden 8 D16 64 5N 15 40 E
Flat →, Canada 72 A3 61 33N 125 18W
Flathead L., U.S.A. 82 C7 47 51N 114 8W
Flattery, C., Australia 62 A4 14 58S 145 21 E
Flattery, C., U.S.A. 84 B2 48 23N 124 29W
Flatwoods, U.S.A. 76 F4 38 31N 82 43W
Fleetwood, U.K. 10 D4 53 55N 3 1W
Fleetwood, U.S.A. 79 F9 40 27N 75 49W
Flekkefjord, Norway 9 G12 58 18N 6 39 E
Flemington, U.S.A. 78 E7 41 7N 77 28W
Flensburg, Germany 16 A5 54 47N 9 27 E
Flers, France 18 B3 48 47N 0 33W
Flesherton, Canada 78 B4 44 16N 80 33W
Flesko, Tanjung, Indonesia 37 D6 0 29N 124 30 E
Fleurieu Pen., Australia 63 F2 35 40S 138 5 E
Flevoland □, Neths. 15 B5 52 30N 5 30 E
Flin Flon, Canada 73 C8 54 46N 101 53W
Flinders →, Australia 62 B3 17 36S 140 36 E
Flinders B., Australia 61 F2 34 19S 115 19 E
Flinders Group, Australia 62 A3 14 11S 144 15 E
Flinders I., S. Austral., Australia 63 E1 33 44S 134 41 E
Flinders I., Tas., Australia 62 G4 40 0S 148 0 E
Flinders Ranges, Australia 63 E2 31 30S 138 30 E
Flinders Reefs, Australia 62 B4 17 37S 148 31 E
Flint, U.K. 10 D4 53 15N 3 8W
Flint, U.S.A. 76 D4 43 1N 83 41W
Flint →, U.S.A. 77 K3 30 57N 84 34W
Flint I., Kiribati 65 J12 11 26S 151 48W
Flintshire □, U.K. 10 D4 53 17N 3 17W
Flodden, U.K. 10 B5 55 37N 2 8W
Floodwood, U.S.A. 80 B8 46 55N 92 55W
Flora, U.S.A. 76 F1 38 40N 88 29W
Florala, U.S.A. 77 K2 31 0N 86 20W
Florence = Firenze, Italy 20 C4 43 46N 11 15 E
Florence, Ala., U.S.A. 77 H2 34 48N 87 41W
Florence, Ariz., U.S.A. 83 K8 33 2N 111 23W
Florence, Colo., U.S.A. 80 F2 38 23N 105 8W
Florence, Oreg., U.S.A. 82 E1 43 58N 124 7W
Florence, S.C., U.S.A. 77 H6 34 12N 79 46W
Florence, L., Australia 63 D2 28 53S 138 9 E
Florencia, Colombia 92 1 36N 75 36W
Florennes, Belgium 15 D4 50 15N 4 35 E
Florenville, Belgium 15 E5 49 40N 5 19 E
Flores, Guatemala 88 C2 16 59N 89 50W
Flores, Indonesia 37 F6 8 35S 121 0 E
Flores I., Canada 72 D3 49 20N 126 10W
Flores Sea, Indonesia 37 F6 6 30S 120 0 E
Floreşti, Moldova 17 E15 47 53N 28 17 E
Floresville, U.S.A. 81 L5 29 8N 98 10W
Floriano, Brazil 93 E10 6 50S 43 0W
Florianópolis, Brazil 95 B6 27 30S 48 30W
Florida, Cuba 88 B4 21 32N 78 14W
Florida, Uruguay 95 C4 34 7S 56 10W
Florida □, U.S.A. 77 L5 28 0N 82 0W
Florida, Straits of, U.S.A. 88 B4 25 0N 80 0W
Florida B., U.S.A. 88 B3 25 0N 80 45W
Florida Keys, U.S.A. 77 N5 24 40N 81 0W
Flórina, Greece 21 D9 40 48N 21 26 E
Florø, Norway 9 F11 61 35N 5 1 E
Flower Station, Canada 79 A8 45 10N 76 41W
Flowerpot I., Canada 78 A3 45 18N 81 38W
Floydada, U.S.A. 81 J4 33 59N 101 20W
Fluk, Indonesia 37 E7 1 42S 127 44 E
Flushing = Vlissingen, Neths. 15 C3 51 26N 3 34 E
Flying Fish, C., Antarctica 5 D15 72 6S 102 29W
Foam Lake, Canada 73 C8 51 40N 103 32W
Foça, Turkey 21 E12 38 39N 26 46 E
Focşani, Romania 17 F14 45 41N 27 15 E
Fóggia, Italy 20 D6 41 27N 15 34 E
Fogo, Canada 71 C9 49 43N 54 17W
Fogo I., Canada 71 C9 49 40N 54 5W
Föhr, Germany 16 A5 54 43N 8 30 E
Foix, France 18 E4 42 58N 1 38 E
Folda, Nord-Trøndelag, Norway 8 D14 64 32N 10 30 E
Folda, Nordland, Norway 8 C16 67 38N 14 50 E
Foley, U.S.A. 77 K2 30 24N 87 41W
Foleyet, Canada 70 C3 48 15N 82 25W
Folgefonni, Norway 9 F12 60 3N 6 23 E
Foligno, Italy 20 C5 42 57N 12 42 E
Folkestone, U.K. 11 F9 51 5N 1 12 E
Folkston, U.S.A. 77 K5 30 50N 82 0W
Follansbee, U.S.A. 78 F4 40 19N 80 35W
Folsom L., U.S.A. 84 G5 38 42N 121 9W
Fond-du-Lac, Canada 73 B7 59 19N 107 12W
Fond du Lac, U.S.A. 80 D10 43 47N 88 27W
Fond-du-Lac →, Canada 73 B7 59 17N 106 0W
Fonda, U.S.A. 79 D10 42 57N 74 22W
Fondi, Italy 20 D5 41 21N 13 25 E
Fongafale, Tuvalu 64 H9 8 31S 179 13 E
Fonsagrada = A Fonsagrada, Spain 19 A2 43 8N 7 4W
Fonseca, G. de, Cent. Amer. 88 D2 13 10N 87 40W
Fontainebleau, France 18 B5 48 24N 2 40 E
Fontana, U.S.A. 85 L9 34 6N 117 26W
Fontas →, Canada 72 B4 58 14N 121 48W
Fonte Boa, Brazil 92 D5 2 33S 66 0W
Fontenay-le-Comte, France 18 C3 46 28N 0 48W
Fontenelle Reservoir, U.S.A. 82 E8 42 1N 110 3W
Fontur, Iceland 8 C6 66 23N 14 32W
Foochow = Fuzhou, China 33 D6 26 5N 119 16 E
Foping, China 34 H5 33 41N 108 0 E
Forbes, Australia 63 E4 33 22S 148 0 E
Forbesganj, India 43 F12 26 17N 87 18 E
Ford City, Calif., U.S.A. 85 K7 35 9N 119 27W
Ford City, Pa., U.S.A. 78 F5 40 46N 79 32W
Førde, Norway 9 F11 61 27N 5 53 E
Ford's Bridge, Australia 63 D4 29 41S 145 29 E
Fordyce, U.S.A. 81 J8 33 49N 92 25W
Forel, Mt., Greenland 4 C6 66 52N 36 55W
Foremost, Canada 72 D6 49 26N 111 34W
Forest, Canada 78 C3 43 6N 82 0W
Forest, U.S.A. 81 J10 32 22N 89 29W
Forest City, Iowa, U.S.A. 80 D8 43 16N 93 39W
Forest City, N.C., U.S.A. 77 H5 35 20N 81 52W
Forest City, Pa., U.S.A. 79 E9 41 39N 75 28W
Forest Grove, U.S.A. 84 E3 45 31N 123 7W
Forestburg, Canada 72 C6 52 35N 112 1W
Foresthill, U.S.A. 84 F6 39 1N 120 49W
Forestier Pen., Australia 62 G4 43 0S 148 0 E
Forestville, Canada 71 C6 48 48N 69 2W
Forestville, Calif., U.S.A. 84 G4 38 28N 122 54W
Forestville, N.Y., U.S.A. 78 D5 42 28N 79 10W
Forfar, U.K. 12 E6 56 39N 2 53W
Forks, U.S.A. 84 C2 47 57N 124 23W
Forksville, U.S.A. 79 E8 41 29N 76 35W
Forlì, Italy 20 B5 44 13N 12 3 E
Forman, U.S.A. 80 B6 46 7N 97 38W
Formby Pt., U.K. 10 D4 53 33N 3 6W
Formentera, Spain 22 C7 38 43N 1 27 E
Formentor, C. de, Spain 22 B10 39 58N 3 13 E
Former Yugoslav Republic of Macedonia = Macedonia ■, Europe 21 D9 41 53N 21 40 E
Fórmia, Italy 20 D5 41 15N 13 37 E
Formosa = Taiwan ■, Asia 33 D7 23 30N 121 0 E
Formosa, Argentina 94 B4 26 15S 58 10W
Formosa, Brazil 93 G9 15 32S 47 20W
Formosa □, Argentina 94 B4 25 0S 60 0W
Formosa, Serra, Brazil 93 F8 12 0S 55 0W
Formosa Bay, Kenya 54 C5 2 40S 40 20 E
Fornells, Spain 22 A11 40 3N 4 7 E
Føroyar, Atl. Oc. 8 F9 62 0N 7 0W
Forres, U.K. 12 D5 57 37N 3 37W
Forrest, Australia 61 F4 30 51S 128 6 E
Forrest, Mt., Australia 61 D4 24 48S 127 45 E
Forrest City, U.S.A. 81 H9 35 1N 90 47W
Forsayth, Australia 62 B3 18 33S 143 34 E
Forssa, Finland 9 F20 60 49N 23 38 E
Forst, Germany 16 C8 51 45N 14 37 E
Forsyth, U.S.A. 82 C10 46 16N 106 41W
Fort Abbas, Pakistan 42 E5 29 12N 72 52 E
Fort Albany, Canada 70 B3 52 15N 81 35W
Fort Ann, U.S.A. 79 C11 43 25N 73 30W
Fort Assiniboine, Canada 72 C6 54 20N 114 45W
Fort Augustus, U.K. 12 D4 57 9N 4 42W
Fort Beaufort, S. Africa 56 E4 32 46S 26 40 E
Fort Benton, U.S.A. 82 C8 47 49N 110 40W
Fort Bragg, U.S.A. 82 G2 39 26N 123 48W
Fort Bridger, U.S.A. 82 F8 41 19N 110 23W
Fort Chipewyan, Canada 73 B6 58 42N 111 8W
Fort Collins, U.S.A. 80 E2 40 35N 105 5W
Fort-Coulonge, Canada 70 C4 45 50N 76 45W
Fort Covington, U.S.A. 79 B10 44 59N 74 29W
Fort Davis, U.S.A. 81 K3 30 35N 103 54W
Fort-de-France, Martinique 89 D7 14 36N 61 2W
Fort Defiance, U.S.A. 83 J9 35 45N 109 5W
Fort Dodge, U.S.A. 80 D7 42 30N 94 11W
Fort Edward, U.S.A. 79 C11 43 16N 73 35W
Fort Erie, Canada 78 D6 42 54N 78 56W
Fort Fairfield, U.S.A. 77 B12 46 46N 67 50W
Fort Frances, Canada 73 D10 48 36N 93 24W
Fort Garland, U.S.A. 83 H11 37 26N 105 26W
Fort George = Chisasibi, Canada 70 B4 53 50N 79 0W
Fort Good-Hope, Canada 68 B7 66 14N 128 40W
Fort Hancock, U.S.A. 83 L11 31 18N 105 51W
Fort Hertz = Putao, Burma 41 F20 27 28N 97 30 E
Fort Hope, Canada 70 B2 51 30N 88 0W
Fort Irwin, U.S.A. 85 K10 35 16N 116 34W
Fort Jameson = Chipata, Zambia 55 E3 13 38S 32 28 E
Fort Kent, U.S.A. 77 B11 47 15N 68 36W
Fort Klamath, U.S.A. 82 E3 42 42N 122 0W
Fort-Lamy = Ndjamena, Chad 51 F8 12 10N 14 59 E
Fort Laramie, U.S.A. 80 D2 42 13N 104 31W
Fort Lauderdale, U.S.A. 77 M5 26 7N 80 8W
Fort Liard, Canada 72 A4 60 14N 123 30W
Fort Liberté, Haiti 89 C5 19 42N 71 51W
Fort Lupton, U.S.A. 80 E2 40 5N 104 49W
Fort Mackay, Canada 72 B6 57 12N 111 41W
Fort Macleod, Canada 72 D6 49 45N 113 30W
Fort McMurray, Canada 72 B6 56 44N 111 7W
Fort McPherson, Canada 68 B6 67 30N 134 55W
Fort Madison, U.S.A. 80 E9 40 38N 91 27W
Fort Meade, U.S.A. 77 M5 27 45N 81 48W
Fort Morgan, U.S.A. 80 E3 40 15N 103 48W
Fort Munro, Pakistan 42 E3 29 54N 69 58 E
Fort Myers, U.S.A. 77 M5 26 39N 81 52W
Fort Nelson, Canada 72 B4 58 50N 122 44W
Fort Nelson →, Canada 72 B4 59 32N 124 0W
Fort Norman = Tulita, Canada 68 B7 64 57N 125 30W
Fort Payne, U.S.A. 77 H3 34 26N 85 43W
Fort Peck, U.S.A. 82 B10 48 1N 106 27W
Fort Peck Dam, U.S.A. 82 C10 48 0N 106 26W
Fort Peck L., U.S.A. 82 C10 48 0N 106 26W
Fort Pierce, U.S.A. 77 M5 27 27N 80 20W
Fort Pierre, U.S.A. 80 C4 44 21N 100 22W
Fort Plain, U.S.A. 79 D10 42 56N 74 37W
Fort Portal, Uganda 54 B3 0 40N 30 20 E
Fort Providence, Canada 72 A5 61 3N 117 40W
Fort Qu'Appelle, Canada 73 C8 50 45N 103 50W
Fort Resolution, Canada 72 A6 61 10N 113 40W
Fort Rixon, Zimbabwe 55 G2 20 2S 29 17 E
Fort Rosebery = Mansa, Zambia 55 E2 11 13S 28 55 E
Fort Ross, U.S.A. 84 G3 38 32N 123 13W
Fort Rousset = Owando, Congo 52 E3 0 29S 15 55 E
Fort Rupert = Waskaganish, Canada 70 B4 51 30N 78 40W
Fort St. James, Canada 72 C4 54 30N 124 10W
Fort St. John, Canada 72 B4 56 15N 120 50W
Fort Sandeman = Zhob, Pakistan 42 D3 31 20N 69 31 E
Fort Saskatchewan, Canada 72 C6 53 40N 113 15W
Fort Scott, U.S.A. 81 G7 37 50N 94 42W
Fort Severn, Canada 70 A2 56 0N 87 40W
Fort Shevchenko, Kazakstan 25 F9 44 35N 50 23 E
Fort Simpson, Canada 72 A4 61 45N 121 15W
Fort Smith, Canada 72 B6 60 0N 111 51W
Fort Smith, U.S.A. 81 H7 35 23N 94 25W
Fort Stockton, U.S.A. 81 K3 30 53N 102 53W
Fort Sumner, U.S.A. 81 H2 34 28N 104 15W
Fort Thompson, U.S.A. 80 C5 44 3N 99 26W
Fort Trinquet = Bir Mogreïn, Mauritania 50 C3 25 10N 11 25W
Fort Valley, U.S.A. 77 J4 32 33N 83 53W
Fort Vermilion, Canada 72 B5 58 24N 116 0W
Fort Walton Beach, U.S.A. 77 K2 30 25N 86 36W
Fort Wayne, U.S.A. 76 E3 41 4N 85 9W
Fort William, U.K. 12 E3 56 49N 5 7W
Fort Worth, U.S.A. 81 J6 32 45N 97 18W
Fort Yates, U.S.A. 80 B4 46 5N 100 38W
Fort Yukon, U.S.A. 68 B5 66 34N 145 16W
Fortaleza, Brazil 93 D11 3 45S 38 35W
Forteau, Canada 71 B8 51 28N 56 58W
Fortescue →, Australia 60 D2 21 0S 116 4 E
Forth →, U.K. 12 E5 56 9N 3 50W
Forth, Firth of, U.K. 12 E6 56 5N 2 55W
Fortrose, U.K. 12 D4 57 35N 4 9W
Fortuna, Calif., U.S.A. 82 F1 40 36N 124 9W
Fortuna, N. Dak., U.S.A. 80 A3 48 55N 103 47W
Fortune, Canada 71 C8 47 4N 55 50W
Fortune B., Canada 71 C8 47 30N 55 22W
Forūr, Iran 45 E7 26 17N 54 32 E
Foshan, China 33 D6 23 4N 113 5 E
Fosna, Norway 8 E14 63 50N 10 20 E
Fosnavåg, Norway 9 E11 62 22N 5 38 E
Fossano, Italy 18 D7 44 33N 7 43 E
Fossil, U.S.A. 82 D3 45 0N 120 9W
Foster, Australia 63 F4 38 40S 146 15 E
Foster, Canada 79 A12 45 17N 72 30W
Foster →, Canada 73 B7 55 47N 105 49W
Fosters Ra., Australia 62 C1 21 35S 133 48 E
Fostoria, U.S.A. 76 E4 41 10N 83 25W
Fougères, France 18 B3 48 21N 1 14W
Foul Pt., Sri Lanka 40 Q12 8 35N 81 18 E
Foula, U.K. 12 A6 60 10N 2 5W
Foulness I., U.K. 11 F8 51 36N 0 55 E
Foulpointe, Madag. 57 B8 17 41S 49 31 E
Foulweather, C., U.S.A. 74 B2 44 50N 124 5W
Foumban, Cameroon 52 C2 5 45N 10 50 E
Fountain, U.S.A. 80 F2 38 41N 104 42W
Fountain Springs, U.S.A. 85 K8 35 54N 118 51W
Fouriesburg, S. Africa 56 D4 28 38S 28 14 E
Foúrnoi, Greece 21 F12 37 36N 26 32 E
Fourth Cataract, Sudan 51 E12 18 47N 32 3 E
Fouta Djalon, Guinea 50 F3 11 20N 12 10W
Foux, Cap-à-, Haiti 89 C5 19 43N 73 27W
Foveaux Str., N.Z. 59 M2 46 42S 168 10 E
Fowey, U.K. 11 G3 50 20N 4 39W
Fowler, Calif., U.S.A. 84 J7 36 38N 119 41W
Fowler, Colo., U.S.A. 80 F3 38 8N 104 2W
Fowlers B., Australia 61 F5 31 59S 132 34 E
Fowman, Iran 45 B6 37 13N 49 19 E
Fox →, Canada 73 B10 56 3N 93 18W
Fox Creek, Canada 72 C5 54 24N 116 48W
Fox Lake, Canada 72 B6 58 28N 114 31W
Fox Valley, Canada 73 C7 50 30N 109 25W
Foxboro, U.S.A. 79 D13 42 4N 71 16W
Foxe Basin, Canada 69 B12 66 0N 77 0W
Foxe Chan., Canada 69 B12 65 0N 80 0W
Foxe Pen., Canada 69 B12 65 0N 76 0W
Foxton, N.Z. 59 J5 40 29S 175 18 E
Foyle, Lough, U.K. 13 A4 55 7N 7 4W
Foynes, Ireland 13 D2 52 37N 9 7W
Fóz do Cunene, Angola 56 B1 17 15S 11 48 E
Foz do Iguaçu, Brazil 95 B5 25 30S 54 30W
Frackville, U.S.A. 79 F8 40 47N 76 14W
Fraile Muerto, Uruguay 95 C5 32 31S 54 32W
Framingham, U.S.A. 79 D13 42 17N 71 25W
Franca, Brazil 93 H9 20 33S 47 30W
Francavilla Fontana, Italy 21 D7 40 32N 17 35 E
France ■, Europe 18 C5 47 0N 3 0 E
Frances, Australia 63 F3 36 41S 140 55 E
Frances →, Canada 72 A3 60 16N 129 10W
Frances L., Canada 72 A3 61 23N 129 30W
Franceville, Gabon 52 E2 1 40S 13 32 E
Franche-Comté, France 18 C6 46 50N 5 55 E
Francis Case, L., U.S.A. 80 D5 43 4N 98 34W
Francisco Beltrão, Brazil 95 B5 26 5S 53 4W
Francisco I. Madero, Coahuila, Mexico 86 B4 25 48N 103 18W
Francisco I. Madero, Durango, Mexico 86 C4 24 32N 104 22W
Francistown, Botswana 57 C4 21 7S 27 33 E
François, Canada 71 C8 47 35N 56 45W
François L., Canada 72 C3 54 0N 125 30W
Franeker, Neths. 15 A5 53 12N 5 33 E
Frankford, Canada 78 B7 44 12N 77 36W
Frankfort, S. Africa 57 D4 27 17S 28 30 E
Frankfort, Ind., U.S.A. 76 E2 40 17N 86 31W
Frankfort, Kans., U.S.A. 80 F6 39 42N 96 25W
Frankfort, Ky., U.S.A. 76 F3 38 12N 84 52W
Frankfort, N.Y., U.S.A. 79 C9 43 2N 75 4W

Grenadines

Goldsworthy, *Australia* .... **60 D2** 20 21 S 119 30 E
Goldthwaite, *U.S.A.* **81 K5** 31 27N 98 34W
Goleniów, *Poland* .... **16 B8** 53 35N 14 50 E
Golestānak, *Iran* .... **45 D7** 30 36N 54 14 E
Goleta, *U.S.A.* **85 L7** 34 27N 119 50W
Golfito, *Costa Rica* **88 E3** 8 41N 83 5W
Golfo Aranci, *Italy* .... **20 D3** 40 59N 9 38 E
Goliad, *U.S.A.* **81 L6** 28 40N 97 23W
Golpāyegān, *Iran* .... **45 C6** 33 27N 50 18 E
Golra, *Pakistan* .... **42 C5** 33 37N 72 56 E
Golspie, *U.K.* **12 D5** 57 58N 3 59W
Goma,
Dem. Rep. of the Congo . **54 C2** 1 37S 29 10 E
Gomal Pass, *Pakistan* ..... **42 D3** 31 56N 69 20 E
Gomati →, *India* .... **43 G10** 25 32N 83 11 E
Gombari,
Dem. Rep. of the Congo . **54 B2** 2 45N 29 3 E
Gombe, *Nigeria* .... **51 F8** 10 19N 11 2 E
Gombe →, *Tanzania* .... **54 C3** 4 38S 31 40 E
Gomel = Homyel, *Belarus* . **17 B16** 52 28N 31 0 E
Gomera, *Canary Is.* **22 F2** 28 7N 17 14W
Gómez Palacio, *Mexico* ... **86 B4** 25 40N 104 0W
Gomīshān, *Iran* .... **45 B7** 37 4N 54 6 E
Gomogomo, *Indonesia* .... **37 F8** 6 39S 134 43 E
Gomoh, *India* .... **41 H15** 23 52N 86 10 E
Gompa = Ganta, *Liberia* .. **50 G4** 7 15N 8 59W
Gonābād, *Iran* .... **45 C8** 34 15N 58 45 E
Gonaïves, *Haiti* **89 C5** 19 20N 72 42W
Gonâve, G. de la, *Haiti* **89 C5** 19 29N 72 42W
Gonâve, I. de la, *Haiti* **89 C5** 18 45N 73 0W
Gonbad-e Kāvūs, *Iran* ..... **45 B7** 37 20N 55 25 E
Gonda, *India* .... **43 F9** 27 9N 81 58 E
Gondal, *India* .... **42 J4** 21 58N 70 52 E
Gonder, *Ethiopia* .... **46 E2** 12 39N 37 30 E
Gondia, *India* .... **40 J12** 21 23N 80 10 E
Gondola, *Mozam.* .... **55 F3** 19 10S 33 37 E
Gönen, *Turkey* .... **21 D12** 40 6N 27 39 E
Gonghe, *China* .... **32 C5** 36 18N 100 32 E
Gongolgon, *Australia* ..... **63 E4** 30 21S 146 54 E
Gongzhuling, *China* ...... **35 C13** 43 30N 124 40 E
Gonzales, *Calif., U.S.A.* **84 J5** 36 30N 121 26W
Gonzales, *Tex., U.S.A.* **81 L6** 29 30N 97 27W
González Chaves, *Argentina* **94 D3** 38 2S 60 5W
Good Hope, C. of, *S. Africa* **56 E2** 34 24S 18 30 E
Gooderham, *Canada* **78 B6** 44 54N 78 21W
Gooding, *U.S.A.* **82 E6** 42 56N 114 43W
Goodland, *U.S.A.* **80 F4** 39 21N 101 43W
Goodlow, *Canada* **72 B4** 56 20N 120 8W
Goodooga, *Australia* ..... **63 D4** 29 3S 147 28 E
Goodsprings, *U.S.A.* **85 K11** 35 49N 115 27W
Goole, *U.K.* **10 D7** 53 42N 0 53W
Goolgowi, *Australia* ...... **63 E4** 33 58S 145 41 E
Goolwa, *Australia* .... **63 F2** 35 30S 138 47 E
Goomalling, *Australia* ..... **61 F2** 31 15S 116 49 E
Goomeri, *Australia* .... **63 D5** 26 12S 152 6 E
Goonda, *Mozam.* .... **55 F3** 19 48S 33 57 E
Goondiwindi, *Australia* .... **63 D5** 28 30S 150 21 E
Goongarrie, L., *Australia* .. **61 F3** 30 3S 121 9 E
Goonyella, *Australia* ..... **62 C4** 21 47S 147 58 E
Goose →, *Canada* **71 B7** 53 20N 60 35W
Goose Creek, *U.S.A.* **77 J5** 32 59N 80 2W
Goose L., *U.S.A.* **82 F3** 41 56N 120 26W
Gop, *India* .... **40 H6** 22 5N 69 50 E
Gopalganj, *India* .... **43 F11** 26 28N 84 30 E
Göppingen, *Germany* ..... **16 D5** 48 42N 9 39 E
Gorakhpur, *India* .... **43 F10** 26 47N 83 23 E
Goražde, *Bos.-H.* .... **21 C8** 43 38N 18 58 E
Gorda, *U.S.A.* **84 K5** 35 53N 121 26W
Gorda, Pta., *Canary Is.* **22 F2** 28 45N 18 0W
Gorda, Pta., *Nic.* **88 D3** 14 20N 83 10W
Gordan B., *Australia* ...... **60 B5** 11 35S 130 10 E
Gordon, *U.S.A.* **80 D3** 42 48N 102 12W
Gordon →, *Australia* .... **62 G4** 42 27S 145 30 E
Gordon L., *Alta., Canada* .. **73 B6** 56 30N 110 25W
Gordon L., *N.W.T., Canada* **72 A6** 63 5N 113 11W
Gordonvale, *Australia* ..... **62 B4** 17 5S 145 50 E
Gore, *Ethiopia* .... **46 F2** 8 12N 35 32 E
Gore, *N.Z.* .... **59 M2** 46 5S 168 58 E
Gore Bay, *Canada* **70 C3** 45 57N 82 28W
Gorey, *Ireland* **13 D5** 52 41N 6 18W
Gorg, *Iran* .... **45 D8** 29 29N 59 43 E
Gorgān, *Iran* .... **45 B7** 36 50N 54 29 E
Gorgona, I., *Colombia* **92 C3** 3 0N 78 10W
Gorham, *U.S.A.* **79 B13** 44 23N 71 10W
Goriganga →, *India* ..... **43 E9** 29 45N 80 23 E
Gorinchem, *Neths.* .... **15 C4** 51 50N 4 59 E
Goris, *Armenia* .... **25 G8** 39 31N 46 22 E
Gorízia, *Italy* .... **20 B5** 45 56N 13 37 E
Gorki = Nizhniy Novgorod,
Russia .... **24 C7** 56 20N 44 0 E
Gorkiy = Nizhniy Novgorod,
Russia .... **24 C7** 56 20N 44 0 E
Gorkovskoye Vdkhr., *Russia* **24 C7** 57 2N 43 4 E
Görlitz, *Germany* .... **16 C8** 51 9N 14 58 E
Gorlovka = Horlivka,
Ukraine .... **25 E6** 48 19N 38 5 E
Gorman, *U.S.A.* **85 L8** 34 47N 118 51W
Gorna Dzhumayo =
Blagoevgrad, *Bulgaria* .. **21 C10** 42 2N 23 5 E
Gorna Oryakhovitsa,
Bulgaria .... **21 C11** 43 7N 25 40 E
Gorno-Altay □, *Russia* .... **26 D9** 51 0N 86 0 E
Gorno-Altaysk, *Russia* .... **26 D9** 51 50N 86 5 E
Gornyatski, *Russia* .... **24 A11** 67 32N 64 3 E
Gornyy, *Russia* .... **30 B6** 44 57N 133 59 E
Gorodenka = Horodenka,
Ukraine .... **17 D13** 48 41N 25 29 E
Gorodok = Horodok,
Ukraine .... **17 D12** 49 46N 23 32 E
Gorokhov = Horokhiv,
Ukraine .... **17 C13** 50 30N 24 45 E
Goromonzi, *Zimbabwe* .... **55 F3** 17 52S 31 22 E
Gorong, Kepulauan,
Indonesia .... **37 E8** 3 59S 131 25 E
Gorongose →, *Mozam.* .. **57 C5** 20 30S 34 40 E
Gorongoza, *Mozam.* ...... **55 F3** 18 44S 34 2 E
Gorongoza, Sa. da, *Mozam.* **55 F3** 18 27S 34 2 E
Gorontalo, *Indonesia* ..... **37 D6** 0 35N 123 5 E
Gort, *Ireland* **13 C3** 53 3N 8 49W
Gortis, *Greece* .... **23 D6** 35 4N 24 58 E
Gorzów Wielkopolski,
Poland .... **16 B8** 52 43N 15 15 E
Gosford, *Australia* .... **63 E5** 33 23S 151 18 E
Goshen, *Calif., U.S.A.* **84 J7** 36 21N 119 25W
Goshen, *Ind., U.S.A.* **76 E3** 41 35N 85 50W
Goshen, *N.Y., U.S.A.* **79 E10** 41 24N 74 20W
Goshogawara, *Japan* ..... **30 D10** 40 48N 140 27 E
Goslar, *Germany* .... **16 C6** 51 54N 10 25 E
Gospič, *Croatia* .... **16 F8** 44 35N 15 23 E
Gosport, *U.K.* **11 G6** 50 48N 1 9W
Gosse →, *Australia* ..... **62 B1** 19 32S 134 37 E
Göta älv →, *Sweden* .... **9 H14** 57 42N 11 54 E
Göta kanal, *Sweden* ...... **9 G16** 58 30N 15 58 E
Götaland, *Sweden* .... **9 G15** 57 30N 14 30 E
Göteborg, *Sweden* .... **9 H14** 57 43N 11 59 E
Gotha, *Germany* .... **16 C6** 50 56N 10 42 E
Gothenburg = Göteborg,
Sweden .... **9 H14** 57 43N 11 59 E
Gothenburg, *U.S.A.* **80 E4** 40 56N 100 10W
Gotland, *Sweden* .... **9 H18** 57 30N 18 33 E
Gotō-Rettō, *Japan* .... **31 H4** 32 55N 129 5 E
Gotska Sandön, *Sweden* .. **9 G18** 58 24N 19 15 E
Gōtsu, *Japan* .... **31 G6** 35 0N 132 14 E
Gott Pk., *Canada* **72 C4** 50 18N 122 16W
Göttingen, *Germany* ...... **16 C5** 51 31N 9 55 E
Gottwaldov = Zlín,
Czech Rep. .... **17 D9** 49 14N 17 40 E
Goubangzi, *China* .... **35 D11** 41 20N 121 52 E
Gouda, *Neths.* .... **15 B4** 52 1N 4 42 E
Goúdhoura, Ákra, *Greece* . **23 E8** 34 59N 26 6 E
Gough I., *Atl. Oc.* **2 G9** 40 10S 9 45W
Gouin, Rés., *Canada* **70 C5** 48 35N 74 40W
Goulburn, *Australia* ...... **63 E4** 34 44S 149 44 E
Goulburn Is., *Australia* .... **62 A1** 11 40S 133 20 E
Goulimine, *Morocco* **50 C3** 28 56N 10 0W
Gourits →, *S. Africa* ..... **56 E3** 34 21S 21 52 E
Goúrnais, *Greece* .... **23 D7** 35 19N 25 16 E
Gouverneur, *U.S.A.* **79 B9** 44 20N 75 28W
Gouviá, *Greece* .... **23 A3** 39 39N 19 50 E
Governador Valadares,
Brazil **93 G10** 18 15S 41 57W
Governor's Harbour,
Bahamas **88 A4** 25 10N 76 14W
Govindgarh, *India* .... **43 G9** 24 23N 81 18 E
Gowan Ra., *Australia* ..... **62 D4** 25 0S 145 0 E
Gowanda, *U.S.A.* **78 D6** 42 28N 78 56W
Gowd-e Zirreh, *Afghan.* ... **40 E3** 29 45N 62 0 E
Gower, *U.K.* **11 F3** 51 35N 4 10W
Gowna, L., *Ireland* **13 C4** 53 51N 7 34W
Goya, *Argentina* **94 B4** 29 10S 59 10W
Goyder Lagoon, *Australia* . **63 D2** 27 3S 138 58 E
Goyllarisquisga, *Peru* **92 F3** 10 31S 76 24W
Goz Beïda, *Chad* .... **51 F10** 12 10N 21 20 E
Gozo, *Malta* .... **23 C1** 36 3N 14 13 E
Graaff-Reinet, *S. Africa* ... **56 E3** 32 13S 24 32 E
Gračac, *Croatia* .... **16 F8** 44 18N 15 57 E
Gracias a Dios, C., *Honduras* **88 D3** 15 0N 83 10W
Graciosa, I., *Canary Is.* **22 E6** 29 15N 13 32W
Grado, *Spain* **19 A2** 43 23N 6 4W
Grady, *U.S.A.* **81 H3** 34 49N 103 19W
Grafham Water, *U.K.* **11 E7** 52 19N 0 18W
Grafton, *Australia* .... **63 D5** 29 38S 152 58 E
Grafton, *N. Dak., U.S.A.* ... **80 A6** 48 25N 97 25W
Grafton, *W. Va., U.S.A.* **76 F5** 39 21N 80 2W
Graham, *Canada* **70 C1** 49 20N 90 30W
Graham, *U.S.A.* **81 J5** 33 6N 98 35W
Graham, Mt., *U.S.A.* **83 K9** 32 42N 109 52W
Graham Bell, Ostrov =
Greem-Bell, Ostrov,
Russia .... **26 A7** 81 0N 62 0 E
Graham I., *B.C., Canada* **72 C2** 53 40N 132 30W
Graham I., *N.W.T., Canada* **68 C6** 77 25N 90 30W
Graham Land, *Antarctica* .. **5 C17** 65 0S 64 0W
Grahamstown, *S. Africa* ... **56 E4** 33 19S 26 31 E
Grahamsville, *U.S.A.* **79 E10** 41 51N 74 33W
Grain Coast, *W. Afr.* **50 H3** 4 20N 10 0W
Grajaú, *Brazil* **93 E9** 5 50S 46 4W
Grajaú →, *Brazil* **93 D10** 3 41S 44 48W
Grampian, *U.S.A.* **78 F6** 40 58N 78 37W
Grampian Highlands =
Grampian Mts., *U.K.* **12 E5** 56 50N 4 0W
Grampian Mts., *U.K.* **12 E5** 56 50N 4 0W
Grampians, The, *Australia* **63 F3** 37 0S 142 20 E
Gran Canaria, *Canary Is.* .. **22 G4** 27 55N 15 35W
Gran Chaco, *S. Amer.* **94 B3** 25 0S 61 0W
Gran Paradiso, *Italy* ...... **18 D7** 45 33N 7 17 E
Gran Sasso d'Itália, *Italy* .. **20 C5** 42 27N 13 42 E
Granada, *Nic.* **88 D2** 11 58N 86 0W
Granada, *Spain* **19 D4** 37 10N 3 35W
Granada, *U.S.A.* **81 F3** 38 4N 102 19W
Granadilla de Abona,
Canary Is. **22 F3** 28 7N 16 33W
Granard, *Ireland* **13 C4** 53 47N 7 30W
Granbury, *U.S.A.* **81 J6** 32 27N 97 47W
Granby, *Canada* **79 A12** 45 25N 72 45W
Granby, *U.S.A.* **82 F11** 40 5N 105 56W
Grand →, *Canada* **78 D5** 42 51N 79 34W
Grand →, *Mo., U.S.A.* **80 F8** 39 23N 93 7W
Grand →, *S. Dak., U.S.A.* . **80 C4** 45 40N 100 45W
Grand Bahama, *Bahamas* .. **88 A4** 26 40N 78 30W
Grand Bank, *Canada* **71 C8** 47 6N 55 48W
Grand Bassam, *Ivory C.* **50 G5** 5 10N 3 49W
Grand-Bourg, *Guadeloupe* . **89 C7** 15 53N 61 19W
Grand Canal = Yun Ho →,
China .... **35 E9** 39 10N 117 10 E
Grand Canyon, *U.S.A.* **83 H7** 36 3N 112 9W
Grand Canyon National
Park, *U.S.A.* **83 H7** 36 15N 112 30W
Grand Cayman, *Cayman Is.* **88 C3** 19 20N 81 20W
Grand Centre, *Canada* **73 C6** 54 25N 110 13W
Grand Coulee, *U.S.A.* **82 C4** 47 57N 119 0W
Grand Coulee Dam, *U.S.A.* **82 C4** 47 57N 118 59W
Grand Erg du Bilma, *Niger* **51 E8** 18 30N 14 0 E
Grand Erg Occidental,
Algeria .... **50 B6** 30 20N 1 0 E
Grand Erg Oriental, *Algeria* **50 B7** 30 0N 6 30 E
Grand Falls, *Canada* **71 C6** 47 3N 67 44W
Grand Falls-Windsor,
Canada **71 C8** 48 56N 55 40W
Grand Forks, *Canada* **72 D5** 49 0N 118 30W
Grand Forks, *U.S.A.* **80 B6** 47 55N 97 3W
Grand Gorge, *U.S.A.* **79 D10** 42 21N 74 29W
Grand Haven, *U.S.A.* **76 D2** 43 4N 86 13W
Grand I., *Mich., U.S.A.* **76 B2** 46 31N 86 40W
Grand I., *N.Y., U.S.A.* **78 D6** 43 0N 78 58W
Grand Island, *U.S.A.* **80 E5** 40 55N 98 21W
Grand Isle, *La., U.S.A.* **81 L9** 29 14N 90 0W
Grand Isle, *Vt., U.S.A.* **79 B11** 44 43N 73 18W
Grand Junction, *U.S.A.* ... **83 G9** 39 4N 108 33W
Grand L., *N.B., Canada* **71 C6** 45 57N 66 7W
Grand L., *Nfld., Canada* **71 C8** 49 0N 57 30W
Grand L., *Nfld., Canada* **71 B7** 53 40N 60 30W
Grand L., *U.S.A.* **81 L8** 29 55N 92 47W
Grand Lake, *U.S.A.* **82 F11** 40 15N 105 49W
Grand Manan I., *Canada* .. **71 D6** 44 45N 66 52W
Grand Marais, *Canada* **80 B9** 47 45N 90 25W
Grand Marais, *U.S.A.* **76 B3** 46 40N 85 59W
Grand-Mère, *Canada* **70 C5** 46 36N 72 40W
Grand Prairie, *U.S.A.* **81 J6** 32 47N 97 0W
Grand Rapids, *Canada* **73 C9** 53 12N 99 19W
Grand Rapids, *Mich., U.S.A.* **76 D2** 42 58N 85 40W
Grand Rapids, *Minn., U.S.A.* **80 B8** 47 14N 93 31W
Grand St-Bernard, Col du,
Europe .... **18 D7** 45 50N 7 10 E
Grand Teton, *U.S.A.* **82 E8** 43 54N 111 50W
Grand Teton National Park,
U.S.A. **82 D8** 43 50N 110 50W
Grand Union Canal, *U.K.* .. **11 E7** 52 7N 0 53W
Grand View, *Canada* **73 C8** 51 10N 100 42W
Grande →, *Jujuy,*
Argentina **94 A2** 24 20S 65 2W
Grande →, *Mendoza,*
Argentina **94 D2** 36 52S 69 45W
Grande →, *Bolivia* **92 G6** 15 51S 64 39W
Grande →, *Bahia, Brazil* . **93 F10** 11 30S 44 30W
Grande →, *Minas Gerais,*
Brazil **93 H8** 20 6S 51 4W
Grande, B., *Argentina* **96 G3** 50 30S 68 20W
Grande, Rio →, *U.S.A.* ... **81 N6** 25 58N 97 9W
Grande Baleine, R. de
la →, *Canada* **70 A4** 55 16N 77 47W
Grande Cache, *Canada* **72 C5** 53 53N 119 8W
Grande-Entrée, *Canada* ... **71 C7** 47 30N 61 40W
Grande Prairie, *Canada* ... **72 B5** 55 10N 118 50W
Grande-Rivière, *Canada* ... **71 C7** 48 26N 64 30W
Grande-Vallée, *Canada* ... **71 C6** 49 14N 65 8W
Grandfalls, *U.S.A.* **81 K3** 31 20N 102 51W
Grandview, *U.S.A.* **82 C4** 46 15N 119 54W
Graneros, *Chile* **94 C1** 34 5S 70 45W
Grangemouth, *U.K.* **12 E5** 56 1N 3 42W
Granger, *U.S.A.* **82 F9** 41 35N 109 58W
Grangeville, *U.S.A.* **82 D5** 45 56N 116 7W
Granisle, *Canada* **72 C3** 54 53N 126 13W
Granite City, *U.S.A.* **80 F9** 38 42N 90 9W
Granite Falls, *U.S.A.* **80 C7** 44 49N 95 33W
Granite L., *Canada* **71 C8** 48 8N 57 5W
Granite Mt., *U.S.A.* **85 M10** 33 5N 116 28W
Granite Pk., *U.S.A.* **82 D9** 45 10N 109 48W
Graniteville, *U.S.A.* **79 B12** 44 8N 72 29W
Granity, *N.Z.* .... **59 J3** 41 39S 171 51 E
Granja, *Brazil* **93 D10** 3 7S 40 50W
Granollers, *Spain* .... **19 B7** 41 39N 2 18 E
Grant, *U.S.A.* **80 E4** 40 53N 101 42W
Grant, Mt., *U.S.A.* **82 G4** 38 34N 118 48W
Grant City, *U.S.A.* **80 E7** 40 29N 94 25W
Grant I., *Australia* .... **60 B5** 11 10S 132 52 E
Grant Range, *U.S.A.* **83 G6** 38 30N 115 25W
Grantham, *U.K.* **10 E7** 52 55N 0 38W
Grantown-on-Spey, *U.K.* .. **12 D5** 57 20N 3 36W
Grants, *U.S.A.* **83 J10** 35 9N 107 52W
Grants Pass, *U.S.A.* **82 E2** 42 26N 123 19W
Grantsville, *U.S.A.* **82 F7** 40 36N 112 28W
Granville, *France* **18 B3** 48 50N 1 35W
Granville, *N. Dak., U.S.A.* ... **80 A4** 48 16N 100 47W
Granville, *N.Y., U.S.A.* **79 C11** 43 24N 73 16W
Granville, *Ohio, U.S.A.* **78 F2** 40 4N 82 31W
Granville L., *Canada* **73 B8** 56 18N 100 30W
Graskop, *S. Africa* .... **57 C5** 24 56S 30 49 E
Grass →, *Canada* **73 B9** 56 3N 96 33W
Grass Range, *U.S.A.* **82 C9** 47 0N 109 0W
Grass River Prov. Park,
Canada **73 C8** 54 40N 100 50W
Grass Valley, *Calif., U.S.A.* . **84 F6** 39 13N 121 4W
Grass Valley, *Oreg., U.S.A.* **82 D3** 45 22N 120 47W
Grasse, *France* .... **18 E7** 43 38N 6 56 E
Grassflat, *U.S.A.* **78 F6** 41 0N 78 6W
Grasslands Nat. Park,
Canada **73 D7** 49 11N 107 38W
Grassy, *Australia* .... **62 G3** 40 3S 144 5 E
Graulhet, *France* .... **18 E4** 43 45N 1 59 E
Gravelbourg, *Canada* **73 D7** 49 50N 106 35W
's-Gravenhage, *Neths.* .... **15 B4** 52 7N 4 17 E
Gravenhurst, *Canada* **78 B5** 44 52N 79 20W
Gravesend, *Australia* ..... **63 D5** 29 35S 150 20 E
Gravesend, *U.K.* .... **11 F8** 51 26N 0 22 E
Gravois, Pointe-à-, *Haiti* ... **89 C5** 18 15N 73 56W
Grayling, *U.S.A.* **76 C3** 44 40N 84 43W
Grays Harbor, *U.S.A.* **82 C1** 46 59N 124 1W
Grays L., *U.S.A.* **82 E8** 43 4N 111 26W
Grays River, *U.S.A.* **84 D3** 46 21N 123 37W
Graz, *Austria* .... **16 E8** 47 4N 15 27 E
Greasy L., *Canada* **72 A4** 62 55N 122 12W
Great Abaco I., *Bahamas* .. **88 A4** 26 25N 77 10W
Great Artesian Basin,
Australia .... **62 C3** 23 0S 144 0 E
Great Australian Bight,
Australia .... **61 F5** 33 30S 130 0 E
Great Bahama Bank,
Bahamas **88 B4** 23 15N 78 0W
Great Barrier I., *N.Z.* ...... **59 G5** 36 11S 175 25 E
Great Barrier Reef, *Australia* **62 B4** 18 0S 146 50 E
Great Barrington, *U.S.A.* .. **79 D11** 42 12N 73 22W
Great Basin, *U.S.A.* **82 G5** 40 0N 117 0W
Great Basin Nat. Park,
U.S.A. **82 G6** 38 55N 114 14W
Great Bear →, *Canada* ... **68 B7** 65 0N 124 0W
Great Bear L., *Canada* **68 B8** 65 30N 120 0W
Great Belt = Store Bælt,
Denmark .... **9 J14** 55 20N 11 0 E
Great Bend, *Kans., U.S.A.* . **80 F5** 38 22N 98 46W
Great Bend, *Pa., U.S.A.* **79 E9** 41 58N 75 45W
Great Blasket I., *Ireland* ... **13 D1** 52 6N 10 32W
Great Britain, *Europe* **6 E5** 54 0N 2 15W
Great Codroy, *Canada* **71 C8** 47 51N 59 16W
Great Dividing Ra., *Australia* **62 C4** 23 0S 146 0 E
Great Driffield = Driffield,
U.K. **10 C7** 54 0N 0 26W
Great Exuma I., *Bahamas* .. **88 B4** 23 30N 75 50W
Great Falls, *U.S.A.* **82 C8** 47 30N 111 17W
Great Fish = Groot Vis →,
S. Africa .... **56 E4** 33 28S 27 5 E
Great Guana Cay, *Bahamas* **88 B4** 24 0N 76 20W
Great Inagua I., *Bahamas* .. **89 B5** 21 0N 73 20W
Great Indian Desert = Thar
Desert, *India* .... **42 F5** 28 0N 72 0 E
Great Karoo, *S. Africa* .... **56 E3** 31 55S 21 0 E
Great Lake, *Australia* ..... **62 G4** 41 50S 146 40 E
Great Lakes, *N. Amer.* **66 E11** 46 0N 84 0W
Great Malvern, *U.K.* **11 E5** 52 7N 2 18W
Great Miami →, *U.S.A.* ... **76 F3** 39 20N 84 40W
Great Ormes Head, *U.K.* ... **10 D4** 53 20N 3 52W
Great Ouse →, *U.K.* ..... **10 E8** 52 48N 0 21 E
Great Palm I., *Australia* ... **62 B4** 18 45S 146 40 E
Great Plains, *N. Amer.* **74 A6** 47 0N 105 0W
Great Ruaha →, *Tanzania* **54 D4** 7 56S 37 52 E
Great Sacandaga Res.,
U.S.A. **79 C10** 43 6N 74 16W
Great Saint Bernard Pass =
Grand St-Bernard, Col du,
Europe .... **18 D7** 45 50N 7 10 E
Great Salt L., *U.S.A.* **82 F7** 41 15N 112 40W
Great Salt Lake Desert,
U.S.A. **82 F7** 40 50N 113 30W
Great Salt Plains L., *U.S.A.* **81 G5** 36 45N 98 8W
Great Sandy Desert,
Australia .... **60 D3** 21 0S 124 0 E
Great Sangi = Sangihe,
Pulau, *Indonesia* .... **37 D7** 3 45N 125 30 E
Great Skellig, *Ireland* **13 E1** 51 47N 10 33W
Great Slave L., *Canada* **72 A5** 61 23N 115 38W
Great Smoky Mts. Nat. Park,
U.S.A. **77 H4** 35 40N 83 40W
Great Snow Mt., *Canada* .. **72 B4** 57 26N 124 0W
Great Stour = Stour →,
U.K. .... **11 F9** 51 18N 1 22 E
Great Victoria Desert,
Australia .... **61 E4** 29 30S 126 30 E
Great Wall, *China* .... **34 E5** 38 30N 109 30 E
Great Whernside, *U.K.* **10 C6** 54 10N 1 58W
Great Yarmouth, *U.K.* ..... **11 E9** 52 37N 1 44 E
Greater Antilles, *W. Indies* . **89 C5** 17 40N 74 0W
Greater London □, *U.K.* ... **11 F7** 51 31N 0 6W
Greater Manchester □, *U.K.* **10 D5** 53 30N 2 15W
Greater Sunda Is., *Indonesia* **36 F4** 7 0S 112 0 E
Greco, C., *Cyprus* .... **23 E13** 34 57N 34 5 E
Gredos, Sierra de, *Spain* .. **19 B3** 40 20N 5 0W
Greece, *U.S.A.* **78 C7** 43 13N 77 41W
Greece ■, *Europe* .... **21 E9** 40 0N 23 0 E
Greeley, *Colo., U.S.A.* **80 E2** 40 25N 104 42W
Greeley, *Nebr., U.S.A.* **80 E5** 41 33N 98 32W
Greem-Bell, Ostrov, *Russia* **26 A7** 81 0N 62 0 E
Green, *U.S.A.* **82 E2** 43 9N 123 22W
Green →, *Ky., U.S.A.* **76 G2** 37 54N 87 30W
Green →, *Utah, U.S.A.* ... **83 G9** 38 11N 109 53W
Green B., *U.S.A.* **76 C2** 45 0N 87 30W
Green Bay, *U.S.A.* **76 C2** 44 31N 88 0W
Green C., *Australia* .... **63 F5** 37 13S 150 1 E
Green Cove Springs, *U.S.A.* **77 L5** 29 59N 81 42W
Green Lake, *Canada* **73 C7** 54 17N 107 47W
Green Mts., *U.S.A.* **79 C12** 43 45N 72 45W
Green River, *Utah, U.S.A.* .. **83 G8** 38 59N 110 10W
Green River, *Wyo., U.S.A.* .. **82 F9** 41 32N 109 28W
Green Valley, *U.S.A.* **83 L8** 31 52N 110 56W
Greenbank, *U.S.A.* **84 B4** 48 6N 122 34W
Greenbush, *Mich., U.S.A.* .. **78 B1** 44 35N 83 19W
Greenbush, *Minn., U.S.A.* .. **80 A6** 48 42N 96 11W
Greencastle, *U.S.A.* **76 F2** 39 38N 86 52W
Greene, *U.S.A.* **79 D9** 42 20N 75 46W
Greenfield, *Calif., U.S.A.* ... **84 J5** 36 19N 121 15W
Greenfield, *Calif., U.S.A.* ... **85 K8** 35 15N 119 0W
Greenfield, *Ind., U.S.A.* **76 F3** 39 47N 85 46W
Greenfield, *Iowa, U.S.A.* ... **80 E7** 41 18N 94 28W
Greenfield, *Mass., U.S.A.* .. **79 D12** 42 35N 72 36W
Greenfield, *Mo., U.S.A.* **81 G8** 37 25N 93 51W
Greenfield Park, *Canada* ... **79 A11** 45 29N 73 29W
Greenland ■, *N. Amer.* **4 C5** 66 0N 45 0W
Greenland Sea, *Arctic* **4 B7** 73 0N 10 0W
Greenock, *U.K.* **12 F4** 55 57N 4 46W
Greenore, *Ireland* **13 B5** 54 2N 6 8W
Greenore Pt., *Ireland* **13 D5** 52 14N 6 19W
Greenough, *Australia* ..... **61 E1** 28 58S 114 43 E
Greenough →, *Australia* .. **61 E1** 28 51S 114 38 E
Greenough Pt., *Canada* ... **78 B3** 44 58N 81 26W
Greenport, *U.S.A.* **79 E12** 41 6N 72 22W
Greensboro, *Ga., U.S.A.* ... **77 J4** 33 35N 83 11W
Greensboro, *N.C., U.S.A.* .. **77 G6** 36 4N 79 48W
Greensboro, *Vt., U.S.A.* **79 B12** 44 36N 72 18W
Greensburg, *Ind., U.S.A.* ... **76 F3** 39 20N 85 29W
Greensburg, *Kans., U.S.A.* . **81 G5** 37 36N 99 18W
Greensburg, *Pa., U.S.A.* ... **78 F5** 40 18N 79 33W
Greenstone Pt., *U.K.* **12 D3** 57 55N 5 37W
Greenvale, *Australia* ...... **62 B4** 18 59S 145 7 E
Greenville, *Ala., U.S.A.* **77 K2** 31 50N 86 38W
Greenville, *Calif., U.S.A.* ... **84 E6** 40 8N 120 57W
Greenville, *Maine, U.S.A.* .. **77 C11** 45 28N 69 35W
Greenville, *Mich., U.S.A.* .. **76 D3** 43 11N 85 15W
Greenville, *Miss., U.S.A.* ... **81 J9** 33 24N 91 4W
Greenville, *Mo., U.S.A.* **81 G9** 37 8N 90 27W
Greenville, *N.C., U.S.A.* **77 H7** 35 37N 77 23W
Greenville, *N.H., U.S.A.* ... **79 D13** 42 46N 71 49W
Greenville, *N.Y., U.S.A.* ... **79 D10** 42 25N 74 1W
Greenville, *Ohio, U.S.A.* ... **76 E3** 40 6N 84 38W
Greenville, *Pa., U.S.A.* **78 E4** 41 24N 80 23W
Greenville, *S.C., U.S.A.* **77 H4** 34 51N 82 24W
Greenville, *Tenn., U.S.A.* ... **77 G4** 36 13N 82 51W
Greenville, *Tex., U.S.A.* **81 J6** 33 8N 96 7W
Greenwater Lake Prov. Park,
Canada **73 C8** 52 32N 103 30W
Greenwich, *U.K.* .... **11 F8** 51 29N 0 1 E
Greenwich, *Conn., U.S.A.* .. **79 E11** 41 2N 73 38W
Greenwich, *N.Y., U.S.A.* ... **79 C11** 43 5N 73 30W
Greenwich, *Ohio, U.S.A.* ... **78 E2** 41 2N 82 31W
Greenwood, *Canada* **72 D5** 49 10N 118 40W
Greenwood, *Ark., U.S.A.* ... **81 H7** 35 13N 94 16W
Greenwood, *Ind., U.S.A.* ... **76 F2** 39 37N 86 7W
Greenwood, *Miss., U.S.A.* .. **81 J9** 33 31N 90 11W
Greenwood, *S.C., U.S.A.* ... **77 H4** 34 12N 82 10W
Greenwood, Mt., *Australia* . **60 B5** 13 48S 130 4 E
Gregory, *U.S.A.* **80 D5** 43 14N 99 20W
Gregory →, *Australia* .... **62 B2** 17 53S 139 17 E
Gregory, L., *S. Austral.,*
Australia .... **63 D2** 28 55S 139 0 E
Gregory, L., *W. Austral.,*
Australia .... **61 E2** 25 38S 119 58 E
Gregory Downs, *Australia* . **62 B2** 18 35S 138 45 E
Gregory L., *Australia* ..... **60 D4** 20 0S 127 40 E
Gregory Ra., *Queens.,*
Australia .... **62 B3** 19 30S 143 40 E
Gregory Ra., *W. Austral.,*
Australia .... **60 D3** 21 20S 121 12 E
Greifswald, *Germany* ..... **16 A7** 54 5N 13 23 E
Greiz, *Germany* .... **16 C7** 50 39N 12 10 E
Gremikha, *Russia* .... **24 A6** 67 59N 39 47 E
Grenå, *Denmark* .... **9 H14** 56 25N 10 53 E
Grenada, *U.S.A.* **81 J10** 33 47N 89 49W
Grenada ■, *W. Indies* **89 D7** 12 10N 61 40W
Grenadier I., *U.S.A.* **79 B8** 44 3N 76 22W
Grenadines, *W. Indies* **89 D7** 12 40N 61 20W

H

Henryville

Hamadān □, Iran 45 C6 35 0N 49 0 E
Hamāh, Syria 44 C3 35 5N 36 40 E
Hamamatsu, Japan 31 G8 34 45N 137 45 E
Hamar, Norway 9 F14 60 48N 11 7 E
Hamâta, Gebel, Egypt 44 E2 24 17N 35 0 E
Hambantota, Sri Lanka 40 R12 6 10N 81 10 E
Hamber Prov. Park, Canada 72 C5 52 20N 118 0W
Hamburg, Germany 16 B5 53 33N 9 59 E
Hamburg, Ark., U.S.A. 81 J9 33 14N 91 48W
Hamburg, N.Y., U.S.A. 78 D6 42 43N 78 50W
Hamburg, Pa., U.S.A. 79 F9 40 33N 75 59W
Ḥamḍ, W. al →, Si. Arabia 44 E3 24 55N 36 20 E
Hamden, U.S.A. 79 E12 41 23N 72 54W
Häme, Finland 9 F20 61 38N 25 10 E
Hämeenlinna, Finland 9 F21 61 0N 24 28 E
Hamelin Pool, Australia 61 E1 26 22S 114 20 E
Hameln, Germany 16 B5 52 6N 9 21 E
Hamerkaz □, Israel 47 C3 32 15N 34 55 E
Hamersley Ra., Australia 60 D2 22 0S 117 45 E
Hamhung, N. Korea 35 E14 39 54N 127 30 E
Hami, China 32 B4 42 55N 93 25 E
Hamilton, Australia 63 F3 37 45S 142 2 E
Hamilton, Canada 78 C5 43 15N 79 50W
Hamilton, N.Z. 59 G5 37 47S 175 19 E
Hamilton, U.K. 12 F4 55 46N 4 2W
Hamilton, Ala., U.S.A. 77 H1 34 9N 87 59W
Hamilton, Mont., U.S.A. 82 C6 46 15N 114 10W
Hamilton, N.Y., U.S.A. 79 D9 42 50N 75 33W
Hamilton, Ohio, U.S.A. 76 F3 39 24N 84 34W
Hamilton, Tex., U.S.A. 81 K5 31 42N 98 7W
Hamilton →, Australia 62 C2 23 30S 139 47 E
Hamilton City, U.S.A. 84 F4 39 45N 122 1W
Hamilton Inlet, Canada 71 B8 54 0N 57 30W
Hamilton Mt., U.S.A. 79 C10 43 25N 74 22W
Hamina, Finland 9 F22 60 34N 27 12 E
Hamirpur, H.P., India 42 D7 31 41N 76 31 E
Hamirpur, Ut. P., India 43 G9 25 57N 80 9 E
Hamlet, U.S.A. 77 H6 34 53N 79 42W
Hamley Bridge, Australia 63 E2 34 17S 138 35 E
Hamlin = Hameln, Germany 16 B5 52 6N 9 21 E
Hamlin, N.Y., U.S.A. 78 C7 43 17N 77 55W
Hamlin, Tex., U.S.A. 81 J4 32 53N 100 8W
Hamm, Germany 16 C4 51 40N 7 50 E
Ḥammār, Hawr al, Iraq 44 D5 30 50N 47 10 E
Hammerfest, Norway 8 A20 70 39N 23 41 E
Hammond, Ind., U.S.A. 76 E2 41 38N 87 30W
Hammond, La., U.S.A. 81 K9 30 30N 90 28W
Hammond, N.Y., U.S.A. 79 B9 44 27N 75 42W
Hammondsport, U.S.A. 78 D7 42 25N 77 13W
Hammonton, U.S.A. 76 F8 39 39N 74 48W
Hampden, N.Z. 59 L3 45 18S 170 50 E
Hampshire □, U.K. 11 F6 51 7N 1 23W
Hampshire Downs, U.K. 11 F6 51 15N 1 10W
Hampton, N.B., Canada 71 C6 45 32N 65 51W
Hampton, Ont., Canada 78 C6 43 58N 78 45W
Hampton, Ark., U.S.A. 81 J8 33 32N 92 28W
Hampton, Iowa, U.S.A. 80 D8 42 45N 93 13W
Hampton, N.H., U.S.A. 79 D14 42 57N 70 50W
Hampton, S.C., U.S.A. 77 J5 32 52N 81 7W
Hampton, Va., U.S.A. 76 G7 37 2N 76 21W
Hampton Bays, U.S.A. 79 F12 40 53N 72 30W
Hampton Tableland, Australia 61 F4 32 0S 127 0 E
Hamyang, S. Korea 35 G14 35 32N 127 42 E
Han Pijesak, Bos.-H. 21 B8 44 5N 18 57 E
Hana, U.S.A. 74 H17 20 45N 155 59W
Hanak, Si. Arabia 44 E3 25 32N 37 0 E
Hanamaki, Japan 30 E10 39 23N 141 7 E
Hanang, Tanzania 54 C4 4 30S 35 25 E
Hanau, Germany 16 C5 50 7N 8 56 E
Hanbogd = Ihbulag, Mongolia 34 C4 43 11N 107 10 E
Hancheng, China 34 G6 35 31N 110 25 E
Hancock, Mich., U.S.A. 80 B10 47 8N 88 35W
Hancock, N.Y., U.S.A. 79 E9 41 57N 75 17W
Handa, Japan 31 G8 34 53N 136 55 E
Handan, China 34 F8 36 35N 114 28 E
Handeni, Tanzania 54 D4 5 25S 38 2 E
Handwara, India 43 B6 34 21N 74 20 E
Hanegev, Israel 47 E4 30 50N 35 0 E
Hanford, U.S.A. 84 J7 36 20N 119 39W
Hang Chat, Thailand 38 C2 18 20N 99 21 E
Hang Dong, Thailand 38 C2 18 41N 98 55 E
Hangang →, S. Korea 35 F14 37 50N 126 30 E
Hangayn Nuruu, Mongolia 32 B4 47 30N 99 0 E
Hangchou = Hangzhou, China 33 C7 30 18N 120 11 E
Hanggin Houqi, China 34 D4 40 58N 107 4 E
Hanggin Qi, China 34 E5 39 52N 108 50 E
Hangu, China 35 E9 39 18N 117 53 E
Hangzhou, China 33 C7 30 18N 120 11 E
Hangzhou Wan, China 33 C7 30 15N 120 45 E
Hanhongor, Mongolia 34 C3 43 55N 104 28 E
Ḥanīdh, Si. Arabia 45 E6 26 35N 48 38 E
Ḥanīsh, Yemen 46 E3 13 45N 42 46 E
Hankinson, U.S.A. 80 B6 46 4N 96 54W
Hanko, Finland 9 G20 59 50N 22 57 E
Hanksville, U.S.A. 83 G8 38 22N 110 43W
Hanle, India 43 C8 32 42N 79 4 E
Hanmer Springs, N.Z. 59 K4 42 32S 172 50 E
Hann →, Australia 60 C4 17 26S 126 17 E
Hann, Mt., Australia 60 C4 15 45S 126 0 E
Hanna, Canada 72 C6 51 40N 111 54W
Hanna, U.S.A. 82 F10 41 52N 106 34W
Hannah B., Canada 70 B4 51 40N 80 0W
Hannibal, Mo., U.S.A. 80 F9 39 42N 91 22W
Hannibal, N.Y., U.S.A. 79 C8 43 19N 76 35W
Hannover, Germany 16 B5 52 22N 9 46 E
Hanoi, Vietnam 32 D5 21 5N 105 55 E
Hanover = Hannover, Germany 16 B5 52 22N 9 46 E
Hanover, Canada 78 B3 44 9N 81 2W
Hanover, S. Africa 56 E3 31 4S 24 29 E
Hanover, N.H., U.S.A. 79 C12 43 42N 72 17W
Hanover, Ohio, U.S.A. 78 F2 40 4N 82 16W
Hanover, Pa., U.S.A. 76 F7 39 48N 76 59W
Hanover, I., Chile 96 G2 51 0S 74 50W
Hansdiha, India 43 G12 24 36N 87 5 E
Hansi, India 42 E6 29 10N 75 57 E
Hanson, L., Australia 63 E2 31 0S 136 15 E
Hantsavichy, Belarus 17 B14 52 49N 26 30 E
Hanumangarh, India 42 E6 29 35N 74 19 E
Hanzhong, China 34 H4 33 10N 107 1 E
Hanzhuang, China 35 G9 34 33N 117 23 E
Haora, India 43 H13 22 37N 88 20 E
Haparanda, Sweden 8 D21 65 52N 24 8 E
Happy, U.S.A. 81 H4 34 45N 101 52W
Happy Camp, U.S.A. 82 F2 41 48N 123 23W
Happy Valley-Goose Bay, Canada 71 B7 53 15N 60 20W
Hapsu, N. Korea 35 D15 41 13N 128 51 E
Hapur, India 42 E7 28 45N 77 45 E
Ḥaql, Si. Arabia 47 F3 29 10N 34 58 E
Har, Indonesia 37 F8 5 16S 133 14 E
Har-Ayrag, Mongolia 34 B5 45 47N 109 16 E
Har Hu, China 32 C4 38 20N 97 38 E
Har Us Nuur, Mongolia 32 B4 48 0N 92 0 E
Har Yehuda, Israel 47 D3 31 35N 34 57 E
Ḥaraḍ, Si. Arabia 46 C4 24 22N 49 0 E
Haranomachi, Japan 30 F10 37 38N 140 58 E
Harare, Zimbabwe 55 F3 17 43S 31 2 E
Harbin, China 35 B14 45 48N 126 40 E
Harbor Beach, U.S.A. 78 C2 43 51N 82 39W
Harbour Breton, Canada 71 C8 47 29N 55 50W
Harbour Deep, Canada 71 B8 50 25N 56 32W
Harda, India 42 H7 22 27N 77 5 E
Hardangerfjorden, Norway 9 F12 60 5N 6 0 E
Hardangervidda, Norway 9 F12 60 7N 7 20 E
Hardap Dam, Namibia 56 C2 24 32S 17 50 E
Hardenberg, Neths. 15 B6 52 34N 6 37 E
Harderwijk, Neths. 15 B5 52 21N 5 38 E
Hardey →, Australia 60 D2 22 45S 116 8 E
Hardin, U.S.A. 82 D10 45 44N 107 37W
Harding, S. Africa 57 E4 30 35S 29 55 E
Harding Ra., Australia 60 C3 16 17S 124 55 E
Hardisty, Canada 72 C6 52 40N 111 18W
Hardoi, India 43 F9 27 26N 80 6 E
Hardwar = Haridwar, India 42 E8 29 58N 78 9 E
Hardwick, U.S.A. 79 B12 44 30N 72 22W
Hardy, Pen., Chile 96 H3 55 30S 68 20W
Hare B., Canada 71 B8 51 15N 55 45W
Hareid, Norway 9 E12 62 22N 6 1 E
Harer, Ethiopia 46 F3 9 20N 42 8 E
Hargeisa, Somali Rep. 46 F3 9 30N 44 2 E
Hari →, Indonesia 36 E2 1 16S 104 5 E
Haria, Canary Is. 22 E6 29 8N 13 32W
Haridwar, India 42 E8 29 58N 78 9 E
Harim, Jabal al, Oman 45 E8 25 58N 56 14 E
Haringhata →, Bangla. 41 J16 22 0N 89 58 E
Harīrūd →, Asia 40 A2 37 24N 60 38 E
Härjedalen, Sweden 9 E15 62 22N 13 5 E
Harlan, Iowa, U.S.A. 80 E7 41 39N 95 19W
Harlan, Ky., U.S.A. 77 G4 36 51N 83 19W
Harlech, U.K. 10 E3 52 52N 4 6W
Harlem, U.S.A. 82 B9 48 32N 108 47W
Harlingen, Neths. 15 A5 53 11N 5 25 E
Harlingen, U.S.A. 81 M6 26 12N 97 42W
Harlow, U.K. 11 F8 51 46N 0 8 E
Harlowton, U.S.A. 82 C9 46 26N 109 50W
Harnai, Pakistan 42 D2 30 6N 67 56 E
Harney Basin, U.S.A. 82 E4 43 30N 119 0W
Harney L., U.S.A. 82 E4 43 14N 119 8W
Harney Peak, U.S.A. 80 D3 43 52N 103 32W
Härnösand, Sweden 9 E17 62 38N 17 55 E
Haroldswick, U.K. 12 A8 60 48N 0 50W
Harp L., Canada 71 A7 55 5N 61 50W
Harper, Liberia 50 H4 4 25N 7 43W
Harrai, India 43 H8 22 37N 79 13 E
Harrand, Pakistan 42 E4 29 28N 70 3 E
Harricana →, Canada 70 B4 50 56N 79 32W
Harriman, U.S.A. 77 H3 35 56N 84 33W
Harrington Harbour, Canada 71 B8 50 31N 59 30W
Harris, U.K. 12 D2 57 50N 6 55W
Harris, Sd. of, U.K. 12 D1 57 44N 7 6W
Harris L., Australia 63 E2 31 10S 135 10 E
Harris Pt., Canada 78 C2 43 6N 82 9W
Harrisburg, Ill., U.S.A. 81 G10 37 44N 88 32W
Harrisburg, Nebr., U.S.A. 80 E3 41 33N 103 44W
Harrisburg, Pa., U.S.A. 78 F8 40 16N 76 53W
Harrismith, S. Africa 57 D4 28 15S 29 8 E
Harrison, Ark., U.S.A. 81 G8 36 14N 93 7W
Harrison, Maine, U.S.A. 79 B14 44 7N 70 39W
Harrison, Nebr., U.S.A. 80 D3 42 41N 103 53W
Harrison, C., Canada 71 B8 54 55N 57 55W
Harrison L., Canada 72 D4 49 33N 121 50W
Harrisonburg, U.S.A. 76 F6 38 27N 78 52W
Harrisonville, U.S.A. 80 F7 38 39N 94 21W
Harriston, Canada 78 C4 43 57N 80 53W
Harrisville, Mich., U.S.A. 78 B1 44 39N 83 17W
Harrisville, N.Y., U.S.A. 79 B9 44 9N 75 19W
Harrisville, Pa., U.S.A. 78 E5 41 8N 80 0W
Harrodsburg, U.S.A. 76 G3 37 46N 84 51W
Harrogate, U.K. 10 C6 54 0N 1 33W
Harrow, U.K. 11 F7 51 35N 0 21W
Harrowsmith, Canada 79 B8 44 24N 76 40W
Harry S. Truman Reservoir, U.S.A. 80 F7 38 16N 93 24W
Harsīn, Iran 44 C5 34 18N 47 33 E
Harstad, Norway 8 B17 68 48N 16 30 E
Harsud, India 42 H7 22 6N 76 44 E
Hart, U.S.A. 76 D2 43 42N 86 22W
Hart, L., Australia 63 E2 31 10S 136 25 E
Hartbees →, S. Africa 56 D3 28 45S 20 32 E
Hartford, Conn., U.S.A. 79 E12 41 46N 72 41W
Hartford, Ky., U.S.A. 76 G2 37 27N 86 55W
Hartford, S. Dak., U.S.A. 80 D6 43 38N 96 57W
Hartford, Wis., U.S.A. 80 D10 43 19N 88 22W
Hartford City, U.S.A. 76 E3 40 27N 85 22W
Hartland, Canada 71 C6 46 20N 67 32W
Hartland Pt., U.K. 11 F3 51 1N 4 32W
Hartlepool, U.K. 10 C6 54 42N 1 13W
Hartlepool □, U.K. 10 C6 54 42N 1 17W
Hartley Bay, Canada 72 C3 53 25N 129 15W
Hartmannberge, Namibia 56 B1 17 0S 13 0 E
Hartney, Canada 73 D8 49 30N 100 35W
Harts →, S. Africa 56 D3 28 24S 24 17 E
Hartselle, U.S.A. 77 H2 34 27N 86 56W
Hartshorne, U.S.A. 81 H7 34 51N 95 34W
Hartstown, U.S.A. 78 E4 41 33N 80 23W
Hartsville, U.S.A. 77 H5 34 23N 80 4W
Hartwell, U.S.A. 77 H4 34 21N 82 56W
Harunabad, Pakistan 42 E5 29 35N 73 8 E
Harvand, Iran 45 D7 28 25N 55 43 E
Harvey, Australia 61 F2 33 5S 115 54 E
Harvey, Ill., U.S.A. 76 E2 41 36N 87 50W
Harvey, N. Dak., U.S.A. 80 B5 47 47N 99 56W
Harwich, U.K. 11 F9 51 56N 1 17 E
Haryana □, India 42 E7 29 0N 76 10 E
Haryn →, Belarus 17 B14 52 7N 27 17 E
Harz, Germany 16 C6 51 38N 10 44 E
Hasa □, Si. Arabia 45 E6 25 50N 49 0 E
Ḥasanābād, Iran 45 C7 32 8N 52 44 E
Hasdo →, India 43 J10 21 44N 82 44 E
Hashimoto, Japan 31 G7 34 19N 135 37 E
Hashtjerd, Iran 45 C6 35 52N 50 40 E
Haskell, U.S.A. 81 J5 33 10N 99 44W
Haslemere, U.K. 11 F7 51 5N 0 43W
Hasselt, Belgium 15 D5 50 56N 5 21 E
Hassi Messaoud, Algeria 50 B7 31 51N 6 1 E
Hässleholm, Sweden 9 H15 56 10N 13 46 E
Hastings, N.Z. 59 H6 39 39S 176 52 E
Hastings, U.K. 11 G8 50 51N 0 35 E
Hastings, Mich., U.S.A. 76 D3 42 39N 85 17W
Hastings, Minn., U.S.A. 80 C8 44 44N 92 51W
Hastings, Nebr., U.S.A. 80 E5 40 35N 98 23W
Hastings Ra., Australia 63 E5 31 15S 152 14 E
Hat Yai, Thailand 39 J3 7 1N 100 27 E
Hatanbulag = Ergel, Mongolia 34 C5 43 8N 109 5 E
Hatay = Antalya, Turkey 25 G5 36 52N 30 45 E
Hatch, U.S.A. 83 K10 32 40N 107 9W
Hatchet L., Canada 73 B8 58 36N 103 40W
Hateruma-Shima, Japan 31 M1 24 3N 123 47 E
Hatfield P.O., Australia 63 E3 33 54S 143 49 E
Hatgal, Mongolia 32 A5 50 26N 100 9 E
Hathras, India 42 F8 27 36N 78 6 E
Hatia, Bangla. 41 H17 22 30N 91 5 E
Hato Mayor, Dom. Rep. 89 C6 18 46N 69 15W
Hatta, India 43 G8 24 7N 79 36 E
Hattah, Australia 63 E3 34 48S 142 17 E
Hatteras, C., U.S.A. 77 H8 35 14N 75 32W
Hattiesburg, U.S.A. 81 K10 31 20N 89 17W
Hatvan, Hungary 17 E10 47 40N 19 45 E
Hau Bon = Cheo Reo, Vietnam 36 B3 13 25N 108 28 E
Hau Duc, Vietnam 38 E7 15 20N 108 13 E
Haugesund, Norway 9 G11 59 23N 5 13 E
Haukipudas, Finland 8 D21 65 12N 25 20 E
Haultain →, Canada 73 B7 55 51N 106 46W
Hauraki G., N.Z. 59 G5 36 35S 175 5 E
Haut Atlas, Morocco 50 B4 32 30N 5 0W
Haut-Zaïre = Orientale □, Dem. Rep. of the Congo 54 B2 2 20N 26 0 E
Hautes Fagnes = Hohe Venn, Belgium 15 D6 50 30N 6 5 E
Hauts Plateaux, Algeria 48 C4 35 0N 1 0 E
Havana = La Habana, Cuba 88 B3 23 8N 82 22W
Havana, U.S.A. 80 E9 40 18N 90 4W
Havant, U.K. 11 G7 50 51N 0 58W
Havasu, L., U.S.A. 85 L12 34 18N 114 28W
Havel →, Germany 16 B7 52 50N 12 3 E
Havelian, Pakistan 42 B5 34 2N 73 10 E
Havelock, Canada 78 B7 44 26N 77 53W
Havelock, N.Z. 59 J4 41 17S 173 48 E
Havelock, U.S.A. 77 H7 34 53N 76 54W
Haverfordwest, U.K. 11 F3 51 48N 4 58W
Haverhill, U.S.A. 79 D13 42 47N 71 5W
Haverstraw, U.S.A. 79 E11 41 12N 73 58W
Havirga, Mongolia 34 B7 45 41N 113 5 E
Havířov, Czech. 17 D10 49 46N 18 20 E
Havlíčkův Brod, Czech Rep. 16 D8 49 36N 15 33 E
Havre, U.S.A. 82 B9 48 33N 109 41W
Havre-Aubert, Canada 71 C7 47 12N 61 56W
Havre-St.-Pierre, Canada 71 B7 50 18N 63 33W
Haw →, U.S.A. 77 H6 35 36N 79 3W
Hawaii □, U.S.A. 74 H16 19 30N 156 30W
Hawaii I., Pac. Oc. 74 J17 20 0N 155 0W
Hawaiian Is., Pac. Oc. 74 H17 20 30N 156 0W
Hawaiian Ridge, Pac. Oc. 65 E11 24 0N 165 0W
Hawarden, U.S.A. 80 D6 43 0N 96 29W
Hawea, L., N.Z. 59 L2 44 28S 169 19 E
Hawera, N.Z. 59 H5 39 35S 174 19 E
Hawick, U.K. 12 F6 55 26N 2 47W
Hawk Junction, Canada 70 C3 48 5N 84 38W
Hawke B., N.Z. 59 H6 39 25S 177 20 E
Hawker, Australia 63 E2 31 59S 138 22 E
Hawkesbury, Canada 70 C5 45 37N 74 37W
Hawkesbury I., Canada 72 C3 53 37N 129 3W
Hawkesbury Pt., Australia 62 A1 11 55S 134 5 E
Hawkinsville, U.S.A. 77 J4 32 17N 83 28W
Hawley, Minn., U.S.A. 80 B6 46 53N 96 19W
Hawley, Pa., U.S.A. 79 E9 41 28N 75 11W
Ḥawrān, W. →, Iraq 44 C4 33 58N 42 34 E
Hawsh Müssá, Lebanon 47 B4 33 45N 35 55 E
Hawthorne, U.S.A. 82 G4 38 32N 118 38W
Hay, Australia 63 E3 34 30S 144 51 E
Hay →, Australia 62 C2 24 50S 138 0 E
Hay →, Canada 72 A5 60 50N 116 26W
Hay, C., Australia 60 B4 14 5S 129 29 E
Hay I., Canada 78 B4 44 53N 80 58W
Hay L., Canada 72 B5 58 50N 118 50W
Hay-on-Wye, U.K. 11 E4 52 5N 3 8W
Hay River, Canada 72 A5 60 51N 115 44W
Hay Springs, U.S.A. 80 D3 42 41N 102 41W
Haya = Tehoru, Indonesia 37 E7 3 19S 129 37 E
Hayachine-San, Japan 30 E10 39 34N 141 29 E
Hayden, U.S.A. 82 F10 40 30N 107 16W
Haydon, Australia 62 B3 18 0S 141 30 E
Hayes, U.S.A. 80 C4 44 23N 101 1W
Hayes →, Canada 70 A1 57 3N 92 12W
Hayes Creek, Australia 60 B5 13 43S 131 22 E
Hayle, U.K. 11 G2 50 11N 5 26W
Hayling I., U.K. 11 G7 50 48N 0 59W
Hayrabolu, Turkey 21 D12 41 12N 27 5 E
Hays, Canada 72 C6 50 6N 111 48W
Hays, U.S.A. 80 F5 38 53N 99 20W
Haysyn, Ukraine 17 D15 48 57N 29 25 E
Hayvoron, Ukraine 17 D15 48 22N 29 52 E
Hayward, Calif., U.S.A. 84 H4 37 40N 122 5W
Hayward, Wis., U.S.A. 80 B9 46 1N 91 29W
Haywards Heath, U.K. 11 G7 51 0N 0 5W
Hazafon □, Israel 47 C4 32 40N 35 20 E
Hazārān, Kūh-e, Iran 45 D8 29 35N 57 20 E
Hazard, U.S.A. 76 G4 37 15N 83 12W
Hazaribag, India 43 H11 23 58N 85 26 E
Hazaribag Road, India 43 G11 24 12N 85 57 E
Hazelton, Canada 72 B3 55 20N 127 42W
Hazelton, U.S.A. 80 B4 46 29N 100 17W
Hazen, U.S.A. 80 B4 47 18N 101 38W
Hazlehurst, Ga., U.S.A. 77 K4 31 52N 82 36W
Hazlehurst, Miss., U.S.A. 81 K9 31 52N 90 24W
Hazlet, U.S.A. 79 F10 40 25N 74 12W
Hazleton, U.S.A. 79 F9 40 57N 75 59W
Hazlett, L., Australia 60 D4 21 30S 128 48 E
Hazro, Turkey 44 B4 38 15N 40 47 E
Head of Bight, Australia 61 F5 31 30S 131 25 E
Headlands, Zimbabwe 55 F3 18 15S 32 2 E
Healdsburg, U.S.A. 84 G4 38 37N 122 52W
Healdton, U.S.A. 81 H6 34 14N 97 29W
Healesville, Australia 63 F4 37 35S 145 30 E
Heard I., Ind. Oc. 3 G13 53 0S 74 0 E
Hearne, U.S.A. 81 K6 30 53N 96 36W
Hearst, Canada 70 C3 49 40N 83 41W
Heart →, U.S.A. 80 B4 46 46N 100 50W
Heart's Content, Canada 71 C9 47 54N 53 27W
Heath Pt., Canada 71 C7 49 8N 61 40W
Heavener, U.S.A. 81 H7 34 53N 94 36W
Hebbronville, U.S.A. 81 M5 27 18N 98 41W
Hebei □, China 34 E9 39 0N 116 0 E
Hebel, Australia 63 D4 28 58S 147 47 E
Heber, U.S.A. 85 N11 32 44N 115 32W
Heber City, U.S.A. 82 F8 40 31N 111 25W
Heber Springs, U.S.A. 81 H9 35 30N 92 2W
Hebert, Canada 73 C7 50 30N 107 10W
Hebgen L., U.S.A. 82 D8 44 52N 111 20W
Hebi, China 34 G8 35 57N 114 7 E
Hebrides, U.K. 6 D4 57 30N 7 0W
Hebron = Al Khalīl, West Bank 47 D4 31 32N 35 6 E
Hebron, Canada 69 C13 58 5N 62 30W
Hebron, N. Dak., U.S.A. 80 B3 46 54N 102 3W
Hebron, Nebr., U.S.A. 80 E6 40 10N 97 35W
Hecate Str., Canada 72 C2 53 10N 130 30W
Heceta I., U.S.A. 72 B2 55 46N 133 40W
Hechi, China 32 D5 24 40N 108 2 E
Hechuan, China 32 C5 30 2N 106 12 E
Hecla, U.S.A. 80 C5 45 53N 98 9W
Hecla I., Canada 73 C9 51 10N 96 43W
Hede, Sweden 9 E15 62 23N 13 30 E
Hedemora, Sweden 9 F16 60 18N 15 58 E
Heerde, Neths. 15 B6 52 24N 6 2 E
Heerenveen, Neths. 15 B5 52 57N 5 55 E
Heerhugowaard, Neths. 15 B4 52 40N 4 51 E
Heerlen, Neths. 18 A6 50 55N 5 58 E
Ḥefa, Israel 47 C4 32 46N 35 0 E
Ḥefa □, Israel 47 C4 32 40N 35 0 E
Hefei, China 33 C6 31 52N 117 18 E
Hegang, China 33 B8 47 20N 130 19 E
Heichengzhen, China 34 F4 36 24N 106 3 E
Heidelberg, Germany 16 D5 49 24N 8 42 E
Heidelberg, S. Africa 56 E3 34 6S 20 59 E
Heilbron, S. Africa 57 D4 27 16S 27 59 E
Heilbronn, Germany 16 D5 49 9N 9 13 E
Heilongjiang □, China 33 B7 48 0N 126 0 E
Heilunkiang = Heilongjiang □, China 33 B7 48 0N 126 0 E
Heimaey, Iceland 8 E3 63 26N 20 17W
Heinola, Finland 9 F22 61 13N 26 2 E
Heinze Is., Burma 41 M20 14 25N 97 45 E
Heishan, China 35 D12 41 40N 122 5 E
Heishui, China 35 C10 42 8N 119 30 E
Hejaz = Ḥijāz □, Si. Arabia 46 C3 24 0N 40 0 E
Hejian, China 34 E9 38 25N 116 5 E
Hejin, China 34 G6 35 35N 110 42 E
Hekimhan, Turkey 44 B3 38 50N 37 55 E
Hekla, Iceland 8 E4 63 56N 19 35W
Hekou, China 32 D5 22 30N 103 59 E
Helan Shan, China 34 E3 38 30N 105 55 E
Helen Atoll, Pac. Oc. 37 D8 2 40N 132 0 E
Helena, Ark., U.S.A. 81 H9 34 32N 90 36W
Helena, Mont., U.S.A. 82 C7 46 36N 112 2W
Helendale, U.S.A. 85 L9 34 44N 117 19W
Helensburgh, U.K. 12 E4 56 1N 4 43W
Helensville, N.Z. 59 G5 36 41S 174 29 E
Helenvale, Australia 62 B4 15 43S 145 14 E
Helgeland, Norway 8 C15 66 7N 13 29 E
Helgoland, Germany 16 A4 54 10N 7 53 E
Heligoland = Helgoland, Germany 16 A4 54 10N 7 53 E
Heligoland B. = Deutsche Bucht, Germany 16 A5 54 15N 8 0 E
Hella, Iceland 8 E3 63 50N 20 24W
Hellertown, U.S.A. 79 F9 40 35N 75 21W
Hellespont = Çanakkale Boğazı, Turkey 21 D12 40 17N 26 32 E
Hellevoetsluis, Neths. 15 C4 51 50N 4 8 E
Hellín, Spain 19 C5 38 31N 1 40W
Helmand □, Afghan. 40 D4 31 20N 64 0 E
Helmand →, Afghan. 40 D2 31 12N 61 34 E
Helmond, Neths. 15 C5 51 29N 5 41 E
Helmsdale, U.K. 12 C5 58 7N 3 39W
Helmsdale →, U.K. 12 C5 58 7N 3 40W
Helong, China 35 C15 42 40N 129 0 E
Helper, U.S.A. 82 G8 39 41N 110 51W
Helsingborg, Sweden 9 H15 56 3N 12 42 E
Helsingfors = Helsinki, Finland 9 F21 60 15N 25 3 E
Helsingør, Denmark 9 H15 56 2N 12 35 E
Helsinki, Finland 9 F21 60 15N 25 3 E
Helston, U.K. 11 G2 50 6N 5 17W
Helvellyn, U.K. 10 C4 54 32N 3 1W
Helwân, Egypt 51 C12 29 50N 31 20 E
Hemel Hempstead, U.K. 11 F7 51 44N 0 28W
Hemet, U.S.A. 85 M10 33 45N 116 58W
Hemingford, U.S.A. 80 D3 42 19N 103 4W
Hemmingford, Canada 79 A11 45 3N 73 35W
Hempstead, U.S.A. 81 K6 30 6N 96 5W
Hemse, Sweden 9 H18 57 15N 18 22 E
Henan □, China 34 H8 34 0N 114 0 E
Henares →, Spain 19 B4 40 24N 3 30W
Henashi-Misaki, Japan 30 D9 40 37N 139 51 E
Henderson, Argentina 94 D3 36 18S 61 43W
Henderson, Ky., U.S.A. 76 G2 37 50N 87 35W
Henderson, N.C., U.S.A. 77 G6 36 20N 78 25W
Henderson, Nev., U.S.A. 85 J12 36 2N 114 59W
Henderson, Tenn., U.S.A. 77 H1 35 26N 88 38W
Henderson, Tex., U.S.A. 81 J7 32 9N 94 48W
Hendersonville, N.C., U.S.A. 77 H4 35 19N 82 28W
Hendersonville, Tenn., U.S.A. 77 G2 36 18N 86 37W
Hendījān, Iran 45 D6 30 14N 49 43 E
Hendorābī, Iran 45 E7 26 40N 53 37 E
Hengcheng, China 34 E4 38 18N 106 28 E
Hengdaohezi, China 35 B15 44 52N 129 0 E
Hengelo, Neths. 15 B6 52 16N 6 48 E
Hengshan, China 34 F5 37 58N 109 5 E
Hengshui, China 34 F8 37 41N 115 40 E
Hengyang, China 33 D6 26 52N 112 33 E
Henlopen, C., U.S.A. 76 F8 38 48N 75 6W
Hennenman, S. Africa 56 D4 27 59S 27 1 E
Hennessey, U.S.A. 81 G6 36 6N 97 54W
Henrietta, U.S.A. 81 J5 33 49N 98 12W
Henrietta, Ostrov = Genriyetty, Ostrov, Russia 27 B16 77 6N 156 30 E
Henrietta Maria, C., Canada 70 A3 55 9N 82 20W
Henry, U.S.A. 80 E10 41 7N 89 22W
Henryetta, U.S.A. 81 H7 35 27N 95 59W
Henryville, Canada 79 A11 45 8N 73 11W

Hensall

Hensall, Canada 78 C3 43 26N 81 30W
Hentiyn Nuruu, Mongolia 33 B5 48 30N 108 30 E
Henty, Australia 63 F4 35 30S 147 0 E
Henzada, Burma 41 L19 17 38N 95 26 E
Heppner, U.S.A. 82 D4 45 21N 119 33W
Hepworth, Canada 78 B3 44 37N 81 9W
Hequ, China 34 E6 39 20N 111 15 E
Héraðsflói, Iceland 8 D6 65 42N 14 12W
Héraðsvötn →, Iceland 8 D4 65 45N 19 25W
Herald Cays, Australia 62 B4 16 58S 149 9 E
Herāt, Afghan. 40 B3 34 20N 62 7 E
Herāt □, Afghan. 40 B3 35 0N 62 0 E
Herbert →, Australia 62 B4 18 31S 146 17 E
Herberton, Australia 62 B4 17 20S 145 25 E
Herceg-Novi, Montenegro, Yug. 21 C8 42 30N 18 33 E
Herchmer, Canada 73 B10 57 22N 94 10W
Herðubreið, Iceland 8 D5 65 11N 16 21W
Hereford, U.K. 11 E5 52 4N 2 43W
Hereford, U.S.A. 81 H3 34 49N 102 24W
Herefordshire □, U.K. 11 E5 52 8N 2 40W
Herentals, Belgium 15 C4 51 12N 4 51 E
Herford, Germany 16 B5 52 7N 8 39 E
Herington, U.S.A. 80 F6 38 40N 96 57W
Herkimer, U.S.A. 79 D10 43 0N 74 59W
Herlong, U.S.A. 84 E6 40 8N 120 8W
Herm, U.K. 11 H5 49 30N 2 28W
Hermann, U.S.A. 80 F9 38 42N 91 27W
Hermannsburg, Australia 60 D5 23 57S 132 45 E
Hermanus, S. Africa 56 E2 34 27S 19 12 E
Hermidale, Australia 63 E4 31 30S 146 42 E
Hermiston, U.S.A. 82 D4 45 51N 119 17W
Hermitage, N.Z. 59 K3 43 44S 170 5 E
Hermite, I., Chile 96 H3 55 50S 68 0W
Hermon, U.S.A. 79 B9 44 28N 75 14W
Hermon, Mt. = Shaykh, J. ash, Lebanon 47 B4 33 25N 35 50 E
Hermosillo, Mexico 86 B2 29 10N 111 0W
Hernád →, Hungary 17 D11 47 56N 21 8 E
Hernandarias, Paraguay 95 B5 25 20S 54 40W
Hernandez, U.S.A. 84 J6 36 24N 120 46W
Hernando, Argentina 94 C3 32 28S 63 40W
Hernando, U.S.A. 81 H10 34 50N 90 0W
Herndon, U.S.A. 78 F8 40 43N 76 51W
Herne, Germany 15 C7 51 32N 7 14 E
Herne Bay, U.K. 11 F9 51 21N 1 8 E
Herning, Denmark 9 H13 56 8N 8 58 E
Heroica = Caborca, Mexico 86 A2 30 40N 112 10W
Heroica Nogales = Nogales, Mexico 86 A2 31 20N 110 56W
Heron Bay, Canada 70 C2 48 40N 86 25W
Herradura, Pta. de la, Canary Is. 22 F5 28 26N 14 8W
Herreid, U.S.A. 80 C4 45 50N 100 4W
Herrin, U.S.A. 81 G10 37 48N 89 2W
Herriot, Canada 73 B8 56 22N 101 16W
Hershey, U.S.A. 79 F8 40 17N 76 39W
Hersonissos, Greece 23 D7 35 18N 25 22 E
Herstal, Belgium 15 D5 50 40N 5 38 E
Hertford, U.K. 11 F7 51 48N 0 4W
Hertfordshire □, U.K. 11 F7 51 51N 0 5W
's-Hertogenbosch, Neths. 15 C5 51 42N 5 17 E
Hertzogville, S. Africa 56 D4 28 9S 25 30 E
Hervey B., Australia 62 C5 25 0S 152 52 E
Herzliyya, Israel 47 C3 32 10N 34 50 E
Ḥeṣār, Fārs, Iran 45 D6 29 52N 50 16 E
Ḥeṣār, Markazī, Iran 45 C6 35 50N 49 12 E
Heshui, China 34 G5 35 48N 108 0 E
Heshun, China 34 F7 37 22N 113 32 E
Hesperia, U.S.A. 85 L9 34 25N 117 18W
Hesse = Hessen □, Germany 16 C5 50 30N 9 0 E
Hessen □, Germany 16 C5 50 30N 9 0 E
Hetch Hetchy Aqueduct, U.S.A. 84 H5 37 29N 122 19W
Hettinger, U.S.A. 80 C3 46 0N 102 42W
Heuvelton, U.S.A. 79 B9 44 37N 75 25W
Hewitt, U.S.A. 81 K6 31 27N 97 11W
Hexham, U.K. 10 C5 54 58N 2 4W
Hexigten Qi, China 35 C9 43 18N 117 30 E
Ḥeydarābād, Iran 45 D7 30 33N 55 38 E
Heysham, U.K. 10 C5 54 3N 2 53W
Heywood, Australia 63 F3 38 8S 141 37 E
Heze, China 34 G8 35 14N 115 20 E
Hi Vista, U.S.A. 85 L9 34 45N 117 46W
Hialeah, U.S.A. 77 N5 25 50N 80 17W
Hiawatha, U.S.A. 80 F7 39 51N 95 32W
Hibbing, U.S.A. 80 B8 47 25N 92 56W
Hibbs B., Australia 62 G4 42 35S 145 15 E
Hibernia Reef, Australia 60 B3 12 0S 123 23 E
Hickman, U.S.A. 81 G10 36 34N 89 11W
Hickory, U.S.A. 77 H5 35 44N 81 21W
Hicks, Pt., Australia 63 F4 37 49S 149 17 E
Hicks L., Canada 73 A9 61 25N 100 0W
Hicksville, U.S.A. 79 F11 40 46N 73 32W
Hida-Gawa →, Japan 31 G8 35 26N 137 3 E
Hida-Sammyaku, Japan 31 F8 36 30N 137 40 E
Hidaka-Sammyaku, Japan 30 C11 42 35N 142 45 E
Hidalgo, Mexico 87 C5 24 15N 99 26W
Hidalgo □, Mexico 87 C5 20 30N 99 10W
Hidalgo, Presa M., Mexico 86 B3 26 30N 108 35W
Hidalgo, Pta. del, Canary Is. 22 F3 28 33N 16 19W
Hidalgo del Parral, Mexico 86 B3 26 58N 105 40W
Hierro, Canary Is. 22 G1 27 44N 18 0W
Higashiajima-San, Japan 30 F10 37 40N 140 10 E
Higashiōsaka, Japan 31 G7 34 40N 135 37 E
Higgins, U.S.A. 81 G4 36 7N 100 2W
Higgins Corner, U.S.A. 84 F5 39 2N 121 5W
High Atlas = Haut Atlas, Morocco 50 B4 32 30N 5 0W
High Bridge, U.S.A. 79 F10 40 40N 74 54W
High Level, Canada 72 B5 58 31N 117 8W
High Point, U.S.A. 77 H6 35 57N 80 0W
High Prairie, Canada 72 B5 55 30N 116 30W
High River, Canada 72 C6 50 30N 113 50W
High Tatra = Tatry, Slovak Rep. 17 D11 49 20N 20 0 E
High Veld, Africa 48 J6 27 0S 27 0 E
High Wycombe, U.K. 11 F7 51 37N 0 45W
Highland □, U.K. 12 D4 57 17N 4 21W
Highland Park, U.S.A. 76 D2 42 11N 87 48W
Highmore, U.S.A. 80 C5 44 31N 99 27W
Highrock L., Canada 73 B8 55 45N 100 30W
Highrock L., Sask., Canada 73 B7 57 5N 105 32W
Higüey, Dom. Rep. 89 C6 18 37N 68 42W
Hiiumaa, Estonia 9 G20 58 50N 22 45 E
Ḥijāz □, Si. Arabia 46 C3 24 0N 40 0 E
Hijo = Tagum, Phil. 37 C7 7 33N 125 53 E
Hikari, Japan 31 H5 33 58N 131 58 E
Hiko, U.S.A. 84 H11 37 32N 115 14W
Hikone, Japan 31 G8 35 15N 136 10 E
Hikurangi, N.Z. 59 F5 35 36S 174 17 E
Hikurangi, Mt., N.Z. 59 H6 38 21S 176 52 E
Hildesheim, Germany 16 B5 52 9N 9 56 E
Hill →, Australia 61 F2 30 23S 115 3 E
Hill City, Idaho, U.S.A. 82 E6 43 18N 115 3W
Hill City, Kans., U.S.A. 80 F5 39 22N 99 51W
Hill City, S. Dak., U.S.A. 80 D3 43 56N 103 35W
Hill Island L., Canada 73 A7 60 30N 109 50W
Hillcrest Center, U.S.A. 85 K8 35 23N 118 57W
Hillegom, Neths. 15 B4 52 18N 4 35 E
Hillerød, Denmark 9 J15 55 56N 12 19 E
Hillsboro, Kans., U.S.A. 80 F6 38 21N 97 12W
Hillsboro, N. Dak., U.S.A. 80 B6 47 26N 97 3W
Hillsboro, N.H., U.S.A. 79 C13 43 7N 71 54W
Hillsboro, Ohio, U.S.A. 76 F4 39 12N 83 37W
Hillsboro, Oreg., U.S.A. 84 E4 45 31N 122 59W
Hillsboro, Tex., U.S.A. 81 J6 32 1N 97 8W
Hillsborough, Grenada 89 D7 12 28N 61 28W
Hillsdale, Mich., U.S.A. 76 E3 41 56N 84 38W
Hillsdale, N.Y., U.S.A. 79 D11 42 11N 73 30W
Hillsport, Canada 70 C2 49 27N 85 34W
Hillston, Australia 63 E4 33 30S 145 31 E
Hilo, U.S.A. 74 J17 19 44N 155 5W
Hilton, U.S.A. 78 C7 43 17N 77 48W
Hilton Head Island, U.S.A. 77 J5 32 13N 80 45W
Hilversum, Neths. 15 B5 52 14N 5 10 E
Himachal Pradesh □, India 42 D7 31 30N 77 0 E
Himalaya, Asia 43 E11 29 0N 84 0 E
Himatnagar, India 40 H8 23 37N 72 57 E
Himeji, Japan 31 G7 34 50N 134 40 E
Himi, Japan 31 F8 36 50N 136 55 E
Ḥimş, Syria 47 A5 34 40N 36 45 E
Ḥimş □, Syria 47 A6 34 30N 37 0 E
Hinche, Haiti 89 C5 19 9N 72 1W
Hinchinbrook I., Australia 62 B4 18 20S 146 15 E
Hinckley, U.K. 11 E6 52 33N 1 22W
Hinckley, U.S.A. 80 B8 46 1N 92 56W
Hindaun, India 42 F7 26 44N 77 5 E
Hindmarsh, L., Australia 63 F3 36 5S 141 55 E
Hindu Bagh, Pakistan 42 D2 30 56N 67 50 E
Hindu Kush, Asia 40 B7 36 0N 71 0 E
Hindubagh, Pakistan 40 D5 30 56N 67 57 E
Hindupur, India 40 N10 13 49N 77 32 E
Hines Creek, Canada 72 B5 56 20N 118 40W
Hinesville, U.S.A. 77 K5 31 51N 81 36W
Hinganghat, India 40 J11 20 30N 78 52 E
Hingham, U.S.A. 82 B8 48 33N 110 25W
Hingir, India 43 J10 21 57N 83 41 E
Hingoli, India 40 K10 19 41N 77 15 E
Hinna = Imi, Ethiopia 46 F3 6 28N 42 10 E
Hinnøya, Norway 8 B16 68 35N 15 50 E
Hinojosa del Duque, Spain 19 C3 38 30N 5 9W
Hinsdale, U.S.A. 79 D12 42 47N 72 29W
Hinton, Canada 72 C5 53 26N 117 34W
Hinton, U.S.A. 76 G5 37 40N 80 54W
Hirado, Japan 31 H4 33 22N 129 33 E
Hirakud Dam, India 41 J13 21 32N 83 45 E
Hiran →, India 43 H8 23 6N 79 21 E
Hirapur, India 43 G8 24 22N 79 13 E
Hiratsuka, Japan 31 G9 35 19N 139 21 E
Hiroo, Japan 30 C11 42 17N 143 19 E
Hirosaki, Japan 30 D10 40 34N 140 28 E
Hiroshima, Japan 31 G6 34 24N 132 30 E
Hiroshima □, Japan 31 G6 34 50N 133 0 E
Hisar, India 42 E6 29 12N 75 45 E
Hisb →, Iraq 44 D5 31 45N 44 17 E
Ḥismá, Si. Arabia 44 D3 28 30N 36 0 E
Hispaniola, W. Indies 89 C5 19 0N 71 0W
Hīt, Iraq 44 C4 33 38N 42 49 E
Hita, Japan 31 H5 33 20N 130 58 E
Hitachi, Japan 31 F10 36 36N 140 39 E
Hitchin, U.K. 11 F7 51 58N 0 16W
Hitoyoshi, Japan 31 H5 32 13N 130 45 E
Hitra, Norway 8 E13 63 30N 8 45 E
Hixon, Canada 72 C4 53 25N 122 35W
Hiyyon, N. →, Israel 47 E4 30 25N 35 10 E
Hjalmar L., Canada 73 A7 61 33N 109 25W
Hjälmaren, Sweden 9 G16 59 18N 15 40 E
Hjørring, Denmark 9 H13 57 29N 9 59 E
Hluhluwe, S. Africa 57 D5 28 1S 32 15 E
Hlyboka, Ukraine 17 D13 48 5N 25 56 E
Ho Chi Minh City = Phanh Bho Ho Chi Minh, Vietnam 39 G6 10 58N 106 40 E
Ho Thuong, Vietnam 38 C5 19 32N 105 48 E
Hoa Da, Vietnam 39 G7 11 16N 108 40 E
Hoa Hiep, Vietnam 39 G5 11 34N 105 51 E
Hoai Nhon, Vietnam 38 E7 14 28N 109 1 E
Hoang Lien Son, Vietnam 38 A4 22 0N 104 0 E
Hoare B., Canada 69 B13 65 17N 62 30W
Hobart, Australia 62 G4 42 50S 147 21 E
Hobart, U.S.A. 81 H5 35 1N 99 6W
Hobbs, U.S.A. 81 J3 32 42N 103 8W
Hobbs Coast, Antarctica 5 D14 74 50S 131 0W
Hobe Sound, U.S.A. 77 M5 27 4N 80 8W
Hoboken, U.S.A. 79 F10 40 45N 74 4W
Hobro, Denmark 9 H13 56 39N 9 46 E
Hoburgen, Sweden 9 H18 56 55N 18 7 E
Hodaka-Dake, Japan 31 F8 36 17N 137 39 E
Hodgeville, Canada 73 C7 50 7N 106 58W
Hodgson, Canada 73 C9 51 13N 97 36W
Hódmezővásárhely, Hungary 17 E11 46 28N 20 22 E
Hodna, Chott el, Algeria 50 A6 35 26N 4 43 E
Hodonín, Czech Rep. 17 D9 48 50N 17 10 E
Hoeamdong, N. Korea 35 C16 42 30N 130 16 E
Hoek van Holland, Neths. 15 C4 52 0N 4 7 E
Hoengsŏng, S. Korea 35 F14 37 29N 127 59 E
Hoeryong, N. Korea 35 C15 42 30N 129 45 E
Hoeyang, N. Korea 35 E14 38 43N 127 36 E
Hof, Germany 16 C6 50 19N 11 55 E
Hofmeyr, S. Africa 56 E4 31 39S 25 50 E
Höfn, Iceland 8 D6 64 15N 15 13W
Hofors, Sweden 9 F17 60 31N 16 15 E
Hofsjökull, Iceland 8 D4 64 49N 18 48W
Hōfu, Japan 31 G5 34 3N 131 34 E
Hogan Group, Australia 63 F4 39 13S 147 1 E
Hogarth, Mt., Australia 62 C2 21 48S 136 58 E
Hoggar = Ahaggar, Algeria 50 D7 23 0N 6 30 E
Hogsty Reef, Bahamas 89 B5 21 41N 73 48W
Hoh →, U.S.A. 84 C2 47 45N 124 29W
Hohe Venn, Belgium 15 D6 50 30N 6 5 E
Hohenwald, U.S.A. 77 H2 35 33N 87 33W
Hohhot, China 34 D6 40 52N 111 40 E
Hóhlakas, Greece 23 D9 35 57N 27 53 E
Hoi An, Vietnam 38 E7 15 30N 108 19 E
Hoisington, U.S.A. 80 F5 38 31N 98 47W
Hōjō, Japan 31 H6 33 58N 132 46 E
Hokianga Harbour, N.Z. 59 F4 35 31S 173 22 E
Hokitika, N.Z. 59 K3 42 42S 171 0 E
Hokkaidō □, Japan 30 C11 43 30N 143 0 E
Holbrook, Australia 63 F4 35 42S 147 18 E
Holbrook, U.S.A. 83 J8 34 54N 110 10W
Holden, U.S.A. 82 G7 39 6N 112 16W
Holdenville, U.S.A. 81 H6 35 5N 96 24W
Holdrege, U.S.A. 80 E5 40 26N 99 23W
Holguín, Cuba 88 B4 20 50N 76 20W
Hollams Bird I., Namibia 56 C1 24 40S 14 30 E
Holland, Mich., U.S.A. 76 D2 42 47N 86 7W
Holland, N.Y., U.S.A. 78 D6 42 38N 78 32W
Hollandale, U.S.A. 81 J9 33 10N 90 51W
Hollandia = Jayapura, Indonesia 37 E10 2 28S 140 38 E
Holley, U.S.A. 78 C6 43 14N 78 2W
Hollidaysburg, U.S.A. 78 F6 40 26N 78 24W
Hollis, U.S.A. 81 H5 34 41N 99 55W
Hollister, Calif., U.S.A. 84 J5 36 51N 121 24W
Hollister, Idaho, U.S.A. 82 E6 42 21N 114 35W
Holly Hill, U.S.A. 77 L5 29 16N 81 3W
Holly Springs, U.S.A. 81 H10 34 46N 89 27W
Hollywood, Calif., U.S.A. 74 D3 34 7N 118 25W
Hollywood, Fla., U.S.A. 77 N5 26 1N 80 9W
Holman, Canada 68 A8 70 42N 117 41W
Holman, N.W.T., Canada 68 A8 70 44N 117 44W
Hólmavík, Iceland 8 D3 65 42N 21 40W
Holmen, U.S.A. 80 D9 43 58N 91 15W
Holmes Reefs, Australia 62 B4 16 27S 148 0 E
Holmsund, Sweden 8 E19 63 41N 20 20 E
Holroyd →, Australia 62 A3 14 10S 141 36 E
Holstebro, Denmark 9 H13 56 22N 8 37 E
Holsworthy, U.K. 11 G3 50 48N 4 22W
Holton, Canada 71 B8 54 31N 57 12W
Holton, U.S.A. 80 F7 39 28N 95 44W
Holtville, U.S.A. 85 N11 32 49N 115 23W
Holwerd, Neths. 15 A5 53 22N 5 54 E
Holy I., Angl., U.K. 10 D3 53 17N 4 37W
Holy I., Northumb., U.K. 10 B6 55 40N 1 47W
Holyhead, U.K. 10 D3 53 18N 4 38W
Holyoke, Colo., U.S.A. 80 E3 40 35N 102 18W
Holyoke, Mass., U.S.A. 79 D12 42 12N 72 37W
Holyrood, Canada 71 C9 47 27N 53 8W
Homa Bay, Kenya 54 C3 0 36S 34 30 E
Homalin, Burma 41 G19 24 55N 95 0 E
Homand, Iran 45 C8 32 28N 59 37 E
Homathko →, Canada 72 C4 51 0N 124 56W
Hombori, Mali 50 E5 15 20N 1 38W
Home B., Canada 69 B13 68 40N 67 10W
Home Hill, Australia 62 B4 19 43S 147 25 E
Homedale, U.S.A. 82 E5 43 37N 116 56W
Homer, Alaska, U.S.A. 68 C4 59 39N 151 33W
Homer, La., U.S.A. 81 J8 32 48N 93 4W
Homer City, U.S.A. 78 F5 40 32N 79 10W
Homestead, Australia 62 C4 20 20S 145 40 E
Homestead, U.S.A. 77 N5 25 28N 80 29W
Homewood, U.S.A. 84 F6 39 4N 120 8W
Homoine, Mozam. 57 C6 23 55S 35 8 E
Homs = Ḥimş, Syria 47 A5 34 40N 36 45 E
Homyel, Belarus 17 B16 52 28N 31 0 E
Hon Chong, Vietnam 39 G5 10 25N 104 30 E
Hon Me, Vietnam 38 C5 19 23N 105 56 E
Honan = Henan □, China 34 H8 34 0N 114 0 E
Honbetsu, Japan 30 C11 43 7N 143 37 E
Honcut, U.S.A. 84 F5 39 20N 121 32W
Hondeklipbaai, S. Africa 56 E2 30 19S 17 17 E
Hondo, Japan 31 H5 32 27N 130 12 E
Hondo, U.S.A. 81 L5 29 21N 99 9W
Hondo →, Belize 87 D7 18 25N 88 21W
Honduras ■, Cent. Amer. 88 D2 14 40N 86 30W
Honduras, G. de, Caribbean 88 C2 16 50N 87 0W
Hønefoss, Norway 9 F14 60 10N 10 18 E
Honesdale, U.S.A. 79 E9 41 34N 75 16W
Honey L., U.S.A. 84 E6 40 15N 120 19W
Honfleur, France 18 B4 49 25N 0 13 E
Hong →, Vietnam 32 D5 22 0N 104 0 E
Hong He →, China 34 H8 32 25N 115 35 E
Hong Kong □, China 33 D6 22 11N 114 14 E
Hongch'ŏn, S. Korea 35 F14 37 44N 127 53 E
Hongjiang, China 33 D5 27 7N 109 59 E
Hongliu He →, China 34 F5 38 0N 109 50 E
Hongor, Mongolia 34 B7 45 45N 112 50 E
Hongsa, Laos 38 C3 19 43N 101 20 E
Hongshui He →, China 33 D5 23 48N 109 30 E
Hongsŏng, S. Korea 35 F14 36 37N 126 38 E
Hongtong, China 34 F6 36 16N 111 40 E
Honguedo, Détroit d', Canada 71 C7 49 15N 64 0W
Hongwon, N. Korea 35 E14 40 0N 127 56 E
Hongze Hu, China 35 H10 33 15N 118 35 E
Honiara, Solomon Is. 64 H7 9 27S 159 57 E
Honiton, U.K. 11 G4 50 47N 3 11W
Honjō, Japan 30 E10 39 23N 140 3 E
Honningsvåg, Norway 8 A21 70 59N 25 59 E
Honolulu, U.S.A. 74 H16 21 19N 157 52W
Honshū, Japan 31 G9 36 0N 138 0 E
Hood, Mt., U.S.A. 82 D3 45 23N 121 42W
Hood, Pt., Australia 61 F2 34 23S 119 34 E
Hood River, U.S.A. 82 D3 45 43N 121 31W
Hoodsport, U.S.A. 84 C3 47 24N 123 9W
Hoogeveen, Neths. 15 B6 52 44N 6 28 E
Hoogezand-Sappemeer, Neths. 15 A6 53 9N 6 45 E
Hooghly = Hugli →, India 43 J13 21 56N 88 4 E
Hooghly-Chinsura = Chunchura, India 43 H13 22 53N 88 27 E
Hook Hd., Ireland 13 D5 52 7N 6 56W
Hook I., Australia 62 C4 20 4S 149 0 E
Hook of Holland = Hoek van Holland, Neths. 15 C4 52 0N 4 7 E
Hooker, U.S.A. 81 G4 36 52N 101 13W
Hooker Creek, Australia 60 C5 18 23S 130 38 E
Hoonah, U.S.A. 72 B1 58 7N 135 27W
Hooper Bay, U.S.A. 68 B3 61 32N 166 6W
Hoopeston, U.S.A. 76 E2 40 28N 87 40W
Hoopstad, S. Africa 56 D4 27 50S 25 55 E
Hoorn, Neths. 15 B5 52 38N 5 4 E
Hoover, U.S.A. 77 J2 33 20N 86 11W
Hoover Dam, U.S.A. 85 K12 36 1N 114 44W
Hooversville, U.S.A. 78 F6 40 9N 78 55W
Hop Bottom, U.S.A. 79 E9 41 42N 75 46W
Hope, Canada 72 D4 49 25N 121 25W
Hope, Ariz., U.S.A. 85 M13 33 43N 113 42W
Hope, Ark., U.S.A. 81 J8 33 40N 93 36W
Hope, L., S. Austral., Australia 63 D2 28 24S 139 18 E
Hope, L., W. Austral., Australia 61 F3 32 35S 120 15 E
Hope I., Canada 78 B4 44 55N 80 11W
Hope Town, Bahamas 88 A4 26 35N 76 57W
Hopedale, Canada 71 A7 55 28N 60 13W
Hopedale, U.S.A. 79 D13 42 8N 71 33W
Hopefield, S. Africa 56 E2 33 3S 18 22 E
Hopei = Hebei □, China 34 E9 39 0N 116 0 E
Hopelchén, Mexico 87 D7 19 46N 89 50W
Hopetoun, Vic., Australia 63 F3 35 42S 142 22 E
Hopetoun, W. Austral., Australia 61 F3 33 57S 120 7 E
Hopetown, S. Africa 56 D3 29 34S 24 3 E
Hopevale, Australia 62 B4 15 16S 145 20 E
Hopewell, U.S.A. 76 G7 37 18N 77 17W
Hopkins, L., Australia 60 D4 24 15S 128 35 E
Hopkinsville, U.S.A. 77 G2 36 52N 87 29W
Hopland, U.S.A. 84 G3 38 58N 123 7W
Hoquiam, U.S.A. 84 D3 46 59N 123 53W
Horden Hills, Australia 60 D5 20 15S 130 0 E
Horinger, China 34 D6 40 28N 111 48 E
Horlick Mts., Antarctica 5 E15 84 0S 102 0W
Horlivka, Ukraine 25 E6 48 19N 38 5 E
Hormak, Iran 45 D9 29 58N 60 51 E
Hormoz, Iran 45 E7 27 35N 55 0 E
Hormoz, Jaz.-ye, Iran 45 E8 27 8N 56 28 E
Hormozgān □, Iran 45 E8 27 30N 56 0 E
Hormuz, Kūh-e, Iran 45 E7 27 27N 55 10 E
Hormuz, Str. of, The Gulf 45 E8 26 30N 56 30 E
Horn, Austria 16 D8 48 39N 15 40 E
Horn, Iceland 8 C2 66 28N 22 28W
Horn →, Canada 72 A5 61 30N 118 1W
Horn, Cape = Hornos, C. de, Chile 96 H3 55 50S 67 30W
Horn Head, Ireland 13 A3 55 14N 8 0W
Horn I., Australia 62 A3 10 37S 142 17 E
Horn Mts., Canada 72 A5 62 15N 119 15W
Hornavan, Sweden 8 C17 66 15N 17 30 E
Hornbeck, U.S.A. 81 K8 31 20N 93 24W
Hornbrook, U.S.A. 82 F2 41 55N 122 33W
Horncastle, U.K. 10 D7 53 13N 0 7W
Hornell, U.S.A. 78 D7 42 20N 77 40W
Hornell L., Canada 72 A5 62 20N 119 25W
Hornepayne, Canada 70 C3 49 14N 84 48W
Hornings Mills, Canada 78 B4 44 9N 80 12W
Hornitos, U.S.A. 84 H6 37 30N 120 14W
Hornos, C. de, Chile 96 H3 55 50S 67 30W
Hornsea, U.K. 10 D7 53 55N 0 11W
Horobetsu, Japan 30 C10 42 24N 141 6 E
Horodenka, Ukraine 17 D13 48 41N 25 29 E
Horodok, Khmelnytskyy, Ukraine 17 D14 49 10N 26 34 E
Horodok, Lviv, Ukraine 17 D12 49 46N 23 32 E
Horokhiv, Ukraine 17 C13 50 30N 24 45 E
Horqin Youyi Qianqi, China 35 A12 46 5N 122 3 E
Horqueta, Paraguay 94 A4 23 15S 56 55W
Horse Creek, U.S.A. 80 E3 41 57N 105 10W
Horse Is., Canada 71 B8 50 15N 55 50W
Horsefly L., Canada 72 C4 52 25N 121 0W
Horseheads, U.S.A. 78 D8 42 10N 76 49W
Horsens, Denmark 9 J13 55 52N 9 51 E
Horsham, Australia 63 F3 36 44S 142 13 E
Horsham, U.K. 11 F7 51 4N 0 20W
Horten, Norway 9 G14 59 25N 10 32 E
Horton, U.S.A. 80 F7 39 40N 95 32W
Horton →, Canada 68 B7 69 56N 126 52W
Horwood L., Canada 70 C3 48 5N 82 20W
Hose, Gunung-Gunung, Malaysia 36 D4 2 5N 114 6 E
Ḥoseynābād, Khuzestān, Iran 45 C6 32 45N 48 20 E
Ḥoseynābād, Kordestān, Iran 44 C5 35 33N 47 8 E
Hoshangabad, India 42 H7 22 45N 77 45 E
Hoshiarpur, India 42 D6 31 30N 75 58 E
Hospet, India 40 M10 15 15N 76 20 E
Hoste, I., Chile 96 H3 55 0S 69 0W
Hot, Thailand 38 C2 18 8N 98 29 E
Hot Creek Range, U.S.A. 82 G6 38 40N 116 20W
Hot Springs, Ark., U.S.A. 81 H8 34 31N 93 3W
Hot Springs, S. Dak., U.S.A. 80 D3 43 26N 103 29W
Hotagen, Sweden 8 E16 63 50N 14 30 E
Hotan, China 32 C2 37 25N 79 55 E
Hotazel, S. Africa 56 D3 27 17S 22 58 E
Hotchkiss, U.S.A. 83 G10 38 48N 107 43W
Hotham, C., Australia 60 B5 12 2S 131 18 E
Hoting, Sweden 8 D17 64 8N 16 15 E
Hotte, Massif de la, Haiti 89 C5 18 30N 73 45W
Hottentotsbaai, Namibia 56 D1 26 8S 14 59 E
Houffalize, Belgium 15 D5 50 8N 5 48 E
Houghton, Mich., U.S.A. 80 B10 47 7N 88 34W
Houghton, N.Y., U.S.A. 78 D6 42 25N 78 10W
Houghton L., U.S.A. 76 C3 44 21N 84 44W
Houhora Heads, N.Z. 59 F4 34 49S 173 9 E
Houlton, U.S.A. 77 B12 46 8N 67 51W
Houma, U.S.A. 81 L9 29 36N 90 43W
Housatonic →, U.S.A. 79 E11 41 10N 73 7W
Houston, Canada 72 C3 54 25N 126 39W
Houston, Mo., U.S.A. 81 G9 37 22N 91 58W
Houston, Tex., U.S.A. 81 L7 29 46N 95 22W
Houtman Abrolhos, Australia 61 E1 28 43S 113 48 E
Hovd, Mongolia 32 B4 48 2N 91 37 E
Hove, U.K. 11 G7 50 50N 0 10W
Hoveyzeh, Iran 45 D6 31 27N 48 4 E
Hövsgöl, Mongolia 34 C5 43 37N 109 39 E
Hövsgöl Nuur, Mongolia 32 A5 51 0N 100 30 E
Howard, Australia 63 D5 25 16S 152 32 E
Howard, Pa., U.S.A. 78 F7 41 1N 77 40W
Howard, S. Dak., U.S.A. 80 C6 44 1N 97 32W
Howe, U.S.A. 82 E7 43 48N 113 0W
Howe, C., Australia 63 F5 37 30S 150 0 E
Howe I., Canada 79 B8 44 16N 76 17W
Howell, U.S.A. 76 D4 42 36N 83 56W
Howick, Canada 79 A11 45 11N 73 51W
Howick, S. Africa 57 D5 29 28S 30 14 E
Howick Group, Australia 62 A4 14 20S 145 30 E
Howitt, L., Australia 63 D2 27 40S 138 40 E
Howland I., Pac. Oc. 64 G10 0 48N 176 38W
Howrah = Haora, India 43 H13 22 37N 88 20 E
Howth Hd., Ireland 13 C5 53 22N 6 3W
Höxter, Germany 16 C5 51 46N 9 22 E
Hoy, U.K. 12 C5 58 50N 3 15W
Høyanger, Norway 9 F12 61 13N 6 4 E

Indonesia

Hoyerswerda, Germany 16 C8 51 26N 14 14 E
Hoylake, U.K. 10 D4 53 24N 3 10W
Hpungan Pass, Burma 41 F20 27 30N 96 55 E
Hradec Králové, Czech Rep. 16 C8 50 15N 15 50 E
Hrodna, Belarus 17 B12 53 42N 23 52 E
Hrodzyanka, Belarus 17 B15 53 31N 28 42 E
Hron →, Slovak Rep. 17 E10 47 49N 18 45 E
Hrvatska = Croatia ■, Europe 16 F9 45 20N 16 0 E
Hrymayliv, Ukraine 17 D14 49 20N 26 5 E
Hsenwi, Burma 41 H20 23 22N 97 55 E
Hsiamen = Xiamen, China 33 D6 24 25N 118 4 E
Hsian = Xi'an, China 34 G5 34 15N 109 0 E
Hsinchu, Taiwan 33 D7 24 48N 120 58 E
Hsinhailien = Lianyungang, China 35 G10 34 40N 119 11 E
Hsüchou = Xuzhou, China 35 G9 34 18N 117 10 E
Hu Xian, China 34 G5 34 8N 108 42 E
Hua Hin, Thailand 38 F2 12 34N 99 58 E
Hua Xian, Henan, China 34 G8 35 30N 114 30 E
Hua Xian, Shaanxi, China 34 G5 34 30N 109 48 E
Huachinera, Mexico 86 A3 30 9N 108 55W
Huacho, Peru 92 F3 11 10S 77 35W
Huade, China 34 D7 41 55N 113 59 E
Huadian, China 35 C14 43 0N 126 40 E
Huai He →, China 33 C6 33 0N 118 30 E
Huai Yot, Thailand 39 J2 7 45N 99 37 E
Huai'an, Hebei, China 34 D8 40 30N 114 20 E
Huai'an, Jiangsu, China 35 H10 33 30N 119 10 E
Huaibei, China 34 G9 34 0N 116 48 E
Huaide = Gongzhuling, China 35 C13 43 30N 124 40 E
Huaidezhen, China 35 C13 43 48N 124 50 E
Huainan, China 33 C6 32 38N 116 58 E
Huairen, China 34 E7 39 48N 113 20 E
Huairou, China 34 D9 40 20N 116 35 E
Huaiyang, China 34 H8 33 40N 114 52 E
Huaiyin, China 35 H10 33 30N 119 2 E
Huaiyuan, China 35 H9 32 55N 117 10 E
Huajianzi, China 35 D13 41 23N 125 20 E
Huajuapan de Leon, Mexico 87 D5 17 50N 97 48W
Hualapai Peak, U.S.A. 83 J7 35 5N 113 54W
Huallaga →, Peru 92 E3 5 15S 75 30W
Huambo, Angola 53 G3 12 42S 15 54 E
Huan Jiang →, China 34 G5 34 28N 109 0 E
Huan Xian, China 34 F4 36 33N 107 7 E
Huancabamba, Peru 92 E3 5 10S 79 15W
Huancane, Peru 92 G5 15 10S 69 44W
Huancavelica, Peru 92 F3 12 50S 75 5W
Huancayo, Peru 92 F3 12 5S 75 12W
Huanchaca, Bolivia 92 H5 20 15S 66 40W
Huang Hai = Yellow Sea, China 35 G12 35 0N 123 0 E
Huang He →, China 35 F10 37 55N 118 50 E
Huang Xian, China 35 F11 37 38N 120 30 E
Huangling, China 34 G5 35 34N 109 15 E
Huanglong, China 34 G5 35 30N 109 59 E
Huangshan, China 33 D6 29 42N 118 25 E
Huangshi, China 33 C6 30 10N 115 3 E
Huangsongdian, China 35 C14 43 45N 127 25 E
Huantai, China 35 F9 36 58N 117 56 E
Huánuco, Peru 92 E3 9 55S 76 15W
Huaraz, Peru 92 E3 9 30S 77 32W
Huarmey, Peru 92 F3 10 5S 78 5W
Huascarán, Peru 92 E3 9 8S 77 36W
Huasco, Chile 94 B1 28 30S 71 15W
Huasco →, Chile 94 B1 28 27S 71 13W
Huasna, U.S.A. 85 K6 35 6N 120 24W
Huatabampo, Mexico 86 B3 26 50N 109 50W
Huauchinango, Mexico 87 C5 20 11N 98 3W
Huautla de Jiménez, Mexico 87 D5 18 8N 96 51W
Huay Namota, Mexico 86 C4 21 56N 104 30W
Huayin, China 34 G6 34 35N 110 5 E
Hubbard, Ohio, U.S.A. 78 E4 41 9N 80 34W
Hubbard, Tex., U.S.A. 81 K6 31 51N 96 48W
Hubbart Pt., Canada 73 B10 59 21N 94 41W
Hubei □, China 33 C6 31 0N 112 0 E
Hubli, India 40 M9 15 22N 75 15 E
Huch'ang, N. Korea 35 D14 41 25N 127 2 E
Hucknall, U.K. 10 D6 53 3N 1 13W
Huddersfield, U.K. 10 D6 53 39N 1 47W
Hudiksvall, Sweden 9 F17 61 43N 17 10 E
Hudson, Canada 70 B1 50 6N 92 9W
Hudson, Mass., U.S.A. 79 D13 42 23N 71 34W
Hudson, N.Y., U.S.A. 79 D11 42 15N 73 46W
Hudson, Wis., U.S.A. 80 C8 44 58N 92 45W
Hudson, Wyo., U.S.A. 82 E9 42 54N 108 35W
Hudson →, U.S.A. 79 F10 40 42N 74 2W
Hudson Bay, N.W.T., Canada 69 C11 60 0N 86 0W
Hudson Bay, Sask., Canada 73 C8 52 51N 102 23W
Hudson Falls, U.S.A. 79 C11 43 18N 73 35W
Hudson Mts., Antarctica 5 D16 74 32S 99 20W
Hudson Str., Canada 69 B13 62 0N 70 0W
Hudson's Hope, Canada 72 B4 56 0N 121 54W
Hue, Vietnam 38 D6 16 30N 107 35 E
Huehuetenango, Guatemala 88 C1 15 20N 91 28W
Huejúcar, Mexico 86 C4 22 21N 103 13W
Huelva, Spain 19 D2 37 18N 6 57W
Huentelauquén, Chile 94 C1 31 38S 71 33W
Huerta, Sa. de la, Argentina 94 C2 31 10S 67 30W
Huesca, Spain 19 A5 42 8N 0 25W
Huetamo, Mexico 86 D4 18 36N 100 54W
Hugh →, Australia 62 D1 25 1S 134 1 E
Hughenden, Australia 62 C3 20 52S 144 10 E
Hughes, Australia 61 F4 30 42S 129 31 E
Hughesville, U.S.A. 79 E8 41 14N 76 44W
Hugli →, India 43 J13 21 56N 88 4 E
Hugo, Colo., U.S.A. 80 F3 39 8N 103 28W
Hugo, Okla., U.S.A. 81 H7 34 1N 95 31W
Hugoton, U.S.A. 81 G4 37 11N 101 21W
Hui Xian = Huixian, China 34 G7 35 27N 113 12 E
Hui Xian, China 34 H4 33 50N 106 4 E
Hui'anbu, China 34 F4 37 28N 106 38 E
Huichapán, Mexico 87 C5 20 24N 99 40W
Huifa He →, China 35 C14 43 0N 127 50 E
Huila, Nevado del, Colombia 92 C3 3 0N 76 0W
Huimin, China 35 F9 37 27N 117 28 E
Huinan, China 35 C14 42 40N 126 2 E
Huinca Renancó, Argentina 94 C3 34 51S 64 22W
Huining, China 34 G3 35 38N 105 0 E
Huinong, China 34 E4 39 5N 106 35 E
Huisache, Mexico 86 C4 22 55N 100 25W
Huiting, China 34 G9 34 5N 116 5 E
Huixian, China 34 G7 35 27N 113 12 E
Huixtla, Mexico 87 D6 15 9N 92 28W
Huize, China 32 D5 26 24N 103 15 E
Hukawng Valley, Burma 41 F20 26 30N 96 30 E
Hukuntsi, Botswana 56 C3 23 58S 21 45 E
Ḥulayfā', Si. Arabia 44 E4 25 58N 40 45 E
Huld = Ulaanjirem, Mongolia 34 B3 45 5N 105 30 E
Hulin He →, China 35 B12 45 0N 122 10 E
Hull = Kingston upon Hull, U.K. 10 D7 53 45N 0 21W
Hull, Canada 79 A9 45 25N 75 44W
Hull →, U.K. 10 D7 53 44N 0 20W
Hulst, Neths. 15 C4 51 17N 4 2 E
Hulun Nur, China 33 B6 49 0N 117 30 E
Humahuaca, Argentina 94 A2 23 10S 65 25W
Humaitá, Brazil 92 E6 7 35S 63 1W
Humaitá, Paraguay 94 B4 27 2S 58 31W
Humansdorp, S. Africa 56 E3 34 2S 24 46 E
Humbe, Angola 56 B1 16 40S 14 55 E
Humber →, U.K. 10 D7 53 42N 0 27W
Humboldt, Canada 73 C7 52 15N 105 9W
Humboldt, Iowa, U.S.A. 80 D7 42 44N 94 13W
Humboldt, Tenn., U.S.A. 81 H10 35 50N 88 55W
Humboldt →, U.S.A. 82 F4 39 59N 118 36W
Humboldt Gletscher, Greenland 4 B4 79 30N 62 0W
Hume, U.S.A. 84 J8 36 48N 118 54W
Hume, L., Australia 63 F4 36 0S 147 5 E
Humenné, Slovak Rep. 17 D11 48 55N 21 50 E
Humphreys, Mt., U.S.A. 84 H8 37 17N 118 40W
Humphreys Peak, U.S.A. 83 J8 35 21N 111 41W
Humptulips, U.S.A. 84 C3 47 14N 123 57W
Hūn, Libya 51 C9 29 2N 16 0 E
Hun Jiang →, China 35 D13 40 50N 125 38 E
Húnaflói, Iceland 8 D3 65 50N 20 50W
Hunan □, China 33 D6 27 30N 112 0 E
Hunchun, China 35 C16 42 52N 130 28 E
Hundewali, Pakistan 42 D5 31 55N 72 38 E
Hundred Mile House, Canada 72 C4 51 38N 121 18W
Hunedoara, Romania 17 F12 45 40N 22 50 E
Hungary ■, Europe 17 E10 47 20N 19 20 E
Hungary, Plain of, Europe 6 F10 47 0N 20 0 E
Hungerford, Australia 63 D3 28 58S 144 24 E
Hŭngnam, N. Korea 35 E14 39 49N 127 45 E
Hunsberge, Namibia 56 D2 27 45S 17 12 E
Hunsrück, Germany 16 D4 49 56N 7 27 E
Hunstanton, U.K. 10 E8 52 56N 0 29 E
Hunter, U.S.A. 79 D10 42 13N 74 13W
Hunter I., Australia 62 G3 40 30S 144 45 E
Hunter I., Canada 72 C3 51 55N 128 0W
Hunter Ra., Australia 63 E5 32 45S 150 15 E
Hunters Road, Zimbabwe 55 F2 19 9S 29 49 E
Hunterville, N.Z. 59 H5 39 56S 175 35 E
Huntingburg, U.S.A. 76 F2 38 18N 86 57W
Huntingdon, Canada 70 C5 45 6N 74 10W
Huntingdon, U.K. 11 E7 52 20N 0 11W
Huntingdon, U.S.A. 78 F6 40 30N 78 1W
Huntington, Ind., U.S.A. 76 E3 40 53N 85 30W
Huntington, Oreg., U.S.A. 82 D5 44 21N 117 16W
Huntington, Utah, U.S.A. 82 G8 39 20N 110 58W
Huntington, W. Va., U.S.A. 76 F4 38 25N 82 27W
Huntington Beach, U.S.A. 85 M9 33 40N 118 5W
Huntington Station, U.S.A. 79 F11 40 52N 73 26W
Huntly, N.Z. 59 G5 37 34S 175 11 E
Huntly, U.K. 12 D6 57 27N 2 47W
Huntsville, Canada 78 A5 45 20N 79 14W
Huntsville, Ala., U.S.A. 77 H2 34 44N 86 35W
Huntsville, Tex., U.S.A. 81 K7 30 43N 95 33W
Hunyani →, Zimbabwe 55 F3 15 57S 30 39 E
Hunyuan, China 34 E7 39 42N 113 42 E
Hunza →, India 43 B6 35 54N 74 20 E
Huo Xian = Huozhou, China 34 F6 36 36N 111 42 E
Huong Hoa, Vietnam 38 D6 16 37N 106 45 E
Huong Khe, Vietnam 38 C5 18 13N 105 41 E
Huonville, Australia 62 G4 43 0S 147 5 E
Huozhou, China 34 F6 36 36N 111 42 E
Hupeh = Hubei □, China 33 C6 31 0N 112 0 E
Ḥūr, Iran 45 D8 30 50N 57 7 E
Hurd, C., Canada 78 A3 45 13N 81 44W
Hure Qi, China 35 C11 42 45N 121 45 E
Hurghada, Egypt 51 C12 27 15N 33 50 E
Hurley, N. Mex., U.S.A. 83 K9 32 42N 108 8W
Hurley, Wis., U.S.A. 80 B9 46 27N 90 11W
Huron, Calif., U.S.A. 84 J6 36 12N 120 6W
Huron, Ohio, U.S.A. 78 E2 41 24N 82 33W
Huron, S. Dak., U.S.A. 80 C5 44 22N 98 13W
Huron, L., U.S.A. 78 B2 44 30N 82 40W
Hurricane, U.S.A. 83 H7 37 11N 113 17W
Hurunui →, N.Z. 59 K4 42 54S 173 18 E
Húsavík, Iceland 8 C5 66 3N 17 21W
Huşi, Romania 17 E15 46 41N 28 7 E
Huskvarna, Sweden 9 H16 57 47N 14 15 E
Hustadvika, Norway 8 E12 63 0N 7 0 E
Hustontown, U.S.A. 78 F6 40 3N 78 2W
Hutchinson, Kans., U.S.A. 81 F6 38 5N 97 56W
Hutchinson, Minn., U.S.A. 80 C7 44 54N 94 22W
Hutte Sauvage, L. de la, Canada 71 A7 56 15N 64 45W
Hutton, Mt., Australia 63 D4 25 51S 148 20 E
Huy, Belgium 15 D5 50 31N 5 15 E
Huzhou, China 33 C7 30 51N 120 8 E
Hvammstangi, Iceland 8 D3 65 24N 20 57W
Hvar, Croatia 20 C7 43 11N 16 28 E
Hvítá →, Iceland 8 D3 64 30N 21 58W
Hwachŏn-chŏsuji, S. Korea 35 E14 38 5N 127 50 E
Hwang Ho = Huang He →, China 35 F10 37 55N 118 50 E
Hwange, Zimbabwe 55 F2 18 18S 26 30 E
Hwange Nat. Park, Zimbabwe 56 B4 19 0S 26 30 E
Hyannis, Mass., U.S.A. 76 E10 41 39N 70 17W
Hyannis, Nebr., U.S.A. 80 E4 42 0N 101 46W
Hyargas Nuur, Mongolia 32 B4 49 0N 93 0 E
Hydaburg, U.S.A. 72 B2 55 15N 132 50W
Hyde Park, U.S.A. 79 E11 41 47N 73 56W
Hyden, Australia 61 F2 32 24S 118 53 E
Hyder, U.S.A. 72 B2 55 55N 130 5W
Hyderabad, India 40 L11 17 22N 78 29 E
Hyderabad, Pakistan 42 G3 25 23N 68 24 E
Hyères, France 18 E7 43 8N 6 9 E
Hyères, Îs. d', France 18 E7 43 0N 6 20 E
Hyesan, N. Korea 35 D15 41 20N 128 10 E
Hyland →, Canada 72 B3 59 52N 128 12W
Hymia, India 43 C8 33 40N 78 2 E
Hyndman Peak, U.S.A. 82 E6 43 45N 114 8W
Hyōgo □, Japan 31 G7 35 15N 134 50 E
Hyrum, U.S.A. 82 F8 41 38N 111 51W
Hysham, U.S.A. 82 C10 46 18N 107 14W
Hythe, U.K. 11 F9 51 4N 1 5 E
Hyūga, Japan 31 H5 32 25N 131 35 E
Hyvinge = Hyvinkää, Finland 9 F21 60 38N 24 50 E
Hyvinkää, Finland 9 F21 60 38N 24 50 E

I

I-n-Gall, Niger 50 E7 16 51N 7 1 E
Iaco →, Brazil 92 E5 9 3S 68 34W
Iakora, Madag. 57 C8 23 6S 46 40 E
Ialomiţa →, Romania 17 F14 44 42N 27 51 E
Iaşi, Romania 17 E14 47 10N 27 40 E
Ib →, India 43 J10 21 34N 83 48 E
Iba, Phil. 37 A6 15 22N 120 0 E
Ibadan, Nigeria 50 G6 7 22N 3 58 E
Ibagué, Colombia 92 C3 4 20N 75 20W
Ibar →, Serbia, Yug. 21 C9 43 43N 20 45 E
Ibaraki □, Japan 31 F10 36 10N 140 10 E
Ibarra, Ecuador 92 C3 0 21N 78 7W
Ibembo, Dem. Rep. of the Congo 54 B1 2 35N 23 35 E
Ibera, L., Argentina 94 B4 28 30S 57 9W
Iberian Peninsula, Europe 6 H5 40 0N 5 0W
Iberville, Canada 79 A11 45 19N 73 17W
Iberville, Lac d', Canada 70 A5 55 55N 73 15W
Ibiá, Brazil 93 G9 19 30S 46 30W
Ibicuí →, Brazil 95 B4 29 25S 56 47W
Ibicuy, Argentina 94 C4 33 55S 59 10W
Ibioapaba, Sa. da, Brazil 93 D10 4 0S 41 30W
Ibiza = Eivissa, Spain 22 C7 38 54N 1 26 E
Ibo, Mozam. 55 E5 12 22S 40 40 E
Ibonma, Indonesia 37 E8 3 29S 133 31 E
Ibotirama, Brazil 93 F10 12 13S 43 12W
Ibrāhīm →, Lebanon 47 A4 34 4N 35 38 E
'Ibrī, Oman 45 F8 23 14N 56 30 E
Ibu, Indonesia 37 D7 1 35N 127 33 E
Ibusuki, Japan 31 J5 31 12N 130 40 E
Ica, Peru 92 F3 14 0S 75 48W
Iça →, Brazil 92 D5 2 55S 67 58W
Içana, Brazil 92 C5 0 21N 67 19W
Içana →, Brazil 92 C5 0 26N 67 19W
İçel = Mersin, Turkey 25 G5 36 51N 34 36 E
Iceland ■, Europe 8 D4 64 45N 19 0W
Ich'ang = Yichang, China 33 C6 30 40N 111 20 E
Ichchapuram, India 41 K14 19 10N 84 40 E
Ichhawar, India 42 H7 23 1N 77 1 E
Ichihara, Japan 31 G10 35 28N 140 5 E
Ichikawa, Japan 31 G9 35 44N 139 55 E
Ichilo →, Bolivia 92 G6 15 57S 64 50W
Ichinohe, Japan 30 D10 40 13N 141 17 E
Ichinomiya, Japan 31 G8 35 18N 136 48 E
Ichinoseki, Japan 30 E10 38 55N 141 8 E
Ichŏn, S. Korea 35 F14 37 17N 127 27 E
Icod, Canary Is. 22 F3 28 22N 16 43W
Ida Grove, U.S.A. 80 D7 42 21N 95 28W
Idabel, U.S.A. 81 J7 33 54N 94 50W
Idaho □, U.S.A. 82 D7 45 0N 115 0W
Idaho City, U.S.A. 82 E6 43 50N 115 50W
Idaho Falls, U.S.A. 82 E7 43 30N 112 2W
Idar-Oberstein, Germany 16 D4 49 43N 7 16 E
Idfû, Egypt 51 D12 24 55N 32 49 E
Ídhi Óros, Greece 23 D6 35 15N 24 45 E
Ídhra, Greece 21 F10 37 20N 23 28 E
Idi, Indonesia 36 C1 5 2N 97 37 E
Idiofa, Dem. Rep. of the Congo 52 E3 4 55S 19 42 E
Idlib, Syria 44 C3 35 55N 36 36 E
Idria, U.S.A. 84 J6 36 25N 120 41W
Idutywa, S. Africa 57 E4 32 8S 28 18 E
Ieper, Belgium 15 D2 50 51N 2 53 E
Ierápetra, Greece 23 E7 35 1N 25 44 E
Iesi, Italy 20 C5 43 31N 13 14 E
Ifakara, Tanzania 52 F7 8 8S 36 41 E
'Ifāl, W. al →, Si. Arabia 44 D2 28 7N 35 3 E
Ifanadiana, Madag. 57 C8 21 19S 47 39 E
Ife, Nigeria 50 G6 7 30N 4 31 E
Iférouâne, Niger 50 E7 19 5N 8 24 E
Iffley, Australia 62 B3 18 53S 141 12 E
Ifni, Morocco 50 C3 29 29N 10 12W
Iforas, Adrar des, Mali 50 E6 19 40N 1 40 E
Ifould, L., Australia 61 F5 30 52S 132 6 E
Iganga, Uganda 54 B3 0 37N 33 28 E
Igarapava, Brazil 93 H9 20 3S 47 47W
Igarka, Russia 26 C9 67 30N 86 33 E
Igatimi, Paraguay 95 A4 24 5S 55 40W
Iggesund, Sweden 9 F17 61 39N 17 10 E
Iglésias, Italy 20 E3 39 19N 8 32 E
Igloolik, Canada 69 B11 69 20N 81 49W
Igluligaarjuk, Canada 69 B10 63 21N 90 42W
Ignace, Canada 70 C1 49 30N 91 40W
İğneada Burnu, Turkey 21 D13 41 53N 28 2 E
Igoumenítsa, Greece 21 E9 39 32N 20 18 E
Iguaçu →, Brazil 95 B5 25 36S 54 36W
Iguaçu, Cat. del, Brazil 95 B5 25 41S 54 26W
Iguaçu Falls = Iguaçu, Cat. del, Brazil 95 B5 25 41S 54 26W
Iguala, Mexico 87 D5 18 20N 99 40W
Igualada, Spain 19 B6 41 37N 1 37 E
Iguassu = Iguaçu →, Brazil 95 B5 25 36S 54 36W
Iguatu, Brazil 93 E11 6 20S 39 18W
Iharana, Madag. 57 A9 13 25S 50 0 E
Ihbulag, Mongolia 34 C4 43 11N 107 10 E
Iheya-Shima, Japan 31 L3 27 4N 127 58 E
Ihosy, Madag. 57 C8 22 24S 46 8 E
Ihotry, L., Madag. 57 C7 21 56S 43 41 E
Ii, Finland 8 D21 65 19N 25 22 E
Ii-Shima, Japan 31 L3 26 43N 127 47 E
Iida, Japan 31 G8 35 35N 137 50 E
Iijoki →, Finland 8 D21 65 20N 25 20 E
Iisalmi, Finland 8 E22 63 32N 27 10 E
Iiyama, Japan 31 F9 36 51N 138 22 E
Iizuka, Japan 31 H5 33 38N 130 42 E
Ijebu-Ode, Nigeria 50 G6 6 47N 3 58 E
IJmuiden, Neths. 15 B4 52 28N 4 35 E
IJssel →, Neths. 15 B5 52 35N 5 50 E
IJsselmeer, Neths. 15 B5 52 45N 5 20 E
Ijuí, Brazil 95 B5 28 23S 53 55W
Ijuí →, Brazil 95 B4 27 58S 55 20W
Ikaluktutiak, Canada 68 B9 69 10N 105 0W
Ikare, Nigeria 50 G7 7 32N 5 40 E
Ikaría, Greece 21 F12 37 35N 26 10 E
Ikeda, Japan 31 G6 34 1N 133 48 E
Ikela, Dem. Rep. of the Congo 52 E4 1 6S 23 6 E
Iki, Japan 31 H4 33 45N 129 42 E
Ikimba L., Tanzania 54 C3 1 30S 31 20 E
Ikopa →, Madag. 57 B8 16 45S 46 40 E
Ikungu, Tanzania 54 C3 1 33S 33 42 E
Ilagan, Phil. 37 A6 17 7N 121 53 E
Īlām, Iran 44 C5 33 36N 46 36 E
Ilam, Nepal 43 F12 26 58N 87 58 E
Ilam □, Iran 44 C5 33 0N 47 0 E
Ilanskiy, Russia 27 D10 56 14N 96 3 E
Ilawa, Poland 17 B10 53 36N 19 34 E
Ile-à-la-Crosse, Canada 73 B7 55 27N 107 53W
Ile-à-la-Crosse, Lac, Canada 73 B7 55 40N 107 45W
Île-de-France □, France 18 B5 49 0N 2 20 E
Ilebo, Dem. Rep. of the Congo 52 E4 4 17S 20 55 E
Ilek, Russia 26 D6 51 32N 53 21 E
Ilek →, Russia 24 D9 51 30N 53 22 E
Ilesha, Nigeria 50 G6 7 37N 4 40 E
Ilford, Canada 73 B9 56 4N 95 35W
Ilfracombe, Australia 62 C3 23 30S 144 30 E
Ilfracombe, U.K. 11 F3 51 12N 4 8W
Ilhéus, Brazil 93 F11 14 49S 39 2W
Ili →, Kazakstan 26 E8 45 53N 77 10 E
Iliamna L., U.S.A. 68 C4 59 30N 155 0W
Iligan, Phil. 37 C6 8 12N 124 13 E
Ilion, U.S.A. 79 D9 43 1N 75 2W
Ilkeston, U.K. 10 E6 52 58N 1 19W
Ilkley, U.K. 10 D6 53 56N 1 48W
Illampu = Ancohuma, Nevada, Bolivia 92 G5 16 0S 68 50W
Illana B., Phil. 37 C6 7 35N 123 45 E
Illapel, Chile 94 C1 32 0S 71 10W
Iller →, Germany 16 D6 48 23N 9 58 E
Illetas, Spain 22 B9 39 32N 2 35 E
Illimani, Nevado, Bolivia 92 G5 16 30S 67 50W
Illinois □, U.S.A. 80 E10 40 15N 89 30W
Illinois →, U.S.A. 75 C8 38 58N 90 28W
Illium = Troy, Turkey 21 E12 39 57N 26 12 E
Illizi, Algeria 50 C7 26 31N 8 32 E
Ilmajoki, Finland 9 E20 62 44N 22 34 E
Ilmen, Ozero, Russia 24 C5 58 15N 31 10 E
Ilo, Peru 92 G4 17 40S 71 20W
Iloilo, Phil. 37 B6 10 45N 122 33 E
Ilorin, Nigeria 50 G6 8 30N 4 35 E
Ilwaco, U.S.A. 84 D2 46 19N 124 3W
Ilwaki, Indonesia 37 F7 7 55S 126 30 E
Imabari, Japan 31 G6 34 4N 133 0 E
Imaloto →, Madag. 57 C8 23 27S 45 13 E
Imandra, Ozero, Russia 24 A5 67 30N 33 0 E
Imari, Japan 31 H4 33 15N 129 52 E
Imatra, Finland 24 B4 61 12N 28 48 E
Imbil, Australia 63 D5 26 22S 152 32 E
imeni 26 Bakinskikh Komissarov = Neftçala, Azerbaijan 25 G8 39 19N 49 12 E
Imeri, Serra, Brazil 92 C5 0 50N 65 25W
Imerimandroso, Madag. 57 B8 17 26S 48 35 E
Imi, Ethiopia 46 F3 6 28N 42 10 E
Imlay, U.S.A. 82 F4 40 40N 118 9W
Imlay City, U.S.A. 78 D1 43 2N 83 5W
Immingham, U.K. 10 D7 53 37N 0 13W
Immokalee, U.S.A. 77 M5 26 25N 81 25W
Ímola, Italy 20 B4 44 20N 11 42 E
Imperatriz, Brazil 93 E9 5 30S 47 29W
Impéria, Italy 18 E8 43 53N 8 3 E
Imperial, Canada 73 C7 51 21N 105 28W
Imperial, Calif., U.S.A. 85 N11 32 51N 115 34W
Imperial, Nebr., U.S.A. 80 E4 40 31N 101 39W
Imperial Beach, U.S.A. 85 N9 32 35N 117 8W
Imperial Dam, U.S.A. 85 N12 32 55N 114 25W
Imperial Reservoir, U.S.A. 85 N12 32 53N 114 28W
Imperial Valley, U.S.A. 85 N11 33 0N 115 30W
Imperieuse Reef, Australia 60 C2 17 36S 118 50 E
Impfondo, Congo 52 D3 1 40N 18 0 E
Imphal, India 41 G18 24 48N 93 56 E
İmroz = Gökçeada, Turkey 21 D11 40 10N 25 50 E
Imuris, Mexico 86 A2 30 47N 110 52W
Imuruan B., Phil. 37 B5 10 40N 119 10 E
In Salah, Algeria 50 C6 27 10N 2 32 E
Ina, Japan 31 G8 35 50N 137 55 E
Inangahua Junction, N.Z. 59 J3 41 52S 171 59 E
Inanwatan, Indonesia 37 E8 2 10S 132 14 E
Iñapari, Peru 92 F5 11 0S 69 40W
Inari, Finland 8 B22 68 54N 27 5 E
Inarijärvi, Finland 8 B22 69 0N 28 0 E
Inawashiro-Ko, Japan 30 F10 37 29N 140 6 E
Inca, Spain 22 B9 39 43N 2 54 E
Inca de Oro, Chile 94 B2 26 45S 69 54W
Incaguasi, Chile 94 B1 29 12S 71 5W
İnce Burun, Turkey 25 F5 42 7N 34 56 E
İncesu, Turkey 44 B2 38 38N 35 11 E
Inch'ŏn, S. Korea 35 F14 37 27N 126 40 E
İncirliova, Turkey 21 F12 37 50N 27 41 E
Incline Village, U.S.A. 82 G4 39 10N 119 58W
Incomáti →, Mozam. 57 D5 25 46S 32 43 E
Indalsälven →, Sweden 9 E17 62 36N 17 30 E
Indaw, Burma 41 G20 24 15N 96 5 E
Independence, Calif., U.S.A. 84 J8 36 48N 118 12W
Independence, Iowa, U.S.A. 80 D9 42 28N 91 54W
Independence, Kans., U.S.A. 81 G7 37 14N 95 42W
Independence, Ky., U.S.A. 76 F3 38 57N 84 33W
Independence, Mo., U.S.A. 80 F7 39 6N 94 25W
Independence Fjord, Greenland 4 A6 82 10N 29 0W
Independence Mts., U.S.A. 82 F5 41 20N 116 0W
Index, U.S.A. 84 C5 47 50N 121 33W
India ■, Asia 40 K11 20 0N 78 0 E
Indian →, U.S.A. 77 M5 27 59N 80 34W
Indian Cabins, Canada 72 B5 59 52N 117 40W
Indian Harbour, Canada 71 B8 54 27N 57 13W
Indian Head, Canada 73 C8 50 30N 103 41W
Indian Lake, U.S.A. 79 C10 43 47N 74 16W
Indian Ocean 28 K11 5 0S 75 0 E
Indian Springs, U.S.A. 85 J11 36 35N 115 40W
Indiana, U.S.A. 78 F5 40 37N 79 9W
Indiana □, U.S.A. 76 F3 40 0N 86 0W
Indianapolis, U.S.A. 76 F2 39 46N 86 9W
Indianola, Iowa, U.S.A. 80 E8 41 22N 93 34W
Indianola, Miss., U.S.A. 81 J9 33 27N 90 39W
Indiga, Russia 24 A8 67 38N 49 9 E
Indigirka →, Russia 27 B15 70 48N 148 54 E
Indio, U.S.A. 85 M10 33 43N 116 13W
Indo-China, Asia 28 H14 15 0N 102 0 E
Indonesia ■, Asia 36 F5 5 0S 115 0 E

Indore

Indore, *India* **42 H6** 22 42N 75 53 E
Indramayu, *Indonesia* **37 G13** 6 20S 108 19 E
Indravati →, *India* **41 K12** 19 20N 80 20 E
Indre →, *France* **18 C4** 47 16N 0 11 E
Indulkana, *Australia* **63 D1** 26 58S 133 5 E
Indus →, *Pakistan* **42 G2** 24 20N 67 47 E
Indus, Mouth of the, *Pakistan* **42 H3** 24 0N 68 0 E
İnebolu, *Turkey* **25 F5** 41 55N 33 40 E
Infiernillo, Presa del, *Mexico* **86 D4** 18 9N 102 0W
Ingenio, *Canary Is.* **22 G4** 27 55N 15 26W
Ingenio Santa Ana, *Argentina* **94 B2** 27 25S 65 40W
Ingersoll, *Canada* **78 C4** 43 4N 80 55W
Ingham, *Australia* **62 B4** 18 43S 146 10 E
Ingleborough, *U.K.* **10 C5** 54 10N 2 22W
Inglewood, *Queens., Australia* **63 D5** 28 25S 151 2 E
Inglewood, *Vic., Australia* **63 F3** 36 29S 143 53 E
Inglewood, *N.Z.* **59 H5** 39 9S 174 14 E
Inglewood, *U.S.A.* **85 M8** 33 58N 118 21W
Ingólfshöfði, *Iceland* **8 E5** 63 48N 16 39W
Ingolstadt, *Germany* **16 D6** 48 46N 11 26 E
Ingomar, *U.S.A.* **82 C10** 46 35N 107 23W
Ingonish, *Canada* **71 C7** 46 42N 60 18W
Ingraj Bazar, *India* **43 G13** 24 58N 88 10 E
Ingrid Christensen Coast, *Antarctica* **5 C6** 69 30S 76 0 E
Ingulec = Inhulec, *Ukraine* **25 E5** 47 42N 33 14 E
Ingushetia □, *Russia* **25 E8** 43 20N 44 50 E
Ingwavuma, *S. Africa* **57 D5** 27 9S 31 59 E
Inhaca, I., *Mozam.* **57 D5** 26 1S 32 57 E
Inhafenga, *Mozam.* **57 C5** 20 36S 33 53 E
Inhambane, *Mozam.* **57 C6** 23 54S 35 30 E
Inhambane □, *Mozam.* **57 C5** 22 30S 34 20 E
Inhaminga, *Mozam.* **55 F4** 18 26S 35 0 E
Inharrime, *Mozam.* **57 C6** 24 30S 35 0 E
Inharrime →, *Mozam.* **57 C6** 24 30S 35 0 E
Inhulec, *Ukraine* **25 E5** 47 42N 33 14 E
Ining = Yining, *China* **26 E9** 43 58N 81 10 E
Inírida →, *Colombia* **92 C5** 3 55N 67 52W
Inishbofin, *Ireland* **13 C1** 53 37N 10 13W
Inisheer, *Ireland* **13 C2** 53 3N 9 32W
Inishfree B., *Ireland* **13 A3** 55 4N 8 23W
Inishkea North, *Ireland* **13 B1** 54 9N 10 11W
Inishkea South, *Ireland* **13 B1** 54 7N 10 12W
Inishmaan, *Ireland* **13 C2** 53 5N 9 35W
Inishmore, *Ireland* **13 C2** 53 8N 9 45W
Inishowen Pen., *Ireland* **13 A4** 55 14N 7 15W
Inishshark, *Ireland* **13 C1** 53 37N 10 16W
Inishturk, *Ireland* **13 C1** 53 42N 10 7W
Inishvickillane, *Ireland* **13 D1** 52 3N 10 37W
Injune, *Australia* **63 D4** 25 53S 148 32 E
Inklin →, *Canada* **72 B2** 58 50N 133 10W
Inle L., *Burma* **41 J20** 20 30N 96 58 E
Inlet, *U.S.A.* **79 C10** 43 45N 74 48W
Inn →, *Austria* **16 D7** 48 35N 13 28 E
Innamincka, *Australia* **63 D3** 27 44S 140 46 E
Inner Hebrides, *U.K.* **12 E2** 57 0N 6 30W
Inner Mongolia = Nei Monggol Zizhiqu □, *China* **34 D7** 42 0N 112 0 E
Inner Sound, *U.K.* **12 D3** 57 30N 5 55W
Innerkip, *Canada* **78 C4** 43 13N 80 42W
Innetalling I., *Canada* **70 A4** 56 0N 79 0W
Innisfail, *Australia* **62 B4** 17 33S 146 5 E
Innisfail, *Canada* **72 C6** 52 0N 113 57W
In'no-shima, *Japan* **31 G6** 34 19N 133 10 E
Innsbruck, *Austria* **16 E6** 47 16N 11 23 E
Inny →, *Ireland* **13 C4** 53 30N 7 50W
Inongo, *Dem. Rep. of the Congo* **52 E3** 1 55S 18 30 E
Inoucdjouac = Inukjuak, *Canada* **69 C12** 58 25N 78 15W
Inowrocław, *Poland* **17 B10** 52 50N 18 12 E
Inpundong, *N. Korea* **35 D14** 41 25N 126 34 E
Inscription, C., *Australia* **61 E1** 25 29S 112 59 E
Insein, *Burma* **41 L20** 16 50N 96 5 E
Inta, *Russia* **24 A11** 66 5N 60 8 E
Intendente Alvear, *Argentina* **94 D3** 35 12S 63 32W
Interlaken, *Switz.* **18 C7** 46 41N 7 50 E
Interlaken, *U.S.A.* **79 D8** 42 37N 76 44W
International Falls, *U.S.A.* **80 A8** 48 36N 93 25W
Intiyaco, *Argentina* **94 B3** 28 43S 60 5W
Inukjuak, *Canada* **69 C12** 58 25N 78 15W
Inútil, B., *Chile* **96 G2** 53 30S 70 15W
Inuvik, *Canada* **68 B6** 68 16N 133 40W
Inveraray, *U.K.* **12 E3** 56 14N 5 5W
Inverbervie, *U.K.* **12 E6** 56 51N 2 17W
Invercargill, *N.Z.* **59 M2** 46 24S 168 24 E
Inverclyde □, *U.K.* **12 F4** 55 55N 4 49W
Inverell, *Australia* **63 D5** 29 45S 151 8 E
Invergordon, *U.K.* **12 D4** 57 41N 4 10W
Inverloch, *Australia* **63 F4** 38 38S 145 45 E
Invermere, *Canada* **72 C5** 50 30N 116 2W
Inverness, *Canada* **71 C7** 46 15N 61 19W
Inverness, *U.K.* **12 D4** 57 29N 4 13W
Inverness, *U.S.A.* **77 L4** 28 50N 82 20W
Inverurie, *U.K.* **12 D6** 57 17N 2 23W
Investigator Group, *Australia* **63 E1** 34 45S 134 20 E
Investigator Str., *Australia* **63 F2** 35 30S 137 0 E
Inya, *Russia* **26 D9** 50 28N 86 37 E
Inyanga, *Zimbabwe* **55 F3** 18 12S 32 40 E
Inyangani, *Zimbabwe* **55 F3** 18 5S 32 50 E
Inyantue, *Zimbabwe* **55 F2** 18 30S 26 40 E
Inyo Mts., *U.S.A.* **84 J9** 36 40N 118 0W
Inyokern, *U.S.A.* **85 K9** 35 39N 117 49W
Inza, *Russia* **24 D8** 53 55N 46 25 E
Iō-Jima, *Japan* **31 J5** 30 48N 130 18 E
Ioánnina, *Greece* **21 E9** 39 42N 20 47 E
Iola, *U.S.A.* **81 G7** 37 55N 95 24W
Iona, *U.K.* **12 E2** 56 20N 6 25W
Ione, *U.S.A.* **84 G6** 38 21N 120 56W
Ionia, *U.S.A.* **76 D3** 42 59N 85 4W
Ionian Is. = Iónioi Nísoi, *Greece* **21 E9** 38 40N 20 0 E
Ionian Sea, *Medit. S.* **21 E7** 37 30N 17 30 E
Iónioi Nísoi, *Greece* **21 E9** 38 40N 20 0 E
Íos, *Greece* **21 F11** 36 41N 25 20 E
Iowa □, *U.S.A.* **80 D8** 42 18N 93 30W
Iowa →, *U.S.A.* **80 E9** 41 10N 91 1W
Iowa City, *U.S.A.* **80 E9** 41 40N 91 32W
Iowa Falls, *U.S.A.* **80 D8** 42 31N 93 16W
Iowa Park, *U.S.A.* **81 J5** 33 57N 98 40W
Ipala, *Tanzania* **54 C3** 4 30S 32 52 E
Ipameri, *Brazil* **93 G9** 17 44S 48 9W
Ipatinga, *Brazil* **93 G10** 19 32S 42 30W
Ipiales, *Colombia* **92 C3** 0 50N 77 37W
Ipin = Yibin, *China* **32 D5** 28 45N 104 32 E
Ipixuna, *Brazil* **92 E4** 7 0S 71 40W
Ipoh, *Malaysia* **39 K3** 4 35N 101 5 E
Ippy, *C.A.R.* **52 C4** 6 5N 21 7 E
İpsala, *Turkey* **21 D12** 40 55N 26 23 E
Ipswich, *Australia* **63 D5** 27 35S 152 40 E
Ipswich, *U.K.* **11 E9** 52 4N 1 10 E
Ipswich, *Mass., U.S.A.* **79 D14** 42 41N 70 50W
Ipswich, *S. Dak., U.S.A.* **80 C5** 45 27N 99 2W
Ipu, *Brazil* **93 D10** 4 23S 40 44W
Iqaluit, *Canada* **69 B13** 63 44N 68 31W
Iquique, *Chile* **92 H4** 20 19S 70 5W
Iquitos, *Peru* **92 D4** 3 45S 73 10W
Irabu-Jima, *Japan* **31 M2** 24 50N 125 10 E
Iracoubo, *Fr. Guiana* **93 B8** 5 30N 53 10W
Īrafshān, *Iran* **45 E9** 26 42N 61 56 E
Iráklion, *Greece* **23 D7** 35 20N 25 12 E
Iráklion □, *Greece* **23 D7** 35 10N 25 10 E
Irala, *Paraguay* **95 B5** 25 55S 54 35W
Iran ■, *Asia* **45 C7** 33 0N 53 0 E
Iran, Gunung-Gunung, *Malaysia* **36 D4** 2 20N 114 50 E
Iran, Plateau of, *Asia* **28 F9** 32 0N 55 0 E
Iran Ra. = Iran, Gunung-Gunung, *Malaysia* **36 D4** 2 20N 114 50 E
Īrānshahr, *Iran* **45 E9** 27 15N 60 40 E
Irapuato, *Mexico* **86 C4** 20 40N 101 30W
Iraq ■, *Asia* **44 C5** 33 0N 44 0 E
Irati, *Brazil* **95 B5** 25 25S 50 38W
Irbid, *Jordan* **47 C4** 32 35N 35 48 E
Irbid □, *Jordan* **47 C5** 32 15N 36 35 E
Ireland ■, *Europe* **13 C4** 53 50N 7 52W
Irhyangdong, *N. Korea* **35 D15** 41 15N 129 30 E
Iri, *S. Korea* **35 G14** 35 59N 127 0 E
Irian Jaya □, *Indonesia* **37 E9** 4 0S 137 0 E
Iringa, *Tanzania* **54 D4** 7 48S 35 43 E
Iringa □, *Tanzania* **54 D4** 7 48S 35 43 E
Iriomote-Jima, *Japan* **31 M1** 24 19N 123 48 E
Iriona, *Honduras* **88 C2** 15 57N 85 11W
Iriri →, *Brazil* **93 D8** 3 52S 52 37W
Irish Republic ■, *Europe* **13 C3** 53 0N 8 0W
Irish Sea, *U.K.* **10 D3** 53 38N 4 48W
Irkutsk, *Russia* **27 D11** 52 18N 104 20 E
Irma, *Canada* **73 C6** 52 55N 111 14W
Irō-Zaki, *Japan* **31 G9** 34 36N 138 51 E
Iron Baron, *Australia* **63 E2** 32 58S 137 11 E
Iron Gate = Portile de Fier, *Europe* **17 F12** 44 44N 22 30 E
Iron Knob, *Australia* **63 E2** 32 46S 137 8 E
Iron Mountain, *U.S.A.* **76 C1** 45 49N 88 4W
Iron River, *U.S.A.* **80 B10** 46 6N 88 39W
Irondequoit, *U.S.A.* **78 C7** 43 13N 77 35W
Ironstone Kopje, *Botswana* **56 D3** 25 17S 24 5 E
Ironton, *Mo., U.S.A.* **81 G9** 37 36N 90 38W
Ironton, *Ohio, U.S.A.* **76 F4** 38 32N 82 41W
Ironwood, *U.S.A.* **80 B9** 46 27N 90 9W
Iroquois, *Canada* **79 B9** 44 51N 75 19W
Iroquois Falls, *Canada* **70 C3** 48 46N 80 41W
Irpin, *Ukraine* **17 C16** 50 30N 30 15 E
Irrara Cr. →, *Australia* **63 D4** 29 35S 145 31 E
Irrawaddy □, *Burma* **41 L19** 17 0N 95 0 E
Irrawaddy →, *Burma* **41 M19** 15 50N 95 6 E
Irricana, *Canada* **72 C6** 51 19N 113 37W
Irtysh →, *Russia* **26 C7** 61 4N 68 52 E
Irumu, *Dem. Rep. of the Congo* **54 B2** 1 32N 29 53 E
Irún, *Spain* **19 A5** 43 20N 1 52W
Irunea = Pamplona, *Spain* **19 A5** 42 48N 1 38W
Irvine, *Canada* **73 D6** 49 57N 110 16W
Irvine, *U.K.* **12 F4** 55 37N 4 41W
Irvine, *Calif., U.S.A.* **85 M9** 33 41N 117 46W
Irvine, *Ky., U.S.A.* **76 G4** 37 42N 83 58W
Irvinestown, *U.K.* **13 B4** 54 28N 7 39W
Irving, *U.S.A.* **81 J6** 32 49N 96 56W
Irvona, *U.S.A.* **78 F6** 40 46N 78 33W
Irwin →, *Australia* **61 E1** 29 15S 114 54 E
Irymple, *Australia* **63 E3** 34 14S 142 8 E
Isa Khel, *Pakistan* **42 C4** 32 41N 71 17 E
Isaac →, *Australia* **62 C4** 22 55S 149 20 E
Isabel, *U.S.A.* **80 C4** 45 24N 101 26W
Isabela, I., *Mexico* **86 C3** 21 51N 105 55W
Isabelia, Cord., *Nic.* **88 D2** 13 30N 85 25W
Isabella, *Phil.* **37 C6** 6 40N 122 10 E
Isabella Ra., *Australia* **60 D3** 21 0S 121 4 E
Ísafjarðardjúp, *Iceland* **8 C2** 66 10N 23 0W
Ísafjörður, *Iceland* **8 C2** 66 5N 23 9W
Isagarh, *India* **42 G7** 24 48N 77 51 E
Isahaya, *Japan* **31 H5** 32 52N 130 2 E
Isaka, *Tanzania* **54 C3** 3 56S 32 59 E
Isan →, *India* **43 F9** 26 51N 80 7 E
Isana = Içana →, *Brazil* **92 C5** 0 26N 67 19W
Isar →, *Germany* **16 D7** 48 48N 12 57 E
Íschia, *Italy* **20 D5** 40 44N 13 57 E
Isdell →, *Australia* **60 C3** 16 27S 124 51 E
Ise, *Japan* **31 G8** 34 25N 136 45 E
Ise-Wan, *Japan* **31 G8** 34 43N 136 43 E
Iseramagazi, *Tanzania* **54 C3** 4 37S 32 10 E
Isère →, *France* **18 D6** 44 59N 4 51 E
Isérnia, *Italy* **20 D6** 41 36N 14 14 E
Isfahan = Eşfahān, *Iran* **45 C6** 32 39N 51 43 E
Ishigaki-Shima, *Japan* **31 M2** 24 20N 124 10 E
Ishikari-Gawa →, *Japan* **30 C10** 43 15N 141 23 E
Ishikari-Sammyaku, *Japan* **30 C11** 43 30N 143 0 E
Ishikari-Wan, *Japan* **30 C10** 43 25N 141 1 E
Ishikawa □, *Japan* **31 F8** 36 30N 136 30 E
Ishim, *Russia* **26 D7** 56 10N 69 30 E
Ishim →, *Russia* **26 D8** 57 45N 71 10 E
Ishinomaki, *Japan* **30 E10** 38 32N 141 20 E
Ishioka, *Japan* **31 F10** 36 11N 140 16 E
Ishkuman, *Pakistan* **43 A5** 36 30N 73 50 E
Ishpeming, *U.S.A.* **76 B2** 46 29N 87 40W
Isil Kul, *Russia* **26 D8** 54 55N 71 16 E
Isiolo, *Kenya* **54 B4** 0 24N 37 33 E
Isiro, *Dem. Rep. of the Congo* **54 B2** 2 53N 27 40 E
Isisford, *Australia* **62 C3** 24 15S 144 21 E
İskenderun, *Turkey* **25 G6** 36 32N 36 10 E
İskenderun Körfezi, *Turkey* **25 G6** 36 40N 35 50 E
Iskŭr →, *Bulgaria* **21 C11** 43 45N 24 25 E
Iskut →, *Canada* **72 B2** 56 45N 131 49W
Isla →, *U.K.* **12 E5** 56 32N 3 20W
Isla Vista, *U.S.A.* **85 L7** 34 25N 119 53W
Islam Headworks, *Pakistan* **42 E5** 29 49N 72 33 E
Islamabad, *Pakistan* **42 C5** 33 40N 73 10 E
Islamgarh, *Pakistan* **42 F4** 27 51N 70 48 E
Islamkot, *Pakistan* **42 G4** 24 42N 70 13 E
Islampur, *India* **43 G11** 25 9N 85 12 E
Island L., *Canada* **73 C10** 53 47N 94 25W
Island Lagoon, *Australia* **63 E2** 31 30S 136 40 E
Island Pond, *U.S.A.* **79 B13** 44 49N 71 53W
Islands, B. of, *Canada* **71 C8** 49 11N 58 15W
Islay, *U.K.* **12 F2** 55 46N 6 10W
Isle →, *France* **18 D3** 44 55N 0 15W
Isle aux Morts, *Canada* **71 C8** 47 35N 59 0W
Isle of Wight □, *U.K.* **11 G6** 50 41N 1 17W
Isle Royale, *U.S.A.* **80 B10** 48 0N 88 54W
Isle Royale National Park, *U.S.A.* **80 B10** 48 0N 88 55W
Isleton, *U.S.A.* **84 G5** 38 10N 121 37W
Ismail = Izmayil, *Ukraine* **17 F15** 45 22N 28 46 E
Ismâ'ilîya, *Egypt* **51 B12** 30 37N 32 18 E
Isogstalo, *India* **43 B8** 34 15N 78 46 E
Isparta, *Turkey* **25 G5** 37 47N 30 30 E
Íspica, *Italy* **20 F6** 36 47N 14 55 E
Israel ■, *Asia* **47 D3** 32 0N 34 50 E
Issoire, *France* **18 D5** 45 32N 3 15 E
Issyk-Kul = Ysyk-Köl, *Kyrgyzstan* **28 E11** 42 26N 76 12 E
Issyk-Kul, Ozero = Ysyk-Köl, Ozero, *Kyrgyzstan* **26 E8** 42 25N 77 15 E
İstanbul, *Turkey* **21 D13** 41 0N 29 0 E
İstanbul Boğazı, *Turkey* **21 D13** 41 10N 29 10 E
Istiaía, *Greece* **21 E10** 38 57N 23 9 E
Istokpoga, L., *U.S.A.* **77 M5** 27 23N 81 17W
Istra, *Croatia* **16 F7** 45 10N 14 0 E
Istres, *France* **18 E6** 43 31N 4 59 E
Istria = Istra, *Croatia* **16 F7** 45 10N 14 0 E
Itá, *Paraguay* **94 B4** 25 29S 57 21W
Itaberaba, *Brazil* **93 F10** 12 32S 40 18W
Itabira, *Brazil* **93 G10** 19 37S 43 13W
Itabirito, *Brazil* **95 A7** 20 15S 43 48W
Itabuna, *Brazil* **93 F11** 14 48S 39 16W
Itacaunas →, *Brazil* **93 E9** 5 21S 49 8W
Itacoatiara, *Brazil* **92 D7** 3 8S 58 25W
Itaipú, Représa de, *Brazil* **95 B5** 25 30S 54 30W
Itaituba, *Brazil* **93 D7** 4 10S 55 50W
Itajaí, *Brazil* **95 B6** 27 50S 48 39W
Itajubá, *Brazil* **95 A6** 22 24S 45 30W
Itaka, *Tanzania* **55 D3** 8 50S 32 49 E
Italy ■, *Europe* **20 C5** 42 0N 13 0 E
Itamaraju, *Brazil* **93 G11** 17 5S 39 31W
Itampolo, *Madag.* **57 C7** 24 41S 43 57 E
Itapecuru-Mirim, *Brazil* **93 D10** 3 24S 44 20W
Itaperuna, *Brazil* **95 A7** 21 10S 41 54W
Itapetininga, *Brazil* **95 A6** 23 36S 48 7W
Itapeva, *Brazil* **95 A6** 23 59S 48 59W
Itapicuru →, *Bahia, Brazil* **93 F11** 11 47S 37 32W
Itapicuru →, *Maranhão, Brazil* **93 D10** 2 52S 44 12W
Itapipoca, *Brazil* **93 D11** 3 30S 39 35W
Itapuá □, *Paraguay* **95 B4** 26 40S 55 40W
Itaquari, *Brazil* **95 A7** 20 20S 40 25W
Itaquí, *Brazil* **94 B4** 29 8S 56 30W
Itararé, *Brazil* **95 A6** 24 6S 49 23W
Itarsi, *India* **42 H7** 22 36N 77 51 E
Itatí, *Argentina* **94 B4** 27 16S 58 15W
Itchen →, *U.K.* **11 G6** 50 55N 1 22W
Itezhi Tezhi, L., *Zambia* **55 F2** 15 30S 25 30 E
Ithaca = Itháki, *Greece* **21 E9** 38 25N 20 40 E
Ithaca, *U.S.A.* **79 D8** 42 27N 76 30W
Itháki, *Greece* **21 E9** 38 25N 20 40 E
Itiquira →, *Brazil* **93 G7** 17 18S 56 44W
Ito, *Japan* **31 G9** 34 58N 139 5 E
Ito Aba I., *S. China Sea* **36 B4** 10 23N 114 21 E
Itoigawa, *Japan* **31 F8** 37 2N 137 51 E
Itonamas →, *Bolivia* **92 F6** 12 28S 64 24W
Ittoqqortoormiit = Scoresbysund, *Greenland* **4 B6** 70 20N 23 0W
Itu, *Brazil* **95 A6** 23 17S 47 15W
Ituiutaba, *Brazil* **93 G9** 19 0S 49 25W
Itumbiara, *Brazil* **93 G9** 18 20S 49 10W
Ituna, *Canada* **73 C8** 51 10N 103 24W
Itunge Port, *Tanzania* **55 D3** 9 40S 33 55 E
Iturbe, *Argentina* **94 A2** 23 0S 65 25W
Ituri →, *Dem. Rep. of the Congo* **54 B2** 1 40N 27 1 E
Iturup, Ostrov, *Russia* **27 E15** 45 0N 148 0 E
Ituxi →, *Brazil* **92 E6** 7 18S 64 51W
Ituyuro →, *Argentina* **94 A3** 22 40S 63 50W
Itzehoe, *Germany* **16 B5** 53 55N 9 31 E
Ivaí →, *Brazil* **95 A5** 23 18S 53 42W
Ivalo, *Finland* **8 B22** 68 38N 27 35 E
Ivalojoki →, *Finland* **8 B22** 68 40N 27 40 E
Ivanava, *Belarus* **17 B13** 52 7N 25 29 E
Ivanhoe, *Australia* **63 E3** 32 56S 144 20 E
Ivanhoe, *Calif., U.S.A.* **84 J7** 36 23N 119 13W
Ivanhoe, *Minn., U.S.A.* **80 C6** 44 28N 96 15W
Ivano-Frankivsk, *Ukraine* **17 D13** 48 40N 24 40 E
Ivano-Frankovsk = Ivano-Frankivsk, *Ukraine* **17 D13** 48 40N 24 40 E
Ivanovo = Ivanava, *Belarus* **17 B13** 52 7N 25 29 E
Ivanovo, *Russia* **24 C7** 57 5N 41 0 E
Ivato, *Madag.* **57 C8** 20 37S 47 10 E
Ivatsevichy, *Belarus* **17 B13** 52 43N 25 21 E
Ivdel, *Russia* **24 B11** 60 42N 60 24 E
Ivindo →, *Gabon* **52 D2** 0 9S 12 9 E
Ivinheima →, *Brazil* **95 A5** 23 14S 53 42W
Ivinhema, *Brazil* **95 A5** 22 10S 53 37W
Ivohibe, *Madag.* **57 C8** 22 31S 46 57 E
Ivory Coast, *Africa* **50 H4** 5 0N 5 0W
Ivory Coast ■, *Africa* **50 G4** 7 30N 5 0W
Ivrea, *Italy* **18 D7** 45 28N 7 52 E
Ivujivik, *Canada* **69 B12** 62 24N 77 55W
Ivybridge, *U.K.* **11 G4** 50 23N 3 56W
Iwaizumi, *Japan* **30 E10** 39 50N 141 45 E
Iwaki, *Japan* **31 F10** 37 3N 140 55 E
Iwakuni, *Japan* **31 G6** 34 15N 132 8 E
Iwamizawa, *Japan* **30 C10** 43 12N 141 46 E
Iwanai, *Japan* **30 C10** 42 58N 140 30 E
Iwata, *Japan* **31 G8** 34 42N 137 51 E
Iwate □, *Japan* **30 E10** 39 30N 141 30 E
Iwate-San, *Japan* **30 E10** 39 51N 141 0 E
Iwo, *Nigeria* **50 G6** 7 39N 4 9 E
Ixiamas, *Bolivia* **92 F5** 13 50S 68 5W
Ixopo, *S. Africa* **57 E5** 30 11S 30 5 E
Ixtepec, *Mexico* **87 D5** 16 32N 95 10W
Ixtlán del Río, *Mexico* **86 C4** 21 5N 104 21W
Iyo, *Japan* **31 H6** 33 45N 132 45 E
Izabal, L. de, *Guatemala* **88 C2** 15 30N 89 10W
Izamal, *Mexico* **87 C7** 20 56N 89 1W
Izena-Shima, *Japan* **31 L3** 26 56N 127 56 E
Izhevsk, *Russia* **24 C9** 56 51N 53 14 E
Izhma →, *Russia* **24 A9** 65 19N 52 54 E
Izmayil, *Ukraine* **17 F15** 45 22N 28 46 E
İzmir, *Turkey* **21 E12** 38 25N 27 8 E
İzmit = Kocaeli, *Turkey* **25 F4** 40 45N 29 50 E
İznik Gölü, *Turkey* **21 D13** 40 27N 29 30 E
Izra, *Syria* **47 C5** 32 51N 36 15 E
Izu-Shotō, *Japan* **31 G10** 34 30N 140 0 E
Izúcar de Matamoros, *Mexico* **87 D5** 18 36N 98 28W
Izumi-sano, *Japan* **31 G7** 34 23N 135 18 E
Izumo, *Japan* **31 G6** 35 20N 132 46 E
Izyaslav, *Ukraine* **17 C14** 50 5N 26 50 E

J

Jabalpur, *India* **43 H8** 23 9N 79 58 E
Jabbūl, *Syria* **44 B3** 36 4N 37 30 E
Jabiru, *Australia* **60 B5** 12 40S 132 53 E
Jablah, *Syria* **44 C3** 35 20N 36 0 E
Jablonec nad Nisou, *Czech Rep.* **16 C8** 50 43N 15 10 E
Jaboatão, *Brazil* **93 E11** 8 7S 35 1W
Jaboticabal, *Brazil* **95 A6** 21 15S 48 17W
Jaca, *Spain* **19 A5** 42 35N 0 33W
Jacareí, *Brazil* **95 A6** 23 20S 46 0W
Jacarèzinho, *Brazil* **95 A6** 23 5S 49 58W
Jackman, *U.S.A.* **77 C10** 45 35N 70 17W
Jacksboro, *U.S.A.* **81 J5** 33 14N 98 15W
Jackson, *Ala., U.S.A.* **77 K2** 31 31N 87 53W
Jackson, *Calif., U.S.A.* **84 G6** 38 21N 120 46W
Jackson, *Ky., U.S.A.* **76 G4** 37 33N 83 23W
Jackson, *Mich., U.S.A.* **76 D3** 42 15N 84 24W
Jackson, *Minn., U.S.A.* **80 D7** 43 37N 95 1W
Jackson, *Miss., U.S.A.* **81 J9** 32 18N 90 12W
Jackson, *Mo., U.S.A.* **81 G10** 37 23N 89 40W
Jackson, *N.H., U.S.A.* **79 B13** 44 10N 71 11W
Jackson, *Ohio, U.S.A.* **76 F4** 39 3N 82 39W
Jackson, *Tenn., U.S.A.* **77 H1** 35 37N 88 49W
Jackson, *Wyo., U.S.A.* **82 E8** 43 29N 110 46W
Jackson B., *N.Z.* **59 K2** 43 58S 168 42 E
Jackson L., *U.S.A.* **82 E8** 43 52N 110 36W
Jacksons, *N.Z.* **59 K3** 42 46S 171 32 E
Jackson's Arm, *Canada* **71 C8** 49 52N 56 47W
Jacksonville, *Ala., U.S.A.* **77 J3** 33 49N 85 46W
Jacksonville, *Ark., U.S.A.* **81 H8** 34 52N 92 7W
Jacksonville, *Calif., U.S.A.* **84 H6** 37 52N 120 24W
Jacksonville, *Fla., U.S.A.* **77 K5** 30 20N 81 39W
Jacksonville, *Ill., U.S.A.* **80 F9** 39 44N 90 14W
Jacksonville, *N.C., U.S.A.* **77 H7** 34 45N 77 26W
Jacksonville, *Tex., U.S.A.* **81 K7** 31 58N 95 17W
Jacksonville Beach, *U.S.A.* **77 K5** 30 17N 81 24W
Jacmel, *Haiti* **89 C5** 18 14N 72 32W
Jacob Lake, *U.S.A.* **83 H7** 36 43N 112 13W
Jacobabad, *Pakistan* **42 E3** 28 20N 68 29 E
Jacobina, *Brazil* **93 F10** 11 11S 40 30W
Jacques Cartier, Dét. de, *Canada* **71 C7** 50 0N 63 30W
Jacques-Cartier, Mt., *Canada* **71 C6** 48 57N 66 0W
Jacques Cartier, Parc Prov., *Canada* **71 C5** 47 15N 71 33W
Jacuí →, *Brazil* **95 C5** 30 2S 51 15W
Jacumba, *U.S.A.* **85 N10** 32 37N 116 11W
Jacundá →, *Brazil* **93 D8** 1 57S 50 26W
Jadotville = Likasi, *Dem. Rep. of the Congo* **55 E2** 10 55S 26 48 E
Jaén, *Peru* **92 E3** 5 25S 78 40W
Jaén, *Spain* **19 D4** 37 44N 3 43W
Jafarabad, *India* **42 J4** 20 52N 71 22 E
Jaffa = Tel Aviv-Yafo, *Israel* **47 C3** 32 4N 34 48 E
Jaffa, C., *Australia* **63 F2** 36 58S 139 40 E
Jaffna, *Sri Lanka* **40 Q12** 9 45N 80 2 E
Jaffrey, *U.S.A.* **79 D12** 42 49N 72 2W
Jagadhri, *India* **42 D7** 30 10N 77 20 E
Jagadishpur, *India* **43 G11** 25 30N 84 21 E
Jagdalpur, *India* **41 K13** 19 3N 82 0 E
Jagersfontein, *S. Africa* **56 D4** 29 44S 25 27 E
Jaghīn →, *Iran* **45 E8** 27 17N 57 13 E
Jagodina, *Serbia, Yug.* **21 C9** 44 5N 21 15 E
Jagraon, *India* **40 D9** 30 50N 75 25 E
Jagtial, *India* **40 K11** 18 50N 79 0 E
Jaguariaíva, *Brazil* **95 A6** 24 10S 49 50W
Jaguaribe →, *Brazil* **93 D11** 4 25S 37 45W
Jagüey Grande, *Cuba* **88 B3** 22 35N 81 7W
Jahanabad, *India* **43 G11** 25 13N 84 59 E
Jahazpur, *India* **42 G6** 25 37N 75 17 E
Jahrom, *Iran* **45 D7** 28 30N 53 31 E
Jaijon, *India* **42 D7** 31 21N 76 9 E
Jailolo, *Indonesia* **37 D7** 1 5N 127 30 E
Jailolo, Selat, *Indonesia* **37 D7** 0 5N 129 5 E
Jaipur, *India* **42 F6** 27 0N 75 50 E
Jais, *India* **43 F9** 26 15N 81 32 E
Jaisalmer, *India* **42 F4** 26 55N 70 54 E
Jaisinghnagar, *India* **43 H8** 23 38N 78 34 E
Jaitaran, *India* **42 F5** 26 12N 73 56 E
Jaithari, *India* **43 H8** 23 14N 78 37 E
Jājarm, *Iran* **45 B8** 36 58N 56 27 E
Jakam →, *India* **42 H6** 23 54N 74 13 E
Jakarta, *Indonesia* **37 G12** 6 9S 106 49 E
Jakhal, *India* **42 E6** 29 48N 75 50 E
Jakhau, *India* **42 H3** 23 13N 68 43 E
Jakobstad = Pietarsaari, *Finland* **8 E20** 63 40N 22 43 E
Jal, *U.S.A.* **81 J3** 32 7N 103 12W
Jalalabad, *Afghan.* **42 B4** 34 30N 70 29 E
Jalalabad, *India* **43 F8** 27 41N 79 42 E
Jalalpur Jattan, *Pakistan* **42 C6** 32 38N 74 11 E
Jalama, *U.S.A.* **85 L6** 34 29N 120 29W
Jalapa, *Guatemala* **88 D2** 14 39N 89 59W
Jalapa Enríquez, *Mexico* **87 D5** 19 32N 96 55W
Jalasjärvi, *Finland* **9 E20** 62 29N 22 47 E
Jalaun, *India* **43 F8** 26 8N 79 25 E
Jaldhaka →, *Bangla.* **43 F13** 26 16N 89 16 E
Jalesar, *India* **42 F8** 27 29N 78 19 E
Jaleswar, *Nepal* **43 F11** 26 38N 85 48 E
Jalgaon, *Maharashtra, India* **40 J10** 21 2N 76 31 E
Jalgaon, *Maharashtra, India* **40 J9** 21 0N 75 42 E
Jalībah, *Iraq* **44 D5** 30 35N 46 32 E
Jalisco □, *Mexico* **86 D4** 20 0N 104 0W
Jalkot, *Pakistan* **43 B5** 35 14N 73 24 E
Jalna, *India* **40 K9** 19 48N 75 38 E
Jalón →, *Spain* **19 B5** 41 47N 1 4W
Jalor, *India* **42 G5** 25 21N 72 37 E
Jalpa, *Mexico* **86 C4** 21 38N 102 58W
Jalpaiguri, *India* **41 F16** 26 32N 88 46 E
Jaluit I., *Marshall Is.* **64 G8** 6 0N 169 30 E

Juruena

Jalūlā, *Iraq* 44 C5 34 16N 45 10 E
Jamaica ■, *W. Indies* 88 C4 18 10N 77 30W
Jamalpur, *Bangla.* 41 G16 24 52N 89 56 E
Jamalpur, *India* 43 G12 25 18N 86 28 E
Jamalpurganj, *India* 43 H13 23 2N 87 59 E
Jamanxim →, *Brazil* 93 D7 4 43S 56 18W
Jambi, *Indonesia* 36 E2 1 38S 103 30 E
Jambi □, *Indonesia* 36 E2 1 30S 102 30 E
Jambusar, *India* 42 H5 22 3N 72 51 E
James →, *S. Dak., U.S.A.* 80 D6 42 52N 97 18W
James →, *Va., U.S.A.* 76 G7 36 56N 76 27W
James B., *Canada* 70 B3 54 0N 80 0W
James Ranges, *Australia* 60 D5 24 10S 132 30 E
James Ross I., *Antarctica* 5 C18 63 58S 57 50W
Jamesabad, *Pakistan* 42 G3 25 17N 69 15 E
Jamestown, *Australia* 63 E2 33 10S 138 32 E
Jamestown, *S. Africa* 56 E4 31 6S 26 45 E
Jamestown, *N. Dak., U.S.A.* 80 B5 46 54N 98 42W
Jamestown, *N.Y., U.S.A.* 78 D5 42 6N 79 14W
Jamestown, *Pa., U.S.A.* 78 E4 41 29N 80 27W
Jamīlābād, *Iran* 45 C6 34 24N 48 28 E
Jamiltepec, *Mexico* 87 D5 16 17N 97 49W
Jamira →, *India* 43 J13 21 35N 88 28 E
Jamkhandi, *India* 40 L9 16 30N 75 15 E
Jammu, *India* 42 C6 32 43N 74 54 E
Jammu & Kashmir □, *India* 43 B7 34 25N 77 0 E
Jamnagar, *India* 42 H4 22 30N 70 6 E
Jamni →, *India* 43 G8 25 13N 78 35 E
Jampur, *Pakistan* 42 E4 29 39N 70 40 E
Jamrud, *Pakistan* 42 C4 33 59N 71 24 E
Jämsä, *Finland* 9 F21 61 53N 25 10 E
Jamshedpur, *India* 43 H12 22 44N 86 12 E
Jamtara, *India* 43 H12 23 59N 86 49 E
Jämtland, *Sweden* 8 E15 63 31N 14 0 E
Jan L., *Canada* 73 C8 54 56N 102 55W
Jan Mayen, *Arctic* 4 B7 71 0N 9 0W
Janakkala, *Finland* 9 F21 60 54N 24 36 E
Janaúba, *Brazil* 93 G10 15 48S 43 19W
Jand, *Pakistan* 42 C5 33 30N 72 6 E
Jandaq, *Iran* 45 C7 34 3N 54 22 E
Jandia, *Canary Is.* 22 F5 28 6N 14 21W
Jandia, Pta. de, *Canary Is.* 22 F5 28 3N 14 31W
Jandola, *Pakistan* 42 C4 32 20N 70 9 E
Jandowae, *Australia* 63 D5 26 45S 151 7 E
Janesville, *U.S.A.* 80 D10 42 41N 89 1W
Janghai, *India* 43 G10 25 33N 82 19 E
Janīn, *West Bank* 47 C4 32 28N 35 18 E
Janjgir, *India* 43 J10 22 1N 82 34 E
Janos, *Mexico* 86 A3 30 45N 108 10W
Januária, *Brazil* 93 G10 15 25S 44 25W
Janubio, *Canary Is.* 22 F6 28 56N 13 50W
Jaora, *India* 42 H6 23 40N 75 10 E
Japan ■, *Asia* 31 G8 36 0N 136 0 E
Japan, Sea of, *Asia* 30 E7 40 0N 135 0 E
Japan Trench, *Pac. Oc.* 28 F18 32 0N 142 0 E
Japen = Yapen, *Indonesia* 37 E9 1 50S 136 0 E
Japla, *India* 43 G11 24 33N 84 1 E
Japurá →, *Brazil* 92 D5 3 8S 65 46W
Jaquarão, *Brazil* 95 C5 32 34S 53 23W
Jaqué, *Panama* 88 E4 7 27N 78 8W
Jarābulus, *Syria* 44 B3 36 49N 38 1 E
Jarama →, *Spain* 19 B4 40 24N 3 32W
Jaranwala, *Pakistan* 42 D5 31 15N 73 26 E
Jarash, *Jordan* 47 C4 32 17N 35 54 E
Jardim, *Brazil* 94 A4 21 28S 56 2W
Jardines de la Reina, Arch. de los, *Cuba* 88 B4 20 50N 78 50W
Jargalang, *China* 35 C12 43 5N 122 55 E
Jargalant = Hovd, *Mongolia* 32 B4 48 2N 91 37 E
Jari →, *Brazil* 93 D8 1 9S 51 54W
Jarīr, W. al →, *Si. Arabia* 44 E4 25 38N 42 30 E
Jarosław, *Poland* 17 C12 50 2N 22 42 E
Jarrahdale, *Australia* 61 F2 32 24S 116 5 E
Jarrahi →, *Iran* 45 D6 30 49N 48 48 E
Jarres, Plaine des, *Laos* 38 C4 19 27N 103 10 E
Jartai, *China* 34 E3 39 45N 105 48 E
Jarud Qi, *China* 35 B11 44 28N 120 50 E
Järvenpää, *Finland* 9 F21 60 29N 25 5 E
Jarvis, *Canada* 78 D4 42 53N 80 6W
Jarvis I., *Pac. Oc.* 65 H12 0 15S 159 55W
Jarwa, *India* 43 F10 27 38N 82 30 E
Jasdan, *India* 42 H4 22 2N 71 12 E
Jashpurnagar, *India* 43 H11 22 54N 84 9 E
Jasidih, *India* 43 G12 24 31N 86 39 E
Jāsimīyah, *Iraq* 44 C5 33 45N 44 41 E
Jasin, *Malaysia* 39 L4 2 20N 102 26 E
Jāsk, *Iran* 45 E8 25 38N 57 45 E
Jasło, *Poland* 17 D11 49 45N 21 30 E
Jaso, *India* 43 G9 24 30N 80 29 E
Jasper, *Alta., Canada* 72 C5 52 55N 118 5W
Jasper, *Ont., Canada* 79 B9 44 52N 75 57W
Jasper, *Ala., U.S.A.* 77 J2 33 50N 87 17W
Jasper, *Fla., U.S.A.* 77 K4 30 31N 82 57W
Jasper, *Ind., U.S.A.* 76 F2 38 24N 86 56W
Jasper, *Tex., U.S.A.* 81 K8 30 56N 94 1W
Jasper Nat. Park, *Canada* 72 C5 52 50N 118 8W
Jasrasar, *India* 42 F5 27 43N 73 49 E
Jászberény, *Hungary* 17 E10 47 30N 19 55 E
Jataí, *Brazil* 93 G8 17 58S 51 48W
Jati, *Pakistan* 42 G3 24 20N 68 19 E
Jatibarang, *Indonesia* 37 G13 6 28S 108 18 E
Jatinegara, *Indonesia* 37 G12 6 13S 106 52 E
Játiva = Xátiva, *Spain* 19 C5 38 59N 0 32W
Jaú, *Brazil* 95 A6 22 10S 48 30W
Jauja, *Peru* 92 F3 11 45S 75 15W
Jaunpur, *India* 43 G10 25 46N 82 44 E
Java = Jawa, *Indonesia* 37 G14 7 0S 110 0 E
Java Barat □, *Indonesia* 37 G12 7 0S 107 0 E
Java Sea, *Indonesia* 36 E3 4 35S 107 15 E
Java Tengah □, *Indonesia* 37 G14 7 0S 110 0 E
Java Timur □, *Indonesia* 37 G15 8 0S 113 0 E
Java Trench, *Ind. Oc.* 36 F3 9 0S 105 0 E
Javhlant = Uliastay, *Mongolia* 32 B4 47 56N 97 28 E
Jawa, *Indonesia* 37 G14 7 0S 110 0 E
Jawad, *India* 42 G6 24 36N 74 51 E
Jay Peak, *U.S.A.* 79 B12 44 55N 72 32W
Jaya, Puncak, *Indonesia* 37 E9 3 57S 137 17 E
Jayanti, *India* 41 F16 26 45N 89 40 E
Jayapura, *Indonesia* 37 E10 2 28S 140 38 E
Jayawijaya, Pegunungan, *Indonesia* 37 F9 5 0S 139 0 E
Jaynagar, *India* 41 F15 26 43N 86 9 E
Jayrūd, *Syria* 44 C3 33 49N 36 44 E
Jayton, *U.S.A.* 81 J4 33 15N 100 34W
Jāz Mūrīān, Hāmūn-e, *Iran* 45 E8 27 20N 58 55 E
Jazīreh-ye Shīf, *Iran* 45 D6 29 4N 50 54 E
Jazminal, *Mexico* 86 C4 24 56N 101 25W
Jazzīn, *Lebanon* 47 B4 33 31N 35 35 E
Jean, *U.S.A.* 85 K11 35 47N 115 20W
Jean Marie River, *Canada* 72 A4 61 32N 120 38W
Jean Rabel, *Haiti* 89 C5 19 50N 73 5W
Jeanerette, *U.S.A.* 81 L9 29 55N 91 40W
Jeanette, Ostrov = Zhannetty, Ostrov, *Russia* 27 B16 76 43N 158 0 E
Jeannette, *U.S.A.* 78 F5 40 20N 79 36W
Jebāl Bārez, Kūh-e, *Iran* 45 D8 28 30N 58 20 E
Jebel, Bahr el →, *Sudan* 51 G12 9 30N 30 25 E
Jedburgh, *U.K.* 12 F6 55 29N 2 33W
Jedda = Jiddah, *Si. Arabia* 46 C2 21 29N 39 10 E
Jeddore L., *Canada* 71 C8 48 3N 55 55W
Jędrzejów, *Poland* 17 C11 50 35N 20 15 E
Jefferson, *Iowa, U.S.A.* 80 D7 42 1N 94 23W
Jefferson, *Ohio, U.S.A.* 78 E4 41 44N 80 46W
Jefferson, *Tex., U.S.A.* 81 J7 32 46N 94 21W
Jefferson, Mt., *Nev., U.S.A.* 82 G5 38 51N 117 0W
Jefferson, Mt., *Oreg., U.S.A.* 82 D3 44 41N 121 48W
Jefferson City, *Mo., U.S.A.* 80 F8 38 34N 92 10W
Jefferson City, *Tenn., U.S.A.* 77 G4 36 7N 83 30W
Jeffersontown, *U.S.A.* 76 F3 38 12N 85 35W
Jeffersonville, *U.S.A.* 76 F3 38 17N 85 44W
Jeffrey City, *U.S.A.* 82 E10 42 30N 107 49W
Jega, *Nigeria* 50 F6 12 15N 4 23 E
Jēkabpils, *Latvia* 9 H21 56 29N 25 57 E
Jekyll I., *U.S.A.* 77 K5 31 4N 81 25W
Jelenia Góra, *Poland* 16 C8 50 50N 15 45 E
Jelgava, *Latvia* 9 H20 56 41N 23 49 E
Jemaja, *Indonesia* 39 L5 3 5N 105 45 E
Jemaluang, *Malaysia* 39 L4 2 16N 103 52 E
Jember, *Indonesia* 37 H15 8 11S 113 41 E
Jembongan, *Malaysia* 36 C5 6 45N 117 20 E
Jena, *Germany* 16 C6 50 54N 11 35 E
Jena, *U.S.A.* 81 K8 31 41N 92 8W
Jenkins, *U.S.A.* 76 G4 37 10N 82 38W
Jenner, *U.S.A.* 84 G3 38 27N 123 7W
Jennings, *U.S.A.* 81 K8 30 13N 92 40W
Jepara, *Indonesia* 37 G14 7 40S 109 14 E
Jeparit, *Australia* 63 F3 36 8S 142 1 E
Jequié, *Brazil* 93 F10 13 51S 40 5W
Jequitinhonha, *Brazil* 93 G10 16 30S 41 0W
Jequitinhonha →, *Brazil* 93 G11 15 51S 38 53W
Jerantut, *Malaysia* 39 L4 3 56N 102 22 E
Jérémie, *Haiti* 89 C5 18 40N 74 10W
Jerez, Punta, *Mexico* 87 C5 22 58N 97 40W
Jerez de García Salinas, *Mexico* 86 C4 22 39N 103 0W
Jerez de la Frontera, *Spain* 19 D2 36 41N 6 7W
Jerez de los Caballeros, *Spain* 19 C2 38 20N 6 45W
Jericho = El Arīḥā, *West Bank* 47 D4 31 52N 35 27 E
Jericho, *Australia* 62 C4 23 38S 146 6 E
Jerilderie, *Australia* 63 F4 35 20S 145 41 E
Jermyn, *U.S.A.* 79 E9 41 31N 75 31W
Jerome, *U.S.A.* 82 E6 42 44N 114 31W
Jerramungup, *Australia* 61 F2 33 55S 118 55 E
Jersey, *U.K.* 11 H5 49 11N 2 7W
Jersey City, *U.S.A.* 79 F10 40 44N 74 4W
Jersey Shore, *U.S.A.* 78 E7 41 12N 77 15W
Jerseyville, *U.S.A.* 80 F9 39 7N 90 20W
Jerusalem, *Israel* 47 D4 31 47N 35 10 E
Jervis B., *Australia* 63 F5 35 8S 150 46 E
Jervis Inlet, *Canada* 72 C4 50 0N 123 57W
Jesselton = Kota Kinabalu, *Malaysia* 36 C5 6 0N 116 4 E
Jessore, *Bangla.* 41 H16 23 10N 89 10 E
Jesup, *U.S.A.* 77 K5 31 36N 81 53W
Jesús Carranza, *Mexico* 87 D5 17 28N 95 1W
Jesús María, *Argentina* 94 C3 30 59S 64 5W
Jetmore, *U.S.A.* 81 F5 38 4N 99 54W
Jetpur, *India* 42 J4 21 45N 70 10 E
Jevnaker, *Norway* 9 F14 60 15N 10 26 E
Jewett, *U.S.A.* 78 F3 40 22N 81 2W
Jewett City, *U.S.A.* 79 E13 41 36N 72 0W
Jeyḥūnābād, *Iran* 45 C6 34 58N 48 59 E
Jeypore, *India* 41 K13 18 50N 82 38 E
Jha Jha, *India* 43 G12 24 46N 86 22 E
Jhabua, *India* 42 H6 22 46N 74 36 E
Jhajjar, *India* 42 E7 28 37N 76 42 E
Jhal, *Pakistan* 42 E2 28 17N 67 27 E
Jhal Jhao, *Pakistan* 40 F4 26 20N 65 35 E
Jhalawar, *India* 42 G7 24 40N 76 10 E
Jhalida, *India* 43 H11 23 22N 85 58 E
Jhalrapatan, *India* 42 G7 24 33N 76 10 E
Jhang Maghiana, *Pakistan* 42 D5 31 15N 72 22 E
Jhansi, *India* 43 G8 25 30N 78 36 E
Jhargram, *India* 43 H12 22 27N 86 59 E
Jharia, *India* 43 H12 23 45N 86 26 E
Jharsuguda, *India* 41 J14 21 56N 84 5 E
Jhelum, *Pakistan* 42 C5 33 0N 73 45 E
Jhelum →, *Pakistan* 42 D5 31 20N 72 10 E
Jhilmilli, *India* 43 H10 23 24N 82 51 E
Jhudo, *Pakistan* 42 G3 24 58N 69 18 E
Jhunjhunu, *India* 42 E6 28 10N 75 30 E
Ji-Paraná, *Brazil* 92 F6 10 52S 62 57W
Ji Xian, *Hebei, China* 34 F8 37 35N 115 30 E
Ji Xian, *Henan, China* 34 G8 35 22N 114 5 E
Ji Xian, *Shanxi, China* 34 F6 36 7N 110 40 E
Jia Xian, *Henan, China* 34 H7 33 59N 113 12 E
Jia Xian, *Shaanxi, China* 34 E6 38 12N 110 28 E
Jiamusi, *China* 33 B8 46 40N 130 26 E
Ji'an, *Jiangxi, China* 33 D6 27 6N 114 59 E
Ji'an, *Jilin, China* 35 D14 41 5N 126 10 E
Jianchang, *China* 35 D11 40 55N 120 35 E
Jianchangying, *China* 35 D10 40 10N 118 50 E
Jiangcheng, *China* 32 D5 22 36N 101 52 E
Jiangmen, *China* 33 D6 22 32N 113 0 E
Jiangsu □, *China* 35 H11 33 0N 120 0 E
Jiangxi □, *China* 33 D6 27 30N 116 0 E
Jiao Xian = Jiaozhou, *China* 35 F11 36 18N 120 1 E
Jiaohe, *Hebei, China* 34 E9 38 2N 116 20 E
Jiaohe, *Jilin, China* 35 C14 43 40N 127 22 E
Jiaozhou, *China* 35 F11 36 18N 120 1 E
Jiaozhou Wan, *China* 35 F11 36 5N 120 10 E
Jiaozuo, *China* 34 G7 35 16N 113 12 E
Jiawang, *China* 35 G9 34 28N 117 26 E
Jiaxiang, *China* 34 G9 35 25N 116 20 E
Jiaxing, *China* 33 C7 30 49N 120 45 E
Jiayi = Chiai, *Taiwan* 33 D7 23 29N 120 25 E
Jibuti = Djibouti ■, *Africa* 46 E3 12 0N 43 0 E
Jicarón, I., *Panama* 88 E3 7 10N 81 50W
Jiddah, *Si. Arabia* 46 C2 21 29N 39 10 E
Jido, *India* 41 E19 29 2N 94 58 E
Jieshou, *China* 34 H8 33 18N 115 22 E
Jiexiu, *China* 34 F6 37 2N 111 55 E
Jiggalong, *Australia* 60 D3 23 21S 120 47 E
Jigni, *India* 43 G8 25 45N 79 25 E
Jihlava, *Czech Rep.* 16 D8 49 28N 15 35 E
Jihlava →, *Czech Rep.* 17 D9 48 55N 16 36 E
Jijiga, *Ethiopia* 46 F3 9 20N 42 50 E
Jilin, *China* 35 C14 43 44N 126 30 E
Jilin □, *China* 35 C14 44 0N 127 0 E
Jilong = Chilung, *Taiwan* 33 D7 25 3N 121 45 E
Jim Thorpe, *U.S.A.* 79 F9 40 52N 75 44W
Jima, *Ethiopia* 46 F2 7 40N 36 47 E
Jiménez, *Mexico* 86 B4 27 10N 104 54W
Jimo, *China* 35 F11 36 23N 120 30 E
Jin Xian = Jinzhou, *China* 34 E8 38 2N 115 2 E
Jin Xian, *China* 35 E11 38 55N 121 42 E
Jinan, *China* 34 F9 36 38N 117 1 E
Jincheng, *China* 34 G7 35 29N 112 50 E
Jind, *India* 42 E7 29 19N 76 22 E
Jindabyne, *Australia* 63 F4 36 25S 148 35 E
Jindřichův Hradec, *Czech Rep.* 16 D8 49 10N 15 2 E
Jing He →, *China* 34 G5 34 27N 109 4 E
Jingbian, *China* 34 F5 37 20N 108 30 E
Jingchuan, *China* 34 G4 35 20N 107 20 E
Jingdezhen, *China* 33 D6 29 20N 117 11 E
Jinggu, *China* 32 D5 23 35N 100 41 E
Jinghai, *China* 34 E9 38 55N 116 55 E
Jingle, *China* 34 E6 38 20N 111 55 E
Jingning, *China* 34 G3 35 30N 105 43 E
Jingpo Hu, *China* 35 C15 43 55N 128 55 E
Jingtai, *China* 34 F3 37 10N 104 6 E
Jingxing, *China* 34 E8 38 2N 114 8 E
Jingyang, *China* 34 G5 34 30N 108 50 E
Jingyu, *China* 35 C14 42 25N 126 45 E
Jingyuan, *China* 34 F3 36 30N 104 40 E
Jingziguan, *China* 34 H6 33 15N 111 0 E
Jinhua, *China* 33 D6 29 8N 119 38 E
Jining, *Nei Mongol Zizhiqu, China* 34 D7 41 5N 113 0 E
Jining, *Shandong, China* 34 G9 35 22N 116 34 E
Jinja, *Uganda* 54 B3 0 25N 33 12 E
Jinjang, *Malaysia* 39 L3 3 13N 101 39 E
Jinji, *China* 34 F4 37 58N 106 8 E
Jinnah Barrage, *Pakistan* 40 C7 32 58N 71 33 E
Jinotega, *Nic.* 88 D2 13 6N 85 59W
Jinotepe, *Nic.* 88 D2 11 50N 86 10W
Jinsha Jiang →, *China* 32 D5 28 50N 104 36 E
Jinxi, *China* 35 D11 40 52N 120 50 E
Jinxiang, *China* 34 G9 35 5N 116 22 E
Jinzhou, *Hebei, China* 34 E8 38 2N 115 2 E
Jinzhou, *Liaoning, China* 35 D11 41 5N 121 3 E
Jiparaná →, *Brazil* 92 E6 8 3S 62 52W
Jipijapa, *Ecuador* 92 D2 1 0S 80 40W
Jiquilpan, *Mexico* 86 D4 19 57N 102 42W
Jishan, *China* 34 G6 35 34N 110 58 E
Jisr ash Shughūr, *Syria* 44 C3 35 49N 36 18 E
Jitarning, *Australia* 61 F2 32 48S 117 57 E
Jitra, *Malaysia* 39 J3 6 16N 100 25 E
Jiu →, *Romania* 17 F12 43 47N 23 48 E
Jiudengkou, *China* 34 E4 39 56N 106 40 E
Jiujiang, *China* 33 D6 29 42N 115 58 E
Jiutai, *China* 35 B13 44 10N 125 50 E
Jiuxiangcheng, *China* 34 H8 33 12N 114 50 E
Jiuxincheng, *China* 34 E8 39 17N 115 59 E
Jixi, *China* 35 B16 45 20N 130 50 E
Jiyang, *China* 35 F9 37 0N 117 12 E
Jiyuan, *China* 34 G7 35 7N 112 57 E
Jīzān, *Si. Arabia* 46 D3 17 0N 42 20 E
Jize, *China* 34 F8 36 54N 114 56 E
Jīzl, Wādī al, *Si. Arabia* 44 E3 25 39N 38 25 E
Jizō-Zaki, *Japan* 31 G6 35 34N 133 20 E
Jizzakh, *Uzbekistan* 26 E7 40 6N 67 50 E
Joaçaba, *Brazil* 95 B5 27 5S 51 31W
João Pessoa, *Brazil* 93 E12 7 10S 34 52W
Joaquín V. González, *Argentina* 94 B3 25 10S 64 0W
Jobat, *India* 42 H6 22 25N 74 34 E
Jodhpur, *India* 42 F5 26 23N 73 8 E
Jodiya, *India* 42 H4 22 42N 70 18 E
Joensuu, *Finland* 24 B4 62 37N 29 49 E
Jōetsu, *Japan* 31 F9 37 12N 138 10 E
Jofane, *Mozam.* 57 C5 21 15S 34 18 E
Jogbani, *India* 43 F12 26 25N 87 15 E
Jõgeva, *Estonia* 9 G22 58 45N 26 24 E
Jogjakarta = Yogyakarta, *Indonesia* 37 G14 7 49S 110 22 E
Johannesburg, *S. Africa* 57 D4 26 10S 28 2 E
Johannesburg, *U.S.A.* 85 K9 35 22N 117 38W
Johilla →, *India* 43 H9 23 37N 81 14 E
John Day, *U.S.A.* 82 D4 44 25N 118 57W
John Day →, *U.S.A.* 82 D3 45 44N 120 39W
John D'Or Prairie, *Canada* 72 B5 58 30N 115 8W
John H. Kerr Reservoir, *U.S.A.* 77 G6 36 36N 78 18W
John o' Groats, *U.K.* 12 C5 58 38N 3 4W
Johnnie, *U.S.A.* 85 J10 36 25N 116 5W
John's Ra., *Australia* 62 C1 21 55S 133 23 E
Johnson, *Kans., U.S.A.* 81 G4 37 34N 101 45W
Johnson, *Vt., U.S.A.* 79 B12 44 38N 72 41W
Johnson City, *N.Y., U.S.A.* 79 D9 42 7N 75 58W
Johnson City, *Tenn., U.S.A.* 77 G4 36 19N 82 21W
Johnson City, *Tex., U.S.A.* 81 K5 30 17N 98 25W
Johnsonburg, *U.S.A.* 78 E6 41 29N 78 41W
Johnsondale, *U.S.A.* 85 K8 35 58N 118 32W
Johnson's Crossing, *Canada* 72 A2 60 29N 133 18W
Johnston, L., *Australia* 61 F3 32 25S 120 30 E
Johnston Falls = Mambilima Falls, *Zambia* 55 E2 10 31S 28 45 E
Johnston I., *Pac. Oc.* 65 F11 17 10N 169 8W
Johnstone Str., *Canada* 72 C3 50 28N 126 0W
Johnstown, *N.Y., U.S.A.* 79 C10 43 0N 74 22W
Johnstown, *Ohio, U.S.A.* 78 F2 40 9N 82 41W
Johnstown, *Pa., U.S.A.* 78 F6 40 20N 78 55W
Johor Baharu, *Malaysia* 39 M4 1 28N 103 46 E
Jõhvi, *Estonia* 9 G22 59 22N 27 27 E
Joinville, *Brazil* 95 B6 26 15S 48 55W
Joinville I., *Antarctica* 5 C18 65 0S 55 30W
Jojutla, *Mexico* 87 D5 18 37N 99 11W
Jokkmokk, *Sweden* 8 C18 66 35N 19 50 E
Jökulsá á Bru →, *Iceland* 8 D6 65 40N 14 16W
Jökulsá á Fjöllum →, *Iceland* 8 C5 66 10N 16 30W
Jolfā, *Āzarbājān-e Sharqī, Iran* 44 B5 38 57N 45 38 E
Jolfā, *Eşfahan, Iran* 45 C6 32 58N 51 37 E
Joliet, *U.S.A.* 76 E1 41 32N 88 5W
Joliette, *Canada* 70 C5 46 3N 73 24W
Jolo, *Phil.* 37 C6 6 0N 121 0 E
Jolon, *U.S.A.* 84 K5 35 58N 121 9W
Jombang, *Indonesia* 37 G15 7 33S 112 14 E
Jonava, *Lithuania* 9 J21 55 8N 24 12 E
Jones Sound, *Canada* 4 B3 76 0N 85 0W
Jonesboro, *Ark., U.S.A.* 81 H9 35 50N 90 42W
Jonesboro, *La., U.S.A.* 81 J8 32 15N 92 43W
Joniškis, *Lithuania* 9 H20 56 13N 23 35 E
Jönköping, *Sweden* 9 H16 57 45N 14 8 E
Jonquière, *Canada* 71 C5 48 27N 71 14W
Joplin, *U.S.A.* 81 G7 37 6N 94 31W
Jora, *India* 42 F6 26 20N 77 49 E
Jordan, *Mont., U.S.A.* 82 C10 47 19N 106 55W
Jordan, *N.Y., U.S.A.* 79 C8 43 4N 76 29W
Jordan ■, *Asia* 47 E5 31 0N 36 0 E
Jordan →, *Asia* 47 D4 31 48N 35 32 E
Jordan Valley, *U.S.A.* 82 E5 42 59N 117 3W
Jorhat, *India* 41 F19 26 45N 94 12 E
Jörn, *Sweden* 8 D19 65 4N 20 1 E
Jorong, *Indonesia* 36 E4 3 58S 114 56 E
Jørpeland, *Norway* 9 G11 59 3N 6 1 E
Jorquera →, *Chile* 94 B2 28 3S 69 58W
Jos, *Nigeria* 50 G7 9 53N 8 51 E
José Batlle y Ordóñez, *Uruguay* 95 C4 33 20S 55 10W
Joseph, L., *Nfld., Canada* 71 B6 52 45N 65 18W
Joseph, L., *Ont., Canada* 78 A5 45 10N 79 44W
Joseph Bonaparte G., *Australia* 60 B4 14 35S 128 50 E
Joshinath, *India* 43 D8 30 34N 79 34 E
Joshua Tree, *U.S.A.* 85 L10 34 8N 116 19W
Joshua Tree National Park, *U.S.A.* 85 M10 33 55N 116 0W
Jostedalsbreen, *Norway* 9 F12 61 40N 6 59 E
Jotunheimen, *Norway* 9 F13 61 35N 8 25 E
Jourdanton, *U.S.A.* 81 L5 28 55N 98 33W
Jovellanos, *Cuba* 88 B3 22 40N 81 10W
Ju Xian, *China* 35 F10 36 35N 118 20 E
Juan Aldama, *Mexico* 86 C4 24 20N 103 23W
Juan Bautista Alberdi, *Argentina* 94 C3 34 26S 61 48W
Juan de Fuca Str., *Canada* 84 B3 48 15N 124 0W
Juan de Nova, *Ind. Oc.* 57 B7 17 3S 43 45 E
Juan Fernández, Arch. de, *Pac. Oc.* 90 G2 33 50S 80 0W
Juan José Castelli, *Argentina* 94 B3 25 27S 60 57W
Juan L. Lacaze, *Uruguay* 94 C4 34 26S 57 25W
Juankoski, *Finland* 8 E23 63 3N 28 19 E
Juárez, *Argentina* 94 D4 37 40S 59 43W
Juárez, *Mexico* 85 N11 32 20N 115 57W
Juárez, Sierra de, *Mexico* 86 A1 32 0N 116 0W
Juàzeiro, *Brazil* 93 E10 9 30S 40 30W
Juàzeiro do Norte, *Brazil* 93 E11 7 10S 39 18W
Juba, *Sudan* 51 H12 4 50N 31 35 E
Jubayl, *Lebanon* 47 A4 34 5N 35 39 E
Jubbah, *Si. Arabia* 44 D4 28 2N 40 56 E
Jubbal, *India* 42 D7 31 5N 77 40 E
Jubbulpore = Jabalpur, *India* 43 H8 23 9N 79 58 E
Jubilee L., *Australia* 61 E4 29 0S 126 50 E
Juby, C., *Morocco* 50 C3 28 0N 12 59W
Júcar = Xúquer →, *Spain* 19 C5 39 5N 0 10W
Júcaro, *Cuba* 88 B4 21 37N 78 51W
Juchitán, *Mexico* 87 D5 16 27N 95 5W
Judaea = Har Yehuda, *Israel* 47 D3 31 35N 34 57 E
Judith →, *U.S.A.* 82 C9 47 44N 109 39W
Judith, Pt., *U.S.A.* 79 E13 41 22N 71 29W
Judith Gap, *U.S.A.* 82 C9 46 41N 109 45W
Jugoslavia = Yugoslavia ■, *Europe* 21 B9 43 20N 20 0 E
Juigalpa, *Nic.* 88 D2 12 6N 85 26W
Juiz de Fora, *Brazil* 95 A7 21 43S 43 19W
Jujuy □, *Argentina* 94 A2 23 20S 65 40W
Julesburg, *U.S.A.* 80 E3 40 59N 102 16W
Juli, *Peru* 92 G5 16 10S 69 25W
Julia Cr. →, *Australia* 62 C3 20 0S 141 11 E
Julia Creek, *Australia* 62 C3 20 39S 141 44 E
Juliaca, *Peru* 92 G4 15 25S 70 10W
Julian, *U.S.A.* 85 M10 33 4N 116 38W
Julian L., *Canada* 70 B4 54 25N 77 57W
Julianatop, *Surinam* 93 C7 3 40N 56 30W
Julianehåb, *Greenland* 4 C5 60 43N 46 0W
Julimes, *Mexico* 86 B3 28 25N 105 27W
Jullundur, *India* 42 D6 31 20N 75 40 E
Julu, *China* 34 F8 37 15N 115 2 E
Jumbo, *Zimbabwe* 55 F3 17 30S 30 58 E
Jumbo Pk., *U.S.A.* 85 J12 36 12N 114 11W
Jumentos Cays, *Bahamas* 88 B4 23 0N 75 40W
Jumilla, *Spain* 19 C5 38 28N 1 19W
Jumla, *Nepal* 43 E10 29 15N 82 13 E
Jumna = Yamuna →, *India* 43 G9 25 30N 81 53 E
Junagadh, *India* 42 J4 21 30N 70 30 E
Junction, *Tex., U.S.A.* 81 K5 30 29N 99 46W
Junction, *Utah, U.S.A.* 83 G7 38 14N 112 13W
Junction B., *Australia* 62 A1 11 52S 133 55 E
Junction City, *Kans., U.S.A.* 80 F6 39 2N 96 50W
Junction City, *Oreg., U.S.A.* 82 D2 44 13N 123 12W
Junction Pt., *Australia* 62 A1 11 45S 133 50 E
Jundah, *Australia* 62 C3 24 46S 143 2 E
Jundiaí, *Brazil* 95 A6 24 30S 47 0W
Juneau, *U.S.A.* 72 B2 58 18N 134 25W
Junee, *Australia* 63 E4 34 53S 147 35 E
Jungfrau, *Switz.* 18 C7 46 32N 7 58 E
Junggar Pendi, *China* 32 B3 44 30N 86 0 E
Jungshahi, *Pakistan* 42 G2 24 52N 67 44 E
Juniata →, *U.S.A.* 78 F7 40 30N 77 40W
Junín, *Argentina* 94 C3 34 33S 60 57W
Junín de los Andes, *Argentina* 96 D2 39 45S 71 0W
Jūniyah, *Lebanon* 47 B4 33 59N 35 38 E
Juntas, *Chile* 94 B2 28 24S 69 58W
Juntura, *U.S.A.* 82 E4 43 45N 118 5W
Jur, Nahr el →, *Sudan* 51 G11 8 45N 29 15 E
Jura = Jura, Mts. du, *Europe* 18 C7 46 40N 6 5 E
Jura = Schwäbische Alb, *Germany* 16 D5 48 20N 9 30 E
Jura, *U.K.* 12 F3 56 0N 5 50W
Jura, Mts. du, *Europe* 18 C7 46 40N 6 5 E
Jura, Sd. of, *U.K.* 12 F3 55 57N 5 45W
Jurbarkas, *Lithuania* 9 J20 55 4N 22 46 E
Jurien, *Australia* 61 F2 30 18S 115 2 E
Jūrmala, *Latvia* 9 H20 56 58N 23 34 E
Juruá →, *Brazil* 92 D5 2 37S 65 44W
Juruena, *Brazil* 92 F7 13 0S 58 10W

Kentucky L.

Kapuas Hulu Ra. = Kapuas Hulu, Pegunungan, *Malaysia* **36 D4** 1 30N 113 30 E
Kapulo, *Dem. Rep. of the Congo* **55 D2** 8 18S 29 15 E
Kapunda, *Australia* **63 E2** 34 20S 138 56 E
Kapuni, *N.Z.* **59 H5** 39 29S 174 8 E
Kapurthala, *India* **42 D6** 31 23N 75 25 E
Kapuskasing, *Canada* **70 C3** 49 25N 82 30W
Kapuskasing →, *Canada* **70 C3** 49 49N 82 0W
Kaputar, *Australia* **63 E5** 30 15S 150 10 E
Kaputir, *Kenya* **54 B4** 2 5N 35 28 E
Kara, *Russia* **26 C7** 69 10N 65 0 E
Kara Bogaz Gol, Zaliv = Garabogazköl Aylagy, *Turkmenistan* **25 F9** 41 0N 53 30 E
Kara Kalpak Republic = Karakalpakstan □, *Uzbekistan* **26 E6** 43 0N 58 0 E
Kara Kum, *Turkmenistan* **26 F7** 39 30N 60 0 E
Kara Sea, *Russia* **26 B8** 75 0N 70 0 E
Karabiğa, *Turkey* **21 D12** 40 23N 27 17 E
Karabük, *Turkey* **25 F5** 41 12N 32 37 E
Karaburun, *Turkey* **21 E12** 38 41N 26 28 E
Karabutak = Qarabutaq, *Kazakstan* **26 E7** 49 59N 60 14 E
Karacabey, *Turkey* **21 D13** 40 12N 28 21 E
Karacasu, *Turkey* **21 F13** 37 43N 28 35 E
Karachey-Cherkessia □, *Russia* **25 F7** 43 40N 41 30 E
Karachi, *Pakistan* **42 G2** 24 53N 67 0 E
Karad, *India* **40 L9** 17 15N 74 10 E
Karaganda = Qaraghandy, *Kazakstan* **26 E8** 49 50N 73 10 E
Karagayly, *Kazakstan* **26 E8** 49 26N 76 0 E
Karaginskiy, Ostrov, *Russia* **27 D17** 58 45N 164 0 E
Karagiye, Vpadina, *Kazakstan* **25 F9** 43 27N 51 45 E
Karagiye Depression = Karagiye, Vpadina, *Kazakstan* **25 F9** 43 27N 51 45 E
Karagola Road, *India* **43 G12** 25 29N 87 23 E
Karaikal, *India* **40 P11** 10 59N 79 50 E
Karaikkudi, *India* **40 P11** 10 5N 78 45 E
Karaj, *Iran* **45 C6** 35 48N 51 0 E
Karak, *Malaysia* **39 L4** 3 25N 102 2 E
Karakalpakstan □, *Uzbekistan* **26 E6** 43 0N 58 0 E
Karakelong, *Indonesia* **37 D7** 4 35N 126 50 E
Karakitang, *Indonesia* **37 D7** 3 14N 125 28 E
Karaklis = Vanadzor, *Armenia* **25 F7** 40 48N 44 30 E
Karakoram Pass, *Pakistan* **43 B7** 35 33N 77 50 E
Karakoram Ra., *Pakistan* **43 B7** 35 30N 77 0 E
Karalon, *Russia* **27 D12** 57 5N 115 50 E
Karama, *Jordan* **47 D4** 31 57N 35 35 E
Karaman, *Turkey* **25 G5** 37 14N 33 13 E
Karamay, *China* **32 B3** 45 30N 84 58 E
Karambu, *Indonesia* **36 E5** 3 53S 116 6 E
Karamea Bight, *N.Z.* **59 J3** 41 22S 171 40 E
Karamnasa →, *India* **43 G10** 25 31N 83 52 E
Karand, *Iran* **44 C5** 34 16N 46 15 E
Karanganyar, *Indonesia* **37 G13** 7 38S 109 37 E
Karanjia, *India* **43 J11** 21 47N 85 58 E
Karasburg, *Namibia* **56 D2** 28 0S 18 44 E
Karasino, *Russia* **26 C9** 66 50N 86 50 E
Karasjok, *Norway* **8 B21** 69 27N 25 30 E
Karasuk, *Russia* **26 D8** 53 44N 78 2 E
Karasuyama, *Japan* **31 F10** 36 39N 140 9 E
Karatau = Qarataū, *Kazakstan* **26 E8** 43 10N 70 28 E
Karatau, Khrebet, *Kazakstan* **26 E7** 43 30N 69 30 E
Karatsu, *Japan* **31 H5** 33 26N 129 58 E
Karaul, *Russia* **26 B9** 70 6N 82 15 E
Karauli, *India* **42 F7** 26 30N 77 4 E
Karavostasi, *Cyprus* **23 D11** 35 8N 32 50 E
Karawang, *Indonesia* **37 G12** 6 30S 107 15 E
Karawanken, *Europe* **16 E8** 46 30N 14 40 E
Karayazı, *Turkey* **25 G7** 39 41N 42 9 E
Karazhal, *Kazakstan* **26 E8** 48 2N 70 49 E
Karbalā', *Iraq* **44 C5** 32 36N 44 3 E
Karcag, *Hungary* **17 E11** 47 19N 20 57 E
Karcha →, *Pakistan* **43 B7** 34 45N 76 10 E
Karchana, *India* **43 G9** 25 17N 81 56 E
Kardhitsa, *Greece* **21 E9** 39 23N 21 54 E
Kärdla, *Estonia* **9 G20** 58 50N 22 40 E
Kareeberge, *S. Africa* **56 E3** 30 59S 21 50 E
Kareha →, *India* **43 G12** 25 44N 86 21 E
Kareima, *Sudan* **51 E12** 18 30N 31 49 E
Karelia □, *Russia* **24 A5** 65 30N 32 30 E
Karelian Republic = Karelia □, *Russia* **24 A5** 65 30N 32 30 E
Karera, *India* **42 G8** 25 32N 78 9 E
Kārevāndar, *Iran* **45 E9** 27 53N 60 44 E
Kargasok, *Russia* **26 D9** 59 3N 80 53 E
Kargat, *Russia* **26 D9** 55 10N 80 15 E
Kargil, *India* **43 B7** 34 32N 76 12 E
Kargopol, *Russia* **24 B6** 61 30N 38 58 E
Karhal, *India* **43 F8** 27 1N 78 57 E
Karīān, *Iran* **45 E8** 26 57N 57 14 E
Kariba, *Zimbabwe* **55 F2** 16 28S 28 50 E
Kariba, L., *Zimbabwe* **55 F2** 16 40S 28 25 E
Kariba Dam, *Zimbabwe* **55 F2** 16 30S 28 35 E
Kariba Gorge, *Zambia* **55 F2** 16 30S 28 50 E
Karibib, *Namibia* **56 C2** 22 0S 15 56 E
Karimata, Kepulauan, *Indonesia* **36 E3** 1 25S 109 0 E
Karimata, Selat, *Indonesia* **36 E3** 2 0S 108 40 E
Karimata Is. = Karimata, Kepulauan, *Indonesia* **36 E3** 1 25S 109 0 E
Karimnagar, *India* **40 K11** 18 26N 79 10 E
Karimunjawa, Kepulauan, *Indonesia* **36 F4** 5 50S 110 30 E
Karin, *Somali Rep.* **46 E4** 10 50N 45 52 E
Karīt, *Iran* **45 C8** 33 29N 56 55 E
Kariya, *Japan* **31 G8** 34 58N 137 1 E
Karkaralinsk = Qarqaraly, *Kazakstan* **26 E8** 49 26N 75 30 E
Karkheh →, *Iran* **44 D5** 31 2N 47 29 E
Karkinitska Zatoka, *Ukraine* **25 E5** 45 56N 33 0 E
Karkinitskiy Zaliv = Karkinitska Zatoka, *Ukraine* **25 E5** 45 56N 33 0 E
Karl-Marx-Stadt = Chemnitz, *Germany* **16 C7** 50 51N 12 54 E
Karlovac, *Croatia* **16 F8** 45 31N 15 36 E
Karlovo, *Bulgaria* **21 C11** 42 38N 24 47 E
Karlovy Vary, *Czech Rep.* **16 C7** 50 13N 12 51 E
Karlsbad = Karlovy Vary, *Czech Rep.* **16 C7** 50 13N 12 51 E
Karlsborg, *Sweden* **9 G16** 58 33N 14 33 E
Karlshamn, *Sweden* **9 H16** 56 10N 14 51 E
Karlskoga, *Sweden* **9 G16** 59 28N 14 33 E
Karlskrona, *Sweden* **9 H16** 56 10N 15 35 E
Karlsruhe, *Germany* **16 D5** 49 0N 8 23 E
Karlstad, *Sweden* **9 G15** 59 23N 13 30 E
Karlstad, *U.S.A.* **80 A6** 48 35N 96 31W
Karmi'el, *Israel* **47 C4** 32 55N 35 18 E
Karnak, *Egypt* **51 C12** 25 43N 32 39 E
Karnal, *India* **42 E7** 29 42N 77 2 E
Karnali →, *Nepal* **43 E9** 28 45N 81 16 E
Karnaphuli Res., *Bangla.* **41 H18** 22 40N 92 20 E
Karnaprayag, *India* **43 D8** 30 16N 79 15 E
Karnataka □, *India* **40 N10** 13 15N 77 0 E
Karnes City, *U.S.A.* **81 L6** 28 53N 97 54W
Karnische Alpen, *Europe* **16 E7** 46 36N 13 0 E
Kärnten □, *Austria* **16 E8** 46 52N 13 30 E
Karoi, *Zimbabwe* **55 F2** 16 48S 29 45 E
Karonga, *Malawi* **55 D3** 9 57S 33 55 E
Karoonda, *Australia* **63 F2** 35 1S 139 59 E
Karor, *Pakistan* **42 D4** 31 15N 70 59 E
Karora, *Sudan* **51 E13** 17 44N 38 15 E
Karpasia □, *Cyprus* **23 D13** 35 32N 34 15 E
Kárpathos, *Greece* **21 G12** 35 37N 27 10 E
Karpinsk, *Russia* **24 C11** 59 45N 60 1 E
Karpogory, *Russia* **24 B7** 64 0N 44 27 E
Karpuz Burnu = Apostolos Andreas, C., *Cyprus* **23 D13** 35 42N 34 35 E
Karratha, *Australia* **60 D2** 20 53S 116 40 E
Kars, *Turkey* **25 F7** 40 40N 43 5 E
Karsakpay, *Kazakstan* **26 E7** 47 55N 66 40 E
Karshi = Qarshi, *Uzbekistan* **26 F7** 38 53N 65 48 E
Karsiyang, *India* **43 F13** 26 56N 88 18 E
Karsog, *India* **42 D7** 31 23N 77 12 E
Kartaly, *Russia* **26 D7** 53 3N 60 40 E
Kartapur, *India* **42 D6** 31 27N 75 32 E
Karthaus, *U.S.A.* **78 E6** 41 8N 78 9W
Karufa, *Indonesia* **37 E8** 3 50S 133 20 E
Karumba, *Australia* **62 B3** 17 31S 140 50 E
Karumo, *Tanzania* **54 C3** 2 25S 32 50 E
Karumwa, *Tanzania* **54 C3** 3 12S 32 38 E
Kārūn →, *Iran* **45 D6** 30 26N 48 10 E
Karungu, *Kenya* **54 C3** 0 50S 34 10 E
Karviná, *Czech Rep.* **17 D10** 49 53N 18 31 E
Karwan →, *India* **42 F8** 27 26N 78 4 E
Karwar, *India* **40 M9** 14 55N 74 13 E
Karwi, *India* **43 G9** 25 12N 80 57 E
Kasache, *Malawi* **55 E3** 13 25S 34 20 E
Kasai →, *Dem. Rep. of the Congo* **52 E3** 3 30S 16 10 E
Kasaï-Oriental □, *Dem. Rep. of the Congo* **54 D1** 5 0S 24 30 E
Kasaji, *Dem. Rep. of the Congo* **55 E1** 10 25S 23 27 E
Kasama, *Zambia* **55 E3** 10 16S 31 9 E
Kasan-dong, *N. Korea* **35 D14** 41 18N 126 55 E
Kasane, *Namibia* **56 B3** 17 34S 24 50 E
Kasanga, *Tanzania* **55 D3** 8 30S 31 10 E
Kasaragod, *India* **40 N9** 12 30N 74 58 E
Kasba L., *Canada* **73 A8** 60 20N 102 10W
Kāseh Garān, *Iran* **44 C5** 34 5N 46 2 E
Kasempa, *Zambia* **55 E2** 13 30S 25 44 E
Kasenga, *Dem. Rep. of the Congo* **55 E2** 10 20S 28 45 E
Kasese, *Uganda* **54 B3** 0 13N 30 3 E
Kasewa, *Zambia* **55 E2** 14 28S 28 53 E
Kasganj, *India* **43 F8** 27 48N 78 42 E
Kashabowie, *Canada* **70 C1** 48 40N 90 26W
Kashaf, *Iran* **45 C9** 35 58N 61 7 E
Kāshān, *Iran* **45 C6** 34 5N 51 30 E
Kashechewan, *Canada* **70 B3** 52 18N 81 37W
Kashi, *China* **32 C2** 39 30N 76 2 E
Kashimbo, *Dem. Rep. of the Congo* **55 E2** 11 12S 26 19 E
Kashipur, *India* **43 E8** 29 15N 79 0 E
Kashiwazaki, *Japan* **31 F9** 37 22N 138 33 E
Kashk-e Kohneh, *Afghan.* **40 B3** 34 55N 62 30 E
Kashkū'īyeh, *Iran* **45 D7** 30 31N 55 40 E
Kāshmar, *Iran* **45 C8** 35 16N 58 26 E
Kashmir, *Asia* **43 C7** 34 0N 76 0 E
Kashmor, *Pakistan* **42 E3** 28 28N 69 32 E
Kashun Noerh = Gaxun Nur, *China* **32 B5** 42 22N 100 30 E
Kasiari, *India* **43 H12** 22 8N 87 14 E
Kasimov, *Russia* **24 D7** 54 55N 41 20 E
Kasinge, *Dem. Rep. of the Congo* **54 D2** 6 15S 26 58 E
Kasiruta, *Indonesia* **37 E7** 0 25S 127 12 E
Kaskaskia →, *U.S.A.* **80 G10** 37 58N 89 57W
Kaskattama →, *Canada* **73 B10** 57 3N 90 4W
Kaskinen, *Finland* **9 E19** 62 22N 21 15 E
Kaslo, *Canada* **72 D5** 49 55N 116 55W
Kasmere L., *Canada* **73 B8** 59 34N 101 10W
Kasongo, *Dem. Rep. of the Congo* **54 C2** 4 30S 26 33 E
Kasongo Lunda, *Dem. Rep. of the Congo* **52 F3** 6 35S 16 49 E
Kásos, *Greece* **21 G12** 35 20N 26 55 E
Kassalâ, *Sudan* **51 E13** 15 30N 36 0 E
Kassel, *Germany* **16 C5** 51 18N 9 26 E
Kassiópi, *Greece* **23 A3** 39 48N 19 53 E
Kasson, *U.S.A.* **80 C8** 44 2N 92 45W
Kastamonu, *Turkey* **25 F5** 41 25N 33 43 E
Kastélli, *Greece* **23 D5** 35 29N 23 38 E
Kastéllion, *Greece* **23 D7** 35 12N 25 20 E
Kasterlee, *Belgium* **15 C4** 51 15N 4 59 E
Kastoría, *Greece* **21 D9** 40 30N 21 19 E
Kasulu, *Tanzania* **54 C3** 4 37S 30 5 E
Kasumi, *Japan* **31 G7** 35 38N 134 38 E
Kasungu, *Malawi* **55 E3** 13 0S 33 29 E
Kasur, *Pakistan* **42 D6** 31 5N 74 25 E
Kataba, *Zambia* **55 F2** 16 5S 25 10 E
Katahdin, Mt., *U.S.A.* **77 C11** 45 54N 68 56W
Katako Kombe, *Dem. Rep. of the Congo* **54 C1** 3 25S 24 20 E
Katale, *Tanzania* **54 C3** 4 52S 31 7 E
Katanda, Katanga, *Dem. Rep. of the Congo* **54 D1** 7 52S 24 13 E
Katanda, Nord-Kivu, *Dem. Rep. of the Congo* **54 C2** 0 55S 29 21 E
Katanga □, *Dem. Rep. of the Congo* **54 D2** 8 0S 25 0 E
Katangi, *India* **40 J11** 21 56N 79 50 E
Katanning, *Australia* **61 F2** 33 40S 117 33 E
Katavi Swamp, *Tanzania* **54 D3** 6 50S 31 10 E
Kateríni, *Greece* **21 D10** 40 18N 22 37 E
Katghora, *India* **43 H10** 22 30N 82 33 E
Katha, *Burma* **41 G20** 24 10N 96 30 E
Katherîna, Gebel, *Egypt* **44 D2** 28 30N 33 57 E
Katherine, *Australia* **60 B5** 14 27S 132 20 E
Katherine Gorge, *Australia* **60 B5** 14 18S 132 28 E
Kathi, *India* **42 J6** 21 47N 74 3 E
Kathiawar, *India* **42 H4** 22 20N 71 0 E
Kathikas, *Cyprus* **23 E11** 34 55N 32 25 E
Kathua, *India* **42 C6** 32 23N 75 34 E
Katihar, *India* **43 G12** 25 34N 87 36 E
Katima Mulilo, *Zambia* **56 B3** 17 28S 24 13 E
Katimbira, *Malawi* **55 E3** 12 40S 34 0 E
Katingan = Mendawai →, *Indonesia* **36 E4** 3 30S 113 0 E
Katiola, *Ivory C.* **50 G4** 8 10N 5 10W
Katmandu, *Nepal* **43 F11** 27 45N 85 20 E
Katni, *India* **43 H9** 23 51N 80 24 E
Káto Arkhánai, *Greece* **23 D7** 35 15N 25 10 E
Káto Khorió, *Greece* **23 D7** 35 3N 25 47 E
Kato Pyrgos, *Cyprus* **23 D11** 35 11N 32 41 E
Katompe, *Dem. Rep. of the Congo* **54 D2** 6 2S 26 23 E
Katonga →, *Uganda* **54 B3** 0 34N 31 50 E
Katoomba, *Australia* **63 E5** 33 41S 150 19 E
Katowice, *Poland* **17 C10** 50 17N 19 5 E
Katrine, L., *U.K.* **12 E4** 56 15N 4 30W
Katrineholm, *Sweden* **9 G17** 59 9N 16 12 E
Katsepe, *Madag.* **57 B8** 15 45S 46 15 E
Katsina, *Nigeria* **50 F7** 13 0N 7 32 E
Katsumoto, *Japan* **31 H4** 33 51N 129 42 E
Katsuura, *Japan* **31 G10** 35 10N 140 20 E
Katsuyama, *Japan* **31 F8** 36 3N 136 30 E
Kattaviá, *Greece* **23 D9** 35 57N 27 46 E
Kattegat, *Denmark* **9 H14** 56 40N 11 20 E
Katumba, *Dem. Rep. of the Congo* **54 D2** 7 40S 25 17 E
Katungu, *Kenya* **54 C5** 2 55S 40 3 E
Katwa, *India* **43 H13** 23 30N 88 5 E
Katwijk, *Neths.* **15 B4** 52 12N 4 24 E
Kauai, *U.S.A.* **74 H15** 22 3N 159 30W
Kauai Channel, *U.S.A.* **74 H15** 21 45N 158 50W
Kaufman, *U.S.A.* **81 J6** 32 35N 96 19W
Kauhajoki, *Finland* **9 E20** 62 25N 22 10 E
Kaukauna, *U.S.A.* **76 C1** 44 17N 88 17W
Kaukauveld, *Namibia* **56 C3** 20 0S 20 15 E
Kaunakakai, *U.S.A.* **74 H16** 21 6N 157 1W
Kaunas, *Lithuania* **9 J20** 54 54N 23 54 E
Kaunia, *Bangla.* **43 G13** 25 46N 89 26 E
Kautokeino, *Norway* **8 B20** 69 0N 23 4 E
Kauwapur, *India* **43 F10** 27 31N 82 18 E
Kavacha, *Russia* **27 C17** 60 16N 169 51 E
Kavalerovo, *Russia* **30 B7** 44 15N 135 4 E
Kavali, *India* **40 M12** 14 55N 80 1 E
Kavála, *Greece* **21 D11** 40 57N 24 28 E
Kavār, *Iran* **45 D7** 29 11N 52 44 E
Kavi, *India* **42 H5** 22 12N 72 38 E
Kavir, Dasht-e, *Iran* **45 C7** 34 30N 55 0 E
Kavos, *Greece* **23 B4** 39 23N 20 3 E
Kaw, *Fr. Guiana* **93 C8** 4 30N 52 15W
Kawagama L., *Canada* **78 A6** 45 18N 78 45W
Kawagoe, *Japan* **31 G9** 35 55N 139 29 E
Kawaguchi, *Japan* **31 G9** 35 52N 139 45 E
Kawaihae, *U.S.A.* **74 H17** 20 3N 155 50W
Kawambwa, *Zambia* **55 D2** 9 48S 29 3 E
Kawanoe, *Japan* **31 G6** 34 1N 133 34 E
Kawardha, *India* **43 J9** 22 0N 81 17 E
Kawasaki, *Japan* **31 G9** 35 35N 139 42 E
Kawasi, *Indonesia* **37 E7** 1 38S 127 28 E
Kawerau, *N.Z.* **59 H6** 38 7S 176 42 E
Kawhia Harbour, *N.Z.* **59 H5** 38 5S 174 51 E
Kawio, Kepulauan, *Indonesia* **37 D7** 4 30N 125 30 E
Kawnro, *Burma* **41 H21** 22 48N 99 8 E
Kawthaung, *Burma* **39 H2** 10 5N 98 36 E
Kawthoolei = Kawthule □, *Burma* **41 L20** 18 0N 97 30 E
Kawthule □, *Burma* **41 L20** 18 0N 97 30 E
Kaya, *Burkina Faso* **50 F5** 13 4N 1 10W
Kayah □, *Burma* **41 K20** 19 15N 97 15 E
Kayan →, *Indonesia* **36 D5** 2 55N 117 35 E
Kaycee, *U.S.A.* **82 E10** 43 43N 106 38W
Kayeli, *Indonesia* **37 E7** 3 20S 127 10 E
Kayenta, *U.S.A.* **83 H8** 36 44N 110 15W
Kayes, *Mali* **50 F3** 14 25N 11 30W
Kayin = Kawthule □, *Burma* **41 L20** 18 0N 97 30 E
Kayoa, *Indonesia* **37 D7** 0 1N 127 28 E
Kayomba, *Zambia* **55 E1** 13 11S 24 2 E
Kayseri, *Turkey* **25 G6** 38 45N 35 30 E
Kaysville, *U.S.A.* **82 F8** 41 2N 111 56W
Kazachye, *Russia* **27 B14** 70 52N 135 58 E
Kazakstan ■, *Asia* **26 E8** 50 0N 70 0 E
Kazan, *Russia* **24 C8** 55 50N 49 10 E
Kazan →, *Canada* **73 A9** 64 3N 95 35W
Kazan-Rettō, *Pac. Oc.* **64 E6** 25 0N 141 0 E
Kazanlŭk, *Bulgaria* **21 C11** 42 38N 25 20 E
Kazatin = Kozyatyn, *Ukraine* **17 D15** 49 45N 28 50 E
Kāzerūn, *Iran* **45 D6** 29 38N 51 40 E
Kazi Magomed = Qazimämmäd, *Azerbaijan* **45 A6** 40 3N 49 0 E
Kazuno, *Japan* **30 D10** 40 10N 140 45 E
Kazym →, *Russia* **26 C7** 63 54N 65 50 E
Kéa, *Greece* **21 F11** 37 35N 24 22 E
Keady, *U.K.* **13 B5** 54 15N 6 42W
Kearney, *U.S.A.* **80 E5** 40 42N 99 5W
Kearny, *U.S.A.* **83 K8** 33 3N 110 55W
Kearsarge, Mt., *U.S.A.* **79 C13** 43 22N 71 50W
Keban, *Turkey* **25 G6** 38 50N 38 50 E
Keban Baraji, *Turkey* **25 G6** 38 41N 38 33 E
Kebnekaise, *Sweden* **8 C18** 67 53N 18 33 E
Kebri Dehar, *Ethiopia* **46 F3** 6 45N 44 17 E
Kebumen, *Indonesia* **37 G13** 7 42S 109 40 E
Kechika →, *Canada* **72 B3** 59 41N 127 12W
Kecskemét, *Hungary* **17 E10** 46 57N 19 42 E
Kėdainiai, *Lithuania* **9 J21** 55 15N 24 2 E
Kedarnath, *India* **43 D8** 30 44N 79 4 E
Kedgwick, *Canada* **71 C6** 47 40N 67 20W
Kédhros Óros, *Greece* **23 D6** 35 11N 24 37 E
Kedia Hill, *Botswana* **56 C3** 21 28S 24 37 E
Kediri, *Indonesia* **37 G15** 7 51S 112 1 E
Keeler, *U.S.A.* **84 J9** 36 29N 117 52W
Keeley L., *Canada* **73 C7** 54 54N 108 8W
Keeling Is. = Cocos Is., *Ind. Oc.* **64 J1** 12 10S 96 55 E
Keelung = Chilung, *Taiwan* **33 D7** 25 3N 121 45 E
Keene, *Canada* **78 B6** 44 15N 78 10W
Keene, *Calif., U.S.A.* **85 K8** 35 13N 118 33W
Keene, *N.H., U.S.A.* **79 D12** 42 56N 72 17W
Keene, *N.Y., U.S.A.* **79 B11** 44 16N 73 46W
Keeper Hill, *Ireland* **13 D3** 52 45N 8 16W
Keer-Weer, C., *Australia* **62 A3** 14 0S 141 32 E
Keeseville, *U.S.A.* **79 B11** 44 29N 73 30W
Keetmanshoop, *Namibia* **56 D2** 26 35S 18 8 E
Keewatin, *Canada* **73 D10** 49 46N 94 34W
Keewatin →, *Canada* **73 B8** 56 29N 100 46W
Kefallinía, *Greece* **21 E9** 38 20N 20 30 E
Kefamenanu, *Indonesia* **37 F6** 9 28S 124 29 E
Kefar Sava, *Israel* **47 C3** 32 11N 34 54 E
Keffi, *Nigeria* **50 G7** 8 55N 7 43 E
Keflavík, *Iceland* **8 D2** 64 2N 22 35W
Keg River, *Canada* **72 B5** 57 54N 117 55W
Kegaska, *Canada* **71 B7** 50 9N 61 18W
Keighley, *U.K.* **10 D6** 53 52N 1 54W
Keila, *Estonia* **9 G21** 59 18N 24 25 E
Keimoes, *S. Africa* **56 D3** 28 41S 20 59 E
Keitele, *Finland* **8 E22** 63 10N 26 20 E
Keith, *Australia* **63 F3** 36 6S 140 20 E
Keith, *U.K.* **12 D6** 57 32N 2 57W
Keizer, *U.S.A.* **82 D2** 44 57N 123 1W
Kejimkujik Nat. Park, *Canada* **71 D6** 44 25N 65 25W
Kejser Franz Joseph Fjord = Kong Franz Joseph Fd., *Greenland* **4 B6** 73 30N 24 30W
Kekri, *India* **42 G6** 26 0N 75 10 E
Kelan, *China* **34 E6** 38 43N 111 31 E
Kelang, *Malaysia* **39 L3** 3 2N 101 26 E
Kelantan →, *Malaysia* **39 J4** 6 13N 102 14 E
Kelkit →, *Turkey* **25 F6** 40 45N 36 32 E
Kellerberrin, *Australia* **61 F2** 31 36S 117 38 E
Kellett, C., *Canada* **4 B1** 72 0N 126 0W
Kelleys I., *U.S.A.* **78 E2** 41 36N 82 42W
Kellogg, *U.S.A.* **82 C5** 47 32N 116 7W
Kells = Ceanannus Mor, *Ireland* **13 C5** 53 44N 6 53W
Kelokedhara, *Cyprus* **23 E11** 34 48N 32 39 E
Kelowna, *Canada* **72 D5** 49 50N 119 25W
Kelseyville, *U.S.A.* **84 G4** 38 59N 122 50W
Kelso, *N.Z.* **59 L2** 45 54S 169 15 E
Kelso, *U.K.* **12 F6** 55 36N 2 26W
Kelso, *U.S.A.* **84 D4** 46 9N 122 54W
Keluang, *Malaysia* **39 L4** 2 3N 103 18 E
Kelvington, *Canada* **73 C8** 52 10N 103 30W
Kem, *Russia* **24 B5** 65 0N 34 38 E
Kem →, *Russia* **24 B5** 64 57N 34 41 E
Kema, *Indonesia* **37 D7** 1 22N 125 8 E
Kemah, *Turkey* **44 B3** 39 32N 39 5 E
Kemaman, *Malaysia* **36 D2** 4 12N 103 18 E
Kemano, *Canada* **72 C3** 53 35N 128 0W
Kemasik, *Malaysia* **39 K4** 4 25N 103 27 E
Kemerovo, *Russia* **26 D9** 55 20N 86 5 E
Kemi, *Finland* **8 D21** 65 44N 24 34 E
Kemi älv = Kemijoki →, *Finland* **8 D21** 65 47N 24 32 E
Kemijärvi, *Finland* **8 C22** 66 43N 27 22 E
Kemijoki →, *Finland* **8 D21** 65 47N 24 32 E
Kemmerer, *U.S.A.* **82 F8** 41 48N 110 32W
Kemmuna = Comino, *Malta* **23 C1** 36 2N 14 20 E
Kemp, L., *U.S.A.* **81 J5** 33 46N 99 9W
Kemp Land, *Antarctica* **5 C5** 69 0S 55 0 E
Kempsey, *Australia* **63 E5** 31 1S 152 50 E
Kempt, L., *Canada* **70 C5** 47 25N 74 22W
Kempten, *Germany* **16 E6** 47 45N 10 17 E
Kempton, *Australia* **62 G4** 42 31S 147 12 E
Kemptville, *Canada* **79 B9** 45 0N 75 38W
Ken →, *India* **43 G9** 25 13N 80 27 E
Kenai, *U.S.A.* **68 B4** 60 33N 151 16W
Kendai, *India* **43 H10** 22 45N 82 37 E
Kendal, *Indonesia* **37 G14** 6 56S 110 14 E
Kendal, *U.K.* **10 C5** 54 20N 2 44W
Kendall, *Australia* **63 E5** 31 35S 152 44 E
Kendall, *U.S.A.* **77 N5** 25 41N 80 19W
Kendall →, *Australia* **62 A3** 14 4S 141 35 E
Kendallville, *U.S.A.* **76 E3** 41 27N 85 16W
Kendari, *Indonesia* **37 E6** 3 50S 122 30 E
Kendawangan, *Indonesia* **36 E4** 2 32S 110 17 E
Kendrapara, *India* **41 J15** 20 35N 86 30 E
Kendrew, *S. Africa* **56 E3** 32 32S 24 30 E
Kene Thao, *Laos* **38 D3** 17 44N 101 10 E
Kenedy, *U.S.A.* **81 L6** 28 49N 97 51W
Kenema, *S. Leone* **50 G3** 7 50N 11 14W
Keng Kok, *Laos* **38 D5** 16 26N 105 12 E
Keng Tawng, *Burma* **41 J21** 20 45N 98 18 E
Keng Tung, *Burma* **41 J21** 21 0N 99 30 E
Kenge, *Dem. Rep. of the Congo* **52 E3** 4 50S 17 4 E
Kengeja, *Tanzania* **54 D4** 5 26S 39 45 E
Kenhardt, *S. Africa* **56 D3** 29 19S 21 12 E
Kenitra, *Morocco* **50 B4** 34 15N 6 40W
Kenli, *China* **35 F10** 37 30N 118 20 E
Kenmare, *Ireland* **13 E2** 51 53N 9 36W
Kenmare, *U.S.A.* **80 A3** 48 41N 102 5W
Kenmare River, *Ireland* **13 E2** 51 48N 9 51W
Kennebago Lake, *U.S.A.* **79 A14** 45 4N 70 40W
Kennebec, *U.S.A.* **80 D5** 43 54N 99 52W
Kennebec →, *U.S.A.* **77 D11** 43 45N 69 46W
Kennebunk, *U.S.A.* **79 C14** 43 23N 70 33W
Kennedy, *Zimbabwe* **55 F2** 18 52S 27 10 E
Kennedy Ra., *Australia* **61 D2** 24 45S 115 10 E
Kennedy Taungdeik, *Burma* **41 H18** 23 15N 93 45 E
Kenner, *U.S.A.* **81 L9** 29 59N 90 15W
Kennet →, *U.K.* **11 F7** 51 27N 0 57W
Kenneth Ra., *Australia* **61 D2** 23 50S 117 8 E
Kennett, *U.S.A.* **81 G9** 36 14N 90 3W
Kennewick, *U.S.A.* **82 C4** 46 12N 119 7W
Kenogami →, *Canada* **70 B3** 51 6N 84 28W
Kenora, *Canada* **73 D10** 49 47N 94 29W
Kenosha, *U.S.A.* **76 D2** 42 35N 87 49W
Kensington, *Canada* **71 C7** 46 28N 63 34W
Kent, *Ohio, U.S.A.* **78 E3** 41 9N 81 22W
Kent, *Tex., U.S.A.* **81 K2** 31 4N 104 13W
Kent, *Wash., U.S.A.* **84 C4** 47 23N 122 14W
Kent □, *U.K.* **11 F8** 51 12N 0 40 E
Kent Group, *Australia* **62 F4** 39 30S 147 20 E
Kent Pen., *Canada* **68 B9** 68 30N 107 0W
Kentau, *Kazakstan* **26 E7** 43 32N 68 36 E
Kentland, *U.S.A.* **76 E2** 40 46N 87 27W
Kenton, *U.S.A.* **76 E4** 40 39N 83 37W
Kentucky □, *U.S.A.* **76 G3** 37 0N 84 0W
Kentucky →, *U.S.A.* **76 F3** 38 41N 85 11W
Kentucky L., *U.S.A.* **77 G2** 37 1N 88 16W

Kosciusko

Kosciusko, *U.S.A.* **81 J10** 33 4N 89 35W
Kosciuszko, Mt., *Australia* **63 F4** 36 27S 148 16 E
Kosha, *Sudan* **51 D12** 20 50N 30 30 E
K'oshih = Kashi, *China* **32 C2** 39 30N 76 2 E
Koshiki-Rettō, *Japan* **31 J4** 31 45N 129 49 E
Kosi, *India* **42 F7** 27 48N 77 29 E
Kosi →, *India* **43 E8** 28 41N 78 57 E
Košice, *Slovak Rep.* **17 D11** 48 42N 21 15 E
Koskhinoú, *Greece* **23 C10** 36 23N 28 13 E
Koslan, *Russia* **24 B8** 63 34N 49 14 E
Kosŏng, *N. Korea* **35 E15** 38 40N 128 22 E
Kosovo □, *Yugoslavia* **21 C9** 42 30N 21 0 E
Kosovska Mitrovica, *Yugoslavia* **21 C9** 42 54N 20 52 E
Kossou, L. de, *Ivory C.* **50 G4** 6 59N 5 31W
Koster, *S. Africa* **56 D4** 25 52S 26 54 E
Kôstî, *Sudan* **51 F12** 13 8N 32 43 E
Kostopil, *Ukraine* **17 C14** 50 51N 26 22 E
Kostroma, *Russia* **24 C7** 57 50N 40 58 E
Kostrzyn, *Poland* **16 B8** 52 35N 14 39 E
Koszalin, *Poland* **16 A9** 54 11N 16 8 E
Kot Addu, *Pakistan* **42 D4** 30 30N 71 0 E
Kot Kapura, *India* **42 D6** 30 35N 74 50 E
Kot Moman, *Pakistan* **42 C5** 32 13N 73 0 E
Kot Sultan, *Pakistan* **42 D4** 30 46N 70 56 E
Kota, *India* **42 G6** 25 14N 75 49 E
Kota Baharu, *Malaysia* **39 J4** 6 7N 102 14 E
Kota Barrage, *India* **42 G6** 25 6N 75 51 E
Kota Belud, *Malaysia* **36 C5** 6 21N 116 26 E
Kota Kinabalu, *Malaysia* **36 C5** 6 0N 116 4 E
Kota Kubu Baharu, *Malaysia* **39 L3** 3 34N 101 39 E
Kota Tinggi, *Malaysia* **39 M4** 1 44N 103 53 E
Kotaagung, *Indonesia* **36 F2** 5 38S 104 29 E
Kotabaru, *Indonesia* **36 E5** 3 20S 116 20 E
Kotabumi, *Indonesia* **36 E2** 4 49S 104 54 E
Kotamobagu, *Indonesia* **37 D6** 0 57N 124 31 E
Kotcho L., *Canada* **72 B4** 59 7N 121 12W
Kotdwara, *India* **43 E8** 29 45N 78 32 E
Kotelnich, *Russia* **24 C8** 58 22N 48 24 E
Kotelnikovo, *Russia* **25 E7** 47 38N 43 8 E
Kotelnyy, Ostrov, *Russia* **27 B14** 75 10N 139 0 E
Kothari →, *India* **42 G6** 25 20N 75 4 E
Kothi, *Mad. P., India* **43 H10** 23 21N 82 3 E
Kothi, *Mad. P., India* **43 G9** 24 45N 80 40 E
Kotiro, *Pakistan* **42 F2** 26 17N 67 13 E
Kotka, *Finland* **9 F22** 60 28N 26 58 E
Kotlas, *Russia* **24 B8** 61 17N 46 43 E
Kotli, *Pakistan* **42 C5** 33 30N 73 55 E
Kotma, *India* **43 H9** 23 12N 81 58 E
Kotmul, *Pakistan* **43 B6** 35 32N 75 10 E
Kotor, *Montenegro, Yug.* **21 C8** 42 25N 18 47 E
Kotovsk, *Ukraine* **17 E15** 47 45N 29 35 E
Kotputli, *India* **42 F7** 27 43N 76 12 E
Kotri, *Pakistan* **42 G3** 25 22N 68 22 E
Kottayam, *India* **40 Q10** 9 35N 76 33 E
Kotturu, *India* **40 M10** 14 45N 76 10 E
Kotuy →, *Russia* **27 B11** 71 54N 102 6 E
Kotzebue, *U.S.A.* **68 B3** 66 53N 162 39W
Koudougou, *Burkina Faso* **50 F5** 12 10N 2 20W
Koufonísi, *Greece* **23 E8** 34 56N 26 8 E
Kougaberge, *S. Africa* **56 E3** 33 48S 23 50 E
Kouilou →, *Congo* **52 E2** 4 10S 12 5 E
Koula Moutou, *Gabon* **52 E2** 1 15S 12 25 E
Koulen = Kulen, *Cambodia* **38 F5** 13 50N 104 40 E
Kouloúra, *Greece* **23 A3** 39 42N 19 54 E
Koúm-bournoú, Ákra, *Greece* **23 C10** 36 15N 28 11 E
Koumala, *Australia* **62 C4** 21 38S 149 15 E
Koumra, *Chad* **51 G9** 8 50N 17 35 E
Kounradskiy, *Kazakstan* **26 E8** 46 59N 75 0 E
Kountze, *U.S.A.* **81 K7** 30 22N 94 19W
Kouris →, *Cyprus* **23 E11** 34 38N 32 54 E
Kourou, *Fr. Guiana* **93 B8** 5 9N 52 39W
Kousseri, *Cameroon* **51 F8** 12 0N 14 55 E
Kouvola, *Finland* **9 F22** 60 52N 26 43 E
Kovdor, *Russia* **24 A5** 67 34N 30 24 E
Kovel, *Ukraine* **17 C13** 51 11N 24 38 E
Kovrov, *Russia* **24 C7** 56 25N 41 25 E
Kowanyama, *Australia* **62 B3** 15 29S 141 44 E
Kowŏn, *N. Korea* **35 E14** 39 26N 127 14 E
Köyceğiz, *Turkey* **21 F13** 36 57N 28 40 E
Koza, *Japan* **31 L3** 26 19N 127 46 E
Kozan, *Turkey* **44 B2** 37 26N 35 50 E
Kozáni, *Greece* **21 D9** 40 19N 21 47 E
Kozhikode = Calicut, *India* **40 P9** 11 15N 75 43 E
Kozhva, *Russia* **24 A10** 65 10N 57 0 E
Kozyatyn, *Ukraine* **17 D15** 49 45N 28 50 E
Kra, Isthmus of = Kra, Kho Khot, *Thailand* **39 G2** 10 15N 99 30 E
Kra, Kho Khot, *Thailand* **39 G2** 10 15N 99 30 E
Kra Buri, *Thailand* **39 G2** 10 22N 98 46 E
Krabi, *Thailand* **39 H2** 8 4N 98 55 E
Kracheh, *Cambodia* **38 F6** 12 32N 106 10 E
Kragan, *Indonesia* **37 G14** 6 43S 111 38 E
Kragerø, *Norway* **9 G13** 58 52N 9 25 E
Kragujevac, *Serbia, Yug.* **21 B9** 44 2N 20 56 E
Krajina, *Bos.-H.* **20 B7** 44 45N 16 35 E
Krakatau = Rakata, Pulau, *Indonesia* **36 F3** 6 10S 105 20 E
Krakatoa = Rakata, Pulau, *Indonesia* **36 F3** 6 10S 105 20 E
Krakor, *Cambodia* **38 F5** 12 32N 104 12 E
Kraków, *Poland* **17 C10** 50 4N 19 57 E
Kralanh, *Cambodia* **38 F4** 13 35N 103 25 E
Kraljevo, *Serbia, Yug.* **21 C9** 43 44N 20 41 E
Kramatorsk, *Ukraine* **25 E6** 48 50N 37 30 E
Kramfors, *Sweden* **9 E17** 62 55N 17 48 E
Kranj, *Slovenia* **16 E8** 46 16N 14 22 E
Krankskop, *S. Africa* **57 D5** 28 0S 30 47 E
Krasavino, *Russia* **24 B8** 60 58N 46 29 E
Kraskino, *Russia* **27 E14** 42 44N 130 48 E
Kraśnik, *Poland* **17 C12** 50 55N 22 15 E
Krasnoarmeysk, *Russia* **26 D5** 51 0N 45 42 E
Krasnodar, *Russia* **25 E6** 45 5N 39 0 E
Krasnokamsk, *Russia* **24 C10** 58 4N 55 48 E
Krasnoperekopsk, *Ukraine* **25 E5** 46 0N 33 54 E
Krasnorechenskiy, *Russia* **30 B7** 44 41N 135 14 E
Krasnoselkup, *Russia* **26 C9** 65 20N 82 10 E
Krasnoturinsk, *Russia* **24 C11** 59 46N 60 12 E
Krasnoufimsk, *Russia* **24 C10** 56 36N 57 38 E
Krasnouralsk, *Russia* **24 C11** 58 21N 60 3 E
Krasnovishersk, *Russia* **24 B10** 60 23N 57 3 E
Krasnovodsk = Türkmenbashi, *Turkmenistan* **25 G9** 40 5N 53 5 E
Krasnoyarsk, *Russia* **27 D10** 56 8N 93 0 E
Krasnyy Kut, *Russia* **25 D8** 50 50N 47 0 E
Krasnyy Luch, *Ukraine* **25 E6** 48 13N 39 0 E
Krasnyy Yar, *Russia* **25 E8** 46 43N 48 23 E
Kratie = Kracheh, *Cambodia* **38 F6** 12 32N 106 10 E
Krau, *Indonesia* **37 E10** 3 19S 140 5 E
Kravanh, Chuor Phnum, *Cambodia* **39 G4** 12 0N 103 32 E
Krefeld, *Germany* **16 C4** 51 20N 6 33 E
Kremen, *Croatia* **16 F8** 44 28N 15 53 E
Kremenchug = Kremenchuk, *Ukraine* **25 E5** 49 5N 33 25 E
Kremenchuk, *Ukraine* **25 E5** 49 5N 33 25 E
Kremenchuksk Vdskh., *Ukraine* **25 E5** 49 20N 32 30 E
Kremenets, *Ukraine* **17 C13** 50 8N 25 43 E
Kremmling, *U.S.A.* **82 F10** 40 4N 106 24W
Krems, *Austria* **16 D8** 48 25N 15 36 E
Kretinga, *Lithuania* **9 J19** 55 53N 21 15 E
Kribi, *Cameroon* **52 D1** 2 57N 9 56 E
Krichev = Krychaw, *Belarus* **17 B16** 53 40N 31 41 E
Kriós, Ákra, *Greece* **23 D5** 35 13N 23 34 E
Krishna →, *India* **41 M12** 15 57N 80 59 E
Krishnanagar, *India* **43 H13** 23 24N 88 33 E
Kristiansand, *Norway* **9 G13** 58 8N 8 1 E
Kristianstad, *Sweden* **9 H16** 56 2N 14 9 E
Kristiansund, *Norway* **8 E12** 63 7N 7 45 E
Kristiinankaupunki, *Finland* **9 E19** 62 16N 21 21 E
Kristinehamn, *Sweden* **9 G16** 59 18N 14 7 E
Kristinestad = Kristiinankaupunki, *Finland* **9 E19** 62 16N 21 21 E
Kríti, *Greece* **23 D7** 35 15N 25 0 E
Kritsá, *Greece* **23 D7** 35 10N 25 41 E
Krivoy Rog = Kryvyy Rih, *Ukraine* **25 E5** 47 51N 33 20 E
Krk, *Croatia* **16 F8** 45 8N 14 40 E
Krokodil →, *Mozam.* **57 D5** 25 14S 32 18 E
Krong Kaoh Kong, *Cambodia* **36 B2** 11 35N 103 0 E
Kronprins Olav Kyst, *Antarctica* **5 C5** 69 0S 42 0 E
Kronshtadt, *Russia* **24 B4** 59 57N 29 51 E
Kroonstad, *S. Africa* **56 D4** 27 43S 27 19 E
Kropotkin, *Russia* **25 E7** 45 28N 40 28 E
Krosno, *Poland* **17 D11** 49 42N 21 46 E
Krotoszyn, *Poland* **17 C9** 51 42N 17 23 E
Kroussón, *Greece* **23 D6** 35 13N 24 59 E
Kruger Nat. Park, *S. Africa* **57 C5** 23 30S 31 40 E
Krugersdorp, *S. Africa* **57 D4** 26 5S 27 46 E
Kruisfontein, *S. Africa* **56 E3** 33 59S 24 43 E
Krung Thep = Bangkok, *Thailand* **38 F3** 13 45N 100 35 E
Krupki, *Belarus* **17 A15** 54 19N 29 8 E
Kruševac, *Serbia, Yug.* **21 C9** 43 35N 21 28 E
Krychaw, *Belarus* **17 B16** 53 40N 31 41 E
Krymskiy Poluostrov = Krymskyy Pivostriv, *Ukraine* **25 F5** 45 0N 34 0 E
Krymskyy Pivostriv, *Ukraine* **25 F5** 45 0N 34 0 E
Kryvyy Rih, *Ukraine* **25 E5** 47 51N 33 20 E
Ksar el Kebir, *Morocco* **50 B4** 35 0N 6 0W
Ksar es Souk = Ar Rachidiya, *Morocco* **50 B5** 31 58N 4 20W
Kuala Belait, *Malaysia* **36 D4** 4 35N 114 11 E
Kuala Berang, *Malaysia* **39 K4** 5 5N 103 1 E
Kuala Dungun = Dungun, *Malaysia* **39 K4** 4 45N 103 25 E
Kuala Kangsar, *Malaysia* **39 K3** 4 46N 100 56 E
Kuala Kelawang, *Malaysia* **39 L4** 2 56N 102 5 E
Kuala Kerai, *Malaysia* **39 K4** 5 30N 102 12 E
Kuala Lipis, *Malaysia* **39 K4** 4 10N 102 3 E
Kuala Lumpur, *Malaysia* **39 L3** 3 9N 101 41 E
Kuala Nerang, *Malaysia* **39 J3** 6 16N 100 37 E
Kuala Pilah, *Malaysia* **39 L4** 2 45N 102 15 E
Kuala Rompin, *Malaysia* **39 L4** 2 49N 103 29 E
Kuala Selangor, *Malaysia* **39 L3** 3 20N 101 15 E
Kuala Sepetang, *Malaysia* **39 K3** 4 49N 100 28 E
Kuala Terengganu, *Malaysia* **39 K4** 5 20N 103 8 E
Kualajelai, *Indonesia* **36 E4** 2 58S 110 46 E
Kualakapuas, *Indonesia* **36 E4** 2 55S 114 20 E
Kualakurun, *Indonesia* **36 E4** 1 10S 113 50 E
Kualapembuang, *Indonesia* **36 E4** 3 14S 112 38 E
Kualasimpang, *Indonesia* **36 D1** 4 17N 98 3 E
Kuancheng, *China* **35 D10** 40 37N 118 30 E
Kuandang, *Indonesia* **37 D6** 0 56N 123 1 E
Kuandian, *China* **35 D13** 40 45N 124 45 E
Kuangchou = Guangzhou, *China* **33 D6** 23 5N 113 10 E
Kuantan, *Malaysia* **39 L4** 3 49N 103 20 E
Kuba = Quba, *Azerbaijan* **25 F8** 41 21N 48 32 E
Kuban →, *Russia* **25 E6** 45 20N 37 30 E
Kubokawa, *Japan* **31 H6** 33 12N 133 8 E
Kucha Gompa, *India* **43 B7** 34 25N 76 56 E
Kuchaman, *India* **42 F6** 27 13N 74 47 E
Kuchinda, *India* **43 J11** 21 44N 84 21 E
Kuching, *Malaysia* **36 D4** 1 33N 110 25 E
Kuchino-eruba-Jima, *Japan* **31 J5** 30 28N 130 12 E
Kuchino-Shima, *Japan* **31 K4** 29 57N 129 55 E
Kuchinotsu, *Japan* **31 H5** 32 36N 130 11 E
Kucing = Kuching, *Malaysia* **36 D4** 1 33N 110 25 E
Kud →, *Pakistan* **42 F2** 26 5N 66 20 E
Kuda, *India* **40 H7** 23 10N 71 15 E
Kudat, *Malaysia* **36 C5** 6 55N 116 55 E
Kudus, *Indonesia* **37 G14** 6 48S 110 51 E
Kudymkar, *Russia* **24 C9** 59 1N 54 39 E
Kueiyang = Guiyang, *China* **32 D5** 26 32N 106 40 E
Kufra Oasis = Al Kufrah, *Libya* **51 D10** 24 17N 23 15 E
Kufstein, *Austria* **16 E7** 47 35N 12 11 E
Kugluktuk, *Canada* **68 B8** 67 50N 115 5W
Kugong I., *Canada* **70 A4** 56 18N 79 50W
Kūhak, *Iran* **40 F3** 27 12N 63 10 E
Kuhan, *Pakistan* **42 E2** 28 19N 67 14 E
Kūhbonān, *Iran* **45 D8** 31 23N 56 19 E
Kūhestak, *Iran* **45 E8** 26 47N 57 2 E
Kuhin, *Iran* **45 B6** 36 22N 49 40 E
Kūhīrī, *Iran* **45 E9** 26 55N 61 2 E
Kūhpāyeh, *Eşfahan, Iran* **45 C7** 32 44N 52 20 E
Kūhpāyeh, *Kermān, Iran* **45 D8** 30 35N 57 15 E
Kūhrān, Kūh-e, *Iran* **45 E8** 26 46N 58 12 E
Kui Buri, *Thailand* **39 F2** 12 3N 99 52 E
Kuito, *Angola* **53 G3** 12 22S 16 55 E
Kuiu I., *U.S.A.* **72 B2** 57 45N 134 10W
Kujang, *N. Korea* **35 E14** 39 57N 126 1 E
Kuji, *Japan* **30 D10** 40 11N 141 46 E
Kujū-San, *Japan* **31 H5** 33 5N 131 15 E
Kukësi, *Albania* **21 C9** 42 5N 20 27 E
Kukup, *Malaysia* **39 M4** 1 20N 103 27 E
Kula, *Turkey* **21 E13** 38 32N 28 40 E
Kulachi, *Pakistan* **42 D4** 31 56N 70 27 E
Kulai, *Malaysia* **39 M4** 1 44N 103 35 E
Kulal, Mt., *Kenya* **54 B4** 2 42N 36 57 E
Kulasekarappattinam, *India* **40 Q11** 8 20N 78 5 E
Kuldīga, *Latvia* **9 H19** 56 58N 21 59 E
Kuldja = Yining, *China* **26 E9** 43 58N 81 10 E
Kulen, *Cambodia* **38 F5** 13 50N 104 40 E
Kulgam, *India* **43 C6** 33 36N 75 2 E
Kulgera, *Australia* **62 D1** 25 50S 133 18 E
Kulim, *Malaysia* **39 K3** 5 22N 100 34 E
Kulin, *Australia* **61 F2** 32 40S 118 2 E
Kŭlob, *Tajikistan* **26 F7** 37 55N 69 50 E
Kulsary, *Kazakstan* **25 E9** 46 59N 54 1 E
Kulti, *India* **43 H12** 23 43N 86 50 E
Kulu, *India* **42 D7** 31 58N 77 6 E
Kulumbura, *Australia* **60 B4** 13 55S 126 35 E
Kulunda, *Russia* **26 D8** 52 35N 78 57 E
Kulungar, *Afghan.* **42 C3** 34 0N 69 2 E
Kūlvand, *Iran* **45 D7** 31 21N 54 35 E
Kulwin, *Australia* **63 F3** 35 0S 142 42 E
Kulyab = Kŭlob, *Tajikistan* **26 F7** 37 55N 69 50 E
Kuma →, *Russia* **25 F8** 44 55N 47 0 E
Kumagaya, *Japan* **31 F9** 36 9N 139 22 E
Kumai, *Indonesia* **36 E4** 2 44S 111 43 E
Kumamba, Kepulauan, *Indonesia* **37 E9** 1 36S 138 45 E
Kumamoto, *Japan* **31 H5** 32 45N 130 45 E
Kumamoto □, *Japan* **31 H5** 32 55N 130 55 E
Kumanovo, *Macedonia* **21 C9** 42 9N 21 42 E
Kumara, *N.Z.* **59 K3** 42 37S 171 12 E
Kumarina, *Australia* **61 D2** 24 41S 119 32 E
Kumasi, *Ghana* **50 G5** 6 41N 1 38W
Kumayri = Gyumri, *Armenia* **25 F7** 40 47N 43 50 E
Kumba, *Cameroon* **52 D1** 4 36N 9 24 E
Kumbakonam, *India* **40 P11** 10 58N 79 25 E
Kumbarilla, *Australia* **63 D5** 27 15S 150 55 E
Kumbhraj, *India* **42 G7** 24 22N 77 3 E
Kumbia, *Australia* **63 D5** 26 41S 151 39 E
Kŭmch'ŏn, *N. Korea* **35 E14** 38 10N 126 29 E
Kumdok, *India* **43 C8** 33 32N 78 10 E
Kume-Shima, *Japan* **31 L3** 26 20N 126 47 E
Kumertau, *Russia* **24 D10** 52 45N 55 57 E
Kumharsain, *India* **42 D7** 31 19N 77 27 E
Kŭmhwa, *S. Korea* **35 E14** 38 17N 127 28 E
Kumi, *Uganda* **54 B3** 1 30N 33 58 E
Kumla, *Sweden* **9 G16** 59 8N 15 10 E
Kumo, *Nigeria* **51 F8** 10 1N 11 12 E
Kumon Bum, *Burma* **41 F20** 26 30N 97 15 E
Kunashir, Ostrov, *Russia* **27 E15** 44 0N 146 0 E
Kunda, *Estonia* **9 G22** 59 30N 26 34 E
Kunda, *India* **43 G9** 25 43N 81 31 E
Kundar →, *Pakistan* **42 D3** 31 56N 69 19 E
Kundian, *Pakistan* **42 C4** 32 27N 71 28 E
Kundla, *India* **42 J4** 21 21N 71 25 E
Kunga →, *Bangla.* **43 J13** 21 46N 89 30 E
Kunghit I., *Canada* **72 C2** 52 6N 131 3W
Kungrad = Qŭnghirot, *Uzbekistan* **26 E6** 43 6N 58 54 E
Kungsbacka, *Sweden* **9 H15** 57 30N 12 5 E
Kungur, *Russia* **24 C10** 57 25N 56 57 E
Kunhar →, *Pakistan* **43 B5** 34 20N 73 30 E
Kuningan, *Indonesia* **37 G13** 6 59S 108 29 E
Kunlong, *Burma* **41 H21** 23 20N 98 50 E
Kunlun Shan, *Asia* **32 C3** 36 0N 86 30 E
Kunming, *China* **32 D5** 25 1N 102 41 E
Kunsan, *S. Korea* **35 G14** 35 59N 126 45 E
Kununurra, *Australia* **60 C4** 15 40S 128 50 E
Kunwari →, *India* **43 F8** 26 26N 79 11 E
Kunya-Urgench = Köneürgench, *Turkmenistan* **26 E6** 42 19N 59 10 E
Kuopio, *Finland* **8 E22** 62 53N 27 35 E
Kupa →, *Croatia* **16 F9** 45 28N 16 24 E
Kupang, *Indonesia* **37 F6** 10 19S 123 39 E
Kupreanof I., *U.S.A.* **72 B2** 56 50N 133 30W
Kupyansk-Uzlovoi, *Ukraine* **25 E6** 49 40N 37 43 E
Kuqa, *China* **32 B3** 41 35N 82 30 E
Kür →, *Azerbaijan* **25 G8** 39 29N 49 15 E
Kür Dili, *Azerbaijan* **45 B6** 39 3N 49 13 E
Kura = Kür →, *Azerbaijan* **25 G8** 39 29N 49 15 E
Kuranda, *Australia* **62 B4** 16 48S 145 35 E
Kuranga, *India* **42 H3** 22 4N 69 10 E
Kurashiki, *Japan* **31 G6** 34 40N 133 50 E
Kurayoshi, *Japan* **31 G6** 35 26N 133 50 E
Kŭrdzhali, *Bulgaria* **21 D11** 41 38N 25 21 E
Kure, *Japan* **31 G6** 34 14N 132 32 E
Kuressaare, *Estonia* **9 G20** 58 15N 22 30 E
Kurgan, *Russia* **26 D7** 55 26N 65 18 E
Kuri, *India* **42 F4** 26 37N 70 43 E
Kuria Maria Is. = Khurīyā Murīyā, Jazā 'ir, *Oman* **46 D6** 17 30N 55 58 E
Kuridala, *Australia* **62 C3** 21 16S 140 29 E
Kurigram, *Bangla.* **41 G16** 25 49N 89 39 E
Kurikka, *Finland* **9 E20** 62 36N 22 24 E
Kuril Is. = Kurilskiye Ostrova, *Russia* **27 E16** 45 0N 150 0 E
Kuril Trench, *Pac. Oc.* **28 E19** 44 0N 153 0 E
Kurilsk, *Russia* **27 E15** 45 14N 147 53 E
Kurilskiye Ostrova, *Russia* **27 E16** 45 0N 150 0 E
Kurino, *Japan* **31 J5** 31 57N 130 43 E
Kurinskaya Kosa = Kür Dili, *Azerbaijan* **45 B6** 39 3N 49 13 E
Kurnool, *India* **40 M11** 15 45N 78 0 E
Kuro-Shima, *Kagoshima, Japan* **31 J4** 30 50N 129 57 E
Kuro-Shima, *Okinawa, Japan* **31 M2** 24 14N 124 1 E
Kurow, *N.Z.* **59 L3** 44 44S 170 29 E
Kurram →, *Pakistan* **42 C4** 32 36N 71 20 E
Kurri Kurri, *Australia* **63 E5** 32 50S 151 28 E
Kurrimine, *Australia* **62 B4** 17 47S 146 6 E
Kurshskiy Zaliv, *Russia* **9 J19** 55 9N 21 6 E
Kursk, *Russia* **24 D6** 51 42N 36 11 E
Kuruçay, *Turkey* **44 B3** 39 39N 38 29 E
Kuruktag, *China* **32 B3** 41 0N 89 0 E
Kuruman, *S. Africa* **56 D3** 27 28S 23 28 E
Kuruman →, *S. Africa* **56 D3** 26 56S 20 39 E
Kurume, *Japan* **31 H5** 33 15N 130 30 E
Kurunegala, *Sri Lanka* **40 R12** 7 30N 80 23 E
Kurya, *Russia* **24 B10** 61 42N 57 9 E
Kus Gölü, *Turkey* **21 D12** 40 10N 27 55 E
Kuşadası, *Turkey* **21 F12** 37 52N 27 15 E
Kusatsu, *Japan* **31 F9** 36 37N 138 36 E
Kusawa L., *Canada* **72 A1** 60 20N 136 13W
Kushalgarh, *India* **42 H6** 23 10N 74 27 E
Kushikino, *Japan* **31 J5** 31 44N 130 16 E
Kushima, *Japan* **31 J5** 31 29N 131 14 E
Kushimoto, *Japan* **31 H7** 33 28N 135 47 E
Kushiro, *Japan* **30 C12** 43 0N 144 25 E
Kushiro-Gawa →, *Japan* **30 C12** 42 59N 144 23 E
Kūshk, *Iran* **45 D8** 28 46N 56 51 E
Kushka = Gushgy, *Turkmenistan* **26 F7** 35 20N 62 18 E
Kūshkī, *Iran* **44 C5** 33 31N 47 13 E
Kushol, *India* **43 C7** 33 40N 76 36 E
Kushtia, *Bangla.* **41 H16** 23 55N 89 5 E
Kushva, *Russia* **24 C10** 58 18N 59 45 E
Kuskokwim B., *U.S.A.* **68 C3** 59 45N 162 25W
Kusmi, *India* **43 H10** 23 17N 83 55 E
Kussharo-Ko, *Japan* **30 C12** 43 38N 144 21 E
Kustanay = Qostanay, *Kazakstan* **26 D7** 53 10N 63 35 E
Kut, Ko, *Thailand* **39 G4** 11 40N 102 35 E
Kütahya, *Turkey* **25 G5** 39 30N 30 2 E
Kutaisi, *Georgia* **25 F7** 42 19N 42 40 E
Kutaraja = Banda Aceh, *Indonesia* **36 C1** 5 35N 95 20 E
Kutch, Gulf of = Kachchh, Gulf of, *India* **42 H3** 22 50N 69 15 E
Kutch, Rann of = Kachchh, Rann of, *India* **42 H4** 24 0N 70 0 E
Kutiyana, *India* **42 J4** 21 36N 70 2 E
Kutno, *Poland* **17 B10** 52 15N 19 23 E
Kutu, *Dem. Rep. of the Congo* **52 E3** 2 40S 18 11 E
Kutum, *Sudan* **51 F10** 14 10N 24 40 E
Kuujjuaq, *Canada* **69 C13** 58 6N 68 15W
Kuujjuarapik, *Canada* **70 A4** 55 20N 77 35W
Kuŭp-tong, *N. Korea* **35 D14** 40 45N 126 1 E
Kuusamo, *Finland* **8 D23** 65 57N 29 8 E
Kuusankoski, *Finland* **9 F22** 60 55N 26 38 E
Kuvango, *Angola* **53 G3** 14 28S 16 20 E
Kuwait = Al Kuwayt, *Kuwait* **44 D5** 29 30N 48 0 E
Kuwait ■, *Asia* **44 D5** 29 30N 47 30 E
Kuwana, *Japan* **31 G8** 35 5N 136 43 E
Kuwana →, *India* **43 F10** 26 25N 83 15 E
Kuybyshev = Samara, *Russia* **24 D9** 53 8N 50 6 E
Kuybyshev, *Russia* **26 D8** 55 27N 78 19 E
Kuybyshevskoye Vdkhr., *Russia* **24 C8** 55 2N 49 30 E
Kuye He →, *China* **34 E6** 38 23N 110 46 E
Kūyeh, *Iran* **44 B5** 38 45N 47 57 E
Kūysanjaq, *Iraq* **44 B5** 36 5N 44 38 E
Kuyto, Ozero, *Russia* **24 B5** 65 6N 31 20 E
Kuyumba, *Russia* **27 C10** 60 58N 96 59 E
Kuzey Anadolu Dağları, *Turkey* **25 F6** 41 30N 35 0 E
Kuznetsk, *Russia* **24 D8** 53 12N 46 40 E
Kuzomen, *Russia* **24 A6** 66 22N 36 50 E
Kvænangen, *Norway* **8 A19** 70 5N 21 15 E
Kvaløy, *Norway* **8 B18** 69 40N 18 30 E
Kvarner, *Croatia* **16 F8** 44 50N 14 10 E
Kvarnerič, *Croatia* **16 F8** 44 43N 14 37 E
Kwa-Nobuhle, *S. Africa* **53 L5** 33 50S 25 22 E
Kwabhaca, *S. Africa* **57 E4** 30 51S 29 0 E
Kwakhanai, *Botswana* **56 C3** 21 39S 21 16 E
Kwakoegron, *Surinam* **93 B7** 5 12N 55 25W
Kwale, *Kenya* **54 C4** 4 15S 39 31 E
KwaMashu, *S. Africa* **57 D5** 29 45S 30 58 E
Kwando →, *Africa* **56 B3** 18 27S 23 32 E
Kwangdaeri, *N. Korea* **35 D14** 40 31N 127 32 E
Kwangju, *S. Korea* **35 G14** 35 9N 126 54 E
Kwango →, *Dem. Rep. of the Congo* **52 E3** 3 14S 17 22 E
Kwangsi-Chuang = Guangxi Zhuangzu Zizhiqu □, *China* **33 D5** 24 0N 109 0 E
Kwangtung = Guangdong □, *China* **33 D6** 23 0N 113 0 E
Kwataboahegan →, *Canada* **70 B3** 51 9N 80 50W
Kwatisore, *Indonesia* **37 E8** 3 18S 134 50 E
KwaZulu Natal □, *S. Africa* **57 D5** 29 0S 30 0 E
Kweichow = Guizhou □, *China* **32 D5** 27 0N 107 0 E
Kwekwe, *Zimbabwe* **55 F2** 18 58S 29 48 E
Kwidzyn, *Poland* **17 B10** 53 44N 18 55 E
Kwinana New Town, *Australia* **61 F2** 32 15S 115 47 E
Kwoka, *Indonesia* **37 E8** 0 31S 132 27 E
Kyabra Cr. →, *Australia* **63 D3** 25 36S 142 55 E
Kyabram, *Australia* **63 F4** 36 19S 145 4 E
Kyaikto, *Burma* **38 D1** 17 20N 97 3 E
Kyakhta, *Russia* **27 D11** 50 30N 106 25 E
Kyancutta, *Australia* **63 E2** 33 8S 135 33 E
Kyangin, *Burma* **41 K19** 18 20N 95 20 E
Kyaukpadaung, *Burma* **41 J19** 20 52N 95 8 E
Kyaukpyu, *Burma* **41 K18** 19 28N 93 30 E
Kyaukse, *Burma* **41 J20** 21 36N 96 10 E
Kyburz, *U.S.A.* **84 G6** 38 47N 120 18W
Kyelang, *India* **42 C7** 32 35N 77 2 E
Kyenjojo, *Uganda* **54 B3** 0 40N 30 37 E
Kyle, *Canada* **73 C7** 50 50N 108 2W
Kyle Dam, *Zimbabwe* **55 G3** 20 15S 31 0 E
Kyle of Lochalsh, *U.K.* **12 D3** 57 17N 5 44W
Kymijoki →, *Finland* **9 F22** 60 30N 26 55 E
Kyneton, *Australia* **63 F3** 37 10S 144 29 E
Kynuna, *Australia* **62 C3** 21 37S 141 55 E
Kyō-ga-Saki, *Japan* **31 G7** 35 45N 135 15 E
Kyoga, L., *Uganda* **54 B3** 1 35N 33 0 E
Kyogle, *Australia* **63 D5** 28 40S 153 0 E
Kyongju, *S. Korea* **35 G15** 35 51N 129 14 E
Kyongpyaw, *Burma* **41 L19** 17 12N 95 10 E
Kyŏngsŏng, *N. Korea* **35 D15** 41 35N 129 36 E
Kyōto, *Japan* **31 G7** 35 0N 135 45 E
Kyōto □, *Japan* **31 G7** 35 15N 135 45 E
Kyparissovouno, *Cyprus* **23 D12** 35 19N 33 10 E
Kyperounda, *Cyprus* **23 E11** 34 56N 32 58 E
Kyrenia, *Cyprus* **23 D12** 35 20N 33 20 E
Kyrgyzstan ■, *Asia* **26 E8** 42 0N 75 0 E
Kyrönjoki →, *Finland* **8 E19** 63 14N 21 45 E
Kystatyam, *Russia* **27 C13** 67 20N 123 10 E
Kythréa, *Cyprus* **23 D12** 35 15N 33 29 E
Kyunhla, *Burma* **41 H19** 23 25N 95 15 E
Kyuquot Sound, *Canada* **72 D3** 50 2N 127 22W
Kyūshū, *Japan* **31 H5** 33 0N 131 0 E
Kyūshū □, *Japan* **31 H5** 33 0N 131 0 E
Kyūshū-Sanchi, *Japan* **31 H5** 32 35N 131 17 E

Lappeenranta

Lappeenranta, Finland 9 F23 61 3N 28 12 E
Lappland, Europe 8 B21 68 7N 24 0 E
Laprida, Argentina 94 D3 37 34S 60 45W
Lapseki, Turkey 21 D12 40 20N 26 41 E
Laptev Sea, Russia 27 B13 76 0N 125 0 E
Lapua, Finland 8 E20 62 58N 23 0 E
L'Áquila, Italy 20 C5 42 22N 13 22 E
Lār, Āzarbājān-e Sharqī, Iran 44 B5 38 30N 47 52 E
Lār, Fārs, Iran 45 E7 27 40N 54 14 E
Laramie, U.S.A. 80 E2 41 19N 105 35W
Laramie →, U.S.A. 82 F11 42 13N 104 33W
Laramie Mts., U.S.A. 80 E2 42 0N 105 30W
Laranjeiras do Sul, Brazil 95 B5 25 23S 52 23W
Larantuka, Indonesia 37 F6 8 21S 122 55 E
Larat, Indonesia 37 F8 7 0S 132 0 E
Larde, Mozam. 55 F4 16 28S 39 43 E
Larder Lake, Canada 70 C4 48 5N 79 40W
Lardhos, Ákra = Líndhos, Ákra, Greece 23 C10 36 4N 28 10 E
Lardhos, Órmos, Greece 23 C10 36 4N 28 2 E
Laredo, U.S.A. 81 M5 27 30N 99 30W
Laredo Sd., Canada 72 C3 52 30N 128 53W
Largo, U.S.A. 77 M4 27 55N 82 47W
Largs, U.K. 12 F4 55 47N 4 52W
Lariang, Indonesia 37 E5 1 26S 119 17 E
Larimore, U.S.A. 80 B6 47 54N 97 38W
Lārīn, Iran 45 C7 35 55N 52 19 E
Lárisa, Greece 21 E10 39 36N 22 27 E
Larkana, Pakistan 42 F3 27 32N 68 18 E
Larnaca, Cyprus 23 E12 34 55N 33 38 E
Larnaca Bay, Cyprus 23 E12 34 53N 33 45 E
Larne, U.K. 13 B6 54 51N 5 51W
Larned, U.S.A. 80 F5 38 11N 99 6W
Larose, U.S.A. 81 L9 29 34N 90 23W
Larrimah, Australia 60 C5 15 35S 133 12 E
Larsen Ice Shelf, Antarctica 5 C17 67 0S 62 0W
Larvik, Norway 9 G14 59 4N 10 2 E
Las Animas, U.S.A. 80 F3 38 4N 103 13W
Las Anod, Somali Rep. 46 F4 8 26N 47 19 E
Las Aves, Is., W. Indies 89 C7 15 45N 63 55W
Las Brenãs, Argentina 94 B3 27 5S 61 7W
Las Cejas, Argentina 96 B4 26 53S 64 44W
Las Chimeneas, Mexico 85 N10 32 8N 116 5W
Las Cruces, U.S.A. 83 K10 32 19N 106 47W
Las Flores, Argentina 94 D4 36 10S 59 7W
Las Heras, Argentina 94 C2 32 51S 68 49W
Las Lajas, Argentina 96 D2 38 30S 70 25W
Las Lomitas, Argentina 94 A3 24 43S 60 35W
Las Palmas, Argentina 94 B4 27 8S 58 45W
Las Palmas, Canary Is. 22 F4 28 7N 15 26W
Las Palmas →, Mexico 85 N10 32 26N 116 54W
Las Piedras, Uruguay 95 C4 34 44S 56 14W
Las Pipinas, Argentina 94 D4 35 30S 57 19W
Las Plumas, Argentina 96 E3 43 40S 67 15W
Las Rosas, Argentina 94 C3 32 30S 61 35W
Las Tablas, Panama 88 E3 7 49N 80 14W
Las Termas, Argentina 94 B3 27 29S 64 52W
Las Toscas, Argentina 94 B4 28 21S 59 18W
Las Truchas, Mexico 86 D4 17 57N 102 13W
Las Varillas, Argentina 94 C3 31 50S 62 50W
Las Vegas, N. Mex., U.S.A. 83 J11 35 36N 105 13W
Las Vegas, Nev., U.S.A. 85 J11 36 10N 115 9W
Lascano, Uruguay 95 C5 33 35S 54 12W
Lashburn, Canada 73 C7 53 10N 109 40W
Lashio, Burma 41 H20 22 56N 97 45 E
Lashkar, India 42 F8 26 10N 78 10 E
Lasíthi, Greece 23 D7 35 11N 25 31 E
Lasíthi □, Greece 23 D7 35 5N 25 50 E
Lāsjerd, Iran 45 C7 35 24N 53 4 E
Lassen Pk., U.S.A. 82 F3 40 29N 121 31W
Lassen Volcanic National Park, U.S.A. 82 F3 40 30N 121 20W
Last Mountain L., Canada 73 C7 51 5N 105 14W
Lastchance Cr. →, U.S.A. 84 E5 40 2N 121 15W
Lastoursville, Gabon 52 E2 0 55S 12 38 E
Lastovo, Croatia 20 C7 42 46N 16 55 E
Lat Yao, Thailand 38 E2 15 45N 99 48 E
Latacunga, Ecuador 92 D3 0 50S 78 35W
Latakia = Al Lādhiqīyah, Syria 44 C2 35 30N 35 45 E
Latchford, Canada 70 C4 47 20N 79 50W
Latehar, India 43 H11 23 45N 84 30 E
Latham, Australia 61 E2 29 44S 116 20 E
Lathi, India 42 F4 27 43N 71 23 E
Lathrop Wells, U.S.A. 85 J10 36 39N 116 24W
Latina, Italy 20 D5 41 28N 12 52 E
Latium = Lazio □, Italy 20 C5 42 10N 12 30 E
Laton, U.S.A. 84 J7 36 26N 119 41W
Latouche Treville, C., Australia 60 C3 18 27S 121 49 E
Latrobe, Australia 62 G4 41 14S 146 30 E
Latrobe, U.S.A. 78 F5 40 19N 79 23W
Latvia ■, Europe 9 H20 56 50N 24 0 E
Lau Group, Fiji 59 C9 17 0S 178 30W
Lauchhammer, Germany 16 C7 51 29N 13 47 E
Laughlin, U.S.A. 83 J6 35 8N 114 35W
Laukaa, Finland 9 E21 62 24N 25 56 E
Launceston, Australia 62 G4 41 24S 147 8 E
Launceston, U.K. 11 G3 50 38N 4 22W
Laune →, Ireland 13 D2 52 7N 9 47W
Launglon Bok, Burma 38 F1 13 50N 97 54 E
Laura, Australia 62 B3 15 32S 144 32 E
Laurel, Miss., U.S.A. 81 K10 31 41N 89 8W
Laurel, Mont., U.S.A. 82 D9 45 40N 108 46W
Laurencekirk, U.K. 12 E6 56 50N 2 28W
Laurens, U.S.A. 77 H4 34 30N 82 1W
Laurentian Plateau, Canada 71 B6 52 0N 70 0W
Lauria, Italy 20 E6 40 2N 15 50 E
Laurie L., Canada 73 B8 56 35N 101 57W
Laurinburg, U.S.A. 77 H6 34 47N 79 28W
Laurium, U.S.A. 76 B1 47 14N 88 27W
Lausanne, Switz. 18 C7 46 32N 6 38 E
Laut, Indonesia 39 K6 4 45N 108 0 E
Laut, Pulau, Indonesia 36 E5 3 40S 116 10 E
Laut Kecil, Kepulauan, Indonesia 36 E5 4 45S 115 40 E
Lautoka, Fiji 59 C7 17 37S 177 27 E
Lavagh More, Ireland 13 B3 54 46N 8 6W
Laval, France 18 B3 48 4N 0 48W
Lavalle, Argentina 94 B2 28 15S 65 15W
Lavant Station, Canada 79 A8 45 3N 76 42W
Lāvar Meydān, Iran 45 D7 30 20N 54 30 E
Laverton, Australia 61 E3 28 44S 122 29 E
Lavras, Brazil 95 A7 21 20S 45 0W
Lávrion, Greece 21 F11 37 40N 24 4 E
Lávris, Greece 23 D6 35 25N 24 40 E
Lavumisa, Swaziland 57 D5 27 20S 31 55 E
Lawas, Malaysia 36 D5 4 55N 115 25 E
Lawele, Indonesia 37 F6 5 16S 123 3 E
Lawng Pit, Burma 41 G20 25 30N 97 25 E
Lawqah, Si. Arabia 44 D4 29 49N 42 45 E
Lawrence, N.Z. 59 L2 45 55S 169 41 E
Lawrence, Kans., U.S.A. 80 F7 38 58N 95 14W
Lawrence, Mass., U.S.A. 79 D13 42 43N 71 10W
Lawrenceburg, Ind., U.S.A. 76 F3 39 6N 84 52W
Lawrenceburg, Tenn., U.S.A. 77 H2 35 14N 87 20W
Lawrenceville, Ga., U.S.A. 77 J4 33 57N 83 59W
Lawrenceville, Pa., U.S.A. 78 E7 41 59N 77 8W
Laws, U.S.A. 84 H8 37 24N 118 20W
Lawton, U.S.A. 81 H5 34 37N 98 25W
Lawu, Indonesia 37 G14 7 40S 111 13 E
Laxford, L., U.K. 12 C3 58 24N 5 6W
Laylá, Si. Arabia 46 C4 22 10N 46 40 E
Laylān, Iraq 44 C5 35 18N 44 31 E
Layton, U.S.A. 82 F7 41 4N 111 58W
Laytonville, U.S.A. 82 G2 39 41N 123 29W
Lazio □, Italy 20 C5 42 10N 12 30 E
Lazo, Russia 30 C6 43 25N 133 55 E
Le Creusot, France 18 C6 46 48N 4 24 E
Le François, Martinique 89 D7 14 38N 60 57W
Le Havre, France 18 B4 49 30N 0 5 E
Le Mans, France 18 C4 48 0N 0 10 E
Le Mars, U.S.A. 80 D6 42 47N 96 10W
Le Mont-St-Michel, France 18 B3 48 40N 1 30W
Le Moule, Guadeloupe 89 C7 16 20N 61 22W
Le Puy-en-Velay, France 18 D5 45 3N 3 52 E
Le Sueur, U.S.A. 80 C8 44 28N 93 55W
Le Thuy, Vietnam 38 D6 17 14N 106 49 E
Le Touquet-Paris-Plage, France 18 A4 50 30N 1 36 E
Le Tréport, France 18 A4 50 3N 1 20 E
Le Verdon-sur-Mer, France 18 D3 45 33N 1 4W
Lea →, U.K. 11 F8 51 31N 0 1 E
Leach, Cambodia 39 F4 12 21N 103 46 E
Lead, U.S.A. 80 C3 44 21N 103 46W
Leader, Canada 73 C7 50 50N 109 30W
Leadville, U.S.A. 83 G10 39 15N 106 18W
Leaf →, U.S.A. 81 K10 30 59N 88 44W
Leaf Rapids, Canada 73 B9 56 30N 99 59W
Leamington, Canada 78 D2 42 3N 82 36W
Leamington, U.S.A. 82 G7 39 32N 112 17W
Leamington Spa = Royal Leamington Spa, U.K. 11 E6 52 18N 1 31W
Leandro Norte Alem, Argentina 95 B4 27 34S 55 15W
Leane, L., Ireland 13 D2 52 2N 9 32W
Learmonth, Australia 60 D1 22 13S 114 10 E
Leask, Canada 73 C7 53 5N 106 45W
Leatherhead, U.K. 11 F7 51 18N 0 20W
Leavenworth, Kans., U.S.A. 80 F7 39 19N 94 55W
Leavenworth, Wash., U.S.A. 82 C3 47 36N 120 40W
Lebak, Phil. 37 C6 6 32N 124 5 E
Lebam, U.S.A. 84 D3 46 34N 123 33W
Lebanon, Ind., U.S.A. 76 E2 40 3N 86 28W
Lebanon, Kans., U.S.A. 80 F5 39 49N 98 33W
Lebanon, Ky., U.S.A. 76 G3 37 34N 85 15W
Lebanon, Mo., U.S.A. 81 G8 37 41N 92 40W
Lebanon, N.H., U.S.A. 79 C12 43 39N 72 15W
Lebanon, Oreg., U.S.A. 82 D2 44 32N 122 55W
Lebanon, Pa., U.S.A. 79 F8 40 20N 76 26W
Lebanon, Tenn., U.S.A. 77 G2 36 12N 86 18W
Lebanon ■, Asia 47 B5 34 0N 36 0 E
Lebec, U.S.A. 85 L8 34 50N 118 52W
Lebel-sur-Quévillon, Canada 70 C4 49 3N 76 59W
Lebomboberge, S. Africa 57 C5 24 30S 32 0 E
Lębork, Poland 17 A9 54 33N 17 46 E
Lebrija, Spain 19 D2 36 53N 6 5W
Lebu, Chile 94 D1 37 40S 73 47W
Lecce, Italy 21 D8 40 23N 18 11 E
Lecco, Italy 18 D8 45 51N 9 23 E
Lech →, Germany 16 D6 48 43N 10 56 E
Lecontes Mills, U.S.A. 78 E6 41 5N 78 17W
Łęczyca, Poland 17 B10 52 5N 19 15 E
Ledong, China 38 C7 18 41N 109 5 E
Leduc, Canada 72 C6 53 15N 113 30W
Lee, U.S.A. 79 D11 42 19N 73 15W
Lee →, Ireland 13 E3 51 53N 8 56W
Lee Vining, U.S.A. 84 H7 37 58N 119 7W
Leech L., U.S.A. 80 B7 47 10N 94 24W
Leechburg, U.S.A. 78 F5 40 37N 79 36W
Leeds, U.K. 10 D6 53 48N 1 33W
Leeds, U.S.A. 77 J2 33 33N 86 33W
Leek, Neths. 15 A6 53 10N 6 24 E
Leek, U.K. 10 D5 53 7N 2 1W
Leeman, Australia 61 E1 29 57S 114 58 E
Leeper, U.S.A. 78 E5 41 22N 79 18W
Leer, Germany 16 B4 53 13N 7 26 E
Leesburg, U.S.A. 77 L5 28 49N 81 53W
Leesville, U.S.A. 81 K8 31 9N 93 16W
Leeton, Australia 63 E4 34 33S 146 23 E
Leetonia, U.S.A. 78 F4 40 53N 80 45W
Leeu Gamka, S. Africa 56 E3 32 47S 21 59 E
Leeuwarden, Neths. 15 A5 53 15N 5 48 E
Leeuwin, C., Australia 61 F2 34 20S 115 9 E
Leeward Is., Atl. Oc. 89 C7 16 30N 63 30W
Lefka, Cyprus 23 D11 35 6N 32 51 E
Lefkoniko, Cyprus 23 D12 35 18N 33 44 E
Lefroy, Canada 78 B5 44 16N 79 34W
Lefroy, L., Australia 61 F3 31 21S 121 40 E
Leganés, Spain 19 B4 40 19N 3 45W
Legazpi, Phil. 37 B6 13 10N 123 45 E
Legendre I., Australia 60 D2 20 22S 116 55 E
Leghorn = Livorno, Italy 20 C4 43 33N 10 19 E
Legionowo, Poland 17 B11 52 25N 20 50 E
Legnago, Italy 20 B4 45 11N 11 18 E
Legnica, Poland 16 C9 51 12N 16 10 E
Leh, India 43 B7 34 9N 77 35 E
Lehigh Acres, U.S.A. 77 M5 26 36N 81 39W
Lehighton, U.S.A. 79 F9 40 50N 75 43W
Lehututu, Botswana 56 C3 23 54S 21 55 E
Leiah, Pakistan 42 D4 30 58N 70 58 E
Leicester, U.K. 11 E6 52 38N 1 8W
Leicester City □, U.K. 11 E6 52 38N 1 8W
Leicestershire □, U.K. 11 E6 52 41N 1 17W
Leichhardt →, Australia 62 B2 17 35S 139 48 E
Leichhardt Ra., Australia 62 C4 20 46S 147 40 E
Leiden, Neths. 15 B4 52 9N 4 30 E
Leie →, Belgium 15 C3 51 2N 3 45 E
Leigh Creek, Australia 63 E2 30 38S 138 26 E
Leine →, Germany 16 B5 52 43N 9 36 E
Leinster, Australia 61 E3 27 51S 120 36 E
Leinster □, Ireland 13 C4 53 3N 7 8W
Leinster, Mt., Ireland 13 D5 52 37N 6 46W
Leipzig, Germany 16 C7 51 18N 12 22 E
Leiria, Portugal 19 C1 39 46N 8 53W
Leirvik, Norway 9 G11 59 47N 5 28 E
Leisler, Mt., Australia 60 D4 23 23S 129 20 E
Leith, U.K. 12 F5 55 59N 3 11W
Leith Hill, U.K. 11 F7 51 11N 0 22W
Leitrim, Ireland 13 B3 54 0N 8 5W
Leitrim □, Ireland 13 B4 54 8N 8 0W
Leizhou Bandao, China 33 D6 21 0N 110 0 E
Lek →, Neths. 15 C4 51 54N 4 35 E
Leka, Norway 8 D14 65 5N 11 35 E
Lékva Óros, Greece 23 D6 35 18N 24 3 E
Leland, Mich., U.S.A. 76 C3 45 1N 85 45W
Leland, Miss., U.S.A. 81 J9 33 24N 90 54W
Leleque, Argentina 96 E2 42 28S 71 0W
Lelystad, Neths. 15 B5 52 30N 5 25 E
Léman, L., Europe 18 C7 46 26N 6 30 E
Lemera, Dem. Rep. of the Congo 54 C2 3 0S 28 55 E
Lemhi Ra., U.S.A. 82 D7 44 30N 113 30W
Lemmer, Neths. 15 B5 52 51N 5 43 E
Lemmon, U.S.A. 80 C3 45 57N 102 10W
Lemon Grove, U.S.A. 85 N9 32 45N 117 2W
Lemoore, U.S.A. 84 J7 36 18N 119 46W
Lemvig, Denmark 9 H13 56 33N 8 20 E
Lena →, Russia 27 B13 72 52N 126 40 E
Léndas, Greece 23 E6 34 56N 24 56 E
Lendeh, Iran 45 D6 30 58N 50 25 E
Lenggong, Malaysia 39 K3 5 6N 100 58 E
Lengua de Vaca, Pta., Chile 94 C1 30 14S 71 38W
Leninabad = Khudzhand, Tajikistan 26 E7 40 17N 69 37 E
Leninakan = Gyumri, Armenia 25 F7 40 47N 43 50 E
Leningrad = Sankt-Peterburg, Russia 24 C5 59 55N 30 20 E
Leninogorsk, Kazakstan 26 D9 50 20N 83 30 E
Leninsk, Russia 25 E8 48 40N 45 15 E
Leninsk-Kuznetskiy, Russia 26 D9 54 44N 86 10 E
Lenkoran = Länkäran, Azerbaijan 25 G8 38 48N 48 52 E
Lenmalu, Indonesia 37 E8 1 45S 130 15 E
Lennox, U.S.A. 80 D6 43 21N 96 53W
Lennoxville, Canada 79 A13 45 22N 71 51W
Lenoir, U.S.A. 77 H5 35 55N 81 32W
Lenoir City, U.S.A. 77 H3 35 48N 84 16W
Lenore L., Canada 73 C8 52 30N 104 59W
Lenox, U.S.A. 79 D11 42 22N 73 17W
Lens, France 18 A5 50 26N 2 50 E
Lensk, Russia 27 C12 60 48N 114 55 E
Lentini, Italy 20 F6 37 17N 15 0 E
Lenwood, U.S.A. 85 L9 34 53N 117 7W
Lenya, Burma 36 B1 11 33N 98 57 E
Leoben, Austria 16 E8 47 22N 15 5 E
Leodhas = Lewis, U.K. 12 C2 58 9N 6 40W
Leola, U.S.A. 80 C5 45 43N 98 56W
Leominster, U.K. 11 E5 52 14N 2 43W
Leominster, U.S.A. 79 D13 42 32N 71 46W
León, Mexico 86 C4 21 7N 101 40W
León, Nic. 88 D2 12 20N 86 51W
León, Spain 19 A3 42 38N 5 34W
Leon, U.S.A. 80 E8 40 44N 93 45W
Leon →, U.S.A. 81 K6 31 14N 97 28W
León, Montes de, Spain 19 A2 42 30N 6 18W
Leonardtown, U.S.A. 76 F7 38 17N 76 38W
Leongatha, Australia 63 F4 38 30S 145 58 E
Leonora, Australia 61 E3 28 49S 121 19 E
Léopold II, Lac = Mai-Ndombe, L., Dem. Rep. of the Congo 52 E3 2 0S 18 20 E
Leopoldina, Brazil 95 A7 21 28S 42 40W
Leopoldsburg, Belgium 15 C5 51 7N 5 13 E
Léopoldville = Kinshasa, Dem. Rep. of the Congo 52 E3 4 20S 15 15 E
Leoti, U.S.A. 80 F4 38 29N 101 21W
Leova, Moldova 17 E15 46 28N 28 15 E
Leoville, Canada 73 C7 53 39N 107 33W
Lepel = Lyepyel, Belarus 24 D4 54 50N 28 40 E
Lépo, L. do, Angola 56 B2 17 0S 19 0 E
Leppävirta, Finland 9 E22 62 29N 27 46 E
Lerdo, Mexico 86 B4 25 32N 103 32W
Leribe, Lesotho 57 D4 28 51S 28 3 E
Lérida = Lleida, Spain 19 B6 41 37N 0 39 E
Lerwick, U.K. 12 A7 60 9N 1 9W
Les Cayes, Haiti 89 C5 18 15N 73 46W
Les Sables-d'Olonne, France 18 C3 46 30N 1 45W
Lesbos = Lésvos, Greece 21 E12 39 10N 26 20 E
Leshan, China 32 D5 29 33N 103 41 E
Leshukonskoye, Russia 24 B8 64 54N 45 46 E
Leskov I., Antarctica 5 B1 56 0S 28 0W
Leskovac, Serbia, Yug. 21 C9 43 0N 21 58 E
Lesopilnoye, Russia 30 A7 46 44N 134 20 E
Lesotho ■, Africa 57 D4 29 40S 28 0 E
Lesozavodsk, Russia 27 E14 45 30N 133 29 E
Lesse →, Belgium 15 D4 50 15N 4 54 E
Lesser Antilles, W. Indies 89 D7 15 0N 61 0W
Lesser Slave L., Canada 72 B5 55 30N 115 25W
Lesser Sunda Is., Indonesia 37 F6 7 0S 120 0 E
Lessines, Belgium 15 D3 50 42N 3 50 E
Lester, U.S.A. 84 C5 47 12N 121 29W
Lestock, Canada 73 C8 51 19N 103 59W
Lesuer I., Australia 60 B4 13 50S 127 17 E
Lésvos, Greece 21 E12 39 10N 26 20 E
Leszno, Poland 17 C9 51 50N 16 30 E
Letchworth, U.K. 11 F7 51 59N 0 13W
Lethbridge, Canada 72 D6 49 45N 112 45W
Lethem, Guyana 92 C7 3 20N 59 50W
Leti, Kepulauan, Indonesia 37 F7 8 10S 128 0 E
Leti Is. = Leti, Kepulauan, Indonesia 37 F7 8 10S 128 0 E
Letiahau →, Botswana 56 C3 21 16S 24 0 E
Leticia, Colombia 92 D5 4 9S 70 0W
Leting, China 35 E10 39 23N 118 55 E
Letjiesbos, S. Africa 56 E3 32 34S 22 16 E
Letlhakeng, Botswana 56 C3 24 0S 24 59 E
Letong, Indonesia 36 D3 2 58N 105 42 E
Letpadan, Burma 41 L19 17 45N 95 45 E
Letpan, Burma 41 K19 19 28N 94 10 E
Letsôk-aw Kyun, Burma 39 G2 11 30N 98 25 E
Letterkenny, Ireland 13 B4 54 57N 7 45W
Leucadia, U.S.A. 85 M9 33 4N 117 18W
Leuser, G., Indonesia 36 D1 3 46N 97 12 E
Leuven, Belgium 15 D4 50 52N 4 42 E
Leuze-en-Hainaut, Belgium 15 D3 50 36N 3 37 E
Levádhia, Greece 21 E10 38 27N 22 54 E
Levanger, Norway 8 E14 63 45N 11 19 E
Levelland, U.S.A. 81 J3 33 35N 102 23W
Leven, U.K. 12 E6 56 12N 3 0W
Leven, L., U.K. 12 E5 56 12N 3 22W
Leven, Toraka, Madag. 57 A8 12 30S 47 45 E
Leveque C., Australia 60 C3 16 20S 123 0 E
Levice, Slovak Rep. 17 D10 48 13N 18 35 E
Levin, N.Z. 59 J5 40 37S 175 18 E
Lévis, Canada 71 C5 46 48N 71 9W
Levis, L., Canada 72 A5 62 37N 117 58W
Levittown, N.Y., U.S.A. 79 F11 40 44N 73 31W
Levittown, Pa., U.S.A. 79 F10 40 9N 74 51W
Levkás, Greece 21 E9 38 40N 20 43 E
Levkímmi, Greece 23 B4 39 25N 20 3 E
Levkímmi, Ákra, Greece 23 B4 39 29N 20 4 E
Levkôsia = Nicosia, Cyprus 23 D12 35 10N 33 25 E
Levskigrad = Karlovo, Bulgaria 21 C11 42 38N 24 47 E
Lewes, U.K. 11 G8 50 52N 0 1 E
Lewes, U.S.A. 76 F8 38 46N 75 9W
Lewis, U.K. 12 C2 58 9N 6 40W
Lewis →, U.S.A. 84 E4 45 51N 122 48W
Lewis, Butt of, U.K. 12 C2 58 31N 6 16W
Lewis Ra., Australia 60 D4 20 3S 128 50 E
Lewis Range, U.S.A. 82 C7 48 5N 113 5W
Lewis Run, U.S.A. 78 E6 41 52N 78 40W
Lewisburg, Pa., U.S.A. 78 F8 40 58N 76 54W
Lewisburg, Tenn., U.S.A. 77 H2 35 27N 86 48W
Lewisburg, W. Va., U.S.A. 76 G5 37 48N 80 27W
Lewisporte, Canada 71 C8 49 15N 55 3W
Lewiston, Idaho, U.S.A. 82 C5 46 25N 117 1W
Lewiston, Maine, U.S.A. 77 C11 44 6N 70 13W
Lewiston, N.Y., U.S.A. 78 C5 43 11N 79 3W
Lewistown, Mont., U.S.A. 82 C9 47 4N 109 26W
Lewistown, Pa., U.S.A. 78 F7 40 36N 77 34W
Lexington, Ill., U.S.A. 80 E10 40 39N 88 47W
Lexington, Ky., U.S.A. 76 F3 38 3N 84 30W
Lexington, Mich., U.S.A. 78 C2 43 16N 82 32W
Lexington, Mo., U.S.A. 80 F8 39 11N 93 52W
Lexington, N.C., U.S.A. 77 H5 35 49N 80 15W
Lexington, N.Y., U.S.A. 79 D10 42 15N 74 22W
Lexington, Nebr., U.S.A. 80 E5 40 47N 99 45W
Lexington, Ohio, U.S.A. 78 F2 40 41N 82 35W
Lexington, Tenn., U.S.A. 77 H1 35 39N 88 24W
Lexington, Va., U.S.A. 76 G6 37 47N 79 27W
Lexington Park, U.S.A. 76 F7 38 16N 76 27W
Leyburn, U.K. 10 C6 54 19N 1 48W
Leyland, U.K. 10 D5 53 42N 2 43W
Leyte, Phil. 37 B7 11 0N 125 0 E
Lezha, Albania 21 D8 41 47N 19 39 E
Lhasa, China 32 D4 29 25N 90 58 E
Lhazê, China 32 D3 29 5N 87 38 E
Lhokkruet, Indonesia 36 D1 4 55N 95 24 E
Lhokseumawe, Indonesia 36 C1 5 10N 97 10 E
L'Hospitalet de Llobregat, Spain 19 B7 41 21N 2 6 E
Lhuntsi Dzong, India 41 F17 27 39N 91 10 E
Li, Thailand 38 D2 17 48N 98 57 E
Li Xian, Gansu, China 34 G3 34 10N 105 5 E
Li Xian, Hebei, China 34 E8 38 30N 115 35 E
Lianga, Phil. 37 C7 8 38N 126 6 E
Liangcheng, Nei Mongol Zizhiqu, China 34 D7 40 28N 112 25 E
Liangcheng, Shandong, China 35 G10 35 32N 119 37 E
Liangdang, China 34 H4 33 56N 106 18 E
Liangpran, Indonesia 36 D4 1 4N 114 23 E
Lianshanguan, China 35 D12 40 53N 123 43 E
Lianshui, China 35 H10 33 42N 119 20 E
Lianyungang, China 35 G10 34 40N 119 11 E
Liao He →, China 35 D11 41 0N 121 50 E
Liaocheng, China 34 F8 36 28N 115 58 E
Liaodong Bandao, China 35 E12 40 0N 122 30 E
Liaodong Wan, China 35 D11 40 20N 121 10 E
Liaoning □, China 35 D12 41 40N 122 30 E
Liaoyang, China 35 D12 41 15N 122 58 E
Liaoyuan, China 35 C13 42 58N 125 2 E
Liaozhong, China 35 D12 41 23N 122 50 E
Liard →, Canada 72 A4 61 51N 121 18W
Liard River, Canada 72 B3 59 25N 126 5W
Liari, Pakistan 42 G2 25 37N 66 30 E
Libau = Liepāja, Latvia 9 H19 56 30N 21 0 E
Libby, U.S.A. 82 B6 48 23N 115 33W
Libenge, Dem. Rep. of the Congo 52 D3 3 40N 18 55 E
Liberal, U.S.A. 81 G4 37 3N 100 55W
Liberec, Czech Rep. 16 C8 50 47N 15 7 E
Liberia, Costa Rica 88 D2 10 40N 85 30W
Liberia ■, W. Afr. 50 G4 6 30N 9 30W
Liberty, Mo., U.S.A. 80 F7 39 15N 94 25W
Liberty, N.Y., U.S.A. 79 E10 41 48N 74 45W
Liberty, Pa., U.S.A. 78 E7 41 34N 77 6W
Liberty, Tex., U.S.A. 81 K7 30 3N 94 48W
Lîbîya, Sahrâ', Africa 51 C10 25 0N 25 0 E
Libobo, Tanjung, Indonesia 37 E7 0 54S 128 28 E
Libode, S. Africa 57 E4 31 33S 29 2 E
Libourne, France 18 D3 44 55N 0 14W
Libramont, Belgium 15 E5 49 55N 5 23 E
Libreville, Gabon 52 D1 0 25N 9 26 E
Libya ■, N. Afr. 51 C9 27 0N 17 0 E
Libyan Desert = Lîbîya, Sahrâ', Africa 51 C10 25 0N 25 0 E
Licantén, Chile 94 D1 35 55S 72 0W
Licata, Italy 20 F5 37 6N 13 56 E
Licheng, China 34 F7 36 28N 113 20 E
Lichfield, U.K. 11 E6 52 41N 1 49W
Lichinga, Mozam. 55 E4 13 13S 35 11 E
Lichtenburg, S. Africa 56 D4 26 8S 26 8 E
Licking →, U.S.A. 76 F3 39 6N 84 30W
Lida, Belarus 9 K21 53 53N 25 15 E
Lidköping, Sweden 9 G15 58 31N 13 7 E
Liebig, Mt., Australia 60 D5 23 18S 131 22 E
Liechtenstein ■, Europe 18 C8 47 8N 9 35 E
Liège, Belgium 15 D5 50 38N 5 35 E
Liège □, Belgium 15 D5 50 32N 5 35 E
Liegnitz = Legnica, Poland 16 C9 51 12N 16 10 E
Lienart, Dem. Rep. of the Congo 54 B2 3 3N 25 31 E
Lienyünchiangshih = Lianyungang, China 35 G10 34 40N 119 11 E
Lienz, Austria 16 E7 46 50N 12 46 E
Liepāja, Latvia 9 H19 56 30N 21 0 E
Lier, Belgium 15 C4 51 7N 4 34 E
Lièvre →, Canada 70 C4 45 31N 75 26W
Liffey →, Ireland 13 C5 53 21N 6 13W
Lifford, Ireland 13 B4 54 51N 7 29W

Longview

Lifudzin, Russia 30 B7 44 21N 134 58 E
Lightning Ridge, Australia 63 D4 29 22S 148 0 E
Ligonier, U.S.A. 78 F5 40 15N 79 14W
Liguria □, Italy 18 D8 44 30N 8 50 E
Ligurian Sea, Medit. S. 20 C3 43 20N 9 0 E
Lihou Reefs and Cays, Australia 62 B5 17 25S 151 40 E
Lihue, U.S.A. 74 H15 21 59N 159 23W
Lijiang, China 32 D5 26 55N 100 20 E
Likasi, Dem. Rep. of the Congo 55 E2 10 55S 26 48 E
Likoma I., Malawi 55 E3 12 3S 34 45 E
Likumburu, Tanzania 55 D4 9 43S 35 8 E
Lille, France 18 A5 50 38N 3 3 E
Lille Bælt, Denmark 9 J13 55 20N 9 45 E
Lillehammer, Norway 9 F14 61 8N 10 30 E
Lillesand, Norway 9 G13 58 15N 8 23 E
Lillian Pt., Australia 61 E4 27 40S 126 6 E
Lillooet, Canada 72 C4 50 44N 121 57W
Lillooet →, Canada 72 D4 49 15N 121 57W
Lilongwe, Malawi 55 E3 14 0S 33 48 E
Liloy, Phil. 37 C6 8 4N 122 39 E
Lim →, Bos.-H. 21 C8 43 45N 19 15 E
Lima, Indonesia 37 E7 3 37S 128 4 E
Lima, Peru 92 F3 12 0S 77 0W
Lima, Mont., U.S.A. 82 D7 44 38N 112 36W
Lima, Ohio, U.S.A. 76 E3 40 44N 84 6W
Lima →, Portugal 19 B1 41 41N 8 50W
Liman, Indonesia 37 G14 7 48S 111 45 E
Limassol, Cyprus 23 E12 34 42N 33 1 E
Limavady, U.K. 13 A5 55 3N 6 56W
Limay →, Argentina 96 D3 39 0S 68 0W
Limay Mahuida, Argentina 94 D2 37 10S 66 45W
Limbang, Brunei 36 D5 4 42N 115 6 E
Limbaži, Latvia 9 H21 57 31N 24 42 E
Limbdi, India 42 H4 22 34N 71 51 E
Limbe, Cameroon 52 D1 4 1N 9 10 E
Limburg, Germany 16 C5 50 22N 8 4 E
Limburg □, Belgium 15 C5 51 2N 5 25 E
Limburg □, Neths. 15 C5 51 20N 5 55 E
Limeira, Brazil 95 A6 22 35S 47 28W
Limerick, Ireland 13 D3 52 40N 8 37W
Limerick, U.S.A. 79 C14 43 41N 70 48W
Limerick □, Ireland 13 D3 52 30N 8 50W
Limestone, U.S.A. 78 D6 42 2N 78 38W
Limestone →, Canada 73 B10 56 31N 94 7W
Limfjorden, Denmark 9 H13 56 55N 9 0 E
Limia = Lima →, Portugal 19 B1 41 41N 8 50W
Limingen, Norway 8 D15 64 48N 13 35 E
Limmen Bight, Australia 62 A2 14 40S 135 35 E
Limmen Bight →, Australia 62 B2 15 7S 135 44 E
Limnos, Greece 21 E11 39 50N 25 5 E
Limoges, Canada 79 A9 45 20N 75 16W
Limoges, France 18 D4 45 50N 1 15 E
Limón, Costa Rica 88 E3 10 0N 83 2W
Limon, U.S.A. 80 F3 39 16N 103 41W
Limousin, France 18 D4 45 30N 1 30 E
Limoux, France 18 E5 43 4N 2 12 E
Limpopo →, Africa 57 D5 25 5S 33 30 E
Limuru, Kenya 54 C4 1 2S 36 35 E
Lin Xian, China 34 F6 37 57N 110 58 E
Linares, Chile 94 D1 35 50S 71 40W
Linares, Mexico 87 C5 24 50N 99 40W
Linares, Spain 19 C4 38 10N 3 40W
Lincheng, China 34 F8 37 25N 114 30 E
Lincoln, Argentina 94 C3 34 55S 61 30W
Lincoln, N.Z. 59 K4 43 38S 172 30 E
Lincoln, U.K. 10 D7 53 14N 0 32W
Lincoln, Calif., U.S.A. 84 G5 38 54N 121 17W
Lincoln, Ill., U.S.A. 80 E10 40 9N 89 22W
Lincoln, Kans., U.S.A. 80 F5 39 3N 98 9W
Lincoln, Maine, U.S.A. 77 C11 45 22N 68 30W
Lincoln, N.H., U.S.A. 79 B13 44 3N 71 40W
Lincoln, N. Mex., U.S.A. 83 K11 33 30N 105 23W
Lincoln, Nebr., U.S.A. 80 E6 40 49N 96 41W
Lincoln City, U.S.A. 82 D1 44 57N 124 1W
Lincoln Hav = Lincoln Sea, Arctic 4 A5 84 0N 55 0W
Lincoln Sea, Arctic 4 A5 84 0N 55 0W
Lincolnshire □, U.K. 10 D7 53 14N 0 32W
Lincolnshire Wolds, U.K. 10 D7 53 26N 0 13W
Lincolnton, U.S.A. 77 H5 35 29N 81 16W
Lind, U.S.A. 82 C4 46 58N 118 37W
Linda, U.S.A. 84 F5 39 8N 121 34W
Linden, Guyana 92 B7 6 0N 58 10W
Linden, Ala., U.S.A. 77 J2 32 18N 87 48W
Linden, Calif., U.S.A. 84 G5 38 1N 121 5W
Linden, Tex., U.S.A. 81 J7 33 1N 94 22W
Lindenhurst, U.S.A. 79 F11 40 41N 73 23W
Lindesnes, Norway 9 H12 57 58N 7 3 E
Líndhos, Greece 23 C10 36 6N 28 4 E
Líndhos, Ákra, Greece 23 C10 36 4N 28 10 E
Lindi, Tanzania 55 D4 9 58S 39 38 E
Lindi □, Tanzania 55 D4 9 40S 38 30 E
Lindi →, Dem. Rep. of the Congo 54 B2 0 33N 25 5 E
Lindsay, Canada 78 B6 44 22N 78 43W
Lindsay, Calif., U.S.A. 84 J7 36 12N 119 5W
Lindsay, Okla., U.S.A. 81 H6 34 50N 97 38W
Lindsborg, U.S.A. 80 F6 38 35N 97 40W
Linesville, U.S.A. 78 E4 41 39N 80 26W
Linfen, China 34 F6 36 3N 111 30 E
Ling Xian, China 34 F9 37 22N 116 30 E
Lingao, China 38 C7 19 56N 109 42 E
Lingayen, Phil. 37 A6 16 1N 120 14 E
Lingayen G., Phil. 37 A6 16 10N 120 15 E
Lingbi, China 35 H9 33 33N 117 33 E
Lingchuan, China 34 G7 35 45N 113 12 E
Lingen, Germany 16 B4 52 31N 7 19 E
Lingga, Indonesia 36 E2 0 12S 104 37 E
Lingga, Kepulauan, Indonesia 36 E2 0 10S 104 30 E
Lingga Arch. = Lingga, Kepulauan, Indonesia 36 E2 0 10S 104 30 E
Lingle, U.S.A. 80 D2 42 8N 104 21W
Lingqiu, China 34 E8 39 28N 114 22 E
Lingshi, China 34 F6 36 48N 111 48 E
Lingshou, China 34 E8 38 20N 114 20 E
Lingshui, China 38 C8 18 27N 110 0 E
Lingtai, China 34 G4 35 0N 107 40 E
Linguère, Senegal 50 E2 15 25N 15 5W
Lingwu, China 34 E4 38 6N 106 20 E
Lingyuan, China 35 D10 41 10N 119 15 E
Linhai, China 33 D7 28 50N 121 8 E
Linhares, Brazil 93 G10 19 25S 40 4W
Linhe, China 34 D4 40 48N 107 20 E
Linjiang, China 35 D14 41 50N 127 0 E
Linköping, Sweden 9 G16 58 28N 15 36 E
Linkou, China 35 B16 45 15N 130 18 E
Linnhe, L., U.K. 12 E3 56 36N 5 25W
Linosa, I., Medit. S. 20 G5 35 51N 12 50 E
Linqi, China 34 G7 35 45N 113 52 E
Linqing, China 34 F8 36 50N 115 42 E
Linqu, China 35 F10 36 25N 118 30 E
Linru, China 34 G7 34 11N 112 52 E
Lins, Brazil 95 A6 21 40S 49 44W
Linton, Ind., U.S.A. 76 F2 39 2N 87 10W
Linton, N. Dak., U.S.A. 80 B4 46 16N 100 14W
Lintong, China 34 G5 34 20N 109 10 E
Linwood, Canada 78 C4 43 35N 80 43W
Linxi, China 35 C10 43 36N 118 2 E
Linxia, China 32 C5 35 36N 103 10 E
Linyanti →, Africa 56 B4 17 50S 25 5 E
Linyi, China 35 G10 35 5N 118 21 E
Linz, Austria 16 D8 48 18N 14 18 E
Linzhenzhen, China 34 F5 36 30N 109 59 E
Linzi, China 35 F10 36 50N 118 20 E
Lion, G. du, France 18 E6 43 10N 4 0 E
Lionárisso, Cyprus 23 D13 35 28N 34 8 E
Lions, G. of = Lion, G. du, France 18 E6 43 10N 4 0 E
Lion's Den, Zimbabwe 55 F3 17 15S 30 5 E
Lion's Head, Canada 78 B3 44 58N 81 15W
Lipa, Phil. 37 B6 13 57N 121 10 E
Lipali, Mozam. 55 F4 15 50S 35 50 E
Lípari, Italy 20 E6 38 26N 14 58 E
Lípari, Is. = Eólie, Ís., Italy 20 E6 38 30N 14 57 E
Lipcani, Moldova 17 D14 48 14N 26 48 E
Lipetsk, Russia 24 D6 52 37N 39 35 E
Lipkany = Lipcani, Moldova 17 D14 48 14N 26 48 E
Lipovcy Manzovka, Russia 30 B6 44 12N 132 26 E
Lipovets, Ukraine 17 D15 49 12N 29 1 E
Lippe →, Germany 16 C4 51 39N 6 36 E
Lipscomb, U.S.A. 81 G4 36 14N 100 16W
Liptrap C., Australia 63 F4 38 50S 145 55 E
Lira, Uganda 54 B3 2 17N 32 57 E
Liria = Lliria, Spain 19 C5 39 37N 0 35W
Lisala, Dem. Rep. of the Congo 52 D4 2 12N 21 38 E
Lisboa, Portugal 19 C1 38 42N 9 10W
Lisbon = Lisboa, Portugal 19 C1 38 42N 9 10W
Lisbon, N. Dak., U.S.A. 80 B6 46 27N 97 41W
Lisbon, N.H., U.S.A. 79 B13 44 13N 71 55W
Lisbon, Ohio, U.S.A. 78 F4 40 46N 80 46W
Lisbon Falls, U.S.A. 77 D10 44 0N 70 4W
Lisburn, U.K. 13 B5 54 31N 6 3W
Liscannor B., Ireland 13 D2 52 55N 9 24W
Lishi, China 34 F6 37 31N 111 8 E
Lishu, China 35 C13 43 20N 124 18 E
Lisianski I., Pac. Oc. 64 E10 26 2N 174 0W
Lisichansk = Lysychansk, Ukraine 25 E6 48 55N 38 30 E
Lisieux, France 18 B4 49 10N 0 12 E
Liski, Russia 25 D6 51 3N 39 30 E
Lismore, Australia 63 D5 28 44S 153 21 E
Lismore, Ireland 13 D4 52 8N 7 55W
Lista, Norway 9 G12 58 7N 6 39 E
Lister, Mt., Antarctica 5 D11 78 0S 162 0 E
Liston, Australia 63 D5 28 39S 152 6 E
Listowel, Canada 78 C4 43 44N 80 58W
Listowel, Ireland 13 D2 52 27N 9 29W
Litani →, Lebanon 47 B4 33 20N 35 15 E
Litchfield, Calif., U.S.A. 84 E6 40 24N 120 23W
Litchfield, Conn., U.S.A. 79 E11 41 45N 73 11W
Litchfield, Ill., U.S.A. 80 F10 39 11N 89 39W
Litchfield, Minn., U.S.A. 80 C7 45 8N 94 32W
Lithgow, Australia 63 E5 33 25S 150 8 E
Líthinon, Ákra, Greece 23 E6 34 55N 24 44 E
Lithuania ■, Europe 9 J20 55 30N 24 0 E
Lititz, U.S.A. 79 F8 40 9N 76 18W
Litoměřice, Czech Rep. 16 C8 50 33N 14 10 E
Little Abaco I., Bahamas 88 A4 26 50N 77 30W
Little Barrier I., N.Z. 59 G5 36 12S 175 8 E
Little Belt Mts., U.S.A. 82 C8 46 40N 110 45W
Little Blue →, U.S.A. 80 F6 39 42N 96 41W
Little Buffalo →, Canada 72 A6 61 0N 113 46W
Little Cayman, I., Cayman Is. 88 C3 19 41N 80 3W
Little Churchill →, Canada 73 B9 57 30N 95 22W
Little Colorado →, U.S.A. 83 H8 36 12N 111 48W
Little Current, Canada 70 C3 45 55N 82 0W
Little Current →, Canada 70 B3 50 57N 84 36W
Little Falls, Minn., U.S.A. 80 C7 45 59N 94 22W
Little Falls, N.Y., U.S.A. 79 C10 43 3N 74 51W
Little Fork →, U.S.A. 80 A8 48 31N 93 35W
Little Grand Rapids, Canada 73 C9 52 0N 95 29W
Little Humboldt →, U.S.A. 82 F5 41 1N 117 43W
Little Inagua I., Bahamas 89 B5 21 40N 73 50W
Little Karoo, S. Africa 56 E3 33 45S 21 0 E
Little Lake, U.S.A. 85 K9 35 56N 117 55W
Little Laut Is. = Laut Kecil, Kepulauan, Indonesia 36 E5 4 45S 115 40 E
Little-Mecatina = Petit-Mécatina →, Canada 71 B8 50 40N 59 30W
Little Minch, U.K. 12 D2 57 35N 6 45W
Little Missouri →, U.S.A. 80 B3 47 36N 102 25W
Little Ouse →, U.K. 11 E9 52 22N 1 12 E
Little Rann, India 42 H4 23 25N 71 25 E
Little Red →, U.S.A. 81 H9 35 11N 91 27W
Little River, N.Z. 59 K4 43 45S 172 49 E
Little Rock, U.S.A. 81 H8 34 45N 92 17W
Little Ruaha →, Tanzania 54 D4 7 57S 37 53 E
Little Sable Pt., U.S.A. 76 D2 43 38N 86 33W
Little Sioux →, U.S.A. 80 E6 41 48N 96 4W
Little Smoky →, Canada 72 C5 54 44N 117 11W
Little Snake →, U.S.A. 82 F9 40 27N 108 26W
Little Valley, U.S.A. 78 D6 42 15N 78 48W
Little Wabash →, U.S.A. 76 G1 37 55N 88 5W
Little White →, U.S.A. 80 D4 43 40N 100 40W
Littlefield, U.S.A. 81 J3 33 55N 102 20W
Littlehampton, U.K. 11 G7 50 49N 0 32W
Littleton, U.S.A. 79 B13 44 18N 71 46W
Liu He →, China 35 D11 40 55N 121 35 E
Liuba, China 34 H4 33 38N 106 55 E
Liugou, China 35 D10 40 57N 118 15 E
Liuhe, China 35 C13 42 17N 125 43 E
Liukang Tenggaja = Sabalana, Kepulauan, Indonesia 37 F5 6 45S 118 50 E
Liuli, Tanzania 55 E3 11 3S 34 38 E
Liuwa Plain, Zambia 53 G4 14 20S 22 30 E
Liuzhou, China 33 D5 24 22N 109 22 E
Liuzhuang, China 35 H11 33 12N 120 18 E
Livadhia, Cyprus 23 E12 34 57N 33 38 E
Live Oak, Calif., U.S.A. 84 F5 39 17N 121 40W
Live Oak, Fla., U.S.A. 77 K4 30 18N 82 59W
Liveras, Cyprus 23 D11 35 23N 32 57 E
Livermore, U.S.A. 84 H5 37 41N 121 47W
Livermore, Mt., U.S.A. 81 K2 30 38N 104 11W
Livermore Falls, U.S.A. 77 C11 44 29N 70 11W
Liverpool, Canada 71 D7 44 5N 64 41W
Liverpool, U.K. 10 D4 53 25N 3 0W
Liverpool, U.S.A. 79 C8 43 6N 76 13W
Liverpool Bay, U.K. 10 D4 53 30N 3 20W
Liverpool Plains, Australia 63 E5 31 15S 150 15 E
Liverpool Ra., Australia 63 E5 31 50S 150 30 E
Livingston, Guatemala 88 C2 15 50N 88 50W
Livingston, U.K. 12 F5 55 54N 3 30W
Livingston, Ala., U.S.A. 77 J1 32 35N 88 11W
Livingston, Calif., U.S.A. 84 H6 37 23N 120 43W
Livingston, Mont., U.S.A. 82 D8 45 40N 110 34W
Livingston, S.C., U.S.A. 77 J5 33 32N 80 53W
Livingston, Tenn., U.S.A. 77 G3 36 23N 85 19W
Livingston, Tex., U.S.A. 81 K7 30 43N 94 56W
Livingston, L., U.S.A. 81 K7 30 50N 95 10W
Livingston Manor, U.S.A. 79 E10 41 54N 74 50W
Livingstone, Zambia 55 F2 17 46S 25 52 E
Livingstone Mts., Tanzania 55 D3 9 40S 34 20 E
Livingstonia, Malawi 55 E3 10 38S 34 5 E
Livny, Russia 24 D6 52 30N 37 30 E
Livonia, Mich., U.S.A. 76 D4 42 23N 83 23W
Livonia, N.Y., U.S.A. 78 D7 42 49N 77 40W
Livorno, Italy 20 C4 43 33N 10 19 E
Livramento, Brazil 95 C4 30 55S 55 30W
Liwale, Tanzania 55 D4 9 48S 37 58 E
Lizard I., Australia 62 A4 14 42S 145 30 E
Lizard Pt., U.K. 11 H2 49 57N 5 13W
Ljubljana, Slovenia 16 E8 46 4N 14 33 E
Ljungan →, Sweden 9 E17 62 18N 17 23 E
Ljungby, Sweden 9 H15 56 49N 13 55 E
Ljusdal, Sweden 9 F17 61 46N 16 3 E
Ljusnan →, Sweden 9 F17 61 12N 17 8 E
Ljusne, Sweden 9 F17 61 13N 17 7 E
Llancanelo, Salina, Argentina 94 D2 35 40S 69 8W
Llandeilo, U.K. 11 F4 51 53N 3 59W
Llandovery, U.K. 11 F4 51 59N 3 48W
Llandrindod Wells, U.K. 11 E4 52 14N 3 22W
Llandudno, U.K. 10 D4 53 19N 3 50W
Llanelli, U.K. 11 F3 51 41N 4 10W
Llanes, Spain 19 A3 43 25N 4 50W
Llangollen, U.K. 10 E4 52 58N 3 11W
Llanidloes, U.K. 11 E4 52 27N 3 31W
Llano, U.S.A. 81 K5 30 45N 98 41W
Llano →, U.S.A. 81 K5 30 39N 98 26W
Llano Estacado, U.S.A. 81 J3 33 30N 103 0W
Llanos, S. Amer. 92 C4 5 0N 71 35W
Llanquihue, L., Chile 96 E1 41 10S 75 50W
Llanwrtyd Wells, U.K. 11 E4 52 7N 3 38W
Llebeig, C. des, Spain 22 B9 39 33N 2 18 E
Lleida, Spain 19 B6 41 37N 0 39 E
Llentrisca, C., Spain 22 C7 38 52N 1 15 E
Llera, Mexico 87 C5 23 19N 99 1W
Lleyn Peninsula, U.K. 10 E3 52 51N 4 36W
Llico, Chile 94 C1 34 46S 72 5W
Lliria, Spain 19 C5 39 37N 0 35W
Llobregat →, Spain 19 B7 41 19N 2 9 E
Lloret de Mar, Spain 19 B7 41 41N 2 53 E
Lloyd B., Australia 62 A3 12 45S 143 27 E
Lloyd L., Canada 73 B7 57 22N 108 57W
Lloydminster, Canada 73 C7 53 17N 110 0W
Llucmajor, Spain 22 B9 39 29N 2 53 E
Llullaillaco, Volcán, S. Amer. 94 A2 24 43S 68 30W
Lo →, Vietnam 38 B5 21 18N 105 25 E
Loa, U.S.A. 83 G8 38 24N 111 39W
Loa →, Chile 94 A1 21 26S 70 41W
Loaita I., S. China Sea 36 B4 10 41N 114 25 E
Loange →, Dem. Rep. of the Congo 52 E4 4 17S 20 2 E
Lobatse, Botswana 56 D4 25 12S 25 40 E
Lobería, Argentina 94 D4 38 10S 58 40W
Lobito, Angola 53 G2 12 18S 13 35 E
Lobos, Argentina 94 D4 35 10S 59 0W
Lobos, I., Mexico 86 B2 27 15N 110 30W
Lobos, I. de, Canary Is. 22 F6 28 45N 13 50W
Loc Binh, Vietnam 38 B6 21 46N 106 54 E
Loc Ninh, Vietnam 39 G6 11 50N 106 34 E
Locarno, Switz. 18 C8 46 10N 8 47 E
Loch Baghasdail = Lochboisdale, U.K. 12 D1 57 9N 7 20W
Loch Garman = Wexford, Ireland 13 D5 52 20N 6 28W
Loch Nam Madadh = Lochmaddy, U.K. 12 D1 57 36N 7 10W
Lochaber, U.K. 12 E3 56 59N 5 1W
Locharbriggs, U.K. 12 F5 55 7N 3 35W
Lochboisdale, U.K. 12 D1 57 9N 7 20W
Loche, L. La, Canada 73 B7 56 30N 109 30W
Lochem, Neths. 15 B6 52 9N 6 26 E
Loches, France 18 C4 47 7N 1 0 E
Lochgilphead, U.K. 12 E3 56 2N 5 26W
Lochinver, U.K. 12 C3 58 9N 5 14W
Lochmaddy, U.K. 12 D1 57 36N 7 10W
Lochnagar, Australia 62 C4 23 33S 145 38 E
Lochnagar, U.K. 12 E5 56 57N 3 15W
Lochy, L., U.K. 12 E4 57 0N 4 53W
Lock, Australia 63 E2 33 34S 135 46 E
Lock Haven, U.S.A. 78 E7 41 8N 77 28W
Lockeford, U.S.A. 84 G5 38 10N 121 9W
Lockeport, Canada 71 D6 43 47N 65 4W
Lockerbie, U.K. 12 F5 55 7N 3 21W
Lockhart, Australia 63 F4 35 14S 146 40 E
Lockhart, U.S.A. 81 L6 29 53N 97 40W
Lockhart, L., Australia 61 F2 33 15S 119 3 E
Lockhart River, Australia 62 A3 12 58S 143 30 E
Lockney, U.S.A. 81 H4 34 7N 101 27W
Lockport, U.S.A. 78 C6 43 10N 78 42W
Lod, Israel 47 D3 31 57N 34 54 E
Lodeinoye Pole, Russia 24 B5 60 44N 33 33 E
Lodge Bay, Canada 71 B8 52 14N 55 51W
Lodge Grass, U.S.A. 82 D10 45 19N 107 22W
Lodgepole Cr. →, U.S.A. 80 E2 41 20N 104 30W
Lodhran, Pakistan 42 E4 29 32N 71 30 E
Lodi, Italy 18 D8 45 19N 9 30 E
Lodi, Calif., U.S.A. 84 G5 38 8N 121 16W
Lodi, Ohio, U.S.A. 78 E3 41 2N 82 0W
Lodja, Dem. Rep. of the Congo 54 C1 3 30S 23 23 E
Lodwar, Kenya 54 B4 3 10N 35 40 E
Łódź, Poland 17 C10 51 45N 19 27 E
Loei, Thailand 38 D3 17 29N 101 35 E
Loengo, Dem. Rep. of the Congo 54 C2 4 48S 26 30 E
Loeriesfontein, S. Africa 56 E2 31 0S 19 26 E
Lofoten, Norway 8 B15 68 30N 14 0 E
Logan, Iowa, U.S.A. 80 E7 41 39N 95 47W
Logan, Ohio, U.S.A. 76 F4 39 32N 82 25W
Logan, Utah, U.S.A. 82 F8 41 44N 111 50W
Logan, W. Va., U.S.A. 76 G5 37 51N 81 59W
Logan, Mt., Canada 68 B5 60 31N 140 22W
Logandale, U.S.A. 85 J12 36 36N 114 29W
Logansport, Ind., U.S.A. 76 E2 40 45N 86 22W
Logansport, La., U.S.A. 81 K8 31 58N 94 0W
Logone →, Chad 51 F9 12 6N 15 2 E
Logroño, Spain 19 A4 42 28N 2 27W
Lohardaga, India 43 H11 23 27N 84 45 E
Loharia, India 42 H6 23 45N 74 14 E
Loharu, India 42 E6 28 27N 75 49 E
Lohja, Finland 9 F21 60 12N 24 5 E
Lohri Wah →, Pakistan 42 F2 27 27N 67 37 E
Loi-kaw, Burma 41 K20 19 40N 97 17 E
Loimaa, Finland 9 F20 60 50N 23 5 E
Loir →, France 18 C3 47 33N 0 32W
Loire →, France 18 C2 47 16N 2 10W
Loja, Ecuador 92 D3 3 59S 79 16W
Loja, Spain 19 D3 37 10N 4 10W
Loji = Kawasi, Indonesia 37 E7 1 38S 127 28 E
Lokandu, Dem. Rep. of the Congo 54 C2 2 30S 25 45 E
Lokeren, Belgium 15 C3 51 6N 3 59 E
Lokichokio, Kenya 54 B3 4 19N 34 13 E
Lokitaung, Kenya 54 B4 4 12N 35 48 E
Lokkan tekojärvi, Finland 8 C22 67 55N 27 35 E
Lokoja, Nigeria 50 G7 7 47N 6 45 E
Lola, Mt., U.S.A. 84 F6 39 26N 120 22W
Loliondo, Tanzania 54 C4 2 2S 35 39 E
Lolland, Denmark 9 J14 54 45N 11 30 E
Lolo, U.S.A. 82 C6 46 45N 114 5W
Lom, Bulgaria 21 C10 43 48N 23 12 E
Lom Kao, Thailand 38 D3 16 53N 101 14 E
Lom Sak, Thailand 38 D3 16 47N 101 15 E
Loma, U.S.A. 82 C8 47 56N 110 30W
Loma Linda, U.S.A. 85 L9 34 3N 117 16W
Lomami →, Dem. Rep. of the Congo 54 B1 0 46N 24 16 E
Lomas de Zamóra, Argentina 94 C4 34 45S 58 25W
Lombadina, Australia 60 C3 16 31S 122 54 E
Lombárdia □, Italy 18 D8 45 40N 9 30 E
Lombardy = Lombárdia □, Italy 18 D8 45 40N 9 30 E
Lomblen, Indonesia 37 F6 8 30S 123 32 E
Lombok, Indonesia 36 F5 8 45S 116 30 E
Lomé, Togo 50 G6 6 9N 1 20 E
Lomela, Dem. Rep. of the Congo 52 E4 2 19S 23 15 E
Lomela →, Dem. Rep. of the Congo 52 E4 0 15S 20 40 E
Lommel, Belgium 15 C5 51 14N 5 19 E
Lomond, Canada 72 C6 50 24N 112 36W
Lomond, L., U.K. 12 E4 56 8N 4 38W
Lomphat, Cambodia 38 F6 13 30N 106 59 E
Lompobatang, Indonesia 37 F5 5 24S 119 56 E
Lompoc, U.S.A. 85 L6 34 38N 120 28W
Lomza, Poland 17 B12 53 10N 22 2 E
Loncoche, Chile 96 D2 39 20S 72 50W
Londa, India 40 M9 15 30N 74 30 E
Londiani, Kenya 54 C4 0 10S 35 33 E
London, Canada 78 D3 42 59N 81 15W
London, U.K. 11 F7 51 30N 0 3W
London, Ky., U.S.A. 76 G3 37 8N 84 5W
London, Ohio, U.S.A. 76 F4 39 53N 83 27W
London, Greater □, U.K. 11 F7 51 36N 0 5W
Londonderry, U.K. 13 B4 55 0N 7 20W
Londonderry □, U.K. 13 B4 55 0N 7 20W
Londonderry, C., Australia 60 B4 13 45S 126 55 E
Londonderry, I., Chile 96 H2 55 0S 71 0W
Londres, Argentina 96 B3 27 43S 67 7W
Londrina, Brazil 95 A5 23 18S 51 10W
Lone Pine, U.S.A. 84 J8 36 36N 118 4W
Long B., U.S.A. 77 J6 33 35N 78 45W
Long Beach, Calif., U.S.A. 85 M8 33 47N 118 11W
Long Beach, N.Y., U.S.A. 79 F11 40 35N 73 39W
Long Beach, Wash., U.S.A. 84 D2 46 21N 124 3W
Long Branch, U.S.A. 79 F11 40 18N 74 0W
Long Creek, U.S.A. 82 D4 44 43N 119 6W
Long Eaton, U.K. 10 E6 52 53N 1 15W
Long I., Australia 62 C4 22 8S 149 53 E
Long I., Bahamas 89 B4 23 20N 75 10W
Long I., Canada 70 B4 54 50N 79 20W
Long I., Ireland 13 E2 51 30N 9 34W
Long I., U.S.A. 79 F11 40 45N 73 30W
Long Island Sd., U.S.A. 79 E12 41 10N 73 0W
Long L., Canada 70 C2 49 30N 86 50W
Long Lake, U.S.A. 79 C10 43 58N 74 25W
Long Point B., Canada 78 D4 42 40N 80 10W
Long Prairie →, U.S.A. 80 C7 46 20N 94 36W
Long Pt., Canada 78 D4 42 35N 80 2W
Long Range Mts., Canada 71 C8 49 30N 57 30W
Long Reef, Australia 60 B4 14 1S 125 48 E
Long Spruce, Canada 73 B10 56 24N 94 21W
Long Str. = Longa, Proliv, Russia 4 C16 70 0N 175 0 E
Long Thanh, Vietnam 39 G6 10 47N 106 57 E
Long Xian, China 34 G4 34 55N 106 55 E
Long Xuyen, Vietnam 39 G5 10 19N 105 28 E
Longa, Proliv, Russia 4 C16 70 0N 175 0 E
Longbenton, U.K. 10 B6 55 1N 1 31W
Longboat Key, U.S.A. 77 M4 27 23N 82 39W
Longde, China 34 G4 35 30N 106 20 E
Longford, Australia 62 G4 41 32S 147 3 E
Longford, Ireland 13 C4 53 43N 7 49W
Longford □, Ireland 13 C4 53 42N 7 45W
Longguan, China 34 D8 40 45N 115 30 E
Longhua, China 35 D9 41 18N 117 45 E
Longido, Tanzania 54 C4 2 43S 36 42 E
Longiram, Indonesia 36 E5 0 5S 115 45 E
Longkou, China 35 F11 37 40N 120 18 E
Longlac, Canada 70 C2 49 45N 86 25W
Longmeadow, U.S.A. 79 D12 42 3N 72 34W
Longmont, U.S.A. 80 E2 40 10N 105 6W
Longnawan, Indonesia 36 D4 1 51N 114 55 E
Longreach, Australia 62 C3 23 28S 144 14 E
Longueuil, Canada 79 A11 45 32N 73 28W
Longview, Tex., U.S.A. 81 J7 32 30N 94 44W

M

Mallaig

McConaughy, L., U.S.A. 80 E4 41 14N 101 40W
McCook, U.S.A. 80 E4 40 12N 100 38W
McCreary, Canada 73 C9 50 47N 99 29W
McCullough Mt., U.S.A. 85 K11 35 35N 115 13W
McCusker —►, Canada 73 B7 55 32N 108 39W
McDame, Canada 72 B3 59 44N 128 59W
McDermitt, U.S.A. 82 F5 41 59N 117 43W
McDonald, U.S.A. 78 F4 40 22N 80 14W
Macdonald, L., Australia 60 D4 23 30S 129 0 E
McDonald Is., Ind. Oc. 3 G13 53 0S 73 0 E
MacDonnell Ranges, Australia 60 D5 23 40S 133 0 E
MacDowell L., Canada 70 B1 52 15N 92 45W
Macduff, U.K. 12 D6 57 40N 2 31W
Macedonia = Makedhonía □, Greece 21 D10 40 39N 22 0 E
Macedonia, U.S.A. 78 E3 41 19N 81 31W
Macedonia ■, Europe 21 D9 41 53N 21 40 E
Maceió, Brazil 93 E11 9 40S 35 41W
Macerata, Italy 20 C5 43 18N 13 27 E
McFarland, U.S.A. 85 K7 35 41N 119 14W
McFarlane —►, Canada 73 B7 59 12N 107 58W
Macfarlane, L., Australia 63 E2 32 0S 136 40 E
McGehee, U.S.A. 81 J9 33 38N 91 24W
McGill, U.S.A. 82 G6 39 23N 114 47W
Macgillycuddy's Reeks, Ireland 13 E2 51 58N 9 45W
McGraw, U.S.A. 79 D8 42 36N 76 8W
McGregor, U.S.A. 80 D9 43 1N 91 11W
McGregor Ra., Australia 63 D3 27 0S 142 45 E
Mach, Pakistan 40 E5 29 50N 67 20 E
Māch Kowr, Iran 45 E9 25 48N 61 28 E
Machado = Jiparaná —►, Brazil 92 E6 8 3S 62 52W
Machagai, Argentina 94 B3 26 56S 60 2W
Machakos, Kenya 54 C4 1 30S 37 15 E
Machala, Ecuador 92 D3 3 20S 79 57W
Machanga, Mozam. 57 C6 20 59S 35 0 E
Machattie, L., Australia 62 C2 24 50S 139 48 E
Machava, Mozam. 57 D5 25 54S 32 28 E
Machece, Mozam. 55 F4 19 15S 35 32 E
Machhu —►, India 42 H4 23 6N 70 46 E
Machias, Maine, U.S.A. 77 C12 44 43N 67 28W
Machias, N.Y., U.S.A. 78 D6 42 25N 78 30W
Machichi —►, Canada 73 B10 57 3N 92 6W
Machico, Madeira 22 D3 32 43N 16 44W
Machilipatnam, India 41 L12 16 12N 81 8 E
Machiques, Venezuela 92 A4 10 4N 72 34W
Machupicchu, Peru 92 F4 13 8S 72 30W
Machynlleth, U.K. 11 E4 52 35N 3 50W
McIlwraith Ra., Australia 62 A3 13 50S 143 20 E
McInnes L., Canada 73 C10 52 13N 93 45W
McIntosh, U.S.A. 80 C4 45 55N 101 21W
McIntosh L., Canada 73 B8 55 45N 105 0W
Macintosh Ra., Australia 61 E4 27 39S 125 32 E
Macintyre —►, Australia 63 D5 28 37S 150 47 E
Mackay, Australia 62 C4 21 8S 149 11 E
Mackay, U.S.A. 82 E7 43 55N 113 37W
MacKay —►, Canada 72 B6 57 10N 111 38W
Mackay, L., Australia 60 D4 22 30S 129 0 E
McKay Ra., Australia 60 D3 23 0S 122 30 E
McKeesport, U.S.A. 78 F5 40 21N 79 52W
McKellar, Canada 78 A5 45 30N 79 55W
McKenna, U.S.A. 84 D4 46 56N 122 33W
Mackenzie, Canada 72 B4 55 20N 123 5W
McKenzie, U.S.A. 77 G1 36 8N 88 31W
Mackenzie —►, Australia 62 C4 23 38S 149 46 E
Mackenzie —►, Canada 68 B6 69 10N 134 20W
McKenzie —►, U.S.A. 82 D2 44 7N 123 6W
Mackenzie Bay, Canada 4 B1 69 0N 137 30W
Mackenzie City = Linden, Guyana 92 B7 6 0N 58 10W
Mackenzie Mts., Canada 68 B7 64 0N 130 0W
Mackinaw City, U.S.A. 76 C3 45 47N 84 44W
McKinlay, Australia 62 C3 21 16S 141 18 E
McKinlay —►, Australia 62 C3 20 50S 141 28 E
McKinley, Mt., U.S.A. 68 B4 63 4N 151 0W
McKinley Sea, Arctic 4 A7 82 0N 0 0 E
McKinney, U.S.A. 81 J6 33 12N 96 37W
Mackinnon Road, Kenya 54 C4 3 40S 39 1 E
McKittrick, U.S.A. 85 K7 35 18N 119 37W
Macklin, Canada 73 C7 52 20N 109 56W
Macksville, Australia 63 E5 30 40S 152 56 E
McLaughlin, U.S.A. 80 C4 45 49N 100 49W
Maclean, Australia 63 D5 29 26S 153 16 E
McLean, U.S.A. 81 H4 35 14N 100 36W
McLeansboro, U.S.A. 80 F10 38 6N 88 32W
Maclear, S. Africa 57 E4 31 2S 28 23 E
Macleay —►, Australia 63 E5 30 56S 153 0 E
McLennan, Canada 72 B5 55 42N 116 50W
McLeod —►, Canada 72 C5 54 9N 115 44W
MacLeod, B., Canada 73 A7 62 53N 110 0W
McLeod, L., Australia 61 D1 24 9S 113 47 E
MacLeod Lake, Canada 72 C4 54 58N 123 0W
McLoughlin, Mt., U.S.A. 82 E2 42 27N 122 19W
McMechen, U.S.A. 78 G4 39 57N 80 44W
McMinnville, Oreg., U.S.A. 82 D2 45 13N 123 12W
McMinnville, Tenn., U.S.A. 77 H3 35 41N 85 46W
McMurdo Sd., Antarctica 5 D11 77 0S 170 0 E
McMurray = Fort McMurray, Canada 72 B6 56 44N 111 7W
McMurray, U.S.A. 84 B4 48 19N 122 14W
Macodoene, Mozam. 57 C6 23 32S 35 5 E
Macomb, U.S.A. 80 E9 40 27N 90 40W
Mâcon, France 18 C6 46 19N 4 50 E
Macon, Ga., U.S.A. 77 J4 32 51N 83 38W
Macon, Miss., U.S.A. 77 J1 33 7N 88 34W
Macon, Mo., U.S.A. 80 F8 39 44N 92 28W
Macossa, Mozam. 55 F3 17 55S 33 56 E
Macoun L., Canada 73 B8 56 32N 103 40W
Macovane, Mozam. 57 C6 21 30S 35 2 E
McPherson, U.S.A. 80 F6 38 22N 97 40W
McPherson Pk., U.S.A. 85 L7 34 53N 119 53W
McPherson Ra., Australia 63 D5 28 15S 153 15 E
Macquarie —►, Australia 63 E4 30 5S 147 30 E
Macquarie Harbour, Australia 62 G4 42 15S 145 23 E
Macquarie Is., Pac. Oc. 64 N7 54 36S 158 55 E
MacRobertson Land, Antarctica 5 D6 71 0S 64 0 E
Macroom, Ireland 13 E3 51 54N 8 57W
MacTier, Canada 78 A5 45 9N 79 46W
Macubela, Mozam. 55 F4 16 53S 37 49 E
Macuiza, Mozam. 55 F3 18 7S 34 29 E
Macusani, Peru 92 F4 14 4S 70 29W
Macuse, Mozam. 55 F4 17 45S 37 10 E
Macuspana, Mexico 87 D6 17 46N 92 36W
Macusse, Angola 56 B3 17 48S 20 23 E
Madadeni, S. Africa 57 D5 27 43S 30 3 E
Madagascar ■, Africa 57 C8 20 0S 47 0 E
Madā'in Sālih, Si. Arabia 44 E3 26 46N 37 57 E
Madama, Niger 51 D8 22 0N 13 40 E
Madame I., Canada 71 C7 45 30N 60 58W
Madaripur, Bangla. 41 H17 23 19N 90 15 E
Madauk, Burma 41 L20 17 56N 96 52 E
Madawaska, Canada 78 A7 45 30N 78 0W
Madawaska —►, Canada 78 A8 45 27N 76 21W
Madaya, Burma 41 H20 22 12N 96 10 E
Maddalena, Italy 20 D3 41 16N 9 23 E
Madeira, Atl. Oc. 22 D3 32 50N 17 0W
Madeira —►, Brazil 92 D7 3 22S 58 45W
Madeleine, Îs. de la, Canada 71 C7 47 30N 61 40W
Madera, Mexico 86 B3 29 12N 108 7W
Madera, Calif., U.S.A. 84 J6 36 57N 120 3W
Madera, Pa., U.S.A. 78 F6 40 49N 78 26W
Madha, India 40 L9 18 0N 75 30 E
Madhavpur, India 42 J3 21 15N 69 58 E
Madhepura, India 43 F12 26 11N 86 23 E
Madhubani, India 43 F12 26 21N 86 7 E
Madhupur, India 43 G12 24 16N 86 39 E
Madhya Pradesh □, India 42 J8 22 50N 78 0 E
Madidi —►, Bolivia 92 F5 12 32S 66 52W
Madikeri, India 40 N9 12 30N 75 45 E
Madill, U.S.A. 81 H6 34 6N 96 46W
Madimba, Dem. Rep. of the Congo 52 E3 4 58S 15 5 E
Ma'din, Syria 44 C3 35 45N 39 36 E
Madingou, Congo 52 E2 4 10S 13 33 E
Madirovalo, Madag. 57 B8 16 26S 46 32 E
Madison, Calif., U.S.A. 84 G5 38 41N 121 59W
Madison, Fla., U.S.A. 77 K4 30 28N 83 25W
Madison, Ind., U.S.A. 76 F3 38 44N 85 23W
Madison, Nebr., U.S.A. 80 E6 41 50N 97 27W
Madison, Ohio, U.S.A. 78 E3 41 46N 81 3W
Madison, S. Dak., U.S.A. 80 D6 44 0N 97 7W
Madison, Wis., U.S.A. 80 D10 43 4N 89 24W
Madison —►, U.S.A. 82 D8 45 56N 111 31W
Madison Heights, U.S.A. 76 G6 37 25N 79 8W
Madisonville, Ky., U.S.A. 76 G2 37 20N 87 30W
Madisonville, Tex., U.S.A. 81 K7 30 57N 95 55W
Madista, Botswana 56 C4 21 15S 25 6 E
Madiun, Indonesia 37 G14 7 38S 111 32 E
Madoc, Canada 78 B7 44 30N 77 28W
Madona, Latvia 9 H22 56 53N 26 5 E
Madrakah, Ra's al, Oman 46 D6 19 0N 57 50 E
Madras = Chennai, India 40 N12 13 8N 80 19 E
Madras = Tamil Nadu □, India 40 P10 11 0N 77 0 E
Madras, U.S.A. 82 D3 44 38N 121 8W
Madre, L., Mexico 87 C5 25 0N 97 30W
Madre, Laguna, U.S.A. 81 M6 27 0N 97 30W
Madre, Sierra, Phil. 37 A6 17 0N 122 0 E
Madre de Dios —►, Bolivia 92 F5 10 59S 66 8W
Madre de Dios, I., Chile 96 G1 50 20S 75 10W
Madre del Sur, Sierra, Mexico 87 D5 17 30N 100 0W
Madre Occidental, Sierra, Mexico 86 B3 27 0N 107 0W
Madre Oriental, Sierra, Mexico 86 C5 25 0N 100 0W
Madri, India 42 G5 24 16N 73 32 E
Madrid, Spain 19 B4 40 25N 3 45W
Madrid, U.S.A. 79 B9 44 45N 75 8W
Madura, Australia 61 F4 31 55S 127 0 E
Madura, Indonesia 37 G15 7 30S 114 0 E
Madura, Selat, Indonesia 37 G15 7 30S 113 20 E
Madurai, India 40 Q11 9 55N 78 10 E
Madurantakam, India 40 N11 12 30N 79 50 E
Mae Chan, Thailand 38 B2 20 9N 99 52 E
Mae Hong Son, Thailand 38 C2 19 16N 97 56 E
Mae Khlong —►, Thailand 38 F3 13 24N 100 0 E
Mae Phrik, Thailand 38 D2 17 27N 99 7 E
Mae Ramat, Thailand 38 D2 16 58N 98 31 E
Mae Rim, Thailand 38 C2 18 54N 98 57 E
Mae Sot, Thailand 38 D2 16 43N 98 34 E
Mae Suai, Thailand 38 C2 19 39N 99 33 E
Mae Tha, Thailand 38 C2 18 28N 99 8 E
Maebashi, Japan 31 F9 36 24N 139 4 E
Maesteg, U.K. 11 F4 51 36N 3 40W
Maestra, Sierra, Cuba 88 B4 20 15N 77 0W
Maevatanana, Madag. 57 B8 16 56S 46 49 E
Mafeking = Mafikeng, S. Africa 56 D4 25 50S 25 38 E
Mafeking, Canada 73 C8 52 40N 101 10W
Mafeteng, Lesotho 56 D4 29 51S 27 15 E
Maffra, Australia 63 F4 37 53S 146 58 E
Mafia I., Tanzania 54 D4 7 45S 39 50 E
Mafikeng, S. Africa 56 D4 25 50S 25 38 E
Mafra, Brazil 95 B6 26 10S 49 55W
Mafra, Portugal 19 C1 38 55N 9 20W
Mafungabusi Plateau, Zimbabwe 55 F2 18 30S 29 8 E
Magadan, Russia 27 D16 59 38N 150 50 E
Magadi, Kenya 54 C4 1 54S 36 19 E
Magadi, L., Kenya 54 C4 1 54S 36 19 E
Magaliesburg, S. Africa 57 D4 26 0S 27 32 E
Magallanes, Estrecho de, Chile 96 G2 52 30S 75 0W
Magangué, Colombia 92 B4 9 14N 74 45W
Magdalen Is. = Madeleine, Îs. de la, Canada 71 C7 47 30N 61 40W
Magdalena, Argentina 94 D4 35 5S 57 30W
Magdalena, Bolivia 92 F6 13 13S 63 57W
Magdalena, Mexico 86 A2 30 50N 112 0W
Magdalena, U.S.A. 83 J10 34 7N 107 15W
Magdalena —►, Colombia 92 A4 11 6N 74 51W
Magdalena —►, Mexico 86 A2 30 40N 112 25W
Magdalena, B., Mexico 86 C2 24 30N 112 10W
Magdalena, Llano de la, Mexico 86 C2 25 0N 111 30W
Magdeburg, Germany 16 B6 52 7N 11 38 E
Magdelaine Cays, Australia 62 B5 16 33S 150 18 E
Magee, U.S.A. 81 K10 31 52N 89 44W
Magelang, Indonesia 37 G14 7 29S 110 13 E
Magellan's Str. = Magallanes, Estrecho de, Chile 96 G2 52 30S 75 0W
Magenta, L., Australia 61 F2 33 30S 119 2 E
Magerøya, Norway 8 A21 71 3N 25 40 E
Maggiore, Lago, Italy 18 D8 45 57N 8 39 E
Maghâgha, Egypt 51 C12 28 38N 30 50 E
Magherafelt, U.K. 13 B5 54 45N 6 37W
Maghreb, N. Afr. 50 B5 32 0N 4 0W
Magistralnyy, Russia 27 D11 56 16N 107 36 E
Magnetic Pole (North) = North Magnetic Pole, Canada 4 B2 77 58N 102 8W
Magnetic Pole (South) = South Magnetic Pole, Antarctica 5 C9 64 8S 138 8 E
Magnitogorsk, Russia 24 D10 53 27N 59 4 E
Magnolia, Ark., U.S.A. 81 J8 33 16N 93 14W
Magnolia, Miss., U.S.A. 81 K9 31 9N 90 28W
Magog, Canada 79 A12 45 18N 72 9W
Magoro, Uganda 54 B3 1 45N 34 12 E
Magosa = Famagusta, Cyprus 23 D12 35 8N 33 55 E
Magouládhes, Greece 23 A3 39 45N 19 42 E
Magoye, Zambia 55 F2 16 1S 27 30 E
Magozal, Mexico 87 C5 21 34N 97 59W
Magpie, L., Canada 71 B7 51 0N 64 41W
Magrath, Canada 72 D6 49 25N 112 50W
Maguarinho, C., Brazil 93 D9 0 15S 48 30W
Mağusa = Famagusta, Cyprus 23 D12 35 8N 33 55 E
Maguse L., Canada 73 A9 61 40N 95 10W
Maguse Pt., Canada 73 A10 61 20N 93 50W
Magvana, India 42 H3 23 13N 69 22 E
Magwe, Burma 41 J19 20 10N 95 0 E
Maha Sarakham, Thailand 38 D4 16 12N 103 16 E
Mahābād, Iran 44 B5 36 50N 45 45 E
Mahabharat Lekh, Nepal 43 E10 28 30N 82 0 E
Mahabo, Madag. 57 C7 20 23S 44 40 E
Mahadeo Hills, India 43 H8 22 20N 78 30 E
Mahaffey, U.S.A. 78 F6 40 53N 78 44W
Mahagi, Dem. Rep. of the Congo 54 B3 2 20N 31 0 E
Mahajamba —►, Madag. 57 B8 15 33S 47 8 E
Mahajamba, Helodranon' i, Madag. 57 B8 15 24S 47 5 E
Mahajan, India 42 E5 28 48N 73 56 E
Mahajanga, Madag. 57 B8 15 40S 46 25 E
Mahajanga □, Madag. 57 B8 17 0S 47 0 E
Mahajilo —►, Madag. 57 B8 19 42S 45 22 E
Mahakam —►, Indonesia 36 E5 0 35S 117 17 E
Mahalapye, Botswana 56 C4 23 1S 26 51 E
Maḩallāt, Iran 45 C6 33 55N 50 30 E
Māhān, Iran 45 D8 30 5N 57 18 E
Mahan —►, India 43 H10 23 30N 82 50 E
Mahanadi —►, India 41 J15 20 20N 86 25 E
Mahananda —►, India 43 G12 25 12N 87 52 E
Mahanoro, Madag. 57 B8 19 54S 48 48 E
Mahanoy City, U.S.A. 79 F8 40 49N 76 9W
Maharashtra □, India 40 J9 20 30N 75 30 E
Mahari Mts., Tanzania 54 D3 6 20S 30 0 E
Mahasham, W. —►, Egypt 47 E3 30 15N 34 10 E
Mahasolo, Madag. 57 B8 19 7S 46 22 E
Mahattat ash Shīdīyah, Jordan 47 F4 29 55N 35 55 E
Mahattat 'Unayzah, Jordan 47 E4 30 30N 35 47 E
Mahaxay, Laos 38 D5 17 22N 105 12 E
Mahbubnagar, India 40 L10 16 45N 77 59 E
Maḩḑah, Oman 45 E7 24 24N 55 59 E
Mahdia, Tunisia 51 A8 35 28N 11 0 E
Mahe, India 43 C8 33 10N 78 32 E
Mahendragarh, India 42 E7 28 17N 76 14 E
Mahenge, Tanzania 55 D4 8 45S 36 41 E
Maheno, N.Z. 59 L3 45 10S 170 50 E
Mahesana, India 42 H5 23 39N 72 26 E
Maheshwar, India 42 H6 22 11N 75 35 E
Mahgawan, India 43 F8 26 29N 78 37 E
Mahi —►, India 42 H5 22 15N 72 55 E
Mahia Pen., N.Z. 59 H6 39 9S 177 55 E
Mahilyow, Belarus 17 B16 53 55N 30 18 E
Mahmud Kot, Pakistan 42 D4 30 16N 71 0 E
Mahnomen, U.S.A. 80 B7 47 19N 95 58W
Mahoba, India 43 G8 25 15N 79 55 E
Mahón = Maó, Spain 22 B11 39 53N 4 16 E
Mahone Bay, Canada 71 D7 44 30N 64 20W
Mahopac, U.S.A. 79 E11 41 22N 73 45W
Mahuva, India 42 J4 21 5N 71 48 E
Mai-Ndombe, L., Dem. Rep. of the Congo 52 E3 2 0S 18 20 E
Mai-Sai, Thailand 38 B2 20 20N 99 55 E
Maicurú —►, Brazil 93 D8 2 14S 54 17W
Maidan Khula, Afghan. 42 C3 33 36N 69 50 E
Maidenhead, U.K. 11 F7 51 31N 0 42W
Maidstone, Canada 73 C7 53 5N 109 20W
Maidstone, U.K. 11 F8 51 16N 0 32 E
Maiduguri, Nigeria 51 F8 12 0N 13 20 E
Maihar, India 43 G9 24 16N 80 45 E
Maijdi, Bangla. 41 H17 22 48N 91 10 E
Maikala Ra., India 41 J12 22 0N 81 0 E
Mailani, India 43 E9 28 17N 80 21 E
Mailsi, Pakistan 42 E5 29 48N 72 15 E
Main —►, Germany 16 C5 50 0N 8 18 E
Main —►, U.K. 13 B5 54 48N 6 18W
Maine, France 18 C3 48 20N 0 15W
Maine □, U.S.A. 77 C11 45 20N 69 0W
Maine —►, Ireland 13 D2 52 9N 9 45W
Maingkwan, Burma 41 F20 26 15N 96 37 E
Mainit, L., Phil. 37 C7 9 31N 125 30 E
Mainland, Orkney, U.K. 12 C5 58 59N 3 8W
Mainland, Shet., U.K. 12 A7 60 15N 1 22W
Mainoru, Australia 62 A1 14 0S 134 6 E
Mainpuri, India 43 F8 27 18N 79 4 E
Maintirano, Madag. 57 B7 18 3S 44 1 E
Mainz, Germany 16 C5 50 1N 8 14 E
Maipú, Argentina 94 D4 36 52S 57 50W
Maiquetía, Venezuela 92 A5 10 36N 66 57W
Mairabari, India 41 F18 26 30N 92 22 E
Maisí, Cuba 89 B5 20 17N 74 9W
Maisí, Pta. de, Cuba 89 B5 20 10N 74 10W
Maitland, N.S.W., Australia 63 E5 32 33S 151 36 E
Maitland, S. Austral., Australia 63 E2 34 23S 137 40 E
Maitland —►, Canada 78 C3 43 45N 81 43W
Maiz, Is. del, Nic. 88 D3 12 15N 83 4W
Maizuru, Japan 31 G7 35 25N 135 22 E
Majalengka, Indonesia 37 G13 6 50S 108 13 E
Majene, Indonesia 37 E5 3 38S 118 57 E
Majorca = Mallorca, Spain 22 B10 39 30N 3 0 E
Makale, Indonesia 37 E5 3 6S 119 51 E
Makamba, Burundi 54 C2 4 8S 29 49 E
Makarikari = Makgadikgadi Salt Pans, Botswana 56 C4 20 40S 25 45 E
Makarovo, Russia 27 D11 57 40N 107 45 E
Makasar = Ujung Pandang, Indonesia 37 F5 5 10S 119 20 E
Makasar, Selat, Indonesia 37 E5 1 0S 118 20 E
Makasar, Str. of = Makasar, Selat, Indonesia 37 E5 1 0S 118 20 E
Makat, Kazakstan 25 E9 47 39N 53 19 E
Makedhonía □, Greece 21 D10 40 39N 22 0 E
Makedonija = Macedonia ■, Europe 21 D9 41 53N 21 40 E
Makena, U.S.A. 74 H16 20 39N 156 27W
Makeyevka = Makiyivka, Ukraine 25 E6 48 0N 38 0 E
Makgadikgadi Salt Pans, Botswana 56 C4 20 40S 25 45 E
Makhachkala, Russia 25 F8 43 0N 47 30 E
Makhmūr, Iraq 44 C4 35 46N 43 35 E
Makian, Indonesia 37 D7 0 20N 127 20 E
Makindu, Kenya 54 C4 2 18S 37 50 E
Makinsk, Kazakstan 26 D8 52 37N 70 26 E
Makiyivka, Ukraine 25 E6 48 0N 38 0 E
Makkah, Si. Arabia 46 C2 21 30N 39 54 E
Makkovik, Canada 71 A8 55 10N 59 10W
Makó, Hungary 17 E11 46 14N 20 33 E
Makokou, Gabon 52 D2 0 40N 12 50 E
Makongo, Dem. Rep. of the Congo 54 B2 3 25N 26 17 E
Makoro, Dem. Rep. of the Congo 54 B2 3 10N 29 59 E
Makrai, India 40 H10 22 2N 77 0 E
Makran Coast Range, Pakistan 40 G4 25 40N 64 0 E
Makrana, India 42 F6 27 2N 74 46 E
Makriyialos, Greece 23 D7 35 2N 25 59 E
Mākū, Iran 44 B5 39 15N 44 31 E
Makunda, Botswana 56 C3 22 30S 20 7 E
Makurazaki, Japan 31 J5 31 15N 130 20 E
Makurdi, Nigeria 50 G7 7 43N 8 35 E
Makūyeh, Iran 45 D7 28 7N 53 9 E
Makwassie, S. Africa 56 D4 27 17S 26 0 E
Mal B., Ireland 13 D2 52 50N 9 30W
Mala, Pta., Panama 88 E3 7 28N 80 2W
Malabar Coast, India 40 P9 11 0N 75 0 E
Malabo = Rey Malabo, Eq. Guin. 52 D1 3 45N 8 50 E
Malacca, Str. of, Indonesia 39 L3 3 0N 101 0 E
Malad City, U.S.A. 82 E7 42 12N 112 15W
Maladzyechna, Belarus 17 A14 54 20N 26 50 E
Málaga, Spain 19 D3 36 43N 4 23W
Malagarasi, Tanzania 54 D3 5 5S 30 50 E
Malagarasi —►, Tanzania 54 D2 5 12S 29 47 E
Malagasy Rep. = Madagascar ■, Africa 57 C8 20 0S 47 0 E
Malahide, Ireland 13 C5 53 26N 6 9W
Malaimbandy, Madag. 57 C8 20 20S 45 36 E
Malakâl, Sudan 51 G12 9 33N 31 40 E
Malakand, Pakistan 42 B4 34 40N 71 55 E
Malakwal, Pakistan 42 C5 32 34N 73 13 E
Malamala, Indonesia 37 E6 3 21S 120 55 E
Malanda, Australia 62 B4 17 22S 145 35 E
Malang, Indonesia 37 G15 7 59S 112 45 E
Malangen, Norway 8 B18 69 24N 18 37 E
Malanje, Angola 52 F3 9 36S 16 17 E
Mälaren, Sweden 9 G17 59 30N 17 10 E
Malargüe, Argentina 94 D2 35 32S 69 30W
Malartic, Canada 70 C4 48 9N 78 9W
Malaryta, Belarus 17 C13 51 50N 24 3 E
Malatya, Turkey 25 G6 38 25N 38 20 E
Malawi ■, Africa 55 E3 11 55S 34 0 E
Malawi, L. = Nyasa, L., Africa 55 E3 12 30S 34 30 E
Malay Pen., Asia 39 J3 7 25N 100 0 E
Malaya Vishera, Russia 24 C5 58 55N 32 25 E
Malaybalay, Phil. 37 C7 8 5N 125 7 E
Malāyer, Iran 45 C6 34 19N 48 51 E
Malaysia ■, Asia 39 K4 5 0N 110 0 E
Malazgirt, Turkey 25 G7 39 10N 42 33 E
Malbon, Australia 62 C3 21 5S 140 17 E
Malbooma, Australia 63 E1 30 41S 134 11 E
Malbork, Poland 17 B10 54 3N 19 1 E
Malcolm, Australia 61 E3 28 51S 121 25 E
Malcolm, Pt., Australia 61 F3 33 48S 123 45 E
Maldah, India 43 G13 25 2N 88 9 E
Maldegem, Belgium 15 C3 51 14N 3 26 E
Malden, Mass., U.S.A. 79 D13 42 26N 71 4W
Malden, Mo., U.S.A. 81 G10 36 34N 89 57W
Malden I., Kiribati 65 H12 4 3S 155 1W
Maldives ■, Ind. Oc. 29 J11 5 0N 73 0 E
Maldonado, Uruguay 95 C5 34 59S 55 0W
Maldonado, Punta, Mexico 87 D5 16 19N 98 35W
Malé, Maldives 29 J11 4 0N 73 28 E
Malé Karpaty, Slovak Rep. 17 D9 48 30N 17 20 E
Maléa, Ákra, Greece 21 F10 36 28N 23 7 E
Malegaon, India 40 J9 20 30N 74 38 E
Malei, Mozam. 55 F4 17 12S 36 58 E
Malek Kandī, Iran 44 B5 37 9N 46 6 E
Malela, Dem. Rep. of the Congo 54 C2 4 22S 26 8 E
Malema, Mozam. 55 E4 14 57S 37 20 E
Máleme, Greece 23 D5 35 31N 23 49 E
Maleny, Australia 63 D5 26 45S 152 52 E
Malerkotla, India 42 D6 30 32N 75 58 E
Máles, Greece 23 D7 35 6N 25 35 E
Malgomaj, Sweden 8 D17 64 40N 16 30 E
Malha, Sudan 51 E11 15 8N 25 10 E
Malhargarh, India 42 G6 24 17N 74 59 E
Malheur —►, U.S.A. 82 D5 44 4N 116 59W
Malheur L., U.S.A. 82 E4 43 20N 118 48W
Mali ■, Africa 50 E5 17 0N 3 0W
Mali —►, Burma 41 G20 25 40N 97 40 E
Mali Kyun, Burma 38 F2 13 0N 98 20 E
Malibu, U.S.A. 85 L8 34 2N 118 41W
Maliku, Indonesia 37 E6 0 39S 123 16 E
Malili, Indonesia 37 E6 2 42S 121 6 E
Malimba, Mts., Dem. Rep. of the Congo 54 D2 7 30S 29 30 E
Malin Hd., Ireland 13 A4 55 23N 7 23W
Malin Pen., Ireland 13 A4 55 20N 7 17W
Malindi, Kenya 54 C5 3 12S 40 5 E
Malines = Mechelen, Belgium 15 C4 51 2N 4 29 E
Malino, Indonesia 37 D6 1 0N 121 0 E
Malinyi, Tanzania 55 D4 8 56S 36 0 E
Malita, Phil. 37 C7 6 19N 125 39 E
Maliwun, Burma 36 B1 10 17N 98 40 E
Maliya, India 42 H4 23 5N 70 46 E
Malkara, Turkey 21 D12 40 53N 26 53 E
Mallacoota Inlet, Australia 63 F4 37 34S 149 40 E
Mallaig, U.K. 12 D3 57 0N 5 50W

Mehndawal

Marmara, Sea of =
Marmara Denizi, Turkey . 21 D13 40 45N 28 15 E
Marmara Denizi, Turkey . . . 21 D13 40 45N 28 15 E
Marmaris, Turkey . . . . 21 F13 36 50N 28 14 E
Marmion, Mt., Australia . . . 61 E2 29 16S 119 50 E
Marmion L., Canada 70 C1 48 55N 91 20W
Marmolada, Mte., Italy . . . . 20 A4 46 26N 11 51 E
Marmora, Canada 78 B7 44 28N 77 41W
Marne →, France . . . . 18 B5 48 48N 2 24 E
Maroala, Madag. . . . . 57 B8 15 23S 47 59 E
Maroantsetra, Madag. . . . . 57 B8 15 26S 49 44 E
Maromandia, Madag. . . . . . 57 A8 14 13S 48 5 E
Marondera, Zimbabwe . . . . 55 F3 18 5S 31 42 E
Maroni →, Fr. Guiana 93 B8 5 30N 54 0W
Maroochydore, Australia . . 63 D5 26 29S 153 5 E
Maroona, Australia . . . . . . 63 F3 37 27S 142 54 E
Marosakoa, Madag. . . . . . . 57 B8 15 26S 46 38 E
Maroua, Cameroon . . . . . . 51 F8 10 40N 14 20 E
Marovoay, Madag. . . . . 57 B8 16 6S 46 39 E
Marquard, S. Africa . . . . . . 56 D4 28 40S 27 28 E
Marquesas Is. = Marquises, Is., Pac. Oc. 65 H14 9 30S 140 0W
Marquette, U.S.A. 76 B2 46 33N 87 24W
Marquises, Is., Pac. Oc. . . . 65 H14 9 30S 140 0W
Marra, Djebel, Sudan . . . . 51 F10 13 10N 24 22 E
Marracuene, Mozam. . . . . . 57 D5 25 45S 32 35 E
Marrakech, Morocco 50 B4 31 9N 8 0W
Marrawah, Australia . . . . . 62 G3 40 55S 144 42 E
Marree, Australia . . . . 63 D2 29 39S 138 1 E
Marrero, U.S.A. 81 L9 29 54N 90 6W
Marrimane, Mozam. . . . . . . 57 C5 22 58S 33 34 E
Marromeu, Mozam. . . . . . . 57 B6 18 15S 36 25 E
Marrowie Cr. →, Australia 63 E4 33 23S 145 40 E
Marrubane, Mozam. . . . . . . 55 F4 18 0S 37 0 E
Marrupa, Mozam. . . . . 55 E4 13 8S 37 30 E
Mars Hill, U.S.A. 77 B12 46 31N 67 52W
Marsá Matrûh, Egypt . . . . . 51 B11 31 19N 27 9 E
Marsabit, Kenya . . . . 54 B4 2 18N 38 0 E
Marsala, Italy . . . . 20 F5 37 48N 12 26 E
Marsalforn, Malta . . . . 23 C1 36 4N 14 15 E
Marsden, Australia . . . . . . 63 E4 33 47S 147 32 E
Marseille, France . . . . 18 E6 43 18N 5 23 E
Marseilles = Marseille, France . . . . 18 E6 43 18N 5 23 E
Marsh I., U.S.A. 81 L9 29 34N 91 53W
Marshall, Ark., U.S.A. 81 H8 35 55N 92 38W
Marshall, Mich., U.S.A. . . . 76 D3 42 16N 84 58W
Marshall, Minn., U.S.A. . . . 80 C7 44 25N 95 45W
Marshall, Mo., U.S.A. 80 F8 39 7N 93 12W
Marshall, Tex., U.S.A. 81 J7 32 33N 94 23W
Marshall →, Australia . . . 62 C2 22 59S 136 59 E
Marshall Is. ■, Pac. Oc. . . . 64 G9 9 0N 171 0 E
Marshalltown, U.S.A. 80 D8 42 3N 92 55W
Marshfield, Mo., U.S.A. . . . 81 G8 37 15N 92 54W
Marshfield, Vt., U.S.A. . . . 79 B12 44 20N 72 20W
Marshfield, Wis., U.S.A. . . . 80 C9 44 40N 90 10W
Marshūn, Iran . . . . 45 B6 36 19N 49 23 E
Märsta, Sweden . . . . 9 G17 59 37N 17 52 E
Mart, U.S.A. 81 K6 31 33N 96 50W
Martaban, Burma . . . . 41 L20 16 30N 97 35 E
Martaban, G. of, Burma . . . 41 L20 16 5N 96 30 E
Martapura, Kalimantan, Indonesia . . . . 36 E4 3 22S 114 47 E
Martapura, Sumatera, Indonesia . . . . 36 E2 4 19S 104 22 E
Martelange, Belgium . . . . . 15 E5 49 49N 5 43 E
Martha's Vineyard, U.S.A. . 79 E14 41 25N 70 38W
Martigny, Switz. . . . . 18 C7 46 6N 7 3 E
Martigues, France . . . . . . 18 E6 43 24N 5 4 E
Martin, Slovak Rep. . . . . . 17 D10 49 6N 18 58 E
Martin, S. Dak., U.S.A. . . . 80 D4 43 11N 101 44W
Martin, Tenn., U.S.A. 81 G10 36 21N 88 51W
Martin L., U.S.A. 77 J3 32 41N 85 55W
Martina Franca, Italy . . . . 20 D7 40 42N 17 20 E
Martinborough, N.Z. . . . . . 59 J5 41 14S 175 29 E
Martinez, Calif., U.S.A. . . . 84 G4 38 1N 122 8W
Martinez, Ga., U.S.A. 77 J4 33 31N 82 4W
Martinique ■, W. Indies . . . 89 D7 14 40N 61 0W
Martinique Passage, W. Indies 89 C7 15 15N 61 0W
Martinópolis, Brazil 95 A5 22 11S 51 12W
Martins Ferry, U.S.A. 78 F4 40 6N 80 44W
Martinsburg, Pa., U.S.A. . . 78 F6 40 19N 78 20W
Martinsburg, W. Va., U.S.A. 76 F7 39 27N 77 58W
Martinsville, Ind., U.S.A. . . 76 F2 39 26N 86 25W
Martinsville, Va., U.S.A. . . 77 G6 36 41N 79 52W
Marton, N.Z. . . . . 59 J5 40 4S 175 23 E
Martos, Spain 19 D4 37 44N 3 58W
Marudi, Malaysia . . . . 36 D4 4 11N 114 19 E
Ma'ruf, Afghan. . . . . 40 D5 31 30N 67 6 E
Marugame, Japan . . . . 31 G6 34 15N 133 40 E
Marunga, Angola . . . . 56 B3 17 28S 20 2 E
Marungu, Mts., Dem. Rep. of the Congo . 54 D3 7 30S 30 0 E
Marv Dasht, Iran . . . . 45 D7 29 50N 52 40 E
Marvast, Iran . . . . 45 D7 30 30N 54 15 E
Marvel Loch, Australia . . . 61 F2 31 28S 119 29 E
Marwar, India . . . . 42 G5 25 43N 73 45 E
Mary, Turkmenistan . . . . . . 26 F7 37 40N 61 50 E
Maryborough = Port Laoise, Ireland 13 C4 53 2N 7 18W
Maryborough, Queens., Australia . . . . 63 D5 25 31S 152 37 E
Maryborough, Vic., Australia 63 F3 37 0S 143 44 E
Maryfield, Canada 73 D8 49 50N 101 35W
Maryland □, U.S.A. 76 F7 39 0N 76 30W
Maryland Junction, Zimbabwe . . . . 55 F3 17 45S 30 31 E
Maryport, U.K. 10 C4 54 44N 3 28W
Mary's Harbour, Canada . . 71 B8 52 18N 55 51W
Marystown, Canada 71 C8 47 10N 55 10W
Marysville, Canada 72 D5 49 35N 116 0W
Marysville, Calif., U.S.A. . . 84 F5 39 9N 121 35W
Marysville, Kans., U.S.A. . . 80 F6 39 51N 96 39W
Marysville, Mich., U.S.A. . . 78 D2 42 54N 82 29W
Marysville, Ohio, U.S.A. . . . 76 E4 40 14N 83 22W
Marysville, Wash., U.S.A. . . 84 B4 48 3N 122 11W
Maryville, Mo., U.S.A. 80 E7 40 21N 94 52W
Maryville, Tenn., U.S.A. . . . 77 H4 35 46N 83 58W
Marzūq, Libya . . . . 51 C8 25 53N 13 57 E
Masahunga, Tanzania . . . . 54 C3 2 6S 33 18 E
Masai Steppe, Tanzania . . . 54 C4 4 30S 36 30 E
Masaka, Uganda . . . . 54 C3 0 21S 31 45 E
Masalembo, Kepulauan, Indonesia . . . . 36 F4 5 35S 114 30 E
Masalima, Kepulauan, Indonesia . . . . 36 F5 5 4S 117 5 E
Masamba, Indonesia . . . . . 37 E6 2 30S 120 15 E
Masan, S. Korea . . . . 35 G15 35 11N 128 32 E
Masandam, Ra's, Oman . . . 45 E8 26 30N 56 30 E
Masasi, Tanzania . . . . 55 E4 10 45S 38 52 E
Masaya, Nic. 88 D2 12 0N 86 7W
Masbate, Phil. . . . . 37 B6 12 21N 123 36 E
Mascara, Algeria . . . . 50 A6 35 26N 0 6 E
Mascota, Mexico 86 C4 20 30N 104 50W
Masela, Indonesia . . . . . . 37 F7 8 9S 129 51 E
Maseru, Lesotho . . . . 56 D4 29 18S 27 30 E
Mashaba, Zimbabwe . . . . . 55 G3 20 2S 30 29 E
Mashābih, Si. Arabia . . . . 44 E3 25 35N 36 30 E
Masherbrum, Pakistan . . . . 43 B7 35 38N 76 18 E
Mashhad, Iran . . . . 45 B8 36 20N 59 35 E
Mashīz, Iran . . . . 45 D8 29 56N 56 37 E
Mashkel, Hamun-i, Pakistan 40 E3 28 20N 62 56 E
Mashki Chāh, Pakistan . . . 40 E3 29 5N 62 30 E
Mashonaland, Zimbabwe . . 53 H6 16 30S 31 0 E
Mashonaland Central □, Zimbabwe . . . . 57 B5 17 30S 31 0 E
Mashonaland East □, Zimbabwe . . . . 57 B5 18 0S 32 0 E
Mashonaland West □, Zimbabwe . . . . 57 B4 17 30S 29 30 E
Mashrakh, India . . . . 43 F11 26 7N 84 48 E
Masindi, Uganda . . . . 54 B3 1 40N 31 43 E
Masindi Port, Uganda . . . . 54 B3 1 43N 32 2 E
Maşīrah, Oman . . . . 46 C6 21 0N 58 50 E
Maşīrah, Khalīj, Oman . . . 46 C6 20 10N 58 10 E
Masisi, Dem. Rep. of the Congo . 54 C2 1 23S 28 49 E
Masjed Soleyman, Iran . . . 45 D6 31 55N 49 18 E
Mask, L., Ireland 13 C2 53 36N 9 22W
Maskin, Oman . . . . 45 F8 23 30N 56 50 E
Masoala, Tanjon' i, Madag. 57 B9 15 59S 50 13 E
Masoarivo, Madag. . . . . . . 57 B7 19 3S 44 19 E
Masohi = Amahai, Indonesia . . . . 37 E7 3 20S 128 55 E
Masomeloka, Madag. . . . . . 57 C8 20 17S 48 37 E
Mason, Nev., U.S.A. 84 G7 38 56N 119 8W
Mason, Tex., U.S.A. 81 K5 30 45N 99 14W
Mason City, U.S.A. 80 D8 43 9N 93 12W
Maspalomas, Canary Is. . . . 22 G4 27 46N 15 35W
Maspalomas, Pta., Canary Is. 22 G4 27 43N 15 36W
Masqat, Oman . . . . 46 C6 23 37N 58 36 E
Massa, Italy . . . . 18 D9 44 1N 10 9 E
Massachusetts □, U.S.A. . . 79 D13 42 30N 72 0W
Massachusetts B., U.S.A. . . 79 D14 42 20N 70 50W
Massakory, Chad . . . . 51 F9 13 0N 15 49 E
Massanella, Spain . . . . 22 B9 39 48N 2 51 E
Massangena, Mozam. . . . . . 57 C5 21 34S 33 0 E
Massango, Angola . . . . 52 F3 8 2S 16 21 E
Massawa = Mitsiwa, Eritrea 46 D2 15 35N 39 25 E
Massena, U.S.A. 79 B10 44 56N 74 54W
Massénya, Chad . . . . 51 F9 11 21N 16 9 E
Masset, Canada 72 C2 54 2N 132 10W
Massif Central, France . . . 18 D5 44 55N 3 0 E
Massillon, U.S.A. 78 F3 40 48N 81 32W
Massinga, Mozam. . . . . . . 57 C6 23 15S 35 22 E
Massingir, Mozam. . . . . . . 57 C5 23 51S 32 4 E
Masson, Canada 79 A9 45 32N 75 25W
Masson I., Antarctica . . . . 5 C7 66 10S 93 20 E
Mastanli = Momchilgrad, Bulgaria . . . . 21 D11 41 33N 25 23 E
Masterton, N.Z. . . . . 59 J5 40 56S 175 39 E
Mastic, U.S.A. 79 F12 40 47N 72 54W
Mastuj, Pakistan . . . . 43 A5 36 20N 72 36 E
Mastung, Pakistan . . . . . . 40 E5 29 50N 66 56 E
Masty, Belarus . . . . 17 B13 53 27N 24 38 E
Masuda, Japan . . . . 31 G5 34 40N 131 51 E
Masvingo, Zimbabwe . . . . . 55 G3 20 8S 30 49 E
Masvingo □, Zimbabwe . . . 55 G3 21 0S 31 30 E
Maşyāf, Syria . . . . 44 C3 35 4N 36 20 E
Matabeleland, Zimbabwe . . 53 H5 18 0S 27 0 E
Matabeleland North □, Zimbabwe . . . . 55 F2 19 0S 28 0 E
Matabeleland South □, Zimbabwe . . . . 55 G2 21 0S 29 0 E
Matachewan, Canada 70 C3 47 56N 80 39W
Matadi, Dem. Rep. of the Congo . 52 F2 5 52S 13 31 E
Matagalpa, Nic. 88 D2 13 0N 85 58W
Matagami, Canada 70 C4 49 45N 77 34W
Matagami, L., Canada 70 C4 49 50N 77 40W
Matagorda B., U.S.A. 81 L6 28 40N 96 0W
Matagorda I., U.S.A. 81 L6 28 15N 96 30W
Matak, Indonesia . . . . 39 L6 3 18N 106 16 E
Mátala, Greece . . . . 23 E6 34 59N 24 45 E
Matam, Senegal 50 E3 15 34N 13 17W
Matamoros, Campeche, Mexico 87 D6 18 50N 90 50W
Matamoros, Coahuila, Mexico 86 B4 25 33N 103 15W
Matamoros, Tamaulipas, Mexico 87 B5 25 50N 97 30W
Ma'ţan as Sarra, Libya . . . . 51 D10 21 45N 22 0 E
Matandu →, Tanzania . . . . 55 D3 8 45S 34 19 E
Matane, Canada 71 C6 48 50N 67 33W
Matanomadh, India . . . . . . 42 H3 23 33N 68 57 E
Matanzas, Cuba 88 B3 23 0N 81 40W
Matapan, C. = Taínaron, Ákra, Greece . . . . 21 F10 36 22N 22 27 E
Matapédia, Canada 71 C6 48 0N 66 59W
Matara, Sri Lanka . . . . 40 S12 5 58N 80 30 E
Mataram, Indonesia . . . . . . 36 F5 8 41S 116 10 E
Matarani, Peru 92 G4 17 0S 72 10W
Mataranka, Australia . . . . . 60 B5 14 55S 133 4 E
Matarma, Râs, Egypt . . . . . 47 E1 30 27N 32 44 E
Mataró, Spain . . . . 19 B7 41 32N 2 29 E
Matatiele, S. Africa . . . . . . 57 E4 30 20S 28 49 E
Mataura, N.Z. . . . . 59 M2 46 11S 168 51 E
Matehuala, Mexico 86 C4 23 40N 100 40W
Mateke Hills, Zimbabwe . . . 55 G3 21 48S 31 0 E
Matera, Italy . . . . 20 D7 40 40N 16 36 E
Matetsi, Zimbabwe . . . . . . 55 F2 18 12S 26 0 E
Mathis, U.S.A. 81 L6 28 6N 97 50W
Mathráki, Greece . . . . 23 A3 39 48N 19 31 E
Mathura, India . . . . 42 F7 27 30N 77 40 E
Mati, Phil. . . . . 37 C7 6 55N 126 15 E
Matiali, India . . . . 43 F13 26 56N 88 49 E
Matias Romero, Mexico . . . 87 D5 16 53N 95 2W
Matibane, Mozam. . . . . . . 55 E5 14 49S 40 45 E
Matima, Botswana . . . . . . 56 C3 20 15S 24 26 E
Matiri Ra., N.Z. . . . . 59 J4 41 38S 172 20 E
Matla →, India . . . . 43 J13 21 40N 88 40 E
Matli, Pakistan . . . . 42 G3 25 2N 68 39 E
Matlock, U.K. 10 D6 53 9N 1 33W
Mato Grosso □, Brazil 93 F8 14 0S 55 0W
Mato Grosso, Planalto do, Brazil 93 G8 15 0S 55 0W
Mato Grosso do Sul □, Brazil 93 G8 18 0S 55 0W
Matochkin Shar, Russia . . . 26 B6 73 10N 56 40 E
Matopo Hills, Zimbabwe . . 55 G2 20 36S 28 20 E
Matopos, Zimbabwe . . . . . 55 G2 20 20S 28 29 E
Matosinhos, Portugal 19 B1 41 11N 8 42W
Maţraḩ, Oman . . . . 46 C6 23 37N 58 30 E
Matsue, Japan . . . . 31 G6 35 25N 133 10 E
Matsumae, Japan . . . . 30 D10 41 26N 140 7 E
Matsumoto, Japan . . . . . . 31 F9 36 15N 138 0 E
Matsusaka, Japan . . . . 31 G8 34 34N 136 32 E
Matsutō, Japan . . . . 31 F8 36 31N 136 34 E
Matsuura, Japan . . . . 31 H4 33 20N 129 49 E
Matsuyama, Japan . . . . . . 31 H6 33 45N 132 45 E
Mattagami →, Canada 70 B3 50 43N 81 29W
Mattancheri, India . . . . . . 40 Q10 9 50N 76 15 E
Mattawa, Canada 70 C4 46 20N 78 45W
Matterhorn, Switz. . . . . . . 18 D7 45 58N 7 39 E
Matthew Town, Bahamas . . 89 B5 20 57N 73 40W
Matthew's Ridge, Guyana . . 92 B6 7 37N 60 10W
Mattice, Canada 70 C3 49 40N 83 20W
Mattituck, U.S.A. 79 F12 40 59N 72 32W
Mattoon, U.S.A. 76 F1 39 29N 88 23W
Matuba, Mozam. . . . . 57 C5 24 28S 32 49 E
Matucana, Peru 92 F3 11 55S 76 25W
Matūn = Khowst, Afghan. . . 42 C3 33 22N 69 58 E
Maturín, Venezuela 92 B6 9 45N 63 11W
Mau, India . . . . 43 G10 25 56N 83 33 E
Mau, Mad. P., India . . . . . . 43 F8 26 17N 78 41 E
Mau, Ut. P., India . . . . 43 G9 25 17N 81 23 E
Mau Escarpment, Kenya . . . 54 C4 0 40S 36 0 E
Mau Ranipur, India . . . . . . 43 G8 25 16N 79 8 E
Maubeuge, France . . . . . . 18 A6 50 17N 3 57 E
Maud, Pt., Australia . . . . . 60 D1 23 6S 113 45 E
Maude, Australia . . . . 63 E3 34 29S 144 18 E
Maudin Sun, Burma . . . . . . 41 M19 16 0N 94 30 E
Maués, Brazil 92 D7 3 20S 57 45W
Mauganj, India . . . . 41 G12 24 50N 81 55 E
Maughold Hd., U.K. 10 C3 54 18N 4 18W
Maui, U.S.A. 74 H16 20 48N 156 20W
Maulamyaing = Moulmein, Burma . . . . 41 L20 16 30N 97 40 E
Maule □, Chile 94 D1 36 5S 72 30W
Maumee, U.S.A. 76 E4 41 34N 83 39W
Maumee →, U.S.A. 76 E4 41 42N 83 28W
Maumere, Indonesia . . . . . 37 F6 8 38S 122 13 E
Maun, Botswana . . . . 56 C3 20 0S 23 26 E
Mauna Kea, U.S.A. 74 J17 19 50N 155 28W
Mauna Loa, U.S.A. 74 J17 19 30N 155 35W
Maungmagan Is., Burma . . . 38 F1 14 0N 97 30 E
Maungmagan Kyunzu, Burma . . . . 41 N20 14 0N 97 48 E
Maupin, U.S.A. 82 D3 45 11N 121 5W
Maurepas, L., U.S.A. 81 K9 30 15N 90 30W
Maurice, L., Australia . . . . 61 E5 29 30S 131 0 E
Mauricie, Parc Nat. de la, Canada 70 C5 46 45N 73 0W
Mauritania ■, Africa 50 E3 20 50N 10 0W
Mauritius ■, Ind. Oc. . . . . . 49 J9 20 0S 57 0 E
Mauston, U.S.A. 80 D9 43 48N 90 5W
Mavli, India . . . . 42 G5 24 45N 73 55 E
Mavuradonha Mts., Zimbabwe . . . . 55 F3 16 30S 31 30 E
Mawa, Dem. Rep. of the Congo . 54 B2 2 45N 26 40 E
Mawai, India . . . . 43 H9 22 30N 81 4 E
Mawana, India . . . . 42 E7 29 6N 77 58 E
Mawand, Pakistan . . . . 42 E3 29 33N 68 38 E
Mawk Mai, Burma . . . . 41 J20 20 14N 97 37 E
Mawlaik, Burma . . . . 41 H19 23 40N 94 26 E
Mawqaq, Si. Arabia . . . . . . 44 E4 27 25N 41 8 E
Mawson Coast, Antarctica . 5 C6 68 30S 63 0 E
Max, U.S.A. 80 B4 47 49N 101 18W
Maxcanú, Mexico 87 C6 20 40N 92 0W
Maxesibeni, S. Africa . . . . 57 E4 30 49S 29 23 E
Maxhamish L., Canada 72 B4 59 50N 123 17W
Maxixe, Mozam. . . . . 57 C6 23 54S 35 17 E
Maxville, Canada 79 A10 45 17N 74 51W
Maxwell, U.S.A. 84 F4 39 17N 122 11W
Maxwelton, Australia . . . . . 62 C3 20 43S 142 41 E
May, C., U.S.A. 76 F8 38 56N 74 58W
May Pen, Jamaica 88 C4 17 58N 77 15W
Maya →, Russia . . . . 27 D14 60 28N 134 28 E
Maya Mts., Belize 87 D7 16 30N 89 0W
Mayaguana, Bahamas 89 B5 22 30N 72 44W
Mayagüez, Puerto Rico . . . 89 C6 18 12N 67 9W
Mayāmey, Iran . . . . 45 B7 36 24N 55 42 E
Mayanup, Australia . . . . . . 61 F2 33 57S 116 27 E
Mayapan, Mexico 87 C7 20 30N 89 25W
Mayarí, Cuba 89 B4 20 40N 75 41W
Maybell, U.S.A. 82 F9 40 31N 108 5W
Maybole, U.K. 12 F4 55 21N 4 42W
Maydān, Iraq . . . . 44 C5 34 55N 45 37 E
Maydena, Australia . . . . . . 62 G4 42 45S 146 30 E
Mayenne →, France 18 C3 47 30N 0 32W
Mayer, U.S.A. 83 J7 34 24N 112 14W
Mayerthorpe, Canada 72 C5 53 57N 115 8W
Mayfield, Ky., U.S.A. 77 G1 36 44N 88 38W
Mayfield, N.Y., U.S.A. 79 C10 43 6N 74 16W
Mayhill, U.S.A. 83 K11 32 53N 105 29W
Maykop, Russia . . . . 25 F7 44 35N 40 10 E
Maymyo, Burma . . . . 38 A1 22 2N 96 28 E
Maynard, Mass., U.S.A. . . . 79 D13 42 26N 71 27W
Maynard, Wash., U.S.A. . . . 84 C4 47 59N 122 55W
Maynard Hills, Australia . . 61 E2 28 28S 119 49 E
Mayne →, Australia . . . . . 62 C3 23 40S 141 55 E
Maynooth, Ireland 13 C5 53 23N 6 34W
Mayo, Canada 68 B6 63 38N 135 57W
Mayo □, Ireland 13 C2 53 53N 9 3W
Mayon Volcano, Phil. . . . . . 37 B6 13 15N 123 41 E
Mayor I., N.Z. . . . . 59 G6 37 16S 176 17 E
Mayotte, I., Mayotte . . . . . 53 G9 12 50S 45 10 E
Maysville, U.S.A. 76 F4 38 39N 83 46W
Mayu, Indonesia . . . . 37 D7 1 30N 126 30 E
Mayumba, Gabon . . . . 52 E2 3 25S 10 39 E
Mayville, N. Dak., U.S.A. . . 80 B6 47 30N 97 20W
Mayville, N.Y., U.S.A. 78 D5 42 15N 79 30W
Mayya, Russia . . . . 27 C14 61 44N 130 18 E
Mazabuka, Zambia . . . . . . 55 F2 15 52S 27 44 E
Mazagán = El Jadida, Morocco 50 B4 33 11N 8 17W
Mazagão, Brazil 93 D8 0 7S 51 16W
Mazán, Peru 92 D4 3 30S 73 0W
Māzandarān □, Iran . . . . . . 45 B7 36 30N 52 0 E
Mazapil, Mexico 86 C4 24 38N 101 34W
Mazara del Vallo, Italy . . . . 20 F5 37 39N 12 35 E
Mazarrón, Spain 19 D5 37 38N 1 19W
Mazaruni →, Guyana 92 B7 6 25N 58 35W
Mazatán, Mexico 86 B2 29 0N 110 8W
Mazatenango, Guatemala . . 88 D1 14 35N 91 30W
Mazatlán, Mexico 86 C3 23 13N 106 25W
Mažeikiai, Lithuania . . . . . 9 H20 56 20N 22 20 E
Māzhān, Iran . . . . 45 C8 32 30N 59 0 E
Mazīnān, Iran . . . . 45 B8 36 19N 56 56 E
Mazoe, Mozam. . . . . 55 F3 16 42S 33 7 E
Mazoe →, Mozam. . . . . 55 F3 16 20S 33 30 E
Mazowe, Zimbabwe . . . . . . 55 F3 17 28S 30 58 E
Mazurian Lakes = Mazurski, Pojezierze, Poland . . . . . 17 B11 53 50N 21 0 E
Mazurski, Pojezierze, Poland 17 B11 53 50N 21 0 E
Mazyr, Belarus . . . . 17 B15 51 59N 29 15 E
Mbabane, Swaziland . . . . . 57 D5 26 18S 31 6 E
Mbaïki, C.A.R. . . . . 52 D3 3 53N 18 1 E
Mbala, Zambia . . . . 55 D3 8 46S 31 24 E
Mbale, Uganda . . . . 54 B3 1 8N 34 12 E
Mbalmayo, Cameroon . . . . 52 D2 3 33N 11 33 E
Mbamba Bay, Tanzania . . . 55 E3 11 13S 34 49 E
Mbandaka, Dem. Rep. of the Congo . 52 D3 0 1N 18 18 E
Mbanza Congo, Angola . . . 52 F2 6 18S 14 16 E
Mbanza Ngungu, Dem. Rep. of the Congo . 52 F2 5 12S 14 53 E
Mbarara, Uganda . . . . 54 C3 0 35S 30 40 E
Mbashe →, S. Africa . . . . . 57 E4 32 15S 28 54 E
Mbenkuru →, Tanzania . . . 55 D4 9 25S 39 50 E
Mberengwa, Zimbabwe . . . 55 G2 20 29S 29 57 E
Mberengwa, Mt., Zimbabwe 55 G2 20 37S 29 55 E
Mbesuma, Zambia . . . . 55 E3 10 0S 32 2 E
Mbeya, Tanzania . . . . 55 D3 8 54S 33 29 E
Mbeya □, Tanzania . . . . . . 54 D3 8 15S 33 30 E
Mbinga, Tanzania . . . . 55 E4 10 50S 35 0 E
Mbini □, Eq. Guin. . . . . . . 52 D2 1 30N 10 0 E
Mbour, Senegal 50 F2 14 22N 16 54W
Mbuji-Mayi, Dem. Rep. of the Congo . 54 D1 6 9S 23 40 E
Mbulu, Tanzania . . . . 54 C4 3 45S 35 30 E
Mburucuyá, Argentina 94 B4 28 1S 58 14W
Mchinja, Tanzania . . . . 55 D4 9 44S 39 45 E
Mchinji, Malawi . . . . 55 E3 13 47S 32 58 E
Mdantsane, S. Africa . . . . . 53 L5 32 56S 27 46 E
Mead, L., U.S.A. 85 J12 36 1N 114 44W
Meade, U.S.A. 81 G4 37 17N 100 20W
Meadow Lake, Canada 73 C7 54 10N 108 26W
Meadow Lake Prov. Park, Canada 73 C7 54 27N 109 0W
Meadow Valley Wash →, U.S.A. 85 J12 36 40N 114 34W
Meadville, U.S.A. 78 E4 41 39N 80 9W
Meaford, Canada 78 B4 44 36N 80 35W
Mealy Mts., Canada 71 B8 53 10N 58 0W
Meander River, Canada . . . 72 B5 59 2N 117 42W
Meares, C., U.S.A. 82 D2 45 37N 124 0W
Mearim →, Brazil 93 D10 3 4S 44 35W
Meath □, Ireland 13 C5 53 40N 6 57W
Meath Park, Canada 73 C7 53 27N 105 22W
Meaux, France . . . . 18 B5 48 58N 2 50 E
Mebechi-Gawa →, Japan . . 30 D10 40 31N 141 31 E
Mecanhelas, Mozam. . . . . . 55 F4 15 12S 35 54 E
Mecca = Makkah, Si. Arabia 46 C2 21 30N 39 54 E
Mecca, U.S.A. 85 M10 33 34N 116 5W
Mechanicsburg, U.S.A. . . . 78 F8 40 13N 77 1W
Mechanicville, U.S.A. 79 D11 42 54N 73 41W
Mechelen, Belgium . . . . . . 15 C4 51 2N 4 29 E
Mecheria, Algeria 50 B5 33 35N 0 18W
Mecklenburg, Germany . . . 16 B6 53 33N 11 40 E
Mecklenburger Bucht, Germany . . . . 16 A6 54 20N 11 40 E
Meconta, Mozam. . . . . 55 E4 14 59S 39 50 E
Medan, Indonesia . . . . 36 D1 3 40N 98 38 E
Medanosa, Pta., Argentina . 96 F3 48 8S 66 0W
Médéa, Algeria . . . . 50 A6 36 12N 2 50 E
Medellín, Colombia 92 B3 6 15N 75 35W
Medelpad, Sweden . . . . . . 9 E17 62 33N 16 30 E
Medemblik, Neths. . . . . . . 15 B5 52 46N 5 8 E
Medford, Mass., U.S.A. . . . 79 D13 42 25N 71 7W
Medford, Oreg., U.S.A. . . . 82 E2 42 19N 122 52W
Medford, Wis., U.S.A. 80 C9 45 9N 90 20W
Medgidia, Romania . . . . . . 17 F15 44 15N 28 19 E
Media Agua, Argentina . . . 94 C2 31 58S 68 25W
Media Luna, Argentina . . . 94 C2 34 45S 66 44W
Medianeira, Brazil 95 B5 25 17S 54 5W
Mediaş, Romania . . . . 17 E13 46 9N 24 22 E
Medicine Bow, U.S.A. 82 F10 41 54N 106 12W
Medicine Bow Pk., U.S.A. . 82 F10 41 21N 106 19W
Medicine Bow Ra., U.S.A. . 82 F10 41 10N 106 25W
Medicine Hat, Canada 73 D6 50 0N 110 45W
Medicine Lake, U.S.A. 80 A2 48 30N 104 30W
Medicine Lodge, U.S.A. . . . 81 G5 37 17N 98 35W
Medina = Al Madīnah, Si. Arabia . . . . 46 C2 24 35N 39 52 E
Medina, N. Dak., U.S.A. . . . 80 B5 46 54N 99 18W
Medina, N.Y., U.S.A. 78 C6 43 13N 78 23W
Medina, Ohio, U.S.A. 78 E3 41 8N 81 52W
Medina →, U.S.A. 81 L5 29 16N 98 29W
Medina del Campo, Spain . . 19 B3 41 18N 4 55W
Medina L., U.S.A. 81 L5 29 32N 98 56W
Medina Sidonia, Spain 19 D3 36 28N 5 57W
Medinipur, India . . . . 43 H12 22 25N 87 21 E
Mediterranean Sea, Europe 6 H7 35 0N 15 0 E
Médoc, France 18 D3 45 10N 0 50W
Medveditsa →, Russia . . . . 25 E7 49 35N 42 41 E
Medvezhi, Ostrava, Russia . 27 B17 71 0N 161 0 E
Medvezhyegorsk, Russia . . 24 B5 63 0N 34 25 E
Medway →, U.K. . . . . 11 F8 51 27N 0 46 E
Medway Towns □, U.K. . . . 11 F8 51 25N 0 32 E
Meekatharra, Australia . . . 61 E2 26 32S 118 29 E
Meeker, U.S.A. 82 F10 40 2N 107 55W
Meelpaeg Res., Canada . . . 71 C8 48 15N 56 33W
Meerut, India . . . . 42 E7 29 1N 77 42 E
Meeteetse, U.S.A. 82 D9 44 9N 108 52W
Mega, Ethiopia . . . . 46 G2 3 57N 38 19 E
Mégara, Greece . . . . 21 F10 37 58N 23 22 E
Megasini, India . . . . 43 J12 21 38N 86 21 E
Meghalaya □, India . . . . . . 41 G17 25 50N 91 0 E
Mégiscane, L., Canada 70 C4 48 35N 75 55W
Meharry, Mt., Australia . . . 60 D2 22 59S 118 35 E
Mehlville, U.S.A. 80 F9 38 30N 90 19W
Mehndawal, India . . . . 43 F10 26 58N 83 5 E

Minigwal, L., *Australia* .... **61 E3** 29 31S 123 14 E
Minilya →, *Australia* .... **61 D1** 23 45S 114 0 E
Minilya Roadhouse, *Australia* .... **61 D1** 23 55S 114 0 E
Minipi L., *Canada* **71 B7** 52 25N 60 45W
Mink L., *Canada* **72 A5** 61 54N 117 40W
Minna, *Nigeria* .... **50 G7** 9 37N 6 30 E
Minneapolis, *Kans., U.S.A.* **80 F6** 39 8N 97 42W
Minneapolis, *Minn., U.S.A.* **80 C8** 44 59N 93 16W
Minnedosa, *Canada* **73 C9** 50 14N 99 50W
Minnesota □, *U.S.A.* **80 B8** 46 0N 94 15W
Minnesota →, *U.S.A.* **80 C8** 44 54N 93 9W
Minnewaukan, *U.S.A.* **80 A5** 48 4N 99 15W
Minnipa, *Australia* .... **63 E2** 32 51S 135 9 E
Minnitaki L., *Canada* **70 C1** 49 57N 92 10W
Mino, *Japan* .... **31 G8** 35 32N 136 55 E
Miño →, *Spain* **19 A2** 41 52N 8 40W
Minorca = Menorca, *Spain* **22 B11** 40 0N 4 0 E
Minot, *U.S.A.* **80 A4** 48 14N 101 18W
Minqin, *China* .... **34 E2** 38 38N 103 20 E
Minsk, *Belarus* .... **17 B14** 53 52N 27 30 E
Mińsk Mazowiecki, *Poland* . **17 B11** 52 10N 21 33 E
Mintabie, *Australia* .... **63 D1** 27 15S 133 7 E
Mintaka Pass, *Pakistan* .... **43 A6** 37 0N 74 58 E
Minteke Daban = Mintaka Pass, *Pakistan* .... **43 A6** 37 0N 74 58 E
Minto, *Canada* **71 C6** 46 5N 66 5W
Minto, L., *Canada* **70 A5** 57 13N 75 0W
Minton, *Canada* **73 D8** 49 10N 104 35W
Minturn, *U.S.A.* **82 G10** 39 35N 106 26W
Minusinsk, *Russia* .... **27 D10** 53 43N 91 20 E
Minutang, *India* .... **41 E20** 28 15N 96 30 E
Miquelon, *Canada* **70 C4** 49 25N 76 27W
Miquelon, *St- P. & M.* **71 C8** 47 8N 56 22W
Mīr Kūh, *Iran* .... **45 E8** 26 22N 58 55 E
Mīr Shahdād, *Iran* .... **45 E8** 26 15N 58 29 E
Mira, *Italy* .... **20 B5** 45 26N 12 8 E
Mira por vos Cay, *Bahamas* **89 B5** 22 9N 74 30W
Miraj, *India* .... **40 L9** 16 50N 74 45 E
Miram Shah, *Pakistan* .... **42 C4** 33 0N 70 2 E
Miramar, *Argentina* **94 D4** 38 15S 57 50W
Miramar, *Mozam.* .... **57 C6** 23 50S 35 35 E
Miramichi, *Canada* **71 C6** 47 2N 65 28W
Miramichi B., *Canada* **71 C7** 47 15N 65 0W
Miranda, *Brazil* **93 H7** 20 10S 56 15W
Miranda →, *Brazil* **92 G7** 19 25S 57 20W
Miranda de Ebro, *Spain* **19 A4** 42 41N 2 57W
Miranda do Douro, *Portugal* **19 B2** 41 30N 6 16W
Mirandópolis, *Brazil* **95 A5** 21 9S 51 6W
Mirango, *Malawi* .... **55 E3** 13 32S 34 58 E
Mirassol, *Brazil* **95 A6** 20 46S 49 28W
Mirbāţ, *Oman* .... **46 D5** 17 0N 54 45 E
Miri, *Malaysia* .... **36 D4** 4 23N 113 59 E
Miriam Vale, *Australia* .... **62 C5** 24 20S 151 33 E
Mirim, L., *S. Amer.* **95 C5** 32 45S 52 50W
Mirnyy, *Russia* .... **27 C12** 62 33N 113 53 E
Mirokhan, *Pakistan* .... **42 F3** 27 46N 68 6 E
Mirond L., *Canada* **73 B8** 55 6N 102 47W
Mirpur, *Pakistan* .... **43 C5** 33 32N 73 56 E
Mirpur Batoro, *Pakistan* .... **42 G3** 24 44N 68 16 E
Mirpur Bibiwari, *Pakistan* .. **42 E2** 28 33N 67 44 E
Mirpur Khas, *Pakistan* .... **42 G3** 25 30N 69 0 E
Mirpur Sakro, *Pakistan* .... **42 G2** 24 33N 67 41 E
Mirtağ, *Turkey* .... **44 B4** 38 23N 41 56 E
Miryang, *S. Korea* .... **35 G15** 35 31N 128 44 E
Mirzapur, *India* .... **43 G10** 25 10N 82 34 E
Mirzapur-cum-Vindhyachal = Mirzapur, *India* .... **43 G10** 25 10N 82 34 E
Misantla, *Mexico* **87 D5** 19 56N 96 50W
Misawa, *Japan* .... **30 D10** 40 41N 141 24 E
Miscou I., *Canada* **71 C7** 47 57N 64 31W
Mish'āb, Ra's al, *Si. Arabia* **45 D6** 28 15N 48 43 E
Mishan, *China* .... **33 B8** 45 37N 131 48 E
Mishawaka, *U.S.A.* **76 E2** 41 40N 86 11W
Mishima, *Japan* .... **31 G9** 35 10N 138 52 E
Misión, *Mexico* **85 N10** 32 6N 116 53W
Misiones □, *Argentina* **95 B5** 27 0S 55 0W
Misiones □, *Paraguay* **94 B4** 27 0S 56 0W
Miskah, *Si. Arabia* .... **44 E4** 24 49N 42 56 E
Miskitos, Cayos, *Nic.* **88 D3** 14 26N 82 50W
Miskolc, *Hungary* .... **17 D11** 48 7N 20 50 E
Misoke, *Dem. Rep. of the Congo* . **54 C2** 0 42S 28 2 E
Misool, *Indonesia* .... **37 E8** 1 52S 130 10 E
Misrātah, *Libya* .... **51 B9** 32 24N 15 3 E
Missanabie, *Canada* **70 C3** 48 20N 84 6W
Missinaibi →, *Canada* **70 B3** 50 43N 81 29W
Missinaibi L., *Canada* **70 C3** 48 23N 83 40W
Mission, *Canada* **72 D4** 49 10N 122 15W
Mission, *S. Dak., U.S.A.* **80 D4** 43 18N 100 39W
Mission, *Tex., U.S.A.* **81 M5** 26 13N 98 20W
Mission Beach, *Australia* .. **62 B4** 17 53S 146 6 E
Mission Viejo, *U.S.A.* **85 M9** 33 36N 117 40W
Missisa L., *Canada* **70 B2** 52 20N 85 7W
Missisicabi →, *Canada* **70 B4** 51 14N 79 31W
Mississagi →, *Canada* **70 C3** 46 15N 83 9W
Mississauga, *Canada* **78 C5** 43 32N 79 35W
Mississippi □, *U.S.A.* **81 J10** 33 0N 90 0W
Mississippi →, *U.S.A.* **81 L10** 29 9N 89 15W
Mississippi L., *Canada* **79 A8** 45 5N 76 10W
Mississippi River Delta, *U.S.A.* **81 L9** 29 10N 89 15W
Mississippi Sd., *U.S.A.* **81 K10** 30 20N 89 0W
Missoula, *U.S.A.* **82 C7** 46 52N 114 1W
Missouri □, *U.S.A.* **80 F8** 38 25N 92 30W
Missouri →, *U.S.A.* **80 F9** 38 49N 90 7W
Missouri City, *U.S.A.* **81 L7** 29 37N 95 32W
Missouri Valley, *U.S.A.* **80 E7** 41 34N 95 53W
Mist, *U.S.A.* **84 E3** 45 59N 123 15W
Mistassibi →, *Canada* **71 B5** 48 53N 72 13W
Mistassini, *Canada* **71 C5** 48 53N 72 12W
Mistassini →, *Canada* **71 C5** 48 42N 72 20W
Mistassini, L., *Canada* **70 B5** 51 0N 73 30W
Mistastin L., *Canada* **71 A7** 55 57N 63 20W
Mistinibi, L., *Canada* **71 A7** 55 56N 64 17W
Misty L., *Canada* **73 B8** 58 53N 101 40W
Misurata = Misrātah, *Libya* **51 B9** 32 24N 15 3 E
Mitchell, *Australia* .... **63 D4** 26 29S 147 58 E
Mitchell, *Canada* **78 C3** 43 28N 81 12W
Mitchell, *Nebr., U.S.A.* **80 E3** 41 57N 103 49W
Mitchell, *Oreg., U.S.A.* **82 D3** 44 34N 120 9W
Mitchell, *S. Dak., U.S.A.* **80 D6** 43 43N 98 2W
Mitchell →, *Australia* .... **62 B3** 15 12S 141 35 E
Mitchell, Mt., *U.S.A.* **77 H4** 35 46N 82 16W
Mitchell Ranges, *Australia* . **62 A2** 12 49S 135 36 E
Mitchelstown, *Ireland* **13 D3** 52 15N 8 16W
Mitha Tiwana, *Pakistan* .... **42 C5** 32 13N 72 6 E
Mithi, *Pakistan* .... **42 G3** 24 44N 69 48 E
Mithrao, *Pakistan* .... **42 F3** 27 28N 69 40 E
Mitilíni, *Greece* .... **21 E12** 39 6N 26 35 E
Mito, *Japan* .... **31 F10** 36 20N 140 30 E
Mitrovica = Kosovska Mitrovica, *Serbia, Yug.* .. **21 C9** 42 54N 20 52 E
Mitsinjo, *Madag.* .... **57 B8** 16 1S 45 52 E
Mitsiwa, *Eritrea* .... **46 D2** 15 35N 39 25 E
Mitsukaidō, *Japan* .... **31 F9** 36 1N 139 59 E
Mittagong, *Australia* .... **63 E5** 34 28S 150 29 E
Mitú, *Colombia* **92 C4** 1 15N 70 13W
Mitumba, *Tanzania* .... **54 D3** 7 8S 31 2 E
Mitumba, Mts., *Dem. Rep. of the Congo* . **54 D2** 7 0S 27 30 E
Mitwaba, *Dem. Rep. of the Congo* . **55 D2** 8 2S 27 17 E
Mityana, *Uganda* .... **54 B3** 0 23N 32 2 E
Mixteco →, *Mexico* **87 D5** 18 11N 98 30W
Miyagi □, *Japan* .... **30 E10** 38 15N 140 45 E
Miyah, W. el →, *Syria* .... **44 C3** 34 44N 39 57 E
Miyake-Jima, *Japan* .... **31 G9** 34 5N 139 30 E
Miyako, *Japan* .... **30 E10** 39 40N 141 59 E
Miyako-Jima, *Japan* .... **31 M2** 24 45N 125 20 E
Miyako-Rettō, *Japan* .... **31 M2** 24 24N 125 0 E
Miyakonojō, *Japan* .... **31 J5** 31 40N 131 5 E
Miyani, *India* .... **42 J3** 21 50N 69 26 E
Miyanoura-Dake, *Japan* .... **31 J5** 30 20N 130 31 E
Miyazaki, *Japan* .... **31 J5** 31 56N 131 30 E
Miyazaki □, *Japan* .... **31 H5** 32 30N 131 30 E
Miyazu, *Japan* .... **31 G7** 35 35N 135 10 E
Miyet, Bahr el = Dead Sea, *Asia* .... **47 D4** 31 30N 35 30 E
Miyoshi, *Japan* .... **31 G6** 34 48N 132 51 E
Miyun, *China* .... **34 D9** 40 28N 116 50 E
Miyun Shuiku, *China* .... **35 D9** 40 30N 117 0 E
Mizdah, *Libya* .... **51 B8** 31 30N 13 0 E
Mizen Hd., *Cork, Ireland* **13 E2** 51 27N 9 50W
Mizen Hd., *Wick., Ireland* **13 D5** 52 51N 6 4W
Mizhi, *China* .... **34 F6** 37 47N 110 12 E
Mizoram □, *India* .... **41 H18** 23 30N 92 40 E
Mizpe Ramon, *Israel* .... **47 E3** 30 34N 34 49 E
Mizusawa, *Japan* .... **30 E10** 39 8N 141 8 E
Mjölby, *Sweden* .... **9 G16** 58 20N 15 10 E
Mjøsa, *Norway* .... **9 F14** 60 40N 11 0 E
Mkata, *Tanzania* .... **54 D4** 5 45S 38 20 E
Mkokotoni, *Tanzania* .... **54 D4** 5 55S 39 15 E
Mkomazi, *Tanzania* .... **54 C4** 4 40S 38 7 E
Mkomazi →, *S. Africa* .... **57 E5** 30 12S 30 50 E
Mkulwe, *Tanzania* .... **55 D3** 8 37S 32 20 E
Mkumbi, Ras, *Tanzania* .... **54 D4** 7 38S 39 55 E
Mkushi, *Zambia* .... **55 E2** 14 25S 29 15 E
Mkushi River, *Zambia* .... **55 E2** 13 32S 29 45 E
Mkuze, *S. Africa* .... **57 D5** 27 10S 32 0 E
Mladá Boleslav, *Czech Rep.* **16 C8** 50 27N 14 53 E
Mlala Hills, *Tanzania* .... **54 D3** 6 50S 31 40 E
Mlange = Mulanje, *Malawi* **55 F4** 16 2S 35 33 E
Mlanje, Pic, *Malawi* .... **53 H7** 15 57S 35 38 E
Mława, *Poland* .... **17 B11** 53 9N 20 25 E
Mljet, *Croatia* .... **20 C7** 42 43N 17 30 E
Mmabatho, *S. Africa* .... **56 D4** 25 49S 25 30 E
Mo i Rana, *Norway* .... **8 C16** 66 20N 14 7 E
Moa, *Cuba* **89 B4** 20 40N 74 56W
Moa, *Indonesia* .... **37 F7** 8 0S 128 0 E
Moab, *U.S.A.* **83 G9** 38 35N 109 33W
Moala, *Fiji* .... **59 D8** 18 36S 179 53 E
Moama, *Australia* .... **63 F3** 36 7S 144 46 E
Moapa, *U.S.A.* **85 J12** 36 40N 114 37W
Moate, *Ireland* **13 C4** 53 24N 7 44W
Moba, *Dem. Rep. of the Congo* . **54 D2** 7 0S 29 48 E
Mobārakābād, *Iran* .... **45 D7** 28 24N 53 20 E
Mobaye, *C.A.R.* .... **52 D4** 4 25N 21 5 E
Mobayi, *Dem. Rep. of the Congo* . **52 D4** 4 15N 21 8 E
Moberley Lake, *Canada* **72 B4** 55 50N 121 44W
Moberly, *U.S.A.* **80 F8** 39 25N 92 26W
Mobile, *U.S.A.* **77 K1** 30 41N 88 3W
Mobile B., *U.S.A.* **77 K2** 30 30N 88 0W
Mobridge, *U.S.A.* **80 C4** 45 32N 100 26W
Mobutu Sese Seko, L. = Albert L., *Africa* .... **54 B3** 1 30N 31 0 E
Moc Chau, *Vietnam* .... **38 B5** 20 50N 104 38 E
Moc Hoa, *Vietnam* .... **39 G5** 10 46N 105 56 E
Mocabe Kasari, *Dem. Rep. of the Congo* . **55 D2** 9 58S 26 12 E
Moçambique, *Mozam.* .... **55 F5** 15 3S 40 42 E
Moçâmedes = Namibe, *Angola* .... **53 H2** 15 7S 12 11 E
Mocanaqua, *U.S.A.* **79 E8** 41 9N 76 8W
Mochudi, *Botswana* .... **56 C4** 24 27S 26 7 E
Mocimboa da Praia, *Mozam.* **55 E5** 11 25S 40 20 E
Moclips, *U.S.A.* **84 C2** 47 14N 124 13W
Mocoa, *Colombia* **92 C3** 1 7N 76 35W
Mococa, *Brazil* **95 A6** 21 28S 47 0W
Mocorito, *Mexico* **86 B3** 25 30N 107 53W
Moctezuma, *Mexico* **86 B3** 29 50N 109 0W
Moctezuma →, *Mexico* **87 C5** 21 59N 98 34W
Mocuba, *Mozam.* .... **55 F4** 16 54S 36 57 E
Mocúzari, Presa, *Mexico* **86 B3** 27 10N 109 10W
Modane, *France* .... **18 D7** 45 12N 6 40 E
Modasa, *India* .... **42 H5** 23 30N 73 21 E
Modder →, *S. Africa* .... **56 D3** 29 2S 24 37 E
Modderrivier, *S. Africa* .... **56 D3** 29 2S 24 38 E
Módena, *Italy* .... **20 B4** 44 40N 10 55 E
Modena, *U.S.A.* **83 H7** 37 48N 113 56W
Modesto, *U.S.A.* **84 H6** 37 39N 121 0W
Módica, *Italy* .... **20 F6** 36 52N 14 46 E
Moe, *Australia* .... **63 F4** 38 12S 146 19 E
Moebase, *Mozam.* .... **55 F4** 17 3S 38 41 E
Moengo, *Surinam* **93 B8** 5 45N 54 20W
Moffat, *U.K.* **12 F5** 55 21N 3 27W
Moga, *India* .... **42 D6** 30 48N 75 8 E
Mogadishu = Muqdisho, *Somali Rep.* .... **46 G4** 2 2N 45 25 E
Mogador = Essaouira, *Morocco* **50 B4** 31 32N 9 42W
Mogalakwena →, *S. Africa* **57 C4** 22 38S 28 40 E
Mogami-Gawa →, *Japan* .. **30 E10** 38 45N 140 0 E
Mogán, *Canary Is.* **22 G4** 27 53N 15 43W
Mogaung, *Burma* .... **41 G20** 25 20N 97 0 E
Mogi das Cruzes, *Brazil* **95 A6** 23 31S 46 11W
Mogi-Guaçu →, *Brazil* **95 A6** 20 53S 48 10W
Mogi-Mirim, *Brazil* **95 A6** 22 29S 47 0W
Mogilev = Mahilyow, *Belarus* .... **17 B16** 53 55N 30 18 E
Mogilev-Podolskiy = Mohyliv-Podilskyy, *Ukraine* .... **17 D14** 48 26N 27 48 E
Mogincual, *Mozam.* .... **55 F5** 15 35S 40 25 E
Mogocha, *Russia* .... **27 D12** 53 40N 119 50 E
Mogok, *Burma* .... **41 H20** 23 0N 96 40 E
Mogollon Rim, *U.S.A.* **83 J8** 34 10N 110 50W
Mogumber, *Australia* .... **61 F2** 31 2S 116 3 E
Mohács, *Hungary* .... **17 F10** 45 58N 18 41 E
Mohales Hoek, *Lesotho* .... **56 E4** 30 7S 27 26 E
Mohall, *U.S.A.* **80 A4** 48 46N 101 31W
Moḩammadābād, *Iran* .... **45 B8** 37 52N 59 5 E
Mohammedia, *Morocco* **50 B4** 33 44N 7 21W
Mohana →, *India* .... **43 G11** 24 43N 85 0 E
Mohanlalganj, *India* .... **43 F9** 26 41N 80 58 E
Mohave, L., *U.S.A.* **85 K12** 35 12N 114 34W
Mohawk →, *U.S.A.* **79 D11** 42 47N 73 41W
Mohenjodaro, *Pakistan* .... **42 F3** 27 19N 68 7 E
Mohicanville Reservoir, *U.S.A.* **78 F3** 40 45N 82 0W
Mohoro, *Tanzania* .... **54 D4** 8 6S 39 8 E
Mohyliv-Podilskyy, *Ukraine* **17 D14** 48 26N 27 48 E
Moidart, L., *U.K.* **12 E3** 56 47N 5 52W
Moira →, *Canada* **78 B7** 44 21N 77 24W
Moires, *Greece* .... **23 D6** 35 4N 24 56 E
Moisaküla, *Estonia* .... **9 G21** 58 3N 25 12 E
Moisie, *Canada* **71 B6** 50 12N 66 1W
Moisie →, *Canada* **71 B6** 50 14N 66 5W
Mojave, *U.S.A.* **85 K8** 35 3N 118 10W
Mojave Desert, *U.S.A.* **85 L10** 35 0N 116 30W
Mojo, *Bolivia* **94 A2** 21 48S 65 33W
Mojokerto, *Indonesia* .... **37 G15** 7 28S 112 26 E
Mokai, *N.Z.* .... **59 H5** 38 32S 175 56 E
Mokambo, *Dem. Rep. of the Congo* . **55 E2** 12 25S 28 20 E
Mokameh, *India* .... **43 G11** 25 24N 85 55 E
Mokelumne →, *U.S.A.* **84 G5** 38 13N 121 28W
Mokelumne Hill, *U.S.A.* **84 G6** 38 18N 120 43W
Mokhós, *Greece* .... **23 D7** 35 16N 25 27 E
Mokhotlong, *Lesotho* .... **57 D4** 29 22S 29 2 E
Mokokchung, *India* .... **41 F19** 26 15N 94 30 E
Mokp'o, *S. Korea* .... **35 G14** 34 50N 126 25 E
Mokra Gora, *Serbia, Yug.* .. **21 C9** 42 50N 20 30 E
Mol, *Belgium* .... **15 C5** 51 11N 5 5 E
Molchanovo, *Russia* .... **26 D9** 57 40N 83 50 E
Mold, *U.K.* **10 D4** 53 9N 3 8W
Moldavia = Moldova ■, *Europe* .... **17 E15** 47 0N 28 0 E
Molde, *Norway* .... **8 E12** 62 45N 7 9 E
Moldova ■, *Europe* .... **17 E15** 47 0N 28 0 E
Moldoveana, Vf., *Romania* . **17 F13** 45 36N 24 45 E
Mole →, *U.K.* **11 F7** 51 24N 0 21W
Mole Creek, *Australia* .... **62 G4** 41 34S 146 24 E
Molepolole, *Botswana* .... **56 C4** 24 28S 25 28 E
Molfetta, *Italy* .... **20 D7** 41 12N 16 36 E
Moline, *U.S.A.* **80 E9** 41 30N 90 31W
Molinos, *Argentina* **94 B2** 25 28S 66 15W
Moliro, *Dem. Rep. of the Congo* . **54 D3** 8 12S 30 30 E
Mollendo, *Peru* **92 G4** 17 0S 72 0W
Mollerin, L., *Australia* .... **61 F2** 30 30S 117 35 E
Molodechno = Maladzyechna, *Belarus* .. **17 A14** 54 20N 26 50 E
Molokai, *U.S.A.* **74 H16** 21 8N 157 0W
Molong, *Australia* .... **63 E4** 33 5S 148 54 E
Molopo →, *Africa* .... **56 D3** 27 30S 20 13 E
Molotov = Perm, *Russia* .. **24 C10** 58 0N 56 10 E
Molson L., *Canada* **73 C9** 54 22N 96 40W
Molteno, *S. Africa* .... **56 E4** 31 22S 26 22 E
Molu, *Indonesia* .... **37 F8** 6 45S 131 40 E
Molucca Sea, *Indonesia* .... **37 E6** 2 0S 124 0 E
Moluccas = Maluku, *Indonesia* .... **37 E7** 1 0S 127 0 E
Moma, *Dem. Rep. of the Congo* . **54 C1** 1 35S 23 52 E
Moma, *Mozam.* .... **55 F4** 16 47S 39 4 E
Mombasa, *Kenya* .... **54 C4** 4 2S 39 43 E
Mombetsu, *Japan* .... **30 B11** 44 21N 143 22 E
Momchilgrad, *Bulgaria* .... **21 D11** 41 33N 25 23 E
Momi, *Dem. Rep. of the Congo* . **54 C2** 1 42S 27 0 E
Mompós, *Colombia* **92 B4** 9 14N 74 26W
Møn, *Denmark* .... **9 J15** 54 57N 12 20 E
Mon →, *Burma* .... **41 J19** 20 25N 94 30 E
Mona, Canal de la, *W. Indies* **89 C6** 18 30N 67 45W
Mona, Isla, *Puerto Rico* **89 C6** 18 5N 67 54W
Mona, Pta., *Costa Rica* **88 E3** 9 37N 82 36W
Monaca, *U.S.A.* **78 F4** 40 41N 80 17W
Monaco ■, *Europe* .... **18 E7** 43 46N 7 23 E
Monadhliath Mts., *U.K.* **12 D4** 57 10N 4 4W
Monadnock, Mt., *U.S.A.* **79 D12** 42 52N 72 7W
Monaghan, *Ireland* **13 B5** 54 15N 6 57W
Monaghan □, *Ireland* **13 B5** 54 11N 6 56W
Monahans, *U.S.A.* **81 K3** 31 36N 102 54W
Monapo, *Mozam.* .... **55 E5** 14 56S 40 19 E
Monar, L., *U.K.* **12 D3** 57 26N 5 8W
Monarch Mt., *Canada* **72 C3** 51 55N 125 57W
Monashee Mts., *Canada* **72 C5** 51 0N 118 43W
Monasterevin, *Ireland* **13 C4** 53 8N 7 4W
Monastir = Bitola, *Macedonia* .... **21 D9** 41 1N 21 20 E
Moncayo, Sierra del, *Spain* **19 B5** 41 48N 1 50W
Monchegorsk, *Russia* .... **24 A5** 67 54N 32 58 E
Mönchengladbach, *Germany* .... **16 C4** 51 11N 6 27 E
Monchique, *Portugal* **19 D1** 37 19N 8 38W
Moncks Corner, *U.S.A.* **77 J5** 33 12N 80 1W
Monclova, *Mexico* **86 B4** 26 50N 101 30W
Moncton, *Canada* **71 C7** 46 7N 64 51W
Mondego →, *Portugal* **19 B1** 40 9N 8 52W
Mondeodo, *Indonesia* .... **37 E6** 3 34S 122 9 E
Mondovì, *Italy* .... **18 D7** 44 23N 7 49 E
Mondrain I., *Australia* .... **61 F3** 34 9S 122 14 E
Monessen, *U.S.A.* **78 F5** 40 9N 79 54W
Monett, *U.S.A.* **81 G8** 36 55N 93 55W
Moneymore, *U.K.* **13 B5** 54 41N 6 40W
Monforte de Lemos, *Spain* **19 A2** 42 31N 7 33W
Mong Hsu, *Burma* .... **41 J21** 21 54N 98 30 E
Mong Kung, *Burma* .... **41 J20** 21 35N 97 35 E
Mong Nai, *Burma* .... **41 J20** 20 32N 97 46 E
Mong Pawk, *Burma* .... **41 H21** 22 4N 99 16 E
Mong Ton, *Burma* .... **41 J21** 20 17N 98 45 E
Mong Wa, *Burma* .... **41 J22** 21 26N 100 27 E
Mong Yai, *Burma* .... **41 H21** 22 21N 98 3 E
Mongalla, *Sudan* .... **51 G12** 5 8N 31 42 E
Mongers, L., *Australia* .... **61 E2** 29 25S 117 5 E
Monghyr = Munger, *India* . **43 G12** 25 23N 86 30 E
Mongibello = Etna, *Italy* .. **20 F6** 37 50N 14 55 E
Mongo, *Chad* .... **51 F9** 12 14N 18 43 E
Mongolia ■, *Asia* .... **27 E10** 47 0N 103 0 E
Mongu, *Zambia* .... **53 H4** 15 16S 23 12 E
Môngua, *Angola* .... **56 B2** 16 43S 15 20 E
Monifieth, *U.K.* **12 E6** 56 30N 2 48W
Monkey Bay, *Malawi* .... **55 E4** 14 7S 35 1 E
Monkey Mia, *Australia* .... **61 E1** 25 48S 113 43 E
Monkey River, *Belize* **87 D7** 16 22N 88 29W
Monkoto, *Dem. Rep. of the Congo* . **52 E4** 1 38S 20 35 E
Monkton, *Canada* **78 C3** 43 35N 81 5W
Monmouth, *U.K.* **11 F5** 51 48N 2 42W
Monmouth, *Ill., U.S.A.* **80 E9** 40 55N 90 39W
Monmouth, *Oreg., U.S.A.* .. **82 D2** 44 51N 123 14W
Monmouthshire □, *U.K.* **11 F5** 51 48N 2 54W
Mono L., *U.S.A.* **84 H7** 38 1N 119 1W
Monolith, *U.S.A.* **85 K8** 35 7N 118 22W
Monólithos, *Greece* .... **23 C9** 36 7N 27 45 E
Monongahela, *U.S.A.* **78 F5** 40 12N 79 56W
Monópoli, *Italy* .... **20 D7** 40 57N 17 18 E
Monroe, *Ga., U.S.A.* **77 J4** 33 47N 83 43W
Monroe, *La., U.S.A.* **81 J8** 32 30N 92 7W
Monroe, *Mich., U.S.A.* **76 E4** 41 55N 83 24W
Monroe, *N.C., U.S.A.* **77 H5** 34 59N 80 33W
Monroe, *N.Y., U.S.A.* **79 E10** 41 20N 74 11W
Monroe, *Utah, U.S.A.* **83 G7** 38 38N 112 7W
Monroe, *Wash., U.S.A.* **84 C5** 47 51N 121 58W
Monroe, *Wis., U.S.A.* **80 D10** 42 36N 89 38W
Monroe City, *U.S.A.* **80 F9** 39 39N 91 44W
Monroeton, *U.S.A.* **79 E8** 41 43N 76 29W
Monroeville, *Ala., U.S.A.* .. **77 K2** 31 31N 87 20W
Monroeville, *Pa., U.S.A.* **78 F5** 40 26N 79 45W
Monrovia, *Liberia* **50 G3** 6 18N 10 47W
Mons, *Belgium* .... **15 D3** 50 27N 3 58 E
Monse, *Indonesia* .... **37 E6** 4 0S 123 10 E
Mont-de-Marsan, *France* .. **18 E3** 43 54N 0 31W
Mont-Joli, *Canada* **71 C6** 48 37N 68 10W
Mont-Laurier, *Canada* **70 C4** 46 35N 75 30W
Mont-Louis, *Canada* **71 C6** 49 15N 65 44W
Mont-St-Michel, Le = Le Mont-St-Michel, *France* . **18 B3** 48 40N 1 30W
Mont Tremblant, Parc Recr. du, *Canada* **70 C5** 46 30N 74 30W
Montagu, *S. Africa* .... **56 E3** 33 45S 20 8 E
Montagu I., *Antarctica* **5 B1** 58 25S 26 20W
Montague, *Canada* **71 C7** 46 10N 62 39W
Montague, I., *Mexico* **86 A2** 31 40N 114 56W
Montague Ra., *Australia* .. **61 E2** 27 15S 119 30 E
Montague Sd., *Australia* .. **60 B4** 14 28S 125 20 E
Montalbán, *Spain* **19 B5** 40 50N 0 45W
Montalvo, *U.S.A.* **85 L7** 34 15N 119 12W
Montana, *Bulgaria* .... **21 C10** 43 27N 23 16 E
Montaña, *Peru* **92 E4** 6 0S 73 0W
Montana □, *U.S.A.* **82 C9** 47 0N 110 0W
Montaña Clara, I., *Canary Is.* **22 E6** 29 17N 13 33W
Montargis, *France* .... **18 C5** 47 59N 2 43 E
Montauban, *France* .... **18 D4** 44 2N 1 21 E
Montauk, *U.S.A.* **79 E13** 41 3N 71 57W
Montauk Pt., *U.S.A.* **79 E13** 41 4N 71 52W
Montbéliard, *France* .... **18 C7** 47 31N 6 48 E
Montceau-les-Mines, *France* **18 C6** 46 40N 4 23 E
Montclair, *U.S.A.* **79 F10** 40 49N 74 13W
Monte Albán, *Mexico* **87 D5** 17 2N 96 45W
Monte Alegre, *Brazil* **93 D8** 2 0S 54 0W
Monte Azul, *Brazil* **93 G10** 15 9S 42 53W
Monte Bello Is., *Australia* .. **60 D2** 20 30S 115 45 E
Monte-Carlo, *Monaco* .... **18 E7** 43 46N 7 23 E
Monte Caseros, *Argentina* . **94 C4** 30 10S 57 50W
Monte Comán, *Argentina* .. **94 C2** 34 40S 67 53W
Monte Cristi, *Dom. Rep.* **89 C5** 19 52N 71 39W
Monte Lindo →, *Paraguay* . **94 A4** 23 56S 57 12W
Monte Patria, *Chile* **94 C1** 30 42S 70 58W
Monte Quemado, *Argentina* **94 B3** 25 53S 62 41W
Monte Rio, *U.S.A.* **84 G4** 38 28N 123 0W
Monte Santu, C. di, *Italy* .. **20 D3** 40 5N 9 44 E
Monte Vista, *U.S.A.* **83 H10** 37 35N 106 9W
Monteagudo, *Argentina* **95 B5** 27 14S 54 8W
Montebello, *Canada* **70 C5** 45 40N 74 55W
Montecito, *U.S.A.* **85 L7** 34 26N 119 40W
Montecristo, *Italy* .... **20 C4** 42 20N 10 19 E
Montego Bay, *Jamaica* **88 C4** 18 30N 78 0W
Montélimar, *France* .... **18 D6** 44 33N 4 45 E
Montello, *U.S.A.* **80 D10** 43 48N 89 20W
Montemorelos, *Mexico* **87 B5** 25 11N 99 42W
Montenegro, *Brazil* **95 B5** 29 39S 51 29W
Montenegro □, *Yugoslavia* **21 C8** 42 40N 19 20 E
Montepuez, *Mozam.* .... **55 E4** 13 8S 38 59 E
Montepuez →, *Mozam.* .... **55 E5** 12 32S 40 27 E
Monterey, *U.S.A.* **84 J5** 36 37N 121 55W
Monterey B., *U.S.A.* **84 J5** 36 45N 122 0W
Montería, *Colombia* **92 B3** 8 46N 75 53W
Monteros, *Argentina* **94 B2** 27 11S 65 30W
Monterrey, *Mexico* **86 B4** 25 40N 100 30W
Montes Claros, *Brazil* **93 G10** 16 30S 43 50W
Montesano, *U.S.A.* **84 D3** 46 59N 123 36W
Montesilvano, *Italy* .... **20 C6** 42 29N 14 8 E
Montevideo, *Uruguay* **95 C4** 34 50S 56 11W
Montevideo, *U.S.A.* **80 C7** 44 57N 95 43W
Montezuma, *U.S.A.* **80 E8** 41 35N 92 32W
Montgomery = Sahiwal, *Pakistan* .... **42 D5** 30 45N 73 8 E
Montgomery, *U.K.* **11 E4** 52 34N 3 8W
Montgomery, *Ala., U.S.A.* .. **77 J2** 32 23N 86 19W
Montgomery, *Pa., U.S.A.* **78 E8** 41 10N 76 53W
Montgomery, *W. Va., U.S.A.* **76 F5** 38 11N 81 19W
Montgomery City, *U.S.A.* .. **80 F9** 38 59N 91 30W
Monticello, *Ark., U.S.A.* **81 J9** 33 38N 91 47W
Monticello, *Fla., U.S.A.* **77 K4** 30 33N 83 52W
Monticello, *Ind., U.S.A.* **76 E2** 40 45N 86 46W
Monticello, *Iowa, U.S.A.* **80 D9** 42 15N 91 12W
Monticello, *Ky., U.S.A.* **77 G3** 36 50N 84 51W
Monticello, *Minn., U.S.A.* .. **80 C8** 45 18N 93 48W
Monticello, *Miss., U.S.A.* .. **81 K9** 31 33N 90 7W
Monticello, *N.Y., U.S.A.* **79 E10** 41 39N 74 42W
Monticello, *Utah, U.S.A.* **83 H9** 37 52N 109 21W
Montijo, *Portugal* **19 C1** 38 41N 8 54W
Montilla, *Spain* **19 D3** 37 36N 4 40W
Montluçon, *France* .... **18 C5** 46 22N 2 36 E
Montmagny, *Canada* **71 C5** 46 58N 70 34W
Montmartre, *Canada* **73 C8** 50 14N 103 27W
Montmorillon, *France* .... **18 C4** 46 26N 0 50 E
Monto, *Australia* .... **62 C5** 24 52S 151 6 E
Montoro, *Spain* **19 C3** 38 1N 4 27W
Montour Falls, *U.S.A.* **78 D8** 42 21N 76 51W

Montoursville

Montoursville, U.S.A. 78 E8 41 15N 76 55W
Montpelier, Idaho, U.S.A. 82 E8 42 19N 111 18W
Montpelier, Vt., U.S.A. 79 B12 44 16N 72 35W
Montpellier, France 18 E5 43 37N 3 52 E
Montréal, Canada 79 A11 45 31N 73 34W
Montreal →, Canada 70 C3 47 14N 84 39W
Montreal L., Canada 73 C7 54 20N 105 45W
Montreal Lake, Canada 73 C7 54 3N 105 46W
Montreux, Switz. 18 C7 46 26N 6 55 E
Montrose, U.K. 12 E6 56 44N 2 27W
Montrose, Colo., U.S.A. 83 G10 38 29N 107 53W
Montrose, Pa., U.S.A. 79 E9 41 50N 75 53W
Monts, Pte. des, Canada 71 C6 49 20N 67 12W
Montserrat ■, W. Indies 89 C7 16 40N 62 10W
Montuiri, Spain 22 B9 39 34N 2 59 E
Monywa, Burma 41 H19 22 7N 95 11 E
Monza, Italy 18 D8 45 35N 9 16 E
Monze, Zambia 55 F2 16 17S 27 29 E
Monze, C., Pakistan 42 G2 24 47N 66 37 E
Monzón, Spain 19 B6 41 52N 0 10 E
Mooers, U.S.A. 79 B11 44 58N 73 35W
Mooi River, S. Africa 57 D4 29 13S 29 50 E
Moonah →, Australia 62 C2 22 3S 138 33 E
Moonda, L., Australia 62 D3 25 52S 140 25 E
Moonie, Australia 63 D5 27 46S 150 20 E
Moonie →, Australia 63 D4 29 19S 148 43 E
Moonta, Australia 63 E2 34 6S 137 32 E
Moora, Australia 61 F2 30 37S 115 58 E
Moorcroft, U.S.A. 80 C2 44 16N 104 57W
Moore →, Australia 61 F2 31 22S 115 30 E
Moore, L., Australia 61 E2 29 50S 117 35 E
Moore Park, Australia 62 C5 24 43S 152 17 E
Moore Reefs, Australia 62 B4 16 0S 149 5 E
Moorefield, U.S.A. 76 F6 39 5N 78 59W
Moores Res., U.S.A. 79 B13 44 45N 71 50W
Moorfoot Hills, U.K. 12 F5 55 44N 3 8W
Moorhead, U.S.A. 80 B6 46 53N 96 45W
Moorpark, U.S.A. 85 L8 34 17N 118 53W
Moorreesburg, S. Africa 56 E2 33 6S 18 38 E
Moose →, Canada 70 B3 51 20N 80 25W
Moose →, U.S.A. 79 C9 43 38N 75 24W
Moose Creek, Canada 79 A10 45 15N 74 58W
Moose Factory, Canada 70 B3 51 16N 80 32W
Moose Jaw, Canada 73 C7 50 24N 105 30W
Moose Jaw →, Canada 73 C7 50 34N 105 18W
Moose Lake, Canada 73 C8 53 43N 100 20W
Moose Lake, U.S.A. 80 B8 46 27N 92 46W
Moose Mountain Prov. Park, Canada 73 D8 49 48N 102 25W
Moosehead L., U.S.A. 77 C11 45 38N 69 40W
Mooselookmeguntic L., U.S.A. 77 C10 44 55N 70 49W
Moosilauke, Mt., U.S.A. 79 B13 44 3N 71 40W
Moosomin, Canada 73 C8 50 9N 101 40W
Moosonee, Canada 70 B3 51 17N 80 39W
Moosup, U.S.A. 79 E13 41 43N 71 53W
Mopeia Velha, Mozam. 55 F4 17 30S 35 40 E
Mopipi, Botswana 56 C3 21 6S 24 55 E
Mopoi, C.A.R. 54 A2 5 6N 26 54 E
Mopti, Mali 50 F5 14 30N 4 0W
Moqor, Afghan. 42 C2 32 50N 67 42 E
Moquegua, Peru 92 G4 17 15S 70 46W
Mora, Sweden 9 F16 61 2N 14 38 E
Mora, Minn., U.S.A. 80 C8 45 53N 93 18W
Mora, N. Mex., U.S.A. 83 J11 35 58N 105 20W
Mora →, U.S.A. 81 H2 35 35N 104 25W
Moradabad, India 43 E8 28 50N 78 50 E
Morafenobe, Madag. 57 B7 17 50S 44 53 E
Moramanga, Madag. 57 B8 18 56S 48 12 E
Moran, Kans., U.S.A. 81 G7 37 55N 95 10W
Moran, Wyo., U.S.A. 82 E8 43 53N 110 37W
Moranbah, Australia 62 C4 22 1S 148 6 E
Morant Cays, Jamaica 88 C4 17 22N 76 0W
Morant Pt., Jamaica 88 C4 17 55N 76 12W
Morar, India 42 F8 26 14N 78 14 E
Morar, L., U.K. 12 E3 56 57N 5 40W
Moratuwa, Sri Lanka 40 R11 6 45N 79 55 E
Morava →, Serbia, Yug. 21 B9 44 36N 21 4 E
Morava →, Slovak Rep. 17 D9 48 10N 16 59 E
Moravia, U.S.A. 79 D8 42 43N 76 25W
Moravian Hts. = Českomoravská Vrchovina, Czech Rep. 16 D8 49 30N 15 40 E
Morawa, Australia 61 E2 29 13S 116 0 E
Morawhanna, Guyana 92 B7 8 30N 59 40W
Moray □, U.K. 12 D5 57 31N 3 18W
Moray Firth, U.K. 12 D5 57 40N 3 52W
Morbi, India 42 H4 22 50N 70 42 E
Morden, Canada 73 D9 49 15N 98 10W
Mordovian Republic = Mordvinia □, Russia 24 D7 54 20N 44 30 E
Mordvinia □, Russia 24 D7 54 20N 44 30 E
Morea, Greece 6 H10 37 45N 22 10 E
Moreau →, U.S.A. 80 C4 45 18N 100 43W
Morecambe, U.K. 10 C5 54 5N 2 52W
Morecambe B., U.K. 10 C5 54 7N 3 0W
Moree, Australia 63 D4 29 28S 149 54 E
Morehead, U.S.A. 76 F4 38 11N 83 26W
Morehead City, U.S.A. 77 H7 34 43N 76 43W
Morel →, India 42 F7 26 13N 76 36 E
Morelia, Mexico 86 D4 19 42N 101 7W
Morella, Australia 62 C3 23 0S 143 52 E
Morella, Spain 19 B5 40 35N 0 5W
Morelos, Mexico 86 B3 26 42N 107 40W
Morelos □, Mexico 87 D5 18 40N 99 10W
Morena, India 42 F8 26 30N 78 4 E
Morena, Sierra, Spain 19 C3 38 20N 4 0W
Moreno Valley, U.S.A. 85 M10 33 56N 117 15W
Moresby I., Canada 72 C2 52 30N 131 40W
Moreton I., Australia 63 D5 27 10S 153 25 E
Morey, Spain 22 B10 39 44N 3 20 E
Morgan, U.S.A. 82 F8 41 2N 111 41W
Morgan City, U.S.A. 81 L9 29 42N 91 12W
Morgan Hill, U.S.A. 84 H5 37 8N 121 39W
Morganfield, U.S.A. 76 G2 37 41N 87 55W
Morganton, U.S.A. 77 H5 35 45N 81 41W
Morgantown, U.S.A. 76 F6 39 38N 79 57W
Morgenzon, S. Africa 57 D4 26 45S 29 36 E
Morghak, Iran 45 D8 29 7N 57 54 E
Morhar →, India 43 G11 25 29N 85 11 E
Moriarty, U.S.A. 83 J10 34 59N 106 3W
Morice L., Canada 72 C3 53 50N 127 40W
Morinville, Canada 72 C6 53 49N 113 41W
Morioka, Japan 30 E10 39 45N 141 8 E
Moris, Mexico 86 B3 28 8N 108 32W
Morlaix, France 18 B2 48 36N 3 52W
Mornington, Australia 63 F4 38 15S 145 5 E
Mornington, I., Chile 96 F1 49 50S 75 30W
Mornington I., Australia 62 B2 16 30S 139 30 E
Moro, Pakistan 42 F2 26 40N 68 0 E
Moro →, Pakistan 42 E2 29 42N 67 22 E
Moro G., Phil. 37 C6 6 30N 123 0 E
Morocco ■, N. Afr. 50 B4 32 0N 5 50W
Morogoro, Tanzania 54 D4 6 50S 37 40 E
Morogoro □, Tanzania 54 D4 8 0S 37 0 E
Moroleón, Mexico 86 C4 20 8N 101 32W
Morombe, Madag. 57 C7 21 45S 43 22 E
Moron, Argentina 94 C4 34 39S 58 37W
Morón, Cuba 88 B4 22 8N 78 39W
Morón de la Frontera, Spain 19 D3 37 6N 5 28W
Morona →, Peru 92 D3 4 40S 77 10W
Morondava, Madag. 57 C7 20 17S 44 17 E
Morongo Valley, U.S.A. 85 L10 34 3N 116 37W
Moroni, Comoros Is. 49 H8 11 40S 43 16 E
Moroni, U.S.A. 82 G8 39 32N 111 35W
Morotai, Indonesia 37 D7 2 10N 128 30 E
Moroto, Uganda 54 B3 2 28N 34 42 E
Moroto Summit, Kenya 54 B3 2 30N 34 43 E
Morpeth, U.K. 10 B6 55 10N 1 41W
Morphou, Cyprus 23 D11 35 12N 32 59 E
Morphou Bay, Cyprus 23 D11 35 15N 32 50 E
Morrilton, U.S.A. 81 H8 35 9N 92 44W
Morrinhos, Brazil 93 G9 17 45S 49 10W
Morrinsville, N.Z. 59 G5 37 40S 175 32 E
Morris, Canada 73 D9 49 25N 97 22W
Morris, Minn., U.S.A. 80 C7 45 35N 95 55W
Morris, N.Y., U.S.A. 79 D9 42 33N 75 15W
Morris, Pa., U.S.A. 78 E7 41 35N 77 17W
Morris, Mt., Australia 61 E5 26 9S 131 4 E
Morrisburg, Canada 79 B9 44 55N 75 7W
Morristown, Ariz., U.S.A. 83 K7 33 51N 112 37W
Morristown, N.J., U.S.A. 79 F10 40 48N 74 29W
Morristown, N.Y., U.S.A. 79 B9 44 35N 75 39W
Morristown, Tenn., U.S.A. 77 G4 36 13N 83 18W
Morrisville, N.Y., U.S.A. 79 D9 42 53N 75 35W
Morrisville, Pa., U.S.A. 79 F10 40 13N 74 47W
Morrisville, Vt., U.S.A. 79 B12 44 34N 72 36W
Morro, Pta., Chile 94 B1 27 6S 71 0W
Morro Bay, U.S.A. 84 K6 35 22N 120 51W
Morro del Jable, Canary Is. 22 F5 28 3N 14 23W
Morro Jable, Pta. de, Canary Is. 22 F5 28 2N 14 20W
Morrosquillo, G. de, Colombia 88 E4 9 35N 75 40W
Morrumbene, Mozam. 57 C6 23 31S 35 16 E
Morshansk, Russia 24 D7 53 28N 41 50 E
Morteros, Argentina 94 C3 30 50S 62 0W
Mortlach, Canada 73 C7 50 27N 106 4W
Mortlake, Australia 63 F3 38 5S 142 50 E
Morton, Tex., U.S.A. 81 J3 33 44N 102 46W
Morton, Wash., U.S.A. 84 D4 46 34N 122 17W
Morundah, Australia 63 E4 34 57S 146 19 E
Moruya, Australia 63 F5 35 58S 150 3 E
Morvan, France 18 C6 47 5N 4 3 E
Morven, Australia 63 D4 26 22S 147 5 E
Morvern, U.K. 12 E3 56 38N 5 44W
Morwell, Australia 63 F4 38 10S 146 22 E
Morzhovets, Ostrov, Russia 24 A7 66 44N 42 35 E
Moscos Is. = Maungmagan Is., Burma 38 F1 14 0N 97 30 E
Moscow = Moskva, Russia 24 C6 55 45N 37 35 E
Moscow, Idaho, U.S.A. 82 C5 46 44N 117 0W
Moscow, Pa., U.S.A. 79 E9 41 20N 75 31W
Mosel →, Europe 18 A7 50 22N 7 36 E
Moselle = Mosel →, Europe 18 A7 50 22N 7 36 E
Moses Lake, U.S.A. 82 C4 47 8N 119 17W
Mosgiel, N.Z. 59 L3 45 53S 170 21 E
Moshi, Tanzania 54 C4 3 22S 37 18 E
Moshupa, Botswana 56 C4 24 46S 25 29 E
Mosjøen, Norway 8 D15 65 51N 13 12 E
Moskenesøya, Norway 8 C15 67 58N 13 0 E
Moskenstraumen, Norway 8 C15 67 47N 12 45 E
Moskva, Russia 24 C6 55 45N 37 35 E
Mosomane, Botswana 56 C4 24 2S 26 19 E
Moson-magyaróvár, Hungary 17 E9 47 52N 17 18 E
Mosquera, Colombia 92 C3 2 35N 78 24W
Mosquero, U.S.A. 81 H3 35 47N 103 58W
Mosquitia, Honduras 88 C3 15 20N 84 10W
Mosquito Coast = Mosquitia, Honduras 88 C3 15 20N 84 10W
Mosquito Creek L., U.S.A. 78 E4 41 18N 80 46W
Mosquito L., Canada 73 A8 62 35N 103 20W
Mosquitos, G. de los, Panama 88 E3 9 15N 81 10W
Moss, Norway 9 G14 59 27N 10 40 E
Moss Vale, Australia 63 E5 34 32S 150 25 E
Mossbank, Canada 73 D7 49 56N 105 56W
Mossburn, N.Z. 59 L2 45 41S 168 15 E
Mosselbaai, S. Africa 56 E3 34 11S 22 8 E
Mossendjo, Congo 52 E2 2 55S 12 42 E
Mossgiel, Australia 63 E3 33 15S 144 5 E
Mossman, Australia 62 B4 16 21S 145 15 E
Mossoró, Brazil 93 E11 5 10S 37 15W
Mossuril, Mozam. 55 E5 14 58S 40 42 E
Most, Czech Rep. 16 C7 50 31N 13 38 E
Mosta, Malta 23 D1 35 54N 14 24 E
Moştafáābād, Iran 45 C7 33 39N 54 53 E
Mostaganem, Algeria 50 A6 35 54N 0 5 E
Mostar, Bos.-H. 21 C7 43 22N 17 50 E
Mostardas, Brazil 95 C5 31 2S 50 51W
Mostiska = Mostyska, Ukraine 17 D12 49 48N 23 4 E
Mosty = Masty, Belarus 17 B13 53 27N 24 38 E
Mostyska, Ukraine 17 D12 49 48N 23 4 E
Mosul = Al Mawşil, Iraq 44 B4 36 15N 43 5 E
Mosŭlpo, S. Korea 35 H14 33 20N 126 17 E
Motagua →, Guatemala 88 C2 15 44N 88 14W
Motala, Sweden 9 G16 58 32N 15 1 E
Moth, India 43 G8 25 43N 78 57 E
Motherwell, U.K. 12 F5 55 47N 3 58W
Motihari, India 43 F11 26 30N 84 55 E
Motozintla de Mendoza, Mexico 87 D6 15 21N 92 14W
Motril, Spain 19 D4 36 31N 3 37W
Mott, U.S.A. 80 B3 46 23N 102 20W
Motueka, N.Z. 59 J4 41 7S 173 1 E
Motueka →, N.Z. 59 J4 41 5S 173 1 E
Motul, Mexico 87 C7 21 0N 89 20W
Mouchalagane →, Canada 71 B6 50 56N 68 41W
Moúdhros, Greece 21 E11 39 50N 25 18 E
Mouila, Gabon 52 E2 1 50S 11 0 E
Moulamein, Australia 63 F3 35 3S 144 1 E
Moulianá, Greece 23 D7 35 10N 25 59 E
Moulins, France 18 C5 46 35N 3 19 E
Moulmein, Burma 41 L20 16 30N 97 40 E
Moulouya, O. →, Morocco 50 B5 35 5N 2 25W
Moultrie, U.S.A. 77 K4 31 11N 83 47W
Moultrie, L., U.S.A. 77 J5 33 20N 80 5W
Mound City, Mo., U.S.A. 80 E7 40 7N 95 14W
Mound City, S. Dak., U.S.A. 80 C4 45 44N 100 4W
Moundou, Chad 51 G9 8 40N 16 10 E
Moundsville, U.S.A. 78 G4 39 55N 80 44W
Moung, Cambodia 38 F4 12 46N 103 27 E
Mount Airy, U.S.A. 77 G5 36 31N 80 37W
Mount Albert, Canada 78 B5 44 8N 79 19W
Mount Barker, S. Austral., Australia 63 F2 35 5S 138 52 E
Mount Barker, W. Austral., Australia 61 F2 34 38S 117 40 E
Mount Beauty, Australia 63 F4 36 47S 147 10 E
Mount Brydges, Canada 78 D3 42 54N 81 29W
Mount Burr, Australia 63 F3 37 34S 140 26 E
Mount Carmel, Ill., U.S.A. 76 F2 38 25N 87 46W
Mount Carmel, Pa., U.S.A. 79 F8 40 47N 76 24W
Mount Charleston, U.S.A. 85 J11 36 16N 115 37W
Mount Clemens, U.S.A. 78 D2 42 35N 82 53W
Mount Coolon, Australia 62 C4 21 25S 147 25 E
Mount Darwin, Zimbabwe 55 F3 16 47S 31 38 E
Mount Desert I., U.S.A. 77 C11 44 21N 68 20W
Mount Dora, U.S.A. 77 L5 28 48N 81 38W
Mount Edziza Prov. Park, Canada 72 B2 57 30N 130 45W
Mount Fletcher, S. Africa 57 E4 30 40S 28 30 E
Mount Forest, Canada 78 C4 43 59N 80 43W
Mount Gambier, Australia 63 F3 37 50S 140 46 E
Mount Garnet, Australia 62 B4 17 37S 145 6 E
Mount Holly, U.S.A. 79 G10 39 59N 74 47W
Mount Holly Springs, U.S.A. 78 F7 40 7N 77 12W
Mount Hope, N.S.W., Australia 63 E4 32 51S 145 51 E
Mount Hope, S. Austral., Australia 63 E2 34 7S 135 23 E
Mount Isa, Australia 62 C2 20 42S 139 26 E
Mount Jewett, U.S.A. 78 E6 41 44N 78 39W
Mount Kisco, U.S.A. 79 E11 41 12N 73 44W
Mount Laguna, U.S.A. 85 N10 32 52N 116 25W
Mount Larcom, Australia 62 C5 23 48S 150 59 E
Mount Lofty Ra., Australia 63 E2 34 35S 139 5 E
Mount Magnet, Australia 61 E2 28 2S 117 47 E
Mount Maunganui, N.Z. 59 G6 37 40S 176 14 E
Mount Molloy, Australia 62 B4 16 42S 145 20 E
Mount Morgan, Australia 62 C5 23 40S 150 25 E
Mount Morris, U.S.A. 78 D7 42 44N 77 52W
Mount Pearl, Canada 71 C9 47 31N 52 47W
Mount Penn, U.S.A. 79 F9 40 20N 75 54W
Mount Perry, Australia 63 D5 25 13S 151 42 E
Mount Pleasant, Iowa, U.S.A. 80 E9 40 58N 91 33W
Mount Pleasant, Mich., U.S.A. 76 D3 43 36N 84 46W
Mount Pleasant, Pa., U.S.A. 78 F5 40 9N 79 33W
Mount Pleasant, S.C., U.S.A. 77 J6 32 47N 79 52W
Mount Pleasant, Tenn., U.S.A. 77 H2 35 32N 87 12W
Mount Pleasant, Tex., U.S.A. 81 J7 33 9N 94 58W
Mount Pleasant, Utah, U.S.A. 82 G8 39 33N 111 27W
Mount Pocono, U.S.A. 79 E9 41 7N 75 22W
Mount Rainier Nat. Park, U.S.A. 84 D5 46 55N 121 50W
Mount Revelstoke Nat. Park, Canada 72 C5 51 5N 118 30W
Mount Robson Prov. Park, Canada 72 C5 53 0N 119 0W
Mount Shasta, U.S.A. 82 F2 41 19N 122 19W
Mount Signal, U.S.A. 85 N11 32 39N 115 37W
Mount Sterling, Ill., U.S.A. 80 F9 39 59N 90 45W
Mount Sterling, Ky., U.S.A. 76 F4 38 4N 83 56W
Mount Surprise, Australia 62 B3 18 10S 144 17 E
Mount Union, U.S.A. 78 F7 40 23N 77 53W
Mount Upton, U.S.A. 79 D9 42 26N 75 23W
Mount Vernon, Ill., U.S.A. 76 F1 38 19N 88 55W
Mount Vernon, Ind., U.S.A. 80 F10 38 17N 88 57W
Mount Vernon, N.Y., U.S.A. 79 F11 40 55N 73 50W
Mount Vernon, Ohio, U.S.A. 78 F2 40 23N 82 29W
Mount Vernon, Wash., U.S.A. 84 B4 48 25N 122 20W
Mountain Ash, U.K. 11 F4 51 40N 3 23W
Mountain Center, U.S.A. 85 M10 33 42N 116 44W
Mountain City, Nev., U.S.A. 82 F6 41 50N 115 58W
Mountain City, Tenn., U.S.A. 77 G5 36 29N 81 48W
Mountain Dale, U.S.A. 79 E10 41 41N 74 32W
Mountain Grove, U.S.A. 81 G8 37 8N 92 16W
Mountain Home, Ark., U.S.A. 81 G8 36 20N 92 23W
Mountain Home, Idaho, U.S.A. 82 E6 43 8N 115 41W
Mountain Iron, U.S.A. 80 B8 47 32N 92 37W
Mountain Pass, U.S.A. 85 K11 35 29N 115 35W
Mountain View, Ark., U.S.A. 81 H8 35 52N 92 7W
Mountain View, Calif., U.S.A. 84 H4 37 23N 122 5W
Mountain View, Hawaii, U.S.A. 74 J17 19 33N 155 7W
Mountainair, U.S.A. 83 J10 34 31N 106 15W
Mountlake Terrace, U.S.A. 84 C4 47 47N 122 19W
Mountmellick, Ireland 13 C4 53 7N 7 20W
Mountrath, Ireland 13 D4 53 0N 7 28W
Moura, Australia 62 C4 24 35S 149 58 E
Moura, Brazil 92 D6 1 32S 61 38W
Moura, Portugal 19 C2 38 7N 7 30W
Mourdi, Dépression du, Chad 51 E10 18 10N 23 0 E
Mourilyan, Australia 62 B4 17 35S 146 3 E
Mourne →, U.K. 13 B4 54 52N 7 26W
Mourne Mts., U.K. 13 B5 54 10N 6 0W
Mourniaí, Greece 23 D6 35 29N 24 1 E
Mournies = Mourniaí, Greece 23 D6 35 29N 24 1 E
Mouscron, Belgium 15 D3 50 45N 3 12 E
Moussoro, Chad 51 F9 13 41N 16 35 E
Moutohara, N.Z. 59 H6 38 27S 177 32 E
Moutong, Indonesia 37 D6 0 28N 121 13 E
Movas, Mexico 86 B3 28 10N 109 25W
Moville, Ireland 13 A4 55 11N 7 3W
Mowandjum, Australia 60 C3 17 22S 123 40 E
Moy →, Ireland 13 B2 54 8N 9 8W
Moyale, Kenya 54 B4 3 30N 39 0 E
Moyen Atlas, Morocco 50 B4 33 0N 5 0W
Moyne, L. le, Canada 71 A6 56 45N 68 47W
Moyo, Indonesia 36 F5 8 10S 117 40 E
Moyobamba, Peru 92 E3 6 0S 77 0W
Moyyero →, Russia 27 C11 68 44N 103 42 E
Moyynty, Kazakstan 26 E8 47 10N 73 18 E
Mozambique = Moçambique, Mozam. 55 F5 15 3S 40 42 E
Mozambique ■, Africa 55 F4 19 0S 35 0 E
Mozambique Chan., Africa 57 B7 17 30S 42 30 E
Mozdok, Russia 25 F7 43 45N 44 48 E
Mozdūrān, Iran 45 B9 36 9N 60 35 E
Mozhnābād, Iran 45 C9 34 7N 60 6 E
Mozyr = Mazyr, Belarus 17 B15 51 59N 29 15 E
Mpanda, Tanzania 54 D3 6 23S 31 1 E
Mpika, Zambia 55 E3 11 51S 31 25 E
Mpulungu, Zambia 55 D3 8 51S 31 5 E
Mpumalanga, S. Africa 57 D5 29 50S 30 33 E
Mpumalanga □, S. Africa 57 B5 26 0S 30 0 E
Mpwapwa, Tanzania 54 D4 6 23S 36 30 E
Msambansovu, Zimbabwe 55 F3 15 50S 30 3 E
M'sila →, Algeria 50 A6 35 30N 4 29 E
Msoro, Zambia 55 E3 13 35S 31 50 E
Mstislavl = Mstsislaw, Belarus 17 A16 54 0N 31 50 E
Mstsislaw, Belarus 17 A16 54 0N 31 50 E
Mtama, Tanzania 55 E4 10 17S 39 21 E
Mtilikwe →, Zimbabwe 55 G3 21 9S 31 30 E
Mtubatuba, S. Africa 57 D5 28 30S 32 8 E
Mtwara-Mikindani, Tanzania 55 E5 10 20S 40 20 E
Mu Gia, Deo, Vietnam 38 D5 17 40N 105 47 E
Mu Us Shamo, China 34 E5 39 0N 109 0 E
Muang Chiang Rai = Chiang Rai, Thailand 38 C2 19 52N 99 50 E
Muang Khong, Laos 36 B3 14 5N 105 52 E
Muang Khong, Laos 38 E5 14 7N 105 51 E
Muang Lamphun, Thailand 38 C2 18 40N 99 2 E
Muar, Malaysia 39 L4 2 3N 102 34 E
Muarabungo, Indonesia 36 E2 1 28S 102 52 E
Muaraenim, Indonesia 36 E2 3 40S 103 50 E
Muarajuloi, Indonesia 36 E4 0 12S 114 3 E
Muarakaman, Indonesia 36 E5 0 2S 116 45 E
Muaratebo, Indonesia 36 E2 1 30S 102 26 E
Muaratembesi, Indonesia 36 E2 1 42S 103 8 E
Muaratewe, Indonesia 36 E4 0 58S 114 52 E
Mubarakpur, India 43 F10 26 6N 83 18 E
Mubarraz = Al Mubarraz, Si. Arabia 45 E6 25 30N 49 40 E
Mubende, Uganda 54 B3 0 33N 31 22 E
Mubi, Nigeria 51 F8 10 18N 13 16 E
Mubur, Pulau, Indonesia 39 L6 3 20N 106 12 E
Mucajaí →, Brazil 92 C6 2 25N 60 52W
Muchachos, Roque de los, Canary Is. 22 F2 28 44N 17 52W
Muchinga Mts., Zambia 55 E3 11 30S 31 30 E
Muck, U.K. 12 E2 56 50N 6 15W
Muckadilla, Australia 63 D4 26 35S 148 23 E
Mucuri, Brazil 93 G11 18 0S 39 36W
Mucusso, Angola 56 B3 18 1S 21 25 E
Muda, Canary Is. 22 F6 28 34N 13 57W
Mudanjiang, China 35 B15 44 38N 129 30 E
Mudanya, Turkey 21 D13 40 25N 28 50 E
Muddy Cr. →, U.S.A. 83 H8 38 24N 110 42W
Mudgee, Australia 63 E4 32 32S 149 31 E
Mudjatik →, Canada 73 B7 56 1N 107 36W
Muecate, Mozam. 55 E4 14 55S 39 40 E
Mueda, Mozam. 55 E4 11 36S 39 28 E
Mueller Ra., Australia 60 C4 18 18S 126 46 E
Muende, Mozam. 55 E3 14 28S 33 0 E
Muerto, Mar, Mexico 87 D6 16 10N 94 10W
Mufulira, Zambia 55 E2 12 32S 28 15 E
Mufumbiro Range, Africa 54 C2 1 25S 29 30 E
Mughal Sarai, India 43 G10 25 18N 83 7 E
Mughayrā', Si. Arabia 44 D3 29 17N 37 41 E
Mugi, Japan 31 H7 33 40N 134 25 E
Mugila, Mts., Dem. Rep. of the Congo 54 D2 7 0S 28 50 E
Muğla, Turkey 21 F13 37 15N 28 22 E
Mugu, Nepal 43 E10 29 45N 82 30 E
Muhammad, Râs, Egypt 44 E2 27 44N 34 16 E
Muhammad Qol, Sudan 51 D13 20 53N 37 9 E
Muhammadabad, India 43 F10 26 4N 83 25 E
Muhesi →, Tanzania 54 D4 7 0S 35 20 E
Mühlhausen, Germany 16 C6 51 12N 10 27 E
Mühlig Hofmann fjell, Antarctica 5 D3 72 30S 5 0 E
Muhos, Finland 8 D22 64 47N 25 59 E
Muhu, Estonia 9 G20 58 36N 23 11 E
Muhutwe, Tanzania 54 C3 1 35S 31 45 E
Muine Bheag, Ireland 13 D5 52 42N 6 58W
Muir, L., Australia 61 F2 34 30S 116 40 E
Mukacheve, Ukraine 17 D12 48 27N 22 45 E
Mukachevo = Mukacheve, Ukraine 17 D12 48 27N 22 45 E
Mukah, Malaysia 36 D4 2 55N 112 5 E
Mukandwara, India 42 G6 24 49N 75 59 E
Mukdahan, Thailand 38 D5 16 32N 104 43 E
Mukden = Shenyang, China 35 D12 41 48N 123 27 E
Mukerian, India 42 D6 31 57N 75 37 E
Mukhtuya = Lensk, Russia 27 C12 60 48N 114 55 E
Mukinbudin, Australia 61 F2 30 55S 118 5 E
Mukishi, Dem. Rep. of the Congo 55 D1 8 30S 24 44 E
Mukomuko, Indonesia 36 E2 2 30S 101 10 E
Mukomwenze, Dem. Rep. of the Congo 54 D2 6 49S 27 15 E
Muktsar, India 42 D6 30 30N 74 30 E
Mukur = Moqor, Afghan. 42 C2 32 50N 67 42 E
Mukutawa →, Canada 73 C9 53 10N 97 24W
Mukwela, Zambia 55 F2 17 0S 26 40 E
Mula, Spain 19 C5 38 3N 1 33W
Mula →, Pakistan 42 F2 27 57N 67 36 E
Mulange, Dem. Rep. of the Congo 54 C2 3 40S 27 10 E
Mulanje, Malawi 55 F4 16 2S 35 33 E
Mulchén, Chile 94 D1 37 45S 72 20W
Mulde →, Germany 16 C7 51 53N 12 15 E
Mule Creek Junction, U.S.A. 80 D2 43 19N 104 8W
Muleba, Tanzania 54 C3 1 50S 31 37 E
Mulejé, Mexico 86 B2 26 53N 112 1W
Muleshoe, U.S.A. 81 H3 34 13N 102 43W
Mulgrave, Canada 71 C7 45 38N 61 31W
Mulhacén, Spain 19 D4 37 4N 3 20W
Mülheim, Germany 33 C6 51 25N 6 54 E

Nanching

Mulhouse, *France* **18 C7** 47 40N 7 20 E
Muling, *China* **35 B16** 44 35N 130 10 E
Mull, *U.K.* **12 E3** 56 25N 5 56W
Mull, Sound of, *U.K.* **12 E3** 56 30N 5 50W
Mullaittivu, *Sri Lanka* **40 Q12** 9 15N 80 49 E
Mullen, *U.S.A.* **80 D4** 42 3N 101 1W
Mullens, *U.S.A.* **76 G5** 37 35N 81 23W
Muller, Pegunungan, *Indonesia* **36 D4** 0 30N 113 30 E
Mullet Pen., *Ireland* **13 B1** 54 13N 10 2W
Mullewa, *Australia* **61 E2** 28 29S 115 30 E
Mulligan →, *Australia* **62 D2** 25 0S 139 0 E
Mullingar, *Ireland* **13 C4** 53 31N 7 21W
Mullins, *U.S.A.* **77 H6** 34 12N 79 15W
Mullumbimby, *Australia* **63 D5** 28 30S 153 30 E
Mulobezi, *Zambia* **55 F2** 16 45S 25 7 E
Mulroy B., *Ireland* **13 A4** 55 15N 7 46W
Multan, *Pakistan* **42 D4** 30 15N 71 36 E
Mulumbe, Mts., *Dem. Rep. of the Congo* **55 D2** 8 40S 27 30 E
Mulungushi Dam, *Zambia* **55 E2** 14 48S 28 48 E
Mulvane, *U.S.A.* **81 G6** 37 29N 97 15W
Mumbai, *India* **40 K8** 18 55N 72 50 E
Mumbwa, *Zambia* **55 F2** 15 0S 27 0 E
Mun →, *Thailand* **38 E5** 15 19N 105 30 E
Muna, *Indonesia* **37 F6** 5 0S 122 30 E
Munabao, *India* **42 G4** 25 45N 70 17 E
Munamagi, *Estonia* **9 H22** 57 43N 27 4 E
München, *Germany* **16 D6** 48 8N 11 34 E
Munchen-Gladbach = Mönchengladbach, *Germany* **16 C4** 51 11N 6 27 E
Muncho Lake, *Canada* **72 B3** 59 0N 125 50W
Munch'ŏn, *N. Korea* **35 E14** 39 14N 127 19 E
Muncie, *U.S.A.* **76 E3** 40 12N 85 23W
Muncoonie, L., *Australia* **62 D2** 25 12S 138 40 E
Mundabbera, *Australia* **63 D5** 25 36S 151 18 E
Munday, *U.S.A.* **81 J5** 33 27N 99 38W
Münden, *Germany* **16 C5** 51 25N 9 38 E
Mundiwindi, *Australia* **60 D3** 23 47S 120 9 E
Mundo Novo, *Brazil* **93 F10** 11 50S 40 29W
Mundra, *India* **42 H3** 22 54N 69 48 E
Mundrabilla, *Australia* **61 F4** 31 52S 127 51 E
Mungallala, *Australia* **63 D4** 26 28S 147 34 E
Mungallala Cr. →, *Australia* **63 D4** 28 53S 147 5 E
Mungana, *Australia* **62 B3** 17 8S 144 27 E
Mungaoli, *India* **42 G8** 24 24N 78 7 E
Mungari, *Mozam.* **55 F3** 17 12S 33 30 E
Mungbere, *Dem. Rep. of the Congo* **54 B2** 2 36N 28 28 E
Mungeli, *India* **43 H9** 22 4N 81 41 E
Munger, *India* **43 G12** 25 23N 86 30 E
Munich = München, *Germany* **16 D6** 48 8N 11 34 E
Munising, *U.S.A.* **76 B2** 46 25N 86 40W
Munku-Sardyk, *Russia* **27 D11** 51 45N 100 20 E
Muñoz Gamero, Pen., *Chile* **96 G2** 52 30S 73 5W
Munroe L., *Canada* **73 B9** 59 13N 98 35W
Munsan, *S. Korea* **35 F14** 37 51N 126 48 E
Münster, *Germany* **16 C4** 51 58N 7 37 E
Munster □, *Ireland* **13 D3** 52 18N 8 44W
Muntadgin, *Australia* **61 F2** 31 45S 118 33 E
Muntok, *Indonesia* **36 E3** 2 5S 105 10 E
Munyama, *Zambia* **55 F2** 16 5S 28 31 E
Muong Et, *Laos* **38 B5** 20 49N 104 1 E
Muong Hiem, *Laos* **38 B4** 20 5N 103 22 E
Muong Kau, *Laos* **38 E5** 15 6N 105 47 E
Muong Khao, *Laos* **38 C4** 19 38N 103 32 E
Muong Liep, *Laos* **38 C3** 18 29N 101 40 E
Muong May, *Laos* **38 E6** 14 49N 106 56 E
Muong Nong, *Laos* **38 D6** 16 22N 106 30 E
Muong Oua, *Laos* **38 C3** 18 18N 101 20 E
Muong Phalane, *Laos* **38 D5** 16 39N 105 34 E
Muong Phieng, *Laos* **38 C3** 19 6N 101 32 E
Muong Phine, *Laos* **38 D6** 16 32N 106 2 E
Muong Saiapoun, *Laos* **38 C3** 18 24N 101 31 E
Muong Sen, *Vietnam* **38 C5** 19 24N 104 8 E
Muong Soui, *Laos* **38 C4** 19 33N 102 52 E
Muong Xia, *Vietnam* **38 B5** 20 19N 104 50 E
Muonio, *Finland* **8 C20** 67 57N 23 40 E
Muonionjoki →, *Finland* **8 C20** 67 11N 23 34 E
Muping, *China* **35 F11** 37 22N 121 36 E
Muqdisho, *Somali Rep.* **46 G4** 2 2N 45 25 E
Mur →, *Austria* **17 E9** 46 18N 16 52 E
Murakami, *Japan* **30 E9** 38 14N 139 29 E
Murallón, Cerro, *Chile* **96 F2** 49 48S 73 30W
Muranda, *Rwanda* **54 C2** 1 52S 29 20 E
Murang'a, *Kenya* **54 C4** 0 45S 37 9 E
Murashi, *Russia* **24 C8** 59 30N 49 0 E
Murat →, *Turkey* **25 G7** 38 46N 40 0 E
Muratlı, *Turkey* **21 D12** 41 10N 27 29 E
Murayama, *Japan* **30 E10** 38 30N 140 25 E
Murban, *U.A.E.* **45 F7** 23 50N 53 45 E
Murchison →, *Australia* **61 E1** 27 45S 114 0 E
Murchison, Mt., *Antarctica* **5 D11** 73 0S 168 0 E
Murchison Falls, *Uganda* **54 B3** 2 15N 31 30 E
Murchison Ra., *Australia* **62 C1** 20 0S 134 10 E
Murchison Rapids, *Malawi* **55 F3** 15 55S 34 35 E
Murcia, *Spain* **19 D5** 38 5N 1 10W
Murcia □, *Spain* **19 D5** 37 50N 1 30W
Murdo, *U.S.A.* **80 D4** 43 53N 100 43W
Murdoch Pt., *Australia* **62 A3** 14 37S 144 55 E
Mureş →, *Romania* **17 E11** 46 15N 20 13 E
Mureşul = Mureş →, *Romania* **17 E11** 46 15N 20 13 E
Murfreesboro, *N.C., U.S.A.* **77 G7** 36 27N 77 6W
Murfreesboro, *Tenn., U.S.A.* **77 H2** 35 51N 86 24W
Murgab = Murghob, *Tajikistan* **26 F8** 38 10N 74 2 E
Murgab →, *Turkmenistan* **45 B9** 38 18N 61 12 E
Murgenella, *Australia* **60 B5** 11 34S 132 56 E
Murgha Kibzai, *Pakistan* **42 D3** 30 44N 69 25 E
Murghob, *Tajikistan* **26 F8** 38 10N 74 2 E
Murgon, *Australia* **63 D5** 26 15S 151 54 E
Muri, *India* **43 H11** 23 22N 85 52 E
Muria, *Indonesia* **37 G14** 6 36S 110 53 E
Muriaé, *Brazil* **95 A7** 21 8S 42 23W
Muriel Mine, *Zimbabwe* **55 F3** 17 14S 30 40 E
Müritz, *Germany* **16 B7** 53 25N 12 42 E
Murka, *Kenya* **54 C4** 3 27S 38 0 E
Murliganj, *India* **43 G12** 25 54N 86 59 E
Murmansk, *Russia* **24 A5** 68 57N 33 10 E
Muro, *Spain* **22 B10** 39 44N 3 3 E
Murom, *Russia* **24 C7** 55 35N 42 3 E
Muroran, *Japan* **30 C10** 42 25N 141 0 E
Muroto, *Japan* **31 H7** 33 18N 134 9 E
Muroto-Misaki, *Japan* **31 H7** 33 15N 134 10 E
Murphy, *U.S.A.* **82 E5** 43 13N 116 33W
Murphys, *U.S.A.* **84 G6** 38 8N 120 28W
Murray, *Ky., U.S.A.* **77 G1** 36 37N 88 19W
Murray, *Utah, U.S.A.* **82 F8** 40 40N 111 53W
Murray →, *Australia* **63 F2** 35 20S 139 22 E
Murray, L., *U.S.A.* **77 H5** 34 3N 81 13W
Murray Bridge, *Australia* **63 F2** 35 6S 139 14 E
Murray Harbour, *Canada* **71 C7** 46 0N 62 28W
Murraysburg, *S. Africa* **56 E3** 31 58S 23 47 E
Murree, *Pakistan* **42 C5** 33 56N 73 28 E
Murrieta, *U.S.A.* **85 M9** 33 33N 117 13W
Murrumbidgee →, *Australia* **63 E3** 34 43S 143 12 E
Murrumburrah, *Australia* **63 E4** 34 32S 148 22 E
Murrurundi, *Australia* **63 E5** 31 42S 150 51 E
Murshidabad, *India* **43 G13** 24 11N 88 19 E
Murtle L., *Canada* **72 C5** 52 8N 119 38W
Murtoa, *Australia* **63 F3** 36 35S 142 28 E
Murungu, *Tanzania* **54 C3** 4 12S 31 10 E
Mururoa, *Pac. Oc.* **65 K14** 21 52S 138 55W
Murwara, *India* **43 H9** 23 46N 80 28 E
Murwillumbah, *Australia* **63 D5** 28 18S 153 27 E
Mürzzuschlag, *Austria* **16 E8** 47 36N 15 41 E
Muş, *Turkey* **25 G7** 38 45N 41 30 E
Mûsa, Gebel, *Egypt* **44 D2** 28 33N 33 59 E
Musa Khel, *Pakistan* **42 D3** 30 59N 69 52 E
Mūsá Qal'eh, *Afghan.* **40 C4** 32 20N 64 50 E
Musaffargarh, *Pakistan* **40 D7** 30 10N 71 10 E
Musafirkhana, *India* **43 F9** 26 22N 81 48 E
Musala, *Bulgaria* **21 C10** 42 13N 23 37 E
Musala, *Indonesia* **36 D1** 1 41N 98 28 E
Musan, *N. Korea* **35 C15** 42 12N 129 12 E
Musangu, *Dem. Rep. of the Congo* **55 E1** 10 28S 23 55 E
Musasa, *Tanzania* **54 C3** 3 25S 31 30 E
Musay'id, *Qatar* **45 E6** 25 0N 51 33 E
Muscat = Masqat, *Oman* **46 C6** 23 37N 58 36 E
Muscat & Oman = Oman ■, *Asia* **46 C6** 23 0N 58 0 E
Muscatine, *U.S.A.* **80 E9** 41 25N 91 3W
Musgrave Harbour, *Canada* **71 C9** 49 27N 53 58W
Musgrave Ranges, *Australia* **61 E5** 26 0S 132 0 E
Mushie, *Dem. Rep. of the Congo* **52 E3** 2 56S 16 55 E
Musi →, *Indonesia* **36 E2** 2 20S 104 56 E
Muskeg →, *Canada* **72 A4** 60 20N 123 20W
Muskegon, *U.S.A.* **76 D2** 43 14N 86 16W
Muskegon →, *U.S.A.* **76 D2** 43 14N 86 21W
Muskegon Heights, *U.S.A.* **76 D2** 43 12N 86 16W
Muskogee, *U.S.A.* **81 H7** 35 45N 95 22W
Muskoka, L., *Canada* **78 B5** 45 0N 79 25W
Muskwa →, *Canada* **72 B4** 58 47N 122 48W
Muslīmiyah, *Syria* **44 B3** 36 19N 37 12 E
Musofu, *Zambia* **55 E2** 13 30S 29 0 E
Musoma, *Tanzania* **54 C3** 1 30S 33 48 E
Musquaro, L., *Canada* **71 B7** 50 38N 61 5W
Musquodoboit Harbour, *Canada* **71 D7** 44 50N 63 9W
Musselburgh, *U.K.* **12 F5** 55 57N 3 2W
Musselshell →, *U.S.A.* **82 C10** 47 21N 107 57W
Mussoorie, *India* **42 D8** 30 27N 78 6 E
Mussuco, *Angola* **56 B2** 17 2S 19 3 E
Mustafakemalpaşa, *Turkey* **21 D13** 40 2N 28 24 E
Mustang, *Nepal* **43 E10** 29 10N 83 55 E
Musters, L., *Argentina* **96 F3** 45 20S 69 25W
Musudan, *N. Korea* **35 D15** 40 50N 129 43 E
Muswellbrook, *Australia* **63 E5** 32 16S 150 56 E
Mût, *Egypt* **51 C11** 25 28N 28 58 E
Mut, *Turkey* **44 B2** 36 40N 33 28 E
Mutanda, *Mozam.* **57 C5** 21 0S 33 34 E
Mutanda, *Zambia* **55 E2** 12 24S 26 13 E
Mutare, *Zimbabwe* **55 F3** 18 58S 32 38 E
Muting, *Indonesia* **37 F10** 7 23S 140 20 E
Mutoray, *Russia* **27 C11** 60 56N 101 0 E
Mutshatsha, *Dem. Rep. of the Congo* **55 E1** 10 35S 24 20 E
Mutsu, *Japan* **30 D10** 41 5N 140 55 E
Mutsu-Wan, *Japan* **30 D10** 41 5N 140 55 E
Muttaburra, *Australia* **62 C3** 22 38S 144 29 E
Mutton I., *Ireland* **13 D2** 52 49N 9 32W
Mutuáli, *Mozam.* **55 E4** 14 55S 37 0 E
Muweilih, *Egypt* **47 E3** 30 42N 34 19 E
Muy Muy, *Nic.* **88 D2** 12 39N 85 36W
Muyinga, *Burundi* **54 C3** 3 14S 30 33 E
Muynak, *Uzbekistan* **26 E6** 43 44N 59 10 E
Muzaffarabad, *Pakistan* **43 B5** 34 25N 73 30 E
Muzaffargarh, *Pakistan* **42 D4** 30 5N 71 14 E
Muzaffarnagar, *India* **42 E7** 29 26N 77 40 E
Muzaffarpur, *India* **43 F11** 26 7N 85 23 E
Muzafirpur, *Pakistan* **42 D3** 30 58N 69 9 E
Muzhi, *Russia* **24 A11** 65 25N 64 40 E
Mvuma, *Zimbabwe* **55 F3** 19 16S 30 30 E
Mvurwi, *Zimbabwe* **55 F3** 17 0S 30 57 E
Mwadui, *Tanzania* **54 C3** 3 26S 33 32 E
Mwambo, *Tanzania* **55 E5** 10 30S 40 22 E
Mwandi, *Zambia* **55 F1** 17 30S 24 51 E
Mwanza, *Dem. Rep. of the Congo* **54 D2** 7 55S 26 43 E
Mwanza, *Tanzania* **54 C3** 2 30S 32 58 E
Mwanza, *Zambia* **55 F1** 16 58S 24 28 E
Mwanza □, *Tanzania* **54 C3** 2 0S 33 0 E
Mwaya, *Tanzania* **55 D3** 9 32S 33 55 E
Mweelrea, *Ireland* **13 C2** 53 39N 9 49W
Mweka, *Dem. Rep. of the Congo* **52 E4** 4 50S 21 34 E
Mwene-Ditu, *Dem. Rep. of the Congo* **52 F4** 6 35S 22 27 E
Mwenezi, *Zimbabwe* **55 G3** 21 15S 30 48 E
Mwenezi →, *Mozam.* **55 G3** 22 40S 31 50 E
Mwenga, *Dem. Rep. of the Congo* **54 C2** 3 1S 28 28 E
Mweru, L., *Zambia* **55 D2** 9 0S 28 40 E
Mweza Range, *Zimbabwe* **55 G3** 21 0S 30 0 E
Mwilambwe, *Dem. Rep. of the Congo* **54 D2** 8 7S 25 5 E
Mwimbi, *Tanzania* **55 D3** 8 38S 31 39 E
Mwinilunga, *Zambia* **55 E1** 11 43S 24 25 E
My Tho, *Vietnam* **39 G6** 10 29N 106 23 E
Myajlar, *India* **42 F4** 26 15N 70 20 E
Myanaung, *Burma* **41 K19** 18 18N 95 22 E
Myanmar = Burma ■, *Asia* **41 J20** 21 0N 96 30 E
Myaungmya, *Burma* **41 L19** 16 30N 94 40 E
Mycenæ, *Greece* **21 F10** 37 39N 22 52 E
Myeik Kyunzu, *Burma* **39 G1** 11 30N 97 30 E
Myers Chuck, *U.S.A.* **72 B2** 55 44N 132 11W
Myerstown, *U.S.A.* **79 F8** 40 22N 76 19W
Myingyan, *Burma* **41 J19** 21 30N 95 20 E
Myitkyina, *Burma* **41 G20** 25 24N 97 26 E
Mykines, *Færoe Is.* **8 E9** 62 7N 7 35W
Mykolayiv, *Ukraine* **25 E5** 46 58N 32 0 E
Mymensingh, *Bangla.* **41 G17** 24 45N 90 24 E
Mynydd Du, *U.K.* **11 F4** 51 52N 3 50W
Mýrdalsjökull, *Iceland* **8 E4** 63 40N 19 6W
Myrtle Beach, *U.S.A.* **77 J6** 33 42N 78 53W
Myrtle Creek, *U.S.A.* **82 E2** 43 1N 123 17W
Myrtle Point, *U.S.A.* **82 E1** 43 4N 124 8W
Myrtou, *Cyprus* **23 D12** 35 18N 33 4 E
Mysia, *Turkey* **21 E12** 39 50N 27 0 E
Mysore = Karnataka □, *India* **40 N10** 13 15N 77 0 E
Mysore, *India* **40 N10** 12 17N 76 41 E
Mystic, *U.S.A.* **79 E13** 41 21N 71 58W
Myszków, *Poland* **17 C10** 50 45N 19 22 E
Mytishchi, *Russia* **24 C6** 55 50N 37 50 E
Mývatn, *Iceland* **8 D5** 65 36N 17 0W
Mzimba, *Malawi* **55 E3** 11 55S 33 39 E
Mzimkulu →, *S. Africa* **57 E5** 30 44S 30 28 E
Mzimvubu →, *S. Africa* **57 E4** 31 38S 29 33 E
Mzuzu, *Malawi* **55 E3** 11 30S 33 55 E

N

Na Hearadh = Harris, *U.K.* **12 D2** 57 50N 6 55W
Na Noi, *Thailand* **38 C3** 18 19N 100 43 E
Na Phao, *Laos* **38 D5** 17 35N 105 44 E
Na San, *Vietnam* **38 B5** 21 12N 104 2 E
Naab →, *Germany* **16 D6** 49 1N 12 2 E
Naantali, *Finland* **9 F19** 60 29N 22 2 E
Naas, *Ireland* **13 C5** 53 12N 6 40W
Nababiep, *S. Africa* **56 D2** 29 36S 17 46 E
Nabadwip = Navadwip, *India* **43 H13** 23 34N 88 20 E
Nabari, *Japan* **31 G8** 34 37N 136 5 E
Nabawa, *Australia* **61 E1** 28 30S 114 48 E
Nabberu, L., *Australia* **61 E3** 25 50S 120 30 E
Naberezhnyye Chelny, *Russia* **24 C9** 55 42N 52 19 E
Nabeul, *Tunisia* **51 A8** 36 30N 10 44 E
Nabha, *India* **42 D7** 30 26N 76 14 E
Nabīd, *Iran* **45 D8** 29 40N 57 38 E
Nabire, *Indonesia* **37 E9** 3 15S 135 26 E
Nabisar, *Pakistan* **42 G3** 25 8N 69 40 E
Nabisipi →, *Canada* **71 B7** 50 14N 62 13W
Nabiswera, *Uganda* **54 B3** 1 27N 32 15 E
Nablus = Nābulus, *West Bank* **47 C4** 32 14N 35 15 E
Naboomspruit, *S. Africa* **57 C4** 24 32S 28 40 E
Nābulus, *West Bank* **47 C4** 32 14N 35 15 E
Nacala, *Mozam.* **55 E5** 14 31S 40 34 E
Nacala-Velha, *Mozam.* **55 E5** 14 32S 40 34 E
Nacaome, *Honduras* **88 D2** 13 31N 87 30W
Nacaroa, *Mozam.* **55 E4** 14 22S 39 56 E
Naches, *U.S.A.* **82 C3** 46 44N 120 42W
Naches →, *U.S.A.* **84 D6** 46 38N 120 31W
Nachicapau, L., *Canada* **71 A6** 56 40N 68 5W
Nachingwea, *Tanzania* **55 E4** 10 23S 38 49 E
Nachna, *India* **42 F4** 27 34N 71 41 E
Nacimiento L., *U.S.A.* **84 K6** 35 46N 120 53W
Naco, *Mexico* **86 A3** 31 20N 109 56W
Nacogdoches, *U.S.A.* **81 K7** 31 36N 94 39W
Nácori Chico, *Mexico* **86 B3** 29 39N 109 1W
Nacozari, *Mexico* **86 A3** 30 24N 109 39W
Nadiad, *India* **42 H5** 22 41N 72 56 E
Nador, *Morocco* **50 B5** 35 14N 2 58W
Nadur, *Malta* **23 C1** 36 2N 14 17 E
Nadūshan, *Iran* **45 C7** 32 2N 53 35 E
Nadvirna, *Ukraine* **17 D13** 48 37N 24 30 E
Nadvoitsy, *Russia* **24 B5** 63 52N 34 14 E
Nadvornaya = Nadvirna, *Ukraine* **17 D13** 48 37N 24 30 E
Nadym, *Russia* **26 C8** 65 35N 72 42 E
Nadym →, *Russia* **26 C8** 66 12N 72 0 E
Nærbø, *Norway* **9 G11** 58 40N 5 39 E
Næstved, *Denmark* **9 J14** 55 13N 11 44 E
Naft-e Safīd, *Iran* **45 D6** 31 40N 49 17 E
Naftshahr, *Iran* **44 C5** 34 0N 45 30 E
Nafud Desert = An Nafūd, *Si. Arabia* **44 D4** 28 15N 41 0 E
Naga, *Phil.* **37 B6** 13 38N 123 15 E
Nagahama, *Japan* **31 G8** 35 23N 136 16 E
Nagai, *Japan* **30 E10** 38 6N 140 2 E
Nagaland □, *India* **41 G19** 26 0N 94 30 E
Nagano, *Japan* **31 F9** 36 40N 138 10 E
Nagano □, *Japan* **31 F9** 36 15N 138 0 E
Nagaoka, *Japan* **31 F9** 37 27N 138 51 E
Nagappattinam, *India* **40 P11** 10 46N 79 51 E
Nagar →, *Bangla.* **43 G13** 24 27N 89 12 E
Nagar Parkar, *Pakistan* **42 G4** 24 28N 70 46 E
Nagasaki, *Japan* **31 H4** 32 47N 129 50 E
Nagasaki □, *Japan* **31 H4** 32 50N 129 40 E
Nagato, *Japan* **31 G5** 34 19N 131 5 E
Nagaur, *India* **42 F5** 27 15N 73 45 E
Nagda, *India* **42 H6** 23 27N 75 25 E
Nagercoil, *India* **40 Q10** 8 12N 77 26 E
Nagina, *India* **43 E8** 29 30N 78 30 E
Nagineh, *Iran* **45 C8** 34 20N 57 15 E
Nagir, *Pakistan* **43 A6** 36 12N 74 42 E
Nagod, *India* **43 G9** 24 34N 80 36 E
Nagoorin, *Australia* **62 C5** 24 17S 151 15 E
Nagorno-Karabakh, *Azerbaijan* **25 F8** 39 55N 46 45 E
Nagornyy, *Russia* **27 D13** 55 58N 124 57 E
Nagoya, *Japan* **31 G8** 35 10N 136 50 E
Nagpur, *India* **40 J11** 21 8N 79 10 E
Nagua, *Dom. Rep.* **89 C6** 19 23N 69 50W
Nagykanizsa, *Hungary* **17 E9** 46 28N 17 0 E
Nagykőrös, *Hungary* **17 E10** 47 5N 19 48 E
Naha, *Japan* **31 L3** 26 13N 127 42 E
Nahan, *India* **42 D7** 30 33N 77 18 E
Nahanni Butte, *Canada* **72 A4** 61 2N 123 31W
Nahanni Nat. Park, *Canada* **72 A4** 61 15N 125 0W
Nahargarh, *Mad. P., India* **42 G6** 24 10N 75 14 E
Nahargarh, *Raj., India* **42 G7** 24 55N 76 50 E
Nahariyya, *Israel* **44 C2** 33 1N 35 5 E
Nahāvand, *Iran* **45 C6** 34 10N 48 22 E
Naicá, *Mexico* **86 B3** 27 53N 105 31W
Naicam, *Canada* **73 C8** 52 30N 104 30W
Naikoon Prov. Park, *Canada* **72 C2** 53 55N 131 55W
Naimisharanya, *India* **43 F9** 27 21N 80 30 E
Nain, *Canada* **71 A7** 56 34N 61 40W
Nā'īn, *Iran* **45 C7** 32 54N 53 0 E
Naini Tal, *India* **43 E8** 29 30N 79 30 E
Nainpur, *India* **40 H12** 22 30N 80 10 E
Nainwa, *India* **42 G6** 25 46N 75 51 E
Nairn, *U.K.* **12 D5** 57 35N 3 53W
Nairobi, *Kenya* **54 C4** 1 17S 36 48 E
Naissaar, *Estonia* **9 G21** 59 34N 24 29 E
Naivasha, *Kenya* **54 C4** 0 40S 36 30 E
Naivasha, L., *Kenya* **54 C4** 0 48S 36 20 E
Najafābād, *Iran* **45 C6** 32 40N 51 15 E
Najd, *Si. Arabia* **46 B3** 26 30N 42 0 E
Najibabad, *India* **42 E8** 29 40N 78 20 E
Najin, *N. Korea* **35 C16** 42 12N 130 15 E
Najmah, *Si. Arabia* **45 E6** 26 42N 50 6 E
Naju, *S. Korea* **35 G14** 35 3N 126 43 E
Nakadōri-Shima, *Japan* **31 H4** 32 57N 129 4 E
Nakalagba, *Dem. Rep. of the Congo* **54 B2** 2 50N 27 58 E
Nakaminato, *Japan* **31 F10** 36 21N 140 36 E
Nakamura, *Japan* **31 H6** 32 59N 132 56 E
Nakano, *Japan* **31 F9** 36 45N 138 22 E
Nakano-Shima, *Japan* **31 K4** 29 51N 129 52 E
Nakashibetsu, *Japan* **30 C12** 43 33N 144 59 E
Nakfa, *Eritrea* **46 D2** 16 40N 38 32 E
Nakhfar al Buşayyah, *Iraq* **44 D5** 30 0N 46 10 E
Nakhichevan = Naxçıvan, *Azerbaijan* **25 G8** 39 12N 45 15 E
Nakhichevan Republic = Naxçıvan □, *Azerbaijan* **25 G8** 39 25N 45 26 E
Nakhl, *Egypt* **47 F2** 29 55N 33 43 E
Nakhl-e Taqī, *Iran* **45 E7** 27 28N 52 36 E
Nakhodka, *Russia* **27 E14** 42 53N 132 54 E
Nakhon Nayok, *Thailand* **38 E3** 14 12N 101 13 E
Nakhon Pathom, *Thailand* **38 F3** 13 49N 100 3 E
Nakhon Phanom, *Thailand* **38 D5** 17 23N 104 43 E
Nakhon Ratchasima, *Thailand* **38 E4** 14 59N 102 12 E
Nakhon Sawan, *Thailand* **38 E3** 15 35N 100 10 E
Nakhon Si Thammarat, *Thailand* **39 H3** 8 29N 100 0 E
Nakhon Thai, *Thailand* **38 D3** 17 5N 100 44 E
Nakhtarana, *India* **42 H3** 23 20N 69 15 E
Nakina, *Canada* **70 B2** 50 10N 86 40W
Nakodar, *India* **42 D6** 31 8N 75 31 E
Nakskov, *Denmark* **9 J14** 54 50N 11 8 E
Naktong →, *S. Korea* **35 G15** 35 7N 128 57 E
Nakuru, *Kenya* **54 C4** 0 15S 36 4 E
Nakuru, L., *Kenya* **54 C4** 0 23S 36 5 E
Nakusp, *Canada* **72 C5** 50 20N 117 45W
Nal, *Pakistan* **42 F2** 27 40N 66 12 E
Nal →, *Pakistan* **42 G1** 25 20N 65 30 E
Nalchik, *Russia* **25 F7** 43 30N 43 33 E
Nalgonda, *India* **40 L11** 17 6N 79 15 E
Nalhati, *India* **43 G12** 24 17N 87 52 E
Naliya, *India* **42 H3** 23 16N 68 50 E
Nallamalai Hills, *India* **40 M11** 15 30N 78 50 E
Nam Can, *Vietnam* **39 H5** 8 46N 104 59 E
Nam-ch'on, *N. Korea* **35 E14** 38 15N 126 26 E
Nam Co, *China* **32 C4** 30 30N 90 45 E
Nam Du, Hon, *Vietnam* **39 H5** 9 41N 104 21 E
Nam Ngum Dam, *Laos* **38 C4** 18 35N 102 34 E
Nam-Phan = Cochin China, *Vietnam* **39 G6** 10 30N 106 0 E
Nam Phong, *Thailand* **38 D4** 16 42N 102 52 E
Nam Tok, *Thailand* **38 E2** 14 21N 99 4 E
Namacunde, *Angola* **56 B2** 17 18S 15 50 E
Namacurra, *Mozam.* **57 B6** 17 30S 36 50 E
Namak, Daryācheh-ye, *Iran* **45 C7** 34 30N 52 0 E
Namak, Kavir-e, *Iran* **45 C8** 34 30N 57 30 E
Namakzār, Daryācheh-ye, *Iran* **45 C9** 34 0N 60 30 E
Namaland, *Namibia* **56 C2** 26 0S 17 0 E
Namangan, *Uzbekistan* **26 E8** 41 0N 71 40 E
Namapa, *Mozam.* **55 E4** 13 43S 39 50 E
Namaqualand, *S. Africa* **56 E2** 30 0S 17 25 E
Namasagali, *Uganda* **54 B3** 1 2N 33 0 E
Namber, *Indonesia* **37 E8** 1 2S 134 49 E
Nambour, *Australia* **63 D5** 26 32S 152 58 E
Nambucca Heads, *Australia* **63 E5** 30 37S 153 0 E
Namcha Barwa, *China* **32 D4** 29 40N 95 10 E
Namche Bazar, *Nepal* **43 F12** 27 51N 86 47 E
Namchonjŏm = Nam-ch'on, *N. Korea* **35 E14** 38 15N 126 26 E
Namecunda, *Mozam.* **55 E4** 14 54S 37 37 E
Nameponda, *Mozam.* **55 F4** 15 50S 39 50 E
Nametil, *Mozam.* **55 F4** 15 40S 39 21 E
Namew L., *Canada* **73 C8** 54 14N 101 56W
Namgia, *India* **43 D8** 31 48N 78 40 E
Namib Desert = Namibwoestyn, *Namibia* **56 C2** 22 30S 15 0 E
Namibe, *Angola* **53 H2** 15 7S 12 11 E
Namibe □, *Angola* **56 B1** 16 35S 12 30 E
Namibia ■, *Africa* **56 C2** 22 0S 18 9 E
Namibwoestyn, *Namibia* **56 C2** 22 30S 15 0 E
Namlea, *Indonesia* **37 E7** 3 18S 127 5 E
Namoi →, *Australia* **63 E4** 30 12S 149 30 E
Nampa, *U.S.A.* **82 E5** 43 34N 116 34W
Namp'o, *N. Korea* **35 E13** 38 52N 125 10 E
Nampō-Shotō, *Japan* **31 J10** 32 0N 140 0 E
Nampula, *Mozam.* **55 F4** 15 6S 39 15 E
Namrole, *Indonesia* **37 E7** 3 46S 126 46 E
Namse Shankou, *China* **41 E13** 30 0N 82 25 E
Namsen →, *Norway* **8 D14** 64 28N 11 37 E
Namsos, *Norway* **8 D14** 64 29N 11 30 E
Namtsy, *Russia* **27 C13** 62 43N 129 37 E
Namtu, *Burma* **41 H20** 23 5N 97 28 E
Namtumbo, *Tanzania* **55 E4** 10 30S 36 4 E
Namu, *Canada* **72 C3** 51 52N 127 50W
Namur, *Belgium* **15 D4** 50 27N 4 52 E
Namur □, *Belgium* **15 D4** 50 17N 5 0 E
Namutoni, *Namibia* **56 B2** 18 49S 16 55 E
Namwala, *Zambia* **55 F2** 15 44S 26 30 E
Namwŏn, *S. Korea* **35 G14** 35 23N 127 23 E
Nan, *Thailand* **38 C3** 18 48N 100 46 E
Nan →, *Thailand* **38 E3** 15 42N 100 9 E
Nan-ch'ang = Nanchang, *China* **33 D6** 28 42N 115 55 E
Nanaimo, *Canada* **72 D4** 49 10N 124 0W
Nanam, *N. Korea* **35 D15** 41 44N 129 40 E
Nanango, *Australia* **63 D5** 26 40S 152 0 E
Nanao, *Japan* **31 F8** 37 0N 137 0 E
Nanchang, *China* **33 D6** 28 42N 115 55 E
Nanching = Nanjing, *China* **33 C6** 32 2N 118 47 E

O

Oshkosh

Ofotfjorden, Norway 8 B17 68 27N 17 0 E
Ōfunato, Japan 30 E10 39 4N 141 43 E
Oga, Japan 30 E9 39 55N 139 50 E
Oga-Hantō, Japan 30 E9 39 58N 139 47 E
Ogaden, Ethiopia 46 F3 7 30N 45 30 E
Ōgaki, Japan 31 G8 35 21N 136 37 E
Ogallala, U.S.A. 80 E4 41 8N 101 43W
Ogasawara Gunto, Pac. Oc. 28 G18 27 0N 142 0 E
Ogbomosho, Nigeria 50 G6 8 1N 4 11 E
Ogden, U.S.A. 82 F7 41 13N 111 58W
Ogdensburg, U.S.A. 79 B9 44 42N 75 30W
Ogeechee →, U.S.A. 77 K5 31 50N 81 3W
Ogilby, U.S.A. 85 N12 32 49N 114 50W
Oglio →, Italy 20 B4 45 2N 10 39 E
Ogmore, Australia 62 C4 22 37S 149 35 E
Ogoki, Canada 70 B2 51 38N 85 58W
Ogoki →, Canada 70 B2 51 38N 85 57W
Ogoki L., Canada 70 B2 50 50N 87 10W
Ogoki Res., Canada 70 B2 50 45N 88 15W
Ogooué →, Gabon 52 E1 1 0S 9 0 E
Ogowe = Ogooué →,
Gabon 52 E1 1 0S 9 0 E
Ogre, Latvia 9 H21 56 49N 24 36 E
Ogurchinskiy, Ostrov,
Turkmenistan 45 B7 38 55N 53 2 E
Ohai, N.Z. 59 L2 45 55S 168 0 E
Ohakune, N.Z. 59 H5 39 24S 175 24 E
Ohata, Japan 30 D10 41 24N 141 10 E
Ohau, L., N.Z. 59 L2 44 15S 169 53 E
Ohio □, U.S.A. 78 F2 40 15N 82 45W
Ohio →, U.S.A. 76 G1 36 59N 89 8W
Ohře →, Czech Rep. 16 C8 50 30N 14 10 E
Ohrid, Macedonia 21 D9 41 8N 20 52 E
Ohridsko Jezero, Macedonia 21 D9 41 8N 20 52 E
Ohrigstad, S. Africa 57 C5 24 39S 30 36 E
Oiapoque, Brazil 93 3 50N 51 50W
Oikou, China 35 E9 38 35N 117 42 E
Oil City, U.S.A. 78 E5 41 26N 79 42W
Oil Springs, Canada 78 D2 42 47N 82 7W
Oildale, U.S.A. 85 K7 35 25N 119 1W
Oise →, France 18 B5 49 0N 2 4 E
Ōita, Japan 31 H5 33 14N 131 36 E
Ōita □, Japan 31 H5 33 15N 131 30 E
Oiticica, Brazil 93 E10 5 3S 41 5W
Ojacaliente, Mexico 86 C4 22 34N 102 15W
Ojai, U.S.A. 85 L7 34 27N 119 15W
Ojinaga, Mexico 86 B4 29 34N 104 25W
Ojiya, Japan 31 F9 37 18N 138 48 E
Ojos del Salado, Cerro,
Argentina 94 B2 27 0S 68 40W
Oka →, Russia 24 C7 56 20N 43 59 E
Okaba, Indonesia 37 F9 8 6S 139 42 E
Okahandja, Namibia 56 C2 22 0S 16 59 E
Okahukura, N.Z. 59 H5 38 48S 175 14 E
Okanagan L., Canada 72 D5 50 0N 119 30W
Okanogan, U.S.A. 82 B4 48 22N 119 35W
Okanogan →, U.S.A. 82 B4 48 6N 119 44W
Okaputa, Namibia 56 C2 20 5S 17 0 E
Okara, Pakistan 42 D5 30 50N 73 31 E
Okarito, N.Z. 59 K3 43 15S 170 9 E
Okaukuejo, Namibia 56 B2 19 10S 16 0 E
Okavango Swamps,
Botswana 56 B3 18 45S 22 45 E
Okaya, Japan 31 F9 36 5N 138 10 E
Okayama, Japan 31 G6 34 40N 133 54 E
Okayama □, Japan 31 G6 35 0N 133 50 E
Okazaki, Japan 31 G8 34 57N 137 10 E
Okeechobee, U.S.A. 77 M5 27 15N 80 50W
Okeechobee, L., U.S.A. 77 M5 27 0N 80 50W
Okefenokee Swamp, U.S.A. 77 K4 30 40N 82 20W
Okehampton, U.K. 11 G4 50 44N 4 0W
Okha, India 42 H3 22 27N 69 4 E
Okha, Russia 27 D15 53 40N 143 0 E
Okhotsk, Russia 27 D15 59 20N 143 10 E
Okhotsk, Sea of, Asia 27 D15 55 0N 145 0 E
Okhotskiy Perevoz, Russia 27 C14 61 52N 135 35 E
Okhtyrka, Ukraine 25 D5 50 25N 35 0 E
Oki-Shotō, Japan 31 F6 36 5N 133 15 E
Okiep, S. Africa 56 D2 29 39S 17 53 E
Okinawa □, Japan 31 L4 26 40N 128 0 E
Okinawa-Guntō, Japan 31 L4 26 40N 128 0 E
Okinawa-Jima, Japan 31 L4 26 32N 128 0 E
Okino-erabu-Shima, Japan 31 L4 27 21N 128 33 E
Oklahoma □, U.S.A. 81 H6 35 20N 97 30W
Oklahoma City, U.S.A. 81 H6 35 30N 97 30W
Okmulgee, U.S.A. 81 H7 35 37N 95 58W
Oknitsa = Ocniţa, Moldova 17 D14 48 25N 27 30 E
Okolo, Uganda 54 B3 2 37N 31 8 E
Okolona, U.S.A. 81 J10 34 0N 88 45W
Okotoks, Canada 72 C6 50 43N 113 58W
Oksibil, Indonesia 37 E10 4 59S 140 35 E
Oksovskiy, Russia 24 B6 62 33N 39 57 E
Oktabrsk = Oktyabrsk,
Kazakstan 25 E10 49 28N 57 25 E
Oktyabrsk, Kazakstan 25 E10 49 28N 57 25 E
Oktyabrskiy = Aktsyabrski,
Belarus 17 B15 52 38N 28 53 E
Oktyabrskiy, Russia 24 D9 54 28N 53 28 E
Oktyabrskoy Revolyutsii,
Ostrov, Russia 27 B10 79 30N 97 0 E
Okuru, N.Z. 59 K2 43 55S 168 55 E
Okushiri-Tō, Japan 30 C9 42 15N 139 30 E
Okwa →, Botswana 56 C3 22 30S 23 0 E
Ola, U.S.A. 81 H8 35 2N 93 13W
Ólafsfjörður, Iceland 8 C4 66 4N 18 39W
Ólafsvík, Iceland 8 D2 64 53N 23 43W
Olancha, U.S.A. 85 J8 36 17N 118 1W
Olancha Pk., U.S.A. 85 J8 36 15N 118 7W
Olanchito, Honduras 88 C2 15 30N 86 30W
Öland, Sweden 9 H17 56 45N 16 38 E
Olary, Australia 63 E3 32 18S 140 19 E
Olascoaga, Argentina 94 D3 35 15S 60 39W
Olathe, U.S.A. 80 F7 38 53N 94 49W
Olavarría, Argentina 94 D3 36 55S 60 20W
Oława, Poland 17 C9 50 57N 17 20 E
Ólbia, Italy 20 D3 40 55N 9 31 E
Olcott, U.S.A. 78 C6 43 20N 78 42W
Old Bahama Chan. =
Bahama, Canal Viejo de,
W. Indies 88 B4 22 10N 77 30W
Old Baldy Pk. = San
Antonio, Mt., U.S.A. 85 L9 34 17N 117 38W
Old Castile = Castilla y
Leon □, Spain 19 B3 42 0N 5 0W
Old Crow, Canada 68 B6 67 30N 139 55W
Old Dale, U.S.A. 85 L11 34 8N 115 47W
Old Forge, N.Y., U.S.A. 79 C10 43 43N 74 58W
Old Forge, Pa., U.S.A. 79 E9 41 22N 75 45W
Old Perlican, Canada 71 C9 48 5N 53 1W
Old Shinyanga, Tanzania 54 C3 3 33S 33 27 E
Old Speck Mt., U.S.A. 79 B14 44 34N 70 57W
Old Town, U.S.A. 77 C11 44 56N 68 39W
Old Washington, U.S.A. 78 F3 40 2N 81 27W
Old Wives L., Canada 73 C7 50 5N 106 0W
Oldbury, U.K. 11 F5 51 38N 2 33W
Oldcastle, Ireland 13 C4 53 46N 7 10W
Oldeani, Tanzania 54 C4 3 22S 35 35 E
Oldenburg, Germany 16 B5 53 9N 8 13 E
Oldenzaal, Neths. 15 B6 52 19N 6 53 E
Oldham, U.K. 10 D5 53 33N 2 7W
Oldman →, Canada 72 D6 49 57N 111 42W
Oldmeldrum, U.K. 12 D6 57 20N 2 19W
Olds, Canada 72 C6 51 50N 114 10W
Oldziyt, Mongolia 34 B5 44 40N 109 1 E
Olean, U.S.A. 78 D6 42 5N 78 26W
Olekma →, Russia 27 C13 60 22N 120 42 E
Olekminsk, Russia 27 C13 60 25N 120 30 E
Oleksandriya, Ukraine 17 C14 50 37N 26 19 E
Olema, U.S.A. 84 G4 38 3N 122 47W
Olenegorsk, Russia 24 A5 68 9N 33 18 E
Olenek, Russia 27 C12 68 28N 112 18 E
Olenek →, Russia 27 B13 73 0N 120 10 E
Oléron, Î. d', France 18 D3 45 55N 1 15W
Oleśnica, Poland 17 C9 51 13N 17 22 E
Olevsk, Ukraine 17 C14 51 12N 27 39 E
Olga, Russia 27 E14 43 50N 135 14 E
Olga, L., Canada 70 C4 49 47N 77 15W
Olga, Mt., Australia 61 E5 25 20S 130 50 E
Olhão, Portugal 19 D2 37 3N 7 48W
Olifants →, Africa 57 C5 23 57S 31 58 E
Olifantshoek, S. Africa 56 D3 27 57S 22 42 E
Ólimbos, Óros, Greece 21 D10 40 6N 22 23 E
Olímpia, Brazil 95 A6 20 44S 48 54W
Olinda, Brazil 93 E12 8 1S 34 51W
Oliva, Argentina 94 C3 32 0S 63 38W
Olivehurst, U.S.A. 84 F5 39 6N 121 34W
Olivenza, Spain 19 C2 38 41N 7 9W
Oliver, Canada 72 D5 49 13N 119 37W
Oliver L., Canada 73 B8 56 56N 103 22W
Ollagüe, Chile 94 A2 21 15S 68 10W
Olney, Ill., U.S.A. 76 F1 38 44N 88 5W
Olney, Tex., U.S.A. 81 J5 33 22N 98 45W
Olomane →, Canada 71 B7 50 14N 60 37W
Olomouc, Czech Rep. 17 D9 49 38N 17 12 E
Olonets, Russia 24 B5 61 0N 32 54 E
Olongapo, Phil. 37 B6 14 50N 120 18 E
Olot, Spain 19 A7 42 11N 2 30 E
Olovyannaya, Russia 27 D12 50 58N 115 35 E
Oloy →, Russia 27 C16 66 29N 159 29 E
Olsztyn, Poland 17 B11 53 48N 20 29 E
Olt →, Romania 17 G13 43 43N 24 51 E
Olteniţa, Romania 17 F14 44 7N 26 42 E
Olton, U.S.A. 81 H3 34 11N 102 8W
Olymbos, Cyprus 23 D12 35 21N 33 45 E
Olympia, Greece 21 F9 37 39N 21 39 E
Olympia, U.S.A. 84 D4 47 3N 122 53W
Olympic Dam, Australia 63 E2 30 30S 136 55 E
Olympic Mts., U.S.A. 84 C3 47 55N 123 45W
Olympic Nat. Park, U.S.A. 84 C3 47 48N 123 30W
Olympus, Cyprus 23 E11 34 56N 32 52 E
Olympus, Mt. = Ólimbos,
Óros, Greece 21 D10 40 6N 22 23 E
Olympus, Mt. = Uludağ,
Turkey 21 D13 40 4N 29 13 E
Olympus, Mt., U.S.A. 84 C3 47 48N 123 43W
Olyphant, U.S.A. 79 E9 41 27N 75 36W
Om →, Russia 26 D8 54 59N 73 22 E
Om Koi, Thailand 38 D2 17 48N 98 22 E
Ōma, Japan 30 D10 41 45N 141 5 E
Ōmachi, Japan 31 F8 36 30N 137 50 E
Omae-Zaki, Japan 31 G9 34 36N 138 14 E
Ōmagari, Japan 30 E10 39 27N 140 29 E
Omagh, U.K. 13 B4 54 36N 7 19W
Omagh □, U.K. 13 B4 54 35N 7 15W
Omaha, U.S.A. 80 E7 41 17N 95 58W
Omak, U.S.A. 82 B4 48 25N 119 31W
Omalos, Greece 23 D5 35 19N 23 55 E
Oman ■, Asia 46 C6 23 0N 58 0 E
Oman, G. of, Asia 45 E8 24 30N 58 30 E
Omaruru, Namibia 56 C2 21 26S 16 0 E
Omaruru →, Namibia 56 C1 22 7S 14 15 E
Omate, Peru 92 G4 16 45S 71 0W
Ombai, Selat, Indonesia 37 F6 8 30S 124 50 E
Omboué, Gabon 52 E1 1 35S 9 15 E
Ombrone →, Italy 20 C4 42 42N 11 5 E
Omdurmân, Sudan 51 E12 15 40N 32 28 E
Omemee, Canada 78 B6 44 18N 78 33W
Omeo, Australia 63 F4 37 6S 147 36 E
Omeonga,
Dem. Rep. of the Congo 54 C1 3 40S 24 22 E
Ometepe, I. de, Nic. 88 D2 11 32N 85 35W
Ometepec, Mexico 87 D5 16 39N 98 23W
Ominato, Japan 30 D10 41 17N 141 10 E
Omineca →, Canada 72 B4 56 3N 124 16W
Omitara, Namibia 56 C2 22 16S 18 2 E
Ōmiya, Japan 31 G9 35 54N 139 38 E
Ommen, Neths. 15 B6 52 31N 6 26 E
Ömnögovĭ □, Mongolia 34 C3 43 15N 104 0 E
Omo →, Ethiopia 46 F2 6 25N 36 10 E
Omodhos, Cyprus 23 E11 34 51N 32 48 E
Omolon →, Russia 27 C16 68 42N 158 36 E
Omono-Gawa →, Japan 30 E10 39 46N 140 3 E
Omsk, Russia 26 D8 55 0N 73 12 E
Omsukchan, Russia 27 C16 62 32N 155 48 E
Ōmu, Japan 30 B11 44 34N 142 58 E
Omul, Vf., Romania 17 F13 45 27N 25 29 E
Ōmura, Japan 31 H4 32 56N 129 57 E
Omuramba Omatako →,
Namibia 53 H4 17 45S 20 25 E
Ōmuta, Japan 31 H5 33 5N 130 26 E
Onaga, U.S.A. 80 F6 39 29N 96 10W
Onalaska, U.S.A. 80 D9 43 53N 91 14W
Onancock, U.S.A. 76 G8 37 43N 75 45W
Onang, Indonesia 37 E5 3 2S 118 49 E
Onaping L., Canada 70 C3 47 3N 81 30W
Onavas, Mexico 86 B3 28 28N 109 30W
Onawa, U.S.A. 80 D6 42 2N 96 6W
Oncócua, Angola 56 B1 16 30S 13 25 E
Onda, Spain 19 C5 39 55N 0 17W
Ondaejin, N. Korea 35 D15 41 34N 129 40 E
Ondangua, Namibia 56 B2 17 57S 16 4 E
Ondjiva, Angola 56 B2 16 48S 15 50 E
Öndörshil, Mongolia 34 B5 45 13N 108 5 E
Öndverðarnes, Iceland 8 D1 64 52N 24 0W
One Tree, Australia 63 E3 34 11S 144 43 E
Onega, Russia 24 B6 64 0N 38 10 E
Onega →, Russia 24 B6 63 58N 38 2 E
Onega, G. of = Onezhskaya
Guba, Russia 24 B6 64 24N 36 38 E
Onega, L. = Onezhskoye
Ozero, Russia 24 B6 61 44N 35 22 E
Onehunga, N.Z. 59 G5 36 55S 174 48 E
Oneida, U.S.A. 79 C9 43 6N 75 39W
Oneida L., U.S.A. 79 C9 43 12N 75 54W
O'Neill, U.S.A. 80 D5 42 27N 98 39W
Onekotan, Ostrov, Russia 27 E16 49 25N 154 45 E
Onema,
Dem. Rep. of the Congo 54 C1 4 35S 24 30 E
Oneonta, U.S.A. 79 D9 42 27N 75 4W
Oneşti, Romania 17 E14 46 15N 26 45 E
Onezhskaya Guba, Russia 24 B6 64 24N 36 38 E
Onezhskoye Ozero, Russia 24 B6 61 44N 35 22 E
Ongarue, N.Z. 59 H5 38 42S 175 19 E
Ongerup, Australia 61 F2 33 58S 118 28 E
Ongjin, N. Korea 35 F13 37 56N 125 21 E
Ongkharak, Thailand 38 E3 14 8N 101 1 E
Ongniud Qi, China 35 C10 43 0N 118 38 E
Ongoka,
Dem. Rep. of the Congo 54 C2 1 20S 26 0 E
Ongole, India 40 M12 15 33N 80 2 E
Ongon = Havirga, Mongolia 34 B7 45 41N 113 5 E
Onida, U.S.A. 80 C4 44 42N 100 4W
Onilahy →, Madag. 57 C7 23 34S 43 45 E
Onitsha, Nigeria 50 G7 6 6N 6 42 E
Onoda, Japan 31 G5 34 2N 131 25 E
Onpyŏng-ni, S. Korea 35 H14 33 25N 126 55 E
Onslow, Australia 60 D2 21 40S 115 12 E
Onslow B., U.S.A. 77 H7 34 20N 77 15W
Ontake-San, Japan 31 G8 35 53N 137 29 E
Ontario, Calif., U.S.A. 85 L9 34 4N 117 39W
Ontario, Oreg., U.S.A. 82 D5 44 2N 116 58W
Ontario □, Canada 70 B2 48 0N 83 0W
Ontario, L., N. Amer. 75 B11 43 20N 78 0W
Ontonagon, U.S.A. 80 B10 46 52N 89 19W
Onyx, U.S.A. 85 K8 35 41N 118 14W
Oodnadatta, Australia 63 D2 27 33S 135 30 E
Ooldea, Australia 61 F5 30 27S 131 50 E
Oombulgurri, Australia 60 C4 15 15S 127 45 E
Oorindi, Australia 62 C3 20 40S 141 1 E
Oost-Vlaanderen □, Belgium 15 C3 51 5N 3 50 E
Oostende, Belgium 15 C2 51 15N 2 54 E
Oosterhout, Neths. 15 C4 51 39N 4 47 E
Oosterschelde →, Neths. 15 C4 51 33N 4 0 E
Oosterwolde, Neths. 15 B6 53 0N 6 17 E
Ootacamund =
Udagamandalam, India 40 P10 11 30N 76 44 E
Ootsa L., Canada 72 C3 53 50N 126 2W
Opala,
Dem. Rep. of the Congo 54 C1 0 40S 24 20 E
Opanake, Sri Lanka 40 R12 6 35N 80 40 E
Opasatika, Canada 70 C3 49 30N 82 50W
Opasquia Prov. Park,
Canada 70 B1 53 33N 93 5W
Opava, Czech Rep. 17 D9 49 57N 17 58 E
Opelika, U.S.A. 77 J3 32 39N 85 23W
Opelousas, U.S.A. 81 K8 30 32N 92 5W
Opémisca, L., Canada 70 C5 49 56N 74 52W
Opheim, U.S.A. 82 B10 48 51N 106 24W
Ophthalmia Ra., Australia 60 D2 23 15S 119 30 E
Opinaca →, Canada 70 B4 52 15N 78 2W
Opinaca, Rés., Canada 70 B4 52 39N 76 20W
Opinnagau →, Canada 70 B3 54 12N 82 25W
Opiscoteo, L., Canada 71 B6 53 10N 68 10W
Opole, Poland 17 C9 50 42N 17 58 E
Oporto = Porto, Portugal 19 B1 41 8N 8 40W
Opotiki, N.Z. 59 H6 38 1S 177 19 E
Opp, U.S.A. 77 K2 31 17N 86 16W
Oppdal, Norway 9 E13 62 35N 9 41 E
Opportunity, U.S.A. 82 C5 47 39N 117 15W
Opua, N.Z. 59 F5 35 19S 174 9 E
Opunake, N.Z. 59 H4 39 26S 173 52 E
Ora, Cyprus 23 E12 34 51N 33 12 E
Oracle, U.S.A. 83 K8 32 37N 110 46W
Oradea, Romania 17 E11 47 2N 21 58 E
Öræfajökull, Iceland 8 D5 64 2N 16 39W
Orai, India 43 G8 25 58N 79 30 E
Oral = Zhayyq →,
Kazakstan 25 E9 47 0N 51 48 E
Oral, Kazakstan 25 D9 51 20N 51 20 E
Oran, Algeria 50 A5 35 45N 0 39W
Orange, Australia 63 E4 33 15S 149 7 E
Orange, France 18 D6 44 8N 4 47 E
Orange, Calif., U.S.A. 85 M9 33 47N 117 51W
Orange, Mass., U.S.A. 79 D12 42 35N 72 19W
Orange, Tex., U.S.A. 81 K8 30 6N 93 44W
Orange, Va., U.S.A. 76 F6 38 15N 78 7W
Orange →, S. Africa 56 D2 28 41S 16 28 E
Orange, C., Brazil 93 C8 4 20N 51 30W
Orange Cove, U.S.A. 84 J7 36 38N 119 19W
Orange Free State = Free
State □, S. Africa 56 D4 28 30S 27 0 E
Orange Grove, U.S.A. 81 M6 27 58N 97 56W
Orange Walk, Belize 87 D7 18 6N 88 33W
Orangeburg, U.S.A. 77 J5 33 30N 80 52W
Orangeville, Canada 78 C4 43 55N 80 5W
Oranienburg, Germany 16 B7 52 45N 13 14 E
Oranje = Orange →,
S. Africa 56 D2 28 41S 16 28 E
Oranje Vrystaat = Free
State □, S. Africa 56 D4 28 30S 27 0 E
Oranjemund, Namibia 56 D2 28 38S 16 29 E
Oranjerivier, S. Africa 56 D3 29 40S 24 12 E
Orapa, Botswana 53 J5 21 15S 25 30 E
Oras, Phil. 37 B7 12 9N 125 28 E
Oraşul Stalin = Braşov,
Romania 17 F13 45 38N 25 35 E
Orbetello, Italy 20 C4 42 27N 11 13 E
Orbisonia, U.S.A. 78 F7 40 15N 77 54W
Orbost, Australia 63 F4 37 40S 148 29 E
Orcas I., U.S.A. 84 B4 48 42N 122 56W
Orchard City, U.S.A. 83 G10 38 50N 107 58W
Orchila, I., Venezuela 89 D6 11 48N 66 10W
Orcutt, U.S.A. 85 L6 34 52N 120 27W
Ord, U.S.A. 80 E5 41 36N 98 56W
Ord →, Australia 60 C4 15 33S 128 15 E
Ord, Mt., Australia 60 C4 17 20S 125 34 E
Orderville, U.S.A. 83 H7 37 17N 112 38W
Ordos = Mu Us Shamo,
China 34 E5 39 0N 109 0 E
Ordu, Turkey 25 F6 40 55N 37 53 E
Ordway, U.S.A. 80 F3 38 13N 103 46W
Ordzhonikidze =
Vladikavkaz, Russia 25 F7 43 0N 44 35 E
Ore,
Dem. Rep. of the Congo 54 B2 3 17N 29 30 E
Ore Mts. = Erzgebirge,
Germany 16 C7 50 27N 12 55 E
Örebro, Sweden 9 G16 59 20N 15 18 E
Oregon, U.S.A. 80 D10 42 1N 89 20W
Oregon □, U.S.A. 82 E3 44 0N 121 0W
Oregon City, U.S.A. 84 E4 45 21N 122 36W
Orekhovo-Zuyevo, Russia 24 C6 55 50N 38 55 E
Orel, Russia 24 D6 52 57N 36 3 E
Orem, U.S.A. 74 B4 40 19N 111 42W
Ören, Turkey 21 F12 37 3N 27 57 E
Orenburg, Russia 24 D10 51 45N 55 6 E
Orense = Ourense, Spain 19 A2 42 19N 7 55W
Orepuki, N.Z. 59 M1 46 19S 167 46 E
Orestiás, Greece 21 D12 41 30N 26 33 E
Orestos Pereyra, Mexico 86 B3 26 31N 105 40W
Orford Ness, U.K. 11 E9 52 5N 1 35 E
Organos, Pta. de los,
Canary Is. 22 F2 28 12N 17 17W
Orgaz, Spain 19 C4 39 39N 3 53W
Orgeyev = Orhei, Moldova 17 E15 47 24N 28 50 E
Orhaneli, Turkey 21 E13 39 54N 28 59 E
Orhangazi, Turkey 21 D13 40 29N 29 18 E
Orhei, Moldova 17 E15 47 24N 28 50 E
Orhon Gol →, Mongolia 32 A5 50 21N 106 0 E
Oriental, Cordillera,
Colombia 92 B4 6 0N 73 0W
Orientale □,
Dem. Rep. of the Congo 54 B2 2 20N 26 0 E
Oriente, Argentina 94 D3 38 44S 60 37W
Orihuela, Spain 19 C5 38 7N 0 55W
Orillia, Canada 78 B5 44 40N 79 24W
Orinoco →, Venezuela 92 B6 9 15N 61 30W
Orion, Canada 73 D6 49 27N 110 49W
Oriskany, U.S.A. 79 C9 43 10N 75 20W
Orissa □, India 41 K14 20 0N 84 0 E
Orissaare, Estonia 9 G20 58 34N 23 5 E
Oristano, Italy 20 E3 39 54N 8 36 E
Oristano, G. di, Italy 20 E3 39 50N 8 29 E
Orizaba, Mexico 87 D5 18 51N 97 6W
Orkanger, Norway 8 E13 63 18N 9 52 E
Orkla →, Norway 8 E13 63 18N 9 51 E
Orkney, S. Africa 56 D4 26 58S 26 40 E
Orkney □, U.K. 12 B5 59 2N 3 13W
Orkney Is., U.K. 12 B6 59 0N 3 0W
Orland, U.S.A. 84 F4 39 45N 122 12W
Orlando, U.S.A. 77 L5 28 33N 81 23W
Orléanais, France 18 C5 48 0N 2 0 E
Orléans, France 18 C4 47 54N 1 52 E
Orleans, U.S.A. 79 B12 44 49N 72 12W
Orléans, I. d', Canada 71 C5 46 54N 70 58W
Ormara, Pakistan 40 G4 25 16N 64 33 E
Ormoc, Phil. 37 B6 11 0N 124 37 E
Ormond, N.Z. 59 H6 38 33S 177 56 E
Ormond Beach, U.S.A. 77 L5 29 17N 81 3W
Ormskirk, U.K. 10 D5 53 35N 2 54W
Ormstown, Canada 79 A11 45 8N 74 0W
Örnsköldsvik, Sweden 8 E18 63 17N 18 40 E
Oro, N. Korea 35 D14 40 1N 127 27 E
Oro →, Mexico 86 B3 25 35N 105 2W
Oro Grande, U.S.A. 85 L9 34 36N 117 20W
Oro Valley, U.S.A. 83 K8 32 26N 110 58W
Orocué, Colombia 92 C4 4 48N 71 20W
Orofino, U.S.A. 82 C5 46 29N 116 15W
Orol Dengizi = Aral Sea,
Asia 26 E7 44 30N 60 0 E
Oromocto, Canada 71 C6 45 54N 66 29W
Orono, Canada 78 C6 43 59N 78 37W
Orono, U.S.A. 77 C11 44 53N 68 40W
Oronsay, U.K. 12 E2 56 1N 6 15W
Oroqen Zizhiqi, China 33 A7 50 34N 123 43 E
Oroquieta, Phil. 37 C6 8 32N 123 44 E
Orosháza, Hungary 17 E11 46 32N 20 42 E
Orotukan, Russia 27 C16 62 16N 151 42 E
Oroville, Calif., U.S.A. 84 F5 39 31N 121 33W
Oroville, Wash., U.S.A. 82 B4 48 56N 119 26W
Oroville, L., U.S.A. 84 F5 39 33N 121 29W
Orroroo, Australia 63 E2 32 43S 138 38 E
Orrville, U.S.A. 78 F3 40 50N 81 46W
Orsha, Belarus 24 D5 54 30N 30 25 E
Orsk, Russia 26 D6 51 12N 58 34 E
Orşova, Romania 17 F12 44 41N 22 25 E
Ortaca, Turkey 21 F13 36 49N 28 45 E
Ortegal, C., Spain 19 A2 43 43N 7 52W
Orthez, France 18 E3 43 29N 0 48W
Ortigueira, Spain 19 A2 43 40N 7 50W
Orting, U.S.A. 84 C4 47 6N 122 12W
Ortles, Italy 18 C9 46 31N 10 33 E
Ortón →, Bolivia 92 F5 10 50S 67 0W
Ortonville, U.S.A. 80 C6 45 19N 96 27W
Orūmīyeh, Iran 44 B5 37 40N 45 0 E
Orūmīyeh, Daryācheh-ye,
Iran 44 B5 37 50N 45 30 E
Oruro, Bolivia 92 G5 18 0S 67 9W
Orust, Sweden 9 G14 58 10N 11 40 E
Oruzgān □, Afghan. 40 C5 33 30N 66 0 E
Orvieto, Italy 20 C5 42 43N 12 7 E
Orwell, N.Y., U.S.A. 79 C9 43 35N 75 50W
Orwell, Ohio, U.S.A. 78 E4 41 32N 80 52W
Orwell →, U.K. 11 F9 51 59N 1 18 E
Orwigsburg, U.S.A. 79 F8 40 38N 76 6W
Oryakhovo, Bulgaria 21 C10 43 40N 23 57 E
Osa, Russia 24 C10 57 17N 55 26 E
Osa, Pen. de, Costa Rica 88 E3 8 0N 84 0W
Osage, U.S.A. 80 D8 43 17N 92 49W
Osage →, U.S.A. 80 F9 38 35N 91 57W
Osage City, U.S.A. 80 F7 38 38N 95 50W
Ōsaka, Japan 31 G7 34 40N 135 30 E
Osan, S. Korea 35 F14 37 11N 127 4 E
Osawatomie, U.S.A. 80 F7 38 31N 94 57W
Osborne, U.S.A. 80 F5 39 26N 98 42W
Osceola, Ark., U.S.A. 81 H10 35 42N 89 58W
Osceola, Iowa, U.S.A. 80 E8 41 2N 93 46W
Oscoda, U.S.A. 78 B1 44 26N 83 20W
Ösel = Saaremaa, Estonia 9 G20 58 30N 22 30 E
Osgoode, Canada 79 A9 45 8N 75 36W
Osh, Kyrgyzstan 26 E8 40 37N 72 49 E
Oshakati, Namibia 53 H3 17 45S 15 40 E
Oshawa, Canada 78 C6 43 50N 78 50W
Oshkosh, Nebr., U.S.A. 80 E3 41 24N 102 21W
Oshkosh, Wis., U.S.A. 80 C10 44 1N 88 33W

151

Penn Yan

Penn Yan, U.S.A. 78 D7 42 40N 77 3W
Pennant, Canada 73 C7 50 32N 108 14W
Penner →, India 40 M12 14 35N 80 10 E
Pennines, U.K. 10 C5 54 45N 2 27W
Pennington, U.S.A. 84 F5 39 15N 121 47W
Pennsburg, U.S.A. 79 F9 40 23N 75 29W
Pennsylvania □, U.S.A. 76 E7 40 45N 77 30W
Penny, Canada 72 C4 53 51N 121 20W
Penobscot →, U.S.A. 77 C11 44 30N 68 48W
Penobscot B., U.S.A. 77 C11 44 35N 68 50W
Penola, Australia 63 F3 37 25S 140 48 E
Penong, Australia 61 F5 31 56S 133 1 E
Penonomé, Panama 88 E3 8 31N 80 21W
Penrith, Australia 63 E5 33 43S 150 38 E
Penrith, U.K. 10 C5 54 40N 2 45W
Penryn, U.K. 11 G2 50 9N 5 7W
Pensacola, U.S.A. 77 K2 30 25N 87 13W
Pensacola Mts., Antarctica 5 E1 84 0S 40 0W
Pense, Canada 73 C8 50 25N 104 59W
Penshurst, Australia 63 F3 37 49S 142 20 E
Penticton, Canada 72 D5 49 30N 119 38W
Pentland, Australia 62 C4 20 32S 145 25 E
Pentland Firth, U.K. 12 C5 58 43N 3 10W
Pentland Hills, U.K. 12 F5 55 48N 3 25W
Penza, Russia 24 D8 53 15N 45 5 E
Penzance, U.K. 11 G2 50 7N 5 33W
Penzhino, Russia 27 C17 63 30N 167 55 E
Penzhinskaya Guba, Russia 27 C17 61 30N 163 0 E
Peoria, Ariz., U.S.A. 83 K7 33 35N 112 14W
Peoria, Ill., U.S.A. 80 E10 40 42N 89 36W
Pepacton Reservoir, U.S.A. 79 D10 42 5N 74 58W
Pera Hd., Australia 62 A3 12 55S 141 37 E
Perabumulih, Indonesia 36 E2 3 27S 104 15 E
Perak →, Malaysia 39 K3 4 0N 100 50 E
Pérama, Kérkira, Greece 23 A3 39 34N 19 54 E
Pérama, Kriti, Greece 23 D6 35 20N 24 40 E
Peräpohjola, Finland 8 C22 66 16N 26 10 E
Percé, Canada 71 C7 48 31N 64 13W
Perche, Collines du, France 18 B4 48 30N 0 40 E
Percival Lakes, Australia 60 D4 21 25S 125 0 E
Percy Is., Australia 62 C5 21 39S 150 16 E
Perdido, Mte., Spain 19 A6 42 40N 0 5 E
Perdu, Mt. = Perdido, Mte., Spain 19 A6 42 40N 0 5 E
Pereira, Colombia 92 C3 4 49N 75 43W
Perenjori, Australia 61 E2 29 26S 116 16 E
Pereyaslav-Khmelnytskyy, Ukraine 25 D5 50 3N 31 28 E
Pérez, I., Mexico 87 C7 22 24N 89 42W
Pergamino, Argentina 94 C3 33 52S 60 30W
Pergau →, Malaysia 39 K3 5 23N 102 2 E
Perham, U.S.A. 80 B7 46 36N 95 34W
Perhentian, Kepulauan, Malaysia 36 C2 5 54N 102 42 E
Péribonca →, Canada 71 C5 48 45N 72 5W
Péribonca, L., Canada 71 B5 50 1N 71 10W
Perico, Argentina 94 A2 24 20S 65 5W
Pericos, Mexico 86 B3 25 3N 107 42W
Périgueux, France 18 D4 45 10N 0 42 E
Perijá, Sierra de, Colombia 92 B4 9 30N 73 3W
Peristerona →, Cyprus 23 D12 35 8N 33 5 E
Perito Moreno, Argentina 96 F2 46 36S 70 56W
Perkasie, U.S.A. 79 F9 40 22N 75 18W
Perlas, Arch. de las, Panama 88 E4 8 41N 79 7W
Perlas, Punta de, Nic. 88 D3 12 30N 83 30W
Perm, Russia 24 C10 58 0N 56 10 E
Pernambuco = Recife, Brazil 93 E12 8 0S 35 0W
Pernambuco □, Brazil 93 E11 8 0S 37 0W
Pernatty Lagoon, Australia 63 E2 31 30S 137 12 E
Pernik, Bulgaria 21 C10 42 35N 23 2 E
Peron Is., Australia 60 B5 13 9S 130 4 E
Peron Pen., Australia 61 E1 26 0S 113 10 E
Perow, Canada 72 C3 54 35N 126 10W
Perpendicular Pt., Australia 63 E5 31 37S 152 52 E
Perpignan, France 18 E5 42 42N 2 53 E
Perris, U.S.A. 85 M9 33 47N 117 14W
Perry, Fla., U.S.A. 77 K4 30 7N 83 35W
Perry, Ga., U.S.A. 77 J4 32 28N 83 44W
Perry, Iowa, U.S.A. 80 E7 41 51N 94 6W
Perry, Okla., U.S.A. 81 G6 36 17N 97 14W
Perryton, U.S.A. 81 G4 36 24N 100 48W
Perryville, U.S.A. 81 G10 37 43N 89 52W
Persepolis, Iran 45 D7 29 55N 52 50 E
Pershotravensk, Ukraine 17 C14 50 13N 27 40 E
Persia = Iran ■, Asia 45 C7 33 0N 53 0 E
Persian Gulf = Gulf, The, Asia 45 E6 27 0N 50 0 E
Perth, Australia 61 F2 31 57S 115 52 E
Perth, Canada 79 B8 44 55N 76 15W
Perth, U.K. 12 E5 56 24N 3 26W
Perth & Kinross □, U.K. 12 E5 56 45N 3 55W
Perth Amboy, U.S.A. 79 F10 40 31N 74 16W
Perth-Andover, Canada 71 C6 46 44N 67 42W
Peru, Ind., U.S.A. 76 E2 40 45N 86 4W
Peru, N.Y., U.S.A. 79 B11 44 35N 73 32W
Peru ■, S. Amer. 92 D4 4 0S 75 0W
Peru-Chile Trench, Pac. Oc. 92 G3 20 0S 72 0W
Perúgia, Italy 20 C5 43 7N 12 23 E
Pervomaysk, Ukraine 25 E5 48 10N 30 46 E
Pervouralsk, Russia 24 C10 56 59N 59 59 E
Pésaro, Italy 20 C5 43 54N 12 55 E
Pescara, Italy 20 C6 42 28N 14 13 E
Peshawar, Pakistan 42 B4 34 2N 71 37 E
Peshkopi, Albania 21 D9 41 41N 20 25 E
Peshtigo, U.S.A. 76 C2 45 4N 87 46W
Pesqueira, Brazil 93 E11 8 20S 36 42W
Petah Tiqwa, Israel 47 C3 32 6N 34 53 E
Petaling Jaya, Malaysia 39 L3 3 4N 101 42 E
Petaloudhes, Greece 23 C10 36 18N 28 5 E
Petaluma, U.S.A. 84 G4 38 14N 122 39W
Pétange, Lux. 15 E5 49 33N 5 55 E
Petaro, Pakistan 42 G3 25 31N 68 18 E
Petatlán, Mexico 86 D4 17 31N 101 16W
Petauke, Zambia 55 E3 14 14S 31 20 E
Petawawa, Canada 70 C4 45 54N 77 17W
Petén Itzá, L., Guatemala 88 C2 16 58N 89 50W
Peter I.s Øy, Antarctica 5 C16 69 0S 91 0W
Peter Pond L., Canada 73 B7 55 55N 108 44W
Peterbell, Canada 70 C3 48 36N 83 21W
Peterborough, Australia 63 E2 32 58S 138 51 E
Peterborough, Canada 78 B6 44 20N 78 20W
Peterborough, U.K. 11 E7 52 35N 0 15W
Peterborough, U.S.A. 79 D13 42 53N 71 57W
Peterborough □, U.K. 11 E7 52 35N 0 15W
Peterculter, U.K. 12 D6 57 6N 2 16W
Peterhead, U.K. 12 D7 57 31N 1 48W
Peterlee, U.K. 10 C6 54 47N 1 20W
Petermann Bjerg, Greenland 66 B17 73 7N 28 25W
Petermann Ranges, Australia 60 E5 26 0S 130 30 E
Petersburg, Alaska, U.S.A. 68 C6 56 48N 132 58W
Petersburg, Pa., U.S.A. 78 F6 40 34N 78 3W
Petersburg, Va., U.S.A. 76 G7 37 14N 77 24W
Petersburg, W. Va., U.S.A. 76 F6 39 1N 79 5W
Petersfield, U.K. 11 F7 51 1N 0 56W
Petit Goâve, Haiti 89 C5 18 27N 72 51W
Petit Jardin, Canada 71 C8 48 28N 59 14W
Petit Lac Manicouagan, Canada 71 B6 51 25N 67 40W
Petit-Mécatina →, Canada 71 B8 50 40N 59 30W
Petit-Mécatina, I. du, Canada 71 B8 50 30N 59 25W
Petitcodiac, Canada 71 C6 45 57N 65 11W
Petite Baleine →, Canada 70 A4 56 0N 76 45W
Petite Saguenay, Canada 71 C5 48 15N 70 4W
Petitot →, Canada 72 A4 60 14N 123 29W
Petitsikapau L., Canada 71 B6 54 37N 66 25W
Petlad, India 42 H5 22 30N 72 45 E
Peto, Mexico 87 C7 20 10N 88 53W
Petone, N.Z. 59 J5 41 13S 174 53 E
Petorca, Chile 94 C1 32 15S 70 56W
Petoskey, U.S.A. 76 C3 45 22N 84 57W
Petra, Jordan 47 E4 30 20N 35 22 E
Petra, Spain 22 B10 39 37N 3 6 E
Petra, Ostrova, Russia 4 B13 76 15N 118 30 E
Petra Velikogo, Zaliv, Russia 30 C6 42 40N 132 0 E
Petrich, Bulgaria 21 D10 41 24N 23 13 E
Petrified Forest National Park, U.S.A. 83 J9 35 0N 109 30W
Petrikov = Pyetrikaw, Belarus 17 B15 52 11N 28 29 E
Petrograd = Sankt-Peterburg, Russia 24 C5 59 55N 30 20 E
Petrolândia, Brazil 93 E11 9 5S 38 20W
Petrolia, Canada 78 D2 42 54N 82 9W
Petrolina, Brazil 93 E10 9 24S 40 30W
Petropavl, Kazakstan 26 D7 54 53N 69 13 E
Petropavlovsk = Petropavl, Kazakstan 26 D7 54 53N 69 13 E
Petropavlovsk-Kamchatskiy, Russia 27 D16 53 3N 158 43 E
Petrópolis, Brazil 95 A7 22 33S 43 9W
Petroşani, Romania 17 F12 45 28N 23 20 E
Petrovaradin, Serbia, Yug. 21 B8 45 16N 19 55 E
Petrovsk, Russia 24 D8 52 22N 45 19 E
Petrovsk-Zabaykalskiy, Russia 27 D11 51 20N 108 55 E
Petrozavodsk, Russia 24 B5 61 41N 34 20 E
Petrus Steyn, S. Africa 57 D4 27 38S 28 8 E
Petrusburg, S. Africa 56 D4 29 4S 25 26 E
Peumo, Chile 94 C1 34 21S 71 12W
Peureulak, Indonesia 36 D1 4 48N 97 45 E
Pevek, Russia 27 C18 69 41N 171 19 E
Pforzheim, Germany 16 D5 48 52N 8 41 E
Phagwara, India 40 D9 31 10N 75 40 E
Phaistós, Greece 23 D6 35 2N 24 50 E
Phala, Botswana 56 C4 23 45S 26 50 E
Phalera = Phulera, India 42 F6 26 52N 75 16 E
Phalodi, India 42 F5 27 12N 72 24 E
Phan, Thailand 38 C2 19 28N 99 43 E
Phan Rang, Vietnam 39 G7 11 34N 109 0 E
Phan Ri = Hoa Da, Vietnam 39 G7 11 16N 108 40 E
Phan Thiet, Vietnam 39 G7 11 1N 108 9 E
Phanat Nikhom, Thailand 38 F3 13 27N 101 11 E
Phangan, Ko, Thailand 39 H3 9 45N 100 0 E
Phangnga, Thailand 39 H2 8 28N 98 30 E
Phanh Bho Ho Chi Minh, Vietnam 39 G6 10 58N 106 40 E
Phanom Sarakham, Thailand 38 F3 13 45N 101 21 E
Phaphund, India 43 F8 26 36N 79 28 E
Pharenda, India 43 F10 27 5N 83 17 E
Pharr, U.S.A. 81 M5 26 12N 98 11W
Phatthalung, Thailand 39 J3 7 39N 100 6 E
Phayao, Thailand 38 C2 19 11N 99 55 E
Phelps, U.S.A. 78 D7 42 58N 77 3W
Phelps L., Canada 73 B8 59 15N 103 15W
Phenix City, U.S.A. 77 J3 32 28N 85 0W
Phet Buri, Thailand 38 F2 13 1N 99 55 E
Phetchabun, Thailand 38 D3 16 25N 101 8 E
Phetchabun, Thiu Khao, Thailand 38 E3 16 0N 101 20 E
Phetchaburi = Phet Buri, Thailand 38 F2 13 1N 99 55 E
Phi Phi, Ko, Thailand 39 J2 7 45N 98 46 E
Phiafay, Laos 38 E6 14 48N 106 0 E
Phibun Mangsahan, Thailand 38 E5 15 14N 105 14 E
Phichai, Thailand 38 D3 17 22N 100 10 E
Phichit, Thailand 38 D3 16 26N 100 22 E
Philadelphia, Miss., U.S.A. 81 J10 32 46N 89 7W
Philadelphia, N.Y., U.S.A. 79 B9 44 9N 75 43W
Philadelphia, Pa., U.S.A. 79 G9 39 57N 75 10W
Philip, U.S.A. 80 C4 44 2N 101 40W
Philippeville, Belgium 15 D4 50 12N 4 33 E
Philippi, U.S.A. 76 F5 39 9N 80 3W
Philippi L., Australia 62 C2 24 20S 138 55 E
Philippines ■, Asia 37 B6 12 0N 123 0 E
Philippolis, S. Africa 56 E4 30 15S 25 16 E
Philippopolis = Plovdiv, Bulgaria 21 C11 42 8N 24 44 E
Philipsburg, Canada 79 A11 45 2N 73 5W
Philipsburg, Mont., U.S.A. 82 C7 46 20N 113 18W
Philipsburg, Pa., U.S.A. 78 F6 40 54N 78 13W
Philipstown = Daingean, Ireland 13 C4 53 18N 7 17W
Philipstown, S. Africa 56 E3 30 28S 24 30 E
Phillip I., Australia 63 F4 38 30S 145 12 E
Phillips, U.S.A. 80 C9 45 42N 90 24W
Phillipsburg, Kans., U.S.A. 80 F5 39 45N 99 19W
Phillipsburg, N.J., U.S.A. 79 F9 40 42N 75 12W
Philmont, U.S.A. 79 D11 42 15N 73 39W
Philomath, U.S.A. 82 D2 44 32N 123 22W
Phimai, Thailand 38 E4 15 13N 102 30 E
Phitsanulok, Thailand 38 D3 16 50N 100 12 E
Phnom Dangrek, Thailand 36 B2 14 20N 104 0 E
Phnom Penh, Cambodia 39 G5 11 33N 104 55 E
Phnum Penh = Phnom Penh, Cambodia 39 G5 11 33N 104 55 E
Phoenicia, U.S.A. 79 D10 42 5N 74 14W
Phoenix, Ariz., U.S.A. 83 K7 33 27N 112 4W
Phoenix, N.Y., U.S.A. 79 C8 43 14N 76 18W
Phoenix Is., Kiribati 64 H10 3 30S 172 0W
Phoenixville, U.S.A. 79 F9 40 8N 75 31W
Phon, Thailand 38 E4 15 49N 102 36 E
Phon Tiou, Laos 38 D5 17 53N 104 37 E
Phong →, Thailand 38 D4 16 23N 102 56 E
Phong Tho, Vietnam 38 A4 22 32N 103 21 E
Phonhong, Laos 38 C4 18 30N 102 25 E
Phonum, Thailand 39 H2 8 49N 98 48 E
Phosphate Hill, Australia 62 C2 21 53S 139 58 E
Photharam, Thailand 38 F2 13 41N 99 51 E
Phra Nakhon Si Ayutthaya, Thailand 38 E3 14 25N 100 30 E
Phra Thong, Ko, Thailand 39 H2 9 5N 98 17 E
Phrae, Thailand 38 C3 18 7N 100 9 E
Phrom Phiram, Thailand 38 D3 17 2N 100 12 E
Phu Dien, Vietnam 38 C5 18 58N 105 31 E
Phu Loi, Laos 38 B4 20 14N 103 14 E
Phu Quoc, Dao, Vietnam 39 G4 10 20N 104 0 E
Phuket, Thailand 39 J2 7 52N 98 22 E
Phuket, Ko, Thailand 39 J2 8 0N 98 22 E
Phul, India 42 D6 30 19N 75 14 E
Phulad, India 42 G5 25 38N 73 49 E
Phulchari, Bangla. 43 G13 25 11N 89 37 E
Phulera, India 42 F6 26 52N 75 16 E
Phulpur, India 43 G10 25 31N 82 49 E
Phun Phin, Thailand 39 H2 9 7N 99 12 E
Piacenza, Italy 18 D8 45 1N 9 40 E
Pian Cr. →, Australia 63 E4 30 2S 148 12 E
Pianosa, Italy 20 C4 42 35N 10 5 E
Piapot, Canada 73 D7 49 59N 109 8W
Piatra Neamţ, Romania 17 E14 46 56N 26 21 E
Piauí □, Brazil 93 E10 7 0S 43 0W
Piaui →, Brazil 93 E10 6 38S 42 42W
Piave →, Italy 20 B5 45 32N 12 44 E
Pibor Post, Sudan 51 G12 6 47N 33 3 E
Picardie, France 18 B5 49 50N 3 0 E
Picardy = Picardie, France 18 B5 49 50N 3 0 E
Picayune, U.S.A. 81 K10 30 32N 89 41W
Pichhor, India 43 G8 25 58N 78 20 E
Pichilemu, Chile 94 C1 34 22S 72 0W
Pichor, India 42 G8 25 11N 78 11 E
Pickerel L., Canada 70 C1 48 40N 91 25W
Pickering, U.K. 10 C7 54 15N 0 46W
Pickering, Vale of, U.K. 10 C7 54 14N 0 45W
Pickle Lake, Canada 70 B1 51 30N 90 12W
Pickwick L., U.S.A. 77 H1 35 4N 88 15W
Pico Truncado, Argentina 96 F3 46 40S 68 0W
Picos, Brazil 93 E10 7 5S 41 28W
Picton, Australia 63 E5 34 12S 150 34 E
Picton, Canada 78 B7 44 1N 77 9W
Picton, N.Z. 59 J5 41 18S 174 3 E
Pictou, Canada 71 C7 45 41N 62 42W
Picture Butte, Canada 72 D6 49 55N 112 45W
Picún Leufú, Argentina 96 D3 39 30S 69 5W
Pidurutalagala, Sri Lanka 40 R12 7 10N 80 50 E
Piedmont = Piemonte □, Italy 18 D7 45 0N 8 0 E
Piedmont, Ala., U.S.A. 77 J3 33 55N 85 37W
Piedmont, S.C., U.S.A. 75 D10 34 0N 81 30W
Piedras Negras, Mexico 86 B4 28 42N 100 31W
Pieksämäki, Finland 9 E22 62 18N 27 10 E
Piemonte □, Italy 18 D7 45 0N 8 0 E
Piercefield, U.S.A. 79 B10 44 13N 74 35W
Pierceland, Canada 73 C7 54 20N 109 46W
Pierpont, U.S.A. 78 E4 41 45N 80 34W
Pierre, U.S.A. 80 C4 44 22N 100 21W
Piet Retief, S. Africa 57 D5 27 1S 30 50 E
Pietarsaari, Finland 8 E20 63 40N 22 43 E
Pietermaritzburg, S. Africa 57 D5 29 35S 30 25 E
Pietersburg, S. Africa 57 C4 23 54S 29 25 E
Pietrosul, Vf., Maramureş, Romania 17 E13 47 35N 24 43 E
Pietrosul, Vf., Suceava, Romania 17 E13 47 12N 25 18 E
Pigeon L., Canada 78 B6 44 27N 78 30W
Piggott, U.S.A. 81 G9 36 23N 90 11W
Pigüe, Argentina 94 D3 37 36S 62 25W
Pihani, India 43 F9 27 36N 80 15 E
Pihlajavesi, Finland 9 F23 61 45N 28 45 E
Pijijiapan, Mexico 87 D6 15 42N 93 14W
Pikangikum Berens, Canada 73 C10 51 49N 94 0W
Pikes Peak, U.S.A. 80 F2 38 50N 105 3W
Piketberg, S. Africa 56 E2 32 55S 18 40 E
Pikeville, U.S.A. 76 G4 37 29N 82 31W
Pikou, China 35 E12 39 18N 122 22 E
Pikwitonei, Canada 73 B9 55 35N 97 9W
Piła, Poland 17 B9 53 10N 16 48 E
Pilani, India 42 E6 28 22N 75 33 E
Pilar, Paraguay 94 B4 26 50S 58 20W
Pilaya →, Bolivia 92 H6 20 55S 64 4W
Pilbara, Australia 60 D2 23 35S 117 25 E
Pilcomayo →, Paraguay 94 B4 25 21S 57 42W
Pilibhit, India 43 E8 28 40N 79 50 E
Pilica →, Poland 17 C11 51 52N 21 17 E
Pilkhawa, India 42 E7 28 43N 77 42 E
Pilliga, Australia 63 E4 30 21S 148 54 E
Pílos, Greece 21 F9 36 55N 21 42 E
Pilot Mound, Canada 73 D9 49 15N 98 54W
Pilot Point, U.S.A. 81 J6 33 24N 96 58W
Pilot Rock, U.S.A. 82 D4 45 29N 118 50W
Pilsen = Plzeň, Czech Rep. 16 D7 49 45N 13 22 E
Pima, U.S.A. 83 K9 32 54N 109 50W
Pimba, Australia 63 E2 31 18S 136 46 E
Pimenta Bueno, Brazil 92 F6 11 35S 61 10W
Pimentel, Peru 92 E3 6 45S 79 55W
Pinang, Malaysia 39 K3 5 25N 100 15 E
Pinar, C. des, Spain 22 B10 39 53N 3 12 E
Pinar del Río, Cuba 88 B3 22 26N 83 40W
Pınarhisar, Turkey 21 D12 41 37N 27 30 E
Pinatubo, Phil. 37 A6 15 8N 120 21 E
Pincher Creek, Canada 72 D6 49 30N 113 57W
Pinchi L., Canada 72 C4 54 38N 124 30W
Pinckneyville, U.S.A. 80 F10 38 5N 89 23W
Pińczów, Poland 17 C11 50 32N 20 32 E
Pindar, Australia 61 E2 28 30S 115 47 E
Pindi Gheb, Pakistan 42 C5 33 14N 72 21 E
Pindos Óros, Greece 21 E9 40 0N 21 0 E
Pindus Mts. = Pindos Óros, Greece 21 E9 40 0N 21 0 E
Pine →, B.C., Canada 72 B4 56 8N 120 43W
Pine →, Sask., Canada 73 B7 58 50N 105 38W
Pine, C., Canada 71 C9 46 37N 53 32W
Pine Bluff, U.S.A. 81 H9 34 13N 92 1W
Pine Bluffs, U.S.A. 80 E2 41 11N 104 4W
Pine City, U.S.A. 80 C8 45 50N 92 59W
Pine Cr. →, U.S.A. 78 E7 41 10N 77 16W
Pine Creek, Australia 60 B5 13 50S 131 50 E
Pine Falls, Canada 73 C9 50 34N 96 11W
Pine Flat Res., U.S.A. 84 J7 36 50N 119 20W
Pine Grove, U.S.A. 79 F8 40 33N 76 23W
Pine Pass, Canada 72 B4 55 25N 122 42W
Pine Point, Canada 72 A6 60 50N 114 28W
Pine Ridge, U.S.A. 80 D3 43 2N 102 33W
Pine River, Canada 73 C8 51 45N 100 30W
Pine River, U.S.A. 80 B7 46 43N 94 24W
Pine Valley, U.S.A. 85 N10 32 50N 116 32W
Pinecrest, U.S.A. 84 G6 38 12N 120 1W
Pinedale, Calif., U.S.A. 84 J7 36 50N 119 48W
Pinedale, Wyo., U.S.A. 82 E9 42 52N 109 52W
Pinega →, Russia 24 B8 64 30N 44 19 E
Pinehill, Australia 62 C4 23 38S 146 57 E
Pinehouse L., Canada 73 B7 55 32N 106 35W
Pineimuta →, Canada 70 B1 52 8N 88 33W
Pinerolo, Italy 18 D7 44 53N 7 21 E
Pinetop, U.S.A. 83 J9 34 8N 109 56W
Pinetown, S. Africa 57 D5 29 48S 30 54 E
Pineville, U.S.A. 81 K8 31 19N 92 26W
Ping →, Thailand 38 E3 15 42N 100 9 E
Pingaring, Australia 61 F2 32 40S 118 32 E
Pingding, China 34 F7 37 47N 113 38 E
Pingdingshan, China 34 H7 33 43N 113 27 E
Pingdong, Taiwan 33 D7 22 39N 120 30 E
Pingdu, China 35 F10 36 42N 119 59 E
Pingelly, Australia 61 F2 32 32S 117 5 E
Pingliang, China 34 G4 35 35N 106 31 E
Pinglu, China 34 E7 39 31N 112 30 E
Pingluo, China 34 E4 38 52N 106 30 E
Pingquan, China 35 D10 41 1N 118 37 E
Pingrup, Australia 61 F2 33 32S 118 29 E
P'ingtung, Taiwan 33 D7 22 38N 120 30 E
Pingwu, China 34 H3 32 25N 104 30 E
Pingxiang, China 32 D5 22 6N 106 46 E
Pingyao, China 34 F7 37 12N 112 10 E
Pingyi, China 35 G9 35 30N 117 35 E
Pingyin, China 34 F9 36 20N 116 25 E
Pingyuan, China 34 F9 37 10N 116 22 E
Pinhal, Brazil 95 A6 22 10S 46 46W
Pinheiro, Brazil 93 D9 2 31S 45 5W
Pinheiro Machado, Brazil 95 C5 31 34S 53 23W
Pinhel, Portugal 19 B2 40 50N 7 1W
Pini, Indonesia 36 D1 0 10N 98 40 E
Piniós →, Greece 21 E10 39 55N 22 41 E
Pinjarra, Australia 61 F2 32 37S 115 52 E
Pink Mountain, Canada 72 B4 57 3N 122 52W
Pinnacles, U.S.A. 84 J5 36 33N 121 19W
Pinnaroo, Australia 63 F3 35 17S 140 53 E
Pinnes, Ákra, Greece 21 D11 40 5N 24 20 E
Pinon Hills, U.S.A. 85 L9 34 26N 117 39W
Pinos, Mexico 86 C4 22 20N 101 40W
Pinos, Mt., U.S.A. 85 L7 34 49N 119 8W
Pinos Pt., U.S.A. 83 H3 36 38N 121 57W
Pinotepa Nacional, Mexico 87 D5 16 19N 98 3W
Pinrang, Indonesia 37 E5 3 46S 119 41 E
Pins, Pte. aux, Canada 78 D3 42 15N 81 51W
Pinsk, Belarus 17 B14 52 10N 26 1 E
Pintados, Chile 92 H5 20 35S 69 40W
Pinyug, Russia 24 B8 60 5N 48 0 E
Pioche, U.S.A. 83 H6 37 56N 114 27W
Piombino, Italy 20 C4 42 55N 10 32 E
Pioner, Ostrov, Russia 27 B10 79 50N 92 0 E
Piorini, L., Brazil 92 D6 3 15S 62 35W
Piotrków Trybunalski, Poland 17 C10 51 23N 19 43 E
Pīp, Iran 45 E9 26 45N 60 10 E
Pipar, India 42 F5 26 25N 73 31 E
Pipar Road, India 42 F5 26 27N 73 27 E
Piparia, Mad. P., India 42 H8 22 45N 78 23 E
Piparia, Mad. P., India 42 J7 21 49N 77 37 E
Pipestone, U.S.A. 80 D6 44 0N 96 19W
Pipestone →, Canada 70 B2 52 53N 89 23W
Pipestone Cr. →, Canada 73 D8 49 38N 100 15W
Piplan, Pakistan 42 C4 32 17N 71 21 E
Piploda, India 42 H6 23 37N 74 56 E
Pipmuacan, Rés., Canada 71 C5 49 45N 70 30W
Pippingarra, Australia 60 D2 20 27S 118 42 E
Piqua, U.S.A. 76 E3 40 9N 84 15W
Piquiri →, Brazil 95 A5 24 3S 54 14W
Pīr Sohrāb, Iran 45 E9 25 44N 60 54 E
Piracicaba, Brazil 95 A6 22 45S 47 40W
Piracuruca, Brazil 93 D10 3 50S 41 50W
Piræus = Piraiévs, Greece 21 F10 37 57N 23 42 E
Piraiévs, Greece 21 F10 37 57N 23 42 E
Pirajuí, Brazil 95 A6 21 59S 49 29W
Piram I., India 42 J5 21 36N 72 21 E
Pirané, Argentina 94 B4 25 42S 59 6W
Pirapora, Brazil 93 G10 17 20S 44 56W
Pirawa, India 42 G7 24 10N 76 2 E
Pírgos, Greece 21 F9 37 40N 21 27 E
Piribebuy, Paraguay 94 B4 25 26S 57 2W
Pirimapun, Indonesia 37 F9 6 45S 138 0 E
Pirin Planina, Bulgaria 21 D10 41 40N 23 30 E
Pírineos = Pyrénées, Europe 18 E4 42 45N 0 18 E
Piripiri, Brazil 93 D10 4 15S 41 46W
Pirmasens, Germany 16 D4 49 12N 7 36 E
Pirot, Serbia, Yug. 21 C10 43 9N 22 33 E
Piru, Indonesia 37 E7 3 4S 128 12 E
Piru, U.S.A. 85 L8 34 25N 118 48W
Pisa, Italy 20 C4 43 43N 10 23 E
Pisagua, Chile 92 G4 19 40S 70 15W
Pisco, Peru 92 F3 13 50S 76 12W
Písek, Czech Rep. 16 D8 49 19N 14 10 E
Pishan, China 32 C2 37 30N 78 33 E
Pīshīn, Iran 45 E9 26 6N 61 47 E
Pishin, Pakistan 42 D2 30 35N 67 0 E
Pishin Lora →, Pakistan 42 E1 29 9N 64 5 E
Pising, Indonesia 37 F6 5 8S 121 53 E
Pismo Beach, U.S.A. 85 K6 35 9N 120 38W
Pissis, Cerro, Argentina 94 B2 27 45S 68 48W
Pissouri, Cyprus 23 E11 34 40N 32 42 E
Pistóia, Italy 20 C4 43 55N 10 54 E
Pistol B., Canada 73 A10 62 25N 92 37W
Pisuerga →, Spain 19 B3 41 33N 4 52W
Pit →, U.S.A. 82 F2 40 47N 122 6W
Pitarpunga, L., Australia 63 E3 34 24S 143 30 E
Pitcairn I., Pac. Oc. 65 K14 25 5S 130 5W
Pite älv →, Sweden 8 D19 65 20N 21 25 E
Piteå, Sweden 8 D19 65 20N 21 25 E
Piteşti, Romania 17 F13 44 52N 24 54 E
Pithapuram, India 41 L13 17 10N 82 15 E
Pithara, Australia 61 F2 30 20S 116 35 E
Pithoragarh, India 43 E9 29 35N 80 13 E
Pithoro, Pakistan 42 G3 25 31N 69 23 E
Pitlochry, U.K. 12 E5 56 42N 3 44W

Q

Râs Timirist

Qal'at al Akhḍar, Si. Arabia 44 E3 28 0N 37 10 E
Qal'at Dīzah, Iraq 44 B5 36 11N 45 7 E
Qal'at Şaliḥ, Iraq 44 D5 31 31N 47 16 E
Qal'at Sukkar, Iraq 44 D5 31 51N 46 5 E
Qal'eh Shaharak, Afghan. 40 B4 34 10N 64 20 E
Qamdo, China 32 C4 31 15N 97 6 E
Qamruddin Karez, Pakistan 42 D3 31 45N 68 20 E
Qandahār, Afghan. 40 D4 31 32N 65 30 E
Qandahār □, Afghan. 40 D4 31 0N 65 0 E
Qapān, Iran 45 B7 37 40N 55 47 E
Qapshaghay, Kazakstan 26 E8 43 51N 77 14 E
Qaqortoq = Julianehåb, Greenland 4 C5 60 43N 46 0W
Qara Qash →, India 43 B8 35 0N 78 30 E
Qarabutaq, Kazakstan 26 E7 49 59N 60 14 E
Qaraghandy, Kazakstan 26 E8 49 50N 73 10 E
Qārah, Si. Arabia 44 D4 29 55N 40 3 E
Qarataū, Kazakstan 26 E8 43 10N 70 28 E
Qareh →, Iran 44 B5 39 25N 47 22 E
Qareh Tekān, Iran 45 B6 36 38N 49 29 E
Qarqan He →, China 32 C3 39 30N 88 30 E
Qarqaraly, Kazakstan 26 E8 49 26N 75 30 E
Qarshi, Uzbekistan 26 F7 38 53N 65 48 E
Qartabā, Lebanon 47 A4 34 4N 35 50 E
Qaryat al Gharab, Iraq 44 D5 31 27N 44 48 E
Qaryat al 'Ulyā, Si. Arabia 44 E5 27 33N 47 42 E
Qasr 'Amra, Jordan 44 D3 31 48N 36 35 E
Qaşr-e Qand, Iran 45 E9 26 15N 60 45 E
Qasr Farâfra, Egypt 51 C11 27 0N 28 1 E
Qatanā, Syria 47 B5 33 26N 36 4 E
Qatar ■, Asia 45 E6 25 30N 51 15 E
Qatlīsh, Iran 45 B8 37 50N 57 19 E
Qattâra, Munkhafed el, Egypt 51 C11 29 30N 27 30 E
Qattâra Depression = Qattâra, Munkhafed el, Egypt 51 C11 29 30N 27 30 E
Qawām al Ḥamzah, Iraq 44 D5 31 43N 44 58 E
Qāyen, Iran 45 C8 33 40N 59 10 E
Qazaqstan = Kazakstan ■, Asia 26 E8 50 0N 70 0 E
Qazimämmäd, Azerbaijan 45 A6 40 3N 49 0 E
Qazvin, Iran 45 B6 36 15N 50 0 E
Qena, Egypt 51 C12 26 10N 32 43 E
Qeqertarsuaq = Disko, Greenland 4 C5 69 45N 53 30W
Qeqertarsuaq = Godhavn, Greenland 4 C5 69 15N 53 38W
Qeshlāq, Iran 44 C5 34 55N 46 28 E
Qeshm, Iran 45 E8 26 55N 56 10 E
Qeys, Iran 45 E7 26 32N 53 58 E
Qezel Owzen →, Iran 45 B6 36 45N 49 22 E
Qezi'ot, Israel 47 E3 30 52N 34 26 E
Qi Xian, China 34 G8 34 40N 114 48 E
Qian Gorlos, China 35 B13 45 5N 124 42 E
Qian Xian, China 34 G5 34 31N 108 15 E
Qianyang, China 34 G4 34 40N 107 8 E
Qibā', Si. Arabia 44 E5 27 24N 44 20 E
Qikiqtarjuaq, Canada 69 B13 67 33N 63 0W
Qila Safed, Pakistan 40 E2 29 0N 61 30 E
Qila Saifullāh, Pakistan 42 D3 30 45N 68 17 E
Qilian Shan, China 32 C4 38 30N 96 0 E
Qin He →, China 34 G7 35 1N 113 22 E
Qin Ling = Qinling Shandi, China 34 H5 33 50N 108 10 E
Qin'an, China 34 G3 34 48N 105 40 E
Qing Xian, China 34 E9 38 35N 116 45 E
Qingcheng, China 35 F9 37 15N 117 40 E
Qingdao, China 35 F11 36 5N 120 20 E
Qingfeng, China 34 G8 35 52N 115 8 E
Qinghai □, China 32 C4 36 0N 98 0 E
Qinghai Hu, China 32 C5 36 40N 100 10 E
Qinghecheng, China 35 D13 41 28N 124 15 E
Qinghemen, China 35 D11 41 48N 121 25 E
Qingjian, China 34 F6 37 8N 110 8 E
Qingjiang = Huaiyin, China 35 H10 33 30N 119 2 E
Qingshui, China 34 G4 34 48N 106 8 E
Qingshuihe, China 34 E6 39 55N 111 35 E
Qingtongxia Shuiku, China 34 F3 37 50N 105 58 E
Qingxu, China 34 F7 37 34N 112 22 E
Qingyang, China 34 F4 36 2N 107 55 E
Qingyuan, China 35 C13 42 10N 124 55 E
Qingyun, China 35 F9 37 45N 117 20 E
Qinhuangdao, China 35 E10 39 56N 119 30 E
Qinling Shandi, China 34 H5 33 50N 108 10 E
Qinshui, China 34 G7 35 40N 112 8 E
Qinyang = Jiyuan, China 34 G7 35 7N 112 57 E
Qinyuan, China 34 F7 36 29N 112 20 E
Qinzhou, China 32 D5 21 58N 108 38 E
Qionghai, China 38 C8 19 15N 110 26 E
Qiongzhou Haixia, China 38 B8 20 10N 110 15 E
Qiqihar, China 27 E13 47 26N 124 0 E
Qiraîya, W. →, Egypt 47 E3 30 27N 34 0 E
Qiryat Ata, Israel 47 C4 32 47N 35 6 E
Qiryat Gat, Israel 47 D3 31 32N 34 46 E
Qiryat Mal'akhi, Israel 47 D3 31 44N 34 44 E
Qiryat Shemona, Israel 47 B4 33 13N 35 35 E
Qiryat Yam, Israel 47 C4 32 51N 35 4 E
Qishan, China 34 G4 34 25N 107 38 E
Qitai, China 32 B3 44 2N 89 35 E
Qixia, China 35 F11 37 17N 120 52 E
Qızılağac Körfäzi, Azerbaijan 45 B6 39 9N 49 0 E
Qojūr, Iran 44 B5 36 12N 47 55 E
Qom, Iran 45 C6 34 40N 51 0 E
Qomolangma Feng = Everest, Mt., Nepal 43 E12 28 5N 86 58 E
Qomsheh, Iran 45 D6 32 0N 51 55 E
Qostanay, Kazakstan 26 D7 53 10N 63 35 E
Quabbin Reservoir, U.S.A. 79 D12 42 20N 72 20W
Quairading, Australia 61 F2 32 0S 117 21 E
Quakertown, U.S.A. 79 F9 40 26N 75 21W
Qualicum Beach, Canada 72 D4 49 22N 124 26W
Quambatook, Australia 63 F3 35 49S 143 34 E
Quambone, Australia 63 E4 30 57S 147 53 E
Quamby, Australia 62 C3 20 22S 140 17 E
Quan Long = Ca Mau, Vietnam 39 H5 9 7N 105 8 E
Quanah, U.S.A. 81 H5 34 18N 99 44W
Quang Ngai, Vietnam 38 E7 15 13N 108 58 E
Quang Tri, Vietnam 38 D6 16 45N 107 13 E
Quantock Hills, U.K. 11 F4 51 8N 3 10W
Quanzhou, China 33 D6 24 55N 118 34 E
Qu'Appelle, Canada 73 C8 50 33N 103 53W
Quaqtaq, Canada 69 B13 60 55N 69 40W
Quaraí, Brazil 94 C4 30 15S 56 20W
Quartu Sant'Élena, Italy 20 E3 39 15N 9 10 E
Quartzsite, U.S.A. 85 M12 33 40N 114 13W
Quatsino Sd., Canada 72 C3 50 25N 127 58W
Quba, Azerbaijan 25 F8 41 21N 48 32 E
Qūchān, Iran 45 B8 37 10N 58 27 E
Queanbeyan, Australia 63 F4 35 17S 149 14 E
Québec, Canada 71 C5 46 52N 71 13W
Québec □, Canada 71 C6 48 0N 74 0W
Queen Alexandra Ra., Antarctica 5 E11 85 0S 170 0 E
Queen Charlotte City, Canada 72 C2 53 15N 132 2W
Queen Charlotte Is., Canada 72 C2 53 20N 132 10W
Queen Charlotte Sd., Canada 72 C3 51 0N 128 0W
Queen Charlotte Strait, Canada 72 C3 50 45N 127 10W
Queen Elizabeth Is., Canada 66 B10 76 0N 95 0W
Queen Elizabeth Nat. Park, Uganda 54 C3 0 0 30 0 E
Queen Mary Land, Antarctica 5 D7 70 0S 95 0 E
Queen Maud G., Canada 68 B9 68 15N 102 30W
Queen Maud Land, Antarctica 5 D3 72 30S 12 0 E
Queen Maud Mts., Antarctica 5 E13 86 0S 160 0W
Queens Chan., Australia 60 C4 15 0S 129 30 E
Queenscliff, Australia 63 F3 38 16S 144 39 E
Queensland □, Australia 62 C3 22 0S 142 0 E
Queenstown, Australia 62 G4 42 4S 145 35 E
Queenstown, N.Z. 59 L2 45 1S 168 40 E
Queenstown, S. Africa 56 E4 31 52S 26 52 E
Queets, U.S.A. 84 C2 47 32N 124 20W
Queguay Grande →, Uruguay 94 C4 32 9S 58 9W
Queimadas, Brazil 93 F11 11 0S 39 38W
Quelimane, Mozam. 55 F4 17 53S 36 58 E
Quellón, Chile 96 E2 43 7S 73 37W
Quelpart = Cheju do, S. Korea 35 H14 33 29N 126 34 E
Quemado, N. Mex., U.S.A. 83 J9 34 20N 108 30W
Quemado, Tex., U.S.A. 81 L4 28 58N 100 35W
Quemú-Quemú, Argentina 94 D3 36 3S 63 36W
Quequén, Argentina 94 D4 38 30S 58 30W
Querétaro, Mexico 86 C4 20 36N 100 23W
Querétaro □, Mexico 86 C5 20 30N 100 0W
Queshan, China 34 H8 32 55N 114 2 E
Quesnel, Canada 72 C4 53 0N 122 30W
Quesnel →, Canada 72 C4 52 58N 122 29W
Quesnel L., Canada 72 C4 52 30N 121 20W
Questa, U.S.A. 83 H11 36 42N 105 36W
Quetico Prov. Park, Canada 70 C1 48 30N 91 45W
Quetta, Pakistan 42 D2 30 15N 66 55 E
Quezaltenango, Guatemala 88 D1 14 50N 91 30W
Quezon City, Phil. 37 B6 14 38N 121 0 E
Qufār, Si. Arabia 44 E4 27 26N 41 37 E
Qui Nhon, Vietnam 38 F7 13 40N 109 13 E
Quibaxe, Angola 52 F2 8 24S 14 27 E
Quibdo, Colombia 92 B3 5 42N 76 40W
Quiberon, France 18 C2 47 29N 3 9W
Quiet L., Canada 72 A2 61 5N 133 5W
Quiindy, Paraguay 94 B4 25 58S 57 14W
Quila, Mexico 86 C3 24 23N 107 13W
Quilán, C., Chile 96 E2 43 15S 74 30W
Quilcene, U.S.A. 84 C4 47 49N 122 53W
Quilimarí, Chile 94 C1 32 5S 71 30W
Quilino, Argentina 94 C3 30 14S 64 29W
Quill Lakes, Canada 73 C8 51 55N 104 13W
Quillabamba, Peru 92 F4 12 50S 72 50W
Quillagua, Chile 94 A2 21 40S 69 40W
Quillaicillo, Chile 94 C1 31 17S 71 40W
Quillota, Chile 94 C1 32 54S 71 16W
Quilmes, Argentina 94 C4 34 43S 58 15W
Quilon, India 40 Q10 8 50N 76 38 E
Quilpie, Australia 63 D3 26 35S 144 11 E
Quilpué, Chile 94 C1 33 5S 71 33W
Quilua, Mozam. 55 F4 16 17S 39 54 E
Quimilí, Argentina 94 B3 27 40S 62 30W
Quimper, France 18 B1 48 0N 4 9W
Quimperlé, France 18 C2 47 53N 3 33W
Quinault →, U.S.A. 84 C2 47 21N 124 18W
Quincy, Calif., U.S.A. 84 F6 39 56N 120 57W
Quincy, Fla., U.S.A. 77 K3 30 35N 84 34W
Quincy, Ill., U.S.A. 80 F9 39 56N 91 23W
Quincy, Mass., U.S.A. 79 D14 42 15N 71 0W
Quincy, Wash., U.S.A. 82 C4 47 22N 119 56W
Quines, Argentina 94 C2 32 13S 65 48W
Quinga, Mozam. 55 F5 15 49S 40 15 E
Quinns Rocks, Australia 61 F2 31 40S 115 42 E
Quintana Roo □, Mexico 87 D7 19 0N 88 0W
Quintanar de la Orden, Spain 19 C4 39 36N 3 5W
Quintero, Chile 94 C1 32 45S 71 30W
Quirihue, Chile 94 D1 36 15S 72 35W
Quirindi, Australia 63 E5 31 28S 150 40 E
Quirinópolis, Brazil 93 G8 18 32S 50 30W
Quissanga, Mozam. 55 E5 12 24S 40 28 E
Quitilipi, Argentina 94 B3 26 50S 60 13W
Quitman, U.S.A. 77 K4 30 47N 83 34W
Quito, Ecuador 92 D3 0 15S 78 35W
Quixadá, Brazil 93 D11 4 55S 39 0W
Quixaxe, Mozam. 55 F5 15 17S 40 4 E
Qul'ân, Jazâ'ir, Egypt 44 E2 24 22N 35 31 E
Qumbu, S. Africa 57 E4 31 10S 28 48 E
Quneitra, Syria 47 B4 33 7N 35 48 E
Qŭnghirot, Uzbekistan 26 E6 43 6N 58 54 E
Quoin I., Australia 60 B4 14 54S 129 32 E
Quoin Pt., S. Africa 56 E2 34 46S 19 37 E
Quorn, Australia 63 E2 32 25S 138 5 E
Qŭqon, Uzbekistan 26 E8 40 30N 70 57 E
Qurnat as Sawdā', Lebanon 47 A5 34 18N 36 6 E
Quşaybā', Si. Arabia 44 E4 26 53N 43 35 E
Qusaybah, Iraq 44 C4 34 24N 40 59 E
Quseir, Egypt 44 E2 26 7N 34 16 E
Qūshchī, Iran 44 B5 37 59N 45 3 E
Quthing, Lesotho 57 E4 30 25S 27 36 E
Qūţīābād, Iran 45 C6 35 47N 48 30 E
Quwo, China 34 G6 35 38N 111 25 E
Quyang, China 34 E8 38 35N 114 40 E
Quynh Nhai, Vietnam 38 B4 21 49N 103 33 E
Quyon, Canada 79 A8 45 31N 76 14W
Quzhou, China 33 D6 28 57N 118 54 E
Quzi, China 34 F4 36 20N 107 20 E
Qyzylorda, Kazakstan 26 E7 44 48N 65 28 E

R

Ra, Ko, Thailand 39 H2 9 13N 98 16 E
Raahe, Finland 8 D21 64 40N 24 28 E
Raalte, Neths. 15 B6 52 23N 6 16 E
Raasay, U.K. 12 D2 57 25N 6 4W
Raasay, Sd. of, U.K. 12 D2 57 30N 6 8W
Raba, Indonesia 37 F5 8 36S 118 55 E
Rába →, Hungary 17 E9 47 38N 17 38 E
Rabai, Kenya 54 C4 3 50S 39 31 E
Rabat, Malta 23 D1 35 53N 14 25 E
Rabat, Morocco 50 B4 34 2N 6 48W
Rabaul, Papua N. G. 64 H7 4 24S 152 18 E
Rābigh, Si. Arabia 46 C2 22 50N 39 5 E
Râbniţa, Moldova 17 E15 47 45N 29 0 E
Rābor, Iran 45 D8 29 17N 56 55 E
Race, C., Canada 71 C9 46 40N 53 5W
Rach Gia, Vietnam 39 G5 10 5N 105 5 E
Rachid, Mauritania 50 E3 18 48N 11 41W
Racibórz, Poland 17 C10 50 7N 18 18 E
Racine, U.S.A. 76 D2 42 41N 87 51W
Rackerby, U.S.A. 84 F5 39 26N 121 22W
Radama, Nosy, Madag. 57 A8 14 0S 47 47 E
Radama, Saikanosy, Madag. 57 A8 14 16S 47 53 E
Rădăuţi, Romania 17 E13 47 50N 25 59 E
Radcliff, U.S.A. 76 G3 37 51N 85 57W
Radekhiv, Ukraine 17 C13 50 25N 24 32 E
Radekhov = Radekhiv, Ukraine 17 C13 50 25N 24 32 E
Radford, U.S.A. 76 G5 37 8N 80 34W
Radhanpur, India 42 H4 23 50N 71 38 E
Radhwa, Jabal, Si. Arabia 44 E3 24 34N 38 18 E
Radisson, Canada 70 B4 53 47N 77 37W
Radisson, Sask., Canada 73 C7 52 30N 107 20W
Radium Hot Springs, Canada 72 C5 50 35N 116 2W
Radnor Forest, U.K. 11 E4 52 17N 3 10W
Radom, Poland 17 C11 51 23N 21 12 E
Radomsko, Poland 17 C10 51 5N 19 28 E
Radomyshl, Ukraine 17 C15 50 30N 29 12 E
Radstock, C., Australia 63 E1 33 12S 134 20 E
Radviliškis, Lithuania 9 J20 55 49N 23 33 E
Radville, Canada 73 D8 49 30N 104 15W
Rae, Canada 72 A5 62 50N 116 3W
Rae Bareli, India 43 F9 26 18N 81 20 E
Rae Isthmus, Canada 69 B11 66 40N 87 30W
Raeren, Belgium 15 D6 50 41N 6 7 E
Raeside, L., Australia 61 E3 29 20S 122 0 E
Raetihi, N.Z. 59 H5 39 25S 175 17 E
Rafaela, Argentina 94 C3 31 10S 61 30W
Rafah, Gaza Strip 47 D3 31 18N 34 14 E
Rafai, C.A.R. 54 B1 4 59N 23 58 E
Rafḥā, Si. Arabia 44 D4 29 35N 43 35 E
Rafsanjān, Iran 45 D8 30 30N 56 5 E
Raft Pt., Australia 60 C3 16 4S 124 26 E
Raga, Sudan 51 G11 8 28N 25 41 E
Ragachow, Belarus 17 B16 53 8N 30 5 E
Ragama, Sri Lanka 40 R11 7 0N 79 50 E
Ragged, Mt., Australia 61 F3 33 27S 123 25 E
Raghunathpalli, India 43 H11 22 14N 84 48 E
Raghunathpur, India 43 H12 23 33N 86 40 E
Raglan, N.Z. 59 G5 37 55S 174 55 E
Ragusa, Italy 20 F6 36 55N 14 44 E
Raha, Indonesia 37 E6 4 55S 123 0 E
Rahaeng = Tak, Thailand 38 D2 16 52N 99 8 E
Rahatgarh, India 43 H8 23 47N 78 22 E
Raḥīmah, Si. Arabia 45 E6 26 42N 50 4 E
Rahimyar Khan, Pakistan 42 E4 28 30N 70 25 E
Rāhjerd, Iran 45 C6 34 22N 50 22 E
Rahon, India 42 D7 31 3N 76 7 E
Raichur, India 40 L10 16 10N 77 20 E
Raiganj, India 43 G13 25 37N 88 10 E
Raigarh, India 41 J13 21 56N 83 25 E
Raijua, Indonesia 37 F6 10 37S 121 36 E
Raikot, India 42 D6 30 41N 75 42 E
Railton, Australia 62 G4 41 25S 146 28 E
Rainbow Lake, Canada 72 B5 58 30N 119 23W
Rainier, U.S.A. 84 D4 46 53N 122 41W
Rainier, Mt., U.S.A. 84 D5 46 52N 121 46W
Rainy L., Canada 73 D10 48 42N 93 10W
Rainy River, Canada 73 D10 48 43N 94 29W
Raippaluoto, Finland 8 E19 63 13N 21 14 E
Raipur, India 41 J12 21 17N 81 45 E
Raisen, India 42 H8 23 20N 77 48 E
Raisio, Finland 9 F20 60 28N 22 11 E
Raj Nandgaon, India 41 J12 21 5N 81 5 E
Raj Nilgiri, India 43 J12 21 28N 86 46 E
Raja, Ujung, Indonesia 36 D1 3 40N 96 25 E
Raja Ampat, Kepulauan, Indonesia 37 E8 0 30S 130 0 E
Rajahmundry, India 41 L12 17 1N 81 48 E
Rajang →, Malaysia 36 D4 2 30N 112 0 E
Rajanpur, Pakistan 42 E4 29 6N 70 19 E
Rajapalaiyam, India 40 Q10 9 25N 77 35 E
Rajasthan □, India 42 F5 26 45N 73 30 E
Rajasthan Canal, India 42 F5 28 0N 72 0 E
Rajauri, India 43 C6 33 25N 74 21 E
Rajgarh, Mad. P., India 42 G7 24 2N 76 45 E
Rajgarh, Raj., India 42 F7 27 14N 76 38 E
Rajgarh, Raj., India 42 E6 28 40N 75 25 E
Rajgir, India 43 G11 25 2N 85 25 E
Rajkot, India 42 H4 22 15N 70 56 E
Rajmahal Hills, India 43 G12 24 30N 87 30 E
Rajpipla, India 40 J8 21 50N 73 30 E
Rajpur, India 42 H6 22 18N 74 21 E
Rajpura, India 42 D7 30 25N 76 32 E
Rajshahi, Bangla. 41 G16 24 22N 88 39 E
Rajshahi □, Bangla. 43 G13 25 0N 89 0 E
Rajula, India 42 J4 21 3N 71 26 E
Rakaia, N.Z. 59 K4 43 45S 172 1 E
Rakaia →, N.Z. 59 K4 43 36S 172 15 E
Rakan, Ra's, Qatar 45 E6 26 10N 51 20 E
Rakaposhi, Pakistan 43 A6 36 10N 74 25 E
Rakata, Pulau, Indonesia 36 F3 6 10S 105 20 E
Rakhiv, Ukraine 17 D13 48 3N 24 12 E
Rakhni, Pakistan 42 D3 30 4N 69 56 E
Rakhni →, Pakistan 42 E3 29 31N 69 36 E
Rakitnoye, Russia 30 B7 45 36N 134 17 E
Rakops, Botswana 56 C3 21 1S 24 28 E
Rakvere, Estonia 9 G22 59 20N 26 25 E
Raleigh, U.S.A. 77 H6 35 47N 78 39W
Raleigh B., U.S.A. 75 D11 34 50N 76 15W
Ralls, U.S.A. 81 J4 33 41N 101 24W
Ralston, U.S.A. 78 E8 41 30N 76 57W
Ram →, Canada 72 A4 62 1N 123 41W
Rām Allāh, West Bank 47 D4 31 55N 35 10 E
Ram Hd., Australia 63 F4 37 47S 149 30 E
Rama, Nic. 88 D3 12 9N 84 15W
Ramakona, India 43 J8 21 43N 78 50 E
Raman, Thailand 39 J3 6 29N 101 18 E
Ramanathapuram, India 40 Q11 9 25N 78 55 E
Ramanetaka, B. de, Madag. 57 A8 14 13S 47 52 E
Ramanujganj, India 43 H10 23 48N 83 42 E
Ramat Gan, Israel 47 C3 32 4N 34 48 E
Ramatlhabama, S. Africa 56 D4 25 37S 25 33 E
Ramban, India 43 C6 33 14N 75 12 E
Rambipuji, Indonesia 37 H15 8 12S 113 37 E
Ramechhap, Nepal 43 F12 27 25N 86 10 E
Ramganga →, India 43 F8 27 5N 79 58 E
Ramgarh, Bihar, India 43 H11 23 40N 85 35 E
Ramgarh, Raj., India 42 F6 27 16N 75 14 E
Ramgarh, Raj., India 42 F4 27 30N 70 36 E
Rāmhormoz, Iran 45 D6 31 15N 49 35 E
Ramīān, Iran 45 B7 37 3N 55 16 E
Ramingining, Australia 62 A2 12 19S 135 3 E
Ramla, Israel 47 D3 31 55N 34 52 E
Ramnad = Ramanathapuram, India 40 Q11 9 25N 78 55 E
Ramnagar, India 43 E8 29 24N 79 7 E
Ramnagar, Jammu & Kashmir, India 43 C6 32 47N 75 18 E
Râmnicu Sărat, Romania 17 F14 45 26N 27 3 E
Râmnicu Vâlcea, Romania 17 F13 45 9N 24 21 E
Ramona, U.S.A. 85 M10 33 2N 116 52W
Ramore, Canada 70 C3 48 30N 80 25W
Ramotswa, Botswana 56 C4 24 50S 25 52 E
Rampur, H.P., India 42 D7 31 26N 77 43 E
Rampur, Mad. P., India 42 H5 23 25N 73 53 E
Rampur, Ut. P., India 43 E8 28 50N 79 5 E
Rampur Hat, India 43 G12 24 10N 87 50 E
Rampura, India 42 G6 24 30N 75 27 E
Ramrama Tola, India 43 J8 21 52N 79 55 E
Ramree I. = Ramree Kyun, Burma 41 K19 19 0N 94 0 E
Ramree Kyun, Burma 41 K19 19 0N 94 0 E
Rāmsar, Iran 45 B6 36 53N 50 41 E
Ramsey, U.K. 10 C3 54 20N 4 22W
Ramsey, U.S.A. 79 E10 41 4N 74 9W
Ramsey L., Canada 70 C3 47 13N 82 15W
Ramsgate, U.K. 11 F9 51 20N 1 25 E
Ramtek, India 40 J11 21 20N 79 15 E
Rana Pratap Sagar Dam, India 42 G6 24 58N 75 38 E
Ranaghat, India 43 H13 23 15N 88 35 E
Ranahu, Pakistan 42 G3 25 55N 69 45 E
Ranau, Malaysia 36 C5 6 2N 116 40 E
Rancagua, Chile 94 C1 34 10S 70 50W
Rancheria →, Canada 72 A3 60 13N 129 7W
Ranchester, U.S.A. 82 D10 44 54N 107 10W
Ranchi, India 43 H11 23 19N 85 27 E
Rancho Cucamonga, U.S.A. 85 L9 34 10N 117 30W
Randalstown, U.K. 13 B5 54 45N 6 19W
Randers, Denmark 9 H14 56 29N 10 1 E
Randfontein, S. Africa 57 D4 26 8S 27 45 E
Randle, U.S.A. 84 D5 46 32N 121 57W
Randolph, Mass., U.S.A. 79 D13 42 10N 71 2W
Randolph, N.Y., U.S.A. 78 D6 42 10N 78 59W
Randolph, Utah, U.S.A. 82 F8 41 40N 111 11W
Randolph, Vt., U.S.A. 79 C12 43 55N 72 40W
Randsburg, U.S.A. 85 K9 35 22N 117 39W
Råne älv →, Sweden 8 D20 65 50N 22 20 E
Rangae, Thailand 39 J3 6 19N 101 44 E
Rangaunu B., N.Z. 59 F4 34 51S 173 15 E
Rangeley, U.S.A. 79 B14 44 58N 70 39W
Rangeley L., U.S.A. 79 B14 44 55N 70 43W
Rangely, U.S.A. 82 F9 40 5N 108 48W
Ranger, U.S.A. 81 J5 32 28N 98 41W
Rangia, India 41 F17 26 28N 91 38 E
Rangiora, N.Z. 59 K4 43 19S 172 36 E
Rangitaiki →, N.Z. 59 G6 37 54S 176 49 E
Rangitata →, N.Z. 59 K3 43 45S 171 15 E
Rangkasbitung, Indonesia 37 G12 6 21S 106 15 E
Rangon →, Burma 41 L20 16 28N 96 40 E
Rangoon, Burma 41 L20 16 45N 96 20 E
Rangpur, Bangla. 41 G16 25 42N 89 22 E
Rangsit, Thailand 38 F3 13 59N 100 37 E
Ranibennur, India 40 M9 14 35N 75 30 E
Raniganj, Ut. P., India 43 F9 27 3N 82 13 E
Raniganj, W. Bengal, India 41 H15 23 40N 87 5 E
Ranikhet, India 43 E8 29 39N 79 25 E
Raniwara, India 40 G8 24 50N 72 10 E
Rāniyah, Iraq 44 B5 36 15N 44 53 E
Ranka, India 43 H10 23 59N 83 47 E
Ranken →, Australia 62 C2 20 31S 137 36 E
Rankin, U.S.A. 81 K4 31 13N 101 56W
Rankin Inlet, Canada 68 B10 62 30N 93 0W
Rankins Springs, Australia 63 E4 33 49S 146 14 E
Rannoch, L., U.K. 12 E4 56 41N 4 20W
Rannoch Moor, U.K. 12 E4 56 38N 4 48W
Ranobe, Helodranon' i, Madag. 57 C7 23 3S 43 33 E
Ranohira, Madag. 57 C8 22 29S 45 24 E
Ranomafana, Toamasina, Madag. 57 B8 18 57S 48 50 E
Ranomafana, Toliara, Madag. 57 C8 24 34S 47 0 E
Ranong, Thailand 39 H2 9 56N 98 40 E
Rānsa, Iran 45 C6 33 39N 48 18 E
Ransiki, Indonesia 37 E8 1 30S 134 10 E
Rantauprapat, Indonesia 36 D1 2 15N 99 50 E
Rantemario, Indonesia 37 E5 3 15S 119 57 E
Rantoul, U.S.A. 76 E1 40 19N 88 9W
Raoyang, China 34 E8 38 15N 115 45 E
Rapa, Pac. Oc. 65 K13 27 35S 144 20W
Rapallo, Italy 18 D8 44 21N 9 14 E
Rapar, India 42 H4 23 34N 70 38 E
Rāpch, Iran 45 E8 25 40N 59 15 E
Raper, C., Canada 69 B13 69 44N 67 6W
Rapid City, U.S.A. 80 D3 44 5N 103 14W
Rapid River, U.S.A. 76 C2 45 55N 86 58W
Rapla, Estonia 9 G21 59 1N 24 52 E
Rapti →, India 43 F10 26 18N 83 41 E
Raquette →, U.S.A. 79 B10 45 0N 74 42W
Raquette Lake, U.S.A. 79 C10 43 49N 74 40W
Rarotonga, Cook Is. 65 K12 21 30S 160 0W
Ra's al 'Ayn, Syria 44 B4 36 45N 40 12 E
Ra's al Khaymah, U.A.E. 45 E8 25 50N 55 59 E
Ra's an Naqb, Jordan 47 F4 30 0N 35 29 E
Ras Dashen, Ethiopia 46 E2 13 8N 38 26 E
Râs Timirist, Mauritania 50 E2 19 21N 16 30W

Rasca, Pta. de la

Rasca, Pta. de la, *Canary Is.* **22 G3** 27 59N 16 41W
Raseiniai, *Lithuania* **9 J20** 55 25N 23 5 E
Rashmi, *India* **42 G6** 25 4N 74 22 E
Rasht, *Iran* **45 B6** 37 20N 49 40 E
Rasi Salai, *Thailand* **38 E5** 15 20N 104 9 E
Rason L., *Australia* **61 E3** 28 45S 124 25 E
Rasra, *India* **43 G10** 25 50N 83 50 E
Rasul, *Pakistan* **42 C5** 32 42N 73 34 E
Rat Buri, *Thailand* **38 F2** 13 30N 99 54 E
Rat Islands, *U.S.A.* **68 C1** 52 0N 178 0 E
Rat L., *Canada* **73 B9** 56 10N 99 40W
Ratangarh, *India* **42 E6** 28 5N 74 35 E
Raţāwī, *Iraq* **44 D5** 30 38N 47 13 E
Ratcatchers L., *Australia* **63 E3** 32 38S 143 10 E
Rath, *India* **43 G8** 25 36N 79 37 E
Rath Luirc, *Ireland* **13 D3** 52 21N 8 40W
Rathdrum, *Ireland* **13 D5** 52 56N 6 14W
Rathenow, *Germany* **16 B7** 52 37N 12 19 E
Rathkeale, *Ireland* **13 D3** 52 32N 8 56W
Rathlin I., *U.K.* **13 A5** 55 18N 6 14W
Rathmelton, *Ireland* **13 A4** 55 2N 7 38W
Ratibor = Racibórz, *Poland* **17 C10** 50 7N 18 18 E
Ratlam, *India* **42 H6** 23 20N 75 0 E
Ratnagiri, *India* **40 L8** 16 57N 73 18 E
Ratodero, *Pakistan* **42 F3** 27 48N 68 18 E
Raton, *U.S.A.* **81 G2** 36 54N 104 24W
Rattaphum, *Thailand* **39 J3** 7 8N 100 16 E
Rattray Hd., *U.K.* **12 D7** 57 38N 1 50W
Ratz, Mt., *Canada* **72 B2** 57 23N 132 12W
Raub, *Malaysia* **39 L3** 3 47N 101 52 E
Rauch, *Argentina* **94 D4** 36 45S 59 5W
Raudales de Malpaso, *Mexico* **87 D6** 17 30N 23 30W
Raufarhöfn, *Iceland* **8 C6** 66 27N 15 57W
Raufoss, *Norway* **9 F14** 60 44N 10 37 E
Raukumara Ra., *N.Z.* **59 H6** 38 5S 177 55 E
Rauma, *Finland* **9 F19** 61 10N 21 30 E
Raurkela, *India* **43 H11** 22 14N 84 50 E
Rausu-Dake, *Japan* **30 B12** 44 4N 145 7 E
Rava-Ruska, *Poland* **17 C12** 50 15N 23 42 E
Rava Russkaya = Rava-Ruska, *Poland* **17 C12** 50 15N 23 42 E
Ravalli, *U.S.A.* **82 C6** 47 17N 114 11W
Ravānsar, *Iran* **44 C5** 34 43N 46 40 E
Rāvar, *Iran* **45 D8** 31 20N 56 51 E
Ravena, *U.S.A.* **79 D11** 42 28N 73 49W
Ravenna, *Italy* **20 B5** 44 25N 12 12 E
Ravenna, *Nebr., U.S.A.* **80 E5** 41 1N 98 55W
Ravenna, *Ohio, U.S.A.* **78 E3** 41 9N 81 15W
Ravensburg, *Germany* **16 E5** 47 46N 9 36 E
Ravenshoe, *Australia* **62 B4** 17 37S 145 29 E
Ravensthorpe, *Australia* **61 F3** 33 35S 120 2 E
Ravenswood, *Australia* **62 C4** 20 6S 146 54 E
Ravenswood, *U.S.A.* **76 F5** 38 57N 81 46W
Ravi →, *Pakistan* **42 D4** 30 35N 71 49 E
Rawalpindi, *Pakistan* **42 C5** 33 38N 73 8 E
Rawāndūz, *Iraq* **44 B5** 36 40N 44 30 E
Rawang, *Malaysia* **39 L3** 3 20N 101 35 E
Rawene, *N.Z.* **59 F4** 35 25S 173 32 E
Rawlinna, *Australia* **61 F4** 30 58S 125 28 E
Rawlins, *U.S.A.* **82 F10** 41 47N 107 14W
Rawlinson Ra., *Australia* **61 D4** 24 40S 128 30 E
Rawson, *Argentina* **96 E3** 43 15S 65 5W
Raxaul, *India* **43 F11** 26 59N 84 51 E
Ray, *U.S.A.* **80 A3** 48 21N 103 10W
Ray, C., *Canada* **71 C8** 47 33N 59 15W
Rayadurg, *India* **40 M10** 14 40N 76 50 E
Rayagada, *India* **41 K13** 19 15N 83 20 E
Raychikhinsk, *Russia* **27 E13** 49 46N 129 25 E
Rāyen, *Iran* **45 D8** 29 34N 57 26 E
Rayleigh, *U.K.* **11 F8** 51 36N 0 37 E
Raymond, *Canada* **72 D6** 49 30N 112 35W
Raymond, *Calif., U.S.A.* **84 H7** 37 13N 119 54W
Raymond, *N.H., U.S.A.* **79 C13** 43 2N 71 11W
Raymond, *Wash., U.S.A.* **84 D3** 46 41N 123 44W
Raymond Terrace, *Australia* **63 E5** 32 45S 151 44 E
Raymondville, *U.S.A.* **81 M6** 26 29N 97 47W
Raymore, *Canada* **73 C8** 51 25N 104 31W
Rayna, *India* **43 H12** 23 5N 87 54 E
Rayón, *Mexico* **86 B2** 29 43N 110 35W
Rayong, *Thailand* **38 F3** 12 40N 101 20 E
Rayville, *U.S.A.* **81 J9** 32 29N 91 46W
Raz, Pte. du, *France* **18 C1** 48 2N 4 47W
Razan, *Iran* **45 C6** 35 23N 49 2 E
Razdel'naya = Rozdilna, *Ukraine* **17 E16** 46 50N 30 2 E
Razdolnoye, *Russia* **30 C5** 43 30N 131 52 E
Razeh, *Iran* **45 C6** 32 47N 48 9 E
Razgrad, *Bulgaria* **21 C12** 43 33N 26 34 E
Razim, Lacul, *Romania* **17 F15** 44 50N 29 0 E
Razmak, *Pakistan* **42 C3** 32 45N 69 50 E
Ré, Î. de, *France* **18 C3** 46 12N 1 30W
Reading, *U.K.* **11 F7** 51 27N 0 58W
Reading, *U.S.A.* **79 F9** 40 20N 75 56W
Reading □, *U.K.* **11 F7** 51 27N 0 58W
Realicó, *Argentina* **94 D3** 35 0S 64 15W
Ream, *Cambodia* **39 G4** 10 34N 103 39 E
Reata, *Mexico* **86 B4** 26 8N 101 5W
Reay Forest, *U.K.* **12 C4** 58 22N 4 55W
Rebi, *Indonesia* **37 F8** 6 23S 134 7 E
Rebiana, *Libya* **51 D10** 24 12N 22 10 E
Rebun-Tō, *Japan* **30 B10** 45 23N 141 2 E
Recherche, Arch. of the, *Australia* **61 F3** 34 15S 122 50 E
Rechna Doab, *Pakistan* **42 D5** 31 35N 73 30 E
Rechytsa, *Belarus* **17 B16** 52 21N 30 24 E
Recife, *Brazil* **93 E12** 8 0S 35 0W
Recklinghausen, *Germany* **15 C7** 51 37N 7 12 E
Reconquista, *Argentina* **94 B4** 29 10S 59 45W
Recreo, *Argentina* **94 B2** 29 25S 65 10W
Red →, *La., U.S.A.* **81 K9** 31 1N 91 45W
Red →, *N. Dak., U.S.A.* **68 C10** 49 0N 97 15W
Red Bank, *U.S.A.* **79 F10** 40 21N 74 5W
Red Bay, *Canada* **71 B8** 51 44N 56 25W
Red Bluff, *U.S.A.* **82 F2** 40 11N 122 15W
Red Bluff L., *U.S.A.* **81 K3** 31 54N 103 55W
Red Cliffs, *Australia* **63 E3** 34 19S 142 11 E
Red Cloud, *U.S.A.* **80 E5** 40 5N 98 32W
Red Creek, *U.S.A.* **79 C8** 43 14N 76 45W
Red Deer, *Canada* **72 C6** 52 20N 113 50W
Red Deer →, *Alta., Canada* **73 C7** 50 58N 110 0W
Red Deer →, *Man., Canada* **73 C8** 52 53N 101 1W
Red Deer L., *Canada* **73 C8** 52 55N 101 20W
Red Hook, *U.S.A.* **79 E11** 41 55N 73 53W
Red Indian L., *Canada* **71 C8** 48 35N 57 0W
Red L., *Canada* **73 C10** 51 3N 93 49W
Red Lake, *Canada* **73 C10** 51 3N 93 49W
Red Lake Falls, *U.S.A.* **80 B6** 47 53N 96 16W
Red Lake Road, *Canada* **73 C10** 49 59N 93 25W
Red Lodge, *U.S.A.* **82 D9** 45 11N 109 15W
Red Mountain, *U.S.A.* **85 K9** 35 37N 117 38W
Red Oak, *U.S.A.* **80 E7** 41 1N 95 14W
Red Rock, *Canada* **70 C2** 48 55N 88 15W
Red Rock, L., *U.S.A.* **80 E8** 41 22N 92 59W
Red Rocks Pt., *Australia* **61 F4** 32 13S 127 32 E
Red Sea, *Asia* **46 C2** 25 0N 36 0 E
Red Slate Mt., *U.S.A.* **84 H8** 37 31N 118 52W
Red Sucker L., *Canada* **70 B1** 54 9N 93 40W
Red Tower Pass = Turnu Roşu, P., *Romania* **17 F13** 45 33N 24 17 E
Red Wing, *U.S.A.* **80 C8** 44 34N 92 31W
Redang, *Malaysia* **36 C2** 5 49N 103 2 E
Redange, *Lux.* **15 E5** 49 46N 5 52 E
Redcar, *U.K.* **10 C6** 54 37N 1 4W
Redcar & Cleveland □, *U.K.* **10 C7** 54 29N 1 0W
Redcliff, *Canada* **73 C6** 50 10N 110 50W
Redcliffe, *Australia* **63 D5** 27 12S 153 0 E
Redcliffe, Mt., *Australia* **61 E3** 28 30S 121 30 E
Reddersburg, *S. Africa* **56 D4** 29 41S 26 10 E
Redding, *U.S.A.* **82 F2** 40 35N 122 24W
Redditch, *U.K.* **11 E6** 52 18N 1 55W
Redfield, *U.S.A.* **80 C5** 44 53N 98 31W
Redford, *U.S.A.* **79 B11** 44 38N 73 48W
Redlands, *U.S.A.* **85 M9** 34 4N 117 11W
Redmond, *Oreg., U.S.A.* **82 D3** 44 17N 121 11W
Redmond, *Wash., U.S.A.* **84 C4** 47 41N 122 7W
Redon, *France* **18 C2** 47 40N 2 6W
Redonda, *Antigua* **89 C7** 16 58N 62 19W
Redondela, *Spain* **19 A1** 42 15N 8 38W
Redondo Beach, *U.S.A.* **85 M8** 33 50N 118 23W
Redruth, *U.K.* **11 G2** 50 14N 5 14W
Redvers, *Canada* **73 D8** 49 35N 101 40W
Redwater, *Canada* **72 C6** 53 55N 113 6W
Redwood, *U.S.A.* **79 B9** 44 18N 75 48W
Redwood City, *U.S.A.* **84 H4** 37 30N 122 15W
Redwood Falls, *U.S.A.* **80 C7** 44 32N 95 7W
Redwood National Park, *U.S.A.* **82 F1** 41 40N 124 5W
Ree, L., *Ireland* **13 C3** 53 35N 8 0W
Reed, L., *Canada* **73 C8** 54 38N 100 30W
Reed City, *U.S.A.* **76 D3** 43 53N 85 31W
Reedley, *U.S.A.* **84 J7** 36 36N 119 27W
Reedsburg, *U.S.A.* **80 D9** 43 32N 90 0W
Reedsport, *U.S.A.* **82 E1** 43 42N 124 6W
Reedsville, *U.S.A.* **78 F7** 40 39N 77 35W
Reefton, *N.Z.* **59 K3** 42 6S 171 51 E
Reese →, *U.S.A.* **82 F5** 40 48N 117 4W
Refugio, *U.S.A.* **81 L6** 28 18N 97 17W
Regensburg, *Germany* **16 D7** 49 1N 12 6 E
Réggio di Calábria, *Italy* **20 E6** 38 6N 15 39 E
Réggio nell'Emília, *Italy* **20 B4** 44 43N 10 36 E
Reghin, *Romania* **17 E13** 46 46N 24 42 E
Regina, *Canada* **73 C8** 50 27N 104 35W
Regina Beach, *Canada* **73 C8** 50 47N 105 0W
Registro, *Brazil* **95 A6** 24 29S 47 49W
Rehar →, *India* **43 H10** 23 55N 82 40 E
Rehli, *India* **43 H8** 23 38N 79 5 E
Rehoboth, *Namibia* **56 C2** 23 15S 17 4 E
Rehovot, *Israel* **47 D3** 31 54N 34 48 E
Reichenbach, *Germany* **16 C7** 50 37N 12 17 E
Reid, *Australia* **61 F4** 30 49S 128 26 E
Reidsville, *U.S.A.* **77 G6** 36 21N 79 40W
Reigate, *U.K.* **11 F7** 51 14N 0 12W
Reims, *France* **18 B6** 49 15N 4 1 E
Reina Adelaida, Arch., *Chile* **96 G2** 52 20S 74 0W
Reindeer →, *Canada* **73 B8** 55 36N 103 11W
Reindeer I., *Canada* **73 C9** 52 30N 98 0W
Reindeer L., *Canada* **73 B8** 57 15N 102 15W
Reinga, C., *N.Z.* **59 F4** 34 25S 172 43 E
Reinosa, *Spain* **19 A3** 43 2N 4 15W
Reitz, *S. Africa* **57 D4** 27 48S 28 29 E
Reivilo, *S. Africa* **56 D3** 27 36S 24 8 E
Reliance, *Canada* **73 A7** 63 0N 109 20W
Remarkable, Mt., *Australia* **63 E2** 32 48S 138 10 E
Rembang, *Indonesia* **37 G14** 6 42S 111 21 E
Remedios, *Panama* **88 E3** 8 15N 81 50W
Remeshk, *Iran* **45 E8** 26 55N 58 50 E
Remich, *Lux.* **15 E6** 49 32N 6 22 E
Remscheid, *Germany* **15 C7** 51 11N 7 12 E
Ren Xian, *China* **34 F8** 37 8N 114 40 E
Rendsburg, *Germany* **16 A5** 54 17N 9 39 E
Renfrew, *Canada* **79 A8** 45 30N 76 40W
Renfrewshire □, *U.K.* **12 F4** 55 49N 4 38W
Rengat, *Indonesia* **36 E2** 0 30S 102 45 E
Rengo, *Chile* **94 C1** 34 24S 70 50W
Reni, *Ukraine* **17 F15** 45 28N 28 15 E
Renmark, *Australia* **63 E3** 34 11S 140 43 E
Rennell Sd., *Canada* **72 C2** 53 23N 132 35W
Renner Springs, *Australia* **62 B1** 18 20S 133 47 E
Rennes, *France* **18 B3** 48 7N 1 41W
Rennie L., *Canada* **73 A7** 61 32N 105 35W
Reno, *U.S.A.* **84 F7** 39 31N 119 48W
Reno →, *Italy* **20 B5** 44 38N 12 16 E
Renovo, *U.S.A.* **78 E7** 41 20N 77 45W
Renqiu, *China* **34 E9** 38 43N 116 5 E
Rensselaer, *Ind., U.S.A.* **76 E2** 40 57N 87 9W
Rensselaer, *N.Y., U.S.A.* **79 D11** 42 38N 73 45W
Rentería, *Spain* **19 A5** 43 19N 1 54W
Renton, *U.S.A.* **84 C4** 47 29N 122 12W
Reotipur, *India* **43 G10** 25 33N 83 45 E
Republic, *Mo., U.S.A.* **81 G8** 37 7N 93 29W
Republic, *Wash., U.S.A.* **82 B4** 48 39N 118 44W
Republican →, *U.S.A.* **80 F6** 39 4N 96 48W
Repulse Bay, *Canada* **69 B11** 66 30N 86 30W
Requena, *Peru* **92 E4** 5 5S 73 52W
Requena, *Spain* **19 C5** 39 30N 1 4W
Reşadiye = Datça, *Turkey* **21 F12** 36 46N 27 40 E
Reserve, *U.S.A.* **83 K9** 33 43N 108 45W
Resht = Rasht, *Iran* **45 B6** 37 20N 49 40 E
Resistencia, *Argentina* **94 B4** 27 30S 59 0W
Reşiţa, *Romania* **17 F11** 45 18N 21 53 E
Resolution I., *Canada* **69 B13** 61 30N 65 0W
Resolution I., *N.Z.* **59 L1** 45 40S 166 40 E
Ressano Garcia, *Mozam.* **57 D5** 25 25S 32 0 E
Reston, *Canada* **73 D8** 49 33N 101 6W
Retalhuleu, *Guatemala* **88 D1** 14 33N 91 46W
Retenue, L. de, *Dem. Rep. of the Congo* **55 E2** 11 0S 27 0 E
Retford, *U.K.* **10 D7** 53 19N 0 56W
Réthímnon, *Greece* **23 D6** 35 18N 24 30 E
Réthímnon □, *Greece* **23 D6** 35 23N 24 28 E
Reti, *Pakistan* **42 E3** 28 5N 69 48 E
Réunion ■, *Ind. Oc.* **49 J9** 21 0S 56 0 E
Reus, *Spain* **19 B6** 41 10N 1 5 E
Reutlingen, *Germany* **16 D5** 48 29N 9 12 E
Reval = Tallinn, *Estonia* **9 G21** 59 22N 24 48 E
Revda, *Russia* **24 C10** 56 48N 59 57 E
Revelganj, *India* **43 G11** 25 50N 84 40 E
Revelstoke, *Canada* **72 C5** 51 0N 118 10W
Reventazón, *Peru* **92 E2** 6 10S 80 58W
Revillagigedo, Is. de, *Pac. Oc.* **86 D2** 18 40N 112 0W
Revuè →, *Mozam.* **55 F3** 19 50S 34 0 E
Rewa, *India* **43 G9** 24 33N 81 25 E
Rewari, *India* **42 E7** 28 15N 76 40 E
Rexburg, *U.S.A.* **82 E8** 43 49N 111 47W
Rey, *Iran* **45 C6** 35 35N 51 25 E
Rey, I. del, *Panama* **88 E4** 8 20N 78 30W
Rey Malabo, *Eq. Guin.* **52 D1** 3 45N 8 50 E
Reyðarfjörður, *Iceland* **8 D6** 65 2N 14 13W
Reyes, Pt., *U.S.A.* **84 H3** 38 0N 123 0W
Reykjahlið, *Iceland* **8 D5** 65 40N 16 55W
Reykjanes, *Iceland* **8 E2** 63 48N 22 40W
Reykjavík, *Iceland* **8 D3** 64 10N 21 57W
Reynolds Ra., *Australia* **60 D5** 22 30S 133 0 E
Reynoldsville, *U.S.A.* **78 E6** 41 5N 78 58W
Reynosa, *Mexico* **87 B5** 26 5N 98 18W
Rēzekne, *Latvia* **9 H22** 56 30N 27 17 E
Rezvān, *Iran* **45 E8** 27 34N 56 6 E
Rhayader, *U.K.* **11 E4** 52 18N 3 29W
Rhein →, *Europe* **15 C6** 51 52N 6 2 E
Rhein-Main-Donau-Kanal, *Germany* **16 D6** 49 15N 11 15 E
Rheine, *Germany* **16 B4** 52 17N 7 26 E
Rheinland-Pfalz □, *Germany* **16 C4** 50 0N 7 0 E
Rhin = Rhein →, *Europe* **15 C6** 51 52N 6 2 E
Rhine = Rhein →, *Europe* **15 C6** 51 52N 6 2 E
Rhinebeck, *U.S.A.* **79 E11** 41 56N 73 55W
Rhineland-Palatinate = Rheinland-Pfalz □, *Germany* **16 C4** 50 0N 7 0 E
Rhinelander, *U.S.A.* **80 C10** 45 38N 89 25W
Rhinns Pt., *U.K.* **12 F2** 55 40N 6 29W
Rhino Camp, *Uganda* **54 B3** 3 0N 31 22 E
Rhir, Cap, *Morocco* **50 B4** 30 38N 9 54W
Rhode Island □, *U.S.A.* **79 E13** 41 40N 71 30W
Rhodes = Ródhos, *Greece* **23 C10** 36 15N 28 10 E
Rhodesia = Zimbabwe ■, *Africa* **55 F3** 19 0S 30 0 E
Rhodope Mts. = Rhodopi Planina, *Bulgaria* **21 D11** 41 40N 24 20 E
Rhodopi Planina, *Bulgaria* **21 D11** 41 40N 24 20 E
Rhön = Rhön, *Germany* **16 C5** 50 24N 9 58 E
Rhön, *Germany* **16 C5** 50 24N 9 58 E
Rhondda, *U.K.* **11 F4** 51 39N 3 31W
Rhondda Cynon Taff □, *U.K.* **11 F4** 51 42N 3 27W
Rhône →, *France* **18 E6** 43 28N 4 42 E
Rhum, *U.K.* **12 E2** 57 0N 6 20W
Rhyl, *U.K.* **10 D4** 53 20N 3 29W
Riachão, *Brazil* **93 E9** 7 20S 46 37W
Riasi, *India* **43 C6** 33 10N 74 50 E
Riau □, *Indonesia* **36 E2** 0 0 102 35 E
Riau, Kepulauan, *Indonesia* **36 D2** 0 30N 104 20 E
Riau Arch. = Riau, Kepulauan, *Indonesia* **36 D2** 0 30N 104 20 E
Ribadeo, *Spain* **19 A2** 43 35N 7 5W
Ribas do Rio Pardo, *Brazil* **93 H8** 20 27S 53 46W
Ribble →, *U.K.* **10 D5** 53 52N 2 25W
Ribe, *Denmark* **9 J13** 55 19N 8 44 E
Ribeira Brava, *Madeira* **22 D2** 32 41N 17 4W
Ribeirão Prêto, *Brazil* **95 A6** 21 10S 47 50W
Riberalta, *Bolivia* **92 F5** 11 0S 66 0W
Riccarton, *N.Z.* **59 K4** 43 32S 172 37 E
Rice, *U.S.A.* **85 L12** 34 5N 114 51W
Rice L., *Canada* **78 B6** 44 12N 78 10W
Rice Lake, *U.S.A.* **80 C9** 45 30N 91 44W
Rich, C., *Canada* **78 B4** 44 43N 80 38W
Richards Bay, *S. Africa* **57 D5** 28 48S 32 6 E
Richardson →, *Canada* **73 B6** 58 25N 111 14W
Richardson Lakes, *U.S.A.* **76 C10** 44 46N 70 58W
Richardson Springs, *U.S.A.* **84 F5** 39 51N 121 46W
Riche, C., *Australia* **61 F2** 34 36S 118 47 E
Richey, *U.S.A.* **80 B2** 47 39N 105 4W
Richfield, *U.S.A.* **83 G8** 38 46N 112 5W
Richfield Springs, *U.S.A.* **79 D10** 42 51N 74 59W
Richford, *U.S.A.* **79 B12** 45 0N 72 40W
Richibucto, *Canada* **71 C7** 46 42N 64 54W
Richland, *Ga., U.S.A.* **77 J3** 32 5N 84 40W
Richland, *Wash., U.S.A.* **82 C4** 46 17N 119 18W
Richland Center, *U.S.A.* **80 D9** 43 21N 90 23W
Richlands, *U.S.A.* **76 G5** 37 6N 81 48W
Richmond, *Australia* **62 C3** 20 43S 143 8 E
Richmond, *N.Z.* **59 J4** 41 20S 173 12 E
Richmond, *U.K.* **10 C6** 54 25N 1 43W
Richmond, *Calif., U.S.A.* **84 H4** 37 56N 122 21W
Richmond, *Ind., U.S.A.* **76 F3** 39 50N 84 53W
Richmond, *Ky., U.S.A.* **76 G3** 37 45N 84 18W
Richmond, *Mich., U.S.A.* **78 D2** 42 49N 82 45W
Richmond, *Mo., U.S.A.* **80 F8** 39 17N 93 58W
Richmond, *Tex., U.S.A.* **81 L7** 29 35N 95 46W
Richmond, *Utah, U.S.A.* **82 F8** 41 56N 111 48W
Richmond, *Va., U.S.A.* **76 G7** 37 33N 77 27W
Richmond, *Vt., U.S.A.* **79 B12** 44 24N 72 59W
Richmond Hill, *Canada* **78 C5** 43 52N 79 27W
Richmond Ra., *Australia* **63 D5** 29 0S 152 45 E
Richwood, *U.S.A.* **76 F5** 38 14N 80 32W
Ridder = Leninogorsk, *Kazakstan* **26 D9** 50 20N 83 30 E
Riddlesburg, *U.S.A.* **78 F6** 40 9N 78 15W
Ridgecrest, *U.S.A.* **85 K9** 35 38N 117 40W
Ridgefield, *Conn., U.S.A.* **79 E11** 41 17N 73 30W
Ridgefield, *Wash., U.S.A.* **84 E4** 45 49N 122 45W
Ridgeland, *U.S.A.* **77 J5** 32 29N 80 59W
Ridgetown, *Canada* **78 D3** 42 26N 81 52W
Ridgewood, *U.S.A.* **79 F10** 40 59N 74 7W
Ridgway, *U.S.A.* **78 E6** 41 25N 78 44W
Riding Mountain Nat. Park, *Canada* **73 C9** 50 50N 100 0W
Ridley, Mt., *Australia* **61 F3** 33 12S 122 7 E
Ried, *Austria* **16 D7** 48 14N 13 30 E
Riesa, *Germany* **16 C7** 51 17N 13 17 E
Riet →, *S. Africa* **56 D3** 29 0S 23 54 E
Rieti, *Italy* **20 C5** 42 24N 12 51 E
Riffe L., *U.S.A.* **84 D4** 46 32N 122 26W
Rifle, *U.S.A.* **82 G10** 39 32N 107 47W
Rift Valley □, *Kenya* **54 B4** 0 20N 36 0 E
Rīga, *Latvia* **9 H21** 56 53N 24 8 E
Riga, G. of, *Latvia* **9 H20** 57 40N 23 45 E
Rīgān, *Iran* **45 D8** 28 37N 58 58 E
Rīgas Jūras Līcis = Riga, G. of, *Latvia* **9 H20** 57 40N 23 45 E
Rigaud, *Canada* **79 A10** 45 29N 74 18W
Rigby, *U.S.A.* **82 E8** 43 40N 111 55W
Rīgestān □, *Afghan.* **40 D4** 30 15N 65 0 E
Riggins, *U.S.A.* **82 D5** 45 25N 116 19W
Rigolet, *Canada* **71 B8** 54 10N 58 23W
Rihand Dam, *India* **43 G10** 24 9N 83 2 E
Riihimäki, *Finland* **9 F21** 60 45N 24 48 E
Riiser-Larsen-halvøya, *Antarctica* **5 C4** 68 0S 35 0 E
Rijeka, *Croatia* **16 F8** 45 20N 14 21 E
Rijssen, *Neths.* **15 B6** 52 19N 6 31 E
Rikuzentakada, *Japan* **30 E10** 39 0N 141 40 E
Riley, *U.S.A.* **82 E4** 43 32N 119 28W
Rimah, Wadi ar →, *Si. Arabia* **44 E4** 26 5N 41 30 E
Rimbey, *Canada* **72 C6** 52 35N 114 15W
Rimersburg, *U.S.A.* **78 E5** 41 3N 79 30W
Rímini, *Italy* **20 B5** 44 3N 12 33 E
Rimouski, *Canada* **71 C6** 48 27N 68 30W
Rimrock, *U.S.A.* **84 D5** 46 38N 121 10W
Rinca, *Indonesia* **37 F5** 8 45S 119 35 E
Rincón de Romos, *Mexico* **86 C4** 22 14N 102 18W
Rinconada, *Argentina* **94 A2** 22 26S 66 10W
Rind →, *India* **43 G9** 25 53N 80 33 E
Ringas, *India* **42 F6** 27 21N 75 34 E
Ringkøbing, *Denmark* **9 H13** 56 5N 8 15 E
Ringvassøy, *Norway* **8 B18** 69 56N 19 15 E
Ringwood, *U.S.A.* **79 E10** 41 7N 74 15W
Rinjani, *Indonesia* **36 F5** 8 24S 116 28 E
Rio Branco, *Brazil* **92 E5** 9 58S 67 49W
Río Branco, *Uruguay* **95 C5** 32 40S 53 40W
Río Bravo del Norte →, *Mexico* **87 B5** 25 57N 97 9W
Rio Brilhante, *Brazil* **95 A5** 21 48S 54 33W
Rio Claro, *Brazil* **95 A6** 22 19S 47 35W
Rio Claro, *Trin. & Tob.* **89 D7** 10 20N 61 25W
Río Colorado, *Argentina* **96 D4** 39 0S 64 0W
Río Cuarto, *Argentina* **94 C3** 33 10S 64 25W
Rio das Pedras, *Mozam.* **57 C6** 23 8S 35 28 E
Rio de Janeiro, *Brazil* **95 A7** 23 0S 43 12W
Rio de Janeiro □, *Brazil* **95 A7** 22 50S 43 0W
Rio do Sul, *Brazil* **95 B6** 27 13S 49 37W
Río Gallegos, *Argentina* **96 G3** 51 35S 69 15W
Rio Grande = Grande, Rio →, *U.S.A.* **81 N6** 25 58N 97 9W
Río Grande, *Argentina* **96 G3** 53 50S 67 45W
Rio Grande, *Brazil* **95 C5** 32 0S 52 20W
Río Grande, *Mexico* **86 C4** 23 50N 103 2W
Río Grande, *Nic.* **88 D3** 12 54N 83 33W
Rio Grande City, *U.S.A.* **81 M5** 26 23N 98 49W
Río Grande de Santiago →, *Mexico* **86 C3** 21 36N 105 26W
Rio Grande del Norte →, *N. Amer.* **75 E7** 26 0N 97 0W
Rio Grande do Norte □, *Brazil* **93 E11** 5 40S 36 0W
Rio Grande do Sul □, *Brazil* **95 C5** 30 0S 53 0W
Río Hato, *Panama* **88 E3** 8 22N 80 10W
Río Lagartos, *Mexico* **87 C7** 21 36N 88 10W
Rio Largo, *Brazil* **93 E11** 9 28S 35 50W
Río Mulatos, *Bolivia* **92 G5** 19 40S 66 50W
Río Muni = Mbini □, *Eq. Guin.* **52 D2** 1 30N 10 0 E
Rio Negro, *Brazil* **95 B6** 26 0S 49 55W
Rio Pardo, *Brazil* **95 C5** 30 0S 52 30W
Rio Rancho, *U.S.A.* **83 J10** 35 14N 106 38W
Río Segundo, *Argentina* **94 C3** 31 40S 63 59W
Río Tercero, *Argentina* **94 C3** 32 15S 64 8W
Rio Verde, *Brazil* **93 G8** 17 50S 51 0W
Río Verde, *Mexico* **87 C5** 21 56N 99 59W
Rio Vista, *U.S.A.* **84 G5** 38 10N 121 42W
Ríobamba, *Ecuador* **92 D3** 1 50S 78 45W
Ríohacha, *Colombia* **92 A4** 11 33N 72 55W
Ríosucio, *Colombia* **92 B3** 7 27N 77 7W
Riou L., *Canada* **73 B7** 59 7N 106 25W
Ripley, *Canada* **78 B3** 44 4N 81 35W
Ripley, *Calif., U.S.A.* **85 M12** 33 32N 114 39W
Ripley, *N.Y., U.S.A.* **78 D5** 42 16N 79 43W
Ripley, *Tenn., U.S.A.* **81 H10** 35 45N 89 32W
Ripley, *W. Va., U.S.A.* **76 F5** 38 49N 81 43W
Ripon, *U.K.* **10 C6** 54 9N 1 31W
Ripon, *Calif., U.S.A.* **84 H5** 37 44N 121 7W
Ripon, *Wis., U.S.A.* **76 D1** 43 51N 88 50W
Rishā', W. ar →, *Si. Arabia* **44 E5** 25 33N 44 5 E
Rishiri-Tō, *Japan* **30 B10** 45 11N 141 15 E
Rishon le Ẓiyyon, *Israel* **47 D3** 31 58N 34 48 E
Rison, *U.S.A.* **81 J8** 33 58N 92 11W
Risør, *Norway* **9 G13** 58 43N 9 13 E
Rita Blanca Cr. →, *U.S.A.* **81 H3** 35 40N 102 29W
Ritter, Mt., *U.S.A.* **84 H7** 37 41N 119 12W
Rittman, *U.S.A.* **78 F3** 40 58N 81 47W
Ritzville, *U.S.A.* **82 C4** 47 8N 118 23W
Riva del Garda, *Italy* **20 B4** 45 53N 10 50 E
Rivadavia, *Buenos Aires, Argentina* **94 D3** 35 29S 62 59W
Rivadavia, *Mendoza, Argentina* **94 C2** 33 13S 68 30W
Rivadavia, *Salta, Argentina* **94 A3** 24 5S 62 54W
Rivadavia, *Chile* **94 B1** 29 57S 70 35W
Rivas, *Nic.* **88 D2** 11 30N 85 50W
River Cess, *Liberia* **50 G4** 5 30N 9 32W
River Jordan, *Canada* **84 B2** 48 26N 124 3W
Rivera, *Argentina* **94 D3** 37 12S 63 14W
Rivera, *Uruguay* **95 C4** 31 0S 55 50W
Riverbank, *U.S.A.* **84 H6** 37 44N 120 56W
Riverdale, *U.S.A.* **84 J7** 36 26N 119 52W
Riverhead, *U.S.A.* **79 F12** 40 55N 72 40W
Riverhurst, *Canada* **73 C7** 50 55N 106 50W
Rivers, *Canada* **73 C8** 50 2N 100 14W
Rivers Inlet, *Canada* **72 C3** 51 42N 127 15W
Riversdale, *S. Africa* **56 E3** 34 7S 21 15 E
Riverside, *U.S.A.* **85 M9** 33 59N 117 22W
Riverton, *Australia* **63 E2** 34 10S 138 46 E
Riverton, *Canada* **73 C9** 51 1N 97 0W
Riverton, *N.Z.* **59 M2** 46 21S 168 0 E
Riverton, *U.S.A.* **82 E9** 43 2N 108 23W
Riverton Heights, *U.S.A.* **84 C4** 47 28N 122 17W
Riviera, *U.S.A.* **85 K12** 35 4N 114 35W
Riviera di Levante, *Italy* **18 D8** 44 15N 9 30 E
Riviera di Ponente, *Italy* **18 D8** 44 10N 8 20 E
Rivière-au-Renard, *Canada* **71 C7** 48 59N 64 23W
Rivière-du-Loup, *Canada* **71 C6** 47 50N 69 30W
Rivière-Pentecôte, *Canada* **71 C6** 49 57N 67 1W

Rzhev

Rivière-Pilote, *Martinique* **89 D7** 14 26N 60 53W
Rivière St. Paul, *Canada* **71 B8** 51 28N 57 45W
Rivne, *Ukraine* **17 C14** 50 40N 26 10 E
Rivoli, *Italy* **18 D7** 45 3N 7 31 E
Rivoli B., *Australia* **63 F3** 37 32S 140 3 E
Riyadh = Ar Riyāḍ, *Si. Arabia* **46 C4** 24 41N 46 42 E
Rize, *Turkey* **25 F7** 41 0N 40 30 E
Rizhao, *China* **35 G10** 35 25N 119 30 E
Rizokarpaso, *Cyprus* **23 D13** 35 36N 34 23 E
Rizzuto, C., *Italy* **20 E7** 38 53N 17 5 E
Rjukan, *Norway* **9 G13** 59 54N 8 33 E
Road Town, *Virgin Is.* **89 C7** 18 27N 64 37W
Roan Plateau, *U.S.A.* **82 G9** 39 20N 109 20W
Roanne, *France* **18 C6** 46 3N 4 4 E
Roanoke, *Ala., U.S.A.* **77 J3** 33 9N 85 22W
Roanoke, *Va., U.S.A.* **76 G6** 37 16N 79 56W
Roanoke →, *U.S.A.* **77 H7** 35 57N 76 42W
Roanoke I., *U.S.A.* **77 H8** 35 55N 75 40W
Roanoke Rapids, *U.S.A.* **77 G7** 36 28N 77 40W
Roatán, *Honduras* **88 C2** 16 18N 86 35W
Robāt Sang, *Iran* **45 C8** 35 35N 59 10 E
Robbins I., *Australia* **62 G4** 40 42S 145 0 E
Robe, *Australia* **63 F2** 37 11S 139 45 E
Robe →, *Australia* **60 D2** 21 42S 116 15 E
Robert Lee, *U.S.A.* **81 K4** 31 54N 100 29W
Robertsdale, *U.S.A.* **78 F6** 40 11N 78 6W
Robertsganj, *India* **43 G10** 24 44N 83 4 E
Robertson, *S. Africa* **56 E2** 33 46S 19 50 E
Robertson I., *Antarctica* **5 C18** 65 15S 59 30W
Robertson Ra., *Australia* **60 D3** 23 15S 121 0 E
Robertstown, *Australia* **63 E2** 33 58S 139 5 E
Roberval, *Canada* **71 C5** 48 32N 72 15W
Robeson Chan., *Greenland* **4 A4** 82 0N 61 30W
Robesonia, *U.S.A.* **79 F8** 40 21N 76 8W
Robinson, *U.S.A.* **76 F2** 39 0N 87 44W
Robinson →, *Australia* **62 B2** 16 3S 137 16 E
Robinson Ra., *Australia* **61 E2** 25 40S 119 0 E
Robinvale, *Australia* **63 E3** 34 40S 142 45 E
Roblin, *Canada* **73 C8** 51 14N 101 21W
Roboré, *Bolivia* **92 G7** 18 10S 59 45W
Robson, *Canada* **72 D5** 49 20N 117 41W
Robson, Mt., *Canada* **72 C5** 53 10N 119 10W
Robstown, *U.S.A.* **81 M6** 27 47N 97 40W
Roca, C. da, *Portugal* **19 C1** 38 40N 9 31W
Roca Partida, I., *Mexico* **86 D2** 19 1N 112 2W
Rocas, I., *Brazil* **93 D12** 4 0S 34 1W
Rocha, *Uruguay* **95 C5** 34 30S 54 25W
Rochdale, *U.K.* **10 D5** 53 38N 2 9W
Rochefort, *Belgium* **15 D5** 50 9N 5 12 E
Rochefort, *France* **18 D3** 45 56N 0 57W
Rochelle, *U.S.A.* **80 E10** 41 56N 89 4W
Rocher River, *Canada* **72 A6** 61 23N 112 44W
Rochester, *U.K.* **11 F8** 51 23N 0 31 E
Rochester, *Ind., U.S.A.* **76 E2** 41 4N 86 13W
Rochester, *Minn., U.S.A.* **80 C8** 44 1N 92 28W
Rochester, *N.H., U.S.A.* **79 C14** 43 18N 70 59W
Rochester, *N.Y., U.S.A.* **78 C7** 43 10N 77 37W
Rock →, *Canada* **72 A3** 60 7N 127 7W
Rock Creek, *U.S.A.* **78 E4** 41 40N 80 52W
Rock Falls, *U.S.A.* **80 E10** 41 47N 89 41W
Rock Hill, *U.S.A.* **77 H5** 34 56N 81 1W
Rock Island, *U.S.A.* **80 E9** 41 30N 90 34W
Rock Rapids, *U.S.A.* **80 D6** 43 26N 96 10W
Rock Sound, *Bahamas* **88 B4** 24 54N 76 12W
Rock Springs, *Mont., U.S.A.* **82 C10** 46 49N 106 15W
Rock Springs, *Wyo., U.S.A.* **82 F9** 41 35N 109 14W
Rock Valley, *U.S.A.* **80 D6** 43 12N 96 18W
Rockall, *Atl. Oc.* **6 D3** 57 37N 13 42W
Rockdale, *Tex., U.S.A.* **81 K6** 30 39N 97 0W
Rockdale, *Wash., U.S.A.* **84 C5** 47 22N 121 28W
Rockefeller Plateau, *Antarctica* **5 E14** 80 0S 140 0W
Rockford, *U.S.A.* **80 D10** 42 16N 89 6W
Rockglen, *Canada* **73 D7** 49 11N 105 57W
Rockhampton, *Australia* **62 C5** 23 22S 150 32 E
Rockingham, *Australia* **61 F2** 32 15S 115 38 E
Rockingham, *U.S.A.* **77 H6** 34 57N 79 46W
Rockingham B., *Australia* **62 B4** 18 5S 146 10 E
Rocklake, *U.S.A.* **80 A5** 48 47N 99 15W
Rockland, *Canada* **79 A9** 45 33N 75 17W
Rockland, *Idaho, U.S.A.* **82 E7** 42 34N 112 53W
Rockland, *Maine, U.S.A.* **77 C11** 44 6N 69 7W
Rockland, *Mich., U.S.A.* **80 B10** 46 44N 89 11W
Rocklin, *U.S.A.* **84 G5** 38 48N 121 14W
Rockport, *Mass., U.S.A.* **79 D14** 42 39N 70 37W
Rockport, *Mo., U.S.A.* **80 E7** 40 25N 95 31W
Rockport, *Tex., U.S.A.* **81 L6** 28 2N 97 3W
Rocksprings, *U.S.A.* **81 K4** 30 1N 100 13W
Rockville, *Conn., U.S.A.* **79 E12** 41 52N 72 28W
Rockville, *Md., U.S.A.* **76 F7** 39 5N 77 9W
Rockwall, *U.S.A.* **81 J6** 32 56N 96 28W
Rockwell City, *U.S.A.* **80 D7** 42 24N 94 38W
Rockwood, *Canada* **78 C4** 43 37N 80 8W
Rockwood, *Maine, U.S.A.* **77 C11** 45 41N 69 45W
Rockwood, *Tenn., U.S.A.* **77 H3** 35 52N 84 41W
Rocky Ford, *U.S.A.* **80 F3** 38 3N 103 43W
Rocky Gully, *Australia* **61 F2** 34 30S 116 57 E
Rocky Harbour, *Canada* **71 C8** 49 36N 57 55W
Rocky Island L., *Canada* **70 C3** 46 55N 83 0W
Rocky Lane, *Canada* **72 B5** 58 31N 116 22W
Rocky Mount, *U.S.A.* **77 H7** 35 57N 77 48W
Rocky Mountain House, *Canada* **72 C6** 52 22N 114 55W
Rocky Mountain National Park, *U.S.A.* **82 F11** 40 25N 105 45W
Rocky Mts., *N. Amer.* **74 C5** 49 0N 115 0W
Rod, *Pakistan* **40 E3** 28 10N 63 5 E
Rødbyhavn, *Denmark* **9 J14** 54 39N 11 22 E
Roddickton, *Canada* **71 B8** 50 51N 56 8W
Rodez, *France* **18 D5** 44 21N 2 33 E
Rodhopoú, *Greece* **23 D5** 35 34N 23 45 E
Ródhos, *Greece* **23 C10** 36 15N 28 10 E
Rodney, *Canada* **78 D3** 42 34N 81 41W
Rodney, C., *N.Z.* **59 G5** 36 17S 174 50 E
Rodriguez, *Ind. Oc.* **3 E13** 19 45S 63 20 E
Roe →, *U.K.* **13 A5** 55 6N 6 59W
Roebling, *U.S.A.* **79 F10** 40 7N 74 47W
Roebourne, *Australia* **60 D2** 20 44S 117 9 E
Roebuck B., *Australia* **60 C3** 18 5S 122 20 E
Roermond, *Neths.* **15 C6** 51 12N 6 0 E
Roes Welcome Sd., *Canada* **69 B11** 65 0N 87 0W
Roeselare, *Belgium* **15 D3** 50 57N 3 7 E
Rogachev = Ragachow, *Belarus* **17 B16** 53 8N 30 5 E
Rogagua, L., *Bolivia* **92 F5** 13 43S 66 50W
Rogatyn, *Ukraine* **17 D13** 49 24N 24 36 E
Rogdhia, *Greece* **23 D7** 35 22N 25 1 E
Rogers, *U.S.A.* **81 G7** 36 20N 94 7W
Rogers City, *U.S.A.* **76 C4** 45 25N 83 49W
Rogersville, *Canada* **71 C6** 46 44N 65 26W
Roggan →, *Canada* **70 B4** 54 24N 79 25W
Roggan L., *Canada* **70 B4** 54 8N 77 50W
Roggeveldberge, *S. Africa* **56 E3** 32 10S 20 10 E
Rogoaguado, L., *Bolivia* **92 F5** 13 0S 65 30W
Rogue →, *U.S.A.* **82 E1** 42 26N 124 26W
Róhda, *Greece* **23 A3** 39 48N 19 46 E
Rohnert Park, *U.S.A.* **84 G4** 38 16N 122 40W
Rohri, *Pakistan* **42 F3** 27 45N 68 51 E
Rohri Canal, *Pakistan* **42 F3** 26 15N 68 27 E
Rohtak, *India* **42 E7** 28 55N 76 43 E
Roi Et, *Thailand* **38 D4** 16 4N 103 40 E
Roja, *Latvia* **9 H20** 57 29N 22 43 E
Rojas, *Argentina* **94 C3** 34 10S 60 45W
Rojo, C., *Mexico* **87 C5** 21 33N 97 20W
Rokan →, *Indonesia* **36 D2** 2 0N 100 50 E
Rokiškis, *Lithuania* **9 J21** 55 55N 25 35 E
Rolândia, *Brazil* **95 A5** 23 18S 51 23W
Rolla, *U.S.A.* **81 G9** 37 57N 91 46W
Rolleston, *Australia* **62 C4** 24 28S 148 35 E
Rollingstone, *Australia* **62 B4** 19 2S 146 24 E
Roma, *Australia* **63 D4** 26 32S 148 49 E
Roma, *Italy* **20 D5** 41 54N 12 29 E
Roma, *Sweden* **9 H18** 57 32N 18 26 E
Roma, *U.S.A.* **81 M5** 26 25N 99 1W
Romain C., *U.S.A.* **77 J6** 33 0N 79 22W
Romaine, *Canada* **71 B7** 50 13N 60 40W
Romaine →, *Canada* **71 B7** 50 18N 63 47W
Roman, *Romania* **17 E14** 46 57N 26 55 E
Romang, *Indonesia* **37 F7** 7 30S 127 20 E
Români, *Egypt* **47 E1** 30 59N 32 38 E
Romania ■, *Europe* **17 F12** 46 0N 25 0 E
Romano, Cayo, *Cuba* **88 B4** 22 0N 77 30W
Romanovka = Basarabeasca, *Moldova* **17 E15** 46 21N 28 58 E
Romans-sur-Isère, *France* **18 D6** 45 3N 5 3 E
Romblon, *Phil.* **37 B6** 12 33N 122 17 E
Rome = Roma, *Italy* **20 D5** 41 54N 12 29 E
Rome, *Ga., U.S.A.* **77 H3** 34 15N 85 10W
Rome, *N.Y., U.S.A.* **79 C9** 43 13N 75 27W
Rome, *Pa., U.S.A.* **79 E8** 41 51N 76 21W
Romney, *U.S.A.* **76 F6** 39 21N 78 45W
Romney Marsh, *U.K.* **11 F8** 51 2N 0 54 E
Rømø, *Denmark* **9 J13** 55 10N 8 30 E
Romorantin-Lanthenay, *France* **18 C4** 47 21N 1 45 E
Romsdalen, *Norway* **9 E12** 62 25N 7 52 E
Romsey, *U.K.* **11 G6** 51 0N 1 29W
Ron, *Vietnam* **38 D6** 17 53N 106 27 E
Rona, *U.K.* **12 D3** 57 34N 5 59W
Ronan, *U.S.A.* **82 C6** 47 32N 114 6W
Roncador, Cayos, *Caribbean* **88 D3** 13 32N 80 4W
Roncador, Serra do, *Brazil* **93 F8** 12 30S 52 30W
Ronda, *Spain* **19 D3** 36 46N 5 12W
Rondane, *Norway* **9 F13** 61 57N 9 50 E
Rondônia □, *Brazil* **92 F6** 11 0S 63 0W
Rondonópolis, *Brazil* **93 G8** 16 28S 54 38W
Rong, Koh, *Cambodia* **39 G4** 10 45N 103 15 E
Ronge, L. la, *Canada* **73 B7** 55 6N 105 17W
Rønne, *Denmark* **9 J16** 55 6N 14 43 E
Ronne Ice Shelf, *Antarctica* **5 D18** 78 0S 60 0W
Ronsard, C., *Australia* **61 D1** 24 46S 113 10 E
Ronse, *Belgium* **15 D3** 50 45N 3 35 E
Roodepoort, *S. Africa* **57 D4** 26 11S 27 54 E
Roof Butte, *U.S.A.* **83 H9** 36 28N 109 5W
Roorkee, *India* **42 E7** 29 52N 77 59 E
Roosendaal, *Neths.* **15 C4** 51 32N 4 29 E
Roosevelt, *U.S.A.* **82 F8** 40 18N 109 59W
Roosevelt →, *Brazil* **92 E6** 7 35S 60 20W
Roosevelt, Mt., *Canada* **72 B3** 58 26N 125 20W
Roosevelt I., *Antarctica* **5 D12** 79 30S 162 0W
Roper →, *Australia* **62 A2** 14 43S 135 27 E
Roper Bar, *Australia* **62 A1** 14 44S 134 44 E
Roque Pérez, *Argentina* **94 D4** 35 25S 59 24W
Roquetas de Mar, *Spain* **19 D4** 36 46N 2 36W
Roraima □, *Brazil* **92 C6** 2 0N 61 30W
Roraima, Mt., *Venezuela* **92 B6** 5 10N 60 40W
Røros, *Norway* **9 E14** 62 35N 11 23 E
Rosa, *Zambia* **55 D3** 9 33S 31 15 E
Rosa, L., *Bahamas* **89 B5** 21 0N 73 30W
Rosa, Monte, *Europe* **18 D7** 45 57N 7 53 E
Rosalia, *U.S.A.* **82 C5** 47 14N 117 22W
Rosamond, *U.S.A.* **85 L8** 34 52N 118 10W
Rosario, *Argentina* **94 C3** 33 0S 60 40W
Rosário, *Brazil* **93 D10** 3 0S 44 15W
Rosario, *Baja Calif., Mexico* **86 B1** 30 0N 115 50W
Rosario, *Sinaloa, Mexico* **86 C3** 23 0N 105 52W
Rosario, *Paraguay* **94 A4** 24 30S 57 35W
Rosario de la Frontera, *Argentina* **94 B3** 25 50S 65 0W
Rosario de Lerma, *Argentina* **94 A2** 24 59S 65 35W
Rosario del Tala, *Argentina* **94 C4** 32 20S 59 10W
Rosário do Sul, *Brazil* **95 C5** 30 15S 54 55W
Rosarito, *Mexico* **85 N9** 32 18N 117 4W
Roscoe, *U.S.A.* **79 E10** 41 56N 74 55W
Roscommon, *Ireland* **13 C3** 53 38N 8 11W
Roscommon □, *Ireland* **13 C3** 53 49N 8 23W
Roscrea, *Ireland* **13 D4** 52 57N 7 49W
Rose →, *Australia* **62 A2** 14 16S 135 45 E
Rose Blanche, *Canada* **71 C8** 47 38N 58 45W
Rose Pt., *Canada* **72 C2** 54 11N 131 39W
Rose Valley, *Canada* **73 C8** 52 19N 103 49W
Roseau, *Domin.* **89 C7** 15 20N 61 24W
Roseau, *U.S.A.* **80 A7** 48 51N 95 46W
Rosebery, *Australia* **62 G4** 41 46S 145 33 E
Rosebud, *S. Dak., U.S.A.* **80 D4** 43 14N 100 51W
Rosebud, *Tex., U.S.A.* **81 K6** 31 4N 96 59W
Roseburg, *U.S.A.* **82 E2** 43 13N 123 20W
Rosedale, *U.S.A.* **81 J9** 33 51N 91 2W
Roseland, *U.S.A.* **84 G4** 38 25N 122 43W
Rosemary, *Canada* **72 C6** 50 46N 112 5W
Rosenberg, *U.S.A.* **81 L7** 29 34N 95 49W
Rosenheim, *Germany* **16 E7** 47 51N 12 7 E
Roses, G. de, *Spain* **19 A7** 42 10N 3 15 E
Rosetown, *Canada* **73 C7** 51 35N 107 59W
Roseville, *Calif., U.S.A.* **84 G5** 38 45N 121 17W
Roseville, *Mich., U.S.A.* **78 D2** 42 30N 82 56W
Rosewood, *Australia* **63 D5** 27 38S 152 36 E
Roshkhvār, *Iran* **45 C8** 34 58N 59 37 E
Rosignano Marittimo, *Italy* **20 C4** 43 24N 10 28 E
Rosignol, *Guyana* **92 B7** 6 15N 57 30W
Roşiori-de-Vede, *Romania* **17 F13** 44 7N 24 59 E
Roskilde, *Denmark* **9 J15** 55 38N 12 3 E
Roslavl, *Russia* **24 D5** 53 57N 32 55 E
Rosmead, *S. Africa* **56 E4** 31 29S 25 8 E
Ross, *Australia* **62 G4** 42 2S 147 30 E
Ross, *N.Z.* **59 K3** 42 53S 170 49 E
Ross I., *Antarctica* **5 D11** 77 30S 168 0 E
Ross Ice Shelf, *Antarctica* **5 E12** 80 0S 180 0 E
Ross L., *U.S.A.* **82 B3** 48 44N 121 4W
Ross-on-Wye, *U.K.* **11 F5** 51 54N 2 34W
Ross River, *Australia* **62 C1** 23 44S 134 30 E
Ross River, *Canada* **72 A2** 62 30N 131 30W
Ross Sea, *Antarctica* **5 D11** 74 0S 178 0 E
Rossall Pt., *U.K.* **10 D4** 53 55N 3 3W
Rossan Pt., *Ireland* **13 B3** 54 42N 8 47W
Rossano, *Italy* **20 E7** 39 36N 16 39 E
Rossburn, *Canada* **73 C8** 50 40N 100 49W
Rosseau, *Canada* **78 A5** 45 16N 79 39W
Rosseau L., *Canada* **78 A5** 45 10N 79 35W
Rosses, The, *Ireland* **13 A3** 55 2N 8 20W
Rossignol, L., *Canada* **70 B5** 52 43N 73 40W
Rossignol Res., *Canada* **71 D6** 44 12N 65 10W
Rossland, *Canada* **72 D5** 49 6N 117 50W
Rosslare, *Ireland* **13 D5** 52 17N 6 24W
Rosso, *Mauritania* **50 E2** 16 40N 15 45W
Rossosh, *Russia* **25 D6** 50 15N 39 28 E
Røssvatnet, *Norway* **8 D16** 65 45N 14 5 E
Røst, *Norway* **8 C15** 67 32N 12 0 E
Rosthern, *Canada* **73 C7** 52 40N 106 20W
Rostock, *Germany* **16 A7** 54 5N 12 8 E
Rostov, *Don, Russia* **25 E6** 47 15N 39 45 E
Rostov, *Yaroslavl, Russia* **24 C6** 57 14N 39 25 E
Roswell, *Ga., U.S.A.* **77 H3** 34 2N 84 22W
Roswell, *N. Mex., U.S.A.* **81 J2** 33 24N 104 32W
Rotan, *U.S.A.* **81 J4** 32 51N 100 28W
Rother →, *U.K.* **11 G8** 50 59N 0 45 E
Rotherham, *U.K.* **10 D6** 53 26N 1 20W
Rothes, *U.K.* **12 D5** 57 32N 3 13W
Rothesay, *Canada* **71 C6** 45 23N 66 0W
Rothesay, *U.K.* **12 F3** 55 50N 5 3W
Roti, *Indonesia* **37 F6** 10 50S 123 0 E
Roto, *Australia* **63 E4** 33 0S 145 30 E
Rotondo Mte., *France* **18 E8** 42 14N 9 8 E
Rotoroa, L., *N.Z.* **59 J4** 41 55S 172 39 E
Rotorua, *N.Z.* **59 H6** 38 9S 176 16 E
Rotorua, L., *N.Z.* **59 H6** 38 5S 176 18 E
Rotterdam, *Neths.* **15 C4** 51 55N 4 30 E
Rotterdam, *U.S.A.* **79 D10** 42 48N 74 1W
Rottnest I., *Australia* **61 F2** 32 0S 115 27 E
Rottumeroog, *Neths.* **15 A6** 53 33N 6 34 E
Rottweil, *Germany* **16 D5** 48 9N 8 37 E
Rotuma, *Fiji* **64 J9** 12 25S 177 5 E
Roubaix, *France* **18 A5** 50 40N 3 10 E
Rouen, *France* **18 B4** 49 27N 1 4 E
Rouleau, *Canada* **73 C8** 50 10N 104 56W
Round Mountain, *U.S.A.* **82 G5** 38 43N 117 4W
Round Mt., *Australia* **63 E5** 30 26S 152 16 E
Round Rock, *U.S.A.* **81 K6** 30 31N 97 41W
Roundup, *U.S.A.* **82 C9** 46 27N 108 33W
Rousay, *U.K.* **12 B5** 59 10N 3 2W
Rouses Point, *U.S.A.* **79 B11** 44 59N 73 22W
Rouseville, *U.S.A.* **78 E5** 41 28N 79 42W
Roussillon, *France* **18 E5** 42 30N 2 35 E
Rouxville, *S. Africa* **56 E4** 30 25S 26 50 E
Rouyn-Noranda, *Canada* **70 C4** 48 20N 79 0W
Rovaniemi, *Finland* **8 C21** 66 29N 25 41 E
Rovereto, *Italy* **20 B4** 45 53N 11 3 E
Rovigo, *Italy* **20 B4** 45 4N 11 47 E
Rovinj, *Croatia* **16 F7** 45 5N 13 40 E
Rovno = Rivne, *Ukraine* **17 C14** 50 40N 26 10 E
Rovuma = Ruvuma →, *Tanzania* **55 E5** 10 29S 40 28 E
Row'ān, *Iran* **45 C6** 35 8N 48 51 E
Rowena, *Australia* **63 D4** 29 48S 148 55 E
Rowley Shoals, *Australia* **60 C2** 17 30S 119 0 E
Roxas, *Phil.* **37 B6** 11 36N 122 49 E
Roxboro, *U.S.A.* **77 G6** 36 24N 78 59W
Roxburgh, *N.Z.* **59 L2** 45 33S 169 19 E
Roxbury, *U.S.A.* **78 F7** 40 6N 77 39W
Roy, *Mont., U.S.A.* **82 C9** 47 20N 108 58W
Roy, *N. Mex., U.S.A.* **81 H2** 35 57N 104 12W
Roy, *Utah, U.S.A.* **82 F7** 41 10N 112 2W
Royal Canal, *Ireland* **13 C4** 53 30N 7 13W
Royal Leamington Spa, *U.K.* **11 E6** 52 18N 1 31W
Royal Tunbridge Wells, *U.K.* **11 F8** 51 7N 0 16 E
Royan, *France* **18 D3** 45 37N 1 2W
Royston, *U.K.* **11 E7** 52 3N 0 0
Rozdilna, *Ukraine* **17 E16** 46 50N 30 2 E
Rozhyshche, *Ukraine* **17 C13** 50 54N 25 15 E
Rtishchevo, *Russia* **24 C7** 52 18N 43 46 E
Ruacaná, *Angola* **56 B1** 17 20S 14 12 E
Ruahine Ra., *N.Z.* **59 H6** 39 55S 176 2 E
Ruapehu, *N.Z.* **59 H5** 39 17S 175 35 E
Ruapuke I., *N.Z.* **59 M2** 46 46S 168 31 E
Ruâq, W. →, *Egypt* **47 F2** 30 0N 33 49 E
Rub' al Khālī, *Si. Arabia* **46 D4** 18 0N 48 0 E
Rubeho Mts., *Tanzania* **54 D4** 6 50S 36 25 E
Rubh a' Mhail, *U.K.* **12 F2** 55 56N 6 8W
Rubha Hunish, *U.K.* **12 D2** 57 42N 6 20W
Rubha Robhanais = Lewis, Butt of, *U.K.* **12 C2** 58 31N 6 16W
Rubicon →, *U.S.A.* **84 G5** 38 53N 121 4W
Rubio, *Venezuela* **92 B4** 7 43N 72 22W
Rubtsovsk, *Russia* **26 D9** 51 30N 81 10 E
Ruby L., *U.S.A.* **82 F6** 40 10N 115 28W
Ruby Mts., *U.S.A.* **82 F6** 40 30N 115 20W
Rubyvale, *Australia* **62 C4** 23 25S 147 42 E
Rūd Sar, *Iran* **45 B6** 37 8N 50 18 E
Rudall, *Australia* **63 E2** 33 43S 136 17 E
Rudall →, *Australia* **60 D3** 22 34S 122 13 E
Rudewa, *Tanzania* **55 E3** 10 7S 34 40 E
Rudnyy, *Kazakstan* **26 D7** 52 57N 63 7 E
Rudolfa, Ostrov, *Russia* **26 A6** 81 45N 58 30 E
Rudyard, *U.S.A.* **76 B3** 46 14N 84 36W
Rufiji →, *Tanzania* **54 D4** 7 50S 39 15 E
Rufino, *Argentina* **94 C3** 34 20S 62 50W
Rufunsa, *Zambia* **55 F2** 15 4S 29 34 E
Rugby, *U.K.* **11 E6** 52 23N 1 16W
Rugby, *U.S.A.* **80 A5** 48 22N 100 0W
Rügen, *Germany* **16 A7** 54 22N 13 24 E
Ruhengeri, *Rwanda* **54 C2** 1 30S 29 36 E
Ruhnu, *Estonia* **9 H20** 57 48N 23 15 E
Ruhr →, *Germany* **16 C4** 51 27N 6 43 E
Ruhuhu →, *Tanzania* **55 E3** 10 31S 34 34 E
Ruidoso, *U.S.A.* **83 K11** 33 20N 105 41W
Ruivo, Pico, *Madeira* **22 D3** 32 45N 16 56W
Rujm Tal'at al Jamā'ah, *Jordan* **47 E4** 30 24N 35 30 E
Ruk, *Pakistan* **42 F3** 27 50N 68 42 E
Rukhla, *Pakistan* **42 C4** 32 27N 71 57 E
Ruki →, *Dem. Rep. of the Congo* **52 E3** 0 5N 18 17 E
Rukwa □, *Tanzania* **54 D3** 7 0S 31 30 E
Rukwa, L., *Tanzania* **54 D3** 8 0S 32 20 E
Rulhieres, C., *Australia* **60 B4** 13 56S 127 22 E
Rum = Rhum, *U.K.* **12 E2** 57 0N 6 20W
Rum Cay, *Bahamas* **89 B5** 23 40N 74 58W
Rum Jungle, *Australia* **60 B5** 13 0S 130 59 E
Rumāḥ, *Si. Arabia* **44 E5** 25 29N 47 10 E
Rumania = Romania ■, *Europe* **17 F12** 46 0N 25 0 E
Rumaylah, *Iraq* **44 D5** 30 47N 47 37 E
Rumbêk, *Sudan* **51 G11** 6 54N 29 37 E
Rumford, *U.S.A.* **77 C10** 44 33N 70 33W
Rumia, *Poland* **17 A10** 54 37N 18 25 E
Rumoi, *Japan* **30 C10** 43 56N 141 39 E
Rumonge, *Burundi* **54 C2** 3 59S 29 26 E
Rumson, *U.S.A.* **79 F11** 40 23N 74 0W
Rumuruti, *Kenya* **54 B4** 0 17N 36 32 E
Runan, *China* **34 H8** 33 0N 114 30 E
Runanga, *N.Z.* **59 K3** 42 25S 171 15 E
Runaway, C., *N.Z.* **59 G6** 37 32S 177 59 E
Runcorn, *U.K.* **10 D5** 53 21N 2 44W
Rundu, *Namibia* **53 H3** 17 52S 19 43 E
Rungwa, *Tanzania* **54 D3** 6 55S 33 32 E
Rungwa →, *Tanzania* **54 D3** 7 36S 31 50 E
Rungwe, *Tanzania* **55 D3** 9 11S 33 32 E
Rungwe, Mt., *Tanzania* **52 F6** 9 8S 33 40 E
Runton Ra., *Australia* **60 D3** 23 31S 123 6 E
Ruoqiang, *China* **32 C3** 38 55N 88 10 E
Rupa, *India* **41 F18** 27 15N 92 21 E
Rupar, *India* **42 D7** 31 2N 76 38 E
Rupat, *Indonesia* **36 D2** 1 45N 101 40 E
Rupen →, *India* **42 H4** 23 28N 71 31 E
Rupert, *U.S.A.* **82 E7** 42 37N 113 41W
Rupert →, *Canada* **70 B4** 51 29N 78 45W
Rupert B., *Canada* **70 B4** 51 35N 79 0W
Rupert House = Waskaganish, *Canada* **70 B4** 51 30N 78 40W
Rupsa, *India* **43 J12** 21 37N 87 1 E
Rurrenabaque, *Bolivia* **92 F5** 14 30S 67 32W
Rusambo, *Zimbabwe* **55 F3** 16 30S 32 4 E
Rusape, *Zimbabwe* **55 F3** 18 35S 32 8 E
Ruschuk = Ruse, *Bulgaria* **21 C12** 43 48N 25 59 E
Ruse, *Bulgaria* **21 C12** 43 48N 25 59 E
Rush, *Ireland* **13 C5** 53 31N 6 6W
Rushan, *China* **35 F11** 36 56N 121 30 E
Rushden, *U.K.* **11 E7** 52 18N 0 35W
Rushmore, Mt., *U.S.A.* **80 D3** 43 53N 103 28W
Rushville, *Ill., U.S.A.* **80 E9** 40 7N 90 34W
Rushville, *Ind., U.S.A.* **76 F3** 39 37N 85 27W
Rushville, *Nebr., U.S.A.* **80 D3** 42 43N 102 28W
Russas, *Brazil* **93 D11** 4 55S 37 50W
Russell, *Canada* **73 C8** 50 50N 101 20W
Russell, *Kans., U.S.A.* **80 F5** 38 54N 98 52W
Russell, *N.Y., U.S.A.* **79 B9** 44 27N 75 9W
Russell, *Pa., U.S.A.* **78 E5** 41 56N 79 8W
Russell L., *Man., Canada* **73 B8** 56 15N 101 30W
Russell L., *N.W.T., Canada* **72 A5** 63 5N 115 44W
Russellkonda, *India* **41 K14** 19 57N 84 42 E
Russellville, *Ala., U.S.A.* **77 H2** 34 30N 87 44W
Russellville, *Ark., U.S.A.* **81 H8** 35 17N 93 8W
Russellville, *Ky., U.S.A.* **77 G2** 36 51N 86 53W
Russia ■, *Eurasia* **27 C11** 62 0N 105 0 E
Russian →, *U.S.A.* **84 G3** 38 27N 123 8W
Russkoye Ustie, *Russia* **4 B15** 71 0N 149 0 E
Rustam, *Pakistan* **42 B5** 34 25N 72 13 E
Rustam Shahr, *Pakistan* **42 F2** 26 58N 66 6 E
Rustavi, *Georgia* **25 F8** 41 30N 45 0 E
Rustenburg, *S. Africa* **56 D4** 25 41S 27 14 E
Ruston, *U.S.A.* **81 J8** 32 32N 92 38W
Rutana, *Burundi* **54 C3** 3 55S 30 0 E
Ruteng, *Indonesia* **37 F6** 8 35S 120 30 E
Ruth, *U.S.A.* **78 C2** 43 42N 82 45W
Rutherford, *U.S.A.* **84 G4** 38 26N 122 24W
Rutland, *U.S.A.* **79 C12** 43 37N 72 58W
Rutland □, *U.K.* **11 E7** 52 38N 0 40W
Rutland Water, *U.K.* **11 E7** 52 39N 0 38W
Rutledge →, *Canada* **73 A6** 61 4N 112 0W
Rutledge L., *Canada* **73 A6** 61 33N 110 47W
Rutshuru, *Dem. Rep. of the Congo* **54 C2** 1 13S 29 25 E
Ruvu, *Tanzania* **54 D4** 6 49S 38 43 E
Ruvu →, *Tanzania* **54 D4** 6 23S 38 52 E
Ruvuma □, *Tanzania* **55 E4** 10 20S 36 0 E
Ruvuma →, *Tanzania* **55 E5** 10 29S 40 28 E
Ruwais, *U.A.E.* **45 E7** 24 5N 52 50 E
Ruwenzori, *Africa* **54 B2** 0 30N 29 55 E
Ruyigi, *Burundi* **54 C3** 3 29S 30 15 E
Ružomberok, *Slovak Rep.* **17 D10** 49 3N 19 17 E
Rwanda ■, *Africa* **54 C3** 2 0S 30 0 E
Ryan, L., *U.K.* **12 G3** 55 0N 5 2W
Ryazan, *Russia* **24 D6** 54 40N 39 40 E
Ryazhsk, *Russia* **24 D7** 53 45N 40 3 E
Rybache = Rybachye, *Kazakstan* **26 E9** 46 40N 81 20 E
Rybachiy Poluostrov, *Russia* **24 A5** 69 43N 32 0 E
Rybachye = Ysyk-Köl, *Kyrgyzstan* **28 E11** 42 26N 76 12 E
Rybachye, *Kazakstan* **26 E9** 46 40N 81 20 E
Rybinsk, *Russia* **24 C6** 58 5N 38 50 E
Rybinskoye Vdkhr., *Russia* **24 C6** 58 30N 38 25 E
Rybnitsa = Râbniţa, *Moldova* **17 E15** 47 45N 29 0 E
Rycroft, *Canada* **72 B5** 55 45N 118 40W
Ryde, *U.K.* **11 G6** 50 43N 1 9W
Ryderwood, *U.S.A.* **84 D3** 46 23N 123 3W
Rye, *U.K.* **11 G8** 50 57N 0 45 E
Rye →, *U.K.* **10 C7** 54 11N 0 44W
Rye Bay, *U.K.* **11 G8** 50 52N 0 49 E
Rye Patch Reservoir, *U.S.A.* **82 F4** 40 28N 118 19W
Ryegate, *U.S.A.* **82 C9** 46 18N 109 15W
Ryley, *Canada* **72 C6** 53 17N 112 26W
Rylstone, *Australia* **63 E4** 32 46S 149 58 E
Ryōtsu, *Japan* **30 E9** 38 5N 138 26 E
Rypin, *Poland* **17 B10** 53 3N 19 25 E
Ryūgasaki, *Japan* **31 G10** 35 54N 140 11 E
Ryūkyū Is. = Ryūkyū-rettō, *Japan* **31 M3** 26 0N 126 0 E
Ryūkyū-rettō, *Japan* **31 M3** 26 0N 126 0 E
Rzeszów, *Poland* **17 C11** 50 5N 21 58 E
Rzhev, *Russia* **24 C5** 56 20N 34 20 E

S

Sa, *Thailand* **38 C3** 18 34N 100 45 E
Sa Canal, *Spain* **22 C7** 38 51N 1 23 E
Sa Conillera, *Spain* **22 C7** 38 59N 1 13 E
Sa Dec, *Vietnam* **39 G5** 10 20N 105 46 E
Sa Dragonera, *Spain* **22 B9** 39 35N 2 19 E
Sa Mesquida, *Spain* **22 B11** 39 55N 4 16 E
Sa Savina, *Spain* **22 C7** 38 44N 1 25 E
Sa'ādatābād, *Fārs, Iran* **45 D7** 30 10N 53 5 E
Sa'ādatābād, *Hormozgān, Iran* **45 D7** 28 3N 55 53 E
Sa'ādatābād, *Kermān, Iran* **45 D7** 29 40N 55 51 E
Saale →, *Germany* **16 C6** 51 56N 11 54 E
Saalfeld, *Germany* **16 C6** 50 38N 11 21 E
Saar →, *Europe* **18 B7** 49 41N 6 32 E
Saarbrücken, *Germany* **16 D4** 49 14N 6 59 E
Saaremaa, *Estonia* **9 G20** 58 30N 22 30 E
Saarijärvi, *Finland* **9 E21** 62 43N 25 16 E
Saariselkä, *Finland* **8 B23** 68 16N 28 15 E
Sab 'Ābar, *Syria* **44 C3** 33 46N 37 41 E
Saba, *W. Indies* **89 C7** 17 42N 63 26W
Šabac, *Serbia, Yug.* **21 B8** 44 48N 19 42 E
Sabadell, *Spain* **19 B7** 41 28N 2 7 E
Sabah □, *Malaysia* **36 C5** 6 0N 117 0 E
Sabak Bernam, *Malaysia* **39 L3** 3 46N 100 58 E
Sabalān, Kūhhā-ye, *Iran* **44 B5** 38 15N 47 45 E
Sabalana, Kepulauan, *Indonesia* **37 F5** 6 45 S 118 50 E
Sábana de la Mar, *Dom. Rep.* **89 C6** 19 7N 69 24W
Sábanalarga, *Colombia* **92 A4** 10 38N 74 55W
Sabang, *Indonesia* **36 C1** 5 50N 95 15 E
Sabará, *Brazil* **93 G10** 19 55 S 43 46W
Sabarmati →, *India* **42 H5** 22 18N 72 22 E
Sabattis, *U.S.A.* **79 B10** 44 6N 74 40W
Saberania, *Indonesia* **37 E9** 2 5 S 138 18 E
Sabhah, *Libya* **51 C8** 27 9N 14 29 E
Sabi →, *India* **42 E7** 28 29N 76 44 E
Sabie, *S. Africa* **57 D5** 25 10 S 30 48 E
Sabinal, *Mexico* **86 A3** 30 58N 107 25W
Sabinal, *U.S.A.* **81 L5** 29 19N 99 28W
Sabinas, *Mexico* **86 B4** 27 50N 101 10W
Sabinas →, *Mexico* **86 B4** 27 37N 100 42W
Sabinas Hidalgo, *Mexico* **86 B4** 26 33N 100 10W
Sabine →, *U.S.A.* **81 L8** 29 59N 93 47W
Sabine L., *U.S.A.* **81 L8** 29 53N 93 51W
Sabine Pass, *U.S.A.* **81 L8** 29 44N 93 54W
Sabinsville, *U.S.A.* **78 E7** 41 52N 77 31W
Sabkhet el Bardawîl, *Egypt* **47 D2** 31 10N 33 15 E
Sablayan, *Phil.* **37 B6** 12 50N 120 50 E
Sable, *Canada* **71 A6** 55 30N 68 21W
Sable, C., *Canada* **71 D6** 43 29N 65 38W
Sable, C., *U.S.A.* **75 E10** 25 9N 81 8W
Sable I., *Canada* **71 D8** 44 0N 60 0W
Sabrina Coast, *Antarctica* **5 C9** 68 0 S 120 0 E
Sabulubbek, *Indonesia* **36 E1** 1 36 S 98 40 E
Sabzevār, *Iran* **45 B8** 36 15N 57 40 E
Sabzvārān, *Iran* **45 D8** 28 45N 57 50 E
Sac City, *U.S.A.* **80 D7** 42 25N 95 0W
Săcele, *Romania* **17 F13** 45 37N 25 41 E
Sachigo →, *Canada* **70 A2** 55 6N 88 58W
Sachigo, L., *Canada* **70 B1** 53 50N 92 12W
Sachsen □, *Germany* **16 C7** 50 55N 13 10 E
Sachsen-Anhalt □, *Germany* **16 C7** 52 0N 12 0 E
Sackets Harbor, *U.S.A.* **79 C8** 43 57N 76 7W
Sackville, *Canada* **71 C7** 45 54N 64 22W
Saco, *Maine, U.S.A.* **77 D10** 43 30N 70 27W
Saco, *Mont., U.S.A.* **82 B10** 48 28N 107 21W
Sacramento, *U.S.A.* **84 G5** 38 35N 121 29W
Sacramento →, *U.S.A.* **84 G5** 38 3N 121 56W
Sacramento Mts., *U.S.A.* **83 K11** 32 30N 105 30W
Sacramento Valley, *U.S.A.* **84 G5** 39 30N 122 0W
Sada-Misaki, *Japan* **31 H6** 33 20N 132 1 E
Sadabad, *India* **42 F8** 27 27N 78 3 E
Sadani, *Tanzania* **54 D4** 5 58 S 38 35 E
Sadao, *Thailand* **39 J3** 6 38N 100 26 E
Sadd el Aali, *Egypt* **51 D12** 23 54N 32 54 E
Saddle Mt., *U.S.A.* **84 E3** 45 58N 123 41W
Sadimi, *Dem. Rep. of the Congo* **55 D1** 9 25 S 23 32 E
Sado, *Japan* **30 F9** 38 0N 138 25 E
Sadon, *Burma* **41 G20** 25 28N 97 55 E
Sadra, *India* **42 H5** 23 21N 72 43 E
Sadri, *India* **42 G5** 25 11N 73 26 E
Sæby, *Denmark* **9 H14** 57 21N 10 30 E
Saegertown, *U.S.A.* **78 E4** 41 43N 80 9W
Şafājah, *Si. Arabia* **44 E3** 26 25N 39 0 E
Säffle, *Sweden* **9 G15** 59 8N 12 55 E
Safford, *U.S.A.* **83 K9** 32 50N 109 43W
Saffron Walden, *U.K.* **11 E8** 52 1N 0 16 E
Safi, *Morocco* **50 B4** 32 18N 9 20W
Şafīābād, *Iran* **45 B8** 36 45N 57 58 E
Safid Dasht, *Iran* **45 C6** 33 27N 48 11 E
Safīd Kūh, *Afghan.* **40 B3** 34 45N 63 0 E
Safid Rūd →, *Iran* **45 B6** 37 23N 50 11 E
Safipur, *India* **43 F9** 26 44N 80 21 E
Safwān, *Iraq* **44 D5** 30 7N 47 43 E
Sag Harbor, *U.S.A.* **79 F12** 41 0N 72 18W
Saga, *Japan* **31 H5** 33 15N 130 16 E
Saga □, *Japan* **31 H5** 33 15N 130 20 E
Sagae, *Japan* **30 E10** 38 22N 140 17 E
Sagamore, *U.S.A.* **78 F5** 40 46N 79 14W
Sagar, *India* **40 M9** 14 14N 75 6 E
Sagar, *Mad. P., India* **43 H8** 23 50N 78 44 E
Sagara, L., *Tanzania* **54 D3** 5 20 S 31 0 E
Saginaw, *U.S.A.* **76 D4** 43 26N 83 56W
Saginaw →, *U.S.A.* **76 D4** 43 39N 83 51W
Saginaw B., *U.S.A.* **76 D4** 43 50N 83 40W
Saglouc = Salluit, *Canada* **69 B12** 62 14N 75 38W
Sagŏ-ri, *S. Korea* **35 G14** 35 25N 126 49 E
Sagua la Grande, *Cuba* **88 B3** 22 50N 80 10W
Saguache, *U.S.A.* **83 G10** 38 5N 106 8W
Saguaro Nat. Park, *U.S.A.* **83 K8** 32 12N 110 38W
Saguenay →, *Canada* **71 C5** 48 22N 71 0W
Sagunt, *Spain* **19 C5** 39 42N 0 18W
Sagunto = Sagunt, *Spain* **19 C5** 39 42N 0 18W
Sagwara, *India* **42 H6** 23 41N 74 1 E
Sahagún, *Spain* **19 A3** 42 18N 5 2W
Saḩam al Jawlān, *Syria* **47 C4** 32 45N 35 55 E
Sahand, Kūh-e, *Iran* **44 B5** 37 44N 46 27 E
Sahara, *Africa* **50 D6** 23 0N 5 0 E
Saharan Atlas = Saharien, Atlas, *Algeria* **50 B6** 33 30N 1 0 E
Saharanpur, *India* **42 E7** 29 58N 77 33 E
Saharien, Atlas, *Algeria* **50 B6** 33 30N 1 0 E
Saharsa, *India* **43 G12** 25 53N 86 36 E
Sahasinaka, *Madag.* **57 C8** 21 49 S 47 49 E
Sahaswan, *India* **43 E8** 28 5N 78 45 E
Sahel, *Africa* **50 E5** 16 0N 5 0 E
Sahibganj, *India* **43 G12** 25 12N 87 40 E
Sāḩilīyah, *Iraq* **44 C4** 33 43N 42 42 E
Sahiwal, *Pakistan* **42 D5** 30 45N 73 8 E
Şahneh, *Iran* **44 C5** 34 29N 47 41 E
Sahuaripa, *Mexico* **86 B3** 29 0N 109 13W
Sahuarita, *U.S.A.* **83 L8** 31 57N 110 58W
Sahuayo, *Mexico* **86 C4** 20 4N 102 43W
Sai →, *India* **43 G10** 25 39N 82 47 E
Sai Buri, *Thailand* **39 J3** 6 43N 101 45 E
Sa'id Bundas, *Sudan* **51 G10** 8 24N 24 48 E
Sa'īdābād, *Kermān, Iran* **45 D7** 29 30N 55 45 E
Sa'īdābād, *Semnān, Iran* **45 B7** 36 8N 54 11 E
Sa'īdīyeh, *Iran* **45 B6** 36 20N 48 55 E
Saidpur, *Bangla.* **41 G16** 25 48N 89 0 E
Saidpur, *India* **43 G10** 25 33N 83 11 E
Saidu, *Pakistan* **43 B5** 34 43N 72 24 E
Saigon = Phanh Bho Ho Chi Minh, *Vietnam* **39 G6** 10 58N 106 40 E
Saijō, *Japan* **31 H6** 33 55N 133 11 E
Saikhoa Ghat, *India* **41 F19** 27 50N 95 40 E
Saiki, *Japan* **31 H5** 32 58N 131 51 E
Sailana, *India* **42 H6** 23 28N 74 55 E
Sailolof, *Indonesia* **37 E8** 1 7 S 130 46 E
Saimaa, *Finland* **9 F23** 61 15N 28 15 E
Şa'in Dezh, *Iran* **44 B5** 36 40N 46 25 E
St. Abb's Head, *U.K.* **12 F6** 55 55N 2 8W
St. Alban's, *Canada* **71 C8** 47 51N 55 50W
St. Albans, *U.K.* **11 F7** 51 45N 0 19W
St. Albans, *Vt., U.S.A.* **79 B11** 44 49N 73 5W
St. Albans, *W. Va., U.S.A.* **76 F5** 38 23N 81 50W
St. Alban's Head, *U.K.* **11 G5** 50 34N 2 4W
St. Albert, *Canada* **72 C6** 53 37N 113 32W
St. Andrew's, *Canada* **71 C8** 47 45N 59 15W
St. Andrews, *U.K.* **12 E6** 56 20N 2 47W
St-Anicet, *Canada* **79 A10** 45 8N 74 22W
St. Ann B., *Canada* **71 C7** 46 22N 60 25W
St. Ann's Bay, *Jamaica* **88 C4** 18 26N 77 15W
St. Anthony, *Canada* **71 B8** 51 22N 55 35W
St. Anthony, *U.S.A.* **82 E8** 43 58N 111 41W
St. Antoine, *Canada* **71 C7** 46 22N 64 45W
St. Arnaud, *Australia* **63 F3** 36 40 S 143 16 E
St-Augustin →, *Canada* **71 B8** 51 16N 58 40W
St-Augustin-Saguenay, *Canada* **71 B8** 51 13N 58 38W
St. Augustine, *U.S.A.* **77 L5** 29 54N 81 19W
St. Austell, *U.K.* **11 G3** 50 20N 4 47W
St. Barbe, *Canada* **71 B8** 51 12N 56 46W
St-Barthélemy, *W. Indies* **89 C7** 17 50N 62 50W
St. Bees Hd., *U.K.* **10 C4** 54 31N 3 38W
St. Bride's, *Canada* **71 C9** 46 56N 54 10W
St. Brides B., *U.K.* **11 F2** 51 49N 5 9W
St-Brieuc, *France* **18 B2** 48 30N 2 46W
St. Catharines, *Canada* **78 C5** 43 10N 79 15W
St. Catherines I., *U.S.A.* **77 K5** 31 40N 81 10W
St. Catherine's Pt., *U.K.* **11 G6** 50 34N 1 18W
St-Chamond, *France* **18 D6** 45 28N 4 31 E
St. Charles, *Ill., U.S.A.* **76 E1** 41 54N 88 19W
St. Charles, *Mo., U.S.A.* **80 F9** 38 47N 90 29W
St. Charles, *Va., U.S.A.* **76 F7** 36 48N 83 4W
St. Christopher-Nevis = St. Kitts & Nevis ■, *W. Indies* **89 C7** 17 20N 62 40W
St. Clair, *Mich., U.S.A.* **78 D2** 42 50N 82 30W
St. Clair, *Pa., U.S.A.* **79 F8** 40 43N 76 12W
St. Clair →, *U.S.A.* **78 D2** 42 38N 82 31W
St. Clair, L., *Canada* **70 D3** 42 30N 82 45W
St. Clair, L., *U.S.A.* **78 D2** 42 27N 82 39W
St. Clairsville, *U.S.A.* **78 F4** 40 5N 80 54W
St. Claude, *Canada* **73 D9** 49 40N 98 20W
St-Clet, *Canada* **79 A10** 45 21N 74 13W
St. Cloud, *Fla., U.S.A.* **77 L5** 28 15N 81 17W
St. Cloud, *Minn., U.S.A.* **80 C7** 45 34N 94 10W
St. Cricq, C., *Australia* **61 E1** 25 17 S 113 6 E
St. Croix, *Virgin Is.* **89 C7** 17 45N 64 45W
St. Croix →, *U.S.A.* **80 C8** 44 45N 92 48W
St. Croix Falls, *U.S.A.* **80 C8** 45 24N 92 38W
St. David's, *Canada* **71 C8** 48 12N 58 52W
St. David's, *U.K.* **11 F2** 51 53N 5 16W
St. David's Head, *U.K.* **11 F2** 51 54N 5 19W
St-Denis, *France* **18 B5** 48 56N 2 22 E
St-Dizier, *France* **18 B6** 48 38N 4 56 E
St. Elias, Mt., *U.S.A.* **68 B5** 60 18N 140 56W
St. Elias Mts., *Canada* **72 A1** 60 33N 139 28W
St. Elias Mts., *U.S.A.* **68 C6** 60 0N 138 0W
St-Étienne, *France* **18 D6** 45 27N 4 22 E
St. Eugène, *Canada* **79 A10** 45 30N 74 28W
St. Eustatius, *W. Indies* **89 C7** 17 20N 63 0W
St-Félicien, *Canada* **70 C5** 48 40N 72 25W
St-Flour, *France* **18 D5** 45 2N 3 6 E
St. Francis, *U.S.A.* **80 F4** 39 47N 101 48W
St. Francis →, *U.S.A.* **81 H9** 34 38N 90 36W
St. Francis, C., *S. Africa* **56 E3** 34 14S 24 49 E
St. Francisville, *U.S.A.* **81 K9** 30 47N 91 23W
St-François, L., *Canada* **79 A10** 45 10N 74 22W
St-Gabriel, *Canada* **70 C5** 46 17N 73 24W
St. Gallen = Sankt Gallen, *Switz.* **18 C8** 47 26N 9 22 E
St-Gaudens, *France* **18 E4** 43 6N 0 44 E
St. George, *Australia* **63 D4** 28 1 S 148 30 E
St. George, *Canada* **71 C6** 45 11N 66 50W
St. George, *S.C., U.S.A.* **77 J5** 33 11N 80 35W
St. George, *Utah, U.S.A.* **83 H7** 37 6N 113 35W
St. George, C., *Canada* **71 C8** 48 30N 59 16W
St. George, C., *U.S.A.* **77 L3** 29 40N 85 5W
St. George Ra., *Australia* **60 C4** 18 40S 125 0 E
St. George's, *Canada* **71 C8** 48 26N 58 31W
St-Georges, *Canada* **71 C5** 46 8N 70 40W
St. George's, *Grenada* **89 D7** 12 5N 61 43W
St. George's B., *Canada* **71 C8** 48 24N 58 53W
St. Georges Basin, *N.S.W., Australia* **63 F5** 35 7S 150 36 E
St. Georges Basin, *W. Austral., Australia* **60 C4** 15 23S 125 2 E
St. George's Channel, *Europe* **13 E6** 52 0N 6 0W
St. Georges Hd., *Australia* **63 F5** 35 12S 150 42 E
St. Gotthard P. = San Gottardo, P. del, *Switz.* **18 C8** 46 33N 8 33 E
St. Helena, *U.S.A.* **82 G2** 38 30N 122 28W
St. Helena ■, *Atl. Oc.* **49 H3** 15 55S 5 44W
St. Helena, Mt., *U.S.A.* **84 G4** 38 40N 122 36W
St. Helena B., *S. Africa* **56 E2** 32 40S 18 10 E
St. Helens, *Australia* **62 G4** 41 20S 148 15 E
St. Helens, *U.K.* **10 D5** 53 27N 2 44W
St. Helens, *U.S.A.* **84 E4** 45 52N 122 48W
St. Helens, Mt., *U.S.A.* **84 D4** 46 12N 122 12W
St. Helier, *U.K.* **11 H5** 49 10N 2 7W
St-Hubert, *Belgium* **15 D5** 50 2N 5 23 E
St-Hyacinthe, *Canada* **70 C5** 45 40N 72 58W
St. Ignace, *U.S.A.* **76 C3** 45 52N 84 44W
St. Ignace I., *Canada* **70 C2** 48 45N 88 0W
St. Ignatius, *U.S.A.* **82 C6** 47 19N 114 6W
St. Ives, *U.K.* **11 G2** 50 12N 5 30W
St. James, *U.S.A.* **80 D7** 43 59N 94 38W
St-Jean →, *Canada* **71 B7** 50 17N 64 20W
St-Jean, L., *Canada* **71 C5** 48 40N 72 0W
St-Jean-Port-Joli, *Canada* **71 C5** 47 15N 70 13W
St-Jean-sur-Richelieu, *Canada* **79 A11** 45 20N 73 20W
St-Jérôme, *Canada* **70 C5** 45 47N 74 0W
St. John, *Canada* **71 C6** 45 20N 66 8W
St. John, *U.S.A.* **81 G5** 38 0N 98 46W
St. John →, *U.S.A.* **77 C12** 45 12N 66 5W
St. John, C., *Canada* **71 C8** 50 0N 55 32W
St. John's, *Antigua* **89 C7** 17 6N 61 51W
St. John's, *Canada* **71 C9** 47 35N 52 40W
St. Johns, *Ariz., U.S.A.* **83 J9** 34 30N 109 22W
St. Johns, *Mich., U.S.A.* **76 D3** 43 0N 84 33W
St. Johns →, *U.S.A.* **77 K5** 30 24N 81 24W
St. John's Pt., *Ireland* **13 B3** 54 34N 8 27W
St. Johnsbury, *U.S.A.* **79 B12** 44 25N 72 1W
St. Johnsville, *U.S.A.* **79 D10** 43 0N 74 43W
St. Joseph, *La., U.S.A.* **81 K9** 31 55N 91 14W
St. Joseph, *Mich., U.S.A.* **75 B9** 42 6N 86 29W
St. Joseph, *Mo., U.S.A.* **80 F7** 39 46N 94 50W
St. Joseph →, *U.S.A.* **76 D2** 42 7N 86 29W
St. Joseph, I., *Canada* **70 C3** 46 12N 83 58W
St. Joseph, L., *Canada* **70 B1** 51 10N 90 35W
St-Jovite, *Canada* **70 C5** 46 8N 74 38W
St. Kilda, *N.Z.* **59 L3** 45 53S 170 31 E
St. Kitts & Nevis ■, *W. Indies* **89 C7** 17 20N 62 40W
St. Laurent, *Canada* **73 C9** 50 25N 97 58W
St. Lawrence, *Australia* **62 C4** 22 16S 149 31 E
St. Lawrence, *Canada* **71 C8** 46 54N 55 23W
St. Lawrence →, *Canada* **71 C6** 49 30N 66 0W
St. Lawrence, Gulf of, *Canada* **71 C7** 48 25N 62 0W
St. Lawrence I., *U.S.A.* **68 B3** 63 30N 170 30W
St. Leonard, *Canada* **71 C6** 47 12N 67 58W
St. Lewis →, *Canada* **71 B8** 52 26N 56 11W
St-Lô, *France* **18 B3** 49 7N 1 5W
St. Louis, *Senegal* **50 E2** 16 8N 16 27W
St. Louis, *U.S.A.* **80 F9** 38 37N 90 12W
St. Louis →, *U.S.A.* **80 B8** 47 15N 92 45W
St. Lucia ■, *W. Indies* **89 D7** 14 0N 60 50W
St. Lucia, L., *S. Africa* **57 D5** 28 5S 32 30 E
St. Lucia Channel, *W. Indies* **89 D7** 14 15N 61 0W
St. Maarten, *W. Indies* **89 C7** 18 0N 63 5W
St. Magnus B., *U.K.* **12 A7** 60 25N 1 35W
St-Malo, *France* **18 B2** 48 39N 2 1W
St-Marc, *Haiti* **89 C5** 19 10N 72 41W
St. Maries, *U.S.A.* **82 C5** 47 19N 116 35W
St-Martin, *W. Indies* **89 C7** 18 0N 63 0W
St. Martin, L., *Canada* **73 C9** 51 40N 98 30W
St. Mary Pk., *Australia* **63 E2** 31 32S 138 34 E
St. Marys, *Australia* **62 G4** 41 35S 148 11 E
St. Marys, *Canada* **78 C3** 43 20N 81 10W
St. Mary's, *Corn., U.K.* **11 H1** 49 55N 6 18W
St. Mary's, *Orkney, U.K.* **12 C6** 58 54N 2 54W
St. Marys, *Ga., U.S.A.* **77 K5** 30 44N 81 33W
St. Marys, *Pa., U.S.A.* **78 E6** 41 26N 78 34W
St. Mary's, C., *Canada* **71 C9** 46 50N 54 12W
St. Mary's B., *Canada* **71 C9** 46 50N 53 50W
St. Marys Bay, *Canada* **71 D6** 44 25N 66 10W
St-Mathieu, Pte., *France* **18 B1** 48 20N 4 45W
St. Matthew I., *U.S.A.* **68 B2** 60 24N 172 42W
St. Matthews, I. = Zadetkyi Kyun, *Burma* **39 H2** 10 0N 98 25 E
St-Maurice →, *Canada* **70 C5** 46 21N 72 31W
St-Nazaire, *France* **18 C2** 47 17N 2 12W
St. Neots, *U.K.* **11 E7** 52 14N 0 15W
St-Niklaas, *Belgium* **15 C4** 51 10N 4 8 E
St-Omer, *France* **18 A5** 50 45N 2 15 E
St-Pamphile, *Canada* **71 C6** 46 58N 69 48W
St. Pascal, *Canada* **71 C6** 47 32N 69 48W
St. Paul, *Canada* **72 C6** 54 0N 111 17W
St. Paul, *Minn., U.S.A.* **80 C8** 44 57N 93 6W
St. Paul, *Nebr., U.S.A.* **80 E5** 41 13N 98 27W
St-Paul →, *Canada* **71 B8** 51 27N 57 42W
St. Paul, I., *Ind. Oc.* **3 F13** 38 55S 77 34 E
St. Paul I., *Canada* **71 C7** 47 12N 60 9W
St. Peter, *U.S.A.* **80 C8** 44 20N 93 57W
St. Peter Port, *U.K.* **11 H5** 49 26N 2 33W
St. Peters, *N.S., Canada* **71 C7** 45 40N 60 53W
St. Peters, *P.E.I., Canada* **71 C7** 46 25N 62 35W
St. Petersburg = Sankt-Peterburg, *Russia* **24 C5** 59 55N 30 20 E
St. Petersburg, *U.S.A.* **77 M4** 27 46N 82 39W
St-Pie, *Canada* **79 A12** 45 30N 72 54W
St-Pierre, *St- P. & M.* **71 C8** 46 46N 56 12W
St-Pierre, L., *Canada* **70 C5** 46 12N 72 52W
St-Pierre et Miquelon □, *St- P. & M.* **71 C8** 46 55N 56 10W
St. Quentin, *Canada* **71 C6** 47 30N 67 23W
St-Quentin, *France* **18 B5** 49 50N 3 16 E
St. Regis, *U.S.A.* **82 C6** 47 18N 115 6W
St. Sebastien, Tanjon' i, *Madag.* **57 A8** 12 26S 48 44 E
St-Siméon, *Canada* **71 C6** 47 51N 69 54W
St. Simons I., *U.S.A.* **77 K5** 31 12N 81 15W
St. Simons Island, *U.S.A.* **77 K5** 31 9N 81 22W
St. Stephen, *Canada* **71 C6** 45 16N 67 17W
St. Thomas, *Canada* **78 D3** 42 45N 81 10W
St. Thomas I., *Virgin Is.* **89 C7** 18 20N 64 55W
St-Tite, *Canada* **70 C5** 46 45N 72 34W
St-Tropez, *France* **18 E7** 43 17N 6 38 E
St. Troud = St. Truiden, *Belgium* **15 D5** 50 48N 5 10 E
St. Truiden, *Belgium* **15 D5** 50 48N 5 10 E
St. Vincent, G., *Australia* **63 F2** 35 0S 138 0 E
St. Vincent & the Grenadines ■, *W. Indies* **89 D7** 13 0N 61 10W
St. Vincent Passage, *W. Indies* **89 D7** 13 30N 61 0W
St-Vith, *Belgium* **15 D6** 50 17N 6 9 E
St. Walburg, *Canada* **73 C7** 53 39N 109 12W
Ste-Agathe-des-Monts, *Canada* **70 C5** 46 3N 74 17W
Ste-Anne, L., *Canada* **71 B6** 50 0N 67 42W
Ste-Anne-des-Monts, *Canada* **71 C6** 49 8N 66 30W
Ste. Genevieve, *U.S.A.* **80 G9** 37 59N 90 2W
Ste-Marguerite →, *Canada* **71 B6** 50 9N 66 36W
Ste-Marie, *Martinique* **89 D7** 14 48N 61 1W
Ste-Marie de la Madeleine, *Canada* **71 C5** 46 26N 71 0W
Ste-Rose, *Guadeloupe* **89 C7** 16 20N 61 45W
Ste. Rose du Lac, *Canada* **73 C9** 51 4N 99 30W
Saintes, *France* **18 D3** 45 45N 0 37W
Saintes, I. des, *Guadeloupe* **89 C7** 15 50N 61 35W
Saintfield, *U.K.* **13 B6** 54 28N 5 49W
Sainthiya, *India* **43 H12** 23 57N 87 40 E
Saintonge, *France* **18 D3** 45 40N 0 50W
Saipan, *Pac. Oc.* **64 F6** 15 12N 145 45 E
Sairang, *India* **41 H18** 23 50N 92 45 E
Sairecábur, Cerro, *Bolivia* **94 A2** 22 43S 67 54W
Saitama □, *Japan* **31 F9** 36 25N 139 30 E
Saiyid, *Pakistan* **42 C5** 33 7N 73 2 E
Sajama, *Bolivia* **92 G5** 18 7S 69 0W
Sajószentpéter, *Hungary* **17 D11** 48 12N 20 44 E
Sajum, *India* **43 C8** 33 20N 79 0 E
Sak →, *S. Africa* **56 E3** 30 52S 20 25 E
Sakai, *Japan* **31 G7** 34 30N 135 30 E
Sakaide, *Japan* **31 G6** 34 15N 133 50 E
Sakaiminato, *Japan* **31 G6** 35 38N 133 11 E
Sakākah, *Si. Arabia* **44 D4** 30 0N 40 8 E
Sakakawea, L., *U.S.A.* **80 B4** 47 30N 101 25W
Sakami →, *Canada* **70 B4** 53 40N 76 40W
Sakami, L., *Canada* **70 B4** 53 15N 77 0W
Sakania, *Dem. Rep. of the Congo* **55 E2** 12 43S 28 30 E
Sakarya, *Turkey* **25 F5** 40 48N 30 25 E
Sakashima-Guntō, *Japan* **31 M2** 24 46N 124 0 E
Sakata, *Japan* **30 E9** 38 55N 139 50 E
Sakchu, *N. Korea* **35 D13** 40 23N 125 2 E
Sakeny →, *Madag.* **57 C8** 20 0S 45 25 E
Sakha □, *Russia* **27 C14** 66 0N 130 0 E
Sakhalin, *Russia* **27 D15** 51 0N 143 0 E
Sakhalinskiy Zaliv, *Russia* **27 D15** 54 0N 141 0 E
Šakiai, *Lithuania* **9 J20** 54 59N 23 2 E
Sakon Nakhon, *Thailand* **38 D5** 17 10N 104 9 E
Sakrand, *Pakistan* **42 F3** 26 10N 68 15 E
Sakri, *India* **43 F12** 26 13N 86 5 E
Sakrivier, *S. Africa* **56 E3** 30 54S 20 28 E
Sakti, *India* **43 H10** 22 2N 82 58 E
Sakuma, *Japan* **31 G8** 35 3N 137 49 E
Sakurai, *Japan* **31 G7** 34 30N 135 51 E
Sala, *Sweden* **9 G17** 59 58N 16 35 E
Sala Consilina, *Italy* **20 D6** 40 23N 15 36 E
Sala-y-Gómez, *Pac. Oc.* **65 K17** 26 28S 105 28W
Salaberry-de-Valleyfield, *Canada* **79 A10** 45 15N 74 8W
Saladas, *Argentina* **94 B4** 28 15S 58 40W
Saladillo, *Argentina* **94 D4** 35 40S 59 55W
Salado →, *Buenos Aires, Argentina* **94 D4** 35 44S 57 22W
Salado →, *La Pampa, Argentina* **96 D3** 37 30S 67 0W
Salado →, *Santa Fe, Argentina* **94 C3** 31 40S 60 41W
Salado →, *Mexico* **81 M5** 26 52N 99 19W
Salaga, *Ghana* **50 G5** 8 31N 0 31W
Sālah, *Syria* **47 C5** 32 40N 36 45 E
Sálakhos, *Greece* **23 C9** 36 17N 27 57 E
Salālah, *Oman* **46 D5** 16 56N 53 59 E
Salamanca, *Chile* **94 C1** 31 46S 70 59W
Salamanca, *Spain* **19 B3** 40 58N 5 39W
Salamanca, *U.S.A.* **78 D6** 42 10N 78 43W
Salāmatābād, *Iran* **44 C5** 35 39N 47 50 E
Salamis, *Cyprus* **23 D12** 35 11N 33 54 E
Salamís, *Greece* **21 F10** 37 56N 23 30 E
Salar de Atacama, *Chile* **94 A2** 23 30S 68 25W
Salar de Uyuni, *Bolivia* **92 H5** 20 30S 67 45W
Salatiga, *Indonesia* **37 G14** 7 19S 110 30 E
Salavat, *Russia* **24 D10** 53 21N 55 55 E
Salaverry, *Peru* **92 E3** 8 15S 79 0W
Salawati, *Indonesia* **37 E8** 1 7S 130 52 E
Salaya, *India* **42 H3** 22 19N 69 35 E
Salayar, *Indonesia* **37 F6** 6 7S 120 30 E
Salcombe, *U.K.* **11 G4** 50 14N 3 47W
Saldanha, *S. Africa* **56 E2** 33 0S 17 58 E
Saldanha B., *S. Africa* **56 E2** 33 6S 18 0 E
Saldus, *Latvia* **9 H20** 56 38N 22 30 E
Sale, *Australia* **63 F4** 38 6S 147 6 E
Salé, *Morocco* **50 B4** 34 3N 6 48W
Sale, *U.K.* **10 D5** 53 26N 2 19W
Salekhard, *Russia* **26 C7** 66 30N 66 35 E
Salem, *India* **40 P11** 11 40N 78 11 E
Salem, *Ill., U.S.A.* **76 F1** 38 38N 88 57W
Salem, *Ind., U.S.A.* **76 F2** 38 36N 86 6W
Salem, *Mass., U.S.A.* **79 D14** 42 31N 70 53W
Salem, *Mo., U.S.A.* **81 G9** 37 39N 91 32W
Salem, *N.H., U.S.A.* **79 D13** 42 45N 71 12W
Salem, *N.J., U.S.A.* **76 F8** 39 34N 75 28W
Salem, *N.Y., U.S.A.* **79 C11** 43 10N 73 20W
Salem, *Ohio, U.S.A.* **78 F4** 40 54N 80 52W
Salem, *Oreg., U.S.A.* **82 D2** 44 56N 123 2W
Salem, *S. Dak., U.S.A.* **80 D6** 43 44N 97 23W
Salem, *Va., U.S.A.* **76 G5** 37 18N 80 3W
Salerno, *Italy* **20 D6** 40 41N 14 47 E
Salford, *U.K.* **10 D5** 53 30N 2 18W
Salgótarján, *Hungary* **17 D10** 48 5N 19 47 E
Salgueiro, *Brazil* **93 E11** 8 4S 39 6W
Salibabu, *Indonesia* **37 D7** 3 51N 126 40 E
Salida, *U.S.A.* **74 C5** 38 32N 106 0W
Salihli, *Turkey* **21 E13** 38 28N 28 8 E
Salihorsk, *Belarus* **17 B14** 52 51N 27 27 E
Salima, *Malawi* **53 G6** 13 47S 34 28 E
Salina, *Italy* **20 E6** 38 34N 14 50 E
Salina, *Kans., U.S.A.* **80 F6** 38 50N 97 37W
Salina, *Utah, U.S.A.* **83 G8** 38 58N 111 51W
Salina Cruz, *Mexico* **87 D5** 16 10N 95 10W
Salinas, *Brazil* **93 G10** 16 10S 42 10W
Salinas, *Chile* **94 A2** 23 31S 69 29W
Salinas, *Ecuador* **92 D2** 2 10S 80 58W
Salinas, *U.S.A.* **84 J5** 36 40N 121 39W
Salinas →, *Guatemala* **87 D6** 16 28N 90 31W
Salinas →, *U.S.A.* **84 J5** 36 45N 121 48W
Salinas, B. de, *Nic.* **88 D2** 11 4N 85 45W
Salinas, Pampa de las, *Argentina* **94 C2** 31 58S 66 42W
Salinas Ambargasta, *Argentina* **94 B3** 29 0S 65 0W

159

Surt, Libya 51 B9 31 11N 16 39 E
Surt, Khalīj, Libya 51 B9 31 40N 18 30 E
Surtanahu, Pakistan 42 F4 26 22N 70 0 E
Surtsey, Iceland 8 E3 63 20N 20 30W
Suruga-Wan, Japan 31 G9 34 45N 138 30 E
Susaki, Japan 31 H6 33 22N 133 17 E
Sūsangerd, Iran 45 D6 31 35N 48 6 E
Susanville, U.S.A. 82 F3 40 25N 120 39W
Susner, India 42 H7 23 57N 76 5 E
Susquehanna, U.S.A. 79 E9 41 57N 75 36W
Susquehanna →, U.S.A. 79 G8 39 33N 76 5W
Susques, Argentina 94 A2 23 35S 66 25W
Sussex, Canada 71 C6 45 45N 65 37W
Sussex, U.S.A. 79 E10 41 13N 74 37W
Sussex, E. □, U.K. 11 G8 51 0N 0 20 E
Sussex, W. □, U.K. 11 G7 51 0N 0 30W
Sustut →, Canada 72 B3 56 20N 127 30W
Susuman, Russia 27 C15 62 47N 148 10 E
Susunu, Indonesia 37 E8 3 20S 133 25 E
Susurluk, Turkey 21 E13 39 54N 28 8 E
Sutherland, S. Africa 56 E3 32 24S 20 40 E
Sutherland, U.S.A. 80 E4 41 10N 101 8W
Sutherland Falls, N.Z. 59 L1 44 48S 167 46 E
Sutherlin, U.S.A. 82 E2 43 23N 123 19W
Suthri, India 42 H3 23 3N 68 55 E
Sutlej →, Pakistan 42 E4 29 23N 71 3 E
Sutter, U.S.A. 84 F5 39 10N 121 45W
Sutter Creek, U.S.A. 84 G6 38 24N 120 48W
Sutton, Canada 79 A12 45 6N 72 37W
Sutton, Nebr., U.S.A. 80 E6 40 36N 97 52W
Sutton, W. Va., U.S.A. 76 F5 38 40N 80 43W
Sutton →, Canada 70 A3 55 15N 83 45W
Sutton Coldfield, U.K. 11 E6 52 35N 1 49W
Sutton in Ashfield, U.K. 10 D6 53 8N 1 16W
Sutton L., Canada 70 B3 54 15N 84 42W
Suttor →, Australia 62 C4 21 36S 147 2 E
Suttsu, Japan 30 C10 42 48N 140 14 E
Suva, Fiji 59 D8 18 6S 178 30 E
Suva Planina, Serbia, Yug. 21 C10 43 10N 22 5 E
Suvorov Is. = Suwarrow Is., Cook Is. 65 J11 15 0S 163 0W
Suwałki, Poland 17 A12 54 8N 22 59 E
Suwannaphum, Thailand 38 E4 15 33N 103 47 E
Suwannee →, U.S.A. 77 L4 29 17N 83 10W
Suwanose-Jima, Japan 31 K4 29 38N 129 43 E
Suwarrow Is., Cook Is. 65 J11 15 0S 163 0W
Suwayq aş Şuqban, Iraq 44 D5 31 32N 46 7 E
Suweis, Khalîg el, Egypt 51 C12 28 40N 33 0 E
Suweis, Qanâ es, Egypt 51 B12 31 0N 32 20 E
Suwŏn, S. Korea 35 F14 37 17N 127 1 E
Suzdal, Russia 24 C7 56 29N 40 26 E
Suzhou, Anhui, China 34 H9 33 41N 116 59 E
Suzhou, Jiangsu, China 33 C7 31 19N 120 38 E
Suzu, Japan 31 F8 37 25N 137 17 E
Suzu-Misaki, Japan 31 F8 37 31N 137 21 E
Suzuka, Japan 31 G8 34 55N 136 36 E
Svalbard, Arctic 4 B8 78 0N 17 0 E
Svappavaara, Sweden 8 C19 67 40N 21 3 E
Svartisen, Norway 8 C15 66 40N 13 50 E
Svay Chek, Cambodia 38 F4 13 48N 102 58 E
Svay Rieng, Cambodia 39 G5 11 9N 105 45 E
Svealand □, Sweden 9 G16 60 20N 15 0 E
Sveg, Sweden 9 E16 62 2N 14 21 E
Svendborg, Denmark 9 J14 55 4N 10 35 E
Sverdlovsk = Yekaterinburg, Russia 26 D7 56 50N 60 30 E
Sverdrup Is., Canada 4 B3 79 0N 97 0W
Svetlaya, Russia 30 A9 46 33N 138 18 E
Svetlogorsk = Svyetlahorsk, Belarus 17 B15 52 38N 29 46 E
Svir →, Russia 24 B5 60 30N 32 48 E
Svishtov, Bulgaria 21 C11 43 36N 25 23 E
Svislach, Belarus 17 B13 53 3N 24 2 E
Svobodnyy, Russia 27 D13 51 20N 128 0 E
Svolvær, Norway 8 B16 68 15N 14 34 E
Svyetlahorsk, Belarus 17 B15 52 38N 29 46 E
Swabian Alps = Schwäbische Alb, Germany 16 D5 48 20N 9 30 E
Swainsboro, U.S.A. 77 J4 32 36N 82 20W
Swakopmund, Namibia 56 C1 22 37S 14 30 E
Swale →, U.K. 10 C6 54 5N 1 20W
Swan →, Australia 61 F2 32 3S 115 45 E
Swan →, Canada 73 C8 52 30N 100 45W
Swan Hill, Australia 63 F3 35 20S 143 33 E
Swan Hills, Canada 72 C5 54 43N 115 24W
Swan Is., W. Indies 88 C3 17 22N 83 57W
Swan L., Canada 73 C8 52 30N 100 40W
Swan Peak, U.S.A. 82 C7 47 43N 113 38W
Swan Ra., U.S.A. 82 C7 48 0N 113 45W
Swan Reach, Australia 63 E2 34 35S 139 37 E
Swan River, Canada 73 C8 52 10N 101 16W
Swanage, U.K. 11 G6 50 36N 1 58W
Swansea, Australia 62 G4 42 8S 148 4 E
Swansea, Canada 78 C5 43 38N 79 28W
Swansea, U.K. 11 F4 51 37N 3 57W
Swansea □, U.K. 11 F3 51 38N 4 3W
Swar →, Pakistan 43 B5 34 40N 72 5 E
Swartberge, S. Africa 56 E3 33 20S 22 0 E
Swartmodder, S. Africa 56 D3 28 1S 20 32 E
Swartruggens, S. Africa 56 D4 25 39S 26 42 E
Swastika, Canada 70 C3 48 7N 80 6W
Swatow = Shantou, China 33 D6 23 18N 116 40 E
Swaziland ■, Africa 57 D5 26 30S 31 30 E
Sweden ■, Europe 9 G16 57 0N 15 0 E
Sweet Home, U.S.A. 82 D2 44 24N 122 44W
Sweetgrass, U.S.A. 82 B8 48 59N 111 58W
Sweetwater, Nev., U.S.A. 84 G7 38 27N 119 9W
Sweetwater, Tenn., U.S.A. 77 H3 35 36N 84 28W
Sweetwater, Tex., U.S.A. 81 J4 32 28N 100 25W
Sweetwater →, U.S.A. 82 E10 42 31N 107 2W
Swellendam, S. Africa 56 E3 34 1S 20 26 E
Świdnica, Poland 17 C9 50 50N 16 30 E
Świdnik, Poland 17 C12 51 13N 22 39 E
Świebodzin, Poland 16 B8 52 15N 15 31 E
Świecie, Poland 17 B10 53 25N 18 30 E
Swift Current, Canada 73 C7 50 20N 107 45W
Swiftcurrent →, Canada 73 C7 50 38N 107 44W
Swilly, L., Ireland 13 A4 55 12N 7 33W
Swindon, U.K. 11 F6 51 34N 1 46W
Swindon □, U.K. 11 F6 51 34N 1 46W
Swinemünde = Świnoujście, Poland 16 B8 53 54N 14 16 E
Swinford, Ireland 13 C3 53 57N 8 58W
Świnoujście, Poland 16 B8 53 54N 14 16 E
Switzerland ■, Europe 18 C8 46 30N 8 0 E
Swords, Ireland 13 C5 53 28N 6 13W
Swoyerville, U.S.A. 79 E9 41 18N 75 53W
Sydenham →, Canada 78 D2 42 33N 82 25W
Sydney, Australia 63 E5 33 53S 151 10 E
Sydney, Canada 71 C7 46 7N 60 7W
Sydney L., Canada 73 C10 50 41N 94 25W
Sydney Mines, Canada 71 C7 46 18N 60 15W
Sydprøven, Greenland 4 C5 60 30N 45 35W
Sydra, G. of = Surt, Khalīj, Libya 51 B9 31 40N 18 30 E
Sykesville, U.S.A. 78 E6 41 3N 78 50W
Syktyvkar, Russia 24 B9 61 45N 50 40 E
Sylacauga, U.S.A. 77 J2 33 10N 86 15W
Sylarna, Sweden 8 E15 63 2N 12 13 E
Sylhet, Bangla. 41 G17 24 54N 91 52 E
Sylt, Germany 16 A5 54 54N 8 22 E
Sylvan Beach, U.S.A. 79 C9 43 12N 75 44W
Sylvan Lake, Canada 72 C6 52 20N 114 3W
Sylvania, U.S.A. 77 J5 32 45N 81 38W
Sylvester, U.S.A. 77 K4 31 32N 83 50W
Sym, Russia 26 C9 60 20N 88 18 E
Symón, Mexico 86 C4 24 42N 102 35W
Synnott Ra., Australia 60 C4 16 30S 125 20 E
Syracuse, Kans., U.S.A. 81 G4 37 59N 101 45W
Syracuse, N.Y., U.S.A. 79 C8 43 3N 76 9W
Syracuse, Nebr., U.S.A. 80 E6 40 39N 96 11W
Syrdarya →, Kazakstan 26 E7 46 3N 61 0 E
Syria ■, Asia 44 C3 35 0N 38 0 E
Syrian Desert = Shâm, Bādiyat ash, Asia 44 C3 32 0N 40 0 E
Syzran, Russia 24 D8 53 12N 48 30 E
Szczecin, Poland 16 B8 53 27N 14 27 E
Szczecinek, Poland 17 B9 53 43N 16 41 E
Szczeciński, Zalew = Stettiner Haff, Germany 16 B8 53 47N 14 15 E
Szczytno, Poland 17 B11 53 33N 21 0 E
Szechwan = Sichuan □, China 32 C5 31 0N 104 0 E
Szeged, Hungary 17 E11 46 16N 20 10 E
Székesfehérvár, Hungary 17 E10 47 15N 18 25 E
Szekszárd, Hungary 17 E10 46 22N 18 42 E
Szentes, Hungary 17 E11 46 39N 20 21 E
Szolnok, Hungary 17 E11 47 10N 20 15 E
Szombathely, Hungary 17 E9 47 14N 16 38 E

T

Ta Khli Khok, Thailand 38 E3 15 18N 100 20 E
Ta Lai, Vietnam 39 G6 11 24N 107 23 E
Tabacal, Argentina 94 A3 23 15S 64 15W
Tabaco, Phil. 37 B6 13 22N 123 44 E
Ţābah, Si. Arabia 44 E4 26 55N 42 38 E
Ţabas, Khorāsān, Iran 45 C9 32 48N 60 12 E
Ţabas, Khorāsān, Iran 45 C8 33 35N 56 55 E
Tabasará, Serranía de, Panama 88 E3 8 35N 81 40W
Tabasco □, Mexico 87 D6 17 45N 93 30W
Tabāsīn, Iran 45 D8 31 12N 57 54 E
Tabatinga, Serra da, Brazil 93 F10 10 30S 44 0W
Taber, Canada 72 D6 49 47N 112 8W
Taberg, U.S.A. 79 C9 43 18N 75 37W
Tablas, Phil. 37 B6 12 25N 122 2 E
Table B. = Tafelbaai, S. Africa 56 E2 33 35S 18 25 E
Table B., Canada 71 B8 53 40N 56 25W
Table Mt., S. Africa 56 E2 34 0S 18 22 E
Table Rock L., U.S.A. 81 G8 36 36N 93 19W
Tabletop, Mt., Australia 62 C4 23 24S 147 11 E
Tábor, Czech Rep. 16 D8 49 25N 14 39 E
Tabora, Tanzania 54 D3 5 2S 32 50 E
Tabora □, Tanzania 54 D3 5 0S 33 0 E
Tabou, Ivory C. 50 H4 4 30N 7 20W
Tabrīz, Iran 44 B5 38 7N 46 20 E
Tabuaeran, Pac. Oc. 65 G12 3 51N 159 22W
Tabūk, Si. Arabia 44 D3 28 23N 36 36 E
Tacámbaro de Codallos, Mexico 86 D4 19 14N 101 28W
Tacheng, China 32 B3 46 40N 82 58 E
Tach'ing Shan = Daqing Shan, China 34 D6 40 40N 111 0 E
Tacloban, Phil. 37 B6 11 15N 124 58 E
Tacna, Peru 92 G4 18 0S 70 20W
Tacoma, U.S.A. 84 C4 47 14N 122 26W
Tacuarembó, Uruguay 95 C4 31 45S 56 0W
Tademaït, Plateau du, Algeria 50 C6 28 30N 2 30 E
Tadjoura, Djibouti 46 E3 11 50N 42 55 E
Tadmor, N.Z. 59 J4 41 27S 172 45 E
Tadoule, L., Canada 73 B9 58 36N 98 20W
Tadoussac, Canada 71 C6 48 11N 69 42W
Tadzhikistan = Tajikistan ■, Asia 26 F8 38 30N 70 0 E
Taechŏn-ni, S. Korea 35 F14 36 21N 126 36 E
Taegu, S. Korea 35 G15 35 50N 128 37 E
Taegwan, N. Korea 35 D13 40 13N 125 12 E
Taejŏn, S. Korea 35 F14 36 20N 127 28 E
Tafalla, Spain 19 A5 42 30N 1 41W
Tafelbaai, S. Africa 56 E2 33 35S 18 25 E
Tafermaar, Indonesia 37 F8 6 47S 134 10 E
Tafí Viejo, Argentina 94 B2 26 43S 65 17W
Tafihān, Iran 45 D7 29 25N 52 39 E
Tafresh, Iran 45 C6 34 45N 49 57 E
Taft, Iran 45 D7 31 45N 54 14 E
Taft, Phil. 37 B7 11 57N 125 30 E
Taft, U.S.A. 85 K7 35 8N 119 28W
Taftān, Kūh-e, Iran 45 D9 28 40N 61 0 E
Taga Dzong, Bhutan 41 F16 27 5N 89 55 E
Taganrog, Russia 25 E6 47 12N 38 50 E
Tagbilaran, Phil. 37 C6 9 39N 123 51 E
Tagish, Canada 72 A2 60 19N 134 16W
Tagish L., Canada 72 A2 60 10N 134 20W
Tagliamento →, Italy 20 B5 45 38N 13 6 E
Tagomago, Spain 22 B8 39 2N 1 39 E
Taguatinga, Brazil 93 F10 12 16S 42 26W
Tagum, Phil. 37 C7 7 33N 125 53 E
Tagus = Tejo →, Europe 19 C1 38 40N 9 24W
Tahakopa, N.Z. 59 M2 46 30S 169 23 E
Tahan, Gunong, Malaysia 39 K4 4 34N 102 17 E
Tahat, Algeria 50 D7 23 18N 5 33 E
Tāherī, Iran 45 E7 27 43N 52 20 E
Tahiti, Pac. Oc. 65 J13 17 37S 149 27W
Tahlequah, U.S.A. 81 H7 35 55N 94 58W
Tahoe, L., U.S.A. 84 G6 39 6N 120 2W
Tahoe City, U.S.A. 84 F6 39 10N 120 9W
Tahoka, U.S.A. 81 J4 33 10N 101 48W
Taholah, U.S.A. 84 C2 47 21N 124 17W
Tahoua, Niger 50 F7 14 57N 5 16 E
Tahrūd, Iran 45 D8 29 26N 57 49 E
Tahsis, Canada 72 D3 49 55N 126 40W
Tahta, Egypt 51 C12 26 44N 31 32 E
Tahulandang, Indonesia 37 D7 2 27N 125 23 E
Tahuna, Indonesia 37 D7 3 38N 125 30 E
Tai Shan, China 35 F9 36 25N 117 20 E
Tai'an, China 35 F9 36 12N 117 8 E
Taibei = T'aipei, Taiwan 33 D7 25 2N 121 30 E
Taibique, Canary Is. 22 G2 27 42N 17 58W
Taibus Qi, China 34 D8 41 54N 115 22 E
T'aichung, Taiwan 33 D7 24 9N 120 37 E
Taieri →, N.Z. 59 M3 46 3S 170 12 E
Taigu, China 34 F7 37 28N 112 30 E
Taihang Shan, China 34 G7 36 0N 113 30 E
Taihape, N.Z. 59 H5 39 41S 175 48 E
Taihe, China 34 H8 33 20N 115 42 E
Taikang, China 34 G8 34 5N 114 50 E
Tailem Bend, Australia 63 F2 35 12S 139 29 E
Taimyr Peninsula = Taymyr, Poluostrov, Russia 27 B11 75 0N 100 0 E
Tain, U.K. 12 D4 57 49N 4 4W
T'ainan, Taiwan 33 D7 23 0N 120 10 E
Taínaron, Ákra, Greece 21 F10 36 22N 22 27 E
T'aipei, Taiwan 33 D7 25 2N 121 30 E
Taiping, Malaysia 39 K3 4 51N 100 44 E
Taipingzhen, China 34 H6 33 35N 111 42 E
Tairbeart = Tarbert, U.K. 12 D2 57 54N 6 49W
Taita Hills, Kenya 54 C4 3 25S 38 15 E
Taitao, Pen. de, Chile 96 F2 46 30S 75 0W
T'aitung, Taiwan 33 D7 22 43N 121 4 E
Taivalkoski, Finland 8 D23 65 33N 28 12 E
Taiwan ■, Asia 33 D7 23 30N 121 0 E
Taïyetos Óros, Greece 21 F10 37 0N 22 23 E
Taiyiba, Israel 47 C4 32 36N 35 27 E
Taiyuan, China 34 F7 37 52N 112 33 E
Taizhong = T'aichung, Taiwan 33 D7 24 9N 120 37 E
Ta'izz, Yemen 46 E3 13 35N 44 2 E
Tājābād, Iran 45 D7 30 2N 54 24 E
Tajikistan ■, Asia 26 F8 38 30N 70 0 E
Tajima, Japan 31 F9 37 12N 139 46 E
Tajo = Tejo →, Europe 19 C1 38 40N 9 24W
Tajrīsh, Iran 45 C6 35 48N 51 25 E
Tak, Thailand 38 D2 16 52N 99 8 E
Takāb, Iran 44 B5 36 24N 47 7 E
Takachiho, Japan 31 H5 32 42N 131 18 E
Takada, Japan 31 F9 37 7N 138 15 E
Takahagi, Japan 31 F10 36 43N 140 45 E
Takaka, N.Z. 59 J4 40 51S 172 50 E
Takamatsu, Japan 31 G7 34 20N 134 5 E
Takaoka, Japan 31 F8 36 47N 137 0 E
Takapuna, N.Z. 59 G5 36 47S 174 47 E
Takasaki, Japan 31 F9 36 20N 139 0 E
Takatsuki, Japan 31 G7 34 51N 135 37 E
Takaungu, Kenya 54 C4 3 38S 39 52 E
Takayama, Japan 31 F8 36 18N 137 11 E
Take-Shima, Japan 31 J5 30 49N 130 26 E
Takefu, Japan 31 G8 35 50N 136 10 E
Takengon, Indonesia 36 D1 4 45N 96 50 E
Takeo, Japan 31 H5 33 12N 130 1 E
Tākestān, Iran 45 C6 36 0N 49 40 E
Taketa, Japan 31 H5 32 58N 131 24 E
Takev, Cambodia 39 G5 10 59N 104 47 E
Takh, India 43 C7 33 6N 77 32 E
Takht-Sulaiman, Pakistan 42 D3 31 40N 69 58 E
Takikawa, Japan 30 C10 43 33N 141 54 E
Takla L., Canada 72 B3 55 15N 125 45W
Takla Landing, Canada 72 B3 55 30N 125 50W
Takla Makan = Taklamakan Shamo, China 32 C3 38 0N 83 0 E
Taklamakan Shamo, China 32 C3 38 0N 83 0 E
Taku →, Canada 72 B2 58 30N 133 50W
Tal Halāl, Iran 45 D7 28 54N 55 1 E
Tala, Uruguay 95 C4 34 21S 55 46W
Talagang, Pakistan 42 C5 32 55N 72 25 E
Talagante, Chile 94 C1 33 40S 70 50W
Talamanca, Cordillera de, Cent. Amer. 88 E3 9 20N 83 20W
Talara, Peru 92 D2 4 38S 81 18W
Talas, Kyrgyzstan 26 E8 42 30N 72 13 E
Talâta, Egypt 47 E1 30 36N 32 20 E
Talaud, Kepulauan, Indonesia 37 D7 4 30N 127 10 E
Talaud Is. = Talaud, Kepulauan, Indonesia 37 D7 4 30N 127 10 E
Talavera de la Reina, Spain 19 C3 39 55N 4 46W
Talayan, Phil. 37 C6 6 52N 124 24 E
Talbandh, India 43 H12 22 3N 86 20 E
Talbot, C., Australia 60 B4 13 48S 126 43 E
Talbragar →, Australia 63 E4 32 12S 148 37 E
Talca, Chile 94 D1 35 28S 71 40W
Talcahuano, Chile 94 D1 36 40S 73 10W
Talcher, India 41 J14 21 0N 85 18 E
Taldy Kurgan = Taldyqorghan, Kazakstan 26 E8 45 10N 78 45 E
Taldyqorghan, Kazakstan 26 E8 45 10N 78 45 E
Ţālesh, Iran 45 B6 37 58N 48 58 E
Ţalesh, Kūhhā-ye, Iran 45 B6 37 42N 48 55 E
Tali Post, Sudan 51 G12 5 55N 30 44 E
Taliabu, Indonesia 37 E6 1 50S 125 0 E
Talibon, Phil. 37 B6 10 9N 124 20 E
Talibong, Ko, Thailand 39 J2 7 15N 99 23 E
Talihina, U.S.A. 81 H7 34 45N 95 3W
Taliwang, Indonesia 36 F5 8 50S 116 55 E
Tall 'Afar, Iraq 44 B4 36 22N 42 27 E
Tall Kalakh, Syria 47 A5 34 41N 36 15 E
Talladega, U.S.A. 77 J2 33 26N 86 6W
Tallahassee, U.S.A. 77 K3 30 27N 84 17W
Tallangatta, Australia 63 F4 36 15S 147 19 E
Tallering Pk., Australia 61 E2 28 6S 115 37 E
Talli, Pakistan 42 E3 29 32N 68 8 E
Tallinn, Estonia 9 G21 59 22N 24 48 E
Tallmadge, U.S.A. 78 E3 41 6N 81 27W
Tallulah, U.S.A. 81 J9 32 25N 91 11W
Taloyoak, Canada 68 B10 69 32N 93 32W
Talpa de Allende, Mexico 86 C4 20 23N 104 51W
Talsi, Latvia 9 H20 57 10N 22 30 E
Taltal, Chile 94 B1 25 23S 70 33W
Taltson →, Canada 72 A6 61 24N 112 46W
Talwood, Australia 63 D4 28 29S 149 29 E
Talyawalka →, Australia 63 E3 32 28S 142 22 E
Tam Chau, Vietnam 39 G5 10 48N 105 12 E
Tam Ky, Vietnam 38 E7 15 34N 108 29 E
Tam Quan, Vietnam 38 E7 14 35N 109 3 E
Tama, U.S.A. 80 E8 41 58N 92 35W
Tamale, Ghana 50 G5 9 22N 0 50W
Tamano, Japan 31 G6 34 29N 133 59 E
Tamanrasset, Algeria 50 D7 22 50N 5 30 E
Tamaqua, U.S.A. 79 F9 40 48N 75 58W
Tamar →, U.K. 11 G3 50 27N 4 15W
Tamarinda, Spain 22 B10 39 55N 3 49 E
Tamashima, Japan 31 G6 34 32N 133 40 E
Tamaulipas □, Mexico 87 C5 24 0N 99 0W
Tamaulipas, Sierra de, Mexico 87 C5 23 30N 98 20W
Tamazula, Mexico 86 C3 24 55N 106 58W
Tamazunchale, Mexico 87 C5 21 16N 98 47W
Tambacounda, Senegal 50 F3 13 45N 13 40W
Tambelan, Kepulauan, Indonesia 36 D3 1 0N 107 30 E
Tambellup, Australia 61 F2 34 4S 117 37 E
Tambo, Australia 62 C4 24 54S 146 14 E
Tambo de Mora, Peru 92 F3 13 30S 76 8W
Tambohorano, Madag. 57 B7 17 30S 43 58 E
Tambora, Indonesia 36 F5 8 12S 118 5 E
Tambov, Russia 24 D7 52 45N 41 28 E
Tambuku, Indonesia 37 G15 7 8S 113 40 E
Tâmega →, Portugal 19 B1 41 5N 8 21W
Tamenglong, India 41 G18 25 0N 93 35 E
Tamiahua, L. de, Mexico 87 C5 21 30N 97 30W
Tamil Nadu □, India 40 P10 11 0N 77 0 E
Tamluk, India 43 H12 22 18N 87 58 E
Tammerfors = Tampere, Finland 9 F20 61 30N 23 50 E
Tammisaari, Finland 9 F20 60 0N 23 26 E
Tamo Abu, Pegunungan, Malaysia 36 D5 3 10N 115 5 E
Tampa, U.S.A. 77 M4 27 57N 82 27W
Tampa B., U.S.A. 77 M4 27 50N 82 30W
Tampere, Finland 9 F20 61 30N 23 50 E
Tampico, Mexico 87 C5 22 20N 97 50W
Tampin, Malaysia 39 L4 2 28N 102 13 E
Tamu, Burma 41 G19 24 13N 94 12 E
Tamworth, Australia 63 E5 31 7S 150 58 E
Tamworth, Canada 78 B8 44 29N 77 0W
Tamworth, U.K. 11 E6 52 39N 1 41W
Tamyang, S. Korea 35 G14 35 19N 126 59 E
Tan An, Vietnam 39 G6 10 32N 106 25 E
Tan-Tan, Morocco 50 C3 28 29N 11 1W
Tana →, Kenya 54 C5 2 32S 40 31 E
Tana →, Norway 8 A23 70 30N 28 14 E
Tana, L., Ethiopia 46 E2 13 5N 37 30 E
Tana River, Kenya 54 C4 2 0S 39 30 E
Tanabe, Japan 31 H7 33 44N 135 22 E
Tanafjorden, Norway 8 A23 70 45N 28 25 E
Tanaga, Pta., Canary Is. 22 G1 27 42N 18 10W
Tanahbala, Indonesia 36 E1 0 30S 98 30 E
Tanahgrogot, Indonesia 36 E5 1 55S 116 15 E
Tanahjampea, Indonesia 37 F6 7 10S 120 35 E
Tanahmasa, Indonesia 36 E1 0 12S 98 39 E
Tanahmerah, Indonesia 37 F10 6 5S 140 16 E
Tanakpur, India 43 E9 29 5N 80 7 E
Tanakura, Japan 31 F10 37 10N 140 20 E
Tanami, Australia 60 C4 19 59S 129 43 E
Tanami Desert, Australia 60 C5 18 50S 132 0 E
Tanana →, U.S.A. 68 B4 65 10N 151 58W
Tananarive = Antananarivo, Madag. 57 B8 18 55S 47 31 E
Tánaro →, Italy 18 D8 44 55N 8 40 E
Tancheng, China 35 G10 34 25N 118 20 E
Tanch'ŏn, N. Korea 35 D15 40 27N 128 54 E
Tanda, Ut. P., India 43 F10 26 33N 82 35 E
Tanda, Ut. P., India 43 E8 28 57N 78 56 E
Tandag, Phil. 37 C7 9 4N 126 9 E
Tandaia, Tanzania 55 D3 9 25S 34 15 E
Tandaué, Angola 56 B2 16 58S 18 5 E
Tandil, Argentina 94 D4 37 15S 59 6W
Tandil, Sa. del, Argentina 94 D4 37 30S 59 0W
Tandlianwala, Pakistan 42 D5 31 3N 73 9 E
Tando Adam, Pakistan 42 G3 25 45N 68 40 E
Tando Allahyar, Pakistan 42 G3 25 28N 68 43 E
Tando Bago, Pakistan 42 G3 24 47N 68 58 E
Tando Mohommed Khan, Pakistan 42 G3 25 8N 68 32 E
Tandou L., Australia 63 E3 32 40S 142 5 E
Tandragee, U.K. 13 B5 54 21N 6 24W
Tane-ga-Shima, Japan 31 J5 30 30N 131 0 E
Taneatua, N.Z. 59 H6 38 4S 177 1 E
Tanen Tong Dan, Burma 38 D2 16 30N 98 30 E
Tanezrouft, Algeria 50 D6 23 9N 0 11 E
Tang, Koh, Cambodia 39 G4 10 16N 103 7 E
Tang, Ra's-e, Iran 45 E8 25 21N 59 52 E
Tang Krasang, Cambodia 38 F5 12 34N 105 3 E
Tanga, Tanzania 54 D4 5 5S 39 2 E
Tanga □, Tanzania 54 D4 5 20S 38 0 E
Tanganyika, L., Africa 54 D3 6 40S 30 0 E
Tanger = Tangier, Morocco 50 A4 35 50N 5 49W
Tangerang, Indonesia 37 G12 6 11S 106 37 E
Tanggu, China 35 E9 39 2N 117 40 E
Tanggula Shan, China 32 C4 32 40N 92 10 E
Tanghe, China 34 H7 32 47N 112 50 E
Tangier, Morocco 50 A4 35 50N 5 49W
Tangorin, Australia 62 C3 21 47S 144 12 E
Tangshan, China 35 E10 39 38N 118 10 E
Tangtou, China 35 G10 35 28N 118 30 E
Tanimbar, Kepulauan, Indonesia 37 F8 7 30S 131 30 E
Tanimbar Is. = Tanimbar, Kepulauan, Indonesia 37 F8 7 30S 131 30 E
Taninthari = Tenasserim □, Burma 38 F2 14 0N 98 30 E
Tanjay, Phil. 37 C6 9 30N 123 5 E
Tanjong Malim, Malaysia 39 L3 3 42N 101 31 E
Tanjore = Thanjavur, India 40 P11 10 48N 79 12 E
Tanjung, Indonesia 36 E5 2 10S 115 25 E
Tanjungbalai, Indonesia 36 D1 2 55N 99 44 E
Tanjungbatu, Indonesia 36 D5 2 23N 118 3 E
Tanjungkarang Telukbetung, Indonesia 36 F3 5 20S 105 10 E
Tanjungpandan, Indonesia 36 E3 2 43S 107 38 E
Tanjungpinang, Indonesia 36 D2 1 5N 104 30 E
Tanjungredeb, Indonesia 36 D5 2 9N 117 29 E
Tanjungselor, Indonesia 36 D5 2 55N 117 25 E
Tank, Pakistan 42 C4 32 14N 70 25 E
Tankhala, India 42 J5 21 58N 73 47 E
Tannersville, U.S.A. 79 E9 41 3N 75 18W
Tannu-Ola, Russia 27 D10 51 0N 94 0 E
Tannum Sands, Australia 62 C5 23 57S 151 22 E

Tha Sala

Tanout, *Niger* **50 F7** 14 50N 8 55 E
Tanta, *Egypt* **51 B12** 30 45N 30 57 E
Tantoyuca, *Mexico* **87 C5** 21 21N 98 10W
Tantung = Dandong, *China* **35 D13** 40 10N 124 20 E
Tanunda, *Australia* **63 E2** 34 30S 139 0 E
Tanzania ■, *Africa* **54 D3** 6 0S 34 0 E
Tanzilla →, *Canada* **72 B2** 58 8N 130 43W
Tao, Ko, *Thailand* **39 G2** 10 5N 99 52 E
Tao'an = Taonan, *China* **35 B12** 45 22N 122 40 E
Tao'er He →, *China* **35 B13** 45 45N 124 5 E
Taolanaro, *Madag.* **57 D8** 25 2S 47 0 E
Taole, *China* **34 E4** 38 48N 106 40 E
Taonan, *China* **35 B12** 45 22N 122 40 E
Taos, *U.S.A.* **83 H11** 36 24N 105 35W
Taoudenni, *Mali* **50 D5** 22 40N 3 55W
Tapa, *Estonia* **9 G21** 59 15N 25 50 E
Tapa Shan = Daba Shan, *China* **33 C5** 32 0N 109 0 E
Tapachula, *Mexico* **87 E6** 14 54N 92 17W
Tapah, *Malaysia* **39 K3** 4 12N 101 15 E
Tapajós →, *Brazil* **93 D8** 2 24S 54 41W
Tapaktuan, *Indonesia* **36 D1** 3 15N 97 10 E
Tapanahoni →, *Surinam* **93 C8** 4 20N 54 25W
Tapanui, *N.Z.* **59 L2** 45 56S 169 18 E
Tapauá →, *Brazil* **92 E6** 5 40S 64 21W
Tapes, *Brazil* **95 C5** 30 40S 51 23W
Tapeta, *Liberia* **50 G4** 6 29N 8 52W
Taphan Hin, *Thailand* **38 D3** 16 13N 100 26 E
Tapirapecó, Serra, *Venezuela* **92 C6** 1 10N 65 0W
Tapuaenuku, Mt., *N.Z.* **59 K4** 42 0S 173 39 E
Tapul Group, *Phil.* **37 C6** 5 35N 120 50 E
Tapurucuará, *Brazil* **92 D5** 0 24S 65 2W
Ţaqţaq, *Iraq* **44 C5** 35 53N 44 35 E
Taquara, *Brazil* **95 B5** 29 36S 50 46W
Taquari →, *Brazil* **92 G7** 19 15S 57 17W
Tara, *Australia* **63 D5** 27 17S 150 31 E
Tara, *Canada* **78 B3** 44 28N 81 9W
Tara, *Russia* **26 D8** 56 55N 74 24 E
Tara, *Zambia* **55 F2** 16 58S 26 45 E
Tara →, *Montenegro, Yug.* **21 C8** 43 21N 18 51 E
Tarabagatay, Khrebet, *Kazakstan* **26 E9** 48 0N 83 0 E
Tarābulus, *Lebanon* **47 A4** 34 31N 35 50 E
Tarābulus, *Libya* **51 B8** 32 49N 13 7 E
Taradehi, *India* **43 H8** 23 18N 79 21 E
Tarajalejo, *Canary Is.* **22 F5** 28 12N 14 7W
Tarakan, *Indonesia* **36 D5** 3 20N 117 35 E
Tarakit, Mt., *Kenya* **54 B4** 2 2N 35 10 E
Tarama-Jima, *Japan* **31 M2** 24 39N 124 42 E
Taran, Mys, *Russia* **9 J18** 54 56N 19 59 E
Taranagar, *India* **42 E6** 28 43N 74 50 E
Taranaki □, *N.Z.* **59 H5** 39 25S 174 30 E
Tarancón, *Spain* **19 B4** 40 1N 3 0W
Taranga Hill, *India* **40 H8** 24 0N 72 40 E
Taransay, *U.K.* **12 D1** 57 54N 7 0W
Táranto, *Italy* **20 D7** 40 28N 17 14 E
Táranto, G. di, *Italy* **20 D7** 40 8N 17 20 E
Tarapacá, *Colombia* **92 D5** 2 56S 69 46W
Tarapacá □, *Chile* **94 A2** 20 45S 69 30W
Tarapoto, *Peru* **92 E3** 6 30S 76 20W
Tararua Ra., *N.Z.* **59 J5** 40 45S 175 25 E
Tarashcha, *Ukraine* **17 D16** 49 30N 30 31 E
Tarauacá, *Brazil* **92 E4** 8 6S 70 48W
Tarauacá →, *Brazil* **92 E5** 6 42S 69 48W
Tarawa, *Kiribati* **64 G9** 1 30N 173 0 E
Tarawera, *N.Z.* **59 H6** 39 2S 176 36 E
Tarawera L., *N.Z.* **59 H6** 38 13S 176 27 E
Tarazona, *Spain* **19 B5** 41 55N 1 43W
Tarbat Ness, *U.K.* **12 D5** 57 52N 3 47W
Tarbela Dam, *Pakistan* **42 B5** 34 8N 72 52 E
Tarbert, *Arg. & Bute, U.K.* **12 F3** 55 52N 5 25W
Tarbert, *W. Isles, U.K.* **12 D2** 57 54N 6 49W
Tarbes, *France* **18 E4** 43 15N 0 3 E
Tarboro, *U.S.A.* **77 H7** 35 54N 77 32W
Tarcoola, *Australia* **63 E1** 30 44S 134 36 E
Tarcoon, *Australia* **63 E4** 30 15S 146 43 E
Taree, *Australia* **63 E5** 31 50S 152 30 E
Tarfaya, *Morocco* **50 C3** 27 55N 12 55W
Târgovişte, *Romania* **17 F13** 44 55N 25 27 E
Târgu-Jiu, *Romania* **17 F12** 45 5N 23 19 E
Târgu Mureş, *Romania* **17 E13** 46 31N 24 38 E
Ţarif, *U.A.E.* **45 E7** 24 3N 53 46 E
Tarifa, *Spain* **19 D3** 36 1N 5 36W
Tarija, *Bolivia* **94 A3** 21 30S 64 40W
Tarija □, *Bolivia* **94 A3** 21 30S 63 30W
Tariku →, *Indonesia* **37 E9** 2 55S 138 26 E
Tarim Basin = Tarim Pendi, *China* **32 B3** 40 0N 84 0 E
Tarim He →, *China* **32 C3** 39 30N 88 30 E
Tarim Pendi, *China* **32 B3** 40 0N 84 0 E
Taritatu →, *Indonesia* **37 E9** 2 54S 138 27 E
Tarka →, *S. Africa* **56 E4** 32 10S 26 0 E
Tarkastad, *S. Africa* **56 E4** 32 0S 26 16 E
Tarkhankut, Mys, *Ukraine* **25 E5** 45 25N 32 30 E
Tarko Sale, *Russia* **26 C8** 64 55N 77 50 E
Tarkwa, *Ghana* **50 G5** 5 20N 2 0W
Tarlac, *Phil.* **37 A6** 15 29N 120 35 E
Tarma, *Peru* **92 F3** 11 25S 75 45W
Tarn →, *France* **18 E4** 44 5N 1 6 E
Târnăveni, *Romania* **17 E13** 46 19N 24 13 E
Tarnobrzeg, *Poland* **17 C11** 50 35N 21 41 E
Tarnów, *Poland* **17 C11** 50 3N 21 0 E
Tarnowskie Góry, *Poland* **17 C10** 50 27N 18 54 E
Ţārom, *Iran* **45 D7** 28 11N 55 46 E
Taroom, *Australia* **63 D4** 25 36S 149 48 E
Taroudannt, *Morocco* **50 B4** 30 30N 8 52W
Tarpon Springs, *U.S.A.* **77 L4** 28 9N 82 45W
Tarragona, *Spain* **19 B6** 41 5N 1 17 E
Tarraleah, *Australia* **62 G4** 42 17S 146 26 E
Tarrasa = Terrassa, *Spain* **19 B7** 41 34N 2 1 E
Tarrytown, *U.S.A.* **79 E11** 41 4N 73 52W
Tarshiha = Me'ona, *Israel* **47 B4** 33 1N 35 15 E
Tarso Emissi, *Chad* **51 D9** 21 27N 18 36 E
Tarsus, *Turkey* **25 G5** 36 58N 34 55 E
Tartagal, *Argentina* **94 A3** 22 30S 63 50W
Tartu, *Estonia* **9 G22** 58 20N 26 44 E
Ţarţūs, *Syria* **44 C2** 34 55N 35 55 E
Tarumizu, *Japan* **31 J5** 31 29N 130 42 E
Tarutao, Ko, *Thailand* **39 J2** 6 33N 99 40 E
Tarutung, *Indonesia* **36 D1** 2 0N 98 54 E
Taseko →, *Canada* **72 C4** 52 8N 123 45W
Tash-Kömür, *Kyrgyzstan* **26 E8** 41 40N 72 10 E
Tash-Kumyr = Tash-Kömür, *Kyrgyzstan* **26 E8** 41 40N 72 10 E
Tashauz = Dashhowuz, *Turkmenistan* **26 E6** 41 49N 59 58 E
Tashi Chho Dzong = Thimphu, *Bhutan* **41 F16** 27 31N 89 45 E
Ţashk, Daryācheh-ye, *Iran* **45 D7** 29 45N 53 35 E
Tashkent = Toshkent, *Uzbekistan* **26 E7** 41 20N 69 10 E
Tashtagol, *Russia* **26 D9** 52 47N 87 53 E
Tasikmalaya, *Indonesia* **37 G13** 7 18S 108 12 E
Tåsjön, *Sweden* **8 D16** 64 15N 15 40 E
Taskan, *Russia* **27 C16** 62 59N 150 20 E
Tasman B., *N.Z.* **59 J4** 40 59S 173 25 E
Tasman Mts., *N.Z.* **59 J4** 41 3S 172 25 E
Tasman Pen., *Australia* **62 G4** 43 10S 148 0 E
Tasman Sea, *Pac. Oc.* **64 L8** 36 0S 160 0 E
Tasmania □, *Australia* **62 G4** 42 0S 146 30 E
Tassili n'Ajjer, *Algeria* **50 C7** 25 47N 8 1 E
Tatabánya, *Hungary* **17 E10** 47 32N 18 25 E
Tatahouine, *Tunisia* **51 B8** 32 56N 10 27 E
Tatar Republic = Tatarstan □, *Russia* **24 C9** 55 30N 51 30 E
Tatarbunary, *Ukraine* **17 F15** 45 50N 29 39 E
Tatarsk, *Russia* **26 D8** 55 14N 76 0 E
Tatarstan □, *Russia* **24 C9** 55 30N 51 30 E
Tateyama, *Japan* **31 G9** 35 0N 139 50 E
Tathlina L., *Canada* **72 A5** 60 33N 117 39W
Tathra, *Australia* **63 F4** 36 44S 149 59 E
Tati →, *India* **40 J8** 21 8N 72 41 E
Tatinnai L., *Canada* **73 A9** 60 55N 97 40W
Tatla L., *Canada* **72 C4** 52 0N 124 20W
Tatnam, C., *Canada* **73 B10** 57 16N 91 0W
Tatra = Tatry, *Slovak Rep.* **17 D11** 49 20N 20 0 E
Tatry, *Slovak Rep.* **17 D11** 49 20N 20 0 E
Tatshenshini →, *Canada* **72 B1** 59 28N 137 45W
Tatsuno, *Japan* **31 G7** 34 52N 134 33 E
Tatta, *Pakistan* **42 G2** 24 42N 67 55 E
Tatuī, *Brazil* **95 A6** 23 25S 47 53W
Tatum, *U.S.A.* **81 J3** 33 16N 103 19W
Tat'ung = Datong, *China* **34 D7** 40 6N 113 18 E
Tatvan, *Turkey* **25 G7** 38 31N 42 15 E
Taubaté, *Brazil* **95 A6** 23 0S 45 36W
Tauern, *Austria* **16 E7** 47 15N 12 40 E
Taumarunui, *N.Z.* **59 H5** 38 53S 175 15 E
Taumaturgo, *Brazil* **92 E4** 8 54S 72 51W
Taung, *S. Africa* **56 D3** 27 33S 24 47 E
Taungdwingyi, *Burma* **41 J19** 20 1N 95 40 E
Taunggyi, *Burma* **41 J20** 20 50N 97 0 E
Taungup, *Burma* **41 K19** 18 51N 94 14 E
Taungup Pass, *Burma* **41 K19** 18 40N 94 45 E
Taungup Taunggya, *Burma* **41 K18** 18 20N 93 40 E
Taunsa, *Pakistan* **42 D4** 30 42N 70 39 E
Taunsa Barrage, *Pakistan* **42 D4** 30 42N 70 50 E
Taunton, *U.K.* **11 F4** 51 1N 3 5W
Taunton, *U.S.A.* **79 E13** 41 54N 71 6W
Taunus, *Germany* **16 C5** 50 13N 8 34 E
Taupo, *N.Z.* **59 H6** 38 41S 176 7 E
Taupo, L., *N.Z.* **59 H5** 38 46S 175 55 E
Taurage, *Lithuania* **9 J20** 55 14N 22 16 E
Tauranga, *N.Z.* **59 G6** 37 42S 176 11 E
Tauranga Harb., *N.Z.* **59 G6** 37 30S 176 5 E
Taureau, Rés., *Canada* **70 C5** 46 46N 73 50W
Taurianova, *Italy* **20 E7** 38 21N 16 1 E
Taurus Mts. = Toros Dağları, *Turkey* **25 G5** 37 0N 32 30 E
Tavda, *Russia* **26 D7** 58 7N 65 8 E
Tavda →, *Russia* **26 D7** 57 47N 67 18 E
Taveta, *Tanzania* **54 C4** 3 23S 37 37 E
Taveuni, *Fiji* **59 C9** 16 51S 179 58W
Tavira, *Portugal* **19 D2** 37 8N 7 40W
Tavistock, *Canada* **78 C4** 43 19N 80 50W
Tavistock, *U.K.* **11 G3** 50 33N 4 9W
Tavoy = Dawei, *Burma* **38 E2** 14 2N 98 12 E
Taw →, *U.K.* **11 F3** 51 4N 4 4W
Tawa →, *India* **42 H8** 22 48N 77 48 E
Tawas City, *U.S.A.* **76 C4** 44 16N 83 31W
Tawau, *Malaysia* **36 D5** 4 20N 117 55 E
Tawitawi, *Phil.* **37 C6** 5 10N 120 0 E
Taxco de Alarcón, *Mexico* **87 D5** 18 33N 99 36W
Taxila, *Pakistan* **42 C5** 33 42N 72 52 E
Tay →, *U.K.* **12 E5** 56 37N 3 38W
Tay, Firth of, *U.K.* **12 E5** 56 25N 3 8W
Tay, L., *Australia* **61 F3** 32 55S 120 48 E
Tay, L., *U.K.* **12 E4** 56 32N 4 8W
Tay Ninh, *Vietnam* **39 G6** 11 20N 106 5 E
Tayabamba, *Peru* **92 E3** 8 15S 77 16W
Taylakova, *Russia* **26 D8** 59 13N 74 0 E
Taylakovy = Taylakova, *Russia* **26 D8** 59 13N 74 0 E
Taylor, *Canada* **72 B4** 56 13N 120 40W
Taylor, *Nebr., U.S.A.* **80 E5** 41 46N 99 23W
Taylor, *Pa., U.S.A.* **79 E9** 41 23N 75 43W
Taylor, *Tex., U.S.A.* **81 K6** 30 34N 97 25W
Taylor, Mt., *U.S.A.* **83 J10** 35 14N 107 37W
Taylorville, *U.S.A.* **80 F10** 39 33N 89 18W
Taymā, *Si. Arabia* **44 E3** 27 35N 38 45 E
Taymyr, Oz., *Russia* **27 B11** 74 20N 102 0 E
Taymyr, Poluostrov, *Russia* **27 B11** 75 0N 100 0 E
Tayport, *U.K.* **12 E6** 56 27N 2 52W
Tayshet, *Russia* **27 D10** 55 58N 98 1 E
Taytay, *Phil.* **37 B5** 10 45N 119 30 E
Taz →, *Russia* **26 C8** 67 32N 78 40 E
Taza, *Morocco* **50 B5** 34 16N 4 6W
Tāzah Khurmātū, *Iraq* **44 C5** 35 18N 44 20 E
Tazawa-Ko, *Japan* **30 E10** 39 43N 140 40 E
Tazin, *Canada* **73 B7** 59 48N 109 55W
Tazin L., *Canada* **73 B7** 59 44N 108 42W
Tazovskiy, *Russia* **26 C8** 67 30N 78 44 E
Tbilisi, *Georgia* **25 F7** 41 43N 44 50 E
Tchad = Chad ■, *Africa* **51 F8** 15 0N 17 15 E
Tchad, L., *Chad* **51 F8** 13 30N 14 30 E
Tch'eng-tou = Chengdu, *China* **32 C5** 30 38N 104 2 E
Tchentlo L., *Canada* **72 B4** 55 15N 125 0W
Tchibanga, *Gabon* **52 E2** 2 45S 11 0 E
Tch'ong-k'ing = Chongqing, *China* **32 D5** 29 35N 106 25 E
Tczew, *Poland* **17 A10** 54 8N 18 50 E
Te Anau, L., *N.Z.* **59 L1** 45 15S 167 45 E
Te Aroha, *N.Z.* **59 G5** 37 32S 175 44 E
Te Awamutu, *N.Z.* **59 H5** 38 1S 175 20 E
Te Kuiti, *N.Z.* **59 H5** 38 20S 175 11 E
Te Puke, *N.Z.* **59 G6** 37 46S 176 22 E
Te Waewae B., *N.Z.* **59 M1** 46 13S 167 33 E
Teague, *U.S.A.* **81 K6** 31 38N 96 17W
Teapa, *Mexico* **87 D6** 18 35N 92 56W
Tebakang, *Malaysia* **36 D4** 1 6N 110 30 E
Tébessa, *Algeria* **50 A7** 35 22N 8 8 E
Tebicuary →, *Paraguay* **94 B4** 26 36S 58 16W
Tebingtinggi, *Indonesia* **36 D1** 3 20N 99 9 E
Tebintingii, *Indonesia* **36 E2** 1 0N 102 45 E
Tecate, *Mexico* **85 N10** 32 34N 116 38W
Tecka, *Argentina* **96 E2** 43 29S 70 48W
Tecomán, *Mexico* **86 D4** 18 55N 103 53W
Tecopa, *U.S.A.* **85 K10** 35 51N 116 13W
Tecoripa, *Mexico* **86 B3** 28 37N 109 57W
Tecuala, *Mexico* **86 C3** 22 23N 105 27W
Tecuci, *Romania* **17 F14** 45 51N 27 27 E
Tecumseh, *Canada* **78 D2** 42 19N 82 54W
Tecumseh, *Mich., U.S.A.* **76 D4** 42 0N 83 57W
Tecumseh, *Okla., U.S.A.* **81 H6** 35 15N 96 56W
Tedzhen = Tejen, *Turkmenistan* **26 F7** 37 23N 60 31 E
Tees →, *U.K.* **10 C6** 54 37N 1 10W
Tees B., *U.K.* **10 C6** 54 40N 1 9W
Teeswater, *Canada* **78 C3** 43 59N 81 17W
Tefé, *Brazil* **92 D6** 3 25S 64 50W
Tegal, *Indonesia* **37 G13** 6 52S 109 8 E
Tegid, L. = Bala, L., *U.K.* **10 E4** 52 53N 3 37W
Tegucigalpa, *Honduras* **88 D2** 14 5N 87 14W
Tehachapi, *U.S.A.* **85 K8** 35 8N 118 27W
Tehachapi Mts., *U.S.A.* **85 L8** 35 0N 118 30W
Tehoru, *Indonesia* **37 E7** 3 19S 129 37 E
Tehrān, *Iran* **45 C6** 35 44N 51 30 E
Tehri, *India* **43 D8** 30 23N 78 29 E
Tehuacán, *Mexico* **87 D5** 18 30N 97 30W
Tehuantepec, *Mexico* **87 D5** 16 21N 95 13W
Tehuantepec, G. de, *Mexico* **87 D5** 15 50N 95 12W
Tehuantepec, Istmo de, *Mexico* **87 D6** 17 0N 94 30W
Teide, *Canary Is.* **22 F3** 28 15N 16 38W
Teifi →, *U.K.* **11 E3** 52 5N 4 41W
Teign →, *U.K.* **11 G4** 50 32N 3 32W
Teignmouth, *U.K.* **11 G4** 50 33N 3 31W
Tejam, *India* **43 E9** 29 57N 80 11 E
Tejen, *Turkmenistan* **26 F7** 37 23N 60 31 E
Tejen →, *Turkmenistan* **45 B9** 37 24N 60 38 E
Tejo →, *Europe* **19 C1** 38 40N 9 24W
Tejon Pass, *U.S.A.* **85 L8** 34 49N 118 53W
Tekamah, *U.S.A.* **80 E6** 41 47N 96 13W
Tekapo, L., *N.Z.* **59 K3** 43 53S 170 33 E
Tekax, *Mexico* **87 C7** 20 11N 89 18W
Tekeli, *Kazakstan* **26 E8** 44 50N 79 0 E
Tekirdağ, *Turkey* **21 D12** 40 58N 27 30 E
Tekkali, *India* **41 K14** 18 37N 84 15 E
Tekoa, *U.S.A.* **82 C5** 47 14N 117 4W
Tel Aviv-Yafo, *Israel* **47 C3** 32 4N 34 48 E
Tel Lakhish, *Israel* **47 D3** 31 34N 34 51 E
Tel Megiddo, *Israel* **47 C4** 32 35N 35 11 E
Tela, *Honduras* **88 C2** 15 40N 87 28W
Telanaipura = Jambi, *Indonesia* **36 E2** 1 38S 103 30 E
Telavi, *Georgia* **25 F8** 42 0N 45 30 E
Telde, *Canary Is.* **22 G4** 27 59N 15 25W
Telegraph Creek, *Canada* **72 B2** 58 0N 131 10W
Telekhany = Tsyelyakhany, *Belarus* **17 B13** 52 30N 25 46 E
Telemark, *Norway* **9 G12** 59 15N 7 40 E
Telén, *Argentina* **94 D2** 36 15S 65 31W
Teleng, *Iran* **45 E9** 25 47N 61 3 E
Teles Pires →, *Brazil* **92 E7** 7 21S 58 3W
Telescope Pk., *U.S.A.* **85 J9** 36 10N 117 5W
Telfer Mine, *Australia* **60 C3** 21 40S 122 12 E
Telford, *U.K.* **11 E5** 52 40N 2 27W
Telford and Wrekin □, *U.K.* **10 E5** 52 45N 2 27W
Telkwa, *Canada* **72 C3** 54 41N 127 5W
Tell City, *U.S.A.* **76 G2** 37 57N 86 46W
Tellicherry, *India* **40 P9** 11 45N 75 30 E
Telluride, *U.S.A.* **83 H10** 37 56N 107 49W
Teloloapán, *Mexico* **87 D5** 18 21N 99 51W
Telpos Iz, *Russia* **24 B10** 63 16N 59 13 E
Telsen, *Argentina* **96 E3** 42 30S 66 50W
Telšiai, *Lithuania* **9 H20** 55 59N 22 14 E
Teluk Anson = Teluk Intan, *Malaysia* **39 K3** 4 3N 101 0 E
Teluk Betung = Tanjungkarang Telukbetung, *Indonesia* **36 F3** 5 20S 105 10 E
Teluk Intan, *Malaysia* **39 K3** 4 3N 101 0 E
Telukbutun, *Indonesia* **39 K7** 4 13N 108 12 E
Telukdalem, *Indonesia* **36 D1** 0 33N 97 50 E
Tema, *Ghana* **50 G5** 5 41N 0 0 E
Temax, *Mexico* **87 C7** 21 10N 88 50W
Temba, *S. Africa* **57 D4** 25 20S 28 17 E
Tembagapura, *Indonesia* **37 E9** 4 20S 137 0 E
Tembe, *Dem. Rep. of the Congo* **54 C2** 0 16S 28 14 E
Temblor Range, *U.S.A.* **85 K7** 35 20N 119 50W
Teme →, *U.K.* **11 E5** 52 11N 2 13W
Temecula, *U.S.A.* **85 M9** 33 30N 117 9W
Temerloh, *Malaysia* **36 D2** 3 27N 102 25 E
Teminabuan, *Indonesia* **37 E8** 1 26S 132 1 E
Temir, *Kazakstan* **25 E10** 49 1N 57 14 E
Temirtau, *Kazakstan* **26 D8** 50 5N 72 56 E
Temirtau, *Russia* **26 D9** 53 10N 87 30 E
Temiscamie →, *Canada* **71 B5** 50 59N 73 5W
Témiscaming, *Canada* **70 C4** 46 44N 79 5W
Témiscamingue, L., *Canada* **70 C4** 47 10N 79 25W
Temosachic, *Mexico* **86 B3** 28 58N 107 50W
Tempe, *U.S.A.* **83 K8** 33 25N 111 56W
Tempiute, *U.S.A.* **84 H11** 37 39N 115 38W
Temple, *U.S.A.* **81 K6** 31 6N 97 21W
Temple B., *Australia* **62 A3** 12 15S 143 3 E
Templemore, *Ireland* **13 D4** 52 47N 7 51W
Templeton, *U.S.A.* **84 K6** 35 33N 120 42W
Templeton →, *Australia* **62 C2** 21 0S 138 40 E
Tempoal, *Mexico* **87 C5** 21 31N 98 23W
Temuco, *Chile* **96 D2** 38 45S 72 40W
Temuka, *N.Z.* **59 L3** 44 14S 171 17 E
Tenabo, *Mexico* **87 C6** 20 2N 90 12W
Tenaha, *U.S.A.* **81 K7** 31 57N 94 15W
Tenakee Springs, *U.S.A.* **72 B1** 57 47N 135 13W
Tenali, *India* **40 L12** 16 15N 80 35 E
Tenancingo, *Mexico* **87 D5** 19 0N 99 33W
Tenango, *Mexico* **87 D5** 19 7N 99 33W
Tenasserim, *Burma* **39 F2** 12 6N 99 3 E
Tenasserim □, *Burma* **38 F2** 14 0N 98 30 E
Tenby, *U.K.* **11 F3** 51 40N 4 42W
Tenda, Colle di, *France* **18 D7** 44 7N 7 36 E
Tendaho, *Ethiopia* **46 E3** 11 48N 40 54 E
Tendukhera, *India* **43 H8** 23 24N 79 33 E
Ténéré, *Niger* **50 E7** 19 0N 10 30 E
Tenerife, *Canary Is.* **22 F3** 28 15N 16 35W
Tenerife, Pico, *Canary Is.* **22 G1** 27 43N 18 1W
Teng Xian, *China* **35 G9** 35 5N 117 10 E
Tengah □, *Indonesia* **37 E6** 2 0S 122 0 E
Tengah, Kepulauan, *Indonesia* **36 F5** 7 5S 118 15 E
Tengchong, *China* **32 D4** 25 0N 98 28 E
Tengchowfu = Penglai, *China* **35 F11** 37 48N 120 42 E
Tenggara □, *Indonesia* **37 E6** 3 0S 122 0 E
Tenggarong, *Indonesia* **36 E5** 0 24S 116 58 E
Tenggol, Pulau, *Malaysia* **39 K4** 4 48N 103 41 E
Tengiz, Ozero, *Kazakstan* **26 D7** 50 30N 69 0 E
Tenino, *U.S.A.* **84 D4** 46 51N 122 51W
Tenkasi, *India* **40 Q10** 8 55N 77 20 E
Tenke, *Katanga, Dem. Rep. of the Congo* **55 E2** 11 22S 26 40 E
Tenke, *Katanga, Dem. Rep. of the Congo* **55 E2** 10 32S 26 7 E
Tennant Creek, *Australia* **62 B1** 19 30S 134 15 E
Tennessee □, *U.S.A.* **77 H2** 36 0N 86 30W
Tennessee →, *U.S.A.* **76 G1** 37 4N 88 34W
Teno, Pta. de, *Canary Is.* **22 F3** 28 21N 16 55W
Tenom, *Malaysia* **36 C5** 5 4N 115 57 E
Tenosique, *Mexico* **87 D6** 17 30N 91 24W
Tenryū-Gawa →, *Japan* **31 G8** 35 39N 137 48 E
Tenterden, *U.K.* **11 F8** 51 4N 0 42 E
Tenterfield, *Australia* **63 D5** 29 0S 152 0 E
Teófilo Otoni, *Brazil* **93 G10** 17 50S 41 30W
Tepa, *Indonesia* **37 F7** 7 52S 129 31 E
Tepalcatepec →, *Mexico* **86 D4** 18 35N 101 59W
Tepehuanes, *Mexico* **86 B3** 25 21N 105 44W
Tepetongo, *Mexico* **86 C4** 22 28N 103 9W
Tepic, *Mexico* **86 C4** 21 30N 104 54W
Teplice, *Czech Rep.* **16 C7** 50 40N 13 48 E
Tepoca, C., *Mexico* **86 A2** 30 20N 112 25W
Tequila, *Mexico* **86 C4** 20 54N 103 47W
Ter →, *Spain* **19 A7** 42 2N 3 12 E
Ter Apel, *Neths.* **15 B7** 52 53N 7 5 E
Teraina, *Kiribati* **65 G11** 4 43N 160 25W
Téramo, *Italy* **20 C5** 42 39N 13 42 E
Terang, *Australia* **63 F3** 38 15S 142 55 E
Tercero →, *Argentina* **94 C3** 32 58S 61 47W
Terebovlya, *Ukraine* **17 D13** 49 18N 25 44 E
Terek →, *Russia* **25 F8** 44 0N 47 30 E
Teresina, *Brazil* **93 E10** 5 9S 42 45W
Terewah, L., *Australia* **63 D4** 29 52S 147 35 E
Teridgerie Cr. →, *Australia* **63 E4** 30 25S 148 50 E
Termez = Termiz, *Uzbekistan* **26 F7** 37 15N 67 15 E
Términi Imerese, *Italy* **20 F5** 37 59N 13 42 E
Términos, L. de, *Mexico* **87 D6** 18 35N 91 30W
Termiz, *Uzbekistan* **26 F7** 37 15N 67 15 E
Térmoli, *Italy* **20 C6** 42 0N 15 0 E
Ternate, *Indonesia* **37 D7** 0 45N 127 25 E
Terneuzen, *Neths.* **15 C3** 51 20N 3 50 E
Terney, *Russia* **27 E14** 45 3N 136 37 E
Terni, *Italy* **20 C5** 42 34N 12 37 E
Ternopil, *Ukraine* **17 D13** 49 30N 25 40 E
Ternopol = Ternopil, *Ukraine* **17 D13** 49 30N 25 40 E
Terowie, *Australia* **63 E2** 33 8S 138 55 E
Terra Bella, *U.S.A.* **85 K7** 35 58N 119 3W
Terra Nova Nat. Park, *Canada* **71 C9** 48 33N 53 55W
Terrace, *Canada* **72 C3** 54 30N 128 35W
Terrace Bay, *Canada* **70 C2** 48 47N 87 5W
Terracina, *Italy* **20 D5** 41 17N 13 15 E
Terralba, *Italy* **20 E3** 39 43N 8 39 E
Terranova = Ólbia, *Italy* **20 D3** 40 55N 9 31 E
Terrassa, *Spain* **19 B7** 41 34N 2 1 E
Terre Haute, *U.S.A.* **76 F2** 39 28N 87 25W
Terrebonne B., *U.S.A.* **81 L9** 29 5N 90 35W
Terrell, *U.S.A.* **81 J6** 32 44N 96 17W
Terrenceville, *Canada* **71 C9** 47 40N 54 44W
Terry, *U.S.A.* **80 B2** 46 47N 105 19W
Terryville, *U.S.A.* **79 E11** 41 41N 73 3W
Terschelling, *Neths.* **15 A5** 53 25N 5 20 E
Teruel, *Spain* **19 B5** 40 22N 1 8W
Tervola, *Finland* **8 C21** 66 6N 24 49 E
Teryaweyna L., *Australia* **63 E3** 32 18S 143 22 E
Teshio, *Japan* **30 B10** 44 53N 141 44 E
Teshio-Gawa →, *Japan* **30 B10** 44 53N 141 45 E
Tesiyn Gol →, *Mongolia* **32 A4** 50 40N 93 20 E
Teslin, *Canada* **72 A2** 60 10N 132 43W
Teslin →, *Canada* **72 A2** 61 34N 134 35W
Teslin L., *Canada* **72 A2** 60 15N 132 57W
Tessalit, *Mali* **50 D6** 20 12N 1 0 E
Test →, *U.K.* **11 G6** 50 56N 1 29W
Testigos, Is. Las, *Venezuela* **89 D7** 11 23N 63 7W
Tetachuck L., *Canada* **72 C3** 53 18N 125 55W
Tetas, Pta., *Chile* **94 A1** 23 31S 70 38W
Tete, *Mozam.* **55 F3** 16 13S 33 33 E
Tete □, *Mozam.* **55 F3** 15 15S 32 40 E
Teterev →, *Ukraine* **17 C16** 51 1N 30 5 E
Teteven, *Bulgaria* **21 C11** 42 58N 24 17 E
Tethul →, *Canada* **72 A6** 60 35N 112 12W
Tetiyev, *Ukraine* **17 D15** 49 22N 29 38 E
Teton →, *U.S.A.* **82 C8** 47 56N 110 31W
Tétouan, *Morocco* **50 A4** 35 35N 5 21W
Tetovo, *Macedonia* **21 C9** 42 1N 20 59 E
Teuco →, *Argentina* **94 B3** 25 35S 60 11W
Teulon, *Canada* **73 C9** 50 23N 97 16W
Teun, *Indonesia* **37 F7** 6 59S 129 8 E
Teutoburger Wald, *Germany* **16 B5** 52 5N 8 22 E
Tevere →, *Italy* **20 D5** 41 44N 12 14 E
Teverya, *Israel* **47 C4** 32 47N 35 32 E
Teviot →, *U.K.* **12 F6** 55 29N 2 38W
Tewantin, *Australia* **63 D5** 26 27S 153 3 E
Tewkesbury, *U.K.* **11 F5** 51 59N 2 9W
Texada I., *Canada* **72 D4** 49 40N 124 25W
Texarkana, *Ark., U.S.A.* **81 J8** 33 26N 94 2W
Texarkana, *Tex., U.S.A.* **81 J7** 33 26N 94 3W
Texas, *Australia* **63 D5** 28 49S 151 9 E
Texas □, *U.S.A.* **81 K5** 31 40N 98 30W
Texas City, *U.S.A.* **81 L7** 29 24N 94 54W
Texel, *Neths.* **15 A4** 53 5N 4 50 E
Texline, *U.S.A.* **81 G3** 36 23N 103 2W
Texoma, L., *U.S.A.* **81 J6** 33 50N 96 34W
Tezin, *Afghan.* **42 B3** 34 24N 69 30 E
Teziutlán, *Mexico* **87 D5** 19 50N 97 22W
Tezpur, *India* **41 F18** 26 40N 92 45 E
Tezzeron L., *Canada* **72 C4** 54 43N 124 30W
Tha-anne →, *Canada* **73 A10** 60 31N 94 37W
Tha Deua, *Laos* **38 D4** 17 57N 102 53 E
Tha Deua, *Laos* **38 C3** 19 26N 101 50 E
Tha Pla, *Thailand* **38 D3** 17 48N 100 32 E
Tha Rua, *Thailand* **38 E3** 14 34N 100 44 E
Tha Sala, *Thailand* **39 H2** 8 40N 99 56 E

Tukuyu

Tukuyu, *Tanzania* . . . . **55 D3** 9 17S 33 35 E
Tula, *Hidalgo, Mexico* **87 C5** 20 5N 99 20W
Tula, *Tamaulipas, Mexico* . **87 C5** 23 0N 99 40W
Tula, *Russia* . . . . **24 D6** 54 13N 37 38 E
Tulancingo, *Mexico* **87 C5** 20 5N 99 22W
Tulare, *U.S.A.* **84 J7** 36 13N 119 21W
Tulare Lake Bed, *U.S.A.* . . . **84 K7** 36 0N 119 48W
Tularosa, *U.S.A.* **83 K10** 33 5N 106 1W
Tulbagh, *S. Africa* . . . . **56 E2** 33 16S 19 6 E
Tulcán, *Ecuador* **92 C3** 0 48N 77 43W
Tulcea, *Romania* . . . . **17 F15** 45 13N 28 46 E
Tulchyn, *Ukraine* . . . . **17 D15** 48 41N 28 49 E
Tūleh, *Iran* . . . . **45 C7** 34 35N 52 33 E
Tulemalu L., *Canada* **73 A9** 62 58N 99 25W
Tuli, *Zimbabwe* . . . . **55 G2** 21 58S 29 13 E
Tulia, *U.S.A.* **81 H4** 34 32N 101 46W
Tulita, *Canada* **68 B7** 64 57N 125 30W
Ţūlkarm, *West Bank* . . . . . . **47 C4** 32 19N 35 2 E
Tulla, *Ireland* **13 D3** 52 53N 8 46W
Tullahoma, *U.S.A.* **77 H2** 35 22N 86 13W
Tullamore, *Australia* . . . . . . **63 E4** 32 39S 147 36 E
Tullamore, *Ireland* **13 C4** 53 16N 7 31W
Tulle, *France* . . . . **18 D4** 45 16N 1 46 E
Tullow, *Ireland* **13 D5** 52 49N 6 45W
Tully, *Australia* . . . . **62 B4** 17 56S 145 55 E
Tully, *U.S.A.* **79 D8** 42 48N 76 7W
Tulsa, *U.S.A.* **81 G7** 36 10N 95 55W
Tulsequah, *Canada* **72 B2** 58 39N 133 35W
Tulua, *Colombia* **92 C3** 4 6N 76 11W
Tulun, *Russia* . . . . **27 D11** 54 32N 100 35 E
Tulungagung, *Indonesia* . . **37 H14** 8 5S 111 54 E
Tuma →, *Nic.* **88 D3** 13 6N 84 35W
Tumaco, *Colombia* **92 C3** 1 50N 78 45W
Tumatumari, *Guyana* **92 B7** 5 20N 58 55W
Tumba, *Sweden* . . . . **9 G17** 59 12N 17 48 E
Tumba, L.,
Dem. Rep. of the Congo . **52 E3** 0 50S 18 0 E
Tumbarumba, *Australia* . . . **63 F4** 35 44S 148 0 E
Tumbaya, *Argentina* **94 A2** 23 50S 65 26W
Tumbes, *Peru* **92 D2** 3 37S 80 27W
Tumbwe,
Dem. Rep. of the Congo . **55 E2** 11 25S 27 15 E
Tumby Bay, *Australia* . . . . . **63 E2** 34 21S 136 8 E
Tumd Youqi, *China* . . . . **34 D6** 40 30N 110 30 E
Tumen, *China* . . . . **35 C15** 43 0N 129 50 E
Tumen Jiang →, *China* . . **35 C16** 42 20N 130 35 E
Tumeremo, *Venezuela* **92 B6** 7 18N 61 30W
Tumkur, *India* . . . . **40 N10** 13 18N 77 6 E
Tump, *Pakistan* . . . . **40 F3** 26 7N 62 16 E
Tumpat, *Malaysia* . . . . **39 J4** 6 11N 102 10 E
Tumu, *Ghana* **50 F5** 10 56N 1 56W
Tumucumaque, Serra, *Brazil* **93 C8** 2 0N 55 0W
Tumut, *Australia* . . . . **63 F4** 35 16S 148 13 E
Tumwater, *U.S.A.* **84 C4** 47 1N 122 54W
Tuna, *India* . . . . **42 H4** 22 59N 70 5 E
Tunas de Zaza, *Cuba* **88 B4** 21 39N 79 34W
Tunbridge Wells = Royal
Tunbridge Wells, *U.K.* . . . . **11 F8** 51 7N 0 16 E
Tuncurry-Forster, *Australia* **63 E5** 32 17S 152 29 E
Tundla, *India* . . . . **42 F8** 27 12N 78 17 E
Tunduru, *Tanzania* . . . . **55 E4** 11 8S 37 25 E
Tundzha →, *Bulgaria* . . . . **21 C11** 41 40N 26 35 E
Tunga Pass, *India* . . . . **41 E19** 29 0N 94 14 E
Tungabhadra →, *India* . . . **40 M11** 15 57N 78 15 E
Tungla, *Nic.* **88 D3** 13 24N 84 21W
Tungsten, *Canada* **72 A3** 61 57N 128 16W
Tunguska, Nizhnyaya →,
Russia . . . . **27 C9** 65 48N 88 4 E
Tunguska,
Podkamennaya →,
Russia . . . . **27 C10** 61 50N 90 13 E
Tunica, *U.S.A.* **81 H9** 34 41N 90 23W
Tunis, *Tunisia* . . . . **51 A8** 36 50N 10 11 E
Tunisia ■, *Africa* . . . . **51 A7** 33 30N 9 10 E
Tunja, *Colombia* **92 B4** 5 33N 73 25W
Tunkhannock, *U.S.A.* **79 E9** 41 32N 75 57W
Tunliu, *China* . . . . **34 F7** 36 13N 112 52 E
Tunnsjøen, *Norway* . . . . . . **8 D15** 64 45N 13 25 E
Tunungayualok I., *Canada* . **71 A7** 56 0N 61 0W
Tunuyán, *Argentina* **94 C2** 33 35S 69 0W
Tunuyán →, *Argentina* . . . **94 C2** 33 33S 67 30W
Tuolumne, *U.S.A.* **84 H6** 37 58N 120 15W
Tuolumne →, *U.S.A.* **84 H5** 37 36N 121 13W
Tūp Āghāj, *Iran* . . . . **44 B5** 36 3N 47 50 E
Tupã, *Brazil* **95 A5** 21 57S 50 28W
Tupelo, *U.S.A.* **77 H1** 34 16N 88 43W
Tupinambaranas, *Brazil* . . . **92 D7** 3 0S 58 0W
Tupiza, *Bolivia* **94 A2** 21 30S 65 40W
Tupman, *U.S.A.* **85 K7** 35 18N 119 21W
Tupper, *Canada* **72 B4** 55 32N 120 1W
Tupper Lake, *U.S.A.* **79 B10** 44 14N 74 28W
Tupungato, Cerro, *S. Amer.* **94 C2** 33 15S 69 50W
Tuquan, *China* . . . . **35 B11** 45 18N 121 38 E
Túquerres, *Colombia* **92 C3** 1 5N 77 37W
Tura, *Russia* . . . . **27 C11** 64 20N 100 17 E
Turabah, *Si. Arabia* . . . . . . **46 C3** 28 20N 43 15 E
Tūrān, *Iran* . . . . **45 C8** 35 39N 56 42 E
Turan, *Russia* . . . . **27 D10** 51 55N 95 0 E
Ţurayf, *Si. Arabia* . . . . **44 D3** 31 41N 38 39 E
Turda, *Romania* . . . . **17 E12** 46 34N 23 47 E
Turek, *Poland* . . . . **17 B10** 52 3N 18 30 E
Turen, *Venezuela* **92 B5** 9 17N 69 6W
Turfan = Turpan, *China* . . . **32 B3** 43 58N 89 10 E
Turfan Depression = Turpan
Hami, *China* . . . . **28 E12** 42 40N 89 25 E
Turgeon →, *Canada* **70 C4** 50 0N 78 56W
Tŭrgovishte, *Bulgaria* . . . . . **21 C12** 43 17N 26 38 E
Turgutlu, *Turkey* . . . . **21 E12** 38 30N 27 43 E
Turia →, *Spain* **19 C5** 39 27N 0 19W
Turiaçu, *Brazil* **93 D9** 1 40S 45 19W
Turiaçu →, *Brazil* **93 D9** 1 36S 45 19W
Turin = Torino, *Italy* . . . . . . **18 D7** 45 3N 7 40 E
Turkana, L., *Africa* . . . . **54 B4** 3 30N 36 5 E
Turkestan = Türkistan,
Kazakstan . . . . **26 E7** 43 17N 68 16 E
Turkey ■, *Eurasia* . . . . **25 G6** 39 0N 36 0 E
Turkey Creek, *Australia* . . . **60 C4** 17 2S 128 12 E
Türkistan, *Kazakstan* . . . . . **26 E7** 43 17N 68 16 E
Türkmenbashi,
Turkmenistan . . . . **25 G9** 40 5N 53 5 E
Turkmenistan ■, *Asia* . . . . . **26 F6** 39 0N 59 0 E
Turks & Caicos Is. ■,
W. Indies **89 B5** 21 20N 71 20W
Turks Island Passage,
W. Indies **89 B5** 21 30N 71 30W
Turku, *Finland* . . . . **9 F20** 60 30N 22 19 E
Turkwel →, *Kenya* . . . . . . **54 B4** 3 6N 36 6 E
Turlock, *U.S.A.* **84 H6** 37 30N 120 51W
Turnagain →, *Canada* **72 B3** 59 12N 127 35W
Turnagain, C., *N.Z.* . . . . **59 J6** 40 28S 176 38 E
Turneffe Is., *Belize* **87 D7** 17 20N 87 50W
Turner, *U.S.A.* **82 B9** 48 51N 108 24W
Turner Pt., *Australia* . . . . . . **62 A1** 11 47S 133 32 E
Turner Valley, *Canada* **72 C6** 50 40N 114 17W
Turners Falls, *U.S.A.* **79 D12** 42 36N 72 33W
Turnhout, *Belgium* . . . . **15 C4** 51 19N 4 57 E
Turnor L., *Canada* **73 B7** 56 35N 108 35W
Tŭrnovo = Veliko Tŭrnovo,
Bulgaria . . . . **21 C11** 43 5N 25 41 E
Turnu Măgurele, *Romania* . **17 G13** 43 46N 24 56 E
Turnu Roşu, P., *Romania* . . **17 F13** 45 33N 24 17 E
Turpan, *China* . . . . **32 B3** 43 58N 89 10 E
Turpan Hami, *China* . . . . . . **28 E12** 42 40N 89 25 E
Turriff, *U.K.* **12 D6** 57 32N 2 27W
Tursāq, *Iraq* . . . . **44 C5** 33 27N 45 47 E
Turtle Head I., *Australia* . . . **62 A3** 10 56S 142 37 E
Turtle L., *Canada* **73 C7** 53 36N 108 38W
Turtle Lake, *U.S.A.* **80 B4** 47 31N 100 53W
Turtleford, *Canada* **73 C7** 53 23N 108 57W
Turukhansk, *Russia* . . . . . . **27 C9** 65 21N 88 5 E
Tuscaloosa, *U.S.A.* **77 J2** 33 12N 87 34W
Tuscany = Toscana □, *Italy* **20 C4** 43 25N 11 0 E
Tuscarawas →, *U.S.A.* . . . **78 F3** 40 24N 81 25W
Tuscarora Mt., *U.S.A.* **78 F7** 40 55N 77 55W
Tuscola, *Ill., U.S.A.* **76 F1** 39 48N 88 17W
Tuscola, *Tex., U.S.A.* **81 J5** 32 12N 99 48W
Tuscumbia, *U.S.A.* **77 H2** 34 44N 87 42W
Tuskegee, *U.S.A.* **77 J3** 32 25N 85 42W
Tustin, *U.S.A.* **85 M9** 33 44N 117 49W
Tuticorin, *India* . . . . **40 Q11** 8 50N 78 12 E
Tutóia, *Brazil* **93 D10** 2 45S 42 20W
Tutong, *Brunei* . . . . **36 D4** 4 47N 114 40 E
Tutrakan, *Bulgaria* . . . . **21 B12** 44 2N 26 40 E
Tuttle Creek L., *U.S.A.* **80 F6** 39 22N 96 40W
Tuttlingen, *Germany* . . . . . . **16 E5** 47 58N 8 48 E
Tutuala, *Indonesia* . . . . **37 F7** 8 25S 127 15 E
Tutuila, *Amer. Samoa* **59 B13** 14 19S 170 50W
Tutume, *Botswana* . . . . **53 J5** 20 30S 27 5 E
Tututepec, *Mexico* **87 D5** 16 9N 97 38W
Tuva □, *Russia* . . . . **27 D10** 51 30N 95 0 E
Tuvalu ■, *Pac. Oc.* . . . . **64 H9** 8 0S 178 0 E
Tuxpan, *Mexico* **87 C5** 20 58N 97 23W
Tuxtla Gutiérrez, *Mexico* . . . **87 D6** 16 50N 93 10W
Tuy = Tui, *Spain* **19 A1** 42 3N 8 39W
Tuy An, *Vietnam* . . . . **38 F7** 13 17N 109 16 E
Tuy Duc, *Vietnam* . . . . **39 F6** 12 15N 107 27 E
Tuy Hoa, *Vietnam* . . . . **38 F7** 13 5N 109 10 E
Tuy Phong, *Vietnam* . . . . . . **39 G7** 11 14N 108 43 E
Tuya L., *Canada* **72 B2** 59 7N 130 35W
Tuyen Hoa, *Vietnam* . . . . . . **38 D6** 17 50N 106 10 E
Tūysarkān, *Iran* . . . . **45 C6** 34 33N 48 27 E
Tuz Gölü, *Turkey* . . . . **25 G5** 38 42N 33 18 E
Ţūz Khurmātū, *Iraq* . . . . . . **44 C5** 34 56N 44 38 E
Tuzla, *Bos.-H.* . . . . **21 B8** 44 34N 18 41 E
Tver, *Russia* . . . . **24 C6** 56 55N 35 55 E
Twain, *U.S.A.* **84 E5** 40 1N 121 3W
Twain Harte, *U.S.A.* **84 G6** 38 2N 120 14W
Tweed, *Canada* **78 B7** 44 29N 77 19W
Tweed →, *U.K.* **12 F6** 55 45N 2 0W
Tweed Heads, *Australia* . . . **63 D5** 28 10S 153 31 E
Tweedsmuir Prov. Park,
Canada **72 C3** 53 0N 126 20W
Twentynine Palms, *U.S.A.* . . **85 L10** 34 8N 116 3W
Twillingate, *Canada* **71 C9** 49 42N 54 45W
Twin Bridges, *U.S.A.* **82 D7** 45 33N 112 20W
Twin Falls, *Canada* **71 B7** 53 30N 64 32W
Twin Falls, *U.S.A.* **82 E6** 42 34N 114 28W
Twin Valley, *U.S.A.* **80 B6** 47 16N 96 16W
Twinsburg, *U.S.A.* **78 E3** 41 18N 81 26W
Twitchell Reservoir, *U.S.A.* . **85 L6** 34 59N 120 19W
Two Harbors, *U.S.A.* **80 B9** 47 2N 91 40W
Two Hills, *Canada* **72 C6** 53 43N 111 52W
Two Rivers, *U.S.A.* **76 C2** 44 9N 87 34W
Two Rocks, *Australia* . . . . . **61 F2** 31 30S 115 35 E
Twofold B., *Australia* . . . . . **63 F4** 37 8S 149 59 E
Tyachiv, *Ukraine* . . . . **17 D12** 48 1N 23 35 E
Tychy, *Poland* . . . . **17 C10** 50 9N 18 59 E
Tyler, *U.S.A.* **75 D7** 32 18N 95 17W
Tyler, *Minn., U.S.A.* **80 C6** 44 18N 96 8W
Tyler, *Tex., U.S.A.* **81 J7** 32 21N 95 18W
Tynda, *Russia* . . . . **27 D13** 55 10N 124 43 E
Tyndall, *U.S.A.* **80 D6** 43 0N 97 50W
Tyne →, *U.K.* **10 C6** 54 59N 1 32W
Tyne & Wear □, *U.K.* **10 B6** 55 6N 1 17W
Tynemouth, *U.K.* **10 B6** 55 1N 1 26W
Tyre = Sūr, *Lebanon* . . . . . **47 B4** 33 19N 35 16 E
Tyrifjorden, *Norway* . . . . . . **9 F14** 60 2N 10 8 E
Tyrol = Tirol □, *Austria* . . . **16 E6** 47 3N 10 43 E
Tyrone, *U.S.A.* **78 F6** 40 40N 78 14W
Tyrone □, *U.K.* **13 B4** 54 38N 7 11W
Tyrrell →, *Australia* . . . . . . **63 F3** 35 26S 142 51 E
Tyrrell, L., *Australia* . . . . . . **63 F3** 35 20S 142 50 E
Tyrrell L., *Canada* **73 A7** 63 7N 105 27W
Tyrrhenian Sea, *Medit. S.* . . **20 E5** 40 0N 12 30 E
Tysfjorden, *Norway* . . . . **8 B17** 68 7N 16 25 E
Tyulgan, *Russia* . . . . **24 D10** 52 22N 56 12 E
Tyumen, *Russia* . . . . **26 D7** 57 11N 65 29 E
Tywi →, *U.K.* **11 F3** 51 48N 4 21W
Tywyn, *U.K.* **11 E3** 52 35N 4 5W
Tzaneen, *S. Africa* . . . . **57 C5** 23 47S 30 9 E
Tzermiádhes, *Greece* . . . . . **23 D7** 35 12N 25 29 E
Tzukong = Zigong, *China* . . **32 D5** 29 15N 104 48 E

U

U Taphao, *Thailand* . . . . . . **38 F3** 12 35N 101 0 E
U.S.A. = United States of
America ■, *N. Amer.* **74 C7** 37 0N 96 0W
Uatumã →, *Brazil* **92 D7** 2 26S 57 37W
Uaupés, *Brazil* **92 D5** 0 8S 67 5W
Uaupés →, *Brazil* **92 C5** 0 2N 67 16W
Uaxactún, *Guatemala* **88 C2** 17 25N 89 29W
Ubá, *Brazil* **95 A7** 21 8S 43 0W
Ubaitaba, *Brazil* **93 F11** 14 18S 39 20W
Ubangi = Oubangi →,
Dem. Rep. of the Congo . **52 E3** 0 30S 17 50 E
Ubauro, *Pakistan* . . . . **42 E3** 28 15N 69 45 E
Ubayyiḍ, W. al →, *Iraq* . . . **44 C4** 32 34N 43 48 E
Ube, *Japan* . . . . **31 H5** 33 56N 131 15 E
Úbeda, *Spain* **19 C4** 38 3N 3 23W
Uberaba, *Brazil* **93 G9** 19 50S 47 55W
Uberlândia, *Brazil* **93 G9** 19 0S 48 20W
Ubolratna Res., *Thailand* . . **38 D4** 16 45N 102 30 E
Ubombo, *S. Africa* . . . . **57 D5** 27 31S 32 4 E
Ubon Ratchathani, *Thailand* **38 E5** 15 15N 104 50 E
Ubondo,
Dem. Rep. of the Congo . **54 C2** 0 55S 25 42 E
Ubort →, *Belarus* . . . . **17 B15** 52 6N 28 30 E
Ubundu,
Dem. Rep. of the Congo . **54 C2** 0 22S 25 30 E
Ucayali →, *Peru* **92 D4** 4 30S 73 30W
Uchiura-Wan, *Japan* . . . . . . **30 C10** 42 25N 140 40 E
Uchquduq, *Uzbekistan* . . . . **26 E7** 41 50N 62 50 E
Uchur →, *Russia* . . . . **27 D14** 58 48N 130 35 E
Ucluelet, *Canada* **72 D3** 48 57N 125 32W
Uda →, *Russia* . . . . **27 D14** 54 42N 135 14 E
Udagamandalam, *India* . . . . **40 P10** 11 30N 76 44 E
Udainagar, *India* . . . . **42 H7** 22 33N 76 13 E
Udaipur, *India* . . . . **42 G5** 24 36N 73 44 E
Udaipur Garhi, *Nepal* . . . . . **43 F12** 27 0N 86 35 E
Udala, *India* . . . . **43 J12** 21 35N 86 34 E
Uddevalla, *Sweden* . . . . **9 G14** 58 21N 11 55 E
Uddjaur, *Sweden* . . . . **8 D17** 65 56N 17 49 E
Uden, *Neths.* . . . . **15 C5** 51 40N 5 37 E
Udgir, *India* . . . . **40 K10** 18 25N 77 5 E
Udhampur, *India* . . . . **43 C6** 33 0N 75 5 E
Údine, *Italy* . . . . **20 A5** 46 3N 13 14 E
Udmurtia □, *Russia* . . . . . . **24 C9** 57 30N 52 30 E
Udon Thani, *Thailand* . . . . . **38 D4** 17 29N 102 46 E
Udupi, *India* . . . . **40 N9** 13 25N 74 42 E
Udzungwa Range, *Tanzania* **55 D4** 9 30S 35 10 E
Ueda, *Japan* . . . . **31 F9** 36 24N 138 16 E
Uedineniya, Os., *Russia* . . . **4 B12** 78 0N 85 0 E
Uele →,
Dem. Rep. of the Congo . **52 D4** 3 45N 24 45 E
Uelen, *Russia* **27 C19** 66 10N 170 0W
Uelzen, *Germany* . . . . **16 B6** 52 57N 10 32 E
Ufa, *Russia* . . . . **24 D10** 54 45N 55 55 E
Ufa →, *Russia* . . . . **24 D10** 54 40N 56 0 E
Ugab →, *Namibia* . . . . **56 C1** 20 55S 13 30 E
Ugalla →, *Tanzania* . . . . . **54 D3** 5 8S 30 42 E
Uganda ■, *Africa* . . . . **54 B3** 2 0N 32 0 E
Ugie, *S. Africa* . . . . **57 E4** 31 10S 28 13 E
Uglegorsk, *Russia* . . . . **27 E15** 49 5N 142 2 E
Ugljan, *Croatia* . . . . **16 F8** 44 12N 15 10 E
Uhrichsville, *U.S.A.* **78 F3** 40 24N 81 21W
Uibhist a Deas = South
Uist, *U.K.* **12 D1** 57 20N 7 15W
Uibhist a Tuath = North
Uist, *U.K.* **12 D1** 57 40N 7 15W
Uig, *U.K.* **12 D2** 57 35N 6 21W
Uíge, *Angola* . . . . **52 F2** 7 30S 14 40 E
Uijŏngbu, *S. Korea* . . . . **35 F14** 37 48N 127 0 E
Ŭiju, *N. Korea* . . . . **35 D13** 40 15N 124 35 E
Uinta Mts., *U.S.A.* **82 F8** 40 45N 110 30W
Uitenhage, *S. Africa* . . . . . . **56 E4** 33 40S 25 28 E
Uithuizen, *Neths.* . . . . **15 A6** 53 24N 6 41 E
Ujh →, *India* . . . . **42 C6** 32 10N 75 18 E
Ujhani, *India* . . . . **43 F8** 28 0N 79 6 E
Uji-guntō, *Japan* . . . . **31 J4** 31 15N 129 25 E
Ujjain, *India* . . . . **42 H6** 23 9N 75 43 E
Ujung Pandang, *Indonesia* . **37 F5** 5 10S 119 20 E
Uka, *Russia* . . . . **27 D17** 57 50N 162 0 E
Ukara I., *Tanzania* . . . . **54 C3** 1 50S 33 0 E
Uke-Shima, *Japan* . . . . **31 K4** 28 2N 129 14 E
Ukerewe I., *Tanzania* . . . . . **54 C3** 2 0S 33 0 E
Ukhrul, *India* . . . . **41 G19** 25 10N 94 25 E
Ukhta, *Russia* . . . . **24 B9** 63 34N 53 41 E
Ukiah, *U.S.A.* **84 F3** 39 9N 123 13W
Ukki Fort, *India* . . . . **43 C7** 33 28N 76 54 E
Ukmergė, *Lithuania* . . . . **9 J21** 55 15N 24 45 E
Ukraine ■, *Europe* . . . . **25 E5** 49 0N 32 0 E
Uku, *Angola* . . . . **53 G2** 11 24S 14 22 E
Ukwi, *Botswana* . . . . **56 C3** 23 29S 20 30 E
Ulaan-Uul, *Mongolia* . . . . . . **34 B6** 44 13N 111 10 E
Ulaanbaatar, *Mongolia* . . . . **27 E11** 47 55N 106 53 E
Ulaangom, *Mongolia* . . . . . . **32 A4** 50 5N 92 10 E
Ulaanjirem, *Mongolia* . . . . . **34 B3** 45 5N 105 30 E
Ulamba,
Dem. Rep. of the Congo . **55 D1** 9 3S 23 38 E
Ulan Bator = Ulaanbaatar,
Mongolia . . . . **27 E11** 47 55N 106 53 E
Ulan Ude, *Russia* . . . . **27 D11** 51 45N 107 40 E
Ulaya, *Morogoro, Tanzania* . **54 D4** 7 3S 36 55 E
Ulaya, *Tabora, Tanzania* . . . **54 C3** 4 25S 33 30 E
Ulcinj, *Montenegro, Yug.* . . . **21 D8** 41 58N 19 10 E
Ulco, *S. Africa* . . . . **56 D3** 28 21S 24 15 E
Ulefoss, *Norway* . . . . **9 G13** 59 17N 9 16 E
Ulhasnagar, *India* . . . . **40 K8** 19 15N 73 10 E
Uliastay, *Mongolia* . . . . **32 B4** 47 56N 97 28 E
Ulithi Atoll, *Pac. Oc.* . . . . . . **37 B9** 10 0N 139 30 E
Ulladulla, *Australia* . . . . **63 F5** 35 21S 150 29 E
Ullapool, *U.K.* **12 D3** 57 54N 5 9W
Ullswater, *U.K.* **10 C5** 54 34N 2 52W
Ullŭng-do, *S. Korea* . . . . **31 F5** 37 30N 130 30 E
Ulm, *Germany* . . . . **16 D5** 48 23N 9 58 E
Ulmarra, *Australia* . . . . **63 D5** 29 37S 153 4 E
Ulonguè, *Mozam.* . . . . **55 E3** 14 37S 34 19 E
Ulricehamn, *Sweden* . . . . . . **9 H15** 57 46N 13 26 E
Ulsan, *S. Korea* . . . . **35 G15** 35 20N 129 15 E
Ulsta, *U.K.* **12 A7** 60 30N 1 9W
Ulster □, *U.K.* **13 B5** 54 35N 6 30W
Ulubat Gölü, *Turkey* . . . . **21 D13** 40 9N 28 35 E
Uludağ, *Turkey* . . . . **21 D13** 40 4N 29 13 E
Uluguru Mts., *Tanzania* . . . . **54 D4** 7 15S 37 40 E
Ulungur He →, *China* . . . . . **32 B3** 47 1N 87 24 E
Uluru = Ayers Rock,
Australia . . . . **61 E5** 25 23S 131 5 E
Uluru Nat. Park, *Australia* . . **61 E5** 25 15S 131 20 E
Ulutau, *Kazakstan* . . . . **26 E7** 48 39N 67 1 E
Ulva, *U.K.* **12 E2** 56 29N 6 13W
Ulverston, *U.K.* **10 C4** 54 13N 3 5W
Ulverstone, *Australia* . . . . . . **62 G4** 41 11S 146 11 E
Ulya, *Russia* . . . . **27 D15** 59 10N 142 0 E
Ulyanovsk = Simbirsk,
Russia . . . . **24 D8** 54 20N 48 25 E
Ulyasutay = Uliastay,
Mongolia . . . . **32 B4** 47 56N 97 28 E
Ulysses, *U.S.A.* **81 G4** 37 35N 101 22W
Umala, *Bolivia* **92 G5** 17 25S 68 5W
Uman, *Ukraine* . . . . **17 D16** 48 40N 30 12 E
Umaria, *India* . . . . **41 H12** 23 35N 80 50 E
Umarkot, *Pakistan* . . . . **40 G6** 25 15N 69 40 E
Umarpada, *India* . . . . **42 J5** 21 27N 73 30 E
Umatilla, *U.S.A.* **82 D4** 45 55N 119 21W
Umba, *Russia* . . . . **24 A5** 66 42N 34 11 E
Umbagog L., *U.S.A.* **79 B13** 44 46N 71 3W
Umbakumba, *Australia* . . . . **62 A2** 13 47S 136 50 E
Umbrella Mts., *N.Z.* . . . . **59 L2** 45 35S 169 5 E
Ume älv →, *Sweden* . . . . . . **8 E19** 63 45N 20 20 E
Umeå, *Sweden* . . . . **8 E19** 63 45N 20 20 E
Umera, *Indonesia* . . . . **37 E7** 0 12S 129 37 E
Umfuli →, *Zimbabwe* . . . . . **55 F2** 17 30S 29 23 E
Umgusa, *Zimbabwe* . . . . **55 F2** 19 29S 27 52 E
Umkomaas, *S. Africa* . . . . . . **57 E5** 30 13S 30 48 E
Umlazi, *S. Africa* . . . . **53 L6** 29 59S 30 54 E
Umm ad Daraj, J., *Jordan* . . **47 C4** 32 18N 35 48 E
Umm al Qaywayn, *U.A.E.* . . . **45 E7** 25 30N 55 35 E
Umm al Qittayn, *Jordan* . . . . **47 C5** 32 18N 36 40 E
Umm Bāb, *Qatar* . . . . **45 E6** 25 12N 50 48 E
Umm el Fahm, *Israel* . . . . . . **47 C4** 32 31N 35 9 E
Umm Keddada, *Sudan* . . . . . **51 F11** 13 36N 26 42 E
Umm Lajj, *Si. Arabia* . . . . . . **44 E3** 25 0N 37 23 E
Umm Ruwaba, *Sudan* . . . . . . **51 F12** 12 50N 31 20 E
Umnak I., *U.S.A.* **68 C3** 53 15N 168 20W
Umniati →, *Zimbabwe* . . . . **55 F2** 16 49S 28 45 E
Umpqua →, *U.S.A.* **82 E1** 43 40N 124 12W
Umreth, *India* . . . . **42 H5** 22 41N 73 4 E
Umtata, *S. Africa* . . . . **57 E4** 31 36S 28 49 E
Umuarama, *Brazil* **95 A5** 23 45S 53 20W
Umvukwe Ra., *Zimbabwe* . . **55 F3** 16 45S 30 45 E
Umzimvubu = Port St.
Johns, *S. Africa* . . . . **57 E4** 31 38S 29 33 E
Umzingwane →,
Zimbabwe . . . . **55 G2** 22 12S 29 56 E
Umzinto, *S. Africa* . . . . **57 E5** 30 15S 30 45 E
Una, *India* . . . . **42 J4** 20 46N 71 8 E
Una →, *Bos.-H.* . . . . **16 F9** 45 0N 16 20 E
Unadilla, *U.S.A.* **79 D9** 42 20N 75 19W
Unalakleet, *U.S.A.* **68 B3** 63 52N 160 47W
Unalaska, *U.S.A.* **68 C3** 53 53N 166 32W
Unalaska I., *U.S.A.* **68 C3** 53 35N 166 50W
'Unayzah, *Si. Arabia* . . . . . . **44 E4** 26 6N 43 58 E
'Unāzah, J., *Asia* . . . . **44 C3** 32 12N 39 18 E
Uncía, *Bolivia* **92 G5** 18 25S 66 40W
Uncompahgre Peak, *U.S.A.* **83 G10** 38 4N 107 28W
Uncompahgre Plateau,
U.S.A. **83 G9** 38 20N 108 15W
Underbool, *Australia* . . . . . . **63 F3** 35 10S 141 51 E
Ungarie, *Australia* . . . . **63 E4** 33 38S 146 56 E
Ungarra, *Australia* . . . . **63 E2** 34 12S 136 2 E
Ungava, Pén. d', *Canada* . . . **69 C12** 60 0N 74 0W
Ungava B., *Canada* **69 C13** 59 30N 67 30W
Ungeny = Ungheni,
Moldova . . . . **17 E14** 47 11N 27 51 E
Unggi, *N. Korea* . . . . **35 C16** 42 16N 130 28 E
Ungheni, *Moldova* . . . . **17 E14** 47 11N 27 51 E
União da Vitória, *Brazil* **95 B5** 26 13S 51 5W
Unimak I., *U.S.A.* **68 C3** 54 45N 164 0W
Union, *Miss., U.S.A.* **81 J10** 32 34N 89 7W
Union, *Mo., U.S.A.* **80 F9** 38 27N 91 0W
Union, *S.C., U.S.A.* **77 H5** 34 43N 81 37W
Union City, *Calif., U.S.A.* . . . **84 H4** 37 36N 122 1W
Union City, *N.J., U.S.A.* **79 F10** 40 45N 74 2W
Union City, *Pa., U.S.A.* **78 E5** 41 54N 79 51W
Union City, *Tenn., U.S.A.* . . . **81 G10** 36 26N 89 3W
Union Gap, *U.S.A.* **82 C3** 46 33N 120 28W
Union Springs, *U.S.A.* **77 J3** 32 9N 85 43W
Uniondale, *S. Africa* . . . . . . **56 E3** 33 39S 23 7 E
Uniontown, *U.S.A.* **76 F6** 39 54N 79 44W
Unionville, *U.S.A.* **80 E8** 40 29N 93 1W
United Arab Emirates ■,
Asia . . . . **45 F7** 23 50N 54 0 E
United Kingdom ■, *Europe* . **7 E5** 53 0N 2 0W
United States of America ■,
N. Amer. **74 C7** 37 0N 96 0W
Unity, *Canada* **73 C7** 52 30N 109 5W
University Park, *U.S.A.* **83 K10** 32 17N 106 45W
Unjha, *India* . . . . **42 H5** 23 46N 72 24 E
Unnao, *India* . . . . **43 F9** 26 35N 80 30 E
Unst, *U.K.* **12 A8** 60 44N 0 53W
Unuk →, *Canada* **72 B2** 56 5N 131 3W
Uozu, *Japan* . . . . **31 F8** 36 48N 137 24 E
Upata, *Venezuela* **92 B6** 8 1N 62 24W
Upemba, L.,
Dem. Rep. of the Congo . **55 D2** 8 30S 26 20 E
Upernavik, *Greenland* **4 B5** 72 49N 56 20W
Upington, *S. Africa* . . . . **56 D3** 28 25S 21 15 E
Upleta, *India* . . . . **42 J4** 21 46N 70 16 E
Upolu, *W. Samoa* **59 A13** 13 58S 172 0W
Upper Alkali L., *U.S.A.* **82 F3** 41 47N 120 8W
Upper Arrow L., *Canada* . . . **72 C5** 50 30N 117 50W
Upper Foster L., *Canada* . . . **73 B7** 56 47N 105 20W
Upper Hutt, *N.Z.* . . . . **59 J5** 41 8S 175 5 E
Upper Klamath L., *U.S.A.* . . . **82 E3** 42 25N 121 55W
Upper Lake, *U.S.A.* **84 F4** 39 10N 122 54W
Upper Musquodoboit,
Canada **71 C7** 45 10N 62 58W
Upper Red L., *U.S.A.* **80 A7** 48 8N 94 45W
Upper Sandusky, *U.S.A.* . . . **76 E4** 40 50N 83 17W
Upper Volta = Burkina
Faso ■, *Africa* **50 F5** 12 0N 1 0W
Uppland, *Sweden* . . . . **9 F17** 59 59N 17 48 E
Uppsala, *Sweden* . . . . **9 G17** 59 53N 17 38 E
Upshi, *India* . . . . **43 C7** 33 48N 77 52 E
Upstart, C., *Australia* . . . . . **62 B4** 19 41S 147 45 E
Upton, *U.S.A.* **80 C2** 44 6N 104 38W
Ur, *Iraq* . . . . **44 D5** 30 55N 46 25 E
Urad Qianqi, *China* . . . . **34 D5** 40 40N 108 30 E
Urakawa, *Japan* . . . . **30 C11** 42 9N 142 47 E
Ural = Zhayyq →,
Kazakstan . . . . **25 E9** 47 0N 51 48 E
Ural, *Australia* . . . . **63 E4** 33 21S 146 12 E
Ural Mts. = Uralskie Gory,
Eurasia . . . . **24 C10** 60 0N 59 0 E
Uralla, *Australia* . . . . **63 E5** 30 37S 151 29 E
Uralsk = Oral, *Kazakstan* . . **25 D9** 51 20N 51 20 E
Uralskie Gory, *Eurasia* . . . . **24 C10** 60 0N 59 0 E
Urambo, *Tanzania* . . . . **54 D3** 5 4S 32 0 E
Urana, *Australia* . . . . **63 F4** 35 15S 146 21 E
Urandangi, *Australia* . . . . . . **62 C2** 21 32S 138 14 E
Uranium City, *Canada* **73 B7** 59 34N 108 37W
Uraricoera →, *Brazil* **92 C6** 3 2N 60 30W
Urawa, *Japan* . . . . **31 G9** 35 50N 139 40 E
Uray, *Russia* . . . . **26 C7** 60 5N 65 15 E
'Uray'irah, *Si. Arabia* . . . . . **45 E6** 25 57N 48 53 E
Urbana, *Ill., U.S.A.* **76 E1** 40 7N 88 12W
Urbana, *Ohio, U.S.A.* **76 E4** 40 7N 83 45W
Urbino, *Italy* . . . . **20 C5** 43 43N 12 38 E
Urbión, Picos de, *Spain* . . . **19 A4** 42 1N 2 52W
Urcos, *Peru* **92 F4** 13 40S 71 38W

Vestfjorden

Vestfjorden, Norway 8 C15 67 55N 14 0 E
Vestmannaeyjar, Iceland 8 E3 63 27N 20 15W
Vestspitsbergen, Svalbard 4 B8 78 40N 17 0 E
Vestvågøy, Norway 8 B15 68 18N 13 50 E
Vesuvio, Italy 20 D6 40 49N 14 26 E
Vesuvius, Mt. = Vesuvio, Italy 20 D6 40 49N 14 26 E
Veszprém, Hungary 17 E9 47 8N 17 57 E
Vetlanda, Sweden 9 H16 57 24N 15 3 E
Vetlugu →, Russia 24 C8 56 36N 46 4 E
Vettore, Mte., Italy 20 C5 42 49N 13 16 E
Veurne, Belgium 15 C2 51 5N 2 40 E
Veys, Iran 45 D6 31 30N 49 0 E
Vezhen, Bulgaria 21 C11 42 50N 24 20 E
Vi Thanh, Vietnam 39 H5 9 42N 105 26 E
Viacha, Bolivia 92 G5 16 39S 68 18W
Viamão, Brazil 95 C5 30 5S 51 0W
Viana, Brazil 93 D10 3 13S 44 55W
Viana do Alentejo, Portugal 19 C2 38 17N 7 59W
Viana do Castelo, Portugal 19 B1 41 42N 8 50W
Vianden, Lux. 15 E6 49 56N 6 12 E
Vianópolis, Brazil 93 G9 16 40S 48 35W
Viaréggio, Italy 20 C4 43 52N 10 14 E
Vibo Valéntia, Italy 20 E7 38 40N 16 6 E
Viborg, Denmark 9 H13 56 27N 9 23 E
Vic, Spain 19 B7 41 58N 2 19 E
Vicenza, Italy 20 B4 45 33N 11 33 E
Vich = Vic, Spain 19 B7 41 58N 2 19 E
Vichada →, Colombia 92 C5 4 55N 67 50W
Vichy, France 18 C5 46 9N 3 26 E
Vicksburg, Ariz., U.S.A. 85 M13 33 45N 113 45W
Vicksburg, Miss., U.S.A. 81 J9 32 21N 90 53W
Victor, India 42 J4 21 0N 71 30 E
Victor, U.S.A. 78 D7 42 58N 77 24W
Victor Harbor, Australia 63 F2 35 30S 138 37 E
Victoria = Labuan, Malaysia 36 C5 5 20N 115 14 E
Victoria, Argentina 94 C3 32 40S 60 10W
Victoria, Canada 72 D4 48 30N 123 25W
Victoria, Chile 96 D2 38 13S 72 20W
Victoria, Malta 23 C1 36 2N 14 14 E
Victoria, Kans., U.S.A. 80 F5 38 52N 99 9W
Victoria, Tex., U.S.A. 81 L6 28 48N 97 0W
Victoria □, Australia 63 F3 37 0S 144 0 E
Victoria →, Australia 60 C4 15 10S 129 40 E
Victoria, Grand L., Canada 70 C4 47 31N 77 30W
Victoria, L., Africa 54 C3 1 0S 33 0 E
Victoria, L., Australia 63 E3 33 57S 141 15 E
Victoria Beach, Canada 73 C9 50 40N 96 35W
Victoria de Durango = Durango, Mexico 86 C4 24 3N 104 39W
Victoria de las Tunas, Cuba 88 B4 20 58N 76 59W
Victoria Falls, Zimbabwe 55 F2 17 58S 25 52 E
Victoria Harbour, Canada 78 B5 44 45N 79 45W
Victoria I., Canada 68 A8 71 0N 111 0W
Victoria L., Canada 71 C8 48 20N 57 27W
Victoria Ld., Antarctica 5 D11 75 0S 160 0 E
Victoria Nile →, Uganda 54 B3 2 14N 31 26 E
Victoria River, Australia 60 C5 16 25S 131 0 E
Victoria Str., Canada 68 B9 69 30N 100 0W
Victoria Taungdeik, Burma 41 J18 21 15N 93 55 E
Victoria West, S. Africa 56 E3 31 25S 23 4 E
Victoriaville, Canada 71 C5 46 4N 71 56W
Victorica, Argentina 94 D2 36 20S 65 30W
Victorville, U.S.A. 85 L9 34 32N 117 18W
Vicuña, Chile 94 C1 30 0S 70 50W
Vicuña Mackenna, Argentina 94 C3 33 53S 64 25W
Vidal, U.S.A. 85 L12 34 7N 114 31W
Vidal Junction, U.S.A. 85 L12 34 11N 114 34W
Vidalia, U.S.A. 77 J4 32 13N 82 25W
Vídho, Greece 23 A3 39 38N 19 55 E
Vidin, Bulgaria 21 C10 43 59N 22 50 E
Vidisha, India 42 H7 23 28N 77 53 E
Vidzy, Belarus 9 J22 55 23N 26 37 E
Viedma, Argentina 96 E4 40 50S 63 0W
Viedma, L., Argentina 96 F2 49 30S 72 30W
Vielsalm, Belgium 15 D5 50 17N 5 54 E
Vienna = Wien, Austria 16 D9 48 12N 16 22 E
Vienna, Ill., U.S.A. 81 G10 37 25N 88 54W
Vienna, Mo., U.S.A. 80 F9 38 11N 91 57W
Vienne, France 18 D6 45 31N 4 53 E
Vienne →, France 18 C4 47 13N 0 5 E
Vientiane, Laos 38 D4 17 58N 102 36 E
Vientos, Paso de los, Caribbean 89 C5 20 0N 74 0W
Vierzon, France 18 C5 47 13N 2 5 E
Vietnam ■, Asia 38 C6 19 0N 106 0 E
Vigan, Phil. 37 A6 17 35N 120 28 E
Vigévano, Italy 18 D8 45 19N 8 51 E
Vigia, Brazil 93 D9 0 50S 48 5W
Vigía Chico, Mexico 87 D7 19 46N 87 35W
Víglas, Ákra, Greece 23 D9 35 54N 27 51 E
Vigo, Spain 19 A1 42 12N 8 41W
Vihowa, Pakistan 42 D4 31 8N 70 30 E
Vihowa →, Pakistan 42 D4 31 8N 70 41 E
Vijayawada, India 41 L12 16 31N 80 39 E
Vik, Iceland 8 E4 63 25N 19 1W
Vikeke, Indonesia 37 F7 8 52S 126 23 E
Viking, Canada 72 C6 53 7N 111 50W
Vikna, Norway 8 D14 64 55N 10 58 E
Vila da Maganja, Mozam. 55 F4 17 18S 37 30 E
Vila de João Belo = Xai-Xai, Mozam. 57 D5 25 6S 33 31 E
Vila do Bispo, Portugal 19 D1 37 5N 8 53W
Vila do Chibuto, Mozam. 57 C5 24 40S 33 33 E
Vila Franca de Xira, Portugal 19 C1 38 57N 8 59W
Vila Gamito, Mozam. 55 E3 14 12S 33 0 E
Vila Gomes da Costa, Mozam. 57 C5 24 20S 33 37 E
Vila Machado, Mozam. 55 F3 19 15S 34 14 E
Vila Mouzinho, Mozam. 55 E3 14 48S 34 25 E
Vila Nova de Gaia, Portugal 19 B1 41 8N 8 37W
Vila Real, Portugal 19 B2 41 17N 7 48W
Vila-real de los Infantes, Spain 19 C5 39 55N 0 3W
Vila Real de Santo António, Portugal 19 D2 37 10N 7 28W
Vila Vasco da Gama, Mozam. 55 E3 14 54S 32 14 E
Vila Velha, Brazil 95 A7 20 20S 40 17W
Vilagarcía de Arousa, Spain 19 A1 42 34N 8 46W
Vilaine →, France 18 C2 47 30N 2 27W
Vilanandro, Tanjona, Madag. 57 B7 16 11S 44 27 E
Vilanculos, Mozam. 57 C6 22 1S 35 17 E
Vilanova i la Geltrú, Spain 19 B6 41 13N 1 40 E
Vileyka, Belarus 17 A14 54 30N 26 53 E
Vilhelmina, Sweden 8 D17 64 35N 16 39 E
Vilhena, Brazil 92 F6 12 40S 60 5W
Viliga, Russia 27 C16 61 36N 156 56 E
Viliya →, Lithuania 9 J21 55 8N 24 16 E
Viljandi, Estonia 9 G21 58 28N 25 30 E
Vilkitskogo, Proliv, Russia 27 B11 78 0N 103 0 E
Vilkovo = Vylkove, Ukraine 17 F15 45 28N 29 32 E
Villa Abecia, Bolivia 94 A2 21 0S 68 18W
Villa Ahumada, Mexico 86 A3 30 38N 106 30W
Villa Ana, Argentina 94 B4 28 28S 59 40W
Villa Ángela, Argentina 94 B3 27 34S 60 45W
Villa Bella, Bolivia 92 F5 10 25S 65 22W
Villa Bens = Tarfaya, Morocco 50 C3 27 55N 12 55W
Villa Cañás, Argentina 94 C3 34 0S 61 35W
Villa Cisneros = Dakhla, W. Sahara 50 D2 23 50N 15 53W
Villa Colón, Argentina 94 C2 31 38S 68 20W
Villa Constitución, Argentina 94 C3 33 15S 60 20W
Villa de María, Argentina 94 B3 29 55S 63 43W
Villa Dolores, Argentina 94 C2 31 58S 65 15W
Villa Frontera, Mexico 86 B4 26 56N 101 27W
Villa Guillermina, Argentina 94 B4 28 15S 59 29W
Villa Hayes, Paraguay 94 B4 25 5S 57 20W
Villa Iris, Argentina 94 D3 38 12S 63 12W
Villa Juárez, Mexico 86 B4 27 37N 100 44W
Villa María, Argentina 94 C3 32 20S 63 10W
Villa Mazán, Argentina 94 B2 28 40S 66 30W
Villa Montes, Bolivia 94 A3 21 10S 63 30W
Villa Ocampo, Argentina 94 B4 28 30S 59 20W
Villa Ocampo, Mexico 86 B3 26 29N 105 30W
Villa Ojo de Agua, Argentina 94 B3 29 30S 63 44W
Villa San José, Argentina 94 C4 32 12S 58 15W
Villa San Martín, Argentina 94 B3 28 15S 64 9W
Villa Unión, Mexico 86 C3 23 12N 106 14W
Villacarlos, Spain 22 B11 39 53N 4 17 E
Villacarrillo, Spain 19 C4 38 7N 3 3W
Villach, Austria 16 E7 46 37N 13 51 E
Villafranca de los Caballeros, Spain 22 B10 39 34N 3 25 E
Villagrán, Mexico 87 C5 24 29N 99 29W
Villaguay, Argentina 94 C4 32 0S 59 0W
Villahermosa, Mexico 87 D6 17 59N 92 55W
Villajoyosa, Spain 19 C5 38 30N 0 12W
Villalba, Spain 19 A2 43 26N 7 40W
Villanueva, U.S.A. 81 H2 35 16N 105 22W
Villanueva de la Serena, Spain 19 C3 38 59N 5 50W
Villanueva y Geltrú = Vilanova i la Geltrú, Spain 19 B6 41 13N 1 40 E
Villarreal = Vila-real de los Infantes, Spain 19 C5 39 55N 0 3W
Villarrica, Chile 96 D2 39 15S 72 15W
Villarrica, Paraguay 94 B4 25 40S 56 30W
Villarrobledo, Spain 19 C4 39 18N 2 36W
Villavicencio, Argentina 94 C2 32 28S 69 0W
Villavicencio, Colombia 92 C4 4 9N 73 37W
Villaviciosa, Spain 19 A3 43 32N 5 27W
Villazón, Bolivia 94 A2 22 0S 65 35W
Ville-Marie, Canada 70 C4 47 20N 79 30W
Ville Platte, U.S.A. 81 K8 30 41N 92 17W
Villena, Spain 19 C5 38 39N 0 52W
Villeneuve-d'Ascq, France 18 A5 50 38N 3 9 E
Villeneuve-sur-Lot, France 18 D4 44 24N 0 42 E
Villiers, S. Africa 57 D4 27 2S 28 36 E
Villingen-Schwenningen, Germany 16 D5 48 3N 8 26 E
Vilna, Canada 72 C6 54 7N 111 55W
Vilnius, Lithuania 9 J21 54 38N 25 19 E
Vilvoorde, Belgium 15 D4 50 56N 4 26 E
Vilyuy →, Russia 27 C13 64 24N 126 26 E
Vilyuysk, Russia 27 C13 63 40N 121 35 E
Viña del Mar, Chile 94 C1 33 0S 71 30W
Vinarós, Spain 19 B6 40 30N 0 27 E
Vincennes, U.S.A. 76 F2 38 41N 87 32W
Vincent, U.S.A. 85 L8 34 33N 118 11W
Vinchina, Argentina 94 B2 28 45S 68 15W
Vindelälven →, Sweden 8 E18 63 55N 19 50 E
Vindeln, Sweden 8 D18 64 12N 19 43 E
Vindhya Ra., India 42 H7 22 50N 77 0 E
Vineland, U.S.A. 76 F8 39 29N 75 2W
Vinh, Vietnam 38 C5 18 45N 105 38 E
Vinh Linh, Vietnam 38 D6 17 4N 107 2 E
Vinh Long, Vietnam 39 G5 10 16N 105 57 E
Vinita, U.S.A. 81 G7 36 39N 95 9W
Vinkovci, Croatia 21 B8 45 19N 18 48 E
Vinnitsa = Vinnytsya, Ukraine 17 D15 49 15N 28 30 E
Vinnytsya, Ukraine 17 D15 49 15N 28 30 E
Vinton, Calif., U.S.A. 84 F6 39 48N 120 10W
Vinton, Iowa, U.S.A. 80 D8 42 10N 92 1W
Vinton, La., U.S.A. 81 K8 30 11N 93 35W
Virac, Phil. 37 B6 13 30N 124 20 E
Virachei, Cambodia 38 F6 13 59N 106 49 E
Virago Sd., Canada 72 C2 54 0N 132 30W
Viramgam, India 42 H5 23 5N 72 0 E
Viranşehir, Turkey 44 B3 37 13N 39 45 E
Virawah, Pakistan 42 G4 24 31N 70 46 E
Virden, Canada 73 D8 49 50N 100 56W
Vire, France 18 B3 48 50N 0 53W
Virgenes, C., Argentina 96 G3 52 19S 68 21W
Virgin →, U.S.A. 83 H6 36 28N 114 21W
Virgin Gorda, Virgin Is. 89 C7 18 30N 64 26W
Virgin Is. (British) ■, W. Indies 89 C7 18 30N 64 30W
Virgin Is. (U.S.) ■, W. Indies 89 C7 18 20N 65 0W
Virginia, S. Africa 56 D4 28 8S 26 55 E
Virginia, U.S.A. 80 B8 47 31N 92 32W
Virginia □, U.S.A. 76 G7 37 30N 78 45W
Virginia Beach, U.S.A. 76 G8 36 51N 75 59W
Virginia City, Mont., U.S.A. 82 D8 45 18N 111 56W
Virginia City, Nev., U.S.A. 84 F7 39 19N 119 39W
Virginia Falls, Canada 72 A3 61 38N 125 42W
Virginiatown, Canada 70 C4 48 9N 79 36W
Viroqua, U.S.A. 80 D9 43 34N 90 53W
Virovitica, Croatia 20 B7 45 51N 17 21 E
Virpur, India 42 J4 21 51N 70 42 E
Virton, Belgium 15 E5 49 35N 5 32 E
Virudunagar, India 40 Q10 9 30N 77 58 E
Vis, Croatia 20 C7 43 4N 16 10 E
Visalia, U.S.A. 84 J7 36 20N 119 18W
Visayan Sea, Phil. 37 B6 11 30N 123 30 E
Visby, Sweden 9 H18 57 37N 18 18 E
Viscount Melville Sd., Canada 4 B2 74 10N 108 0W
Visé, Belgium 15 D5 50 44N 5 41 E
Višegrad, Bos.-H. 21 C8 43 47N 19 17 E
Viseu, Brazil 93 D9 1 10S 46 5W
Viseu, Portugal 19 B2 40 40N 7 55W
Vishakhapatnam, India 41 L13 17 45N 83 20 E
Visnagar, India 42 H5 23 45N 72 32 E
Viso, Mte., Italy 18 D7 44 38N 7 5 E
Visokoi I., Antarctica 5 B1 56 43S 27 15W
Vista, U.S.A. 85 M9 33 12N 117 14W
Vistula = Wisla →, Poland 17 A10 54 22N 18 55 E
Vitebsk = Vitsyebsk, Belarus 24 C5 55 10N 30 15 E
Viterbo, Italy 20 C5 42 25N 12 6 E
Viti Levu, Fiji 59 C7 17 30S 177 30 E
Vitigudino, Spain 19 B2 41 1N 6 26W
Vitim, Russia 27 D12 59 28N 112 35 E
Vitim →, Russia 27 D12 59 26N 112 34 E
Vitória, Brazil 93 H10 20 20S 40 22W
Vitória da Conquista, Brazil 93 F10 14 51S 40 51W
Vitória de São Antão, Brazil 93 E11 8 10S 35 20W
Vitoria-Gasteiz, Spain 19 A4 42 50N 2 41W
Vitsyebsk, Belarus 24 C5 55 10N 30 15 E
Vittória, Italy 20 F6 36 57N 14 32 E
Vittório Véneto, Italy 20 B5 45 59N 12 18 E
Viveiro, Spain 19 A2 43 39N 7 38W
Vivian, U.S.A. 81 J8 32 53N 93 59W
Vizcaíno, Desierto de, Mexico 86 B2 27 40N 113 50W
Vizcaíno, Sierra, Mexico 86 B2 27 30N 114 0W
Vize, Turkey 21 D12 41 34N 27 45 E
Vizianagaram, India 41 K13 18 6N 83 30 E
Vjosa →, Albania 21 D8 40 37N 19 24 E
Vlaardingen, Neths. 15 C4 51 55N 4 21 E
Vladikavkaz, Russia 25 F7 43 0N 44 35 E
Vladimir, Russia 24 C7 56 15N 40 30 E
Vladimir Volynskiy = Volodymyr-Volynskyy, Ukraine 17 C13 50 50N 24 18 E
Vladivostok, Russia 27 E14 43 10N 131 53 E
Vlieland, Neths. 15 A4 53 16N 4 55 E
Vlissingen, Neths. 15 C3 51 26N 3 34 E
Vlóra, Albania 21 D8 40 32N 19 28 E
Vltava →, Czech Rep. 16 D8 50 21N 14 30 E
Vo Dat, Vietnam 39 G6 11 9N 107 31 E
Voe, U.K. 12 A7 60 21N 1 16W
Vogelkop = Doberai, Jazirah, Indonesia 37 E8 1 25S 133 0 E
Vogelsberg, Germany 16 C5 50 31N 9 12 E
Voghera, Italy 18 D8 44 59N 9 1 E
Vohibinany, Madag. 57 B8 18 49S 49 4 E
Vohimarina = Iharana, Madag. 57 A9 13 25S 50 0 E
Vohimena, Tanjon' i, Madag. 57 D8 25 36S 45 8 E
Vohipeno, Madag. 57 C8 22 22S 47 51 E
Voi, Kenya 54 C4 3 25S 38 32 E
Voiron, France 18 D6 45 22N 5 35 E
Voisey B., Canada 71 A7 56 15N 61 50W
Vojmsjön, Sweden 8 D17 64 55N 16 40 E
Vojvodina □, Serbia, Yug. 21 B9 45 20N 20 0 E
Volborg, U.S.A. 80 C2 45 51N 105 41W
Volcano Is. = Kazan-Rettō, Pac. Oc. 64 E6 25 0N 141 0 E
Volda, Norway 9 E12 62 9N 6 5 E
Volga →, Russia 25 E8 46 0N 48 30 E
Volga Hts. = Privolzhskaya Vozvyshennost, Russia 25 D8 51 0N 46 0 E
Volgodonsk, Russia 25 E7 47 33N 42 5 E
Volgograd, Russia 25 E7 48 40N 44 25 E
Volgogradskoye Vdkhr., Russia 25 E8 50 0N 45 20 E
Volkhov →, Russia 24 B5 60 8N 32 20 E
Volkovysk = Vawkavysk, Belarus 17 B13 53 9N 24 30 E
Volksrust, S. Africa 57 D4 27 24S 29 53 E
Volochanka, Russia 27 B10 71 0N 94 28 E
Volodymyr-Volynskyy, Ukraine 17 C13 50 50N 24 18 E
Vologda, Russia 24 C6 59 10N 39 45 E
Vólos, Greece 21 E10 39 24N 22 59 E
Volovets, Ukraine 17 D12 48 43N 23 11 E
Volozhin = Valozhyn, Belarus 17 A14 54 3N 26 30 E
Volsk, Russia 24 D8 52 5N 47 22 E
Volta →, Ghana 48 F4 5 46N 0 41 E
Volta, L., Ghana 50 G6 7 30N 0 0 E
Volta Redonda, Brazil 95 A7 22 31S 44 5W
Voltaire, C., Australia 60 B4 14 16S 125 35 E
Volterra, Italy 20 C4 43 24N 10 51 E
Volturno →, Italy 20 D5 41 1N 13 55 E
Volzhskiy, Russia 25 E7 48 56N 44 46 E
Vondrozo, Madag. 57 C8 22 49S 47 20 E
Vopnafjörður, Iceland 8 D6 65 45N 14 50W
Vóriai Sporádhes, Greece 21 E10 39 15N 23 30 E
Vorkuta, Russia 24 A11 67 48N 64 20 E
Vormsi, Estonia 9 G20 59 1N 23 13 E
Voronezh, Russia 25 D6 51 40N 39 10 E
Voroshilovgrad = Luhansk, Ukraine 25 E6 48 38N 39 15 E
Voroshilovsk = Alchevsk, Ukraine 25 E6 48 30N 38 45 E
Võrts Järv, Estonia 9 G22 58 16N 26 3 E
Võru, Estonia 9 H22 57 48N 26 54 E
Vosges, France 18 B7 48 20N 7 10 E
Voss, Norway 9 F12 60 38N 6 26 E
Vostok I., Kiribati 65 J12 10 5S 152 23W
Votkinsk, Russia 24 C9 57 0N 53 55 E
Votkinskoye Vdkhr., Russia 24 C10 57 22N 55 12 E
Votsuri-Shima, Japan 31 M1 25 45N 123 29 E
Vouga →, Portugal 19 B1 40 41N 8 40W
Voúxa, Ákra, Greece 23 D5 35 37N 23 32 E
Vozhe, Ozero, Russia 24 B6 60 45N 39 0 E
Voznesensk, Ukraine 25 E5 47 35N 31 21 E
Voznesenye, Russia 24 B6 61 0N 35 28 E
Vrangelya, Ostrov, Russia 27 B19 71 0N 180 0 E
Vranje, Serbia, Yug. 21 C9 42 34N 21 54 E
Vratsa, Bulgaria 21 C10 43 15N 23 30 E
Vrbas →, Bos.-H. 20 B7 45 8N 17 29 E
Vrede, S. Africa 57 D4 27 24S 29 6 E
Vredefort, S. Africa 56 D4 27 0S 27 22 E
Vredenburg, S. Africa 56 E2 32 56S 18 0 E
Vredendal, S. Africa 56 E2 31 41S 18 35 E
Vrindavan, India 42 F7 27 37N 77 40 E
Vrises, Greece 23 D6 35 23N 24 13 E
Vršac, Serbia, Yug. 21 B9 45 8N 21 20 E
Vryburg, S. Africa 56 D3 26 55S 24 45 E
Vryheid, S. Africa 57 D5 27 45S 30 47 E
Vu Liet, Vietnam 38 C5 18 43N 105 23 E
Vukovar, Croatia 21 B8 45 21N 18 59 E
Vulcan, Canada 72 C6 50 25N 113 15W
Vulcan, Romania 17 F12 45 23N 23 17 E
Vulcaneşti, Moldova 17 F15 45 41N 28 18 E
Vulcano, Italy 20 E6 38 24N 14 58 E
Vulkaneshty = Vulcaneşti, Moldova 17 F15 45 41N 28 18 E
Vunduzi →, Mozam. 55 F3 18 56S 34 1 E
Vung Tau, Vietnam 39 G6 10 21N 107 4 E
Vyatka = Kirov, Russia 24 C8 58 35N 49 40 E
Vyatka →, Russia 24 C9 55 37N 51 28 E
Vyatskiye Polyany, Russia 24 C9 56 14N 51 5 E
Vyazemskiy, Russia 27 E14 47 32N 134 45 E
Vyazma, Russia 24 C5 55 10N 34 15 E
Vyborg, Russia 24 B4 60 43N 28 47 E
Vychegda →, Russia 24 B8 61 18N 46 36 E
Vychodné Beskydy, Europe 17 D11 49 20N 22 0 E
Vyg-ozero, Russia 24 B5 63 47N 34 29 E
Vylkove, Ukraine 17 F15 45 28N 29 32 E
Vynohradiv, Ukraine 17 D12 48 9N 23 2 E
Vyrnwy, L., U.K. 10 E4 52 48N 3 31W
Vyshniy Volochek, Russia 24 C5 57 30N 34 30 E
Vyškov, Czech Rep. 17 D9 49 17N 17 0 E
Vytegra, Russia 24 B6 61 0N 36 27 E

W

W.A.C. Bennett Dam, Canada 72 B4 56 2N 122 6W
Waal →, Neths. 15 C5 51 37N 5 0 E
Waalwijk, Neths. 15 C5 51 42N 5 4 E
Wabana, Canada 71 C9 47 40N 53 0W
Wabasca →, Canada 72 B5 58 22N 115 20W
Wabasca-Desmarais, Canada 72 B6 55 57N 113 56W
Wabash, U.S.A. 76 E3 40 48N 85 49W
Wabash →, U.S.A. 76 G1 37 48N 88 2W
Wabigoon L., Canada 73 D10 49 44N 92 44W
Wabowden, Canada 73 C9 54 55N 98 38W
Wabuk Pt., Canada 70 A2 55 20N 85 5W
Wabush, Canada 71 B6 52 55N 66 52W
Waco, U.S.A. 81 K6 31 33N 97 9W
Waconichi, L., Canada 70 B5 50 8N 74 0W
Wad Hamid, Sudan 51 E12 16 30N 32 45 E
Wâd Medanî, Sudan 51 F12 14 28N 33 30 E
Wad Thana, Pakistan 42 F2 27 22N 66 23 E
Wadai, Africa 48 E5 12 0N 19 0 E
Wadayama, Japan 31 G7 35 19N 134 52 E
Waddeneilanden, Neths. 15 A5 53 20N 5 10 E
Waddenzee, Neths. 15 A5 53 6N 5 10 E
Waddington, U.S.A. 79 B9 44 52N 75 12W
Waddington, Mt., Canada 72 C3 51 23N 125 15W
Waddy Pt., Australia 63 C5 24 58S 153 21 E
Wadebridge, U.K. 11 G3 50 31N 4 51W
Wadena, Canada 73 C8 51 57N 103 47W
Wadena, U.S.A. 80 B7 46 26N 95 8W
Wadeye, Australia 60 B4 14 28S 129 52 E
Wadhams, Canada 72 C3 51 30N 127 30W
Wādī as Sīr, Jordan 47 D4 31 56N 35 49 E
Wadi Halfa, Sudan 51 D12 21 53N 31 19 E
Wadsworth, Nev., U.S.A. 82 G4 39 38N 119 17W
Wadsworth, Ohio, U.S.A. 78 E3 41 2N 81 44W
Waegwan, S. Korea 35 G15 35 59N 128 23 E
Wafangdian, China 35 E11 39 38N 121 58 E
Wafrah, Si. Arabia 44 D5 28 33N 47 56 E
Wageningen, Neths. 15 C5 51 58N 5 40 E
Wager B., Canada 69 B11 65 26N 88 40W
Wagga Wagga, Australia 63 F4 35 7S 147 24 E
Waghete, Indonesia 37 E9 4 10S 135 50 E
Wagin, Australia 61 F2 33 17S 117 25 E
Wagner, U.S.A. 80 D5 43 5N 98 18W
Wagon Mound, U.S.A. 81 G2 36 1N 104 42W
Wagoner, U.S.A. 81 H7 35 58N 95 22W
Wah, Pakistan 42 C5 33 45N 72 40 E
Wahai, Indonesia 37 E7 2 48S 129 35 E
Wahiawa, U.S.A. 74 H15 21 30N 158 2W
Wâḥid, Egypt 47 E1 30 48N 32 21 E
Wahnai, Afghan. 42 C1 32 40N 65 50 E
Wahoo, U.S.A. 80 E6 41 13N 96 37W
Wahpeton, U.S.A. 80 B6 46 16N 96 36W
Wai, Koh, Cambodia 39 H4 9 55N 102 55 E
Waiau →, N.Z. 59 K4 42 47S 173 22 E
Waibeem, Indonesia 37 E8 0 30S 132 59 E
Waigeo, Indonesia 37 E8 0 20S 130 40 E
Waihi, N.Z. 59 G5 37 23S 175 52 E
Waihou →, N.Z. 59 G5 37 15S 175 40 E
Waika, Dem. Rep. of the Congo 54 C2 2 22S 25 42 E
Waikabubak, Indonesia 37 F5 9 45S 119 25 E
Waikari, N.Z. 59 K4 42 58S 172 41 E
Waikato →, N.Z. 59 G5 37 23S 174 43 E
Waikerie, Australia 63 E3 34 9S 140 0 E
Waikokopu, N.Z. 59 H6 39 3S 177 52 E
Waikouaiti, N.Z. 59 L3 45 36S 170 41 E
Wailuku, U.S.A. 74 H16 20 53N 156 30W
Waimakariri →, N.Z. 59 K4 43 24S 172 42 E
Waimate, N.Z. 59 L3 44 45S 171 3 E
Wainganga →, India 40 K11 18 50N 79 55 E
Waingapu, Indonesia 37 F6 9 35S 120 11 E
Waini →, Guyana 92 B7 8 20N 59 50W
Wainwright, Canada 73 C6 52 50N 110 50W
Waiouru, N.Z. 59 H5 39 28S 175 41 E
Waipara, N.Z. 59 K4 43 3S 172 46 E
Waipawa, N.Z. 59 H6 39 56S 176 38 E
Waipiro, N.Z. 59 H7 38 2S 178 22 E
Waipu, N.Z. 59 F5 35 59S 174 29 E
Waipukurau, N.Z. 59 J6 40 1S 176 33 E
Wairakei, N.Z. 59 H6 38 37S 176 6 E
Wairarapa, L., N.Z. 59 J5 41 14S 175 15 E
Wairoa, N.Z. 59 H6 39 3S 177 25 E
Waitaki →, N.Z. 59 L3 44 56S 171 7 E
Waitara, N.Z. 59 H5 38 59S 174 15 E
Waitsburg, U.S.A. 82 C5 46 16N 118 9W
Waiuku, N.Z. 59 G5 37 15S 174 45 E
Wajima, Japan 31 F8 37 30N 137 0 E
Wajir, Kenya 54 B5 1 42N 40 5 E
Wakasa, Japan 31 G7 35 20N 134 24 E
Wakasa-Wan, Japan 31 G7 35 40N 135 30 E
Wakatipu, L., N.Z. 59 L2 45 5S 168 33 E
Wakaw, Canada 73 C7 52 39N 105 44W
Wakayama, Japan 31 G7 34 15N 135 15 E
Wakayama □, Japan 31 H7 33 50N 135 30 E
Wake Forest, U.S.A. 77 H6 35 59N 78 30W

West Ice Shelf

Wake I., Pac. Oc. 64 F8 19 18N 166 36 E
WaKeeney, U.S.A. 80 F5 39 1N 99 53W
Wakefield, N.Z. 59 J4 41 24S 173 5 E
Wakefield, U.K. 10 D6 53 41N 1 29W
Wakefield, Mass., U.S.A. 79 D13 42 30N 71 4W
Wakefield, Mich., U.S.A. 80 B10 46 29N 89 56W
Wakema, Burma 41 L19 16 30N 95 11 E
Wakkanai, Japan 30 B10 45 28N 141 35 E
Wakkerstroom, S. Africa 57 D5 27 24S 30 10 E
Wakool, Australia 63 F3 35 28S 144 23 E
Wakool →, Australia 63 F3 35 5S 143 33 E
Wakre, Indonesia 37 E8 0 19S 131 5 E
Wakuach, L., Canada 71 A6 55 34N 67 32W
Walamba, Zambia 55 E2 13 30S 28 42 E
Walbrzych, Poland 16 C9 50 45N 16 18 E
Walbury Hill, U.K. 11 F6 51 21N 1 28W
Walcha, Australia 63 E5 30 55S 151 31 E
Walcheren, Neths. 15 C3 51 30N 3 35 E
Walcott, U.S.A. 82 F10 41 46N 106 51W
Walcz, Poland 16 B9 53 17N 16 27 E
Waldburg Ra., Australia 61 D2 24 40S 117 35 E
Walden, Colo., U.S.A. 82 F10 40 44N 106 17W
Walden, N.Y., U.S.A. 79 E10 41 34N 74 11W
Waldport, U.S.A. 82 D1 44 26N 124 4W
Waldron, U.S.A. 81 H7 34 54N 94 5W
Walebing, Australia 61 F2 30 41S 116 13 E
Wales □, U.K. 11 E3 52 19N 4 43W
Walgett, Australia 63 E4 30 0S 148 5 E
Walgreen Coast, Antarctica 5 D15 75 15S 105 0W
Walker, U.S.A. 80 B7 47 6N 94 35W
Walker, L., Canada 71 B6 50 20N 67 11W
Walker L., Canada 73 C9 54 42N 95 57W
Walker L., U.S.A. 82 G4 38 42N 118 43W
Walkerston, Australia 62 C4 21 11S 149 8 E
Walkerton, Canada 78 B3 44 10N 81 10W
Wall, U.S.A. 80 D3 44 0N 102 8W
Walla Walla, U.S.A. 82 C4 46 4N 118 20W
Wallace, Idaho, U.S.A. 82 C6 47 28N 115 56W
Wallace, N.C., U.S.A. 77 H7 34 44N 77 59W
Wallaceburg, Canada 78 D2 42 34N 82 23W
Wallachia = Valahia, Romania 17 F13 44 35N 25 0 E
Wallal, Australia 63 D4 26 32S 146 7 E
Wallam Cr. →, Australia 63 D4 28 40S 147 20 E
Wallambin, L., Australia 61 F2 30 57S 117 35 E
Wallan, Australia 63 F3 37 26S 144 59 E
Wallangarra, Australia 63 D5 28 56S 151 58 E
Wallaroo, Australia 63 E2 33 56S 137 39 E
Wallenpaupack, L., U.S.A. 79 E9 41 25N 75 15W
Wallingford, U.S.A. 79 E12 41 27N 72 50W
Wallis & Futuna, Is., Pac. Oc. 64 J10 13 18S 176 10W
Wallowa, U.S.A. 82 D5 45 34N 117 32W
Wallowa Mts., U.S.A. 82 D5 45 20N 117 30W
Walls, U.K. 12 A7 60 14N 1 33W
Wallula, U.S.A. 82 C4 46 5N 118 54W
Wallumbilla, Australia 63 D4 26 33S 149 9 E
Walmsley, L., Canada 73 A7 63 25N 108 36W
Walney, I. of, U.K. 10 C4 54 6N 3 15W
Walnut Creek, U.S.A. 84 H4 37 54N 122 4W
Walnut Ridge, U.S.A. 81 G9 36 4N 90 57W
Walpole, Australia 61 F2 34 58S 116 44 E
Walpole, U.S.A. 79 D13 42 9N 71 15W
Walsall, U.K. 11 E6 52 35N 1 58W
Walsenburg, U.S.A. 81 G2 37 38N 104 47W
Walsh, U.S.A. 81 G3 37 23N 102 17W
Walsh →, Australia 62 B3 16 31S 143 42 E
Walterboro, U.S.A. 77 J5 32 55N 80 40W
Walters, U.S.A. 81 H5 34 22N 98 19W
Waltham, U.S.A. 79 D13 42 23N 71 14W
Waltman, U.S.A. 82 E10 43 4N 107 12W
Walton, U.S.A. 79 D9 42 10N 75 8W
Walton-on-the-Naze, U.K. 11 F9 51 51N 1 17 E
Walvis Bay, Namibia 56 C1 23 0S 14 28 E
Walvisbaai = Walvis Bay, Namibia 56 C1 23 0S 14 28 E
Wamba, Dem. Rep. of the Congo 54 B2 2 10N 27 57 E
Wamba, Kenya 54 B4 0 58N 37 19 E
Wamego, U.S.A. 80 F6 39 12N 96 18W
Wamena, Indonesia 37 E9 4 4S 138 57 E
Wamsutter, U.S.A. 82 F9 41 40N 107 58W
Wamulan, Indonesia 37 E7 3 27S 126 7 E
Wan Xian, China 34 E8 38 47N 115 7 E
Wana, Pakistan 42 C3 32 20N 69 32 E
Wanaaring, Australia 63 D3 29 38S 144 9 E
Wanaka, N.Z. 59 L2 44 42S 169 9 E
Wanaka L., N.Z. 59 L2 44 33S 169 7 E
Wanapitei L., Canada 70 C3 46 45N 80 40W
Wandel Sea = McKinley Sea, Arctic 4 A7 82 0N 0 0 E
Wanderer, Zimbabwe 55 F3 19 36S 30 1 E
Wandhari, Pakistan 42 F2 27 42N 66 48 E
Wandoan, Australia 63 D4 26 5S 149 55 E
Wanfu, China 35 D12 40 8N 122 38 E
Wang →, Thailand 38 D2 17 8N 99 2 E
Wang Noi, Thailand 38 E3 14 13N 100 44 E
Wang Saphung, Thailand 38 D3 17 18N 101 46 E
Wang Thong, Thailand 38 D3 16 50N 100 26 E
Wanga, Dem. Rep. of the Congo 54 B2 2 58N 29 12 E
Wangal, Indonesia 37 F8 6 8S 134 9 E
Wanganella, Australia 63 F3 35 6S 144 49 E
Wanganui, N.Z. 59 H5 39 56S 175 3 E
Wangaratta, Australia 63 F4 36 21S 146 19 E
Wangary, Australia 63 E2 34 35S 135 29 E
Wangdu, China 34 E8 38 40N 115 7 E
Wangerooge, Germany 16 B4 53 47N 7 54 E
Wangi, Kenya 54 C5 1 58S 40 58 E
Wangiwangi, Indonesia 37 F6 5 22S 123 37 E
Wangqing, China 35 C15 43 12N 129 42 E
Wankaner, India 42 H4 22 35N 71 0 E
Wanless, Canada 73 C8 54 11N 101 21W
Wanning, Taiwan 38 C8 23 15N 121 17 E
Wanon Niwat, Thailand 38 D4 17 38N 103 46 E
Wanquan, China 34 D8 40 50N 114 40 E
Wanrong, China 34 G6 35 25N 110 50 E
Wantage, U.K. 11 F6 51 35N 1 25W
Wanxian, China 33 C5 30 42N 108 20 E
Wapakoneta, U.S.A. 76 E3 40 34N 84 12W
Wapato, U.S.A. 82 C3 46 27N 120 25W
Wapawekka L., Canada 73 C8 54 55N 104 40W
Wapikopa L., Canada 70 B2 52 56N 87 53W
Wapiti →, Canada 72 B5 55 5N 118 18W
Wappingers Falls, U.S.A. 79 E11 41 36N 73 55W
Wapsipinicon →, U.S.A. 80 E9 41 44N 90 19W
Warangal, India 40 L11 17 58N 79 35 E
Waraseoni, India 43 J9 21 45N 80 2 E
Waratah, Australia 62 G4 41 30S 145 30 E
Waratah B., Australia 63 F4 38 54S 146 5 E
Warburton, Vic., Australia 63 F4 37 47S 145 42 E
Warburton, W. Austral., Australia 61 E4 26 8S 126 35 E
Warburton Ra., Australia 61 E4 25 55S 126 28 E
Ward, N.Z. 59 J5 41 49S 174 11 E
Ward →, Australia 63 D4 26 28S 146 6 E
Ward Mt., U.S.A. 84 H8 37 12N 118 54W
Warden, S. Africa 57 D4 27 50S 29 0 E
Wardha, India 40 J11 20 45N 78 39 E
Wardha →, India 40 K11 19 57N 79 11 E
Ware, Canada 72 B3 57 26N 125 41W
Ware, U.S.A. 79 D12 42 16N 72 14W
Waregem, Belgium 15 D3 50 53N 3 27 E
Wareham, U.S.A. 79 E14 41 46N 70 43W
Waremme, Belgium 15 D5 50 43N 5 15 E
Warialda, Australia 63 D5 29 29S 150 33 E
Wariap, Indonesia 37 E8 1 30S 134 5 E
Warin Chamrap, Thailand 38 E5 15 12N 104 53 E
Warkopi, Indonesia 37 E8 1 12S 134 9 E
Warm Springs, U.S.A. 83 G5 38 10N 116 20W
Warman, Canada 73 C7 52 19N 106 30W
Warmbad, Namibia 56 D2 28 25S 18 42 E
Warmbad, S. Africa 57 C4 24 51S 28 19 E
Warminster, U.K. 11 F5 51 12N 2 10W
Warminster, U.S.A. 79 F9 40 12N 75 6W
Warner Mts., U.S.A. 82 F3 41 40N 120 15W
Warner Robins, U.S.A. 77 J4 32 37N 83 36W
Waroona, Australia 61 F2 32 50S 115 58 E
Warracknabeal, Australia 63 F3 36 9S 142 26 E
Warragul, Australia 63 F4 38 10S 145 58 E
Warrego →, Australia 63 E4 30 24S 145 21 E
Warrego Ra., Australia 62 C4 24 58S 146 0 E
Warren, Australia 63 E4 31 42S 147 51 E
Warren, Ark., U.S.A. 81 J8 33 37N 92 4W
Warren, Mich., U.S.A. 76 D4 42 30N 83 0W
Warren, Minn., U.S.A. 80 A6 48 12N 96 46W
Warren, Ohio, U.S.A. 78 E4 41 14N 80 49W
Warren, Pa., U.S.A. 78 E5 41 51N 79 9W
Warrenpoint, U.K. 13 B5 54 6N 6 15W
Warrensburg, Mo., U.S.A. 80 F8 38 46N 93 44W
Warrensburg, N.Y., U.S.A. 79 C11 43 29N 73 46W
Warrenton, S. Africa 56 D3 28 9S 24 47 E
Warrenton, U.S.A. 84 D3 46 10N 123 56W
Warri, Nigeria 50 G7 5 30N 5 41 E
Warrina, Australia 63 D2 28 12S 135 50 E
Warrington, U.K. 10 D5 53 24N 2 35W
Warrington, U.S.A. 77 K2 30 23N 87 17W
Warrington □, U.K. 10 D5 53 24N 2 35W
Warrnambool, Australia 63 F3 38 25S 142 30 E
Warroad, U.S.A. 80 A7 48 54N 95 19W
Warruwi, Australia 62 A1 11 36S 133 20 E
Warsa, Indonesia 37 E9 0 47S 135 55 E
Warsak Dam, Pakistan 42 B4 34 11N 71 19 E
Warsaw = Warszawa, Poland 17 B11 52 13N 21 0 E
Warsaw, Ind., U.S.A. 76 E3 41 14N 85 51W
Warsaw, N.Y., U.S.A. 78 D6 42 45N 78 8W
Warsaw, Ohio, U.S.A. 78 F3 40 20N 82 0W
Warszawa, Poland 17 B11 52 13N 21 0 E
Warta →, Poland 16 B8 52 35N 14 39 E
Warthe = Warta →, Poland 16 B8 52 35N 14 39 E
Waru, Indonesia 37 E8 3 30S 130 36 E
Warwick, Australia 63 D5 28 10S 152 1 E
Warwick, U.K. 11 E6 52 18N 1 35W
Warwick, N.Y., U.S.A. 79 E10 41 16N 74 22W
Warwick, R.I., U.S.A. 79 E13 41 42N 71 28W
Warwickshire □, U.K. 11 E6 52 14N 1 38W
Wasaga Beach, Canada 78 B4 44 31N 80 1W
Wasagaming, Canada 73 C9 50 39N 99 58W
Wasatch Ra., U.S.A. 82 F8 40 30N 111 15W
Wasbank, S. Africa 57 D5 28 15S 30 9 E
Wasco, Calif., U.S.A. 85 K7 35 36N 119 20W
Wasco, Oreg., U.S.A. 82 D3 45 36N 120 42W
Waseca, U.S.A. 80 C8 44 5N 93 30W
Wasekamio L., Canada 73 B7 56 45N 108 45W
Wash, The, U.K. 10 E8 52 58N 0 20 E
Washago, Canada 78 B5 44 45N 79 20W
Washburn, N. Dak., U.S.A. 80 B4 47 17N 101 2W
Washburn, Wis., U.S.A. 80 B9 46 40N 90 54W
Washim, India 40 J10 20 3N 77 0 E
Washington, U.K. 10 C6 54 55N 1 30W
Washington, D.C., U.S.A. 76 F7 38 54N 77 2W
Washington, Ga., U.S.A. 77 J4 33 44N 82 44W
Washington, Ind., U.S.A. 76 F2 38 40N 87 10W
Washington, Iowa, U.S.A. 80 E9 41 18N 91 42W
Washington, Mo., U.S.A. 80 F9 38 33N 91 1W
Washington, N.C., U.S.A. 77 H7 35 33N 77 3W
Washington, N.J., U.S.A. 79 F10 40 46N 74 59W
Washington, Pa., U.S.A. 78 F4 40 10N 80 15W
Washington, Utah, U.S.A. 83 H7 37 8N 113 31W
Washington □, U.S.A. 82 C3 47 30N 120 30W
Washington, Mt., U.S.A. 79 B13 44 16N 71 18W
Washington Court House, U.S.A. 76 F4 39 32N 83 26W
Washington I., U.S.A. 76 C2 45 23N 86 54W
Washougal, U.S.A. 84 E4 45 35N 122 21W
Wasian, Indonesia 37 E8 1 47S 133 19 E
Wasilla, U.S.A. 68 B5 61 35N 149 26W
Wasior, Indonesia 37 E8 2 43S 134 30 E
Waskaganish, Canada 70 B4 51 30N 78 40W
Waskaiowaka, L., Canada 73 B9 56 33N 96 23W
Waskesiu Lake, Canada 73 C7 53 55N 106 5W
Wasserkuppe, Germany 16 C5 50 29N 9 55 E
Waswanipi, Canada 70 C4 49 40N 76 29W
Waswanipi, L., Canada 70 C4 49 35N 76 40W
Watampone, Indonesia 37 E6 4 29S 120 25 E
Water Park Pt., Australia 62 C5 22 56S 150 47 E
Water Valley, U.S.A. 81 H10 34 10N 89 38W
Waterberge, S. Africa 57 C4 24 10S 28 0 E
Waterbury, Conn., U.S.A. 79 E11 41 33N 73 3W
Waterbury, Vt., U.S.A. 79 B12 44 20N 72 46W
Waterbury L., Canada 73 B8 58 10N 104 22W
Waterdown, Canada 78 C5 43 20N 79 53W
Waterford, Canada 78 D4 42 56N 80 17W
Waterford, Ireland 13 D4 52 15N 7 8W
Waterford, Calif., U.S.A. 84 H6 37 38N 120 46W
Waterford, Pa., U.S.A. 78 E5 41 57N 79 59W
Waterford □, Ireland 13 D4 52 10N 7 40W
Waterford Harbour, Ireland 13 D5 52 8N 6 58W
Waterhen L., Canada 73 C9 52 10N 99 40W
Waterloo, Belgium 15 D4 50 43N 4 25 E
Waterloo, Ont., Canada 78 C4 43 30N 80 32W
Waterloo, Qué., Canada 79 A12 45 22N 72 32W
Waterloo, Ill., U.S.A. 80 F9 38 20N 90 9W
Waterloo, Iowa, U.S.A. 80 D8 42 30N 92 21W
Waterloo, N.Y., U.S.A. 78 D8 42 54N 76 52W
Watersmeet, U.S.A. 80 B10 46 16N 89 11W
Waterton Nat. Park, U.S.A. 82 B7 48 45N 115 0W
Watertown, Conn., U.S.A. 79 E11 41 36N 73 7W
Watertown, N.Y., U.S.A. 79 C9 43 59N 75 55W
Watertown, S. Dak., U.S.A. 80 C6 44 54N 97 7W
Watertown, Wis., U.S.A. 80 D10 43 12N 88 43W
Waterval-Boven, S. Africa 57 D5 25 40S 30 18 E
Waterville, Canada 79 A13 45 16N 71 54W
Waterville, Maine, U.S.A. 77 C11 44 33N 69 38W
Waterville, N.Y., U.S.A. 79 D9 42 56N 75 23W
Waterville, Pa., U.S.A. 78 E7 41 19N 77 21W
Waterville, Wash., U.S.A. 82 C3 47 39N 120 4W
Watervliet, U.S.A. 79 D11 42 44N 73 42W
Wates, Indonesia 37 G14 7 51S 110 10 E
Watford, Canada 78 D3 42 57N 81 53W
Watford, U.K. 11 F7 51 40N 0 24W
Watford City, U.S.A. 80 B3 47 48N 103 17W
Wathaman →, Canada 73 B8 57 16N 102 59W
Wathaman L., Canada 73 B8 56 58N 103 44W
Watheroo, Australia 61 F2 30 15S 116 0 E
Wating, China 34 G4 35 40N 106 38 E
Watkins Glen, U.S.A. 78 D8 42 23N 76 52W
Watling I. = San Salvador I., Bahamas 89 B5 24 0N 74 40W
Watonga, U.S.A. 81 H5 35 51N 98 25W
Watrous, Canada 73 C7 51 40N 105 25W
Watrous, U.S.A. 81 H2 35 48N 104 59W
Watsa, Dem. Rep. of the Congo 54 B2 3 4N 29 30 E
Watseka, U.S.A. 76 E2 40 47N 87 44W
Watson, Australia 61 F5 30 29S 131 31 E
Watson, Canada 73 C8 52 10N 104 30W
Watson Lake, Canada 72 A3 60 6N 128 49W
Watsontown, U.S.A. 78 E8 41 5N 76 52W
Watsonville, U.S.A. 84 J5 36 55N 121 45W
Wattiwarriganna Cr. →, Australia 63 D2 28 57S 136 10 E
Watuata = Batuata, Indonesia 37 F6 6 12S 122 42 E
Watubela, Kepulauan, Indonesia 37 E8 4 28S 131 35 E
Watubela Is. = Watubela, Kepulauan, Indonesia 37 E8 4 28S 131 35 E
Wau, Sudan 49 F6 7 45N 28 1 E
Waubamik, Canada 78 A4 45 27N 80 1W
Waubay, U.S.A. 80 C6 45 20N 97 18W
Wauchope, N.S.W., Australia 63 E5 31 28S 152 45 E
Wauchope, N. Terr., Australia 62 C1 20 36S 134 15 E
Waukarlycarly, L., Australia 60 D3 21 18S 121 56 E
Waukegan, U.S.A. 75 B9 42 22N 87 50W
Waukesha, U.S.A. 76 D1 43 1N 88 14W
Waukon, U.S.A. 80 D9 43 16N 91 29W
Waupaca, U.S.A. 80 C10 44 21N 89 5W
Waupun, U.S.A. 80 D10 43 38N 88 44W
Waurika, U.S.A. 81 H6 34 10N 98 0W
Wausau, U.S.A. 80 C10 44 58N 89 38W
Wautoma, U.S.A. 80 C10 44 4N 89 18W
Wauwatosa, U.S.A. 76 D2 43 3N 88 0W
Waveney →, U.K. 11 E9 52 35N 1 39 E
Waverley, N.Z. 59 H5 39 46S 174 37 E
Waverly, Iowa, U.S.A. 80 D8 42 44N 92 29W
Waverly, N.Y., U.S.A. 79 E8 42 1N 76 32W
Wavre, Belgium 15 D4 50 43N 4 38 E
Wâw, Sudan 51 G11 7 45N 28 1 E
Wāw al Kabīr, Libya 51 C9 25 20N 16 43 E
Wawa, Canada 70 C3 47 59N 84 47W
Wawanesa, Canada 73 D9 49 36N 99 40W
Wawona, U.S.A. 84 H7 37 32N 119 39W
Waxahachie, U.S.A. 81 J6 32 24N 96 51W
Way, L., Australia 61 E3 26 45S 120 16 E
Waycross, U.S.A. 77 K4 31 13N 82 21W
Wayland, U.S.A. 78 D7 42 34N 77 35W
Wayne, Nebr., U.S.A. 80 D6 42 14N 97 1W
Wayne, W. Va., U.S.A. 76 F4 38 13N 82 27W
Waynesboro, Ga., U.S.A. 77 J4 33 6N 82 1W
Waynesboro, Miss., U.S.A. 77 K1 31 40N 88 39W
Waynesboro, Pa., U.S.A. 76 F7 39 45N 77 35W
Waynesboro, Va., U.S.A. 76 F6 38 4N 78 53W
Waynesburg, U.S.A. 76 F5 39 54N 80 11W
Waynesville, U.S.A. 77 H4 35 28N 82 58W
Waynoka, U.S.A. 81 G5 36 35N 98 53W
Wazirabad, Pakistan 42 C6 32 30N 74 8 E
We, Indonesia 36 C1 5 51N 95 18 E
Weald, The, U.K. 11 F8 51 4N 0 20 E
Wear →, U.K. 10 C6 54 55N 1 23W
Weatherford, Okla., U.S.A. 81 H5 35 32N 98 43W
Weatherford, Tex., U.S.A. 81 J6 32 46N 97 48W
Weaverville, U.S.A. 82 F2 40 44N 122 56W
Webb City, U.S.A. 81 G7 37 9N 94 28W
Webequie, Canada 70 B2 52 59N 87 21W
Webster, Mass., U.S.A. 79 D13 42 3N 71 53W
Webster, N.Y., U.S.A. 78 C7 43 13N 77 26W
Webster, S. Dak., U.S.A. 80 C6 45 20N 97 31W
Webster City, U.S.A. 80 D8 42 28N 93 49W
Webster Springs, U.S.A. 76 F5 38 29N 80 25W
Weda, Indonesia 37 D7 0 21N 127 50 E
Weda, Teluk, Indonesia 37 D7 0 30N 127 50 E
Weddell I., Falk. Is. 96 G4 51 50S 61 0W
Weddell Sea, Antarctica 5 D1 72 30S 40 0W
Wedderburn, Australia 63 F3 36 26S 143 33 E
Wedgeport, Canada 71 D6 43 44N 65 59W
Wedza, Zimbabwe 55 F3 18 40S 31 33 E
Wee Waa, Australia 63 E4 30 11S 149 26 E
Weed, U.S.A. 82 F2 41 25N 122 23W
Weed Heights, U.S.A. 84 G7 38 59N 119 13W
Weedsport, U.S.A. 79 C8 43 3N 76 35W
Weedville, U.S.A. 78 E6 41 17N 78 30W
Weenen, S. Africa 57 D5 28 48S 30 7 E
Weert, Neths. 15 C5 51 15N 5 43 E
Wei He →, Hebei, China 34 F8 36 10N 115 45 E
Wei He →, Shaanxi, China 34 G6 34 38N 110 15 E
Weichang, China 35 D9 41 58N 117 49 E
Weichuan, China 34 G7 34 20N 113 59 E
Weiden, Germany 16 D7 49 41N 12 10 E
Weifang, China 35 F10 36 44N 119 7 E
Weihai, China 35 F12 37 30N 122 6 E
Weimar, Germany 16 C6 50 58N 11 19 E
Weinan, China 34 G5 34 31N 109 29 E
Weipa, Australia 62 A3 12 40S 141 50 E
Weir →, Australia 63 D4 28 20S 149 50 E
Weir →, Canada 73 B10 56 54N 93 21W
Weir River, Canada 73 B10 56 49N 94 6W
Weirton, U.S.A. 78 F4 40 24N 80 35W
Weiser, U.S.A. 82 D5 44 10N 117 0W
Weishan, China 35 G9 34 47N 117 5 E
Weiyuan, China 34 G3 35 7N 104 10 E
Wejherowo, Poland 17 A10 54 35N 18 12 E
Wekusko L., Canada 73 C9 54 40N 99 50W
Welch, U.S.A. 76 G5 37 26N 81 35W
Welkom, S. Africa 56 D4 28 0S 26 46 E
Welland, Canada 78 D5 43 0N 79 15W
Welland →, U.K. 11 E7 52 51N 0 5W
Wellesley Is., Australia 62 B2 16 42S 139 30 E
Wellingborough, U.K. 11 E7 52 19N 0 41W
Wellington, Australia 63 E4 32 35S 148 59 E
Wellington, Canada 78 C7 43 57N 77 20W
Wellington, N.Z. 59 J5 41 19S 174 46 E
Wellington, S. Africa 56 E2 33 38S 19 1 E
Wellington, Somst., U.K. 11 G4 50 58N 3 13W
Wellington, Telford & Wrekin, U.K. 11 E5 52 42N 2 30W
Wellington, Colo., U.S.A. 80 E2 40 42N 105 0W
Wellington, Kans., U.S.A. 81 G6 37 16N 97 24W
Wellington, Nev., U.S.A. 84 G7 38 45N 119 23W
Wellington, Ohio, U.S.A. 78 E2 41 10N 82 13W
Wellington, Tex., U.S.A. 81 H4 34 51N 100 13W
Wellington, I., Chile 96 F2 49 30S 75 0W
Wellington, L., Australia 63 F4 38 6S 147 20 E
Wells, U.K. 11 F5 51 13N 2 39W
Wells, Maine, U.S.A. 79 C14 43 20N 70 35W
Wells, N.Y., U.S.A. 79 C10 43 24N 74 17W
Wells, Nev., U.S.A. 82 F6 41 7N 114 58W
Wells, L., Australia 61 E3 26 44S 123 15 E
Wells, Mt., Australia 60 C4 17 25S 127 8 E
Wells Gray Prov. Park, Canada 72 C4 52 30N 120 15W
Wells-next-the-Sea, U.K. 10 E8 52 57N 0 51 E
Wells River, U.S.A. 79 B12 44 9N 72 4W
Wellsboro, U.S.A. 78 E7 41 45N 77 18W
Wellsburg, U.S.A. 78 F4 40 16N 80 37W
Wellsville, N.Y., U.S.A. 78 D7 42 7N 77 57W
Wellsville, Ohio, U.S.A. 78 F4 40 36N 80 39W
Wellsville, Utah, U.S.A. 82 F8 41 38N 111 56W
Wellton, U.S.A. 83 K6 32 40N 114 8W
Wels, Austria 16 D8 48 9N 14 1 E
Welshpool, U.K. 11 E4 52 39N 3 8W
Welwyn Garden City, U.K. 11 F7 51 48N 0 12W
Wem, U.K. 10 E5 52 52N 2 44W
Wembere →, Tanzania 54 C3 4 10S 34 15 E
Wemindji, Canada 70 B4 53 0N 78 49W
Wen Xian, China 34 G7 34 55N 113 5 E
Wenatchee, U.S.A. 82 C3 47 25N 120 19W
Wenchang, China 38 C8 19 38N 110 42 E
Wenchi, Ghana 50 G5 7 46N 2 8W
Wenchow = Wenzhou, China 33 D7 28 0N 120 38 E
Wenden, U.S.A. 85 M13 33 49N 113 33W
Wendeng, China 35 F12 37 15N 122 5 E
Wendesi, Indonesia 37 E8 2 30S 134 17 E
Wendover, U.S.A. 82 F6 40 44N 114 2W
Wenlock →, Australia 62 A3 12 2S 141 55 E
Wenshan, China 32 D5 23 20N 104 18 E
Wenshang, China 34 G9 35 45N 116 30 E
Wenshui, China 34 F7 37 26N 112 1 E
Wensleydale, U.K. 10 C6 54 17N 2 0W
Wensu, China 32 B3 41 15N 80 10 E
Wensum →, U.K. 10 E8 52 40N 1 15 E
Wentworth, Australia 63 E3 34 2S 141 54 E
Wentzel L., Canada 72 B6 59 2N 114 28W
Wenut, Indonesia 37 E8 3 11S 133 19 E
Wenxi, China 34 G6 35 20N 111 10 E
Wenxian, China 34 H3 32 43N 104 36 E
Wenzhou, China 33 D7 28 0N 120 38 E
Weott, U.S.A. 82 F2 40 20N 123 55W
Wepener, S. Africa 56 D4 29 42S 27 3 E
Werda, Botswana 56 D3 25 24S 23 15 E
Weri, Indonesia 37 E8 3 10S 132 38 E
Werra →, Germany 16 C5 51 24N 9 39 E
Werrimull, Australia 63 E3 34 25S 141 38 E
Werris Creek, Australia 63 E5 31 18S 150 38 E
Weser →, Germany 16 B5 53 36N 8 28 E
Wesiri, Indonesia 37 F7 7 30S 126 30 E
Weslemkoon L., Canada 78 A7 45 2N 77 25W
Wesleyville, Canada 71 C9 49 8N 53 36W
Wesleyville, U.S.A. 78 D4 42 9N 80 0W
Wessel, C., Australia 62 A2 10 59S 136 46 E
Wessel Is., Australia 62 A2 11 10S 136 45 E
Wessington Springs, U.S.A. 80 C5 44 5N 98 34W
West, U.S.A. 81 K6 31 48N 97 6W
West →, U.S.A. 79 D12 42 52N 72 33W
West Baines →, Australia 60 C4 15 38S 129 59 E
West Bank □, Asia 47 C4 32 6N 35 13 E
West Bend, U.S.A. 76 D1 43 25N 88 11W
West Bengal □, India 43 H13 23 0N 88 0 E
West Berkshire □, U.K. 11 F6 51 25N 1 17W
West Beskids = Západné Beskydy, Europe 17 D10 49 30N 19 0 E
West Branch, U.S.A. 76 C3 44 17N 84 14W
West Branch Susquehanna →, U.S.A. 79 F8 40 53N 76 48W
West Bromwich, U.K. 11 E6 52 32N 1 59W
West Burra, U.K. 12 A7 60 5N 1 21W
West Canada Cr. →, U.S.A. 79 C10 43 1N 74 58W
West Cape Howe, Australia 61 G2 35 8S 117 36 E
West Chazy, U.S.A. 79 B11 44 49N 73 28W
West Chester, U.S.A. 79 G9 39 58N 75 36W
West Columbia, U.S.A. 81 L7 29 9N 95 39W
West Covina, U.S.A. 85 L9 34 4N 117 54W
West Des Moines, U.S.A. 80 E8 41 35N 93 43W
West Dunbartonshire □, U.K. 12 F4 55 59N 4 30W
West End, Bahamas 88 A4 26 41N 78 58W
West Falkland, Falk. Is. 96 G5 51 40S 60 0W
West Fargo, U.S.A. 80 B6 46 52N 96 54W
West Farmington, U.S.A. 78 E4 41 23N 80 58W
West Fjord = Vestfjorden, Norway 8 C15 67 55N 14 0 E
West Fork Trinity →, U.S.A. 81 J6 32 48N 96 54W
West Frankfort, U.S.A. 80 G10 37 54N 88 55W
West Hartford, U.S.A. 79 E12 41 45N 72 44W
West Haven, U.S.A. 79 E12 41 17N 72 57W
West Hazleton, U.S.A. 79 F9 40 58N 76 0W
West Helena, U.S.A. 81 H9 34 33N 90 38W
West Hurley, U.S.A. 79 E10 41 59N 74 7W
West Ice Shelf, Antarctica 5 C7 67 0S 85 0 E

Yeysk

Woodend, *Australia* **63 F3** 37 20S 144 33 E
Woodford, *Australia* **63 D5** 26 58S 152 47 E
Woodfords, *U.S.A.* **84 G7** 38 47N 119 50W
Woodlake, *U.S.A.* **84 J7** 36 25N 119 6W
Woodland, *Calif., U.S.A.* **84 G5** 38 41N 121 46W
Woodland, *Maine, U.S.A.* **77 C12** 45 9N 67 25W
Woodland, *Pa., U.S.A.* **78 F6** 40 59N 78 21W
Woodland, *Wash., U.S.A.* **84 E4** 45 54N 122 45W
Woodland Caribou Prov. Park, *Canada* **73 C10** 51 0N 94 45W
Woodridge, *Canada* **73 D9** 49 20N 96 9W
Woodroffe, Mt., *Australia* **61 E5** 26 20S 131 45 E
Woods, L., *Australia* **62 B1** 17 50S 133 30 E
Woods, L. of the, *Canada* **73 D10** 49 15N 94 45W
Woodside, *Australia* **63 F4** 38 31S 146 52 E
Woodstock, *Australia* **62 B4** 19 35S 146 50 E
Woodstock, *N.B., Canada* **71 C6** 46 11N 67 37W
Woodstock, *Ont., Canada* **78 C4** 43 10N 80 45W
Woodstock, *U.K.* **11 F6** 51 51N 1 20W
Woodstock, *Ill., U.S.A.* **80 D10** 42 19N 88 27W
Woodstock, *Vt., U.S.A.* **79 C12** 43 37N 72 31W
Woodsville, *U.S.A.* **79 B13** 44 9N 72 2W
Woodville, *N.Z.* **59 J5** 40 20S 175 53 E
Woodville, *Miss., U.S.A.* **81 K9** 31 6N 91 18W
Woodville, *Tex., U.S.A.* **81 K7** 30 47N 94 25W
Woodward, *U.S.A.* **81 G5** 36 26N 99 24W
Woody, *U.S.A.* **85 K8** 35 42N 118 50W
Woody →, *Canada* **73 C8** 52 31N 100 51W
Woolamai, C., *Australia* **63 F4** 38 30S 145 23 E
Wooler, *U.K.* **10 B5** 55 33N 2 1W
Woolgoolga, *Australia* **63 E5** 30 6S 153 11 E
Woomera, *Australia* **63 E2** 31 5S 136 50 E
Woonsocket, *R.I., U.S.A.* **79 E13** 42 0N 71 31W
Woonsocket, *S. Dak., U.S.A.* **80 C5** 44 3N 98 17W
Wooramel →, *Australia* **61 E1** 25 47S 114 10 E
Wooramel Roadhouse, *Australia* **61 E1** 25 45S 114 17 E
Wooster, *U.S.A.* **78 F3** 40 48N 81 56W
Worcester, *S. Africa* **56 E2** 33 39S 19 27 E
Worcester, *U.K.* **11 E5** 52 11N 2 12W
Worcester, *Mass., U.S.A.* **79 D13** 42 16N 71 48W
Worcester, *N.Y., U.S.A.* **79 D10** 42 36N 74 45W
Worcestershire □, *U.K.* **11 E5** 52 13N 2 10W
Workington, *U.K.* **10 C4** 54 39N 3 33W
Worksop, *U.K.* **10 D6** 53 18N 1 7W
Workum, *Neths.* **15 B5** 52 59N 5 26 E
Worland, *U.S.A.* **82 D10** 44 1N 107 57W
Worms, *Germany* **16 D5** 49 37N 8 21 E
Worsley, *Canada* **72 B5** 56 31N 119 8W
Wortham, *U.S.A.* **81 K6** 31 47N 96 28W
Worthing, *U.K.* **11 G7** 50 49N 0 21W
Worthington, *Minn., U.S.A.* **80 D7** 43 37N 95 36W
Worthington, *Pa., U.S.A.* **78 F5** 40 50N 79 38W
Wosi, *Indonesia* **37 E7** 0 15S 128 0 E
Wou-han = Wuhan, *China* **33 C6** 30 31N 114 18 E
Wousi = Wuxi, *China* **33 C7** 31 33N 120 18 E
Wowoni, *Indonesia* **37 E6** 4 5S 123 5 E
Wrangel I. = Vrangelya, Ostrov, *Russia* **27 B19** 71 0N 180 0 E
Wrangell, *U.S.A.* **72 B2** 56 28N 132 23W
Wrangell Mts., *U.S.A.* **68 B5** 61 30N 142 0W
Wrath, C., *U.K.* **12 C3** 58 38N 5 1W
Wray, *U.S.A.* **80 E3** 40 5N 102 13W
Wrekin, The, *U.K.* **11 E5** 52 41N 2 32W
Wrens, *U.S.A.* **77 J4** 33 12N 82 23W
Wrexham, *U.K.* **10 D4** 53 3N 3 0W
Wrexham □, *U.K.* **10 D5** 53 1N 2 58W
Wright, *U.S.A.* **80 D2** 43 47N 105 30W
Wright Pt., *Canada* **78 C3** 43 48N 81 44W
Wrightson Mt., *U.S.A.* **83 L8** 31 42N 110 51W
Wrightwood, *U.S.A.* **85 L9** 34 21N 117 38W
Wrigley, *Canada* **68 B7** 63 16N 123 37W
Wrocław, *Poland* **17 C9** 51 5N 17 5 E
Września, *Poland* **17 B9** 52 21N 17 36 E
Wu Jiang →, *China* **32 D5** 29 40N 107 20 E
Wu'an, *China* **34 F8** 36 40N 114 15 E
Wubin, *Australia* **61 F2** 30 6S 116 37 E
Wubu, *China* **34 F6** 37 28N 110 42 E
Wuchang, *China* **35 B14** 44 55N 127 5 E
Wucheng, *China* **34 F9** 37 12N 116 20 E
Wuchuan, *China* **34 D6** 41 5N 111 28 E
Wudi, *China* **35 F9** 37 40N 117 35 E
Wuding He →, *China* **34 F6** 37 2N 110 23 E
Wudinna, *Australia* **63 E2** 33 0S 135 22 E
Wudu, *China* **34 H3** 33 22N 104 54 E
Wuhan, *China* **33 C6** 30 31N 114 18 E
Wuhe, *China* **35 H9** 33 10N 117 50 E
Wuhsi = Wuxi, *China* **33 C7** 31 33N 120 18 E
Wuhu, *China* **33 C6** 31 22N 118 21 E
Wukari, *Nigeria* **50 G7** 7 51N 9 42 E
Wulajie, *China* **35 B14** 44 6N 126 33 E
Wulanbulang, *China* **34 D6** 41 5N 110 55 E
Wular L., *India* **43 B6** 34 20N 74 30 E
Wulian, *China* **35 G10** 35 40N 119 12 E
Wuliaru, *Indonesia* **37 F8** 7 27S 131 0 E
Wuluk'omushih Ling, *China* **32 C3** 36 25N 87 25 E
Wulumuchi = Ürümqi, *China* **26 E9** 43 45N 87 45 E
Wundowie, *Australia* **61 F2** 31 47S 116 23 E
Wunnummin L., *Canada* **70 B2** 52 55N 89 10W
Wuntho, *Burma* **41 H19** 23 55N 95 45 E
Wuppertal, *Germany* **16 C4** 51 16N 7 12 E
Wuppertal, *S. Africa* **56 E2** 32 13S 19 12 E
Wuqing, *China* **35 E9** 39 23N 117 4 E
Wurtsboro, *U.S.A.* **79 E10** 41 35N 74 29W
Würzburg, *Germany* **16 D5** 49 46N 9 55 E
Wushan, *China* **34 G3** 34 43N 104 53 E
Wusuli Jiang = Ussuri →, *Asia* **30 A7** 48 27N 135 0 E
Wutai, *China* **34 E7** 38 40N 113 12 E
Wuting = Huimin, *China* **35 F9** 37 27N 117 28 E
Wutonghaolai, *China* **35 C11** 42 50N 120 5 E
Wutongqiao, *China* **32 D5** 29 22N 103 50 E
Wuwei, *China* **32 C5** 37 57N 102 34 E
Wuxi, *China* **33 C7** 31 33N 120 18 E
Wuxiang, *China* **34 F7** 36 49N 112 50 E
Wuyang, *China* **34 H7** 33 25N 113 35 E
Wuyi, *China* **34 F8** 37 46N 115 56 E
Wuyi Shan, *China* **33 D6** 27 0N 117 0 E
Wuyuan, *China* **34 D5** 41 2N 108 20 E
Wuzhai, *China* **34 E6** 38 54N 111 48 E
Wuzhi Shan, *China* **38 C7** 18 45N 109 45 E
Wuzhong, *China* **34 E4** 38 2N 106 12 E
Wuzhou, *China* **33 D6** 23 30N 111 18 E
Wyaaba Cr. →, *Australia* **62 B3** 16 27S 141 35 E
Wyalkatchem, *Australia* **61 F2** 31 8S 117 22 E
Wyalusing, *U.S.A.* **79 E8** 41 40N 76 16W
Wyandotte, *U.S.A.* **76 D4** 42 12N 83 9W
Wyandra, *Australia* **63 D4** 27 12S 145 56 E
Wyangala Res., *Australia* **63 E4** 33 54S 149 0 E
Wyara, L., *Australia* **63 D3** 28 42S 144 14 E
Wycheproof, *Australia* **63 F3** 36 5S 143 17 E
Wye →, *U.K.* **11 F5** 51 38N 2 40W
Wyemandoo, *Australia* **61 E2** 28 28S 118 29 E
Wymondham, *U.K.* **11 E9** 52 35N 1 7 E
Wymore, *U.S.A.* **80 E6** 40 7N 96 40W
Wyndham, *Australia* **60 C4** 15 33S 128 3 E
Wyndham, *N.Z.* **59 M2** 46 20S 168 51 E
Wynne, *U.S.A.* **81 H9** 35 14N 90 47W
Wynyard, *Australia* **62 G4** 41 5S 145 44 E
Wynyard, *Canada* **73 C8** 51 45N 104 10W
Wyola L., *Australia* **61 E5** 29 8S 130 17 E
Wyoming, *Canada* **78 D2** 42 57N 82 7W
Wyoming □, *U.S.A.* **82 E10** 43 0N 107 30W
Wyomissing, *U.S.A.* **79 F9** 40 20N 75 59W
Wyong, *Australia* **63 E5** 33 14S 151 24 E
Wytheville, *U.S.A.* **76 G5** 36 57N 81 5W

X

Xaçmaz, *Azerbaijan* **25 F8** 41 31N 48 42 E
Xai-Xai, *Mozam.* **57 D5** 25 6S 33 31 E
Xainza, *China* **32 C3** 30 58N 88 35 E
Xangongo, *Angola* **56 B2** 16 45S 15 5 E
Xankändi, *Azerbaijan* **25 G8** 39 52N 46 49 E
Xánthi, *Greece* **21 D11** 41 10N 24 58 E
Xanxerê, *Brazil* **95 B5** 26 53S 52 23W
Xapuri, *Brazil* **92 F5** 10 35S 68 35W
Xar Moron He →, *China* **35 C11** 43 25N 120 35 E
Xátiva, *Spain* **19 C5** 38 59N 0 32W
Xau, L., *Botswana* **56 C3** 21 15S 24 44 E
Xavantina, *Brazil* **95 A5** 21 15S 52 48W
Xenia, *U.S.A.* **76 F4** 39 41N 83 56W
Xeropotamos →, *Cyprus* **23 E11** 34 42N 32 33 E
Xhora, *S. Africa* **57 E4** 31 55S 28 38 E
Xhumo, *Botswana* **56 C3** 21 7S 24 35 E
Xi Jiang →, *China* **33 D6** 22 5N 113 20 E
Xi Xian, *China* **34 F6** 36 41N 110 58 E
Xia Xian, *China* **34 G6** 35 8N 111 12 E
Xiachengzi, *China* **35 B16** 44 40N 130 18 E
Xiaguan, *China* **32 D5** 25 32N 100 16 E
Xiajin, *China* **34 F9** 36 56N 116 0 E
Xiamen, *China* **33 D6** 24 25N 118 4 E
Xi'an, *China* **34 G5** 34 15N 109 0 E
Xian Xian, *China* **34 E9** 38 12N 116 6 E
Xiang Jiang →, *China* **33 D6** 28 55N 112 50 E
Xiangcheng, *Henan, China* **34 H8** 33 29N 114 52 E
Xiangcheng, *Henan, China* **34 H7** 33 50N 113 27 E
Xiangfan, *China* **33 C6** 32 2N 112 8 E
Xianggang = Hong Kong □, *China* **33 D6** 22 11N 114 14 E
Xianghuang Qi, *China* **34 C7** 42 2N 113 50 E
Xiangning, *China* **34 G6** 35 58N 110 50 E
Xiangquan, *China* **34 F7** 36 30N 113 1 E
Xiangquan He = Sutlej →, *Pakistan* **42 E4** 29 23N 71 3 E
Xiangshui, *China* **35 G10** 34 12N 119 33 E
Xiangtan, *China* **33 D6** 27 51N 112 54 E
Xianyang, *China* **34 G5** 34 20N 108 40 E
Xiao Hinggan Ling, *China* **33 B7** 49 0N 127 0 E
Xiao Xian, *China* **34 G9** 34 15N 116 55 E
Xiaoyi, *China* **34 F6** 37 8N 111 48 E
Xiawa, *China* **35 C11** 42 35N 120 38 E
Xiayi, *China* **34 G9** 34 15N 116 10 E
Xichang, *China* **32 D5** 27 51N 102 19 E
Xichuan, *China* **34 H6** 33 0N 111 30 E
Xieng Khouang, *Laos* **38 C4** 19 17N 103 25 E
Xifei He →, *China* **34 H9** 32 45N 116 40 E
Xifeng, *Gansu, China* **34 G4** 35 40N 107 40 E
Xifeng, *Liaoning, China* **35 C13** 42 42N 124 45 E
Xifengzhen = Xifeng, *China* **34 G4** 35 40N 107 40 E
Xigazê, *China* **32 D3** 29 5N 88 45 E
Xihe, *China* **34 G3** 34 2N 105 20 E
Xihua, *China* **34 H8** 33 45N 114 30 E
Xiliao He →, *China* **35 C12** 43 32N 123 35 E
Xin Xian = Xinzhou, *China* **34 E7** 38 22N 112 46 E
Xinavane, *Mozam.* **57 D5** 25 2S 32 47 E
Xinbin, *China* **35 D13** 41 40N 125 2 E
Xing Xian, *China* **34 E6** 38 27N 111 7 E
Xing'an, *China* **33 D6** 25 38N 110 40 E
Xingcheng, *China* **35 D11** 40 40N 120 45 E
Xinghe, *China* **34 D7** 40 55N 113 55 E
Xinghua, *China* **35 H10** 32 58N 119 48 E
Xinglong, *China* **35 D9** 40 25N 117 30 E
Xingping, *China* **34 G5** 34 20N 108 28 E
Xingtai, *China* **34 F8** 37 3N 114 32 E
Xingu →, *Brazil* **93 D8** 1 30S 51 53W
Xingyang, *China* **34 G7** 34 45N 112 52 E
Xinhe, *China* **34 F8** 37 30N 115 15 E
Xining, *China* **32 C5** 36 34N 101 40 E
Xinjiang, *China* **34 G6** 35 34N 111 11 E
Xinjiang Uygur Zizhiqu □, *China* **32 C3** 42 0N 86 0 E
Xinjin = Pulandian, *China* **35 E11** 39 25N 121 58 E
Xinkai He →, *China* **35 C12** 43 32N 123 35 E
Xinle, *China* **34 E8** 38 25N 114 40 E
Xinlitun, *China* **35 D12** 42 0N 122 8 E
Xinmin, *China* **35 D12** 41 59N 122 50 E
Xintai, *China* **35 G9** 35 55N 117 45 E
Xinxiang, *China* **34 G7** 35 18N 113 50 E
Xinzhan, *China* **35 C14** 43 50N 127 18 E
Xinzheng, *China* **34 G7** 34 20N 113 45 E
Xinzhou, *China* **34 E7** 38 22N 112 46 E
Xiong Xian, *China* **34 E9** 38 59N 116 8 E
Xiongyuecheng, *China* **35 D12** 40 12N 122 5 E
Xiping, *Henan, China* **34 H8** 33 22N 114 5 E
Xiping, *Henan, China* **34 H6** 33 25N 111 8 E
Xique-Xique, *Brazil* **93 F10** 10 50S 42 40W
Xisha Qundao = Paracel Is., *S. China Sea* **36 A4** 15 50N 112 0 E
Xiuyan, *China* **35 D12** 40 18N 123 11 E
Xixabangma Feng, *China* **41 E14** 28 20N 85 40 E
Xixia, *China* **34 H6** 33 25N 111 29 E
Xixiang, *China* **34 H4** 33 0N 107 44 E
Xiyang, *China* **34 F7** 37 38N 113 38 E
Xizang Zizhiqu □, *China* **32 C3** 32 0N 88 0 E
Xlendi, *Malta* **23 C1** 36 1N 14 12 E
Xuan Loc, *Vietnam* **39 G6** 10 56N 107 14 E
Xuanhua, *China* **34 D8** 40 40N 115 2 E
Xuchang, *China* **34 G7** 34 2N 113 48 E
Xun Xian, *China* **34 G8** 35 42N 114 33 E
Xunyang, *China* **34 H5** 32 48N 109 22 E
Xunyi, *China* **34 G5** 35 8N 108 20 E
Xúquer →, *Spain* **19 C5** 39 5N 0 10W
Xushui, *China* **34 E8** 39 2N 115 40 E
Xuyen Moc, *Vietnam* **39 G6** 10 34N 107 25 E
Xuzhou, *China* **35 G9** 34 18N 117 10 E
Xylophagou, *Cyprus* **23 E12** 34 54N 33 51 E

Y

Ya Xian, *China* **38 C7** 18 14N 109 29 E
Yaamba, *Australia* **62 C5** 23 8S 150 22 E
Yaapeet, *Australia* **63 F3** 35 45S 142 3 E
Yablonovy Ra. = Yablonovyy Khrebet, *Russia* **27 D12** 53 0N 114 0 E
Yablonovyy Khrebet, *Russia* **27 D12** 53 0N 114 0 E
Yabrai Shan, *China* **34 E2** 39 40N 103 0 E
Yabrūd, *Syria* **47 B5** 33 58N 36 39 E
Yacheng, *China* **33 E5** 18 22N 109 6 E
Yacuiba, *Bolivia* **94 A3** 22 0S 63 43W
Yacuma →, *Bolivia* **92 F5** 13 38S 65 23W
Yadgir, *India* **40 L10** 16 45N 77 5 E
Yadkin →, *U.S.A.* **77 H5** 35 29N 80 9W
Yaeyama-Rettō, *Japan* **31 M1** 24 30N 123 40 E
Yagodnoye, *Russia* **27 C15** 62 33N 149 40 E
Yahila, *Dem. Rep. of the Congo* **54 B1** 0 13N 24 28 E
Yahk, *Canada* **72 D5** 49 6N 116 10W
Yahuma, *Dem. Rep. of the Congo* **52 D4** 1 0N 23 10 E
Yaita, *Japan* **31 F9** 36 48N 139 56 E
Yaiza, *Canary Is.* **22 F6** 28 57N 13 46W
Yakima, *U.S.A.* **82 C3** 46 36N 120 31W
Yakima →, *U.S.A.* **82 C3** 47 0N 120 30W
Yakobi I., *U.S.A.* **72 B1** 58 0N 136 30W
Yakovlevka, *Russia* **30 B6** 44 26N 133 28 E
Yaku-Shima, *Japan* **31 J5** 30 20N 130 30 E
Yakumo, *Japan* **30 C10** 42 15N 140 16 E
Yakutat, *U.S.A.* **68 C6** 59 33N 139 44W
Yakutia = Sakha □, *Russia* **27 C14** 66 0N 130 0 E
Yakutsk, *Russia* **27 C13** 62 5N 129 50 E
Yala, *Thailand* **39 J3** 6 33N 101 18 E
Yale, *U.S.A.* **78 C2** 43 8N 82 48W
Yalgoo, *Australia* **61 E2** 28 16S 116 39 E
Yalinga, *C.A.R.* **52 C4** 6 33N 23 10 E
Yalkubul, Punta, *Mexico* **87 C7** 21 32N 88 37W
Yalleroi, *Australia* **62 C4** 24 3S 145 42 E
Yalobusha →, *U.S.A.* **81 J9** 33 33N 90 10W
Yalong Jiang →, *China* **32 D5** 26 40N 101 55 E
Yalova, *Turkey* **21 D13** 40 41N 29 15 E
Yalta, *Ukraine* **25 F5** 44 30N 34 10 E
Yalu Jiang →, *China* **35 E13** 40 0N 124 22 E
Yam Ha Melaḥ = Dead Sea, *Asia* **47 D4** 31 30N 35 30 E
Yam Kinneret, *Israel* **47 C4** 32 45N 35 35 E
Yamada, *Japan* **31 H5** 33 33N 130 49 E
Yamagata, *Japan* **30 E10** 38 15N 140 15 E
Yamagata □, *Japan* **30 E10** 38 30N 140 0 E
Yamaguchi, *Japan* **31 G5** 34 10N 131 32 E
Yamaguchi □, *Japan* **31 G5** 34 20N 131 40 E
Yamal, Poluostrov, *Russia* **26 B8** 71 0N 70 0 E
Yamal Pen. = Yamal, Poluostrov, *Russia* **26 B8** 71 0N 70 0 E
Yamanashi □, *Japan* **31 G9** 35 40N 138 40 E
Yamantau, Gora, *Russia* **24 D10** 54 15N 58 6 E
Yamba, *Australia* **63 D5** 29 26S 153 23 E
Yambarran Ra., *Australia* **60 C5** 15 10S 130 25 E
Yâmbiô, *Sudan* **51 H11** 4 35N 28 16 E
Yambol, *Bulgaria* **21 C12** 42 30N 26 30 E
Yamdena, *Indonesia* **37 F8** 7 45S 131 20 E
Yame, *Japan* **31 H5** 33 13N 130 35 E
Yamethin, *Burma* **41 J20** 20 29N 96 18 E
Yamma-Yamma, L., *Australia* **63 D3** 26 16S 141 20 E
Yamoussoukro, *Ivory C.* **50 G4** 6 49N 5 17W
Yampa →, *U.S.A.* **82 F9** 40 32N 108 59W
Yampi Sd., *Australia* **60 C3** 16 8S 123 38 E
Yampil, *Moldova* **17 D15** 48 15N 28 15 E
Yampol = Yampil, *Moldova* **17 D15** 48 15N 28 15 E
Yamuna →, *India* **43 G9** 25 30N 81 53 E
Yamunanagar, *India* **42 D7** 30 7N 77 17 E
Yamzho Yumco, *China* **32 D4** 28 48N 90 35 E
Yana →, *Russia* **27 B14** 71 30N 136 0 E
Yanagawa, *Japan* **31 H5** 33 10N 130 24 E
Yanai, *Japan* **31 H6** 33 58N 132 7 E
Yan'an, *China* **34 F5** 36 35N 109 26 E
Yanaul, *Russia* **24 C10** 56 25N 55 0 E
Yanbu 'al Baḥr, *Si. Arabia* **46 C2** 24 0N 38 5 E
Yanchang, *China* **34 F6** 36 43N 110 1 E
Yancheng, *Henan, China* **34 H8** 33 35N 114 0 E
Yancheng, *Jiangsu, China* **35 H11** 33 23N 120 8 E
Yanchep Beach, *Australia* **61 F2** 31 33S 115 37 E
Yanchi, *China* **34 F4** 37 48N 107 20 E
Yanchuan, *China* **34 F6** 36 51N 110 10 E
Yanco, *Australia* **63 E4** 34 38S 146 27 E
Yanco Cr. →, *Australia* **63 F4** 35 14S 145 35 E
Yandoon, *Burma* **41 L19** 17 0N 95 40 E
Yang Xian, *China* **34 H4** 33 15N 107 30 E
Yangambi, *Dem. Rep. of the Congo* **54 B1** 0 47N 24 20 E
Yangcheng, *China* **34 G7** 35 28N 112 22 E
Yangch'ü = Taiyuan, *China* **34 F7** 37 52N 112 33 E
Yanggao, *China* **34 D7** 40 21N 113 55 E
Yanggu, *China* **34 F8** 36 8N 115 43 E
Yangliuqing, *China* **35 E9** 39 2N 117 5 E
Yangon = Rangoon, *Burma* **41 L20** 16 45N 96 20 E
Yangpingguan, *China* **34 H4** 32 58N 106 5 E
Yangquan, *China* **34 F7** 37 58N 113 31 E
Yangtse = Chang Jiang →, *China* **33 C7** 31 48N 121 10 E
Yangtze Kiang = Chang Jiang →, *China* **33 C7** 31 48N 121 10 E
Yangyang, *S. Korea* **35 E15** 38 4N 128 38 E
Yangyuan, *China* **34 D8** 40 1N 114 10 E
Yangzhou, *China* **33 C6** 32 21N 119 26 E
Yanji, *China* **35 C15** 42 59N 129 30 E
Yankton, *U.S.A.* **80 D6** 42 53N 97 23W
Yanonge, *Dem. Rep. of the Congo* **54 B1** 0 35N 24 38 E
Yanqi, *China* **32 B3** 42 5N 86 35 E
Yanqing, *China* **34 D8** 40 30N 115 58 E
Yanshan, *China* **35 E9** 38 4N 117 22 E
Yanshou, *China* **35 B15** 45 28N 128 22 E
Yantabulla, *Australia* **63 D4** 29 21S 145 0 E
Yantai, *China* **35 F11** 37 34N 121 22 E
Yanzhou, *China* **34 G9** 35 35N 116 49 E
Yao Xian, *China* **34 G5** 34 55N 108 59 E
Yao Yai, Ko, *Thailand* **39 J2** 8 0N 98 35 E
Yaoundé, *Cameroon* **52 D2** 3 50N 11 35 E
Yaowan, *China* **35 G10** 34 15N 118 3 E
Yap I., *Pac. Oc.* **64 G5** 9 30N 138 10 E
Yapen, *Indonesia* **37 E9** 1 50S 136 0 E
Yapen, Selat, *Indonesia* **37 E9** 1 20S 136 10 E
Yapero, *Indonesia* **37 E9** 4 59S 137 11 E
Yappar →, *Australia* **62 B3** 18 22S 141 16 E
Yaqui →, *Mexico* **86 B2** 27 37N 110 39W
Yar-Sale, *Russia* **26 C8** 66 50N 70 50 E
Yaraka, *Australia* **62 C3** 24 53S 144 3 E
Yaransk, *Russia* **24 C8** 57 22N 47 49 E
Yare →, *U.K.* **11 E9** 52 35N 1 38 E
Yaremcha, *Ukraine* **17 D13** 48 27N 24 33 E
Yarensk, *Russia* **24 B8** 62 11N 49 15 E
Yarí →, *Colombia* **92 D4** 0 20S 72 20W
Yarkand = Shache, *China* **32 C2** 38 20N 77 10 E
Yarker, *Canada* **79 B8** 44 23N 76 46W
Yarkhun →, *Pakistan* **43 A5** 36 17N 72 30 E
Yarmouth, *Canada* **71 D6** 43 50N 66 7W
Yarmūk →, *Syria* **47 C4** 32 42N 35 40 E
Yaroslavl, *Russia* **24 C6** 57 35N 39 55 E
Yarqa, W. →, *Egypt* **47 F2** 30 0N 33 49 E
Yarra Yarra Lakes, *Australia* **61 E2** 29 40S 115 45 E
Yarram, *Australia* **63 F4** 38 29S 146 39 E
Yarraman, *Australia* **63 D5** 26 50S 152 0 E
Yarras, *Australia* **63 E5** 31 25S 152 20 E
Yartsevo, *Russia* **27 C10** 60 20N 90 0 E
Yarumal, *Colombia* **92 B3** 6 58N 75 24W
Yasawa Group, *Fiji* **59 C7** 17 0S 177 23 E
Yaselda, *Belarus* **17 B14** 52 7N 26 28 E
Yasin, *Pakistan* **43 A5** 36 24N 73 23 E
Yasinski, L., *Canada* **70 B4** 53 16N 77 35W
Yasinya, *Ukraine* **17 D13** 48 16N 24 21 E
Yasothon, *Thailand* **38 E5** 15 50N 104 10 E
Yass, *Australia* **63 E4** 34 49S 148 54 E
Yatağan, *Turkey* **21 F13** 37 20N 28 10 E
Yates Center, *U.S.A.* **81 G7** 37 53N 95 44W
Yathkyed L., *Canada* **73 A9** 62 40N 98 0W
Yatsushiro, *Japan* **31 H5** 32 30N 130 40 E
Yatta Plateau, *Kenya* **54 C4** 2 0S 38 0 E
Yavari →, *Peru* **92 D4** 4 21S 70 2W
Yávaros, *Mexico* **86 B3** 26 42N 109 31W
Yavatmal, *India* **40 J11** 20 20N 78 15 E
Yavne, *Israel* **47 D3** 31 52N 34 45 E
Yavoriv, *Ukraine* **17 D12** 49 55N 23 20 E
Yavorov = Yavoriv, *Ukraine* **17 D12** 49 55N 23 20 E
Yawatahama, *Japan* **31 H6** 33 27N 132 24 E
Yazd, *Iran* **45 D7** 31 55N 54 27 E
Yazd □, *Iran* **45 D7** 32 0N 55 0 E
Yazd-e Khvāst, *Iran* **45 D7** 31 31N 52 7 E
Yazman, *Pakistan* **42 E4** 29 8N 71 45 E
Yazoo →, *U.S.A.* **81 J9** 32 22N 90 54W
Yazoo City, *U.S.A.* **81 J9** 32 51N 90 25W
Yding Skovhøj, *Denmark* **9 J13** 55 59N 9 46 E
Ye Xian = Laizhou, *China* **35 F10** 37 8N 119 57 E
Ye Xian, *China* **34 H7** 33 35N 113 25 E
Yebyu, *Burma* **38 E2** 14 15N 98 13 E
Yechŏn, *S. Korea* **35 F15** 36 39N 128 27 E
Yecla, *Spain* **19 C5** 38 35N 1 5W
Yécora, *Mexico* **86 B3** 28 20N 108 58W
Yedintsy = Edineţ, *Moldova* **17 D14** 48 9N 27 18 E
Yegros, *Paraguay* **94 B4** 26 20S 56 25W
Yehuda, Midbar, *Israel* **47 D4** 31 35N 35 15 E
Yei, *Sudan* **51 H12** 4 9N 30 40 E
Yekaterinburg, *Russia* **26 D7** 56 50N 60 30 E
Yekaterinodar = Krasnodar, *Russia* **25 E6** 45 5N 39 0 E
Yelarbon, *Australia* **63 D5** 28 33S 150 38 E
Yelets, *Russia* **24 D6** 52 40N 38 30 E
Yelizavetgrad = Kirovohrad, *Ukraine* **25 E5** 48 35N 32 20 E
Yell, *U.K.* **12 A7** 60 35N 1 5W
Yell Sd., *U.K.* **12 A7** 60 33N 1 15W
Yellow Sea, *China* **35 G12** 35 0N 123 0 E
Yellowhead Pass, *Canada* **72 C5** 52 53N 118 25W
Yellowknife, *Canada* **72 A6** 62 27N 114 29W
Yellowknife →, *Canada* **72 A6** 62 31N 114 19W
Yellowstone →, *U.S.A.* **80 B3** 47 59N 103 59W
Yellowstone L., *U.S.A.* **82 D8** 44 27N 110 22W
Yellowstone National Park, *U.S.A.* **82 D9** 44 40N 110 30W
Yelsk, *Belarus* **17 C15** 51 50N 29 10 E
Yemen ■, *Asia* **46 E3** 15 0N 44 0 E
Yenangyaung, *Burma* **41 J19** 20 30N 95 0 E
Yenbo = Yanbu 'al Baḥr, *Si. Arabia* **46 C2** 24 0N 38 5 E
Yenda, *Australia* **63 E4** 34 13S 146 14 E
Yenice, *Turkey* **21 E12** 39 55N 27 17 E
Yenisey →, *Russia* **26 B9** 71 50N 82 40 E
Yeniseysk, *Russia* **27 D10** 58 27N 92 13 E
Yeniseyskiy Zaliv, *Russia* **26 B9** 72 20N 81 0 E
Yennádhi, *Greece* **23 C9** 36 2N 27 56 E
Yenyuka, *Russia* **27 D13** 57 57N 121 15 E
Yeo →, *U.K.* **11 G5** 51 2N 2 49W
Yeo, L., *Australia* **61 E3** 28 0S 124 30 E
Yeo I., *Canada* **78 A3** 45 24N 81 48W
Yeola, *India* **40 J9** 20 2N 74 30 E
Yeoryioúpolis, *Greece* **23 D6** 35 20N 24 15 E
Yeovil, *U.K.* **11 G5** 50 57N 2 38W
Yeppoon, *Australia* **62 C5** 23 5S 150 47 E
Yerbent, *Turkmenistan* **26 F6** 39 30N 58 50 E
Yerbogachen, *Russia* **27 C11** 61 16N 108 0 E
Yerevan, *Armenia* **25 F7** 40 10N 44 31 E
Yerington, *U.S.A.* **82 G4** 38 59N 119 10W
Yermak, *Kazakstan* **26 D8** 52 2N 76 55 E
Yermo, *U.S.A.* **85 L10** 34 54N 116 50W
Yerólakkos, *Cyprus* **23 D12** 35 11N 33 15 E
Yeropol, *Russia* **27 C17** 65 15N 168 40 E
Yeropótamos →, *Greece* **23 D6** 35 3N 24 50 E
Yeroskipos, *Cyprus* **23 E11** 34 46N 32 28 E
Yershov, *Russia* **25 D8** 51 23N 48 27 E
Yerushalayim = Jerusalem, *Israel* **47 D4** 31 47N 35 10 E
Yes Tor, *U.K.* **11 G4** 50 41N 4 0W
Yesan, *S. Korea* **35 F14** 36 41N 126 51 E
Yeso, *U.S.A.* **81 H2** 34 26N 104 37W
Yessey, *Russia* **27 C11** 68 29N 102 10 E
Yetman, *Australia* **63 D5** 28 56S 150 48 E
Yeu, Î. d', *France* **18 C2** 46 42N 2 20W
Yevpatoriya, *Ukraine* **25 E5** 45 15N 33 20 E
Yeysk, *Russia* **25 E6** 46 40N 38 12 E

Yezd = Yazd, Iran 45 D7 31 55N 54 27 E
Yhati, Paraguay 94 B4 25 45S 56 35W
Yhú, Paraguay 95 B4 25 0S 56 0W
Yi →, Uruguay 94 C4 33 7S 57 8W
Yi 'Allaq, G., Egypt 47 E2 30 22N 33 32 E
Yi He →, China 35 G10 34 10N 118 8 E
Yi Xian, Hebei, China 34 E8 39 20N 115 30 E
Yi Xian, Liaoning, China 35 D11 41 30N 121 22 E
Yialiás →, Cyprus 23 D12 35 9N 33 44 E
Yialousa, Cyprus 23 D13 35 32N 34 10 E
Yianisádhes, Greece 23 D8 35 20N 26 10 E
Yiannitsa, Greece 21 D10 40 46N 22 24 E
Yibin, China 32 D5 28 45N 104 32 E
Yichang, China 33 C6 30 40N 111 20 E
Yicheng, China 34 G6 35 42N 111 40 E
Yichuan, China 34 F6 36 2N 110 10 E
Yichun, China 33 B7 47 44N 128 52 E
Yidu, China 35 F10 36 43N 118 28 E
Yijun, China 34 G5 35 28N 109 8 E
Yıldız Dağları, Turkey 21 D12 41 48N 27 36 E
Yilehuli Shan, China 33 A7 51 20N 124 20 E
Yimianpo, China 35 B15 45 7N 128 2 E
Yinchuan, China 34 E4 38 30N 106 15 E
Yindarlgooda, L., Australia 61 F3 30 40S 121 52 E
Ying He →, China 34 H9 32 30N 116 30 E
Ying Xian, China 34 E7 39 32N 113 10 E
Yingkou, China 35 D12 40 37N 122 18 E
Yining, China 26 E9 43 58N 81 10 E
Yinmabin, Burma 41 H19 22 10N 94 55 E
Yiofiros →, Greece 23 D7 35 20N 25 6 E
Yirga Alem, Ethiopia 46 F2 6 48N 38 22 E
Yirrkala, Australia 62 A2 12 14S 136 56 E
Yishan, China 32 D5 24 28N 108 38 E
Yishui, China 35 G10 35 47N 118 30 E
Yíthion, Greece 21 F10 36 46N 22 34 E
Yitiaoshan, China 34 F3 37 5N 104 2 E
Yitong, China 35 C13 43 13N 125 20 E
Yiyang, Henan, China 34 G7 34 27N 112 10 E
Yiyang, Hunan, China 33 D6 28 35N 112 18 E
Yli-Kitka, Finland 8 C23 66 8N 28 30 E
Ylitornio, Finland 8 C20 66 19N 23 39 E
Ylivieska, Finland 8 D21 64 4N 24 28 E
Yoakum, U.S.A. 81 L6 29 17N 97 9W
Yog Pt., Phil. 37 B6 14 6N 124 12 E
Yogyakarta, Indonesia 37 G14 7 49S 110 22 E
Yoho Nat. Park, Canada 72 C5 51 25N 116 30W
Yojoa, L. de, Honduras 88 D2 14 53N 88 0W
Yŏju, S. Korea 35 F14 37 20N 127 35 E
Yokadouma, Cameroon 52 D2 3 26N 14 55 E
Yokkaichi, Japan 31 G8 34 55N 136 38 E
Yoko, Cameroon 52 C2 5 32N 12 20 E
Yokohama, Japan 31 G9 35 27N 139 28 E
Yokosuka, Japan 31 G9 35 20N 139 40 E
Yokote, Japan 30 E10 39 20N 140 30 E
Yola, Nigeria 51 G8 9 10N 12 29 E
Yolaina, Cordillera de, Nic. 88 D3 11 30N 84 0W
Yoloten, Turkmenistan 45 B9 37 18N 62 21 E
Yom →, Thailand 36 A2 15 35N 100 1 E
Yonago, Japan 31 G6 35 25N 133 19 E
Yonaguni-Jima, Japan 31 M1 24 27N 123 0 E
Yŏnan, N. Korea 35 F14 37 55N 126 11 E
Yonezawa, Japan 30 F10 37 57N 140 4 E
Yong Peng, Malaysia 39 M4 2 0N 103 3 E
Yong Sata, Thailand 39 J2 7 8N 99 41 E
Yongamp'o, N. Korea 35 E13 39 56N 124 23 E
Yongcheng, China 34 H9 33 55N 116 20 E
Yŏngch'ŏn, S. Korea 35 G15 35 58N 128 56 E
Yongdeng, China 34 F2 36 38N 103 25 E
Yŏngdŏk, S. Korea 35 F15 36 24N 129 22 E
Yŏngdŭngpo, S. Korea 35 F14 37 31N 126 54 E
Yonghe, China 34 F6 36 46N 110 38 E
Yŏnghŭng, N. Korea 35 E14 39 31N 127 18 E
Yongji, China 34 G6 34 52N 110 28 E
Yŏngju, S. Korea 35 F15 36 50N 128 40 E
Yongnian, China 34 F8 36 47N 114 29 E
Yongning, China 34 E4 38 15N 106 14 E
Yongqing, China 34 E9 39 25N 116 28 E
Yŏngwŏl, S. Korea 35 F15 37 11N 128 28 E
Yonibana, S. Leone 50 G3 8 30N 12 19W
Yonkers, U.S.A. 79 F11 40 56N 73 54W
Yonne →, France 18 B5 48 23N 2 58 E
York, Australia 61 F2 31 52S 116 47 E
York, U.K. 10 D6 53 58N 1 6W
York, Nebr., U.S.A. 80 E6 40 52N 97 36W
York, Pa., U.S.A. 76 F7 39 58N 76 44W
York, C., Australia 62 A3 10 42S 142 31 E
York, City of □, U.K. 10 D6 53 58N 1 6W
York, Kap, Greenland 4 B4 75 55N 66 25W
York, Vale of, U.K. 10 C6 54 15N 1 25W
York Haven, U.S.A. 78 F8 40 7N 76 46W
York Sd., Australia 60 C4 15 0S 125 5 E
Yorke Pen., Australia 63 E2 34 50S 137 40 E
Yorketown, Australia 63 F2 35 0S 137 33 E
Yorkshire Wolds, U.K. 10 C7 54 8N 0 31W
Yorkton, Canada 73 C8 51 11N 102 28W
Yorkville, U.S.A. 84 G3 38 52N 123 13W
Yoro, Honduras 88 C2 15 9N 87 7W
Yoron-Jima, Japan 31 L4 27 2N 128 26 E
Yos Sudarso, Pulau = Dolak, Pulau, Indonesia 37 F9 8 0S 138 30 E
Yosemite National Park, U.S.A. 84 H7 37 45N 119 40W
Yosemite Village, U.S.A. 84 H7 37 45N 119 35W
Yoshkar Ola, Russia 24 C8 56 38N 47 55 E
Yŏsu, S. Korea 35 G14 34 47N 127 45 E
Yotvata, Israel 47 F4 29 55N 35 2 E
Youbou, Canada 84 B2 48 53N 124 13W
Youghal, Ireland 13 E4 51 56N 7 52W
Youghal B., Ireland 13 E4 51 55N 7 49W
Young, Australia 63 E4 34 19S 148 18 E
Young, Canada 73 C7 51 47N 105 45W
Young, Uruguay 94 C4 32 44S 57 36W
Younghusband, L., Australia 63 E2 30 50S 136 5 E
Younghusband Pen., Australia 63 F2 36 0S 139 25 E
Youngstown, Canada 73 C6 51 35N 111 10W
Youngstown, N.Y., U.S.A. 78 C5 43 15N 79 3W
Youngstown, Ohio, U.S.A. 78 E4 41 6N 80 39W
Youngsville, U.S.A. 78 E5 41 51N 79 19W
Youngwood, U.S.A. 78 F5 40 14N 79 34W
Youyu, China 34 D7 40 10N 112 20 E
Yozgat, Turkey 25 G5 39 51N 34 47 E
Ypané →, Paraguay 94 A4 23 29S 57 19W
Ypres = Ieper, Belgium 15 D2 50 51N 2 53 E
Yreka, U.S.A. 82 F2 41 44N 122 38W
Ystad, Sweden 9 J15 55 26N 13 50 E
Ysyk-Köl, Kyrgyzstan 28 E11 42 26N 76 12 E
Ysyk-Köl, Ozero, Kyrgyzstan 26 E8 42 25N 77 15 E
Ythan →, U.K. 12 D7 57 19N 1 59W
Ytyk Kyuyel, Russia 27 C14 62 30N 133 45 E
Yu Jiang →, China 33 D6 23 22N 110 3 E
Yu Xian = Yuzhou, China 34 G7 34 10N 113 28 E
Yu Xian, Hebei, China 34 E8 39 50N 114 35 E
Yu Xian, Shanxi, China 34 E7 38 5N 113 20 E
Yuan Jiang →, China 33 D6 28 55N 111 50 E
Yuanqu, China 34 G6 35 18N 111 40 E
Yuanyang, China 34 G7 35 3N 113 58 E
Yuba →, U.S.A. 84 F5 39 8N 121 36W
Yuba City, U.S.A. 84 F5 39 8N 121 37W
Yūbari, Japan 30 C10 43 4N 141 59 E
Yūbetsu, Japan 30 B11 44 13N 143 50 E
Yucatán □, Mexico 87 C7 21 30N 86 30W
Yucatán, Canal de, Caribbean 88 B2 22 0N 86 30W
Yucatán, Península de, Mexico 66 H11 19 30N 89 0W
Yucatán Basin, Cent. Amer. 66 H11 19 0N 86 0W
Yucatan Str. = Yucatán, Canal de, Caribbean 88 B2 22 0N 86 30W
Yucca, U.S.A. 85 L12 34 52N 114 9W
Yucca Valley, U.S.A. 85 L10 34 8N 116 27W
Yucheng, China 34 F9 36 55N 116 32 E
Yuci, China 34 F7 37 42N 112 46 E
Yuendumu, Australia 60 D5 22 16S 131 49 E
Yugoslavia ■, Europe 21 B9 43 20N 20 0 E
Yukon →, U.S.A. 68 B3 62 32N 163 54W
Yukon Territory □, Canada 68 B6 63 0N 135 0W
Yukta, Russia 27 C11 63 26N 105 42 E
Yukuhashi, Japan 31 H5 33 44N 130 59 E
Yulara, Australia 61 E5 25 10S 130 55 E
Yule →, Australia 60 D2 20 41S 118 17 E
Yuleba, Australia 63 D4 26 37S 149 24 E
Yulin, Shaanxi, China 34 E5 38 20N 109 30 E
Yulin, Shensi, China 38 C7 38 15N 109 30 E
Yuma, Ariz., U.S.A. 85 N12 32 43N 114 37W
Yuma, Colo., U.S.A. 80 E3 40 8N 102 43W
Yuma, B. de, Dom. Rep. 89 C6 18 20N 68 35W
Yumbe, Uganda 54 B3 3 28N 31 15 E
Yumbi, Dem. Rep. of the Congo 54 C2 1 12S 26 15 E
Yumen, China 32 C4 39 50N 97 30 E
Yun Ho →, China 35 E9 39 10N 117 10 E
Yuna, Australia 61 E2 28 20S 115 0 E
Yuncheng, Henan, China 34 G8 35 36N 115 57 E
Yuncheng, Shanxi, China 34 G6 35 2N 111 0 E
Yungas, Bolivia 92 G5 17 0S 66 0W
Yungay, Chile 94 D1 37 10S 72 5W
Yunnan □, China 32 D5 25 0N 102 0 E
Yunta, Australia 63 E2 32 34S 139 36 E
Yunxi, China 34 H6 33 0N 110 22 E
Yupyongdong, N. Korea 35 D15 41 49N 128 53 E
Yurga, Russia 26 D9 55 42N 84 51 E
Yurimaguas, Peru 92 E3 5 55S 76 7W
Yuryung Kaya, Russia 27 B12 72 48N 113 23 E
Yuscarán, Honduras 88 D2 13 58N 86 45W
Yushe, China 34 F7 37 4N 112 58 E
Yushu, Jilin, China 35 B14 44 43N 126 38 E
Yushu, Qinghai, China 32 C4 33 5N 96 55 E
Yutai, China 34 G9 35 0N 116 45 E
Yutian, China 35 E9 39 53N 117 45 E
Yuxan Qarabağ = Nagorno-Karabakh, Azerbaijan 25 F8 39 55N 46 45 E
Yuxi, China 32 D5 24 30N 102 35 E
Yuzawa, Japan 30 E10 39 10N 140 30 E
Yuzhno-Sakhalinsk, Russia 27 E15 46 58N 142 45 E
Yuzhou, China 34 G7 34 10N 113 28 E
Yvetot, France 18 B4 49 37N 0 44 E

Z

Zaanstad, Neths. 15 B4 52 27N 4 50 E
Zāb al Kabīr →, Iraq 44 C4 36 1N 43 24 E
Zāb aş Şagīr →, Iraq 44 C4 35 17N 43 29 E
Zabaykalsk, Russia 27 E12 49 40N 117 25 E
Zābol, Iran 45 D9 31 0N 61 32 E
Zābolī, Iran 45 E9 27 10N 61 35 E
Zabrze, Poland 17 C10 50 18N 18 50 E
Zacapa, Guatemala 88 D2 14 59N 89 31W
Zacapu, Mexico 86 D4 19 50N 101 43W
Zacatecas, Mexico 86 C4 22 49N 102 34W
Zacatecas □, Mexico 86 C4 23 30N 103 0W
Zacatecoluca, El Salv. 88 D2 13 29N 88 51W
Zachary, U.S.A. 81 K9 30 39N 91 9W
Zacoalco, Mexico 86 C4 20 14N 103 33W
Zacualtipán, Mexico 87 C5 20 39N 98 36W
Zadar, Croatia 16 F8 44 8N 15 14 E
Zadetkyi Kyun, Burma 39 H2 10 0N 98 25 E
Zafarqand, Iran 45 C7 33 11N 52 29 E
Zafra, Spain 19 C2 38 26N 6 30W
Żagań, Poland 16 C8 51 39N 15 22 E
Zagaoua, Chad 51 E10 15 30N 22 24 E
Zagazig, Egypt 51 B12 30 40N 31 30 E
Zāgheh, Iran 45 C6 33 30N 48 42 E
Zagorsk = Sergiyev Posad, Russia 24 C6 56 20N 38 10 E
Zagreb, Croatia 16 F9 45 50N 15 58 E
Zāgros, Kūhhā-ye, Iran 45 C6 33 45N 48 5 E
Zagros Mts. = Zāgros, Kūhhā-ye, Iran 45 C6 33 45N 48 5 E
Zāhedān, Fārs, Iran 45 D7 28 46N 53 52 E
Zāhedān, Sīstān va Balūchestān, Iran 45 D9 29 30N 60 50 E
Zahlah, Lebanon 47 B4 33 52N 35 50 E
Zaïre = Congo →, Africa 52 F2 6 4S 12 24 E
Zaječar, Serbia, Yug. 21 C10 43 53N 22 18 E
Zakamensk, Russia 27 D11 50 23N 103 17 E
Zakhodnaya Dzvina = Daugava →, Latvia 9 H21 57 4N 24 3 E
Zākhū, Iraq 44 B4 37 10N 42 50 E
Zákinthos, Greece 21 F9 37 47N 20 57 E
Zakopane, Poland 17 D10 49 18N 19 57 E
Zákros, Greece 23 D8 35 6N 26 10 E
Zalaegerszeg, Hungary 17 E9 46 53N 16 47 E
Zalău, Romania 17 E12 47 12N 23 3 E
Zaleshchiki = Zalishchyky, Ukraine 17 D13 48 45N 25 45 E
Zalew Wiślany, Poland 17 A10 54 20N 19 50 E
Zalingei, Sudan 51 F10 12 51N 23 29 E
Zalishchyky, Ukraine 17 D13 48 45N 25 45 E
Zama L., Canada 72 B5 58 45N 119 5W
Zambeke, Dem. Rep. of the Congo 54 B2 2 8N 25 17 E
Zambeze →, Africa 55 F4 18 35S 36 20 E
Zambezi = Zambeze →, Africa 55 F4 18 35S 36 20 E
Zambezi, Zambia 53 G4 13 30S 23 15 E
Zambezia □, Mozam. 55 F4 16 15S 37 30 E
Zambia ■, Africa 55 F2 15 0S 28 0 E
Zamboanga, Phil. 37 C6 6 59N 122 3 E
Zamora, Mexico 86 D4 20 0N 102 21W
Zamora, Spain 19 B3 41 30N 5 45W
Zamość, Poland 17 C12 50 43N 23 15 E
Zandvoort, Neths. 15 B4 52 22N 4 32 E
Zanesville, U.S.A. 78 G2 39 56N 82 1W
Zangābād, Iran 44 B5 38 26N 46 44 E
Zangue →, Mozam. 55 F4 17 50S 35 21 E
Zanjān, Iran 45 B6 36 40N 48 35 E
Zanjān □, Iran 45 B6 37 20N 49 30 E
Zanjān →, Iran 45 B6 37 8N 47 47 E
Zante = Zákinthos, Greece 21 F9 37 47N 20 57 E
Zanthus, Australia 61 F3 31 2S 123 34 E
Zanzibar, Tanzania 54 D4 6 12S 39 12 E
Zaouiet El-Kala = Bordj Omar Driss, Algeria 50 C7 28 10N 6 40 E
Zaouiet Reggane, Algeria 50 C6 26 32N 0 3 E
Zaozhuang, China 35 G9 34 50N 117 35 E
Zap Suyu = Zāb al Kabīr →, Iraq 44 C4 36 1N 43 24 E
Zapadnaya Dvina = Daugava →, Latvia 9 H21 57 4N 24 3 E
Západné Beskydy, Europe 17 D10 49 30N 19 0 E
Zapala, Argentina 96 D2 39 0S 70 5W
Zapaleri, Cerro, Bolivia 94 A2 22 49S 67 11W
Zapata, U.S.A. 81 M5 26 55N 99 16W
Zapolyarnyy, Russia 24 A5 69 26N 30 51 E
Zaporizhzhya, Ukraine 25 E6 47 50N 35 10 E
Zaporozhye = Zaporizhzhya, Ukraine 25 E6 47 50N 35 10 E
Zara, Turkey 44 B3 39 58N 37 43 E
Zaragoza, Coahuila, Mexico 86 B4 28 30N 101 0W
Zaragoza, Nuevo León, Mexico 87 C5 24 0N 99 46W
Zaragoza, Spain 19 B5 41 39N 0 53W
Zarand, Kermān, Iran 45 D8 30 46N 56 34 E
Zarand, Markazī, Iran 45 C6 35 18N 50 25 E
Zaranj, Afghan. 40 D2 30 55N 61 55 E
Zarasai, Lithuania 9 J22 55 40N 26 20 E
Zarate, Argentina 94 C4 34 7S 59 0W
Zard, Kūh-e, Iran 45 C6 32 22N 50 4 E
Zāreh, Iran 45 C6 35 7N 49 9 E
Zaria, Nigeria 50 F7 11 0N 7 40 E
Zarneh, Iran 44 C5 33 55N 46 10 E
Zarós, Greece 23 D6 35 8N 24 54 E
Zarqā', Nahr az →, Jordan 47 C4 32 10N 35 37 E
Zarrin, Iran 45 C7 32 46N 54 37 E
Zaruma, Ecuador 92 D3 3 40S 79 38W
Żary, Poland 16 C8 51 37N 15 10 E
Zarzis, Tunisia 51 B8 33 31N 11 2 E
Zaskar →, India 43 B7 34 13N 77 20 E
Zaskar Mts., India 43 C7 33 15N 77 30 E
Zastron, S. Africa 56 E4 30 18S 27 7 E
Zavāreh, Iran 45 C7 33 29N 52 28 E
Zavitinsk, Russia 27 D13 50 10N 129 20 E
Zavodovski, I., Antarctica 5 B1 56 0S 27 45W
Zawiercie, Poland 17 C10 50 30N 19 24 E
Zāwiyat al Bayḍā = Al Bayḍā, Libya 51 B10 32 50N 21 44 E
Zāyā, Iraq 44 C5 33 33N 44 13 E
Zāyandeh →, Iran 45 C7 32 35N 52 0 E
Zaysan, Kazakstan 26 E9 47 28N 84 52 E
Zaysan, Oz., Kazakstan 26 E9 48 0N 83 0 E
Zayü, China 32 D4 28 48N 97 27 E
Zbarazh, Ukraine 17 D13 49 43N 25 44 E
Zdolbuniv, Ukraine 17 C14 50 30N 26 15 E
Zduńska Wola, Poland 17 C10 51 37N 18 59 E
Zeballos, Canada 72 D3 49 59N 126 50W
Zebediela, S. Africa 57 C4 24 20S 29 17 E
Zeebrugge, Belgium 15 C3 51 19N 3 12 E
Zeehan, Australia 62 G4 41 52S 145 25 E
Zeeland □, Neths. 15 C3 51 30N 3 50 E
Zeerust, S. Africa 56 D4 25 31S 26 4 E
Zefat, Israel 47 C4 32 58N 35 29 E
Zeil, Mt., Australia 60 D5 23 30S 132 23 E
Zeila, Somali Rep. 46 E3 11 21N 43 30 E
Zeist, Neths. 15 B5 52 5N 5 15 E
Zeitz, Germany 16 C7 51 2N 12 7 E
Zelenograd, Russia 24 C6 56 1N 37 12 E
Zelenogradsk, Russia 9 J19 54 53N 20 29 E
Zelienople, U.S.A. 78 F4 40 48N 80 8W
Zémio, C.A.R. 54 A2 5 2N 25 5 E
Zemun, Serbia, Yug. 21 B9 44 51N 20 25 E
Zenica, Bos.-H. 21 B7 44 10N 17 57 E
Žepče, Bos.-H. 21 B8 44 28N 18 2 E
Zevenaar, Neths. 15 C6 51 56N 6 5 E
Zeya, Russia 27 D13 53 48N 127 14 E
Zeya →, Russia 27 D13 51 42N 128 53 E
Zêzere →, Portugal 19 C1 39 28N 8 20W
Zghartā, Lebanon 47 A4 34 21N 35 53 E
Zgorzelec, Poland 16 C8 51 10N 15 0 E
Zhabinka, Belarus 17 B13 52 13N 24 2 E
Zhailma, Kazakstan 26 D7 51 37N 61 33 E
Zhambyl, Kazakstan 26 E8 42 54N 71 22 E
Zhangaqazaly, Kazakstan 26 E7 45 48N 62 6 E
Zhangbei, China 34 D8 41 10N 114 45 E
Zhangguangcai Ling, China 35 B15 45 0N 129 0 E
Zhangjiakou, China 34 D8 40 48N 114 55 E
Zhangwu, China 35 C12 42 43N 123 52 E
Zhangye, China 32 C5 38 50N 100 23 E
Zhangzhou, China 33 D6 24 30N 117 35 E
Zhanhua, China 35 F10 37 40N 118 8 E
Zhanjiang, China 33 D6 21 15N 110 20 E
Zhannetty, Ostrov, Russia 27 B16 76 43N 158 0 E
Zhanyi, China 32 D5 25 38N 103 48 E
Zhanyu, China 35 B12 44 30N 122 30 E
Zhao Xian, China 34 F8 37 43N 114 45 E
Zhaocheng, China 34 F6 36 22N 111 38 E
Zhaotong, China 32 D5 27 20N 103 44 E
Zhaoyuan, Heilongjiang, China 35 B13 45 27N 125 0 E
Zhaoyuan, Shandong, China 35 F11 37 20N 120 23 E
Zhashkiv, Ukraine 17 D16 49 15N 30 5 E
Zhashui, China 34 H5 33 40N 109 8 E
Zhayyq →, Kazakstan 25 E9 47 0N 51 48 E
Zhdanov = Mariupol, Ukraine 25 E6 47 5N 37 31 E
Zhecheng, China 34 G8 34 7N 115 20 E
Zhejiang □, China 33 D7 29 0N 120 0 E
Zheleznodorozhnyy, Russia 24 B9 62 35N 50 55 E
Zheleznogorsk-Ilimskiy, Russia 27 D11 56 34N 104 8 E
Zhen'an, China 34 H5 33 27N 109 9 E
Zhengding, China 34 E8 38 8N 114 32 E
Zhengzhou, China 34 G7 34 45N 113 34 E
Zhenlai, China 35 B12 45 50N 123 5 E
Zhenping, China 34 H7 33 10N 112 16 E
Zhenyuan, China 34 G4 35 35N 107 30 E
Zhetiqara, Kazakstan 26 D7 52 11N 61 12 E
Zhezqazghan, Kazakstan 26 E7 47 44N 67 40 E
Zhidan, China 34 F5 36 48N 108 48 E
Zhigansk, Russia 27 C13 66 48N 123 27 E
Zhilinda, Russia 27 C12 70 0N 114 20 E
Zhitomir = Zhytomyr, Ukraine 17 C15 50 20N 28 40 E
Zhlobin, Belarus 17 B16 52 55N 30 0 E
Zhmerinka = Zhmerynka, Ukraine 17 D15 49 2N 28 2 E
Zhmerynka, Ukraine 17 D15 49 2N 28 2 E
Zhob, Pakistan 42 D3 31 20N 69 31 E
Zhob →, Pakistan 42 C3 32 4N 69 50 E
Zhodino = Zhodzina, Belarus 17 A15 54 5N 28 17 E
Zhodzina, Belarus 17 A15 54 5N 28 17 E
Zhokhova, Ostrov, Russia 27 B16 76 4N 152 40 E
Zhongdian, China 32 D4 27 48N 99 42 E
Zhongning, China 34 F3 37 29N 105 40 E
Zhongtiao Shan, China 34 G6 35 0N 111 10 E
Zhongwei, China 34 F3 37 30N 105 12 E
Zhongyang, China 34 F6 37 20N 111 11 E
Zhoucun, China 35 F9 36 47N 117 48 E
Zhouzhi, China 34 G5 34 10N 108 12 E
Zhuanghe, China 35 E12 39 40N 123 0 E
Zhucheng, China 35 G10 36 0N 119 27 E
Zhugqu, China 34 H3 33 40N 104 30 E
Zhumadian, China 34 H8 32 59N 114 2 E
Zhuo Xian = Zhuozhou, China 34 E8 39 28N 115 58 E
Zhuolu, China 34 D8 40 20N 115 12 E
Zhuozhou, China 34 E8 39 28N 115 58 E
Zhuozi, China 34 D7 41 0N 112 25 E
Zhytomyr, Ukraine 17 C15 50 20N 28 40 E
Ziārān, Iran 45 B6 36 7N 50 32 E
Ziarat, Pakistan 42 D2 30 25N 67 49 E
Zibo, China 35 F10 36 47N 118 3 E
Zichang, China 34 F5 37 18N 109 40 E
Zielona Góra, Poland 16 C8 51 57N 15 31 E
Zierikzee, Neths. 15 C3 51 40N 3 55 E
Zigey, Chad 51 F9 14 43N 15 50 E
Zigong, China 32 D5 29 15N 104 48 E
Ziguinchor, Senegal 50 F2 12 35N 16 20W
Zihuatanejo, Mexico 86 D4 17 38N 101 33W
Žilina, Slovak Rep. 17 D10 49 12N 18 42 E
Zillah, Libya 51 C9 28 30N 17 33 E
Zima, Russia 27 D11 54 0N 102 5 E
Zimapán, Mexico 87 C5 20 54N 99 20W
Zimba, Zambia 55 F2 17 20S 26 11 E
Zimbabwe, Zimbabwe 55 G3 20 16S 30 54 E
Zimbabwe ■, Africa 55 F3 19 0S 30 0 E
Zimnicea, Romania 17 G13 43 40N 25 22 E
Zinder, Niger 50 F7 13 48N 9 0 E
Zinga, Tanzania 55 D4 9 16S 38 49 E
Zion National Park, U.S.A. 83 H7 37 15N 113 5W
Ziros, Greece 23 D8 35 5N 26 8 E
Zitácuaro, Mexico 86 D4 19 28N 100 21W
Zitundo, Mozam. 57 D5 26 48S 32 47 E
Ziway, L., Ethiopia 46 F2 8 0N 38 50 E
Ziyang, China 34 H5 32 32N 108 31 E
Zlatograd, Bulgaria 21 D11 41 22N 25 7 E
Zlatoust, Russia 24 C10 55 10N 59 40 E
Zlin, Czech Rep. 17 D9 49 14N 17 40 E
Zmeinogorsk, Kazakstan 26 D9 51 10N 82 13 E
Znojmo, Czech Rep. 16 D9 48 50N 16 2 E
Zobeyrī, Iran 44 C5 34 10N 46 40 E
Zobia, Dem. Rep. of the Congo 54 B2 3 0N 25 59 E
Zoetermeer, Neths. 15 B4 52 3N 4 30 E
Zolochev = Zolochiv, Ukraine 17 D13 49 45N 24 51 E
Zolochiv, Ukraine 17 D13 49 45N 24 51 E
Zomba, Malawi 55 F4 15 22S 35 19 E
Zongo, Dem. Rep. of the Congo 52 D3 4 20N 18 35 E
Zonguldak, Turkey 25 F5 41 28N 31 50 E
Zonqor Pt., Malta 23 D2 35 51N 14 34 E
Zorritos, Peru 92 D2 3 43S 80 40W
Zou Xiang, China 34 G9 35 30N 116 58 E
Zouar, Chad 51 D9 20 30N 16 32 E
Zouérate = Zouîrât, Mauritania 50 D3 22 44N 12 21W
Zouîrât, Mauritania 50 D3 22 44N 12 21W
Zoutkamp, Neths. 15 A6 53 20N 6 18 E
Zrenjanin, Serbia, Yug. 21 B9 45 22N 20 23 E
Zufār, Oman 46 D5 17 40N 54 0 E
Zug, Switz. 18 C8 47 10N 8 31 E
Zugspitze, Germany 16 E6 47 25N 10 59 E
Zuid-Holland □, Neths. 15 C4 52 0N 4 35 E
Zuidbeveland, Neths. 15 C3 51 30N 3 50 E
Zuidhorn, Neths. 15 A6 53 15N 6 23 E
Zula, Eritrea 46 D2 15 17N 39 40 E
Zumbo, Mozam. 55 F3 15 35S 30 26 E
Zumpango, Mexico 87 D5 19 48N 99 6W
Zunhua, China 35 D9 40 18N 117 58 E
Zuni, U.S.A. 83 J9 35 4N 108 51W
Zunyi, China 32 D5 27 42N 106 53 E
Zuoquan, China 34 F7 37 5N 113 22 E
Zurbātīyah, Iraq 44 C5 33 9N 46 3 E
Zürich, Switz. 18 C8 47 22N 8 32 E
Zutphen, Neths. 15 B6 52 9N 6 12 E
Zuwārah, Libya 51 B8 32 58N 12 1 E
Zūzan, Iran 45 C8 34 22N 59 53 E
Zverinogolovskoye, Russia 26 D7 54 26N 64 50 E
Zvishavane, Zimbabwe 55 G3 20 17S 30 2 E
Zvolen, Slovak Rep. 17 D10 48 33N 19 10 E
Zwelitsha, S. Africa 53 L5 32 55S 27 22 E
Zwettl, Austria 16 D8 48 35N 15 9 E
Zwickau, Germany 16 C7 50 44N 12 30 E
Zwolle, Neths. 15 B6 52 31N 6 6 E
Zwolle, U.S.A. 81 K8 31 38N 93 39W
Żyrardów, Poland 17 B11 52 3N 20 28 E
Zyryan, Kazakstan 26 E9 49 43N 84 20 E
Zyryanka, Russia 27 C16 65 45N 150 51 E
Zyryanovsk = Zyryan, Kazakstan 26 E9 49 43N 84 20 E
Żywiec, Poland 17 D10 49 42N 19 10 E
Zyyi, Cyprus 23 E12 34 43N 33 20 E

World: Regions in the News

YUGOSLAVIA
Population 10,500,000
(Serb 62.6%, Albanian 16.5%,
Montenegrin 5%, Hungarian 3.3%,
Muslim 3.2%)
 Serbia Population: 5,799,800
 (Serb 87.7%, excluding the
 provinces of Kosovo and
 Vojvodina)
 Kosovo Population: 2,084,4000
 (Albanian 81.6%, Serb 9.9%)
 Vojvodena Population: 1,980,800
 (Serb 56.8%, Hungarian 16.9%)
 Montenegro Population: 635,000
 (Montenegrin 61.9%, Muslim
 14.6%, Albanian 7%)

CROATIA
Population: 4,672,000
(Croat 78.1%, Serb 12.2%)

SLOVENIA
Population: 1,972,000
(Slovene 88%, Croat 3%, Serb 2%)

MACEDONIA (F. Y. R. O. M.)
Population: 2,009,000
(Macedonian 64%, Albanian 21.7%,
Turkish 5%, Romanian 3%,
Serb 2%)

BOSNIA-HERZEGOVINA
Population: 3,366,000
(Muslim 49%, Serb 31.2%,
Croat 17.2%)

LEGEND (Former Yugoslavia map)
- – – – International boundaries
- – · – · Republic boundaries
- – – – Province boundaries
- ■ Capital cities
- ——— Dayton Peace Agreement Boundary
- Muslim–Croat Federation
- Bosnian Serb Republic

FORMER YUGOSLAVIA AND KOSOVO

The former Yugoslavia, a federation of six republics, split apart in 1991–2. Fearing Serb domination, Croatia, Slovenia, Macedonia and Bosnia-Herzegovina declared themselves independent. This left two states, Serbia and Montenegro, to continue as Yugoslavia. The presence in Croatia and Bosnia-Herzegovina of Orthodox Christian Serbs, Roman Catholic Croats, and Muslims led to civil war and 'ethnic cleansing'. In 1995, the war ended when the Dayton Peace Accord affirmed Bosnia-Herzegovina as a single state partitioned into a Muslim-Croat Federation and a Serbian Republic.

But the status of Kosovo, a former autonomous Yugoslav region, remained unresolved. Kosovo's autonomy had been abolished in 1989 and the Albanian-speaking, Muslim Kosovars were forced to accept direct Serbian rule. After 1995, support grew for the rebel Kosovo Liberation Army. The Serbs hit back and thousands of Kosovars were forced to flee their homes. In March 1999, NATO launched an aerial offensive against Serbia in an attempt to halt the 'ethnic cleansing'. A Serb military withdrawal from Kosovo was finally agreed in June.

KOSOVO
- ■ Capital city
- ● Other towns
- – · – · International boundaries

THE EURO

The euro (€) is the single currency which will eventually replace the national currencies of the countries of the European Economic and Monetary Union (EMU). Euro notes and coins will come into circulation in January 2000. The euro will be used alongside national currencies until July 2002 when it will become the sole legal tender in the EMU countries.

1 euro (€) = US$ 1.66* = £ 0.66*
*market rate 24.05.99

EURO–ZONE
- Euro-zone January 1999
- ● Non-EU members
- Opted for later entry

NO-FLY ZONE
- ■ Capital cities
- ● Cities
- Kurdish region
- No-fly zone

CONGO

The Congo gained independence from Belgium in 1960 and was renamed Zaïre in 1971. Ethnic rivalries caused instability until 1965, when the country became a one-party state, ruled by President Mobuto. The government allowed the formation of political parties in 1990, but elections were repeatedly postponed. In 1996, fighting broke out in eastern Zaïre, as the Tutsi-Hutu conflict in Burundi and Rwanda spilled over. The rebel leader Laurent Kabila took power in 1997, ousting Mobutu and renaming the country. A rebellion against Kabila broke out in 1998. Rwanda and Uganda supported the rebels, while Angola, Chad, Namibia and Zimbabwe sent troops to assist Kabila.

THE CONGO
- ■ Capital cities
- ● Cities
- – · – · International boundaries
- Neighbouring countries involved in the conflict in the Congo

THE NEAR EAST
- – – – 1949 Armistice Line
- —— 1974 Cease-fire Line
- *Efrata* Main Jewish settlements in the West Bank and Gaza Strip
- ■ Halhul Main Palestinian Arab towns in the West Bank and Gaza Strip
- ■ Capital cities

ISRAEL
Population: 5,644,000 (inc. East Jerusalem and Jewish settlers in the areas under Israeli administration. Jewish 82%, Arab Muslim 13.8%, Arab Christian 2.5%, Druze 1.7%)

West Bank
Population: 1,122,900 (Palestinian Arabs 97% [of whom Arab Muslim 85%, Jewish 7%, Christian 8%])

Gaza Strip
Population: 748,400 (Arab 98%)

JORDAN
Population: 4,435,000 (Arab 99% [of whom about 50% are Palestinian Arab])

LEBANON
Population: 3,506,000 (Arab 93% [of whom 83% are Lebanese Arab and 10% Palestinian Arab])

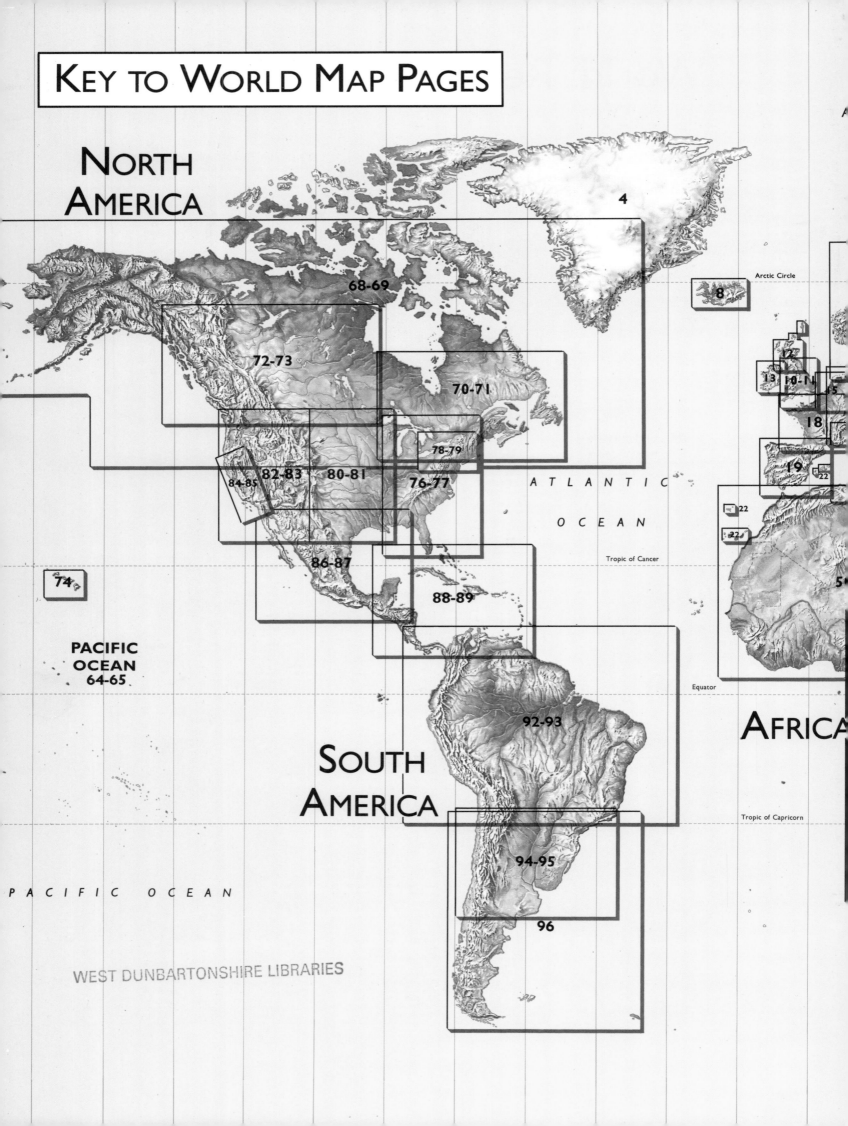

KEY TO WORLD MAP PAGES

NORTH AMERICA

4

Arctic Circle

8

68-69

72-73

70-71

12

13 **10-11**

15

18

78-79

ATLANTIC

19

22

84-85 **82-83** **80-81** **76-77**

OCEAN

22

22

Tropic of Cancer

86-87

74

88-89

5

PACIFIC
OCEAN
64-65

Equator

AFRICA

92-93

SOUTH AMERICA

Tropic of Capricorn

PACIFIC OCEAN

94-95

96

WEST DUNBARTONSHIRE LIBRARIES